Programming
Microsoft® ASP.NET 3.5

Dino Esposito

PUBLISHED BY
Microsoft Press
A Division of Microsoft Corporation
One Microsoft Way
Redmond, Washington 98052-6399

Library of Congress Control Number: 2007942079

Printed and bound in the United States of America.

1 2 3 4 5 6 7 8 9   QWT   3 2 1 0 9 8

Distributed in Canada by H.B. Fenn and Company Ltd.

A CIP catalogue record for this book is available from the British Library.

Microsoft Press books are available through booksellers and distributors worldwide. For further information about international editions, contact your local Microsoft Corporation office or contact Microsoft Press International directly at fax (425) 936-7329. Visit our Web site at www.microsoft.com/mspress. Send comments to mspinput@microsoft.com.

Acquisitions Editor: Ben Ryan
Developmental Editor: Lynn Finnel
Project Editor: Lynn Finnel
Editorial Production: Waypoint Press
Technical Reviewer: Ken Scribner; Technical Review services provided by Content Master, a member of CM Group, Ltd.
Cover: Tom Draper Design

Body Part No. X14-40163

To Silvia, Francesco, and Michela who wait for me and keep me busy.
But I'm happy only when I'm busy.

Contents at a Glance

Table of Contents

What do you think of this book? We want to hear from you!

Microsoft is interested in hearing your feedback so we can continually improve our books and learning resources for you. To participate in a brief online survey, please visit:

www.microsoft.com/learning/booksurvey

Part II   Adding Data in an ASP.NET Site

Part IV ASP.NET AJAX Extensions

Acknowledgements

A good ensemble of people made this book happen: Ben Ryan, Lynn Finnel, Kenn Scribner, Roger LeBlanc, and Steve Sagman. To all of them, I owe a monumental "Thank You" for being so kind, patient, and accurate. They reviewed, edited, reworked, and tested all the text and code this book is made of. Working with you is a privilege and a pleasure. It makes me a better author each time. And I still have a long line of books to write until I can confess to myself, in front of the mirror, that I feel like I'm a good book author.

—Dino

Introduction

The beginning of Web development dates back to about fifteen years ago. Since then, numerous technologies have crossed our life at different speeds and have left different memories. We had meteors like ActiveX Documents and vivid stars like Active Server Pages (ASP). ASP in particular—I believe—marked the watershed; that was around 1997. ASP made it clear that real-world Web development was possible only through a rich and powerful server-side programming model.

Just as Microsoft Visual Basic did for Microsoft Windows development, ASP provided a set of server tools to build dynamic applications quickly and effectively and showed the way ahead. ASP.NET is the culmination of Web development technologies that have rapidly followed one another in the past fifteen years—one building on another, and each filling the gaps of its predecessor. As a result, ASP.NET is currently the most technologically advanced, feature-rich, and powerful platform for building distributed applications transported by HTTP.

The more one works with ASP.NET, the more he or she realizes that even more is needed. ASP.NET simplifies a number of tasks and presents itself as a sort of programming paradise, especially for developers coming from classic ASP. ASP.NET 1.1 just whetted the appetite of the developer community. Thus, after the first months of working with it and assessing it, members of the developer community started asking and wishing for more—in fact, much more.

ASP.NET 2.0 was a major upgrade to the platform, even though it didn't introduce any new or revolutionary programming paradigm to learn. It had no radically new approach to code design and implementation, and there was no new syntax model for developers to become familiar with. Nonetheless, ASP.NET 2.0 represented a fundamental milestone in the Microsoft Web development roadmap.

ASP.NET 2.0 made new practices emerge as best practices. Its new programming techniques required attention from architects and lead developers, and its new system features provided native solutions to known issues with earlier versions.

The recently released upgrade to ASP.NET that goes with the .NET Framework 3.5 doesn't add much to the existing platform. ASP.NET 3.5 is just ASP.NET 2.0 plus a few extensions. You have a few new server controls such as the *ListView* and *DataPager*. You have facilities to work with new .NET Framework improvements—in particular, LINQ and Linq-to-SQL. And, more importantly, you have AJAX extensions.

ASP.NET 3.5 is a complete platform for developing AJAX-enabled applications, as it incorporates an improved version of the ASP.NET AJAX Extensions 1.0 toolkit that was released in early 2007 as an add-on for ASP.NET 2.0. In addition to covering ASP.NET AJAX and Windows Communication Foundation (WCF) services, this book also adds one more ingredient to the recipe that will serve up rich Internet applications—Silverlight.

This book covers the state of the art in Web programming with Microsoft .NET technologies. It is updated to ASP.NET 3.5, but you'll find it useful whatever version of ASP.NET you use.

A book that attempts to detail the state of the art of ASP.NET programming can't do that in much less than 2000 pages. This book is ultimately a reference for the core ASP.NET topics—those you need to learn first in order to be productive—for example, HTTP runtime, security, caching, state management, pages, controls, data binding, and data access.

An excellent companion to this book is an earlier book of mine *Programming Microsoft ASP.NET 2.0 Applications: Advanced Topics* (Microsoft Press, 2006). In spite of the name, which clearly targets the 2.0 platform, the *Advanced Topics* book is still valid and up to date.

None of the topics covered there underwent changes in ASP.NET 3.5. And anything that is new to ASP.NET 3.5 or—like Silverlight—is worth a look is covered in the book you hold in your hands.

Who Is This Book For?

To avoid beating around the bush, let's state it clearly: this is not a book for novice developers. This book is not appropriate if you have only a faint idea of ASP.NET and are looking for a book to get you started quickly and effectively. If you feel you need a step-by-step guide to learn ASP.NET, you're better off looking at other references specifically for the novice ASP.NET developer. Once you have grabbed hold of ASP.NET principles and features and are looking for guidance as to their proper application, you enter into the realm of knowledge covered by this book.

You won't find screen shots here illustrating Visual Studio 2008 wizards, and there is no mention of selecting or unselecting options to get a certain behavior from your code. Of course, this doesn't mean that I hate Visual Studio 2008 and certainly doesn't mean that I'm not recommending Visual Studio 2008 to develop ASP.NET applications. Visual Studio 2008 is a great tool to write ASP.NET applications; however, judged from an ASP.NET perspective, it is merely a working tool. This book, instead, is all about the ASP.NET technology itself.

I do recommend this book to developers who have a knowledge of the basic steps required to build simple ASP.NET pages and know how to easily manage the fundamentals of Web development. Beginners need not apply, even though this book is also a useful and persistent reference to keep on your desk.

System Requirements

You'll need the following hardware and software to build and run the code samples for this book:

- Microsoft Windows Vista, Microsoft Windows XP with Service Pack 2, Microsoft Windows Server 2003 with Service Pack 1, or Microsoft Windows 2000 with Service Pack 4.

- Microsoft Visual Studio 2008 Professional or Standard Edition or Microsoft Visual Studio 2008 Web Developer Express Edition.

- Internet Information Services (IIS) is not strictly required, but it is helpful for testing sample applications in a realistic runtime environment.

- Microsoft SQL Server 2005 Express (included with Visual Studio 2008) or Microsoft SQL Server 2005.

- The Northwind database of Microsoft SQL Server 2000 is used in most examples in this book to demonstrate data-access techniques. You can obtain the Northwind database from the Microsoft Download Center (*http://www.microsoft.com/downloads/details. aspx?FamilyID=06616212-0356-46A0-8DA2-EEBC53A68034&displaylang=en*).

- 766-MHz Pentium or compatible processor (1.5-GHz Pentium recommended).

- 256-MB RAM (512 MB or more recommended).

- Video (800 x 600 or higher resolution) monitor with at least 256 colors (1024 x 768 High Color 16-bit recommended).

- CD-ROM or DVD-ROM drive.

- Microsoft Mouse or compatible pointing device.

Find Additional Content Online

As new or updated material becomes available that complements this book, it will be posted online on the Microsoft Press Online Developer Tools Web site. The type of material you might find includes updates to book content, articles, links to companion content, errata, sample chapters, and more. This Web site will be available soon at *http://www.microsoft.com/ learning/books/online/developer*, and it will be updated periodically.

The Companion Web Site

This book features a companion Web site that makes available to you all the code used in the book. This code is organized by chapter, and you can download it from the companion site at this address: *http://www.microsoft.com/mspress/companion/9780735625273/*.

Support for This Book

Every effort has been made to ensure the accuracy of this book and the companion content. As corrections or changes are collected, they will be added to a Microsoft Knowledge Base article.

Microsoft Press provides support for books and companion content at the following Web site:

http://www.microsoft.com/learning/support/books/

Questions and Comments

If you have comments, questions, or ideas regarding the book or the companion content, or questions that are not answered by visiting the sites above, please send them to Microsoft Press via e-mail to

mspinput@microsoft.com

Or via postal mail to

Microsoft Press
Attn: *Programming Microsoft ASP.NET 3.5* Editor
One Microsoft Way
Redmond, WA 98052-6399

Please note that Microsoft software product support is not offered through the above addresses.

Part I
Building an ASP.NET Page

Chapter 1
The ASP.NET Programming Model

ASP.NET is a Web development platform that provides services, a programming model, and the software infrastructure necessary to build enterprise-class applications. As part of the Microsoft .NET platform, ASP.NET provides a component-based, largely extensible, and easy-to-use way to build, deploy, and run Web applications that target any browser or mobile device.

ASP.NET is the culmination of Web development technologies that have rapidly followed one another in the past ten years—one building on another, and each filling the gaps of its predecessor. As a result, ASP.NET is currently the most technologically advanced, feature-rich, and powerful platform for building distributed applications transported by the HTTP proto-col. ASP.NET simplifies a number of tasks and is sort of a programming paradise, especially for developers coming from classic ASP, Internet Server Application Programming Interface (ISAPI) programming, or other Web platforms.

Released in late 2005, ASP.NET 2.0 introduced significant changes for application architects as well as for developers. Many of the constituent classes have been reworked, and some un-derwent face-lift operations. Several new controls have been added for the sake of produc-tivity, and a bunch of new and enhanced system modules made the run-time pipeline more customizable, flexible, robust, and secure. As a result, new practices have emerged as best practices, new programming techniques became available to architects and lead developers, and new system features provided native solutions to known issues with earlier versions.

ASP.NET 3.5 is the next milestone in the evolution of the ASP.NET platform. In this version, ASP.NET features Asynchronous JavaScript and XML (AJAX) capabilities, integration with the Windows Communication Foundation (WCF) service platform, Language INtegrated Query (LINQ) support and a few new server controls to fill existing functional gaps, such as in the area of rich graphical layout.

To maximize the benefits of using ASP.NET, you should first look at the overall model—the components, programmability, and infrastructure. And a close look at the overall model is exactly what this chapter provides. To start out, let's examine some basic concepts of the ASP.NET platform and its programming model.

What's ASP.NET, Anyway?

Prior to the advent of ASP.NET, three main technologies and platforms were available to develop Web applications: ASP, Java Server Pages (JSP), and the open source Web platform commonly referred to as LAMP (Linux plus Apache plus MySQL plus either Perl, Python, or PHP as the programming language).

> **Note** For completeness, we should also mention a couple of platform-specific, lower-level technologies that ASP and JSP rely on. ASP is actually an ISAPI extension, whereas JSP is imple-mented as a special *servlet* application. ISAPI extensions on Internet Information Services (IIS) based platforms and servlets on Java-based systems let you create server-side, Web-deployed applications using a more classic approach. You write a module that builds and renders the page rather than declaratively design the page using a mix of markup text and embedded code.

Although each has language-specific and architecture-specific features, all these Web development platforms are designed to create interactive pages as part of a Web-based application. To some extent, all enable developers to separate programming logic from the page layout through the use of components that the page itself is responsible for calling and rendering. Aside from this common ultimate goal, significant differences exist among those platforms, most of which relate to the programming model and languages they promote and support. For example, JSP exploits the Java framework of classes and, with JavaBeans, provides an effective extensibility model for reusing components. In addition, JSP supports tag customization and lets developers associate code with a custom tag definition. Finally, because it's a key element of the Java Enterprise Edition 5.0 (J5EE) platform, JSP relies on the Java language   a first-class, compiled language   as opposed to the scripting languages used by both ASP and LAMP platforms.

So how does ASP.NET fit in exactly?

Like other Web development environments, ASP.NET also works on top of the HTTP protocol and takes advantage of HTTP commands and policies to set up two-way, browser-to-server communication and cooperation. What really differentiates ASP.NET from the plethora of other Web development technologies is the abstract programming model it propounds, the Web Forms model. In addition, the whole ASP.NET platform comes as a native part of the Microsoft .NET Framework. To be sure you grasp the importance of this last point, let me explain. ASP.NET applications are compiled pieces of code, are made of reusable and extensible components, can be authored with first-class languages (including C#, Microsoft Visual Basic .NET, Microsoft JScript .NET, and J#), and can access the entire hierarchy of classes in the .NET Framework.

> **Note** In the future, there's a distinct possibility that you can also use dynamic languages to build ASP.NET pages such as Python and Ruby. Dynamic languages should be considered just one more option you have to build Web pages, and they are far away from replacing statically compiled languages such as C#. The Dynamic Language Runtime (DLR) environment—where dynamically languages are hosted—is currently under development and should be integrated in the next version of Microsoft Silverlight, which is a plug-in for supporting a subset of the Windows Presentation Foundation (WPF) in a browser environment. Chances are that the DLR will be integrated in the ASP.NET runtime in a future release. Should this happen, developers will be allowed to also use Python or Ruby to create ASP.NET applications. For more information on the background technology, read the white paper at *http://www.asp.net/IronPython/WhitePaper.aspx*.

In short, ASP.NET delivers a wealth of goodies, tools, and powerful system features that can be effectively grouped within the blanket expression *tools for abstracting the HTTP programming model*. Lots of programmer-friendly classes let you develop pages using typical desktop methods. The Web Forms model promotes an overall event-driven approach, but it is deployed over the Web. In addition, AJAX capabilities make the platform even more powerful and dramatically improve the user's experience.

> **Note** ASP.NET is supported on a variety of server platforms, including Microsoft Windows 2000 with at least Service Pack 2, Windows Server 2003, and newer operating system versions. To develop ASP.NET server applications, Internet Information Services (IIS) version 5.0 or later is also required. Other software you need—for example, Microsoft Data Access Components (MDAC) 2.7—is automatically installed when you set up the .NET Framework. In terms of performance, robustness, and security, the ideal combination of current system software for hosting ASP.NET applications appears to be Windows Server 2003 (preferably with at least Service Pack 1 applied) and IIS 6.0. Windows Server 2008 and IIS 7.0 are just around the corner, though.

Programming in the Age of Web Forms

The rationale behind the ASP.NET Web Forms model is directly related to the search for a better strategy to deal with the growing demand for cheap but powerful Web interaction. As a matter of fact, the HTTP protocol represents the major strength and weakness of Web applications. The stateless nature of the HTTP protocol introduces vastly different programming concepts that are foreign to many desktop developers—first and foremost among these concepts is session state management. On the other hand, the inherent simplicity and scalability of HTTP is the key to its worldwide adoption and effectiveness—in short, we probably couldn't have the Internet as we know it without a protocol like HTTP. Yet, as demand for rich and powerful applications increases, programmers have to devise better ways of setting up easy and effective communication from the client to the server and vice versa. The advent of AJAX is just a clear sign of this need.

The Web Forms model is the ASP.NET implementation of the typical Web paradigm where the browser submits a form to the Web server and receives a full markup page in return. The growing complexity of today's Web pages, full of multimedia, graphic contents and sophisti- cated layouts, makes a paradigm shift necessary. AJAX is the new paradigm that ASP.NET 3.5 fully supports. When AJAX is enabled, an ASP.NET page uses script code under the control of the page developer to send a request for data to the Web server and receive other data as a response. Unlike the Web Forms, the AJAX model doesn't cause full replacement of the current page and results in smoother page transitions and flicker-free page updates. I'll cover AJAX programming in ASP.NET in Chapter 19 and Chapter 20.

Event-Driven Programming over HTTP

ASP.NET Web Forms bring the event-driven model of interaction to the Web. Implementing an event model over the Web requires any data related to the client-side user's activity to be forwarded to the server for corresponding and *stateful* processing. The server processes the output of client actions and triggers reactions. The state of the application contains two types of information: the state of the client and the state of the session. The state of the client—mostly the contents of form input fields collectively referred to as the *page state*—is easily accessible through the server-side collections that store posted values. But what about the overall state of the session? The client expects that sending information to the server through one page is naturally related to any other page he or she might view later, such as when adding items to a shopping cart. Who remembers what a particular user has in the shopping cart? By itself, HTTP is incapable of keeping track of this information; that's where session state and a proper server-side infrastructure surrounding and integrating HTTP fit in.

I can't emphasize enough the importance of understanding the concepts involved with *stateless programming* when developing Web applications. As mentioned, HTTP is a stateless protocol, which means two successive requests across the same session have no knowledge of each other. They are resolved by newly instantiated environments in which no session- specific information is automatically maintained, except all the information the application itself might have stored in some of its own global objects.

The ASP.NET runtime carries the page state back and forth across page requests. When generating HTML code for a given page, ASP.NET encodes and stuffs the state of server-side objects into a few hidden, and transparently created, fields. When the page is requested, the same ASP.NET runtime engine checks for embedded state information—the hidden fields— and uses any decoded information to set up newly created instances of server-side objects. The net effect of such a mechanism is not unlike the Windows Forms model on the desktop and is summarized in Figure 1-1.

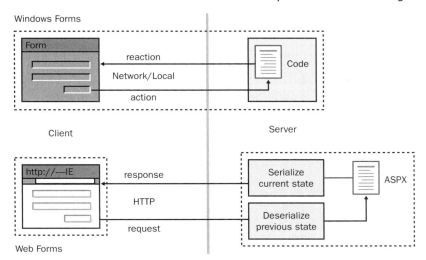

FIGURE 1-1 Comparing the Windows Forms and Web Forms models in the .NET Framework.

The Windows Forms model stems from the typical event-driven desktop programming style. No matter what connectivity exists between the client and server components, the server always works in reaction to the client's input. The server is aware of the overall application state and operates in a two-tier, connected manner. The Web Forms model needs some machinery to support the same event-driven programming model. In Figure 1-1, the needed *machinery* is represented by the state deserialization that occurs when the page is requested and the state serialization performed when the HTML response is being generated.

In charge of this filtering work is the ASP.NET HTTP runtime—a piece of code that extends and specializes the overall capabilities of the hosting Web server. Hidden fields are the low-level tools used to perform the trick. Such a model wouldn't be as effective without a server-side, rich object model spanning the entire content of the server page. This component model is crucial to the building and effective working of the ASP.NET development platform.

The ASP.NET component model identifies and describes the building blocks of ASP.NET pages. It is implemented through an object model that provides a server-side counterpart to virtually any HTML page element, such as HTML tags like *<form>* and *<input>*. In addition, the ASP.NET object model includes numerous components (called server controls or Web controls) that represent more complex elements of the user interface (UI). Some of these controls have no direct mapping with individual HTML elements but are implemented by combining multiple HTML tags. Typical examples of complex UI elements are the *Calendar* control and the *GridView* control.

In the end, an ASP.NET page is made of any number of server controls mixed with verbatim text, markup, and images. Sensitive data excerpted from the page and controls state is unobtrusively stored in hidden fields, and it forms the context of that page request. The association between an instance of the page and its state is unambiguous, not programmatically modifiable, and controlled by the ASP.NET HTTP runtime.

The ASP.NET component model is the first stop on the way to the full understanding of the ASP.NET platform. The component model supports you through the whole development cycle, including the phase of page authoring and run-time system configuration, as shown in Figure 1-2.

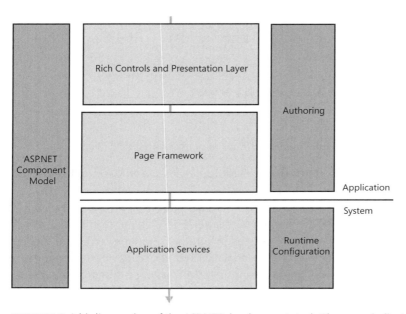

FIGURE 1-2 A bird's-eye view of the ASP.NET development stack. The arrow indicates the typical top-down application perspective, starting with the user interface and traversing through to the system services.

Before we dive into the various elements shown in Figure 1-2, let's briefly review the basics of the HTTP protocol, which remains the foundation of Web interaction. After that, we'll move on to describe the structure of an ASP.NET page and how to write and deploy ASP.NET applications.

The HTTP Protocol

This section provides a quick overview of the way Web applications operate. If you already have a working knowledge of the Web underpinnings, feel free to jump ahead to the section "Structure of an ASP.NET Page."

The acronym *HTTP* has become so familiar to us developers that we sometimes don't remember exactly what it stands for. Actually, *HTTP* stands for Hypertext Transfer Protocol.

HTTP is a text-based protocol that defines how Web browsers and Web servers com-municate. The format of HTTP packets is fully described in RFC 2068 and is available for download from *http://www.w3.org/Protocols/rfc2068/rfc2068.txt*. HTTP packets travel over a Transmission Control Protocol (TCP) connection directed toward default port 80 at the target Internet Protocol (IP) address.

The HTTP Request

When you point the browser to a URL, it uses the available Domain Name System (DNS) to translate the server name you provided with the URL into an IP address. Next, the browser opens a socket and connects to port 80 at that address. For example, the packet with the download request for *http://www.contoso.com/default.aspx* can take the following simple form:

```
GET /default.aspx HTTP/1.1
Host: www.contoso.com
```

The first line of text in a request is the *start line* of the request. It must contain the name of the HTTP command to execute (*GET* in this case), the URL of the resource, plus the version of the HTTP protocol you want to use.

An HTTP request can contain, and usually does contain, a number of headers. An HTTP header is a line of text that provides additional information about the request. In the HTTP request just shown, the line beginning with "Host:" is an HTTP header. Headers that can be found in an HTTP request include the following:

- **User-Agent**   Identifies the type of browser that originated the request
- **Connection**   Closes a connection or keeps a connection alive
- **If-Modified-Since**   Provides client-side cache validation

GET and *POST* are the most commonly used HTTP commands or verbs. The *GET* verb means retrieve whatever information is identified by the request URL. The *POST* verb is used to request that the origin server accept the content enclosed in the request and process it. Typically, the *POST* verb is used to provide a block of data (that is, the result of submitting a form) to a data-handling process.

> **Note** The HTTP protocol is not limited to *GET* and *POST* verbs to express commands. Other options are available, such as *PUT* and *DELETE* to update and delete Web resources, respectively. These verbs, though, are never used in a typical browser session. The set of verbs supported by the HTTP protocol is a topic being revamped these days as the AJAX paradigm takes root and architects explore the most effective ways to build script-callable, server-based services for pages.

The HTTP Response

The server's response includes a *status line* made from the message's protocol version and an exit code (indicating success or that an error has occurred). The status line is followed by a bunch of headers—typically the page content type and length—and the body content. A blank line separates the body content from the rest of the message, as shown in the following response:

```
HTTP/1.1 200 OK
Server: Microsoft-IIS/6.0
Content-Type: text/html
Content-Length: 55

<html><body><h1>ASP.NET 3.5 is cool!</h1></body></html>
```

The preceding code illustrates the simple HTML output returned by the Web server. Requests and responses are strings formatted according to the HTTP schema, and they travel over a TCP connection. The code *200* means that all went OK with the request. The specified Web server processes the request and returns content of a certain length expressed in the given Multipurpose Internet Mail Extensions (MIME) type (*text/html*). HTTP codes that could be returned are listed in the HTTP specification, available at the aforementioned URL. In addition, it should be noted that the blank line between the last header and the content of the HTTP response is not just formatting—the carriage-return and line-feed pair are required and are very much a part of the standard.

What happens next mostly depends on the MIME type and the local browser's capabilities. As long as the MIME type is *text/html*, the browser displays the content as HTML. If the MIME type is, say, *text/xml*, some browsers will render the content as plain text, while others (for example, Microsoft Internet Explorer 6.0 and newer versions) will apply a built-in style sheet.

Building a Server-Side Abstraction Layer

Every conversation between browsers and Web servers consists of an exchange of packets similar to the ones we have just examined. If the requested URL is an HTML page, the Web server typically reads the contents of the *.html* file and flushes it into the body of the response packet. If the URL is an ASP.NET page, a special IIS module gets involved. The module is an IIS ISAPI plug-in, called an *ISAPI extension*.

An ISAPI extension is a dynamic-link library (DLL) registered on a per-file extension basis. An ISAPI extension registered to handle *.aspx* files gets involved whenever a request comes in for this type of resource. The ISAPI extension analyzes the request and configures the server-side environment that will actually process the source of the page. When the state for the request has been successfully retrieved and restored completely, the page is allowed to run and produce the expected output.

Submitting Forms

The HTML *<form>* tag is the only element authorized to transmit client-side data to the server. When the user clicks on a button of type "submit," by design the browser stuffs the current content of all the controls that belong to the form into a string. The string is then passed to the server as part of the *GET* or *POST* command, depending on the attribute set on the *<form>* tag.

The following HTML snippet illustrates a simple form containing a text box and submit button. As you can see, the form is associated with the *POST* command and the default.aspx URL:

```
<form method="post" action="default.aspx">
    <input type="text" name="EmpCode" />
    <input type="submit" value="Send" />
</form>
```

The following request shows the *POST* command that hits the Web server when the user enters **1001** for the employee code and then clicks the submit button:

```
POST /default.aspx HTTP/1.1
Host: www.contoso.com
Content-Type: application/x-www-form-urlencoded
Content-Length: 12

EmpCode=1001
```

While processing the page request, the ISAPI extension parses the body of the request and exposes any information found through a more programmer-friendly object model. For example, instead of remaining a simple name/value string, the *EmpCode* variable is moved to an application-wide collection—the *Request.Form* collection. This represents a first level of abstraction built over the raw HTTP programming model. Objects such as *Request*, *Response*, and *Server* form the HTTP context for the call and, as such, represent the minimum set of objects you find in most Web development platforms, including JSP and ASP. In ASP.NET, though, you find much more.

Structure of an ASP.NET Page

An ASP.NET page is a server-side text file saved with the *.aspx* extension. The internal structure of the page is extremely modular and comprises three distinct sections—page directives, code, and page layout:

- **Page directives**   Page directives set up the environment in which the page will run, specify how the HTTP runtime should process the page, and determine which assumptions about the page are safe to make. Directives also let you import namespaces to simplify coding, load assemblies not currently in the global assembly cache (GAC), and register new controls with custom tag names and namespace prefixes.

■ **Code section**   The code section contains handlers for page and control events, plus optional helper routines. Any source code pertinent to the page can be inserted inline or attached to the page through a separate file. If inserted inline, the code goes into a tag with the misleading name of <script>. (The name <script> has been chosen for backward-compatibility reasons.) Server-side <script> tags are distinguished from client-side <script> tags by the use of the runat=server attribute. (More on this in a moment.) Any page code is always compiled before execution. Starting with version 2.0 of ASP.NET, it can also be precompiled and deployed in the form of a binary assembly.

■ **Page layout**   The page layout represents the skeleton of the page. It includes server controls, literal text, inline JavaScript, and HTML tags. The user interface of the server controls can be fleshed out a bit using declared attributes and control properties.

For the page to work, you don't need to specify all sections. Although real-world pages include all the sections mentioned, perfectly valid and functional pages can include only the code section or page layout. In some special cases, you can even have an ASP.NET page made of a single directive.

In Chapter 2, and even more in Chapter 3, we'll delve deep into the features of a page and its building blocks.

A Sample ASP.NET Page

It is about time we see what an ASP.NET page looks like. To start, a simple text editor will suffice; so let's open Notepad and let the sleeping giant (Microsoft Visual Studio) lie. The following code implements a simple ASP.NET page that lets you enter a string and then changes it to uppercase letters after you click a button. For the sake of simplicity, we use inline code. (As you'll learn later in the book, this is *not* what you'll be doing in real-world applications or in pages with any complexity.)

```
<!-- Directives -->
<% @Page Language="C#" %>

<!-- Code Section -->
<script runat="server">
private void MakeUpper(object sender, EventArgs e)
{
    string buf = TheString.Value;
    TheResult.InnerHtml = buf.ToUpper();
}
</script>

<!-- Layout -->
<html>
<head><title>UpperCase</title></head>
<body>
<h1>Make It Upper</h1>
```

```
<form runat="server">
    <input runat="server" id="TheString" type="text" />
    <input runat="server" id="Button1" type="submit" value="Proceed..."
        OnServerClick="MakeUpper" />
    <hr>
    <h3>Results:</h3>
    <span runat="server" id="TheResult" />
</form>
</body>
</html>
```

Blank lines and comments in the preceding listing separate the three sections—directives, code, and page layout. Notice the unsparing use of the *runat* attribute—it's one of the most important pieces of the whole ASP.NET jigsaw puzzle. In the next section, we'll discuss *runat* in more detail. For now, it suffices to say that the *runat* attribute promotes an otherwise lifeless server-side tag to the rank of a component instance.

The page layout is made of literals and HTML tags, some of which contain the aforementioned *runat* attribute. Everything flagged this way, despite appearances, is not really an HTML element. More precisely, it is the markup placeholder of a server-side component—an ASP.NET control—that is actually responsible for the final markup served to the browser. In an ASP.NET source, every tag marked with the *runat* attribute is not output as-is, but undergoes a transformation process on the server at the end of which the real markup is generated. The ASP.NET runtime is in charge of mapping tags to control instances. Let's quickly review the code.

Quick Review of the Code

Thanks to the *runat* attribute the input text field becomes an instance of the *HtmlInputControl* class when the page is processed on the server. The *Value* property of the class determines the default text to assign to the input field. When the user clicks the submit button, the page automatically posts back to itself. The magic is performed by the *runat* attribute set for the *<form>* tag. Once on the server, the posted value of the input field is read and automatically assigned to the *Value* property of a newly created instance of the *HtmlInputControl*. Next, the code associated with the *OnServerClick* event runs. This code takes the current content of the text box—the posted string—and converts it to uppercase letters. Finally, the uppercase string is assigned it to the *InnerHtml* property of the server-side control bound to the HTML *<span>* tag. When the *MakeUpper* event handler completes, the page is ready for rendering. At this point, updated HTML code is sent to the browser.

To test the page, copy the *.aspx* file to your Web server's root directory. Normally, this is *c:\inetpub\wwwroot*. If you want, create an ad hoc virtual directory using the built-in IIS administration tools. Let's assume the page is named *upper.aspx*. Next, point the browser to the page. Figure 1-3 shows what you get.

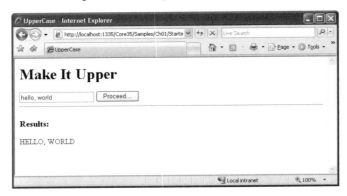

FIGURE 1-3 Our first (and rather simple) ASP.NET page in action.

It would be useful to take a look at the HTML source of the page when it is first displayed to the user—that is, before the user clicks to make the text uppercase.

```
<!-- Directives -->

<!-- Code Section -->

<!-- Layout -->
<html>
<head><title>UpperCase</title></head>
<body>
<h1>Make It Upper</h1>
<form method="post" action="upper.aspx" id="Form1">
<div>
    <input type="hidden" name="__EVENTTARGET" value="" />
    <input type="hidden" name="__EVENTARGUMENT" value="" />
    <input type="hidden" name="__VIEWSTATE" value="/wEPDwUJNzM4N…==" />
</div>

<script type="text/javascript">
<!--
var theForm = document.forms['Form1'];
if (!theForm) {
    theForm = document.Form1;
}
function __doPostBack(eventTarget, eventArgument) {
    if (!theForm.onsubmit || (theForm.onsubmit() != false)) {
        theForm.__EVENTTARGET.value = eventTarget;
        theForm.__EVENTARGUMENT.value = eventArgument;
        theForm.submit();
    }
}
// -->
</script>
```

```
<input name="TheString" type="text" id="TheString" value="Hello, world" />
<input name="Button1" type="submit" id="Button1" value="Proceed ..." />
<hr>
<h3>Results:</h3>
<span id="TheResult"></span>

<div>
    <input type="hidden" name="__EVENTVALIDATION" value="/wEWAwL+nL...o90" />
</div>
</form>
</body>
</html>
```

Within the *<form>* tag, a hard-coded *action* attribute has been added to force posting to the same page. This is by design and is very characteristic of ASP.NET. The various hidden fields you see are essential to the implementation of the postback mechanism and are generated automatically. The same can be said for the embedded script code. The *<input>* tags are nearly identical to their counterpart in the *.aspx* source—only the *runat* attribute disappeared.

Now that we've dirtied our hands with some ASP.NET code, let's step back and review the layers that actually make ASP.NET pages work in the context of an application.

The ASP.NET Component Model

ASP.NET is the key enabling technology for all Web-related functionality provided by the .NET Framework. The .NET Framework is made entirely of an object-oriented hierarchy of classes that span all programming topics for Windows operating systems. Generally speaking, a Web application is made of pages the user requests from a server and that the server processes and returns as markup code—mostly HTML. How the requested resource is processed, and therefore how the markup is generated, is server-specific. In particular, when the resource happens to have an *.aspx* extension, IIS delegates any further processing to the ASP.NET runtime system.

The ASP.NET runtime transforms the source code of the requested *.aspx* page into the living instance of a .NET Framework class that inherits from a base class named *Page*. At the end of the day, a running ASP.NET page is an object, and so it is for some of its components—the server-side controls.

A large number of new ASP.NET features are just a direct or an indirect propagation of the .NET infrastructure. ASP.NET benefits from cross-language integration and exception handling, garbage collection and code access security, deployment and configuration, and an incredibly rich class library. All these features aren't the products of a self-contained engine, they are available to you because ASP.NET applications are a special breed of a .NET application.

A Model for Component Interaction

Any element in an ASP.NET page that is marked with the *runat* attribute can be given a unique ID, allowing you to access that element from your server-side code. Two factors make this approach possible:

- The component-based architecture of the .NET platform, and the fact that ASP.NET is a constituent part of that platform
- The ASP.NET built-in mechanism for the application's state management

The component-based design of .NET makes component interaction easy and effective in all environments including ASP.NET applications. ASP.NET components access page features and interact by calling one another's methods and setting properties.

The fact that all elements in the page are true components, and not simply parsable text, provides a flexible and powerful extensibility model. Creating new controls is as easy as deriving a new class; building a page inheritance hierarchy is as easy as specifying a parent class different from the base *Page* class.

The *runat* Attribute

The *runat* attribute is what determines whether a piece of markup text is to be emitted verbatim at render time or transformed into a stateful instance of a particular .NET class. In the latter case, the class makes itself responsible for emitting the related markup. In an ASP.NET page, all markup elements that have the *runat* attribute set to *server* are considered server-side controls. The control class exposes methods and properties that let you configure the state of the component. The control is responsible for emitting HTML code when the page is rendered to the browser. Let's consider the following simple code that renders an anchor element in the client page:

```
Response.Write("<A id=myAnchor href=www.asp.net>Click me</A>")
```

The anchor element is created programmatically and is not defined in the page layout. In classic ASP, code blocks and the *Response.Write* method are the only ways you have to create or configure controls dynamically. In some development environments, such as Microsoft Visual InterDev, *design-time controls* provided an object-based way to output dynamically generated HTML. Design-time controls, though, were just what the name indicates—that is, controls you can use at design-time to generate markup and script code. In ASP.NET, you have a kind of *run-time controls* to mark the contrast with design-time controls.

Working with Server-Side Controls

Within an ASP page, there's no way for you to code against the *myAnchor* element. It's just frozen, lifeless text, only good for sending to the browser. Once on a client, the *myAnchor* element comes to life and can accept script instructions. Suppose now that you need to set the *href* attribute of the anchor based on run-time conditions. In classic ASP, you could first obtain the value for the *href* attribute and then call *Response.Write*:

```
strHref = "www.asp.net"
strHtml = "<A id=myAnchor "
strHtml = strHtml + "href=" + strHref
strHtml = strHtml + ">Click me</A>"
Response.Write(strHtml)
```

This code will work unchanged in an ASP.NET page but is certainly not the best you can do. By declaring the *<A>* tag with the *runat* attribute, you can give life to the anchor element on the server too:

```
<A runat="server" id="myAnchor">Click me</A>
```

When the page is loaded, the ASP.NET runtime parses the source code and creates instances of all controls marked with the *runat* attribute. Throughout the page, the *myAnchor* ID identifies an instance of the server-side control mapped to the *<A>* tag. The following code can be used to set the *href* attribute programmatically when the page loads:

```
<script runat="server" language="C#">
void Page_Load(object sender, EventArgs e)
{
    myAnchor.HRef = "http://www.asp.net";
}
</script>
```

The markup elements whose name matches an HTML element are mapped to the corresponding HTML server control. Note that not all feasible HTML tags have corresponding ASP.NET controls; for those that don't, a generic control is used. The list of tags and their associated controls is hard-coded in the ASP.NET runtime. Elements that belong to the *<asp>* namespace are mapped to Web server controls. Other markup elements are mapped to the assembly and class name declared by using an *@Register* directive.

Pagewide Tags

The *runat* attribute can also be used with pagewide tags such as *<body>*. These tags are represented through an instance of the *HtmlGenericControl* class. *HtmlGenericControl* is the .NET class used to represent an HTML server-side tag not directly represented by a .NET Framework class. The list of such tags also includes *<span>*, *<font>*, and *<iframe>*.

In the following page, the background color is set programmatically when the page loads:

```
<%@ Page Language="C#" %>
<script runat="server">
private void Page_Load(object sender, EventArgs e)
{
    TheBody.Style[HtmlTextWriterStyle.BackgroundColor] = "lightblue";
}
</script>
<html>
<head><title>Background color</title></head>
<body id="TheBody" runat="server">
    <h3>The background color of this page has been set programmatically.
        Open View|Source menu to see the source code.</h3>
</body>
</html>
```

The resulting HTML code is as follows:

```
<html>
<head><title>Background color</title></head>
<body id="TheBody" style="background-color:lightblue;">
    <h3>The background color of this page has been set programmatically.
        Open View|Source menu to see the source code.</h3>
</body>
</html>
```

Likewise, you can set any of the attributes of the *<body>* tag, thus deciding programmatically, say, which style sheet or background image to use. You use the *HtmlGenericControl*'s *Attributes* collection to create attributes on the tag:

```
TheBody.Attributes["Background"] = "/proaspnet20/images/body.gif";
```

We'll discuss the programming interface of the *HtmlGenericControl* class in more detail in Chapter 4.

> **Note**   Starting with ASP.NET 2.0, the contents of the *<head>* tag can be accessed programmatically as long as it is flagged with the *runat* attribute. The background class for the *<head>* tag is named *HtmlHead*. Through the facilities of the *HtmlHead* control, you can set the page title and link to external style sheets programmatically.

Unknown Tags

In case of unknown tags, namely tags that are neither predefined in the current schema nor user-defined, the ASP.NET runtime can behave in two different ways. If the tag doesn't contain namespace information, ASP.NET treats it like a generic HTML control. The empty namespace, in fact, evaluates to the HTML namespace, thereby leading the ASP.NET runtime to believe the tag is really an HTML element. No exception is raised, and markup text is generated on the server. For example, let's consider the following ASP.NET page:

```
<%@ Page Language="C#" %>
<script runat="server">
void Page_Load(object sender, EventArgs e)
{
    dinoe.Attributes["FavoriteFood"] = "T-bone steak";
}
</script>
<html>
<head><title>Unknown tags</title></head>
<body>
<form runat="server">
  <Person id="dinoe" runat="server" />
  Click the <b>View|Source</b> menu item...
</form>
</body>
</html>
```

The *<Person>* tag is still processed as if it was a regular HTML tag, and the *FavoriteFood* attribute is added. Figure 1-4 shows what the HTML code for this page actually is. In the preceding sample, the type of the *dinoe* object is *HtmlGenericControl*.

FIGURE 1-4 The HTML source code of the sample page

ASP.NET also processes namespace-less custom tags, mapping them to the *HtmlGenericControl* class. If the tag does contain namespace information, it is acceptable as long as the namespace is *<asp>* or a namespace explicitly associated with the tag name using an *@Register* directive. If the namespace is unknown, a compile error occurs.

ASP.NET Server Controls

There are basically two families of ASP.NET server controls. They are HTML server controls and Web server controls. *System.Web.UI.HtmlControls* is the namespace of HTML server controls. *System.Web.UI.WebControls* groups all the Web server controls.

HTML Server Controls

HTML server controls are classes that represent a standard HTML tag supported by most browsers. The set of properties of an HTML server control matches a commonly used set of attributes of the corresponding tag. The control features properties such as *InnerText*, *InnerHtml*, *Style*, and *Value* plus collections such as *Attributes*. Instances of HTML server controls are automatically created by the ASP.NET runtime each time the corresponding HTML tag marked with *runat="server"* is found in the page source.

As mentioned, the available set of HTML server controls doesn't cover all possible HTML tags of any given version of the HTML schema. Only most commonly used tags found their way to the *System.Web.UI.HtmlControls* namespace. Tags such as *<iframe>*, *<frameset>*, *<body>*, and *<hn>* have been left out as well as less frequently used tags such as *<fieldset>*, *<marquee>*, and *<pre>*.

The lack of a specialized server control, however, doesn't limit your programming power when it comes to using and configuring those tags on the server. You only have to use a more generic programming interface—the *HtmlGenericControl* class, which we looked at briefly in this section.

Web Server Controls

Web server controls are controls with more features than HTML server controls. Web server controls include not only input controls such as buttons and text boxes, but also special-purpose controls such as a calendar, an ad rotator, a drop-down list, a tree view, and a data grid. Web server controls also include components that closely resemble some HTML server controls. Web server controls, though, are more abstract than the corresponding HTML server controls in that their object model doesn't necessarily reflect the HTML syntax. For example, let's compare the HTML server text control and the Web server *TextBox* control. The HTML server text control has the following markup:

```
<input runat="server" id="FirstName" type="text" value="Dino" />
```

The Web server *TextBox* control has the following markup:

```
<asp:textbox runat="server" id="FirstName" text="Dino" />
```

Both controls generate the same HTML markup code. However, the programming interface of the HTML server text control matches closely that of the HTML *<input>* tag, while methods and properties of the Web server *TextBox* control are named in a more abstract way that coincides with how similar controls are named in the .NET Framework, for consistency. For example, to set the content of an HTML server text control you must use the *Value* property because *Value* is the corresponding HTML attribute name. If you work with the Web server *TextBox* control, you must resort to *Text*. With very few exceptions (that I'll discuss in Chapter 3), using HTML server controls or Web server controls to represent HTML elements is only a matter of preference and ease of development and maintenance.

The ASP.NET Development Stack

At the highest level of abstraction, the development of an ASP.NET application passes through two phases—page authoring and run-time configuration. You build the pages that form the application, implement its user's requirements, and then fine-tune the surrounding run-time environment to make it serve pages effectively and securely. As Figure 1-2 shows, the ASP.NET component model is the bedrock of all ASP.NET applications and their building blocks. With Figure 1-2 in mind, let's examine the various logical layers to see what they contain and why they contain it.

The Presentation Layer

An ASP.NET page is made of controls, free text, and markup. When the source code is transformed into a living instance of a page class, the ASP.NET runtime makes no further distinction between verbatim text, markup, and server controls—everything is a control, including literal text and carriage-return characters. At run time, any ASP.NET page is a mere graph of controls.

Rich Controls

The programming richness of ASP.NET springs from the wide library of server controls that covers the basic tasks of HTML interaction—for example, collecting text through input tags—as well as more advanced functionalities such as grid-based data display. The native set of controls is large enough to let you fulfill virtually any set of requirements. In addition, the latest version of ASP.NET adds a few new rich controls to take developer's productivity close to its upper limit.

In ASP.NET 3.5, you find controls to create list views, Web wizards, collapsible views of hierarchical data, advanced data reports, commonly used forms, declarative data binding, menus, and site navigation. You even find a tiny API to create portal-like pages. Availability of rich controls means reduction of development time and coding errors, more best practices implemented, and more advanced functionalities delivered to end users. We'll specifically cover controls in Chapter 4, Chapter 6, and later on in Chapter 11.

Custom Controls

ASP.NET core controls provide you with a complete set of tools to build Web functionalities. The standard set of controls can be extended and enhanced by adding custom controls. The underlying ASP.NET component model greatly simplifies the task by applying the common principles and rules of object-oriented programming.

You can build new controls by enhancing an existing control or aggregating two or more controls together to form a new one. ASP.NET 3.5 comes with a small set of base classes to build brand new controls on. This set of classes includes base classes to simplify the development of new data-bound controls. For more in-depth coverage of control development, take a look at my book *"Programming Microsoft ASP.NET 2.0 Applications—Advanced Topics"*, in particular chapters 11 through 15. Although the book is labeled with ASP.NET 2.0 and Visual Studio 2005, there's really nothing in it that doesn't work or is now considered wrong when working with ASP.NET 3.5.

Adaptive Rendering

Starting with version 2.0, ASP.NET ships a new control adapter architecture that allows any server control to create alternate renderings for a variety of browsers. Note, though, that the new adaptive rendering model doesn't apply to *mobile controls*. Mobile controls are a special family of Web controls designed to build applications for mobile devices. ASP.NET mobile controls still use the old adapter model, which was available since ASP.NET 1.1, for controls that inherit from *MobileControl* and are hosted on pages that inherit from *MobilePage*. In short, if you need to write a mobile application with ASP.NET 2.0, you should use the mobile controls, as you would have done with ASP.NET 1.1.

So what's the added value of the new adapter model? With this form of adaptive rendering, you can write control adapters to customize server controls for individual browsers. For example, you can write a control adapter to generate a different HTML markup for the *Calendar* control for a given desktop browser. In addition, by simply replacing the adapter component you can fix bugs that relate to rendering and, to the extent that it is possible, customize a solution to a given client. As an example, consider that Microsoft leveraged the adaptive rendering engine to deliver a CSS-friendly version of some native ASP.NET controls that use cascading style sheet (CSS) layout features instead of plain tables. For more information, check out *http://www.asp.net/cssadapters*.

The Page Framework

Any ASP.NET page works as an instance of a class that descends from the *Page* class. The *Page* class is the ending point of a pipeline of modules that process any HTTP request. The various system components that work on the original request build step by step all the information needed to locate the page object to generate the markup. The page object model sports several features and capabilities that could be grouped in terms of events, scripting, personalization, styling, and prototyping.

Page Events

The life cycle of a page in the ASP.NET runtime is marked by a series of events. By wiring their code up to these events, developers can dynamically modify the page output and the state of constituent controls. In ASP.NET 1.x, a page fires events such as *Init*, *Load*, *PreRender*, and *Unload* that punctuate the key moments in the life of the page. In ASP.NET 2.0 and 3.5 a few new events have been added to allow developers to follow the request processing more closely and precisely. In particular, you find new events to signal the beginning and end of the initialization and loading phase. The page life cycle will be thoroughly examined in Chapter 3.

Page Scripting

The page scripting object model lets developers manage script code and hidden fields to be injected in client pages. This object model generates JavaScript code used to glue together the HTML elements generated by server controls, thus providing features otherwise impossible to program on the server. For example, in this way you can set the input focus to a particular control when the page displays in the client browser.

ASP.NET 2.0 pages can be architected to issue client calls to server methods without performing a full postback and subsequently refresh the whole displayed page. The ASP.NET 2.0 callback mechanism is supplanted by ASP.NET AJAX extensions in ASP.NET 3.5. With AJAX capabilities onboard, you can choose to just enhance your existing ASP.NET 2.0 applications with flicker-free page updates or build pages according to a new paradigm that leverages a set of script-callable Web services. I'll return to AJAX enhancements in Chapter 19 and Chapter 20.

Cross-page posting is another feature that the community of ASP.NET developers loudly demanded. It allows the posting of content of a form to another page. Sounds like teaching old tricks to a new dog? Maybe. As mentioned earlier in this chapter, one defining characteristic of ASP.NET is that each page contains just one *<form>* tag, which continuously posts to itself. That's the way ASP.NET has been designed, and it results in several advantages.

In previous versions of ASP.NET, cross-page posting could be implemented the same way as in classic ASP—that is, posting through an HTML pure *<form>* not marked with the *runat* attribute. This method works fine, but it leaves you far from the object-oriented and strongly typed world of ASP.NET. Cross-page posting as implemented in ASP.NET 2.0 and newer versions just fills the gap.

Page Personalization

Starting with ASP.NET 2.0, you can store and retrieve user-specific information and preferences without the burden of having to write the infrastructural code. The application defines its own model of personalized data, and the ASP.NET runtime does the rest by parsing and compiling that model into a class. Each member of the personalized class data corresponds to a piece of information specific to the current user. Loading and saving personalized data is completely transparent to end users and doesn't even require the page author to know much about the internal plumbing. The user personalized information is available to the page author through a page property. Each page can consume previously saved information and save new information for further requests.

Page Styling

Much like Microsoft Windows XP themes, ASP.NET themes assign a set of styles and visual attributes to elements of the site that can be customized. These elements include control properties, page style sheets, images, and templates on the page. A theme is the union of all visual styles for all customizable elements in the pages—a sort of super–CSS file. A theme is identified by name and consists of CSS files, images, and control skins. A *control skin* is a text file that contains default control declarations in which visual properties are set for the control. With this feature enabled, if the developer adds, say, a *Calendar* control to a page, the control is rendered with the default appearance defined in the theme.

Themes are a great new feature because they allow you to change the look and feel of pages in a single shot and, perhaps more importantly, give all pages a consistent appearance.

Page Prototyping

Almost all Web sites today contain pages with a similar layout. For some sites, the layout is as simple as a header and footer; others sites might contain sophisticated navigational menus and widgets that wrap content. In ASP.NET 1.x, the recommended approach for developers was to wrap these UI blocks in user controls and reference them in each content page. As you can imagine, this model works pretty well when the site contains only a few pages; unfortunately, it becomes unmanageable if the site happens to contain hundreds of pages. An approach based on user controls presents several key issues for content-rich sites. For one thing, you have duplicate code in content pages to reference user controls. Next, application of new templates requires the developer to touch every page. Finally, HTML elements that span the content area are likely split between user controls.

Starting with ASP.NET 2.0, page prototyping is greatly enhanced thanks to *master pages*. Developers working on Web sites where many pages share some layout and functionality can now author any shared functionality in one master file, instead of adding the layout information to each page or separating the layout among several user controls. Based on the shared master, developers can create any number of similar-looking *content pages* simply by referencing the master page through a new attribute. We'll cover master pages in Chapter 6.

The HTTP Runtime Environment

The process by which a Web request becomes plain HTML text for the browser is not much different in any version of ASP.NET. The request is picked up by IIS, given an identity token, and passed to the ASP.NET ISAPI extension (*aspnet_isapi.dll*)—the entry point for any ASP.NET-related processing. This is the general process, but a number of key details depend on the underlying version of IIS and the process model in use.

The process model is the sequence of operations needed to process a request. When the ASP.NET runtime runs on top of IIS 5.x, the process model is based on a separate worker process named *aspnet_wp.exe*. This Microsoft Win32 process receives control directly from IIS through the hosted ASP.NET ISAPI extension. The extension is passed any request for ASP.NET resources, and it hands them over to the worker process. The worker process loads the common language runtime (CLR) and starts the pipeline of managed objects that transform the original request from an HTTP payload into a full-featured page for the browser. The *aspnet_isapi* module and the worker process implement advanced features such as process recycling, page output caching, memory monitoring, and thread pooling. Each Web application runs in a distinct AppDomain within the worker process. By default, the worker process runs under a restricted, poorly privileged account named ASPNET.

> **Note** In the CLR, an application domain (AppDomain) provides isolation, unloading, and security boundaries for executing managed code. An AppDomain is a kind of lightweight, CLR-specific process where multiple assemblies are loaded and secured to execute code. Multiple AppDomains can run in a single CPU process. There is not a one-to-one correlation between AppDomains and threads. Several threads can belong to a single AppDomain, and while a given thread is not confined to a single application domain, at any given time, a thread executes in a single AppDomain.

When ASP.NET runs under IIS version 6.0 or later, the default process model is different and the *aspnet_wp.exe* process is not used. The worker process in use is the standard IIS worker process (*w3wp.exe*) implemented by IIS 6.0 and 7.0. It looks up the URL of the request and loads a specific ISAPI extension. For example, it loads *aspnet_isapi.dll* for ASP.NET-related requests. Under the IIS 6.0 process model, the *aspnet_isapi* extension is responsible for loading the CLR and starting the HTTP pipeline.

Once in the ASP.NET HTTP pipeline, the request passes through various system and user-defined components that work on it until a valid page class is found and successfully instantiated. Developers can modify and adapt the run-time environment to some extent. This can happen in a variety of ways: changing the list of installed HTTP modules, configuration files, state and personalization providers, and other application services.

System HTTP Modules

HTTP modules are the ASP.NET counterpart of ISAPI filters. An HTTP module is a .NET Framework class that implements a particular interface. All ASP.NET applications inherit a few system HTTP modules as defined in the *machine.config* file. Preinstalled modules provide features such as authentication, authorization, and session-related services. Generally speaking, an HTTP module can preprocess and postprocess a request, and it intercepts and handles system events as well as events raised by other modules.

The good news is that you can write and register your own HTTP modules and make them plug into the ASP.NET runtime pipeline, handle system events, and fire their own events. In addition, you can adapt on a per-application basis the list of default HTTP modules. You can add custom modules and remove those that you don't need.

Application Configuration

The behavior of ASP.NET applications is subject to a variety of parameters; some are system-level settings, and some depend on the characteristics of the application. The common set of system parameters are defined in two files—*machine.config* and a machine level (global) *web.config*. All together, the two files contain machine-specific values for all supported settings. Machine settings are normally controlled by the system administrator, and applications should not be given write access to both files. These files are located outside the Web space of the application and, as such, cannot be reached even if an attacker succeeds in injecting malicious code into the system.

Note In ASP.NET 1.x, you have only one machine configuration file named machine.config. The original content of this file has been split between the two files I mentioned starting with ASP.NET 2.0.

Any application can override most of the default values stored in the machine configuration files by creating one or more application-specific *web.config* files. Almost all applications create a *web.config* file in their root folder. This file contains a subset of the machine settings and is written according to the same XML schema. The goal of the application-specific *web.config* is to override some of the default settings. Be aware, however, that not all settings that are defined at the machine level can be overridden in a child configuration file.

If the application contains child directories, you can define a *web.config* file for each directory. The scope of each configuration file is determined in a hierarchical, top-down manner. The settings that are valid for a page are determined by the sum of the changes that the various *web.config* files found along the way applied to the original machine configuration.

Any *web.config* file can extend, restrict, and override any type of settings defined at an upper level, including the machine level. If no configuration file exists in an application folder, the settings that are valid at the upper level are applied.

Application Services

Authentication, state management, and caching are all examples of essential services that the ASP.NET runtime environment supplies to running applications. Starting with ASP.NET 2.0, other services have been added to the list—including membership, role management, and personalization—as shown in Figure 1-5.

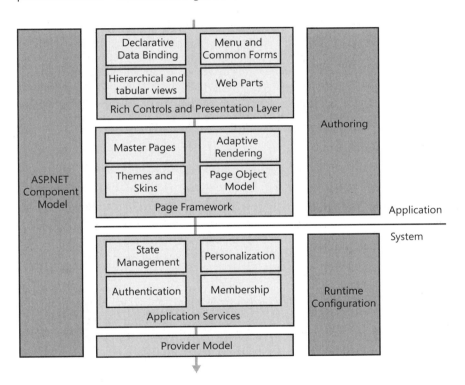

FIGURE 1-5 A more detailed view of the ASP.NET development stack. The arrow indicates the typical top-down application perspective, going down from the user interface to the system services.

Most application services must persist and retrieve some data for internal purposes. While doing so, a service chooses a data model and a storage medium, and it gets to the data through a particular sequence of steps. Applications based on these services are constrained by the design to using those settings—which usually include a fixed data schema, a pre-defined storage medium, or a hard-coded behavior. What if you don't like or don't want these restrictions?

Run-time configuration, as achieved through *machine.config* and *web.config* files, adds some more flexibility to your code. However, run-time configuration does not provide a definitive solution that is flexible enough to allow full customization of the service that would make it extensible and smooth to implement. A more definitive solution is provided in version 2.0 of ASP.NET, which formalizes and integrates into the overall framework of classes a design pattern that was originally developed and used in several ASP.NET Starter Kits. Known as the *provider model*, this pattern defines a common API for a variety of operations—each known as the *provider*. At the same time, the provider's interface contains several hooks for developers to take complete control over the internal behavior of the API, data schema used, and storage medium.

Important   The provider model is one of the most important and critical aspects of ASP.NET. A good understanding of it is crucial to conduct effective design and implementation of cutting-edge applications. The provider model is formalized starting with ASP.NET 2.0, but it is simply the implementation of a design pattern. As such, it is completely decoupled at its core from any platform and framework. So once you understand the basic idea, you can start using it in any application, even outside the boundaries of ASP.NET.

The ASP.NET Provider Model

There's a well-known design pattern behind the ASP.NET provider model—the *strategy* pattern. Defined, the strategy pattern indicates an expected behavior (say, sorting) that can be implemented through a variety of interchangeable algorithms (say, Quicksort or Mergesort). Each application then selects the algorithm that best fits while keeping the public, observable behavior and programming API intact.

The most notable feature of the strategy pattern is that it provides a way for an object, or an entire subsystem, to expose its internals so that a client can unplug the default implementation of a given feature and plug his own in. This is exactly what happens in ASP.NET for a number of services, including membership, roles, state management, personalization, and site navigation. The ASP.NET provider model is the ASP.NET implementation of the strategy pattern.

The Rationale Behind the Provider Model

The provider model is not an application feature that end users can see with their own eyes. In itself, it doesn't make an application show richer content, run faster, or be more responsive. The provider model is an infrastructural feature that improves an application's architecture by enabling developers and architects to operate under the hood of some system components.

At the same time, it enables developers to build new components that expose hooks for clients to plug in and customize behavior and settings. Implementing the strategy pattern doesn't transform an application into an open-source project, allowing anybody to modify anything. It simply means that you have a simple, elegant, and effective pattern to make certain parts of your application customizable by clients. At the same time, the ASP.NET implementation of the pattern—the provider model—makes you capable of customizing certain parts of the ASP.NET runtime environment through special classes, named providers, from which you can derive your own.

Exemplifying the Provider Model

To see an example of the provider model and its major benefits, let's look at Figure 1-6. The figure outlines the classic schema for authenticating a user. The blocks of the diagram follow closely the flow of operations in ASP.NET 1.1 and any Web applications on whatever platform and framework available.

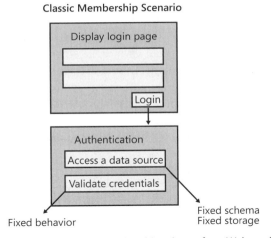

FIGURE 1-6 Classic membership schema for a Web application.

The user who attempts to connect to a protected page is shown a login page and invited to provide their credentials. Next, the name and password are passed on to a function, which is ultimately responsible for validating the user. ASP.NET can automatically check users against Windows accounts or, perhaps, a list of names in the *web.config* file. None of these approaches work well in a realistic Web application; in most cases, developers just end up writing a custom piece of code to validate credentials against a homemade data source. The schema and storage medium of the data source are fixed and determined by the developer. Likewise, the algorithm employed to validate credentials is constrained by the design.

Is there anything wrong with this solution? Not necessarily. It works just fine, puts you in control of everything, and can be adapted to work in other applications. The rub is that there's no well-defined pattern that emerges from this solution. Sure, you can port it from one application to the next, but overall the solution relates to the adapter pattern mostly like cut-and-paste relates to object-oriented inheritance.

Let's briefly consider another scenario—session state management. In ASP.NET 1.x, you can store the session state in a process separate from the running application—be it SQL Server or a Windows service (the ASP.NET state server). If you do so, though, you're constrained to using the data schema that ASP.NET hard-codes for you. Furthermore, imagine you're not a SQL Server customer. In this case, either you abandon the idea of storing session state to a database or you buy a set of licenses for SQL Server. Finally, there's nothing you can do about the internal behavior of the ASP.NET session module. If you don't like the way it, say, serializes data to the out-of-process storage, you can't change it. Take it or leave it—there's no intermediate choice.

Can you see the big picture? There are modules in ASP.NET that force you to take a fixed schema of data, a fixed storage medium, and a fixed internal behavior. The most that you can do is (sometimes) avoid using those modules and write your own from scratch, as we outlined in the membership example. However, rolling your own replacement is not necessarily a smart move. You end up with a proprietary and application-specific system that is not automatically portable from one application to another. In addition, if you hire new people, you have to train those people before they get accustomed to using your API. Finally, you have to put forth a lot of effort to build and test such a proprietary API and make it general enough to be reusable and extensible in a variety of contexts. (Otherwise, you get to reinvent the wheel time after time.)

In which way is the provider model a better solution? In the first place, it supplies a well-documented and common programming interface to perform common tasks. In addition, you gain the ability to completely control the internal business and data access logic of each API that falls under its umbrella.

In the end, in ASP.NET 1.1 you often have no other choice than writing your own API to roll certain functions the way you want. Starting with ASP.NET 2.0, the provider model offers a much better alternative. So much better that it's practically a crime not to use it.

Figure 1-7 revisits Figure 1-6 in light of the provider model.

Provider-based Scenario

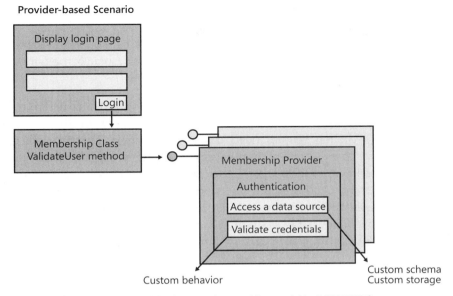

FIGURE 1-7 Membership revisited to use the provider model in ASP.NET 2.0.

ASP.NET 2.0 makes available a bunch of static methods on a global class—*Membership*. (We'll cover the membership API in great detail in Chapter 17.) At the application level, you always invoke the same method to perform the same operation (for example, validating user credentials, creating new users, changing passwords). Below this common API, though, you can plug in your own provider to do the job just the way you want. Writing a new provider is as easy as deriving a new class from a known base and overriding a few well-known methods. The selection of the current provider for a given task takes place in the configuration file.

Benefits of the Provider Model

In the ASP.NET implementation, the strategy pattern brings you two major benefits: extensive customization of the application's run-time environment, and code reusability. Several areas in ASP.NET are affected by the provider model. You can write providers to handle user membership and roles, persist session state, manage user profiles through personalization, and load site map information from a variety of sources. For example, by writing a provider you can change the schema of the data used to persist credentials and store this data in an Oracle or DB2 database. This level of customization of system components is unprecedented, and it opens up a new world of possibilities for application developers. At the same time, it gives you an excellent starting point for writing new providers and even extending the model to your own components.

If you look at ASP.NET 3.5 from the perspective of existing version 1.x applications, the provider model gains even more technical relevance because it is the key to code reuse and subsequent preservation of investments in programming and development time. As I pointed out, a realistic membership system in ASP.NET 1.1 requires you to roll your own API as far as validation and user management are concerned. What should you do when the decision to upgrade to ASP.NET 2.0 or 3.5 is made? Should you drop all that code to embrace the new dazzling membership API of the newest ASP.NET platforms? Or would you be better sticking to the old-fashioned and proprietary API for membership?

The provider model delivers the answer (and a good answer, indeed) in its unique ability to switch the underlying algorithm while preserving the overall behavior. This ability alone wouldn't be sufficient, though. You also need to adapt your existing code to make it pluggable in the new runtime environment. Another popular pattern helps out here—the adapter pattern. The declared intent of the adapter pattern is to convert a class A to an interface B that a client C understands. You wrap the existing code into a new provider class that can be seamlessly plugged into the existing ASP.NET 3.5 framework. You change the underlying implementation of the membership API, and you use your own schema and storage medium while keeping the top-level interface intact. And, more importantly, you get to fully reuse your code.

A Quick Look at the ASP.NET Implementation

The implementation of the ASP.NET provider model consists of three distinct elements—the provider class, configuration layer, and storage layer. The provider class is the component you plug into the existing framework to provide a desired functionality the way you want. The configuration layer supplies information used to identify and instantiate the actual provider. The storage layer is the physical medium where data is stored. Depending on the feature, it can be Active Directory, an Oracle or SQL Server table, an XML file, or whatever else.

The Provider Class

A provider class implements an interface known to its clients. In this way, the class provides clients with the functionality promised by that interface. Clients are not required to know anything about the implementation details of the interface. This code opacity allows for the magic of code driving other code it doesn't even know about. In the ASP.NET provider model, the only variation to the original definition of the strategy pattern is that base classes are used instead of interfaces.

In ASP.NET, a provider class can't just be any class that implements a given interface. Quite the reverse, actually. A provider class must inherit from a well-known base class. There is a base class for each supported type of provider. The base class defines the programming interface of the provider through a bunch of abstract methods.

All provider base classes derive from a common class named *ProviderBase*. This base class provides one overridable method—*Initialize*—through which the run-time environment passes any pertinent settings from configuration files. Figure 1-8 outlines the hierarchy of provider classes.

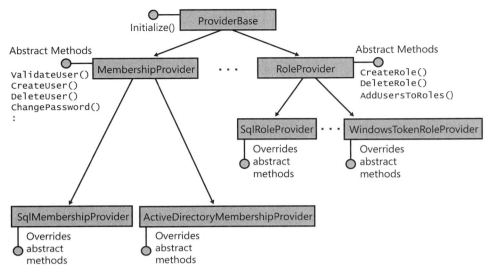

FIGURE 1-8 The hierarchy of provider classes.

Interfaces vs. Base Classes

Raise your hand if you are a developer who has never been involved in hours and hours of debate on the subject of interfaces versus base classes. It's a discussion that rarely comes to an end and always leave folks from different camps firmly holding to their respective positions. Should you use interfaces, or are base classes better? Which considerations is your answer based on? Consider the following fact, first.

Early builds of ASP.NET 2.0—the first version of ASP.NET to support the provider model—implemented the provider model literally with the definition of the strategy pattern   that is, through interfaces. In the Beta 1 timeframe, interfaces were replaced with base classes, and so it was with the released version. The ASP.NET team seemingly came to a conclusion on the issue, did it not?

An interface is a collection of logically related methods that contains only member definitions and no code. An interface type is a partial description of a type, which multiple classes can potentially support. In other words, a good interface is one that is implemented by a number of different types and encapsulates a useful, generalized piece of functionality that clients want to use. That's why many interfaces just end with the suffix "able", such as *IDisposable*, *IComparable*, and *IFormattable*. If an interface has only one useful implementing class, it is likely the offspring of a bad design choice. As a practical rule, new interfaces should be introduced sparingly and with due forethought.

A base class defines a common behavior and a common programming interface for a tree of child classes. Classes are more flexible than interfaces and support versioning.

If you add a new method to version 2.0 of a class, any existing derived classes continue to function unchanged, as long as the new method is not abstract. This is untrue for interfaces.

In light of these considerations, the emerging rule is that one should use base classes instead of interfaces whenever possible (which doesn't read as, "always use base classes"). To me, base classes appear to be an excellent choice, as far as the provider model is concerned.

In more general terms, the debate between base classes and interfaces has no easy answer. In some application-specific cases, in fact, one could argue that using a base class for a behavior that can be described with an interface takes away the option of deriving that new class from a custom base class that could lead to an overall better design. ASP.NET uses base classes for its provider model, and that is the pattern you must follow.

The Configuration Layer

Each supported provider type is assigned a section in the configuration file, which is where the default provider for the feature is set and all available providers are listed. If the provider sports public properties, default values for these properties can be specified through attributes. The contents of the section are passed as an argument to the *Initialize* method of the *ProviderBase* class—the only method that all providers have in common. Within this method, each provider uses the passed information to initialize its own state. Here's a snapshot of the configuration section for the membership provider.

```
<membership defaultProvider="AspNetSqlProvider">
    <providers>
        <add name="AspNetSqlProvider"
            type="System.Web.Security.SqlMembershipProvider, System.Web"
            connectionStringName="LocalSqlServer"
            enablePasswordRetrieval="false"
            enablePasswordReset="true"
            requiresQuestionAndAnswer="true"
            ...
            passwordFormat="Hashed" />
        ...
    </providers>
</membership>
```

The Storage Layer

All providers need to read and write information to a persistent storage medium. In many cases, two providers of the same type differ only by the storage they employ. Details of the storage medium are packed in the attributes of the provider in the *<providers>* section, as shown in the preceding code sample. For example, the preceding *AspNetSqlProvider* provider is the predefined membership provider that reads and writes to a SQL Server table. The connection string for the provider is specified through the *connectionStringName* attribute, which in turn refers to another centralized section of the configuration files that lists all available connection strings.

For the provider to work, any needed infrastructure (that is, database, tables, relationships) must exist. Setting up the working environment is a task typically accomplished at deployment time. ASP.NET makes it a breeze thanks to the Web site administration console, which is shown in Figure 1-9.

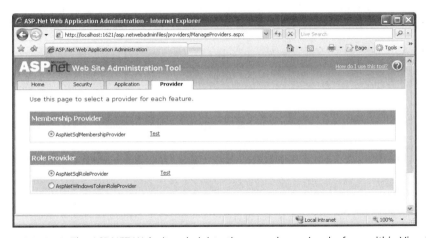

FIGURE 1-9 The ASP.NET Web site administration console you invoke from within Visual Studio.

Available Types of Providers

The provider model is used to achieve several tasks, the most important of which are as follows:

- The implementation of a read/write mechanism to persist the user profile
- The creation of a user-defined repository of user credentials that supports most common operations, such as checking a user for existence, adding and deleting users, and changing passwords
- The creation of a user-defined repository for user roles
- The definition of the site map
- The introduction of newer types of data storage for the session state

Table 1-1 shows the list of the provider classes available in ASP.NET.

TABLE 1-1 Available ASP.NET Provider Base Classes

Class	Description
MembershipProvider	Base class for membership providers used to manage user account information.
PersonalizationProvider	Base class for managing personalization for Web Parts components.
ProfileProvider	Base class for personalization providers used to persist and retrieve a user's profile information.
ProtectedConfigurationProvider	Base class for encryption providers used to encrypt information in configuration files.
RoleProvider	Base class for role providers used to manage user role information.
SessionStateStoreProviderBase	Base class for session state store providers. These providers are used to save and retrieve session state information from persistent storage media.
SiteMapProvider	Base class for managing site map information.
WebEventProvider	Base class for health monitoring providers that process system events.

The classes listed in Table 1-1 define an abstract method for each aspect that's customizable in the feature they represent. For example, regarding membership management, the class *MembershipProvider* exposes methods such as *ValidateUser*, *CreateUser*, *DeleteUser*, *ChangePassword*, and so forth. Note that you'll never use *MembershipProvider* in your code just because it's an abstract class. Instead, you'll use a derived class such as *SqlMembershipProvider* or, perhaps, *ActiveDirectoryMembershipProvider*. The same holds true for other types of providers.

Finally, if you're going to write a custom membership provider that wraps your existing code, you create a class that inherits from *MembershipProvider* or similar classes if other provider-based features are involved.

Note The provider architecture is one of ASP.NET 2.0's most important new features and also one of the most delicate with regard to applications. To prevent developers from producing buggy providers, the ASP.NET team supplies a made-to-measure provider toolkit that details what you can and cannot do in a provider, plus lots of sample code to serve as a guide. Writing a custom provider can be tricky for at least a couple of reasons. First, ASP.NET providers must be thread-safe. Second, their initialization step can lead you straight into a deadly reentrancy. Be sure you download the ASP.NET provider toolkit from the ASP.NET Developer Center (*msdn2.microsoft.com/en-us/asp.net/aa336558.aspx*) before you leap into a new provider project.

Conclusion

As part of the .NET Framework, ASP.NET allows you to take full advantage of features of the common-language runtime (CLR), such as type safety, inheritance, language interoperability, and versioning. ASP.NET builds on the successes of a variety of other platforms, including classic ASP, JSP, and LAMP and promotes a programming model that, although built on top of the stateless HTTP protocol, appears to be stateful and event-driven to programmers. ASP.NET 3.5, in particular, extends previous versions of the Microsoft Web platform with key additions such as WCF, LINQ, and AJAX support.

In this chapter, we first analyzed the component model that backs up ASP.NET Web pages and then went through the development stack from top (presentation layer and rich controls) to bottom (infrastructure and providers). The provider model—in the end, an implementation of the strategy pattern—is a key element in the new ASP.NET architecture and a pillar of support for new applications. Extensively applied, it allows you to customize several low-level aspects of the application's run-time environment and reuse large portions of existing code. Fully understood, it gives you a way to build new components that are flexible and extensible beyond imagination and, as such, seamless to plug in to a variety of projects and easier to customize for clients.

 ## Just the Facts

- In ASP.NET, you take full advantage of all CLR features such as type safety, inheritance, code access security, and language interoperability.

- At execution time, ASP.NET pages are represented by an instance of a class that descends from the Page class.

- The Page class is the ending point of a pipeline of modules that process any HTTP request.

- Only elements in an ASP.NET page marked with the runat attribute can be programmatically accessed when the page is executed on the server.

- Page elements devoid of the runat attribute are not processed on the server and are emitted verbatim.

- The runat attribute applies to virtually any possible tags you can use in an ASP.NET page, including custom and unknown tags.

- The process model is the sequence of operations needed to process a request. The selected process model determines which worker process takes care of running ASP.NET applications and under which account.

- ASP.NET applications run under a poorly privileged account.

■ The behavior of ASP.NET applications can be configured through a bunch of configuration files.

■ The ASP.NET provider model is an infrastructural feature that improves an application's architecture by enabling developers and architects to operate under the hood of some system components.

■ The ASP.NET provider model brings you two major benefits: extensive customization of the application's run-time environment and code reusability.

Chapter 2
Web Development in Microsoft Visual Studio 2008

No matter how you design and implement a Web application, at the end of the day it always consists of a number of pages bound to a public URL. The inexorable progress of Web-related technologies has not changed this basic fact, for the simple reason that it is the natural outcome of the simplicity of the HTTP protocol. As long as HTTP remains the under-lying transportation protocol, a Web application can't be anything radically different from a number of publicly accessible pages. When the application is anything different from this—for example, a Flash-powered site—it takes the serious risk of becoming an opaque box to search engines such as Google and Windows Search.

What's the role of Microsoft ASP.NET and Visual Studio 2008 in the development of Web applications?

ASP.NET provides an abstraction layer on top of HTTP with which developers build Web sites and Web-based front ends for enterprise systems. Thanks to ASP.NET, developers can work with high-level entities such as classes and components within the object-oriented paradigm. Development tools assist developers during their work and help to make the interaction with the ASP.NET framework as seamless and productive as possible. Development tools are ulti-mately responsible for the application or the front end being created and deployed to users. They offer their own programming model and force developers to play by those rules.

The key development tool for building ASP.NET applications and front ends is Visual Studio 2008—the successor to Visual Studio 2005. It has a lot of new features and goodies expressly designed for Web developers to overcome some of the limitations that surfaced from using previous versions.

In this chapter, we'll review the main characteristics and features of Visual Studio 2008 as far as ASP.NET applications are concerned. We'll see how to create and edit projects and how you can target a particular .NET platform. We'll tour around integrated development environment (IDE) features and deployment capabilities, and also explore some new keywords in the supported languages.

Introducing Visual Studio 2008

Visual Studio is a container environment that integrates the functionality of multiple visual designers. You have a designer for building Windows applications, one for building Web sites, one for building Windows Communication Foundation (WCF) services, and so on. All items required by your work—such as references, connectors to data sources, folders, and files—are grouped at two levels: solutions and projects. A solution container contains multiple projects, whereas a project container typically stores multiple items. Using these containers, you manage settings for your solution as a whole or for individual projects. Each item in the project displays its own set of properties through a secondary window—the Properties window.

Let's start with a quick summary of the principal characteristics of Visual Studio 2008 that have been inherited from its predecessor.

Visual Studio Highlights

The version of Visual Studio labeled with the 2005 attribute marked a milestone in the history of the product. Visual Studio 2005 matched a long list of user requirements to really provide a simpler and more friendly way to create ASP.NET applications. Here's some highlights of features that have been maintained, if not improved, in Visual Studio 2008.

No IIS Dependency

Internet Information Services (IIS) is not strictly required for Visual Studio to work. Visual Studio 2008 ships, in fact, with a local Web server that makes IIS optional, at least for quick testing and debugging purposes. Figure 2-1 shows the user interface of the embedded Web server.

Note that the local Web server represents only the default option. If you open the project from an existing IIS virtual directory, Visual Studio 2008 uses IIS to run and test the application.

The embedded Web server is only a small piece of executable code and can't replace all the features of a full-blown Web server such as IIS. It works only with individual pages and doesn't include any of the extra features of IIS, such as the metabase.

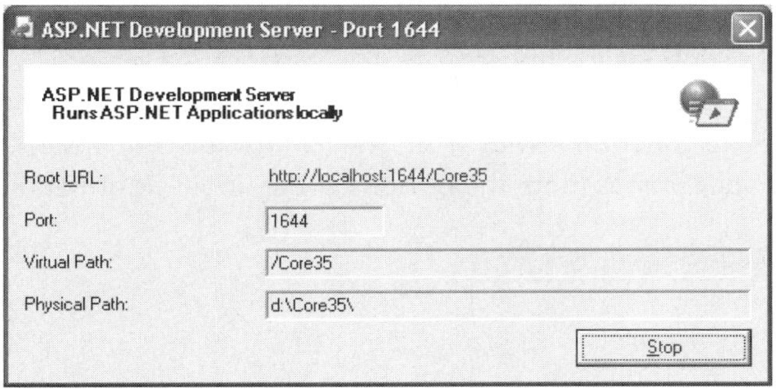

FIGURE 2-1 The local Web server in action in Visual Studio 2008.

Multiple Ways to Access Web Sites

Visual Studio 2008 supports multiple ways to open Web sites. In addition to using FrontPage Server Extensions (FPSE) to connect to a remote Web site, you can access your source files by using FTP or a direct file system path. You can also directly access the local installation of IIS, browse the existing hierarchy of virtual directories, and access existing virtual roots or create new ones. You can open your Web site using a file system path or an IIS virtual directory. In the former case, the local Web server is used to test the site, as Figure 2-2 shows.

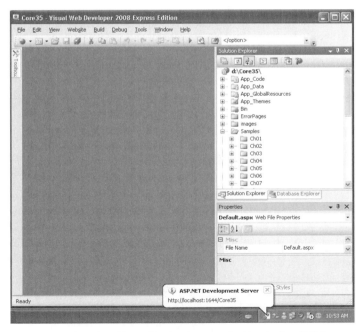

FIGURE 2-2 The ASP.NET application is controlled by the local Web server if the Web site is opened from a file system path.

The interaction with IIS is greatly simplified too, as Figure 2-3 shows. When you try to open a Web site, you are given a few options to choose from. You can locate a project by using a file system path, using the IIS hierarchy of virtual directories (only the local IIS), using FTP, or by just typing the URL of the site configured with FPSE. The IIS tab also contains buttons to create new virtual roots and applications (note the buttons in the upper right-hand corner).

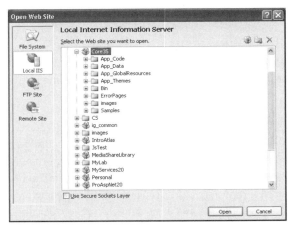

FIGURE 2-3 Navigating your way through the IIS hierarchy to locate an existing virtual directory to open.

Note You can open existing Web sites using the FTP protocol and then create and edit files. However, you must have access to the FTP server and read and write permissions for a particular FTP directory. The directory must already exist because Visual Studio 2008 cannot create a new Web site via FTP.

Project Output Build Options

The old Visual Studio 2005 originally shipped with a project model that didn't compile everything in the site into a single assembly, as its predecessor Visual Studio 2003 did. Instead, it was built on the modified ASP.NET 2.0 compilation model and given the ability to dynamically recognize file types based on the folder they belong to. In this way, not only are changes to *.aspx* files immediately caught, but so are those made to constituent *.cs* or *.vb* files and a variety of accessory resource files. This model results in a sort of dynamic compilation for code-behind classes.

There are pros and cons about the ASP.NET 2.0 compilation model, and some additional parameters need to be considered thoroughly before one can come to a reasonable conclusion about the model. A few months later, Microsoft released a Web Application Project (WAP) extension to Visual Studio 2005 to enable it to maintain projects by compiling everything into a single assembly. (WAP was later incorporated into the Visual Studio 2005 Service Pack 1.)

In Visual Studio 2008, WAP is natively part of the product, although you won't find it available in the Web site menu. If you want to create an ASP.NET Web site based on the ASP.NET 2.0 compilation model, you choose the Web Site option from the File|New menu. If you want to create a WAP, instead, you pick up the Project option from the File|New menu and then select an ASP.NET Web Application.

Solution files (*.sln) are mandatory for WAPs but optional in the other case (ASP.NET Web sites). For ASP.NET Web sites, the root Web directory defines a Web project; you just add files to the directory and they are in the project. If a file doesn't immediately show up, you right-click on the Solution Explorer window and select Refresh Folder. Solution files are still useful to manage multiple projects, but they don't need to live in the Web directory.

Copying a Web Project

Another long-awaited feature worth a mention is the *Copy Web Site* feature. In earlier versions of Visual Studio, duplicating and synchronizing a Web project onto another machine, or simply moving it to another location within the same machine, was not a hassle-free task. Basically, it was completely up to you and to any FTP-based tool you could come up with. If your server host supported FPSE, you could go through an integrated wizard. Otherwise, the most viable solution was using raw File Transfer Protocol (FTP). (Moving a Web site within the same network or machine is a similar experience, except that you can use Windows Explorer.)

Sure the overall procedure was not smooth; but it was hardly a mission-impossible task because only a brute-force copy is required. But what if, with good reason, you wanted to move modified files only? Or only files that match given criteria? In these cases, you were left alone to find and copy only these files. (On the other hand, I'd say, who's better qualified than you for this kind of task?)

Starting with Visual Studio 2005, by selecting a menu item you can copy your current Web site to another local or remote location. The Copy Web Site function is a sort of integrated FTP tool that enables you to easily move files around. Figure 2-4 shows a glimpse of the feature in the latest Visual Studio 2008.

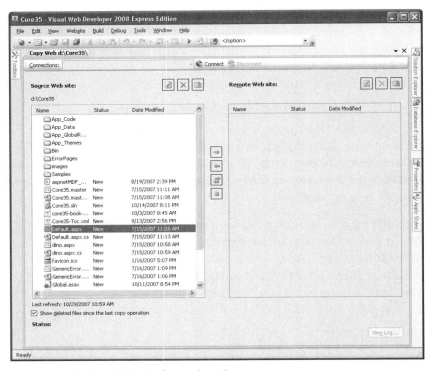

FIGURE 2-4 The Copy Web Site feature in action.

You connect to the target destination, select the desired copy mode—either Overwrite Source To Target Files, Target To Source Files, or Sync Up Source And Target Projects—and then proceed with the physical copying of files. As Figure 2-5 shows, you can copy files to and from virtual and physical folders, within or across the machine's boundaries.

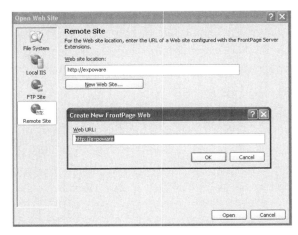

FIGURE 2-5 Connecting to a remote site to make a copy of the local project.

As you can see yourself, the Copy Web Site function is ideal for deployment especially in hosting environment scenarios in which you need to manage live server files. In addition, the Visual Studio 2008 tool can operate as a synchronization tool, which is helpful to quickly test applications in different scenarios and configurations.

Smarter Editing with Microsoft IntelliSense

Visual Studio 2008 supports standalone file editing and doesn't require a project to edit a single file on disk. So if you double-click an *.aspx* file in Windows Explorer, Visual Studio 2008 starts up and lets you edit the source code. Unlike with some previous versions, IntelliSense and related syntax-coloring work effectively. The page can be viewed live in the embedded browser through the local Web server.

Note that IntelliSense now works everywhere within the source file, including within data-binding expressions, page directives, and code inline in *.aspx* files. (See Figure 2-6.)

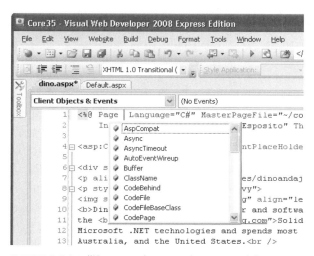

FIGURE 2-6 IntelliSense works everywhere around the source code of the page.

Visual Studio 2008–Specific New Features

The true added value of Visual Studio 2008—and perhaps the primary reason to consider upgrades—is the boost it gives to the developer's productivity. Lots of wizards, smart and context-sensitive popup windows, effective debuggers, and visual designers are all examples of facilities that might not necessarily make any code automatically smarter, but will certainly help developers to focus on key points while skimming over chores, repetitive tasks, and overzealous procedures.

The recipe of Visual Studio is always the same, although it's perfected a bit more each time: improving the developer productivity using the latest technologies, supporting the newest .NET Framework, and aiming at improving the management of the entire application life cycle.

Multitarget Projects

As you might have noticed, past releases of Visual Studio supported only one specific version of the .NET Framework. For years, my desktop was swarming with shortcuts to different versions of Visual Studio based on the projects I maintained at the time: Visual Studio 2002 for .NET Framework 1.0 applications, Visual Studio 2003 for .NET Framework 1.1, and Visual Studio 2005 for .NET Framework 2.0 applications. Finally, Visual Studio 2008 introduces a very cool feature called *multitargeting*. Quite simply, it is the loudly-demanded capability of creating applications for various versions of the .NET Framework.

Multitargeting brings two main benefits to the table. First, you no longer need to install side-by-side two or even three different versions of Visual Studio to deal with the various clients and projects you maintain. Second, you are no longer subliminally invited to upgrade to the next, super-cool version of the .NET Framework because of the new, super-cool time-saving features of the next Visual Studio. One IDE fits all .NET Frameworks, you could say. All frameworks? Really? Well, not exactly. (See Figure 2-7.)

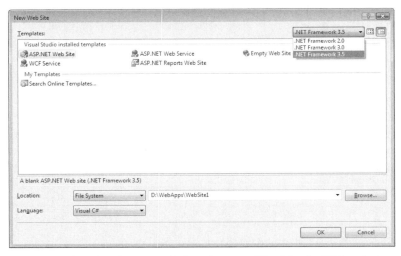

FIGURE 2-7 Choosing the target platform for a new Visual Studio 2008 project on a Windows Vista machine.

Multitargeting in Visual Studio 2008 starts with the .NET Framework 2.0 and should continue for most of the foreseeable future versions. Significant changes in the common language runtime (CLR) that occurred between version 1.1 and 2.0 of the .NET Framework made it impossible to extend multitargeting to any older versions of the framework.

 Warning The multitarget option is not available on Visual Studio 2008 Web Express Edition. You can work only on .NET 3.5 Web sites.

The nice thing about multitargeting is that any piece of the Visual Studio 2008 user interface adapts to the target platform. The toolbox of controls, compiler settings, the list of assemblies to reference, IntelliSense on objects and, of course, binaries are all specific to the selected platform.

The target platform is not a definitive choice. At any moment, in fact, you can upgrade or downgrade to any of the supported targets. You do this from the property pages of the project in the Solution Explorer, as shown in Figure 2-8.

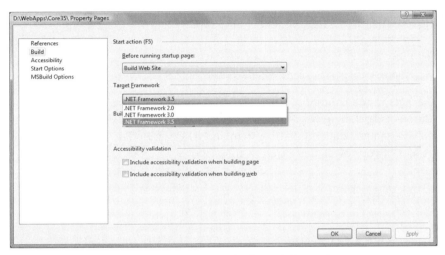

FIGURE 2-8 Upgrade the target .NET Framework of an existing project.

Should you install Visual Studio 2008 if you're mostly maintaining existing .NET Framework 2.0 applications? Clearly, the big news about Visual Studio 2008 is the support it offers for 3.x .NET applications. However, even from a platform-agnostic perspective it has something to offer to developers. Precisely, it's the largely improved set of facilities for developers, with particular attention paid to Web developers. The JavaScript debugger, cascading style sheet (CSS) and master pages designer, LINQ helper tools, and IntelliSense for JavaScript are all features available independently from the target platform.

The JavaScript Debugger

The Visual Studio 2008 debugger has been enhanced in various ways, including the remote debugging support for Windows Vista and debugging support for LINQ queries and WCF services. Web developers, in particular, welcome the better support for script debugging. You can set a breakpoint in JavaScript code and proceed from there step by step. (See Figure 2-9.)

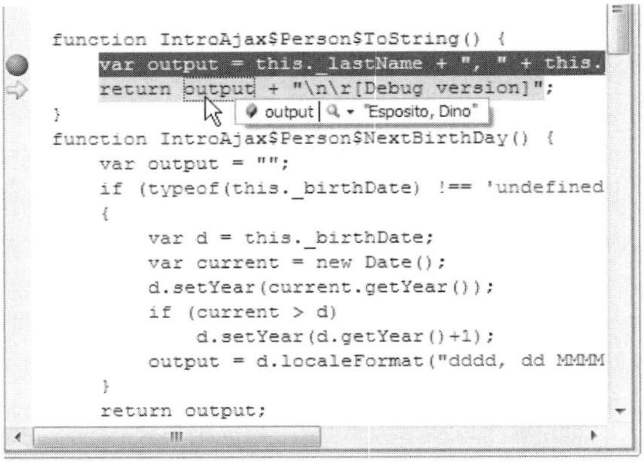

```
function IntroAjax$Person$ToString() {
    var output = this._lastName + ", " + this.
    return output + "\n\r[Debug version]";
}                        ⚙ output  Q ▾  "Esposito, Dino"
function IntroAjax$Person$NextBirthDay() {
    var output = "";
    if (typeof(this._birthDate) !== 'undefined
    {
        var d = this._birthDate;
        var current = new Date();
        d.setYear(current.getYear());
        if (current > d)
            d.setYear(d.getYear()+1);
        output = d.localeFormat("dddd, dd MMMM
    }
    return output;
```

FIGURE 2-9 Setting a breakpoint in a referenced script file.

You have access to the content of each JavaScript variable using the same interface in use for managed objects, including watch windows and data tips. When you're stepping through the debugger, you can navigate inside of system and AJAX script files as well as any referenced JavaScript files of your own. (See Figure 2-10.)

FIGURE 2-10 Stepping through system JavaScript files.

Note that for the script debugger to work, you must ensure that script debugging is not disabled in the browser you're testing. For Internet Explorer, you check this setting by bringing up the Options dialog box, selecting the Advanced tab, and looking for the Disable Script Debugging (Internet Explorer) check box.

IntelliSense for JavaScript

JavaScript objects are now fully discovered and explored by IntelliSense. When you hit the dot (.) key following the name of a JavaScript variable, a small and familiar window pops up with the list of callable members on that object. (See Figure 2-11.)

It works for both native objects (for example, the *Date* object in Figure 2-11) and user-defined JavaScript objects, including ASP.NET AJAX JavaScript objects.

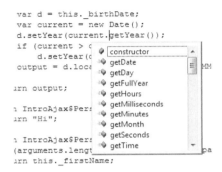

FIGURE 2-11 IntelliSense on JavaScript objects.

CSS Designer

One of the most pleasant surprises that Web developers will find in Visual Studio 2008 is its significantly improved HTML and CSS designer. When an ASP.NET page is being edited, a Format menu appears on the menu bar that contains a Manage Styles item. The subsequent tool window shows all the cascading style sheets and their corresponding rules for the page you are currently editing. It is required that the page be in design mode or at least in a combined view of markup and source (split view). (See Figure 2-12.)

When you select an HTML element or ASP.NET server control, the CSS designer window shows you all the settings currently applied to it. The designer also gives you a chance to modify any of the values using the CSS property grid.

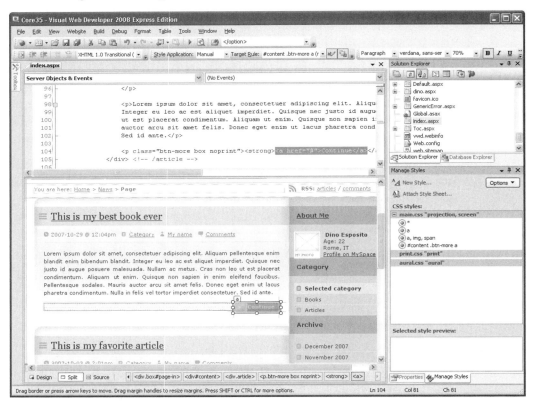

FIGURE 2-12 The CSS designer in action.

New Language Features

In Visual Studio 2008, the C# compiler supports a richer language with some interesting new features. Some are time-saving features that basically move onto the compiler the burden of creating some required code; some are just new capabilities added to the language and backed by the underlying .NET Framework.

I'm illustrating the new language features with respect to C#. It should be noted, though, that analogous features also exist in Visual Basic .NET.

Extension Methods

Extension methods are a way to extend the contract of a class by adding new methods without creating a derived class and without resorting to a related set of partial classes. Extension methods add a *duck-typing* flavor to a strongly typed, compiled environment such as the

CLR. The expression *duck-typing* refers to a programming style typical of many dynamic languages (for example, Python, Ruby, JavaScript) where you pay more attention to the actual set of methods and properties exposed by an object rather than its inheritance from a particular class. The expression *duck-typing*, in fact, descends from the following test: *If it walks like a duck and quacks like a duck, then call it a duck*. In a duck-typed language, you can call a given method on an object of any type. If the object lacks the method, you then get a run-time error.

In practice, you use extension methods to add helpful methods to a given class, regardless of the original contract exposed by the class and known to perspective callers. If you have no access to the source code of the class and still want to extend it, in Visual Studio 2008 you define an extension. Extension methods can be defined for any class, including native classes of the .NET Framework. Here's how to extend the *System.String* class with new methods such as *IsDate* and *ToDate*:

```
public static class StringExtensions
{
    public static bool IsDate(this string content)
    {
        DateTime date;
        bool result = DateTime.TryParse(content, out date);
        return result;
    }

    public static DateTime ToDate(this string content)
    {
        DateTime date;
        bool result = DateTime.TryParse(content, out date);
        if (result)
            return date;
        else
            return DateTime.MinValue;
    }
}
```

An extension method is defined as a static method on a static class. The binding between the method (say, *IsDate*) and type (say, *System.String*) is established through the keyword *this* in the method's prototype:

```
public static bool IsDate(this string content)
```

The type that follows the keyword *this* is treated as the type to extend. Figure 2-13 shows IntelliSense in action on the extended *System.String* type.

```
public partial class Samples_Ch02_ExtMet_TestExt : System.Web.UI.Page
{
    protected void Page_Load(object sender, EventArgs e)
    {
    }

    public void Button1_Click(object sender, EventArgs e)
    {
        string content = TextBox1.Text;
        if (content.IsDate())
        {
            DateT   IndexOf              t.ToDate();
            Label   IndexOfAny           Days(1).ToString("dd MMMM yyyy");
                    Insert
        }           IsDate               (extension) bool string.IsDate()
        else        IsInt32
        {           IsNormalized
            Label   LastIndexOf          alid date.";
        }           LastIndexOfAny
    }               Length
}                   Normalize
```

FIGURE 2-13 IntelliSense shows dynamic extensions to the *String* type.

The following code snippet illustrates how you can use these new methods in your code:

```
void Button1_Click(object sender, EventArgs e)
{
    string content = TextBox1.Text;
    if (content.IsDate())
    {
        DateTime date = content.ToDate();
        Label1.Text = date.AddDays(1).ToString("dd MMMM yyyy");
    }
    else
        Label1.Text = "Not a valid date.";
}
```

Extension methods are checked at compile time and can also be applied to any parent class or interface in the .NET Framework.

Note Extension methods can be used to implement a feature that looks very similar to mixins. Overall, a mixin is a sort of interface with some implemented methods. A class that implements a mixin includes, but does not inherit, all the members on the mixin's interface. Latest versions of C# and Visual Basic .NET don't natively support mixins, even though instructing the compilers to produce the code for it didn't appear to be a huge effort for the developers of the latest versions of C# and Visual Basic .NET. With extension methods, you can simulate mixins in the latest versions of C# and Visual Basic .NET by creating groups of methods and adding them to an existing class without the mechanism of partial classes or inheritance. Why are mixins superior or just preferable to an abstract class? You implement a mixin; you inherit an abstract class. By using mixins, you import the benefit of an existing piece of code without employing a base class.

Automatic Properties

Automatic properties is a feature that instructs the compiler to automatically add a default implementation for the *get/set* methods of a class property. The following code is valid in an interface in previous versions of C#. It is perfectly legal, instead, in a class compiled with the newest C# compiler:

```
public string CompanyName { get; set;}
```

The compiler automatically expands the code as shown here:

```
private string companyName;
public string CompanyName
{
    get { return companyName; }
    set { companyName = value; }
}
```

It is worth noting that automatically generated *get/set* properties are *not* equivalent to public fields. From a metadata perspective, properties and fields are quite different entities. The code generated for each is different. The key thing that is going on here is that you delegate the creation of some repetitive code to the compiler. Automatic properties are clearly not an option when you need to do more than just store a value in the *get/set* methods. Using automatic properties is not a non-return option: at any later time, you can always come back and provide your own *get/set* methods that contain any logic you need.

Object Initializers

Object initializers are another great piece of syntactic sugar that might speed up the creation of the code needed to initialize an object. Instead of going through a potentially long list of assignment instructions, you can code as shown here:

```
Person person = new Person { FirstName="John", LastName="Doe", Age=24 };
```

The idea can be extended to collections, as in the following code snippet:

```
List<Person> friends = new List<Person> {
    new Person { FirstName="Nancy", LastName="Davolio", Age=28 },
    new Person { FirstName="Andrew", LastName="Fuller", Age=35 },
    :
};
```

Compared to the syntax required in Visual Studio 2005, the savings is pretty clear and, for large procedures, can easily add up to dozens of lines of code.

Type Inference and Anonymous Types

The *var* keyword is another interesting new entry in the latest version of C#. Used to qualify a variable, it doesn't indicate a late-bound reference, as its rather popular JavaScript counterpart does. Instead, it merely indicates that the developer doesn't know the type of the variable at the time he's writing the code. However, the type won't be determined at run time (late-binding); instead, the compiler will infer the type from the expression assigned to the *var* variable. For this reason, an initial value assignment is required to avoid a compiler error. When the *var* keyword is used, a strongly typed reference is always generated.

The *var* keyword enables another cool feature of the latest C# language—anonymous types. Quite simply, an anonymous type is an unnamed type that you define using the same object initializer syntax mentioned earlier:

```
var person = new { FirstName="Nancy", LastName="Davolio", Age=28 };
```

For the CLR, anonymous and named types are exactly the same entity. Anonymous types can be used in a variety of scenarios, but they have been introduced primarily to support LINQ queries.

LINQ Operators

As I'll cover in more detail in Chapter 10, both C# and Visual Basic .NET feature a set of SQL-like language operators specifically designed to back queries. Currently, developers have to use a different application programming interface (API) to retrieve data from different repositories. It will be SQL for relational databases, XQuery and XPath for XML documents, and methods on some interface (for example, *ICollection*) for collections and arrays. The main goal of LINQ is unifying this model by providing an ad hoc framework. Nicely enough, this query framework is wired to some new keywords in C# and Visual Basic. The following code snippet gives you a valuable glimpse of LINQ in action:

```
int[] fiboNumbers = new int[] {0,1,1,2,3,5,8,13,21,34};
var data = from n in fiboNumbers
           where n % 2 == 0
           select n;
```

As weird as it might seem, this is C# code that compiles in Visual Studio 2008. The new keywords are *from*, *where*, and *select*. Their meaning is really close to the meaning that analogous keywords have in SQL. Translated to a human language, the query assigns to the resulting variable all elements in the queryable object (a collection, in this case) that match the specified condition (all even numbers in this case). We'll return to LINQ queries and syntax in Chapter 10.

Create an ASP.NET Web Site Project

Let's go further and create a sample ASP.NET Web site project with Visual Studio 2008. You first create a new Web site by choosing the corresponding command on the File, New menu. The dialog box that appears prompts you for the

If you select the Web Site option, Visual Studio generates the minimum number of files for building a Web site. Basically, it creates a default *.aspx* page and an empty *App_Data* directory. The root directory of the site implicitly defines a Web project. Any file or folder added or created under the root is automatically part of the project.

Page Design Features

The ASP.NET front end of an application can include several types of entities, the most important of which are pages. To edit a Web page, you can choose between three views—Design, Split, and Source. The Design view displays the HTML layout, lets you select and edit controls and static elements, and provides a graphical preview of the page. The Source view shows the HTML markup along with the inline code. The markup is syntax-colored and enriched by features such as IntelliSense, tips, and autocompletion. Finally, the Split view splits the screen real estate in two and provides both design and source views.

You choose the template of the item to add to the site from the menu shown in Figure 2-14.

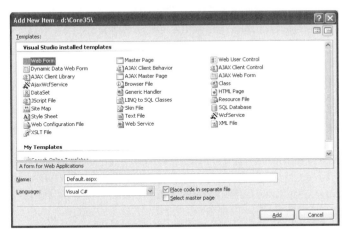

FIGURE 2-14 Item templates supported by Visual Studio 2008.

Note the two check boxes that appear at the bottom of the window. You can choose to keep the code of the page in a separate file and to associate the current page with a master page. Master pages are a feature of ASP.NET that we'll discuss thoroughly in Chapter 6. Before we get to add some code to build a sample page, let's review some design-time features of the page.

Master Pages

The master page is a single file that defines the template for a set of pages. Similar to an ordinary *.aspx* page, the master contains replaceable sections that are each marked with a unique ID. Pages in an application that will inherit the structure defined in the master reference the master page in their *@Page* directive or even programmatically. A page based on a master is said to be a *content page*. One master page can be bound to any number of content pages. Master pages are completely transparent to end users. When working with an application, a user sees and invokes only the URL of content pages. If a content page is requested, the ASP.NET runtime applies a different compilation algorithm and builds the dynamic class as the merge of the master and the content page.

By using master pages, a developer can create a Web site in which various physical pages share a common layout. You code the shared user interface and functionality in the master page and make the master contain named placeholders for content that the derived page will provide. The key advantage is that shared information is stored in a single place—the master page—instead of being replicated in each page. Second, the contract between the master and content page is fixed and determined by the ASP.NET Framework. No change in the application or constituent controls can ever break the link established between master and content.

> **Important** ASP.NET master pages are *one* way of building Web pages. In no way are master pages the only or preferred way of building Web sites. You should use master pages only if you need to duplicate portions of your user interface or if your application lends itself to being (re) designed in terms of master and content pages.

Nested Master Pages

Master pages can be nested, meaning that you can have one master page reference another page as its master. For example, in a large site an overall master page can define the look of the site and then content areas can be created using distinct masters that each partner or content manager can populate and personalize. Another good example is when you have sites that users can customize and choose, say, between a single-column or two-column layout. In this case, you can have a global master to create the look and feel and then a child master for the layout of choice.

Nested master pages are supported since ASP.NET 2.0. The catch is that Visual Studio 2005 didn't support the design of nested masters very well. Thankfully, this capability changes radically with Visual Studio 2008, where nested master pages are fully supported in the page designer.

Content Pages

The master defines the common parts of a certain group of pages and leaves placeholders for customizable regions. Each content page, in turn, defines what the content of each region has to be for a particular *.aspx* page. A content page is a special type of ASP.NET page, as it is allowed to contain only *<asp:Content>* tags. Any classic HTML tags—including client-side *<script>* and comments—are not allowed and, if used, raise compile errors.

The reason for this lies in the implementation of the master page feature. Because the content regions are substituted into the master page placeholders, the destination for any literal markup (that is, comments, script, or other tags) would be ambiguous, because the same kind of content is also allowed in the master.

Visual Studio offers a special Design view of content pages, as Figure 2-15 demonstrates. The view contains as many drawing surfaces as there are content regions in the master. At the same time, the master layout is displayed in the background grayed out to indicate that it's there but you can't access it.

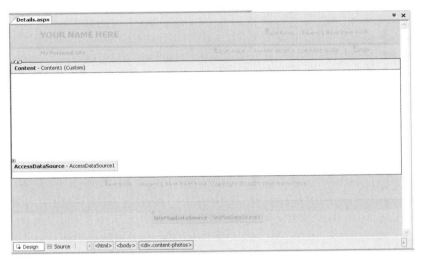

FIGURE 2-15 Content pages in Visual Studio 2008.

 Important Content pages can be used only in conjunction with master pages. A Web Forms page silently becomes a content page when you check the Select Master Page option in the dialog box shown in Figure 2-14.

Code-Behind Classes

When you add new Web Forms and require code and layout separation, a C# (or Visual Basic) class file is created along with the *.aspx* file in the same folder. The class file is named after the .aspx resource simply by adding a language extension. For example, if the Web Forms is named *WebForm1.aspx*, the corresponding code-behind class is named *WebForm1.aspx.cs*. This name is just the default name, and it obeys the default naming convention. Although it is not recommended for the sake of consistency, you should feel free to rename the class file to whatever name you like.

Nothing bad can happen to your application if you make it use inline code instead of code and layout separation. Nonetheless, real-world pages need a good amount of server code, and appending all that code to the *<script>* tag of the *.aspx* file makes the file significantly harder to read, edit, and maintain. Code-behind, on the other hand, is based on the idea that each Web Forms page is bound to a separate class file that contains any code that is relevant to the page. The code-behind class ends up being the basis of the dynamically generated page class that the ASP.NET runtime creates for each requested .aspx resource. All the server code you need to associate to the .aspx resource flows into the code-behind class. The code-behind model promotes object orientation, leads to modular code, and supports code and layout separation, allowing developers and designers to work concurrently to some extent.

The Toolbox of Controls

A Web Forms page is mostly made of controls—either predefined HTML and Web controls, user controls, or custom controls. Except for user controls (*.ascx* files), all the others are conveniently listed in the editor's toolbox. (See Figure 2-16.) The toolbox can be toggled on and off, and it is an easy way to pick up the control of choice and drop it onto the Web form via a drag-and-drop operation. The toolbox is visible only if *.aspx* resources are selected in whatever view mode.

The toolbox is widely customizable and supports the addition of new controls as well as the creation of new user-defined tabs. Controls defined in a project within the current solution are automatically added to the toolbox.

FIGURE 2-16 The Visual Studio 2008 toolbox.

Editor's Special Capabilities

The Visual Studio 2008 code editor presents some interesting features that prove the development team's commitment to excellence and creating satisfaction among all users. I'd like to call your attention to a few of them: markup preservation, improved tab insertion logic and indentation, and target schema validation.

Visual Studio 2008 preserves the formatting of your HTML edits and doesn't even attempt to reformat the source as you switch between views. At the same time, it comes with powerful features for indentation and tag formatting that you can optionally turn on.

In Figure 2-17, you see the list of supported client targets.

FIGURE 2-17 The list of client targets for which Visual Studio can cross-check your markup.

Once you select a target, the whole editing process is adapted to the features of the specified device. Want a quick example? Imagine you select Netscape Navigator 4.0 (NN4) as the client target. NN4 doesn't recognize the *<iframe>* tag; instead, it sports the *<layer>* tag with nearly the same characteristics. As Figure 2-18 shows, Visual Studio detects the difference and handles it correctly. IntelliSense doesn't list *iframe* but prompts you for *layer*. If you are insistent and type in *<iframe>*, anyway, a squiggle shows up to catch your attention.

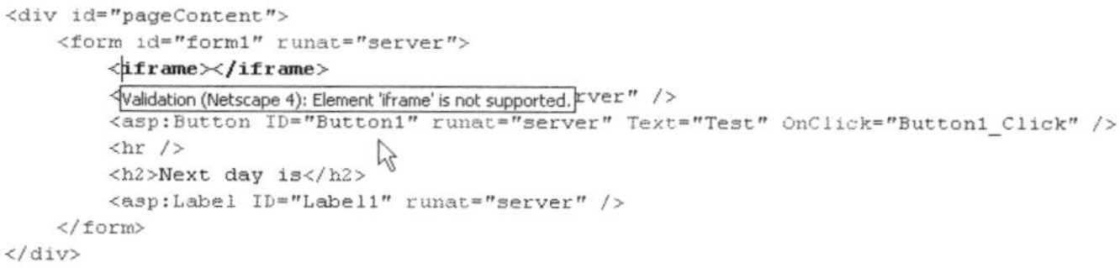

```
<div id="pageContent">
    <form id="form1" runat="server">
        <iframe></iframe>
        Validation (Netscape 4): Element 'iframe' is not supported. ver" />
        <asp:Button ID="Button1" runat="server" Text="Test" OnClick="Button1_Click" />
        <hr />
        <h2>Next day is</h2>
        <asp:Label ID="Label1" runat="server" />
    </form>
</div>
```

FIGURE 2-18 The code editor is sensitive to the selected client target schema.

Code Refactoring

When a *.vb* or a *.cs* file is open for editing in Visual Studio 2008, a new menu appears on the top-most menu strip—the Refactor menu, shown in Figure 2-19.

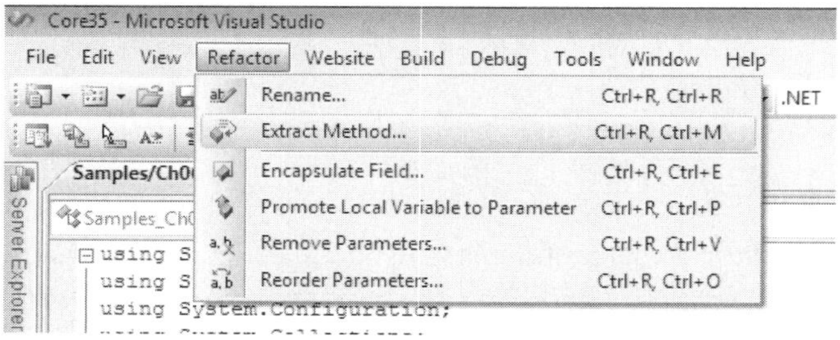

FIGURE 2-19 The new menu for helping developers quickly refactor the code of classes. This menu has fewer items in the Visual Studio 2008 Express Edition.

As you can see, the menu provides advanced facilities for code editing. Among other things, you can extract a block of code and transform it into a new method or rename a member all the way through. The refactor feature doesn't disappoint when it comes to managing properties. Admittedly, one of most boring tasks when writing classes is turning a field into a property with *get* and *set* accessors. Imagine you have a field like the following one:

```
private int _counters;
```

At a certain point, you might realize that a full-featured property would be better. Instead of typing code yourself, you just select the line and refactor to encapsulate the field. Needless to say, the menu item is *Refactor|Encapsulate field*. With the power of a click, the old code becomes the following:

```
public int Counters
{
    get
    {
        return _counters;
    }

    set
    {
        _counters = value;
    }
}
```

You are free to change the public name of the property and, of course, to flesh out the bodies of the *get/set* accessors.

Import/Export of IDE Features

It is common for developers to move a project from one machine to another. This happens for a variety of reasons. For example, you might use multiple machines for test purposes; you continually swing between the client's site and your own office; you are an absolute workaholic who just can't spend a night home without working.

Typically, the various machines have Visual Studio installed with the same set of features, and although it's not necessary, they share the same set of IDE settings. To feel comfortable with the environment, you might have developed macros, reordered menus and toolbars, added new controls to the toolbox, created new project templates, and assigned preferences for colors and fonts. This wealth of information is not easy to catalog, organize, and persist if you have to do that manually.

Figure 2-20 shows the new Import And Export Settings Wizard associated with the Tools menu. You select the IDE settings you want to persist and save them to a file. The file can be created anywhere and is given a *.vssettings* extension. In spite of the extension, it is an XML file.

FIGURE 2-20 The wizard for importing and exporting IDE settings.

Adding Code to the Project

Adding code to the project mostly means that you added Web Forms to the project and now need to hook up some of the page events or events that controls in the form generate. In addition, you might want to add some classes to the project that represent tailor-made functionalities not otherwise available.

Filling a Web Forms page is easy and intuitive. You open the form in layout mode and drag and drop controls from the toolbox onto it. Next, you move elements around and configure their properties. If needed, you can switch to the Source view and manually type the HTML markup the way you want it to be.

A pleasant surprise for many developers is that you can drag and drop controls from the toolbox directly into the Source view; instead of viewing the control graphically rendered, you see the corresponding markup code. Similarly, you can edit the properties of a server control by selecting it in the Design view or highlighting the related HTML in the Source view. (The Split view offers both options at the same time.) Each control deployed on the form can have its own design-time user interface through which you can configure properties for the run time.

Defining Event Handlers

Adding code to a Web Form page means handling some page's or control's events. How do you write an event handler for a particular page element? To try it out, place a button on a form and double-click. Visual Studio switches to the Source view and creates an empty event handler for the control's default event. For a button control, it is the *Click* event. The code you get looks similar to the following:

```
void Button1_Click(object sender, EventArgs e)
{
    ...
}
```

The HTML markup is automatically modified to contain an additional *OnClick* attribute:

```
<asp:button runat="server" id="Button1"
    text="Click"
    OnClick="Button1_Click" />
```

Notice that event binding is always done declaratively in the body of the *.aspx* page. If you're dealing with a code-behind page, the event handler is defined in the code-behind class instead of being placed inline.

When you double-click on a control or on the body of the page, a handler for the default page or control event is generated. What if you need to write a handler for another event? You select the desired control and click on the Events icon in the Properties window. You get a view like that in Figure 2-21 and pick up the event you need.

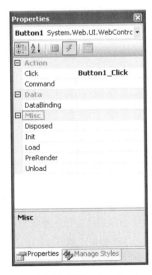

FIGURE 2-21 The Events view in the Properties window.

Writing Helper Classes

Writing helper classes is as easy as adding a new class to the project. The class file can define any number of classes, even partial class definitions, and will actually be compiled to an assembly. Where should you deploy this class file in your project? You have two options: either you create an additional project to generate a DLL component library, or you drop the class file in a special folder below the application's virtual root—the *App_Code* folder.

In the former case, you add another project to the solution by using the File|Add menu. From the list of available projects, you pick up a Class Library project and then add any class files to it. When you're done, you reference the library project in the Web site project and go. Pleasantly enough, IntelliSense will just detect new classes and work as expected.

What's the *App_Code* folder, then? It is an application's subdirectory that has a special meaning to the ASP.NET runtime. The *App_Code* folder is designed to contain reusable components that are automatically compiled and linked to the page code. The folder stores source class files (*.vb* or *.cs*) that the ASP.NET runtime engine dynamically compiles to an assembly upon execution. Created in a predefined path visible to all pages in the site, the resulting assembly is updated whenever any of the source files are updated. It is important to note that any file copied to the *App_Code* folder is deployed as source code on the production box. (I'll say more about special ASP.NET directories in the next section.)

Building a Sample Shared Class

To experience the advantages of reusable source components, let's design a page that makes use of a nontrivial component that would be annoying to insert inline in each page that needs it. The page looks like the one in Figure 2-22.

FIGURE 2-22 The PswdGen.aspx page to generate a new "strong" password of the specified length.

Many products and services available over the Web require a strong password. The definition of a "strong password" is specific to the service, but normally it refers to a password at least eight characters long with at least one character from each of the following groups: uppercase, lowercase, digits, and special characters. We'll use that definition here. The sample page you will build asks the user for the desired length of the password and suggests one built according to the rules just mentioned. You create a new file named *StrongPassword.cs* and place it in the purposely created *App_Code* subdirectory. The class outline is shown here:

```
public class StrongPassword
{
    public StrongPassword()
    {...}

    public string Generate()
    {...}
    public string Generate(int passwordLength)
    {...}
}
```

The class features one method—*Generate*—that will actually generate a new strong password. Of course, the definition of a "strong password" is arbitrary. Once placed in the *App_Code* directory, this class is compiled on demand and made available to all pages. In the sample page, the code to generate and validate a password becomes simpler and more readable:

```
void buttonGenerate_Click(object sender, System.EventArgs e)
{
    // Gets the desired length of the password and ensures
    // it is really expressed as a number. (This is a simple but
    // effective pattern to prevent code/data injection.)
    string text = PswdLength.Text;
    int pswdLen = 8;

    // Use extension methods to do the job
    if (text.IsInt32())
        pswdLen = text.ToInt32();

    // Create and display the new password
    StrongPassword pswd = new StrongPassword();
    labelPassword.Text = pswd.Generate(pswdLen);
}
```

Figure 2-22 shows the page in action. Note that the same functionality can also be achieved by placing the code inline or packing the *StrongPassword* class in a separate assembly.

A Look at the *web.config* File

The behavior of an ASP.NET application is affected by the settings defined in various configuration files—*machine.config* and *web.config*. The *machine.config* file contains default and machine-specific values for all supported settings. Machine settings are normally con-trolled by the system administrator, and applications should never be given write access to it. An application can override most default values stored in the *machine.config* file by creating one or more *web.config* files.

At a minimum, an application creates a *web.config* file in its root folder. The *web.config* file is a subset of *machine.config*, written according to the same XML schema. Although *web.config* allows you to override some of the default settings, you cannot override all settings defined in *machine.config*.

If the application contains child directories, it can define a *web.config* file for each folder. The scope of each configuration file is determined in a hierarchical, top-down manner. The settings actually applied to a page are determined by the sum of the changes that the various *web.config* files on the way from *machine.config* to the page's directory carry. Any *web.config* file can locally extend, restrict, and override any type of settings defined at an upper level. If no configuration file exists in an application folder, the settings valid at the upper level are applied.

Visual Studio usually generates a default *web.config* file for you. The *web.config* file is not strictly necessary for an application to run. Without a *web.config* file, though, you can't debug the application.

ASP.NET Protected Folders

ASP.NET uses a number of special directories below the application root to maintain application content and data. In ASP.NET 1.x, only the Bin directory was used. Starting with version 2.0, ASP.NET introduces a few additional protected directories. None of these directories are automatically created by ASP.NET or Visual Studio 2008, nor are the directories necessarily required to exist. Each directory needs to be created either manually by developers or on demand through Visual Studio when a feature that requires it is enabled.

Additional Application Directories

Table 2-1 lists all the additional directories you can take advantage of. Note that the directories will be there only if they are required by your specific application. Don't be too worried about the number of new directories (that is, seven) you can potentially have. A reasonable estimate is that only two or three (out of seven) additional directories will be present in an average ASP.NET application.

TABLE 2-1 Special Protected Directories in ASP.NET Applications

Directory Name	Intended Goal
Bin	Contains all precompiled assemblies needed by the application.
App_Browsers	Contains browser capability information.
App_Code	Contains source class files (*.vb* or *.cs*) used by pages. All the files must be in the same language; you can't have both C# and VB.NET files in the folder.

Directory Name	Intended Goal
App_Data	Contains data files for the application. These can include XML files and Microsoft Access databases to store personalization data.
App_GlobalResources	Contains .resx resource files global to the application.
App_LocalResources	Contains all .resx resource files that are specific to a particular page.
App_Themes	Contains the definition of the themes supported by the application. (I'll say more about themes in Chapter 6.)
App_WebReferences	Contains .wsdl files linking Web services to the application.

The content in all the directories listed in Table 2-1 won't be accessible via HTTP requests to the server. The only exception is the content of the *App_Themes* folder.

> **Important** The names of these folders aren't customizable. The reason is related to the way the ISAPI filter in charge of blocking HTTP requests to these folders works. For performance reasons, the ISAPI filter can't just access the *web.config* file to read about directory names to look for. That would require the filter to parse the XML file on *any* request and, as you can easily imagine, would be a major performance hit. Alternately, the names of the directories can be written in the registry, which would make for much faster and more affordable access. Unfortunately, a registry-based approach would break XCopy deployment and introduce a major breaking change in the ASP.NET architecture. (See the "Application Deployment" section for more information on XCopy deployment.)

The contents of many folders listed in Table 2-1 are compiled to a dynamic assembly when the request is processed for the first time. This is the case for themes, code, resources, and Web references. (See the "The Resource Directories" section for more information on the ASP.NET compilation model.)

The *App_Code* Directory

As mentioned, you can use the server *App_Code* directory to group your helper and business classes. You deploy them as source files, and the ASP.NET runtime ensures that classes will be automatically compiled on demand. Furthermore, any changes to these files will be detected, causing the involved classes to recompile. The resulting assembly is automatically referenced in the application and shared between all pages participating in the site.

You should put only components into the *App_Code* directory. Do not put pages, Web user controls, or other noncode files containing noncode elements into the subdirectory. The resulting assembly has application scope and is created in the *Temporary ASP.NET Files* folder—well outside the Web application space.

> **Note** If you're worried about deploying valuable C# or VB.NET source files to the Web server, bear in mind that any (repeat, *any*) access to the *App_Code* folder conducted via HTTP is monitored and blocked by the aforementioned ASP.NET ISAPI filter.

Note that all class files in the *App_Code* folder, or in a child folder, must be written in the same language—be it Visual Basic .NET or C#—because they are all compiled to a single assembly and processed by a single compiler. To use different languages, you must organize your class files in subfolders and add some entries to the configuration file to tell the build system to create distinct assemblies—one per language.

Here's an example. Suppose you have two files named source.cs and source.vb. Because they're written in different languages, they can't stay together in the *App_Code* folder. You can then create two subfolders—say, *App_Code/VB* and *App_Code/CS*—and move the files to the subfolder that matches the language. Next you can add the following entries to the *web.config* file:

```
<configuration>
<system.web>
<compilation>
    <codeSubDirectories>
        <add directoryName="VB" />
        <add directoryName="CS" />
    </codeSubDirectories>
</compilation>
</system.web>
</configuration>
```

Note that the *<codeSubDirectories>* section is valid only if it is set in the *web.config* file in the application root. Each section instructs the build system to create a distinct assembly. This means that all the files in the specified directory must be written in the same language, but different directories can target different languages.

> **Note** The *App_Code* directory can also contain XSD files, like those generated for typed *DataSets*. An XSD file represents the strongly typed schema of a table of data. In the .NET Framework 1.1, a typed *DataSet* must be manually created using the *xsd.exe* tool. Starting with ASP.NET 2.0, all you have to do is drop the source XSD file in the *App_Code* folder.

The Resource Directories

A localizable Web page uses resources instead of hard-coded text to flesh out the user interface of contained controls. Once a resource assembly is linked to the application, ASP.NET can select the correct property at run time according to the user's language and culture. In ASP.NET 1.x, developers had to create satellite assemblies manually. Starting with version 2.0, ASP.NET 2.0 creates resource assemblies, parsing and compiling any resource files found in the two supported folders—*App_LocalResources* and *App_GlobalResources*.

A local resource is a resource file specific to a page. A simple naming convention binds the file to the page. If the page is named *sample.aspx*, its corresponding resource file is *sample. aspx.resx*. To be precise, this resource file is language neutral and has no culture defined. To create a resource assembly for a specific culture—say, Italian—you need to name the resource file as follows: *sample.aspx.it.resx*. Generally, the *it* string should be replaced with any other equivalent string that identifies a culture, such as *fr* for French or *en* for English. Figure 2-23 shows a sample local resource folder.

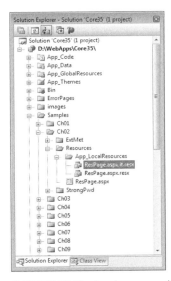

FIGURE 2-23 The local resource directory for the respage.aspx page.

Local resources provide a sort of implicit localization where the page itself automatically ensures that each contained control is mapped to a particular entry in the *.resx* file. Here's how a simple page changes once you add support for local resources:

```
<%@ Page Language="C#"
    meta:resourcekey="TestRes_aspx_PageID"
    UICulture="auto" %>

<html>
<head runat="server">
    <title>Localized Resources</title>
</head>
<body>
<form id="Form1" runat="server">
    <h1>
    <asp:Label runat="server" id="Label1"
        meta:resourcekey="Label1_ResourceID" />
    </h1>
    <asp:Button ID="btn" runat="server"
        meta:resourcekey="Button1_ResourceID" />
</form>
</body>
</html>
```

The page itself and each constituent control are given a resource key. The *.resx* file contains entries in the form *ResourceKey.PropertyName*. For example, the *Text* property of the button is implicitly bound to the *Button1_ResourceID.Text* entry in the *.resx* file. You don't have to write a single line of code for this mapping to take place. You are only requested to populate the resource files as outlined. The *UICulture* attribute set to *auto* tells the ASP.NET runtime to use the current browser's language setting to select the right set of resources.

> **Tip** To quickly test a page against different languages, you open the Internet Explorer Tools menu and click the Languages button. Next, you add the language of choice to the list box of supported languages and move the language of choice to the first position in the list. Click OK and exit. From this point on, Internet Explorer sends the selected language ID with each served request.

Figure 2-24 shows how the same page looks when different languages are set.

Implicit localization works automatically, meaning that you don't need to specify how to read information about each property from a resource file. However, at times you need more direct control over how properties are set. For this, you turn to global resources. When you choose to add a resource file to the application, Visual Studio creates the *App_GlobalResources* directory and places a new *.resx* file in it. You can rename this file at will and fill it with strings, images, sounds, and whatever else is suitable to you. (See Figure 2-25.)

FIGURE 2-24 The *testres.aspx* file in Italian and English.

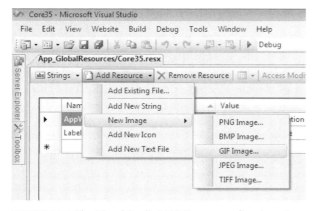

FIGURE 2-25 The Visual Studio2008 Resource editor in action.

Within the page or controls code, you reference resources using an expression, as in the following code:

```
<asp:Label runat="server" ID="Label2"
          Text="<%$ Resources:Core35, Label2_ResourceID %>" />
```

Resources is the keyword that triggers the loading of the value from the resource file. Instead, *Core35* is the name of the *.resx* file that contains the resources. Finally, *Label2_ResourceID* is the name of the entry to read from the resource file. Explicit localization is useful when you have large bodies of text or custom messages you want to localize.

> **Note** The resulting resource assembly for the neutral culture has application scope and is therefore referenced from other assemblies generated in the application.

Linked Web Services

When you add a reference to a Web service, the *.wsdl* file for the Web service is downloaded and copied to the *App_WebReferences* directory. At runtime, any WSDL file found in the Web reference directory is dynamically compiled in a C# or Visual Basic .NET proxy class in much the same way as business classes in the *App_Code* directory are processed.

If you can obtain a WSDL file in other ways (that is, you don't download it through the Add Web Reference Wizard), you can add it manually to the *App_WebReferences* directory.

Available Themes

The *App_Themes* directory defines one or more themes for controls. A *theme* is a set of skins and associated files such as style sheets and images that can be used within an application to give a consistent user interface to controls. In the *App_Themes* directory, each theme occupies a single subdirectory, which has the same name as the theme. All related files are stored in this directory.

When a theme is loaded, the contents of the theme directory are parsed and compiled into a class that inherits from a common base class. Any theme defined outside the *App_Themes* directory is ignored by the ASP.NET build system.

Build the ASP.NET Project

To build and run the ASP.NET application, you simply click the Start button on the toolbar (or press F5) and wait for a browser window to pop up. In Visual Studio 2008, no compile step takes place to incorporate code-behind and helper classes (unless you opt for the WAP project option). All the dynamically generated assemblies, and all precompiled assemblies deployed into the *Bin* folder, are linked to the application used to visit pages.

Once any needed assemblies have been successfully built, Visual Studio auto-attaches to the ASP.NET run-time process—typically, *w3wp.exe*—for debugging purposes. Next, it opens the start page of the application.

> **Important** The ASP.NET run-time process might differ based on the process model in use. The process model is configurable; the default model, though, depends on the underlying operating systems and Web server settings. If your Web server runs Windows 2000 Server, or perhaps any version of Windows XP for whatever reason, the run-time process is *aspnet_wp.exe*. It runs under a weak user account named ASPNET and is designed to interact with IIS 5.x. If you run Windows 2003 Server and IIS 6.0 and don't change the default process model, the run-time process is *w3wp.exe*, which is the standard worker process of IIS 6.0. The *w3wp.exe* process runs under the NETWORK SERVICE account. This process doesn't know anything about ASP.NET, but its behavior is aptly customized by a version-specific copy of the ASP.NET ISAPI extension. Under IIS 6.0, you can even switch back to the IIS 5 process model. If you do so, though, you lose a lot in terms of performance. The default settings for IIS 6.0 and Windows 2003 Server apply to the newest Windows 2008 Server and IIS 7.0, and even to Windows Vista.

When you build the project, Visual Studio 2008 might complain about a missing *web.config* file, which is necessary if you want to debug the code. If you just want to run the page without debugging it, click the Run button in the message box you get. Otherwise, you let Visual Studio generate a proper *web.config* file for you. If you create your own *web.config* file, make sure it contains the following string to enable debugging:

```
<compilation debug="true" />
```

Once this is done, you can commence your debugging session.

Debugging Features

As long as you compiled the project in debug mode (which is, indeed, the default), you can set a few breakpoints in your source files and step into the code, as shown in Figure 2-26.

```
12 public partial class PswdGen_aspx
13 {
14     void buttonGenerate_Click(Object sender, System.EventArgs e)
15     {
16         // Get the password length
17         int pswdLen = 8;
18         bool result = Int32.TryParse(PswdLength.Text, out pswdLen);
19
20         StrongPassword pswd = new StrongPassword();
21         labelPassword.Text = pswd.Generate(pswdLen);
22     }
23 }
24
```

FIGURE 2-26 Stepping into the code of the page by using the Visual Studio integrated debugger.

The Debug menu offers you choices as far as exceptions and breakpoints are concerned. In particular, you can configure the IDE so that it automatically breaks when an exception is thrown. The feature can be fine-tuned to let you focus on any exceptions, any exceptions in a specified set, or all exceptions not handled by the current application.

Breakpoints can be set at an absolute particular location or in a more relative way when the execution reaches a given function. Braveheart debuggers also have the chance to break the code when the memory at a specified address changes.

Watch windows feature a richer user interface centered around the concept of visualizers. A visualizer is a popup window designed to present certain types of data in a more friendly and readable manner—XML, text, or *DataSets*. (See Figure 2-27.)

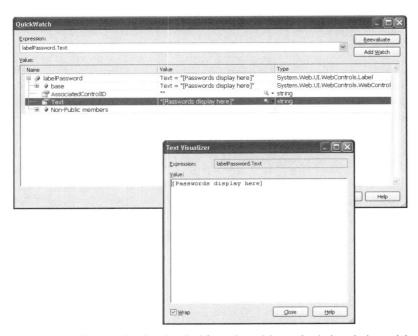

FIGURE 2-27 The text visualizer invoked from the quick-watch window during a debug session.

Visualizers are also active from within code tip windows. A code tip is the made-to-measure ToolTip that previews the value of variables during a debug session. (See Figure 2-28.)

```
public partial class PswdGen_aspx : Page
{
    protected void buttonGenerate_Click(Object sender, System.EventArgs e)
    {
        // Get the password length
        int pswdLen = 8;
        bool result = Int32.TryParse(PswdLength.Text, out pswdLen);

        StrongPassword pswd = new StrongPassword();
        labelPassword.Text = pswd.Generate(pswdLen);
    }
}
                        labelPassword.Text  🔍 ▾ "[Passwords display here]"
                             ✓ Text Visualizer
                               XML Visualizer
                               HTML Visualizer
```

FIGURE 2-28 Invoking a visualizer from within a code tip.

Visualizers are defined for a few types of data. Personally, I just love the *DataSet* visualizer. Checking what's in a *DataSet* instance couldn't be easier.

Testing the Application

There are two ways of testing pages in Visual Studio 2008. You can have pages served by IIS (if installed) or by the embedded local Web server. By default, Visual Studio uses IIS if you open the project as a Web site and indicate its URL; otherwise, it defaults to the local Web server. An important point to consider about the embedded Web server concerns the security context. Under IIS, an ASP.NET application is served by a worker process running under the *real* account defined for the application—typically, a highly restricted account such as ASP.NET or NETWORK SERVICE.

In contrast, the embedded Web server takes the security token of the currently logged-on user—that is, you. This means that if the developer is currently logged on as an administrator—a much more common scenario than it should be—the application receives administrative privileges. The problem here is not a risk of being attacked; the real problem is that you are actually testing the application in a scenario significantly different from the real one. Things that work great under the local Web server might fail miserably under IIS.

For simple applications that only read and run ASP.NET pages, this problem is not that relevant. However, the results of your testing under the local server becomes less reliable if you access files other than Web pages, files located on other machines, files in the Windows registry, or files on a local or remote database. In all these cases, you must make sure that the real ASP.NET account has sufficient permissions to work with those resources.

The bottom line is that even though you can use the local Web server to test pages, it sometimes doesn't offer a realistic test scenario.

Application Deployment

Installing a .NET application in general, and an ASP.NET application in particular, is a matter of performing an *XCopy*—that is, a recursive copy of all the files—to the target folder on the target machine. Often used to describe setup procedures in .NET, the *XCopy deployment* expression communicates the gist of .NET deployment: you don't need to do much more than copy files. In particular, there's no need to play with the registry, no components to set up, and no local files to create. Or, at least, nothing of the kind is needed just because the .NET Framework mandates it.

XCopy Deployment

The deployment of a Web application is a task that can be accomplished in various ways, depending on the context. As far as copy is concerned, you can use any of the following: FTP transfer, any server management tools providing forms of smart replication on a remote site, or an MSI installer application. In Visual Studio 2008, you can even use the *Copy Web Site* function that we discussed earlier in this chapter.

Each option has pros and cons, and the best fit can only be found once you know exactly the runtime host scenario and the purpose of the application is clearly delineated. Be aware that if you're going to deploy the application on an ISP host, you might be forced to play by the rules (read, "use the tools") that your host has set. If you're going to deliver a front end for an existing system to a variety of servers, you might find it easier to create a setup project. On the other hand, FTP is great for general maintenance and for applying quick fixes. Ad hoc tools, on the other hand, could give you automatic sync-up features. Guess what? Choosing the right technique is strictly application-specific and is ultimately left to you.

Copying Files

FTP gives you a lot of freedom, and it lets you modify and replace individual files. It doesn't represent a solution that is automatic, however: whatever you need to do must be accomplished manually. Assuming that you have gained full access to the remote site, using FTP is not much different than using Windows Explorer in the local network. I believe that with the Copy Web Site functionality the need for raw FTP access is going to lessen. If nothing else, the new Copy Web Site function operates as an integrated FTP-like tool to access remote locations.

The new copy function also provides synchronization capabilities too. It is not like the set of features that a specifically designed server management tool would supply, but it can certainly work well through a number of realistic situations. At the end of the day, a site replication tool doesn't do much more than merely transfer files from end to end. Its plusses are the user interface, and the intelligence, built around and atop this basic capability. So a replication tool maintains a database of files with timestamps, attributes, and properties and it can sync up versions of the site in a rather automated way, minimizing the work on your end.

Building a Setup Project

Another common scenario involves using an out-of-the-box installer file. Deploying a Web application this way is a two-step operation. First, create and configure the virtual directory; next, copy the needed files. Visual Studio makes creating a Web setup application a snap. You just create a new type of project—a Web Setup Project—select the files to copy, and build the project.

You create a Web application folder to represent the virtual directory of the new application on the target machine. The Properties box lets you configure the settings of the new virtual directory. For example, the *AllowDirectoryBrowsing* property lets you assign browsing permission to the IIS virtual folder you will create. You can also control the virtual directory name, application execute permissions, the level of isolation, and the default page. The *Bin* subfolder is automatically created, but you can ask the setup to create and populate as many subfolders as you need.

When you build the project, you obtain a Windows Installer *.msi* file that constitutes the setup to ship to your clients. The default installer supports repairing and uninstalling the application. The setup you obtain in this way—which is the simplest you can get—does not contain the .NET Framework, which must be installed on the target machine or explicitly included in the setup project itself.

What Else Do You Need to Do?

One of the coolest features of .NET assemblies is that they are self-describing components. An application that wants to know about the internal characteristics of an assembly has only to ask! The .NET reflection of an API is the programming interface by which a client can interrogate an assembly. This fact eliminates the need to use the registry (or any other sort of centralized repository) to track paths and attributes of binary components. Another pleasant effect of the assembly's structure is that side-by-side execution is now a snap, and ASP.NET applications take advantage of it on a regular basis. In practice, whenever you update a page, two versions of the "same" assembly live side by side for awhile without interference and conflict.

So the XCopy deployment model rocks. Is there something more you need to do to finalize the deployment of your application? Sure there is. Let's detail some additional tasks.

If you use read/write files (XML files, configuration files, Access databases), you need to grant proper file write permission to the application. Likewise, if your application or control generates temporary files, you need to make accommodations for a proper folder with proper file write permissions. These tasks must be accomplished in one way or another before the application goes live. Note that in an ISP scenario you are normally given an isolated disk subtree with full write permissions granted to the ASP.NET account. You must design your applications to be flexible enough to support a configurable path for all their temporary files.

 Note We're not saying anything specific about database configuration here. We're simply assuming that all required databases are in place, properly working, and entirely configured. If this is not the case, you might want to add this task to the list too. The same holds true for any remote application and network services you might need, including Web services and COM+ components.

Configuring the Runtime Environment

Another aspect to consider is runtime configuration. When you develop the ASP.NET code, you test it on a machine with its own pair of *machine.config* and system *web.config* files. When you deploy the application on a production box, you might not be able to restore the same settings. One possible reason is that the administrator does not want you to modify the current settings because they proved to be great for other applications. (This is especially true in an ISP host scenario.)

You can work around the issue by simply replicating any needed settings to the application's root *web.config*. However, if you are deploying your code to a service provider, you might find that many system settings have been locked down and cannot be overridden. In this case, you should ask (or more exactly, beg) the administrator to let you tweak the server's configuration in a way that suits you without hurting other applications. This normally entails creating an application-specific *<location>* section in the *web.config* file.

Deploying an ASP.NET application in a Web-farm scenario poses a few extra configuration issues you must be aware of. All configuration files in the Web farm must be synchronized to the value of a few attributes. You can achieve this in two ways, the simplest of which is packing all attribute values in the application's *web.config*. This approach greatly simplifies the deployment because you only have to run the setup on all machines and no other changes are needed. If any of the required sections are locked down (once more, this is likely to happen in an ISP scenario), you find yourself in the situation described previously, that of begging the administrator to create a new *<location>* section for you.

Note The *<location>* section can be used in both *machine.config* and *web.config* to limit Web settings to the specified application path. In a deployment scenario, the section assumes particular importance in the *machine.config* file and subsequently requires administrative privileges. The *<location>* section is normally used in a *web.config* file in case of a deployment with a main application and a bunch of subapplications.

Site Precompilation

As mentioned, dynamically created assemblies are placed in an internal folder managed by the ASP.NET runtime. Unless source files are modified, the compilation step occurs only once per page—when the page is first requested. Although in many cases the additional overhead is no big deal, removing it still is a form of optimization. Site precompilation consists of deploying the whole site functionality through assemblies. A precompiled application is still made up of source files, but all pages and resources are fictitiously accessed before deployment and compiled to assemblies. The dynamically created assemblies are then packaged and installed on the target machine. As you can see, site precompilation also saves you from deploying valuable source files, thus preserving the intellectual property.

Important Source files, like C# classes or WSDL scripts, are protected against HTTP access. However, they are at the mercy of a hacker in the case of a successful exploitation that allows the attacker to take control of the Web directories.

Site precompilation was possible in ASP.NET 1.x, but starting with version 2.0 it reached the rank of a system tool, fully supported by the framework. In summary, site precompilation offers two main advantages:

- Requests to the site do not cause any delay because the pages and code are compiled to assemblies.

- Sites can be deployed without any source code, thus preserving and protecting the intellectual property of the solutions implemented.

Precompilation can take two forms: in-place precompilation and deployment precompilation.

> **Note** To protect intellectual property, you can also consider obfuscation in addition to site precompilation. *Obfuscation* is a technique that nondestructively changes names in the assembly metadata, thus preventing potential code-crackers from scanning your files for sensitive strings. Obfuscation does not affect the way the code runs, except that it compacts the executable, making it load a bit faster. If decompiled, an obfuscated assembly generates a much less readable intermediate code. Although applicable to all .NET applications, there is nothing wrong with obfuscating your ASP.NET assemblies in case of hacker access for the very same reasons. Visual Studio 2008 provides the community edition of a commercial tool—Dotfuscator.

In-Place Precompilation

In-place precompilation allows a developer or a site administrator to access each page in the application as if it were being used by end users. This means each page is compiled as if for ordinary use. The site is fully compiled before entering production, and no user will experience a first-hit compilation delay, as in version 1.x. In-place precompilation takes place after the site is deployed but before it goes public. To precompile a site in-place, you use the following command, where */core35* indicates the virtual folder of the application:

```
aspnet_compiler -v /core35
```

If you precompile the site again, the compiler skips pages that are up to date and only new or changed files are processed and those with dependencies on new or changed files. Because of this compiler optimization, it is practical to compile the site after even minor updates.

Precompilation is essentially a batch compilation that generates all needed assemblies in the fixed ASP.NET directory on the server machine. If any file fails compilation, precompilation will fail on the application.

Precompilation for Deployment

Precompilation for deployment generates a file representation of the site made of assemblies, static files, and configuration files—a sort of manifest. This representation is generated on a target machine and can also be packaged as MSI and then copied and installed to a production machine. This form of precompilation doesn't require source code to be left on the target machine.

Precompilation for deployment also requires the use of the *aspnet_compiler* command-line tool:

```
aspnet_compiler -m metabasePath
                -c virtualPath
                -p physicalPath
                targetPath
```

The role of each supported parameter is explained in Table 2-2.

TABLE 2-2 Parameters of the *aspnet_compiler* Tool

Switch	Description
-aptca	If this switch is specified, compiled assemblies will allow partially trusted callers.
-c	If this switch is specified, the precompiled application is fully rebuilt.
-d	If this switch is specified, the debug information is emitted during compilation.
-delaysign	If this switch is specified, compiled assemblies are not fully signed when created.
-errorstack	Shows extra debugging information.
-m	Indicates the full IIS metabase path of the application.
-f	Indicates that the target directory will be overwritten if it already exists and existing contents will be lost.
-fixednames	If this switch is specified, the compiled assemblies will be given fixed names.
-keycontainer	Indicates the name of the key container for strong names.
-keyfile	Indicates the physical path to the key file for strong names.
-p	Indicates the physical path of the application to be compiled. If this switch is missing, the IIS metabase is used to locate the application. This switch must be combined with -v.
-u	If this switch is specified, it indicates that the precompiled application is updatable.
-v	Indicates the virtual path of the application to be compiled. If no virtual path is specified, the application is assumed to be in the default site: W3SVC/1/Root.

If no target path is specified, the precompilation takes place in the virtual path of the application, and source files are therefore preserved. If a different target is specified, only assemblies are copied, and the new application runs with no source file in the production environment. The following command line precompiles *Core35* to the specified disk path:

```
aspnet_compiler -v /Core35 c:\ServerPath
```

Static files such as images, *web.config*, and HTML pages are not compiled—they are just copied to the target destination.

> **Warning** If you don't want to deploy HTML pages as clear text, rename them to *.aspx* and compile them. A similar approach can be used for image files. Note, however, that if you hide images and HTML pages behind ASP.NET extensions, you lose in terms of performance because IIS is used to process static files more efficiently than ASP.NET.

Precompilation for deployment comes in two slightly different forms—with or without support for updates. Sites packaged for deployment only are not sensitive to file changes. When a change is required, you modify the original files, recompile the whole site, and redeploy the new layout. The only exception is the site configuration; you can update *web.config* on the production server without having to recompile the site.

Sites precompiled for deployment and update are made of assemblies obtained from all files that normally produce assemblies, such as class and resource files. The compiler, though, doesn't touch *.aspx* page files and simply copies them as part of the final layout. In this way, you are allowed to make limited changes to the ASP.NET pages after compiling them. For example, you can change the position of controls or settings regarding colors, fonts, and other visual parameters. You can also add new controls to existing pages, as long as they do not require event handlers or other code.

In no case can new pages be added to a precompiled site without recompiling it from scratch.

Of the two approaches to precompilation for deployment, the former clearly provides the greatest degree of protection for pages and the best performance at startup. The option that provides for limited updates still requires some further compilation when the site runs the first time. In the end, opting for the deployment and update is nearly identical to the compilation and deployment model of ASP.NET 1.1, where *.aspx* files are deployed in the source and all classes (including code-behind classes) are compiled to assemblies.

Administering an ASP.NET Application

In addition to working pages, well-done graphics, and back-end services and components, a real-world Web application also requires a set of administrative tools to manage users, security, and configuration. In most cases, these tools consist of a passable and quickly arranged user interface built around a bunch of database tables; application developers are ultimately responsible for building them. To save time, these tools are often created as Windows Forms applications. If the application is properly designed, some business and data access objects created for the site can be reused. Are these external and additional applications always necessary?

Although an ad hoc set of utility applications might be desired in some cases, having an integrated, rich, and further customizable tool built into Visual Studio would probably be helpful and sufficient in many cases. In Visual Studio 2008, you find available a whole Web application to administer various aspects of the site. The application, known as the Web Site Administration Tool (WSAT), is available through the Web site menu (or the Solution Explorer toolbar) and is extensively based on the ASP.NET provider model.

The Web Site Administration Tool

Figure 2-29 presents the administration tool in its full splendor. The tool is articulated in three blocks (plus the home), each covering a particular area of administration—membership, user profiles, application settings, and providers.

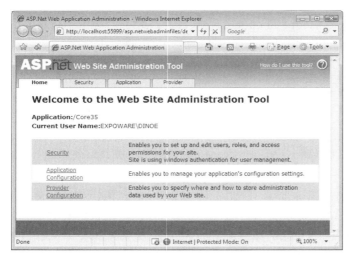

FIGURE 2-29 The Visual Studio 2008 ASP.NET Administration Tool.

As mentioned, WSAT is a distinct application that the ASP.NET setup installs with full source. You find it under the *ASP.NETWebAdminFiles* directory, below the ASP.NET build installation path. This path is

```
C:\WINDOWS\Microsoft.NET\Framework\[version]
```

You can also run the tool from outside Visual Studio 2008. In this case, though, you must indicate a parameter to select the application to configure. Here's the complete URL to type in the browser's address bar for an application named Core35:

```
http://localhost:XXXX/asp.netwebadminfiles/default.aspx
      ?applicationUrl=/Core35
```

The *XXXX* indicates the port used by the local Web server. The WSAT application, in fact, is not publicly exposed through IIS for obvious security reasons. Table 2-3 details what you can expect to do with the tool.

TABLE 2-3 Classes of Settings Defined Through WSAT

Configuration Tab	Description
Security	Enables you to set up and edit users, roles, and access permissions for your site
Application	Enables you to manage your application's configuration settings, such as debugging and SMTP options
Provider	Enables you to select the provider to use for each ASP.NET feature that supports providers

Membership and Role Management

The Security tab of WSAT lets you manage all the security settings for your application. You can choose the authentication method, set up users and passwords, create roles and groups of users, and create rules for controlling access to specific parts of your application. A wizard will guide you through the steps needed to set up individual users and roles. By default, membership and roles information are stored in a local SQL Server database (aspnetdb.mdf) stored in the *App_Data* folder of your Web site. If you want to store user information in a different storage medium, use the Provider tab to select a different provider.

In ASP.NET 1.1, it was fairly common to have a custom database store credentials for authorized users. The point is that this database had to be filled out at some time; in addition, the site administrator had to be able to manage users, especially roles. In ASP.NET 1.1, you have a few options: charge your developers with this additional task, be charged by external consultants with this extra cost, or buy a third-party product. If you can find the product that suits you to perfection in terms of functionalities and costs, you're probably better off buying this instead of building code yourself. With homebrewed code, you end up with a smaller set of features, often renounce the implementation of important security guidelines (for example, force password change every *n* days), and usually spend at least as much money, if not more, for a system with fewer capabilities and likely less reliability.

On the other hand, a WSAT-like tool doesn't sound like a mission-impossible task. However, it is the kind of cost that you might cut out of your budget. Finding a WSAT-like tool integrated in the development environment sounds like the perfect fit. It lets you accomplish basic administration tasks at no extra cost; and if you need more features, you can always turn to third-party products or, because you have the source code, you can inject your own extensions quite seamlessly.

Application Settings Management

Sometimes ASP.NET applications consume information (UI settings, favorites, general preferences, and connection strings) that you don't want to hard-code into pages. While applications can work out their own solutions for keeping data as configurable as possible (for example, databases or XML files), still the *<appSettings>* section in the *web.config* file provides an easy way out. The *<appSettings>* section, in fact, is specifically designed to store application-specific settings that can be expressed in a simple name/value fashion. The WSAT Application tab provides a convenient way to edit this section and create or edit entries.

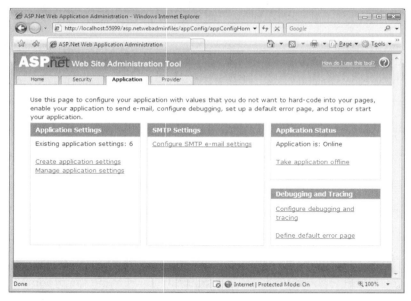

FIGURE 2-30 The Application tab in the Web Site Administration Tool.

As you can see in Figure 2-30, you can use the Application tab also to set debugging/tracing options and manage SMTP settings. In particular, mail settings determine how your Web application sends e-mail. If your e-mail server requires you to log on before you can send messages, you'll use the page to specify the type of authentication that the server requires and, if necessary, any required credentials.

The Application tab also contains a page for you to set error pages to show for particular HTTP errors.

Selecting and Configuring Providers

Profile and membership information require a persistent storage medium for user-specific data. The ASP.NET provider model (discussed in Chapter 1) supplies a plug-in mechanism for you to choose the right support for storing data. ASP.NET installs predefined providers for membership, roles, and personalization based on SQL Server local files. Extensibility, though, is the awesome feature of providers, and it gives you a way to write and plug in your own providers.

If you want to change the default provider for a particular feature, you use the Provider tab. You also use the same page to register a new provider, as shown in Figure 2-31.

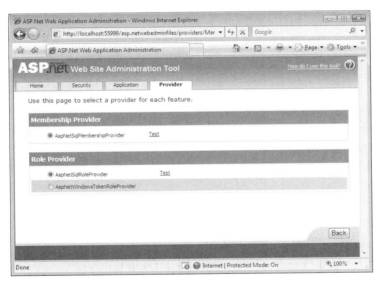

FIGURE 2-31 The Provider tab in the Web Site Administration Tool.

Editing ASP.NET Configuration Files

WSAT is mostly an administrative tool and, although it allows you to edit certain areas of the configuration files, you can't truly consider it to be a *web.config* editor. Visual Studio 2008 has improved the text editor that takes care of *web.config* files and has made it offer full IntelliSense support. Even though IntelliSense helps quite a bit, editing *web.config* through the IDE still requires a lot of tapping on the keyboard and typing many angle brackets on your own. Where else can you turn to edit *web.config* files more seamlessly?

A Visual Editor for *web.config* Files

Starting with version 2.0, ASP.NET provides an interactive tool for configuring the runtime environment and ultimately editing the *web.config* file. The tool is an extension (that is, a custom property page) to the IIS Microsoft Management Console (MMC) snap-in. As a result, a new property page (named ASP.NET) is added to each Web directory node. (See Figure 2-32.)

FIGURE 2-32 The ASP.NET MMC snap-in for IIS 6.0.

To reach the aforementioned property page, you open the IIS MMC snap-in (from the Control Panel) and select the desired Web application in the specified Web site. Next, you right-click to see the properties of this application and select the tab named ASP.NET. At this point, you should get what's presented in Figure 2-32. To start the *web.config* editor, click the Edit Configuration button. At this point, you get a new set of property pages that together supply an interactive user interface for editing the *web.config* files. The code behind this ASP.NET administrative tool leverages the new configuration API that allows you to read and write the contents of *.config* files.

If you use IIS 7.0, you get editing applets right in the IIS Manager, as shown in Figure 2-33.

The editor lets you edit virtually everything you might ever need to change in a *web.config* file. Any changes you enter are saved to a *web.config* file in the current directory—be it the application's root or the subdirectory from where you clicked. In other words, if you want to create or edit the *web.config* file of a subdirectory, locate that directory in the IIS snap-in tree, right-click to turn the editor on, and edit the local configuration.

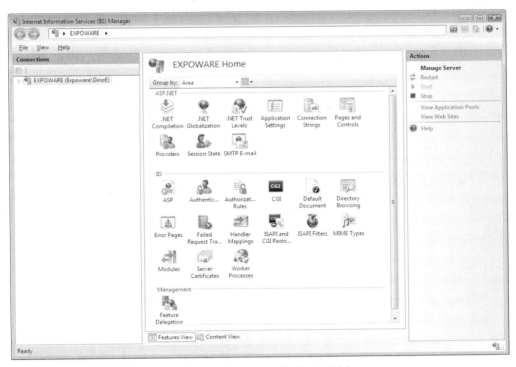

FIGURE 2-33 The bolted-on visual editor for the *web.config* file in IIS 7.0.

Conclusion

Visual Studio 2008 is the made-to-measure tool to build ASP.NET applications. Built to integrate the functionality of multiple visual designers in a common container environment, Visual Studio is capable of providing a unique editing experience to Web and Windows developers.

In this chapter, we traversed the main phases of Web application development through Visual Studio 2008—the page design, maintenance, and evolution of a Web project; and the deployment and administration of the final set of pages, files, and assemblies. The goal of this chapter was to provide the details of ASP.NET development with Visual Studio 2008—what's great, what's been improved, what's new, and what you should know. I also spent some time discussing themes such as deployment and administration. Both are essential steps in finalizing a project, but both steps are often overlooked and often end up forcing developers and customers to swallow bitter pills. In some cases, deployment and administration require ad hoc tools; in as many other cases, though, a small handful of applications can let developers and administrators do their work smoothly and effectively.

Just the Facts

- IIS is no longer a strict requirement for developing ASP.NET applications, as Visual Studio 2008 incorporates a local, mini Web server to be used only for testing during the development cycle.

- Visual Studio 2008 supports multiple ways to open Web sites. In addition to using FPSE, you can access your source files by using FTP, IIS, and even the file system path.

- Visual Studio 2008 supports multitargeting and can create and edit applications written against any version of the .NET Framework, starting with version 2.0.

- An ASP.NET 2.0 application can be made of folders that receive special treatment from the ASP.NET runtime—for example, *App_Code* for classes, *App_Themes* for themes, and *App_GlobalResources* for satellite assemblies.

- Even though you can use the local Web server to test pages, be aware that it doesn't offer a realistic test scenario (different account, different settings). Don't rely on it to determine your application works as expected.

- ASP.NET supports two forms of site precompilation: in-place precompilation and deployment precompilation.

- In-place precompilation applies to deployed applications and simply precompiles all pages to save the first-hit compilation delay.

- Precompilation for deployment creates a file representation of the site made of assemblies and static files. This representation can be generated on any machine, and it can be packaged to MSI and deployed.

- Visual Studio 2008 provides richer support for IntelliSense and debugging in the context of client JavaScript code and offers new capabilities as far as programming languages (C#, Visual Basic .NET) are concerned.

Chapter 3
Anatomy of an ASP.NET Page

ASP.NET pages are dynamically compiled on demand when first required in the context of a Web application. Dynamic compilation is not specific to ASP.NET pages (*.aspx* files); it also occurs with .NET Web Services (.asmx files), Web user controls (.ascx files), HTTP handlers (.ashx files), and a few more ASP.NET application files such as the *global.asax* file. A pipeline of run-time modules takes care of the incoming HTTP packet and makes it evolve from a simple protocol-specific payload up to the rank of a server-side ASP.NET object—precisely, an instance of a class derived from the system's *Page* class. The ASP.NET HTTP runtime processes the page object and causes it to generate the markup to insert in the response. The generation of the response is marked by several events handled by user code and collectively known as the *page life cycle*.

In this chapter, we'll review how an HTTP request for an *.aspx* resource is mapped to a page object, the programming interface of the *Page* class, and how to control the generation of the markup by handling events of the page life cycle.

Invoking a Page

Let's start by examining in detail how the *.aspx* page is converted into a class and then compiled into an assembly. Generating an assembly for a particular *.aspx* resource is a two-step process. First, the source code of the resource file is parsed and a corresponding class is created that inherits either from *Page* or another class that, in turn, inherits from *Page*. Second, the dynamically generated class is compiled into an assembly and cached in an ASP.NET-specific temporary directory.

The compiled page remains in use as long as no changes occur to the linked *.aspx* source file or the whole application is restarted. Any changes to the linked *.aspx* file invalidates the current page-specific assembly and forces the HTTP runtime to create a new assembly on the next request for page.

> **Note** Editing files such as *web.config* and *global.asax* causes the whole application to restart. In this case, all the pages will be recompiled as soon as each page is requested. The same happens if a new assembly is copied or replaced in the application's *Bin* folder.

The Runtime Machinery

All resources that you can access on an Internet Information Services (IIS)–based Web server are grouped by file extension. Any incoming request is then assigned to a particular run-time module for actual processing. Modules that can handle Web resources within the context of IIS are Internet Server Application Programming Interface (ISAPI) extensions—that is, plain old Win32 dynamic-link libraries (DLLs) that expose, much like an interface, a bunch of API functions with predefined names and prototypes. IIS and ISAPI extensions use these DLL entries as a sort of private communication protocol. When IIS needs an ISAPI extension to accomplish a certain task, it simply loads the DLL and calls the appropriate function with valid arguments. Although the ISAPI documentation doesn't mention an ISAPI extension as an interface, it is just that—a module that implements a well-known programming interface.

When the request for a resource arrives, IIS first verifies the type of the resource. Static resources such as images, text files, HTML pages, and scriptless ASP pages are resolved directly by IIS without the involvement of any external modules. IIS accesses the file on the local Web server and flushes its contents to the output console so that the requesting browser can get it. Resources that require server-side elaboration are passed on to the registered module. For example, ASP pages are processed by an ISAPI extension named *asp.dll*. In general, when the resource is associated with executable code, IIS hands the request to that executable for further processing. Files with an *.aspx* extension are assigned to an ISAPI extension named *aspnet_isapi.dll*, as shown in Figure 3-1.

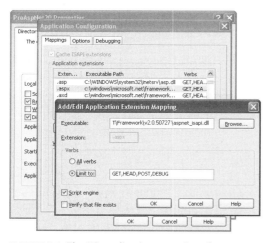

FIGURE 3-1 The IIS application mappings for resources with an *.aspx* extension.

Resource mappings are stored in the IIS *metabase*, which is an IIS-specific configuration database. Upon installation, ASP.NET modifies the IIS metabase to make sure that *aspnet_isapi.dll* can handle some typical ASP.NET resources. Table 3-1 lists some of these resources.

TABLE 3-1 IIS Application Mappings for aspnet_isapi.dll

Extension	Resource Type
.asax	ASP.NET application files such as *global.asax*.. The mapping is there to ensure that *global.asax* can't be requested directly.
.ascx	ASP.NET user control files.
.ashx	HTTP handlers, namely managed modules that interact with the low-level request and response services of IIS.
.asmx	Files that implement .NET Web services.
.aspx	Files that represent ASP.NET pages.
.axd	Extension that identifies internal HTTP handlers used to implement system features such as application-level tracing (*trace.axd*) or script injection (*webresource.axd*).

In addition, the *aspnet_isapi.dll* extension handles other typical Microsoft Visual Studio extensions, such as *.cs*, *.csproj*, *.vb*, *.vbproj*, *.config*, and *.resx*.

As mentioned in Chapter 1, the exact behavior of the ASP.NET ISAPI extension depends on the process model selected for the application. There are two options, as described in the following sections.

IIS 5.0 Process Model

The IIS 5.0 process model is the only option you have if you host your ASP.NET application on any version of Microsoft Windows prior to Windows 2003 Server. According to this processing model, *aspnet_isapi.dll* doesn't process the *.aspx* file, but instead acts as a dispatcher. It collects all the information available about the invoked URL and the underlying resource, and then it routes the request toward another distinct process—the ASP.NET worker process named *aspnet_wp.exe*. The communication between the ISAPI extension and worker process takes place through named pipes.

The whole model is illustrated in Figure 3-2.

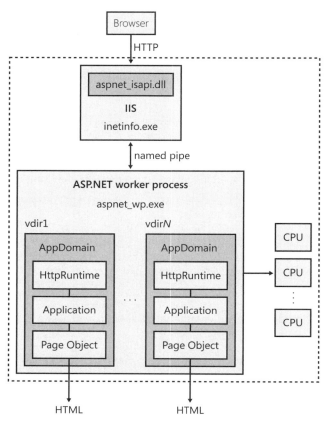

FIGURE 3-2 The ASP.NET runtime environment according to the IIS 5.0 process model.

A single copy of the worker process runs all the time and hosts all the active Web applications. The only exception to this situation is when you have a Web server with multiple CPUs. In this case, you can configure the ASP.NET runtime so that multiple worker processes run, one per each available CPU. A model in which multiple processes run on multiple CPUs in a single-server machine is known as a *Web garden* and is controlled by attributes on the *<processModel>* section in the *machine.config* file.

When a single worker process is used by all CPUs and controls all Web applications, it doesn't necessarily mean that no process isolation is achieved. Each Web application is, in fact, identified with its virtual directory and belongs to a distinct *application domain*, commonly referred to as an AppDomain. A new AppDomain is created within the ASP.NET worker process whenever a client addresses a virtual directory for the first time. After creating the new AppDomain, the ASP.NET runtime loads all the needed assemblies and passes control to the hosted HTTP pipeline to actually service the request.

If a client requests a page from an already running Web application, the ASP.NET runtime simply forwards the request to the existing AppDomain associated with that virtual directory. If the assembly needed to process the page is not loaded in the AppDomain, it will be created on the fly; otherwise, if it was already created upon the first call, it will be simply used.

IIS 6.0 Process Model

The IIS 6.0 process model is the default option for ASP.NET when the Web server operating system is Windows 2003 Server or newer. As the name of the process model clearly suggests, this model requires IIS 6.0. However, on a Windows 2003 Server machine you can still have ASP.NET play by the rules of the IIS 5.0 process model. If this is what you want, explicitly enable the model by tweaking the *<processModel>* section of the *machine.config* file, as shown here:

```
<processModel enable="true">
```

Be aware that switching back to the old IIS 5.0 process model is not a recommended practice, although it is perfectly legal. The main reason lies in the fact that IIS 6.0 employs a different pipeline of internal modules to process an inbound request and can mimic the behavior of IIS 5.0 only if running in emulation mode. The IIS 6.0 pipeline is centered around a generic worker process named *w3wp.exe*. A copy of this executable is shared by all Web applications assigned to the same application pool. In the IIS 6.0 jargon, an application pool is a group of Web applications that share the same copy of the worker process. IIS 6.0 lets you customize the application pools to achieve the degree of isolation that you need for the various applications hosted on a Web server.

The *w3wp.exe* worker process loads *aspnet_isapi.dll*; the ISAPI extension, in turn, loads the common language runtime (CLR) and starts the ASP.NET runtime pipeline to process the request. When the IIS 6.0 process model is in use, the built-in ASP.NET worker process is disabled.

> **Note** Only ASP.NET version 1.1 and later takes full advantage of the IIS 6.0 process model. If you install ASP.NET 1.0 on a Windows 2003 Server machine, the process model will default to the IIS 5.0 process model. This happens because only the version of *aspnet_isapi.dll* that ships with ASP.NET 1.1 is smart enough to recognize its host and load the CLR if needed. The *aspnet_isapi. dll* included in ASP.NET 1.0 is limited to forwarding requests to the ASP.NET worker process and never loads the CLR.

Figure 3-3 shows how ASP.NET applications and other Web applications are processed in IIS 6.0.

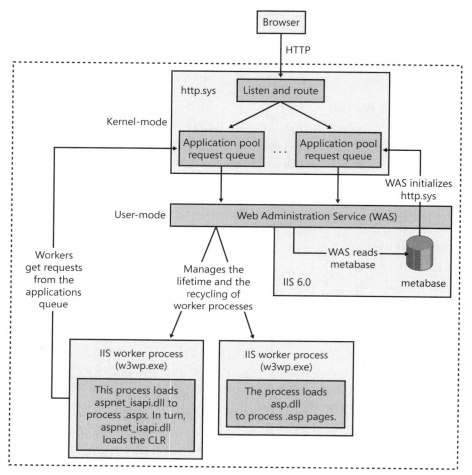

FIGURE 3-3 How ASP.NET and Web applications are processed in IIS 6.0.

IIS 6.0 implements its HTTP listener as a kernel-level module. As a result, all incoming requests are first managed by a driver—*http.sys*. No third-party code ever interacts with the listener, and no user-mode crashes will ever affect the stability of IIS. The *http.sys* driver listens for requests and posts them to the request queue of the appropriate application pool. A module called the Web Administration Service (WAS) reads from the IIS metabase and instructs the *http.sys* driver to create as many request queues as there are application pools registered in the metabase.

In summary, in the IIS 6.0 process model, ASP.NET runs even faster because no interprocess communication between *inetinfo.exe* (the IIS executable) and the worker process is required. The HTTP request is delivered directly at the worker process that hosts the CLR. Furthermore, the ASP.NET worker process is not a special process but simply a copy of the IIS worker process. This fact shifts to IIS the burden of process recycling, page output caching, and health checks.

In the IIS 6.0 process model, ASP.NET ignores most of the contents of the *<processModel>* section from the *machine.config* file. Only thread and deadlock settings are read from that section of *machine.config*. Everything else goes through the metabase and can be configured only by using the IIS Manager. (Other configuration information continues to be read from *.config* files.)

Representing the Requested Page

Each incoming request that refers to an *.aspx* resource is mapped to, and served through, a *Page*-derived class. The ASP.NET HTTP runtime environment first determines the name of the class that will be used to serve the request. A particular naming convention links the URL of the page to the name of the class. If the requested page is, say, default.aspx, the associated class turns out to be *ASP.default_aspx*. If no class exists with that name in any of the assemblies currently loaded in the AppDomain, the HTTP runtime orders that the class be created and compiled. The source code for the class is created by parsing the source code of the *.aspx* resource, and it's temporarily saved in the ASP.NET temporary folder. Next, the class is compiled and loaded in memory to serve the request. When a new request for the same page arrives, the class is ready and no compile step will ever take place. (The class will be re-created and recompiled only if the source code of the *.aspx* source changes.)

The *ASP.default_aspx* class inherits from *Page* or, more likely, from a class that in turn inherits from *Page*. More precisely, the base class for *ASP.default_aspx* will be a combination of the code-behind, partial class created through Visual Studio and a second partial class dynamically arranged by the ASP.NET HTTP runtime. Figure 3-4 provides a graphical demonstration of how the source code of the dynamic page class is built.

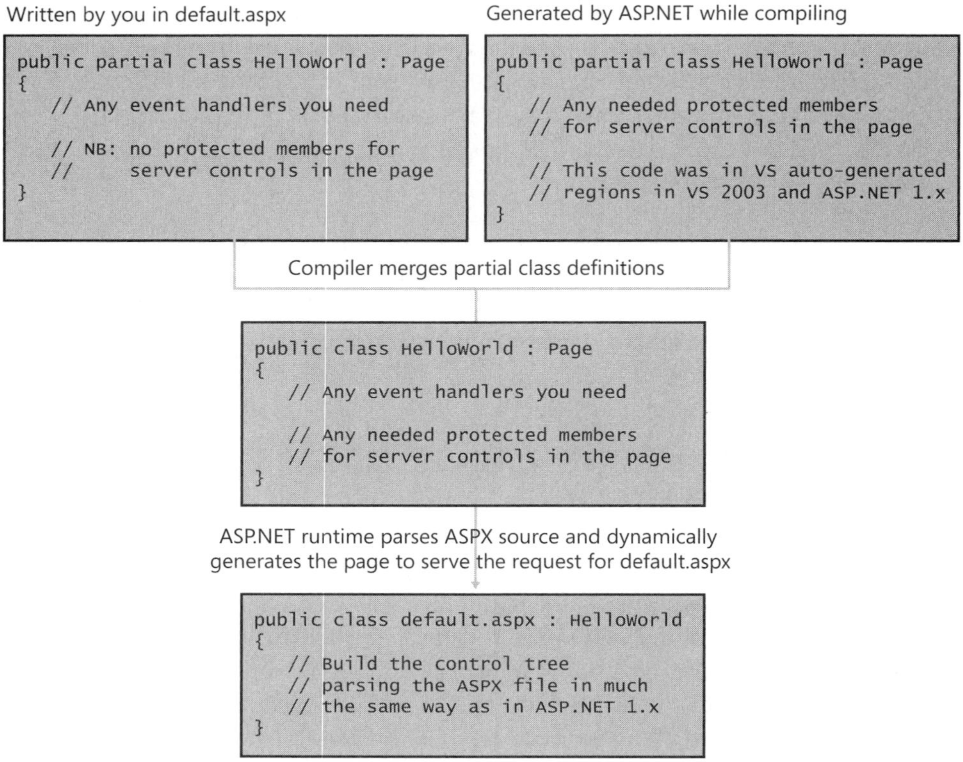

Written by you in default.aspx

```
public partial class HelloWorld : Page
{
    // Any event handlers you need

    // NB: no protected members for
    //     server controls in the page
}
```

Generated by ASP.NET while compiling

```
public partial class HelloWorld : Page
{
    // Any needed protected members
    // for server controls in the page

    // This code was in VS auto-generated
    // regions in VS 2003 and ASP.NET 1.x
}
```

Compiler merges partial class definitions

```
public class HelloWorld : Page
{
    // Any event handlers you need

    // Any needed protected members
    // for server controls in the page
}
```

ASP.NET runtime parses ASPX source and dynamically
generates the page to serve the request for default.aspx

```
public class default.aspx : HelloWorld
{
    // Build the control tree
    // parsing the ASPX file in much
    // the same way as in ASP.NET 1.x
}
```

FIGURE 3-4 ASP.NET generates the source code for the dynamic class that will serve a request.

Partial classes are a hot feature of the latest .NET compilers (version 2.0 and later). When partially declared, a class has its source code split over multiple source files, each of which appears to contain an ordinary class definition from beginning to end. The new keyword *partial*, though, informs the compiler that the class declaration being processed is incomplete. To get full and complete source code, the compiler must look into other files specified on the command line.

Partial Classes in ASP.NET Projects

Ideal for team development, partial classes simplify coding and avoid manual file synchronization in all situations in which a mix of user-defined and tool-generated code is used. Want an illustrious example? ASP.NET projects developed with Visual Studio 2003.

Partial classes are a compiler feature specifically designed to overcome the brittleness of tool-generated code in many Visual Studio 2003 projects, including ASP.NET projects. A savvy use of partial classes allows you to eliminate all those weird, auto-generated, semi-hidden regions of code that Visual Studio 2003 inserts to support page designers.

Generally, partial classes are a source-level, assembly-limited, non-object-oriented way to extend the behavior of a class. A number of advantages are derived from intensive use of partial classes. For example, you can have multiple teams at work on the same component at the same time. In addition, you have a neat and elegant way to add functionality to a class incrementally. In the end, this is just what the ASP.NET runtime does.

The ASPX markup defines server controls that will be handled by the code in the code-behind class. For this model to work, the code-behind class needs to incorporate references to these server controls as internal members—typically, protected members. In Visual Studio 2003, these declarations are added by the integrated development environment (IDE) as you save your markup and stored in semi-hidden regions. In Visual Studio 2005, the code-behind class is a partial class that just lacks member declaration. Missing declarations are incrementally added at run time via a second partial class created by the ASP.NET HTTP runtime. The compiler of choice (C#, Microsoft Visual Basic .NET, or whatever) will then merge the two partial classes to create the real parent of the dynamically created page class.

> **Note** In Visual Studio 2008 and the .NET Framework 3.5 partial classes are partnered with extension methods as a way to add new capabilities to existing .NET classes. By creating a class with extension methods you can extend, say, the System.String class with a *ToInt32* method that returns an integer if the content of the string can be converted to an integer. Once you added to the project the class with extension methods, any string in the project features the new methods. IntelliSense fully supports this feature.

Processing the Request

To serve a request for a page named *default.aspx*, the ASP.NET runtime needs to get a reference to a class *ASP.default_aspx*. As you recall, if this class doesn't exist in any of the assemblies currently loaded in the AppDomain, it will be created. Next, the HTTP runtime environment invokes the class through the methods of a well-known interface—*IHttpHandler*. The root *Page* class implements this interface, which includes a couple of members—the *ProcessRequest* method and the Boolean *IsReusable* property. Once the HTTP runtime has obtained an instance of the class that represents the requested resource, invoking the *ProcessRequest* method—a public method—gives birth to the process that culminates in the generation of the final response for the browser. As mentioned, the steps and events that execute and trigger out of the call to *ProcessRequest* are collectively known as the page life cycle.

Although serving pages is the ultimate goal of the ASP.NET runtime, the way in which the resultant markup code is generated is much more sophisticated than in other platforms and involves many objects. The ASP.NET worker process—be it *w3wp.exe* or *aspnet_wp.exe*—passes any incoming HTTP requests to the so-called HTTP pipeline. The HTTP pipeline is a fully extensible chain of managed objects that works according to the classic concept of a pipeline. All these objects form what is often referred to as the *ASP.NET HTTP runtime environment*.

The *HttpRuntime* Object

A page request passes through a pipeline of objects that process the original HTTP payload and, at the end of the chain, produce some markup code for the browser. The entry point in this pipeline is the *HttpRuntime* class. The ASP.NET worker process activates the HTTP pipeline in the beginning by creating a new instance of the *HttpRuntime* class and then calling its *ProcessRequest* method for each incoming request. For the sake of clarity, note that despite the name, *HttpRuntime.ProcessRequest* has nothing to do with the *IHttpHandler* interface.

The *HttpRuntime* class contains a lot of private and internal methods and only three public static methods: *Close*, *ProcessRequest*, and *UnloadAppDomain*, as detailed in Table 3-2.

TABLE 3-2 Public Methods in the *HttpRuntime* Class

Method	Description
Close	Removes all items from the ASP.NET cache, and terminates the Web application. This method should be used only when your code implements its own hosting environment. There is no need to call this method in the course of normal ASP.NET request processing.
ProcessRequest	Drives all ASP.NET Web processing execution.
UnloadAppDomain	Terminates the current ASP.NET application. The application restarts the next time a request is received for it.

It is important to note that all the methods shown in Table 3-2 have limited applicability in user applications. In particular, you're not supposed to use *ProcessRequest* in your own code, whereas *Close* is useful only if you're hosting ASP.NET in a custom application. Of the three methods in Table 3-2, only *UnloadAppDomain* can be considered for use if, under certain run-time conditions, you realize you need to restart the application. (See the sidebar "What Causes Application Restarts?" later in this chapter.)

Upon creation, the *HttpRuntime* object initializes a number of internal objects that will help carry out the page request. Helper objects include the cache manager and the file system monitor used to detect changes in the files that form the application. When the *ProcessRequest* method is called, the *HttpRuntime* object starts working to serve a page to the browser. It creates a new empty context for the request and initializes a specialized text writer object in which the markup code will be accumulated. A context is given by an instance of the *HttpContext* class, which encapsulates all HTTP-specific information about the request.

After that, the *HttpRuntime* object uses the context information to either locate or create a Web application object capable of handling the request. A Web application is searched using the virtual directory information contained in the URL. The object used to find or create a new Web application is *HttpApplicationFactory*—an internal-use object responsible for returning a valid object capable of handling the request.

Before we get to discover more about the various components of the HTTP pipeline, a look at Figure 3-5 is in order.

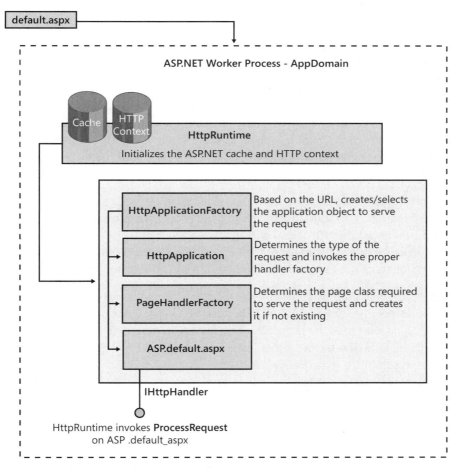

FIGURE 3-5 The HTTP pipeline processing for a page.

The Application Factory

During the lifetime of the application, the *HttpApplicationFactory* object maintains a pool of *HttpApplication* objects to serve incoming HTTP requests. When invoked, the application factory object verifies that an AppDomain exists for the virtual folder the request targets. If the application is already running, the factory picks an *HttpApplication* out of the pool of available objects and passes it the request. A new *HttpApplication* object is created if an existing object is not available.

If the virtual folder has not yet been called for the first time, a new *HttpApplication* object for the virtual folder is created in a new AppDomain. In this case, the creation of an *HttpApplication* object entails the compilation of the *global.asax* application file, if one is present, and the creation of the assembly that represents the actual page requested. This event is actually equivalent to the start of the application. An *HttpApplication* object is used to process a single page request at a time; multiple objects are used to serve simultaneous requests.

The *HttpApplication* Object

HttpApplication is the base class that represents a running ASP.NET application. A running ASP.NET application is represented by a dynamically created class that inherits from *HttpApplication*. The source code of the dynamically generated application class is created by parsing the contents of the *global.asax* file, if any is present. If *global.asax* is available, the application class is built and named after it: *ASP.global_asax*. Otherwise, the base *HttpApplication* class is used.

An instance of an *HttpApplication*-derived class is responsible for managing the entire lifetime of the request it is assigned to. The same instance can be reused only after the request has been completed. The *HttpApplication* maintains a list of HTTP module objects that can filter and even modify the content of the request. Registered modules are called during various moments of the elaboration as the request passes through the pipeline.

The *HttpApplication* object determines the type of object that represents the resource being requested—typically, an ASP.NET page, a Web service, or perhaps a user control. *HttpApplication* then uses the proper handler factory to get an object that represents the requested resource. The factory either instantiates the class for the requested resource from an existing assembly or dynamically creates the assembly and then an instance of the class. A handler factory object is a class that implements the *IHttpHandlerFactory* interface and is responsible for returning an instance of a managed class that can handle the HTTP request—an HTTP handler. An ASP.NET page is simply a handler object—that is, an instance of a class that implements the *IHttpHandler* interface.

The Page Factory

The *HttpApplication* class determines the type of object that must handle the request and delegates the type-specific handler factory to create an instance of that type. Let's see what happens when the resource requested is a page.

Once the *HttpApplication* object in charge of the request has figured out the proper handler, it creates an instance of the handler factory object. For a request that targets a page, the factory is a class named *PageHandlerFactory*. To find the appropriate handler, *HttpApplication* uses the information in the *<httpHandlers>* section of the configuration file. Table 3-3 contains a brief list of the main handlers registered.

TABLE 3-3 Handler Factory Classes in the .NET Framework

Handler Factory	Type	Description
HttpRemotingHandlerFactory	*.rem; *.soap	Instantiates the object that will take care of a .NET Remoting request routed through IIS. Instantiates an object of type *HttpRemotingHandler*.
PageHandlerFactory	*.aspx	Compiles and instantiates the type that represents the page. The source code for the class is built while parsing the source code of the *.aspx* file. Instantiates an object of a type that derives from *Page*.
SimpleHandlerFactory	*.ashx	Compiles and instantiates the specified HTTP handler from the source code of the .ashx file. Instantiates an object that implements the *IHttpHandler* interface.
WebServiceHandlerFactory	*.asmx	Compiles the source code of a Web service, and translates the SOAP payload into a method invocation. Instantiates an object of the type specified in the Web service file.

Bear in mind that handler factory objects do not compile the requested resource each time it is invoked. The compiled code is stored in an ASP.NET temporary directory on the Web server and used until the corresponding resource file is modified. (This bit of efficiency is the primary reason the factory pattern is followed in this case.)

So when the request is received, the page handler factory creates an instance of an object that represents the particular requested page. As mentioned, this object inherits from the *System.Web.UI.Page* class, which in turn implements the *IHttpHandler* interface. The page object is returned to the application factory, which passes that back to the *HttpRuntime* object. The final step accomplished by the ASP.NET runtime is calling the *IHttpHandler*'s *ProcessRequest* method on the page object. This call causes the page to execute the user-defined code and generate the markup for the browser.

In Chapter 14, we'll return to the initialization of an ASP.NET application, the contents of *global.asax*, and the information stuffed into the HTTP context—a container object that, created by the *HttpRuntime* class, is populated and passed along the pipeline and finally bound to the page handler.

What Causes Application Restarts?

There are a few reasons why an ASP.NET application can be restarted. For the most part, an application is restarted to ensure that latent bugs or memory leaks don't affect in the long run the overall behavior of the application. Another reason is that too many dynamic changes to ASPX pages may have caused too large a number of assemblies (typically, one per page) to be loaded in memory. Any application that consumes more than a certain share of virtual memory is killed and restarted. The ASP.NET runtime environment implements a good deal of checks and automatically restarts an application if any the following scenarios occur:

- The maximum limit of dynamic page compilations is reached. This limit is configurable through the *web.config* file.

- The physical path of the Web application has changed, or any directory under the Web application folder is renamed.

- Changes occurred in *global.asax*, *machine.config*, or *web.config* in the application root, or in the *Bin* directory or any of its subdirectories.

- Changes occurred in the code-access security policy file, if one exists.

- Too many files are changed in one of the content directories. (Typically, this happens if files are generated on the fly when requested.)

- Changes occurred to settings that control the restart/shutdown of the ASP. NET worker process. These settings are read from *machine.config* if you don't use Windows 2003 Server with the IIS 6.0 process model. If you're taking full advantage of IIS 6.0, an application is restarted if you modify properties in the *Application Pools* node of the IIS manager.

In addition to all this, in ASP.NET an application can be restarted programmatically by calling *HttpRuntime.UnloadAppDomain*.

The Processing Directives of a Page

Processing directives configure the runtime environment that will execute the page. In ASP. NET, directives can be located anywhere in the page, although it's a good and common practice to place them at the beginning of the file. In addition, the name of a directive is case-insensitive and the values of directive attributes don't need to be quoted. The most important and most frequently used directive in ASP.NET is *@Page*. The complete list of ASP. NET directives is shown in Table 3-4.

TABLE 3-4 Directives Supported by ASP.NET Pages

Directive	Description
@ Assembly	Links an assembly to the current page or user control.
@ Control	Defines control-specific attributes that guide the behavior of the control compiler.
@ Implements	Indicates that the page, or the user control, implements a specified .NET Framework interface.
@ Import	Indicates a namespace to import into a page or user control.
@ Master	Identifies an ASP.NET master page. (See Chapter 6.) *This directive is not available with ASP.NET 1.x.*
@ MasterType	Provides a way to create a strongly typed reference to the ASP.NET master page when the master page is accessed from the *Master* property. (See Chapter 6.) *This directive is not available with ASP.NET 1.x.*
@ OutputCache	Controls the output caching policies of a page or user control. (See Chapter 16.)
@ Page	Defines page-specific attributes that guide the behavior of the page compiler and the language parser that will preprocess the page.
@ PreviousPageType	Provides a way to get strong typing against the previous page, as accessed through the *PreviousPage* property.
@ Reference	Links a page or user control to the current page or user control.
@ Register	Creates a custom tag in the page or the control. The new tag (prefix and name) is associated with the namespace and the code of a user-defined control.

With the exception of *@Page*, *@PreviousPageType*, *@Master*, *@MasterType*, and *@Control*, all directives can be used both within a page and a control declaration. *@Page* and *@Control* are mutually exclusive. *@Page* can be used only in *.aspx* files, while the *@Control* directive can be used only in user control *.ascx* files. *@Master*, in turn, is used to define a very special type of page—the master page.

The syntax of a processing directive is unique and common to all supported types of directives. Multiple attributes must be separated with blanks, and no blank can be placed around the equal sign (=) that assigns a value to an attribute, as the following line of code demonstrates:

```
<%@ Directive_Name attribute="value" [attribute="value"...] %>
```

Each directive has its own closed set of typed attributes. Assigning a value of the wrong type to an attribute, or using a wrong attribute with a directive, results in a compilation error.

> **Important** The content of directive attributes is always rendered as plain text. However, attributes are expected to contain values that can be rendered to a particular .NET Framework type, specific to the attribute. When the ASP.NET page is parsed, all the directive attributes are extracted and stored in a dictionary. The names and number of attributes must match the expected schema for the directive. The string that expresses the value of an attribute is valid as long as it can be converted into the expected type. For example, if the attribute is designed to take a Boolean value, *true* and *false* are its only feasible values.

The @*Page* Directive

The @*Page* directive can be used only in .*aspx* pages, and it generates a compile error if used with other types of ASP.NET pages, such as controls and Web services. Each .*aspx* file is allowed to include at most one @*Page* directive. Although not strictly necessary from the syntax point of view, the directive is realistically required by all pages of some complexity.

@*Page* features about 30 attributes that can be logically grouped in three categories: compilation (defined in Table 3-5), overall page behavior (defined in Table 3-6), and page output (defined in Table 3-7). Each ASP.NET page is compiled upon first request, and the HTML actually served to the browser is generated by the methods of the dynamically generated class. Attributes listed in Table 3-5 let you fine-tune parameters for the compiler and choose the language to use.

TABLE 3-5 @*Page* **Attributes for Page Compilation**

Attribute	Description
ClassName	Specifies the name of the class name that will be dynamically compiled when the page is requested. Must be a class name without namespace information.
CodeFile	Indicates the path to the code-behind class for the current page. The source class file must be deployed to the Web server. *Not available with ASP.NET 1.x.*
CodeBehind	Attribute consumed by Visual Studio .NET 2003, indicates the path to the code-behind class for the current page. The source class file will be compiled to a deployable assembly. (Note that for ASP.NET version 2.0 and later, the *CodeFile* attribute should be used.)
CodeFileBaseClass	Specifies the type name of a base class for a page and its associated code-behind class. The attribute is optional, but when it is used the *CodeFile* attribute must also be present. *Not available with ASP.NET 1.x.*

Attribute	Description
CompilationMode	Indicates whether the page should be compiled at run time. *Not available with ASP.NET 1.x.*
CompilerOptions	A sequence of compiler command-line switches used to compile the page.
Debug	A Boolean value that indicates whether the page should be compiled with debug symbols.
Explicit	A Boolean value that determines whether the page is compiled with the Visual Basic *Option Explicit* mode set to *On. Option Explicit* forces the programmer to explicitly declare all variables. The attribute is ignored if the page language is not Visual Basic .NET.
Inherits	Defines the base class for the page to inherit. It can be any class derived from the *Page* class.
Language	Indicates the language to use when compiling inline code blocks (<% ... %>) and all the code that appears in the page *<script>* section. Supported languages include Visual Basic .NET, C#, JScript .NET, and J#. If not otherwise specified, the language defaults to Visual Basic .NET.
LinePragmas	Indicates whether the runtime should generate line pragmas in the source code
MasterPageFile	Indicates the master page for the current page. *Not available with ASP.NET 1.x.*
Src	Indicates the source file that contains the implementation of the base class specified with *Inherits*. The attribute is not used by Visual Studio and other rapid application development (RAD) designers.
Strict	A Boolean value that determines whether the page is compiled with the Visual Basic *Option Strict* mode set to *On.* When enabled, *Option Strict* permits only type-safe conversions and prohibits implicit conversions in which loss of data is possible. (In this case, the behavior is identical to that of C#.) The attribute is ignored if the page language is not Visual Basic .NET.
Trace	A Boolean value that indicates whether tracing is enabled. If tracing is enabled, extra information is appended to the page's output. The default is *false.*
TraceMode	Indicates how trace messages are to be displayed for the page when tracing is enabled. Feasible values are *SortByTime* and *SortByCategory.* The default, when tracing is enabled, is *SortByTime.*
WarningLevel	Indicates the compiler warning level at which you want the compiler to abort compilation for the page. Possible values are *0* through *4.*

Notice that the default values of the *Explicit* and *Strict* attributes are read from the application's configuration settings. The configuration settings of an ASP.NET application are obtained by merging all machine-wide settings with application-wide and even folder-wide settings. This means you can also control what the default values for the *Explicit* and *Strict* attributes are. Unless you change the default configuration settings—the configuration files are created when the .NET Framework is installed—both *Explicit* and *Strict* default to *true*. Should the related settings be removed from the configuration files, both attributes would default to *false* instead.

Attributes listed in Table 3-6 allow you to control to some extent the overall behavior of the page and the supported range of features. For example, you can set a custom error page, disable session state, and control the transactional behavior of the page.

> **Note** The schema of attributes supported by the *@Page* is not as strict as for other directives. In particular, you can list as a *@Page* attribute, and initialize, any public properties defined on the page class.

TABLE 3-6 *@Page* **Attributes for Page Behavior**

Attribute	Description
AspCompat	A Boolean attribute that, when set to *true*, allows the page to be executed on a single-threaded apartment (STA) thread. The setting allows the page to call COM+ 1.0 components and components developed with Microsoft Visual Basic 6.0 that require access to the unmanaged ASP built-in objects. (I'll cover this topic in Chapter 14.)
Async	If set to *true*, the generated page class derives from *IHttpAsyncHandler* rather than having *IHttpHandler* add some built-in asynchronous capabilities to the page. *Not available with ASP.NET 1.x.*
AsyncTimeOut	Defines the timeout in seconds used when processing asynchronous tasks. The default is 45 seconds. *Not available with ASP.NET 1.x.*
AutoEventWireup	A Boolean attribute that indicates whether page events are automatically enabled. Set to *true* by default. Pages developed with Visual Studio .NET have this attribute set to *false*, and page events are individually tied to handlers.
Buffer	A Boolean attribute that determines whether HTTP response buffering is enabled. Set to *true* by default.
Description	Provides a text description of the page. The ASP.NET page parser ignores the attribute, which subsequently has only a documentation purpose.
EnableEventValidation	A Boolean value that indicates whether the page will emit a hidden field to cache available values for input fields that support event data validation. Set to *true* by default. *Not available with ASP.NET 1.x.*

Attribute	Description
EnableSessionState	Defines how the page should treat session data. If set to *true*, the session state can be read and written. If set to *false*, session data is not available to the application. Finally, if set to *ReadOnly*, the session state can be read but not changed.
EnableViewState	A Boolean value that indicates whether the page *view state* is maintained across page requests. The view state is the page call context—a collection of values that retain the state of the page and are carried back and forth. View state is enabled by default. (I'll cover this topic in Chapter 15.)
EnableTheming	A Boolean value that indicates whether the page will support themes for embedded controls. Set to *true* by default. *Not available in ASP.NET 1.x.*
EnableViewStateMac	A Boolean value that indicates ASP.NET should calculate a machine-specific authentication code and append it to the view state of the page (in addition to Base64 encoding). The *Mac* in the attribute name stands for *machine authentication check*. When the attribute is *true*, upon postbacks ASP.NET will check the authentication code of the view state to make sure that it hasn't been tampered with on the client.
ErrorPage	Defines the target URL to which users will be automatically redirected in case of unhandled page exceptions.
MaintainScrollPosition-OnPostback	Indicates whether to return the user to the same scrollbar position in the client browser after postback. The default is false.
SmartNavigation	A Boolean value that indicates whether the page supports the Microsoft Internet Explorer 5 or later smart navigation feature. Smart navigation allows a page to be refreshed without losing scroll position and element focus.
Theme, StyleSheetTheme	Indicates the name of the theme (or style-sheet theme) selected for the page. *Not available with ASP.NET 1.x.*
Transaction	Indicates whether the page supports or requires transactions. Feasible values are: *Disabled, NotSupported, Supported, Required*, and *RequiresNew*. Transaction support is disabled by default.
ValidateRequest	A Boolean value that indicates whether request validation should occur. If this value is set to *true*, ASP.NET checks all input data against a hard-coded list of potentially dangerous values. This functionality helps reduce the risk of cross-site scripting attacks for pages. The value is *true* by default. *This feature is not supported in ASP.NET 1.0.*
ViewStateEncryption-Mode	Indicates how view state is encrypted, with three possible enumerated values: Auto, Always, or Never. The default is Auto meaning that the viewstate is encrypted only if a control requests that. Note that using encryption over the viewstate adds some overhead to the processing of the page on the server for each request.

Attributes listed in Table 3-7 allow you to control the format of the output being generated for the page. For example, you can set the content type of the page or localize the output to the extent possible.

TABLE 3-7 @*Page* Directives for Page Output

Attribute	Description
ClientTarget	Indicates the target browser for which ASP.NET server controls should render content.
CodePage	Indicates the code page value for the response. Set this attribute only if you created the page using a code page other than the default code page of the Web server on which the page will run. In this case, set the attribute to the code page of your development machine. A code page is a character set that includes numbers, punctuation marks, and other glyphs. Code pages differ on a per-language basis.
ContentType	Defines the content type of the response as a standard MIME type. Supports any valid HTTP content type string.
Culture	Indicates the culture setting for the page. Culture information includes the writing and sorting system, calendar, and date and currency formats. The attribute must be set to a non-neutral culture name, which means it must contain both language and country information. For example, *en-US* is a valid value, unlike *en* alone, which is considered country-neutral.
LCID	A 32-bit value that defines the locale identifier for the page. By default, ASP.NET uses the locale of the Web server.
ResponseEncoding	Indicates the character encoding of the page. The value is used to set the *CharSet* attribute on the content type HTTP header. Internally, ASP.NET handles all strings as Unicode.
Title	Indicates the title of the page. Not really useful for regular pages which would likely use the *<title>* HTML tag, the attribute has been defined to help developers add a title to content pages where access to the *<title>* attribute may not be possible. (This actually depends on how the master page is structured.)
UICulture	Specifies the default culture name used by the Resource Manager to look up culture-specific resources at run time.

As you can see, many attributes discussed in Table 3-7 are related to page localization. Building multilanguage and international applications is a task that ASP.NET, and the .NET Framework in general, greatly simplify. In Chapter 5, we'll delve into the topic.

The @*Assembly* Directive

The @*Assembly* directive links an assembly to the current page so that its classes and interfaces are available for use on the page. When ASP.NET compiles the page, a few assemblies are linked by default. So you should resort to the directive only if you need linkage to a non-default assembly. Table 3-8 lists the .NET assemblies that are automatically provided to the compiler.

TABLE 3-8 **Assemblies Linked by Default**

Assembly File Name	Description
Mscorlib.dll	Provides the core functionality of the .NET Framework, including types, AppDomains, and run-time services.
System.dll	Provides another bunch of system services, including regular expressions, compilation, native methods, file I/O, and networking.
System.Configuration.dll	Defines classes to read and write configuration data. *Not included in ASP.NET 1.x.*
System.Data.dll	Defines data container and data access classes, including the whole ADO.NET framework.
System.Drawing.dll	Implements the GDI+ features.
System.EnterpriseServices.dll	Provides the classes that allow for serviced components and COM+ interaction.
System.Web.dll	The assembly implements the core ASP.NET services, controls, and classes.
System.Web.Mobile.dll	The assembly implements the core ASP.NET mobile services, controls, and classes. *Not included if version 1.0 of the .NET Framework is installed.*
System.Web.Services.dll	Contains the core code that makes Web services run.
System.Xml.dll	Implements the .NET Framework XML features.
System.Runtime.Serialization	Defines the API for .NET serialization. This was one of the additional assemblies that was most frequently added by developers in ASP.NET 2.0 applications. *Only included in ASP.NET 3.5.*
System.ServiceModel	Defines classes and structure for Windows Communication Foundation (WCF) services. *Only included in ASP.NET 3.5.*
System.ServiceModel.Web	Defines the additional classes required by ASP.NET and AJAX to support WCF services. *Only included in ASP.NET 3.5.*
System.WorkflowServices	Defines classes for making workflows and WCF services interact. *Only included in ASP.NET 3.5.*

In addition to these assemblies, the ASP.NET runtime automatically links to the page all the assemblies that reside in the Web application *Bin* subdirectory. Note that you can modify, extend, or restrict the list of default assemblies by editing the global settings set in the global machine-level *web.config* file. In this case, changes apply to all ASP.NET applications run on that Web server. Alternately, you can modify the assembly list on a per-application basis by editing the application's specific *web.config* file. To prevent all assemblies found in the *Bin* directory from being linked to the page, remove the following line from the root configuration file:

```
<add assembly="*" />
```

> **Warning** For an ASP.NET application, the whole set of configuration attributes is set at the machine level. Initially, all applications hosted on a given server machine share the same settings. Then individual applications can override some of those settings in their own *web.config* files. Each application can have a *web.config* file in the root virtual folder and other copies of specialized *web.config* files in application-specific subdirectories. Each page is subject to settings as determined by the configuration files found in the path from the machine to the containing folder. In ASP.NET 1.x, the *machine.config* file contains the complete tree of default settings. In ASP.NET 2.0, the configuration data that specifically refers to Web applications has been moved to a *web.config* file installed in the same system folder as *machine.config*. The folder is named CONFIG and located below the installation path of ASP.NET—that is, *%WINDOWS%\Microsoft. Net\Framework\[version]*.

To link a needed assembly to the page, use the following syntax:

```
<%@ Assembly Name="AssemblyName" %>
<%@ Assembly Src="assembly_code.cs" %>
```

The *@Assembly* directive supports two mutually exclusive attributes: *Name* and *Src*. *Name* indicates the name of the assembly to link to the page. The name cannot include the path or the extension. *Src* indicates the path to a source file to dynamically compile and link against the page. The *@Assembly* directive can appear multiple times in the body of the page. In fact, you need a new directive for each assembly to link. *Name* and *Src* cannot be used in the same *@Assembly* directive, but multiple directives defined in the same page can use either.

> **Note** In terms of performance, the difference between *Name* and *Src* is minimal, although *Name* points to an existing and ready-to-load assembly. The source file referenced by *Src* is compiled only the first time it is requested. The ASP.NET runtime maps a source file with a dynamically compiled assembly and keeps using the compiled code until the original file undergoes changes. This means that after the first application-level call the impact on the page performance is identical whether you use *Name* or *Src*.

The *@Import* Directive

The *@Import* directive links the specified namespace to the page so that all the types defined can be accessed from the page without specifying the fully qualified name. For example, to create a new instance of the ADO.NET *DataSet* class, you either import the *System.Data* namespace or specify the fully qualified class name whenever you need it, as in the following code:

```
System.Data.DataSet ds = new System.Data.DataSet();
```

Once you've imported the *System.Data* namespace into the page, you can use more natural coding, as shown here:

```
DataSet ds = new DataSet();
```

The syntax of the *@Import* directive is rather self-explanatory:

```
<%@ Import namespace="value" %>
```

@Import can be used as many times as needed in the body of the page. The *@Import* directive is the ASP.NET counterpart of the C# *using* statement and the Visual Basic .NET *Imports* statement. Looking back at unmanaged C/C++, we could say the directive plays a role nearly identical to the *#include* directive.

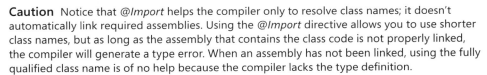

> **Caution** Notice that *@Import* helps the compiler only to resolve class names; it doesn't automatically link required assemblies. Using the *@Import* directive allows you to use shorter class names, but as long as the assembly that contains the class code is not properly linked, the compiler will generate a type error. When an assembly has not been linked, using the fully qualified class name is of no help because the compiler lacks the type definition.
>
> You might have noticed that, more often than not, assembly and namespace names coincide. Bear in mind it only happens by chance and that assemblies and namespaces are radically different entities, each requiring the proper directive.

For example, to be able to connect to a SQL Server database and grab some disconnected data, you need to import the following two namespaces:

```
<%@ Import namespace="System.Data" %>
<%@ Import namespace=" System.Data.SqlClient" %>
```

You need the *System.Data* namespace to work with the *DataSet* and *DataTable* classes, and you need the *System.Data.SqlClient* namespace to prepare and issue the command. In this case, you don't need to link against additional assemblies because the *System.Data.dll* assembly is linked by default.

The *@Implements* Directive

The *@Implements* directive indicates that the current page implements the specified .NET Framework interface. An interface is a set of signatures for a logically related group of functions and is a sort of contract that shows the component's commitment to expose that group of functions. Unlike abstract classes, an interface doesn't provide code or executable functionality. When you implement an interface in an ASP.NET page, you declare any required methods and properties within the *<script>* section. The syntax of the *@Implements* directive is as follows:

```
<%@ Implements interface="InterfaceName" %>
```

The @*Implements* directive can appear multiple times in the page if the page has to implement multiple interfaces. Note that if you decide to put all the page logic in a separate class file, you can't use the directive to implement interfaces. Instead, you implement the interface in the code-behind class.

The @*Reference* Directive

The @*Reference* directive is used to establish a dynamic link between the current page and the specified page or user control. This feature has significant consequences regarding the way in which you set up cross-page communication. It also lets you create strongly typed instances of user controls. Let's review the syntax.

The directive can appear multiple times in the page and features two mutually exclusive attributes—*Page* and *Control*. Both attributes are expected to contain a path to a source file:

```
<%@ Reference page="source_page" %>
<%@ Reference control="source_user_control" %>
```

The *Page* attribute points to an *.aspx* source file, whereas the *Control* attribute contains the path of an *.ascx* user control. In both cases, the referenced source file will be dynamically compiled into an assembly, thus making the classes defined in the source programmatically available to the referencing page. When running, an ASP.NET page is an instance of a .NET Framework class with a specific interface made of methods and properties. When the referencing page executes, a referenced page becomes a class that represents the *.aspx* source file and can be instantiated and programmed at will. Notice that for the directive to work the referenced page must belong to the same domain as the calling page. Cross-site calls are not allowed, and both the *Page* and *Control* attributes expect to receive a relative virtual path.

> **Note** Starting with ASP.NET 2.0, you are better off using cross-page posting to enable communication between pages.

The *Page* Class

In the .NET Framework, the *Page* class provides the basic behavior for all objects that an ASP. NET application builds by starting from *.aspx* files. Defined in the *System.Web.UI* namespace, the class derives from *TemplateControl* and implements the *IHttpHandler* interface:

```
public class Page : TemplateControl, IHttpHandler
```

In particular, *TemplateControl* is the abstract class that provides both ASP.NET pages and user controls with a base set of functionality. At the upper level of the hierarchy, we find the *Control* class. It defines the properties, methods, and events shared by all ASP.NET server-side elements—pages, controls, and user controls.

Derived from a class—*TemplateControl*—that implements *INamingContainer*, *Page* also serves as the naming container for all its constituent controls. In the .NET Framework, the naming container for a control is the first parent control that implements the *INamingContainer* interface. For any class that implements the naming container interface, ASP.NET creates a new virtual namespace in which all child controls are guaranteed to have unique names in the overall tree of controls. (This is also a very important feature for iterative data-bound controls, such as *DataGrid*, for user controls, and controls that fire server-side events.)

The *Page* class also implements the methods of the *IHttpHandler* interface, thus qualifying as the handler of a particular type of HTTP requests—those for *.aspx* files. The key element of the *IHttpHandler* interface is the *ProcessRequest* method, which is the method the ASP.NET runtime calls to start the page processing that will actually serve the request.

 Note *INamingContainer* is a marker interface that has no methods. Its presence alone, though, forces the ASP.NET runtime to create an additional namespace for naming the child controls of the page (or the control) that implements it. The *Page* class is the naming container of all the page's controls, with the clear exception of those controls that implement the *INamingContainer* interface themselves or are children of controls that implement the interface.

Properties of the *Page* Class

The properties of the *Page* object can be classified in three distinct groups: intrinsic objects, worker properties, and page-specific properties. The tables in the following sections enumerate and describe them.

Intrinsic Objects

Table 3-9 lists all properties that return a helper object that is intrinsic to the page. In other words, objects listed here are all essential parts of the infrastructure that allows for the page execution.

TABLE 3-9 ASP.NET Intrinsic Objects in the *Page* Class

Property	Description
Application	Instance of the *HttpApplicationState* class; represents the state of the application. It is functionally equivalent to the ASP intrinsic *Application* object.
Cache	Instance of the *Cache* class; implements the cache for an ASP.NET application. More efficient and powerful than *Application*, it supports item priority and expiration.
Profile	Instance of the *ProfileCommon* class; represents the user-specific set of data associated with the request.
Request	Instance of the *HttpRequest* class; represents the current HTTP request. It is functionally equivalent to the ASP intrinsic *Request* object.
Response	Instance of the *HttpResponse* class; sends HTTP response data to the client. It is functionally equivalent to the ASP intrinsic *Response* object.
Server	Instance of the *HttpServerUtility* class; provides helper methods for processing Web requests. It is functionally equivalent to the ASP intrinsic *Server* object.
Session	Instance of the *HttpSessionState* class; manages user-specific data. It is functionally equivalent to the ASP intrinsic *Session* object.
Trace	Instance of the *TraceContext* class; performs tracing on the page.
User	An *IPrincipal* object that represents the user making the request.

We'll cover *Request*, *Response*, and *Server* in Chapter 14; *Application* and *Session* in Chapter 15; *Cache* will be the subject of Chapter 16. Finally, *User* and security will be the subject of Chapter 17.

Worker Properties

Table 3-10 details page properties that are both informative and provide the grounds for functional capabilities. You can hardly write code in the page without most of these properties.

TABLE 3-10 Worker Properties of the *Page* Class

Property	Description
ClientScript	Gets a *ClientScriptManager* object that contains the client script used on the page. *Not available with ASP.NET 1.x.*
Controls	Returns the collection of all the child controls contained in the current page.
ErrorPage	Gets or sets the error page to which the requesting browser is redirected in case of an unhandled page exception.
Form	Returns the current *HtmlForm* object for the page. *Not available with ASP.NET 1.x.*

Property	Description
Header	Returns a reference to the object that represents the page's header. The object implements *IPageHeader*. *Not available with ASP.NET 1.x.*
IsAsync	Indicates whether the page is being invoked through an asynchronous handler. *Not available with ASP.NET 1.x.*
IsCallback	Indicates whether the page is being loaded in response to a client script callback. *Not available with ASP.NET 1.x.*
IsCrossPagePostBack	Indicates whether the page is being loaded in response to a postback made from within another page. *Not available with ASP.NET 1.x.*
IsPostBack	Indicates whether the page is being loaded in response to a client postback or whether it is being loaded for the first time.
IsValid	Indicates whether page validation succeeded.
Master	Instance of the *MasterPage* class; represents the master page that determines the appearance of the current page. *Not available with ASP. NET 1.x.*
MasterPageFile	Gets and sets the master file for the current page. *Not available with ASP.NET 1.x.*
NamingContainer	Returns *null*.
Page	Returns the current *Page* object.
PageAdapter	Returns the adapter object for the current *Page* object.
Parent	Returns *null*.
PreviousPage	Returns the reference to the caller page in case of a cross-page postback. *Not available with ASP.NET 1.x.*
TemplateSourceDirectory	Gets the virtual directory of the page.
Validators	Returns the collection of all validation controls contained in the page.
ViewStateUserKey	String property that represents a user-specific identifier used to hash the view-state contents. This trick is a line of defense against one-click attacks. *Not available with ASP.NET 1.0.*

In the context of an ASP.NET application, the *Page* object is the root of the hierarchy. For this reason, inherited properties such as *NamingContainer* and *Parent* always return *null*. The *Page* property, on the other hand, returns an instance of the same object (*this* in C# and *Me* in Visual Basic .NET).

The *ViewStateUserKey* property that has been added with version 1.1 of the .NET Framework deserves a special mention. A common use for the user key is to stuff user-specific information that would then be used to hash the contents of the view state along with other information. (See Chapter 15.) A typical value for the *ViewStateUserKey* property is the name of the authenticated user or the user's session ID. This contrivance reinforces the security level for the view state information and further lowers the likelihood of attacks. If you employ a user-specific key, an attacker can't construct a valid view state for your user account unless the attacker can also authenticate as you. With this configuration, you have another barrier against one-click attacks. This technique, though, might not be effective for Web sites that allow anonymous access, unless you have some other unique tracking device running.

Note that if you plan to set the *ViewStateUserKey* property, you must do that during the *Page_Init* event. If you attempt to do it later (for example, when *Page_Load* fires), an exception will be thrown.

Context Properties

Table 3-11 lists properties that represent visual and nonvisual attributes of the page, such as the URL's query string, the client target, the title, and the applied style sheet.

TABLE 3-11 **Page-Specific Properties of the *Page* Class**

Property	Description
ClientID	Always returns the empty string.
ClientQueryString	Gets the query string portion of the requested URL. *Not available with ASP.NET 1.x.*
ClientTarget	Set to the empty string by default; allows you to specify the type of the browser the HTML should comply with. Setting this property disables automatic detection of browser capabilities.
EnableViewState	Indicates whether the page has to manage view-state data. You can also enable or disable the view-state feature through the *EnableViewState* attribute of the *@Page* directive.
EnableViewStateMac	Indicates whether ASP.NET should calculate a machine-specific authentication code and append it to the page view state.
EnableTheming	Indicates whether the page supports themes. *Not available with ASP.NET 1.x.*
ID	Always returns the empty string.
MaintainScrollPositionOnPostback	Indicates whether to return the user to the same position in the client browser after postback. *Not available with ASP.NET 1.x.*
SmartNavigation	Indicates whether smart navigation is enabled. Smart navigation exploits a bunch of browser-specific capabilities to enhance the user's experience with the page.
StyleSheetTheme	Gets or sets the name of the style sheet applied to this page. *Not available with ASP.NET 1.x.*

Property	Description
Theme	Gets and sets the theme for the page. Note that themes can be programmatically set only in the *PreInit* event. *Not available with ASP.NET 1.x.*
Title	Gets or sets the title for the page. *Not available with ASP.NET 1.x.*
TraceEnabled	Toggles page tracing on and off. *Not available with ASP.NET 1.x.*
TraceModeValue	Gets or sets the trace mode. *Not available with ASP.NET 1.x.*
UniqueID	Always returns the empty string.
ViewStateEncryptionMode	Indicates if and how the view state should be encrypted.
Visible	Indicates whether ASP.NET has to render the page. If you set *Visible* to *false*, ASP.NET doesn't generate any HTML code for the page. When *Visible* is *false*, only the text explicitly written using *Response.Write* hits the client.

The three ID properties (*ID*, *ClientID*, and *UniqueID*) always return the empty string from a *Page* object. They make sense only for server controls.

Methods of the *Page* Class

The whole range of *Page* methods can be classified in a few categories based on the tasks each method accomplishes. A few methods are involved with the generation of the markup for the page; others are helper methods to build the page and manage the constituent controls. Finally, a third group collects all the methods that have to do with client-side scripting.

Rendering Methods

Table 3-12 details the methods that are directly or indirectly involved with the generation of the markup code.

TABLE 3-12 Methods for Markup Generation

Method	Description
DataBind	Binds all the data-bound controls contained in the page to their data sources. The *DataBind* method doesn't generate code itself but prepares the ground for the forthcoming rendering.
RenderControl	Outputs the HTML text for the page, including tracing information if tracing is enabled.
VerifyRenderingInServerForm	Controls call this method when they render to ensure that they are included in the body of a server form. The method does not return a value, but it throws an exception in case of error.

In an ASP.NET page, no control can be placed outside a *<form>* tag with the *runat* attribute set to *server*. The *VerifyRenderingInServerForm* method is used by Web and HTML controls to ensure that they are rendered correctly. In theory, custom controls should call this method during the rendering phase. In many situations, the custom control embeds or derives an existing Web or HTML control that will make the check itself.

Not directly exposed by the *Page* class, but strictly related to it, is the *GetWebResourceUrl* method on the *ClientScriptManager* class in ASP.NET 2.0 and higher. The method provides a long-awaited feature to control developers. When you develop a control, you often need to embed static resources such as images or client script files. You can make these files be separate downloads but, even though it's effective, the solution looks poor and inelegant. Visual Studio .NET 2003 and newer versions allow you to embed resources in the control assembly, but how would you retrieve these resources programmatically and bind them to the control? For example, to bind an assembly-stored image to an <IMG> tag, you need a URL for the image. The *GetWebResourceUrl* method returns a URL for the specified resource. The URL refers to a new Web Resource service (*webresource.axd*) that retrieves and returns the requested resource from an assembly.

```
// Bind the <IMG> tag to the given GIF image in the control's assembly
img.ImageUrl = Page.GetWebResourceUrl(typeof(TheControl), GifName));
```

GetWebResourceUrl requires a *Type* object, which will be used to locate the assembly that contains the resource. The assembly is identified with the assembly that contains the definition of the specified type in the current AppDomain. If you're writing a custom control, the type will likely be the control's type. As its second argument, the *GetWebResourceUrl* method requires the name of the embedded resource. The returned URL takes the following form:

```
WebResource.axd?a=assembly&r=resourceName&t=timestamp
```

The timestamp value is the current timestamp of the assembly, and it is added to make the browser download resources again should the assembly be modified.

Controls-Related Methods

Table 3-13 details a bunch of helper methods on the *Page* class that are architected to let you manage and validate child controls and resolve URLs.

TABLE 3-13 Helper Methods of the *Page* Object

Method	Description
DesignerInitialize	Initializes the instance of the *Page* class at design time, when the page is being hosted by RAD designers such as Visual Studio.
FindControl	Takes a control's ID and searches for it in the page's naming container. The search doesn't dig out child controls that are naming containers themselves.

Method	Description
GetTypeHashCode	Retrieves the hash code generated by ASP.xxx_aspx page objects at run time. In the base Page class, the method implementation simply returns 0; significant numbers are returned by classes used for actual pages.
GetValidators	Returns a collection of control validators for a specified validation group. Not available with ASP.NET 1.x.
HasControls	Determines whether the page contains any child controls.
LoadControl	Compiles and loads a user control from an .ascx file, and returns a Control object. If the user control supports caching, the object returned is PartialCachingControl.
LoadTemplate	Compiles and loads a user control from an .ascx file, and returns it wrapped in an instance of an internal class that implements the ITemplate interface. The internal class is named SimpleTemplate.
MapPath	Retrieves the physical, fully qualified path that an absolute or relative virtual path maps to.
ParseControl	Parses a well-formed input string, and returns an instance of the control that corresponds to the specified markup text. If the string contains more controls, only the first is taken into account. The runat attribute can be omitted. The method returns an object of type Control and must be cast to a more specific type.
RegisterRequiresControlState	Registers a control as one that requires control state. Not available with ASP.NET 1.x.
RegisterRequiresPostBack	Registers the specified control to receive a postback handling notice, even if its ID doesn't match any ID in the collection of posted data. The control must implement the IPostBackDataHandler interface.
RegisterRequiresRaiseEvent	Registers the specified control to handle an incoming postback event. The control must implement the IPostBackEventHandler interface.
RegisterViewStateHandler	Mostly for internal use, the method sets an internal flag causing the page view state to be persisted. If this method is not called in the prerendering phase, no view state will ever be written. Typically, only the HtmlForm server control for the page calls this method. There's no need to call it from within user applications.
ResolveUrl	Resolves a relative URL into an absolute URL based on the value of the TemplateSourceDirectory property.
Validate	Instructs any validation controls included on the page to validate their assigned information. ASP.NET 2.0 supports validation groups.

The methods *LoadControl* and *LoadTemplate* share a common code infrastructure but return different objects, as the following pseudocode shows:

```
public Control LoadControl(string virtualPath) {
    Control ascx = GetCompiledUserControlType(virtualPath);
    ascx.InitializeAsUserControl();
    return ascx;
}
public ITemplate LoadTemplate(string virtualPath) {
    Control ascx = GetCompiledUserControlType(virtualPath);
    return new SimpleTemplate(ascx);
}
```

Both methods differ from *ParseControl* in that the latter never causes compilation but simply parses the string and infers control information. The information is then used to create and initialize a new instance of the control class. As mentioned, the *runat* attribute is unnecessary in this context. In ASP.NET, the *runat* attribute is key, but in practice, it has no other role than marking the surrounding markup text for parsing and instantiation. It does not contain information useful to instantiate a control, and for this reason it can be omitted from the strings you pass directly to *ParseControl*.

Script-Related Methods

Table 3-14 enumerates all the methods in the *Page* class that have to do with HTML and script code to be inserted in the client page.

TABLE 3-14 Script-Related Methods

Method	Description
GetCallbackEventReference	Obtains a reference to a client-side function that, when invoked, initiates a client call back to server-side events. *Not available with ASP.NET 1.x.*
GetPostBackClientEvent	Calls into *GetCallbackEventReference*.
GetPostBackClientHyperlink	Appends *javascript:* to the beginning of the return string received from *GetPostBackEventReference*. `javascript:__doPostBack('CtlID','')`
GetPostBackEventReference	Returns the prototype of the client-side script function that causes, when invoked, a postback. It takes a *Control* and an argument, and it returns a string like this: `__doPostBack('CtlID','')`
IsClientScriptBlockRegistered	Determines whether the specified client script is registered with the page. *Marked as obsolete.*
IsStartupScriptRegistered	Determines whether the specified client startup script is registered with the page. *Marked as obsolete.*

Method	Description
RegisterArrayDeclaration	Use this method to add an ECMAScript array to the client page. This method accepts the name of the array and a string that will be used verbatim as the body of the array. For example, if you call the method with arguments such as *theArray* and *"'a', 'b'"*, you get the following JavaScript code: `var theArray = new Array('a', 'b');` *Marked as obsolete.*
RegisterClientScriptBlock	An ASP.NET page uses this method to emit client-side script blocks in the client page just after the opening tag of the HTML *<form>* element. *Marked as obsolete.*
RegisterHiddenField	Use this method to automatically register a hidden field on the page. *Marked as obsolete.*
RegisterOnSubmitStatement	Use this method to emit client script code that handles the client *OnSubmit* event. The script should be a JavaScript function call to client code registered elsewhere. *Marked as obsolete.*
RegisterStartupScript	An ASP.NET page uses this method to emit client-side script blocks in the client page just before closing the HTML *<form>* element. *Marked as obsolete.*
SetFocus	Sets the browser focus to the specified control. *Not available with ASP.NET 1.x.*

As you can see, some methods in Table 3-14, which are defined and usable in ASP.NET 1.x, are marked obsolete. In ASP.NET 3.5 applications, you should avoid calling them and resort to methods with the same name exposed out of the *ClientScript* property. (See Table 3-10.)

```
// Avoid this in ASP.NET 3.5
Page.RegisterArrayDeclaration(…);
// Use this in ASP.NET 3.5
Page.ClientScript.RegisterArrayDeclaration(…);
```

We'll return to *ClientScript* in Chapter 5.

Methods listed in Table 3-14 let you emit JavaScript code in the client page. When you use any of these methods, you actually tell the page to insert that script code when the page is rendered. So when any of these methods execute, the script-related information is simply cached in internal structures and used later when the page object generates its HTML text.

Events of the *Page* Class

The *Page* class fires a few events that are notified during the page life cycle. As Table 3-15 shows, some events are orthogonal to the typical life cycle of a page (initialization, postback, rendering phases) and are fired as extra-page situations evolve. Let's briefly review the events and then attack the topic with an in-depth discussion on the page life cycle.

TABLE 3-15 Events That a Page Can Fire

Event	Description
AbortTransaction	Occurs for ASP.NET pages marked to participate in an automatic transaction when a transaction aborts.
CommitTransaction	Occurs for ASP.NET pages marked to participate in an automatic transaction when a transaction commits.
DataBinding	Occurs when the *DataBind* method is called on the page to bind all the child controls to their respective data sources.
Disposed	Occurs when the page is released from memory, which is the last stage of the page life cycle.
Error	Occurs when an unhandled exception is thrown.
Init	Occurs when the page is initialized, which is the first step in the page life cycle.
InitComplete	Occurs when all child controls and the page have been initialized. *Not available in ASP.NET 1.x.*
Load	Occurs when the page loads up, after being initialized.
LoadComplete	Occurs when the loading of the page is completed and server events have been raised. *Not available in ASP.NET 1.x.*
PreInit	Occurs just before the initialization phase of the page begins. *Not available in ASP.NET 1.x.*
PreLoad	Occurs just before the loading phase of the page begins. *Not available in ASP.NET 1.x.*
PreRender	Occurs when the page is about to render.
PreRenderComplete	Occurs just before the pre-rendering phase begins. *Not available in ASP.NET 1.x.*
SaveStateComplete	Occurs when the view state of the page has been saved to the persistence medium. *Not available in ASP.NET 1.x.*
Unload	Occurs when the page is unloaded from memory but not yet disposed.

The Eventing Model

When a page is requested, its class and the server controls it contains are responsible for executing the request and rendering HTML back to the client. The communication between the client and the server is stateless and disconnected because of the HTTP protocol. Real-world applications, though, need some state to be maintained between successive calls made to the same page. With ASP, and with other server-side development platforms such as Java Server Pages and Linux-based systems (for example, LAMP), the programmer is entirely responsible for persisting the state. In contrast, ASP.NET provides a built-in infrastructure that saves and restores the state of a page in a transparent manner. In this way, and in spite of the underlying stateless protocol, the client experience appears to be that of a continuously executing process. It's just an illusion, though.

Introducing the View State

The illusion of continuity is created by the view state feature of ASP.NET pages and is based on some assumptions about how the page is designed and works. Also, server-side Web controls play a remarkable role. Briefly, before rendering its contents to HTML, the page encodes and stuffs into a persistence medium (typically, a hidden field) all the state information that the page itself and its constituent controls want to save. When the page posts back, the state information is deserialized from the hidden field and used to initialize instances of the server controls declared in the page layout.

The view state is specific to each instance of the page because it is embedded in the HTML. The net effect of this is that controls are initialized with the same values they had the last time the view state was created—that is, the last time the page was rendered to the client. Furthermore, an additional step in the page life cycle merges the persisted state with any updates introduced by client-side actions. When the page executes after a postback, it finds a stateful and up-to-date context just as it is working over a continuous point-to-point connection.

Two basic assumptions are made. The first assumption is that the page always posts to itself and carries its state back and forth. The second assumption is that the server-side controls have to be declared with the *runat=server* attribute to spring to life once the page posts back.

The Single Form Model

Admittedly, for programmers whose experience is with ASP or JSP, the single form model of ASP.NET can be difficult to make sense of at first. These programmers frequently ask questions on forums and newsgroups such as, "Where's the *Action* property of the form?" and "Why can't I redirect to a particular page when a form is submitted?"

ASP.NET pages are built to support exactly one server-side *<form>* tag. The form must include all the controls you want to interact with on the server. Both the form and the controls must be marked with the *runat* attribute; otherwise, they will be considered as plain text to be output verbatim. A server-side form is an instance of the *HtmlForm* class. The *HtmlForm* class does not expose any property equivalent to the *Action* property of the HTML *<form>* tag. The reason is that an ASP.NET page always posts to itself. Unlike the *Action* property, other common form properties such as *Method* and *Target* are fully supported.

Valid ASP.NET pages are also those that have no server-side forms and those that run HTML forms—a *<form>* tag without the *runat* attribute. In an ASP.NET page, you can also have both HTML and server forms. In no case, though, can you have more than one *<form>* tag with the *runat* attribute set to *server*. HTML forms work as usual and let you post to any page in the application. The drawback is that in this case no state will be automatically restored. In other words, the ASP.NET Web Forms model works only if you use exactly one server *<form>* element. We'll return to this topic in Chapter 5.

Asynchronous Pages

ASP.NET pages are served by an HTTP handler like an instance of the *Page* class. Each request takes up a thread in the ASP.NET thread pool and releases it only when the request completes. What if a frequently requested page starts an external and particularly lengthy task? The risk is that the ASP.NET process is idle but has no free threads in the pool to serve incoming requests for other pages. This is mostly due to the fact that HTTP handlers, including page classes, work synchronously. To alleviate this issue, ASP.NET supports asynchronous handlers since version 1.0 through the *IHTTPAsyncHandler* interface. Starting with ASP.NET 2.0, creating asynchronous pages is even easier thanks to specific support from the framework.

Two aspects characterize an asynchronous ASP.NET page: a new attribute on the *@Page* directive, and one or more tasks registered for asynchronous execution. The asynchronous task can be registered in either of two ways. You can define a *Begin/End* pair of asynchronous handlers for the *PreRenderComplete* event or create a *PageAsyncTask* object to represent an asynchronous task. This is generally done in the *Page_Load* event, but any time is fine provided that it happens before the *PreRender* event fires.

In both cases, the asynchronous task is started automatically when the page has progressed to a well-known point. Let's dig out more details.

 Note An ASP.NET asynchronous page is still a class that derives from *Page*. There are no special base classes to inherit for building asynchronous pages.

The *Async* Attribute

The new *Async* attribute on the *@Page* directive accepts a Boolean value to enable or disable asynchronous processing. The default value is *false*.

```
<%@ Page Async="true" ... %>
```

The *Async* attribute is merely a message for the page parser. When used, the page parser implements the *IHttpAsyncHandler* interface in the dynamically generated class for the *.aspx* resource. The *Async* attribute enables the page to register asynchronous handlers for the *PreRenderComplete* event. No additional code is executed at run time as a result of the attribute.

Let's consider a request for a *TestAsync.aspx* page marked with the *Async* directive attribute. The dynamically created class, named *ASP.TestAsync_aspx*, is declared as follows:

```
public class TestAsync_aspx : TestAsync, IHttpHandler, IHttpAsyncHandler
{
    ...
}
```

TestAsync is the code file class and inherits from *Page*, or a class that in turn inherits from *Page*. *IHttpAsyncHandler* is the canonical interface used for serving resources asynchronously since ASP.NET 1.0.

The *AddOnPreRenderCompleteAsync* Method

The *AddOnPreRenderCompleteAsync* method adds an asynchronous event handler for the page's *PreRenderComplete* event. An asynchronous event handler consists of a *Begin/End* pair of event handler methods, as shown here:

```
AddOnPreRenderCompleteAsync (
    new BeginEventHandler(BeginTask),
    new EndEventHandler(EndTask)
);
```

The *BeginEventHandler* and *EndEventHandler* are delegates defined as follows:

```
IAsyncResult BeginEventHandler(
    object sender,
    EventArgs e,
    AsyncCallback cb,
    object state)
void EndEventHandler(
    IAsyncResult ar)
```

In the code file, you place a call to *AddOnPreRenderCompleteAsync* as soon as you can, and always earlier than the *PreRender* event can occur. A good place is usually the *Page_Load* event. Next, you define the two asynchronous event handlers.

The *Begin* handler is responsible for starting any operation you fear can block the underlying thread for too long. The handler is expected to return an *IAsyncResult* object to describe the state of the asynchronous task. The *End* handler completes the operation and updates the page's user interface and controls. Note that you don't necessarily have to create your own object that implements the *IAsyncResult* interface. In most cases, in fact, to start lengthy operations you just use built-in classes that already implement the asynchronous pattern and provide *IAsyncResult* ready-made objects.

> **Important** The *Begin* and *End* event handlers are called at different times and generally on different pooled threads. In between the two methods calls, the lengthy operation takes place. From the ASP.NET runtime perspective, the *Begin* and *End* events are similar to serving distinct requests for the same page. It's as if an asynchronous request is split in two distinct steps—a *Begin* and *End* step. Each request is always served by a pooled thread. Typically, the *Begin* step is served by a thread picked up from the ASP.NET worker thread pool. The *End* step is served by a thread selected from the completion thread pool.

The page progresses up to entering the *PreRenderComplete* stage. You have a pair of asynchronous event handlers defined here. The page executes the *Begin* event, starts the lengthy operation, and is then suspended until the operation terminates. When the work has been completed, the HTTP runtime processes the request again. This time, though, the request processing begins at a later stage than usual. In particular, it begins exactly where it left off—that is, from the *PreRenderComplete* stage. The *End* event executes, and the page finally completes the rest of its life cycle, including view-state storage, markup generation, and unloading.

The Significance of *PreRenderComplete*

So an asynchronous page executes up until the *PreRenderComplete* stage is reached and then blocks while waiting for the asynchronous operation to complete. When the operation is finally accomplished, the page execution resumes from the *PreRenderComplete* stage. A good question to ask would be the following: "Why *PreRenderComplete*?" What makes *PreRenderComplete* such a special event?

By design, in ASP.NET there's a single unwind point for asynchronous operations (also familiarly known as the *async point*). This point is located between the *PreRender* and *PreRenderComplete* events. When the page receives the *PreRender* event, the async point hasn't been reached yet. When the page receives *PreRenderComplete*, the async point has passed.

Building a Sample Asynchronous Page

Let's roll a first asynchronous test page to download and process some RSS feeds. The page markup is quite simple indeed:

```
<%@ Page Async="true" Language="C#" AutoEventWireup="true"
        CodeFile="TestAsync.aspx.cs" Inherits="TestAsync" %>
<html>
<body>
    <form id="form1" runat="server">
        <% = rssData %>
    </form>
</body>
</html>
```

The code file is shown next, and it attempts to download the RSS feed from my personal blog:

```
public partial class TestAsync : System.Web.UI.Page
{
    const string RSSFEED = "http://weblogs.asp.net/despos/rss.aspx";
    private WebRequest req;
    public string rssData;

    void Page_Load (object sender, EventArgs e)
    {
        AddOnPreRenderCompleteAsync (
            new BeginEventHandler(BeginTask),
            new EndEventHandler(EndTask));
    }

    IAsyncResult BeginTask(object sender,
                            EventArgs e, AsyncCallback cb, object state)
    {
        // Trace
        Trace.Warn("Begin async: Thread=" +
                    Thread.CurrentThread.ManagedThreadId.ToString());

        // Prepare to make a Web request for the RSS feed
        req = WebRequest.Create(RSSFEED);

        // Begin the operation and return an IAsyncResult object
        return req.BeginGetResponse(cb, state);
    }

    void EndTask(IAsyncResult ar)
    {
        // This code will be called on a pooled thread

        string text;
        using (WebResponse response = req.EndGetResponse(ar))
        {
            StreamReader reader;
            using (reader = new StreamReader(response.GetResponseStream()))
            {
                text = reader.ReadToEnd();
            }

            // Process the RSS data
            rssData = ProcessFeed(text);
        }

        // Trace
        Trace.Warn("End async: Thread=" +
                    Thread.CurrentThread.ManagedThreadId.ToString());
```

```
        // The page is updated using an ASP-style code block in the ASPX
        // source that displays the contents of the rssData variable
    }

    string ProcessFeed(string feed)
    {
        // Build the page output from the XML input
        ...
    }
}
```

As you can see, such an asynchronous page differs from a standard one only for the aforementioned elements—the *Async* directive attribute and the pair of asynchronous event handlers. Figure 3-6 shows the sample page in action.

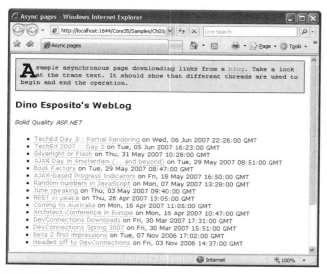

FIGURE 3-6 A sample asynchronous page downloading links from an RSS feed.

It would also be interesting to take a look at the messages traced by the page. Figure 3-7 provides visual clues of it. The Begin and End stages are served by different threads and take place at different times.

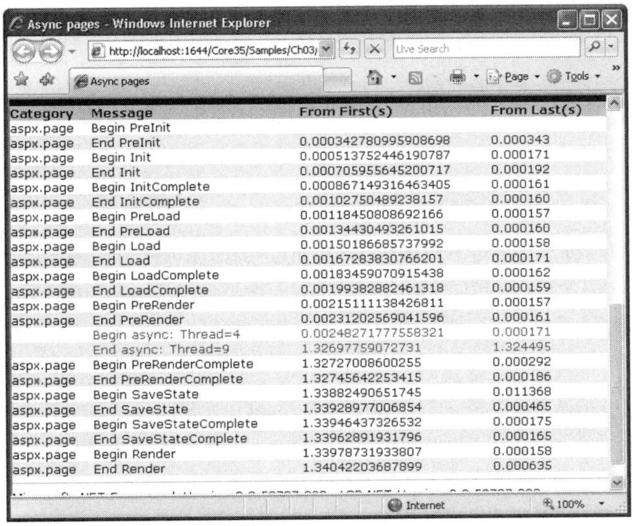

FIGURE 3-7 The traced request details clearly show the two steps needed to process a request asynchronously.

Note the time elapsed between the time we enter *BeginTask* and exit *EndTask* stages (indicated by the elapsed time between the "Begin async" and "End async" entries shown in Figure 3-7). It is much longer than intervals between any other two consecutive operations. It's in that interval that the lengthy operation—in this case, downloading and processing the RSS feed—took place. The interval also includes the time spent to pick up another thread from the pool to serve the second part of the original request.

The *RegisterAsyncTask* Method

The *AddOnPreRenderCompleteAsync* method is not the only tool you have to register an asynchronous task. The *RegisterAsyncTask* method is, in most cases, an even better solution. *RegisterAsyncTask* is a void method and accepts a *PageAsyncTask* object. As the name suggests, the *PageAsyncTask* class represents a task to execute asynchronously.

The following code shows how to rework the sample page that reads some RSS feed and make it use the *RegisterAsyncTask* method:

```
void Page_Load (object sender, EventArgs e)
{
    PageAsyncTask task = new PageAsyncTask(
        new BeginEventHandler(BeginTask),
        new EndEventHandler(EndTask),
        null,
        null);

    RegisterAsyncTask(task);
}
```

The constructor accepts up to five parameters, as shown in the following code:

```
public PageAsyncTask(
    BeginEventHandler beginHandler,
    EndEventHandler endHandler,
    EndEventHandler timeoutHandler,
    object state,
    bool executeInParallel)
```

The *beginHandler* and *endHandler* parameters have the same prototype as the correspond-ing handlers we use for the *AddOnPreRenderCompleteAsync* method. Compared to the *AddOnPreRenderCompleteAsync* method, *PageAsyncTask* lets you specify a timeout function and an optional flag to enable multiple registered tasks to execute in parallel.

The timeout delegate indicates the method that will get called if the task is not completed within the asynchronous timeout interval. By default, an asynchronous task times out if not completed within 45 seconds. You can indicate a different timeout in either the configuration file or the *@Page* directive. Here's what you need if you opt for the *web.config* file:

```
<system.web>
    <pages asyncTimeout="30" />
</system.web>
```

The *@Page* directive contains an integer *AsyncTimeout* attribute that you set to the desired number of seconds. Note that configuring the asynchronous timeout in *web.config* causes all asynchronous pages to use the same timeout value. Individual pages are still free to set their own timeout value in their *@Page* directive.

Just as with the *AddOnPreRenderCompleteAsync* method, you can pass some state to the delegates performing the task. The *state* parameter can be any object.

The execution of all tasks registered is automatically started by the *Page* class code just be-fore the async point is reached. However, by placing a call to the *ExecuteRegisteredAsyncTasks* method on the *Page* class, you can take control of this aspect.

Choosing the Right Approach

When should you use *AddOnPreRenderCompleteAsync*, and when is *RegisterAsyncTask* a better option? Functionally speaking, the two approaches are nearly identical. In both cases, the execution of the request is split in two parts—before and after the async point. So where's the difference?

The first difference is logical. *RegisterAsyncTask* is an API designed to run tasks asyn-chronously from within a page—and not just asynchronous pages with *Async=true*. *AddOnPreRenderCompleteAsync* is an API specifically designed for asynchronous pages. This said, a couple of further differences exist.

One is that *RegisterAsyncTask* executes the *End* handler on a thread with a richer context than *AddOnPreRenderCompleteAsync*. The thread context includes impersonation and HTTP context information that is missing in the thread serving the *End* handler of a classic asynchronous page. In addition, *RegisterAsyncTask* allows you to set a timeout to ensure that any task doesn't run for more than a given number of seconds.

The other difference is that *RegisterAsyncTask* makes significantly easier the implementation of multiple calls to remote sources. You can have parallel execution by simply setting a Boolean flag, and you don't need to create and manage your own *IAsyncResult* object.

The bottom line is that you can use either approach for a single task, but you should opt for *RegisterAsyncTask* when you have multiple tasks to execute simultaneously.

Note For more information on asynchronous pages, check out Chapter 5 of my book *Programming Microsoft ASP.NET 2.0 Applications: Advanced Topics* (Microsoft Press 2006).

Async-Compliant Operations

Which required operations force, or at least strongly suggest, the adoption of an asynchronous page? Any operation can be roughly labeled in either of two ways: CPU bound or I/O bound. CPU bound indicates an operation whose completion time is mostly determined by the speed of the processor and amount of available memory. I/O bound indicates the opposite situation, where the CPU mostly waits for other devices to terminate.

The need for asynchronous processing arises when an excessive amount of time is spent getting data in to and out of the computer in relation to the time spent processing it. In such situations, the CPU is idle or underused and spends most of its time waiting for something to happen. In particular, I/O-bound operations in the context of ASP.NET applications are even more harmful because serving threads are blocked too, and the pool of serving threads is a finite and critical resource. You get real performance advantages if you use the asynchronous model on I/O-bound operations.

Typical examples of I/O-bound operations are all operations that require access to some sort of remote resource or interaction with external hardware devices. Operations on non-local databases and non-local Web service calls are the most common I/O-bound operations for which you should seriously consider building asynchronous pages.

The Page Life Cycle

A page instance is created on every request from the client, and its execution causes itself and its contained controls to iterate through their life-cycle stages. Page execution begins when the HTTP runtime invokes *ProcessRequest*, which kicks off the page and control life cycles. The life cycle consists of a sequence of stages and steps. Some of these stages can be controlled through user-code events; some require a method override. Some other stages, or more exactly sub-stages, are simply not marked as public and are out of the developer's control. They are mentioned here mostly for completeness.

The page life cycle is articulated in three main stages: setup, postback, and finalization. Each stage might have one or more substages and is composed of one or more steps and points where events are raised. The life cycle as described here includes all possible paths. Note that there are modifications to the process depending upon cross-page posts, script callbacks, and postbacks.

Page Setup

When the HTTP runtime instantiates the page class to serve the current request, the page constructor builds a tree of controls. The tree of controls ties into the actual class that the page parser created after looking at the ASPX source. It is important to note that when the request processing begins, all child controls and page intrinsic objects such as HTTP context, request objects, and response objects are set.

The very first step in the page lifetime is determining why the runtime is processing the page request. There are various possible reasons: a normal request, postback, cross-page postback, or callback. The page object configures its internal state based on the actual reason, and it prepares the collection of posted values (if any) based on the method of the request—either *GET* or *POST*. After this first step, the page is ready to fire events to the user code.

The *PreInit* Event

Introduced with ASP.NET 2.0, this event is the entry point in the page life cycle. When the event fires, no master page and no theme have been associated with the page as yet. Furthermore, the page scroll position has been restored, posted data is available, and all page controls have been instantiated and default to the property values defined in the ASPX source. (Note that at this time controls have no ID, unless it is explicitly set in the *.aspx* source.) Changing the master page or the theme programmatically is possible only at this time. This event is available only on the page. *IsCallback*, *IsCrossPagePostback*, and *IsPostBack* are set at this time.

The *Init* Event

The master page and theme, if each exists, have been set and can't be changed anymore. The page processor—that is, the *ProcessRequest* method on the *Page* class—proceeds and iterates over all child controls to give them a chance to initialize their state in a context-sensitive way. All child controls have their *OnInit* method invoked recursively. For each control in the control collection, the naming container and a specific ID are set, if not assigned in the source.

The *Init* event reaches child controls first and the page later. At this stage, the page and controls typically begin loading some parts of their state. At this time, the view state is not restored yet.

The *InitComplete* Event

Introduced with ASP.NET 2.0, this page-only event signals the end of the initialization substage. For a page, only one operation takes place in between the *Init* and *InitComplete* events: tracking of view-state changes is turned on. Tracking view state is the operation that ultimately enables controls to *really* persist in the storage medium any values that are programmatically added to the *ViewState* collection. Simply put, for controls not tracking their view state, any values added to their *ViewState* are lost across postbacks.

All controls turn on view-state tracking immediately after raising their *Init* event, and the page is no exception. (After all, isn't the page just a control?)

> **Important** In light of the previous statement, note that any value written to the *ViewState* collection before *InitComplete* won't be available on the next postback. In ASP.NET 1.x, you must wait for the *Load* event to start writing safely to the page or any control view state.

View-State Restoration

If the page is being processed because of a postback—that is, if the *IsPostBack* property is *true*—the contents of the *__VIEWSTATE* hidden field are restored. The *__VIEWSTATE* hidden field is where the view state of all controls is persisted at the end of a request. The overall view state of the page is a sort of call context and contains the state of each constituent control the last time the page was served to the browser.

At this stage, each control is given a chance to update its current state to make it identical to what it was on last request. There's no event to wire up to handle the view-state restoration. If something needs be customized here, you have to resort to overriding the *LoadViewState* method, defined as protected and virtual on the *Control* class.

Processing Posted Data

All the client data packed in the HTTP request—that is, the contents of all input fields defined with the *<form>* tag—are processed at this time. Posted data usually takes the following form:

```
TextBox1=text&DropDownList1=selectedItem&Button1=Submit
```

It's an &-separated string of name/value pairs. These values are loaded into an internal-use collection. The page processor attempts to find a match between names in the posted collection and ID of controls in the page. Whenever a match is found, the processor checks whether the server control implements the *IPostBackDataHandler* interface. If it does, the methods of the interface are invoked to give the control a chance to refresh its state in light of the posted data. In particular, the page processor invokes the *LoadPostData* method on the interface. If the method returns *true*—that is, the state has been updated—the control is added to a separate collection to receive further attention later.

If a posted name doesn't match any server controls, it is left over and temporarily parked in a separate collection, ready for a second try later.

The *PreLoad* Event

Introduced with ASP.NET 2.0, the *PreLoad* event merely indicates that the page has terminated the system-level initialization phase and is going to enter the phase that gives user code in the page a chance to further configure the page for execution and rendering. This event is raised only for pages.

The *Load* Event

The *Load* event is raised for the page first and then recursively for all child controls. At this time, controls in the page tree are created and their state fully reflects both the previous state and any data posted from the client. The page is ready to execute any initialization code that has to do with the logic and behavior of the page. At this time, access to control properties and view state is absolutely safe.

Handling Dynamically Created Controls

When all controls in the page have been given a chance to complete their initialization before display, the page processor makes a second try on posted values that haven't been matched to existing controls. The behavior described earlier in the "Processing Posted Data" section is repeated on the name/value pairs that were left over previously. This apparently weird approach addresses a specific scenario—the use of dynamically created controls.

Imagine adding a control to the page tree dynamically—for example, in response to a certain user action. As mentioned, the page is rebuilt from scratch after each postback, so any information about the dynamically created control is lost. On the other hand, when the page's form is submitted, the dynamic control there is filled with legal and valid information that is regularly posted. By design, there can't be any server control to match the ID of the dynamic control the first time posted data is processed. However, the ASP.NET framework recognizes that some controls could be created in the *Load* event. For this reason, it makes sense to give it a second try to see whether a match is possible after the user code has run for a while.

If the dynamic control has been re-created in the *Load* event, a match is now possible and the control can refresh its state with posted data.

Handling the Postback

The postback mechanism is the heart of ASP.NET programming. It consists of posting form data to the same page using the view state to restore the call context—that is, the same state of controls existing when the posting page was last generated on the server.

After the page has been initialized and posted values have been taken into account, it's about time that some server-side events occur. There are two main types of events. The first type of event signals that certain controls had the state changed over the postback. The second type of event executes server code in response to the client action that caused the post.

Detecting Control State Changes

The ASP.NET machinery works around an implicit assumption: there must be a one-to-one correspondence between some HTML input tags that operate in the browser and some other ASP.NET controls that live and thrive in the Web server. The canonical example of this correspondence is between *<input type="text">* and *TextBox* controls. To be more technically precise, the link is given by a common ID name. When the user types some new text into an input element and then posts it, the corresponding *TextBox* control—that is, a server control with the same ID as the input tag—is called to handle the posted value. I described this step in the "Processing Posted Data" section earlier in the chapter.

For all controls that had the *LoadPostData* method return *true*, it's now time to execute the second method of the *IPostBackDataHandler* interface: the *RaisePostDataChangedEvent* method. The method signals the control to notify the ASP.NET application that the state of the control has changed. The implementation of the method is up to each control. However, most controls do the same thing: raise a server event and give page authors a way to kick in and execute code to handle the situation. For example, if the *Text* property of a *TextBox* changes over a postback, the *TextBox* raises the *TextChanged* event to the host page.

Executing the Server-Side Postback Event

Any page postback starts with some client action that intends to trigger a server-side action. For example, clicking a client button posts the current contents of the displayed form to the server, thus requiring some action and new, refreshed page output. The client button con-trol—typically, a hyperlink or a submit button—is associated with a server control that imple-ments the *IPostBackEventHandler* interface.

The page processor looks at the posted data and determines the control that caused the postback. If this control implements the *IPostBackEventHandler* interface, the processor invokes the *RaisePostBackEvent* method. The implementation of this method is left to the control and can vary quite a bit, at least in theory. In practice, though, any posting control raises a server event that allows page authors to write code in response to the postback. For example, the *Button* control raises the *onclick* event.

There are two ways a page can post back to the server—by using a submit button (that is, *<input type="submit">*) or through script. A submit HTML button is generated through the *Button* server control. The *LinkButton* control, along with a few other postback controls, in-serts some script code in the client page to bind an HTML event (for example, *onclick*) to the form's *submit* method in the browser's HTML object model. We'll return to this topic in the next chapter.

> **Note** Starting with ASP.NET 2.0, a new property, *UseSubmitBehavior*, exists on the *Button* class to let page developers control the client behavior of the corresponding HTML element as far as form submission is concerned. In ASP.NET 1.x, the *Button* control always outputs an *<input type="submit">* element. In ASP.NET 2.0 and beyond, by setting *UseSubmitBehavior* to *false*, you can change the output to *<input type="button">* but at the same time the *onclick* property of the client element is bound to predefined script code that just posts back.

The *LoadComplete* Event

Introduced in ASP.NET 2.0, the page-only *LoadComplete* event signals the end of the page-preparation phase. It is important to note that no child controls will ever receive this event. After firing *LoadComplete*, the page enters its rendering stage.

Page Finalization

After handling the postback event, the page is ready for generating the output for the browser. The rendering stage is divided in two parts—pre-rendering and markup generation. The pre-rendering sub-stage is in turn characterized by two events for pre-processing and post-processing.

The *PreRender* Event

By handling this event, pages and controls can perform any updates before the output is ren-dered. The *PreRender* event fires for the page first and then recursively for all controls. Note that at this time the page ensures that all child controls are created. This step is important especially for composite controls.

The *PreRenderComplete* Event

Because the *PreRender* event is recursively fired for all child controls, there's no way for the page author to know when the pre-rendering phase has been completed. For this reason, in ASP.NET 2.0 a new event has been added and raised only for the page. This event is *PreRenderComplete*.

The *SaveStateComplete* Event

The next step before each control is rendered out to generate the markup for the page is saving the current state of the page to the view-state storage medium. It is important to note that every action taken after this point that modifies the state could affect the rendering, but it is not persisted and won't be retrieved on the next postback. Saving the page state is a recursive process in which the page processor walks its way through the whole page tree calling the *SaveViewState* method on constituent controls and the page itself. *SaveViewState* is a protected and virtual (that is, overridable) method that is responsible for persisting the content of the *ViewState* dictionary for the current control. (We'll come back to the *ViewState* dictionary in Chapter 14.)

Starting with ASP.NET 2.0, controls provide a second type of state, known as a "control state." A control state is a sort of private view state that is not subject to the application's control. In other words, the *control state* of a control can't be programmatically disabled as is the case with the view state. The control state is persisted at this time, too. Control state is another state storage mechanism whose contents are maintained across page postbacks much like view state, but the purpose of control state is to maintain necessary information for a control to function properly. That is, state behavior property data for a control should be kept in control state, while user interface property data (such as the control's contents) should be kept in view state.

Introduced with ASP.NET 2.0, the *SaveStateComplete* event occurs when the state of controls on the page have been completely saved to the persistence medium.

> **Note** The view state of the page and all individual controls is accumulated in a unique memory structure and then persisted to storage medium. By default, the persistence medium is a hidden field named *__VIEWSTATE*. Serialization to, and deserialization from, the persistence medium is handled through a couple of overridable methods on the *Page* class: *SavePageStateToPersistenceMedium* and *LoadPageStateFromPersistenceMedium*. For example, by overriding these two methods you can persist the page state in a server-side database or in the session state, dramatically reducing the size of the page served to the user. Hold on, though. This option is not free of issues, and we'll talk more about it in Chapter 15.

Generating the Markup

The generation of the markup for the browser is obtained by calling each constituent control to render its own markup, which will be accumulated into a buffer. Several overridable methods allow control developers to intervene in various steps during the markup generation—begin tag, body, and end tag. No user event is associated with the rendering phase.

The *Unload* Event

The rendering phase is followed by a recursive call that raises the *Unload* event for each control, and finally for the page itself. The *Unload* event exists to perform any final clean-up before the page object is released. Typical operations are closing files and database connections.

Note that the unload notification arrives when the page or the control is being unloaded but has not been disposed of yet. Overriding the *Dispose* method of the *Page* class, or more simply handling the page's *Disposed* event, provides the last possibility for the actual page to perform final clean up before it is released from memory. The page processor frees the page object by calling the method *Dispose*. This occurs immediately after the recursive call to the handlers of the *Unload* event has completed.

Conclusion

ASP.NET is a complex technology built on top of a substantially simple—and, fortunately, solid and stable—Web infrastructure. To provide highly improved performance and a richer programming toolset, ASP.NET builds a desktop-like abstraction model, but it still has to rely on HTTP and HTML to hit the target and meet end-user expectations.

There are two relevant aspects in the ASP.NET Web Forms model: the process model, including the Web server process model, and the page object model. Each request of a URL that ends with *.aspx* is assigned to an application object working within the CLR hosted by the worker process. The request results in a dynamically compiled class that is then instantiated and put to work. The *Page* class is the base class for all ASP.NET pages. An instance of this class runs behind any URL that ends with *.aspx*. In most cases, you won't just build your ASP.NET pages from the *Page* class directly, but you'll rely on derived classes that contain event handlers and helper methods, at the very minimum. These classes are known as code-behind classes.

The class that represents the page in action implements the ASP.NET eventing model based on two pillars, the single form model (page reentrancy) and server controls. The page life cycle, fully described in this chapter, details the various stages (and related sub-stages) a page passes through on the way to generate the markup for the browser. A deep understanding of the page life cycle and eventing model is key to diagnosing possible problems and implementing advanced features quickly and efficiently.

In this chapter, we mentioned controls several times. Server controls are components that get input from the user, process the input, and output a response as HTML. In the next chapter, we'll explore various server controls, which include Web controls, HTML controls, and validation controls.

 ## Just the Facts

- A pipeline of run-time modules receive from IIS an incoming HTTP packet and make it evolve from a protocol-specific payload up to an instance of a class derived from *Page*.

- The page class required to serve a given request is dynamically compiled on demand when first required in the context of a Web application.

- The page class compiled to an assembly remains in use as long as no changes occur to the linked *.aspx* source file or the whole application is restarted.

- Each page class is an HTTP handler—that is, a component that the run time uses to service requests of a certain type.

- The ASP.NET code-behind model employs partial classes to generate missing declarations for protected members that represent server controls. This code was auto-generated by old versions of Visual Studio and placed in hidden regions.

- ASP.NET pages always post to themselves and use the view state to restore the state of controls existing when the page was last generated on the server.

- The view state creates the illusion of a stateful programming model in a stateless environment.

- Processing the page on the server entails handling a bunch of events that collectively form the page life cycle. A deep understanding of the page life cycle is key to diagnosing possible problems and implementing advanced features quickly and efficiently.

Chapter 4
ASP.NET Core Server Controls

ASP.NET pages are made of code, markup tags, literal text, and server controls. Based on the request, the server controls generate the right markup language. The ASP.NET runtime combines the output of all controls and serves the client a page to display in a browser. The programming richness of ASP.NET springs from the wide library of server controls that covers the basic tasks of HTML interaction—for example, collecting text through input tags—as well as more advanced functionalities such as calendaring, menus, tree views, and grid-based data display.

Key to ASP.NET control programming is the *runat* attribute. If a tag in the *.aspx* source is declared without the *runat* attribute, it is considered plain text and is output verbatim. Otherwise, the contents of the tag are mapped to a server control and processed during the page life cycle. Back in Chapter 1, we identified two main families of server controls—HTML server controls and Web server controls. HTML controls map to HTML tags and are implemented through server-side classes whose programming interface faithfully represents the standard set of attributes for the corresponding HTML tag. Web controls, in turn, are a more abstract library of controls in which adherence of the proposed API to HTML syntax is much less strict. As a result, Web and HTML controls share a large common subset of functionalities and, in spite of a few exceptions, we could say that Web controls, functionally speaking, are a superset of HTML controls. Web controls also feature a richer development environment with a larger set of methods, properties and events, and they participate more actively in the page life cycle.

As we'll see in more detail in the following pages, a second and more thoughtful look at the characteristics of the server controls in ASP.NET reveals the existence of more than just two families of controls. In real-world ASP.NET applications, you'll end up using controls from at least the following functional categories: HTML controls, core Web controls, validation controls, data-bound controls, user controls, mobile controls, and custom controls. Validation controls are a special subset of Web controls and deserve to be treated in a separate section.

Data-bound controls refer to data binding and therefore to the control's capability of connecting some of its properties to particular data sources. Hence, data-bound controls deserve a section of their own because of the difference in how they're used. User controls are visual aggregates of existing Web and HTML controls that appear as individual, encapsulated, programmable controls to external callers. Mobile controls are used when creating Web applications that target mobile devices. Custom controls refer to server controls you create entirely with code (not visually, as with a user control) that derive from a base control class.

In this chapter, we'll cover HTML controls, Web controls, and validation controls. Data-bound controls will be covered in Chapter 9. User controls, mobile controls, and custom controls find their place in my book —*Programming Microsoft ASP.NET 2.0 Applications: Advanced Topics* (Microsoft Press, 2006), which is written for advanced users as a companion book to this one. As mentioned, the content of my *Advanced Topics* book is not significantly affected by the release of ASP.NET 3.5.

Generalities of ASP.NET Server Controls

All ASP.NET server controls, including HTML and Web controls plus any custom controls you create or download, descend from the *Control* class. The class is defined in the *System.Web.UI* namespace and, as we discussed in Chapter 3, it also is the foundation of all ASP.NET pages. The *Control* class is declared as follows:

```
public class Control : IComponent, IDisposable, IParserAccessor,
    IUrlResolutionService, IDataBindingsAccessor,
    IControlBuilderAccessor, IControlDesignerAccessor,
    IExpressionsAccessor
```

The *IComponent* interface defines the way in which the control interacts with the other components running in the common language runtime (CLR), whereas *IDisposable* implements the common pattern for releasing managed objects deterministically. Table 4-1 explains the role of the other interfaces that the *Control* class implements.

TABLE 4-1 Interfaces Implemented by the *Control* Class

Interface	Goal
IControlBuilderAccessor	Internal use interface; provides members to support the page parser in building a control and the child controls it contains. *Not available in ASP.NET 1.x.*
IControlDesignerAccessor	Internal use interface; provides members to make the control interact with the designer. *Not available in ASP.NET 1.x.*
IDataBindingsAccessor	Makes the control capable of supporting data-binding expressions at design time.
IExpressionsAccessor	Internal use interface; defines the properties a class must implement to support collections of expressions. *Not available in ASP.NET 1.x.*

Interface	Goal
IParserAccessor	Enables the control to work as the container of child controls and to be notified when a block of child markup is parsed.
IUrlResolutionService	Provides members to resolve relative URLs both at runtime and design time. *Not available in ASP.NET 1.x.*

The *IDataBindingsAccessor* interface defines a read-only collection—the *DataBindings* property—that contains all the data bindings for the controls available to rapid application development (RAD) designers such as Microsoft Visual Studio 2008. Note that the collection of data bindings exist only at design time and, as such, is useful only if you write a RAD designer for the control.

Properties of the *Control* Class

The properties of the *Control* class have no user interface–specific features. The class, in fact, represents the minimum set of functionalities expected from a server control. The list of properties for the *Control* class is shown in Table 4-2.

TABLE 4-2 Properties Common to All Server Controls

Property	Description
BindingContainer	Gets the control that represents the logical parent of the current control as far as data binding is concerned. *Not available in ASP.NET 1.x.*
ClientID	Gets the ID assigned to the control in the HTML page. The string is a slightly different version of the UniqueID property. UniqueID can contain the dollar symbol ($), but this symbol is not accepted in ClientID and is replaced with the underscore (_).
Controls	Gets a collection filled with references to all the child controls.
EnableTheming	Indicates whether themes apply to the control. *Not available in ASP. NET 1.x.*
EnableViewState	Gets or sets whether the control should persist its view state—and the view state of any child controls across multiple requests—to the configured medium (for example, HTML hidden field, session state, and server-side databases or files).
ID	Gets or sets the name that will be used to programmatically identify the control in the page.
NamingContainer	Gets a reference to the control's naming container. The naming container for a given control is the parent control above it in the hierarchy that implements the *INamingContainer* interface. If no such control exists, the naming container is the host page.
Page	Gets a reference to the *Page* instance that contains the control.
Parent	Gets a reference to the parent of the control in the page hierarchy.

Property	Description
Site	Gets information about the container that hosts the current control when rendered on a design surface. For example, you use this property to access the Visual Studio designer when the control is being composed in a Web form.
SkinID	Gets or sets the name of the skin to apply to the control. A skin is a particular subset of attributes in a theme. *Not available in ASP.NET 1.x.*
TemplateControl	Gets a reference to the template that contains the current control. *Not available in ASP.NET 1.x.*
TemplateSourceDirectory	Gets the virtual directory of the host page.
UniqueID	Gets a hierarchically qualified ID for the control.
Visible	Gets or sets whether ASP.NET has to render the control.

The *Control* class is the ideal base class for new controls that have no user interface and don't require style information.

Identifying a Server Control

The client ID of a control is generated from the value of the *UniqueID* property—the truly server-side identifier that ASP.NET generates for each control. The contents of the *ClientID* property differ from *UniqueID* simply in that all occurrences of the dollar symbol ($), if any, are replaced with the underscore (_). Dollar symbols in the *UniqueID* string are possible only if the control belongs to a naming container different from the page.

ASP.NET generates the value for the *UniqueID* property based on the value of the *ID* property that the programmer indicates. If no *ID* has been specified, ASP.NET auto-generates a name such as *_ctlX*, where *X* is a progressive 0-based index. If the control's naming container is the host page, *UniqueID* simply takes the value of *ID*. Otherwise, the value of *ID* is prefixed with the string representing the naming container and the result is assigned to *UniqueID*.

Naming Containers

A naming container is primarily a control that acts as a container for other controls. In doing so, the naming container generates a sort of virtual namespace so that ASP.NET roots the actual ID of contained controls in the ID of the naming container. To fully understand the role and importance of naming containers, consider the following example.

Imagine you have a composite control, such as a user control, that includes a child control like a button. Entirely wrapped by the user control, the button is not directly accessible by the page code and can't be given a distinct and per-instance ID. In the end, the ID of the button is hard-coded in the outermost control that creates it. What happens when two or more instances of the composite control are placed on a page? Are you going to have two button child controls with the same ID? This is exactly what will happen unless you configure the composite control to be a naming container.

The importance of naming containers doesn't end here. Imagine you have an instance of a composite control named *Control1* . Imagine also that the embedded button is named *Trigger*. The full name of the child button will be *Control1$Trigger*. Suppose you click on the button and cause the page to post back. If the name of the posting control contains the $ symbol, the ASP.NET runtime recognizes a known pattern: tokenize the name and locate the postback control correctly, no matter its depth in the page tree.

On the other hand, if the button is contained in a control not marked to be a naming container, the ID of the clicked button is not prefixed and will simply be, say, *Trigger*. In this case, the ASP.NET runtime will look for it as a direct child of the form. The search will obviously fail—the button is a child of a top-level control—and the postback event will pass unnoticed.

Note Starting with version 2.0, ASP.NET uses the dollar ($) symbol to separate the various parts to form the ID of a control rooted in a naming container. In ASP.NET 1.x, the colon (:) symbol is used for the same purpose.

Binding Containers

Starting with ASP.NET 2.0, a new kind of container is introduced—the binding container. The binding container—the *BindingContainer* property—indicates which control in the page hierarchy represents the parent of a control as far as data binding is concerned. In other words, the binding container is the control that receives bound data from the host (typically, the page) and that passes it down to child controls.

As you can easily imagine, binding and naming containers often coincide. The only exception is when the control is part of a template. In that case, the *NamingContainer* property is generally set to the physical parent of the control, namely a control in the template. *BindingContainer*, instead, will point to the control that defines the template.

Visibility of a Server Control

If you set *Visible* to *false*, ASP.NET doesn't generate any markup code for the control. However, having *Visible* set to *false* doesn't really mean that no path in the control's code can output text. The control is still an active object that exposes methods and handles events. If a method, or an event handler, sends text directly to the output console through *Response. Write*, this text will be displayed to the user anyway. A control with the *Visible* attribute set to *false* is still part of the page and maintains its position in the control tree.

Methods of the *Control* Class

The methods of the *Control* class are listed and described in Table 4-3.

TABLE 4-3 Public Methods of a Server Control

Method	Description
ApplyStyleSheetSkin	Applies the properties defined in the page style sheet to the control. The skin properties used depend on the *SkinID* property. *Not available in ASP.NET 1.x.*
DataBind	Fires the *OnDataBinding* event and then invokes the *DataBind* method on all child controls.
Dispose	Gives the control a chance to perform clean-up tasks before it gets released from memory.
Focus	Sets the input focus to the control. *Not available in ASP.NET 1.x.*
FindControl	Looks for the specified control in the collection of child controls. Child controls not in the *Controls* collection of the current controls—that is, not direct children—are not retrieved.
HasControls	Indicates whether the control contains any child controls.
RenderControl	Generates the HTML output for the control.
ResolveClientUrl	Use the method to return a URL suitable for use by the client to access resources on the Web server, such as image files, links to additional pages, and so on. Can return a relative path. The method is sealed and can't be overridden in derived classes.
ResolveUrl	Resolves a relative URL to an absolute URL based on the value passed to the *TemplateSourceDirectory* property.
SetRenderMethodDelegate	Internal use method, assigns a delegate to render the control and its content into the parent control.

Each control can have child controls. All children are stored in the *Controls* collection, an object of type *ControlCollection*. This collection class has a few peculiarities. In particular, it post-processes controls that are added to, and removed from, the collection. When a control is added, its view state is restored if needed and view state tracking is turned on. When a control is removed, the *Unload* event is fired.

Events of the *Control* Class

The *Control* class also defines a set of base events that all server controls in the .NET Framework support.

TABLE 4-4 **Events of a Server Control**

Event	Description
DataBinding	Occurs when the *DataBind* method is called on a control and the control is binding to a data source.
Disposed	Occurs when a control is released from memory—the last stage in the control life cycle.
Init	Occurs when the control is initialized—the first step in the life cycle.
Load	Occurs when the control is loaded into the page. Occurs after *Init*.
PreRender	Occurs when the control is about to render its content.
Unload	Occurs when the control is unloaded from memory.

All server controls are rendered to HTML using the *RenderControl* method and, when this happens, the *PreRender* event is fired.

Other Features

Starting with ASP.NET 2.0, server controls gained some new features that are more architectural than related to programming capabilities. These features are the offspring of significant changes in the underpinnings of the controls.

Adaptive Rendering

Adaptive rendering is the process that enables controls to generate different markup for individual browsers. This result is obtained by delegating the generation of the markup to an external component—the adapter. When each control is about to render, it figures out its current adapter and hands the request over to that adapter. Nicely enough, a control adapter is a configurable component that you can declaratively unplug in any application to roll your own.

The selected adapter depends on the current browser. The adapter for a control is resolved by looking at the browser capabilities as configured in the ASP.NET browser database. If the browser record includes an adapter class for a given control, the class is instantiated and used. Otherwise, the default adapter for the control is used, which is an instance of the *ControlAdapter* class. The *ControlAdapter* class is a generic adapter and simply generates the markup for a control by calling the rendering methods on the control itself.

Note The ASP.NET database used for storing browser information is not a real database. It is, instead, a list of text files with a *.browser* extension located under the ASP.NET installation folder on the Web server. The exact path is the following: *%WINDOWS%\Microsoft.NET\Framework\ [version]\CONFIG\Browsers*.

The data located in this folder is used to return browser capabilities.

A control holds a reference to the mapped adapter instance through the (protected) *Adapter* property. Each control has an associated adapter unless it is a composite control that defers to its children for rendering.

All ASP.NET controls have an entry point into the rendering engine in the *Render* method. Here's the method's signature:

```
protected virtual void Render(HtmlTextWriter writer)
{
    ...
}
```

The *Render* method ends up calling into an internal method whose implementation is nearly identical to the following pseudocode:

```
void RenderControlInternal(HtmlTextWriter writer, ControlAdapter adapter)
{
    if (adapter != null)
    {
        adapter.BeginRender(writer);
        adapter.Render(writer);
        adapter.EndRender(writer);
    }
    else
    {
        this.Render(writer);
    }
}
```

As you can see, if defined, a control adapter is used to generate the markup for the control. The adapter can be declaratively specified and is an external component that can be made to measure for your needs. Using an adapter to alter the markup of a given class of controls is an unobtrusive option that doesn't require any changes to existing pages using the control. It only requires you to add a browser definition file.

Browser definition files have a *.browser* extension and contain definitions that apply to a specific browser. At run time, ASP.NET determines the browser being used, uses the configuration file to determine the capabilities of the browser, and based on that figures out how to render markup to that browser. Here's a snippet that illustrates how to register a control adapter for the *Menu* for whatever browsers the user will employ:

```
<browsers>
  <browser refID="Default">
    <controlAdapters>
      <adapter controlType="System.Web.UI.WebControls.Menu"
               adapterType="Core35.MenuAdapter" />
      ...
    <controlAdapters>
  </browser>
</browsers>
```

Saved to a *.browser* file, the preceding snippet is deployed to the *App_Browsers* folder of an ASP.NET application, version 2.0 or newer.

An adapter class looks like the following class:

```
public class MenuAdapter :
            System.Web.UI.WebControls.Adapters.MenuAdapter
{
    ...
}
```

The class commonly overrides methods such as *Init*, *RenderBeginTag*, *RenderEndTag*, and *RenderContents*.

To write an adapter effectively, though, you must reasonably know a lot of details about the internal workings of the control you're hooking up. For more information on the architecture of control adapters, you might want to take a look at *http://msdn2.microsoft.com/en-us/library/67276kc5.aspx*.

> **Note** The markup that too many ASP.NET server controls return makes excessive use of *<table>* tags (often nested) and limited use of CSS styling. Based on the community feedback, the ASP.NET team released a free toolkit to enable a few built-in controls to output CSS-friendly markup where the *<table>* tag is not used or used less and in accordance with XHTML rules. The CSS Control Adapter Toolkit (CSSCAT) can be downloaded from *http://www.asp.net/cssadapters*. It comes with full source code and a permissive license that allows for unlimited further customization of the code. CSSCAT is built atop the control adapter architecture that in ASP.NET 2.0, and newer versions, makes it possible for developers to unplug the default rendering engine to roll their own. CSSCAT defines CSS-friendly adapters for the following controls: *Menu, TreeView, DetailsView, FormView, DataList, GridView, PasswordRecovery, ChangePassword, Login, LoginStatus*, and *CreateUserWizard*. You can freely edit the built-in *.browser* file to limit the number of CSS-friendly controls in your application. At the same time, by using the source code of CSSCAT as a base, you can start developing new adapters for other controls. For more information on the CSSCAT logic and internal architecture, pay a visit to *http://www.asp.net/cssadapters/whitepaper.aspx*.

Browser-Sensitive Rendering

In ASP.NET 2.0 and newer versions, you can declaratively assign a browser-specific value to all control properties. Here's a quick example:

```
<asp:Button ID="Button1" runat="server" Text="I'm a Button"
    ie:Text="IE Button"
    mozilla:Text="Firefox Button" />
```

The *Text* property of the button will contain "IE button" if the page is viewed through Internet Explorer and "Firefox button" if the page goes through Firefox. If another browser is used, the value of the unprefixed *Text* attribute is used. All properties you can insert in a tag declaration can be flagged with a browser ID. Each supported browser has a unique ID. As in the preceding code, *ie* is for Internet Explorer and *mozilla* is for Firefox. Unique IDs exist for various versions of Netscape browsers and mobile devices.

Browser-specific filtering is supported also for master pages. We'll return to this feature in Chapter 6 and present a table with the most common browser IDs. However, browser IDs are interspersed in *.browser* files, which you can find at this path:

```
%windows%\Microsoft.NET\Framework\[version]\CONFIG\Browsers
```

XHTML Compliance

XHTML is a World Wide Web Consortium (W3C) standard that defines Web pages as XML documents. This approach guarantees that the elements in the pages are well formed and more forward-compatible with browsers in the near future. By default, the markup produced by ASP.NET controls conforms to the XHTML standard with very few exceptions. This compliance with standards produces a number of observable features in the final markup served to browsers. For example, each element either includes an explicit closing tag or is self-closing (with */>*) and is always enclosed in a container element. For example, the view state hidden field is surrounded by a *<div>* tag and the *name* attribute has been removed from the *<form>* element:

```
<form method="post" action="default.aspx" id="MainForm">
<div>
    <input type="hidden" name="__VIEWSTATE" id="__VIEWSTATE" value="..." />
</div>
    ...
</form>
```

In addition, any script tags rendered into the page include an appropriate *type* attribute and are rendered in *CDATA* elements.

It's clear that some of these changes might break existing old pages as you upgrade to ASP.NET 3.5. What if, say, you have a page that relies on the *name* attribute on the form? To smooth migration of ASP.NET 1.x pages, you can add the following setting to the *web.config* file, which forces ASP.NET to render controls as in ASP.NET 1.x:

```
<system.web>
    <XHTML11Conformance enableObsoleteRendering="true" />
</system.web>
```

The option to disable XHTML rendering is provided primarily to assist you in upgrading existing pages. You should not abuse it, as it might not be supported in future versions of ASP.NET. Moreover, you should be migrating to XHTML anyway; ASP.NET 3.5 just gives you one more reason to do it now, if possible.

> **Note** The generation of XHTML-compliant output is guaranteed only for the vast majority of core ASP.NET server controls. Controls such as *HyperLink*, *BulletedList*, and *AdRotator* generate non-XHTML-compliant markup regardless of the settings you choose. *GridView* and *TreeView* controls are also at risk if they incorporate *HyperLinkColumn* and *TreeNode* components. You should avoid using these controls in pages where XHTML compliance is a strict requirement. If you make use of third-party controls, you should always check with the vendor to see whether they generate XHTML markup. Finally, note that ASP.NET is unable to fix XHTML errors that occur in the literal part of the pages. If your page contains static text or HTML elements, the responsibility of ensuring that they are XHTML compliant is entirely yours.

How can you make sure that a given page, or a given custom control, renders XHTML markup? You must use a service that runs the page and checks its output. For example, you can use the W3C Markup Validation Service at *http://validator.w3.org*. You can use the validator in two ways: by entering the URL of your page and having it request and check the page, or by uploading the page to the validator's site.

Themeable Controls

In the ASP.NET jargon, a *theme* is a named collection of property settings that can be applied to controls to make them look consistent across pages. You can apply theme settings to an entire Web site, to a page and its controls, or to an individual control. A theme is identified by name and consists of cascading style sheet (CSS) files, images, and control skins. A *control skin* is a text file that contains predefined values for some control properties. Applied together, these settings contribute to change the look and feel of the control and give the whole site a consistent (and, you hope, appealing) user interface. In addition, because themes are a sort of monolithic attribute, you can easily export that look from one application to the next. With themes enabled, if the developer adds, say, a *DataGrid* control to a page, the control is rendered with the default appearance defined in the currently selected theme.

Server controls can dynamically accept or deny theming through a Boolean property named *EnableTheming*, set to *true* by default. As a general rule, themes affect only properties that relate to the control's appearance. Properties that explicitly specify a behavior or imply an action should not be made themeable. Each control has the power to state which properties are themeable and which are not. This happens at compile time through attributes—in particular, the *Themeable* attribute. We'll return to themes in Chapter 6. I cover custom control development in *Programming Microsoft ASP.NET 2.0 Applications: Advanced Topics* (Microsoft Press, 2006).

Control State

Some ASP.NET controls require that some state be kept across requests. Examples of this type of state information include the current page of a paged control and the current sort order of a sortable data control. In ASP.NET 1.x, there is only one container in which this data can be stored—the view state. However, the view state is mainly designed to maintain settings set by the application and, more importantly, it can be turned off. What would happen to control-specific state in this case? For this reason, starting with ASP.NET 2.0 Microsoft introduced the notion of the "control state" and managed to keep it separate from the view state. So it's clear that control state is a vital piece of the control infrastructure.

Control state is a collection of critical view-state data that controls need to function. Because of its critical role, control state data is contained in separate member variables from normal view state and is not affected when view state is disabled. Unlike view state, control state requires extra implementation steps to use.

For one thing, each control needs to signal to the page that it requires control state. Next, there's no unique container to store data, such as *ViewState*; but the data can be retrieved from any object you want—arrays, collections, or a slew of instance variables. Each control persists and loads its control state using a pair of overridable methods, as shown here:

```
protected override object SaveControlState()
protected override void LoadControlState(object state)
```

Control state works similarly to view state and is saved and loaded at the same stage of the pipeline that view state is processed. Ultimately, control state is persisted in the same hidden field as the view state.

Input Focus

A useful feature that ASP.NET 1.x lacks is the ability to quickly assign the input focus to a particular control when the page is displayed. This feature can be coded in not much time by a seasoned developer and can be easily engineered into a company-wide framework for building controls and pages.

As we saw in Chapter 3, the *Page* class of ASP.NET 2.0 provides the *SetFocus* method to assign the input focus to any control you want. The following code shows how to set the focus to a *TextBox* control named *txtLastName*:

```
void Page_Load(object sender, EventArgs e)
{
    if (!IsPostBack)
        SetFocus("txtLastName");
}
```

The *SetFocus* method caches the ID of the control and forces the *Page* class to generate ad hoc script code when the page is rendered. Each control can also reclaim the input focus for itself by calling its new *Focus* method. Starting with version 2.0, all ASP.NET controls benefit from this feature.

HTML Controls

At first sight, HTML server controls look like HTML tags except for the extra *runat=server* attribute. Although it's true that they look the same, the additional *runat* attribute makes a huge difference. As mentioned, in ASP.NET by simply adding the *runat* attribute, you can bring to life otherwise-dead HTML text. Once transformed into a living instance of a server-side component, the original tag can be configured programmatically using an object-oriented approach. By design, HTML controls expose a set of methods and properties that carefully reflect the HTML syntax. For example, to set the default text of an input form field you use a property named *Value* instead of the more expressive *Text*. The name of the server control is determined by the value of the *ID* attribute. The following code snippet shows how to define a server-side input tag named *lastName*:

```
<input runat="server" id="lastName" type="text" />
```

The tag declaration does not include an explicit and static value for the *Value* attribute, which can be configured programmatically as follows:

```
void Page_Load(object sender, EventArgs e)
{
    lastName.Value = "Esposito";
}
```

After being processed by the ASP.NET runtime, the preceding declaration generates the following HTML code:

```
<input name="myName" id="myName" type="text" value="Esposito" />
```

Notice that a server-side *ID* attribute expands to a pair of HTML attributes—*Name* and *ID*. Be aware that this happens for browser compatibility. In no way does this mean that on the server *Name* and *ID* can be interchangeably used to name the server instance of the control. The name of the server control instance is given by *ID*. If you specify both *Name* and *ID* on a server-side tag, the value assigned to *Name* will be silently overridden.

Generalities of HTML Controls

The .NET Framework provides predefined server controls for commonly used HTML elements such as *<form>*, *<input>*, and *<select>*, as well as for tables, images, and hyperlinks. All the predefined HTML server controls inherit from the same base class—the *HtmlControl* class. In addition, each control then provides its own set of specific properties and its own events.

Controls typically supply properties that allow you to manipulate the HTML attributes programmatically from within server code. HTML controls integrate well with data-binding and the ASP.NET state maintenance, and they also provide full support for postback events and client scripting. For example, for a button that gets clicked, you can have some JavaScript code running on the client responding to the *onclick* event as well as some code that handles the event on the server if the page posts back as the result of that event.

HTML controls are defined in the *System.Web.UI.HtmlControls* namespace. Most, but not all, HTML tags have a direct class counterpart in the .NET Framework. HTML elements that don't map to a made-to-measure class are rendered through the *HtmlGenericControl* class and have attributes set using generic collections rather than direct properties. Generic controls include *<iframe>*, *<hr>*, *<font>*, and *<body>*. In general, you should bear in mind that every element that can appear in an HTML page can be marked as *runat="server"* and programmed and styled on the server.

The *HtmlControl* Base Class

The *HtmlControl* class inherits from *Control* and defines the methods, properties, and events common to all HTML controls. Actually, many properties and all methods and events are simply inherited from the base class. Table 4-5 shows the list of properties specific to HTML controls.

TABLE 4-5 Specific Properties of an HTML Control

Property	Description
Attributes	Gets a collection object representing all the attributes set on the control with the corresponding value
Disabled	Gets or sets a Boolean value, which indicates whether the HTML control is disabled
Style	Gets a collection object representing all CSS properties applied to the control
TagName	Gets the name of the HTML tag behind the control

A disabled HTML server control is visible and always gets generated as HTML code. If the *Disabled* property is set to *true*, the *disabled* HTML attribute is inserted in the HTML output for the control. As mentioned earlier, if the *Visible* property is set to *false*, HTML is not generated for the control.

> **Note** The *disabled* HTML attribute applies only to HTML input elements. It has no effect on, say, anchor tags.

Working with HTML Attributes

Each HTML control features more properties than those listed in Table 4-5. Properties of HTML server controls map to HTML attributes, and the values assigned to the properties are replicated in the HTML output. For controls that don't have an HTML direct counterpart, the *Attributes* collection is used to set attributes on the resulting HTML tag. This collection can also be used to set properties not mapped by the control's interface and, if needed, to define custom HTML attributes. Any content of the *Attributes* collection is managed as a string.

Given the following HTML code snippet, let's see how to programmatically set some attributes on the *<body>* tag:

```
<script>
function Init() {
    alert("Hello");
}
</script>

<script runat=server language="C#">
void Page_Load(object sender, EventArgs e) {
    theBody.Attributes["onload"] = "Init()";
}
</script>

<html>
<body runat="server" id="theBody">
</body>
</html>
```

You bind a JavaScript script to the *onload* attribute of the *<body>* tag. The resulting HTML code that the browser displays is as follows:

```
<script>
function Init() {
    alert("Hello");
}
</script>

<html>
<body id="theBody" onload="Init()">
</body>
</html>
```

The *Attributes* property is rendered through a special type of class named *AttributeCollection*. In spite of the name, the content of the class is not directly enumerable using the *for...each* statement because the *IEnumerable* interface is not supported. The *AttributeCollection* class provides ad hoc methods to render attributes of a text writer object and to add and remove elements. Interestingly, if you add an attribute named *Style*, the class is smart enough to reroute the assigned content to the *Style* collection.

Hierarchy of HTML Controls

Most HTML controls can be grouped into two main categories—container and input controls. A few controls, though, cannot be easily catalogued in either of the two groups. They are *HtmlImage*, *HtmlLink*, *HtmlMeta*, and *HtmlTitle*, and they are the ASP.NET counterpart of the *<img>*, *<link>*, *<meta>*, and *<title>* tags. Figure 4-1 shows the tree of HTML controls.

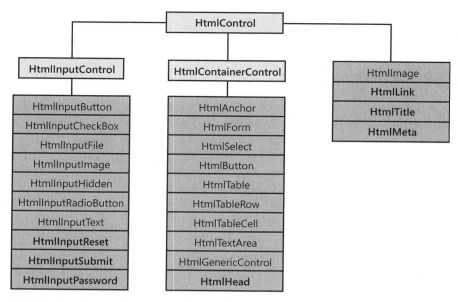

FIGURE 4-1 A diagram that groups all HTML controls by looking at their base class. Controls in boldface type require ASP.NET version 2.0 or later.

The input controls category includes all possible variations of the *<input>* tag, from submit buttons to check boxes and from text fields to radio buttons. The container controls category lists anchors, tables, forms, and in general, all HTML tags that might contain child elements.

HTML Container Controls

The base class for container controls is the *HtmlContainerControl* class, which descends directly from *HtmlControl*. The HTML elements addressed by this tag are elements that must have a closing tag—that is, forms, selection boxes, and tables, as well as anchors and text areas. Compared to the *HtmlControl* class, a container control features a couple of additional string properties—*InnerHtml* and *InnerText*.

Both properties manipulate the reading and writing of literal content found between the opening and closing tags of the element. Note that you cannot get the inner content of a control if the content includes server controls. *InnerHtml* and *InnerText* work only in the presence of all literal content. The tag itself is not considered for the output. Unlike *InnerText*, though, *InnerHtml* lets you work with HTML rich text and doesn't automatically encode and decode text. In other words, *InnerText* retrieves and sets the content of the tag as plain text, whereas *InnerHtml* retrieves and sets the same content but in HTML format.

Table 4-6 lists the HTML container controls defined in ASP.NET.

TABLE 4-6 HTML Container Controls

Class	Description
HtmlAnchor	Represents an HTML anchor—specifically, the *<a>* tag.
HtmlButton	Represents the HTML *<button>* tag. The *<button>* element is defined in the HTML 4.0 specification and supported only in Internet Explorer version 4.0 and later.
HtmlForm	Represents the *<form>* tag, but can be used only as a container of interactive server controls on a Web page. Cannot really be used to create HTML forms programmable on the server.
HtmlGenericControl	Represents an HTML tag for which the .NET Framework does not provide a direct class. Sample tags include *<font>*, *<hr>*, and *<iframe>*. You program these controls by using the *Attributes* collection and set attributes indirectly.
HtmlHead	Represents the *<head>* tag, and allows you to control meta tags, the style sheet, and the page title programmatically. *Not available in ASP.NET 1.x.*
HtmlSelect	Represents the *<select>* tag—that is, an HTML selection box.
HtmlTable	Represents an HTML table—specifically, the *<table>* tag.
HtmlTableCell	Represents the *<td>* HTML tag—that is, a cell in a table.
HtmlTableRow	Represents the *<tr>* HTML tag—that is, a row in a table.
HtmlTextArea	Represents a multiline text box, and maps the *<textarea>* HTML tag.

Note that the *HtmlButton* control is different than *HtmlInputButton*, which represents the button variation of the *<input>* tag. The *HtmlButton* control represents the HTML 4.0–specific *<button>* tag. We'll say more about buttons in the next section while discussing the Web controls.

Server-side forms play a key role in the economy of ASP.NET applications, as they are the means for implementing postbacks and guaranteeing state maintenance. For this reason, the *HtmlForm* control is not simply a form element you can program on the server. In particular, the *HtmlForm* hides the *Action* property and cannot be used to post content to a page different than the content that generated the HTML for the browser. We will cover HTML forms in great detail in Chapter 5.

Managing Header Information

An instance of the *HtmlHead* control is automatically created if the page contains a *<head>* tag marked with the attribute *runat=server*. Note that this setting is the default when you add a new page to a Visual Studio 2008 Web project, as shown in the following snippet:

```
<head runat="server">
    <title>Untitled Page</title>
</head>
```

The header of the page is returned through the new *Header* property of the *Page* class. The property returns *null* if the *<head>* tag is missing, or if it is present but lacks the *runat* attribute.

The *HtmlHead* control implements the *IPageHeader* interface, which consists of three collection properties—*Metadata*, *LinkedStylesheet*, and *Stylesheet*—and a string property—*Title*. The *Metadata* property is a dictionary that collects all the desired child *<meta>* tags of the header:

```
Header.Metadata.Add("CODE-LANGUAGE", "C#");
```

The code results in the following markup:

```
<meta name="CODE-LANGUAGE" content="C#" />
```

To express other common metadata such as *Http-Equiv*, you can resort to the newest *HtmlMeta* control, as shown here:

```
void Page_Init(object sender, EventArgs e)
{
    HtmlMeta meta = new HtmlMeta();
    meta.HttpEquiv = "refresh";
    meta.Content = Int32.Parse(TextBox1.Text).ToString();
    ((Control)Header).Controls.Add(meta);
}
```

The preceding code creates a *<meta>* tag dynamically and adds it to the *<head>* section of the page during the initialization phase. You can also manipulate an existing *<meta>* programmatically, as long as it is flagged with the *runat* attribute.

Tip In Internet Explorer only, the *<meta>* tag can be used to smooth the transition from one page to the next, and also when you move back to a previously visited page. When navigating from page to page in the browser, the current page usually disappears all of a sudden and the new page shows up in its place. By using the following two meta tags, you can make them fade away smoothly:

```
<meta http-equiv="Page-Enter"
content="progid:DXImageTransform.Microsoft.Fade(duration=.5)" />
<meta http-equiv="Page-Exit"
content="progid:DXImageTransform.Microsoft.Fade(duration=.5)" />
```

Needless to say, the tags can be created and managed programmatically in ASP.NET 2.0 and newer versions.

Note To add a *<meta>* tag programmatically in ASP.NET 1.x, you must resort to a trick. You create the string as a literal control and add it to the *Controls* collection of the header.

```
string meta = "<meta http-equiv='refresh' content='3' />";
LiteralControl equiv = new LiteralControl(meta);
((Control) Header).Controls.Add(equiv);
```

Notice that you must explicitly cast the object returned by the *Header* property to *Control*. This is because the *Header* property is declared as type *IPageHeader*, which has no *Controls* property defined.

To link a style sheet file, you use the following code:

```
Header.LinkedStyleSheets.Add("MyStyles.css");
```

Alternatively, you can resort to the *HtmlLink* control. The *HtmlLink* control represents the *<link>* element. Unlike *<a>*, the *<link>* tag can appear only in the *<head>* section of a document, although it might appear any number of times.

Finally, the *HtmlHead* control features the *Title* property, through which you can retrieve and set the title of the page:

```
Header.Title = "This is the title";
```

Note that this property returns the correct page title only if the *<title>* tag is correctly placed within the *<head>* tag. Some browsers, in fact, are quite forgiving on this point and allow developers to define the title outside the header. To manipulate the *<title>* tag independently from the header, use the *HtmlTitle* control and mark the *<title>* tag with the *runat* attribute.

Navigating to a URL

The *HtmlAnchor* class is the programmatic way of accessing and configuring the *<a>* tag. With respect to the other container controls, the *HtmlAnchor* class provides a few extra properties such as *HRef*, *Name*, *Target*, and *Title*. The *HRef* property sets the target of the hyperlink and can be used to navigate to the specified location. The *Name* property names a section in the ASP.NET page that can be reached from anywhere on the same page through #-prefixed *HRef*s. The following code demonstrates a bookmarked anchor named *MoreInfo*:

```
<a name="MoreInfo" />
```

This anchor can be reached using the following hyperlink:

```
<a href="#MoreInfo">Get More Info</a>
```

The *Target* property identifies the target window or the frame where the linked URL will be loaded. Common values for *Target* are *_self*, *_top*, *_blank*, and *_parent*, as well as any other name that refers to a page-specific frame. Although the feature is mostly browser dependent, you should always consider these special names as lowercase. Finally, the *Title* property contains the text that virtually all browsers display as a ToolTip when the mouse hovers over the anchor's area.

Handling Events on the Server

In addition to being used for navigating to a different page, the anchor control—as well as the *HtmlButton* control—can be used to post back the page. Key to this behavior is the *ServerClick* event, which lets you define the name of the method that will handle, on the server, the event generated when the user clicks the control. The following code demonstrates an anchor in which the click event is handled on both the client and server:

```
<a runat=server onclick="Run()" onserverclick="DoSomething">
Click
</a>
```

The *onclick* attribute defines the client-side event handler written using JavaScript; the *onserverclick* attribute refers to the server-side code that will run after the page posts back. Of course, if both event handlers are specified, the client-side handler executes first before the post back occurs.

The *HtmlSelect* Control

The *HtmlSelect* control represents a list of options from which you choose one or more. You control the appearance and behavior of the control by setting the *Size* and *Multiple* properties. The *Size* property specifies the number of rows to be displayed by the control, whereas the *Multiple* property indicates whether more than one item can be selected in the control. Internal items are grouped in the *Items* collection, and each element is represented by a *ListItem* object. Interestingly, the *ListItem* class is not defined in the *HtmlControls* namespace but lives instead in the *WebControls* namespace. To specify the text for each selectable item, you can either set the *Text* property of the *ListItem* or simply define a series of *<option>* tags within the opening and closing tags of the *<select>* element.

By default, the *HtmlSelect* control shows up as a drop-down list. However, if multiple selections are allowed or the height is set to more than one row, the control is displayed as a list box. The index of the selected item in a single-selection control is returned through the *SelectedIndex* property. If the multiple selection is enabled, you just loop through the *Items* collection and check the *Selected* property on individual list items.

The *HtmlSelect* control supports data binding through additional properties. The *DataSource* property lets you set the data source, which can be any .NET object that implements the *IEnumerable* interface. If the data source contains multiple bindable tables (for example, a *DataSet* object), by using the *DataMember* property you can choose a particular one. Finally, the *DataTextField* and *DataValueField* properties are used to bind the list item's *Text* and *Value* properties to columns in the data source. (We'll cover data binding in Chapter 9.)

HTML Tables

In ASP.NET, HTML tables provide a minimum set of functions when rendered using the *HtmlTable* control. In most cases, you don't need to use server-side tables because you typically rely on richer list and grid controls to do the job of displaying tables or records. So you resort to tables when you need to define a fixed layout for graphical elements of the page, but this is not a feature that requires a server-side table.

Until ASP.NET 3.5, server-side tables were not as powerful as pure HTML tables—which are created by using the *<table>* tag. The main limitation was that the *HtmlTable* class did not support HTML elements such as *<caption>*, *<col>*, *<colgroup>*, *<tbody>*, *<thead>*, and *<tfoot>*. If you used these elements in your ASP.NET 2.0 code, no run-time exception or compile error was ever thrown, but those elements were silently removed from the HTML code being generated.

In ASP.NET 3.5, table sections like *<tbody>*, *<thead>*, and *<tfoot>* are fully supported by all flavors of table controls—both *HtmlTable* and *Table*—the control behind the *<asp:Table>* server tag.

The *HtmlTextArea* Control

The *HtmlTextArea* control corresponds to the *<textarea>* HTML element and allows you to programmatically create and configure a multiline text box. The *HtmlTextArea* class provides the *Rows* and *Cols* properties to control the number of rows and columns of the text box. The *Value* property can be used to assign some text to display in the control area.

The *HtmlTextArea* class also provides a *ServerChange* event that fires during a postback and allows you to validate on the server the data contained in the control. Note that the *HtmlTextArea* control does not fire the event itself and does not directly cause the page to post back. Rather, when the page posts back in response to a click on a link or submit button, the *HtmlTextArea* control intervenes in the server-side chain of events and gives the programmer a chance to run some code if the internal content of the control is changed between two successive postbacks.

All ASP.NET controls that, like *HtmlTextArea*, implement the *IPostBackDataHandler* interface can invoke user-defined code when the control's internal state changes. As discussed in Chapter 3, controls can fire custom events by overriding the *RaisePostDataChangedEvent* method on the aforementioned interface. The following pseudocode shows what happens in the method's implementation of *HtmlTextArea*:

```
void System.Web.UI.IPostBackDataHandler.RaisePostDataChangedEvent()
{
    this.OnServerChange(EventArgs.Empty);
}
```

Finally, note that the control raises the event only if the state has changed between two successive posts. To determine whether that has happened, the control needs to track the content it had the time before. This value can be stored only in the view state. Of course, the *ServerChange* even won't fire if you disable the view state for the host page or the control.

HTML Input Controls

In HTML, the *<input>* element has several variations and can be used to provide a submit button as well as a check box or text box. In ASP.NET, each possible instance of the *<input>* element is mapped to a specific class. All input classes derive from the *HtmlInputControl* class. *HtmlInputControl* is the abstract class that defines the common programming interface for all input controls. The class inherits from *HtmlControl* and simply adds three custom properties—*Name*, *Type*, and *Value*—to the inherited interface.

The *Name* property returns the name assigned to the control. In ASP.NET, this property is peculiar because, although it's marked as read/write, it actually works as a read-only property. The *get* accessor returns the control's *UniqueID* property, while the *set* accessor is just void. As a result, whatever value you assign to the property, either programmatically or declaratively, is just ignored and no exception or compile error is ever thrown.

The *Type* property mirrors the *type* attribute of the HTML input elements. The property is read-only. Finally, the *Value* property is read/write and represents the content of the input field.

Table 4-7 lists the HTML input controls defined in ASP.NET.

TABLE 4-7 HTML Input Controls

Class	Description
HtmlInputButton	Represents the various flavors of a command button supported by HTML. Feasible values for the *Type* attribute are *button*, *submit*, and *reset*.
HtmlInputCheckBox	Represents an HTML check box—that is, the *<input>* tag with a type equal to *checkbox*.
HtmlInputFile	Represents the file uploader—that is, the *<input>* tag with a type equal to *file*.
HtmlInputHidden	Represents a hidden buffer of text data—that is, the *<input>* tag with a type equal to *hidden*.
HtmlInputImage	Represents a graphic button—that is, the *<input>* tag with a type equal to *image*. Note that this tag is supported by all browsers.
HtmlInputPassword	Represents a protected text field—that is, the *<input>* tag with a type of *password*. *Not available in ASP.NET 1.x.*

Class	Description
HtmlInputRadioButton	Represents a radio button—that is, the *<input>* tag with a type equal to *radio*.
HtmlInputReset	Represents a reset command button. *Not available in ASP.NET 1.x.*
HtmlInputSubmit	Represents a submit command button. *Not available in ASP.NET 1.x.*
HtmlInputText	Represents a text field—that is, the *<input>* tag with a type of either *password* or *text*.

The hidden and text input controls are nearly identical, and the contents of both are posted back. Essentially, they differ only in that hidden fields are not displayed and, subsequently, they don't provide some UI-related properties such as *MaxLength* and *Size*.

Command Buttons

The *HtmlInputButton* class is the most flexible button class in the .NET Framework. It differs from the *HtmlButton* class in that it renders through the *<input>* tag rather than the Internet Explorer–specific *<button>* tag. This fact ensures for the control much wider support from browsers.

The HTML input button controls support the *ServerClick* event, which allows you to set the code to run on the server after the button is clicked. Note that if you set the button type to *Button* and the *ServerClick* event handler is specified, the control automatically adds the postback script code to the *onclick* HTML attribute. In this way, any click causes the page to post back and the code to execute. Let's consider the following ASP.NET code:

```
<input runat="server" type="button" id="btn" value="Click"
    onserverclick="buttonClicked" />
```

The corresponding HTML code is as follows:

```
<input language="javascript" onclick="__doPostBack('btn','')"
    name="btn"
    type="button"
    value="Click" />
```

The client-side *__doPostBack* script function is the standard piece of code generated by ASP. NET to implement the postback. If the button type is set to *Submit*—that is, a value that would always cause a postback—no client-side script code is generated and the *onclick* attribute is not set.

In ASP.NET 2.0 and newer versions, more specific controls have been added to render submit and reset buttons. The controls are *HtmlInputSubmit* and *HtmlInputReset*.

> **Note** The *HtmlInputImage* control supports a nearly identical pattern for handling server-side events and validation. The *HtmlInputImage* control features a few more properties specific to the image it shows. In particular, you can set the alternate text for the image, the border, and the alignment with respect to the rest of the page. The *ServerClick* event handler has a slightly different form and looks like the following:
>
> ```
> void ImageClickEventHandler(object sender, ImageClickEventArgs e);
> ```
>
> When an image button is clicked, the coordinates of the click are determined by using the *X* and *Y* properties of the *ImageClickEventArgs* data structure.

Controlling Validation

The *HtmlInputButton* class, as well as the *HtmlButton* class, support a Boolean property named *CausesValidation*. The property indicates whether the content of the input fields should be validated when the button is clicked. By default, the property is set to *true*, meaning the validation always takes place. We'll examine data validation later in the chapter. For now, it suffices to say, you can programmatically enable or disable the validation step by using the *CausesValidation* property.

Typically, you might want to disable validation if the button that has been clicked doesn't perform a concrete operation but simply clears the user interface or cancels an ongoing operation. By design, in fact, server-side page validation takes place just before the *ServerClick* event handler is executed. Setting the *CausesValidation* property to *false* is the only means you have to prevent an unnecessary validation.

Detecting State Changes of Controls

Earlier in this chapter, while discussing the features of the *HtmlTextArea* control, we ran into the *ServerChange* event and described it as the mechanism to detect and validate changes in the control's state between two successive postbacks. The *ServerChange* event is not an exclusive feature of the *HtmlTextArea* control but is also supported by other input controls such as *HtmlInputCheckBox*, *HtmlInputRadioButton*, *HtmlInputHidden*, and *HtmlInputText*. Let's look at an example in which we use the *ServerChange* event to detect which elements have been checked since last time the control was processed on the server.

We build a page with a list of check boxes and a button to let the user post back to the server when finished. Notice, in fact, that neither the *HtmlInputCheckBox* control nor any other input control except buttons, post back to the server when clicked. For this reason, you must provide another control on the Web page that supports posting to the server—for example, an *HtmlButton* or an *HtmlInputButton* control. The following code implements the page shown in Figure 4-2:

```
<%@ Page Language="C#" %>
<html>
<script runat="server">
public void DetectChange(object sender, EventArgs e) {
    HtmlInputCheckBox cb = (HtmlInputCheckBox) sender;
    Response.Write("Control <b>" + cb.UniqueID + "</b> changed<br>");
}
</script>

<body>
<form runat="server">
    <input runat="server" type="checkbox" id="one"
        OnServerChange="DetectChange" />One<br />
    <input runat="server" type="checkbox" id="two"
        OnServerChange="DetectChange" />Two<br />
    <input runat="server" type="checkbox" id="three"
        OnServerChange="DetectChange" />Three<br />
    <input runat="server" type="submit" value="Submit" />
</form>
</body>
</html>
```

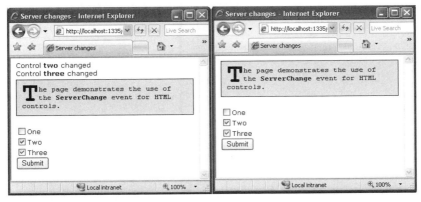

FIGURE 4-2 The *ServerChange* event fires only if the status of the control has changed since the last time the control was processed on the server.

The *ServerChange* event is fired only if the state of the control results changed after two postbacks. To get the first screen shot, you select the element and then submit. Next, if you submit again without selecting or deselecting anything, you get the second screen shot.

As mentioned in Chapter 3, by implementing the *IPostBackDataHandler* interface, each server control gets a chance to update its current state with data posted by the client. I cover this interface in detail in the *Programming Microsoft ASP.NET 2.0 Applications: Advanced Topics* (Microsoft Press, 2006).

Uploading Files

The *HtmlInputFile* control is the HTML tool for uploading files from a browser to the Web server. To take advantage of the *HtmlInputFile* control, you should first ensure that the server form's *Enctype* property is set to *multipart/form-data*. Note, though, that starting with ASP. NET 2.0, the proper *EncType* is automatically set care of the *HtmlInputFile* control before the control's markup is rendered:

```
<form runat="server" enctype="multipart/form-data">
    <input runat="server" type="file" id="upLoader" >
    <input runat="server" type="submit" value="Upload..." />
</form>
```

The way in which the *HtmlInputFile* control is rendered to HTML is browser-specific, but it normally consists of a text box and a Browse button. The user selects a file from the local machine and then clicks the button to submit the page to the server. When this occurs, the browser uploads the selected file to the server, as shown in Figure 4-3.

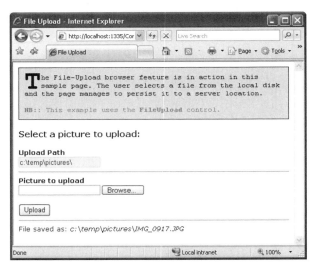

FIGURE 4-3 A new file has been uploaded to the Web server and copied to the destination folder.

> **Note** Prior to ASP.NET, a server-side process—the posting acceptor—was required to run in the background to handle *multipart/form-data* submissions. In ASP.NET, the role of the posting acceptor is no longer necessary, as it is carried out by the ASP.NET runtime itself.

On the server, the file is parked into an object of type *HttpPostedFile* and stays there until explicitly processed—for example, saved to disk or to a database. The *HttpPostedFile* object provides properties and methods to get information on an individual file and to read and save the file. The following code shows how to save a posted file to a particular folder to disk:

```
<%@ Page language="C#" %>
<%@ Import Namespace="System.IO" %>

<script runat="server">
    void UploadButton_Click(object sender, EventArgs e)
    {
        // *** ASSUME THE PATH EXISTS ***
        string savePath = @"c:\temp\pictures\";
        if (!Directory.Exists(savePath)) {
            string msg = "<h1>Upload path doesn't exist: {0}</h1>";
            Response.Write(String.Format(msg, savePath));
            Response.End();
        }

        // Verify that a file has been posted
        if (FileUpload1.PostedFile != null)
        {
            // Save the uploaded file to the specified path
            string fileName = Path.GetFileName(FileUpload1.Value);
            savePath += fileName;
            FileUpload1.PostedFile.SaveAs(savePath);

            // Notify the user of the name the file was saved under.
            UploadStatusLabel.InnerText = "File saved as: " + savePath;
        }
        else
        {
            // Notify the user that a file was not uploaded.
            UploadStatusLabel.InnerText = "No file specified.";
        }
    }
</script>

<html>
<head runat="server">
    <title>File Upload</title>
</head>
<body>
    <form runat="server">
      <h3>Select a picture to upload:</h3>
        <hr />
        <b>Picture to upload</b><br />
        <input type="file" id="FileUpload1" runat="server" />
        <br><br>
        <input runat="server" id="UploadButton" type="submit"
            value="Upload" onserverclick="UploadButton_Click" />
        <hr />
        <span runat="server" id="UploadStatusLabel" />
    </form>
</body>
</html>
```

You can also use the *InputStream* property of the *HttpPostedFile* object to read the posted data before persisting or processing. The *HttpInputFile* control also allows you to restrict the file types that can be uploaded to the server. You do this by setting the *Accept* property with a comma-separated list of MIME types.

> **Caution** When you use the *SaveAs* method, you should pay attention to specify the full path to the output file. If a relative path is provided, ASP.NET attempts to place the file in the system directory. This practice can result in an access denied error. Furthermore, make sure to provide write permission for the account used by ASP.NET for the directory where you want to store the file.

ASP.NET exercises some control on the amount of data being uploaded. The *maxRequest-Length* attribute in the *<httpRuntime>* section of the configuration file sets the maximum allowable file size. An error is generated in the browser when the file exceeds the specified size—4 MB by default. Uploading large files might also generate another runtime error as a result of an excessive consumption of system memory.

The *HtmlImage* Control

The *HtmlImage* class is the ASP.NET counterpart of the *<img>* tag. You can use it to configure on the server the display of an image. Possible parameters you can set are the size of the image, the border, and the alternate text. An instance of *HtmlImage* is created only when the *runat* attribute is added to the *<img>* tag. If you simply need to display an image within a page, and the image is not dynamically determined or configured, there is no need to resort to the *HtmlImage* control, which would add unnecessary overhead to the page.

The following code snippet shows how to configure a server-side *<img>* tag called to display an image whose name is determined based on run-time conditions:

```
theImg.Width = 100;
theImg.Height = 100;
theImg.Src = GetImageUrl(Request); // assume GetImageUrl is a method of yours
```

The *HtmlImage* control should be used to programmatically manipulate the image to change the source file, the width and height, or the alignment of the image relative to other page elements. The majority of properties of the *HtmlImage* control are implemented as strings, including *Src*—the URL of the image—and *Align*. Feasible values of *Align* are only a small set of words such as *left*, *right*, *top*, and so forth. These words would have been more appropriately grouped in a custom enumerated type, thus providing for a strongly typed programming model. If you think so, too, you just got the gist of the difference between HTML and Web server controls! HTML controls just mirror HTML tags; Web controls attempt to provide a more consistent and effective programming interface by exploiting the characteristics of the .NET Framework.

Literal Controls

Literal controls are a special type of server control that ASP.NET creates and uses whenever it encounters plain text that doesn't require server-side processing. In general, everything that appears in the context of an ASP.NET page is treated like a control. If a tag includes the *runat="server"* attribute, ASP.NET creates an instance of a specific class; otherwise, if no *runat* attribute has been specified, the text is compiled into a *LiteralControl* object. Literal controls are simple text holders that are added to and removed from pages using the same programming interface defined for other server controls.

Note that a literal control is created for each sequence of characters placed between two successive server controls, including carriage returns. Using a new line to separate distinct server controls and increase code readability actually affects the number of server controls being created to serve the page. Writing the page as a single string without carriage returns produces the smallest number of server controls.

Web Controls

Web controls are defined in the *System.Web.UI.WebControls* namespace and represent an alternative approach to HTML server controls. Like HTML controls, Web controls are server-side components that spring to life thanks to the *runat="server"* attribute. Unlike HTML controls, Web controls provide a programming interface that refactors the classic set of HTML attributes and events. For this reason, Web controls sometimes appear to be more consistent and abstract in the API design and richer in functionality, but they still generate valid markup. When hosted in *.aspx* pages, Web controls are characterized by the *asp* namespace prefix.

To a large degree, Web controls and HTML controls overlap and generate almost the same markup, although they do it through different programming interfaces. For example, the Web controls namespace defines the *TextBox* control and makes it available through the *<asp:textbox>* tag; similarly, the HTML controls namespace provides the *HtmlInputText* control and declares it using the *<input>* tag. Using either is mostly a matter of preference; only in a few cases will you run into slight functionality differences.

Generalities of Web Controls

The *WebControl* class is the base class from which all Web controls inherit. *WebControl* inherits from *Control*. The class defines several properties and methods that are shared, but not necessarily implemented, by derived controls. Most properties and methods are related to the look and feel of the controls (font, style, colors, CSS) and are subject to browser and

HTML versions. For example, although all Web controls provide the ability to define a border, not all underlying HTML tags actually support a border.

Properties of Web Controls

Table 4-8 lists the properties available on the *WebControl* class.

TABLE 4-8 Specific Properties of Web Controls

Property	Description
AccessKey	Gets or sets the letter to press (together with Alt) to quickly set focus to the control in a Web form. Supported on Internet Explorer 4.0 and newer.
Attributes	Gets the collection of attributes that do not correspond to properties on the control. Attributes set in this way will be rendered as HTML attributes in the resulting page.
BackColor	Gets or sets the background color of the Web control.
BorderColor	Gets or sets the border color of the Web control.
BorderStyle	Gets or sets the border style of the Web control.
BorderWidth	Gets or sets the border width of the Web control.
ControlStyle	Gets the style of the Web server control. The style is an object of type *Style*.
ControlStyleCreated	Gets a value that indicates whether a *Style* object has been created for the *ControlStyle* property.
CssClass	Get or sets the name of the cascading style sheet (CSS) class associated with the client.
Enabled	Gets or sets whether the control is enabled.
Font	Gets the font properties associated with the Web control.
ForeColor	Gets or sets the foreground color of the Web control mostly used to draw text.
Height	Gets or sets the height of the control. The height is expressed as a member of type *Unit*.
Style	Gets a *CssStyleCollection* collection object made of all the attributes assigned to the outer tag of the Web control.
TabIndex	Gets or sets the tab index of the control.
ToolTip	Gets or sets the text displayed when the mouse pointer hovers over the control.
Width	Gets or sets the width of the control. The width is expressed as a member of type *Unit*.

The *ControlStyle* and *ControlStyleCreated* properties are used primarily by control developers, while the *Style* property is what application developers would typically use to set CSS attributes on the outer tag of the control. The *Style* property is implemented using an instance of the class *CssStyleCollection*. The *CssStyleCollection* class is a simple collection of strings like those you would assign to the HTML *style* attribute.

Styling Web Controls

The *ControlStyle* property evaluates to an object of type *Style*—a class that encapsulates the appearance properties of the control. The *Style* class groups together some of the properties that were shown in Table 4-8, and it works as the repository of the graphical and cosmetic attributes that characterize all Web controls. The grouped properties are *BackColor*, *BorderColor*, *BorderStyle*, *BorderWidth*, *CssClass*, *Font*, *ForeColor*, *Height*, and *Width*. All properties of the *Style* class are strongly typed. The properties just mentioned are not persisted to the view state individually, but they benefit from the serialization machinery supported by the *Style* object.

It should be clear by now that the *Style* class is quite different from the *Style* property, whose type is *CssStyleCollection*. Note that style values set through the *Style* property are not automatically reflected by the (strongly typed) values in the *Style* object. For example, you can set the CSS *border-style* through the *Style* property, but that value won't be reflected by the value of the *BorderStyle* property.

```
// Set the border color through a CSS attribute
MyControl.Style["border-color"] = "blue";

// Set the border color through an ASP.NET style property
MyControl.BorderColor = Color.Red;
```

So what happens if you run the preceding code snippet? Which setting would win? When a control is going to render, the contents of both *ControlStyle* and *Style* properties are rendered to HTML *style* attributes. The *ControlStyle* property is processed first, so in case of overlapping settings the value stuffed in *Style*, which is processed later, would win, as shown by the following markup:

```
style="border-color:Red;border-color:blue;    "
```

Managing the Style of Web Controls

The style properties of a Web control can be programmatically manipulated to some extent. For example, in the *Style* class, you can count on a *CopyFrom* method to duplicate the object and on the *MergeWith* method to combine two style objects.

```
currentStyle.MergeStyle(newStyle);
```

The *MergeWith* method joins the properties of both objects. In doing so, it does not replace any property that is already set in the base object but limits itself to defining uninitialized properties. Finally, the *Reset* method clears all current attributes in the various properties of the style object.

Methods of Web Controls

The *WebControl* class supports a few additional methods that are not part of the base *Control* class. These methods are listed in Table 4-9.

TABLE 4-9 Specific Methods of Web Controls

Method	Description
ApplyStyle	Copies any nonempty elements of the specified style object to the control. Existing style properties are overwritten.
CopyBaseAttributes	Imports from the specified Web control the properties *AccessKey*, *Enabled*, *ToolTip*, *TabIndex*, and *Attributes*. Basically, it copies all the properties not encapsulated in the *Style* object.
MergeStyle	Like *ApplyStyle*, copies any nonempty elements of the specified style to the control. Existing style properties are *not* overwritten, though.
RenderBeginTag	Renders the HTML opening tag of the control into the specified writer. The method is called right before the control's *RenderControl* method.
RenderEndTag	Renders the HTML closing tag of the control into the specified writer. The method is called right after the control's *RenderControl* method.

All these methods are rarely of interest to application developers. They are mostly designed to support control developers.

Core Web Controls

The set of Web controls can be divided into various categories according to the provided functionality—input and button controls, validators, data-bound controls, security-related controls, grid and view controls, plus a few miscellaneous controls that provide ad hoc functions and are as common on the Web as they are hard to catalogue (for example, calendar, ad rotator, and so forth).

In this chapter, we're focused on covering the most common and essential Web controls, such as the controls for capturing and validating the user's input and posting data to the server. We'll cover the various types of data-bound controls in Chapter 11, Chapter 12, and Chapter 13. Security-related controls, on the other hand, are slated for Chapter 17. Table 4-10 details the core server controls of ASP.NET.

TABLE 4-10 Core Web Controls

Control	Description
Button	Implements a push button through the *<input>* tag.
CheckBox	Implements a check box through the *<input>* tag.
FileUpload	Allows users to select a file to upload to the server. *Not available in ASP.NET 1.x.*
HiddenField	Implements a hidden field. *Not available in ASP.NET 1.x.*
HyperLink	Implements an anchor *<a>* tag, and lets you specify either the location to jump to or the script code to execute.
Image	Implements a picture box through the *<img>* tag.
ImageButton	Displays an image and responds to mouse clicks on the image like a real button.
ImageMap	Displays an image and optionally defines clickable hot spots on it. *Not available in ASP.NET 1.x.*
Label	Represents a static, nonclickable piece of text. Implemented through the *<span>* tag.
LinkButton	Implements an anchor *<a>* tag that uses only the ASP.NET postback mechanism to post back. It is a special type of hyperlink where the programmer can't directly set the target URL.
MultiView	Represents a control that acts as a container for a group of child *View* controls. *Not available in ASP.NET 1.x.*
Panel	Implements an HTML container using the *<div>* block element. In ASP.NET 2.0, the container supports scrolling. Note that in down-level browsers the control renders out as a *<table>*.
RadioButton	Implements a single radio button through the *<input>* tag.
Table	Implements the outer table container. Equivalent to the HTML *<table>* element.
TableCell	A table cell; is equivalent to the HTML *<td>* element.
TableRow	A table row; is equivalent to the HTML *<tr>* element.
TextBox	Implements a text box using the *<input>* or *<textarea>* tag as appropriate and according to the requested text mode. Can work in single-line, multiline, or password mode.
View	Acts as a container for a group of controls. A *View* control must always be contained within a *MultiView* control. *Not available in ASP.NET 1.x.*

Most controls in Table 4-10 look like HTML controls. Compared to HTML controls, their programming model is certainly richer and more abstract, but in the end it still generates valid and legal markup. If a given feature can't be obtained with raw HTML, there's no way a custom Web control can provide it. No matter how complex the programming model is, all Web controls must produce valid HTML for both up-level and down-level browsers.

Button Controls

Starting with ASP.NET 2.0, controls that provide button functions are characterized by a new interface—*IButtonControl*. Core controls that implement the interface are *Button*, *ImageButton*, and *LinkButton*. In general, by implementing *IButtonControl* any custom control can act like a button on a form.

The *IButtonControl* interface is a clear example of the refactoring process that the entire ASP. NET Framework went through in the transition from 1.x to 2.0. The interface now groups a few properties that most button controls (including some HTML button controls) support since ASP.NET 1.x. In addition to this, a few new properties heralding new functions have been added, such as *PostBackUrl* and *ValidationGroup*. Table 4-11 details the *IButtonControl* interface.

TABLE 4-11 **The *IButtonControl* Interface**

Name	Description
CausesValidation	Boolean value, indicates whether validation is performed when the control is clicked.
CommandArgument	Gets or sets an optional parameter passed to the button's *Command* event along with the associated *CommandName*.
CommandName	Gets or sets the command name associated with the button that is passed to the *Command* event.
PostBackUrl	Indicates the URL that will handle the postback triggered through the button control. This feature is known as cross-page postback. (We'll cover this further in Chapter 5.)
Text	Gets or sets the caption of the button.
ValidationGroup	Gets or sets the name of the validation group that the button belongs to.
Visible	Boolean value, indicates whether the button control is rendered.

In addition to the properties defined by the *IButtonControl* interface, the *Button* class features two new properties in ASP.NET 2.0—*OnClientClick* and *UseSubmitBehavior*. The former standardizes a common practice that many developers used countless times in ASP.NET 1.x projects. *OnClientClick* lets you define the name of the JavaScript function to run when the client-side *onclick* event is fired. The following two statements are perfectly legal and equivalent:

```
// For ASP.NET 2.0 and newer versions
Button1.OnClientClick = "ShowMessage()";

// Equivalent in ASP.NET 1.x
Button1.Attributes["onclick"] = "ShowMessage()";
```

The *OnClientClick* property is also available on *LinkButton* and *ImageButton* controls.

By default, the *Button* class is rendered through an *<input type=submit>* tag. In this way, it takes advantage of the browser's submit mechanism to post back. The *UseSubmitBehavior* property allows you to change the default behavior. Set the *UseSubmitBehavior* property to *false* and the control will render out through an *<input type=button>* tag. Also in this case, though, the *Button* control remains a postback button. When *UseSubmitBehavior* is *false*, the control's *onclick* client event handler is bound to a piece of JavaScript code (the __*do-PostBack* function) that provides the ASP.NET postback mechanism just like for *LinkButton* or *ImageButton* controls.

> **Important** Buttons are not the only controls that can trigger a postback. Text boxes and check boxes (plus a few more data-bound list controls, which we'll see in Chapter 9) also can start a postback if their *AutoPostBack* property is set to *true*. (Note that the default setting is *false*.) When this happens, the control wires up to a client-side event—*onchange* for text boxes and *onclick* for check boxes—and initiates a postback operation via script. In fact, because this mechanism is available to server-side code, virtually any control can be modified to post back.

HyperLinks

The *HyperLink* control creates a link to another Web page and is typically displayed through the text stored in the *Text* property. Alternatively, the hyperlink can be displayed as an image; in this case, the URL of the image is stored in the *ImageUrl* property. Note that if both the *Text* and *ImageUrl* properties are set, the *ImageUrl* property takes precedence. In this case, the content of the *Text* property is displayed as a ToolTip when the mouse hovers over the control's area.

The *NavigateUrl* property indicates the URL the hyperlink is pointing to. The *Target* property is the name of the window or frame that will contain the output of the target URL.

Images and Image Buttons

The *Image* control displays an image on the Web page. The path to the image is set through the *ImageUrl* property. Image URLs can be either relative or absolute, with most programmers showing a clear preference for relative URLs because they make a Web site inherently easier to move. You can also specify alternate text to display when the image is not available or when the browser doesn't render the image for some reason. The property to use in this case is *AlternateText*. The image alignment with respect to other elements on the page is set by using the *ImageAlign* property. Feasible values are taken from the homonymous *enum* type (i.e.: *ImageAlign.Left*, *ImageAlign.Middle*, and so forth).

The *Image* control is not a clickable component and is simply limited to displaying an image. If you need to capture mouse clicks on the image, use the *ImageButton* control instead. The *ImageButton* class descends from *Image* and extends it with a couple of events—*Click* and *Command*—that are raised when the control is clicked. The *OnClick* event handler provides you with an *ImageClickEventArgs* data structure that contains information about the coordinates for the location at which the image is clicked.

The *OnCommand* event handler makes the *ImageButton* control behave like a command button. A command button has an associated name that you can control through the *CommandName* property. If you have multiple *ImageButton* controls on the same page, the command name allows you to distinguish which one is actually clicked. The *CommandArgument* property can be used to pass additional information about the command and the control.

Another new entry in ASP.NET 2.0 is the *ImageMap* control. In its simplest and most commonly used form, the control displays an image on a page. However, when a hot-spot region defined within the control is clicked, the control either generates a post back to the server or navigates to a specified URL. The hot spot is a clickable region within the displayed image. The hot spot is implemented with a class that inherits from the *HotSpot* class. There are three predefined types of hot spots—polygons, circles, and rectangles.

Check Boxes and Radio Buttons

Check boxes and radio buttons are implemented through the *<input>* tag and the *type* attribute set to *checkbox* or *radio*. Unlike the HTML control versions, the Web control versions of check boxes and radio buttons let you specify the associated text as a property. The HTML elements and corresponding HTML controls lack an attribute whose content becomes the text near the check box or radio button. In HTML, to make the text near the check box or radio button clickable, you have to resort to the *<label>* tag with the *for* attribute:

```
<input type="checkbox" id="ctl" />
<label for="ctl">Check me</label>
```

Neither the *HtmlInputCheckBox* nor the *HtmlInputRadioButton* control adds a label, which leaves you responsible for doing that. The counterparts to these Web controls, on the other hand, are not bound to the HTML syntax and do precisely that—they automatically add a *Text* property, which results in an appropriate *<label>* tag. For example, consider the following ASP.NET code:

```
<asp:checkbox runat="server" id="ctl" text="Check me" />
```

It results in the following HTML code:

```
<input type="checkbox" id="ctl" />
<label for="ctl">Check me</label>
```

Scrollable Panels

The *Panel* control groups controls in a *<div>* tag. It allows developers to add and remove controls, and it supports style information. Panels support horizontal and vertical scrollbars implemented through the *overflow* CSS style. Here's an example that demonstrates a scrollable panel:

```
<asp:Panel ID="Panel1" runat="server" Height="85px" Width="400px"
        ScrollBars="Auto" BorderStyle="Solid">
    <h2>Choose a technology</h2>
    <asp:CheckBox ID="ChkBox1" runat="server" Text="ASP.NET" />
<br />
    <asp:CheckBox ID="ChkBox2" runat="server" Text="AJAX" />
<br />
    <asp:CheckBox ID="ChkBox3" runat="server" Text="Web Services" />
<br />
    <asp:CheckBox ID="ChkBox4" runat="server" Text="XML" />
<br />
    <asp:CheckBox ID="ChkBox5" runat="server" Text="WCF Services" />
<br />
    <asp:CheckBox ID="ChkBox6" runat="server" Text="Silverlight" />
<br />
</asp:Panel>
```

Figure 4-4 shows the page in action.

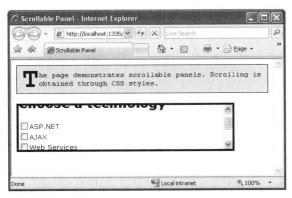

FIGURE 4-4 A page that uses a scrollable panel.

Text Controls

The fastest way to insert text in a Web page is through literals—that is, static text inserted directly in the *.aspx* source. This text will still be compiled to a control but, at least, the number of dynamically created literal controls is the minimum possible because any sequence of consecutive characters are grouped into a single literal. If you need to identify and manipulate particular strings of text programmatically, you can resort to a *Literal* control or, better yet, to the richer *Label* control. Modifiable text requires a *TextBox*.

Some minor changes occurred to these controls starting with ASP.NET 2.0. First, a few new interfaces have been introduced to logically group capabilities. They are *ITextControl* and *IEditableTextControl*. The former includes the sole *Text* property and is implemented by

Literal, Label, TextBox, and list controls. The latter interface defines the *TextChanged* event and is specific to *TextBox* and list controls.

It is worth mentioning a new accessibility feature of the *Label* control—the *AssociatedControlID* property. The property takes the ID of a control in the page—typically, an input control such as a *TextBox*—that you want to associate with the label. *AssociatedControlID* changes the way the *Label* control renders out. It is a *<span>* tag if no associated control is specified; it is a *<label>* tag otherwise. Let's consider the following example:

```
<asp:Label ID="Label1" runat="server" Text="Sample text" />
<asp:TextBox ID="TextBox1" runat="server" />
```

As is, it generates the following markup:

```
<span id="Label1">Sample text</span>
<input name="TextBox1" type="text" id="TextBox1" />
```

If you set the label's *AssociatedControlID* property to *TextBox1*, the markup changes as shown here:

```
<label for="TextBox1" id="Label1">Sample text</label>
<input name="TextBox1" type="text" id="TextBox1" />
```

The runtime behavior changes a bit because now any click on the label text will be extended to the associated control. For example, clicking on the label will move the input focus to a text box, or it will select or deselect a check box.

> **Note** *AssociatedControlID* is a feature designed to improve the accessibility of the resulting page. In Visual Studio 2008, you can check any page for accessibility rules (both WCAG and Section 508) by clicking on the *Tools|Check Accessibility* menu item.

Hidden Fields and File Upload

If you're looking for a more comfortable programming interface to create hidden fields and upload files, two Web controls might help. The *HiddenField* and *FileUpload* controls add no new functionality to the ASP.NET programmer's bag, but they have been added to the toolbox for completeness. A hidden field can be created in two other ways that work with ASP.NET 1.x too. For example, you can use the *RegisterHiddenField* method on the *Page* class:

```
// Works in ASP.NET 1.x but is obsolete starting with 2.0
RegisterHiddenField("HiddenField1", "Great book!");
```

Note that the *RegisterHiddenField* method has been flagged as obsolete in ASP.NET 2.0. The recommended code analogous to the previous snippet is shown next:

```
// Recommended code in ASP.NET 2.0 and beyond
ClientScriptManager.RegisterHiddenField("HiddenField1", "Great book!");
```

In addition, to create a hidden field you can resort to the HTML markup, adding a *runat* attribute if you need to set the value programmatically:

```
<input runat="server" id="HiddenField1" type="hidden" value="..." />
```

Analogous considerations can be made for the *FileUpload* control, which provides the same capabilities as the *HtmlInputFile* control that we discussed earlier. In this case, though, the programming interface is slightly different and perhaps more intuitive. The *HasFile* property and *SaveAs* method hide any reference to the object that represents the posted file. Likewise, the *FileName* property provides a more immediate name for the name of the posted file. The code to upload a file can be rewritten as follows:

```
if (FileUpload1.HasFile)
{
    // Get the name of the file to upload.
    string fileName = FileUpload1.FileName;
    string targetPath = GetSavePath(fileName);
    FileUpload1.SaveAs(targetPath);
}
```

Whether you use *FileUpload* or *HtmlInputFile* is mostly a matter of preference.

Miscellaneous Web Controls

The *WebControls* namespace also includes a few controls that provide useful functionality that is common in Web applications. In particular, we'll examine the *AdRotator* control, which works like an advertisement banner, and the *Calendar* control, which is a flexible and highly interactive control used to specify a date.

The *AdRotator* Control

Abstractly speaking, the *AdRotator* control displays an automatically sized image button and updates both the image and the URL each time the page refreshes. The image to display and other information is read from an XML file written according to a specific schema. More concretely, you use the *AdRotator* control to create an advertisement banner on a Web Forms page. The control actually inserts an image and hyperlink in the page and makes them point to the advertisement page selected. The image is sized by the browser to the dimensions of the *AdRotator* control, regardless of its actual size. The following code shows a typical XML advertisement file:

```
<Advertisements>
<Ad>
    <ImageUrl>6235.gif</ImageUrl>
    <NavigateUrl>www.microsoft.com/MSPress/books/6235.asp</NavigateUrl>
    <AlternateText>Introducing ASP.NET AJAX</AlternateText>
    <Impressions>50</Impressions>
</Ad>
<Ad>
    <ImageUrl>5727.gif</ImageUrl>
    <NavigateUrl>www.microsoft.com/MSPress/books/5727.asp</NavigateUrl>
    <AlternateText>Programming ASP.NET Applications</AlternateText>
    <Impressions>50</Impressions>
</Ad>
</Advertisements>
```

The *<Advertisement>* root node contains multiple *<Ad>* elements, one for each image to show. The advertisement file must reside in the same application as the *AdRotator* control. The syntax of the *AdRotator* control is as follows:

```
<%@ Page Language="C#" %>
<html>
<head><title>Ad Rotators</title></head>
<body>
    <form runat="server">
        <h1>Dino Esposito's Books</h1>
        <asp:AdRotator runat="server" id="bookRotator"
            AdvertisementFile="MyBooks.xml" />
    </form>
</body>
</html>
```

In the XML advertisement file, you use the *<ImageUrl>* node to indicate the image to load and the *<NavigateUrl>* node to specify where to go in case of a click. The *<AlternateText>* node indicates the alternate text to use if the image is unavailable, whereas *<Impressions>* indicates how often an image should be displayed in relation to other images in the advertisement file. The higher the impression value (as compared to the other values in the advertisement file), the higher the frequency its associated ad image is displayed. The sum of all the impressions in the advertisement file may not exceed 2,047,999,999 or the *AdRotator* control will throw an exception. Finally, each image can also be associated with a keyword through the *<Keyword>* node. Of all the elements, only *<ImageUrl>* is required.

Once per roundtrip, the *AdRotator* control fires the server-side *AdCreated* event. The event occurs before the page is rendered. The event handler receives an argument of type *AdCreatedEventArgs*, which contains information about the image, navigation URL, alternate text, and any custom properties associated with the advertisement. The *AdCreated* event can be used to programmatically select the image to show. The XML schema of the advertisement is not fixed and can be extended with custom elements. All nonstandard elements associated with the selected advertisement will be passed to the *AdCreated* event handler stuffed in the *AdProperties* dictionary member of the *AdCreatedEventArgs* class.

> **Note** Starting with ASP.NET 2.0, the *AdRotator* control has undergone a significant change. It is derived from *WebControl* in ASP.NET 1.x, but it inherits from *DataBoundControl* in ASP.NET 2.0 and beyond. Among other things, this means that the advertisement feed can also be provided through an XML or a relational data source. Image and navigation URLs, as well as the alternate text, can be read from fields belonging to the data source. The control cannot be bound to more than one data source at a time. If more than one property—*AdvertisementFile*, *DataSourceID*, or *DataSource*—is set, an exception will be thrown.

The *Calendar* Control

The *Calendar* control (shown in Figure 4-5) displays a one-month calendar and allows you to choose dates and navigate backward and forward through the months of the year. The control is highly customizable both for appearance and functionality. For example, by setting the *SelectionMode* property, you can decide what the user can select—that is, whether a single date, week, or month can be selected.

```
<asp:calendar runat="server" id="hireDate"
    SelectedDate="2007-08-16" VisibleDate="2007-08-16" />
```

FIGURE 4-5 The *Calendar* control in action.

The *VisibleDate* property sets a date that must be visible in the calendar, while *SelectedDate* sets with a different style the date that is rendered as selected. The control also fires three ad hoc events: *DayRender*, *SelectionChanged*, and *VisibleMonthChanged*. The *DayRender* event signals that the control has just created a new day cell. You can hook the event if you think you need to customize the cell output. The *SelectionChanged* event fires when the selected date changes, while *VisibleMonthChanged* is raised whenever the user moves to another month using the control's selector buttons.

The *Calendar* control originates a roundtrip for each selection you make. Although it is cool and powerful on its own, for better performance you might also want to provide a plain text box for manually typing dates.

The *Xml* Control

The *Xml* control, defined by the *<asp:Xml>* tag, is used to inject the content of an XML document directly into an ASP.NET page. The control can display the source XML as-is or as the results of an XSL transformation (XSLT). The *Xml* control is a sort of declarative counterpart for the *XslTransform* class and can make use of the .NET Framework XSLT transform class internally.

You use the *Xml* control when you need to embed XML documents in a Web page. For example, the control is extremely handy when you need to create XML data islands for the client to consume. The control lets you specify a document to work with and, optionally, a transformation to apply. The XML document can be specified in a variety of formats—an XML document object model, string, or file name. The XSLT transformation can be defined through either an already configured instance of the .NET Framework *XslTransform* class or a file name.

```
<asp:xml runat="server"
    documentsource="document.xml"
    transformsource="transform.xsl" />
```

If you're going to apply some transformation to the XML data, you could also embed it inline between the opening and closing tags of the control. The control also makes it easier to accomplish a common task: apply browser-dependent transformations to portions of the page expressed in an XML meta language. In this case, you exploit the programming interface of the control as follows:

```
<asp:xml runat="server" id="theXml" documentsource="document.xml" />
```

In the *Page_Load* event, you just check the browser capabilities and decide which transformation should be applied.

```
void Page_Load(object sender, EventArgs e)
{
    if (IsInternetExplorer(Request.Browser))
        theXml.TransformSource = "ie5.xsl";
    else
        theXml.TransformSource = "downlevel.xsl";
}
```

The *PlaceHolder* Control

The *PlaceHolder* control is one of the few controls in the *WebControls* namespace that isn't derived from the *WebControl* class. It inherits from *Control* and is used only as a container for other controls in the page. The *PlaceHolder* control does not produce visible output of its own and is limited to containing child controls dynamically added through the *Controls* collection. The following code shows how to embed a placeholder control in a Web page:

```
<asp:placeholder runat="server" id="theToolbar" />
```

Once you have a placeholder, you can add controls to it. As mentioned, the placeholder does not add extra functionality, but it provides for grouping and easy and direct identification of a group of related controls. The following code demonstrates how to create a new button and add it to an existing placeholder:

```
Button btn = new Button();
btn.Text = "Click me";
theToolbar.Controls.Add(btn);
```

The *PlaceHolder* control reserves a location in the control tree and can be extremely helpful in identifying specific areas of the page to customize and extend by adding controls programmatically.

> **Important**   Note that each control dynamically added to the *Controls* collection of a parent control is not restored on postback. If the control generates some input elements on the client, the client data is regularly posted but there will be no server-side control to handle that. To avoid this, you must "remember" that you created a certain control dynamically and re-create it while the page loads on postbacks. To remember that a certain control was added to a parent, you can create a custom entry in the view state or use a hidden field.

View Controls

ASP.NET provides two related controls to create a group of interchangeable panels of child controls. The *MultiView* control defines a group of views, each represented with an instance of the *View* class. Only one view is active at a time and rendered to the client. The *View* control can't be used as a standalone component and can only be placed inside a *MultiView* control. Here's an example:

```
<asp:MultiView runat="server" id="Tables">
    <asp:View runat="server" id="Employees">
        . . .
    </asp:View>
    <asp:View runat="server" id="Products">
        ...
    </asp:View>
```

```
    <asp:View runat="server" id="Customers">
        ...
    </asp:View>
</asp:MultiView>
```

You change the active view through postback events when the user clicks buttons or links embedded in the current view. To indicate the new view, you can either set the *ActiveViewIndex* property or pass the view object to the *SetActiveView* method.

Figure 4-6 shows a sample page in action. You select the page from the drop-down list and refresh the view.

```
void Page_Load(object sender, EventArgs e)
{
    // Views is an auto-postback drop-down list
    Tables.ActiveViewIndex = Views.SelectedIndex;
}
```

FIGURE 4-6 A multiview control in action.

The combination of *View* and *MultiView* controls lends itself very well to implementing wizards. In fact, the new ASP.NET *Wizard* control uses a *MultiView* control internally. We'll cover the *Wizard* control in Chapter 6.

Validation Controls

A key rule for writing more secure applications is to get the data right, before you use it. Getting the data right requires you to apply a validation step to any external input. In ASP.NET, validation controls provide an easy-to-use mechanism to perform a variety of validation tasks, including testing for valid types, values within a given range, or required fields.

Validation controls inherit from the *BaseValidator* class which, in turn, descends from *Label*. All validators defined on a page are automatically grouped in the *Validators* collection of the *Page* class. You can validate them all in a single shot using the *Validate* method in the page class or individually by calling the *Validate* method on each validator. The *Validate* method sets the *IsValid* property both on the page and on the individual validator. The *IsValid* property indicates whether the user's entries match the requirements of the validators. Other than explicitly using the *Validate* method, the user's entry is also automatically validated whenever the page posts back.

> **Note** Typical control members involved with input validation have been grouped in the *IValidator* interface that the *BaseValidator* class implements. The interface includes the *Validate* method and the *IsValid* and *ErrorMessage* properties.

The .NET Framework also provides complete client-side implementation for validation controls. This allows Dynamic HTML–enabled browsers (such as Internet Explorer version 4.0 and later) to perform validation on the client as soon as the user tabs out of a monitored input field.

Generalities of Validation Controls

Each validation control references an input control located elsewhere on the page. When the page is going to be submitted, the contents of the monitored server control is passed to the validator for further processing. Each validator would perform a different type of verification. Table 4-12 shows the types of validation supported by the .NET Framework.

TABLE 4-12 Validator Controls in the .NET Framework

Validator	Description
CompareValidator	Compares the user's entry against a fixed value by using a comparison operator such as *LessThan*, *Equal*, or *GreaterThan*. Can also compare against the value of a property in another control on the same page.
CustomValidator	Employs a programmatically defined validation logic to check the validity of the user's entry. You use this validator when the other validators cannot perform the necessary validation and you want to provide custom code that validates the input.
RangeValidator	Ensures that the user's entry falls within a specified range. Lower and upper boundaries can be expressed as numbers, strings, or dates.
RegularExpressionValidator	Validates the user's entry only if it matches a pattern defined by a regular expression.
RequiredFieldValidator	Ensures that the user specifies a value for the field.

Multiple validation controls can be used with an individual input control to validate according to different criteria. For example, you can apply multiple validation controls on a text box that is expected to contain an e-mail address. In particular, you can impose that the field is not skipped (*RequiredFieldValidator*) and that its content matches the typical format of e-mail addresses (*RegularExpressionValidator*).

Table 4-12 lacks a reference to the *ValidationSummary* control. The control does not perform validation tasks itself. Instead, it displays a label to summarize all the validation error messages found on a Web page as the effect of other validators. We'll cover the *ValidationSummary* control later in the chapter.

The *BaseValidator* Class

Table 4-13 details the specific properties of validation controls. Some properties—such as *ForeColor*, *Enabled*, and *Text*—are overridden versions of base properties on base classes.

TABLE 4-13 Basic Properties of Validators

Property	Description
ControlToValidate	Gets or sets the input control to validate. The control is identified by name—that is, by using the value of the *ID* attribute.
Display	If client-side validation is supported and enabled, gets or sets how the space for the error message should be allocated—either statically or dynamically. In case of server-side validation, this property is ignored. A *Static* display is possible only if the browser supports the *display* CSS style. The default is *Dynamic*.
EnableClientScript	True by default; gets or sets whether client-side validation is enabled.
Enabled	Gets or sets whether the validation control is enabled.
ErrorMessage	Gets or sets the text for the error message.
ForeColor	Gets or sets the color of the message displayed when validation fails.
IsValid	Gets or sets whether the associated input control passes validation.
SetFocusOnError	Indicates whether the focus is moved to the control where validation failed. *Not available in ASP.NET 1.x.*
Text	Gets or sets the description displayed for the validator in lieu of the error message. Note, though, this text does not replace the contents of *ErrorMessage* in the summary text.
ValidationGroup	Gets or sets the validation group that this control belongs to. *Not available in ASP.NET 1.x.*

All validation controls inherit from the *BaseValidator* class except for compare validators, for which a further intermediate class—the *BaseCompareValidator* class—exists. The *BaseCompareValidator* class serves as the foundation for validators that perform typed comparisons. An ad hoc property, named *Type*, is used to specify the data type the values are converted to before being compared. The *CanConvert* static method determines whether the user's entry can be converted to the specified data type. Supported types include string, integer, double, date, and currency. The classes acting as compare validators are *RangeValidator* and *CompareValidator*.

Associating Validators with Input Controls

The link between each validator and its associated input control is established through the *ControlToValidate* property. The property must be set to the ID of the input control. If you do not specify a valid input control, an exception will be thrown when the page is rendered. The association validator/control is between two controls within the same container—be it a page, user control, or template.

Not all server controls can be validated, only those that specify their validation property through an attribute named *[ValidationProperty]*. The attribute takes the name of the property that contains the user's entry to check. For example, the validation property for a *TextBox* is *Text* and is indicated as follows:

```
[ValidationProperty("Text")]
public class TextBox : WebControl, ITextControl
{
    ...
}
```

The list of controls that support validation includes *TextBox*, *DropDownList*, *ListBox*, *RadioButtonList*, *FileUpload*, plus a bunch of HTML controls such as *HtmlInputFile*, *HtmlInputText*, *HtmlInputPassword*, *HtmlTextArea*, and *HtmlSelect*. Custom controls can be validated too, as long as they are marked with the aforementioned *[ValidationProperty]* attribute.

Note If the validation property of the associated input control is left empty, all validators accept the value and pass the test. The *RequiredFieldValidator* control represents a rather natural exception to this rule, as it has been specifically designed to detect fields the user skipped and left blank.

Gallery of Controls

Let's take a closer look at the various types of validation controls that you'll use in ASP.NET Web forms.

The *CompareValidator* Control

The *CompareValidator* control lets you compare the value entered by the user with a constant value or the value specified in another control in the same naming container. The behavior of the control is characterized by the following additional properties:

- *ControlToCompare*   Represents the ID of the control to compare with the current user's entry. You should avoid setting the *ControlToCompare* and *ValueToCompare* properties at the same time. They are considered mutually exclusive; if you set both, the *ControlToCompare* property takes precedence.

- *Operator*   Specifies the comparison operation to perform. The list of feasible operations is defined in the *ValidationCompareOperator* enumeration. The default operator is *Equal*; feasible operators are also *LessThan*, *GreaterThan*, and their variations. The *DataTypeCheck* operator is useful when you want to make sure that certain input data can be converted to a certain type. When the *DataTypeCheck* operator is specified, both *ControlToCompare* and *ValueToCompare* are ignored. In this case, the test is made on the type of the input data and succeeds if the specified data can be converted to the expected type. Supported types are expressed through the following keywords: *String*, *Integer*, *Double*, *Date*, and *Currency* (decimal).

- *ValueToCompare*   Indicates the value to compare the user's input against. If the *Type* property is set, the *ValueToCompare* property must comply with it.

The following code demonstrates the typical markup of the *CompareValidator* control when the control is called to validate an integer input from a text box representing someone's age:

```
<asp:CompareValidator runat="server" id="ageValidator"
    ControlToValidate="ageTextBox"
    ValueToCompare="18"
    Operator="GreaterThanEqual"
    Type="Integer"
    ErrorMessage="Must specify an age greater than 17." />
```

The *CustomValidator* Control

The *CustomValidator* control is a generic and totally user-defined validator that uses custom validation logic to accomplish its task. You typically resort to this control when none of the other validators seems appropriate or, more simply, when you need to execute your own code in addition to that of the standard validators.

To set up a custom validator, you can indicate a client-side function through the *ClientValidationFunction* property. If client-side validation is disabled or not supported, simply omit this setting. Alternatively, or in addition to client validation, you can define some managed code to execute on the server. You do this by defining a handler for the *ServerValidate* event. The code will be executed when the page is posted back in response to a click on a button control. The following code snippet shows how to configure a custom validator to check the value of a text box against an array of feasible values:

```
<asp:CustomValidator runat="server" id="membershipValidator"
    ControlToValidate="membership"
    ClientValidationFunction="CheckMembership"
    OnServerValidate="ServerValidation"
    ErrorMessage="Membership can be Normal, Silver,
                  Gold, or Platinum." />
```

If specified, the client validation function takes a mandatory signature and looks like this:

```
function CheckMembership(source, arguments)
{ ... }
```

The *source* argument references the HTML tag that represents the validator control—usually, a *<span>* tag. The *arguments* parameter references an object with two properties, *IsValid* and *Value*. The *Value* property is the value stored in the input control to be validated. The *IsValid* property must be set to *false* or *true* according to the result of the validation.

The *CustomValidator* control is not associated in all cases with a single input control in the current naming container. For this type of validator, setting the *ControlToValidate* property is not mandatory. For example, if the control has to validate the contents of multiple input fields, you do not simply set the *ControlToValidate* property and the *arguments.Value* variable evaluates to the empty string. In this case, you write the validation logic so that any needed values are dynamically retrieved. With client-side script code, this can be done by accessing the members of the document's form, as shown in the following code:

```
function CheckMembership(source, arguments)
{
    // Retrieve the current value of the element
    // with the specified ID
    var membership = document.getElementById("membership").value;
    ...
}
```

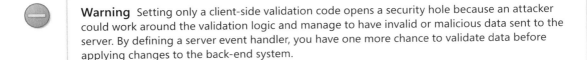

Warning Setting only a client-side validation code opens a security hole because an attacker could work around the validation logic and manage to have invalid or malicious data sent to the server. By defining a server event handler, you have one more chance to validate data before applying changes to the back-end system.

To define a server-side handler for a custom validator, use the *ServerValidate* event.

```
void ServerValidation(object source, ServerValidateEventArgs e)
{
    ...
}
```

The *ServerValidateEventArgs* structure contains two properties—*IsValid* and *Value*—with the same meaning and goal as in the client validation function. If the control is not bound to a particular input field, the *Value* property is empty and you retrieve any needed value using the ASP.NET object model. For example, the following code shows how to check the status of a check box on the server:

```
void ServerValidation (object source, ServerValidateEventArgs e) {
    e.IsValid = (CheckBox1.Checked == true);
}
```

The *CustomValidator* control is the only option you have to validate controls that are not marked with the *[ValidationProperty]* attribute—for example, calendars and check-box controls.

The *RegularExpressionValidator* Control

Regular expressions are an effective way to ensure that a predictable and well-known sequence of characters form the user's entry. For example, using regular expressions you can validate the format of zip codes, Social Security numbers, e-mail addresses, phone numbers, and so on. When using the *RegularExpressionValidator* control, you set the *ValidationExpression* property with the regular expression, which will be used to validate the input.

The following code snippet shows a regular expression validator that ensures the user's entry is an e-mail address:

```
<asp:RegularExpressionValidator runat="server" id="emailValidator"
    ControlToValidate="email"
    ValidationExpression="[a-zA-Z_0-9.-]+\@[a-zA-Z_0-9.-]+\.\w+"
    ErrorMessage="Must be a valid email address." />
```

The regular expression just shown specifies that valid e-mail addresses are formed by two nonzero sequences of letters, digits, dashes, and dots separated by an @ symbol and followed by a dot (.) and an alphabetic string. (This might not be the perfect regular expression for e-mail addresses, but it certainly incorporates the majority of e-mail address formats.)

Note The regular expression validation syntax is slightly different on the client than on the server. The *RegularExpressionValidator* control uses JScript regular expressions on the client and the .NET Framework *Regex* object on the server. Be aware that the JScript regular expression syntax is a subset of the *Regex* model. Whenever possible, try to use the regular expression syntax supported by JScript so that the same result is obtained for both the client and server.

The *RangeValidator* Control

The *RangeValidator* control lets you verify that a given value falls within a specified range. The type of the values involved in the check is specified dynamically and picked from a short list that includes strings, numbers, and dates. The following code shows how to use a range validator control:

```
<asp:RangeValidator runat="server" id="hiredDateValidator"
    ControlToValidate="hired"
    MinimumValue="2000-1-4"
    MaximumValue="9999-12-31"
    Type="Date"
    ErrorMessage="Must be a date after <b>Jan 1, 1999</b>." />
```

The key properties are *MinimumValue* and *MaximumValue*, which together clearly denote the lower and upper boundaries of the interval. Note that an exception is thrown if the strings assigned *MinimumValue* or *MaximumValue* cannot be converted to the numbers or dates according to the value of the *Type* property.

If the type is set to *Date*, but no specific culture is set for the application, you should specify dates using a culture-neutral format, such as *yyyy-MM-dd*. If you don't do so, the chances are good that the values will not be interpreted correctly.

> **Note** The *RangeValidator* control extends the capabilities of the more basic *CompareValidator* control by checking for a value in a fixed interval. In light of this, the *RangeValidator* control might raise an exception if either *MinimumValue* or *MaximumValue* is omitted. Whether the exception is thrown or not depends on the type chosen and its inherent ability to interpret the empty string. For example, an empty string on a *Date* type causes an exception. If you want to operate on an unbound interval—whether lower or upper unbound—either you resort to the *GreaterThan* (or *LessThan*) operator on the *CompareValidator* control or simply use a virtually infinite value such as the 9999-12-31 value.

The *RequiredFieldValidator* Control

To catch when a user skips a mandatory field in an input form, you use the *RequiredFieldValidator* control to show an appropriate error message:

```
<asp:RequiredFieldValidator runat="server" id="lnameValidator"
    ControlToValidate="lname"
    ErrorMessage="Last name is mandatory" />
```

As long as you're using an up-level browser and client-side scripting is enabled for each validator, which is the default, invalid input will display error messages without performing a postback.

> **Important** Note that just tabbing through the controls is not a condition that raises an error; the validator gets involved only if you type blanks or if the field is blank when the page is posted back.

How can you determine whether a certain field is really empty? In many cases, the empty string is sufficient, but this is not a firm rule. The *InitialValue* property specifies the initial value of the input control. The validation fails only if the value of the control equals *InitialValue* upon losing focus. By default, *InitialValue* is initialized with the empty string.

Special Capabilities

The primary reason why you place validation controls on a Web form is to catch errors and inconsistencies in the user's input. But how do you display error messages? Are you interested in client-side validation and, if you are, how would you set it up? Finally, what if you want to validate only a subset of controls when a given button is clicked? Special capabilities of validation controls provide a valid answer to all these issues.

Displaying Error Information

The *ErrorMessage* property determines the static message that each validation control will display in case of error. It is important to know that if the *Text* property is also set, it would take precedence over *ErrorMessage*. *Text* is designed to display inline where the validation control is located; *ErrorMessage* is designed to display in the validation summary. (Strategies for using *Text* and *ErrorMessage* will be discussed more in the next section, "The *ValidationSummary* Control.") Because all validation controls are labels, no other support or helper controls are needed to display any message. The message will be displayed in the body of the validation controls and, subsequently, wherever the validation control is actually placed. The error message is displayed as HTML, so it can contain any HTML formatting attribute.

Validators that work in client mode can create the *<span>* tag for the message either statically or dynamically. You can control this setting by using the *Display* property of the validator. When the display mode is set to *Static* (the default), the *<span>* element is given the following style:

```
style="color:Red;visibility:hidden;"
```

The CSS *visibility* style attribute, when set to *Hidden*, causes the browser not to display the element but reserves space for it. If the *Display* property contains *Dynamic*, the style string changes as follows:

```
style="color:Red;display:none;"
```

The CSS *display* attribute, when set to *none*, simply hides the element, which will take up space on the page only if displayed. The value of the *Display* property becomes critical when you have multiple validators associated with the same input control. (See Figure 4-7.)

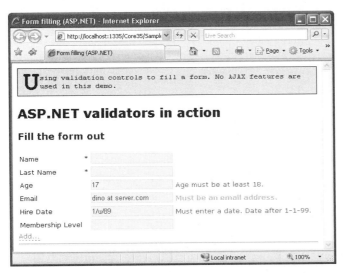

FIGURE 4-7 Input controls in the form are validated on the client.

As you can see, the hire text box is first validated to ensure it contains a valid date and then to verify the specified date is later than 1-1-1999. If the *Display* property is set to *Static* for the first validator, and the date is outside the specified range, you get a page like the one shown in Figure 4-8.

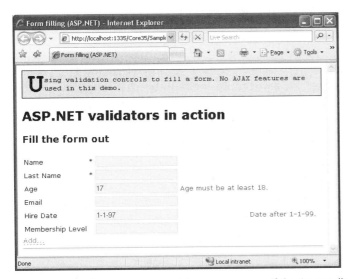

FIGURE 4-8 Static error messages take up space even if they're not displayed.

The full source code of the page in the figure is available on the Web at the following address: *http://www.microsoft.com/mspress/companion/9780735625273/*.

> **Note** You can associate multiple validators with a single input control. The validation takes place in order, and each validation control generates and displays its own error message. The content of the input control is considered valid if all the validators return *true*. If an input control has multiple valid patterns—for example, an ID field can take the form of a Social Security number or a European VAT number—you can either validate by using custom code or regular expressions.

The *ValidationSummary* Control

The *ValidationSummary* control is a label that summarizes and displays all the validation error messages found on a Web page after a postback. The summary is displayed in a single location formatted in a variety of ways. The *DisplayMode* property sets the output format, which can be a list, a bulleted list, or a plain text paragraph. By default, it is a bulleted list. The feasible values are grouped in the *ValidationSummaryDisplayMode* enumeration.

Whatever the format is, the summary can be displayed as text in the page, in a message box, or in both. The Boolean properties *ShowSummary* and *ShowMessageBox* let you decide. The output of the *ValidationSummary* control is not displayed until the page posts back no matter what the value of the *EnableClientScript* property is. The *HeaderText* property defines the text that is displayed atop the summary.

```
<asp:ValidationSummary runat="server"
    ShowMessageBox="true"
    ShowSummary="true"
    HeaderText="The following errors occurred:"
    DisplayMode="BulletList" />
```

This code snippet originates the screen shown in Figure 4-9.

The validation summary is displayed only if there's at least one pending error. Notice that, in the default case, the labels near the input controls are updated anyway, along with the summary text. In summary, you can control the error information in the following ways:

- **Both in-place and summary information**   This is the default scenario. Use the *ValidationSummary* control, and accept all default settings on the validator controls. If you want to leverage both places to display information, a recommended approach consists of minimizing the in-place information by using the *Text* property rather than *ErrorMessage*. If you set both, *Text* is displayed in-place while *ErrorMessage* shows up in the validation summary. For example, you can set *Text* with a glyph or an exclamation mark and assign *ErrorMessage* with more detailed text.

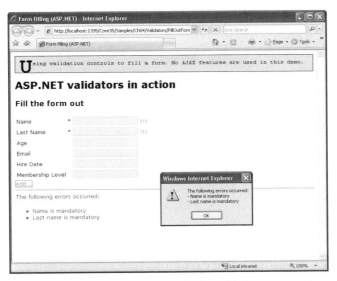

FIGURE 4-9 After the page posts back, the validation summary is updated and a message box pops up to inform the user of the errors.

- **Only in-place information** Do not use the *ValidationSummary* control, and set the *ErrorMessage* property in each validation control you use. The messages appear after the page posts back.

- **Only summary information** Use the *ValidationSummary* control, and set the *ErrorMessage* property on individual validation controls. Set the *Display* property of validators to *None* so that no in-place error message will ever be displayed.

- **Custom error information** You don't use the *ValidationSummary* control, and you set the *Display* property of the individual validators to *None*. In addition, you collect the various error messages through the *ErrorMessage* property on the validation controls and arrange your own feedback for the user.

Enabling Client Validation

As mentioned earlier, the verification normally takes place on the server as the result of the postback event or after the *Validate* method is called. If the browser supports Dynamic HTML, though, you can also activate the validation process on the client, with a significant gain in responsiveness. To be precise, ASP.NET automatically enables client-side validation if it detects a browser with enough capabilities. While ASP.NET 1.x limits its client-side support only to Internet Explorer 4.0 or higher, starting with ASP.NET 2.0 validation controls also work fine on the client with Mozilla Firefox, Netscape 6.x, and Safari 1.2. Figure 4-10 shows the previous sample page in action in Mozilla Firefox.

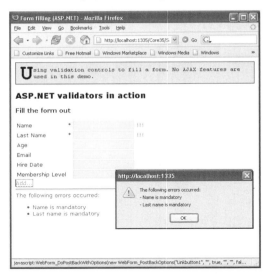

FIGURE 4-10 Client-side validation active also in Mozilla Firefox.

If client-side validation is turned on, the page won't post back until all the input fields contain valid data. To run secure code and prevent malicious and underhanded attacks, you might want to validate data on the server too. Consider also that not all types of validation can be accomplished on the client. In fact, if you need to validate against a database, there's no other option than posting back to the server. (AJAX facilities which we'll explore in Chapter 19 and Chapter 20 may provide a relief for this problem.)

Client validation can be controlled on a per-validation control basis by using the *EnableClientScript* Boolean property. By default, the property is set to *true*, meaning client validation is enabled as long as the browser supports it. By default, the code in the *BaseValidator* class detects the browser's capabilities through the *Request.Browser* property. If the browser is considered up-level, the client validation will be implemented. Browsers and client devices that are considered up-level support at least the following:

- ECMAScript (including JScript and JavaScript) version 1.2

- HTML version 4.0

- The Microsoft Document Object Model

- Cascading style sheets

For down-level browsers, the only requirement is HTML version 3.2. You can also control the client validation at the page level by using the *ClientTarget* attribute on the *@Page* directive.

The following code disables client validation by specifying that any code in the page should target a down-level browser:

```
<% @Page ClientTarget="DownLevel" %>
```

The *ClientTarget* attribute overrides the type of browser that ASP.NET should target when generating the page. When the *ClientTarget* attribute is set, ASP.NET doesn't detect the actual browser's capabilities but loads the capabilities for the specified browser from the browser database.

Validation Groups

In ASP.NET 1.x, control validation occurs in an all-or-nothing kind of way. For example, if you have a set of input and validation controls and two buttons on the form, clicking either button will always validate all controls. In other words, there's no way to validate some controls when one button is clicked, and some others when the other button is clicked. The *CausesValidation* property on button controls allows you to disable validation on a button, but that is not the point here. What is missing is the ability to do validation on a group of controls. This is exactly what the *ValidationGroup* property provides in ASP.NET 2.0 and newer versions. The property is available on validators, input controls, and button controls.

Using the *ValidationGroup* property is simple; just define it for all the validation controls that you want to group together, and then assign the same name to the *ValidationGroup* property of the button that you want to fire the validation. Here's an example:

```
<asp:textbox runat="server" id="TextBox1"  />
<asp:RequiredFieldValidator runat="server"
    ValidationGroup="Group1"
    ControlToValidate="TextBox1"
    ErrorMessage="TextBox1 is mandatory" />
<asp:textbox runat="server" id="TextBox2"  />
<asp:RequiredFieldValidator runat="server"
    ValidationGroup="Group2"
    ControlToValidate="TextBox2"
    ErrorMessage="TextBox2 is mandatory" />
<asp:Button runat="server" Text="Check Group1"
    ValidationGroup="Group1" />
<asp:Button runat="server" Text="Check Group2"
    ValidationGroup="Group2" />
```

The two *RequiredFieldValidator* controls belong to distinct validation groups—*Group1* and *Group2*. The first button validates only the controls defined within Group1; the second button takes care of the input associated with Group2. In this way, the validation process can be made as granular as needed.

> **Important**   The *ValidationGroup* property can also be defined optionally on input controls. This is required only if you use the *CustomValidator* control as a way to check whether a given input control belongs to the right validation group.

The validation group feature gets especially helpful when combined with cross-page postbacks—a feature that we'll cover in the next chapter. Cross-page postback allows a button to post the contents of the current form to another page, in a certain way overriding the single-form model of ASP.NET. Imagine you have a search box in your page, and you want to post its contents directly to a search page without passing through the classic postback mechanism and an additional redirect. Validation groups allow you to check only the contents of the search text box prior to posting to the search page.

Validation groups are also reflected on the server-side, where the *Validate* method of the *Page* class now features an overload that lets you select the group according to which the page must be validated.

Conclusion

In ASP.NET pages, server controls are vital components and transform the programming model of ASP.NET from a mere factory of HTML strings to a more modern and effective component-based model. ASP.NET features a long list of control classes. Looking at the namespaces involved, we should conclude that only two families of controls exist—HTML and Web controls. Controls in the former group simply mirror the set of elements in the HTML syntax. Each constituent control has as many properties as there are attributes in the corresponding HTML tag. Names and behavior have been kept as faithful to the originals as possible. The ultimate goal of the designers of HTML controls is to make the transition from ASP to ASP.NET as seamless as possible—just add *runat="server"* and refresh the page.

The overall design of Web controls is more abstract and much less tied to HTML. In general, Web controls do not promote a strict one-to-one correspondence between controls and HTML tags. However, the capabilities of Web and HTML controls overlap. All ASP.NET server controls render in HTML, but Web controls render to more complex HTML representation than HTML controls.

In the family of core Web controls, we can identify interesting and powerful families of controls—for example, validators. Validators let you put declarative boundaries around input controls so that any user's input is filtered and validated both on the client and server. This alone is not sufficient to certify an application as secure, but it is a quantum leap in the right direction.

Just The Facts

- In ASP.NET, there are two big families of controls: HTML controls and Web controls. The former group includes controls that are in 1:1 correspondence with HTML elements. The controls in the latter group offer a more abstract programming model and richer functionalities not specifically bound to one HTML element.

- If made invisible, ASP.NET controls don't generate any markup code but are activated and processed nonetheless.

- Adaptive rendering is the process that enables controls to generate different markup for individual browsers.

- ASP.NET controls let you declaratively assign a browser-specific value to properties. For example, you can use one style for Internet Explorer and another one for Mozilla Firefox.

- The vast majority of ASP.NET controls can generate XHTML-compliant markup. Non XHTML mode is supported for backward compatibility.

- New controls let you fully manage programmatically the *<head>* tag of a page.

- Everything you put on a page is ultimately processed as a control, including literal text, blanks, and carriage returns. Contiguous characters are conveyed to a single control instance.

- Validation controls let you test for valid types, values within a given range, regular expressions, and required fields.

- Validators let you put declarative boundaries around input controls so that any user's input is filtered and validated both on the client and server.

- Group validation allows you to validate only certain controls when the page posts back.

Chapter 5
Working with the Page

Although formless pages are still accepted and correctly handled, the typical ASP.NET page contains a single *<form>* tag decorated with the *runat* attribute set to *server*. On the server, the *<form>* tag is mapped to an instance of the *HtmlForm* class. The *HtmlForm* class acts as the outermost container of all server controls and wraps them in an HTML *<form>* element when the page is rendered. The obtained HTML form posts to the same page URL and for this reason is said to be *reentrant*. The default method used to submit form data is *POST*, but *GET* can be used as well.

In most cases, the server form is the outermost tag of the page and is contained directly in *<body>*. In general, though, the server *<form>* tag can be the child of any other server container control such as *<table>*, *<div>*, *<body>*, and any other HTML generic control. (We covered HTML controls and Web controls in Chapter 4.) If any noncontainer controls (for example, a *TextBox*) are placed outside the form tag, an exception is thrown. Notice, though, that no check is made at compile time. The exception is raised by the control itself when the host page asks to render. Noncontainer Web controls, in fact, check whether they are being rendered within the boundaries of a server form and throw an *HttpException* if they are not. A call to the *Page*'s *VerifyRenderingInServerForm* method does the job. (Be aware of this virtuous behavior when you get to write custom controls.)

In this chapter, we'll examine some aspects of form-based programming in ASP.NET, including how to use multiple forms in the same page and post data to a different page. We'll touch on localization and personalization and end by discussing tools and effective techniques to debug, trace, and handle errors.

Programming with Forms

One of the most common snags Web developers face when they first approach the ASP.NET lifestyle is the fact that managed Web applications support the single-form interface (SFI) model.

> **Note** If you've never heard anyone use the SFI acronym, there's no reason for you to panic. It's an acronym I've purposely created to mimic other more popular acronyms that, although used in different contexts, describe similar programming models—the single-document interface (SDI) and its opposite, the multiple-document interface (MDI).

In the SFI model, each page always posts to itself and doesn't supply any hook for developers to set the final destination of the postback. What in HTML and ASP programming was the *Action* property of the form is simply not defined on the ASP.NET *HtmlForm* class. As a result, the SFI model is a built-in feature that is so integrated with the ASP.NET platform that you have only two choices: take it, or code the old ASP way without server forms. Note that starting with ASP.NET 2.0, posting form data to different pages is possible, but the implementation of the feature passes through some new capabilities of button controls—the cross-page posting API.

Unlike the action URL, the HTTP method and the target frame of the post can be programmatically adjusted using ad hoc *HtmlForm* properties—*Method* and *Target*.

The *HtmlForm* Class

The *HtmlForm* class inherits from *HtmlContainerControl*, which provides the form with the capability of containing child controls. This capability is shared with other HTML control classes, such as *HtmlTable*, characterized by child elements and a closing tag.

Properties of the *HtmlForm* Class

The *HtmlForm* class provides programmatic access to the HTML *<form>* element on the server through the set of properties shown in Table 5-1. Note that the table includes only a few of the properties *HtmlForm* inherits from the root class *Control*.

TABLE 5-1 Form Properties

Property	Description
Attributes	Inherited from *Control*, gets a name/value collection with all the attributes declared on the tag.
ClientID	Inherited from *Control*, gets the value of *UniqueID*.
Controls	Inherited from *Control*, gets a collection object that represents the child controls of the form.
DefaultButton	String property, gets or sets the button control to display as the default button on the form. *Not available in ASP.NET 1.x.*
DefaultFocus	String property, gets or sets the button control to give input focus when the form is displayed. *Not available in ASP.NET 1.x.*
Disabled	Gets or sets a value indicating whether the form is disabled. Matches the *disabled* HTML attribute.
EncType	Gets or sets the encoding type. Matches the *enctype* HTML attribute.
ID	Inherited from *Control*, gets or sets the programmatic identifier of the form.
InnerHtml	Inherited from *HtmlContainerControl*, gets or sets the markup content found between the opening and closing tags of the form.
InnerText	Inherited from *HtmlContainerControl*, gets or sets the text between the opening and closing tags of the form.
Method	Gets or sets a value that indicates how a browser posts form data to the server. The default value is *POST*. Can be set to *GET* if needed.
Name	Gets the value of *UniqueID*.
Style	Gets a collection of all cascading style sheet (CSS) properties applied to the form.
SubmitDisabledControls	Indicates whether to force controls disabled on the client to submit their values, allowing them to preserve their values after the page posts back to the server. *False* by default. *Not available in ASP.NET 1.x.*
TagName	Returns "form".
Target	Gets or sets the name of the frame or window to render the HTML generated for the page.
UniqueID	Inherited from *Control*, gets the unique, fully qualified name of the form.
Visible	Gets or sets a value that indicates whether the form is rendered. If *false*, the form is not rendered to HTML.

The form must have a unique name. If the programmer doesn't assign the name, ASP.NET generates one by using a built-in algorithm. The default name follows the pattern *CtlX*, in which *X* is a unique integer—typically the index of the control in the page. The programmer can set the form's identifier by using either the *ID* or *Name* property. If both are set, the *ID* attribute takes precedence. (Note, though, that any reliance on the *Name* attribute compromises the XHTML compliance of the page.)

The parent object of the form is the outer container control with the *runat* attribute. If such a control doesn't exist, the page object is set as the parent. Typical containers for the server form are *<table>* and *<div>* if they are marked as server-side objects.

By default, the *Method* property is set to *POST*. The value of the property can be modified programmatically. If the form is posted through the *GET* method, all form data is passed on the URL's query string. However, if you choose the *GET* method, make sure the size allowed for a *GET* request does not affect the integrity of your application or raise security issues.

> **Warning**   RFC 2068, which was mentioned in Chapter 1), defines the format of HTTP packets but doesn't dictate a minimum or maximum URL length. However, browsers set a limitation on the size of the URL that ends up affecting GET requests where the URL is completed with query string parameters. On the Windows platform, the Opera browser accepts up to 4000 characters, Internet Explorer no more than 2 KB. The same for Mozilla-based browsers such as Netscape. In general, 2 KB is an important threshold not to exceed.

Methods of the *HtmlForm* Class

Table 5-2 lists the methods available on the *HtmlForm* class that you'll be using more often. All the methods listed in the table are inherited from the base *System.Web.UI.Control* class.

TABLE 5-2 Form Methods

Method	Description
ApplyStyleSheetSkin	Applies the style properties defined in the page style sheet. *Not available in ASP.NET 1.x.*
DataBind	Calls the *DataBind* method on all child controls.
FindControl	Retrieves and returns the control that matches the specified ID.
Focus	Set input focus to a control. *Not available in ASP.NET 1.x.*
HasControls	Indicates whether the form contains any child controls.
RenderControl	Outputs the HTML code for the form. If tracing is enabled, caches tracing information to be rendered later, at the end of the page.

It is important to note that the *FindControl* method searches only among the form's direct children. Controls belonging to an inner naming container, or that are a child of a form's child control, are not found.

Multiple Forms

As mentioned, the SFI model is the default in ASP.NET and plays a key role in the automatic view state management mechanism we described in Chapter 3. Generally speaking, the ASP.NET's enforcement of the SFI model does not significantly limit the programming power, and all things considered, doing without multiple forms is not a big sacrifice. Some pages, though, would have a more consistent and natural design if they could define multiple *logical* forms. In this context, a *logical* form is a logically related group of input controls. For example, think of a page that provides some information to users but also needs to supply an additional form such as a search or login box.

You can incorporate search and login capabilities in ad hoc classes and call those classes from within the page the user has displayed. This might or might not be the right way to factor your code, though. Especially if you're porting some old code to ASP.NET, you might find it easier to insulate login or search code in a dedicated page. Well, to take advantage of form-based login, how do you post input data to this page?

Using HTML Forms

As mentioned, ASP.NET prevents you from having multiple *<form>* tags flagged with the *runat* attribute. However, nothing prevents you from having one server-side *<form>* tag and multiple client HTML *<form>* elements in the body of the same Web form. Here's an example:

```
<body>
    <table><tr><td>
        <form id="form1" runat="server">
        <h2>Ordinary contents for an ASP.NET page</h2>
        </form>
    </td>
    <td>
        <form method="post" action="search.aspx">
            <table><tr>
                <td>Keyword</td>
                <td><input type="text" id="Keyword" name="Keyword" /></td>
            </tr><tr>
                <td><input type="submit" id="Go" value="Search" /></td>
            </tr></table>
        </form>
    </td>
    </tr></table>
</body>
```

The page contains two forms, one of which is a classic HTML form devoid of the *runat* attribute and, as such, completely ignored by ASP.NET. The markup served to the browser simply contains two *<form>* elements, each pointing to a different action URL.

This code works just fine but has a major drawback: you can't use the ASP.NET programming model to retrieve posted data in the action page of the client form. When writing search. aspx, in fact, you can't rely on view state to retrieve posted values. To know what's been posted, you must resort to the old-fashioned, but still effective, ASP model, as shown in the following code sample:

```
public partial class Search : System.Web.UI.Page
{
    protected void Page_Load(object sender, EventArgs e)
    {
        // Use the Request object to retrieve posted data
        string textToSearch = Request.Form["Keyword"].ToString();
        ...

        // Use standard ASP.NET programming model to populate the page UI
        KeywordBeingUsed.Text = textToSearch;
    }
}
```

You use the protocol-specific collections of the *Request* object to retrieve posted data—*Form* if POST is used, and *QueryString* in case of GET. In addition, you have to use the *name* attribute to identify input elements. Overall, this is perhaps not a recommended approach, but it definitely works. Figure 5-1 shows the page in action.

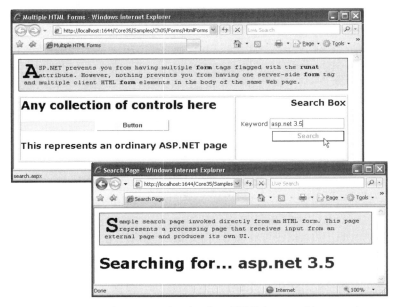

FIGURE 5-1 A server form control and a client HTML form working together.

When the user clicks the search button, the *search.aspx* page is invoked, it receives only the values posted through the HTML form, and it uses them to proceed.

Multiple *<form>* Tags on a Page

The preceding code works because we have only one server form control at a time. If multiple server forms are declared in the same Web form, an exception is thrown. A little-known fact is that a Web form can actually contain as many server-side forms as needed as long as only one at a time is visible. For example, a page with, say, three *<form runat=server>* tags is allowed, but only one form can be actually rendered. Given the dynamics of page rendering, an exception is thrown if more than one *HtmlForm* control attempts to render. By playing with the *Visible* property of the *HtmlForm* class, you can change the active server form during the page lifetime. This trick doesn't really solve the problem of having multiple active forms, but it can be helpful sometimes.

Let's consider the following ASP.NET page:

```
<body>
    <form id="step0" runat="server" visible="true">
        <h1>Welcome</h1>
        <asp:textbox runat="server" id="Textbox1" />
        <asp:button ID="Button1" runat="server" text="Step #1"
            OnClick="Button1_Click" />
    </form>

    <form id="step1" runat="server" visible="false">
        <h1>Step #1</h1>
        <asp:textbox runat="server" id="Textbox2" />
        <asp:button ID="Button2" runat="server" text="Previous step"
            OnClick="Button2_Click" />
        <asp:button ID="Button3" runat="server" text="Step #2"
            OnClick="Button3_Click" />
    </form>

    <form id="step2" runat="server" visible="false">
        <h1>Finalizing</h1>
        <asp:button ID="Button4" runat="server" text="Finish"
            OnClick="Button4_Click" />
    </form>
</body>
```

As you can see, all *<form>* tags are marked as *runat*, but only the first one is visible. Mutually exclusive forms are great at implementing wizards in ASP.NET 1.x. By toggling a form's visibility in button event handlers, you can obtain a wizard-like behavior, as shown in Figure 5-2.

```
public partial class MultipleForms : System.Web.UI.Page
{
    protected void Page_Load(object sender, EventArgs e)
    {
        Title = "Welcome";
    }
```

```
protected void Button1_Click(object sender, EventArgs e)
{
    Title = "Step 1";
    step0.Visible = false;
    step1.Visible = true;
}
protected void Button2_Click(object sender, EventArgs e)
{
    step0.Visible = true;
    step1.Visible = false;
}
protected void Button3_Click(object sender, EventArgs e)
{
    Title = "Finalizing";
    step1.Visible = false;
    step2.Visible = true;
}
protected void Button4_Click(object sender, EventArgs e)
{
    Title = "Done";
    step2.Visible = false;
    Response.Write("<h1>Successfully done.</h1>");
}
}
```

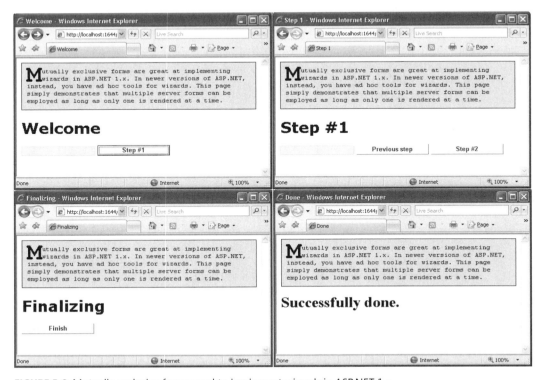

FIGURE 5-2 Mutually exclusive forms used to implement wizards in ASP.NET 1.x.

Multiple View and Wizards

If you're writing an ASP.NET 2.0 or ASP.NET 3.5 application, you don't need to resort to the preceding trick. You find two new controls—*MultiView* and *Wizard*—ready for the job. The *MultiView* control employs logic nearly identical to that of multiple exclusive forms, except that it relies on panels rather than full forms.

The *MultiView* control allows you to define multiple and mutually exclusive HTML panels. The control provides an application programming interface (API) for you to toggle the visibility of the various panels and ensure that exactly one is active and visible at a time. The *MultiView* control doesn't provide a built-in user interface. The *Wizard* control is just that—a *MultiView* control plus some wizard-like predefined user interface (UI) blocks. We'll cover the *Wizard* control in great detail in the next chapter.

Cross-Page Postings

Starting with version 2.0, the ASP.NET framework offers a built-in mechanism to override the normal processing cycle and prevent the page from posting back to itself.

In general, postbacks occur in either of two ways—through a submit button or via script. The client browser usually takes on any post conducted through a button and automatically points to the page that the *action* attribute of the posting form indicates. More flexibility is possible when the post occurs via script. In ASP.NET 2.0, you can configure certain page controls—in particular, those that implement the *IButtonControl* interface—to post to a different target page. This is referred to as cross-page posting.

Posting Data to Another Page

Authoring a Web page that can post data to another page requires only a couple of steps. First, you choose the controls that can cause postback and set their *PostBackUrl* property. A page can include one or more button controls and, generally, any combination of button controls and submit buttons. Notice that in this context a button control is any server control that implements *IButtonControl*. (We fully covered the *IButtonControl* interface in Chapter 4.) The following code snippet shows how to proceed:

```
<form id="Form1" runat="server">
    <asp:textbox runat="server" id="Data" />
    <asp:button runat="server" id="buttonPost"
            Text="Click"
            PostTargetUrl="target.aspx" />
</form>
```

When the *PostBackUrl* property is set, the ASP.NET runtime binds the corresponding HTML element of the button control to a new JavaScript function. Instead of using our old acquaintance __*doPostback*, it uses the new *WebForm_DoPostBackWithOptions* function. The button renders the following markup:

```
<input type="submit" name="buttonPost" id="buttonPost"
    value="Click"
    onclick="javascript:WebForm_DoPostBackWithOptions(
        new WebForm_PostBackOptions("buttonPost", "",
            false, "", "target.aspx", false, false))" />
```

As a result, when the user clicks the button, the current form posts its content to the specified target page. What about the view state? When the page contains a control that does cross-page posting, a new hidden field is also created—__*PREVIOUSPAGE*. The field contains the view state information to be used to serve the request. This view state information is transparently used in lieu of the original view state of the page being posted to.

You use the *PreviousPage* property to reference the posting page and all of its controls. Here's the code behind a sample target page that retrieves the content of a text box defined in the form:

```
protected void Page_Load(object sender, EventArgs e)
{
    // Retrieves posted data
    TextBox txt = (TextBox) PreviousPage.FindControl("TextBox1");
    ...
}
```

By using the *PreviousPage* property on the *Page* class, you can access any input control defined on the posting page. Access to input controls is weakly typed and occurs indirectly through the services of the *FindControl* method. The problem here lies in the fact that the target page doesn't know anything about the type of the posting page. *PreviousPage* is declared as a property of type *Page* and, as such, it can't provide access to members specific to a derived page class.

Furthermore, note that *FindControl* looks up controls only in the current naming container. If the control you are looking for lives inside another control (say, a template), you must first get a reference to the container, and then search the container to find the control. To avoid using *FindControl* altogether, a different approach is required.

The *@PreviousPageType* Directive

Let's say it up front. To retrieve values on the posting page, *FindControl* is your only safe option if you don't know in advance which page will be invoking your target. However, when using cross-page posting in the context of an application, chances are good that you know exactly who will be calling the page and how. In this case, you can take advantage of the *@PreviousPageType* directive to cause the target page's *PreviousPage* property to be typed to the source page class.

In the target page, you add the following directive:

```
<%@ PreviousPageType VirtualPath="crosspagewithtype.aspx" %>
```

The directive can accept either of two attributes—*VirtualPath* or *TypeName*. The former points to the URL of the posting page; the latter indicates the type of the calling page. The directive just shown makes the *PreviousPage* property on the target page class be of the same type as the page at the given path (or the specified type). This fact alone, though, is not sufficient to let you access input controls directly. In Chapter 2 and Chapter 3, we pointed out that each page class contains protected members that represent child controls; unfortunately, you can't call a protected member of a class from an external class. (Only derived classes can access protected members of the parent class.)

To work around the issue, in the caller page you must add public properties that expose any information you want posted pages to access. For example, imagine that *crosspostpage.aspx* contains a *TextBox* named _textBox1. To make it accessible from within a target page, you add the following code to the code-behind class:

```
public TextBox TextBox1
{
    get { return _textBox1; }
}
```

The new *TextBox1* property on the page class wraps and exposes the internal text-box control. In light of this code, the target page can now execute the following code:

```
Response.Write(PreviousPage.TextBox1.Text);
```

Detecting Cross-Page Postings

Being the potential target of a cross-page call doesn't automatically make a target page a different kind of page all of a sudden. There's always the possibility that the target page is invoked on its own—for example, via hyperlinking. When this happens, the *PreviousPage* property returns *null* and other postback-related properties, such as *IsPostBack*, assume the usual values.

If you have such a dual page, you should insert some extra code to discern the page behavior. The following example shows a page that allows only cross-page access:

```
if (PreviousPage == null)
{
    Response.Write("Sorry, that's the wrong way to invoke me.");
    Response.End();
    return;
}
```

The *IsCrossPagePostBack* property on the *Page* class deserves a bit of attention. The property returns *true* if the current page has called another ASP.NET page. It goes without saying that

IsCrossPagePostBack on the target page always returns *false*. Therefore, the following code is *not* equivalent to the one seen before:

```
if (!IsCrossPagePostBack)
{
    ...
}
```

To know whether the current page is being called from another page, you have to test the value of *IsCrossPagePostBack* on the page object returned by *PreviousPage*:

```
// PreviousPage is null in case of a normal request
if (!PreviousPage.IsCrossPagePostBack)
{
    ...
}
```

However, this code will inevitably throw an exception if the page is invoked in a normal way (that is, from the address bar or via hyperlinking since *PreviousPage* is *null*). In the end, the simplest and most effective way to see whether a page is being invoked through cross-page postbacks is by checking *PreviousPage* against *null*.

Dealing with Validation

What if the original page contains validators? Imagine a page with a text box whose value is to be posted to another page. You don't want the post to occur if the text box is empty. To obtain this, you add a *RequiredFieldValidator* control and bind it to the text box:

```
<asp:TextBox ID="TextBox1" runat="server"></asp:TextBox>
<asp:RequiredFieldValidator ID="Validator1" runat="server"
    ControlToValidate="TextBox1" Text="*" />
<asp:Button ID="Button1" runat="server" Text="Apply request..."
    OnClick="Button1_Click" PostBackUrl="target.aspx" />
```

As expected, when you click the button the page won't post if the text box is empty; and a red asterisk (plus an optional message) is displayed to mark the error. This is because by default button controls validate the input controls before proceeding with the post. Is that all, or is there more to dig out?

In most cases, the *RequiredFieldValidator* benefits the client-side capabilities of the browser. This means that, in the case of empty text boxes, the button doesn't even attempt to make the post. Let's work with a *CustomValidator* control, which instead requires that some server-side code be run to check the condition. Can you imagine the scenario? You're on, say, *post.aspx* and want to reach *target.aspx*; to make sure you post only under valid conditions, though, you first need a trip to *post.aspx* to perform some validation. Add this control, write the server validation handler, and put a breakpoint in its code:

```
<asp:CustomValidator ID="CustomValidator1" runat="server" Text="*"
    ControlToValidate="TextBox1" OnServerValidate="ServerValidate" />
```

Debugging this sample page reveals that posting to another page is a two-step operation. First, a classic postback is made to run any server-side code registered with the original page (for example, server-side validation code or code associated with the click of the button). Next, the cross-page call is made to reach the desired page.

```
void ServerValidate(object source, ServerValidateEventArgs args)
{
    args.IsValid = false;
    if (String.Equals(args.Value, "Dino"))
        args.IsValid = true;
}
```

The preceding code sets the page's *IsValid* property to *false* if the text box contains anything other than "Dino." However, this fact alone doesn't prevent the transition to the target page. In other words, you could still have invalid input data posted to the target page.

Fortunately, this issue has an easy workaround, as shown in the following code:

```
if (!PreviousPage.IsValid)
{
    Response.Write("Sorry, the original page contains invalid input.");
    Response.End();
    return;
}
```

In the target page, you test the *IsValid* property on the *PreviousPage* property and terminate the request in the case of a negative answer.

Redirecting Users to Another Page

In addition to the *PostBackUrl* property of button controls, ASP.NET provides another mechanism for transferring control and values from one page to another—you can use the *Server.Transfer* method.

The URL of the new page is not reflected by the browser's address bar because the transfer takes place entirely on the server. The following code shows how to use the method to direct a user to another page:

```
protected void Button1_Click(object sender, EventArgs e)
{
    Server.Transfer("target.aspx");
}
```

Note that all the code that might be following the call to *Transfer* in the page is never executed. In the end, *Transfer* is just a page redirect method. However, it is particularly efficient for two reasons. First, no roundtrip to the client is requested as is the case, for example, with *Response.Redirect*. Second, the same *HttpApplication* that was serving the caller request is reused, thus limiting the impact on the ASP.NET infrastructure.

In ASP.NET 1.x, the spawned page can access the page object representing its caller by using the *Handler* property of the HTTP context, as follows:

```
Page caller = (Page) Context.Handler;
```

Because *Handler* returns a valid instance of the referrer page object, the spawned page can access all of its properties and methods. It cannot directly access the controls because of the protection level, though. This programming model also works in ASP.NET 2.0 and newer versions.

However, in ASP.NET 2.0 and newer versions things are simplified and using *Handler* is no longer necessary. You can use the same programming model of cross-page postings and rely on a non-null *PreviousPage* property and the *@PreviousPageType* directive for strongly typed access to input fields. How can a page detect whether it's being called through a server transfer or through a cross-page postback? In both cases, *PreviousPage* is not null but the *IsCrossPagePostBack* on the *PreviousPage* object is *true* for a cross-page posting and *false* in the case of a server transfer. (This and all other techniques related to form posting are demonstrated in great detail in the sample companion code.)

> **Important** Passing values from one page to another is a task that can be accomplished in a variety of ways—using cross-page posting, server transfer, HTML forms, or query strings. Which one is the most effective? Cross-page posting and server transfer offer a familiar programming model but potentially move a significant chunk of data through the __*PREVIOUSPAGE* field. Whether this information is really needed depends on the characteristics of the target page. In many cases, the target page just needs to receive a few parameters to start working. If this is the case, HTML client forms might be more effective in terms of data being moved. HTML forms, though, require an ASP-like programming model.

Dealing with Page Errors

Just like other .NET applications, ASP.NET applications can take advantage of exceptions to catch and handle runtime errors that occur in the code. Exceptions, though, should be just what their name suggests—that is, exceptional events in the life of the application, raised when something happens that violates an assumption. A typical bad programming practice is to rely on exceptions to catch any possible error resulting from an operation. Admittedly, wrapping a piece of code with a *try/catch* block makes programming much simpler while offering a single point of control for errors. However, employing this technique on a large scale can result in a dramatic loss of performance. Exceptions are meant to target exceptional events that aren't predictable in other ways. Exceptions should not be used to control the normal flow of the program. If there is a way to detect possible inconsistent situations, by all means use that other method and use exceptions as the last resort.

This said, bear in mind that exceptions are the official tool to handle errors in .NET applications. They're not lightweight and should not be overused, but they provide a solid, modern, and effective way of catching errors and recovering from them. They're not evil, but they're not manna from heaven either.

When an exception occurs in an ASP.NET application, the common language runtime (CLR) tries to find a block of code willing to catch it. Exceptions walk their way up the stack until the root of the current application is reached. If no proper handler shows up along the way, the exception gains the rank of unhandled exception and causes the CLR to throw a system-level exception. Users are shown a standard error page that some developers familiarly call YSOD (yellow-screen-of-death), which is a spin-off of the just as illustrious BSOD (blue-screen-of-death) that we all have come to know after years of experience with the Microsoft Windows operating system.

An unhandled exception originates an error and stops the application. As a developer, how should you deal with unhandled exceptions in ASP.NET applications?

Basics of Error Handling

Any ASP.NET application can incur various types of errors. There are configuration errors caused by some invalid syntax or structure in one of the application's *web.config* files and parser errors that occur when the syntax on a page is malformed. In addition, you can run into compilation errors when statements in the page's code-behind class are incorrect. Finally, there are runtime errors that show up during the page's execution.

Default Error Pages

When an unrecoverable error occurs in an ASP.NET page, the user always receives a page that, more or less nicely, informs the user that something went wrong at a certain point. ASP.NET catches any unhandled exception and transforms it into a page for the user, as shown in Figure 5-3.

The typical error page differs for local and remote users. By default, local users—namely, any user accessing the application through the local host—receive the page shown in Figure 5-3. The page includes the call stack—the chain of method calls leading up to the exception—and a brief description of the error. Additional source code information is added if the page runs in debug mode. For security reasons, remote users receive a less detailed page, like the one shown in Figure 5-4.

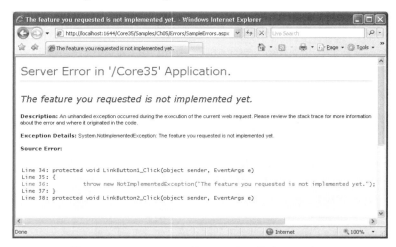

FIGURE 5-3 The error page generated by an unhandled exception.

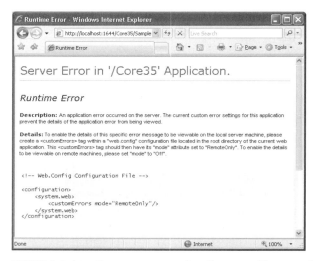

FIGURE 5-4 A runtime error occurred on the server. The page does not provide information about the error, but it still can't be called a user-friendly page!

Exception handling is a powerful mechanism used to trap code anomalies and recover or degrade gracefully. By design, though, exception handling requires you to know exactly the points in the code where a given exception, or a given set of exceptions, can occur. Exceptions raised outside any interception points you might have arranged become unhandled exceptions and originate the YSOD.

ASP.NET provides a couple of global interception points for you to handle errors programmatically, at either the page level or the application level. As mentioned in Chapter 3, the *Page* base class exposes an *Error* event, which you can override in your pages to catch any unhandled exceptions raised during the execution of the page. Likewise, an *Error* event exists on the *HttpApplication* class, too, to catch any unhandled exception thrown within the application.

Page-Level Error Handling

To catch any unhandled exceptions wandering around a particular page, you define a handler for the *Error* event. Here's an example:

```
protected void Page_Error(object sender, EventArgs e)
{
    // Capture the error
    Exception ex = Server.GetLastError();

    // Resolve the error page based on the exception that occurred
    // and redirect to the appropriate page
    if (ex is NotImplementedException)
        Server.Transfer("/errorpages/notimplementedexception.aspx");
    else
        Server.Transfer("/errorpages/apperror.aspx");

    // Clear the error
    Server.ClearError();
}
```

You know about the raised exception through the *GetLastError* method of the *Server* object. In the *Error* handler, you can transfer control to a particular page and show a personalized and exception-specific message to the user. The control is transferred to the error page, and the URL in the address bar of the browser doesn't change. If you use *Server.Transfer* to pass control, the exception information is maintained and the error page itself can call into *GetLastError* and display more detailed information. Finally, once the exception is fully handled, you clear the error by calling *ClearError*.

> **Important** When displaying error messages, pay attention not to hand out sensitive informa- tion that a malicious user might use against your system. Sensitive data includes user names, file system paths, connection strings, and password-related information. You can make error pages smart enough to determine whether the user is local, or whether a custom header is defined, and display more details that can be helpful to diagnose errors.
>
> ```
> if (Request.UserHostAddress == "127.0.0.1") {
>     ...
> }
> ```
>
> You can also use the *Request.Headers* collection to check for custom headers added only by a particular Web server machine. To add a custom header, you open the Properties dialog box of the application's Internet Information Services (IIS) virtual folder and click the HTTP Headers tab.

Global Error Handling

A page *Error* handler catches only errors that occur within a particular page. This means that each page that requires error handling must point to a common piece of code or define its own handler. Such a fine-grained approach is not desirable when you want to share the same generic error handler for all the pages that make up the application. In this case, you can create a global error handler at the application level that catches all unhandled exceptions and routes them to the specified error page.

The implementation is nearly identical to page-level error handlers except that you will be handling the *Error* event on the *HttpApplication* object that represents your application. To do that, you add a *global.asax* file to your application and write code in the predefined *Application_Error* stub:

```
void Application_Error(object sender, EventArgs e)
{
    . . .
}
```

In Microsoft Visual Studio, to generate the *global.asax* file, you select Add New Item and pick up a *Global Application Class* item.

> **Note** You can have at most one *global.asax* file per ASP.NET application. In older versions of Visual Studio, an empty *global.asax* file is generated when you create a Web application project. In Visual Studio 2008, if your Web site project already contains a *global.asax* file, the corresponding selection is removed from the list of available items when you click the Add New Item menu.

You could do something useful in this event handler, such as sending an e-mail to the site administrator or writing to the Windows event log to say that the page failed to execute properly. ASP.NET provides a set of classes in the *System.Net.Mail* namespace for just this purpose. (Note that a similar set of classes exist for ASP.NET 1.x in the *System.Web.Mail* namespace, which is obsolete in ASP.NET 2.0 and newer).

```
MailMessage mail = new MailMessage();
mail.From = new MailAddress("automated@contoso.com");
mail.To.Add(new MailAddress("administrator@contoso.com"));
mail.Subject = "Site Error at " + DateTime.Now;
mail.Body = "Error Description: " + ex.Message;
SmtpClient server = new SmtpClient();
server.Host = "your.smtp.server";
server.Send(mail);
```

The code to use for ASP.NET 1.x is slightly different, doesn't require you to explicitly set the host, and uses the *SmtpMail* class.

To write an entry to the Windows event log, you can use the following code:

```
void Application_Error(object sender, EventArgs e)
{
    // Obtain the URL of the request
    string url = Request.Path;

    // Obtain the Exception object describing the error
    Exception error = Server.GetLastError();

    // Build the message --> [Error occurred. XXX at url]
    StringBuilder text = new StringBuilder("Error occurred. ");
    text.Append(error.Message);
    text.Append(" at ");
    text.Append(url);

    // Write to the Event Log
    EventLog log = new EventLog();
    log.Source = "Core35 Log";
    log.WriteEntry(text.ToString(), EventLogEntryType.Error);
}
```

> **Note** The Event Log *Source* must exist prior to its use in an ASP.NET application, in this case in the *Application_Error* method in *global.asax*. Typical ASPNET account credentials are established such that the ASP.NET account does not have Event Log source creation rights. You'll need to make sure the log is created first on each Web server your code will execute within prior to actually running your Web application.

Robust Error Handling

A good strategy for robust and effective error handling is based on the following three guidelines:

- Anticipate problems by wrapping all blocks of code that might fail in try/catch/finally blocks. This alone doesn't guarantee that no exceptions will ever show up, but at least you'll correctly handle the most common ones.

- Don't leave any exceptions unhandled. By following this guideline, even if you did not anticipate a problem, at least users won't see an exception page. You can do this both at the page and application levels. Needless to say, an application-level error handler takes precedence over page-level handlers.

- Make sure that error pages don't give away any sensitive information. If necessary, distinguish between local and remote users and show detailed messages only to the former. A local user is defined as the user that accesses the application from the Web server machine.

Outlined in this way, error handling is mostly a matter of writing the right code in the right place. However, ASP.NET provides developers with a built-in mechanism to automatically redirect users to error-specific pages. This mechanism is entirely declarative and can be controlled through the *web.config* file.

> **Warning** As we delve deeper into the various topics of ASP.NET, we'll be making extensive use of the information stored in configuration files. Configuration files were briefly introduced in Chapter 1, but you won't find in this book a chapter expressly dedicated to them. For appropriate coverage, you might want to take a look at *Programming Microsoft ASP.NET 2.0 Applications: Advanced Topics* (Microsoft Press, 2006).

Mapping Errors to Pages

When an unhandled exception reaches the root of the stack, ASP.NET renders a default page, displaying the previously mentioned "yellow screen of death." Developers can customize this aspect of ASP.NET to a large extent through the *<customErrors>* section in the application's *web.config* file.

The *<customErrors>* Section

You turn on custom error messages for an ASP.NET application by acting on the *<customErrors>* section. Here's an example:

```
<configuration>
    <system.web>
        ...
        <customErrors mode="RemoteOnly" />
    </system.web>
</configuration>
```

The *mode* attribute specifies whether custom errors are enabled, disabled, or shown only to remote clients. The attribute is required. When the *mode* attribute is set to *RemoteOnly* (the default setting) remote users receive a generic error page that informs them that something went wrong on the server. (See Figure 5-4.) Local users, on the other hand, receive pages that show lots of details about the ASP.NET error. (See Figure 5-3.)

The error-handling policy can be changed at will. In particular, ASP.NET can be instructed to display detailed pages to all local and remote users. To activate this functionality, you change the value of the *mode* attribute to *Off*. For obvious security reasons, *Off* should not be used in production environments—it might reveal critical information to potential attackers.

Using Custom Error Pages

Overall, whatever your choice is for the *mode* attribute, all users have a good chance to be served a rather inexpressive and uninformative error page. To display a more professional, friendly, and apologetic page that has a look and feel consistent with the site, you set *web. config* as follows. Figure 5-5 gives an idea of the results you can get.

```
<configuration>
    <system.web>
        <customErrors mode="On"
            defaultRedirect="/GenericError.aspx" />
    </system.web>
</configuration>
```

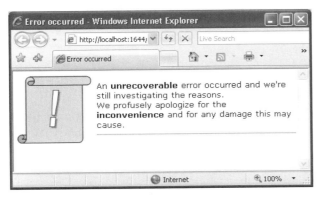

FIGURE 5-5 A nicer looking and more friendly error page.

Whatever the error is, ASP.NET now redirects the user to the *GenericError.aspx* page, whose contents and layout are completely under your control. This look is obtained by adding an optional attribute such as *defaultRedirect*, which indicates the error page to use to notify users. If *mode* is set to *On*, the default redirect takes on the standard error pages for all local and remote users. If *mode* is set to *RemoteOnly*, remote users will receive the custom error page while local users (typically, the developers) still receive the default page with the ASP. NET error information.

In most cases, the custom error page is made of plain HTML so that no error could recursively be raised. However, should the error page, in turn, originate another error, the default generic page of ASP.NET will be shown.

> **Note** When a default redirect is used, the browser receives an HTTP 302 status code and is invited to issue a new request to the specified error page. This fact has a key consequence: any information about the original exception is lost and *GetLastError*, which is called from within the custom error page, returns *null*.

Handling Common HTTP Errors

A generic error page invoked for each unhandled exception can hardly be context-sensitive—especially if you consider that there's no immediate way for the page author to access the original exception. We'll return to this point in a moment.

In addition to redirecting users to a common page for all errors, ASP.NET enables you to customize pages to show when certain HTTP errors occur. The mapping between error pages and specific HTTP status codes is defined in the *web.config* file. The *<customErrors>* section supports an inner *<error>* tag, which you can use to associate HTTP status codes with custom error pages.

```
<configuration>
  <system.web>
    <customErrors mode="On" defaultRedirect="/GenericError.aspx">
        <error statusCode="404" redirect="/ErrorPages/Error404.aspx" />
        <error statusCode="500" redirect="/ErrorPages/Error500.aspx" />
    </customErrors>
  </system.web>
</configuration>
```

The *<error>* element indicates the page to redirect the user to when the specified HTTP error occurs. The attribute *statusCode* denotes the HTTP error. Figure 5-6 shows what happens when the user mistypes the name of the URL and the error HTTP 404 (resource not found) is generated.

FIGURE 5-6 A custom page for the popular HTTP 404 error.

When invoked by the ASP.NET infrastructure, pages are passed the URL that caused the error on the query string. The following code shows the code-behind of a sample HTTP 404 error page:

```
public partial class Error404 : System.Web.UI.Page
{
    protected void Page_Load(object sender, EventArgs e)
    {
```

```
        string errPath = "<i>No error path information is available.</i>";
        object o = Request.QueryString["AspxErrorPath"];
        if (o != null)
            errPath = (string) o;

        // Update the UI
        ErrorPath.InnerHtml = errPath;
    }
}
```

Getting Information About the Exception

As mentioned, when you configure ASP.NET to redirect to a particular set of error pages, you lose any information about the internal exception that might have caused the error. Needless to say, no internal exception is involved in an HTTP 404 or HTTP 302 error. Unhandled exceptions are the typical cause of HTTP 500 internal errors. How do you make the page show context-sensitive information, at least to local users?

You get access to the exception in the *Error* event both at the page and application levels. One thing you can do is this: write a page-level error handler, capture the exception, and store the exception (or only the properties you're interested in) to the session state. The default redirect will then retrieve any context information from the session state.

```
protected void Page_Error(object sender, EventArgs e)
{
    // Captures the error and stores exception data
    Exception ex = Server.GetLastError();

    // Distinguish local and remote users
    if (Request.UserHostAddress == "127.0.0.1")
        Session["LastErrorMessage"] = ex.Message;
    else
        Session["LastErrorMessage"] = "Internal error.";

    // Clear the error
    Server.ClearError();
}
```

The preceding code checks the host address and stores exception-related information (limited to the message for simplicity) only for local users. The following code should be added to the *Page_Load* method of the page that handles the HTTP 500 error:

```
string msg = "No additional information available.";
object extraInfo = Session["LastErrorMessage"];
if (extraInfo != null)
    msg = (string) extraInfo;
ExtraInfo.InnerHtml = msg;
Session["LastErrorMessage"] = null;
```

Figure 5-7 shows the result.

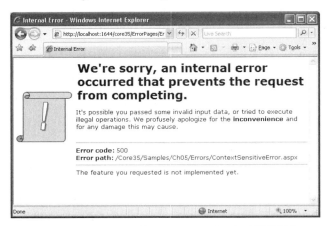

FIGURE 5-7 A context-sensitive error page for the HTTP 500 status code.

Writing context-sensitive error pages requires a page-level *Error* handler to cache the original exception. This means that you should write the same handler for every page that requires context-sensitive errors. You can either resort to a global error handler or write a new *Page*-derived class that incorporates the default *Error* handler. All the pages that require that functionality will derive their code file from this class instead of *Page*.

> **Note** What takes precedence if you have an application-level error handler, a page-level handler, and a bunch of redirects? The application-level handler takes precedence over the others. The page-level code runs later, followed by any code that handles HTTP 500 internal errors. Note that HTTP errors other than 500 are not caught by *Error* page and application events because they're handled by the Web server and don't go through the ASP.NET error-handling mechanism described here.

Debugging Options

Debugging an ASP.NET page is possible only if the page is compiled in debug mode. An assembly compiled in debug mode incorporates additional information for a debugger tool to step through the code. You can enable debug mode on individual pages as well as for all the pages in a given application. The *<compilation>* section in the *web.config* file controls this setting. In particular, you set the *Debug* attribute to *true* to enable debug activity for all pages in the application. The default is *false*. To enable debugging for a single page, you add the *Debug* attribute to the *@Page* directive:

```
<% @Page Debug="true" %>
```

ASP.NET compiles the contents of any *.aspx* resource before execution. The contents of the *.aspx* resource is parsed to obtain a C# (or Microsoft Visual Basic .NET) class file, which is then handed out to the language compiler. When a page is flagged with the *Debug* attribute, ASP.NET doesn't delete the temporary class file used to generate the page assembly. This file is available on the Web server for you to peruse and investigate. The file is located under the Windows folder at the following path: *Microsoft.NET\Framework\[version]\Temporary ASP.NET Files*.

Debug mode is important for testing applications and diagnosing their problems. Note, though, that running applications in debug mode has a significant performance overhead. You should make sure that an application has debugging disabled before deploying it on a production server.

ASP.NET Tracing

Error handling and tool-assisted debugging are essential instruments to make an application run without anomalies and recover gracefully from unexpected exceptions. Tools for tracing complete the kit. Tracing refers to the ability to output messages commenting on the execution of the code. This feature is extremely useful for tracking data inconsistencies, monitoring the flow, asserting conditions, and even gathering profiling information.

The .NET Framework comes with a rather feature-rich set of tools for tracing applications. In particular, the *Systems.Diagnostics* namespace defines two classes, named *Trace* and *Debug*, whose methods can be used to trace the code. The *Trace* and *Debug* classes are essentially identical and work on top of more specialized modules known as "listeners." The listener acts like a driver, collects tracing messages, and stores the messages in a particular medium such as the Windows event log, an application window, or a text file. Each application can have its own set of listeners, which will receive all emitted messages.

ASP.NET comes with a made-to-measure subsystem to provide applications with diagnostic information about individual requests. The tracing subsystem is part of the infrastructure, and all that an application or a page has to do is enable it.

Tracing the Execution Flow in ASP.NET

Tracing lets developers write and leave debug statements in the code and turn them on and off through an attribute, and they can do this even once the application is deployed to a production server. When tracing for a page is enabled, ASP.NET appends diagnostic information to the page's output or sends it to a trace viewer application. For the most part, trace information has a fixed layout and fixed content, but page and control authors can customize it to some extent.

Enabling Page Tracing

Although a *<trace>* configuration section does exist in the *web.config* file to let you configure tracing at the application level, you typically want to control tracing on a per-page basis. However, for large projects you can toggle on and off the trace attribute by using the following code in the application's *web.config* file:

```
<configuration>
    <system.web>
        <trace enabled="true" pageOutput="true" />
    </system.web>
</configuration>
```

The *enabled* attribute enables tracing on the application, while the *pageOutput* attribute permits output to appear in the page. If *pageOutput* is set to *false* (the default setting), the tracing output is automatically routed to the ASP.NET tracer tool— *trace.axd*. At the end of the project, you simply drop the *<trace>* element from the *web.config* file or set both attributes to *false*. In this way, you eliminate at the root the risk of inadvertently leaving tracing enabled on one of the application pages.

The *trace* attribute in the *@Page* directive defaults to *false*; if set to *true*, it enables tracing information to appear at the bottom of pages, as shown in Figure 5-8.

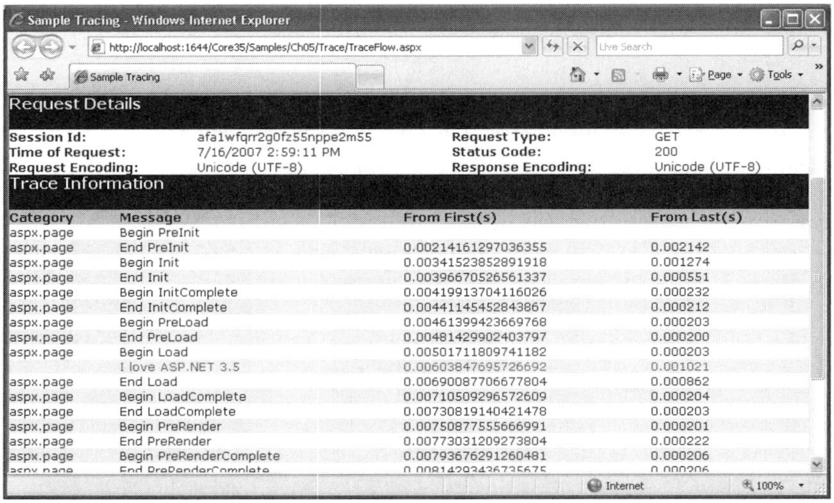

FIGURE 5-8 ASP.NET tracing in action.

The trace information is part of the page and, as such, displays through any type of browser that accesses the page. Several tables of information show up along with the trace information generated by the page. Additional tables display request details, the control tree, and some useful collections such as cookies, headers, form values, and server variables. If the session and the application state are not empty, the contents of the *Session* and *Application* intrinsic properties are also included in the view.

The *@Page* directive also supplies the *TraceMode* attribute to let you choose the order in which the information should be displayed. Feasible values are *SortByCategory* and *SortByTime*. By default, the trace messages appear in the order in which they are emitted. If you set the *TraceMode* attribute to the *SortByCategory* value, the rows appearing in the Trace Information section are sorted by category name. The category to which each row belongs is determined by the method used to emit the message.

Enabling Tracing Programmatically

The *Page* class provides two properties to control tracing programmatically. They are *TraceModeValue* and *TraceEnabled*. As the names suggest, both are the programmatic counterpart of the aforementioned *@Page* directive attributes. *TraceEnabled* is a read-write Boolean property that turns tracing on and off for the specified page. *TraceModeValue* gets and sets a value in the *TraceMode* enumeration to indicate the desired tracing mode of the page—either sort by category or time.

To be honest, enabling and disabling output trace programmatically is not a feature that many applications require in a production scenario. The feature, though, might be valuable during the development cycle.

Writing Trace Messages

A third property on the *Page* class that is relevant to tracing is *Trace*—an instance of the *TraceContext* class. An ASP.NET page populates its trace log using methods on the *TraceContext* class. An instance of this class is created when the HTTP request is set up for execution. The trace object is then exposed through the *Trace* property of the *HttpContext* class and is mirrored by the *Trace* property on the *Page* class.

The *TraceContext* Class

The *TraceContext* class has a simple interface and features a couple of properties and as many methods. The properties are *IsEnabled* and *TraceMode*. The *IsEnabled* property is a read-only Boolean property that indicates whether tracing is enabled or not. The value that this property returns is affected by the *trace* attribute on the *@Page* directive as well as the *enabled* attribute in the *<trace>* section of the *web.config* file. The *TraceMode* property gets and sets the order in which the traced rows will be displayed in the page. The property is of type *TraceMode*—an enumeration that includes values such as *SortByCategory* and *SortByTime*.

Emitting Trace Messages

To emit messages, you can use either of two methods: *Write* or *Warn*. Both methods have three overloads, which all behave in the same way. *Write* and *Warn* are nearly identical methods—the only visible difference is that *Warn* always outputs messages in red.

```
public void Write(string);
public void Write(string, string);
public void Write(string, string, Exception);
```

The simplest overload just emits the specified text in the Message column. (See Figure 5-8.) In the second overload, the first string argument represents the name of the category you want to use for the message—the second argument. The category name can be used to sort trace information and is any name that makes sense to the application to better qualify the message. Finally, the third overload adds an extra *Exception* object in case the message is tracing an error. In this case, the text in the Message column is the concatenation of the specified text and the exception's message.

> **Note** Although the text being passed to both *Write* and *Warn* methods is meant to be displayed in HTML pages, no HTML formatting tag is ever processed. The text is written as plain text so that if you attempt to use boldface characters your only result is having a trace message with ** and ** substrings output directly into your message.

Tracing from External Classes

The ASP.NET *Trace* object is accessible without a fully qualified name from the source code of the page or from the code file class. Custom controls embedded in the page, and their code file classes, can also access the tracing subsystem directly. Other classes don't have the same possibility, though.

Suppose your code-behind class delegates an external class to accomplish some tasks. How can the worker class trace in the ASP.NET page? In the context of the worker class, the *Trace* object is unavailable, or at least not in its unqualified form. External classes that want to emit text in the trace log of the current HTTP request can do that using the following expression:

```
System.Web.HttpContext.Current.Trace.Write(category, msg);
```

Starting with ASP.NET 2.0, you can configure the tracing subsystem to automatically forward messages to the .NET Framework tracing infrastructure, for any listeners registered to display diagnostic messages. To enable this, you add the following code to the *web.config* file:

```
<system.web>
    <trace enabled="true" writeToDiagnosticsTrace="true" />
</system.web>
```

New to ASP.NET 2.0, the *writeToDiagnosticsTrace* attribute defaults to *false*. Listeners that can receive any messages output to the ASP.NET trace context are those listed in the *<trace>* section under the *<system.diagnostics>* section.

The Trace Viewer

ASP.NET also supports application-level tracing through the trace viewer tool. Once tracing has been enabled for the application, each page request routes all the page-specific trace information to the viewer. You can view the trace viewer by requesting *trace.axd* from the root application directory. The trace viewer is shown in Figure 5-9.

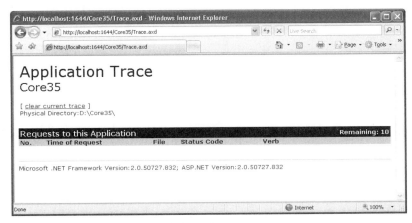

FIGURE 5-9 The trace viewer ready for action.

To enable the viewer, you need to have a *<trace>* section in your application *web.config* file—that is, the configuration file deployed in the root folder:

```
<configuration>
    <system.web>
        <trace enabled="true" />
    </system.web>
</configuration>
```

The *<trace>* section supports a few attributes. The *pageOutput* attribute, for example, indicates whether the trace output should be visible to the individual pages too or accessible only through the viewer. By default, *pageOutput* is *false* and only the viewer receives trace information. However, each page can individually override this setting by using the *Trace* attribute on the *@Page* directive. The trace viewer caches no more than the number of requests specified by the *requestLimit* attribute (which is 10 by default).

In short, the ASP.NET trace viewer acts as a centralized console and gathers all the trace information generated by the pages in a certain application. Each request, up to the maximum number fixed by *requestLimit*, is identified by a row in the viewer's interface and can be consulted until the viewer's cache is cleared, as shown in Figure 5-10.

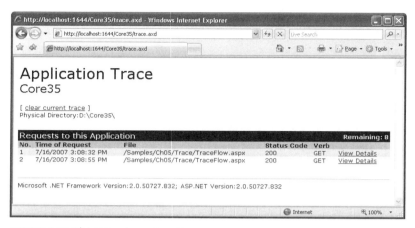

FIGURE 5-10 The trace viewer in action.

The trace viewer automatically tracks all requests and caches the full trace for each. When the request limit is reached, no other request will be cached until the log is manually cleared.

Page Personalization

ASP.NET pages do not necessarily require a rich set of personalization features. However, if you can build an effective personalization layer into your Web application, final pages will be friendlier, more functional, and more appealing to use. For some applications (such as portals and shopping centers), though, personalization is crucial. For others, it is mostly a way to improve visual appearance. In ASP.NET 2.0 and 3.5, personalization comes in two comple-mentary forms: user profiles and themes.

The user profile is designed for persistent storage of structured data using a friendly and type-safe API. The application defines its own model of personalized data, and the ASP.NET runtime does the rest by parsing and compiling that model into a class. Each member of the personalized class data corresponds to a piece of information specific to the current user. Loading and saving personalized data is completely transparent to end users and doesn't even require the page author to know much about the internal plumbing.

Themes assign a set of styles and visual attributes to elements of the site that can be customized. These elements include control properties, page style sheets, images, and templates on the page. A theme is the union of all visual styles for all customizable elements in the pages—a sort of super–CSS file. We'll work on themes in the next chapter.

Creating the User Profile

At the highest level of abstraction, a user profile is a collection of properties that the ASP.NET runtime groups into a dynamically generated class. Any profile data is persisted on a per-user basis and is permanently stored until someone with administrative privileges deletes it. When the application runs and a page is displayed, ASP.NET dynamically creates a profile object that contains, properly typed, the properties you have defined in the data model. The object is then added to the current *HttpContext* object and is available to pages through the *Profile* property.

The data storage is hidden from the user and, to some extent, from the programmers. The user doesn't need to know how and where the data is stored; the programmer simply needs to indicate what type of profile provider he wants to use. The profile provider determines the database to use—typically, a Microsoft SQL Server database—but custom providers and custom data storage models can also be used.

Note In ASP.NET 3.5, the default profile provider is based on SQL Express, a lightweight version of SQL Server 2005. The physical storage medium is a local file named *aspnetdb.mdf*, which is located in the App_Data folder of the Web application.

Definition of the Data Model

To use the ASP.NET profile API, you first decide on the structure of the data model you want to use. Then you attach the data model to the page through the configuration file. The layout of the user profile is defined in the *web.config* file and consists of a list of properties that can take any of the .NET common language runtime (CLR) types. The data model is a block of XML data that describe properties and related .NET Framework types.

The simplest way to add properties to the profile storage medium is through name/value pairs. You define each pair by adding a new property tag to the *<properties>* section of the configuration file. The *<properties>* section is itself part of the larger *<profile>* section, which also includes provider information. The *<profile>* section is located under *<system.web>*. Here's an example of a user profile section:

```
<profile>
    <properties>
        <add name="BackColor" type="string" />
        <add name="ForeColor" type="string" />
    </properties>
</profile>
```

All the properties defined through an *<add>* tag become members of a dynamically created class that is exposed as part of the HTTP context of each page. The *type* attribute indicates the type of the property. If no type information is set, the type defaults to *System.String*.

Any valid CLR type is acceptable. Table 5-3 lists the valid attributes for the *<add>* element. Only *name* is mandatory.

TABLE 5-3 Attributes of the *<add>* Element

Attribute	Description
allowAnonymous	Allows storing values for anonymous users. *False* by default.
defaultValue	Indicates the default value of the property.
customProviderData	Contains data for a custom profile provider.
name	Name of the property.
provider	Name of the provider to use to read and write the property.
readOnly	Specifies whether the property value is read-only. *False* by default.
serializeAs	Indicates how to serialize the value of the property. Possible values are *Xml*, *Binary*, *String*, and *ProviderSpecific*.
type	The .NET Framework type of the property. It is a string object by default.

The User Profile Class Representation

As a programmer, you don't need to know how data is stored or retrieved from the personalization store. However, you must create and configure the store. We skirted this step, but we'll discuss it in detail shortly. The following code snippet gives you an idea of the class being generated to represent the profile's data model:

```
namespace ASP
{
    public class ProfileCommon : ProfileBase
    {
        public virtual string BackColor
        {
            get {(string) GetPropertyValue("BackColor");}
            set {SetPropertyValue("BackColor", value);}
        }
        public virtual string ForeColor
        {
            get {(string) GetPropertyValue("ForeColor");}
            set {SetPropertyValue("ForeColor", value);}
        }
        public virtual ProfileCommon GetProfile(string username)
        {
            object o = ProfileBase.Create(username);
            return (ProfileCommon) o;
        }
        ...
    }
}
```

An instance of this class is associated with the *Profile* property of the page class and is accessed programmatically as follows:

```
// Use the BackColor property to paint the page background
theBody.Attributes["bgcolor"] = Profile.BackColor;
```

There's a tight relationship between user accounts and profile information. We'll investigate this in a moment—for now, you need to take note of this because anonymous users are supported as well.

Using Collection Types

In the previous example, we worked with single, scalar values. However, the personalization engine fully supports more advanced scenarios, such as using collections or custom types. Let's tackle collections first. The following code demonstrates a property *Links* that is a collection of strings:

```
<properties>
    <add name="Links"
        type="System.Collections.Specialized.StringCollection" />
</properties>
```

Nonscalar values such as collections and arrays must be serialized to fit in a data storage medium. The *serializeAs* attribute simply specifies how. As mentioned, acceptable values are *String*, *Xml*, *Binary*, and *ProviderSpecific*. If the *serializeAs* attribute is not present on the *<properties>* definition, the *String* type is assumed. A collection is normally serialized as XML or in a binary format.

Using Custom Types

You can use a custom type with the ASP.NET personalization layer as long as you mark it as a serializable type. You simply author a class and compile it down to an assembly. The name of the assembly is added to the type information for the profile property:

```
<properties>
    <add name="ShoppingCart"
        type="My.Namespace.DataContainer, MyAssem"
        serializeAs="Binary" />
</properties>
```

The assembly that contains the custom type must be available to the ASP.NET application. You obtain this custom type by placing the assembly in the application's *Bin* directory or by registering it within the global assembly cache (GAC).

Grouping Properties

The *<properties>* section can also accept the *<group>* element. The *<group>* element allows you to group a few related properties as if they are properties of an intermediate object. The following code snippet shows an example of grouping:

```
<properties>
    ...
    <group name="Font">
        <add name="Name" type="string" defaultValue="verdana" />
        <add name="SizeInPoints" type="int" defaultValue="8" />
    </group>
</properties>
```

The font properties have been declared children of the *Font* group. This means that from now on any access to *Name* or *SizeInPoints* passes through the *Font* name, as shown here:

```
string fontName = Profile.Font.Name;
```

> **Note** Default values are not saved to the persistence layer. Properties declared with a default value make their debut in the storage medium only when the application assigns them a value different from the default one.

Interacting with the Page

To enable or disable profile support, you set the *enabled* attribute of the *<profile>* element in the *web.config* file. If the property is *true* (the default), personalization features are enabled for all pages. If personalization is disabled, the *Profile* property isn't available to pages.

Creating the Profile Database

As mentioned earlier, profile works strictly on a per-user basis and is permanently stored. Enabling the feature simply turns any functionality on, but it doesn't create the needed infrastructure for user membership and data storage.

Starting with version 2.0, ASP.NET comes with an administrative tool—the ASP.NET Web Site Administration Tool (WSAT)—that is fully integrated in Visual Studio 2005 and Visual Studio 2008. (See Figure 5-11.) You invoke the tool by choosing ASP.NET Configuration from the *Website* menu.

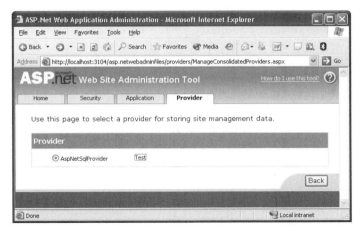

FIGURE 5-11 The ASP.NET Web Site Administration Tool, which is used to select the profile provider.

You can use this tool to create a default database to store profile data. The default database is a SQL Server 2005 Express file named *aspnetdb.mdf*, which is located in the *App_Data* special folder of the ASP.NET application. Tables and schema of the database are fixed. The same database contains tables to hold membership and role information. The use of a membership database with users and roles is important because personalization is designed to be user-specific and because a user ID—either a local Windows account or an application-specific logon—is necessary to index data.

Profile data has no predefined duration and is permanently stored. It is up to the Web site administrator to delete the information when convenient.

Needless to say, WSAT is just one option—and not the only one—for setting up the profile infrastructure. For example, if you're using a custom provider, the setup of your application is responsible for preparing any required storage infrastructure—be it a SQL Server table, an Oracle database, or whatever else. We'll cover the setup of profile providers in the next section.

Working with Anonymous Users

Although user profiles are designed primarily for authenticated users, anonymous users can also store profile data. In this case, though, a few extra requirements must be fulfilled. In particular, you have to turn on the *anonymousIdentification* feature, which is disabled by default:

```
<anonymousIdentification enabled="true" />
```

The purpose of anonymous user identification is to assign a unique identity to users who are not authenticated and recognize and treat all of them as an additional registered user.

> **Note** Anonymous identification in no way affects the identity of the account that is processing the request. Nor does it affect any other aspects of security and user authentication. Anonymous identification is simply a way to give a "regular" ID to unauthenticated users so that they can be tracked as authenticated, "regular" users.

In addition, to support anonymous identification you must mark properties in the data model with the special Boolean attribute named *allowAnonymous*. Properties not marked with the attribute are not made available to anonymous users.

```
<anonymousIdentification enabled="true" />
<profile enabled="true">
    <properties>
        <add name="BackColor"
            type="System.Drawing.Color"
            allowAnonymous="true" />
        <add name="Links"
            type="System.Collections.Specialized.StringCollection"
            serializeAs="Xml" />
    </properties>
</profile>
```

In the preceding code snippet, anonymous users can set the background color but cannot add new links.

Accessing Profile Properties

Before the request begins its processing cycle, the *Profile* property of the page is set with an instance of a dynamically created class that was created after the user profile defined in the *web.config* file. When the page first loads, the profile properties are set with their default values (if any) or are empty objects. They are never null. When custom or collection types are used to define properties, assigning default values might be hard. The code just shown defines a string collection object—the property *Links*—but giving that a default value expressed as a string is virtually impossible. At run time, though, the *Links* property won't be null—it will equal an empty collection. So how can you manage default values for these properties?

Properties that don't have a default value can be initialized in the *Page_Load* event when the page is not posting back. Here's how you can do that:

```
if (!IsPostBack)
{
    // Add some default links to the Links property
    if (Profile.Links.Count == 0) {
        Profile.Links.Add("http://www.contoso.com");
        Profile.Links.Add("http://www.northwind.com");
    }
}
```

Let's consider some sample code. Imagine a page like the one in Figure 5-12 that displays a list of favorite links in a panel. Users can customize the links as well as a few other visual attributes, such as colors and font.

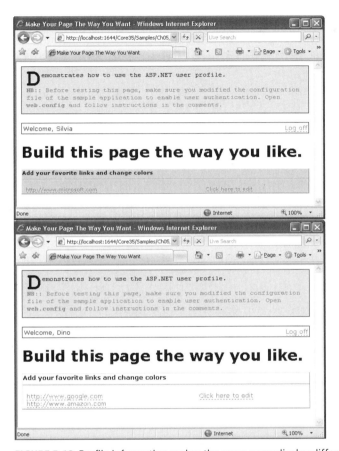

FIGURE 5-12 Profile information makes the same page display differently for different users.

The profile data is expressed by the following XML:

```
<profile enabled="true">
    <properties>
        <add name="BackColor" type="string" />
        <add name="ForeColor" type="string" />
        <add name="Links"
            type="System.Collections.Specialized.StringCollection"/>
        <group name="Font">
            <add name="Name" type="string" />
            <add name="SizeInPoints" type="int" defaultValue="12" />
        </group>
    </properties>
</profile>
```

The page uses the profile data to adjust its own user interface, as shown in the following code:

```
private void ApplyPagePersonalization()
{
    // Set colors in the panel
    InfoPanel.ForeColor = ColorTranslator.FromHtml(Profile.ForeColor);
    InfoPanel.BackColor = ColorTranslator.FromHtml(Profile.BackColor);

    // Set font properties in panel
    InfoPanel.Font.Name = Profile.Font.Name;
    InfoPanel.Font.Size = FontUnit.Point(Profile.Font.SizeInPoints);

    // Create links
    Favorites.Controls.Clear();
    if(Profile.Links.Count == 0)
        Favorites.Controls.Add(new LiteralControl("No links available."));
    else
        foreach (object o in Profile.Links) {
            HyperLink h = new HyperLink ();
            h.Text = o.ToString ();
            h.NavigateUrl = o.ToString ();
            Favorites.Controls.Add(h);
            Favorites.Controls.Add(new LiteralControl("<br />"));
        }
}
```

The *ApplyPagePersonalization* method is invoked from *Page_Load*.

```
protected void Page_Load(object sender, EventArgs e)
{
    if (!IsPostBack) {
        // Initialize profile properties as needed
    }
    ApplyPagePersonalization();
}
```

Initialization is an important phase, but it's strictly application specific. For example, the first time a user requests the page no colors are set and no links are defined. Because we enumerate the contents of the collections, an empty collection is just fine and there's no need to further initialize it. (Note that the framework guarantees that reference objects are always instantiated.) What about color properties? If you specify a default value in the *web.config* file, the framework uses that value to initialize the corresponding property the first time a user requests the page; otherwise, you take care of finding a good default value in *Page_Load*.

At the end of the request, the contents of the profile object are flushed into the profile storage medium and retrieved the next time the page is invoked. When this happens, no uninitialized properties result unless the site administrator has deleted some data offline.

Note that pages that make intensive use of personalization should also provide a user interface to let users modify settings and personalize the visual appearance of the page. The sample page of Figure 5-12 uses a *MultiView* control to switch between the menu-like view that invites you to edit and the editor-like view in Figure 5-13.

FIGURE 5-13 The page incorporates a little editor to let users personalize the page's look and feel.

The full source code for the page is included with the book's sample code.

> **Note** The personalization data of a page is all set when the *Page_Init* event fires. However, when the *Page_PreInit* event arrives no operation has been accomplished yet on the page, not even the loading of personalization data.

Personalization Events

As mentioned, the personalization data is added to the HTTP context of a request before the request begins its processing route. But which system component is in charge of loading personalization data? ASP.NET employs a new HTTP module for this purpose named *ProfileModule*.

The module attaches itself to a couple of HTTP events and gets involved after a request has been authorized and when the request is about to end. If the personalization feature is off, the module returns immediately. Otherwise, it fires the *Personalize* event to the application and then loads personalization data from the current user profile. When the *Personalize* event fires, the personalization data hasn't been loaded yet. Handlers for events fired by an HTTP module must be written to the *global.asax* file.

```
void Profile_Personalize(object sender, ProfileEventArgs e)
{
    ProfileCommon profile = null;

    // Exit if it is the anonymous user
    if (User == null) return;

    // Determine the profile based on the role. The profile database
    // contains a specific entry for a given role.
    if (User.IsInRole("Administrators"))
        profile = (ProfileCommon) ProfileBase.Create("Administrator");
    else if (User.IsInRole("Users"))
        profile = (ProfileCommon) ProfileBase.Create("User");
    else if (User.IsInRole("Guests"))
        profile = (ProfileCommon) ProfileBase.Create("Guest");

    // Make the HTTP profile module use THIS profile object
    if (profile != null)
        e.Profile = profile;
}
```

The personalization layer is not necessarily there for the end user's amusement. You should look at it as a general-purpose tool to carry user-specific information. User-specific information, though, indicates information that applies to the user, not necessarily information entered by the user.

The personalization layer employs the identity of the current user as an index to retrieve the proper set of data, but what about roles? What if you have hundreds of users with different names but who share the same set of profile data (such as menu items, links, and UI settings)? Maintaining hundreds of nearly identical database entries is out of the question. But the standard profile engine doesn't know how to handle roles. That's why you sometimes need to handle the *Personalize* event or perhaps roll your own profile provider.

The code shown previously overrides the process that creates the user profile object and ensures that the returned object is filled with user-specific information accessed through the user role. The static method *Create* on the *ProfileBase* class takes the user name and creates an instance of the profile object specific to that user. *ProfileCommon* is the common name of the dynamically created class that contains the user profile.

The handler of the *Personalize* event receives data through the *ProfileEventArgs* class. The class has a read-write member, named *Profile*. When the event handler returns, the profile HTTP module checks this member. If it is null, the module proceeds as usual and creates a profile object based on the user's identity. If not, it simply binds the current value of the *Profile* member as the profile object of the page.

Migrating Anonymous Data

As mentioned, anonymous users can store and retrieve settings that are persisted using an anonymous unique ID. However, if at a certain point a hitherto anonymous user decides to create an account with the Web site, you might need to migrate to her account all the settings that she made as an anonymous user. This migration doesn't occur automatically.

When a user who has been using your application anonymously logs in, the personalization module fires an event—*MigrateAnonymous*. Properly handled, this global event allows you to import anonymous settings into the profile of an authenticated user. The following pseudo-code demonstrates how to handle the migration of an anonymous profile:

```
void Profile_MigrateAnonymous(object sender, ProfileMigrateEventArgs e)
{
    // Load the profile of the anonymous user
    ProfileCommon anonProfile;
    anonProfile = Profile.GetProfile(e.AnonymousId);

    // Migrate the properties to the new profile
    Profile.BackColor = anonProfile.BackColor;
    ...
}
```

You get the profile for the anonymous user and extract the value of any property you want to import. Next you copy the value to the profile of the currently logged-on user.

Profile Providers

In ASP.NET, the profile API is composed of two distinct elements—the access layer and the storage layer.

The access layer provides a strongly typed model to get and set property values and also manages user identities. It guarantees that the data is retrieved and stored on behalf of the currently logged-on user.

The second element of the profile system is the data storage. The system uses ad hoc providers to perform any tasks involved with the storage and retrieval of values. ASP.NET comes with a profile provider that uses SQL Server 2005 Express as the data engine. If necessary, you can also write custom providers. The profile provider writes data into the storage medium of choice and is responsible for the final schema of the data. A profile provider must be able to either serialize the type (by using XML serialization and binary object serialization, for example) or know how to extract significant information from it.

> **Important** As discussed in Chapter 1, an ASP.NET provider is defined as a pluggable component that extends or replaces a given system functionality. The profile provider is just one implementation of the ASP.NET provider model. Other examples of providers are the membership provider and role manager provider, both of which we'll discuss in Chapter 16. At its core, the provider infrastructure allows customers to change the underlying implementation of some out-of-the-box system functionalities while keeping the top-level interface intact. Providers are relatively simple components with as few methods and properties as possible. Only one instance of the provider exists per application domain.

Configuring Profile Providers

All features, such as user profiling, that have providers should have a default provider. Normally, the default provider is indicated via a *defaultProvider* attribute in the section of the configuration file that describes the specific feature. By default, if a preferred provider is not specified, the first item in the collection is considered the default.

The default profile provider is named *AspNetSqlProfileProvider* and uses SQL Server 2005 Express for data storage. Providers are registered in the *<providers>* section of the configuration file under the main node *<profile>*, as shown here:

```
<profile>
    <providers>
        <add name="AspNetSqlProfileProvider"
            connectionStringName="LocalSqlServer" applicationName="/"
            type="System.Web.Profile.SqlProfileProvider" />
    </providers>
</profile>
```

The *<add>* nodes within the *<providers>* section list all the currently registered providers. The previous code is an excerpt from the *machine.config* file. Attributes such as *name* and *type* are common to all types of providers. Other properties are part of the provider's specific configuration mechanism. Tightly connected with this custom interface is the set of extra properties—in this case, *connectionStringName* and *description*. The *description* attribute is simply text that describes what the provider does.

The *connectionStringName* attribute defines the information needed to set up a connection with the underlying database engine of choice. However, instead of being a plain connection string, the attribute contains the name of a previously registered connection string. For example, *LocalSqlServer* is certainly not the connection string to use for a local or remote connection to an instance of SQL Server. Instead, it is the name of an entry in the new *<connectionStrings>* section of the configuration file. That entry contains any concrete information needed to connect to the database.

The *LocalSqlServer* connection string placeholder is defined in *machine.config* as follows:

```
<connectionStrings>
    <add name="LocalSqlServer"
        connectionString="data source=.\SQLEXPRESS;
                          Integrated Security=SSPI;
                          AttachDBFilename=|DataDirectory|aspnetdb.mdf;
                          User Instance=true"
        providerName="System.Data.SqlClient" />
</connectionStrings>
```

As you can see, the connection string refers to an instance of SQL Server named SQLEXPRESS and attaches to the aspnetdb.mdf database located in the application's data directory—the App_Data folder.

Structure of AspNetDb.mdf

As a developer, you don't need to know much about the layout of the table and the logic that governs it; instead, you're responsible for ensuring that any needed infrastructure is created. To do so, you use the Website menu in Visual Studio .NET 2005 to start the ASP.NET site administration tool.

A view of the tables in the database is shown in Figure 5-14.

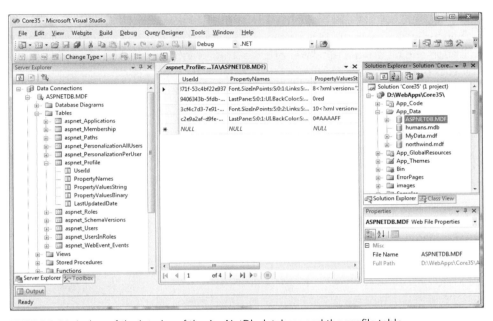

FIGURE 5-14 A view of the interior of the AspNetDb database and the profile table.

Note that the AspNetDb database isn't specific to the personalization infrastructure. As you can see in the figure, it groups all provider-related tables, including those for membership, roles, and users. The internal structure of each database is specific to the mission of the underlying provider.

> **Important** The default profile provider uses the ADO.NET managed provider for SQL Server and is in no way limited to SQL Express. By changing the connection string, you can make it work with a database handled by the full version of SQL Server 2000 and SQL Server 2005. Using SQL Express is recommended for small applications in Internet scenarios or if you simply want to experiment with the functionality.

Custom Profile Providers

The SQL Server profile provider is good at building new applications and is useful for profile data that is inherently tabular. In many cases, though, you won't start an ASP.NET application from scratch but will instead migrate an existing application. You often already have data to integrate with the ASP.NET profile layer. If this data doesn't get along with the relational model, or if it is already stored in a storage medium other than SQL Server, you can write a custom profile provider. An helpful link is the following: *http://msdn.microsoft.com/msdnmag/issues/07/03/ASPNET2/default.aspx*.

Profile providers push the idea that existing data stores can be integrated with the personalization engine using a thin layer of code. This layer of code abstracts the physical characteristics of the data store and exposes its content through a common set of methods and properties. A custom personalization provider is a class that inherits *ProfileProvider*.

> **Note** A custom provider can be bound to one or more profile properties through the property's *provider* attribute:
>
> ```
> <properties>
>     <add name="BackColor" type="string" provider="MyProvider" />
>     . . .
> </properties>
> ```
>
> As of the preceding code, the *BackColor* property is read and written through the *MyProvider* provider. It goes without saying that the provider name must correspond to one of the entries in the *<providers>* section.

Conclusion

In this chapter, we examined three issues you might face when building pages and interacting with them—forms, errors, and user profiles.

Form-based programming is fundamental in Web applications because it's the only way to have users and applications interact. ASP.NET pages can have only one server-side form with a fixed *action* property. Although you can still change the *action* property on the fly with a bit of client script code, this often results in a view state corruption error. ASP.NET 2.0 and ASP.NET 3.5 support cross-page posting as a way to let users post data from one page to another.

Often, good programs do bad things and raise errors. In the Web world, handling errors is a task architecturally left to the runtime environment that is running the application. The ASP.NET runtime is capable of providing two types of error pages, both of which are not very practical for serious and professional applications, although for different reasons. When a user who is locally connected to the application does something that originates an error, by default ASP.NET returns a "geek" page with the stack trace and the full transcript of the exception that occurred. The remote user, on the other hand, receives a less compromising page, but certainly not a user-friendly one. Fortunately, though, the ASP.NET framework is flexible enough to let you change the error pages, even to the point of distinguishing between HTTP errors.

The third aspect that relates to users and pages that we covered in this chapter is personalization. Personalization allows you to write pages that persist user preferences and parametric data from a permanent medium in a totally automated way. As a programmer, you're in charge of setting up the personalization infrastructure, but you need not know anything about the internal details of storage. All you do is call a provider component using the methods of a well-known interface. Personalization is a feature that is not supported by ASP.NET versions prior to version 2.0.

In the next chapter, we'll take page authoring to the next level by exploring powerful and effective ways to build pages, including master pages, themes, and wizards.

Just The Facts

- The typical ASP.NET page contains a single *<form>* tag decorated with the *runat* attribute set. Multiple server-side forms are not allowed to be visible at the same time.

- Starting with ASP.NET 2.0, controls that implement the *IButtonControl* interface are allowed to post to a different target page. The runtime takes care of posting the viewstate and arranges the post.

- Exceptions remain the official .NET way to handle anomalies, but exceptions should be kept to handling exceptional events in the life of the application, raised when something happens that violates an assumption

- When an unrecoverable error occurs in an ASP.NET page, the message a user receives varies based on its local or remote location. Remote users will get a generic error message; local users get details and the call stack.

- As a developer, you can customize the page being displayed both programmatically and declaratively. In the latter case, you can automatically bind a custom page to the HTTP status code.

- ASP.NET pages can be attached to an additional context property—the profile object. The profile is an instance of a class dynamically built around the data model specified in the configuration file.

■ When the profile is active, pages persist user preferences and parametric data to and from a permanent medium in a totally automated way. Developers have no need to know where and how.

■ A common profile is available for anonymous users that has the possibility of migrating the user data to the real profile object when the user logs in.

■ Pages that take advantage of the user profile object should consider adding some UI blocks to let end users modify parameters on the fly.

■ Page personalization is tightly coupled with membership.

Chapter 6
Rich Page Composition

A large number of Web sites these days contain similar-looking, rich pages that share the same graphics, appearance, user interface (UI) widgets, and perhaps some navigational menus or search forms. These pages are rich in content and functionality, are visually appealing, and more importantly, have an overall look and feel that abides by the golden rule of Web usability: "Be consistent." What's the recommended approach for building such pages and Web sites?

One possibility is wrapping these UI elements in user controls and referencing them in each page. Although such a model is extremely powerful and produces modular code, when you have hundreds of pages to work with, it soon becomes unmanageable. Both classic ASP and ASP.NET 1.x provide some workarounds for this type of issue, but neither tackles such a scenario openly and provides a definitive, optimal solution. Starting with version 2.0, ASP. NET faces up to the task through a new technology—*master pages*—and basically benefits from the ASP.NET Framework's ability to merge a "supertemplate" with user-defined content replacements.

With themes, you can easily give the whole site a consistent (and, you hope, appealing) user interface and easily export that look from one application to the next. Much like Microsoft Windows XP themes, ASP.NET themes assign a set of styles and visual attributes to elements of the site that can be customized. Themes are a superset of cascading style sheets (CSS) and are not supported in versions of ASP.NET prior to 2.0.

A recurring task in Web development is collecting user input by using forms. When the input to collect is large and pretty much articulated (read, easy to categorize), multiple forms are typically used to accomplish the task. The whole procedure is divided into various steps, each of which takes care of collecting and validating a particular subset of the expected data. This multistep procedure is often called a "wizard." With version 2.0, ASP.NET introduces a new view control that makes building wizards a snap.

Overall, building rich pages is a much more approachable task in ASP.NET today than it was with previous versions. With master pages, you build pages based on an existing template of code and markup; with themes, you use skins to control pages and achieve visual consistency as well as profile capabilities. Finally, with wizards you add rich functionality to pages.

Working with Master Pages

As a matter of fact, since the beginning ASP.NET and Microsoft Visual Studio greatly simplified the process of authoring Web pages and Web sites and made it affordable to a wide range of people with different skills. However, after a few months of real-world experience, many developers recognized that something was missing in the ASP.NET approach to page authoring. While building simple sites is easy, architecting real-world sites with hundreds of complex and rich pages still requires additional work and, more importantly, key decisions to be made without guidance.

Almost all Web sites use a similar graphical layout for all their pages. This doesn't happen by chance—it grows out of accepted guidelines for design and usability. A consistent layout is characteristic of all cutting-edge Web sites, no matter how complex. For some Web sites, the layout consists of the header, body, and footer; for others, it is a more sophisticated aggregation of navigational menus, buttons, and panels that contain and render the actual content. Needless to say, manual duplication of code and HTML elements is simply out of the question. Making code automatically reusable clearly represents a better approach, but how do you implement it *in practice*?

Authoring Rich Pages in ASP.NET 1.x

In ASP.NET 1.x, the best approach to authoring pages with a common layout is to employ *user controls*. User controls are aggregates of ASP.NET server controls, literal text, and code. (We'll cover user controls in my other book *Programming Microsoft ASP.NET 2.0 Applications: Advanced Topics* (Microsoft Press, 2006) The ASP.NET runtime exposes user controls to the outside world as programmable components. The idea is that you employ user controls to tailor your own user interface components and share them among the pages of the Web site. For example, all the pages that need a navigational menu can reference and configure the user control that provides that feature.

What's Good About User Controls

User controls are like embeddable pages. Turning an existing ASP.NET page into a user control requires only a few minor changes. User controls can be easily linked to any page that needs their services. Furthermore, changes to a user control's implementation do not affect the referencing page and only require you (or the runtime) to recompile the user control into an assembly.

What's Bad About User Controls

If you change the *internal* implementation of the user control, no referencing page will be affected. However, if you alter any aspect of the control's *public* interface (such as the class name, properties, methods, or events), all the pages that reference the control must be updated. This means you must manually retouch all the pages in the application that use the control. Then you must recompile these pages and deploy the assemblies. In addition, the next time a user views each page, the ASP.NET runtime will take a while to respond because the dynamic assembly for the page must be re-created.

Architecturally speaking, the solution based on user controls works just fine. In practice, though, it is not a very manageable model for large-scale applications—its effectiveness decreases as the complexity of the application (the number of pages involved) increases. If your site contains hundreds of pages, handling common elements through user controls can quickly become inefficient and unmanageable.

Visual Inheritance

ASP.NET pages are built as instances of special classes—code-behind or code file classes. Because pages are ultimately classes, what happens if you stuff part of the common UI in some base class and inherit new pages from there? This approach resembles the visual inheritance feature that Windows Forms developers have been familiar with for a long time.

Pure visual inheritance *à la* Windows Forms is impractical in ASP.NET. This is because ASP.NET pages are made of code *and* markup. The markup determines the position of the controls, while code adds logic and functionality. Building predefined graphic templates in the base class doesn't pose issues, but how would you import those standard UI blocks in derived pages and, more importantly, how would you merge those with controls local to the derived page?

In Windows Forms, controls have an absolute position that the designer reproduces, making it easy for developers to insert new controls anywhere. Web Forms, though, typically use relative positioning, which leads to either of the next two design choices. Option one is to supply predefined and named UI blocks in base classes and have derived classes load them in matching placeholders. Option two involves using master pages as defined in ASP.NET 2.0. To implement the former technique do the following:

1. Derive your page from a base class that knows how to create special UI blocks such as toolbars, headers, and footers. Each of these UI blocks has a unique name.

2. Add *<asp:placeholder>* controls to the derived page whose ID matches any of the predefined names. The base class contains the code to explore the control's tree and expand placeholders with predefined UI blocks.

This approach exploits inheritance but provides no WYSIWYG facilities, and it forces you to create UI blocks in code-only mode with no markup. This option is demonstrated in the companion code, but it should be considered only for ASP.NET 1.x applications. The second option mentioned—using master pages—is described in the following section.

Writing a Master Page

Available in ASP.NET 2.0 and newer versions, a *master page* is a distinct file referenced at the application level, as well as at the page level, that contains the static layout of the page. Regions that each "derived" page can customize are referenced in the master page with a special placeholder control. A derived page is simply a collection of blocks the runtime will use to fill the holes in the master. True visual inheritance *à la* Windows Forms is not a goal of ASP.NET master pages. The contents of a master page are merged into the content page, and they dynamically produce a new page class that is served to the user upon request. The merge process takes place at compile time and only once. In no way do the contents of the master serve as a base class for the content page.

What's a Master Page, Anyway?

A master page is similar to an ordinary ASP.NET page except for the top *@Master* directive and the presence of one or more *ContentPlaceHolder* server controls. A *ContentPlaceHolder* control defines a region in the master page that can be customized in a derived page. A master page without content placeholders is technically correct and will be processed correctly by the ASP.NET runtime. However, a placeholderless master fails in its primary goal—to be the supertemplate of multiple pages that look alike. A master page devoid of placeholders works like an ordinary Web page but with the extra burden required to process master pages. Here is a simple master page:

```
<%@ Master Language="C#" CodeFile="Simple.master.cs" Inherits="Simple" %>
<html>
<head runat="server">
    <title>Hello, master pages</title>
</head>
<body>
    <form id="form1" runat="server">
        <asp:Panel ID="HeaderPanel" runat="server"
            BackImageUrl="images/bkgnd.png" Width="100%">
            <asp:Label ID="TitleBox" runat="server"
                Text="Programming ASP.NET 3.5" />
        </asp:Panel>

        <asp:contentplaceholder id="PageBody" runat="server">
          <!-- derived pages will define content for this placeholder -->
        </asp:contentplaceholder>
```

```
        <asp:Panel ID="FooterPanel" runat="server"
            BackImageUrl="images/footer_bkgnd.png">
            <asp:Label ID="SubTitleBox" runat="server"
                Text="Dino Esposito" />
        </asp:Panel>
    </form>
</body>
</html>
```

As you can see, the master page looks like a standard ASP.NET page. Aside from the identifying *@Master* directive, the only key differences are *ContentPlaceHolder* controls. A page bound to this master automatically inherits all the contents of the master (the header and footer, in this case) and can attach custom markup and server controls to each defined placeholder. The content placeholder element is fully identified by its *ID* property and normally doesn't require other attributes.

The *@Master* Directive

The *@Master* directive distinguishes master pages from content pages and allows the ASP. NET runtime to properly handle each. A master page file is compiled to a class that derives from the *MasterPage* class. The *MasterPage* class, in turn, inherits *UserControl*. So, at the end of the day, a master page is treated as a special kind of ASP.NET user control.

The *@Master* directive supports quite a few attributes. For the most part, though, they are the same attributes that we reviewed in Chapter 3 for the *@Page* directive. Table 6-1 details the attributes that have a special meaning to master pages.

TABLE 6-1 Attributes of the *@Master* Directive

Attribute	Description
ClassName	Specifies the name for the class that will be created to render the master page. This value can be any valid class name but should not include a namespace. By default, the class name for simple.master is *ASP.simple_master*.
CodeFile	Indicates the URL to the file that contains any source code associated with the master page.
Inherits	Specifies a code-behind class for the master page to inherit. This can be any class derived from *MasterPage*.
MasterPageFile	Specifies the name of the master page file that this master refers to. A master can refer to another master through the same mechanisms a page uses to attach to a master. If this attribute is set, you will have nested masters.

The master page is associated with a code file that looks like the following:

```
public partial class Simple : System.Web.UI.MasterPage
{
    protected void Page_Load(object sender, EventArgs e)
    {
        ...
    }
    ...
}
```

The @*Master* directive doesn't override attributes set at the @*Page* directive level. For example, you can have the master set the language to Visual Basic .NET and one of the content pages can use C#. The language set at the master page level never influences the choice of the language at the content page level. You can use other ASP.NET directives in a master page—for example, @*Import*. However, the scope of these directives is limited to the master file and does not extend to child pages generated from the master.

The *ContentPlaceHolder* Container Control

The *ContentPlaceHolder* control acts as a container placed in a master page. It marks places in the master where related pages can insert custom content. A content placeholder is uniquely identified by an ID. Here's an example:

```
<asp:contentplaceholder runat="server" ID="PageBody" />
```

A content page is an ASP.NET page that contains only *<asp:Content>* server tags. This element corresponds to an instance of the *Content* class that provides the actual content for a particular placeholder in the master. The link between placeholders and content is established through the ID of the placeholder. The content of a particular instance of the *Content* server control is written to the placeholder whose ID matches the value of the *ContentPlaceHolderID* property, as shown here:

```
<asp:Content runat="server" contentplaceholderID="PageBody">
    ...
</asp:Content>
```

In a master page, you define as many content placeholders as there are customizable regions in the page. A content page doesn't have to fill all the placeholders defined in the bound master. However, a content page can't do more than just fill placeholders defined in the master.

Note A placeholder can't be bound to more than one content region in a single content page. If you have multiple *<asp:Content>* server tags in a content page, each must point to a distinct placeholder in the master.

Specifying Default Content

A content placeholder can be assigned default content that will show up if the content page fails to provide a replacement. Each *ContentPlaceHolder* control in the master page can contain default content. If a content page does not reference a given placeholder in the master, the default content will be used. The following code snippet shows how to define default content:

```
<asp:contentplaceholder runat="server" ID="PageBody">
    <!-- Use the following markup if no custom
        content is provided by the content page -->
    ...
</asp:contentplaceholder>
```

The default content is completely ignored if the content page populates the placeholder. The default content is never merged with the custom markup provided by the content page.

 Note A *ContentPlaceHolder* control can be used only in a master page. Content placeholders are not valid on regular ASP.NET pages. If such a control is found in an ordinary Web page, a parser error occurs.

Writing a Content Page

The master page defines the skeleton of the resulting page. If you need to share the layout or any UI block among all the pages, placing it in a master page will greatly simplify management of the pages in the application. You create the master and then think of your pages in terms of a delta from the master. The master defines the common parts of a certain group of pages and leaves placeholders for customizable regions. Each *content page*, in turn, defines what the content of each region has to be for a particular ASP.NET page. Figure 6-1 shows how to create a content page in Visual Studio.

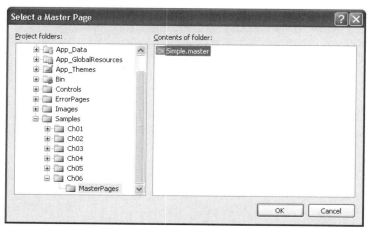

FIGURE 6-1 Adding a content page to a Visual Studio project.

The *Content* Control

The key part of a content page is the *Content* control—a mere container for other controls. The *Content* control is used only in conjunction with a corresponding *ContentPlaceHolder* and is not a standalone control. The master file that we considered earlier defines a single placeholder named *PageBody*. This placeholder represents the body of the page and is placed right below an HTML table that provides the page's header. Figure 6-2 shows a sample content page based on the aforementioned master page.

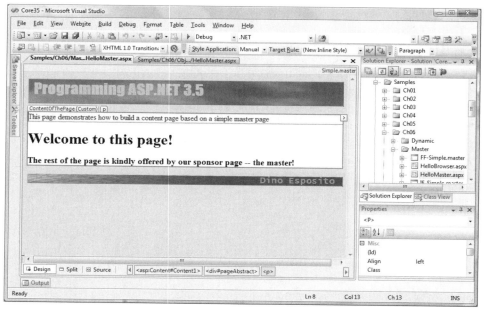

FIGURE 6-2 A preview of the content page. Notice the layout of the master page grayed out in the background.

Let's take a look at the source code of the content page:

```
<%@ Page Language="C#" MasterPageFile="Simple.master"
        CodeFile="HelloMaster.aspx.cs" Inherits="HelloMaster" %>

<asp:Content ID="Content1" ContentPlaceHolderID="PageBody" runat="server">
    <h1>Welcome to this page!</h1>
    <h3>The rest of the page is kindly offered by our sponsor
        page -- the master!</h3>
</asp:Content>
```

The content page is the resource that users invoke through the browser. When the user points her or his browser to this page, the output in Figure 6-3 is shown.

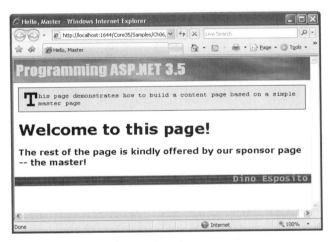

FIGURE 6-3 The sample page in action.

The replaceable part of the master is filled with the corresponding content section defined in the derived pages. A content page—that is, a page bound to a master—is a special breed of page in that it can *only* contain *<asp:Content>* controls. A content page is not permitted to host server controls outside of an *<asp:Content>* tag.

Let's explore the attachment of pages to masters in a bit more detail.

Attaching Pages to a Master

In the previous example, the content page is bound to the master by using the *MasterPageFile* attribute in the *@Page* directive. The attribute contains a string representing the path to the master page. Page-level binding is just one possibility—although it is the most common one.

You can also set the binding between the master and the content at the application or folder level. Application-level binding means that you link all the pages of an application to the same master. You configure this behavior by setting the *Master* attribute in the *<pages>* element of the principal *web.config* file:

```
<configuration>
    <system.web>
        <pages master="MyApp.master" />
    </system.web>
</configuration>
```

If the same setting is expressed in a child *web.config* file—a *web.config* file stored in a site subdirectory—all ASP.NET pages in the folder are bound to a specified master page.

Note that if you define binding at the application or folder level, all the Web pages in the application (or the folder) must have *Content* controls mapped to one or more placeholders in the master page. In other words, application-level binding prevents you from having (or later adding) a page to the site that is not configured as a content page. Any classic ASP.NET page in the application (or folder) that contains server controls will throw an exception.

Device-Specific Masters

Like all ASP.NET pages and controls, master pages can detect the capabilities of the underlying browser and adapt their output to the specific device in use. ASP.NET makes choosing a device-specific master easier than ever. If you want to control how certain pages of your site appear on a particular browser, you can build them from a common master and design the master to address the specific features of the browser. In other words, you can create multiple versions of the same master, each targeting a different type of browser.

How do you associate a particular version of the master and a particular browser? In the content page, you define multiple bindings using the same *MasterPageFile* attribute, but you prefix it with the identifier of the device. For example, suppose you want to provide ad hoc support for Microsoft Internet Explorer and Netscape browsers and use a generic master for any other browsers that users employ to visit the site. You use the following syntax:

```
<%@ Page masterpagefile="Base.master"
    ie:masterpagefile="ieBase.master"
    netscape6to9:masterpagefile="nsBase.master" %>
```

The *ieBase.master* file will be used for Internet Explorer; the *nsBase.master*, on the other hand, will be used if the browser belongs to the Netscape family, version 6.x to 9.0. In any other case, a device-independent master (*base.master*) will be used. When the page runs, the ASP.NET runtime automatically determines which browser or device the user is using and selects the corresponding master page, as shown in Figure 6-4.

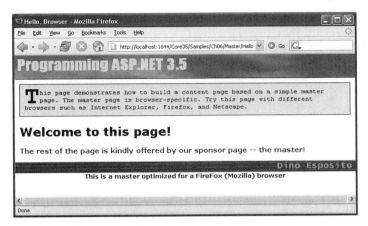

FIGURE 6-4 Browser-specific master pages.

The prefixes you can use to indicate a particular type of browser are those defined in the ASP. NET configuration files for browsers. Table 6-2 lists the most commonly used IDs.

TABLE 6-2 ID of Most Common Browsers

Browser ID	Browser Name
IE	Any version of Internet Explorer
Netscape3	Netscape Navigator 3.x
Netscape4	Netscape Communicator 4.x
Netscape6to9	Any version of Netscape higher than 6.0
Mozilla	Firefox
Opera	Opera
Up	Openwave-powered devices

It goes without saying that you can distinguish not just between up-level and down-level browsers but also between browsers and other devices such as cellular phones and personal digital assistants (PDAs). If you use device-specific masters, you must also indicate a device-independent master.

Warning Browser information is stored differently in ASP.NET 1.x and ASP.NET 2.0 and newer versions. In ASP.NET 1.x, you find it in the *<browserCaps>* section of the *machine.config* file. In newer versions, it is stored in text files with a *.browser* extension located in the *Browsers* folder under the ASP.NET installation path on the Web server. It's the same folder that contains *machine.config* and *WINDOWS%\Microsoft.NET\Framework\[version]\Config\Browsers*.

Setting the Title of a Page

As a collection of *<asp:Content>* tags, a content page is not allowed to include any markup that can specify the title of the page. Using the *<title>* tag is possible in the master page, but the master page—by design—works as the base for a variety of pages, each requiring its own title. The trick to setting the title is in using the *Title* property of the *@Page* directive in the content page:

```
<@Page MasterPageFile="simple.master" Title="Hello, master" %>
```

Note, though, setting the title of the page is possible only if the *<title>* or *<head>* tag in the master is flagged as *runat=server*. When adding a new master page to you Web solution, Visual Studio 2008 automatically marks both tags with the *runat=server* attribute.

Processing Master and Content Pages

The use of master pages slightly changes how pages are processed and compiled. For one thing, a page based on a master has a double dependency—on the *.aspx* source file (the content page) and on the *.master* file (the master page). If either of these pages changes, the dynamic page assembly will be re-created. Although the URL that users need is the URL of the content page, the page served to the browser results from the master page fleshed out with any replacement provided by the content page.

Compiling Master Pages

When the user requests an *.aspx* resource mapped to a content page—that is, a page that references a master—the ASP.NET runtime begins its job by tracking the dependency between the source *.aspx* file and its master. This information is persisted in a local file created in the ASP.NET temporary files folder. Next, the runtime parses the master page source code and creates a Visual Basic .NET or C# class, depending on the language set in the master page. The class inherits *MasterPage*, or the master's code file, and is then compiled to an assembly.

If multiple *.master* files are found in the same directory, they are all processed at the same time. Thus a dynamic assembly is generated for any master files found, even if only one of them is used by the ASP.NET page whose request triggered the compilation process. Therefore, don't leave unused master files in your Web space—they will be compiled anyway. Also note that the compilation tax is paid only the first time a content page is accessed within the application. When a user accesses another page that requires the second master, the response is faster because the previously compiled master is cached.

Serving the Page to Users

As mentioned, any ASP.NET page bound to a master page must have a certain structure—no server controls or literal text is allowed outside the *<asp:Content>* tag. As a result, the layout of the page looks like a plain collection of content elements, each bound to a particular placeholder in the master. The connection is established through the ID property. The *<asp:Content>* element works like a control container, much like the *Panel* control of ASP.NET or the HTML *<div>* tag. All the markup text is compiled to a template and associated with the corresponding placeholder property on the master class.

The master page is a special kind of user control with some templated regions. It's not coincidental, in fact, that the *MasterPage* class inherits from the *UserControl* class. Once instantiated as a user control, the master page is completed with templates generated from the markup defined in the content page. Next, the resulting control is added to the control tree of the current page. No other controls are present in the final page except those brought in by the master. Figure 6-5 shows the skeleton of the final page served to the user.

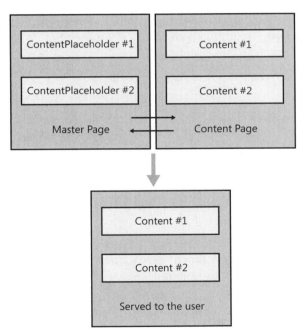

FIGURE 6-5 The structure of the final page in which the master page and the content page are merged.

Nested Master Pages

So far we've seen a pretty simple relationship between a master and a collection of content pages. However, the topology of the relationship can be made as complex and sophisticated as needed. A master can, in fact, be associated with another master and form a hierarchical, nested structure. When nested masters are used, any child master is seen and implemented as a plain content page in which extra *ContentPlaceHolder* controls are defined for an extra level of content pages. Put another way, a child master is a kind of content page that contains a combination of *<asp:Content>* and *<asp:ContentPlaceHolder>* elements. Like any other content page, a child master points to a master page and provides content blocks for its parent's placeholders. At the same time, it makes available new placeholders for its child pages.

> **Note** There's no architectural limitation in the number of nesting levels you can implement in your Web sites. Performance-wise, the depth of the nesting has a negligible impact on the overall functionality and scalability of the solution. The final page served to the user is always compiled on demand and never modified as long as dependent files are not touched.

Let's expand on the previous example to add an intermediate master page. The root master page—named *parent.master*—defines the header, the footer, and a replaceable region. Except for the class names, the source code is identical to the example we considered earlier. Let's have a closer look at the intermediate master—named *content.master*:

```
<%@ Master Language="C#" MasterPageFile="Parent.master"
    CodeFile="Content.master.cs" Inherits="ContentMaster" %>

<asp:Content runat="Server" ContentPlaceHolderID="ContentOfThePage" >
    <table width="100%"><tr>
        <td>
            <h1>Welcome to this page!</h1>
            <h3>The rest of the page is kindly offered by our
                sponsor page -- the master!</h3>
        </td>
        <td align="center">
            <h2>Select Your Favorite Chapter</h2>
            <asp:ContentPlaceHolder runat="server" ID="ChapterMenu" />
        </td>
    </tr></table>
</asp:Content>
```

As you can see, the master contains both a collection of *<asp:Content>* and *<asp:ContentPlaceHolder>* tags. The top directive is that of a master but contains the *MasterPageFile* attribute, which typically characterizes a content page.

The *content.master* resource is not directly viewable because it contains a virtual region. If you're familiar with object-oriented programming (OOP) terminology, I'd say that an intermediate master class is much like an intermediate virtual class that overrides some methods on the parent but leaves other abstract methods to be implemented by another derived class. Just as abstract classes can't be instantiated, nested master pages can't be viewed through a browser. In any case, the *content.master* resource is undoubtedly a master class, and its code file contains a class that inherits from *MasterPage*.

Warning Visual Studio 2008 is currently the only Microsoft tool capable of fully supporting nested master pages. If you're using older versions, you have to create an intermediate master page as a content page and then change the top directive to *@Master*, remove the *Title* attribute and, last but not least, change the base class of the code file to *MasterPage*.

The following code illustrates a content page that builds on two masters:

```
<%@ Page Language="C#" MasterPageFile="Content.master"
        CodeFile="SearchBook.aspx.cs" Inherits="SearchBook"
        Title="Book Viewer" %>

<asp:Content ContentPlaceHolderID="ChapterMenu" runat="server">

    <small>This is the nested master</small><hr />
    <asp:TextBox runat="server" Text="[Enter keywords]" />
    <asp:LinkButton runat="server" Text="Search ..." />
</asp:Content>
```

Figure 6-6 shows the results.

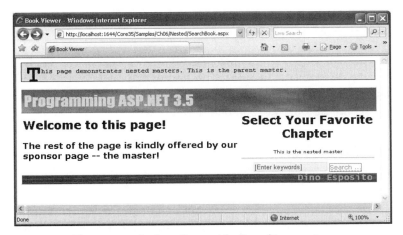

FIGURE 6-6 The page results from the combination of two master pages.

Admittedly, there's nothing in the figure that clearly indicates the existence of two masters; for your information, the innermost master controls the left-most area where the drop-down list is laid out. This means that writing another page that offers an alternative technique to find a chapter is particularly easy. Have a look at the code and Figure 6-7:

```
<%@ Page Language="C#" MasterPageFile="Content.master"
    CodeFile="ViewBook.aspx.cs" Inherits="ViewBook" %>

<asp:Content ContentPlaceHolderID="ChapterMenu" runat="server">
    <asp:DropDownList runat="server">

        ...

    </asp:DropDownList>
</asp:Content>
```

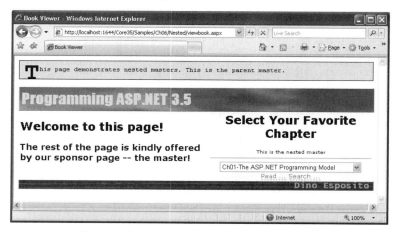

FIGURE 6-7 A slightly different page requires slightly different code!

A sapient use of master and content pages leads straight to an obvious conclusion: slightly different pages require slightly different code.

Programming the Master Page

You can use code in content pages to reference properties, methods, and controls in the master page, with some restrictions. The rule for properties and methods is that you can reference them if they are declared as public members of the master page. This includes public page-scope variables, public properties, and public methods.

Exposing Master Properties

To give an identity to a control in the master, you simply set the *runat* attribute and give the control an ID. Can you then access the control from within a content page? Not directly. The only way to access the master page object model is through the *Master* property. Note, though, that the *Master* property of the *Page* class references the master page object for the content page. This means that only public properties and methods defined on the master page class are accessible.

The following code enhances the previous master page to make it expose the text of the header as a public property:

```
public partial class SimpleWithProp : System.Web.UI.MasterPage
{
    protected void Page_Load(object sender, EventArgs e)
    {
    }
```

```
    public string TitleBoxText
    {
        get { return TitleBox.Text; }
        set { TitleBox.Text = value; }
    }
}
```

The header text of Figure 6-3 (shown earlier) is represented by a *Label* control named *TitleBox*. The control's protection level makes it inaccessible from the outside world, but the public property *TitleBoxText* defined in the preceding code represents a public wrapper around the *Label*'s *Text* property. In the end, the master page has an extra public property through which programmers can set the text of the header.

Invoking Properties on the Master

The *Master* property is the only point of contact between the content page and its master. The bad news is that the *Master* property is defined to be of type *MasterPage*; as such, it doesn't know anything about any property or method definition specific to the master you're really working with. In other words, the following code wouldn't compile because no *TitleBoxText* property is defined on the *MasterPage* class:

```
public partial class HelloMaster : System.Web.UI.Page
{
    protected void Page_Load(object sender, EventArgs e)
    {
        Master.TitleBoxText = "Programming ASP.NET 3.5";
    }
}
```

What's the real type behind the *Master* property?

The *Master* property represents the master page object as compiled by the ASP.NET runtime engine. This class follows the same naming convention as regular pages—*ASP.XXX_master*, where *XXX* is the name of the master file. Developers can override the default class name by setting the *ClassName* attribute on the @*Master* directive. The attribute lets you assign a user-defined name to the master page class:

```
<%@ Master Inherits="SimpleWithProp" ... Classname="MasterWithProp" %>
```

In light of this, to be able to call custom properties or methods, you must first cast the object returned by the *Master* property to the actual type:

```
    ((ASP.MasterWithProp)Master).TitleBoxText = "Programming ASP.NET 3.5";
```

Interestingly enough, Visual Studio provides some facilities to let you identify the right dynamically generated type already at design time. See Figure 6-8.

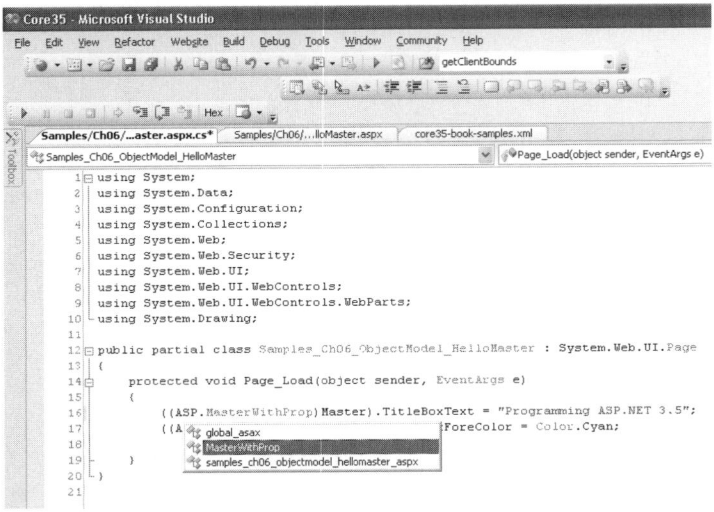

FIGURE 6-8 Visual Studio pops up names of classes that will be created only during the page execution.

The *ASP* namespace is the system namespace that all system dynamically defined types belong to. In Visual Studio, that namespace is properly recognized and handled by IntelliSense.

The *@MasterType* Directive

By adding the *@MasterType* directive in the content page, you can avoid all the casting just shown. The *@MasterType* informs the compiler about the real type of the *Master* property. The *Master* property is declared of the right type in the dynamically created page class, and this allows you to write strong-typed code, as follows:

```
<%@ Page Language="C#" MasterPageFile="SimpleWithProp.master"
    CodeFile="HelloMasterType.aspx.cs" Inherits="HelloMasterType" %>
<%@ MasterType VirtualPath="SimpleWithProp.master" %>
```

In the code file, you can have the following statements:

```
protected void Page_Load(object sender, EventArgs e)
{
    Master.TitleBoxText = "Programming ASP.NET 3.5";
}
```

The *@MasterType* directive supports two mutually exclusive attributes—*VirtualPath* and *TypeName*. Both serve to identify the master class to use. The former does it by URL; the latter by type name.

Changing the Master Page Dynamically

To associate an ASP.NET content page with a master page—keeping in mind that in no case can you associate a classic ASP.NET page with a master—you use the *MasterPageFile* attribute of the *@Page* directive. *MasterPageFile*, though, is also a read-write property on the *Page* class that points to the name of the master page file. Can you dynamically select the master page via code and based on runtime conditions?

Using a dynamically changing master page is definitely possible in ASP.NET and is suitable, for example, for applications that can present themselves to users through different skins. However, programmatically selecting the master page is not a task that you can accomplish at any time. To be precise, you can set the *MasterPageFile* property only during the *PreInit* page event—that is, before the runtime begins working on the request.

```
protected void Page_PreInit(object sender, EventArgs e)
{
    MasterPageFile = "simple2.master";
}
```

If you try to set the *MasterPageFile* property in *Init* or *Load* event handlers, an exception is raised.

> **Note** The *Master* property represents the current instance of the master page object, is a read-only property, and can't be set programmatically. The *Master* property is set by the runtime after loading the content of the file referenced by the *MasterPageFile* property.

Working with Themes

For years, CSS styles have helped site developers to easily and efficiently design pages with a common and consistent look and feel. Although page developers can select the CSS file programmatically on the server, at its core CSS remains an inherent client-side technology, devised and implemented to apply skins to HTML elements. When you build ASP.NET pages, though, you mostly work with server controls.

CSS styles can be used to style server controls, but they're not the right tool for the job. The main issue here is that ASP.NET controls can have properties that are not the direct emanation of a CSS style property. The appearance of an ASP.NET control can be affected by an array of resources—images, strings, templates, markup, combinations of various CSS styles. To properly apply skins to ASP.NET server controls, CSS files are necessary but not sufficient. Enter ASP.NET themes.

ASP.NET themes are closely related to Windows XP themes. Setting a theme is as simple as setting a property, and all the settings the theme contains are applied in a single shot. Themes can be applied to individual controls and also to a page or an entire Web site.

Understanding ASP.NET Themes

More often than not, when you author a page you don't just focus on the tasks a certain set of controls must be able to accomplish. You also consider their appearance. Most of the time, you end up setting visual attributes such as colors, font, borders, and images. The more sophisticated the control, the more time you spend making it look nice rather than just functional.

In ASP.NET, the *DataGrid* control—one of the most popular and customizable controls—provides a gallery of predefined styles from which you choose the most appealing. This gallery of predefined styles is the *DataGrid*'s auto-format feature. *DataGrid*'s built-in styles are implemented through a set of predefined settings that Visual Studio applies to the control at design time. The auto-format feature saves testing and typing and lets you choose the style visually. Added as a time-saving feature, auto-format addresses the issue only partially, as it has two main drawbacks. First, a lot of visual attributes are still persisted to the *.aspx* source file, making rich pages hard to read and maintain. Second, the list of available formats is kind of closed and can't be further extended or personalized if you're not writing Visual Studio ad hoc designers for the specific control.

Wouldn't it be great if you could compose your pages just by picking controls off the toolbox and connecting them, without even bothering about their final look? Wouldn't it be nice if you could then simply create an additional file in the project to define visual attributes for each type of control? In this way, the *.aspx* source file would be free of verbose visual attributes and you could change the style of controls at will, even dynamically, while performing little or no modifications to the original page. ASP.NET themes provide exactly this capability.

What's a Theme, Anyway?

A *theme* is a set of *skins* and associated auxiliary files such as style sheets and images—a sort of super CSS file. Once enabled, the theme determines the appearance of all controls under its jurisdiction. Consider the following simple markup:

```
<asp:Calendar ID="Calendar1" runat="server" />
```

Without themes, the calendar will look grayish, spare, and spartan. With a theme added, the same markup renders a more colorful and appealing calendar. As you can see, a neat separation exists between the page contents and formatting rules. Look at Figure 6-9. Which do you think is the unthemed calendar?

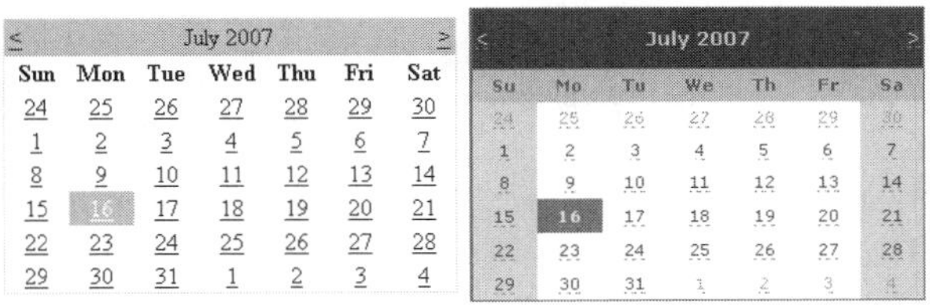

FIGURE 6-9 The same controls, with and without themes.

To fully understand ASP.NET themes, you must be familiar with a few terms, which are detailed in Table 6-3.

TABLE 6-3 ASP.NET Themes Terminology

Term	Definition
Skin	A named set of properties and templates that can be applied to one or more controls on a page. A skin is always associated with a specific control type.
Style sheet	A CSS or server-side style sheet file that can be used by pages on a site.
StyleSheet Theme	A theme used to abstract control properties from controls. The application of this theme means that the control can still override the theme.
Customization Theme	A theme used to abstract control properties from controls, but the theme overrides the control and any style sheet theme.

Imagine you are creating a new Web site and would like it to be visually appealing from the start. Instead of having to learn all the available style properties of each employed control, you just use ASP.NET themes. Using a built-in theme in a page is as easy as setting a property, as we'll see in a moment. With this change, pages automatically inherit a new, and hopefully attractive, appearance. For example, if you add a *Calendar* control to a page, it automatically renders with the default appearance defined in the theme.

Selecting a theme for one or more pages doesn't necessarily bind you to the settings of that theme. Through the Visual Studio designer, you can review the pages and manually adjust some styles in a control if you want to.

> **Note** The following convention holds true in this book and, in general, in related literature. Unless otherwise suggested by the context, the word "theme" indicates a customization theme. A style sheet theme is usually referred to as "a style sheet theme."

Structure of a Theme

Themes are expressed as the union of various files and folders living under a common root directory. Themes can be global or local. Global themes are visible to all Web applications installed on a server machine. Local themes are visible only to the application that defines them. Global themes are contained in child directories located under the following path. The name of the directory is the name of the theme.

```
%WINDOWS%\Microsoft.NET\Framework\[version]\ASP.NETClientFiles\Themes
```

Local themes are specialized folders that live under the *App_Themes* folder at the root of the application. Figure 6-10 shows a sample theme (named Core35-Basic) in a Web application.

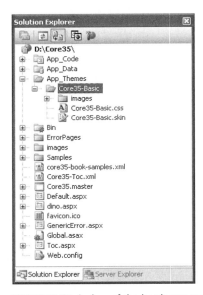

FIGURE 6-10 A view of the book companion code's official theme in Visual Studio.

As you can see, the theme in the figure consists of a *.css* file and a *.skin* file, plus a subdirectory of images. Generally, themes can contain a mix of the following resources:

- **CSS files**   Also known as *style sheets*, CSS files contain style definitions to be applied to elements in an HTML document. Written according to a tailormade syntax, CSS styles define how elements are displayed and where they are positioned on your page. Web browsers that support only HTML 3.2 and earlier will not apply CSS styles. The World Wide Web Consortium (W3C) maintains and constantly evolves CSS standards. Visit *http://www.w3.org* for details on current CSS specifications. CSS files are located in the root of the theme folder.

- **Skin files**   A skin file contains the theme-specific markup for a given set of controls. A skin file is made by a sequence of control definitions that include predefined values for most visual properties and supported templates. Each skin is control-specific and has a unique name. You can define multiple skins for a given control. A skinned control has the original markup written in the *.aspx* source file modified by the content of the skin. The way the modification occurs depends on whether a customization or a style sheet theme is used. Skin files are located in the root of the theme folder.

■ **Image files**   Feature-rich ASP.NET controls might require images. For example, a pageable *DataGrid* control might want to use bitmaps for first or last pages that are graphically compliant to the skin. Images that are part of a skin are typically located in an *Images* directory under the theme folder. (You can change the name of the folder as long as the name is correctly reflected by the skin's attributes.)

■ **Templates**   A control skin is not limited to graphical properties but extends to define the layout of the control—for templated controls that support this capability. By stuffing template definitions in a theme, you can alter the internal structure of a control while leaving the programming interface and behavior intact. Templates are defined as part of the control skin and persisted to skin files.

The content types just listed are not exhaustive, but they do cover the most commonly used data you might want to store in a theme. You can have additional subdirectories filled with any sort of data that makes sense to skinned controls. For example, imagine you have a custom control that displays its own user interface through the services of an external ASP.NET user control (*.ascx*). Skinning this control entails, among other things, indicating the URL to the user control. The user control becomes an effective part of the theme and must be stored under the theme folder. Where exactly? That is up to you, but opting for a *Controls* subdirectory doesn't seem to be a bad idea. We'll return to this point later when building a sample theme.

Customization Themes vs. Style Sheet Themes

There are two forms of themes—customization themes and style sheet themes. Customization themes are used for post customization of a site. The theme overrides any property definition on the control found in the *.aspx* source. By changing the page's theme, you entirely modify the appearance of the page without touching the source files. If you opt for customization theming, you just need minimal markup for each control in the ASP.NET page.

Style sheet themes are similar to CSS style sheets, except that they operate on control properties rather than on HTML element styles. Style sheet themes are applied immediately after the control is initialized and before the attributes in the *.aspx* file are applied. In other words, with a style sheet theme developers define default values for each control that are in fact overridden by settings in the *.aspx* source.

Important Customization themes and style sheet themes use the same source files. They differ only in how the ASP.NET runtime applies them to a page. The same theme can be applied as a customization theme or a style sheet theme at different times.

The difference between customization and style sheet themes is purely a matter of which takes priority over which. Let's review the resultant form of a control when a customization theme and style sheet theme are applied. Imagine you have the following markup:

```
<asp:Calendar ID="Calendar1" runat="server" backcolor="yellow" />
```

If the page that contains this markup is bound to a customization theme, the calendar shows up as defined in the theme. In particular, the background of the calendar will be of the color defined by the theme.

If the page is bound to a style sheet theme, instead, the background color of the calendar is yellow. The other properties are set in accordance with the theme.

Theming Pages and Controls

You can apply themes at various levels—application, folder, and individual pages. In addition, within the same theme you can select different skins for the same type of control.

Setting a theme at the application level affects all the pages and controls in the application. It's a feature you configure in the application's *web.config* file:

```
<system.web>
    <pages theme="Core35-Basic" />
</system.web>
```

The *theme* attribute sets a customization theme, while the *styleSheetTheme* attribute sets a style sheet theme. Note that the case is important in the *web.config*'s schema. Likewise, a theme can be applied to all the pages found in a given folder and below that folder. To do so, you create a new *web.config* file in an application's directory and add the section just shown to it. All the pages in that directory and below it will be themed accordingly. Finally, you can select the theme at the page level and have styles and skins applied only to that page and all its controls.

Enabling Themes on a Page

To associate a theme with a page, you set the *Theme* or *StyleSheetTheme* attribute on the @ *Page* directive, and you're all set:

```
<% @Page Language="C#" Theme="Core35-Basic" %>
<% @Page Language="C#" StyleSheetTheme="Core35-Basic" %>
```

Also in this case, *Theme* sets a customization theme, whereas *StyleSheetTheme* indicates a style sheet theme.

Bear in mind that the name of the selected theme must match the name of a subdirectory under the *App_Themes* path or the name of a global theme. If a theme with a given name exists both locally to the application and globally to the site, the local theme takes precedence. Figure 6-11 shows IntelliSense support for themes in Visual Studio.

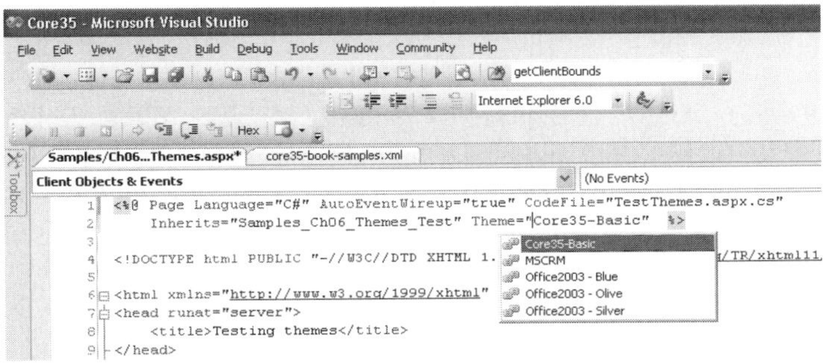

FIGURE 6-11 IntelliSense support for themes in Visual Studio.

While we're speaking of precedence, it is important to note that themes have a hierarchical nature: directory-level themes takes precedence over application-level themes, and page-level themes override any other themes defined around the application. This hierarchy is independent of which attributes are used—*Theme* or *StyleSheetTheme*—to enable theming.

Note Setting both *Theme* and *StyleSheetTheme* attributes is not prohibited, even though it is not a recommended practice. There's a behavioral gap between the two forms of themes that should make clear which one you need in any situation. However, if you set both attributes, consider that both themes will be applied—first the style sheet theme and then the customization theme. The results depend on the CSS cascading mechanism and ultimately is determined by the CSS settings of each theme.

Applying Skins

A skin file looks like a regular ASP.NET page as it is populated by control declaration and import directives. Each control declaration defines the default appearance of a particular control. Consider the following excerpt from a skin file:

```
<!-- This is a possible skin for a Button control -->
<asp:Button runat="server"
    BorderColor="darkgray"
    Font-Bold="true"
    BorderWidth="1px"
    BorderStyle="outset"
    ForeColor="DarkSlateGray"
    BackColor="gainsboro" />
```

The net effect of the skin is that every *Button* control in a themed page will be rendered as defined by the preceding markup. If the theme is applied as a style sheet, the settings just shown will be overridable by the developer; if the theme is a customization theme, those settings determine the final look and feel of the control. Properties that the theme leaves blank are set according to the control's defaults or the *.aspx* source.

> **Important** Whatever theme you apply—customization or style sheet—control properties can always be modified through code in page events such as *Init* and *Load*.

A theme can contain multiple skins for a given control, each identified with a unique name—the *SkinID* attribute. When the *SkinID* attribute is set, the skin is said to be a *named skin*. A theme can contain any number of named skins per control, but just one unnamed (default) skin. You select the skin for a control in an ASP.NET themed page by setting the control's *SkinID* property. The value of the control's *SkinID* property should match an existing skin in the current theme. If the page theme doesn't include a skin that matches the *SkinID* property, the default skin for that control type is used. The following code shows two named skins for a button within the same theme:

```
<!-- Place these two definitions in the same .skin file -->
<asp:button skinid="skinClassic" BackColor="gray" />
<asp:button skinid="skinTrendy" BackColor="lightcyan" />
```

When you enable theming on a page, by default all controls in that page will be themed except controls, and individual control properties, that explicitly disable theming.

> **Note** The automatic application of themes to all controls in a page makes it easy to customize a page that has no knowledge of skins, including existing pages written for ASP.NET 1.x.

Taking Control of Theming

The ASP.NET theming infrastructure provides the *EnableTheming* Boolean property to disable skins for a control and all its children. You can configure a page or control to ignore themes by setting the *EnableTheming* property to *false*. The default value of the property is *true*. *EnableTheming* is defined on the *Control* class and inherited by all server controls and pages. If you want to disable theme support for all controls in a page, you can set the *EnableTheming* attribute on the *@Page* directive.

> **Important** Note that the *EnableTheming* property can be set only in the *Page_PreInit* event for static controls—that is, controls defined in the *.aspx* source. For dynamic controls—that is, controls created programmatically—you must have set the property before adding the control to the page's control tree. A control is added to the page's control tree when you add to the *Controls* collection of the parent control—typically, the form or another control in the form.

When is disabling themes useful? Themes are great at ensuring that all page controls have a consistent look and feel, but at the same time themes override the visual attributes of any control for which a skin is defined. You can control the overriding mechanism a bit by switching style sheet and customization themes. However, when you want a control or page to maintain its predefined look, you just disable themes for that page or control.

Note that disabling themes affects *only* skins, not CSS styles. When a theme includes one or more CSS style-sheet files, they are linked to the *<head>* tag of the resulting HTML document and, after that, are handled entirely by the browser. As you can easily guess, there's not much a Web browser can know about ASP.NET themes!

Theming Controls

Themes style server controls to the degree that each control allows. By default, all control properties are themeable. Theming can be disabled on a particular property by applying the *Themeable* attribute on the property declaration, as follows:

```
[Themeable(false)]
public virtual bool CausesValidation
{
    get { ... }
    set { ... }
}
```

You can't change the *Themeable* attribute for built-in server controls. You have that option for custom controls instead. Moreover, for custom controls you should use the *Themeable* attribute to prevent theming of behavioral properties such as the *CausesValidation* property just shown. Themes should be used only on visual properties that uniquely affect the appearance of the control. Finally, the *Themeable* attribute can be applied to the class declaration of a custom control to stop it from ever bothering about themes:

```
[Themeable(false)]
public MyControl : Control
{
    ...
}
```

Putting Themes to Work

Finding a bunch of themes that suit your needs, free or for a small fee, shouldn't be a problem. However, this is a bad reason for not learning how to build your own themes. As mentioned, themes consist of several supporting files, including CSS style sheets and control skins to decorate HTML elements and server controls, respectively, and any other supporting images or files that make up the final expected result.

I firmly believe that building nice-looking, consistent, usable themes is not a programmer's job. It is a task that designers and graphics people can easily accomplish ten times better and faster. However, themes are more than CSS files, and what's more, they are in the area of control properties—exactly the realm of the developer. In short, developers should provide guidance to theme designers much more than we did in the past with CSS authors.

As a first step, let's review the key differences between CSS files and themes.

CSS vs. Themes

Themes are similar to CSS style sheets in that both apply a set of common attributes to any page where they are declared. Themes differ from CSS style sheets in a few key ways, however.

First and foremost, themes work on control properties, whereas CSS style sheets operate on styles of HTML elements. Because of this, with themes you can include auxiliary files and specify standard images for a *TreeView* or *Menu* control, the paging template of a *DataGrid*, or the layout of a *Login* control. In addition, themes can optionally force overriding of local property values (customization themes) and not cascade as CSS style sheets do.

Because themes incorporate CSS style-sheet definitions and apply them along with other property settings, there's no reason for preferring CSS style sheets over themes in new ASP. NET applications.

> **Note** In Visual Studio 2008, you'll find a brand new, and extremely effective, CSS Designer tool. The tool allows you to manage CSS styles applied to the various elements of a page. It is interesting to note, though, that the tool doesn't capture CSS styles applied through a stylesheet defined in a theme. It works perfectly with CSS, however, when you link to the page using the *<head>* node and from a non-theme folder.

Creating a Theme

To create a new theme in a Visual Studio ASP.NET solution, you start by creating a new folder under *App_Themes*. The simplest way to do this is by right-clicking on the *App_Themes* node and selecting a theme folder. Next, you add theme files to the folder, and when you're done, you can even move the entire directory to the root path of global themes on the Web server.

Typical auxiliary files that form a theme are listed in Figure 6-12. They are CSS style-sheet files, skin files, XML or text files, and extensible style-sheet files (XSLT). Empty files of the specified type are created in the theme folder and edited through more or less specialized text editors in Visual Studio.

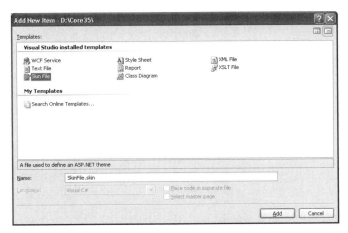

FIGURE 6-12 Adding auxiliary files to an ASP.NET theme.

A skin file is a collection of a control's markup chunks, optionally named through the *SkinID* attribute. You can create a skin file by cutting and pasting the markup of controls you visually configured in a sample page. If some properties of the skinned controls require resources, you can point them to a path inside the theme folder. Here's an example:

```
<asp:BulletedList runat="server"
    Font-Names="Verdana"
    BulletImageURL="Images/smokeandglass_bullet2.gif"
    BulletStyle="CustomImage"
    BackColor="transparent"
    ForeColor="#585880" />
```

This skin of the *BulletedList* control points to a theme-specific URL for the bullet image. The directory *Images* is intended to be relative to the theme folder. Needless to say, the name *Images* is totally arbitrary. Should the skin require other external files, you could group them in other theme subdirectories.

A skin file can define the appearance of built-in server controls as well as custom controls. To skin a custom control, though, you must first reference it in the skin file (just as you would reference it in a typical page file), as follows.

```
<%@ Register TagPrefix="x"
             Namespace="Samples.Core35.Controls"
             Assembly="Core35.Controls" %>
```

Next, you add the desired default markup for any control defined in the specified assembly and namespace.

Loading Themes Dynamically

You can apply themes dynamically, but this requires a bit of care. The ASP.NET runtime loads theme information immediately after the *PreInit* event fires. When the *PreInit* event fires, the name of any theme referenced in the *@Page* directive is already known and will be used unless it is overridden during the event. If you want to enable your users to change themes on the fly, you create a *Page_PreInit* event handler. The following code shows the code file of a sample page that changes themes dynamically:

```
public partial class TestThemes : System.Web.UI.Page
{
    protected void Page_Load(object sender, EventArgs e)
    {
        if (!IsPostBack) {
            ThemeList.DataSource = GetAvailableThemes();
            ThemeList.DataBind();
        }
    }

    void Page_PreInit(object sender, EventArgs e)
    {
        string theme = "";
        if (Page.Request.Form.Count > 0)
            theme = Page.Request["ThemeList"].ToString();
        if (theme == "None")
            theme = "";
        this.Theme = theme;
    }

    protected StringCollection GetAvailableThemes()
    {
        string path = Request.PhysicalApplicationPath + @"App_Themes";
        DirectoryInfo dir = new DirectoryInfo(path);
        StringCollection themes = new StringCollection();
        foreach (DirectoryInfo di in dir.GetDirectories())
            themes.Add(di.Name);

        return themes;
    }
}
```

Figure 6-13 shows the page in action. The drop-down list control enumerates the installed application themes and lets you choose the one to apply. The selected theme is then applied in the *PreInit* event and immediately reflected. In the *PreInit* event, no view state has been restored yet; so *Request.Form* is the only safe way to access a posted value like the selected theme.

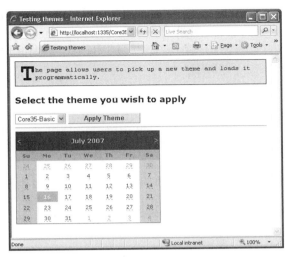

FIGURE 6-13 Changing themes dynamically in a sample page.

Working with Wizards

Master pages and themes give you the power of building similar-looking, rich pages that share graphics, control layout, and even some functionality. A special type of rich page is the page that implements a wizard. More common in Windows desktop applications than in Web scenarios, wizards are typically used to break up large forms to collect user input. A wizard is a sequence of related steps, each associated with an input form and a user interface. Users move through the wizard sequentially, but they are normally given a chance to skip a step or jump back to modify some of the entered values. A wizard is conceptually pretty simple, but implementing it over HTTP connections can be tricky. Everybody involved with serious Web development can only heartily welcome the introduction of the *Wizard* control.

An Overview of the *Wizard* Control

The *Wizard* control supports both linear and nonlinear navigation. It allows you to move backward to change values and to skip steps that are unnecessary due to previous settings or because users don't want to fill those fields. Like many other ASP.NET controls, the *Wizard* supports themes, styles, and templates.

The *Wizard* is a composite control and automatically generates some constituent controls such as navigation buttons and panels. As you'll see in a moment, the programming interface of the control has multiple templates that provide for in-depth customization of the overall user interface. The control also guarantees that state is maintained no matter where you move—backward, forward, or to a particular page. All the steps of a wizard must be declared within the boundaries of the same *Wizard* control. In other words, the wizard must be self-contained and not provide page-to-page navigation.

Structure of a Wizard

As shown in Figure 6-14, a wizard has four parts: header, view, navigation bar, and sidebar.

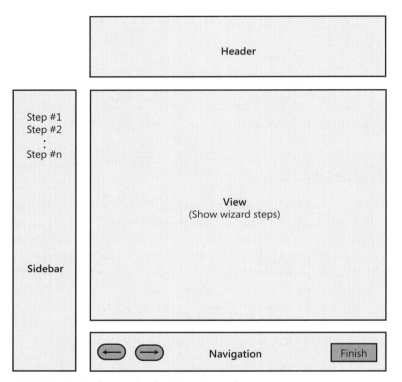

FIGURE 6-14 The four parts of a *Wizard* control.

The header consists of text you can set through the *HeaderText* property. You can change the default appearance of the header text by using its style property; you can also change the structure of the header by using the corresponding header template property. If *HeaderText* is empty and no custom template is specified, no header is shown for the wizard.

The view displays the contents of the currently active step. The wizard requires you to define each step in an *<asp:wizardstep>* element. An *<asp:wizardstep>* element corresponds to a *WizardStep* control. Different types of wizard steps are supported; all wizard step classes inherit from a common base class named *WizardStepBase*.

All wizard steps must be grouped in a single *<wizardsteps>* tag, as shown in the following code:

```
<asp:wizard runat="server" DisplaySideBar="true">
  <wizardsteps>
    <asp:wizardstep runat="server" steptype="auto" id="step1">
      First step
    </asp:wizardstep>
    <asp:wizardstep runat="server" steptype="auto" id="step2">
      Second step
    </asp:wizardstep>
    <asp:wizardstep runat="server" steptype="auto" id="finish">
      Final step
    </asp:wizardstep>
  </wizardsteps>
</asp:wizard>
```

The navigation bar consists of auto-generated buttons that provide any needed functionality—typically, going to the next or previous step or finishing. You can modify the look and feel of the navigation bar by using styles and templates.

The optional sidebar is used to display content in the left side of the control. It provides an overall view of the steps needed to accomplish the wizard's task. By default, it displays a description of each step, with the current step displayed in boldface type. You can customize the sidebar using styles and templates. Figure 6-15 shows the default user interface. Each step is labeled using the ID of the corresponding *<asp:wizardstep>* tag.

FIGURE 6-15 A wizard with the default sidebar on the left side.

Wizard Styles and Templates

You can style all the various parts and buttons of a *Wizard* control by using the properties listed in Table 6-4.

TABLE 6-4 The *Wizard* Control's Style Properties

Style	Description
CancelButtonStyle	Sets the style properties for the wizard's Cancel button
FinishCompleteButtonStyle	Sets the style properties for the wizard's Finish button
FinishPreviousButtonStyle	Sets the style properties for the wizard's Previous button when at the finish step
HeaderStyle	Sets the style properties for the wizard's header
NavigationButtonStyle	Sets the style properties for navigation buttons
NavigationStyle	Sets the style properties for the navigation area
SideBarButtonStyle	Sets the style properties for the buttons on the sidebar
SideBarStyle	Sets the style properties for the wizard's sidebar
StartStepNextButtonStyle	Sets the style properties for the wizard's Next button when at the start step
StepNextButtonStyle	Sets the style properties for the wizard's Next button
StepPreviousButtonStyle	Sets the style properties for the wizard's Previous button
StepStyle	Sets the style properties for the area where steps are displayed

The contents of the header, sidebar, and navigation bar can be further customized with templates. Table 6-5 lists the available templates.

TABLE 6-5 The *Wizard* Control's Template Properties

Style	Description
FinishNavigationTemplate	Specifies the navigation bar shown before the last page of the wizard. By default, the navigation bar contains the Previous and Finish buttons.
HeaderTemplate	Specifies the title bar of the wizard.
SideBarTemplate	Used to display content in the left side of the wizard control.
StartNavigationTemplate	Specifies the navigation bar for the first view in the wizard. By default, it contains only the Next button.
StepNavigationTemplate	Specifies the navigation bar for steps other than first, finish, or complete. By default, it contains Previous and Next buttons.

In addition to using styles and templates, you can control the programming interface of the *Wizard* control through a few properties.

The Wizard's Programming Interface

Table 6-6 lists the properties of the *Wizard* control, excluding style and template properties and properties defined on base classes.

TABLE 6-6 Main Properties of the *Wizard* Control

Property	Description
ActiveStep	Returns the current wizard step object. The object is an instance of the *WizardStep* class.
ActiveStepIndex	Gets and sets the 0-based index of the current wizard step.
DisplayCancelButton	Toggles the visibility of the *Cancel* button. The default value is *false*.
DisplaySideBar	Toggles the visibility of the sidebar. The default value is *false*.
HeaderText	Gets and sets the title of the wizard.
SkipLinkText	The ToolTip string that the control associates with an invisible image, as a hint to screen readers. The default value is "Skip Navigation Links" and is localized based on the server's current locale.
WizardSteps	Returns a collection containing all the *WizardStep* objects defined in the control.

A wizard in action is fully represented by its collection of step views and buttons. In particular, you'll recognize the following buttons: *StartNext*, *StepNext*, *StepPrevious*, *FinishComplete*, *FinishPrevious*, and *Cancel*. Each button is characterized by properties to get and set the button's image URL, caption, type, and destination URL after a click. The name of a property is the name of the button followed by a suffix. The available suffixes are listed in Table 6-7.

TABLE 6-7 Suffix of Button Properties

Suffix	Description
ButtonImageUrl	Gets and sets the URL of the image used to render the button
ButtonText	Gets and sets the text for the button
ButtonType	Gets and sets the type of the button: push button, image, or link button
DestinationPageUrl	Gets and sets the URL to jump to once the button is clicked

Note that names in Table 6-7 do not correspond to real property names. You have the four properties in this table for each distinct type of wizard button. The real name is composed by the name of the button followed by any of the suffixes—for example, *CancelButtonText*, *FinishCompleteDestinationPageUrl*, and so on.

The *Wizard* control also supplies a few interesting methods—for example, *GetHistory*, which is defined as follows:

```
public ICollection GetHistory()
```

GetHistory returns a collection of *WizardStepBase* objects. The order of the items is determined by the order in which the wizard's pages were accessed by the user. The first object returned—the one with an index of 0—is the currently selected wizard step. The second object represents the view before the current one, and so on.

The second method, *MoveTo*, is used to move to a particular wizard step. The method's prototype is described here:

```
public void MoveTo(WizardStepBase step)
```

The method requires you to pass a *WizardStepBase* object, which can be problematic. However, the method is a simple wrapper around the setter of the *ActiveStepIndex* property. If you want to jump to a particular step and not hold an instance of the corresponding *WizardStep* object, setting *ActiveStepIndex* is just as effective.

Table 6-8 lists the key events in the life of a *Wizard* control in an ASP.NET page.

TABLE 6-8 Events of the *Wizard* Control

Event	Description
ActiveViewChanged	Raised when the active step changes
CancelButtonClick	Raised when the *Cancel* button is clicked
FinishButtonClick	Raised when the *Finish Complete* button is clicked
NextButtonClick	Raised when any *Next* button is clicked
PreviousButtonClick	Raised when any *Previous* button is clicked
SideBarButtonClick	Raised when a button on the sidebar is clicked

As you can see, there's a common click event for all *Next* and *Previous* buttons you can find on your way. A *Next* button can be found on the *Start* page as well as on all step pages. Likewise, a *Previous* button can be located on the *Finish* page too. Whenever a *Next* button is clicked, the page receives a *NextButtonClick* event; whenever a *Previous* button is clicked, the control raises a *PreviousButtonClick* event.

Adding Steps to a Wizard

A *WizardStep* object represents one of the child views that the wizard can display. The *WizardStep* class ultimately derives from *View* and adds just a few public properties to it. A *View* object represents a control that acts as a container for a group of controls. A view is hosted within a *MultiView* control. (See Chapter 4.) To create its output, the wizard makes internal use of a *MultiView* control. However, the wizard is not derived from the *MultiView* class.

You define the views of a wizard through distinct instances of the *WizardStep* class, all grouped under the *<WizardSteps>* tag. The *<WizardSteps>* tag corresponds to the *WizardSteps* collection property exposed by the *Wizard* control:

```
<WizardSteps>
    <asp:WizardStep>
        . . .
    </asp:WizardStep>
    <asp:WizardStep>
        . . .
    </asp:WizardStep>
</WizardSteps>
```

Each wizard step is characterized by a title and a type. The *Title* property provides a brief description of the view. This information is not used unless the sidebar is enabled. If the sidebar is enabled, the title of each step is used to create a list of steps. If the sidebar is enabled but no title is provided for the various steps, the ID of the *WizardStep* objects is used to populate the sidebar, as shown earlier in Figure 6-15.

While defining a step, you can also set the *AllowReturn* property, which indicates whether the user is allowed to return to the current step from a subsequent step. The default value of the property is *true*.

Types of Wizard Steps

The *StepType* property indicates how a particular step should be handled and rendered within a wizard. Acceptable values for the step type come from the *WizardStepType* enumeration, as listed in Table 6-9.

TABLE 6-9 Wizard Step Types

Property	Description
Auto	The default setting, which forces the wizard to determine how each contained step should be treated.
Complete	The last page that the wizard displays, usually after the wizard has been completed. The navigation bar and the sidebar aren't displayed.
Finish	The last page used for collecting user data. It lacks the *Next* button, and it shows the *Previous* and *Finish* buttons.
Start	The first screen displayed, with no *Previous* button.
Step	All other intermediate pages, in which the *Previous* and *Next* buttons are displayed.

When the wizard is in automatic mode—the default type *Auto*—it determines the type of each step based on the order in which the steps appear in the source code. For example, the first step is considered to be of type *Start* and the last step is marked as *Finish*. No *Complete* step is assumed. If you correctly assign step types to your wizard steps yourself, rather than use the *Auto* type, the order in which you declare your steps in the *.aspx* source is not relevant.

Creating an Input Step

The following code shows a sample wizard step used to collect the provider name and the connection string to connect to a database and search for some data. For better graphical results, the content of the step is encapsulated in a fixed-height *<div>* tag. If all the steps are configured in this way, users navigating through the wizard won't experience sudden changes in the overall page size and layout.

```
<asp:wizardstep ID="Wizardstep1" runat="server" title="Connect">
    <div>
        <table>
            <tr><td>Provider</td><td>
                <asp:textbox runat="server" id="ProviderName"
                            text="System.Data.SqlClient" />
            </td></tr>
            <tr><td>Connection String</td><td>
                <asp:textbox runat="server" id="ConnString"
                    text="SERVER=(local);DATABASE=northwind;... " />
            </td></tr>
            <tr><td height="100px"></td></tr>
        </table>
    </div>
</asp:wizardstep>
```

Figure 6-16 shows a preview of the step. As you can guess, the step is recognized as a *Start* step. As a result, the wizard is added only to the *Next* button.

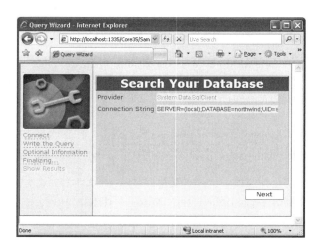

FIGURE 6-16 A sample *Start* wizard step.

A wizard is usually created for collecting input data, so validation becomes a critical is-sue. You can validate the input data in two nonexclusive ways—using validators and using transition event handlers.

The first option involves placing validator controls in the wizard step. This guarantees that invalid input—empty fields or incompatible data types—is caught quickly and, optionally, already on the client.

```
<asp:requiredfieldvalidator ID="RequiredField1" runat="server"
    text="*"
    errormessage="Must indicate a connection string"
    setfocusonerror="true"
    controltovalidate="ConnString" />
```

If you need to access server-side resources to validate the input data, you're better off using transition event handlers. A transition event is an event the wizard raises when it is about to switch to another view. For example, the *NextButtonClick* event is raised when the user clicks the *Next* button to jump to the subsequent step. You can intercept this event, do any required validation, and cancel the transition if necessary. We'll return to this topic in a moment.

Defining the Sidebar

The sidebar is a left-side panel that lists buttons to quickly and randomly reach any step of the wizard. It's a sort of quick-launch menu for the various steps that form the wizard. You control the sidebar's visibility through the Boolean *DisplaySideBar* attribute and define its contents through the *SideBarTemplate* property.

Regardless of the template, the internal layout of the sidebar is not left entirely to your imagination. In particular, the *<SideBarTemplate>* tag must contain a *DataList* control with a well-known ID—*SideBarList*. In addition, the *<ItemTemplate>* block must contain a but-ton object with the name of *SideBarButton*. The button object must be any object that implements the *IButtonControl* interface.

> **Note** For better graphical results, you might want to use explicit heights and widths for all steps and the sidebar as well. Likewise, the push buttons in the navigation bar might look better if they are made the same size. You do this by setting the *Width* and *Height* properties on the *NavigationButtonStyle* object.

Navigating Through the Wizard

When a button is clicked to move to another step, an event is fired to the hosting page. It's up to you to decide when and how to perform any critical validation, such as deciding whether or not conditions exist to move to the next step.

In most cases, you'll want to perform server-side validation only when the user clicks the Finish button to complete the wizard. You can be sure that whatever route the user has taken within the wizard, clicking the Finish button will complete it. Any code you bind to the *FinishButtonClick* event is executed only once, and only when strictly necessary.

By contrast, any code bound to the *Previous* or *Next* button executes when the user moves back or forward. The page posts back on both events.

Filtering Page Navigation with Events

You should perform server-side validation if what the user can do next depends on the data he or she entered in the previous step. This means that in most cases you just need to write a *NextButtonClick* event handler:

```
<asp:wizard runat="server" id="QueryWizard"
    OnNextButtonClick="OnNext">
    ...
</asp:wizard>
```

If the user moves back to a previously visited page, you can usually ignore any data entered in the current step and avoid validation. Because the user is moving back, you can safely assume he or she is not going to use any fresh data. When a back movement is requested, you can assume that any preconditions needed to visit that previous page are verified. This happens by design if your users take a sequential route.

If the wizard's sidebar is enabled, users can jump from page to page in any order. If the logic you're implementing through the wizard requires that preconditions be met before a certain step is reached, you should write a *SideBarButtonClick* event handler and ensure that the requirements have been met.

A wizard click event requires a *WizardNavigationEventHandler* delegate (which is defined for you by ASP.NET):

```
public delegate void WizardNavigationEventHandler(
    object sender,
    WizardNavigationEventArgs e);
```

The *WizardNavigationEventArgs* structure contains two useful properties that inform you about the 0-based indexes of the page being left and the page being displayed. The *CurrentStepIndex* property returns the index of the last page visited; the *NextStepIndex* returns the index of the next page. Note that both properties are read-only.

The following code shows a sample handler for the Next button. The handler prepares a summary message to show when the user is going to the *Finish* page.

```
void OnNext(object sender, WizardNavigationEventArgs e)
{
    // Collect the input data if going to the last page
    // -1 because of 0-based indexing, add -1 if you have a Complete page
    if (e.NextStepIndex == QueryWizard.WizardSteps.Count - 2)
        PrepareFinalStep();
}
void PrepareFinalStep()
{
    string cmdText = DetermineCommandText();

    // Show a Ready-to-go message
    StringBuilder sb = new StringBuilder("");
    sb.AppendFormat("You're about to run: <br><br>{0}<hr>", cmdText);
    sb.Append("<b><br>Ready to go?</b>");
    ReadyMsg.Text = sb.ToString();
}

string DetermineCommandText()
{
    // Generate and return command text here
}
```

Each page displayed by the wizard is a kind of panel (actually, a view) defined within a parent control—the wizard. This means that all child controls used in all steps must have a unique ID. It also means that you can access any of these controls just by name. For example, if one of the pages contains a text box named, say, ProviderName, you can access it from any event handler by using the ProviderName identifier.

The preceding code snippet is an excerpt from a sample wizard that collects input and runs a database query. The first step picks up connection information, whereas the second step lets users define tables, fields, and optionally a WHERE clause. The composed command is shown in the *Finish* page, where the wizard asks for final approval. (See Figure 6-17.)

The full source code of the wizard is in the companion code for this book.

FIGURE 6-17 Two successive pages of the sample wizard: query details and the *Finish* step.

Canceling Events

The *WizardNavigationEventArgs* structure also contains a read/write Boolean property named *Cancel*. If you set this property to *true*, you just cancel the ongoing transition to the destination page. The following code shows how to prevent the display of the next step if the user is on the *Start* page and types in **sa** as the user ID:

```
void OnNext(object sender, WizardNavigationEventArgs e)
{
    if (e.CurrentStepIndex == 0 &&
        ConnString.Text.IndexOf("UID=sa") > -1)
    {
        e.Cancel = true;
        return;
    }
}
```

You can cancel events from within any transition event handler and not just from the *NextButtonClick* event handler. This trick is useful to block navigation if the server-side validation of the input data has failed. If you do cause a step to fail, though, you're responsible for showing some feedback to the user.

> **Note** You can't cancel navigation from within the *ActiveViewChanged* event. This event follows any transition events, such as the *NextButtonClick* or *PreviousButtonClick* event, and occurs when the transition has completed. Unlike transition events, the *ActiveViewChanged* event requires a simpler, parameterless handler—*EventHandler*.

Finalizing the Wizard

All wizards have some code to execute to finalize the task. If you use the ASP.NET *Wizard* control, you place this code in the *FinishButtonClick* event handler. Figure 6-18 shows the final step of a wizard that completed successfully.

```
void OnFinish(object sender, WizardNavigationEventArgs e)
{
    string finalMsg = "The operation completed successfully.";
    try
    {
        // Complete the wizard (compose and run the query)
        string cmd = DetermineCommandText();
        DataTable table = ExecuteCommand(ConnString.Text, cmd);
        grid.DataSource = table;
        grid.DataBind();

        // OK color
        FinalMsg.ForeColor = Color.Blue;
    }
```

```
    catch (Exception ex) {
        FinalMsg.ForeColor = Color.Red;
        finalMsg = String.Format("The operation cannot be completed
                                due to:<br />{0}", ex.Message);
    }
    finally {
        FinalMsg.Text = finalMsg;
    }
}

string DetermineCommandText()
{
    // Generate and return command text here
}

DataTable ExecuteCommand()
{
    // Execute database query here
}
```

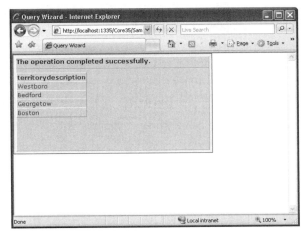

FIGURE 6-18 The final step of a wizard that completed successfully.

If the wizard contains a *Complete* step, that page should be displayed after the Finish button is clicked and the final task has completed. If something goes wrong with the update, you should either cancel the transition to prevent the *Complete* page from even appearing or adapt the user interface of the completion page to display an appropriate error message. Which option you choose depends on the expected behavior of the implemented operation. If the wizard's operation can fail or succeed, you let the wizard complete and display an error message in case something went wrong. If the wizard's operation must complete successfully unless the user quits, you should not make the transition to the *Complete* page; instead, provide users with feedback on what went wrong and give them a chance to try again.

Conclusion

Since version 1.0, ASP.NET has been characterized by a well-balanced mix of low-level and feature-rich tools. Using low-level tools such as events, HTTP modules, and HTTP handlers, you can plug into the ASP.NET pipeline to influence the processing of requests at every stage. At the same time, ASP.NET offers a wealth of feature-rich components for those who don't need control over every little step.

Starting with ASP.NET 2.0, the quantity and quality of application services has grown significantly. The introduction of rich composition tools for building pages like the ones we examined in this chapter is just a confirmation of the trend. In this chapter, we explored master pages to create content pages based on a predefined template made of graphics and, optionally, code. Master pages are not pure object-oriented visual inheritance *à la* Windows Forms; instead, they benefit from aggregation and let derived pages personalize well-known regions of the master. With full support from the Visual Studio environment, master pages are a time-saving feature that brings concrete added value to ASP.NET solutions.

Likewise, themes let developers code pages and controls that allow users to apply skins at will. ASP.NET themes work like Windows XP themes, and overall they're a superset of CSS that covers control properties in addition to HTML element styles. Themes work well in conjunction with the user profile API we discussed in Chapter 5. Using both, developers can let end users choose the theme and persist its name back to the personalization storage layer.

Finally, wizards are made-to-measure controls to quickly and efficiently write multistep input forms that divide complex operations into simple steps.

With this chapter, we completed the first part of the book, dedicated to building ASP.NET pages. With the next chapter, we approach the world of data access and explore ways to add data to a Web site.

 ## Just the Facts

- A master page is a distinct file referenced at the application or page level that contains the static layout of the page.

- A master page contains regions that each *derived* page can customize.

- A *derived* page, or named content page, is a collection of markup blocks that the runtime will use to fill the regions in the master page.

- Content pages can't contain information other than contents for the master's placeholders.

- Regions in the master page can have a default content to be used if the content page doesn't provide any.

- You can define various masters for a page and have the system automatically pick up a particular one based on the browser's user agent string.

- Master pages can be nested and expose a strongly-typed object model.

- Themes are a collection of settings spread over various files that the ASP.NET runtime uses to give the whole site (or page) a consistent user interface.

- Themes become a kind of attribute and can be exported from one application to the next and applied to pages on the fly.

- Themes differ from CSS files because they let you style ASP.NET control properties and not just HTML elements.

- A theme contains skin files, CSS files, images, plus any other auxiliary file you might find useful.

- A skin file is a collection of ASP.NET control declarations. The system ensures that after instantiation each control of that type in the page will have exactly the same set of attributes.

- The wizard control manages multiple views inside a single control and provides an auto-generated user interface for you to move back and forth like in a desktop wizard.

Programming Microsoft® ASP.NET 3.5

Part II
Adding Data in an ASP.NET Site

Chapter 7
ADO.NET Data Providers

ADO.NET is a data-access subsystem in the Microsoft .NET Framework. It was heavily inspired by ActiveX Data Objects (ADO), which has been for years a very successful object model for writing data-aware applications. The key design criteria for ADO.NET are simplicity and performance. Those criteria typically work against each other, but with ADO.NET you get the power and performance of a low-level interface combined with the simplicity of a modern object model. Unlike ADO, though, ADO.NET has been purposely designed to observe general, rather than database-oriented, guidelines.

Several syntactical differences exist between the object models of ADO and ADO.NET. In spite of this, the functionalities of ADO and ADO.NET look much the same. This is because Microsoft put a lot of effort into aligning some programming aspects of the ADO.NET object model with ADO. In this way, seasoned data developers new to .NET don't need to become familiar with too many new concepts and can work with a relatively short learning curve. With ADO.NET, you probably won't be able to reuse much of your existing code. You'll certainly be able, though, to reuse all your skills. At the same time, novice developers face a relatively simple and easy-to-understand model, with a consistent design and a powerful set of features.

The ADO.NET framework is made of two distinct, but closely related, sets of classes—data providers and data containers. We tackle providers in this chapter and reserve containers for the next.

.NET Data Access Infrastructure

ADO.NET is the latest in a long line of database access technologies that began with the Open Database Connectivity (ODBC) API several years ago. Written as a C-style library, ODBC was designed to provide a uniform API to issue SQL calls to various database servers. In the ODBC model, database-specific drivers hide any difference and discrepancy between the SQL language used at the application level and the internal query engine. Next, COM landed in the database territory and started a colonization process that culminated with OLE DB.

OLE DB has evolved from ODBC and, in fact, the open database connectivity principle emerges somewhat intact in it. OLE DB is a COM-based API aimed at building a common lay-er of code for applications to access any data source that can be exposed as a tabular rowset of data. The OLE DB architecture is composed of two elements—a consumer and a provider. The consumer is incorporated in the client and is responsible for setting up COM-based com-munication with the data provider. The OLE DB data provider, in turn, receives calls from the consumer and executes commands on the data source. Whatever the data format and storage medium are, an OLE DB provider returns data formatted in a tabular layout—that is, with rows and columns. OLE DB uses COM to make client applications and data sources communicate.

Because it isn't especially easy to use and is primarily designed for coding from within C++ applications, OLE DB never captured the heart of programmers, even though it could guar-antee a remarkable mix of performance and flexibility. Next came ADO—roughly, a COM au-tomation version of OLE DB—just to make the OLE DB technology accessible from Microsoft Visual Basic and classic Active Server Pages (ASP) applications. When used, ADO acts as the real OLE DB consumer embedded in the host applications. ADO was invented in the age of connected, 2-tier applications, and the object model design reflects that. ADO makes a point of programming redundancy: it usually provides more than just one way of accomplishing key tasks, and it contains a lot of housekeeping code. For all these reasons, although it's in-credibly easy to use, an ADO-based application doesn't perform as efficiently as a pure OLE DB application.

> **Note** Using ADO in .NET applications is still possible, but for performance and consistency reasons its use should be limited to a few very special cases. For example, ADO is the only way you have to work with server cursors. In addition, ADO provides a schema management API to .NET Framework 1.x applications. On the other hand, ADO recordsets can't be directly bound to ASP.NET or Microsoft Windows Forms data-bound controls. We'll cover ASP.NET data binding in Chapter 9.

.NET Managed Data Providers

A key architectural element in the ADO.NET infrastructure is the *managed provider*, which can be considered as the .NET counterpart of the OLE DB provider. A managed data provider enables you to connect to a data source and retrieve and modify data. Compared to the OLE DB provider, a .NET managed provider has a simplified data access architecture made of a smaller set of interfaces and based on .NET Framework data types.

Note The .NET Framework 3.5 introduces new language features fully supported by Visual Studio 2008. One of the most important is the .NET Language Integrated Query, or LINQ for short. Essentially, LINQ helps make querying data a first-class programming concept. Developers can use LINQ with any data source and can express query behavior natively in the language of choice, optionally transforming query results into whatever format is desired. LINQ-enabled languages, such as the newest versions of C# and Visual Basic .NET, provide full type-safety and compile-time checking of query expressions. The .NET Framework 3.5 ships with built-in libraries that enable LINQ queries against collections, XML, and databases. In particular, LINQ-to-SQL is an object/relational mapping (O/RM) implementation that allows you to model a relational database (for example, a SQL Server database) using .NET classes. As a result, you can query the database tables and views using the LINQ syntax, and you can update, insert, and delete data from it. In addition, LINQ-to-SQL fully supports transactions and stored procedures. I'll cover LINQ-to-SQL in Chapter 10. However, for a wider and deeper coverage of the whole LINQ platform, you might want to take a look at the book *Introducing Microsoft LINQ* (Microsoft Press, 2007).

Building Blocks of a .NET Data Provider

The classes in the managed provider interact with the specific data source and return data to the application using the data types defined in the .NET Framework. The logical components implemented in a managed provider are those graphically featured in Figure 7-1.

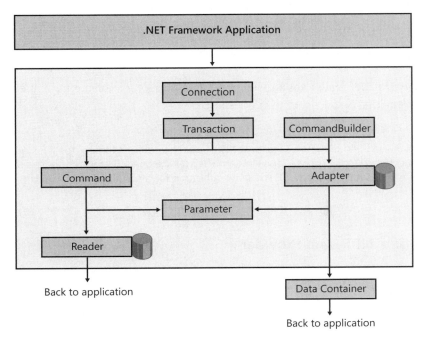

FIGURE 7-1 The .NET Framework classes that form a typical managed provider and their interconnections.

The functionalities supplied by a .NET data provider fall into a couple of categories:

- Support for disconnected data—that is, the capability of populating ADO.NET container classes with fresh data

- Support for connected data access, which includes the capability of setting up a connection and executing a command

Table 7-1 details the principal components of a .NET data provider.

TABLE 7-1 Principal Components of a .NET Data Provider

Component	Description
Connection	Creates a connection with the specified data source, including SQL Server, Oracle, and any data source for which you can indicate either an OLE DB provider or an ODBC driver
Transaction	Represents a transaction to be made in the source database server
Command	Represents a command that hits the underlying database server
Parameter	Represents a parameter you can pass to the command object
DataAdapter	Represents a database command that executes on the specified database server and returns a disconnected set of records
CommandBuilder	Represents a helper object that automatically generates commands and parameters for a *DataAdapter*
DataReader	Represents a read-only, forward-only cursor created on the underlying database server

Each managed provider that wraps a real-world database server implements all the objects in Table 7-1 in a way that is specific to the data source.

Caution You won't find in the .NET Framework any class named *Connection*. You'll find instead several connection-like classes, one for each supported .NET managed provider (for example, *SqlConnection* and *OracleConnection*). The same holds true for the other objects listed in the table.

Interfaces of a .NET Data Provider

The components listed in Table 7-1 are implemented based on methods and properties defined by the interfaces you see in Table 7-2.

TABLE 7-2 Interfaces of .NET Data Providers

Interface	Description
IDbConnection	Represents a unique session with a data source
IDbTransaction	Represents a local, nondistributed transaction
IDbCommand	Represents a command that executes when connected to a data source
IDataParameter	Allows implementation of a parameter to a command
IDataReader	Reads a forward-only, read-only stream of data created after the execution of a command
IDataAdapter	Populates a *DataSet* object, and resolves changes in the *DataSet* object back to the data source
IDbDataAdapter	Supplies methods to execute typical operations on relational databases (such as insert, update, select, and delete)

Note that all these interfaces except *IDataAdapter* are officially considered to be optional. However, any realistic data provider that manages a database server would implement them all.

> **Note** Individual managed providers are in no way limited to implementing all and only the interfaces listed in Table 7-2. Based on the capabilities of the underlying data source and its own level of abstraction, each managed provider can expose more components. A good example of this is the data provider for Microsoft SQL Server that you get in .NET Framework 2.0 and newer versions. It adds several additional classes to handle special operations, such as bulk copy, data dependency, and connection string building.

Managed Providers vs. OLE DB Providers

OLE DB providers and managed data providers are radically different types of components that share a common goal—to provide a unique and uniform programming interface for data access. The differences between OLE DB providers and .NET data providers can be summarized in the following points:

- **Component Technology**   OLE DB providers are in-process COM servers that expose a suite of COM interfaces to consumer modules. The dialog between consumers and providers takes place through COM and involves a number of interfaces. A .NET data provider is a suite of managed classes whose overall design looks into one *particular* data source rather than blinking at an abstract and universal data source, as is the case with OLE DB.

- **Internal Implementation**   Both types of providers end up making calls into the data-source programming API. In doing so, though, they provide a dense layer of code that separates the data source from the calling application. Learning from the OLE DB experience, Microsoft designed .NET data providers to be more agile and simple. Fewer interfaces are involved, and the conversation between the caller and the callee is more direct and as informal as possible.

- **Application Integration**   Another aspect of .NET that makes the conversation between caller and callee more informal is the fact that managed providers return data using the same data structures that the application would use to store it. In OLE DB, the data-retrieval process is more flexible, but it's also more complex because the provider packs data in flat memory buffers and leaves the consumer responsible for mapping that data into usable data structures.

Calling into an OLE DB provider from within a .NET application is more expensive because of the data conversion necessary to make the transition from the managed environment of the common language runtime (CLR) to the COM world. Calling a COM object from within a .NET application is possible through the COM interop layer, but doing so comes at a cost. In general, to access a data source from within a .NET application, you should always use a managed provider instead of OLE DB providers or ODBC drivers. You should be doing this primarily because of the transition costs, but also because managed providers are normally more modern tools based on an optimized architecture.

Some data sources, though, might not have a .NET data provider available. In these cases, resorting to old-fashioned OLE DB providers or ODBC drivers is a pure necessity. For this reason, the .NET Framework encapsulates in managed wrapper classes the logic needed to call into a COM-style OLE DB provider or a C-style ODBC driver.

Data Sources You Access Through ADO.NET

The .NET data provider is the managed component of choice for database vendors to expose their data in the most effective way. Ideally, each database vendor should provide a .NET-compatible API that is seamlessly callable from within managed applications. Unfortunately, this is not always the case. However, at least for the major database management systems (DBMS), a managed data provider can be obtained from either Microsoft or third-party vendors.

As of version 3.5, the .NET Framework supports the data providers listed in Table 7-3.

TABLE 7-3 Managed Data Providers in .NET

Data Source	Namespace	Description
SQL Server	*System.Data.SqlClient*	Targets various versions of SQL Server, including SQL Server 7.0, SQL Server 2000, and the newest SQL Server 2005
SQL Server CE	*Microsoft.SqlServerCe.Client*	Targets SQL Server 2005 Mobile Edition
OLE DB providers	*System.Data.OleDb*	Targets OLE DB providers, including SQLOLEDB, MSDAORA, and the Jet engine

Data Source	Namespace	Description
ODBC drivers	*System.Data.Odbc*	Targets several ODBC drivers, including those for SQL Server, Oracle, and the Jet engine
Oracle	*System.Data.OracleClient*	Targets Oracle 9i, and supports all of its data types

The OLE DB and ODBC managed providers listed in Table 7-3 are not specific to a physical database server, but rather they serve as a bridge that gives instant access to a large number of existing OLE DB providers and ODBC drivers. When you call into OLE DB providers, your .NET applications jumps out of the managed environment and issues COM calls through the COM interop layer.

Accessing SQL Server

As mentioned, Microsoft supplies a managed provider for SQL Server 7.0 and newer versions. Using the classes contained in this provider is by far the most effective way of accessing SQL Server. Figure 7-2 shows how SQL Server is accessed by .NET and COM clients.

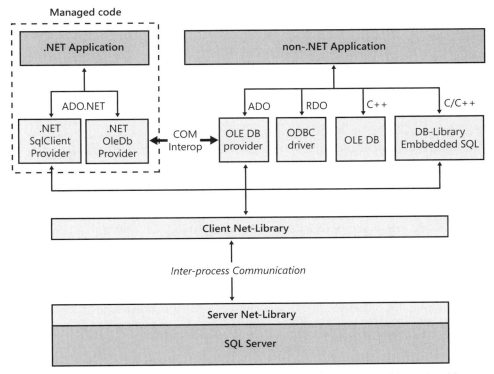

FIGURE 7-2 Accessing SQL Server by using the managed provider for OLE DB adds overhead because the objects called must pass through the COM interop layer.

A .NET application should always access a SQL Server database using the native data provider. Although it's possible to do so, you should have a good reason to opt for an alternative approach like using the OLE DB provider for SQL Server (named SQLOLEDB). A possible good reason is the need to use ADO rather than ADO.NET as the data-access library. The SQL Server native provider not only avoids paying the performance tax of going down to COM, it also implements some little optimizations when preparing the command for SQL Server.

Accessing Oracle Databases

The .NET Framework includes a managed provider for Oracle databases. The classes are located in the *System.Data.OracleClient* namespace in the *System.Data.OracleClient* assembly. Instead of using the managed provider, you can resort to the COM-based OLE DB provider (named MSDAORA) or the ODBC driver. Note, though, that the Microsoft OLE DB provider for Oracle does not support Oracle 9i and its specific data types. In contrast, Oracle 9i data types are fully supported by the .NET managed provider. So by using the .NET component to connect to Oracle, you not only get a performance boost but also increased programming power.

> **Note** The .NET data provider for Oracle requires Oracle client software (version 8.1.7 or later) to be installed on the system before you can use it to connect to an Oracle data source.

Microsoft is not the only company to develop a .NET data provider for Oracle databases. Data Direct, Core Lab, and Oracle itself also ship one. Each provider has its own set of features; for example, the Oracle provider (named ODP.NET) has many optimizations for retrieving and manipulating Oracle native types, such as any flavor of large objects (LOBs) and REF cursors. ODP.NET can participate in transactional applications, with the Oracle database acting as the resource manager and the Microsoft Distributed Transaction Coordinator (DTC) coordinating transactions.

Using OLE DB Providers

The .NET data provider for OLE DB providers is a data-access bridge that allows .NET applications to call into data sources for which a COM OLE DB provider exists. While this approach is architecturally less effective than using native providers, it is the only way to access those data sources when no managed providers are available.

The classes in the *System.Data.OleDb* namespace, though, don't support all types of OLE DB providers and have been optimized to work with only a few of them, as listed in Table 7-4.

TABLE 7-4 OLE DB Providers Tested

Name	Description
Microsoft.Jet.OLEDB.4.0	The OLE DB provider for the Jet engine implemented in Microsoft Access
MSDAORA	The Microsoft OLE DB provider for Oracle 7 that partially supports some features in Oracle 8
SQLOLEDB	The OLE DB provider for SQL Server 6.5 and newer

The preceding list does not include all the OLE DB providers that really work through the OLE DB .NET data provider. However, only the components in Table 7-4 are guaranteed to work well in .NET. In particular, the classes in the *System.Data.OleDb* namespace don't support OLE DB providers that implement any of the OLE DB 2.5 interfaces for semistructured and hierarchical rowsets. This includes the OLE DB providers for Exchange (EXOLEDB) and for Internet Publishing (MSDAIPP).

In general, what really prevents existing OLE DB providers from working properly within the .NET data provider for OLE DB is the set of interfaces they really implement. Some OLE DB providers—for example, those written using the Active Template Library (ATL) or with Visual Basic and the OLE DB Simple Provider Toolkit—are likely to miss one or more COM interfaces that the .NET wrapper requires.

Using ODBC Drivers

The .NET data provider for ODBC lets you access ODBC drivers from managed, ADO.NET-driven applications. Although the ODBC .NET data provider is intended to work with all compliant ODBC drivers, it is guaranteed to work well only with the drivers for SQL Server, Oracle, and Jet. Although ODBC might appear to now be an obsolete technology, it is still used in several production environments, and for some vendors it is still the only way to connect to their products.

You can't access an ODBC driver through an OLE DB provider. There's no technical reason behind this limitation—it's just a matter of common sense. In fact, calling the MSDASQL OLE DB provider from within a .NET application would drive your client through a double data-access bridge—one going from .NET to the OLE DB provider, and one going one level down to the actual ODBC driver.

The Provider Factory Model

ADO.NET takes into careful account the particularity of each DBMS and provides a programming model tailor-made for each one. All .NET data providers share a limited set of common features, but each has unique capabilities. The communication between the user code and the DBMS takes place more directly using ADO.NET. This model works better and faster and is probably clearer to most programmers.

But until version 2.0 of the .NET Framework, ADO.NET has one key snag. Developers must know in advance the data source they're going to access. Generic programming—that is, programming in which the same code targets different data sources at different times—is hard (but not impossible) to do. You can create a generic command object and a generic data reader, but not a generic data adapter and certainly not a generic connection. However, through the *IDbConnection* interface, you can work with a connection object without knowing the underlying data source. But you can never create a connection object in a weakly typed manner—that is, without the help of the *new* operator.

Instantiating Providers Programmatically

Starting with version 2.0, ADO.NET enhances the provider architecture and introduces the factory class. Each .NET data provider encompasses a factory class derived from the base class *DbProviderFactory*. A factory class represents a common entry point for a variety of services specific to the provider. Table 7-5 lists the main methods of a factory class.

TABLE 7-5 Principal Methods of a Factory Class

Method	Description
CreateCommand	Returns a provider-specific command object
CreateCommandBuilder	Returns a provider-specific command builder object
CreateConnection	Returns a provider-specific connection object
CreateDataAdapter	Returns a provider-specific data adapter object
CreateParameter	Returns a provider-specific parameter object

How do you get the factory of a particular provider? By using a new class, *DbProviderFactories*, that has a few static methods. The following code demonstrates how to obtain a factory object for the SQL Server provider:

```
DbProviderFactory fact;
fact = DbProviderFactories.GetFactory("System.Data.SqlClient");
```

The *GetFactory* method takes a string that represents the invariant name of the provider. This name is hard-coded for each provider in the configuration file where it is registered. By convention, the provider name equals its unique namespace.

GetFactory enumerates all the registered providers and gets assembly and class name information for the matching invariant name. The factory class is not instantiated directly. Instead, the method uses reflection to retrieve the value of the static *Instance* property of the factory class. The property returns the instance of the factory class to use. Once you hold a factory object, you can call any of the methods listed earlier in Table 7-5.

The following pseudocode gives you an idea of the internal implementation of the *CreateConnection* method for the *SqlClientFactory* class—the factory class for the SQL Server .NET data provider:

```
public DbConnection CreateConnection()
{
    return new SqlConnection();
}
```

Enumerating Installed Data Providers

You can use all .NET data providers registered in the configuration file. The following excerpt is from the *machine.config* file:

```
<system.data>
  <DbProviderFactories>
    <add name="SqlClient Data Provider"
        invariant="System.Data.SqlClient"
        description=".Net Framework Data Provider for SqlServer"
        type="System.Data.SqlClient.SqlClientFactory, System.Data "/>
    <add name="OracleClient Data Provider"
        invariant="System.Data.OracleClient"
        description=".Net Framework Data Provider for Oracle"
        type="System.Data.OracleClient.OracleFactory,
              System.Data.OracleClient" />
    ...
  </DbProviderFactories>
</system.data>
```

Each provider is characterized by an invariant name, a description, and a type that contains assembly and class information. The *GetFactoryClasses* method on the *DbProviderFactories* class returns this information packed in an easy-to-use *DataTable* object. The following sample page demonstrates how to get a quick list of the installed providers:

```
<%@ page language="C#" %>
<%@ import namespace="System.Data" %>
<%@ import namespace="System.Data.Common" %>

<script runat="server">
    void Page_Load (object sender, EventArgs e)
    {
        DataTable providers = DbProviderFactories.GetFactoryClasses();
        provList.DataSource = providers;
        provList.DataBind();
    }
</script>
```

```
<html>
<head runat="server"><title>List Factory Objects</title></head>
<body>
    <form runat="server">
        <asp:datagrid runat="server" id="provList" />
    </form>
</body>
</html>
```

The final page is shown in Figure 7-3.

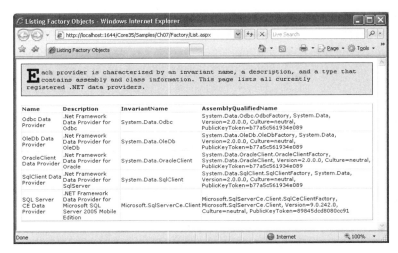

FIGURE 7-3 The list of the installed .NET data providers.

Database-Agnostic Pages

Let's write out some sample code to demonstrate how to craft database-agnostic pages. The sample page will contain three text boxes to collect the name of the provider, connection string, and command text.

```
protected void RunButton_Click(object sender, EventArgs e)
{
    string provider = ProviderNameBox.Text;
    string connString = ConnectionStringBox.Text;
    string commandText = CommandTextBox.Text;

    // Get the provider
    DbProviderFactory fact = DbProviderFactories.GetFactory(provider);

    // Create the connection
    DbConnection conn = fact.CreateConnection();
    conn.ConnectionString = connString;
```

```
    // Create the data adapter
    DbDataAdapter adapter = fact.CreateDataAdapter();
    adapter.SelectCommand = conn.CreateCommand();
    adapter.SelectCommand.CommandText = commandText;

    // Run the query
    DataTable table = new DataTable();
    adapter.Fill(table);

    // Shows the results
    Results.DataSource = table;
    Results.DataBind();
}
```

By changing the provider name and properly adapting the connection string and command, the same core code can now be used to work on other database servers.

> **Caution** Nothing presented here is invented; no magic and no tricks apply. This said, though, don't be fooled by the apparent simplicity of this approach. Be aware that in real-world applications data access is normally insulated in the boundaries of the Data Access Layer (DAL), and that practice suggests you have one DAL per supported data source. This is because the complexity of real problems need to be addressed by getting the most out of each data server. In the end, you need optimized data access code to take advantage of all the features of a given DBMS rather than generic code that you write once and which queries everywhere and everything.

Connecting to Data Sources

The ADO.NET programming model is based on a relatively standard and database-independent sequence of steps. You first create a connection, then prepare and execute a command, and finally process the data retrieved. As far as basic operations and data types are involved, this model works for most providers. Some exceptions are BLOB fields management for Oracle databases and perhaps bulk copy and XML data management for SQL Server databases.

In the rest of the chapter, we'll mostly discuss how ADO.NET data classes work with SQL Server (from version 7.0 onward). However, we'll promptly point out any aspect that is significantly different than other .NET data providers. To start out, let's see how connections take place.

> **More Info** For in-depth coverage of ADO.NET 2.0, see *Programming Microsoft ADO.NET 2.0 Applications: Advanced Topics* by Glenn Johnson (Microsoft Press, 2005) and *Programming ADO.NET 2.0 Core Reference* by David Sceppa (Microsoft Press, 2005)

The *SqlConnection* Class

The first step in working with an ADO.NET-based application is setting up the connection with the data source. The class that represents a physical connection to SQL Server is *SqlConnection*, and it is located in the *System.Data.SqlClient* namespace. The class is sealed (that is, not inheritable) and implements the *IDbConnection* interface. In ADO.NET, the interface is implemented through the intermediate base class *DbConnection*, which also provides additional features shared by all providers. (In fact, adding new members to the interface would have broken existing code.)

The *SqlConnection* class features two constructors, one of which is the default parameterless constructor. The second class constructor, on the other hand, takes a string containing the connection string:

```
public SqlConnection();
public SqlConnection(string);
```

The following code snippet shows the typical way to set up and open a SQL Server connection:

```
string connString = "SERVER=...;DATABASE=...;UID=...;PWD=...";
SqlConnection conn = new SqlConnection(connString);
conn.Open();
...
conn.Close();
```

Properties of the *SqlConnection* Class

Table 7-6 details the public properties defined on the *SqlConnection* class.

TABLE 7-6 Properties of the *SqlConnection* Class

Property	*IDbConnection* Interface Property?	Description
ConnectionString	Yes	Gets or sets the string used to open the database.
ConnectionTimeout	Yes	Gets the number of seconds to wait while trying to establish a connection.
Database	Yes	Gets the name of the database to be used.
DataSource		Gets the name of the instance of SQL Server to connect to. It corresponds to the *Server* connection string attribute.
PacketSize	No	Gets the size in bytes of network packets used to communicate with SQL Server. Set to 8192, it can be any value in the range from 512 through 32,767.

Property	IDbConnection Interface Property?	Description
ServerVersion	No	Gets a string containing the version of the current instance of SQL Server. The version string is in the form of *major.minor.release*.
State	Yes	Gets the current state of the connection: open or closed. Closed is the default.
StatisticsEnabled	No	Enables the retrieval of statistical information over the current connection. *Not available in ADO.NET 1.x.*
WorkStationId	No	Gets the network name of the client, which normally corresponds to the *WorkStation ID* connection string attribute.

An important characteristic to note about the properties of the connection classes is that they are all read-only except *ConnectionString*. In other words, you can configure the connection only through the tokens of the connection string, but you can read attributes back through handy properties.

> **Note** This characteristic of connection class properties in ADO.NET is significantly different than what you find in ADO, where many of the connection properties—for example, *ConnectionTimeout* and *Database*—were read/write.

Methods of the *SqlConnection* Class

Table 7-7 shows the methods available in the *SqlConnection* class.

TABLE 7-7 Methods of the *SqlConnection* Class

Method	IDbConnection Interface Method?	Description
BeginTransaction	Yes	Begins a database transaction. Allows you to specify a name and an isolation level.
ChangeDatabase	Yes	Changes the current database on the connection. Requires a valid database name.
Close	Yes	Closes the connection to the database. Use this method to close an open connection.
CreateCommand	Yes	Creates and returns a *SqlCommand* object associated with the connection.
Dispose	No	Calls *Close*.

Method	*IDbConnection* Interface Method?	Description
EnlistDistributedTransaction	No	If auto-enlistment is disabled, enlists the connection in the specified distributed Enterprise Services DTC transaction. *Not available in ADO.NET 1.0.*
EnlistTransaction	No, but defined on *DbConnection*	Enlists the connection on the specified local or distributed transaction. *Not available in ADO.NET 1.x.*
GetSchema	No, but defined on *DbConnection*	Retrieve schema information for the specified scope (that is, tables, databases). *Not available in ADO.NET 1.x.*
ResetStatistics	No	Resets the statistics service. *Not available in ADO.NET 1.x.*
RetrieveStatistics	No	Gets a hash table filled with the information about the connection, such as data transferred, user details, and transactions. *Not available in ADO.NET 1.x.*
Open	Yes	Opens a database connection.

Note that if the connection goes out of scope, it is not automatically closed. The garbage collector will eventually pick up the object instance, but the connection won't be closed because the garbage collector can't recognize the peculiarity of the object and handle it properly. Therefore, you must explicitly close the connection by calling *Close* or *Dispose* before the object goes out of scope.

> **Note**   Like many other disposable objects, connection classes implement the *IDisposable* interface, thus providing a programming interface for developers to dispose of the object. The dispose pattern entails the sole *Dispose* method; *Close* is not officially part of the pattern, but most classes implement it as well.

Changing Passwords

The *SqlConnection* class provides a static method named *ChangePassword* to let developers change the SQL Server password for the user indicated in the supplied connection string:

```
public static void ChangePassword(
    string connectionString, string newPassword)
```

An exception will be thrown if the connection string requires integrated security (that is, *Integrated Security=True* or an equivalent setting). The method opens a new connection to the server, requests the password change, and closes the connection once it has completed. The connection used to change the password is not taken out of the connection pool. The new password must comply with any password security policy set on the server, including minimum length and requirements for specific characters.

Note that *ChangePassword* works only on SQL Server 2005.

Accessing Schema Information

In ADO.NET 2.0 and beyond, all managed providers are expected to implement a *GetSchema* method for retrieving schema information. The standard providers offer the following over-loads of the method:

```
public override DataTable GetSchema();
public override DataTable GetSchema(string collection);
public override DataTable GetSchema(string collection, string[] filterVal)
```

The schema information you can retrieve is specific to the back-end system. For the full list of valid values, call *GetSchema* with no parameters. The following code shows how to retrieve all available collections and bind the results to a drop-down list:

```
// Get schema collections
SqlConnection conn = new SqlConnection(connString);
conn.Open();
DataTable table = conn.GetSchema();
conn.Close();

// Display their names
CollectionNames.DataSource = table;
CollectionNames.DataTextField = "collectionname";
CollectionNames.DataBind();
```

Figure 7-4 shows the available schema collections for a SQL Server 2000 machine. (For SQL Server 2005, it adds only a *UserDefinedTypes* collection.) Call *GetSchema* on, say, the *Databases* collection and you will get the list of all databases for the instance of SQL Server you are connected to. Likewise, if you call it on *Tables*, you will see the tables in the connected database.

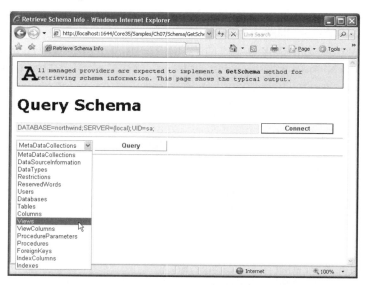

FIGURE 7-4 The list of available schema collections for a SQL Server database

Note The preceding code snippet introduces the *DataTable* class as well as data binding. We will cover the *DataTable* class—one of the most important ADO.NET container classes—in the next chapter. Data binding, on the other hand, will be the subject of Chapter 10.

The list of schema collections is expressed as a *DataTable* object with three columns— *CollectionName* is the column with names. The following code shows how to retrieve schemainformation regarding the collection name currently selected in the drop-down list—the *Views*:

```
string coll = CollectionNames.SelectedValue;
string connString = ConnStringBox.Text;
SqlConnection conn = new SqlConnection(connString);
conn.Open();
DataTable table = conn.GetSchema(coll);
conn.Close();
GridView1.DataSource = table;
GridView1.DataBind();
```

As Figure 7-5 demonstrates, the data is then bound to a grid for display.

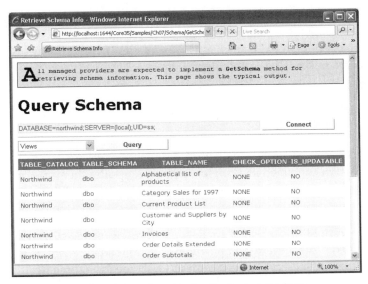

FIGURE 7-5 The list of views found in the Northwind database.

In ADO.NET 2.0 and beyond, all connection objects support *GetSchema* methods, as they are part of the new intermediate *DbConnection* class. In ADO.NET 1.x, you have different approaches depending on the target source. If you work with OLE DB, you get schema information through the OLE DB native provider calling the *GetOleDbSchemaTable* method. The following code shows how to get table information:

```
OleDbConnection conn = new OleDbConnection(connString);
conn.Open();
DataTable schema = cConn.GetOleDbSchemaTable(
    OleDbSchemaGuid.Tables,
    new object[] {null, null, null, "TABLE"});
conn.Close();
```

GetOleDbSchemaTable takes an *OleDbSchemaGuid* argument that identifies the schema information to return. In addition, it takes an array of values to restrict the returned columns. *GetOleDbSchemaTable* returns a *DataTable* populated with the schema information. Alternately, you can get information on available databases, tables, views, constraints, and so on through any functionality provided by the specific data source, such as stored procedures and views.

```
SqlConnection conn = new SqlConnection(connString);
SqlDataAdapter adapter = new SqlDataAdapter(
    "SELECT * FROM INFORMATION_SCHEMA.TABLES " +
        "WHERE TABLE_TYPE = 'BASE TABLE' " +
        "ORDER BY TABLE_TYPE", conn);
DataTable schema = new DataTable();
adapter.Fill(schema);
```

The *GetSchema* method unifies the approach for retrieving schema information. The *SqlDataAdapter* class that appears in the preceding code snippet is a special type of command that we'll explore in depth in the next chapter. One of its key characteristics is that it returns disconnected data packed in a *DataTable* or *DataSet*.

Connection Strings

To connect to a data source, you need a connection string. Typically made of semicolon-separated pairs of names and values, a connection string specifies settings for the database runtime. Typical information contained in a connection string includes the name of the database, location of the server, and user credentials. Other more operational information, such as connection timeout and connection pooling settings, can be specified too.

In many enterprise applications, the usage of connection strings is related to a couple of issues: how to store and protect them, and how to build and manage them. The .NET Framework provides excellent solutions to both issues as we'll see in a moment.

Needless to say, connection strings are database specific, although huge differences don't exist between, say, a connection string for SQL Server and Oracle databases. In this chapter, we mainly focus on SQL Server but point out significant differences.

Configuring Connection Properties

The *ConnectionString* property of the connection class can be set only when the connection is closed. Many connection string values have corresponding read-only properties in the connection class. These properties are updated when the connection string is set. The contents of the connection string are checked and parsed immediately after the *ConnectionString* property is set. Attribute names in a connection string are not case sensitive, and if a given name appears multiple times, the value of the last occurrence is used. Table 7-8 lists the keywords that are supported.

TABLE 7-8 Connection String Keywords for SQL Server

Keyword	Description
Application Name	Name of the client application as it appears in the SQL Profiler. Defaults to *.Net SqlClient Data Provider*.
Async	When *true*, enables asynchronous operation support. *Not supported in ADO.NET 1.x.*
AttachDBFileName or Initial File Name	The full path name of the file (.mdf) to use as an attachable database file.
Connection Timeout	The number of seconds to wait for the connection to take place. Default is 15 seconds.

Keyword	Description
Current Language	The SQL Server language name.
Database or Initial Catalog	The name of the database to connect to.
Encrypt	Indicates whether Secure Sockets Layer (SSL) encryption should be used for all data sent between the client and server. Needs a certificate installed on the server. Default is *false*.
Failover Partner	The name of the partner server to access in case of errors. Connection failover allows an application to connect to an alternate, or backup, database server if the primary database server is unavailable. *Not supported in ADO.NET 1.x.*
Integrated Security or Trusted_ Connection	Indicates whether current Windows account credentials are used for authentication. When set to *false*, explicit user ID and password need to be provided. The special value *sspi* equals *true*. Default is *false*.
MultipleActiveResultSets	When *true*, an application can maintain multiple active result sets. Set to *true* by default, this feature requires SQL Server 2005. *Not supported in ADO.NET 1.x.*
Network Library or Net	Indicates the network library used to establish a connection to SQL Server. Default is *dbmssocn*, which is based on TCP/IP.
Packet Size	Bytes that indicate the size of the packet being exchanged. Default is 8192.
Password or pwd	Password for the account logging on.
Persist Security Info	Indicates whether the managed provider should include password information in the string returned as the connection string. Default is *false*.
Server or Data Source	Name or network address of the instance of SQL Server to connect to.
User ID or uid	User name for the account logging on.
Workstation ID	Name of the machine connecting to SQL Server.

The network dynamic-link library (DLL) specified by the *Network Library* keyword must be installed on the system to which you connect. If you use a local server, the default library is *dbmslpcn*, which uses shared memory. For a list of options, consult the MSDN documentation.

Any attempt to connect to an instance of SQL Server should not exceed a given time. The *Connection Timeout* keyword controls just this. Note that a connection timeout of 0 causes the connection attempt to wait indefinitely; it does not indicate no wait time.

You normally shouldn't change the default packet size, which has been determined based on average operations and workload. However, if you're going to perform bulk operations in which large objects are involved, increasing the packet size can be of help because it decreases the number of reads and writes.

Some of the attributes you see listed in Table 7-8 are specific to ADO.NET 2.0 (and newer versions) and address features that have been introduced lately. They are asynchronous commands and multiple active result sets (MARS). MARS, in particular, removes a long-time constraint of the SQL Server programming model—that is, the constraint of having at most one pending request on a given session at a time. Before ADO.NET 2.0 and SQL Server 2005, several approaches have been tried to work around this limitation, the most common of which is using server-side cursors through ADO. We'll return to MARS later, in the section dedicated to SQL Server 2005.

Connection String Builders

How do you build the connection string to be used in an application? In many cases, you just consider it constant and read it out of a secured source. In other cases, though, you might need to construct it based on user input—for example, when retrieving user ID and password information from a dialog box. In ADO.NET 1.x, you can build the string only by blindly concatenating any name/value pairs. There are two major drawbacks with this technique. One is, the use of wrong keywords is caught only when the application goes under testing. More serious than the lack of a compile-time check, though, is that a blind pair concatenation leaves room for undesired data injections to attach users to a different database or to change in some way the final goal of the connection. Any measures to fend off injections and check the syntax should be manually coded, resulting in a specialized builder class—just like the brand new connection string builder classes you find in ADO.NET.

All default data providers support connection string builders in a guise that perfectly applies to the underlying provider. The following code snippet (and its result, shown in Figure 7-6) builds and displays a connection string for SQL Server:

```
SqlConnectionStringBuilder builder = new SqlConnectionStringBuilder();
builder.DataSource = serverName;
builder.UserID = userid;
builder.Password = pswd;
NewConnString.Text = builder.ConnectionString;
```

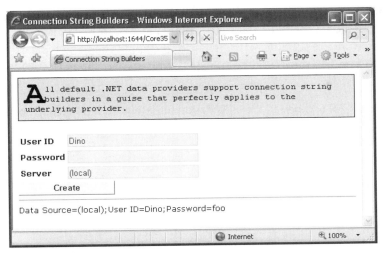

FIGURE 7-6 Building connection strings programmatically and securely.

By using connection string builders, you gain a lot in terms of security because you dramatically reduce injection. Imagine that a malicious user types in the password: *Foo;Trusted_Connection=true*. If you blindly concatenate strings, you might get the following:

```
Password=Foo;Trusted_Connection=true
```

Because the last pair wins, the connection will be opened based on the credentials of the logged-on user. If you use the builder class, you get the following appropriately quoted string:

```
Password="Foo;Trusted_Connection=true"
```

In addition, the builder class exposes all the supported 20+ keywords through easier-to-remember properties recognized by Microsoft IntelliSense.

Storing and Retrieving Connection Strings

Savvy developers avoid hard-coding connection strings in the compiled code. Configuration files (such as the *web.config* file) purposely support the *<appSettings>* named section, which is used to store custom data through name/value pairs. All these values populate the *AppSettings* collection and can be easily retrieved programmatically, as shown here:

```
string connString = ConfigurationSettings.AppSettings["NorthwindConn"];
```

This approach is far from perfect for two reasons. First, connection strings are not just data—they're a special kind of data not to be mixed up with general-purpose application settings. Second, connection strings are a critical parameter for the application and typically contain sensitive data. Therefore, at a minimum they need transparent encryption. Let's tackle storage first.

In the .NET Framework 2.0 and beyond, configuration files define a new section specifically designed to contain connection strings. The section is named *<connectionStrings>* and is laid out as follows:

```
<connectionStrings>
    <add name="NWind"
        connectionString="SERVER=...;DATABASE=...;UID=...;PWD=...;"
        providerName="System.Data.SqlClient" />
</connectionStrings>
```

You can manipulate the contents of the section by using *<add>*, *<remove>*, and *<clear>* nodes. You use an *<add>* node to add a new connection string to the current list, *<remove>* to remove a previously defined connection, and *<clear>* to reset all connections and create a new collection. By placing a *web.config* file in each of the application's directories, you can customize the collection of connection strings that are visible to the pages in the directory. Configuration files located in child directories can remove, clear, and extend the list of connection strings defined at the upper level. Note that each stored connection is identified with a name. This name references the actual connection parameters throughout the application. Connection names are also used within the configuration file to link a connection string to other sections, such as the *<providers>* section of *<membership>* and *<profile>* nodes.

All the connection strings defined in the *web.config* file are loaded into the new *ConfigurationManager.ConnectionStrings* collection. To physically open a connection based on a string stored in the *web.config* file, use following code:

```
string connStr;
connStr = ConfigurationManager.ConnectionStrings["NWind"].ConnectionString;
SqlConnection conn = new SqlConnection(connStr);
```

The full support from the configuration API opens up an interesting possibility for consuming connection strings—declarative binding. As we'll see in Chapter 9, ASP.NET 2.0 supports quite a few data source objects. A data source object is a server control that manages all aspects of data source interaction, including connection setup and command execution. You bind data source objects to data-bound controls and instruct the data source to retrieve data from a specific source. The great news is that you can now indicate the connection string declaratively, as follows:

```
<asp:SqlDataSource id="MySource" runat="server"
  ProviderName="System.Data.SqlClient"
  ConnectionString='<%#
    ConfigurationSettings.ConnectionStrings["NWind"].ConnectionString %>'
  SelectCommand="SELECT * FROM employees">
```

There's a lot more to be known about this feature, though, and we'll delve deeply into that later in the book. For now, it suffices to say that connection strings are much more than strings in the .NET Framework 2.0 and beyond.

Protecting Connection Strings

Starting with version 2.0, ASP.NET introduces a system for protecting sensitive data stored in the configuration system. It uses industry-standard XML encryption to encrypt specific sections of configuration files that might contain sensitive data. XML encryption (which you can learn more about at *http://www.w3.org/TR/xmlenc-core*) is a way to encrypt data and represent the result in XML. Prior to version 2.0, only a few specific ASP.NET sections that contain sensitive data support protection of this data using a machine-specific encryption in a registry key. This approach requires developers to come up with a utility to protect their own secrets—typically connection strings, credentials, and encryption keys.

In the newest versions of the .NET Framework, encryption of configuration sections is optional, and you can enable it for any configuration sections you want by referencing the name of the section in the *<protectedData>* section of the *web.config* file, as shown here:

```
<protectedData>
    <protectedDataSections>
        <add name="connectionStrings"
            provider="RSAProtectedConfigurationProvider" />
    </protectedDataSections>
</protectedData>
```

You can specify the type of encryption you want by selecting the appropriate provider from the list of available encryption providers. The .NET Framework comes with two predefined providers:

- **DPAPIProtectedConfigurationProvider**   Uses the Windows Data Protection API (DPAPI) to encrypt and decrypt data

- **RSAProtectedConfigurationProvider**   Default provider, uses the RSA encryption algorithm to encrypt and decrypt data

Being able to protect data stored in *web.config* is not a feature specific to connection strings. It applies, instead, to all sections, with very few exceptions. This said, let's see how to encrypt connection strings stored in the *web.config* file.

You can use the newest version of a popular system tool—*aspnet_regiis.exe*—or write your own tool by using the ASP.NET configuration API. If you use *aspnet_regiis*, examine the following code, which is a sample usage to encrypt connection strings for the Core35 application:

```
aspnet_regiis.exe -pe connectionStrings -app /core35
```

Note that the section names are case-sensitive. Note also that connection strings are stored in a protected area that is completely transparent to applications, which continue working as before. If you open the *web.config* file after encryption, you see something like the following:

```
<configuration>
  <protectedData>
    <protectedDataSections>
      <add name="connectionStrings"
           provider="RSAProtectedConfigurationProvider" />
    </protectedDataSections>
  </protectedData>
  <connectionStrings>
    <EncryptedData …>
      ...
      <CipherData>
        <CipherValue>cQyofWFQ ... =</CipherValue>
      </CipherData>
    </EncryptedData>
  </connectionStrings>
</configuration>
```

To restore the *web.config* to its original clear state, you use the **–pd** switch in lieu of **–pe** in the aforementioned command line.

> **Caution** Any page that uses protected sections works like a champ as long as you run it inside the local Web server embedded in Visual Studio. You might get an RSA provider configuration error if you access the same page from within a canonical (and much more realistic) IIS virtual folder. What's up with that?
>
> The RSA-based provider—the default protection provider—needs a key container to work. A default key container is created upon installation and is named *NetFrameWorkConfigurationKey*. The *aspnet_regiis.exe* utility provides a lot of command-line switches for you to add, remove, and edit key containers. The essential point is that you have a key container created before you dump the RSA-protected configuration provider. The container must not only exist, but it also needs to be associated with the user account attempting to call it. The system account (running the local Web server) is listed with the container; the ASP.NET account on your Web server might not be. Assuming you run ASP.NET under the NETWORK SERVICE account (the default on Windows Server 2003 machines), you need the following code to add access to the container for the user:
>
> ```
> aspnet_regiis.exe -pa "NetFrameworkConfigurationKey"
>                   "NT AUTHORITY\NETWORK SERVICE"
> ```
>
> It is important that you specify a complete account name, as in the preceding code. Note that granting access to the key container is necessary only if you use the RSA provider.

Both the RSA and DPAPI providers are great options for encrypting sensitive data. The DPAPI provider dramatically simplifies the process of key management—keys are generated based on machine credentials and can be accessed by all processes running on the machine. For the same reason, the DPAPI provider is not ideal to protect sections in a Web farm scenario where the same encrypted *web.config* file will be deployed to several servers. In this case, either you manually encrypt all *web.config* files on each machine or you copy the same container key to all servers. To accomplish this, you create a key container for the application, export it to an XML file, and import it on each server that will need to decrypt the encrypted *web.config* file. To create a key container you do as follows:

```
aspnet_regiis.exe -pc YourContainerName -exp
```

Next, you export the key container to an XML file:

```
aspnet_regiis.exe -px YourContainerName YourXmlFile.xml
```

Next, you move the XML file to each server and import it as follows:

```
aspnet_regiis.exe -pi YourContainerName YourXmlFile.xml
```

As a final step, grant the ASP.NET account permission to access the container (again using *aspnet_regiis.exe* with the **–pa** option as just shown).

> **Note** We won't cover the .NET Framework configuration API in this book. You can find deep coverage of the structure of configuration files and related APIs in my book, *Programming Microsoft ASP.NET 2.0 Applications: Advanced Topics* (Microsoft Press, 2006).

Connection Pooling

Connection pooling is a fundamental aspect of high-performance, scalable applications. For local or intranet desktop applications that are not multithreaded, connection pooling is no big deal—you'll get nearly the same performance with and without pooling. Furthermore, using a nonpooled connection gives you more control over the lifetime. For multithreaded applications, the use of connection pooling is a necessity for performance reasons and to avoid nasty, hardware-dependent bugs. Finally, if ASP.NET applications are involved, every millisecond that the connection is idle steals valuable resources from other requests. Not only should you rely on connection pooling, but you should also open the connection as late as possible and close it as soon as you can.

Using connection pooling makes it far less expensive for the application to open and close the connection to the database, even if that is done frequently. (We'll cover more about this topic later.) All standard .NET data providers have pooling support turned on by default. The .NET data providers for SQL Server and Oracle manage connection pooling internally using ad hoc classes. For the OLE DB data provider, connection pooling is implemented through the OLE DB service infrastructure for session pooling. Connection-string arguments (for example, *OLE DB Service*) can be used to enable or disable various OLE DB services, including pooling. A similar situation occurs with ODBC, in which pooling is controlled by the ODBC driver manager.

Configuring Pooling

Some settings in the connection string directly affect the pooling mechanism. The parameters you can control to configure the SQL Server environment are listed in Table 7-9.

TABLE 7-9 SQL Server Connection Pooling Keywords

Keyword	Description
Connection Lifetime	Sets the maximum duration in seconds of the connection object in the pool. This keyword is checked only when the connection is returned to the pool. If the time the connection has been open is greater than the specified lifetime, the connection object is destroyed. (We'll cover more about this topic later.)
Connection Reset	Determines whether the database connection is reset when being drawn from the pool. Default is *true*.
Enlist	Indicates that the pooler automatically enlists the connection in the creation thread's current transaction context. Default is *true*.
Max Pool Size	Maximum number of connections allowed in the pool. Default is 100.
Min Pool Size	Minimum number of connections allowed in the pool. Default is 0.
Pooling	Indicates that the connection object is drawn from the appropriate pool or, if necessary, is created and added to the appropriate pool. Default is *true*.

With the exception of *Connection Reset*, all the keywords listed in Table 7-9 are acceptable to the Oracle managed provider too.

As far as SQL Server and Oracle providers are concerned, connection pooling is automatically enabled; to disable it, you need to set *Pooling* to *false* in the connection string. To control pooling for an ODBC data source, you use the ODBC Data Source Administrator in the Control Panel. The Connection Pooling tab allows you to specify connection pooling parameters for each ODBC driver installed. Note that any changes to a specific driver affect all applications that make use of it. The .NET data provider for OLE DB automatically pools connections using OLE DB session pooling. You can disable pooling by setting the *OLE DB Services* keyword to -4.

In ADO.NET 2.0 and newer versions, auto enlistment (the *Enlist* keyword) works in the connection strings of all standard data providers, including providers for OLE DB and ODBC. In ADO.NET 1.x, only managed providers for SQL Server and Oracle support auto-enlistment because they are made of native managed code instead of being wrappers around existing code. The new *EnlistTransaction* method on connection classes allows you to enlist a connection object programmatically, be it pooled or not.

Getting and Releasing Objects

Each connection pool is associated with a distinct connection string and the transaction context. When a new connection is opened, if the connection string does not exactly match an existing pool, a new pool is created. Once created, connection pools are not destroyed until the process ends. This behavior does not affect the system performance because maintenance of inactive or empty pools requires only minimal overhead.

When a pool is created, multiple connection objects are created and added so that the minimum size is reached. Next, connections are added to the pool on demand, up to the maximum pool size. Adding a brand new connection object to the pool is the really expensive operation here, as it requires a roundtrip to the database. Next, when a connection object is requested, it is drawn from the pool as long as a usable connection is available. A usable connection must currently be unused, have a matching or null transaction context, and have a valid link to the server. If no usable connection is available, the pooler attempts to create a new connection object. When the maximum pool size is reached, the request is queued and served as soon as an existing connection object is released to the pool.

Connections are released when you call methods such as *Close* or *Dispose*. Connections that are not explicitly closed might not be returned to the pool unless the maximum pool size has been reached and the connection is still valid.

A connection object is removed from the pool if the lifetime has expired (which will be explained further in a moment) or if a severe error has occurred. In these cases, the connection is marked as invalid. The pooler periodically scavenges the various pools and permanently removes invalid connection objects.

Important Connection pools in ADO.NET are created based on the connection string applying an exact match algorithm. In other words, to avoid the creation of an additional connection pool you must ensure that two connection strings carrying the same set of parameters are expressed by two byte-per-byte identical strings. A different order of keywords, or blanks interspersed in the text, are not ignored and end up creating additional pools and therefore additional overhead.

To make connection pooling work effectively, it is extremely important that connection objects are returned to the pool as soon as possible. It is even more important, though, that connections are returned. Note that a connection object that goes out of scope is not closed and, therefore, not immediately returned. For this reason, it is highly recommended that you work with connection objects according to the following pattern:

```
SqlConnection conn = new SqlConnection(connString);
try {
    conn.Open();
    // Do something here
}
```

```
catch {
    // Trap errors here
}
finally {
    conn.Close();
}
```

Alternately, you can resort to the C# *using* statement, as follows:

```
using (SqlConnection conn = new SqlConnection(connString))
{
    // Do something here
    // Trap errors here
}
```

The *using* statement is equivalent to the preceding *try/catch/finally* block in which *Close* or *Dispose* is invoked in the *finally* block. You can call either *Close* or *Dispose* or even both—they do the same thing. *Dispose* cleans the connection string information and then calls *Close*. In addition, note that calling each one multiple times doesn't result in runtime troubles, as closing or disposing of an already closed or disposed of connection is actually a no-operation.

> **Note** Before the .NET Framework 2.0, there was no sort of *using* statement in Visual Basic .NET. Now, you can rely on a shortcut keyword for *try/catch/finally* blocks also in Visual Basic .NET. The keyword is *Using ... End Using*.
>
> ```
> Using conn As New SqlConnection()
>    ...
> End Using
> ```

Detecting Connections Leaks

In ADO.NET 2.0 and newer, you can easily figure out whether you're leaking connections thanks to some new performance counters. In particular, you can monitor the *NumberOfReclaimedConnections* counter, and if you see it going up, you have the evidence that your application is making poor use of connection objects. A good symptom of connection leaking is when you get an invalid operation exception that claims the timeout period elapsed prior to obtaining a connection from the pool. You can make this exception disappear or, more exactly, become less frequent by tweaking some parameters in the connection string. Needless to say, this solution doesn't remove the leak; it simply changes runtime conditions to make it happen less frequently. Here's a quick list of things you should not do that relate to connection management:

- **Do not turn connection pooling off**   With pooling disabled, a new connection object is created every time. No timeout can ever occur, but you lose a lot in performance and, more importantly, you are still leaking connections.

- **Do not shrink the connection lifetime**   Reducing the lifetime of the connection will force the pooler to renew connection objects more frequently. A short lifetime (a few seconds) will make the timeout exception extremely unlikely, but it adds significant overhead and doesn't solve the real problem. Let's say that it is only a little better than turning pooling off.

- **Do not increase the connection timeout**   You tell the pooler to wait a longer time before throwing the timeout exception. Whatever value you set here, ASP.NET aborts the thread after 3 minutes. In general, this option worsens performance without alleviating the problem.

- **Do not increase the pool size**   If you set the maximum pool size high enough (how high depends on the context), you stop getting timeout exceptions while keeping pooling enabled. The drawback is that you greatly reduce your application's scalability because you force your application to use a much larger number of connections than is actually needed.

To avoid leaking connections, you need to guarantee *only* that the connection is closed or disposed of when you're done, and preferably soon after you're done with it.

In the previous section, I emphasized the importance of writing code that guarantees the connection is always closed. However, there might be nasty cases in which your code places a call to *Close*, but it doesn't get called. Let's see why. Consider the following code:

```
SqlConnection conn = new SqlConnection(connString);
conn.Open();
SqlCommand cmd = new SqlCommand(cmdText, conn);
cmd.ExecuteNonQuery();
conn.Close();
```

What if the command throws an exception? The *Close* method is not called, and the connection is not returned to the pool. Wrapping the code in a *using* statement would do the trick because it ensures that *Dispose* is always invoked on the object being used. Here's the correct version of the code:

```
using (SqlConnection conn = new SqlConnection(connString))
{
    conn.Open();
    SqlCommand cmd = new SqlCommand(cmdText, conn);
    cmd.ExecuteNonQuery();
    conn.Close();  // Not called in case of exception
}  // Dispose always called
```

Wrapping your connection in such protected code sections is the only way to avoid connection leaking. (Note that *try/catch/finally* can also be used if you're interested in dealing with any exceptions yourself as close to the source of the problem, if that involves opening the connection or making the database query.)

Managing Connection Lifetime

The *Connection Lifetime* keyword indicates in seconds the time a connection object is considered valid. When the time has elapsed, the connection object should be disposed of. But why on earth should you get rid of a perfectly good connection object? This keyword is useful only in a well-known situation, and it should never be used otherwise. Imagine you have a cluster of servers sharing the workload. At some point, you realize the load is too high and you turn on an additional server. With good reason, you expect the workload to be distributed among all servers. However, this might not happen—the newly added server is idle.

A plausible and common reason for this is that middle-tier components cache the connections and never open new ones. By disposing of working connections, you force the middle-tier applications to create new connections. Needless to say, new connections will be assigned to the least loaded server. In the end, you should set *Connection Lifetime* only if you're in a cluster scenario. Finally, note that in ADO.NET 2.0 the connection builder classes use a different (and more intuitive) name to address the keyword—*LoadBalanceTimeout*.

> **Note**   *LoadBalanceTimeout* is not a newly supported attribute for a connection string. If you use the *SqlConnectionStringBuilder* class to programmatically build the connection string, you'll find a *LoadBalanceTimeout* property to set the *Connection Lifetime* attribute.

Clearing the Connection Pool

Until ADO.NET 2.0, there was no way to programmatically clear the pool of open connections. Admittedly, this is not an operation you need to perform often, but it becomes essential in case the database server goes down for whatever reason. Consider the following scenario: your ASP.NET pages open and then successfully close some connections out of the same pool. Next, the server suddenly goes down and is restarted. As a result, all connection objects in the pool are now invalid because each of them holds a reference to a server connection that no longer exists. What happens when a new page request is issued?

The answer is that the pooler returns an apparently valid connection object to the page, and the page runs the command. Unfortunately, the connection object is not recognized by the database server, resulting in an exception. The connection object is removed from the pool and replaced. The exception will be raised for each command as long as there are connection objects in the pool. In summary, shutting down the server without shutting down the application brings the connection pool into an inconsistent, corrupted state.

This situation is common for applications that deal with server reboots, like a failover cluster. Only one solution is possible—flushing the connection pool. It is not as easy to implement as it might seem at first, though. An easier workaround is catching the exception and changing the connection string slightly to force the use of a new connection pool.

ADO.NET is smart enough to recognize when an exception means that the pool is corrupted. When an exception is thrown during the execution of a command, ADO.NET realizes whether the exception means that the pool is corrupted. In this case, it walks down the pool and marks each connection as obsolete. When does an exception indicate pool corruption? It has to be a fatal exception raised from the network layer on a previously opened connection. All other exceptions are ignored and bubble up as usual.

Two new static methods—*ClearPool* and *ClearAllPools* defined for both *SqlConnection* and *OracleConnection*—can be used to programmatically clear the pool, if you know that the server has been stopped and restarted. These methods are used internally by ADO.NET to clear the pool as described earlier.

Executing Commands

Once you have a physical channel set up between your client and the database, you can start preparing and executing commands. The ADO.NET object model provides two types of command objects—the traditional one-off command and the data adapter. The one-off command executes a SQL command or a stored procedure and returns a sort of cursor. Using that, you then scroll through the rows and read data. While the cursor is in use, the connection is busy and open. The data adapter, on the other hand, is a more powerful object that internally uses a command and a cursor. It retrieves and loads the data into a data container class—*DataSet* or *DataTable*. The client application can then process the data while disconnected from the source.

We'll cover container classes and data adapters in the next chapter. Let's focus on one-off commands, paying particular attention to SQL Server commands.

The *SqlCommand* Class

The *SqlCommand* class represents a SQL Server statement or stored procedure. It is a cloneable and sealed class that implements the *IDbCommand* interface. In ADO.NET, it derives from *DbCommand* which, in turn, implements the interface. A command executes in the context of a connection and, optionally, a transaction. This situation is reflected by the constructors available in the *SqlCommand* class:

```
public SqlCommand();
public SqlCommand(string);
public SqlCommand(string, SqlConnection);
public SqlCommand(string, SqlConnection, SqlTransaction);
```

The string argument denotes the text of the command to execute (and it can be a stored procedure name), whereas the *SqlConnection* parameter is the connection object to use. Finally, if specified, the *SqlTransaction* parameter represents the transactional context in which the command has to run. ADO.NET command objects never implicitly open a connection. The connection must be explicitly assigned to the command by the programmer and opened and closed with direct operations. The same holds true for the transaction.

Properties of the *SqlCommand* Class

Table 7-10 shows the attributes that make up a command in the .NET data provider for SQL Server.

TABLE 7-10 Properties of the *SqlCommand* Class

Property	*IDbCommand* Interface Property?	Description
CommandText	Yes	Gets or sets the statement or the stored procedure name to execute.
CommandTimeout	Yes	Gets or sets the seconds to wait while trying to execute the command. The default is 30.
CommandType	Yes	Gets or sets how the *CommandText* property is to be interpreted. Set to *Text* by default, which means the *CommandText* property contains the text of the command.
Connection	Yes	Gets or sets the connection object used by the command. It is null by default.
Notification	No	Gets or sets the *SqlNotificationRequest* object bound to the command. *This property requires SQL Server 2005.*
NotificationAutoEnlist	No	Indicates whether the command will automatically enlist the SQL Server 2005 notification service. *This property requires SQL Server 2005.*
Parameters	Yes	Gets the collection of parameters associated with the command.
Transaction	Yes	Gets or sets the transaction within which the command executes. The transaction must be connected to the same connection as the command.
UpdatedRowSource	Yes	Gets or sets how query command results are applied to the row being updated. The value of this property is used only when the command runs within the *Update* method of the data adapter. Acceptable values are in the *UpdateRowSource* enumeration.

Commands can be associated with parameters, and each parameter is rendered using a provider-specific object. For the SQL Server managed provider, the parameter class is

SqlParameter. The command type determines the role of the *CommandText* property. The possible values for *CommandType* are as follows:

- **Text**   The default setting, which indicates the property contains Transact-SQL text to execute directly.

- **StoredProcedure**   Indicates that the content of the property is intended to be the name of a stored procedure contained in the current database.

- **TableDirect**   Indicates the property contains a comma-separated list containing the names of the tables to access. All rows and columns of the tables will be returned. It is supported only by the data provider for OLE DB.

To execute a stored procedure, you need the following:

```
using (SqlConnection conn = new SqlConnection(ConnString))
{
    SqlCommand cmd = new SqlCommand(sprocName, conn);
    cmd.CommandType = CommandType.StoredProcedure;
    cmd.Connection.Open();
    cmd.ExecuteNonQuery();
}
```

In ADO.NET 2.0, commands have two main new features—asynchronous executors and support for notification services. We'll cover both later.

Methods of the *SqlCommand* Class

Table 7-11 details the methods available for the *CommandText* class.

TABLE 7-11 Methods of the *CommandText* Class

Property	*IDbCommand* Interface Method?	Description
BeginExecuteNonQuery	No	Executes a nonquery command in a nonblocking manner. *Not supported in ADO.NET 1.x.*
BeginExecuteReader	No	Executes a query command in a nonblocking manner. *Not supported in ADO.NET 1.x.*
BeginExecuteXmlReader	No	Executes an XML query command in a nonblocking manner. *Not supported in ADO.NET 1.x.*
Cancel	Yes	Attempts to cancel the execution of the command. No exception is generated if the attempt fails.
CreateParameter	Yes	Creates a new instance of a *SqlParameter* object.
EndExecuteNonQuery	No	Completes a nonquery command executed asynchronously. *Not supported in ADO.NET 1.x.*

Property	IDbCommand Interface Method?	Description
EndExecuteReader	No	Completes a query command executed asynchronously. *Not supported in ADO.NET 1.x.*
EndExecuteXmlReader	No	Completes an XML query command executed asynchronously. *Not supported in ADO.NET 1.x.*
ExecuteNonQuery	Yes	Executes a nonquery command, and returns the number of rows affected.
ExecuteReader	Yes	Executes a query, and returns a forward-only, read-only cursor—the data reader—to the data.
ExecuteScalar	Yes	Executes a query, and returns the value in the 0,0 position (first column of first row) in the result set. Extra data is ignored.
ExecuteXmlReader	No	Executes a query that returns XML data and builds an *XmlReader* object.
Prepare	Yes	Creates a prepared version of the command in an instance of SQL Server.
ResetCommandTimeout	No	Resets the command timeout to the default.

Parameterized commands define their own arguments using instances of the *SqlParameter* class. Parameters have a name, value, type, direction, and size. In some cases, parameters can also be associated with a source column. A parameter is associated with a command by using the *Parameters* collection:

```
SqlParameter parm = new SqlParameter();
parm.ParameterName = "@employeeid";
parm.DbType = DbType.Int32;
parm.Direction = ParameterDirection.Input;
cmd.Parameters.Add(parm);
```

The following SQL statement uses a parameter:

```
SELECT * FROM employees WHERE employeeid=@employeeid
```

The .NET data provider for SQL Server identifies parameters by name, using the @ symbol to prefix them. In this way, the order in which parameters are associated with the command is not critical.

 Note Named parameters are supported by the managed provider for Oracle but not by the providers for OLE DB and ODBC data sources. The OLE DB and ODBC data sources use positional parameters identified with the question mark (?) placeholder. The order of parameters for these data sources is important.

Ways to Execute

As Table 7-11 shows, a *SqlCommand* object can be executed either synchronously or asynchronously. Let's focus on synchronous execution, which is supported on all .NET platforms. Execution can happen in four different ways: *ExecuteNonQuery*, *ExecuteReader*, *ExecuteScalar*, and *ExecuteXmlReader*. The various executors work in much the same way, but they differ in the return values. Typically, you use the *ExecuteNonQuery* method to perform update operations such as those associated with UPDATE, INSERT, and DELETE statements. In these cases, the return value is the number of rows affected by the command. For other types of statements, such as SET or CREATE, the return value is -1.

The *ExecuteReader* method is expected to work with query commands, and it returns a data reader object—an instance of the *SqlDataReader* class. The data reader is a sort of read-only, forward-only cursor that client code scrolls and reads from. If you execute an update statement through *ExecuteReader*, the command is successfully executed but no affected rows are returned. We'll return to data readers in a moment.

The *ExecuteScalar* method helps considerably when you have to retrieve a single value. It works great with SELECT COUNT statements or for commands that retrieve aggregate values. If you call the method on a regular query statement, only the value in the first column of the first row is read and all the rest is discarded. Using *ExecuteScalar* results in more compact code than you'd get by executing the command and manually retrieving the value in the top-left corner of the rowset.

These three executor methods are common to all command objects. The *SqlCommand* class also features the *ExecuteXmlReader* method. It executes a command that returns XML data and builds an XML reader so that the client application can easily navigate through the XML tree. The *ExecuteXmlReader* method is ideal to use with query commands that end with the FOR XML clause or with commands that query for text fields filled with XML data. Note that while the *XmlReader* object is in use, the underlying connection is busy.

ADO.NET Data Readers

The data reader class is specific to a DBMS and works like a firehose-style cursor. It allows you to scroll through and read one or more result sets generated by a command. The data reader operates in a connected way and moves in a forward-only direction. A data reader is instantiated during the execution of the *ExecuteReader* method. The results are stored in a buffer located on the client and are made available to the reader.

By using the data reader object, you access data one record at a time as soon as it becomes available. An approach based on the data reader is effective both in terms of system overhead and performance. Only one record is cached at any time, and there's no wait time to have the entire result set loaded in memory.

Table 7-12 shows the properties of the *SqlDataReader* class—that is, the data reader class for SQL Server.

TABLE 7-12 Properties of the *SqlDataReader* Class

Property	Description
Depth	Indicates the depth of nesting for the current row. For the *SqlDataReader* class, it always returns 0.
FieldCount	Gets the number of columns in the current row.
HasRows	Gets a value that indicates whether the data reader contains one or more rows. *Not supported in ADO.NET 1.0.*
IsClosed	Gets a value that indicates whether the data reader is closed.
Item	Indexer property, gets the value of a column in the original format.
RecordsAffected	Gets the number of rows modified by the execution of a batch command.

The *Depth* property is meant to indicate the level of nesting for the current row. The depth of the outermost table is always 0; the depth of inner tables grow by one. Most data readers, including the *SqlDataReader* and *OracleDataReader* classes, do not support multiple levels of nesting so that the *Depth* property always returns 0.

The *RecordsAffected* property is not set until all rows are read and the data reader is closed. The default value of *RecordsAffected* is -1. Note that *IsClosed* and *RecordsAffected* are the only properties you can invoke on a closed data reader.

Table 7-13 lists the methods of the SQL Server data reader class.

TABLE 7-13 Methods of the *SqlDataReader* Class

Methods	Description
Close	Closes the reader object. Note that closing the reader does not automatically close the underlying connection.
GetBoolean	Gets the value of the specified column as a Boolean.
GetByte	Gets the value of the specified column as a byte.
GetBytes	Reads a stream of bytes from the specified column into a buffer. You can specify an offset both for reading and writing.
GetChar	Gets the value of the specified column as a single character.
GetChars	Reads a stream of characters from the specified column into a buffer. You can specify an offset both for reading and writing.
GetDataTypeName	Gets the name of the back-end data type in the specified column.
GetDateTime	Gets the value of the specified column as a *DateTime* object.
GetDecimal	Gets the value of the specified column as a decimal.
GetDouble	Gets the value of the specified column as a double-precision floating-point number.

Methods	Description
GetFieldType	Gets the *Type* object for the data in the specified column.
GetFloat	Gets the value of the specified column as a single-precision floating-point number.
GetGuid	Gets the value of the specified column as a globally unique identifier (GUID).
GetInt16	Gets the value of the specified column as a 16-bit integer.
GetInt32	Gets the value of the specified column as a 32-bit integer.
GetInt64	Gets the value of the specified column as a 64-bit integer.
GetName	Gets the name of the specified column.
GetOrdinal	Given the name of the column, returns its ordinal number.
GetSchemaTable	Returns a *DataTable* object that describes the metadata for the columns managed by the reader.
GetString	Gets the value of the specified column as a string.
GetValue	Gets the value of the specified column in its original format.
GetValues	Copies the values of all columns in the supplied array of objects.
IsDbNull	Indicates whether the column contains null values. The type for a null column is *System.DBNull*.
NextResult	Moves the data reader pointer to the beginning of the next result set, if any.
Read	Moves the data reader pointer to the next record, if any.

The SQL Server data reader also features a variety of other DBMS-specific *get* methods. They include methods such as *GetSqlDouble*, *GetSqlMoney*, *GetSqlDecimal*, and so on. The difference between the *GetXXX* and *GetSqlXXX* methods is in the return type. With the *GetXXX* methods, a base .NET Framework type is returned; with the *GetSqlXXX* methods, a .NET Framework wrapper for a SQL Server type is returned—such as *SqlDouble*, *SqlMoney*, or *SqlDecimal*. The SQL Server types belong to the *SqlDbType* enumeration.

All the *GetXXX* methods that return a value from a column identify the column through a 0-based index. Note that the methods don't even attempt a conversion; they simply return data as is and just make a cast to the specified type. If the actual value and the type are not compatible, an exception is thrown.

> **Note** The *GetBytes* method is useful to read large fields one step at a time. However, the method can also be used to obtain the length in bytes of the data in the column. To get this information, pass a buffer that is a null reference and the return value of the method will contain the length.

Reading Data with the Data Reader

The key thing to remember when using a data reader is that you're working while connected. The data reader represents the fastest way to read data out of a source, but you should read your data as soon as possible and release the connection. One row is available at a time, and you must move through the result set by using the *Read* method. The following code snippet illustrates the typical loop you implement to read all the records of a query:

```
using (SqlConnection conn = new SqlConnection(connString))
{
    string cmdText = "SELECT * FROM customers";
    SqlCommand cmd = new SqlCommand(cmdText, conn);
    cmd.Connection.Open();
    SqlDataReader reader = cmd.ExecuteReader();
    while (reader.Read())
        CustomerList.Items.Add(reader["companyname"].ToString());
    reader.Close();
}
```

You have no need to explicitly move the pointer ahead and no need to check for the end of the file. The *Read* method returns *false* if there are no more records to read. A data reader is great if you need to consume data by processing the records in some way. If you need to cache values for later use, the data reader is not appropriate. You need a container object in this case, as we'll see in Chapter 8.

> **Note** Although accessing row fields by name is easy to read and understand, it is not the fastest approach. Internally, in fact, the data reader needs to resolve the name to a 0-based index. If you provide the index directly, you get slightly faster code.
>
> ```
> const int Customers_CustomerID = 0;
> ...
> Response.Write(reader[Customers_CustomerID].ToString());
> ```
>
> The preceding code shows that using constants turns out to be a good compromise between speed and readability.

Command Behaviors

When calling the *ExecuteReader* method on a command object—on any command object regardless of the underlying DBMS—you can require a particular working mode known as a command behavior. *ExecuteReader* has a second overload that takes an argument of type *CommandBehavior*:

```
cmd.ExecuteReader(CommandBehavior.CloseConnection);
```

CommandBehavior is an enumeration. Its values are listed in Table 7-14.

TABLE 7-14 Command Behaviors for the Data Reader

Behavior	Description
CloseConnection	Automatically closes the connection when the data reader is closed.
Default	No special behavior is required. Setting this option is functionally equivalent to calling *ExecuteReader* without parameters.
KeyInfo	The query returns only column metadata and primary key information. The query is executed without any locking on the selected rows.
SchemaOnly	The query returns only column metadata and does not put any lock on the database rows.
SequentialAccess	Enables the reader to load data as a sequential stream. This behavior works in conjunction with methods such as *GetBytes* and *GetChars*, which can be used to read bytes or characters having a limited buffer size for the data being returned.
SingleResult	The query is expected to return only the first result set.
SingleRow	The query is expected to return a single row.

The sequential access mode applies to all columns in the returned result set. This means you can access columns only in the order in which they appear in the result set. For example, you cannot read column #2 before column #1. More exactly, if you read or move past a given location, you can no longer read or move back. Combined with the *GetBytes* method, sequential access can be helpful in cases in which you must read binary large objects (BLOB) with a limited buffer.

Note You can specify *SingleRow* also when executing queries that are expected to return multiple result sets. In this case, all the generated result sets are correctly returned, but each result set has a single row. *SingleRow* and *SingleResult* serve the purpose of letting the underlying provider machinery know about the expected results so that some internal optimization can optionally be made.

Closing the Reader

The data reader is not a publicly creatable object. It does have a constructor, but not one that is callable from within user applications. The data reader constructor is marked as internal and can be invoked only from classes defined in the same assembly—*System.Data*. The data reader is implicitly instantiated when the *ExecuteReader* method is called. Opening and closing the reader are operations distinct from instantiation and must be explicitly invoked by the application. The *Read* method advances the internal pointer to the next readable record in the current result set. The *Read* method returns a Boolean value indicating whether or not more records can be read. While records are being read, the connection is busy and no operation, other than closing, can be performed on the connection object.

The data reader and the connection are distinct objects and should be managed and closed independently. Both objects provide a *Close* method that should be called twice—once on the data reader (first) and once on the connection. When the *CloseConnection* behavior is required, closing the data reader also closes the underlying connection. In addition, the data reader's *Close* method fills in the values for any command output parameters and sets the *RecordsAffected* property.

> **Tip** Because of the extra work *Close* always performs on a data reader class, closing a reader with success can sometimes be expensive, especially in cases of long-running and complicated queries. In situations in which you need to squeeze out every bit of performance, and where the return values and number of records affected are not significant, you can invoke the *Cancel* method of the associated *SqlCommand* object instead of closing the reader. *Cancel* aborts the operation and closes the reader faster. Aside from this, you're still responsible for properly closing the underlying connection.

Accessing Multiple Result Sets

Depending on the syntax of the query, multiple result sets can be returned. By default, the data reader is positioned on the first of them. You use the *Read* method to scroll through the various records in the current result set. When the last record is found, the *Read* method returns *false* and does not advance further. To move to the next result set, you should use the *NextResult* method. The method returns *false* if there are no more result sets to read. The following code shows how to access all records in all returned result sets:

```
using (SqlConnection conn = new SqlConnection(connString))
{
    string cmdText = Query.Text;
    SqlCommand cmd = new SqlCommand(cmdText, conn);
    cmd.Connection.Open();
    SqlDataReader reader = cmd.ExecuteReader();

    do {
        // Move through the first result set
        while (reader.Read())
            sb.AppendFormat("{0}, {1}<br/>", reader[0], reader[1]);

        // Separate result sets
        sb.Append("<hr />");
    } while (reader.NextResult());

    reader.Close();
}

// Display results in the page
Results.Text = sb.ToString();
```

Figure 7-7 shows the output generated by the sample page based on this code.

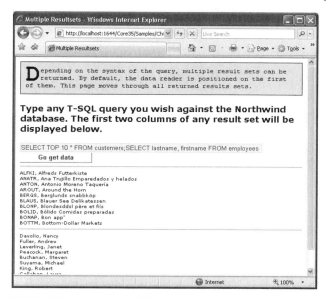

FIGURE 7-7 Processing multiple result sets.

Note The .NET Framework version 1.1 extends the programming interface of data readers by adding the *HasRows* method, which returns a Boolean value indicating whether or not there are more rows to read. However, the method does not tell anything about the number of rows available. Similarly, there is no method or trick to know in advance how many result sets have been returned.

Asynchronous Commands

A database operation is normally a synchronous operation—the caller regains control of the application only after the interaction with the database is completed. This approach can lead to performance and scalability issues in lengthy operations—a common scenario when you interact with a DBMS. The .NET Framework 1.x supports asynchronous operations, but the model is implemented around user-level code. In other words, you can implement your own procedures asynchronously and connect to databases and run commands as part of the code, but connection management and command execution remain atomic operations that execute synchronously.

The .NET data provider for SQL Server in ADO.NET 2.0 (and beyond) provides true asynchronous support for executing commands. This offers a performance advantage because you can perform other actions until the command completes. However, this is not the only benefit. The support for asynchronous operations is built into the *SqlCommand* class and is limited to executing nonquery commands and getting a reader or an XML reader. You can use three different approaches to build commands that work asynchronously. They are nonblocking, polling, and callback.

Setting Up Asynchronous Commands

To enable asynchronous commands, you must set the new *Async* attribute to *true* in the connection string. You'll receive an exception if any of the asynchronous methods are called over a connection that doesn't have asynchronous capabilities explicitly turned on. Enabling asynchronous commands does have a cost in terms of overall performance; for this reason, you're better off using the *Async* keyword only with connection objects that execute asynchronous operations only.

If you need both synchronous and asynchronous commands, employ different connections wherever possible. Note, though, that you can still call synchronous methods over connections enabled to support asynchronous operations. However, you'll only end up using more resources than needed and experience a performance degradation.

> **Note** Asynchronous commands are not implemented by creating a new thread and blocking execution on it. Among other things, ADO.NET is not thread-safe and blocking threads would be a serious performance hit. When asynchronous commands are enabled, ADO.NET opens the TCP socket to the database in overlapped mode and binds it to an I/O completion port. In light of this, synchronous operations execute as the emulation of asynchronous operations, and this explains why they're more expensive than asynchronous-enabled connections.

Nonblocking Commands

Nonblocking commands are the simplest case of asynchronous commands. The code starts the operation and continues executing other unrelated methods; then it comes back to get the results. Whatever the model of choice happens to be, the first step of an asynchronous command is calling one of the *BeginExecuteXXX* methods. For example, if you want to execute a reading command, you call *BeginExecuteReader*:

```
// Start a non-blocking execution
IAsyncResult iar = cmd.BeginExecuteReader();

// Do something else meanwhile
...

// Block the execution until done
SqlDataReader reader = cmd.EndExecuteReader(iar);

// Process data here ...
ProcessData(reader);
```

The *BeginExecuteReader* function returns an *IAsyncResult* object you will use later to complete the call. Note that *EndExecuteReader* is called to finish the operation and will block execution until the ongoing command terminates. The *EndExecuteReader* function will automatically sync up the command with the rest of the application, blocking the code whenever the results of the command are not ready.

As an alternative to the aforementioned approach, the client code might want to check the status of a running asynchronous operation and poll for completion. The following code illustrates the polling option with a query statement:

```
// Executes a query statement
IAsyncResult iar = cmd.BeginExecuteReader();
do {
    // Do something here
} while (!iar.IsCompleted);

// Sync up
SqlDataReader reader = cmd.EndExecuteReader(iar);
ProcessData(reader);
```

It is important to note that if *iar.IsCompleted* returns *true*, the *EndExecuteReader* method will not block the application.

The third option for nonblocking commands has the client code start the database operation and continue without waiting. Later on, when the operation is done, it receives a call. In this case, you pass a delegate to a *BeginExecuteXXX* method and any information that constitutes the state of the particular call. The state is any information you want to pass to the callback function. In this case, you pass the command object:

```
// Begin executing the command
IAsyncResult ar = cmd.BeginExecuteReader(
    new AsyncCallback(ProcessData), cmd);
```

After initiating the asynchronous operation, you can forget about it and do any other work. The specified callback function is invoked at the end of the operation. The callback must have the following layout:

```
public void ProcessData(IAsyncResult ar)
{
    // Retrieve the context of the call
    SqlCommand cmd = (SqlCommand) iar.AsyncState;

    // Complete the async operation
    SqlDataReader reader = cmd.EndExecuteReader(iar);
    ...
}
```

The context of the call you specified as the second argument to *BeingExecuteReader* is packed in the *AsyncState* property of the *IAsyncResult* object.

> **Note** The callback will be called in a thread-pool thread, which is likely to be different from the thread that initiated the operation. Proper thread synchronization might be needed, depending on the application. This also poses a problem with the user interface of applications, especially Windows Forms applications. Ensuring that the UI is refreshed in the right thread is up to you. Windows Forms controls and forms provide mechanisms for deciding if the correct thread is currently executing and for accessing the correct thread if it isn't. You should consult the MSDN documentation or a good Windows Forms programming book for more information regarding multithreaded Windows Forms programming. Note that if you fail to use the threading model correctly, your application will almost certainly lock up and quite possibly even crash.

Executing Parallel Commands in an ASP.NET Page

Having asynchronous commands available is not necessarily a good reason for using them without due forethought. Let's examine a couple of scenarios where asynchronous commands are useful for building better Web pages. The first scenario we'll consider is the execution of multiple SQL statements in parallel, either against the same or different database servers.

Imagine your page displays information about a particular customer—both personal and accounting data. The former block of data comes from the client's database; the latter is excerpted from the accounting database. You can fire both queries at the same time and have them execute in parallel on distinct machines—thus benefitting from true parallelism. Here's an example:

```
protected void QueryButton_Click(object sender, EventArgs e)
{
  string custID = CustomerList.SelectedValue;

  using (SqlConnection conn1 = new SqlConnection(ConnString1))
  using (SqlConnection conn2 = new SqlConnection(ConnString2))
  {
    // Fire the first command: get customer info
    SqlCommand cmd1 = new SqlCommand(CustomerInfoCmd, conn1);
    cmd1.Parameters.Add("@customerid", SqlDbType.Char, 5).Value = custID;
    conn1.Open();
    IAsyncResult arCustomerInfo = cmd1.BeginExecuteReader();

    // Fire the second command: get order info
    SqlCommand cmd2 = new SqlCommand(CustomerOrderHistory, conn2);
    cmd2.CommandType = CommandType.StoredProcedure;
    cmd2.Parameters.Add("@customerid", SqlDbType.Char, 5).Value = custID;
    conn2.Open();
    IAsyncResult arOrdersInfo = cmd2.BeginExecuteReader();

    // Prepare wait objects to sync up
    WaitHandle[] handles = new WaitHandle[2];
    handles[0] = arCustomerInfo.AsyncWaitHandle;
    handles[1] = arOrdersInfo.AsyncWaitHandle;
    SqlDataReader reader;
```

```
// Wait for all commands to terminate (no longer than 5 secs)
for (int i=0; i<2; i++)
{
  StringBuilder builder = new StringBuilder();
  int index = WaitHandle.WaitAny(handles, 5000, false);
      if (index == WaitHandle.WaitTimeout)
          throw new Exception("Timeout expired");

  if (index == 0) {     // Customer info
    reader = cmd1.EndExecuteReader(arCustomerInfo);
    if (!reader.Read())
      continue;

    builder.AppendFormat("{0}<br>", reader["companyname"]);
    builder.AppendFormat("{0}<br>", reader["address"]);
    builder.AppendFormat("{0}<br>", reader["country"]);
    Info.Text = builder.ToString();
    reader.Close();
  }
  if (index == 1) {     // Orders info
    reader = cmd2.EndExecuteReader(arOrdersInfo);
    gridOrders.DataSource = reader;
    gridOrders.DataBind();
    reader.Close();
  }
 }
}
}
```

The page fires the two commands and then sits waiting for the first command to terminate. The *AsyncWaitHandle* object of each *IAsyncResult* is stored in an array and passed to the *WaitAny* method of the *WaitHandle* class. *WaitAny* signals out when any of the commands terminates, but the surrounding *for* statement reiterates the wait until all pending commands terminate. You could have more easily opted for the *WaitAll* method. In this case, though, you can process results as they become available. This fact ensures a performance gain, especially for long-running stored procedures.

> **Note** You can implement the same behavior in ADO.NET 1.x without asynchronous commands by simply assigning each command to a different thread—either a user-defined one or one from the thread pool. In this case, though, each command would have blocked a thread. Blocking threads is fine for client-side applications, but it might compromise scalability in server-side applications such as ASP.NET applications.

Nonblocking Data-Driven ASP.NET Pages

Imagine a data-driven ASP.NET page that employs long-running, synchronous commands. The more the page is requested, the more likely it is that a large share of system threads are blocked while waiting for the database to return results. The paradoxical effect of this is that the Web server is virtually idle (with almost no CPU and network usage) but can't accept new requests because it has very few threads available.

To address this problem, since version 1.0 ASP.NET supports asynchronous HTTP handlers—that is, a special breed of page classes that implement the *IHttpAsyncHandler* interface instead of *IHttpHandler*. Asynchronous HTTP handlers take care of a request and produce a response in an asynchronous manner. In the .NET Framework 2.0, asynchronous handlers can combine with asynchronous commands to boost data-driven pages.

The *IHttpAsyncHandler* interface has *BeginProcessRequest* and *EndProcessRequest* methods. In the former method, you connect to the database and kick off the query. *BeginProcessRequest* receives a callback function directly from ASP.NET; the same callback is used to detect the completion of the asynchronous command.

When *BeginProcessRequest* returns, the page gives the control back to ASP.NET as if it was served. ASP.NET is now free to reuse the thread to process another request while the database server proceeds. When the query is complete, the signaling mechanism ends up invoking the *EndProcessRequest* method, although not necessarily on the same thread as the rest of the page, so to speak. The *EndProcessRequest* method is where you simply collect the data and render the page out.

I cover asynchronous handlers in my other ASP.NET book, *Programming Microsoft ASP.NET 2.0 Applications: Advanced Topics* (Microsoft Press, 2006).

> **Note** A fair number of methods work synchronously even in the context of asynchronous commands. The list includes *BeginXXX* methods and most methods of the data reader class, such as *GetXXX* methods, *Read*, *Close*, and *Dispose*.

Working with Transactions

In ADO.NET, you can choose between two types of transactions: local and distributed. A local transaction involves a single resource—typically, the database you're connected to. You begin the transaction, attach one or more commands to its context, and decide whether the whole operation was successful or whether it failed. The transaction is then committed or rolled back accordingly. This approach is functionally similar to simply running a SQL stored procedure that groups a few commands under the same transaction. Using ADO.NET code makes it more flexible but doesn't change the final effect.

A distributed transaction spans multiple heterogeneous resources and ensures that if the entire transaction is committed or rolled back, all modifications made at the various steps are committed or rolled back as well. A distributed transaction requires a Transaction Processing (TP) monitor. The Distributed Transaction Coordinator (DTC) is the TP monitor for Microsoft Windows 2000 and later.

In ADO.NET 1.x, you manage a local transaction through a bunch of database-specific transaction objects—for example, *SqlTransaction* for SQL Server transactions. You begin the transaction, associate commands to it, and decide about the outcome. For distributed transactions, you need Enterprise Services and serviced components. You can enlist database connections to Enterprise Services DTC managed transactions by using the aforementioned *EnlistDistributedTransaction* method on the connection class.

In ADO.NET 2.0 and beyond, local and distributed transactions can also be managed (more easily, actually) through the new classes defined in the *System.Transactions* namespace—specifically, with the *TransactionScope* class.

Managing Local Transactions as in ADO.NET 1.x

You start a new local transaction through the *BeginTransaction* method of the connection class. You can give the transaction a name and an isolation level. The method maps to the SQL Server implementation of *BEGIN TRANSACTION*. The following code snippet shows the typical flow of a transactional piece of code:

```
SqlTransaction tran;
tran = conn.BeginTransaction();
SqlCommand cmd1 = new SqlCommand(cmdText1);
cmd1.Connection = conn;
cmd1.Transaction = tran;
...
SqlCommand cmd2 = new SqlCommand(cmdText2);
cmd2.Connection = conn;
cmd2.Transaction = tran;
...
try {
   cmd1.ExecuteNonQuery();
   cmd2.ExecuteNonQuery();
   tran.Commit();
}
catch {
   tran.Rollback();
}
finally {
   conn.Close();
}
```

The newly created transaction object operates on the same connection represented by the connection object you used to create it. To add commands to the transaction, you set the *Transaction* property of command objects. Note that if you set the *Transaction* property of a command to a transaction object that is not connected to the same connection, an exception will be thrown as you attempt to execute a statement. Once all the commands have terminated, you call the *Commit* method of the transaction object to complete the transaction, or you call the *Rollback* method to cancel the transaction and undo all changes.

The isolation level of a transaction indicates the locking behavior for the connection. Common values are as follows: *ReadCommitted* (default), *ReadUncommitted*, *RepeatableRead*, and *Serializable*. Imagine a situation in which one transaction changes a value that a second transaction might need to read. *ReadCommitted* locks the row and prevents the second transaction from reading until the change is committed. *ReadUncommitted* doesn't hold locks, thus improving the overall performance. In doing so, though, it allows the second transaction to read a modified row before the original change is committed or rolled back. This is a "dirty read" because if the first transaction rolls the change back, the read value is invalid and there's nothing you can do about it. (Of course, you set *ReadUncommitted* only if dirty reads are not a problem in your scenario.) Note also that disallowing dirty reads also decreases overall system concurrency.

Imagine one transaction reads a committed row; next, another transaction modifies or deletes the row and commits the change. At this point, if the first transaction attempts to read the row again, it will obtain different results. To prevent this, you set the isolation level to *RepeatableRead*. *RepeatableRead* prevents further updates and dirty reads but not other operations that can generate phantom rows. Imagine that a transaction runs a query; next, another transaction does something that modifies the results of the previous query. When the first transaction ends, it returns an inconsistent result to the client. The *Serializable* level prevents concurrent transactions from updating or inserting rows until a given transaction is complete. Table 7-15 summarizes the isolation levels.

TABLE 7-15 Isolation Levels

Level	Dirty Reads	Nonrepeatable	Phantom Rows
ReadUncommitted	Yes	Yes	Yes
ReadCommitted	No	Yes	Yes
RepeatableRead	No	No	Yes
Serializable	No	No	No

The highest isolation level, *Serializable*, provides a high degree of protection against concurrent transactions, but it requires that each transaction complete before any other transaction is allowed to work on the database.

The isolation level can be changed at any time and remains in effect until explicitly changed. If the level is changed during a transaction, the server is expected to apply the new locking level to all statements remaining.

You terminate a transaction explicitly by using the *Commit* or *Rollback* method. The *SqlTransaction* class supports named savepoints in the transaction that can be used to roll back a portion of the transaction. Named savepoints exploit a specific SQL Server feature—the *SAVE TRANSACTION* statement.

This approach to local transactions is possible only in ADO.NET 1.x and is, of course, fully supported in ADO.NET 2.0 and later versions. Let's explore alternative approaches.

Introducing the *TransactionScope* Object

The preceding code based on *BeginTransaction* ties you to a specific database and requires you to start a new transaction to wrap a few database commands. What if you need to work with distinct databases and then, say, send a message to a message queue? In ADO.NET 1.x, you typically create a distributed transaction in Enterprise Services. In ADO.NET 2.0 and beyond, you can perform both local and distributed transactions through a new object— *TransactionScope*. Here's the code:

```
using (TransactionScope ts = new TransactionScope())
{
  using (SqlConnection conn = new SqlConnection(ConnString))
  {
    SqlCommand cmd = new SqlCommand(cmdText, conn);
    cmd.Connection.Open();
    try {
      cmd.ExecuteNonQuery();
    }
    catch (SqlException ex) {
      // Error handling code goes here
      lblMessage.Text = ex.Message;
    }
  }

  // Must call to complete; otherwise abort
  ts.Complete();
}
```

The connection object is defined within the scope of the transaction, so it automatically participates in the transaction. The only thing left to do is commit the transaction, which you do by placing a call to the method *Complete*. If you omit that call, the transaction fails and rolls back no matter what really happened with the command or commands. Needless to say, any exceptions will abort the transaction.

> **Important** You must guarantee that the *TransactionScope* object will be disposed of. By design, the transaction scope commits or rolls back on disposal. Waiting for the garbage collector to kick in and dispose of the transaction scope can be expensive because distributed transactions have a one-minute timeout by default. Keeping multiple databases locked for up to a minute is an excellent scalability killer. Calling *TransactionScope.Dispose* manually in the code might not be enough, as it won't be called in case of exceptions. You should either opt for a *using* statement or a *try/catch/finally* block.

Distributed Transactions with *TransactionScope*

Let's consider a transaction that includes operations on different databases—the Northwind database of SQL Server 2000 and a custom *MyData.mdf* file managed through SQL Server 2005 Express. The file is available in the *app_Data* directory of the sample project in the book's sample code. The sample table we're interested in here can be created with the following command:

```
CREATE TABLE Numbers (ID int, Text varchar(50))
```

You create a unique and all-encompassing *TransactionScope* instance and run the various commands even on different connections. You track the outcome of the various operations and call *Complete* if all went fine. Here's an example:

```
using (TransactionScope ts = new TransactionScope())
{
    // *************************************************************
    // Update Northwind on SQL Server 2000
    using (SqlConnection conn = new SqlConnection(ConnString))
    {
        SqlCommand cmd = new SqlCommand(UpdateCmd, conn);
        cmd.Connection.Open();
        cmd.ExecuteNonQuery(); // note exception aborts transaction
    }

    // *************************************************************
    // Update Numbers on SQL Server 2005
    using (SqlConnection conn = new SqlConnection(ConnString05))
    {
        SqlCommand cmd = new SqlCommand(InsertCmd, conn);
        cmd.Connection.Open();
        cmd.ExecuteNonQuery(); // note exception aborts transaction
    }

    // Must call to complete; otherwise abort
    ts.Complete();
}
```

If an error occurs, say, on the SQL Server 2005 database, any changes successfully entered on the SQL Server 2000 database are automatically rolled back.

TransactionScope is a convenience class that supports the dispose pattern, and internally it simply sets the current transaction, plus it has some state to track scoping. By wrapping everything in a *TransactionScope* object, you're pretty much done, as the object takes care of everything else for you. For example, it determines whether you need a local or distributed transaction, enlists any necessary distributed resources, and proceeds with local processing otherwise. As the code reaches a point where it won't be running locally, *TransactionScope* escalates your transaction to the DTC as appropriate.

Which objects can be enlisted with a transaction? Anything that implements the required interface—*ITransaction*—can be enlisted. ADO.NET 2.0 and later versions ship all standard data providers with support for *System.Transactions*. MSMQ works in compatibility mode.

When some code invokes the *Complete* method, it indicates that all operations in the scope are completed successfully. Note that the method does not physically terminate the distributed transaction, as the commit operation will still happen on *TransactionScope* disposal. However, after calling the method, you can no longer use the distributed transaction.

> **Note** There are a number of differences between *System.Transactions* and Enterprise Services as far as distributed transactions are concerned. First, *System.Transactions* is a transaction framework designed specifically for the managed environment, so it fits more naturally into .NET applications. Of course, internally the classes of the *System.Transactions* namespace might end up delegating some work to DTC and COM+, but that is nothing more than an implementation detail. Another important difference between the two is the existence of a lightweight transaction manager implemented on the managed side that allows for a number of optimizations, including presenting several enlistments as only one for DTC and support for promotable transactions.

Enlisting in a Distributed Transaction in ADO.NET 1.x

If your code uses *TransactionScope*, there's no need for a connection object to explicitly enlist in a transaction. However, if needed, the *EnlistTransaction* method provides you with exactly that capability.

Manually enlisting connections into distributed transactions is a feature already available in ADO.NET 1.1 through the *EnlistDistributedTransaction* method of the connection class. The method manually enlists the connection into a transaction being managed by the Enterprise Services DTC. In this case, you work with a distributed transaction that is defined elsewhere and takes direct advantage of the DTC.

> **Note** *EnlistDistributedTransaction* is useful when you have pooled business objects with an open connection. In this case, enlistment occurs only when the connection is opened. If the object participates in multiple transactions, the connection for that object is not reopened and therefore has no way to automatically enlist in new transactions. In this case, you can disable automatic transaction enlistment and enlist the connection explicitly by using *EnlistDistributedTransaction*.

SQL Server 2005–Specific Enhancements

The .NET data provider for SQL Server also has new features that are tied to the enhancements in SQL Server 2005. SQL Server 2005 introduces significant enhancements in various areas, including data type support, query dependency and notification, and multiple active result sets (MARS).

Support for CLR Types

SQL Server 2005 supports any CLR types. In addition to default types, you can store into and retrieve from SQL Server tables any object that is a valid .NET type. This includes both system types—such as a *Point*—and user-defined classes. This extended set of capabilities is reflected in the ADO.NET provider for SQL Server.

CLR types appear as objects to the data reader, and parameters to commands can be instances of CLR types. The following code snippet demonstrates how to retrieve a value from the MyCustomers table that corresponds to an instance of the user-defined *Customer* class:

```
string cmdText = "SELECT CustomerData FROM MyCustomers";
SqlConnection conn = new SqlConnection(connStr);
using (conn)
{
  SqlCommand cmd = new SqlCommand(cmdText, conn);
  cmd.Connection.Open();
  SqlDataReader reader = cmd.ExecuteReader();
  while(reader.Read())
  {
    Customer cust = (Customer) reader[0];
    // Do some work
  }
  cmd.Connection.Close();
}
```

A SQL Server 2005 user-defined type is stored as a binary stream of bytes. The *get* accessor of the data reader gets the bytes and deserializes them to a valid instance of the original class. The reverse process (serialization) takes place when a user-defined object is placed in a SQL Server column.

Support for XML as a Native Type

SQL Server 2005 natively supports the XML data type, which means you can store XML data in columns. At first glance, this feature seems to be nothing new because XML data is plain text and to store XML data in a column you only need the column to accept text. Native XML support in SQL Server 2005, however, means something different—you can declare the type of a given column as native XML, not plain text adapted to indicate markup text.

In ADO.NET 1.x, the *ExecuteXmlReader* method allows you to process the results of a query as an XML stream. The method builds an *XmlTextReader* object on top of the data coming from SQL Server. Therefore, for the method to work, the entire result set must be XML. Scenarios in which this method is useful include when the *FOR XML* clause is appended or when you query for a scalar value that happens to be XML text.

In ADO.NET 2.0 and beyond, when SQL Server 2005 is up and running, you can obtain an *XmlTextReader* object for each table cell (row, column) whose type is XML. You obtain a *SqlDataReader* object and have it return XML to you using the new *GetSqlXml* method. The following code snippet provides a useful example:

```
string cmdText = " SELECT * FROM MyCustomers";
SqlCommand cmd = new SqlCommand(cmdText, conn);
SqlDataReader reader = cmd.ExecuteReader();
while(reader.Read())
{
  // Assume that field #3 contains XML data

  // Get data and do some work
  SqlXml xml = reader.GetSqlXml(3);
  ProcessData(xml.Value);
}
```

The *SqlXml* class represents the XML data type. The *Value* property of the class returns the XML text as a string.

SQL Notifications and Dependencies

Applications that display volatile data or maintain a cache would benefit from friendly server notification whenever their data changes. SQL Server 2005 offers this feature—it notifies client applications about dynamic changes in the result set generated by a given query. Suppose your application manages the results of a query. If you register for a notification, your application is informed if something happens at the SQL Server level that modifies the result set generated by that query. This means that if a record originally selected by your query is updated or deleted, or if a new record is added that meets the criteria of the query, you're notified. Note, though, the notification reaches your application only if it is still up and running—which poses a clear issue with ASP.NET pages. But let's move forward one step at a time.

The SQL Server provider in ADO.NET provides two ways to use this notification feature and two related classes—*SqlDependency* and *SqlNotificationRequest*. *SqlNotificationRequest* is a lower-level class that exposes server-side functionality, allowing you to execute a command with a notification request. When a T-SQL statement is executed in SQL Server 2005, the notification mechanism keeps track of the query, and if it detects a change that might cause the result set to change, it sends a message to a queue. A queue is a new SQL Server 2005 database object that you create and manage with a new set of T-SQL statements. How the queue is polled and how the message is interpreted is strictly application-specific.

The *SqlDependency* class provides a high-level abstraction of the notification mechanism, and it allows you to set an application-level dependency on the query so that changes in the server can be immediately communicated to the client application through an event. The following code binds a command to a SQL dependency:

```
SqlCommand cmd = new SqlCommand("SELECT * FROM Employees", conn);
SqlDependency dep = new SqlDependency(cmd);
dep.OnChange += new OnChangeEventHandler(OnDependencyChanged);
SqlDataReader reader = cmd.ExecuteReader();
```

The *OnChange* event on the *SqlDependency* class fires whenever the class detects a change that affects the result set of the command. Here's a typical handler:

```
void OnDependencyChanged(object sender, SqlNotificationsEventArgs e)
{
    ...
}
```

When the underlying machinery detects a change, it fires the event to the application.

As mentioned, using notifications in this way is not particularly interesting from an ASP.NET perspective because the page returns immediately after running the query. However, the caching API of ASP.NET 2.0 (and newer versions) provides a similar feature that automatically tracks the results of a query via the ASP.NET cache. What you have in ASP.NET is a custom type of cache dependency that monitors the results of a query for both SQL Server 2000 and SQL Server 2005, although in radically different ways. You create a dependency on a command or a table and place it in the ASP.NET *Cache* object. The cache item will be invalidated as soon as a change in the monitored command or table is detected. If a SQL Server 2000 instance is involved, you can detect changes to only one of the tables touched by the query; if SQL Server 2005 is involved, you get finer control and can track changes to the result set of the query. We'll cover ASP.NET caching in great detail in Chapter 16.

Multiple Active Result Sets

Version 1.x of the SQL Server managed provider, along with the SQL Server ODBC driver, supports only one active result set per connection. The (unmanaged) OLE DB provider and the outermost ADO library appear to support multiple active result sets, but this is an illusion. In OLE DB, the effect is obtained by opening additional and nonpooled connections.

In SQL Server 2005, the MARS feature is natively implemented and allows an application to have more than one *SqlDataReader* open on a connection, each started from a separate command. Having more than one data reader open on a single connection offers a potential performance improvement because multiple readers are much less expensive than multiple connections. At the same time, MARS adds some hidden per-operation costs that are a result of its implementation. Considering the trade-offs and making a thoughtful decision is up to you.

The canonical use of MARS is when you get a data reader to walk through a result set while using another command on the same connection to issue update statements to the database. The following code demonstrates a sample page that walks through a data reader and updates the current record using a second command. If you try this approach in ADO. NET 1.x, or in ADO.NET 2.0 and later with MARS disabled, you get an exception complaining that the data reader associated with this connection is open and should be closed first.

```
using (SqlConnection conn = new SqlConnection(connString))
{
    SqlCommand cmd1 = new SqlCommand("SELECT * FROM employees", conn);
    cmd1.Connection.Open();
    SqlDataReader reader = cmd1.ExecuteReader();

    // Walks the data reader
    while (reader.Read())
    {
        // Reverses the first name
        string firstNameReversed = reader["firstname"].ToString();
        char[] buf = firstNameReversed.ToCharArray();
        Array.Reverse(buf);
        firstNameReversed = new string(buf);

        // Set the new first name on the same connection
        int id = (int)reader["employeeid"];
        SqlCommand cmd2 = new SqlCommand(
                "UPDATE employees SET firstname=@newFirstName WHERE
                  employeeid=@empID", conn);
        cmd2.Parameters.AddWithValue("@newFirstName", firstNameReversed);
        cmd2.Parameters.AddWithValue("empID", id);
        cmd2.ExecuteNonQuery();
    }
    reader.Close();

    // Get a new reader to refresh the UI
    grid.DataSource = cmd1.ExecuteReader();
    grid.DataBind();
    cmd1.Connection.Close();
}
```

Note that for MARS to work, you must use a distinct *SqlCommand* object, as shown in the preceding code. If you use a third command object to re-execute the query to get up-to-date records, there's no need to close the reader explicitly.

Another big benefit of MARS is that, if you're engaged in a transaction, it lets you execute code in the same isolation-level scope of the original connection. You won't get this benefit if you open a second connection under the covers.

The MARS feature is enabled by default when SQL Server 2005 is the database server. To disable MARS, you set the *MultipleActiveResultSets* attribute to *false* in the connection string. There are some hidden costs associated with MARS. First, MARS requires the continuous creation of *SqlCommand* objects. To deal with this issue, a pool of command objects is constituted and maintained. Second, there is a cost in the network layer due to multiplexing the I/O stream of data. Most of these costs are structural, and you should not expect a great performance improvement by disabling the MARS feature. So what's the purpose of the *MultipleActiveResultSets* attribute? The attribute appears mostly for backward compatibility. In this way, applications that expect an exception when more than one result set is used can continue working.

> **Note** MARS-like behavior is available in the .NET Framework 2.0 (and newer) versions of the OLE DB and Oracle managed providers. The Oracle provider doesn't support the MARS attribute on the connection string, but it enables the feature automatically. The OLE DB provider doesn't support the connection string attribute either—it simulates multiple result sets when you connect to earlier versions of SQL Server or when the Microsoft Data Access Components (MDAC 9.0) library is not available. When you operate through OLE DB on a version of SQL Server 2005 equipped with MDAC 9.0, multiple result sets are active and natively implemented.

Conclusion

The .NET data access subsystem is made of two main subtrees—the managed providers and the database-agnostic container classes. ADO.NET managed providers are a new type of data source connectors and replace the COM-based OLE DB providers of ADO and ASP. As of this writing, the .NET Framework includes two native providers—one for SQL Server and one for Oracle—and support for all OLE DB providers and ODBC drivers. Third-party vendors also support MySQL, DB2, and Sybase, and they have alternate providers for Oracle.

A managed provider is faster and more appropriate than any other database technology for data-access tasks in .NET. Especially effective with SQL Server, a managed provider hooks up at the wire level and removes any sort of abstraction layer. In this way, a managed provider makes it possible for ADO.NET to return to callers the same data types they would use to refresh the user interface. A managed provider supplies objects to connect to a data source, execute a command, start a transaction, and then grab or set some data.

In this chapter, we focused on establishing a connection to the data source and setting up commands and transactions. In the next chapter, we'll complete our look at ADO.NET by exploring data container classes such as *DataSet* and *DataTable*.

Just The Facts

- ADO.NET is a data-access subsystem in the Microsoft .NET Framework and is made of two distinct, but closely related, sets of classes—data providers and data containers.

- The functionalities supplied by a .NET data provider fall into a couple of categories: capability of populating container classes, and capability of setting up a connection and executing commands.

- The .NET Framework comes with data providers for SQL Server, Oracle, and all OLE DB and ODBC data sources.

- A data provider is faster and more appropriate than any other database technology for data-access tasks in .NET. Especially effective with SQL Server, a managed data provider hooks up at the wire level and removes any sort of abstraction layer.

- The data provider supplies an object to establish and manage the connection to a data source. This object implements connection pooling.

- In .NET applications, connection strings can be stored in a special section of the configuration file and encrypted if required.

- The data provider supplies an object to execute commands on an open connection and optionally within a transaction. The command object lists various execute methods to account for query and nonquery commands. Commands can execute either synchronously or asynchronously.

- Data returned by a query command are cached in a data reader object, which is a kind of optimized read-only, forward-only cursor.

- Local and distributed transactions can be managed through the TransactionScope class introduced with ADO.NET 2.0 and also supported by newer versions.

Chapter 8
ADO.NET Data Containers

To enhance aggregation and delivery of data across the tiers of distributed enterprise systems, ADO.NET introduces a new breed of object that looks and acts like the in-memory version of a modern powerful database—the *DataSet*. At its core, the *DataSet* is merely a data container—a sort of super dictionary—specifically designed to manage tabular data expressed in terms of tables, columns, and rows. Nothing in the *DataSet* is tied to a physical database—be it Microsoft SQL Server, Microsoft Access, or even Oracle databases. The *DataSet* has no notion of the provider that served its data; it is a mere data container that is serializable, feature-rich, and tightly integrated with ADO.NET providers. *DataSet* and related objects—such as *DataTable*, *DataView*, and *DataRelation*—form the second leg of the ADO. NET framework—that is, smart containers of data filled by enabled managed providers.

ADO.NET containers expose an API to let application developers populate them with any sort of data. In many cases, though, you want a *DataSet* to contain the results of a database query. This entails various steps: running the query, processing the results, filling the container, closing the connection, and so forth. To get the results, you need a command and a data reader; next, you need some code to walk through the reader and copy the records in a proper table layout. All this behavior (and much more, actually) is incorporated in a made-to-measure ADO.NET object—the data adapter. Without further ado, let's start the second part of our ADO.NET exploration with a look at adapters. Next, we'll take the plunge and dive into *DataSet*, *DataTable*, and *DataView* classes. As their names suggest, these classes mimic the behavior of well-known database objects but remain database-agnostic—that is, they exist as purely in-memory objects.

Data Adapters

In ADO.NET, the data adapter object acts as a two-way bridge between a data source and the *DataSet* object. The *DataSet* is a disconnected container of data, and the adapter takes care of filling it and submitting its data back to a particular data source. From an abstract point of view, a data adapter is similar to a command and represents another way of executing a command against the data source.

> **Note** In a certain way, the concepts of a *command*, *data reader*, and *data adapter* are the results of the ADO *Recordset* split. Born to be a simple COM wrapper around an SQL result set, the ADO *Recordset* soon became a rather bloated object incorporating three types of cursors—read-only, disconnected, and server. Compared to ADO, the ADO.NET object model is simpler overall and, more importantly, made of simpler objects. Instead of providing a big monolithic object such as the *Recordset*, ADO.NET supplies three smaller and highly specialized objects—the command, data reader, and *DataSet*. The data reader is generated only by a direct query command; the *DataSet* is filled only by a data adapter. To complete the comparison, note that ADO.NET has no native support for database server cursors.

The big difference between commands and data adapters is just in the way each one returns the retrieved data. A query command returns a read-only, forward-only cursor—the data reader. The data adapter performs its data access, grabs all the data, and packs it into an in-memory container—the *DataSet* or *DataTable*. Under the hood, the data adapter is just an extra layer of abstraction built on top of the command/data reader pair. Internally, in fact, the data adapter just uses a command to query and a data reader to walk its way through the records and fill a user-provided *DataSet*.

Like commands and data readers, data adapters are specific to each data provider. So expect to find a data adapter class for SQL Server, one for Oracle, and so on. To come to grips with data adapters, let's examine the SQL Server adapter.

The *SqlDataAdapter* Class

By definition, a data adapter is a class that implements the *IDataAdapter* interface. However, looking at the actual implementation of the adapters in the supported providers, you can see that multiple layers of code are used. In particular, all data adapter classes inherit from a base class named *DbDataAdapter* and implement the *IDbDataAdapter* interface. The relationship is shown in Figure 8-1.

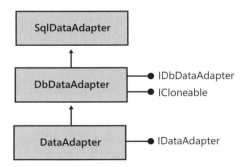

FIGURE 8-1 The hierarchy of data adapters and implemented interfaces.

Programming the SQL Server Data Adapter

Table 8-1 shows the properties of the *SqlDataAdapter* class—that is, the data adapter class for SQL Server.

TABLE 8-1 Properties of the *SqlDataAdapter* Class

Property	Description
AcceptChangesDuringFill	Indicates whether or not insertions of a row during a fill operation should be committed. *True* by default.
AcceptChangesDuringUpdate	Indicates whether or not changed rows processed during a batch update operation should be committed. *True* by default. *Not supported in ADO.NET 1.x.*
ContinueUpdateOnError	Indicates whether in case of row conflicts the batch update continues or an exception is generated.
DeleteCommand	Gets or sets a statement or stored procedure to delete records from the database during batch update. Is a member of the *IDbDataAdapter* interface.
FillLoadOption	Indicates how retrieved values will be applied to existing rows. *Not supported in ADO.NET 1.x.*
InsertCommand	Gets or sets a statement or stored procedure to insert new records in the database during batch update. Is a member of the *IDbDataAdapter* interface.
MissingMappingAction	Determines the action to take when a table or column in the source data is not mapped to a corresponding element in the in-memory structure. Is a member of the *IDataAdapter* interface.
MissingSchemaAction	Determines the action to take when source data does not have a matching table or column in the corresponding in-memory structure. Is a member of the *IDataAdapter* interface.
ReturnProviderSpecificTypes	Indicates whether or not provider-specific types should be used to create table layouts to contain result sets during a fill operation. *Not supported in ADO.NET 1.x.*
SelectCommand	Gets or sets a statement or stored procedure to select records from the database. During batch update, the method is used to download metadata; it is used to select records in a query statement. Is a member of the *IDbDataAdapter* interface.
TableMappings	Gets a collection that provides the mappings between a source table and an in-memory table. Is a member of the *IDataAdapter* interface.
UpdateBatchSize	Indicates the size of the blocks of records submitted at a time during the batch update. Set to 1 by default. *Not supported in ADO.NET 1.x.*
UpdateCommand	Gets or sets a statement or stored procedure to update records in the database during batch update. Is a member of the *IDbDataAdapter* interface.

One thing is essential to know about a data adapter. It is a two-way channel used to read data from a data source into a memory table and to write in-memory data back to a data source. The data source used in both cases is likely to be the same, but it's not necessarily the same. These two operations, known as *fill* and *update*, can be clearly identified in the preceding list of properties.

The four *xxxCommand* members of the *IDbDataAdapter* interface are used to control how in-memory data is written to the database during an *update* operation. This is not entirely true of *SelectCommand*. Although *SelectCommand* plays a role in the batch update process, it is the key member in performing the *fill* operation. The *MissingXXX* properties, *TableMappings* collection, and—in ADO.NET 2.0 and beyond—*FillLoadOption* and *ReturnProviderSpecificTypes* indicate how data read out of the data source is mapped onto client memory.

Once loaded in memory, the (disconnected) data is available for client-side updates performed by a Windows application or an ASP.NET page. Client updates consist of adding new rows and deleting or updating existing ones. A batch update is the data provider procedure that, triggered by the client application, posts all the pending in-memory changes back to a data source. In carrying out this procedure, a bunch of database management system (DBMS)–specific commands are required to carry out the three basic operations—insert, update, and delete. The *InsertCommand*, *UpdateCommand*, and *DeleteCommand* properties are *SqlCommand* objects that do just this.

> **Important** ADO.NET batch updates consist of a series of commands sequentially submitted to the database, by means of the data adapter. As a developer, you fire the batch update process with a single command. Bear in mind that conceptually ADO.NET batch updates don't equate to a series of queries submitted in a single command. "Batch update" doesn't really mean that a batch of commands and data is moved on the DBMS and executes there.
>
> Using a batch update is a powerful approach, but it's not particularly suited to ASP.NET applications. The difficulty lies in the fact that Web applications work over a stateless protocol such as HTTP. So to make the whole scheme work well, you should cache the in-memory table in the session, which is not something all applications can afford. In addition, note that using a batch update saves you from a lot of coding and can be easily configured to serve complex update scenarios. Using a batch update, though, doesn't necessarily give you significant performance advantages because each update requires its own command in ADO.NET 1.x. Starting with ADO.NET 2.0, you can group more updates in a unique command instead through the new *UpdateBatchSize* property.

Table 8-2 lists the methods of the data adapter objects.

TABLE 8-2 Methods of the *SqlDataAdapter* Class

Method	Description
Fill	Populates an in-memory table with rows read from the source.
FillSchema	Configures an in-memory table so that the schema matches the schema in the data source.
GetFillParameters	Returns the parameters the user set on the query statement.
Update	Updates the data source based on the current content of the specified in-memory table. It works by calling the respective INSERT, UPDATE, or DELETE statements for each inserted, updated, or deleted row, respectively, in the table.

The data adapter uses the *SelectCommand* property to retrieve schema and data from the data source. The connection object associated with the *SelectCommand* does not need to be open. If the connection is closed before the reading occurs, it is opened to retrieve data and then closed. If the connection is open when the adapter works, it remains open.

Filling a *DataSet* Using a Data Adapter

A data adapter object uses the *Fill* method to populate an in-memory object with data retrieved through a query. The in-memory structure is a *DataSet* or *DataTable* object. As we'll see more clearly in a moment, the *DataSet* is the in-memory counterpart of a DBMS database. It might contain multiple tables (that is, multiple *DataTable* objects) and set up relationships and constraints between tables. Each table, in turn, is made of a number of columns and rows.

Filling a *DataSet* object ultimately means filling one of its tables. The data adapter can create a new table for each result set generated by the query. The table mapping code decides how. (If the table exists already, it is updated.) Mapping a result set to a *DataSet* is a process articulated in two phases: table mapping and column mapping. During the first step, the data adapter determines the name of the *DataTable* that will contain the rows in the current result set. Each *DataTable* is given a default name you can change at will.

> **Note** Just because you can fill a *DataTable* with any kind of data from any existing source, the name of the table doesn't necessarily have to reflect the name of a database table, even when the data comes out of a database query. The *DataTable*'s table name serves only to identify the object. Changing the name of a *DataTable* doesn't have any impact on the name of the database table that might have been used to fill it.

The default name of the *DataTable* depends on the signature of the *Fill* method that was used for the call. For example, let's consider the following two *Fill* calls:

```
DataSet ds = new DataSet();
adapter.Fill(ds);
adapter.Fill(ds, "MyTable");
```

In the first call, the name of the first result set generated by the query defaults to "Table". If the query produces multiple result sets, additional tables will be named Table1, Table2, and so on, appending a progressive index to the default name. In the second call, the first result set is named MyTable and the others are named after it: MyTable1, MyTable2, and so forth. The procedure is identical; what really changes in the two cases is the base name.

The names of the tables can be changed at two different moments. You can change them after the *DataSet* has been populated or, when using table mapping, you can define settings that will be used to name the tables upon creation. You define a table mapping on a data adapter object by using the *TableMappings* property.

> **Note** You can also use the *Fill* method to populate a single *DataTable*. In this case, only the first result set is taken into account and only one mapping phase occurs—column mapping.
>
> ```
> DataTable dt = new DataTable();
> adapter.Fill(dt);
> ```
>
> The preceding code shows how to use the *Fill* method to populate a *DataTable*.

Loading Options

In ADO.NET 2.0 and beyond, you can better control the way data is loaded into the various data tables during a fill operation. By setting the *FillLoadOption* property, you indicate how rows already in a *DataTable* combine with rows being loaded. The *FillLoadOption* property accepts a value from the *LoadOption* enumeration. Table 8-3 describes the feasible values.

TABLE 8-3 Values from the *LoadOption* Enumeration

Value	Description
OverwriteChanges	Updates the current and original versions of the row with the value of the incoming row.
PreserveChanges	Default option. Updates the original version of the row with the value of the incoming row.
Upsert	Updates the current version of the row with the value of the incoming row.

In each case, the description indicates the behavior when the primary key of a row in the incoming data matches the primary key of an existing row.

OverwriteChanges addresses the need to initialize tables with fresh data. *PreserveChanges*, on the other hand, is useful when you are in the process of synchronizing existing in-memory data with the current state of the database. In this case, you want to preserve any changes you entered on the client—that is, the current values you're working with and that you plan to submit back to the database later. At the same time, you might want to update the values in the *DataSet* that represent the original values read from the database. Finally, *Upsert* simply overwrites the current value, leaving the original value intact.

It is important to note that in-memory rows maintain two distinct values—current and original. The current value is the value that you receive when you read the content of a cell. The original value is the last value stored in the cell that was committed. When you assign a value to a newly created row, you set the current value. The original value is null. The assigned value must be committed to become an effective part of the row. You commit a row by invoking the *AcceptChanges* method (which will be discussed in more detail later). When this happens, the current value is duplicated as the original value and the overall state of the row is modified to *unchanged*. The row has no pending changes.

A *DataSet* populated with a fill operation presents all committed rows where current and original values coincide. Or at least this is the default behavior that you can alter by setting the *AcceptChangesDuringFill* property. Once the data is downloaded on the client, the client application can work with it and enter changes, as shown here:

```
// _data is a filled DataSet object
DataTable table = _data.Tables[0];
DataRow row = table.Rows[0];
row["firstname"] = "Lucy";
```

The assignment simply alters the current value of the row; the original value remains set to null or what it was before the assignment. To make "Lucy" become the effective original value of the row, you have to explicitly accept or commit the change:

```
// Accept all pending (uncommitted) changes on the row
row.AcceptChanges();
```

Uncommitted changes are important because only pending uncommitted changes are taken into account during a batch update operation. To read the current value of a row value, you do as follows:

```
Response.Write(row["firstname"].ToString());
```

To read the original value, you resort to the following:

```
Response.Write(row["firstname", DataRowVersion.Original].ToString());
```

Figure 8-2 shows the output of the sample page that illustrates the *FillLoadOption* property and the adapter's *Fill* method.

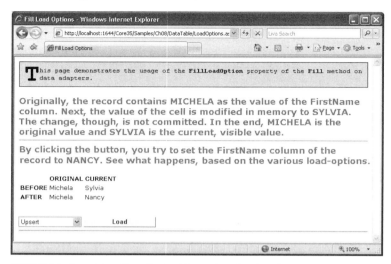

FIGURE 8-2 Examining the effect of the various load options.

As you can see, the *Upsert* option replaces the current value, leaving the original intact.

> **Note** In ADO.NET 1.x, the default behavior is *OverwriteChanges*; if *AcceptChangesDuringFill* is *false*, the actual behavior you get is *Upsert*. You never preserve client changes in ADO.NET 1.x. In ADO.NET 2.0 and beyond, the value of *AcceptChangesDuringFill* is taken into account only for rows added, not for existing rows that get updated by the fill operation.

The *DataSet* is an empty container that a data adapter fills with the results of a query. But what about the number and structure of the child tables? The number of tables depends on the number of result sets. The structure of the tables depends on the table-mapping mechanism.

The Table-Mapping Mechanism

The .NET data provider assigns a default name to each result set generated by the query. The default name is *Table* or any name specified by the programmer in the call to *Fill*. The adapter looks up its *TableMappings* collection for an entry that matches the default name of the result set being read. If a match is found, the data adapter reads the mapped name. Next, it attempts to locate in the *DataSet* a *DataTable* object with the name specified in the mapping, as shown in Figure 8-3.

If the result set named *Table* has been mapped to Employees, a table named Employees is searched in the *DataSet*. If no such *DataTable* object exists, it gets created and filled. If such a *DataTable* exists in the *DataSet*, its content is merged with the contents of the result set.

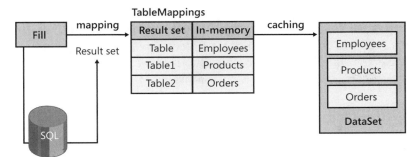

FIGURE 8-3 Mapping a result set onto a *DataSet* object.

The *TableMappings* property represents a collection object of type
DataTableMappingCollection. Each contained *DataTableMapping* object defines a pair of
names: a source table name and an in-memory table name. Here's how to configure a few
table mappings:

```
DataSet ds = new DataSet();
DataTableMapping dtm1, dtm2, dtm3;
dtm1 = adapter.TableMappings.Add("Table", "Employees");
dtm2 = adapter.TableMappings.Add("Table1", "Products");
dtm3 = adapter.TableMappings.Add("Table2", "Orders");
adapter.Fill(ds);
```

It goes without saying that the default names you map onto your own names must coincide
with the default names originated by the call to the *Fill* method. In other words, suppose you
change the last line of the previous code snippet with the following one:

```
adapter.Fill(ds, "MyTable");
```

In this case, the code won't work any longer because the default names will now be MyTable,
MyTable1, and MyTable2. For these names, the *TableMappings* collection would have no entries defined. Finally, bear in mind you can have any number of table mappings. The overall
number of mappings doesn't necessarily have to be related to the expected number of result
sets.

The Column-Mapping Mechanism

If table mapping ended here, it wouldn't be such a big deal for us. In fact, if your goal is simply to give a mnemonic name to your *DataSet* tables, use the following code. The final effect
is exactly the same.

```
DataSet ds = new DataSet();
adapter.Fill(ds);
ds.Tables["Table"].TableName = "Employees";
ds.Tables["Table1"].TableName = "Products";
```

The mapping mechanism, though, has another, rather interesting, facet: column mapping. Column mapping establishes a link between a column in the result set and a column in the mapped *DataTable* object. Column mappings are stored in the *ColumnMappings* collection property defined in the *DataTableMapping* class. The following code shows how to create a column mapping:

```
DataSet ds = new DataSet();
DataTableMapping dtm1;
dtm1 = adapter.TableMappings.Add("Table", "Employees");
dtm1.ColumnMappings.Add("employeeid", "ID");
dtm1.ColumnMappings.Add("firstname", "Name");
dtm1.ColumnMappings.Add("lastname", "FamilyName");
adapter.Fill(ds);
```

Figure 8-4 extends the previous diagram (Figure 8-3) and includes details of the column-mapping mechanism.

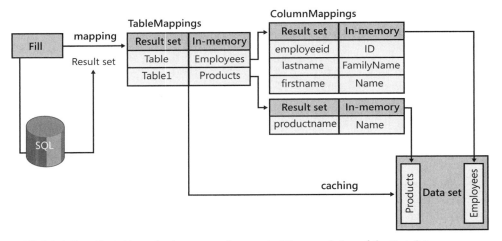

FIGURE 8-4 How the table and column mappings control the population of the *DataSet*.

In the preceding code, the source column *employeeid* is renamed to *ID* and placed in a *DataTable* named *Employees*. The name of the column is the only argument you can change at this level. Bear in mind that all this mapping takes place automatically within the body of the *Fill* method. When *Fill* terminates, each column in the source result set has been transformed into a *DataTable* column object—an instance of the *DataColumn* class.

Missing Mapping Action

The *Fill* method accomplishes two main operations. First, it maps the source result sets onto in-memory tables. Second, it fills the tables with the data fetched from the physical data source. While accomplishing either of these tasks, the *Fill* method could raise some special exceptions. An exception is an anomalous situation that needs to be specifically addressed codewise. When the adapter can't find a table or column mapping, or when a required *DataTable* or *DataColumn* can't be found, the data adapter throws a kind of lightweight exception.

Unlike real exceptions that must be resolved in code, this special breed of data adapter exceptions has to be resolved declaratively by choosing an action from a small set of allowable options. Data adapters raise two types of lightweight exceptions: missing mapping actions and missing schema actions.

A missing mapping action is required in two circumstances that can occur when the data adapter is collecting data to fill the *DataSet*. You need it if a default name is not found in the *TableMappings* collection, or if a column name is not available in the table's *ColumnMappings* collection. The data adapter's *MissingMappingAction* property is the tool you have to customize the behavior of the data adapter in the face of such exceptions. Allowable values for the property come from the *MissingMappingAction* enumeration and are listed in Table 8-4.

TABLE 8-4 The *MissingMappingAction* Enumeration

Value	Description
Error	An exception is generated if a missing column or table is detected.
Ignore	The unmapped column or table is ignored.
Passthrough	Default option. It adds the missing table or column to the structure.

Unless you explicitly set the *MissingMappingAction* property prior to filling the data adapter, the property assumes a default value of *Passthrough*. As a result, missing tables and columns are added using the default name. If you set the *MissingMappingAction* property to *Ignore*, any unmapped table or column is simply ignored. No error is detected, but there will be no content for the incriminating result set (or one of its columns) in the target *DataSet*. If the *MissingMappingAction* property is set to *Error*, the adapter is limited to throwing an exception whenever a missing mapping is detected.

Once the data adapter is done with the mapping phase, it takes care of actually populating the target *DataSet* with the content of the selected result sets. Any required *DataTable* or *DataColumn* object that is not available in the target *DataSet* triggers another lightweight exception and requires another declarative action: the missing schema action.

Missing Schema Action

A missing schema action is required if the *DataSet* does not contain a table with the name that has been determined during the table-mapping step. Similarly, the same action is required if the *DataSet* table does not contain a column with the expected mapping name. *MissingSchemaAction* is the property you set to indicate the action you want to be taken in case of an insufficient table schema. Allowable values for the property come from the *MissingSchemaAction* enumeration and are listed in Table 8-5.

TABLE 8-5 The *MissingSchemaAction* Enumeration

Value	Description
Error	Generates an exception if a missing column or table is detected.
Ignore	Ignores the unmapped column or table.
Add	The default option. Completes the schema by adding any missing item.
AddWithKey	Also adds primary key and constraints.

By default, the *MissingSchemaAction* property is set to *Add*. As a result, the *DataSet* is completed by adding any constituent item that is missing—*DataTable* or *DataColumn*. Bear in mind, though, that the schema information added in this way for each column is very limited. It simply includes name and type. If you want extra information—such as the primary key, autoincrement, read-only, and allow-null settings—use the *AddWithKey* option instead.

Note that even if you use the *AddWithKey* option, not all available information about the column is really loaded into the *DataColumn*. For example, *AddWithKey* marks a column as autoincrement but does not set the related seed and step properties. Also the default value for the source column, if any, is not automatically copied. Only the primary key is imported; any additional indexes you might have set in the database are not. As for the other two options, *Ignore* and *Error*, they work exactly as they do with the *MissingMappingAction* property.

Prefilling the Schema

MissingMappingAction and *MissingSchemaAction* are not as expensive as real exceptions, but they still affect your code. Put another way, filling a *DataSet* that already contains all the needed schema information results in faster code. The advantage of this approach is more evident if your code happens to repeatedly fill an empty *DataSet* with a fixed schema. In this case, using a global *DataSet* object pre-filled with schema information helps to prevent all those requests for recovery actions. The *FillSchema* method just ensures that all the required objects are created beforehand.

```
DataTable[] FillSchema(DataSet ds, SchemaType mappingMode);
```

FillSchema takes a *DataSet* and adds as many tables to it as needed by the query command associated with the data adapter. The method returns an array with all the *DataTable* objects created (only schema, no data). The mapping-mode parameter can be one of the values defined in the *SchemaType* enumeration. The *SchemaType* enumeration values are listed in Table 8-6.

TABLE 8-6 The *SchemaType* Enumeration

Value	Description
Mapped	Apply any existing table mappings to the incoming schema. Configure the *DataSet* with the transformed schema. Recommended option.
Source	Ignore any table mappings on the data adapter. Configure the *DataSet* using the incoming schema without applying any transformations.

The *Mapped* option describes what happens when mappings are defined. *Source*, on the other hand, deliberately ignores any mappings you might have set. In this case, the tables in the *DataSet* retain their default name and all the columns maintain the original name they were given in the source tables.

How Batch Update Works

Batch update consists of the submission of an entire set of changes to the database. The batch update basically repeats the user actions that produced the changes that have the database—rather than the *DataSet*—as the target. Batch update assumes that the application enters its changes to the data set in an offline manner. In a multiuser environment, this might pose design problems if users concurrently access on the server the same data you're editing offline. When you post your changes on a record that another person has modified in the meantime, whose changes win out?

Data Conflicts and Optimistic Lock

The possibility of data conflicts represents a design issue, but it isn't necessarily a problem for the application. Batch update in a multiuser environment creates conflict only if the changes you enter are somewhat implied by the original values you have read. In such a case, if someone else has changed the rows in the time elapsed between your fetch and the batch update, you might want to reconsider or reject your most recent updates. Conflicts detected at update time might introduce significant overhead that could make the batch update solution much less exciting. In environments with a low degree of data contention, batch updates can be effective because they allow for disconnected architectures, higher scalability, and considerably simpler coding.

To submit client changes to the server, use the data adapter's *Update* method. Data can be submitted only on a per-table basis. If you call *Update* without specifying any table name, a default name of Table is assumed. If no table exists with that name, an exception is raised.

```
adapter.Update(ds, "MyTable");
```

The *Update* method prepares and executes a tailor-made *INSERT, UPDATE,* or *DELETE* statement for each inserted, updated, or deleted row in the specified table. Rows are processed according to their natural order, and the row state determines the operation to accomplish. The *Update* method has several overloads and returns an integer, which represents the number of rows successfully updated.

When a row being updated returns an error, an exception is raised and the batch update process is stopped. You can prevent this from happening by setting the *ContinueUpdateOnError* property to *true*. In this case, the batch update terminates only when all the rows have been processed. Rows for which the update completed successfully are committed and marked as unchanged in the *DataSet*. For other rows, the application must decide what to do and re-start the update if needed.

> **Note**   The batch update is a loop that executes one user-defined database command for each inserted, modified, or deleted row in the *DataSet*. In no way does the batch update process send the whole *DataSet* to the database for server-side processing.

Command Builders

The data adapter provides a bunch of command properties—*InsertCommand, DeleteCommand,* and *UpdateCommand*—to let the programmer control and customize the way in which in-memory updates are submitted to the database server. These properties represent a quantum leap from ADO, in which update commands were SQL commands silently generated by the library. If you don't quite see the importance of this change, consider that with ADO.NET you can use stored procedures to perform batch updates and even work with non-SQL data providers.

The commands can also be generated automatically and exposed directly to the data-adapter engine. Command builder objects do that for you. A command builder object—for example, the *SqlCommandBuilder* class—cannot be used in all cases. The automatic generation of commands can take place only under certain circumstances. In particular, command builders do not generate anything if the table is obtained by joining columns from more than one table and if calculated—or aggregate—columns are detected. Command builders are extremely helpful and code-saving only when they are called to deal with single-table updates. How can a command builder generate update statements for a generic table? This is where the fourth command property—the *SelectCommand* property—fits in.

A command builder employs *SelectCommand* to obtain all the metadata necessary to build the update commands. To use command builders, you must set *SelectCommand* with a query string that contains a primary key and a few column names. Only those fields will be used for the update, and the insertion and key fields will be used to uniquely identify rows to update or delete. Note that the command text of *SelectCommand* runs in the provider-specific way that makes it return only metadata and no rows.

The association between the data adapter and the command builder is established through the builder's constructor, as shown in the following code:

```
SqlCommand cmd = new SqlCommand();
cmd.CommandText = "SELECT employeeid, lastname FROM Employees";
cmd.Connection = conn;
adapter.SelectCommand = cmd;
SqlCommandBuilder builder = new SqlCommandBuilder(adapter);
```

The builder requests metadata and generates the commands the first time they are required and then caches them. Each command is exposed through a particular method—*GetInsert-Command*, *GetUpdateCommand*, and *GetDeleteCommand*. Note that using the command builder *does not* automatically set the corresponding command properties on the data adapter.

Note The behavior of data adapters and command builders for other managed providers does not differ in a relevant way from what we described here for the SQL Server .NET data provider.

In-Memory Data Container Objects

The *System.Data* namespace contains several collection-like objects that, combined, provide an in-memory representation of the DBMS relational programming model. The *DataSet* class looks like a catalog, whereas the *DataTable* maps to an individual table. The *DataRelation* class represents a relationship between tables, and the *DataView* creates a filtered view of a table's data. In addition, the *System.Data* namespace also supports constraints and a relatively simple model of indexing.

The facilities of the memory-resident database model tout a programming model in which disconnection is a key feature rather than a precise requirement. Using the *DataSet* model, for example, you can filter and sort the data on the client before it gets to the middle tier. Having such facilities available within the *DataSet* means that once the data is there, you don't need to go back to the database to get a different view on the data. The data stored in the *DataSet* is self-sufficient, which makes the whole model inherently disconnected.

Note An interesting use of the *DataSet* that makes sense both for Web and desktop scenarios is in moving data around between components and tiers. The *DataSet* is great at encapsulating tables of data and relationships. It can also be passed around between tiers as a monolithic object. Finally, it can be serialized, meaning that data and related schema can be moved between tiers in a loosely coupled manner.

The *DataSet* class is the principal component in the ADO.NET object model, but several others are satellite classes that play a fundamental role. ADO.NET container classes are listed Table 8-7.

TABLE 8-7 ADO.NET Container Classes

Class	Description
DataSet	An in-memory cache of data made of tables, relations, and constraints. Serializable and remotable, it can be filled from a variety of data sources and works regardless of which one is used.
DataTable	Represents a relational table of data with a collection of columns and rows.
DataColumn	Represents a column in a *DataTable* object.
DataRow	Represents a row in a *DataTable* object.
DataView	Defined on top of a particular table, it creates a filtered view of data. It can be configured to support editing and sorting. The data view is not a copy of the data—just a mask.
DataRelation	Represents a relationship between two tables in the same *DataSet*. The relationship is set on a common column.

A key point to remember about ADO.NET container classes is that they work regardless of the data source used. You can populate the tables in a *DataSet* using the results of a SQL Server query as well as file system information or data read out of a real-time device. Even more importantly, none of the ADO.NET container classes retains information about the source. Like array or collection objects, they just contain data. Unlike array or collection objects, though, they provide facilities to relate and manage data in a database-like fashion.

The *DataSet* Object

The *DataSet* class implements three important interfaces—*IListSource* makes it possible to return a data-bound list of elements, *ISerializable* makes the class capable of controlling how its data is serialized to a .NET formatter, and *IXmlSerializable* guarantees the class can serialize itself to XML. Table 8-8 lists the properties of the *DataSet* class.

TABLE 8-8 Properties of the *DataSet* Class

Property	Description
CaseSensitive	Gets or sets a value that indicates whether string comparisons within *DataTable* objects are case sensitive.
DataSetName	Gets or sets the name of the *DataSet*.
DefaultViewManager	Gets the default view manager object—an instance of the *DefaultViewManager* class—that contains settings for each table in the *DataSet*.

Property	Description
EnforceConstraints	Gets or sets a value that indicates whether constraint rules are enforced when attempting any update operation.
ExtendedProperties	Gets the collection of customized user information associated with the *DataSet*.
HasErrors	Gets whether there are errors in any of the child *DataTable* objects.
Locale	Gets or sets the locale information used to compare strings within the tables.
Namespace	Gets or sets the namespace of the *DataSet*.
Prefix	Gets or sets the prefix that aliases the namespace of the *DataSet*.
Relations	Gets the collection of the relations set between pairs of child tables.
RemotingFormat	Indicates the desired serialization format—binary or XML. *Not supported in ADO.NET 1.x.*
SchemaSerializationMode	Indicates whether or not schema should be included in the serialized data. *Not supported in ADO.NET 1.x.*
Tables	Gets the collection of contained tables.

The *Namespace* and *Prefix* properties affect the way in which the *DataSet* serializes itself to XML. The name of the *DataSet* is also used to set the root node of the XML representation. If the *DataSetName* is empty, the *NewDataSet* string is used. The methods of the class are listed in Table 8-9.

TABLE 8-9 Methods of the *DataSet* Class

Method	Description
AcceptChanges	Commits all the changes made to all the tables in the *DataSet* since it was loaded or since the last time the method was called.
Clear	Removes all rows in all tables.
Clone	Copies the structure of the *DataSet*, including all table schemas, relations, and constraints. No data is copied.
Copy	Makes a deep copy of the object, including schema and data.
CreateDataReader	Returns a *DataTable*-specific data reader object with one result set per table, in the same sequence as they appear in the *Tables* collection. *Not supported in ADO.NET 1.x.*
GetChanges	Returns a copy of the *DataSet* containing only the changes made to it since it was last loaded or since *AcceptChanges* was called.
GetXml	Returns the XML representation of the data stored.
GetXmlSchema	Returns the XSD schema for the XML string representing the data stored in the *DataSet*.

Method	Description
HasChanges	Indicates whether there are new, deleted, or modified rows in any of the contained tables.
InferXmlSchema	Replicates into the *DataSet* the table structure inferred from the specified XML document.
Merge	Merges the specified ADO.NET object (*DataSet*, *DataTable*, or array of *DataRow* objects) into the current *DataSet*.
ReadXml	Populates the *DataSet* by reading schema and data from the specified XML document.
ReadXmlSchema	Replicates into the *DataSet* the table structure read from the specified XML schema.
RejectChanges	Rolls back all the changes made to all the tables since it was created or since the last time *AcceptChanges* was called.
Reset	Empties tables, relations, and constraints, resetting the *DataSet* to its default state.
WriteXml	Serializes the *DataSet* contents to XML.
WriteXmlSchema	Writes the *DataSet* structure as an XML schema.

To make a full, deep copy of the *DataSet*, you must resort to the *Copy* method—except that in this case you duplicate the object. The following code does not duplicate the object:

```
DataSet tmp = ds;
```

If you simply assign the current *DataSet* reference to another variable, you duplicate the reference but not the object. Use the following code to duplicate the object:

```
DataSet tmp = ds.Copy();
```

The *Copy* method creates and returns a new instance of the *DataSet* object, and it ensures that all the tables, relations, and constraints are duplicated. The *Clone* method is limited to returning a new *DataSet* object in which all the properties have been replicated but no data in the tables is copied.

Reading Stored Data

*DataSet*s and data readers are often presented as mutually exclusive and alternative ways to read data in ADO.NET applications. At its core, in ADO.NET there's just one physical way of reading data—using data readers. *DataSet*s are disconnected containers automatically filled using a reader, and they are ideal for caching data. Data readers are ideal tools for consuming data as you walk your way through the result set.

Imagine now that you have access to some previously cached data—say, a *DataSet* stored in the session state. How do you find and read a particular record? You typically indicate the coordinates of the record (row and column) and perform a random access to it. If you need to read two or more records, you just repeat the operation. In ADO.NET 2.0 and beyond, there's a better way—using in-memory, disconnected readers that you create through the *CreateDataReader* method. A reader obtained in this way is different from the connected, cursor-like data reader you get out of the *ExecuteReader* method on the command class. What you get here is a *DataTableReader* object, good at scrolling the contents of an in-memory data table using the same cursor-like programming interface of data readers. Here's an example:

```
DataSet data = new DataSet();
SqlDataAdapter adapter = new SqlDataAdapter(
    "SELECT * FROM employees;SELECT * FROM customers",
    ConfigurationManager.ConnectionStrings["LocalNWind"].ConnectionString);
adapter.Fill(data);

// Access the whole data set, record by record
DataTableReader reader = data.CreateDataReader();
do
{
    while (reader.Read()) {
        // reader[1] indicates the second column
        Response.Write(String.Format("{0} <br>", reader[1]));
    }
    Response.Write("<hr>");
} while (reader.NextResult());

reader.Close();
```

The *do* statement loops through all the result sets and lists the content of the second field for the record. This code is not really different from the code we examined in Chapter 7 for multiple result sets except that all this code runs in-memory without any connection to the database.

What's the purpose of table readers? Your code runs faster when repeated reads of many consecutive records should be performed.

Merging *DataSet* Objects

A merge operation is typically accomplished by a client application to update an existing *DataSet* object with the latest changes read from the data source. The *Merge* method should be used to fuse together two *DataSet* objects that have nearly identical schemas. The two schemas, though, are not strictly required to be identical.

The first step in the merge operation compares the schemas of the involved *DataSet* objects to see whether they match. If the *DataSet* to be imported contains new columns or a new table source, what happens depends on the missing schema action specified. By default, any missing schema element is added to the target *DataSet*, but you can change the behavior by choosing the *Merge* overload that allows for a *MissingSchemaAction* parameter.

At the second step, the *Merge* method attempts to merge the data by looking at the changed rows in the *DataSet* to be imported. Any modified or deleted row is matched to the corresponding row in the existing *DataSet* by using the primary key value. Added rows are simply added to the existing *DataSet* and retain their primary key value.

The merge operation is an atomic operation that must guarantee integrity and consistency only at its end. For this reason, constraints are disabled during a merge operation. However, if at the end of the merge the original constraints can't be restored—for example, a unique constraint is violated—an exception is thrown, but no uploaded data gets lost. In this case, the *Merge* method completely disables constraints in the *DataSet*. It sets the *EnforceConstraints* property to *false* and marks all invalid rows in error. To restore constraints, you must first resolve errors.

The *DataSet* Commit Model

When the *DataSet* is first loaded, all the rows in all tables are marked as unchanged. (All rows are marked *Added* if the *AcceptChangesDuringFill* property is *false* on the adapter used to fill the *DataSet*.) The state of a table row is stored in a property named *RowState*. Allowable values for the row state are in the *DataRowState* enumeration listed in Table 8-10.

TABLE 8-10 States of a Table Row

Value	Description
Added	The row has been added to the table.
Deleted	The row is marked for deletion from the parent table.
Detached	Either the row has been created but not yet added to the table or the row has been removed from the rows collection.
Modified	Some columns within the row have been changed.
Unchanged	No changes have been made since the last call to *AcceptChanges*. This is also the state of all rows when the table is first created.

Each programmatic operation accomplished on a *DataSet* member changes the state of the involved rows. All changes remain pending in an uncommitted state until a specific call is made to make the changes persistent. The *AcceptChanges* method has the power to commit all the changes and accept the current values as the new original values of the table. After *AcceptChanges* is called, all changes are cleared and rows incorporate the changed values and appear as unchanged. The *RejectChanges* method, on the other hand, rolls back all the pending changes and restores the original values. Note that the *DataSet* retains original values until changes are committed or rejected.

The commit model is applicable at various levels. In particular, by calling *AcceptChanges* or *RejectChanges* on the *DataSet* object, you commit or roll back changes for all the rows in all the contained tables. If you call the same methods on a *DataTable* object, the effect applies to all the rows in the specified table. Finally, you can also accept or reject changes for an individual row in a particular table.

Serializing Contents to XML

The contents of a *DataSet* object can be serialized as XML in two ways, which I'll call *stateless* and *stateful*. Although these expressions are not common throughout the ADO.NET documentation, I feel that they perfectly describe the gist of the two possible approaches. A stateless representation takes a snapshot of the current instance of the data and renders it according to a particular XML schema—the ADO.NET normal form—which is shown in the following code:

```
<MyDataSet>
    <Employees>
        <ID>...</ID>
        <Name>...</Name>
    </Employees>
    ...
    <Orders>
        <OrderID>...</OrderID>
        <OrderDate>...</OrderDate>
        <Amount>...</Amount>
    </Orders>
</MyDataSet>
```

The root node appears after the *DataSetName* property. Nodes one level deeper represent rows of all tables and are named as the table. Each row node contains as many children as there are columns in the row. This code snippet refers to a *DataSet* with two tables—Employees and Orders—with two and three columns, respectively. That kind of string is what the *GetXml* method returns and what the *WriteXml* method writes out when the default write mode is chosen.

```
dataSet.WriteXml(fileName);
dataSet.WriteXml(fileName, mode);
```

A stateful representation, on the other hand, contains the history of the data in the object and includes information about changes as well as pending errors. Table 8-11 summarizes the writing options available for use with *WriteXml* through the *WriteXmlMode* enumeration.

TABLE 8-11 **The *WriteXmlMode* Enumeration**

Write Mode	Description
IgnoreSchema	Writes the contents of the *DataSet* as XML data without schema.
WriteSchema	Writes the contents of the *DataSet*, including an inline XSD schema. The schema cannot be inserted as XDR, nor can it be added as a reference.
DiffGram	Writes the contents of the *DataSet* as a DiffGram, including original and current values

IgnoreSchema is the default option. The following code demonstrates the typical way to serialize a *DataSet* to an XML file:

```
StreamWriter sw = new StreamWriter(fileName);
dataset.WriteXml(sw);    // defaults to XmlWriteMode.IgnoreSchema
sw.Close();
```

A DiffGram is an XML serialization format that includes both the original values and current values of each row in each table. In particular, a DiffGram contains the current instance of rows with the up-to-date values plus a section where all the original values for changed rows are grouped. Each row is given a unique identifier that is used to track changes between the two sections of the DiffGram. This relationship looks a lot like a foreign-key relationship. The following listing outlines the structure of a DiffGram:

```
<diffgr:diffgram
    xmlns:msdata="urn:schemas-microsoft-com:xml-msdata"
    xmlns:diffgr="urn:schemas-microsoft-com:xml-diffgram-v1">
    <DataSet>
    ...
    </DataSet>

    <diffgr:before>
    ...
    </diffgr:before>

    <diffgr:errors>
    ...
    </diffgr:errors>
</diffgr:diffgram>
```

The *<diffgr:diffgram>* root node can have up to three children. The first is the *DataSet* object with its current contents, including newly added rows and modified rows (but not deleted rows). The actual name of this subtree depends on the *DataSetName* property of the source *DataSet* object. If the *DataSet* has no name, the subtree's root is *NewDataSet*. The subtree rooted in the *<diffgr:before>* node contains enough information to restore the original state of all modified rows. For example, it still contains any row that has been deleted as well as the original content of any modified row. All columns affected by any change are tracked in the *<diffgr:before>* subtree. The last subtree is *<diffgr:errors>*, and it contains information about any errors that might have occurred on a particular row.

Serialization and Remoting Format

In addition to XML serialization, the *DataSet* class fully supports .NET binary serialization. Marked with the *[Serializable]* attribute, the *DataSet* object implements the *ISerializable* interface and gains full control over the serialization process. Put another way, the *DataSet* itself embeds the code that generates the stream of bytes saved as the serialized version of the object.

In ADO.NET 1.x, the *DataSet* serializes as XML even when binary serialization is requested through a .NET formatter. Worse yet, the *DataSet* uses the fairly verbose DiffGram format, topped with any related schema information. All .NET distributed systems that make intensive use of disconnected data (as Microsoft's architecture patterns and practices suggests) are sensitive to the size of serialized data. The larger the *DataSet*, the more these systems suffer from consumption of CPU, memory, and bandwidth. Nicely enough, starting with version 2.0 ADO.NET provides a great fix for this limitation through the *RemotingFormat* property.

The property accepts values from the *SerializationFormat* enum type: *Xml* (the default) or *Binary*. When a *DataSet* instance is being serialized through a .NET formatter (say, in a .NET Remoting scenario), it looks at the value of the *RemotingFormat* property and decides about the persistence format. Needless to say, if you set *RemotingFormat* to *Binary* you get a much more compact output:

```
DataSet ds = GetData();
ds.RemotingFormat = SerializationFormat.Binary;
StreamWriter writer = new StreamWriter(BinFile);
BinaryFormatter bin = new BinaryFormatter();
bin.Serialize(writer.BaseStream, ds);
writer.Close();
```

The preceding code shows how to serialize to disk a *DataSet* in a truly binary format. If you omit the statement that sets the remoting format, you obtain the same behavior as in ADO. NET 1.x. If you're passing a *DataSet* through a .NET Remoting channel, the only thing you have to do is set the *RemotingFormat* property.

The *DataTable* Object

The *DataTable* object represents one table of in-memory data. Mostly used as a container of data within a *DataSet*, the *DataTable* object is also valid as a stand-alone object that contains tabular data. The *DataTable* and *DataSet* are the only ADO.NET objects that can be remoted and serialized. Just as with a *DataSet*, a *DataTable* can be created programmatically. In this case, you first define its schema and then add new rows. The following code snippet shows how to create a new table within a *DataSet*:

```
DataSet ds = new DataSet();
DataTable tableEmp = new DataTable("Employees");
tableEmp.Columns.Add("ID", typeof(int));
tableEmp.Columns.Add("Name", typeof(string));
ds.Tables.Add(tableEmp);
```

The table is named Employees and features two columns—ID and Name. The table is empty because no rows have been added yet. To add rows, you first create a new row object by using the *NewRow* method:

```
DataRow row = tableEmp.NewRow();
row["ID"] = 1;
row["Name"] = "Joe Users";
tableEmp.Rows.Add(row);
```

The *DataTable* contains a collection of constraint objects that can be used to ensure the integrity of the data and signals changes to its data-firing events. Let's have a closer look at the programming interface of the *DataTable*, beginning with properties. Table 8-12 lists the properties of the *DataTable* class.

TABLE 8-12 Properties of the *DataTable* Class

Property	Description
CaseSensitive	Gets or sets whether string comparisons are case-sensitive.
ChildRelations	Gets the collection of child relations for this table.
Columns	Gets the collection of columns that belong to this table.
Constraints	Gets the collection of constraints maintained by this table.
DataSet	Gets the *DataSet* this table belongs to.
DefaultView	Gets the default *DataView* object for this table.
DisplayExpression	Gets or sets a display string for the table. Used in the *ToString* method together with *TableName*.
ExtendedProperties	Gets the collection of customized user information.
HasErrors	Gets a value that indicates whether there are errors in any of the rows.
Locale	Gets or sets locale information used to compare strings.
MinimumCapacity	Gets or sets the initial starting size for the table.
Namespace	Gets or sets the namespace for the XML representation of the table.
ParentRelations	Gets the collection of parent relations for this table.
Prefix	Gets or sets the prefix that aliases the table namespace.
PrimaryKey	Gets or sets an array of columns that function as the primary key for the table.
RemotingFormat	Indicates the desired serialization format—binary or XML. *Not supported in ADO.NET 1.x.*
Rows	Gets the collection of rows that belong to this table.
TableName	Gets or sets the name of the *DataTable* object.

Shared by several ADO.NET objects, the *ExtendedProperties* collection manages name/value pairs and accepts values of type *object*. You can use this collection as a generic cargo variable in which to store any user information. The methods of the *DataTable* class are listed in Table 8-13.

TABLE 8-13 **Methods of the *DataTable* Class**

Method	Description
AcceptChanges	Commits all the pending changes made to the table.
BeginInit	Begins the initialization of the table. Used when the table is used on a form or by another component.
BeginLoadData	Turns off notifications, index maintenance, and constraints while loading data.
Clear	Removes all the data from the table.
Clone	Clones the structure of the table. Copies constraints and schema, but doesn't copy data.
Compute	Computes the given expression on the rows that meet the specified filter criteria. Returns the result of the computation as an object.
Copy	Copies both the structure and data for the table.
CreateDataReader	Returns a *DataTableReader* object for the current table. *Not supported in ADO.NET 1.x.*
EndInit	Ends the initialization of the table. Closes the operation started with *BeginInit*.
EndLoadData	Turns on notifications, index maintenance, and constraints after loading data.
GetChanges	Gets a copy of the table containing all changes made to it since it was last loaded or since *AcceptChanges* was called.
GetErrors	Gets an array of all the *DataRow* objects that contain errors.
ImportRow	Performs a deep copy of a *DataRow*, and loads it into the table. Settings, including original and current values, are preserved.
LoadDataRow	Finds and updates a specific row. If no matching row is found, a new row is created using the given values. Uses the primary keys to locate the row.
NewRow	Creates a new *DataRow* object with the schema as the table.
ReadXml	Populates the *DataTable* reading schema and data from the specified XML document. *Not supported in ADO.NET 1.x.*
ReadXmlSchema	Replicates into the *DataTable* the table structure read from the specified XML schema. *Not supported in ADO.NET 1.x.*
RejectChanges	Rolls back all changes that have been made to the table since it was loaded or since the last time *AcceptChanges* was called.
Reset	Resets the *DataTable* object to its default state.

Method	Description
Select	Gets the array of *DataRow* objects that match the criteria.
WriteXml	Serializes the *DataTable* contents to XML. *Not supported in ADO.NET 1.x.*
WriteXmlSchema	Writes the *DataTable* structure as an XML schema. *Not supported in ADO.NET 1.x.*

In ADO.NET 2.0, the *DataTable* implements the *IXmlSerializable* interface and provides public methods to load and save its contents from and to XML streams. The implementation of the interface is also the key that now allows *DataTable* to be used as parameters and return values from .NET Web service methods.

Any row in the *DataTable* is represented by a *DataRow* object, whereas the *DataColumn* object represents a column. The *Select* method implements a simple but effective query engine for the rows of the table. The result set is an array of *DataRow* objects. The filter string is expressed in an internal language that looks like that used to build *WHERE* clauses in a SQL *SELECT* statement. The following line of code is a valid expression that selects all records in which the ID is greater than 5 and the name begins with A:

```
tableEmp.Select("ID >5 AND Name LIKE 'A%'");
```

Refer to the .NET Framework documentation for the full syntax supported by the *Select* method. Note that it is the same language you can use to define expression-based *DataTable* columns.

Performing Computations

The *Compute* method of the *DataTable* class calculates a value by applying a given expression to the table rows that match a specified filter. Expressions can include any sort of Boolean and arithmetic operators, but they can also include more interesting aggregate functions such as *Min*, *Max*, *Count*, and *Sum*, plus a few more statistical operators such as average, standard deviation, and variance. The following code counts the rows in which the Name column begins with A:

```
int numRecs = (int) tableEmp.Compute("Count(ID)", " Name LIKE 'A%'");
```

The *Compute* method has two possible overloads—one that takes only the expression to compute and one that also adds a filter string, as shown in the preceding code. Note that all aggregate functions can operate on a single column. This means you can directly compute the sum on two columns, as in the following pseudocode:

```
Sum(quantity * price)
```

To compute functions on multiple columns, you can leverage the capabilities of the *DataColumn* object and, in particular, its support for dynamic expressions. For example, you can define an in-memory column named *order_item_price* as follows:

```
tableEmp.Columns.Add("order_item_price", typeof(double), "quantity*price");
```

At this point, you can compute the sum of that column using the following expression:

```
Sum(order_item_price)
```

Columns of a Table

A *DataColumn* object represents the schema of a column in a *DataTable* object. It provides properties that describe the characteristics and capabilities of the column. The *DataColumn* properties include *AllowDBNull*, *Unique*, *ReadOnly*, *DefaultValue*, and *Expression*. As discussed earlier, some of these properties are automatically set with the corresponding information read from the data source—at least when the data source is a database.

A *DataColumn* object has a name and type; sometimes it can also have an associated expression. The content of an expression-based column is a function of one or more columns combined with operators and aggregates to form a full expression. When an expression-based column is created, ADO.NET precalculates and caches all the values for the column as if they were native data. At the same time, ADO.NET tracks the columns involved and monitors them for changes. It does so by registering an internal handler for the *DataTable*'s *RowChanged* event. When a row changes in one of the columns involved in the expression, the computed column is automatically refreshed.

Expression-based columns are extremely powerful for setting up more effective and practical forms of data binding. In addition, expression-based columns work side by side with table relations and, using both, you can implement really powerful features. We'll demonstrate this later in the "Data Relations" section.

Rows of a Table

The data in a table is represented with a collection of *DataRow* objects. A row has a state, an array of values, and possibly error information. The *DataTable* maintains various versions of the row. You can query for a particular version at any time using the *Item* accessor property. The following code snippet shows how to read the original value of a column in a particular *DataRow* object. By default, you are returned the current value.

```
Response.Write(row["Name", DataRowVersion.Original].ToString());
```

All the values in a row can be accessed either individually or as a whole. When accessing all the values in a row, you use the *ItemArray* property, which passes you an array of objects, one for each column. The *ItemArray* property is a quick way to read values from a row and to set all the columns on a row in a single shot.

The *DataRow* class doesn't have a public constructor. As a result, a data row can be created only implicitly using the *NewRow* method on a base table. The *NewRow* method populates the *DataRow* object with as many entries as there are columns in the *DataTable*. In this case, the table provides the schema for the row, but the row is in no way a child of the table. To add a row to a *DataTable*, you must explicitly add it to the *Rows* collection:

```
tableEmp.Rows.Add(row);
```

Note that a *DataRow* object cannot be associated with more than one table at a time. To load a row into another table, you can use the *ImportRow* method, which basically duplicates the *DataRow* object and loads it into the specified table. A row can be detached from its parent table by using the *Remove* method. If you use the *Delete* method, on the other hand, the row will be marked for deletion but still remain part of the table.

> **Note** Objects removed from a parent collection are not automatically destroyed or, at least, not until they go out of scope and become fodder for the garbage collector. This consideration holds true for several ADO.NET objects including, but not limited to, the *DataRow*. A *DataTable*, for example, can be detached from the *DataSet* by simply removing it from the *Tables* collection. However, this doesn't mean that the *DataTable* is automatically deleted as an object.

Table Constraints

A constraint is a logical rule set on a table to preserve the integrity of the data. For example, a constraint determines what happens when you delete a record in a table that is related to another one. The .NET Framework supports two types of constraints—*ForeignKeyConstraint* and *UniqueConstraint*.

In particular, the *ForeignKeyConstraint* class sets the rules that govern how the table propagates, updates, and deletes child tables. For example, suppose you have two related tables, one with employees and one with orders. What happens when an employee is deleted? Should you delete all the related records too? The *ForeignKeyConstraint* object associated with the Employees table will determine what is related to it in the Orders table. You create a *ForeignKeyConstraint* object as shown here:

```
DataColumn c1 = tableEmp.Columns("empID");
DataColumn c2 = tableOrd.Columns("empID");
ForeignKeyConstraint fk = new ForeignKeyConstraint("EmpOrders", c1, c2);

// Run some code to configure the constraint object
...

tableOrd.Constraints.Add(fk);
```

The *ForeignKeyConstraint* constructor takes the name of the object plus two *DataColumn* objects. The first *DataColumn* object represents the column (or the columns) on the parent table; the second *DataColumn* object represents the column (or the columns) in the child table. The constraint is added to the child table and is configured using the *UpdateRule, DeleteRule,* and *AcceptRejectRule* properties. While setting the *UpdateRule* and *DeleteRule* properties, you use values taken from the *Rule* enumeration. The *AcceptRejectRule* is the enumeration used to look for the property with the same name. For updates and deletions, the child table can cascade the change or set the involved rows to null or default values. Alternatively, the child table can simply ignore the changes. The *AcceptRejectRule* property is processed when the *AcceptChanges* method is called on the parent row to commit changes. The choices for the constraint are limited to either cascading or ignoring changes.

The *UniqueConstraint* class ensures that a single column (or an array of columns) have unique, nonduplicated values. There are several ways to set a unique constraint. You can create one explicitly by using the class constructor and adding the resulting object to the *Constraints* collection of the *DataTable*:

```
UniqueConstraint uc;
uc = new UniqueConstraint(tableEmp.Columns("empID"));
tableEmp.Constraints.Add(uc);
```

A unique constraint can also be created implicitly by setting the *Unique* property of the column to *true.* In contrast, setting the *Unique* property to *false* resets the constraint. In addition, adding a column to the in-memory primary key for a table automatically creates a unique constraint for the column. Note that a primary key on a *DataTable* object is an array of *DataColumn* objects that is used to index and sort the rows. The *Select* method on the *DataTable* benefits from the index as much as other methods on the *DataView* class do.

> **Note**   When you define a *DataColumn* as the primary key for a *DataTable* object, the table automatically sets the *AllowDBNull* property of the column to *false* and the *Unique* property to *true.* If the primary key is made of multiple columns, only the *AllowDBNull* property is automatically set to *false.*

Data Relations

A data relation represents a parent/child relationship between two *DataTable* objects in the same *DataSet.* In the .NET Framework, a data relation is represented by a *DataRelation* object. You set a relation between two tables based on matching columns in the parent and child tables. The matching columns in the two related tables can have different names, but they must have the same type. All the relations for the tables in a *DataSet* are stored in the *Relations* collection. Table 8-14 lists the properties of the *DataRelation* class.

TABLE 8-14 Properties of the *DataRelation* Class

Property	Description
ChildColumns	Gets the child *DataColumn* objects for the relation.
ChildKeyConstraint	Gets the *ForeignKeyConstraint* object for the relation.
ChildTable	Gets the child *DataTable* object for the relation.
DataSet	Gets the *DataSet* to which the relation belongs.
ExtendedProperties	Gets the collection that stores user information.
Nested	Gets or sets a value that indicates whether the relation should render its data as nested subtrees when the *DataSet* is rendered to XML. (More on this later in the "Serializing a Data Relation" section.)
ParentColumns	Gets the parent *DataColumn* objects for the relation.
ParentKeyConstraint	Gets the *UniqueConstraint* object that ensures unique values on the parent column of the relation.
ParentTable	Gets the parent *DataTable* object for the relation.
RelationName	Gets or sets the name of the *DataRelation* object. The name is used to identify the relation in the *Relations* collection of the parent *DataSet* object.

When a *DataRelation* is created, two constraints are silently created. A foreign-key constraint is set on the child table, using the two columns that form the relation as arguments. In addition, the parent table is given a unique constraint that prevents it from containing duplicates. The constraints are created by default, but by using a different constructor you can instruct the *DataRelation* to skip that step. The *DataRelation* class has no significant methods.

Creating a Data Relation

The *DataRelation* class can be seen as the memory counterpart of a database table relationship. However, when a *DataSet* is loaded from a database, DBMS-specific relationships are not processed and loaded. As a result, data relations are exclusively in-memory objects that must be created explicitly with code. The following snippet shows how:

```
DataColumn c1 = tableEmp.Columns("empID");
DataColumn c2 = tableOrd.Columns("empID");
DataRelation rel = new DataRelation("Emp2Orders", c1, c2);
DataSet.Relations.Add(rel);
```

Given two tables, Employees and Orders, the preceding code sets up a relationship between the two based on the values of the common column *empID*. What are the practical advantages of such a relation? After the relation is set, the parent *DataTable* knows that each row might be a bunch of child related rows. In particular, each employee in the Employees table has an array of related rows in the Orders table. The child rows are exactly those where the value of the *Orders.empID* column matches the empID column on the current Employees row.

ADO.NET provides an automatic mechanism to facilitate the retrieval of these related rows. The method is *GetChildRows* and is exposed by the *DataRow* class. *GetChildRows* takes a relation and returns an array filled with all the *DataRow* objects that match:

```
foreach(DataRow childRow in parentRow.GetChildRows("Emp2Orders"))
{
    // Process the child row
}
```

Another important facility ADO.NET provides for data relations has to do with table calculations and expression-based columns.

Performing Calculations on Relations

A common task in many real-world applications entails that you manage two related tables and process, given a parent row, the subset of child records. In many situations, processing the child rows just means performing some aggregate computations on them. This is just one of the facilities that ADO.NET and relations provide for free. Let's suppose that, given the previous employees-to-orders relation, you need to compute the total of orders issued by a given employee. You could simply add a dynamically computed column to the parent table and bind it to the data in the relation:

```
tableEmp.Columns.Add("Total", typeof(int),
    "Sum(child(Emp2Orders).Amount)");
```

The new column Total contains, for each employee, a value that represents the sum of all the values in the Amount column for the child rows of the relation. In other words, now you have a column that automatically computes the total of orders issued by each employee. The keyword *child* is a special syntax element of the language that ADO.NET expressions support. Basically, the *child* keyword takes a relation name and returns an array of *DataRow* objects that is the child of that relation.

Serializing a Data Relation

The *Nested* property on the *DataRelation* object affects the way in which the parent *DataSet* is rendered to XML. By default, the presence of a relation doesn't change the XML schema used to serialize a *DataSet*. All the tables are therefore rendered sequentially under the root node. A nested relation changes this default schema. In particular, a nested relation is rendered hierarchically with child rows nested under the parent row.

A *DataSet* with Employees and Orders tables is rendered according to the following pattern:

```
<MyDataSet>
    <Employees empid="1" name="Joe Users" />
    ...
    <Orders empid="1" amount="6897" ... />
    <Orders empid="1" amount="19713" ... />
    ...
</MyDataSet>
```

If a relation exists between the tables and is set as nested, the XML schema changes as follows:

```
<MyDataSet>
    <Employees empid="1" name="Joe Users">
        <Orders empid="1" amount="6897" ... />
        <Orders empid="1" amount="19713" ... />
    </Employees>
    ...
</MyDataSet>
```

The child rows are taken out of their natural place and placed within the subtree that represents the parent row.

The *DataView* Object

The *DataView* class represents a customized view of a *DataTable*. The relationship between *DataTable* and *DataView* objects is governed by the rules of a well-known design pattern: the document/view model. The *DataTable* object acts as the document, whereas the *DataView* behaves as the view. At any moment, you can have multiple, different views of the same underlying data. More importantly, you can manage each view as an independent object with its own set of properties, methods, and events.

The view is implemented by maintaining a separate array with the indexes of the original rows that match the criteria set on the view. By default, the table view is unfiltered and contains all the records included in the table. By using the *RowFilter* and *RowStateFilter* properties, you can narrow the set of rows that fit into a particular view. Using the *Sort* property, you can apply a sort expression to the rows in the view. Table 8-15 lists the properties of the *DataView* class.

TABLE 8-15 **Properties of the *DataView* Class**

Property	Description
AllowDelete	Gets or sets a value that indicates whether deletes are allowed in the view.
AllowEdit	Gets or sets a value that indicates whether edits are allowed in the view.
AllowNew	Gets or sets a value that indicates whether new rows can be added through the view.
ApplyDefaultSort	Gets or sets a value that indicates whether to use the default sort.
Count	Gets the number of rows in the view after the filter has been applied.
DataViewManager	Gets the *DataViewManager* object associated with this view.

Property	Description
Item	An indexer property. Gets a row of data from the underlying table.
RowFilter	Gets or sets the expression used to filter out rows in the view.
RowStateFilter	Gets or sets the row state filter used in the view.
Sort	Gets or sets the sorting of the view in terms of columns and order.
Table	Gets or sets the source *DataTable* for the view.

The filter can be an expression, the state of the rows, or both. The *RowStateFilter* property, in particular, takes its acceptable values from the *DataViewRowState* enumeration and allows you to filter based on the original or current values of the row, or on modified, added, or deleted rows. The *RowFilter* property supports the same syntax as the *DataTable*'s *Select* method.

A *DataView* does not contain copies of the table's rows. It is limited to storing an array of indexes that is updated whenever any of the filter properties are set. The *DataView* object is already connected to the underlying *DataTable*, of which it represents a possibly filtered and/or sorted view. The *AllowXXX* properties let you control only whether the view is editable or not. By default, the view is fully editable. Table 8-16 lists the methods of the *DataView* class.

TABLE 8-16 **Methods of the *DataView* Class**

Method	Description
AddNew	Adds a new row to the view and the underlying table.
BeginInit	Begins the initialization of the view.
CopyTo	Copies items from the view into an array.
Delete	Deletes the row at the specified index in the view. The row is deleted from the table too.
EndInit	Ends the initialization of the view.
Find	Finds a row in the view by the specified key value.
FindRows	Returns an array of row objects that match the specified key value.
GetEnumerator	Returns an enumerator object for the *DataView*.

Both the *AddNew* and *Delete* methods affect the underlying *DataTable* object. Multiple changes can be grouped using the pair *BeginInit/EndInit*.

Navigating the View

The contents of a *DataView* object can be scrolled through a variety of programming interfaces, including collections, lists, and enumerators. The *GetEnumerator* method, in particular, ensures that you can walk your way through the records in the view by using the familiar *for...each* statement. The following code shows how to access all the rows that fit into the view:

```
DataView myView = new DataView(table);
foreach(DataRowView rowview in myView)
{
    // dereferences the DataRow object
    DataRow row = rowview.Row;
    ...
}
```

When client applications access a particular row in the view, the *DataView* class expects to find it in an internal cache of rows. If the cache is not empty, the specified row is returned to the caller via an intermediate *DataRowView* object. The *DataRowView* object is a kind of wrapper for the *DataRow* object that contains the actual data. You access row data through the *Row* property. If the row cache is empty, the *DataView* class fills it up with an array of *DataRowView* objects, each of which references an original *DataRow* object. The row cache is refreshed whenever the sort expression or the filter string is updated. The row cache can be empty either because it has never been used or because the sort expression or the filter string has been changed in the meantime. Figure 8-5 illustrates the internal architecture of a *DataView* object.

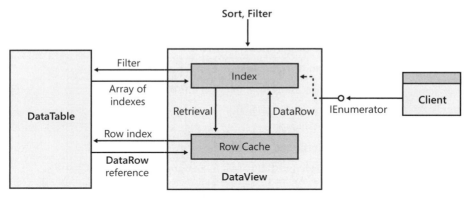

FIGURE 8-5 The internal structure of a *DataView* object.

Finding Rows

The link between the *DataTable* and the *DataView* is typically established at creation time through the constructor:

```
public DataView(DataTable table);
```

However, you could also create a new view and associate it with a table at a later time using the *DataView*'s *Table* property—for example:

```
DataView dv = new DataView();
dv.Table = dataSet.Tables["Employees"];
```

You can also obtain a *DataView* object from any table. In fact, the *DefaultView* property of a *DataTable* object just returns a *DataView* object initialized to work on that table.

```
DataView dv = dt.DefaultView;
```

Originally, the view is unfiltered and the index array contains as many elements as the rows in the table. To quickly find a row, you can use either the *Find* or *FindRows* method. The *Find* method takes one or more values and returns an array with the indexes of the rows that match. The *FindRows* method works in much the same way, but it returns an array of *DataRowView* objects rather than indexes. Both methods accept a sort key value to identify the rows to return.

> **Note** The contents of a *DataView* can be sorted by multiple fields by using the *Sort* property. You can assign to *Sort* a comma-separated list of column names, and even append them with *DESC* or *ASC* to indicate the direction.

Conclusion

Centered around the disconnected model, ADO.NET incorporates a made-to-measure API to let developers store and consume data through special in-memory containers with two key capabilities. First, they behave like real databases and provide interface and functions similar to those of a server DBMS. Second, they're serializable and implement a commit model for you to handle changes in an extremely flexible way.

Classes such as *DataSet* and *DataTable* are ideal to package data to be moved across the tiers of a distributed system. They offer advanced, database-like features such as referential integrity, optimistic locking, constraints, indexing, and filtering. They lend themselves to operate well in batch-update scenarios, where client code connects to a back-end database and submits changes. *DataSet* objects don't know anything about databases and, in general, data providers. They're sort of super-arrays enriched with advanced and database-like features. *DataSet* objects can be filled programmatically with any data that can be represented in a tabular manner. Adapters are special command objects that fill *DataSet* and *DataTable* objects with the results of a query. Likewise, adapters take care of moving the contents of ADO. NET containers back to a connected database table with a compatible layout.

DataSet and *DataTable* are frequently used for binding data to data-bound controls. In the next chapter, we'll address this.

Just The Facts

- ADO.NET data container classes such as *DataSet* and *DataTable* have no notion of the provider that served them data. They are serializable, feature-rich classes and offer a bunch of database-like functions, such as referential integrity, optimistic locking, constraints, indexing, and filtering.

- The data adapter is a command-like object that performs data access, grabs all the data, and packs it into a data container. Like commands and data readers, data adapters are specific to each data provider.

- The *Fill* method of the data adapter maps the source result sets onto in-memory tables and fills the tables with the data fetched from the physical data source.

- In ADO.NET 2.0 and beyond, you can better control the way data is loaded into the various data tables during a fill operation. You can choose, for example, to override current or underlying values.

- The *DataSet* is great at encapsulating tables of data and relationships and moving it between the tiers of an application in a loosely coupled manner.

- ADO.NET batch update consists of a series of commands that the data adapter submits sequentially to the database. Batch update is triggered by a single instruction but doesn't necessarily equate to a series of queries submitted in a single command.

- Batch update is particularly effective in environments with a low degree of data contention because it allows for disconnected architectures, higher scalability, and considerably simpler code.

- In ADO.NET 2.0 and beyond, the *DataSet* can be serialized in a true binary format, which gets you a much more compact output.

- In ADO.NET 2.0 and beyond, the *DataTable* implements the *IXmlSerializable* interface and provides public methods to load and save its contents from and to XML streams. The implementation of the interface also enables the *DataTable* to be used as a parameter and return value from .NET Web service methods.

Chapter 9
The Data-Binding Model

To write effective ASP.NET 1.x data-driven applications, you need a deep understanding of ADO.NET objects. You have to be familiar with connections, commands, transactions, parameters, and all the objects we dealt with in the previous two chapters. In ASP.NET 2.0, the role of ADO.NET object is more blurred because of the introduction of a new family of data-related and more programmer-friendly components—the data source objects. In ASP.NET 2.0, you use ADO.NET objects directly much less frequently. In the .NET Framework 3.5, managed languages support natively the Language Integrated Query (LINQ) engine, meaning that you can use a LINQ-based set of operators to deal with result sets and back-end data stores. Connections, transactions, and procedures are managed in the backstage shielding developers from a lot of SQL and ADO.NET details. We'll delve deep into LINQ-related topics in the next chapter.

In general, complex and sophisticated enterprise systems typically isolate data access code (be it ADO.NET- or LINQ-based) in the data tier, and they often have it wrapped up by an additional layer of helper libraries such as the Microsoft Data Access Application Block. Realistic pages belonging to similar systems never call ADO.NET objects directly, like we did in the demonstration pages of the past two chapters. Starting with ASP.NET 2.0, ADO.NET objects are still essential pieces of the .NET Framework, but they have been pushed into the back-end infrastructure of most common data-binding operations. Starting with version 2.0, ASP.NET offers the possibility of writing data access code that hides many essential steps from view and buries them in the framework's code. Basically, what many ASP.NET 1.x developers called "that boring ADO.NET boilerplate code" has been packed into a bunch of new data source controls and a LINQ-based syntax.

Overall, the data-binding model of ASP.NET is founded on three pillars—data-binding expressions, classic data source–based binding, and data source controls. What's the role of LINQ in ASP.NET 3.5? You can use the subset of LINQ specific to Microsoft SQL Server (named LINQ-to-SQL) either as an enumerable data source or through a made-to-measure data source object. In the end, the data-binding model of ASP.NET 3.5 is the same as in previous versions. It just has one more programming application programming interface (API) that we'll examine in detail in the next chapter. Let's start our tour of the data-binding model with data source-based binding, which is probably the most common and flexible of all.

Data Source-Based Data Binding

Web applications are, for the most part, just data-driven applications. For this reason, the ability to bind HTML elements such as drop-down lists or tables to structured data is a key feature for any development platform. Data binding is the process that retrieves data from a fixed source and dynamically associates this data to properties on server controls. Valid target controls are those that have been specifically designed to support data binding—that is, data-bound controls. Data-bound controls are not another family of controls; they're simply server controls that feature a few well-known data-related properties and feed them using a well-known set of collection objects.

Feasible Data Sources

Many .NET classes can be used as data sources—and not just those that have to do with database content. In ASP.NET, any object that exposes the *IEnumerable* interface is a valid bindable data source. The *IEnumerable* interface defines the minimal API to enumerate the contents of the data source:

```
public interface IEnumerable
{
    IEnumerator GetEnumerator();
}
```

Many bindable objects, though, actually implement more advanced versions of *IEnumerable*, such as *ICollection* and *IList*. In particular, you can bind a Web control to the following classes:

- ADO.NET container classes such as *DataSet*, *DataTable*, and *DataView*
- Data readers
- Custom collections, dictionaries, and arrays

To be honest, I should note that the *DataSet* and *DataTable* classes don't actually implement *IEnumerable* or any other interfaces that inherit from it. However, both classes do store collections of data internally. These collections are accessed using the methods of an intermediate interface—*IListSource*—which performs the trick of making *DataSet* and *DataTable* classes look like they implement a collection.

ADO.NET Classes

As we saw in Chapter 8, ADO.NET provides a bunch of data container classes that can be filled with any sort of data, including results of a database query. These classes represent excellent resources for filling data-bound controls such as lists and grids. If having memory-based classes such as the *DataSet* in the list is no surprise, it's good to find data readers there too. An open data reader can be passed to the data-binding engine of a control. The control will then walk its way through the reader and populate the user interface while keeping the connection to the database busy.

> **Note** Data binding works differently for Web pages and Microsoft Windows desktop applications. Aside from the internal implementations, both Web and Windows forms can share the same data source objects with the exception of the data reader. You can bind a data reader only to ASP.NET controls. Likewise, only Windows Forms controls can be bound to instances of the *DataViewManager* class that we briefly mentioned in Chapter 8 (see Table 8-15).

The *DataSet* class can contain more than one table; however, only one table at a time can be associated with standard ASP.NET data-bound controls. If you bind the control to a *DataSet*, you then need to set an additional property to select a particular table within the *DataSet*. Be aware that this limitation is not attributable to ASP.NET as a platform; it is a result of the implementation of the various data-bound controls. In fact, you could write a custom control that accepts a *DataSet* as its sole data-binding parameter.

DataSet and *DataTable* act as data sources through the *IListSource* interface; *DataView* and data readers, on the other hand, implement *IEnumerable* directly.

Collection-Based Classes

At the highest level of abstraction, a collection serves as a container for instances of other classes. All collection classes implement the *ICollection* interface, which in turn implements the *IEnumerable* interface. As a result, all collection classes provide a basic set of functionalities. All collection classes have a *Count* property to return the number of cached items; they have a *CopyTo* method to copy their items, in their entirety or in part, to an external array; they have a *GetEnumerator* method that instantiates an enumerator object to loop through the child items. *GetEnumerator* is the method behind the curtain whenever you call the *foreach* statement in C# and the *For...Each* statement in Microsoft Visual Basic.

IList and *IDictionary* are two interfaces that extend *ICollection*, giving a more precise characterization to the resultant collection class. *ICollection* provides only basic and minimal functionality for a collection. For example, *ICollection* does not have any methods to add or remove items. Add and remove functions are exactly what the *IList* interface provides. In the *IList* interface, the *Add* and *Insert* methods place new items at the bottom of the collection or at the specified index. The *Remove* and *RemoveAt* methods remove items, while *Clear* empties the collection. Finally, *Contains* verifies whether an item with a given value belongs to the collection, and *IndexOf* returns the index of the specified item. Commonly used container classes that implement both *ICollection* and *IList* are *Array*, *ArrayList*, *StringCollection*, and generics.

The *IDictionary* interface defines the API that represents a collection of key/value pairs. The interface exposes methods similar to *IList*, but with different signatures. Dictionary classes also feature two extra properties, *Keys* and *Values*. They return collections of keys and values, respectively, found in the dictionary. Typical dictionary classes are *ListDictionary*, *Hashtable*, and *SortedList*.

You'll likely use custom collection classes in ASP.NET data-binding scenarios more often than you'll use predefined collection classes. The simplest way to code a custom collection in .NET 1.x is to derive a new class from *CollectionBase* and override at least the method *Add* and the *Item* property, as shown in the following code snippet:

```
public class OrderCollection : CollectionBase
{
    public OrderCollection()
    {
    }

    // Add method
    public void Add(OrderInfo o)
    {
        InnerList.Add(o);
    }

    // Indexer property
    public OrderInfo this[int index]
    {
        get { return (OrderInfo) InnerList[index]; }
        set { InnerList[index] = value; }
    }
}
public class OrderInfo
{
    private int _id;
    public int ID
    {
        get { return _id; }
        set { _id = value; }
    }
    private DateTime _date;
    public DateTime Date
    {
        get { return _date; }
        set { _date = value; }
    }
    ...
}
```

It is important that the element class—*OrderInfo*, in the preceding code—implements data members as properties, instead of fields.

```
public class OrderInfo
{
    public int ID;
    public DateTime Date;
}
```

Data members coded as fields are certainly faster to write, but they are not discovered at run time unless the class provides a custom type descriptor (read, it implements the *ICustomTypeDescriptor* interface) that exposes fields as properties.

In ASP.NET 2.0 and newer versions, the advent of generics greatly simplifies the development of custom collections. In some cases, the code to write reduces to the following:

```
using System.Collections.ObjectModel;
public class OrderCollection : Collection<OrderInfo>
{
    // Optional:: Add methods overrides
}
```

Data-Binding Properties

In ASP.NET, there are two main categories of data-bound controls—list and iterative controls. As we'll see in detail later on, list controls repeat a fixed template for each item found in the data source. Iterative controls are more flexible and let you define the template to repeat explicitly, as well as other templates that directly influence the final layout of the control.

All data-bound controls implement the *DataSource* and *DataSourceID* properties, plus a few more, as detailed in Figure 9-1.

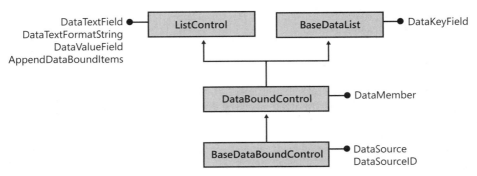

FIGURE 9-1 Class diagram for data binding in ASP.NET.

Note that in ASP.NET 1.x, there's no *DataSourceID* property. Likewise, no intermediate classes such as *BaseDataBoundControl* and *DataBoundControl* exist in versions of ASP.NET prior to 2.0. *ListControl* and *BaseDataList* form the common base for list and iterative controls.

> **Note** For some reason, the *Repeater* control—a low-level iterative control—doesn't inherit from either of the classes in the diagram. It inherits directly from the *Control* class.

The *DataSource* Property

The *DataSource* property lets you specify the data source object the control is linked to. Note that this link is logical and does not result in any overhead or underlying operation until you explicitly order to bind the data to the control. As mentioned, you activate data binding on a control by calling the *DataBind* method. When the method executes, the control actually loads data from the associated data source, evaluates the data-bound properties (if any), and generates the markup to reflect changes.

```
public virtual object DataSource {get; set;}
```

The *DataSource* property is declared of type *object* and can ultimately accept objects that implement either *IEnumerable* (including data readers) or *IListSource*. By the way, only *DataSet* and *DataTable* implement the *IListSource* interface.

The *DataSource* property of a data-bound control is generally set programmatically. However, nothing prevents you from adopting a kind of declarative approach as follows:

```
<asp:DropDownList runat="server" id="theList"
    DataSource="<%# GetData() %>"
    ...
/>
```

In this example, *GetData* is a public or protected member of the code-behind page class that returns a bindable object.

> **Note** How can a data-bound control figure out which object it is actually bound to? Is it a collection, a data reader, or perhaps a *DataTable*? All standard data-bound controls are designed to work only through the *IEnumerable* interface. For this reason, any object bound to *DataSource* is normalized to an object that implements *IEnumerable*. In some cases, the normalization is as easy (and fast) as casting the object to the *IEnumerable* interface. In other cases—specifically, when *DataTable* and *DataSet* are involved—an extra step is performed to locate a particular named collection of data that corresponds to the value assigned to the *DataMember* property. There's no public function to do all this work, although a similar helper class exists in the ASP.NET framework but is flagged as internal. What this helper class does, though, can be easily replicated by custom code: it just combines an array of *if* statements to check types and does casting and conversion as appropriate.

The *DataSourceID* Property

Introduced with ASP.NET 2.0, the *DataSourceID* property gets or sets the ID of the data source component from which the data-bound control retrieves its data. This property is the point of contact between data-bound controls and the new family of data source controls that includes *SqlDataSource* and *ObjectDataSource*. (I'll cover these controls in more detail later in the chapter.)

```
public virtual string DataSourceID {get; set;}
```

By setting *DataSourceID*, you tell the control to turn to the associated data source control for any needs regarding data—retrieval, paging, sorting, counting, or updating.

Like *DataSource*, *DataSourceID* is available on all data-bound controls. The two properties are mutually exclusive. If both are set, you get an invalid operation exception at run time. Note, though, that you also get an exception if *DataSourceID* is set to a string that doesn't correspond to an existing data source control.

The *DataMember* Property

The *DataMember* property gets or sets the name of the data collection to extract when data binding to a data source:

```
public virtual string DataMember {get; set;}
```

You use the property to specify the name of the *DataTable* to use when the *DataSource* property is bound to a *DataSet* object:

```
DataSet data = new DataSet();
SqlDataAdapter adapter = new SqlDataAdapter(cmdText, connString);
adapter.Fill(data);

// Table is the default name of the first table in a
// DataSet filled by an adapter
grid.DataMember = "Table";
grid.DataSource = data;
grid.DataBind();
```

DataMember and *DataSource* can be set in any order, provided that both are set before *DataBind* is invoked. *DataMember* has no relevance if you bind to data using *DataSourceID* with standard data source components.

> **Note** This is not a limitation of the binding technology, but rather a limitation of standard data source components, which don't support multiple views. We'll return to this point later when discussing data source components.

The *DataTextField* Property

Typically used by list controls, the *DataTextField* property specifies which property of a data-bound item should be used to define the display text of the nth element in a list control:

```
public virtual string DataTextField {get; set;}
```

For example, for a drop-down list control the property feeds the displayed text of each item in the list. The following code creates the control shown in Figure 9-2:

```
CountryList.DataSource = data;
CountryList.DataTextField = "country";
CountryList.DataBind();
```

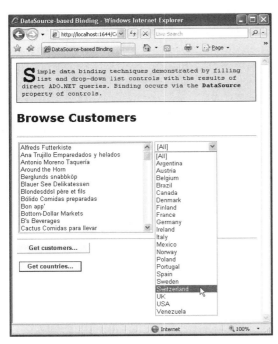

FIGURE 9-2 A drop-down list control filled with the *country* column of a database table.

The same happens for *ListBox*, *CheckBoxList*, and other list controls. Unlike *DataMember*, the *DataTextField* property is necessary also in case the binding is operated by data source components.

Note List controls can automatically format the content of the field bound through the *DataTextField* property. The format expression is indicated via the *DataTextFormatString* property.

The *DataValueField* Property

Similar to *DataTextField*, the *DataValueField* property specifies which property of a data-bound item should be used to identify the nth element in a list control:

```
public virtual string DataValueField {get; set;}
```

To understand the role of this property, consider the markup generated for a drop-down list, set as in the code snippet shown previously:

```
<select name="CountryList" id="CountryList">
    <option selected="selected" value="[All]">[All]</option>
    <option value="Argentina">Argentina</option>
    <option value="Austria">Austria</option>
    ...
</select>
```

The text of each *<option>* tag is determined by the field specified through *DataTextField*; the value of the *value* attribute is determined by *DataValueField*. Consider the following code that fills a *ListBox* with customer names:

```
CustomerList.DataMember = "Table";
CustomerList.DataTextField = "companyname";
CustomerList.DataValueField = "customerid";
CustomerList.DataSource = data;
CustomerList.DataBind();
```

If *DataValueField* is left blank, the value of the *DataTextField* property is used instead. Here's the corresponding markup generated by the preceding code snippet:

```
<select size="4" name="CustomerList" id="CustomerList">
    <option value="BOTTM">Bottom-Dollar Markets</option>
    <option value="LAUGB">Laughing Bacchus Wine Cellars</option>
    ...
</select>
```

As you can see, the *value* attribute now is set to the customer ID—the unique, invisible value determined by the *customerid* field. The content of the *value* attribute for the currently selected item is returned by the *SelectedValue* property of the list control. If you want to access programmatically the displayed text of the current selection, use the *SelectedItem.Text* expression.

The *AppendDataBoundItems* Property

Introduced in ASP.NET 2.0, this Boolean property indicates whether the data-bound items should be appended to the existing contents of the control or whether they should overwrite them. By default, *AppendDataBoundItems* is set to *false*, meaning that data-bound contents replace any existing contents. This behavior is the same as you have in ASP.NET 1.x, where this property doesn't exist.

```
public virtual bool AppendDataBoundItems {get; set;}
```

AppendDataBoundItems is useful when you need to combine constant items with data-bound items. For example, imagine you need to fill a drop-down list with all the distinct countries in which you have a customer. The user selects a country and sees the list of customers who live there. To let users see all the customers in any country, you add an unbound element, such as *[All]*:

```
<asp:DropDownList runat="server" ID="CountryList"
    AppendDataBoundItems="true">
    <asp:ListItem Text="[All]" />
</asp:DropDownList>
```

With *AppendDataBoundItems* set to *false* (which is the default behavior in ASP.NET 1.x), the *[All]* item will be cleared before data-bound items are added. In ASP.NET 1.x, you need to add it programmatically after the binding operation completes.

> **Note** Using additional items not generated by the data-binding process can pose some issues when you consider that users might repeatedly click the button that fills a given user-interface element. In Figure 9-2, a user who clicks the Get Countries button twice will double the country names in the control. To avoid that, you typically clear the *Items* collection of the *DropDownList* control before rebinding. In doing so, though, items added outside of data binding will also be removed. Do not forget to add them back or provide some code that configures the content of the data-bound control before display.

The *DataKeyField* Property

The *DataKeyField* property gets or sets the key field in the specified data source. The property serves the needs of grid-like controls and lets them (uniquely) identify a particular record. Note that the identification of the record is univocal only if the field is unique-constrained in the original data source.

```
public virtual string DataKeyField {get; set;}
```

The *DataKeyField* property is coupled with the *DataKeys* array property. When *DataKeyField* is set, *DataKeys* contains the value of the specified key field for all the control's data items currently displayed in the page. We'll cover this in more detail in Chapter 11 when we talk about *DataGrid* controls.

The new grid control of ASP.NET (the *GridView* control) extends the *DataKeyField* to an array of strings and renames it to *DataKeyNames*. The *DataKeys* property is maintained, though it's defined differently, as we'll see better in Chapter 11.

List Controls

List controls display (or at least need to have in memory) many items at the same time—specifically, the contents of the data source. Depending on its expected behavior, the control picks the needed items from memory and properly formats and displays them. List controls include *DropDownList*, *CheckBoxList*, *RadioButtonList*, *ListBox*, and *BulletedList*. All list controls inherit from the base *ListControl* class.

The *DropDownList* Control

The *DropDownList* control enables users to select one item from a single-selection drop-down list. You can specify the size of the control by setting its height and width in pixels, but you can't control the number of items displayed when the list drops down. Table 9-1 lists the most commonly used properties of the control.

TABLE 9-1 Properties of the *DropDownList* Control

Property	Description
AppendDataBoundItems	Indicates whether statically defined items should be maintained or cleared when adding data-bound items. *Not supported in ASP.NET 1.x.*
AutoPostBack	Indicates whether the control should automatically post back to the server when the user changes the selection.
DataMember	The name of the table in the *DataSource* to bind.
DataSource	The data source that populates the items of the list.
DataSourceID	ID of the data source component to provide data. *Not supported in ASP.NET 1.x.*
DataTextField	Name of the data source field to supply the text of list items.
DataTextFormatString	Formatting string used to visually format list items to be displayed.
DataValueField	Name of the data source field used to supply the value of a list item.
Items	Gets the collection of items in the list control.
SelectedIndex	Gets or sets the index of the selected item in the list.
SelectedItem	Gets the selected item in the list.
SelectedValue	Gets the value of the selected item in the list.

The programming interface of the *DropDownList* also features three properties to configure the border of the drop-down list—the *BorderColor*, *BorderStyle*, and *BorderWidth* properties. Although the properties are correctly transformed in cascading style sheet (CSS) style properties, most browsers won't use them to change the appearance of the final drop-down list.

The *DataTextField* and *DataValueField* properties don't accept expressions, only plain column names. To combine two or more fields of the data source, you can use a calculated column. You can either use a column computed by the database or exploit the power of the ADO. NET object model and add an in-memory column. The following SQL query returns a column obtained by concatenating *lastname* and *firstname*:

```
SELECT lastname + ', ' + firstname AS 'EmployeeName' FROM Employees
```

The same result can also be obtained without the involvement of the database. Once you've filled a *DataTable* object with the result of the query, you add a new column to its *Columns* collection. The content of the column is based on an expression. The following code adds an *EmployeeName* column to the data source that concatenates the last name and first name:

```
dataTable.Columns.Add("EmployeeName",
    typeof(string),
    "lastname + ', ' + firstname");
```

An expression-based column does not need to be filled explicitly. The values for all the cells in the column are calculated and cached when the column is added to the table. The table tracks any dependencies and updates the calculated column whenever any of the constituent columns are updated.

The *CheckBoxList* Control

The *CheckBoxList* control is a single monolithic control that groups a collection of selectable list items with an associated check box, each of which is rendered through an individual *CheckBox* control. The properties of the child check boxes are set by reading the associated data source. You insert a check box list in a page as follows:

```
<asp:CheckBoxList runat="server" id="employeesList">
```

Table 9-2 lists the specific properties of the *CheckBoxList* control.

TABLE 9-2 Properties of the *CheckBoxList* Control

Property	Description
AppendDataBoundItems	Indicates whether statically defined items should be maintained or cleared when adding data-bound items. *Not supported in ASP.NET 1.x.*
AutoPostBack	Indicates whether the control should automatically post back to the server when the user changes the selection.
CellPadding	Indicates pixels between the border and contents of the cell.
CellSpacing	Indicates pixels between cells.

Property	Description
DataMember	The name of the table in the *DataSource* to bind.
DataSource	The data source that populates the items of the list.
DataSourceID	ID of the data source component to provide data. *Not supported in ASP.NET 1.x.*
DataTextField	Name of the data source field to supply the text of list items.
DataTextFormatString	Formatting string used to visually format list items to be displayed.
DataValueField	Name of the data source field used to supply the value of a list item.
Items	Gets the collection of items in the list control.
RepeatColumns	Gets or sets the number of columns to display in the control.
RepeatDirection	Gets or sets a value that indicates whether the control displays vertically or horizontally.
RepeatLayout	Gets or sets the layout of the check boxes (table or flow).
SelectedIndex	Gets or sets the index of the first selected item in the list—the one with the lowest index.
SelectedItem	Gets the first selected item.
SelectedValue	Gets the value of the first selected item.
TextAlign	Gets or sets the text alignment for the check boxes.

The *CheckBoxList* does not supply any properties that know which items have been selected. But this aspect is vital for any Web application that uses selectable elements. The *CheckBoxList* can have any number of items selected, but how can you retrieve them?

Any list control has an *Items* property that contains the collection of the child items. The *Items* property is implemented through the *ListItemCollection* class and makes each contained item accessible via a *ListItem* object. The following code loops through the items stored in a *CheckBoxList* control and checks the *Selected* property of each of them:

```
foreach (ListItem item in chkList.Items)
{
    if (item.Selected) {
        // this item is selected
    }
}
```

Figure 9-3 shows a sample page that lets you select some country names and composes an ad hoc query to list all the customers from those countries.

FIGURE 9-3 A horizontally laid out *CheckBoxList* control in action.

Note that the *SelectedXXX* properties work in a slightly different manner for a *CheckBoxList* control. The *SelectedIndex* property indicates the lowest index of a selected item. By setting *SelectedIndex* to a given value, you state that no items with a lower index should be selected any longer. As a result, the control automatically deselects all items with an index lower than the new value of *SelectedIndex*. Likewise, *SelectedItem* returns the first selected item, and *SelectedValue* returns the value of the first selected item.

The *RadioButtonList* Control

The *RadioButtonList* control acts as the parent control for a collection of radio buttons. Each of the child items is rendered through a *RadioButton* control. By design, a *RadioButtonList* can have zero or one item selected. The *SelectedItem* property returns the selected element as a *ListItem* object. Note, though, that there is nothing to guarantee that only one item is selected at any time. For this reason, be extremely careful when you access the *SelectedItem* of a *RadioButtonList* control—it could be *null*.

```
if (radioButtons.SelectedValue != null)
{
    // Process the selection here
    ...
}
```

The control supports the same set of properties as the *CheckBoxList* control and, just like it, accepts some layout directives. In particular, you can control the rendering process of the list with the *RepeatLayout* and *RepeatDirection* properties. By default, the list items are rendered within a table, which ensures the vertical alignment of the companion text. The property that governs the layout is *RepeatLayout*. The alternative is to display the items as free HTML text, using blanks and breaks to guarantee some sort of minimal structure. *RepeatDirection* is the property that controls the direction in which, with or without a tabular structure, the items flow. Feasible values are *Vertical* (the default) and *Horizontal*. *RepeatColumns* is the property that determines how many columns the list should have. By default, the value is *0*, which means all the items will be displayed in a single row, vertical or horizontal, according to the value of *RepeatDirection*.

The *ListBox* Control

The *ListBox* control represents a vertical sequence of items displayed in a scrollable window. The *ListBox* control allows single-item or multiple-item selection and exposes its contents through the usual *Items* collection, as shown in the following code:

```
<asp:listbox runat="server" id="theListBox"
    rows="5" selectionmode="Multiple" />
```

You can decide the height of the control through the *Rows* property. The height is measured in number of rows rather than pixels or percentages. When it comes to data binding, the *ListBox* control behaves like the controls discussed earlier in the chapter.

Two properties make this control slightly different than other list controls—the *Rows* property, which represents the number of visible rows in the control, and the *SelectionMode* property, which determines whether one or multiple items can be selected. The programming interface of the list box also contains the set of *SelectedXXX* properties we considered earlier. In this case, they work as they do for the *CheckBoxList* control—that is, they return the selected item with the lowest index.

 Note All the list controls examined so far support the *SelectedIndexChanged* event, which is raised when the selection from the list changes and the page posts back to the server. You can use this event to execute server-side code whenever a control is selected or deselected.

The *BulletedList* Control

The *BulletedList* control is a programming interface built around the *<ul>* and *<ol>* HTML tags, with some extra features such as the bullet style, data binding, and support for custom images. The *BulletedList* control is not supported in ASP.NET 1.x. The following example uses a custom bullet object:

```
<asp:bulletedlist runat="server" bulletstyle="Square">
    <asp:listitem>One</asp:listitem>
    <asp:listitem>Two</asp:listitem>
    <asp:listitem>Three</asp:listitem>
</asp:bulletedlist>
```

The bullet style lets you choose the style of the element that precedes the item. You can use numbers, squares, circles, and uppercase and lowercase letters. The child items can be rendered as plain text, hyperlinks, or buttons. Table 9-3 details the main properties of a *BulletedList* control.

TABLE 9-3 Properties of the *BulletedList* Control

Property	Description
AppendDataBoundItems	Indicates whether statically defined items should be maintained or cleared when adding data-bound items
BulletImageUrl	Gets or sets the path to the image to use as the bullet
BulletStyle	Determines the style of the bullet
DataMember	The name of the table in the *DataSource* to bind
DataSource	The data source that populates the items of the list
DataSourceID	ID of the data source component to provide data
DataTextField	Name of the data source field to supply the text of list items
DataTextFormatString	Formatting string used to visually format list items to be displayed
DataValueField	Name of the data source field to supply the value of a list item
DisplayMode	Determines how to display the items: as plain text, link buttons, or hyperlinks
FirstBulletNumber	Gets or sets the value that starts the numbering
Items	Gets the collection of items in the list control
Target	Indicates the target frame in the case of hyperlink mode

The items of a *BulletedList* control support a variety of graphical styles—disc, circle, custom image, plus a few types of numberings including roman numbering. The initial number can be programmatically set through the *FirstBulletNumber* property. The *DisplayMode* property determines how to display the content of each bullet—plain text (the default), link button, or hyperlink. In the case of link buttons, the *Click* event is fired on the server to let you handle the event when the page posts back. In the case of hyperlinks, the browser displays the target page in the specified frame—the *Target* property. The target URL coincides with the contents of the field specified by *DataValueField*.

Figure 9-4 shows a sample page that includes a *RadioButtonList* and *BulletedList* control. The radio-button list is bound to the contents of a system enumerated type—*BulletStyle*—and displays as selectable radio buttons the various bullet styles. To bind the contents of an enumerated type to a data-bound control, you do as follows:

```
BulletOptions.DataSource = Enum.GetValues(typeof(BulletStyle));
BulletOptions.SelectedIndex = 0;
BulletOptions.DataBind();
```

To retrieve and set the selected value, use the following code:

```
BulletStyle style = (BulletStyle) Enum.Parse(typeof(BulletStyle),
                                        BulletOptions.SelectedValue);
BulletedList1.BulletStyle = style;
```

FIGURE 9-4 A sample page to preview the style of a *BulletedList* control.

Iterative Controls

Iterative controls are a special type of data-bound controls that supply a template-based mechanism to create free-form user interfaces. Iterative controls take a data source, loop through the items, and iteratively apply user-defined HTML templates to each row. This basic behavior is common to all three ASP.NET iterators—*Repeater*, *DataList*, and *DataGrid*. Beyond that, iterative controls differ from each other in terms of layout capabilities and functionality.

Iterative controls differ from list controls because of their greater rendering flexibility. An iterative control lets you apply an ASP.NET template to each row in the bound data source. A list control, on the other hand, provides a fixed and built-in template for each data item. List controls are customizable to some extent, but you can't change anything other than the text displayed. No changes to layout are supported. On the other hand, using a list control is considerably easier than setting up an iterative control, as we'll see in a moment. Defining templates requires quite a bit of declarative code, and if accomplished programmatically, it requires that you write a class that implements the *ITemplate* interface. A list control requires only that you go through a few data-binding properties.

We'll take a look at *DataGrid* controls in Chapter 11. Meanwhile, let's briefly meet each control. When they are properly customized and configured, there's no graphical structure—be it flat or hierarchical—that *Repeater* and *DataList* controls can't generate.

> **Note** More space for lower-level iterators such as *Repeater* and *DataList* is reserved in my other related book, *Programming Microsoft ASP.NET 2.0 Applications: Advanced Topics* (Microsoft Press, 2006).

The *Repeater* Control

The *Repeater* displays data using user-provided layouts. It works by repeating a specified ASP.NET template for each item displayed in the list. The *Repeater* is a rather basic templated data-bound control. It has no built-in layout or styling capabilities. All formatting and layout information must be explicitly declared and coded using HTML tags and ASP.NET classes.

The *Repeater* class acts as a naming container by implementing the marker interface *INamingContainer*. (See Chapter 3.) Table 9-4 lists the main properties exposed by the control, not counting those inherited from the base class.

TABLE 9-4 Properties of the *Repeater* Control

Property	Description
AlternatingItemTemplate	Template to define how every other item is rendered.
DataMember	The name of the table in the *DataSource* to bind.
DataSource	The data source that populates the items of the list.
DataSourceID	ID of the data source component to provide data. *Not supported in ASP.NET 1.x.*
FooterTemplate	Template to define how the footer is rendered.
HeaderTemplate	Template to define how the header is rendered.
Items	Gets a *RepeaterItemCollection* object—that is, a collection of *RepeaterItem* objects. Each element of the collection represents a displayed data row in the *Repeater*.
ItemTemplate	Template to define how items are rendered.
SeparatorTemplate	Template to define how the separator between items is to be rendered.

For the most part, properties are the template elements that form the control's user interface. The *Repeater* populates the *Items* collection by enumerating all the data items in the bound data source. For each data-bound item (for example, a table record), it creates a *RepeaterItem* object and adds it to the *Items* collection. The *RepeaterItemCollection* class is a plain collection class with no special or peculiar behavior. The *RepeaterItem* class represents a displayed element within the overall structure created by the *Repeater*. The *RepeaterItem* contains properties to point to the bound data item (such as a table record), the index, and the type of the item (regular item, alternating item, header, footer, and so on). Here's a quick example of a *Repeater*:

```
<asp:Repeater ID="Repeater1" runat="server">
    <HeaderTemplate>
        <h2>We have customers in the following cities</h2>
        <hr />
    </HeaderTemplate>
    <SeparatorTemplate>
        <hr noshade style="border:dashed 1px blue" />
    </SeparatorTemplate>
    <ItemTemplate>
        <%# Eval("City")%>   <b><%# Eval("Country")%></b>
    </ItemTemplate>
    <FooterTemplate>
        <hr />
        <%# CalcTotal() %> cities
    </FooterTemplate>
</asp:Repeater>
```

Bound to the output of the following query, the structure produces what's shown in Figure 9-5:

```
SELECT DISTINCT country, city FROM customers WHERE country=@TheCountry
```

The *@TheCountry* parameter is the name of the country picked from the drop-down list.

```
data = new DataTable();
SqlDataAdapter adapter = new SqlDataAdapter(cmdText, connString);
adapter.SelectCommand.Parameters.AddWithValue("@TheCountry",
                                Countries.SelectedValue);
adapter.Fill(data);
Repeater1.DataSource = data;
Repeater1.DataBind();
```

FIGURE 9-5 A sample *Repeater* control in action. No predefined list control can generate such a free-form output.

Of all the templates, only *ItemTemplate* and *AlternatingItemTemplate* are data-bound, meaning that they are repeated for each item in the data source. You need a mechanism to access public properties on the data item (such as a table record) from within the template. The *Eval* method takes the name of the property (for example, the name of the table column) and returns the content. We'll learn more about *Eval* and *<%# ... %>* code blocks in a moment when discussing data-binding expressions.

The *DataList* Control

The *DataList* is a data-bound control that begins where the *Repeater* ends and terminates a little before the starting point of the *DataGrid* control. In some unrealistically simple cases, you can even take some code that uses a *Repeater*, replace the control, and not even notice any difference. The *DataList* overtakes the *Repeater* in several respects, mostly in the area of graphical layout. The *DataList* supports directional rendering, meaning that items can flow horizontally or vertically to match a specified number of columns. Furthermore, it provides facilities to retrieve a key value associated with the current data row and has built-in support for selection and in-place editing. (I discuss these features in *Programming Microsoft ASP.NET 2.0 Applications: Advanced Topics*.)

In addition, the *DataList* control supports more templates and can fire some extra events beyond those of the *Repeater*. Data binding and the overall behavior are nearly identical for the *Repeater* and *DataList* controls.

The *DataList* works by making some assumptions about the expected results. This is both good and bad news for you as a programmer. It means that in some cases much less code is needed to accomplish the same effect; on the other hand, it also indicates that you should know the behavior of the control very well to govern it. The *DataList* assumes that no HTML tag is split across templates and renders its entire output as an HTML table.

In addition to being a naming container, the *DataList* class implements the *IRepeatInfoUser* interface. The *IRepeatInfoUser* interface defines the properties and methods that must be implemented by any list control that repeats a list of items. This interface is also supported by the *CheckBoxList* and *RadioButtonList* controls and is the brains behind the *RepeatXXX* properties we met earlier. Here's how to rewrite the previous example to get stricter control over the output:

```
<asp:DataList ID="DataList1" runat="server" RepeatColumns="5"
    GridLines="Both">
  <FooterStyle Font-Bold="true" ForeColor="blue" />
  <HeaderTemplate>
     <h2>We have customers in the following cities</h2>
  </HeaderTemplate>
  <ItemTemplate>
     <%# Eval("City") %>   <b><%# Eval("Country")%></b>
  </ItemTemplate>
  <FooterTemplate>
     <%# CalcTotal() %> cities
  </FooterTemplate>
</asp:DataList>
```

The output is shown in Figure 9-6. Note the *FooterStyle* tag; the *DataList* also lets you explicitly style the content of each supported template. In this case, we're going to get boldface and blue text in the footer panel.

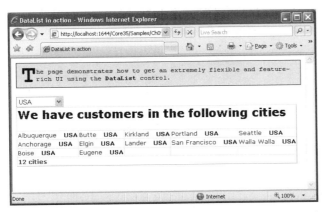

FIGURE 9-6 A sample *DataList* control in action. Note the extended layout capabilities that let you divide items by columns by simply setting a property.

The *DataGrid* Control

The *DataGrid* is an extremely versatile data-bound control that is a fixed presence in any real-world ASP.NET application. While fully supported, in ASP.NET 2.0 the *DataGrid* is pushed into the background by the introduction of a new and much more powerful grid control—the *GridView*. We'll cover both controls in more detail in Chapter 11.

The *DataGrid* control renders a multicolumn, fully templated grid and provides a highly customizable, Microsoft Office Excel–like user interface. In spite of the rather advanced programming interface and the extremely rich set of attributes, the *DataGrid* simply generates an HTML table with interspersed hyperlinks to provide interactive functionalities such as sorting, paging, selection, and in-place editing.

The *DataGrid* is a column-based control and supports various types of data-bound columns, including text columns, templated columns, and command columns. You associate the control with a data source using the *DataSource* property. Just as for other data-bound controls, no data will be physically loaded and bound until the *DataBind* method is called. The simplest way of displaying a table of data using the ASP.NET grid is as follows:

```
<asp:DataGrid runat="server" id="grid" />
```

The control will then automatically generate an HTML table column for each property available in the bound data source. This is only the simplest scenario, however. If needed, you can specify which columns should be displayed and style them at will.

```
grid.DataSource = data;
grid.DataBind();
```

Figure 9-7 demonstrates the grid's output for a sample that returns three fields. As mentioned, we'll cover the *DataGrid* control in much greater detail in Chapter 11.

FIGURE 9-7 A sample *DataGrid* control in action.

Data-Binding Expressions

What we have examined so far is the most common form of data binding that involves list and iterative controls and collections of data. It is important to note that any of the ASP. NET controls support some minimal form of data binding, including text boxes and labels, through the *DataBind* method. In its simplest form, a binding is a connection between one piece of data and a server control property. This simple form of binding is established through a special expression that gets evaluated when the code in the page calls the *DataBind* method on the control.

Simple Data Binding

A data-binding expression is any executable code wrapped by <% ... %> and prefixed by the symbol #. Typically, you use data-binding expressions to set the value of an attribute in the opening tag of a server control. A data-binding expression is programmatically managed via an instance of the *DataBoundLiteralControl* class.

> **Note** The binding expression is really any executable code that can be evaluated at run time. Its purpose is to generate data that the control can use to bind for display or editing. Typically, the code retrieves data from the data source, but there is no requirement that this be the case. Any executable code is acceptable so long as it returns data for binding. A data-binding expression is evaluated only when something happens that fires the control's *DataBinding* event.

The following code snippet shows how to set the text of a label with the current time:

```
<asp:label runat="server" Text='<%# DateTime.Now %>' />
```

Within the delimiters, you can invoke user-defined page methods, static methods, and properties and methods of any other page component. The following code demonstrates a label bound to the name of the currently selected element in a drop-down list control:

```
<asp:label runat="server" Text='<%# dropdown.SelectedItem.Text %>' />
```

Note that if you're going to use quotes within the expression, you should wrap the expression itself with single quotes. The data-binding expression can accept a minimal set of operators, mostly for concatenating subexpressions. If you need more advanced processing and use external arguments, resort to a user-defined method. The only requirement is that the method is declared public or protected.

> **Important** Any data-bound expression you define in the page is evaluated only after *DataBind* is called. You can either call *DataBind* on the page object or on the specific control. If you call *DataBind* on the page object, it will recursively call *DataBind* on all controls defined in the page. If *DataBind* is not called, no <%# ...%> expressions will ever be evaluated.

Binding in Action

Data-binding expressions are particularly useful to update, in a pure declarative manner, properties of controls that depend on other controls in the same page. For example, suppose you have a drop-down list of colors and a label and that you want the text of the label to reflect the selected color.

```
<asp:DropDownList ID="SelColors" runat="server" AutoPostBack="True">
    <asp:ListItem>Orange</asp:ListItem>
    <asp:ListItem>Green</asp:ListItem>
    <asp:ListItem>Red</asp:ListItem>
    <asp:ListItem>Blue</asp:ListItem>
</asp:DropDownList>
<asp:Label runat="server" ID="lblColor"
    Text='<%# "<b>You selected: </b>" + SelColors.SelectedValue %>' />
```

Note that in the <%# ... %> expression you can use any combination of methods, constants, and properties as long as the final result matches the type of the bound property. Also note that the evaluation of the expression requires a postback and a call to *DataBind*. We set the *AutoPostBack* property to *true* just to force a postback when the selection changes in the drop-down list. At the same time, a call to the page's or label's *DataBind* method is required for the refresh to occur.

```
protected void Page_Load(object sender, EventArgs e)
{
    DataBind();
}
```

You can bind to expressions virtually any control properties regardless of the type. Let's see how to bind the *ForeColor* property of the *Label* control to the color string picked from the drop-down list:

```
ForeColor='<%# Color.FromName(SelColors.SelectedValue) %>'
```

Note that you can't just set *ForeColor* to an expression that evaluates to a color string, such as "orange".

```
ForeColor='<%# SelColors.SelectedValue %>'
```

The preceding code won't compile because of the impossible automatic conversion between a string (your expression) and a color (the type of the *ForeColor* property). Interestingly enough, of the following statements only the second will work fine:

```
ForeColor='<%# "orange" %>'
ForeColor="orange"
```

The upshot is that a data-binding expression requires that the return type match the type of the property represented via an attribute. Using a plain constant string is fine, on the other hand, because the page parser recognizes the expression and seamlessly inserts proper conversion code, if such a conversion is possible. Figure 9-8 shows the sample page in action.

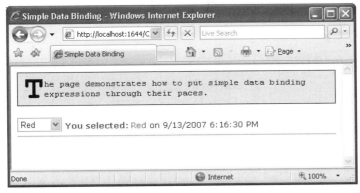

FIGURE 9-8 Drop-down list and label tied up together using a data-binding expression.

Implementation of Data-Binding Expressions

What really happens when a data-binding expression is found in a Web page? How does the ASP.NET runtime process it? Let's consider the following code:

```
<asp:label runat="server" id="today" text='<%# DateTime.Now %>' />
```

When the page parser takes care of the *.aspx* source code, it generates a class where each server control has a factory method. The factory method simply maps the tag name to a server-side control class and transforms attributes on the tag into property assignments. In addition, if a data-binding expression is found, the parser adds a handler for the *DataBinding* event of the control—a *Label* in this case. Here's some pseudocode to illustrate the point:

```
private Control __BuildControlToday() {
    Label __ctrl = new Label();
    this.today = __ctrl;
    __ctrl.ID = "today";

    __ctrl.DataBinding += new EventHandler(this.__DataBindToday);
    return __ctrl;
}
```

The handler assigns the data-binding expression verbatim to the property:

```
public void __DataBindToday(object sender, EventArgs e) {
    Label target;
    target = (Label) sender;
    target.Text = Convert.ToString(DateTime.Now);
}
```

If the value returned by the data-binding expression doesn't match the expected type, you generally get a compile error. However, if the expected type is *string*, the parser attempts a standard conversion through the *Convert.ToString* method. (All .NET Framework types are convertible to a string because they inherit the *ToString* method from the root *object* type.)

The *DataBinder* Class

Earlier in this chapter, we met <%# ... %> expressions in the context of templates, along with the *Eval* method. The *Eval* method is a kind of tailormade operator you use in data-binding expressions to access a public property on the bound data item. The *Eval* method as used earlier is an ASP.NET 2.0-only feature and will generate a compile error if used in ASP.NET 1.x applications. For all versions of ASP.NET, you can use a functionally equivalent method, also named *Eval*, but from another class—*DataBinder*.

> **Important** Through the *Eval* method—even if it comes from *DataBinder* or *Page*—you can access public properties on the bound data item. Let me clarify what public properties are in this context and why I insist on calling them properties. Any class that implements *IEnumerable* can be bound to a control. The list of actual classes certainly includes *DataTable* (where a data item logically corresponds to a table record), but it also includes custom collections (where a data item corresponds to an instance of a given class). The *Eval* method ends up querying the data item object for its set of properties. The object that represents a table record will return descriptors for its columns; other objects will return their set of public properties.

The *DataBinder* class supports generating and parsing data-binding expressions. Of particular importance is its overloaded static method *Eval*. The method uses reflection to parse and evaluate an expression against a runtime object. Clients of the *Eval* method include rapid application development (RAD) tools such as Microsoft Visual Studio .NET designers and Web controls that declaratively place calls to the method to feed dynamically changing values to properties.

The *Eval* Method

The syntax of *DataBinder.Eval* typically looks like this:

```
<%# DataBinder.Eval(Container.DataItem, expression) %>
```

A third, optional parameter is omitted in the preceding snippet. This parameter is a string that contains formatting options for the bound value. The *Container.DataItem* expression references the object on which the expression is evaluated. The expression is typically a string with the name of the field to access on the data item object. It can be an expression that includes indexes and property names. The *DataItem* property represents the object within the current container context. Typically, a container is the current instance of the item object—for example, a *DataGridItem* object—that is about to be rendered.

The code shown earlier is commonly repeated, always in the same form. Only the expression and the format string change from page to page.

A More Compact *Eval*

The original syntax of the *DataBinder.Eval* can be simplified in ASP.NET 2.0 and newer versions, as we already saw earlier in the *Repeater* example. You can use

```
<%# Eval(expression) %>
```

wherever the following expression is accepted in ASP.NET 1.x:

```
<%# DataBinder.Eval(Container.DataItem, expression) %>
```

It goes without saying that the *DataBinder* object is fully supported also in ASP.NET 2.0 and newer versions.

Any piece of code that appears within the <%# ... %> delimiters enjoys special treatment from the ASP.NET runtime. Let's briefly look at what happens with this code. When the page is compiled for use, the *Eval* call is inserted in the source code of the page as a standalone call. The following code gives you an idea of what happens:

```
object o = Eval("lastname");
string result = Convert.ToString(o);
```

The result of the call is converted to a string and is assigned to a data-bound literal control—an instance of the *DataBoundLiteralControl* class. Then the data-bound literal is inserted in the page's control tree.

The *TemplateControl* class—the parent of *Page*—is actually enriched with a new protected (but not virtual) method named *Eval*. The following pseudocode illustrates how the method works:

```
protected object Eval(string expression)
{
    if (Page == null)
        throw new InvalidOperationException(…);
    return DataBinder.Eval(Page.GetDataItem(), expression);
}
```

As you can see, *Eval* is a simple wrapper built around the *DataBinder.Eval* method. The *DataBinder.Eval* method is invoked using the current container's data item. Quite obviously, the current container's data is null outside a data-binding operation—that is, in the stack of calls following a call to *DataBind*. This fact brings up a key difference between *Eval* and *DataBinder.Eval*.

> **Important**   The *TemplateControl*'s *Eval* is a data-binding method and can be used only in the context of a data-bound control during a data-binding operation. On the other hand, *DataBinder.Eval* is a fully fledged method that can be used anywhere in the code. Typically, you use it in the implementation of custom data-bound controls. I show this in the *Programming Microsoft ASP.NET 2.0 Applications: Advanced Topics* book.

Getting the Default Data Item

The pseudocode that illustrates the behavior of the page's *Eval* method shows a *GetDataItem* method from the *Page* class. What is it? As mentioned, the simplified syntax assumes a default *Container.DataItem* context object. *GetDataItem* is simply the function that returns that object.

More precisely, *GetDataItem* is the endpoint of a stack-based mechanism that traces the current binding context for the page. Each control in the control tree is pushed onto this stack at the time the respective *DataBind* method is called. When the *DataBind* method returns, the control is popped from the stack. If the stack is empty, and you attempt to call *Eval* programmatically, *GetDataItem* throws an invalid operation exception. In summary, you can use the *Eval* shortcut only in templates; if you need to access properties of a data item anywhere else in the code, resort to *DataBinder.Eval* and indicate the data item object explicitly.

> **Tip**   As mentioned, you generally need to call *DataBinder.Eval* directly only in the code of custom data-bound controls. (I cover custom controls in *Programming Microsoft ASP.NET 2.0 Applications: Advanced Topics*.) When this happens, though, you might want to save a few internal calls and CPU cycles by calling *DataBinder.GetPropertyValue* instead. This is exactly what *DataBinder.Eval* does in the end.

Other Data-Binding Methods

In ASP.NET, data-binding expressions go far beyond a read-only evaluation of enumerable and tabular data. In addition to *DataBinder*, ASP.NET provides a class that can bind to the result of XPath expressions that are executed against an object that implements the *IXPathNavigable* interface. This class is named *XPathBinder*; it plays the same role as *DataBinder*, except it works on XML data. The *XPathBinder* class backs up a new data-binding method named *XPath*.

ASP.NET also supports declarative two-way data binding, meaning that you can read and write data item properties through a new data-binding method named *Bind*.

Finally, ASP.NET supports user-defined expressions that operate outside the boundaries of data-binding operations. It might sound weird that I discuss non-data-binding expressions in a section explicitly dedicated to data-binding expressions. The reason I mention this option here is to avoid confusion, as the syntax for custom expressions is nearly identical.

The *XPath* Method

Starting with ASP.NET 2.0, data-bound controls can be associated with raw XML data. You can bind XML data in version 1.x, but you have to first fit XML data into a relational structure such as a *DataSet*. When a templated control such as *DataList* or *Repeater* is bound to an XML data source (such as the new *XmlDataSource* control, which we'll cover later in the chapter), individual XML fragments can be bound inside the template using the *XPathBinder* object.

The *XPathBinder.Eval* method accepts an *XmlNode* object along with an XPath expression, and it evaluates and returns the result. The output string can be formatted if a proper format string is specified. *XPathBinder.Eval* casts the container object to *IXPathNavigable*. This is a prerequisite to applying the XPath expression. If the object doesn't implement the interface, an exception is thrown. The *IXPathNavigable* interface is necessary because in the .NET Framework the whole XPath API is built for, and works only with, objects that provide a navigator class. The goal of the interface is to create an XPath navigator object for the query to run.

Like *DataBinder*, the *XPathBinder* class supports a simplified syntax for its evaluator method. The syntax assumes a default container context that is the same object that is tracked for the data binder. The following example demonstrates using the simplified XPath data-binding syntax:

```
<%# XPath("Orders/Order/Customer/LastName") %>
```

The output value is the object returned by *XPathBinder.Eval* converted to a string. Internally, *XPathBinder.Eval* gets a navigator object from the data source and evaluates the expression. The managed XPath API is used.

> **Note** In this book, we don't cover XML classes in the .NET Framework. A good reference is my book *Applied XML with the .NET Framework* (Microsoft Press. 2003). The book covers .NET Framework 1.x, but as far as XPath is concerned, what you can learn from that source is exactly what you need to know.

The *XPathSelect* Method

The *XPathBinder* class also features a *Select* method. The method executes an XPath query and retrieves a nodeset—an enumerable collection of XML nodes. This collection can be assigned as a late-bound value to data-bound controls (such as the *Repeater* control). An equivalent simplified syntax exists for this scenario, too:

```
<asp:Repeater runat="server" DataSource='<%# XPathSelect("orders/order/summary") %>'>
    ...
</asp:Repeater>
```

XPathSelect is the keyword you use in data-binding expressions to indicate the results of an XPath query run on the container object. If the container object does not implement *IXPathNavigable*, an exception is thrown. Like *Eval* and *XPath*, *XPathSelect* assumes a default data item context object.

The *Bind* Method

As we'll see in Chapter 13, ASP.NET supports two-way data binding—that is, the capability to bind data to controls and submit changes back to the database. The *Eval* method is representative of a one-way data binding that automates data reading but not data writing. The new *Bind* method can be used whenever *Eval* is accepted and through a similar syntax:

```
<asp:TextBox Runat="server" ID="TheNotes" Text='<%# Bind("notes") %>' />
```

The big difference is that *Bind* works in both directions—reading and writing. For example, when the *Text* property is being set, *Bind* behaves exactly like *Eval*. In addition, when the *Text* property is being read, *Bind* stores the value into a collection. Enabled ASP.NET data-bound controls (for example, the new *FormView* control and other templated controls) automatically retrieve these values and use them to compose the parameter list of the insert or edit command to run against the data source. The argument passed to *Bind* must match the name of a parameter in the command. For example, the text box just shown provides the value for the *@notes* parameter.

User-Defined Dynamic Expressions

Data-binding expressions are not really dynamic expressions because they are evaluated only within the context of a data-binding call. ASP.NET provides a made-to-measure infrastructure for dynamic expressions based on a new breed of components—the expression builders. (I cover expression builders in *Programming Microsoft ASP.NET 2.0 Applications: Advanced Topics*.)

Dynamic expressions have a syntax that is similar to data binding, except that they use the *$* prefix instead of #. Dynamic expressions are evaluated when the page compiles. The content of the expression is extracted, transformed into code, and injected into the code created for the page. A few predefined expression builders exist, as listed in Table 9-5.

TABLE 9-5 Custom Expressions

Syntax	Description
AppSettings:XXX	Returns the value of the specified setting from the *<appSettings>* section of the configuration file.
ConnectionStrings:XXX[.YYY]	Returns the value of the specified XXX string from the *<connectionStrings>* section of the configuration file. The optional YYY parameter indicates which attribute is read from the section. It can be either *connectionString* (default) or *providerName*.
Resources:XXX, YYY	Returns the value of the YYY global resource read from the XXX resource file (*.resx*).

To declaratively bind a control property to the value of the expression, you follow the schema shown here:

```
<%$ expression %>
```

The exact syntax is defined by the builder associated with each expression. Note, though, that literal expressions are not permitted in the body of the page. In other words, you can use expressions only to set a control property. You can't have the following:

```
<h1><%$ AppSettings:AppVersionNumber %></h1>
```

Instead, you should wrap the expression in a server control, the simplest of which would be the *Literal* control. The following code generates the page in Figure 9-9:

```
<h1><asp:Literal runat="server"
        Text="<%$ Resources:Resource, AppWelcome %>" /></h1>
<hr />
<b>Code version <asp:Literal runat="server"
      Text="<%$ AppSettings:AppVersionNumber %>" /></b>
```

Needless to say, you need to have an *AppWelcome* string resource in the *App_GlobalResource* and an *AppVersionNumber* setting in the *web.config* file.

```
<appSettings>
    <add key="AppVersionNumber" value="8.2.2001" />
</appSettings>
```

FIGURE 9-9 The heading text and the version number are obtained through declarative expressions.

The remaining expression—*ConnectionStrings*—is extremely helpful with data source controls to avoid hard-coding the connection string in the *.aspx* file.

> **Note** Microsoft provides the few built-in expression builders listed in Table 9-5. Developers can define others by simply writing new classes that inherit from *ExpressionBuilder*. To be recognized and properly handled, custom expression builders must be registered in the *web.config* file. I'll touch on this topic in *Programming Microsoft ASP.NET 2.0 Applications: Advanced Topics* (Microsoft Press, 2006).

Data Source Components

ASP.NET 1.x has an extremely flexible and generic data-binding architecture that gives developers full control of the page life cycle. Developers can link data-bound controls such as the *DataGrid* to any enumerable collection of data. While this approach represents a quantum leap from classic ASP, it still requires page developers to learn a lot of architectural details to create even relatively simple read-only pages. This is a problem for Web developers with limited skills because they soon get into trouble if left alone to decide how (or whether) to implement paging, sorting, updates, or perhaps a master/detail view. But this is also a (different) problem for experienced developers, as they have to continually re-implement the same pattern to access data sources, get data, and make the data consistent with the programming interface of data controls.

The key issue with ASP.NET 1.x data binding is a lack of a higher-level and possibly declarative model for data fetching and data manipulation. As a result, an ASP.NET 1.x data access layer is boring to write and requires hundreds of lines of code even for relatively simple scenarios. Enter ASP.NET data source components.

Overview of Data Source Components

A data source component is a server control designed to interact with data-bound controls and hide the complexity of the manual data-binding pattern. Data source components not only provide data to controls, they also support data-bound controls in the execution of other common operations such as insertions, deletions, sorting, and updates. Each data source component wraps a particular data provider—relational databases, XML documents, or custom classes. The support for custom classes means that you can now directly bind your controls to existing classes—for example, classes in your business or data access layer. (I'll say more about this later.)

Existing ASP.NET 1.x controls have been extended in ASP.NET 2.0 and newer versions to support binding to data source controls as far as data retrieval is concerned. The *DataSourceID* property represents the point of contact between old-style data-bound controls and the new data source components. Starting with ASP.NET 2.0, you can successfully bind a *DataGrid* to a data source control without writing a single line of code—not even the ritual call to *DataBind*. However, achieving codeless programming is not the primary goal of data source controls. Think of data source controls as the natural tool to achieve a less complex and semi-automatic interaction between a variety of data sources and controls.

Existing controls such as *DataGrid* and *Repeater* don't take full advantage of data source components. Only controls introduced with ASP.NET 2.0 such as *GridView*, *FormView*, and *DetailsView* (plus the *ListView* control in ASP.NET 3.5) benefit from the true power of data source controls. This is because new controls have a different internal structure specifically designed to deal with data source controls and share with them the complexity of the data-binding pattern.

A Click in the Life of *DataGrid*

To understand the primary goal of data source components, consider what happens when the user performs an action on some data displayed through a *DataGrid*. Imagine you display an editable grid—that is, a grid that contains an edit column. Users click a cell to edit the corresponding row; the *DataGrid* posts back and fires an event. Page authors handle the event by writing some code to switch the *DataGrid* control to edit mode. A pair of OK/Cancel buttons replace the edit button. The user edits the contents of the row and then clicks to save or cancel changes. What happens at this point?

The *DataGrid* control captures the event, validates the user-provided data, and then fires the *UpdateCommand* event. The page author is in charge of handling the event, collecting new data, and building and running any required command against the data source. All these steps require code. The same thing happens if you need to sort data, view a new page, or drill down into the currently selected record.

A Click in the Life of *GridView*

Let's see what happens if you use the successor to the *DataGrid* control—the *GridView* control—which is specifically designed to adhere to the data source model. Let's assume the same scenario: the user clicks, and the control enters edit mode. The first difference is that you don't need to write any code to turn on the *GridView*'s edit mode. If you click on a cell within an edit column, the control "knows" what you want to do and intelligently takes the next step and executes the requested action—turning on the edit mode.

When the user clicks to save changes, again the *GridView* control anticipates the user's next action and talks to the data source control to have it perform the requested operation (update) on the data source. All this requires no code from the page author; only a few settings, such as the command text and the connection string, are required and they can be set declaratively.

The combination of data source controls and new, smarter data-bound controls shows off its true power when your code addresses relatively common scenarios, which it probably does 70 to 80 percent of the time. If you need to have things done in a particular way, just work the old way and take full control of the page life cycle. This said, you'll find that data source controls have much more than just a deep understanding of the page life cycle. Data source controls support declarative parameters, transparent data caching, server-side paging ability, hierarchical data support, and the ability to work asynchronously. Implementing all these features manually would require quite a bit of code.

Internals of Data Source Controls

A data source control represents one or more named views of data. Each view manages a collection of data. The data associated with a data source control is managed through SQL-like operations such as SELECT, INSERT, DELETE, and COUNT and through capabilities such as sorting and paging. Data source controls come in two flavors—tabular and hierarchical. Tabular controls are described in Table 9-6.

TABLE 9-6 Tabular Data Source Controls

Class	Description
AccessDataSource	Represents a connection to a Microsoft Access database. Inherits from the SqlDataSource control, but points to an MDB file and uses the Jet 4.0 OLE DB provider to connect to the database.
LinqDataSource	Allows binding to the results of a Linq-to-SQL query. The control offers properties for you to specify the data context, table name, projection parameters, and *where* clause. *This control is supported only in ASP.NET 3.5.*
ObjectDataSource	Allows binding to a custom .NET business object that returns data. The class is expected to follow a specific design pattern and include, for example, a parameterless constructor and methods that behave in a certain way.
SqlDataSource	Represents a connection to an ADO.NET data provider that returns SQL data, including data sources accessible through OLE DB and ODBC. The name of the provider and the connection string are specified through properties.

Note that the *SqlDataSource* class is *not* specific to SQL Server. It can connect to any ADO.NET provider that manages relational data. Hierarchical data source controls are listed in Table 9-7.

TABLE 9-7 Hierarchical Data Source Controls

Class	Description
SiteMapDataSource	Allows binding to any provider that supplies site map information. The default provider supplies site map data through an XML file in the root folder of the application.
XmlDataSource	Allows binding to XML files and strings with or without schema information.

Note that data source controls have no visual rendering. They are implemented as controls to allow for "declarative persistence" (automatic instantiation during the request processing) as a native part of the *.aspx* source code and to gain access to the page view state.

Data Source Views

A named view is represented by a data source view object—an instance of the *DataSourceView* class. These classes represent a customized view of data in which special settings for sorting, filtering, and other data operations have been defined. The *DataSourceView* class is the base class for all views associated with a data source control. The number of views in a data source control depends on the connection string, characteristics and actual contents of the underlying data source. In ASP.NET 2.0 and newer versions, built-in data source controls support only one view, the default view. Table 9-8 lists the properties of the *DataSourceView* class.

TABLE 9-8 Properties of the *DataSourceView* Class

Property	Description
CanDelete	Indicates whether deletions are allowed on the underlying data source. The deletion is performed by invoking the *Delete* method.
CanInsert	Indicates whether insertions are allowed on the underlying data source. The insertion is performed by invoking the *Insert* method.
CanPage	Indicates whether the data in the view can be paged.
CanRetrieveTotalRowCount	Indicates whether information about the total row count is available.
CanSort	Indicates whether the data in the view can be sorted.
CanUpdate	Indicates whether updates are allowed on the underlying data source. The update is performed by invoking the *Update* method.
Name	Returns the name of the current view.

The *CanXXX* properties indicate not only whether the data source control is capable of performing the specified operation but also whether that operation is appropriate given the current status of the data. Table 9-9 lists all the methods supported by the class.

TABLE 9-9 Methods of the *DataSourceView* Class

Method	Description
Delete	Performs a delete operation on the data associated with the view
Insert	Performs an insert operation on the data associated with the view
Select	Returns an enumerable object filled with the data contained in the underlying data storage
Update	Performs an update operation on the data associated with the view

All data source view objects support data retrieval through the *Select* method. The method returns an object that implements the *IEnumerable* interface. The real type of the object depends on the data source control and the attributes set on it.

Interaction with Data-Bound Controls

Figure 9-10 shows the interaction between a data source control and data-bound control in ASP.NET 2.0 and newer versions.

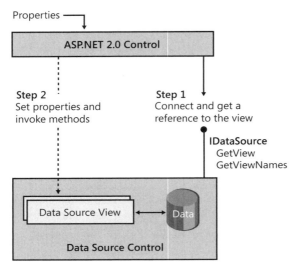

FIGURE 9-10 The data-bound control gets a view object and supports data binding capabilities and operations.

Most ASP.NET controls are aware of the full potential of data source controls, and they use the methods of *IDataSource* to connect to the underlying data repository. Implementing the interface is the only official requirement for a control that intends to behave like a data source control. Once it gets a hold of a data source view object, the control can call the properties and methods shown earlier in Table 9-8 and Table 9-9 to perform required tasks.

Hierarchical Data Source Views

Unlike tabular data source controls, which typically have only one named view, hierarchical data source controls support a view for each level of data that the data source control represents. Hierarchical and tabular data source controls share the same conceptual specification of a consistent and common programming interface for data-bound controls. The only difference is the nature of the data they work with—hierarchical vs. flat and tabular.

The view class is different and is named *HierarchicalDataSourceView*. The class features only one method—*Select*—which returns an enumerable hierarchical object. Hierarchical data source controls are, therefore, read-only.

The *SqlDataSource* Control

The *SqlDataSource* control is a data source control that represents a connection to a relational data store such as SQL Server or Oracle or any data source accessible through OLE DB and Open Database Connectivity (ODBC) bridges.

You set up the connection to the data store using two main properties, *ConnectionString* and *ProviderName*. The former represents the connection string and contains enough information to open a session with the underlying engine. The latter specifies the namespace of the ADO.NET managed provider to use for the operation. The *ProviderName* property defaults to *System.Data.SqlClient*, which means that the default data store is SQL Server. On the other hand, to target any OLE DB provider, use the *System.Data.OleDb* string instead.

The control can retrieve data using either a data adapter or a command object. Depending on your choice, fetched data will be packed in a *DataSet* object or a data reader. The following code snippet shows the minimal code necessary to activate a SQL data source control bound to a SQL Server database:

```
<asp:SqlDataSource runat="server" ID="MySqlSource"
    ProviderName='<%$ ConnectionStrings:LocalNWind.ProviderName %>'
    ConnectionString='<%$ ConnectionStrings:LocalNWind %>'
    SelectCommand="SELECT * FROM employees" />
<asp:DataGrid runat="server" ID="grid" DataSourceID="MySqlSource" />
```

Programming Interface of *SqlDataSource*

The data operations supported by the associated view class are provided by the related sets of properties listed in Table 9-10.

TABLE 9-10 Properties for Configuring Data Operations

Property Group	Description
DeleteCommand, DeleteParameters, DeleteCommandType	Gets or sets the SQL statement, related parameters, and type (text or stored procedure) used to delete rows in the underlying data store.
FilterExpression, FilterParameters	Gets or sets the string (and related parameters) to create a filter on top of the data retrieved using the *Select* command. It works only if the control manages data through a *DataSet*.
InsertCommand, InsertParameters, InsertCommandType	Gets or sets the SQL statement, related parameters, and type (text or stored procedure) used to insert new rows in the underlying data store.
SelectCommand, SelectParameters, SelectCommandType	Gets or sets the SQL statement, related parameters, and type (text or stored procedure) used to retrieve data from the underlying data store.

Property Group	Description
SortParameterName	Gets or sets the name of an input parameter that a command's stored procedure will use to sort data. (The command in this case must be a stored procedure.) It raises an exception if the parameter is missing.
UpdateCommand, UpdateParameters, UpdateCommandType	Gets or sets the SQL statement, related parameters, and type (text or stored procedure) used to update rows in the underlying data store.

Each command property is a string that contains the SQL text to be used. The command can optionally contain the parameters listed in the associated parameter collection. The managed provider and its underlying relational engine determine the exact syntax of the SQL to use and the syntax of the embedded parameters. For example, if the data source control points to SQL Server, command parameter names must be prefixed with the @ symbol. If the target data source is an OLE DB provider, parameters are unnamed, identified with a *?* placeholder symbol, and located by position. The following code snippet shows a more complex data source control in which parametric delete and update commands have been enabled:

```
<asp:SqlDataSource runat="server" ID="MySqlSource"
    ConnectionString='<%$ ConnectionStrings:LocalNWind %>'
    SelectCommand="SELECT * FROM employees"
    UpdateCommand="UPDATE employees SET lastname=@lname"
    DeleteCommand="DELETE FROM employees WHERE employeeid=@TheEmp"
    FilterExpression="employeeid > 3">
    <!-- parameters go here -->
</asp:SqlDataSource>
```

The syntax used for the *FilterExpression* property is the same as the syntax used for the *RowFilter* property of the *DataView* class (Chapter 8), which in turn is similar to that used with the SQL *WHERE* clause. If the *FilterExpression* property needs to be parametric, you can indicate parameters through the *FilterParameters* collection. Filtering is enabled only when *DataSourceMode* is set to *DataSet*.

 Note Note the difference between filter expressions and parameters on the *Select* command. Parameters on the command influence the result set returned by the data store; a filter expression restricts the display to the result set returned through the *Select* command.

Table 9-11 details other operational properties defined on the *SqlDataSource* class. The list doesn't include cache-related properties, which we'll cover in a moment.

TABLE 9-11 **Other Properties on** *SqlDataSource*

Property	Description
CancelSelectOnNullParameter	Indicates whether a data-retrieval operation is canceled if a parameter evaluates to *null*. The default value is *true*.
ConflictDetection	Determines how the control should handle data conflicts during a delete or update operation. By default, changes that occurred in the meantime are overwritten.
ConnectionString	The connection string to connect to the database.
DataSourceMode	Indicates how data should be returned—via a *DataSet* or data reader.
OldValuesParameterFormatString	Gets or sets a format string to apply to the names of any parameters passed to the *Delete* or *Update* method.
ProviderName	Indicates the namespace of the ADO.NET managed provider to use.

It is interesting to note that many of these properties mirror identical properties defined on the actual view class, as illustrated earlier in Figure 9-10.

The *SqlDataSource* object features a few methods and events, which in most cases are common to all data source components. The methods are *Delete*, *Insert*, *Select*, and *Update*, and they're implemented as mere wrappers around the corresponding methods of the underlying data source view class. Events exist in pairs—*Deleting/Deleted*, *Inserting/Inserted*, *Selecting/Selected*, and *Updating/Updated*—and fire before and after any of the methods just mentioned. The beginning of a filtering operation is signaled through the *Filtering* event.

As mentioned, only specific ASP.NET controls can really take advantage of the capabilities of data source controls. For this reason, in the upcoming chapters devoted to *GridView*, *DetailsView*, *FormView*, and *ListView* controls we'll see a lot of sample code showing how to use the *SqlDataSource* control for selecting, updating, paging, and sorting. In this chapter, we need to spend more time discussing other features of the control that can be particularly useful in real-world applications.

Declarative Parameters

Each command property has its own collection of parameters—an instance of a collection class named *ParameterCollection*. ASP.NET supports quite a few parameter types, which are listed in Table 9-12.

TABLE 9-12 Parameter Types for Data Source Controls

Parameter	Description
ControlParameter	Gets the parameter value from any public property of a server control
CookieParameter	Sets the parameter value based on the content of the specified HTTP cookie
FormParameter	Gets the parameter value from the specified input field in the HTTP request form
Parameter	Gets the parameter value assigned by the code
ProfileParameter	Gets the parameter value from the specified property name in the profile object created from the application's personalization scheme
QueryStringParameter	Gets the parameter value from the specified variable in the request query string
SessionParameter	Sets the parameter value based on the content of the specified session state slot

Each parameter class has a *Name* property and a set of properties specific to its role and implementation. To understand declarative parameters in data source controls, take a look at the following code:

```
<asp:SqlDataSource runat="server" ID="MySource"
    ConnectionString='<%$ ConnectionStrings:LocalNWind %>'
    SelectCommand="SELECT * FROM employees WHERE employeeid > @MinID">
    <SelectParameters>
        <asp:ControlParameter Name="MinID" ControlId="EmpID"
            PropertyName="Text" />
    </SelectParameters>
</asp:SqlDataSource>
```

The query contains a placeholder named *@MinID*. The data source control automatically populates the placeholder with the information returned by the *ControlParameter* object. The value of the parameter is determined by the value of a given property on a given control. The name of the property is specified by the *PropertyName* attribute. The ID of the control is in the *ControlId* attribute. For the previous code to work, page developers must guarantee that the page contains a control with a given ID and property; otherwise, an exception is thrown. In the example, the value of the property *Text* on the *EmpID* control is used as the value for the matching parameter.

The binding between formal parameters (the placeholders in the command text) and actual values depends on how the underlying managed provider handles and recognizes parameters. If the provider type supports named parameters—as is the case with SQL Server and Oracle—the binding involves matching the names of placeholders with the names of the parameters. Otherwise, the matching is based on the position. Hence, the first placeholder is bound to the first parameter, and so on. This is what happens if OLE DB is used to access the data.

Conflicts Detection

The *SqlDataSource* control can optionally perform database-intrusive operations such as deletions and updates. It is not a far-fetched idea to have the data read, perhaps modified on the client, and then updated. In a situation in which multiple users are using the same page, what should the behavior of the update/delete methods be if the record they attempt to work on has been modified in the meantime by another user?

The *SqlDataSource* control uses the *ConflictDetection* property to determine what to do when performing update and delete operations. The property is declared as type *ConflictOptions*—an enum type. The default value is *OverwriteChanges*, which means that any intrusive operation happens regardless of whether values in the row have changed since they were last read. The alternative is the *CompareAllValues* value, which simply ensures that the *SqlDataSource* control passes the original data read from the database to the *Delete* or *Update* method of the underlying view class.

It is important to note that changing the value of *ConflictDetection* doesn't produce any significant effect unless you write your delete or update statements in such a way that the command fails if the data in the row doesn't match the data that was initially read. To get this behavior, you should define the command as follows:

```
UPDATE employees SET firstname=@firstname
WHERE employeeid=@employeeid AND firstname=@original_firstname
```

In other words, you must explicitly add to the command an extra clause to check whether the current value of the field being modified still matches the value that was initially read. In this way, intermediate changes entered by concurrent users make the *WHERE* clause fail and make the command fail. You are in charge of tweaking the command text yourself; setting *ConflictDetection* to *CompareAllValues* is not enough.

How would you format the name of the parameters that represent old values? The *SqlDataSource* control uses the *OldValuesParameterFormatString* property to format these parameter names. The default value is *original_{0}*.

When you use the *CompareAllValues* option, you can handle the *Deleted* or *Updated* event on the data source control to check how many rows are affected. If no rows are affected by the operation, a concurrency violation might have occurred.

```
void OnUpdated(object sender, SqlDataSourceStatusEventArgs e)
{
    if (e.AffectedRows == 0) {
        // Concurrency violation: notify the user …
        ...
    }
}
```

Caching Behavior

The data binding between a data-bound control and its data source component is automatic and takes place on each postback caused by the data-bound control. Imagine a page with a grid, a data source control, and a button. If you turn on the grid in edit mode, the *Select* command on the data source control is run; if you click the button, the UI of the grid is rebuilt from the view state and no *Select* statement is run.

To save a query on postbacks, you can ask the data source control to cache the result set for a given duration. While data is cached, the *Select* method retrieves data from the cache rather than from the underlying database. When the cache expires, the *Select* method retrieves data from the underlying database and stores the fresh data back to the cache. The caching behavior of the *SqlDataSource* control is governed by the properties in Table 9-13.

TABLE 9-13 Caching Properties on *SqlDataSource*

Property	Description
CacheDuration	Indicates, in seconds, how long the data should be maintained in the cache.
CacheExpirationPolicy	Indicates if the cache duration is absolute or sliding. If the duration is absolute, data is invalidated after the specified number of seconds. If the duration is sliding, data is invalidated if not used for the specified duration.
CacheKeyDependency	Indicates the name of a user-defined cache key that is linked to all cache entries created by the data source control. By having the key expire, you can clear the control's cache.
EnableCaching	Enables or disables caching support.
SqlCacheDependency	Gets or sets a semicolon-delimited string that indicates which databases and tables to use for the SQL Server cache dependency.

A single cache entry is created for each distinct combination of *SelectCommand*, *ConnectionString*, and *SelectParameters*. Multiple *SqlDataSource* controls can share the same cache entries if they happen to load the same data from the same database. You can take control of cache entries managed by the data source control through the *CacheKeyDependency* property. If set to a non-null string, the property forces the *SqlDataSource* control to create a dependency between that key and all cache entries created by the control. At this point, to clear the control's cache, you only have to assign a new value to the dependency key:

```
// Give the entry a default value to be changed later
Cache["_ClearAll"] = anyInitializationValue;
SqlDataSource1.CacheKeyDependency = "_ClearAll";
...

// Clear the data source control's internal cache
Cache["_ClearAll"] = anyOtherValue;
```

The *SqlDataSource* control can cache data only when working in *DataSet* mode. You get an exception if *DataSourceMode* is set to *DataReader* and caching is enabled.

Finally, the *SqlCacheDependency* property links the *SqlDataSource* cached data with the contents of the specified database table (typically, the same table where the cached data comes from):

```
<asp:SqlDataSource ID="SqlDataSource1" runat="server"
  CacheDuration="1200"
  ConnectionString="<%$ ConnectionStrings:LocalNWind %>"
  EnableCaching="true"
  SelectCommand="SELECT * FROM employees"
  SqlCacheDependency="Northwind:Employees">
</asp:SqlDataSource>
```

Whenever the underlying table changes, the cached data is automatically flushed. We'll cover SQL cache dependencies in detail in Chapter 16.

The *AccessDataSource* Class

The *AccessDataSource* control is a data source control that represents a connection to an Access database. It is based on the *SqlDataSource* control and provides a simpler, made-to-measure programming interface. As a derived class, *AccessDataSource* inherits all members defined on its parent and overrides a few of them. In particular, the control replaces the *ConnectionString* and *ProviderName* properties with a more direct *DataFile* property. You set this property to the *.mdb* database file of choice. The data source control resolves the file path at run time and uses the Microsoft Jet 4 OLE DB provider to connect to the database.

> **Note** *AccessDataSource* actually inherits from *SqlDataSource*, and for this reason it can't make base members disappear, as hinted at earlier. *AccessDataSource* doesn't really replace the *ConnectionString* and *ProviderName* properties; it overrides them so that an exception is thrown whenever someone attempts to set their value. Another property overridden only to throw exceptions is *SqlCacheDependency*. This feature, of course, is not supported by the Access database.

Working with an Access Database

The following code shows how to use the *AccessDataSource* control to open an .mdb file and bind its content to a drop-down list control. Note that the control opens Access database files in read-only mode by default.

```
<asp:AccessDataSource runat="server" ID="MyAccessSource"
    DataFile="~/App_Data/nwind.mdb"
    SelectCommand="SELECT * FROM Customers" />
Select a Customer:
<asp:DropDownList runat="server" DataSourceId="MyAccessSource" />
```

Several features of the *AccessDataSource* control are inherited from the base class, *SqlDataSource*. In fact, the Access data source control is basically a SQL data source control optimized to work with Access databases. Like its parent control, the *AccessDataSource* control supports two distinct data source modes—*DataSet* and *DataReader*, depending on the ADO.NET classes used to retrieve data. Filtering can be applied to the selected data only if the fetch operation returns a *DataSet*. Caching works as on the parent class except for the *SqlCacheDependency* feature.

Updating an Access Database

The *AccessDataSource* can also be used to perform insert, update, or delete operations against the associated database. This is done using ADO.NET commands and parameter collections. Updates are problematic for Access databases when performed from within an ASP.NET application because an Access database is a plain file and the default account of the ASP.NET process (ASPNET or NetworkService, depending on the host operating system) might not have sufficient permission to write to the database file. For the data source updates to work, you should grant write permission to the ASP.NET account on the database file. Alternatively, you can use a different account with adequate permission.

> **Note** Most Internet Service Providers normally give you one directory in which ASPNET and NetworkService accounts have been granted the write permission. In this case, you just place your Access file in this directory and you can read and write seamlessly. In general, though, Access databases are plain files and, as such, are subject to the security rules of ASP.NET.

The *ObjectDataSource* Control

The *ObjectDataSource* class enables user-defined classes to associate the output of their methods to data-bound controls. Like other data source controls, *ObjectDataSource* supports declarative parameters to allow developers to pass page-level variables to the object's methods. The *ObjectDataSource* class makes some assumptions about the objects it wraps. As a consequence, an arbitrary class can't be used with this data source control. In particular, bindable classes are expected to have a default constructor, be stateless, and have methods that easily map to select, update, insert, and delete semantics. Also, the object must perform updates one item at a time; objects that update their state using batch operations are not supported. The bottom line is that managed objects that work well with *ObjectDataSource* are designed with this data source class in mind.

Programming Interface of *ObjectDataSource*

The *ObjectDataSource* component provides nearly the same programmatic interface (events, methods, properties, and associated behaviors) as the *SqlDataSource*, with the addition of three new events and a few properties. The events the *ObjectDataSource* fires are related to the lifetime of the underlying business object the *ObjectDataSource* is bound to—*ObjectCreating*, *ObjectCreated*, and *ObjectDisposing*. Table 9-14 lists other key properties of *ObjectDataSource*.

TABLE 9-14 Main Properties of *ObjectDataSource*

Property	Description
ConvertNullToDBNull	Indicates whether null parameters passed to insert, delete, or update operations are converted to *System.DBNull*. This property is set to *false* by default.
DataObjectTypeName	Gets or sets the name of a class that is to be used as a parameter for a *Select*, *Insert*, *Update*, or *Delete* operation.
DeleteMethod, DeleteParameters	Gets or sets the name of the method and related parameters used to perform a delete operation.
EnablePaging	Indicates whether the control supports paging.
FilterExpression, FilterParameters	Indicates the filter expression (and parameters) to filter the output of a select operation.
InsertMethod, InsertParameters	Gets or sets the name of the method and related parameters used to perform an insert operation.
MaximumRowsParameterName	If the *EnablePaging* property is set to *true*, indicates the parameter name of the *Select* method that accepts the value for the number of records to retrieve.
OldValuesParameterFormatString	Gets or sets a format string to apply to the names of any parameters passed to the *Delete* or *Update* methods.
SelectCountMethod	Gets or sets the name of the method used to perform a select count operation.
SelectMethod, SelectParameters	Gets or sets the name of the method and related parameters used to perform a select operation.
SortParameterName	Gets or sets the name of an input parameter used to sort retrieved data. It raises an exception if the parameter is missing.
StartRowIndexParameterName	If the *EnablePaging* property is set to *true*, indicates the parameter name of the *Select* method that accepts the value for the starting record to retrieve.
UpdateMethod, UpdateParameters	Gets or sets the name of the method and related parameters used to perform an update operation.

The *ObjectDataSource* control uses reflection to locate and invoke the method to handle the specified operation. The *TypeName* property returns the fully qualified name of the assembly that defines the class to call. If the class is defined in the *App_Code* directory, you don't need to indicate the assembly name. Otherwise, you use a comma-separated string in the form of *[classname, assembly]*. Let's see an example.

> **Warning** Having too many classes in the *App_Code* directory can become a nightmare at development time because any changes to any files will cause Visual Studio .NET to recompile the whole set of files in the project. If you prefer, it's completely reasonable to encapsulate your business object in a separate assembly and have your Web application simply reference that assembly.

Implementing Data Retrieval

The following code snippet illustrates a class that can be used with an object data source. The class represents employees and takes advantage of two other helper classes (at the very minimum): *Employee* and *EmployeeCollection*. The class *Employee* contains information about the entity being represented; the class *EmployeeCollection* represents a collection of employees. The behavior of the entity "employee" is codified in a bunch of methods exposed out of the gateway class—*Employees*.

```
public class Employees
{
    public static string ConnectionString {
        ...
    }
    public static void Load(int employeeID) {
        ...
    }
    public static EmployeeCollection LoadAll() {
        ...
    }
    public static EmployeeCollection LoadByCountry(string country) {
        ...
    }
    public static void Save(Employee emp) {
        ...
    }
    public static void Insert(Employee emp) {
        ...
    }
    public static void Delete(int employeeID) {
        ...
    }
    ...
}
```

If you don't use static methods, the worker class you use with *ObjectDataSource* must have a default parameterless constructor. Furthermore, the class should not maintain any state.

> **Warning** Using static methods in classes that represent the gateway to a database table is fine from an architectural viewpoint, but it might pose practical problems with unit testing. What if you test a business class that calls the data access layer (DAL) internally and the DAL fails? Can you figure out what really happened? Does the business class work or not?
>
> To effectively test a business layer that calls into a DAL, you need to focus on the object under test. Mock objects come to the rescue. Mock objects are programmable polymorphic objects that present themselves as others. So you can use mock objects to wrap the DAL and make it always return valid results. In this way, any anomalies are the result of non-DAL classes. The point is that toolkits that provide mock objects typically don't like static methods. That's why instance methods might be preferable in gateway classes of a DAL.

The worker class must be accessible from within the *.aspx* page and can be bound to the *ObjectDataSource* control, as shown here:

```
<asp:ObjectDataSource runat="server" ID="MyObjectSource"
    TypeName="Core35.DAL.Employees"
    SelectMethod="LoadAll" />
```

When the HTTP runtime encounters a similar block in a Web page, it generates code that calls the *LoadAll* method on the specified class. The returned data—an instance of the *EmployeeCollection*—is bound to any control that links to *MyObjectSource* via the *DataSourceID* property. Let's take a brief look at the implementation of the *LoadAll* method:

```
public static EmployeeCollection LoadAll()
{
    EmployeeCollection coll = new EmployeeCollection();

    using (SqlConnection conn = new SqlConnection(ConnectionString))
    {
        SqlCommand cmd = new SqlCommand("SELECT * FROM employees", conn);
        conn.Open();
        SqlDataReader reader = cmd.ExecuteReader();
        HelperMethods.FillEmployeeList(coll, reader);
        reader.Close();
        conn.Close();
    }
    return coll;
}
```

Although it's a bit oversimplified so that it can fit in this section, the preceding code remains quite clear: you execute a command, fill in a custom collection class, and return it to the data-bound control. The only piece of code you need to write is the worker class—you don't need to put any code in the code-behind class of the page.

```
<asp:DataGrid ID="grid" runat="server"
    DataSourceID="MyObjectSource" />
```

The *DataGrid* receives a collection of *Employee* objects defined as follows:

```
public class EmployeeCollection : Collection<Employee>
{
}
```

Binding is totally seamless, even without ADO.NET container objects. (See the companion code for full details.)

The method associated with the *SelectMethod* property must return any of the following: an *IEnumerable* object such as a collection, a *DataSet*, a *DataTable*, or an *Object*. Preferably, the *Select* method is not overloaded, although *ObjectDataSource* doesn't prevent you from using an overloaded method in your business classes.

Using Parameters

In most cases, methods require parameters. *SelectParameters* is the collection you use to add input parameters to the select method. Imagine you have a method to load employees by country. Here's the code you need to come up with:

```
<asp:ObjectDataSource ID="ObjectDataSource1" runat="server"
    TypeName="Core35.DAL.Employees"
    SelectMethod="LoadByCountry">
    <SelectParameters>
        <asp:ControlParameter Name="country" ControlID="Countries"
            PropertyName="SelectedValue" />
    </SelectParameters>
</asp:ObjectDataSource>
```

The preceding code snippet is the declarative version of the following pseudocode, where *Countries* is expected to be a drop-down list filled with country names:

```
string country = Countries.SelectedValue;
EmployeeCollection coll = Employees.LoadByCountry(country);
```

The *ControlParameter* class automates the retrieval of the actual parameter value and the binding to the parameter list of the method. What if you add an *[All Countries]* entry to the drop-down list? In this case, if the All Countries option is selected, you need to call *LoadAll* without parameters; otherwise, if a particular country is selected, you need to call *LoadByCountry* with a parameter. Declarative programming works great in the simple scenarios; otherwise, you just write code.

```
void Page_Load(object sender, EventArgs e)
{
    // Must be cleared every time (or disable the viewstate)
    ObjectDataSource1.SelectParameters.Clear();

    if (Countries.SelectedIndex == 0)
        ObjectDataSource1.SelectMethod = "LoadAll";
```

```
    else
    {
        ObjectDataSource1.SelectMethod = "LoadByCountry";
        ControlParameter cp = new ControlParameter("country",
            "Countries", "SelectedValue");
        ObjectDataSource1.SelectParameters.Add(cp);
    }
}
```

Note that data source controls are like ordinary server controls and can be programmatically configured and invoked. In the code just shown, you first check the selection the user made and if it matches the first option (All Countries), configure the data source control to make a parameterless call to the *LoadAll* method.

You must clean up the content of the *SelectParameters* collection upon page loading. The data source control (more precisely, the underlying view control) caches most of its properties to the view state. As a result, *SelectParameters* is not empty when you refresh the page after changing the drop-down list selection. The preceding code clears only the *SelectParameters* collection; performancewise, it could be preferable to disable the view state altogether on the data source control. However, if you disable the view state, all collections will be empty on the data source control upon loading.

> **Important** *ObjectDataSource* allows data to be retrieved and updated while keeping data access and business logic separate from the user interface. The use of the *ObjectDataSource* class doesn't automatically transform your system into a well-designed, effective n-tiered system. Data source controls are mostly a counterpart to data-bound controls so that the latter can work more intelligently. To take full advantage of *ObjectDataSource*, you need to have your DAL already in place. It doesn't work the other way around. *ObjectDataSource* doesn't necessarily have to be bound to the root of the DAL, which could be on a remote location and perhaps behind a firewall. In this case, you write a local intermediate object and connect it to *ObjectDataSource* on one end and to the DAL on the other end. The intermediate object acts as an application-specific proxy and works according to the application's specific rules. *ObjectDataSource* doesn't break n-tiered systems, nor does it transform existing systems into truly n-tier systems. It greatly benefits, instead, from existing business and data layers.

Caching Data and Object Instances

The *ObjectDataSource* component supports caching only when the specified select method returns a *DataSet* or *DataTable* object. If the wrapped object returns a custom collection (as in the example we're considering), an exception is thrown. Custom object caching is something you must do on your own.

ObjectDataSource is designed to work with classes in the business layer of the application. An instance of the business class is created for each operation performed and is destroyed shortly after the operation is completed. This model is the natural offspring of the stateless programming model that ASP.NET promotes. In the case of business objects that are particularly expensive to initialize, you can resort to static classes or static methods in instance classes. (If you do so, bear in mind what we said earlier regarding unit testing classes with static methods.)

Instances of the business object are not automatically cached or pooled. Both options, though, can be manually implemented by properly handling the *ObjectCreating* and *ObjectDisposing* events on an *ObjectDataSource* control. The *ObjectCreating* event fires when the data source control needs to get an instance of the business class. You can write the handler to retrieve an existing instance of the class and return that to the data source control:

```
// Handle the ObjectCreating event on the data source control
public void BusinessObjectBeingCreated(object sender,
        ObjectDataSourceEventArgs e)
{
    BusinessObject bo = RetrieveBusinessObjectFromPool();
    if (bo == null)
        bo = new BusinessObject();
    e.ObjectInstance = bo;
}
```

Likewise, in *ObjectDisposing* you store the instance again and cancel the disposing operation being executed:

```
// Handle the ObjectDisposing event on the data source control
public void BusinessObjectBeingDisposed(object sender,
        ObjectDataSourceDisposingEventArgs e)
{
    ReturnBusinessObjectToPool(e.ObjectInstance);
    e.Cancel = true;
}
```

The *ObjectDisposing* event allows you to perform cleanup actions in your business object before the *ObjectDataSource* calls the business object's *Dispose* method. If you're caching the business object, as the preceding code has done, be sure to set the cancel flag so that the business object's *Dispose* method isn't invoked and the cached object isn't as a result stored in a disposed state.

Setting Up for Paging

Three properties shown earlier in Table 9-14 participate in paging—*EnablePaging*, *StartRowIndexParameterName*, and *MaximumRowsParameterName*. As the name clearly suggests, *EnablePaging* toggles support for paging on and off. The default value is *false*, meaning that paging is not turned on automatically. *ObjectDataSource* provides an infrastructure for paging, but actual paging must be implemented in the class bound to *ObjectDataSource*. In the following code snippet, the *Customers* class has a method, *LoadByCountry*, that takes two additional parameters to indicate the page size and the index of the first record in the page. The names of these two parameters must be assigned to *MaximumRowsParameterName* and *StartRowIndexParameterName*, respectively.

```
<asp:ObjectDataSource ID="ObjectDataSource1" runat="server"
    TypeName="Core35.DAL.Customers"
    StartRowIndexParameterName="firstRow"
    MaximumRowsParameterName="totalRows"
    SelectMethod="LoadByCountry">
  <SelectParameters>
    <asp:ControlParameter Name="country" ControlID="Countries"
        PropertyName="SelectedValue" />
    <asp:ControlParameter Name="totalRows" ControlID="PageSize"
        PropertyName="Text" />
    <asp:ControlParameter Name="firstRow" ControlID="FirstRow"
        PropertyName="Text" />
  </SelectParameters>
</asp:ObjectDataSource>
```

The implementation of paging is up to the method and must be coded manually. *LoadByCountry* provides two overloads, one of which supports paging. Internally, paging is actually delegated to *FillCustomerList*.

```
public static CustomerCollection LoadByCountry(string country)
{
    return LoadByCountry(country, -1, 0);
}
public static CustomerCollection LoadByCountry(string country,
        int totalRows, int firstRow)
{
    CustomerCollection coll = new CustomerCollection();

    using (SqlConnection conn = new SqlConnection(ConnectionString))
    {
        SqlCommand cmd;
        cmd = new SqlCommand(CustomerCommands.cmdLoadByCountry, conn);
        cmd.Parameters.AddWithValue("@country", country);

        conn.Open();
        SqlDataReader reader = cmd.ExecuteReader();
        HelperMethods.FillCustomerList(coll, reader, totalRows, firstRow);
        reader.Close();
        conn.Close();
    }

    return coll;
}
```

As you can see in the companion source code, *FillCustomerList* simply scrolls the whole result set using a reader and discards all the records that don't belong in the requested range. You could perhaps improve upon this approach to make paging smarter. What's important here is that paging is built into your business object and exposed by data source controls to the pageable controls through a well-known interface.

Updating and Deleting Data

To update underlying data using *ObjectDataSource*, you need to define an update/insert/
delete method. All the actual methods you use must have semantics that are well suited to
implement such operations. Here are some good prototypes for the update operations:

```
public static void Save(Employee emp)
public static void Insert(Employee emp)
public static void Delete(Employee emp)
public static void Delete(int id)
```

More so than with select operations, update operations require parameters. To update
a record, you need to pass new values and one or more old values to make sure the right
record to update is located and to take into account the possibility of data conflicts. To
delete a record, you need to identify it by matching a supplied primary key parameter. To
specify input parameters, you can use command collections such as *UpdateParameters*,
InsertParameters, or *DeleteParameters*. Let's examine update/insert scenarios first.

To update an existing record or insert a new one, you need to pass new values. This can be
done in either of two ways—listing parameters explicitly or aggregating all parameters in an
all-encompassing data structure. The prototypes shown previously for *Save* and *Insert* follow
the latter approach. An alternative might be the following:

```
void Save(int id, string firstName, string lastName, ...)
void Insert(string firstName, string lastName, ...)
```

You can use command parameter collections only if the types involved are simple types—
numbers, strings, dates.

To make a custom class such as *Employee* acceptable to the *ObjectDataSource* control, you
need to set the *DataObjectTypeName* property:

```
<asp:ObjectDataSource ID="RowDataSource" runat="server"
    TypeName="Core35.DAL.Employees"
    SelectMethod="Load"
    UpdateMethod="Save"
    DataObjectTypeName="Core35.DAL.Employee">
  <SelectParameters>
      <asp:ControlParameter Name="id" ControlID="GridView1"
          PropertyName="SelectedValue" />
  </SelectParameters>
</asp:ObjectDataSource>
```

The preceding *ObjectDataSource* control saves rows through the *Save* method, which
takes an *Employee* object. Note that when you set the *DataObjectTypeName* property, the
UpdateParameters collection is ignored. The *ObjectDataSource* instantiates a default instance
of the object before the operation is performed and then attempts to fill its public members

with the values of any matching input fields found around the bound control. Because this work is performed using reflection, the names of the input fields in the bound control must match the names of public properties exposed by the object in the *DataObjectTypeName* property. A practical limitation you must be aware of is the following: you can't define the *Employee* class using complex data types, as follows:

```
public class Employee {
    public string LastName {...}
    public string FirstName {...}
    ...
    public Address HomeAddress {...}
}
```

Representing individual values (*strings* in the sample), the *LastName* and *FirstName* members have good chances to match an input field in the bound control. The same can't be said for the *HomeAddress* member, which is declared with a custom aggregate type such as *Address*. If you go with this schema, all the members in *Address* will be ignored; any related information won't be carried into the *Save* method, with resulting null parameters. All the members in the *Address* data structure should become members of the *Employee* class.

> **Note** Recall that data source controls work at their fullest only with a few ASP.NET controls, such as *GridView* and *DetailsView*. We'll return to the topic of the internal mechanism of parameter binding later in the book. For now, it suffices to say that as a page author you're responsible for making input fields and member names match in the following way: columns in *GridView* and rows in *DetailsView* have a *DataField* attribute pointing to the data source field to use (that is, *lastname*, where *lastname* is typically a database column retrieved by the select operation). The data field name must match (keep in mind that it is case-insensitive) a public property in the class used as a parameter in the update/insert operation. In this case, I'm referring to the *Employee* class, but this holds true for any business object you create as well.

Unlike the insert operation, the update operation also requires a primary key value to uniquely identify the record being updated. If you use an explicit parameter listing, you just append an additional parameter to the list to represent the ID, as follows:

```
<asp:ObjectDataSource runat="server" ID="MyObjectSource"
      TypeName="Core35.SimpleBusinessObject"
      SelectMethod="GetEmployees"
      UpdateMethod="SetEmployee">
  <UpdateParameters>
      <asp:Parameter Name="employeeid" Type="Int32" />
      <asp:Parameter Name="firstname" Type="string" />
      <asp:Parameter Name="lastname" Type="string" />
      <asp:Parameter Name="country" Type="string" DefaultValue="null" />
  </UpdateParameters>
</asp:ObjectDataSource>
```

Note that by setting the *DefaultValue* attribute to *null*, you can make a parameter optional. A null value for a parameter must then be gracefully handled by the business object method that implements the update.

There's an alternative method to set the primary key—through the *DataKeyNames* property of *GridView* and *DetailsView* controls. I'll briefly mention it here and cover it in much greater detail in the next two chapters:

```
<asp:GridView runat="server" ID="grid1"
    DataKeyNames="employeeid"
    DataSourceId="MyObjectSource"
    AutoGenerateEditButton="true">
...
</asp:GridView>
```

When *DataKeyNames* is set on the bound control, data source controls automatically add a parameter to the list of parameters for update and delete commands. The default name of the parameter is *original_XXX*, where *XXX* stands for the value of *DataKeyNames*. For the operation to succeed, the method (or the SQL command if you're using *SqlDataSource*) must handle a parameter with the same name. Here's an example:

```
UPDATE employees SET lastname=@lastname
    WHERE employeeid=@original_employeeid
```

The name format of the key parameter can be changed at will through the *OldValuesParameterFormatString* property. For example, a value of '{0}' assigned to the property would make the following command acceptable:

```
UPDATE employees SET lastname=@lastname
    WHERE employeeid=@employeeid
```

Setting the *DataKeyNames* property on the bound control (hold on, it's *not* a property on the data source control) is also the simplest way to configure a delete operation. For a delete operation, in fact, you don't need to specify a whole record with all its fields; the key is sufficient.

> **Note** In data-bound controls such as *GridView* and *DetailsView*, the *DataKeyNames* property replaces *DataKeyField*, which we found on *DataGrid* and *DataList* controls in ASP.NET 1.x. The difference between the two is that *DataKeyNames* supports keys based on multiple fields. If *DataKeyNames* is set to multiple fields (for example, *id,name*), two parameters are added: *original_id* and *original_name*.

Configuring Parameters at Runtime

When using *ObjectDataSource* with an ASP.NET made-to-measure control (for example, *GridView*), most of the time the binding is totally automatic and you don't have to deal with it. If you need it, though, there's a back door you can use to take control of the update process—the *Updating* event:

```
protected void Updating(object sender,
        ObjectDataSourceMethodEventArgs e)
{
    Employee emp = (Employee) e.InputParameters[0];
    emp.LastName = "WhosThisGuy";
}
```

The event fires before the update operation climaxes. The *InputParameters* collection lists the parameters being passed to the update method. The collection is read-only, meaning that you can't add or delete elements. However, you can modify objects being transported, as the preceding code snippet demonstrates.

This technique is useful when, for whatever reasons, the *ObjectDataSource* control doesn't load all the data its method needs to perform the update. A similar approach can be taken for deletions and insertions as well.

The *LinqDataSource* Class

In the .NET Framework 3.5, Language Integrated Query (LINQ) is a set of syntax extensions that add query capabilities to managed languages such as C# and Visual Basic. With LINQ, .NET applications can query and transform data using a SQL-like set of new operators natively embedded in the language syntax and backed up by a new set of framework classes. ASP.NET applications are no exception. ASP.NET 3.5 applications can take advantage of a subset of the LINQ capabilities through a made-to-measure data source control—the *LinqDataSource* control.

What's Linq-to-SQL, Anyway?

As we'll see in a much greater detail in the next chapter, LINQ establishes the query as a first-class object in .NET 3.5 languages such as C#. At the same time, LINQ builds up a new programming model to query different types of data using a common set of operators such as *from*, *select*, and *where*. What kind of data? There are four distinct flavors of LINQ, with a fifth ready to join the group with the first service pack or upgrade to the .NET Framework 3.5. They are: Linq-to-SQL, Linq-to-Objects, Linq-to-XML, and Linq-to-DataSets, and to follow shortly, Linq-to-Entities. As the name might suggest, Linq-to-SQL queries and transforms relational data stored in a SQL Server database. Note that this is a SQL Server-only feature and other databases are not supported. Linq-to-Objects queries enumerable collections of .NET objects, whereas Linq-to-XML allows you to explore and manipulate the content of XML documents. Finally, Linq-to-DataSets adds a powerful search engine on top of ADO.NET *DataSet* and *DataTable* objects. For more information about LINQ, refer to *Introducing Microsoft LINQ* by Paolo Pialorsi and Marco Russo (Microsoft Press, 2007). For the purposes of this book, I'll cover only Linq-to-SQL in the next chapter.

In general, Linq-to-SQL can be presented as a higher level language to query and transform database tables and records. Compared to the SQL Server native T-SQL, Linq-to-SQL employs an object-based vision of the query, manages strongly-typed data, and automatically resolves foreign keys and relationships (that is, one-to-many relationships) between tables. Unlike T-SQL, a Linq-to-SQL expression relies on language native operators and doesn't present itself as opaque text to be processed through a connection, a command, or perhaps a transaction or reader. With Linq-to-SQL, you still go through ADO.NET objects and T-SQL strings; however, all of this is hidden from view and managed internally by the framework. From a developer's perspective, Linq-to-SQL is a kind of new query language that is easier to understand and code than T-SQL.

The Goal of *LinqDataSource*

The *LinqDataSource* control makes LINQ capabilities available to Web developers through the popular data-source control architecture. Conceptually, the *LinqDataSource* control is similar to *SqlDataSource* in that both controls require that you specify the query directly in the markup of the page. It should be noted, though, that *LinqDataSource* doesn't require connection information. Instead, you bind the data source to a dynamically created class—the data context class—created with the help of the Visual Studio 2008 Object/Relational (O/R) designer. Compared to *ObjectDataSource*, the *LinqDataSource* is simpler and quicker to use, as it doesn't require any manual coding of the business class; at the same time, the requested behavior is expressed through the LINQ language rather than with a method name. Note that this approach can be considered a weakness as well as a strength of the control—it all depends on how much abstraction you need in the design of the domain model and whether you're looking for a quick or a well-architected solution. I'll expand on this concept later in the chapter in the *"LinqDataSource vs ObjectDataSource vs SqlDataSource"* section.

LinqDataSource is not limited to querying and manipulating SQL Server data. You can use it to access data defined in any referenced .NET class through a public property. The following code snippet shows how to populate a drop-down list with the contents of the *AvailableGenres* property of the *BookLibrary* class:

```
<asp:LinqDataSource runat="server" ID="LinqDataSource1"
    ContextTypeName="BookLibrary"
    TableName="AvailableGenres" />
<asp:DropDownList runat="server" ID="DropDownList1"
    DataSourceID="LinqDataSource1" />
```

You can see what the *BookLibrary* class looks like in the following code snippet:

```
public class BookLibrary
{
    string[] _availableGenres = { "Fiction", "Thriller", "Biography" };
```

```
    public BookLibrary()
    {
    }

    public string[] AvailableGenres
    {
        get { return _availableGenres; }
    }
}
```

It goes without saying that the *ContextTypeName* and *TableName* properties are perhaps more naturally assigned with the name of the class generated by the Visual Studio 2008 O/R designer to represent the current data model and the name of the table in that model, respectively, that you want to work with.

The *LinqDataSource* declarative syntax lets you also specify criteria for displaying, filtering, and ordering data. If the target store is a SQL Server database, you can also configure the control to handle updates, inserts, and deletions of records. More importantly, you can do that without having to write the related SQL commands.

Programming Interface of the *LinqDataSource* Control

Table 9-15 lists the key properties defined on the *LinqDataSource* control. By using these properties, you can, as a developer, declaratively set attributes on the control tag in the *.aspx* source.

TABLE 9-15 Properties of the *LinqDataSource* Control

Property	Description
AutoGenerateOrderByClause	Boolean property, instructs the control to automatically generate the *OrderBy* clause of the *Select* statement to include all parameters listed in the *OrderByParameters* collection. It is set to *false* by default.
AutoGenerateWhereClause	Boolean property, instructs the control to automatically generate the *Where* clause of the *Select* statement to include all parameters listed in the *WhereParameters* collection. The automation, though, is limited to testing for equality and requires that parameters in the list have names that exactly match the column names in the table being searched. It is set to *false* by default.
AutoPage	Boolean property, enables the user to page through the returned data. When you set this property to *true*, the data source lets data-bound controls know that paging is supported. In this case, say, a *GridView* control would subsequently set its *AllowPaging* property to *true*. This property is set to *true* by default.

Property	Description
AutoSort	Boolean property, enables the user to sort the data dynamically. When you set this property to *true*, the data source lets data-bound controls know that sorting is supported. In this case, say, a *GridView* control would subsequently set its *AllowSorting* property to *true*. This property is set to *true* by default.
ContextTypeName	Indicates the type of the class being used as the central repository of the data. If the *LinqDataSource* control is bound to a SQL Server table, the type passed as an argument here is the root object of the model created by the Visual Studio 2008 O/R designer. If the control is bound to an object, the property indicates the class name.
EnableDelete	Boolean property, lets data-bound controls know that the data source supports data deletion. This property is set to *false* by default.
EnableInsert	Boolean property, lets data-bound controls know that the data source supports data insertion. This property is set to *false* by default.
EnableUpdate	Boolean property, lets data-bound controls know that the data source supports data updates. This property is set to *false* by default.
GroupBy	Indicates the value of the *GroupBy* LINQ operator used to group selected records by the specified set of columns.
OrderBy	Indicates the value of the *OrderBy* LINQ operator used to sort returned records. To sort by multiple fields, separate column names with a comma.
Select	Indicates the value of the *Select* projection LINQ operator. The content of this property defines the shape of the result set being returned.
StoreOriginalValuesInViewState	Boolean property, indicates whether the control should store in the view state all the values that could be used to enforce conflict detection during updates. This property is set to *true* by default.
TableName	Indicates the name of the table to bind to. If the control is associated to an in-memory object, *TableName* then indicates the property on the object that contains the data to work on.
Where	Indicates the value of the *Where* LINQ operator to filter the set of records being retrieved.

The *LinqDataSource* control also features a few collection properties used to hold values for parametric clauses such as *Where* and *OrderBy* and parametric query and update operations. The list of collection properties includes *DeleteParameters*, *GroupByParameters*, *InsertParameters*, *OrderByParameters*, *SelectParameters*, *UpdateParameters*, and *WhereParameters*.

Along with *TableName* and *ContextTypeName*, the *Select* property is the key to the *LinqDataSource* control. Through the *Select* property, in fact, you specify the projection of data you want properly ordered, filtered, or grouped using the *OrderBy*, *Where*, and *GroupBy* clauses.

Events of the *LinqDataSource* Control

The control supports associated sets of related of events for each key storage operation. In addition, it provides three events for the creation and disposal of the data context object. See Table 9-16 for details.

TABLE 9-16 Events of the *LinqDataSource* Control

Event	Description
ContextCreating, *ContextCreated*, *ContextDisposing*	The *ContextCreating* event fires before the data context object is created, whereas the *ContextCreated* event is raised immediately after. The *ContextDisposing* event is raised before the data context object is disposed of.
Deleting, *Deleted*	The *Deleting* event is raised before the *Delete* operation is executed; the *Deleted* event is raised after the *Delete* operation has been successfully completed.
Inserting, *Inserted*	The *Inserting* event is raised before the *Insert* operation is executed; the *Inserted* event is raised after the *Insert* operation has been successfully completed.
Selecting, *Selected*	The *Selecting* event is raised before the *Select* operation is executed; the *Selected* event is raised after the *Select* operation has been successfully completed.
Updating, *Updated*	The *Updating* event is raised before the *Update* operation is executed; the *Updated* event is raised after the *Update* operation has been successfully completed.

It should be noted that the *LinqDataSource* control doesn't create its own internal copy of the data context object if a *Select* operation is executed in the *Selecting* event. In this case, the control reasonably assumes that you're using your own data context object (for example, a global member of the code-behind class) and hence doesn't proceed with the creation of an object that will likely be a duplicate. Put another way, if you want to take control of the query yourself without relying on the *Select* property, you must also create the data context manually. A good question is, when would you want to do this? Perhaps when the *Select* property of the *LinqDataSource* control might not be appropriate for a query? Just read on.

Selecting, Sorting, and Filtering Data

The *Select* property of the *LinqDataSource* control allows you to decide which of the properties in the data-entity record will be retrieved. If you leave the property to its default value—the empty string—all properties in the data-entity record will be retrieved. This means that, if the data context is a database table, the Linq-to-SQL runtime will be running for you a kind of *SELECT * FROM table* query. To restrict the set of properties retrieved, you can use the following syntax:

```
<asp:LinqDataSource ID="LinqDataSource1" runat="server"
    ContextTypeName="NorthwindDataContext"
    TableName="Customers"
    Select="new (CustomerID, CompanyName, Country)" />
```

The *LinqDataSource* control returns a *List<T>* collection that contains instances of a dynamically created class that just includes the properties whose names have been passed as an argument to the *new* function.

What if you need to order data by one or more properties? You just use the *OrderBy* property, as shown here:

```
<asp:LinqDataSource ID="LinqDataSource2" runat="server"
    ContextTypeName="NorthwindDataContext"
    TableName="Customers"
    Select="new (CustomerID, CompanyName)"
    OrderBy="CompanyName DESC, CustomerID">
 ...
</asp:LinqDataSource>
```

The example selects *CustomerID* and *CompanyName* properties out of the bound list of customers and then sorts them by company name (in descending order, as indicated) and ID.

How about filtering data by applying some criteria? That's exactly the purpose of the *Where* clause. You can specify a static clause where any value to use is known beforehand, or you can put placeholders in the clause to be filled dynamically using parameters. Here's an example of a static *Where* clause:

```
<asp:LinqDataSource ID="LinqDataSource2" runat="server"
    ContextTypeName="NorthwindDataContext"
    TableName="Customers"
    Select="new (CustomerID, CompanyName)"
    OrderBy="customerid, companyname desc"
    Where='Country == "Germany"'>
```

Note that if you intend to use a literal string in the *Where* clause, you have to wrap the string with double quotes and use single quotes for the query string. The clause can also be parametric. In this case, the value assigned to the *Where* property references a parameter name whose details and bindings are detailed in the *WhereParameters* section, as shown next:

```
<asp:LinqDataSource ID="LinqDataSource1" runat="server"
    ContextTypeName="NorthwindDataContext"
    TableName="Customers"
    Select="new (CustomerID, CompanyName)"
```

```
        OrderBy="customerid, companyname desc"
        Where="Country == @Country">
        <WhereParameters>
            <asp:ControlParameter Name="Country"
                Type="String"
                ControlID="CountryList"
                PropertyName="SelectedValue" />
        </WhereParameters>
</asp:LinqDataSource>
<asp:DropDownList ID="CustomerList" runat="server"
        AutoPostBack="true"
        DataSourceID="LinqDataSource1"
        DataTextField="CompanyName"
        DataValueField="CompanyName" />
```

The @Country parameter is bound to the *SelectedValue* property of a list control in the page named *CountryList*.

When you have several parameters to take into account in the *Where* clause, there's a short-cut you can take—at least in some relatively simple cases. You leave the *Where* property blank and set the *AutoGenerateWhereClause* property to *true*, and the *LinqDataSource* control automatically generates the clause for you. All that you have to do is list required parameters in the *WhereParameters* section of the control's markup. This is beneficial because you don't have to specify all criteria in the *Where* property and you can have the control prepare an ad hoc *Where* clause that includes each listed parameter.

At the same time, you can't just expect the *LinqDataSource* control to read your mind and auto-generate all possible types of filters. The effects of the *AutoGenerateWhereClause* property are limited to testing parameters for equality and to do so in the context of an AND operation. In addition, parameter names must exactly match property names on the target data-entity objects. For any other needs, you just write the *Where* clause manually and leave the *AutoGenerateWhereClause* property set to its default value of *false*. Note that you'll receive an exception if the *Where* property is non-empty and *AutoGenerateWhereClause* is *true*.

When the *Select* Property Is Not Enough

The LINQ syntax is fairly rich, as we'll see in the next chapter. Not all the possibilities it offers, though, can be expressed as a plain string and assigned to the *Select* property of the *LinqDataSource* control. In general, this happens as the complexity of the query grows beyond a certain threshold. Popular examples are when you need to use JOINs or, as we'll see in a moment, DISTINCT queries. The LINQ syntax fully supports JOINs and DISTINCT queries, but the parser of the string assigned to the *Select* property just doesn't recognize these operators.

The workaround is quite simple and straightforward: you leave the *Select* property blank and add an event handler for the data source's *Selecting* event:

```
<asp:LinqDataSource ID="LinqDataSource1" runat="server"
    ContextTypeName="NorthwindDataContext"
    TableName="Customers"
    OnSelecting="LinqDataSource1_Selecting" />
```

This can be done either declaratively as just shown or programmatically in the *Init* event of the page:

```
protected void Page_Init(object sender, EventArgs e)
{
    LinqDataSource1.Selecting +=
        new EventHandler<LinqDataSourceSelectEventArgs>(
            LinqDataSource1_Selecting);
}
```

In the body of the handler, you can use the full LINQ syntax to run the query without being limited by the string format and the capabilities of the embedded data source parser. Here's how to distinctively select all countries in which you have customers:

```
private NorthwindDataContext db;
protected void Page_Init(object sender, EventArgs e)
{
    db = new NorthwindDataContext();
}
protected void LinqDataSource1_Selecting(object sender,
                                LinqDataSourceSelectEventArgs e)
{
    var countries = (from c in db.Customers
                     select new { c.Country }).Distinct();
    e.Result = countries;
}
```

The *Result* property on the *LinqDataSourceSelectEventArgs* class holds the list of objects that the data source will share with its bound controls.

It is key to note that, when defined, the *Selecting/Selected* events fire before the *ContextCreating/ContextCreated* pair. However, if in the *Selecting* event you set the *Result* property of the event data structure, no data context object is ever created and no related events are fired. What does this mean to you? If you need to use your own LINQ query, you should also worry about creating the data context object manually. A good place to create the data context manually is in the *Page_Init* method. Figure 9-11 shows a sample page in action that gets the list of countries and then lets users see how that list is related to customers.

FIGURE 9-11 Data-bound controls filled using Linq-to-SQL queries.

Lazy Loading and Prefetch

Although the language-to-SQL mapping layer in Linq-to-SQL is nicely designed and optimized, there might be situations in which too many database roundtrips will occur. Hold on, though. I'm certainly not here to say that Linq-to-SQL is broken or unreliable. What I mean is that, especially for quite complex and spanned queries, the system might end up performing too many roundtrips. This mostly depends on the data that is initially fetched and the use you make of it. For example, if you first select a data set (say, customers) and then loop through the selected records and access child fields (say, orders), it might happen that the Linq-to-SQL engine needs to go back to the database for each step to load the related record. To avoid this overhead, you can decide to prefetch a given related table. You typically do this in the *ContextCreated* event, as shown here:

```
void LinqDataSource1_ContextCreated(object sender,
                                LinqDataSourceStatusEventArgs e)
{
    DataLoadOptions options = new DataLoadOptions();

    // Prefetch the Order Details table
    options.LoadWith<Order>(Order => Order.Order_Details);
    (e.Result as NorthwindDataContext).LoadOptions = options;
}
```

Prefetching some related tables makes the first query more complex, but it might save a good number of subsequent roundtrips.

> **Important**   Note, though, that Linq-to-SQL automatically expands only the deepest association that it finds in the query. This is a precise design choice that was made to reduce the complexity and amount of data returned by joined queries. In general, if you are going to have more than one level of data association, be ready to deal with a number of queries being executed as you access individual records. To see if some sort of optimization is necessary, always run the SQL Profiler and keep an eye on what Linq-to-SQL is really doing for you.

Updating Data

When you set to *true* the value of any *EnableUpdate*, *EnableInsert*, or *EnableDelete* properties, the *LinqDataSource* control creates the commands for updating, inserting, and deleting data. The following example demonstrates how to use a *FormView* control bound to a Linq-to-SQL source to edit the address of a customer:

```
<asp:LinqDataSource ID="LinqDataSource1" runat="server"
    EnableUpdate="true"
    ContextTypeName="NorthwindDataContext"
    TableName="Customers"
    Where="CustomerID == @CustomerID">
    <WhereParameters>
        <asp:ControlParameter Name="CustomerID"
            ControlID="DropDownList1"
            PropertyName="SelectedValue" />
    </WhereParameters>
</asp:LinqDataSource>

<asp:FormView ID="FormView1" runat="server"
    DefaultMode="Edit"
    DataSourceID="LinqDataSource1"
    DataKeyNames="CustomerID">
    <EditItemTemplate>
        <h2>Change the Address</h2>
        <asp:TextBox ID="NewAddress" runat="server"
            Text='<%# Bind("Address") %>' />
        <asp:Button ID="Button1" runat="server"
            Text="Update Address"
            CommandName="Update" />
    </EditItemTemplate>
</asp:FormView>
```

For the code to work, there should be a one-to-one correspondence between bindable properties (for example, *Address*) and public properties on the data-entity object being displayed. In other words, the preceding code will work only if the objects bound to the *LinqDataSource*—the *Customer* class—feature a writable property named *Address*. If you need to programmatically control any values to be updated, you create handlers for events such as *Updating*, *Inserting*, or *Deleting*. Here's an example of how to validate a value being assigned:

```
void LinqDataSource1_Updating(object sender,
                              LinqDataSourceUpdateEventArgs e)
{
    if (!Validate((e.OriginalObject as Customer).Address))
    {
        // Invalid data, cancel the operation
        e.Cancel = true;
    }
}
bool Validate(object member)
{
    ...
}
```

The *OriginalObject* property of the *LinqDataSourceUpdateEventArgs* object contains the data-entity object being updated. You can replace it using the *NewObject* property, or you can cancel the operation via the *Cancel* property.

> **Note** A *LinqDataSource* that supports update commands needs to have the *Select* property left blank. Setting the *Select* property, in fact, causes the *LinqDataSource* control to return an instance of a dynamically created class rather than an instance of the data-entity class.

LinqDataSource vs ObjectDataSource vs SqlDataSource

The difference between *SqlDataSource* and *ObjectDataSource* should be fairly clear. The first leads you to add SQL code directly in the markup of ASP.NET pages or, at best, in the code-behind class. Although the resulting page might still work just great, it's obviously not a best practice to recommend. It might be an effective shortcut for simple sites or temporary pages; however, for the sake of layer separation, you should not use *SqlDataSource* in any ASP.NET applications with a domain model of any significant complexity.

ObjectDataSource is exactly the opposite. It pushes the use of objects and makes the binding between presentation data-bound controls and data sources happen through the mediation of made-to-measure objects. In most cases, the objects bound to *ObjectDataSource* won't be just the top-layer objects of your business tier. But *ObjectDataSource* allows you to preserve—and, to a good extent, it mandates you to have—a well-designed business tier. It might just require that you add a thin façade on top of it to fulfill the control's contract with bound objects.

What about *LinqDataSource*, instead? To me, it falls somewhere in between the other two. As we'll see in the next chapter, to enable Linq-to-SQL you must create a data model—and it's by far easier if you do this through the O/R designer embedded in Visual Studio 2008. This data model is rooted in a data context class and initially contains only data container classes with data but no behavior. The idea behind *LinqDataSource* is that you use the auto-generated object model to manage data, and you provide any required behavior through direct injections of Linq-to-SQL commands in the various properties of the control. In the end, the pattern behind *LinqDataSource* and *SqlDataSource* is nearly the same; the only difference is the language you use—Linq-to-SQL in one case, and raw SQL in the other. Another important difference that must be noted between *SqlDataSource* and *LinqDataSource* is that *SqlDataSource* can accommodate any relational data source, whereas *LinqDataSource* is limited to SQL Server.

The *LinqDataSource* control is not designed to accept methods to call to execute queries or updates. So it requires an underlying object model, but it uses this object model only to back up a query language of a higher level than SQL. The purposes of *LinqDataSource* and *ObjectDataSource* are clearly different. *ObjectDataSource* enables you to take advantage of RAD data binding on top of your existing middle tier. *LinqDataSource* and related tools give you, instead, a quick way to build an extremely thin and, to some extent, anemic object model, Additionally, it can be quite difficult to deploy on a physically different tier without significant refactoring.

The bottom line that I see is that you should consider *ObjectDataSource* for enterprise-class applications and wherever the complexity of the domain model is significant. *LinqDataSource* is a much smarter replacement for *SqlDataSource*, with the current technological limitation of being restricted to use with SQL Server.

The *SiteMapDataSource* Class

Site maps are a common feature of cutting-edge Web sites. A site map is the graph that represents all the pages and directories found in a Web site. Site map information is used to show users the logical coordinates of the page they are visiting, allow users to access site locations dynamically, and render all the navigation information in a graphical fashion (as shown in Figure 9-12).

FIGURE 9-12 The graphical layout that the MSDN Magazine Web site uses to represent the location of a page in the site hierarchy.

ASP.NET contains a rich navigation infrastructure that allows developers to specify the site structure. I cover site navigation in detail in *Programming Microsoft ASP.NET 2.0 Applications: Advanced Topics* (Microsoft Press, 2006). For now, it suffices to say that the site map is a hierarchical piece of information that can be used as input for a hierarchical data source control such as *SiteMapDataSource*. The output of *SiteMapDataSource* can be bound to hierarchical data-bound controls such as *Menu*.

Displaying Site Map Information

The sitemap information can appear in many ways, the simplest of which is to place an XML file named *web.sitemap* in the root of the application. To give you the essence of site maps and site map data sources, let's briefly review a few usage scenarios. Suppose you're writing a Web site and your client asks for a sequence of hyperlinks that indicates the location of the page in the site map. In ASP.NET 1.x, you have to create your own infrastructure to hold site map information and render the page location. (Typically, you would use a configuration file and a user control.) Starting with version 2.0, ASP.NET provides richer support for site maps. You start by creating a configuration file named *web.sitemap* in the root of the Web application. The file describes the relationship between pages on the site. Your next step depends on the expected output.

If the common representation shown in Figure 9-12 (a sequence of hyperlinks with a separator) is what you need, add a *SiteMapPath* control to the page. This control retrieves the site map and produces the necessary HTML markup. In this simple case, there is no need to resort to a site map data source control. If you need to build a more complex hierarchical layout—for example, a tree-based representation—you need the *SiteMapDataSource* control.

The *SiteMapDataSource* control pumps site map information to a hierarchical data-bound control (for example, the new *TreeView* control) so that it can display the site's structure. Here's a quick example:

```
<%@ Page Language="C#" %>
<html>
<body>
    <form runat="server">
        <asp:SiteMapDataSource runat="server" ID="MySiteMapSource" />
        <asp:TreeView runat="server" DataSourceId="MySiteMapSource" />
    </form>
</body>
</html>
```

Figure 9-13 shows the final output as it appears to the end user.

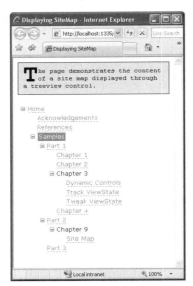

FIGURE 9-13 The site map information rendered through a *TreeView* control.

The site map information might look like the following:

```
<siteMap>
    <siteMapNode title="Home" url="default.aspx" >
        <siteMapNode title="Acknowledgements" url="ack.aspx"/>
        <siteMapNode title="References" url="ref.aspx" />
        <siteMapNode title="Samples">
            <siteMapNode title="Part 1">
                <siteMapNode title="Chapter 1" />
                <siteMapNode title="Chapter 2" />
                <siteMapNode title="Chapter 3">
                    <siteMapNode title="Dynamic Controls"
                                 url=".../dynctls.aspx" />
                    <siteMapNode title="ViewState"
                                 url=".../viewstate.aspx" />
                </siteMapNode>
                <siteMapNode title="Chapter 4" />
            </siteMapNode>
            <siteMapNode title="Part 2">
                <siteMapNode title="Chapter 9">
                    <siteMapNode title="Site map"
                                 url=".../sitemapinfo.aspx" />
                </siteMapNode>
            </siteMapNode>
            <siteMapNode title="Part 3"
                         url="samples.aspx?partid=3" />
        </siteMapNode>
    </siteMapNode>
</siteMap>
```

Note that the *url* attribute is optional. If the attribute is not defined, the node is intended to be an inert container and won't be made clickable.

> **Note** As mentioned, with version 2.0 ASP.NET introduces a new type of data-bound control that was completely unsupported in previous versions—the hierarchical data-bound control. A new base class is defined to provide a minimum set of capabilities—*HierarchicalDataBoundControl*. The *TreeView* and *Menu* controls fall into this category.

Programming Interface of *SiteMapDataSource*

Table 9-17 details the properties available in the *SiteMapDataSource* class.

TABLE 9-17 Properties of *SiteMapDataSource*

Property	Description
Provider	Indicates the site map provider object associated with the data source control.
ShowStartingNode	*True* by default, indicates whether the starting node is retrieved and displayed.
SiteMapProvider	Gets and sets the name of the site map provider associated with the instance of the control.
StartFromCurrentNode	*False* by default, indicates whether the node tree is retrieved relative to the current page.
StartingNodeOffset	Gets and sets a positive or negative offset from the starting node that determines the root hierarchy exposed by the control. This property is set to *0* by default.
StartingNodeUrl	Indicates the URL in the site map in which the node tree is rooted.

By default, the starting node is the root node of the hierarchy, but you can change the starting node through a pair of mutually exclusive properties—*StartFromCurrentNode* and *StartingNodeUrl*. If you explicitly indicate the URL of the page that should appear as the root of the displayed hierarchy, make sure the *StartFromCurrentNode* property is *false*. Likewise, if you set *StartFromCurrentNode* to *true*, ensure the *StartingNodeUrl* property evaluates to the empty string.

When properly used, the *StartingNodeOffset* property lets you restrict the nodes of the site map that are actually displayed. The default value of *0* indicates that the root hierarchy exposed by the *SiteMapDataSource* control is the same as the starting node. A value greater than *0* goes that number of levels down in the hierarchy, proceeding from the root to the requested node, and uses the node found as the root. Looking at the sample site map we considered earlier, if you request *sitemapinfo.aspx* with an offset of *1*, the displayed hierarchy will be rooted in the *Samples* node—that is, one level down the real root. If you set it to *2*, the effective root will be the *Part 2* node. A negative offset, on the other hand, ensures that the specified number of child levels will be displayed if possible.

The *SiteMapDataSource* class features a couple of properties that relate to the site map provider—*SiteMapProvider* and *Provider*. The former specifies the name of the site map provider to use; the latter returns a reference to the object.

The *XmlDataSource* Class

The *XmlDataSource* control is a special type of data source control that supports both tabular and hierarchical views of data. The tabular view of XML data is just a list of nodes at a given level of a hierarchy, whereas the hierarchical view shows the complete hierarchy. An XML node is an instance of the *XmlNode* class; the complete hierarchy is an instance of the *XmlDocument* class. The XML data source supports only read-only scenarios.

> **Important** The *XmlDataSource* control is unique in that it is the only built-in data source control to implement both *IDataSource* and *IHierarchicalDataSource* interfaces. For both inter-faces, though, the control doesn't go further than implementing the *Select* method. Hence, the *XmlDataSource* control is not suitable for Web applications using read/write XML data stores, as it doesn't support methods such as *Delete*, *Insert*, and *Update*.

Programming Interface of *XmlDataSource*

Table 9-18 details the properties of the *XmlDataSource* control.

TABLE 9-18 Properties of *XmlDataSource*

Property	Description
CacheDuration	Indicates, in seconds, how long the data should be maintained in the cache.
CacheExpirationPolicy	Indicates whether the cache duration is absolute or sliding. If the duration is absolute, data is invalidated after the specified number of seconds. If the duration is sliding, data is invalidated if it is not used for the specified duration.
CacheKeyDependency	Indicates the name of a user-defined cache key that is linked to all cache entries created by the data source control. By letting the key expire, you can clear the control's cache.
Data	Contains a block of XML text for the data source control to bind.
DataFile	Indicates the path to the file that contains data to display.
EnableCaching	Enables or disables caching support.
Transform	Contains a block of XSLT text that will be used to transform the XML data bound to the control.
TransformArgumentList	A list of input parameters for the XSLT transformation to apply to the source XML.
TransformFile	Indicates the path to the *.xsl* file that defines an XSLT transformation to be performed on the source XML data.
XPath	Indicates an XPath query to be applied to the XML data.

The *XmlDataSource* control can accept XML input data as a relative or absolute filename assigned to the *DataFile* property or as a string containing the XML content assigned to the *Data* property. If both properties are set, *DataFile* takes precedence. Note that the *Data* property can also be set declaratively through the *<Data>* tag. Furthermore, the contents assigned to *Data*—a potentially large chunk of text—are stored in the view state regardless of the caching settings you might have. If you bind the control to static text, the risk is that you move the XML data back and forth with the page view state while keeping it also stored in the cache for faster access. If you use *Data* and enable caching, consider disabling the view state for the control. (It should be noted, though, that disabling the view state on a control usually affects more than one property.)

If caching is enabled and you change the value of the *DataFile* or *Data* property, the cache is discarded. The *DataSourceChanged* event notifies pages of the event.

Displaying XML Data

The *XmlDataSource* control is commonly bound to a hierarchical control, such as the *TreeView* or *Menu*. (These are the only two built-in hierarchical controls we have in ASP.NET, but others can be created by developers and third-party vendors.)

To understand how the XML data source works, consider a file that is a kind of home-grown XML representation of a *DataSet*—the Employees table of Northwind:

```
<MyDataSet>
    <NorthwindEmployees>
        <Employee>
            <employeeid>1</employeeid>
            <lastname>Davolio</lastname>
            <firstname>Nancy</firstname>
            <title>Sales Representative</title>
        </Employee>
        ...
    <NorthwindEmployees>
<MyDataSet>
```

Next you bind this file to an instance of the *XmlDataSource* control and the data source to a tree view:

```
<asp:XmlDataSource runat="server" ID="XmlSource"
    DataFile="~/App_Data/employees.xml" />
<asp:TreeView runat="server" DataSourceId="XmlSource">
</asp:TreeView>
```

The result (which is not as useful as it could be) is shown in Figure 9-14.

FIGURE 9-14 The layout (rather than contents) of the bound XML file displayed using a *TreeView* control.

To display data in a way that is really helpful to users, you need to configure node bindings in the tree view:

```
<asp:TreeView runat="server" DataSourceId="XmlSource">
    <DataBindings>
        <asp:TreeNodeBinding Depth="3" DataMember="employeeid"
            TextField="#innertext" />
        <asp:TreeNodeBinding Depth="3" DataMember="lastname"
            TextField="#innertext" />
        <asp:TreeNodeBinding Depth="3" DataMember="firstname"
            TextField="#innertext" />
        <asp:TreeNodeBinding Depth="3" DataMember="title"
            TextField="#innertext" />
    </DataBindings>
</asp:TreeView>
```

The *<DataBindings>* section of the *TreeView* control lets you control the layout and the contents of the tree nodes. The *<TreeNodeBinding>* node indicates the 0-based depth (attribute *Depth*) of the specified XML node (attribute *DataMember*), as well as which attributes determine the text displayed for the node in the tree view and the value associated with the node. The *TextField* attribute can be set to the name of the attribute to bind or *#innertext* if you want to display the body of the node. Figure 9-15 provides a preview.

There's a lot more to know about the *TreeView* configuration. I delve into that in *Programming Microsoft ASP.NET 2.0 Applications: Advanced Topics*.

FIGURE 9-15 XML data bound to a *TreeView* control.

The contents returned by the *XmlDataSource* control can be filtered using XPath expressions:

```
<asp:xmldatasource runat="server" ID="XmlSource"
    DataFile="~/App_Data/employees.xml"
    XPath="MyDataSet/NorthwindEmployees/Employee" />
```

The preceding expression displays only the *<Employee>* nodes, with no unique root node in the tree view. XPath expressions are case-sensitive.

> **Note** The *XmlDataSource* control automatically caches data, as the *EnableCaching* property is set to *true* by default. Note also that by default the cache duration is set to *0*, which means an infinite stay for data. In other words, the data source will cache data until the XML file that it depends on is changed.

Transforming XML Data

The *XmlDataSource* class can also transform its data using Extensible Stylesheet Language Transformations (XSLT). You set the transform file by using the *TransformFile* property or by assigning the XSLT content to the string property named *Transform*. Using the *TransformArgumentList* property, you can also pass arguments to the style sheet to be used during the XSL transformation. An XSL transformation is often used when the structure of an XML document does not match the structure needed to process the XML data. Note that once the data is transformed, the *XmlDataSource* becomes read-only and the data cannot be modified or saved back to the original source document.

Conclusion

ASP.NET data binding has three faces—classic source-based binding (as in ASP.NET 1.x), data source controls, and data-binding expressions. Data-binding expressions serve a different purpose than the other two binding techniques. Expressions are used declaratively and within templated controls. They represent calculated values bindable to any property. Starting with ASP.NET 2.0, support for expressions has been empowered to go beyond the boundaries of classic data binding. ASP.NET supports custom expressions that are evaluated when the page loads, not when the data-binding process is triggered.

The old data-binding model of ASP.NET 1.x is maintained intact with enumerable collections of data bound to controls through the *DataSource* property and a few related others. In addition, a new family of controls makes its debut—data source controls. By virtue of being implemented as a control, a data source component can be declaratively persisted into a Web page without any further effort in code. In addition, data source controls can benefit from other parts of the page infrastructure, such as the view state and ASP.NET cache. Data source controls accept parameters, prepare and execute a command, and return results (if any). Commands include the typical data operations—select, insert, update, delete, and total count.

The most interesting consequence of data source controls is the tight integration with some new data-bound controls. These smarter data-bound controls (*GridView*, *FormView*, *DetailsView*) contain logic to automatically bind at appropriate times on behalf of the page developer, and they interact with the underlying data source intelligently, requiring you to write much less code. Existing data-bound controls have been extended to support data source controls, but only for select operations.

Data source controls make declarative, codeless programming easier and likely to happen in reality. Data source controls, though, are just tools and not necessarily the right tool for the job you need to do. Use your own good judgement on a per-case basis.

In the next chapter, we take a tour of Language Integrated Queries (LINQ), with special emphasis on its relationship to relational databases. Further on, we'll continue our examination of data binding from the perspective of data-bound controls.

Just the Facts

- In ASP.NET, all data-bound controls support two binding mechanisms: the classic binding done through enumerable data source objects and data source controls.

- Data source controls are regular server controls with no user interface that intelligently cooperate with the control they're bound to as far as querying for and updating data the bound control requires.

- Data source controls simplify programming by reducing the code you need to write in a good number of scenarios.

- Old-style data-bound controls have been modified to support data source controls; they have not been redesigned to take full advantage of data source controls. For this reason, new controls, such as *GridView* and *DetailsView*, have been added.

- A new type of expression ($-expression) partners data-binding expressions to provide for declarative expressions to be used primarily in the design-time configuration of data source controls.

- $-expressions differ from #-expressions because they are evaluated at parse time and their output becomes part of the page source.

- *ObjectDataSource* is the most compelling of the data source controls because it can bridge your presentation layer to the DAL, even remotely. The *ObjectDataSource* control takes advantage of existing tiers, and overall, it promotes a domain-based design over a purely tiered design.

- *LinqDataSource* allows you to connect data-bound controls directly to a Linq-to-SQL expression. This is not recommended, though, in scenarios where a complex domain logic is present. In this case, you're better off having a full object-oriented business layer connected to the presentation via *ObjectDataSource*. Inside the data access layer, then, you can use Linq-to-SQL to go down to the data. *LinqDataSource* is for quick applications or for applications with a simple domain model

- *XmlDataSource* is both a hierarchical and tabular data source, but it supports only read-only scenarios

Chapter 10
The Linq-to-SQL Programming Model

Linq-to-SQL is an Object/Relational (O/R) mapping implementation that allows developers and architects to model a relational database using .NET classes. At the top of the Linq-to-SQL layer, the code recognizes and operates on classes according to an object-oriented model; at the other end, operations on classes are translated to commands for Create|Read|Update|Delete (CRUD) statements that modify the underlying database through a regular connection.

Essentially, Linq-to-SQL maps classes and methods to database objects, including tables, relationships, views, transactions, stored procedures and user-defined functions. Based on a set of .NET classes that mirror the domain model, the Linq-to-SQL implementation in the .NET Framework 3.5 also provides a way to integrate data validation and some business logic rules into the data model.

The Linq-to-SQL data model is referred to as the *data context* and is usually created via ad hoc tools in Microsoft Visual Studio 2008—specifically, the O/R designer. By default, the classes in the data context are plain containers with data, but no behavior. So you typically end up having, say, a *Customer* class full of descriptive properties (for example, *ID*, *CompanyName*, *Address*) but lacking methods to perform any operations, such as *Load*, *LoadAll*, *Save*, *Validate*. However, the classes in the data context are marked as partial and as such they leave a lot of room for any custom extensions you may wish to include.

In the absence of a codified behavior, developers can operate on the data context using elements of the Language Integrated Query (LINQ) syntax. LINQ is a set of extensions to the .NET Framework 3.5 and its managed languages that basically sets the query as a first-class object. LINQ defines a common syntax and a programming model to query different types of data using a common language.

In the previous chapter, you saw LINQ in action already, but it was through a very special lens—the *LinqDataSource* control. In this chapter, we'll take a look at the LINQ technology, examine its common syntax and, finally, discuss how to use it to operate on Microsoft SQL Server databases.

LINQ In Brief

The whole idea of LINQ originates from a simple fact. The vast majority of applications—desktop and Web—are centered around some sort of data repository; most of the time, that repository is a relational database. For years, architects have been designing applications modeling the domain of the problem through objects. Inside these objects, then, there were connections to data access components—commonly referred to as the data access layer (DAL)—doing the hard and dirty work of interfacing the database and persisting an object model to a relational schema. While this approach is still the most recommended one for complex, large, durable, and enterprise-class applications, it might be too costly for simpler scenarios. And applications that fall under the umbrella of "simpler scenarios" are probably more numerous and are used more frequently.

LINQ was created to address the need these applications have for a powerful, yet simple, set of tools to operate on data stores at a higher conceptual level. LINQ was created to give applications a chance to stop having to deal with opaque command strings and replace them with native operators in the programming language. So the C# and Microsoft Visual Basic compilers in the .NET Framework 3.5 support a new extended syntax that makes it possible to query a configured data store without resorting to an ad hoc application programming interface (API) such as ADO.NET.

> **Note** In my last sentence, I should have said "without *apparently* resorting to" because, under the hood, LINQ operators are mapped to a general-purpose query infrastructure built into the framework. This infrastructure translates LINQ elements into code that interfaces databases and other repositories. When the data store is SQL Server, this infrastructure just translates LINQ query commands into T-SQL commands; and when the data store is an XML document, the infrastructure translates LINQ query commands into calls to XQuery paths.

Language-Integrated Tools for Data Operations

As much as a picture is worth a thousand words, a code snippet may perhaps illustrate the goal of LINQ more quickly and effectively than a whole section of explanatory words. So here's what a LINQ query looks like in C#:

```
var data = from c in dataContext.Customers
           where c.Country == "Spain"
           select c;
```

Can you believe that what you see here compiles perfectly in the newest iteration of the C# language? The text in boldface simply identifies new keywords in the C# language. Similar new keywords also exist in Visual Basic .NET for the .NET Framework 3.5. Here's an example:

```
Dim data = From c In dataContext.Customers _
           Where c.Country = "Spain" _
           Select c
```

Making Sense of LINQ

The preceding LINQ statement makes use of a bunch of new keywords that I'll discuss in more detail later in the chapter. However, it is helpful to scratch the surface of these keywords just to grab the sense of the preceding statement right away. Conceptually, the statement reads like this:

1. The *from* keyword logically loops through the contents of the specified collection (*customers* in the example). The *c* variable plays the same role here as an indexer variable in a classic *for* loop.

2. The expression associated with the *where* keyword is evaluated for each object in the collection.

3. If the criterion is met, the *select* statement adds the currently evaluated object to the list being returned.

4. The variable labeled with the *var* keyword is the designated container of the results of the query. The exact type of the object might not be known in advance, so the *var* keyword indicates that type information will be inferred dynamically once the LINQ expression has been expanded and compiled.

 Note The *var* keyword is the offspring of a new .NET 3.5 language feature called *local type inference*. Essentially, it allows you to declare a variable without specifying its real type. The compiler will infer the actual type from the value you assign to the variable in code. No run-time operation is involved with type inference such as boxing and unboxing. What's going on here is simply that the compiler—and therefore this is all accomplished before the code runs—figures out the real type you would have used and emits a correct and type-safe declaration for that variable in the intermediate language (IL) code. Local type inference, though, works only for local variables and can't be used for type members or in the prototype of a method.

It is not a mere chance that database-like keywords have been used, such as *from*, *where*, and *select*. Even though LINQ is not just about database queries, its overall design was highly influenced by the structure of database queries.

The *dataContext.Customers* collection is actually the sequence of data elements to query. Its contents might or might not come from a database, and its model might or might not have been created after some database schema. This fact is related to two key benefits. First, you can use LINQ to express an efficient query behavior with a variety of data sources and languages. The underlying engine, buried in the .NET Framework 3.5, then transforms results into any format, mostly typed collections of objects. Second, the particular *dataContext.Customers* object is not just a .NET collection. It is, rather, a .NET collection exposed through the services of a very special LINQ class—the *DataContext* class. This class uses a connection string to load data into an in-memory object and reflects a database schema. The *DataContext* class—more precisely, a dynamically created class that inherits *DataContext*—is the missing link between LINQ and Linq-to-SQL that we'll discuss further in the chapter.

Currently, there are a few different flavors of LINQ for distinct data sources: SQL Server databases, XML documents, *DataSet* objects, and managed collections. The LINQ engine is extensible too; so expect third-party vendors to soon provide LINQ interfaces on top of their own products and data sources. For example, an eagerly awaited extension is Linq-to-Oracle to map elements of the LINQ syntax on top of Oracle's internal programming language.

Linq-to-SQL

As mentioned, Linq-to-SQL is an O/R implementation through which you model a SQL Server database using .NET classes. The Linq-to-SQL framework is specific to SQL Server and, unlike ADO.NET, can't be used to address other relational databases.

LINQ operators such as *from*, *where*, and *select* work on collections of objects—the data context—which are created to model the schema of a particular database. Linq-to-SQL requires a data model that can be automatically built from a simple connection string. In Visual Studio 2008, you find a tool—the O/R designer—purposely created to automate the creation of the data model. (See Figure 10-1.) The root class of the data model—the data-context class—inherits from a system-provided base class and implements a fixed contract.

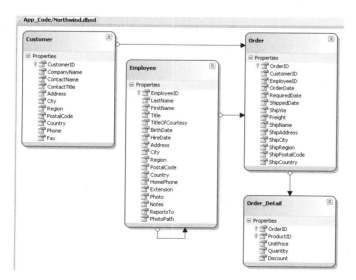

FIGURE 10-1 The O/R designer of Visual Studio 2008 in action on a section of the Northwind database

From the programmer's perspective, it should be noted that the data context is filled up with data as you access objects, and any changes to the model (deletions, updates, insertions) are saved back to the database as you call a submit method on the data-context class. Lazy-loading and prefetch options give you a way to fine-tune the data loading to optimize the overall behavior of the application.

Linq-to-XML

Linq-to-XML is an alternate new way to manipulate XML data in the .NET Framework. Linq-to-XML doesn't replace any of the existing XML libraries (such as XML DOM and XML reader/writer); instead, it provides the same overall set of capabilities through a superior and more developer-friendly syntax. With Linq-to-XML, you can create new documents and transform and query an XML document without resorting to any additional syntax such as XPath or XSLT.

Linq-to-XML provides its own model for manipulating XML documents regardless of the source—be it a stream, a disk file, a database result set, or perhaps manually created, in-memory XML data. The principal types you work with are *XDocument*, *XElement*, and *XAttribute*. Consider the following code:

```
XElement data = new XElement("Books",
    new XElement("Book", new XAttribute("id", "1"),
            new XElement("Title", "Programming ASP.NET 3.5"),
            new XElement("Author", Dino Esposito")
    ),
    new XElement("Book", new XAttribute("id", "2"),
            new XElement("Title", "Introducing ASP.NET AJAX"),
            new XElement("Author", Dino Esposito")
    )
);
```

It creates an XML document like the one shown here:

```
<Books>
  <Book id="1">
    <Title>Programming ASP.NET 3.5</Title>
    <Author>Dino Esposito</Author>
  </Book>
  <Book id="2">
    <Title>Introducing ASP.NET AJAX</Title>
    <Author>Dino Esposito</Author>
  </Book>
</Books>
```

To query, you can use the same syntax just shown for Linq-to-SQL.

```
var data = XDocument.Load(@"Books.xml");
var selectedBooks = from b in data.Book
            where b.Author == "Dino Esposito"
            select b.Title;
```

You loop through the collection of *Book* nodes and compare the inner text of the *Author* node against the provided literal. If a match is found, you add the node to the result set. What about the format of the result set? In this case, you get a collection of strings, each of which refers to the title of a selected book. By using the *new {}* operator (more on this later), you can return a collection of custom objects.

Linq-to-DataSets

Hoards of .NET developers have been using *DataSet* objects in their business and data access layers for the past five years or so. The *DataSet* operates as an in-memory database that exposes tables, indexes, and relationships to the world outside. You can manually populate a *DataSet* with data or use an ADO.NET adapter to work against a relational database. Once the *DataSet* has been filled, you work entirely in memory in a disconnected fashion. So what if you need to search for some data or join together two or more in-memory tables? The *Select* method on the *DataTable* class allows you to employ a declarative syntax to do some of the smart things you can do with the SQL language in a true database. Other *DataTable* methods, along with in-memory relationships, allow you to build the matrix of data you need and resolve any foreign key you happen to have in the data. So what's the purpose of Linq-to-DataSets?

Linq-to-DataSets enables developers to use the LINQ query syntax over the contents of ADO.NET *DataSet* and *DataTable* objects. You don't need to refresh any of the existing code you might have that is based on (typed) *DataSet* and table adapters. In addition, you can enhance it with a terser query syntax.

Let's see how to pick up from the Northwind database all orders that have been placed in the first ten days of January 1998 while expanding the customer ID to the effective company name:

```
DataSet ds = LoadCustomersAndOrders();
var customers = ds.Tables[0].AsEnumerable();
var orders = ds.Tables[1].AsEnumerable();

var data = from o in orders
           join c in customers
           on o.Field<string>("CustomerID")
              equals c.Field<string>("CustomerID")
           where o.Field<DateTime>("OrderDate").Year == 1998 &&
                 o.Field<DateTime>("OrderDate").Month == 1 &&
                 o.Field<DateTime>("OrderDate").Day < 10
           select new {OrderID=o.Field<int>("OrderID"),
                       Company=c.Field<string>("CompanyName")};

DataSet LoadCustomersAndOrders()
{
    // Use ADO.NET to query for data
    // and return a DataSet
}
```

As you saw in Chapter 8, ADO.NET data containers are not natively enumerable data containers. In the .NET Framework 3.5, the new *AsEnumerable* method just converts them into classic *IEnumerable* containers. You can't use plain properties to address the content of table columns; everything in the collection is still a *DataRow* object. For this reason, the *Field<T>* selector must be used to locate a particular value. The *new {}* operator builds up a new object type that will be returned in the resulting collection for whatever purpose you need, including data binding.

Linq-to-Objects

Linq-to-Objects enables you to perform even complex queries over any .NET type that implements *IEnumerable* and *IQueryable*. The list of supported data types is fairly long, as it includes arrays as well as *Collection<T>* collections.

The huge benefit that Linq-to-Objects delivers to developers is the extreme simplification of the query process. With Linq-to-Objects, one no longer needs to arrange loops that go through lists of data checking for conditions and tracking aggregate functions or creating a subset to return. Any of these common operations can be easily accomplished through the innovative LINQ syntax shown here:

```
int[] fiboNumbers = new int[] {0,1,1,2,3,5,8,13,21,34};
var data = from n in fiboNumbers
           where n % 2 == 0
           select n;
```

The query extracts even numbers from the list of the first 10 Fibonacci numbers. As you can see, the developer experience is greatly improved. Developers don't need to worry about instantiating a collection to hold numbers and about setting up a filter through one or more *if* statements. One query language fits all. Have a look at the following code snippet:

```
var data = (from n in fiboNumbers
           where n % 2 == 0 && n < 10
           select n).Sum();
Response.Write(data);
```

The same LINQ syntax allows you to apply a variety of aggregate functions, such as *Sum*, *Average*, *Max*, and *Min*. The preceding code snippet shows how to sum up only even Fibonacci numbers in the original array whose value is less than 10.

A Common Query Syntax

LINQ makes a query a first-class construct in .NET languages, at the same logical level of classes and methods. It does that through a new set of keywords that have been added to C# and Visual Basic .NET purposely. LINQ expressions can be used both to query and update data from any supported data source. Every variable that appears in a LINQ expression is strongly typed. In many cases, though, the actual type of the variable is not set explicitly by the developer but is inferred by the compiler.

There are two ways of expressing LINQ operations: through query expressions based on a new set of language constructs (for example, *from*, *select*, and *where*) and through method calls. It should be noted that all query expressions are mapped to method calls at compile time. Either approach is fine, and both are equivalent functionally and performancewise. It goes without saying, however, that query expressions are more readable and often less verbose. As an example, consider the following query expression:

```
// Using LINQ query expressions
var data = from c in db.Customers
           where c.Country == "Spain"
           select c;
```

It is fully equivalent to the method call shown next, with conversion rules between operators and methods set by the language specification:

```
// Using Standard Query Operator method call
var data = db.Customers.Where(c => c.Country == "Spain")
```

The => operator indicates a *lambda expression*—that is, an inline expression that can be used wherever a delegate type is expected. The => operator is read as "goes to" or "such that." Its left side indicates input parameters, whereas the block of statements to execute occupy the right side of the lambda operator. Lambda expressions are used in LINQ as a convenient way to create delegates. You need to use lambdas in LINQ only if you work with method calls. However, note that the set of methods is larger than the set of operators. So in some cases, your only option is using methods and, whenever required, lambda expressions.

> **Note** In the beginning of the .NET Framework, there were just delegates. Compared to the previous age when pointers laid down the law, it was just great. A delegate is an object-oriented wrapper for a function pointer. And, more importantly, it points to an existing and named function on a class. In the .NET Framework 2.0, managed languages got to support a new powerful construct—anonymous methods. Instead of having a named method to reference from within a delegate, you can have an unnamed method defined inline just where it needs be. The return type is inferred, external variables can still be accessed, and you can shave a lot of private methods off your classes. Lambda expressions are just a further refinement of the idea of an anonymous method, but less verbose and niftier.

Let's proceed now by reviewing the fundamentals of the LINQ query syntax and explore the main families of operators.

Projection Operators

The *Select* operator is perhaps the most popular of all, as it is used to project any contents from the data source to memory. You use it always in combination with the *from* keyword. In the code snippet in this section, I'll generically assume we query a collection of user-defined objects:

```
var data = from c in customers
           select c;
```

The *from* operator binds to a collection of data, whereas the *select* operator specifies the content of each selected object. The projection can be further refined by using the *where* and *orderby* operators to filter and sort the returned objects:

```
var data = from c in customers
           where c.Country == "Spain"
           orderby c.CompanyName, c.ContactName
           select c;
```

The *where* operator takes a Boolean expression where you express the criteria you need to be fulfilled using *Not*, *And*, and *Or* and equality operators. The *orderby* operator accepts a comma-separated list of properties to sort by. By default, the sorting order is ascending; you use the *descending* keyword to invert it:

```
var data = from c in customers
           where c.Country == "Spain"
           orderby c.CompanyName, c.ContactName descending
           select c;
```

Once you have selected a bunch of objects, you hold an enumerable collection. At this point, there are quite a few additional operations you can accomplish just on this collection before it is returned to the caller. For example, you can count the objects or, better yet, you can reverse their order. Here's how to do it:

```
var data = (from c in customers
           where c.Country == "Spain"
           orderby c.CompanyName, c.ContactName descending
           select c).Reverse();
```

The collection being returned to the caller is made of objects found in the *customers* collection. According to the data model, it'll be made of *Customer* objects.

> **Warning** The *Reverse* method is not supported in Linq-to-SQL because of the inherent unordered nature of the result sets you get from a database. It works when the sequence being queried is an enumerable in-memory collection, including an XML document or a *DataSet*.

It is common in database queries to restrict the number of columns you return. How can you manage to select only a subset of the columns in the query? You need to use a variation of the *select* operator, as shown here:

```
var data = from c in customers
           where c.Country == "Spain"
           orderby c.CompanyName, c.ContactName descending
           select new {c.CompanyName, c.ContactName};
```

The *new {}* operator tells the underlying system to generate objects on the fly that feature only the listed properties. The generated type is anonymous, and all of its properties are given a default name that matches the requested property name. However, if you're using calculated properties or if you just want to change the name, use the following syntax:

```
select new {c.CompanyName, YourPropertyName=c.ContactName};
```

Here's an even more interesting example in which one of the properties is obtained from a joined table:

```
var data = from c in customers
           where c.Country == "Spain"
           orderby c.CompanyName
           select new {
               c.CustomerID,
               c.CompanyName,
               c.Country,
               OrdersCount = c.Orders.Count
           };
```

Another variation of the *Select* operator is also worth a look—the *SelectMany* operator. Simply put, the difference between *Select* and *SelectMany* is that the former can return a hierarchy of objects, whereas the latter always returns a flattened set of records. To fully grasp the difference, though, let's consider a realistic scenario where we have a relationship between data sources—say, Customers-to-Orders. What do you think the following query is going to return?

```
var data = from c in customers
           where c.Country == "Spain"
           select (c.Orders);
```

It serves you back a collection with one object for each customer that matches the *where* criterion. Each object, though, is an array of *Order* objects. Let's consider the same query run through the *SelectMany* operator:

```
var data = (from c in customers
            where c.Country == "Spain"
            select c).SelectMany(c => c.Orders);
```

In this case, you get a flat array of order records where the customer ID information, upon which the relationship is built, is repeated. In the case of related tables, by using *Select* you have an extra level of indirection when getting at the same information.

Joining and Grouping

LINQ provides a couple of database-like operators to perform common operations such as joining and grouping collections of objects. In particular, the *Join* operator executes an inner join of two collections using a matching key that the two collections share:

```
var data = from c in customers
           join o in orders
               on c.CustomerID equals o.CustomerID
           select new {c.Name, o.OrderNumber};
```

Unlike SQL languages, the order of items in the *on* clause of a *join* does matter in LINQ. The first item must always come from the outer sequence, whereas the second—the right side of the *equals* operator—must belong to the inner sequence. If you fail in this, you'll get a compile error.

The purpose of the *join* operator can be summarized as follows. It loops through all elements of the outer collection (in the preceding code, *customers*) and adds a new element to the resulting collection for each element in the joined collection (*orders*, in the previous case) that matches the criterion. Joining is a popular operation in databases; with LINQ, you can do the same also on any other supported data containers.

Other join behaviors (for example, *outer*) are supported too. In particular, an *outer join* provides a resulting table in which outer elements with no match with any inner elements are also returned. For example, if you join customers and orders as we did previously, you receive a table with one element for each order placed by any customer. Customers who didn't place any orders are not listed. In an outer join scenario, all customers are listed regardless of the total number of orders they placed. Here's a sample query that demonstrates an outer join:

```
var data = from c in customers
           join o in (from orderInJan97 in orders
                      where orderInJan97.OrderDate.Value.Year == 1997 &&
                            orderInJan97.OrderDate.Value.Month == 1
                      select orderInJan97)
               on c.CustomerID equals o.CustomerID into groupOrders
           select new { c.CompanyName, OrderTotal = groupOrders.Count() };
```

The *customers* collection is joined with the subset of orders placed in January 1997. Each group of orders per customer are temporarily saved into the *groupOrders* container. This group is empty if no match is found on the joining key. The resulting table lists one record per customer, with the total number of orders each placed in a given timeframe:

```
select new { c.CompanyName, Orders = groupOrders };
```

By returning the *groupOrders* property, as in the preceding code snippet, you end up having a collection with the customer name and the list of orders.

The *group* clause returns a sequence of root objects, known as grouping objects, that contain zero or more items that match the key value for the group. For this reason, the output of a grouping operation might not immediately be bindable to tabular data-bound controls such as a *GridView*.

```
var data = from c in customers
           group c.ContactName by
             new {City = c.City, Region = c.Region} into g
           where g.Count() >1 ;
           select g
```

In the example, you group customers by city and region and add to the resulting data the contact name. In addition, you select only the customers with more than one contact in each pair of city and region. When executing such a query, LINQ loops through the source collection and creates groups of related objects that share the same value for the properties listed after the *by* clause. Note that you have to use an anonymous type (the *new* operator) if you need to group by multiple properties. Once a group is found, it is wrapped up in a grouping object and added to the response. You can use the *where* clause to restrict the grouping objects being returned. If you want to apply additional conditions to the grouping operation (like the *HAVING* clause in T-SQL), you just express any criteria in the *by* clause. The next example considers only cities with at least five characters in their name:

```
var data = from c in customers
           group c.ContactName by
             new {City = c.City, Length = c.City.Length >5} into g
           where g.Count() >1 ;
           select g
```

Note that anything that follows the *by* clause is taken into account literally. This means, for instance, that the preceding statement is quite different from the following:

```
var data = from c in customers
           group c.ContactName by
             new {City = c.City >5} into g
           where g.Count() >1 ;
           select g
```

In this case, the criteria to be met is that the name of the city is longer than five characters. No match will be checked, though, on the characters in the city name. As a result, contacts in Rome are ignored but contacts in London and New York are grouped together.

Aggregation

A number of operators are available to aggregate objects and make predefined calculations. LINQ provides common-use operators such as *Count*, *Sum*, *Average*, *Min*, and *Max* whose usage and purpose is self-explanatory. In a previous code snippet, you already met the *Count* operator. The next snippet shows how to use the *Sum* operator to get the total amount of an order in an Order-Details database table:

```
var data = from od in dataContext.Order_Details
           where od.OrderID == 10250
           select new {
               od.OrderID,
               OrderAmount = Sum(od.Quantity * od.UnitPrice)
           };
```

An interesting operator is *Aggregate*, which invokes a given function over the elements of a collection. Each iteration can save a value into an internal buffer; at the end of the loop, the current value is returned.

```
var data = from c in customers
   join o in orders
       on c.CustomerID equals o.CustomerID
           select new {
               c.CompanyName,
               MaxAmount = orders.Aggregate(
                       (t,s) => t.OrderDate > s.OrderDate ? t :s)
           };
```

The code returns a collection of objects where the company name is paired with the date of the most recent order placed.

> **Warning** The *Aggregate* method is not supported in Linq-to-SQL.

Partitioning

LINQ also enables you to pick up a particular sequence of consecutive objects from a collection. You use the *Take* operator to return a given number of elements in a sequence:

```
var data = (from c in customers
            select c).
            Take(10);
```

The sample query just retrieves the first ten objects in the *customers* collection. The *Take* operator doesn't have a built-in language construct such as *from* or *select*. It is, instead, a method on the class that represents the projection of the query. This means that you have to group the query in parentheses and then invoke the *Take* method, as in the preceding snippet.

In addition to the *Take* operator, you can also use the *Skip* operator to jump over a given number of elements in a sequence. *Take* and *Skip* can be combined to go to a particular position, pick up only a subset, and then skip over the remainder:

```
var data = (from c in customers
            select c).
            Skip(30).
            Take(10);
```

If you only use the *Skip* operator, you skip over a given number of elements in a sequence and then return the remainder.

It should be noted that *Skip* and *Take* operators might not have direct counterparts in the underlying data store. For example, in T-SQL they are implemented using *NOT EXISTS*, unless SQL Server 2005 is used where more specific operators exist. This means that the resulting T-SQL query—in case you use this feature in Linq-to-SQL—might not be as optimized as it should be. Whenever you use *Take* or *Skip* make sure you check the effectiveness of the underlying command and the overall performance. If you don't like it that much, feel free to find a specific workaround, such as writing a plain T-SQL query yourself.

Note   In Linq-to-SQL, you can always figure out the underlying T-SQL commands being used by using the SQL Server Profiler. In this way, you can modify LINQ queries to generate different T-SQL statements or decide to go with ADO.NET directly, thus bypassing LINQ.

Identifying Elements

How would identify a single element of a collection? Typically, you either proceed by position and pick up the element at a given index or go through a query and select the element that matches some given criteria. LINQ provides the *First* and *Single* operators to return the first or the single matching element.

The *First* operator uses either a predicate or an index to locate an element in a collection. As the name of the operator implies, it stops at the first element that matches. If you're searching by criteria, you can have any number of matching elements—zero, one, or more. If you employ a positional rule, at most one element will match. The following code selects the first customer from the USA that placed an order in May 1998:

```
var data = (from c in dataContext.Customers
            join o in (from t in dataContext.Orders
                       where t.OrderDate.Value.Year == 1998 &&
                             t.OrderDate.Value.Month == 5
                       select t)
              on c.CustomerID equals o.CustomerID
            select new { Company=c.CompanyName,
                         Country=c.Country,
                         OrderDate=o.OrderDate}
            ).First(x => x.Country == "USA");
```

The query restricts the results to the list of customers who placed orders in the specified timeframe and then picks up the first customer (represented via an anonymous type) whose country is USA. The *data* variable is assigned an instance of the anonymous type defined by the *new {}* operator.

What if no matching object is found? A query that uses *First* throws an exception if it is going to return an empty data set. To avoid that, you use the *FirstOrDefault* operator through the exact same syntax. As a result, the data variable is set to *null*—a value that your code can check against and hence use to recover gracefully. Both operators can be used with a Boolean predicate or can just be parameterless. In this case, the first positional element found in the resulting collection is picked up.

The *First* operator works fine regardless of whether one or more objects are found that match the predicate. The *Single* operator, instead, also ensures that exactly one object exists but raises an exception otherwise. The *SingleOrDefault* operator can prevent an exception only if the resulting sequence is empty. If multiple matching elements are found, an invalid operation exception is still raised. Here's a possible way of dealing with this situation:

```
try
{
    var data = (from c in dataContext.Customers
                join o in (from t in dataContext.Orders
                           where t.OrderDate.Value.Year == 1998 &&
                                 t.OrderDate.Value.Month == 5
                           select t)
                    on c.CustomerID equals o.CustomerID
                select new { Company=c.CompanyName,
                             Country=c.Country,
                             OrderDate=o.OrderDate}
                ).First(x => x.Country == "USA");
    if (data == null)
        ProcessNoCustomerFound();
    else
        ProcessCustomer(data);
}
catch (InvalidOperationException ex)
{
    ProcessMultipleCustomersFound();
}
```

The *try/catch* block does a good job of trapping any invalid-operation exceptions and recovers from the error. If the logical exception of no matching customers was already internally caught by the *SingleOrDefault* method, *data* is *null* and user-defined code can detect the condition and proceed.

> **Warning** Unfortunately, the preceding code snippet will not work, even though it is logically correct and carefully designed. The problem is that you can't pass *var*-declared variables around. As mentioned, the *var* keyword only enables type inference for local variables; it can't be used for formal parameters or return values of a function. This restriction invalidates the preceding code snippet and leaves a key point unanswered: how can you pass any collection that results from LINQ queries around from method to method if not across tiers? The answer is fairly simple and, let me say it, quite obvious too: just use explicit types. So you can quickly create a data-transfer class (say, *SimpleCustomerDTO*) with only the members in the *new {}* operator and initialize the object using the following syntax:
>
> ```
> select new SimpleCustomerDTO {
>                     Company = c.CompanyName, ... })
> ```

The Mechanics of LINQ

The list of LINQ operators is a bit longer than we've discussed to this point. For more information, I suggest you check the online documentation or have a look at "Introducing Microsoft LINQ" by Pablo Pialorsi and Marco Russo (Microsoft Press, 2007). As mentioned, LINQ is a set of language extensions to integrate query capabilities natively in .NET languages such as C# and Visual Basic .NET. From this viewpoint, LINQ is not necessarily bound to a particular data store but can deal with relational data as well as XML documents. It goes without saying, though, that to be data agnostic LINQ requires an underlying layer of code that maps from the high-level common syntax down to the actual query syntax of the data store. Let's have a brief look at some LINQ internals.

The Layers of LINQ

LINQ query operators can work on in-memory instances of any .NET type that is queryable. A .NET type is queryable only if it implements the *IEnumerable* interface or a derived generic interface such as *IQueryable<T>*. Arrays, *List*, *Dictionary*, and any other type of collection in the .NET Framework, including custom collection classes, are inherently queryable because they're enumerable. No sort of transformation is required on these types to make them queryable.

An XML document or a *DataSet*, though, are not immediately queryable because they do not implement the *IEnumerable* interface. For this reason, they require some special treatment before use. This is what happens when you invoke the *AsEnumerable* method on a *DataSet* or preprocess an XML file with the *XDocument.Load* method. Once these methods return, you are served up valid objects that can be used to define the query.

You formalize the query using a common syntax that has no direct mapping to the programming interface of the .NET objects being queried. To query a collection, you must employ ad hoc *for* statements along with predefined methods such as indexers, *Contains*, and *IndexOf*. To query a *DataSet*, you can use the *Select* method of contained *DataTable* objects. To query an XML document, you might want to use XQuery and XPath. As a developer, you don't need to be exposed to all these details. Moreover, exposing developers to this level of detail would negate the primary goal of LINQ—raising the bar of abstraction when it comes to querying for particular subsets of data. So there's a visible layer of LINQ that allows developers to express the query and another underlying layer that maps the parameters of the query to the queryable type. What about the data to query?

As long as we talk about in-memory objects such as collections or *DataSet*s, the data we need to query is available because it is already loaded in memory. But what about databases? More generally, what about situations in which the data to work with is not held in memory?

There's a third layer of LINQ that is charged with the fundamental task of retrieving the data to work with. As far as databases are concerned, this layer is responsible for establishing the connection to the database and mapping the formalized query to the query language (usually, a SQL dialect) of the database. Figure 10-2 shows the layers of LINQ.

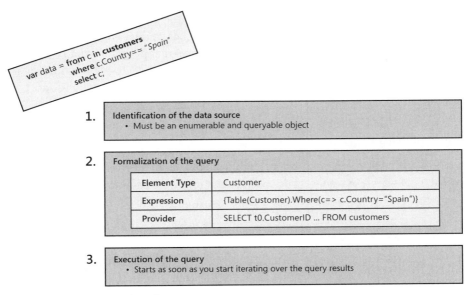

FIGURE 10-2 The layers of LINQ

Mapping to the Data Source

The .NET Framework 3.5 provides the mapping layer for in-memory collections, XML documents, *DataSet*s, and the SQL Server database. As you might have figured out yourself, these feasible data containers just correspond to the various flavors of LINQ. When you query collections, XML documents, or *DataSet* objects, your data model is the same as that which results from the programming interface of the data source. Again, what about databases?

Mapping to SQL Server requires a data model that describes the tables and their relationships. You first create a set of classes that meet LINQ query requirements and then use the LINQ syntax to express your queries. As a result, through Linq-to-SQL you end up using the LINQ syntax to retrieve data from relational tables rather than T-SQL. From this change, two key benefits descend. First, you get a terser and more readable syntax. Second, the query syntax is checked at compile time and is no longer opaque text to the code.

Linq-to-SQL shields you entirely from the intricacies of the T-SQL language, which is mostly good news. In doing so, though, you sign a contract where you declare you fully trust the T-SQL being generated by the LINQ mapping layers. If you have good reasons to doubt the effectiveness of the T-SQL employed, use the SQL Profiler to check which T-SQL commands are actually sent to the database and find a workaround otherwise. Finding a workaround mostly means refactoring that portion of your code so that different commands are generated or avoiding the use of LINQ altogether and resorting to plain old ADO.NET instead.

To extend LINQ with another data container, you need to write a special provider that is way more sophisticated than just an ADO.NET data provider. In a nutshell, this component must be able to remap on the native programming model of its own environment all the supported LINQ operators. A hypothetical Linq-to-Oracle mapping, for example, would express all LINQ operators through a set of commands written in PL/SQL—Oracle's query language. Depending on the type of data source you're going to extend with LINQ support, this operation might not be a picnic.

Executing the Query

A query is just what its name implies—the formalization of a series of operations that will produce a collection of values. Let's consider the following sample LINQ query:

```
var data = from c in dataContext.Customers
           where c.Country == "Spain"
           select c;
```

What do you think the *data* variable contains once the statement has completed? Abstractly speaking, the *from ... select* statement is not much different from an instance of the ADO.NET *SqlCommand* class fully configured to run. Technically speaking, the *from ... select* statement corresponds to an instance of the generic *DataQuery<T>* class that fully describes the query to execute. In both cases, no connection to the database has been established yet and no access to data has been performed.

Just as with *SqlCommand* objects in ADO.NET, the fundamental point is that you must execute the query in order to retrieve any data—just declaring the query is not enough. Unlike with *SqlCommand* objects, though, the execution of the query is started implicitly as soon as you start operating on the data. In other words, no explicit *execute* command is ever necessary, but the execution is automatically deferred until a point in the code is reached where the result of the query is required for proceeding. This feature is referred to as *deferred execution* of a query. How would start operating on the results of a query?

The most common way to request that live data is pumped into memory is by running a loop on the variable designated to contain the results of the query—the *data* variable in the preceding code snippet. The loop can be implemented through any loop statement the language supports—*for, foreach, while*. Another frequently used way to trigger the execution of the query is through data binding:

```
// This statement merely associates data with the data-bound control
GridView1.DataSource = data;

// This statement physically pumps data into the control; this is the
// real trigger that commands the execution of the query
GridView1.DataBind();
```

The query is executed immediately without delay if you use the *ToList* or *ToArray* method to load data into a .NET object:

```
// This query executes immediately
var data = (from c in dataContext.Customers
            where c.Country == "Spain"
            select c).ToList();

// At this point, the results of the query
// are already in memory
GridView1.DataSource = data;
GridView1.DataBind();
```

Finally, note that only queries that produce collections are deferred. If the query is designed to return a scalar value, it gets executed immediately.

Working with SQL Server

Linq-to-SQL brings LINQ query capabilities to SQL Server databases and translates your queries into T-SQL queries. The standard ADO.NET provider—*System.Data.SqlClient*—then takes care of executing the query. Results are returned via a data reader and, finally, loaded into an *IQueryable* collection of entity objects. The "entity objects" are the key element. They form a data model based on the database schema through which you operate on the data.

Important One thing should be said up front and kept in mind: Linq-to-SQL is not a tool to build your middle tier. Don't be fooled by the fact it uses objects. It should be seen, instead, as a powerful tool to build a data access layer using objects and a high-level query syntax rather than using result sets and T-SQL statements. In other words, Linq-to-SQL is used to access the database but not to entirely replace the functionality of a complete data access layer.

The Data Context

Visual Studio 2008 comes with an O/R designer tool that automatically generates a bunch of classes for you to model the schema of the database you connect to. Put another way, the O/R designer (formerly known as *SQLMetal*) gets a connection string as input and generates the data model for the database. The data model contains entity classes as well as a central console class—the data context—that exposes methods to execute specific operations on the tables.

Creating the Data Context

You start creating a Linq-to-SQL data model through the dialog box shown in Figure 10-3. The window pops up when you choose to add a new item to the project.

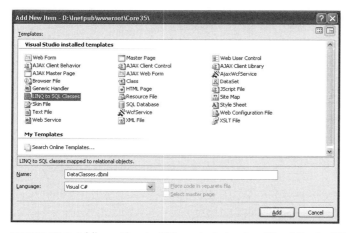

FIGURE 10-3 Adding a Linq-to-SQL context class to a Visual Studio 2008 project

The LINQ to SQL Classes option adds a DBML file to the App_Code folder of the ASP.NET project. The DBML file is an XML document that registers the connection string to the physical database, any tables you want to bring in the in-memory model, and its related entity class. Here's an excerpt:

```xml
<Database Name="Northwind" Class="NorthwindDataContext">
  <Connection ConnectionString="..." Provider="System.Data.SqlClient" />
  <Table Name="dbo.Customers" Member="Customers">
    <Type Name="Customer">
      <Column Name="CustomerID"
              Type="System.String"
              DbType="NChar(5) NOT NULL"
              IsPrimaryKey="true"
              CanBeNull="false" />
      <Column Name="CompanyName"
              Type="System.String"
              DbType="NVarChar(40) NOT NULL"
              CanBeNull="false" />
    ...
```

```
        <Association Name="Customer_Order"
                     Member="Orders"
                     OtherKey="CustomerID"
                     Type="Order" />
     </Type>
   </Table>
   ...
</Database>
```

The *Database* node sets the type name of the root data-context class through its *Class* attribute. The *Connection* node stores all details about the physical connection to the database. Next, you find an array of *Table* nodes, each describing an existing table in the database that you want to add to your model. In the code snippet, you're adding the *dbo. Customers* table as a member on the data-context class named *Customers*. This just defined member is a collection of entity objects as defined later via the *Type* node. The *Type* node contains *Column* child nodes to define members of the entity class. Finally, the *Association* node defines an additional *Orders* member on the *Customer* entity class to represent the one-to-many relationship between *Customers* and *Orders*, as set in the database schema.

As a result, you no longer work with generic tables of records, but use instead a strongly typed collection of entity objects. You can write all this code yourself, but the built-in O/R designer provides a nice user interface around it. All that you have to do is set up a connection string, open the Database Explorer panel in Visual Studio 2008, and then use a drag-and-drop operation to pick up physical tables to add to the context. (See Figure 10-1.)

Generating the Code

The DBML file counts two companion files—one to persist the data-context layout as in Figure 10-1, and one to actually contain the source code for the data context and entity classes. These companion files can be seen in Figure 10-4.

FIGURE 10-4 Companion files for a DBML document

The designer file contains the definition of the *NorthwindDataContext* class as well as all entity classes, including *Customer*, *Order*, and one for any other table you add to the layout through the O/R designer.

The *NorthwindDataContext* class contains a member for each table added (for example, Customers, Orders) plus a method for each stored procedure or user-defined function (UDF) you want to add. All classes can be further extended through the mechanism of partial classes.

Any class in the data model is marked as partial, meaning that you can add another class in the same project with the same signature that the compiler will fuse together at compile time. For example, using partial classes you can add a new member to the *Customer* class to, say, precalculate the total number of orders placed.

Linq-to-SQL entity classes (for example, *Customer*) are designed as a kind of data-transfer objects. They contain data but provide no behavior, not even for their basic I/O. Persistence and loading of entity objects is managed at the data-context level, as we'll see in a moment. You can use partial classes to add behavior to entity classes.

Analyzing the Generated Code

The data-context class is the entry point in the Linq-to-SQL data model being created for a given connection. It represents the gateway through which you connect to the database. Arbitrarily named, the class inherits from *System.Data.Linq.DataContext*. It has a few con-structors, mostly falling down into base constructors, plus a bunch of read-only properties as shown here:

```
public System.Data.Linq.Table<Customer> Customers
{
    get { return this.GetTable<Customer>(); }
}
```

In particular, you find one property for each table that was added to the model.

The LINQ's *Table* type represents a table of data and endows it with methods to filter and query its contents the LINQ way: *Where*, *Distinct*, *First*, *GroupBy*, and the like. Basically, the language-specific keywords we considered so far—such as *from*, *select*, *where*, and so forth—are mapped to methods on a *Table*-derived object.

Entity classes list properties that map to columns in the source database and offer just *get* and *set* methods. The *get* method just returns the stored value. The *set* method is a bit more sophisticated, as you can see:

```
[Column(Storage="_CustomerID", DbType="NChar(5) NOT NULL",
 CanBeNull=false, IsPrimaryKey=true)]
public string CustomerID
{
```

```
   get { return this._CustomerID; }
   set {
      if ((this._CustomerID != value))
      {
         this.OnCustomerIDChanging(value);
         this.SendPropertyChanging();
         this._CustomerID = value;
         this.SendPropertyChanged("CustomerID");
         this.OnCustomerIDChanged();
      }
   }
}
```

The *set* method returns immediately if the value you're going to assign is not different from the current value. Next, it fires a couple of events before and after the actual assignment of the new value, and it invokes extensibility methods for you to customize the operation to the extent that is needed.

The *SendPropertyChanging* and *SendPropertyChanged* methods take care of raising the *PropertyChanging* and *PropertyChanged* events to any event handlers that might be listening. These events are simple notifications and do not carry additional information about the whys and wherefores of the change.

What if you need to hook up the assignment of a new value to a particular property? That's where predefined extensibility methods fit in.

Extensibility Methods in the Generated Code

What's an extensibility method, anyway? Each property on an entity class has a pair of methods with the following prototypes:

```
partial void OnCustomerIDChanging(string value);
partial void OnCustomerIDChanged();
```

In addition, the entity class features three general-purpose extensibility methods as shown here:

```
partial void OnLoaded();
partial void OnValidate();
partial void OnCreated();
```

As the names suggest, you use these methods whenever you need to do something before or after the property is assigned a new value or upon loading or creation.

The goal of extensibility methods is to let developers roll their own code in particular moments of the object's life cycle. The point is, why not use overridable methods? Isn't it object-oriented programming, after all? Or, better yet, why not just write code in the *set* method of a given property?

Overridable methods require a derived class. This means you work with a *MyCustomer* class derived from *Customer* where you override methods to control value assignments. That's just out of the question. Why not simply write the code you need straight in the *set* method of the property? The fact is that the source of entity classes is auto-generated by the O/R designer, and it is automatically refreshed as you modify the model adding a new table or modify the underlying schema. If you enter your own code in the *set* method, all of your changes would be lost with the first event that happens to modify the schema or the model.

Extensibility methods leverage the mechanics of *partial methods*—another cool feature of the latest .NET languages. Partial methods are declared as partial in the entity class, and a call to them is automatically placed in the code. If no body for the method is actually provided, the compiler just skips the method invocation. To provide a body for the method, you add a partial class and define the partial method. Here's an example:

```
public partial class Customer
{
    partial void OnCustomerIDChanging(string value)
    {
        // You're not allowed to set CustomerID to KOEN2
        if (value.Equals("KOEN2"))
        {
            throw new InvalidExpressionException("...");
        }
    }
}
```

Partial methods are subject to some restrictions. In particular, a partial method always returns void, can't have output parameters, is considered as implicitly private, and can't be decorated as virtual. Also, you can't create a delegate to it.

Extensibility methods are extremely helpful for validation. If you need to validate the value of a single property, you can use the pair *OnXxxChanging* and *OnXxxChanged*, where *Xxx* indicates the name of a particular property. If you're just looking for a global point for validating the state of an entity, you use the *OnValidate* method instead. Because the *OnValidate* method is defined on the entity class, you use the *this* keyword to retrieve the current value of supported properties.

The *OnValidate* method is invoked just before the entity is persisted back to the database. The *OnXxxChanging/OnXxxChanged* methods are invoked as soon as the value is assigned to the property.

Querying for Data

Earlier in the chapter, we already examined the typical structure of a LINQ command that queries for data. The structure of a Linq-to-SQL query is not really different from a query that targets, say, an XML document. Preparing the query, though, might require different operations.

Preparing the Query

A LINQ query targets an in-memory queryable object. If your final data store is a SQL Server database, you first need to get a queryable object—the data context. Just adding proper files to the project is not enough, though. You also need to explicitly instantiate the data context. In ASP.NET, you normally do it in the *Page_Load* event handler:

```
private NorthwindDataContext dataContext;

protected void Page_Load(object sender, EventArgs e)
{
    dataContext = new NorthwindDataContext();
}
```

Note that in this case the information about the connection string is hard-coded in the *NorthwindDataContext* class, which reads it out of the *web.config* file. This depends on the steps you take within the wizard that starts after you terminate the dialog box shown earlier in Figure 10-3. However, if you need to make the connection string parametric, be aware that the data-context class features several constructors with which you can pass the connection string or, directly, an ADO.NET *IDbConnection* object.

> **Note** The data-context object must be created for each request, as it is not automatically persisted in any way across requests. You can certainly consider caching the object, but that is entirely your responsibility. The data-content is a lightweight object so creating it whenever you need one does pose particular performance issues.

Inside a Sample Query

Once you have the data context up and running, you can start executing queries using the syntax we examined earlier in the chapter. Let's briefly review the main facts with an example. Suppose you want to display a drop-down list containing the name of all the countries where you have customers. In plain T-SQL, you use the following statement:

```
SELECT DISTINCT country FROM customers
```

In the LINQ syntax, though, the *Distinct* keyword doesn't exist; at least, it doesn't exist as a language keyword. Thankfully, a *Distinct* method exists on the *Table* object. So here's how to lay out a query:

```
var data = (from c in dataContext.Customers
            select c.Country).Distinct();
```

This code just prepares the query and extracts any piece of information that may be used later to actually load data. You are instructing LINQ to loop through the contents of the *Customers* in-memory table on the data context and add the string stored in the *Country* property of the entity object to the results. When you're done, you filter out from the results all duplicates. Clearly, in Linq-to-SQL this description is just an abstract summary of what you get. In reality, the Linq-to-SQL mapping layer translates the preceding expression in the following T-SQL statement:

```
SELECT DISTINCT [t0].[Country] FROM [dbo].[Customers] AS [t0]
```

Next, as soon as the results of the query are needed, it runs the command and assigns the response to the *data* variable.

When is *dataContext.Customers* filled up? All in all, I feel that the best answer is, "Never, until it's necessary." To express a query, filling up *dataContext.Customers* is never necessary. All that it adds to the query is a link to a physical table. In no way are all customers loaded in memory to calculate the distinct countries. However, any code you might have in your pages that accesses the *Customers* collection forces a query to fill the collection at the time the collection is actually accessed. Imagine you have the following in *Page_Load*:

```
// FYI: there are 91 customers in Northwind
Response.Write(dataContext.Customers.Count());
```

What do you think the response will be? 91 or perhaps 0? The *Customers* collection is empty a moment before this instruction is processed. However, *dataContext.Customers* is not a plain *IEnumerable* collection, and therefore the *Count* method doesn't just count the in-memory elements. This is a key difference between Linq-To-SQL and, say, Linq-to-Objects.

Does it mean that the collection gets filled to count 91 elements before the response is output? The answer is no; but still 91 is output. The SQL Profiler clarifies things. Each call to *Count* fires a T-SQL command as shown here:

```
SELECT COUNT(*) FROM customers
```

The collection is never populated, but the total of objects is counted each time you invoke *Count*. Yes, this means that the following code would originate three database roundtrips:

```
Response.Write(dataContext.Customers.Count());
Response.Write(dataContext.Customers.Count());
Response.Write(dataContext.Customers.Count());
```

To fill the collection entirely, you need either to employ a *foreach* statement or use a conversion method such as *ToArray* or *ToList*. Smartly enough, though, the following code doesn't originate 91 roundtrips, but just one:

```
foreach(Customer c in dataContext.Customers)
{
    Response.Write(c.CustomerID + ", ");
}
```

What about the following, instead?

```
// Always the first customer ID is output, but we're making
// a different point here ...
for (int i=0; i<91; i++)
{
    Customer c = dataContext.Customers.Take(i+1).First();
    Response.Write(c.CustomerID + ", ");
}
```

Each execution of the *Take* method requires a roundtrip. You can't use positional rules, such as "take the element at position #5 in T-SQL." So if you need to loop over the records in a table, opt for *foreach*. The *foreach* statement is smart enough to force a *SELECT * FROM* customers query that minimizes the roundtrips to the database.

The bottom line is that with Linq-to-SQL you really work with *System.Data.Linq.Table* objects, not plain .NET in-memory collections. Hence, any operation involves the underlying database table rather than cached data in memory.

Flat and Hierarchical Results

T-SQL result sets are tabular in nature. You can build complex stored procedures to return a sequence of result sets to model nontabular data, but this doesn't change the basic fact—a result set is tabular.

In Linq-to-SQL, associations between tables are automatically resolved by adding collection properties. For example, the *Customer* entity class features an *Orders* property that contains all orders related to the customer. The *Orders* collection is a LINQ Table filled with *Order* objects. What about the following query?

```
var data = from c in dataContext.Customers
           group c.ContactName by new { City = c.City, Region = c.Region }
                into g
           where g.Count() > 1
           select g;
```

Translated in human language, the query groups all contacts operating in the same city and region. What's the structure of the returned data in the output variable?

The structure is not flat and tabular; it's hierarchical instead. The first level contains the key on which the grouping operation occurred—city and region. The second level contains all contacts operating in that city and region. This data format can't just be displayed through a grid. It requires more elaboration, as shown next:

```
foreach(var contacts in data)
{
    Response.Write(contacts.Key.City + ", " + contacts.Key.Region);
    Response.Write("<hr/>");
    foreach(var contact in contacts)
```

```
    {
        Response.Write(contact);
        Response.Write("<br/>");
    }
    Response.Write("<br/>");
    Response.Write("<br/>");
}
```

Figure 10-5 shows the output of the sample page.

FIGURE 10-5 Grouped sequences of records

Each element in a grouped query result has a *Key* property that represents the key of the grouping. If a composite key is used, the *Key* property is an object. Each element in the result set is also a list in which each object contains all the properties listed after the *group* keyword.

Imagine a scenario where you have a relationship between two tables—say, Customers and Orders. The following query uses the *select* keyword and returns an array of objects with the listed set of properties:

```
var data = from c in dataContext.Customers
           where c.Country == "Spain"
           select new { c.CompanyName, c.Orders };
```

The *Orders* property is an array of *Order* objects—all orders placed by the selected customers. A tabular data-bound control is not able to bind that data. Unfortunately, not even a hierarchical control like the *TreeView* is able to accept that data. In this latter case, it is because of a restriction within ASP.NET hierarchical controls, which only accept a data source that implements the *IHierarchicalEnumerable* interface. In the end, you need to navigate through the data set yourself to produce any user interface:

```
StringBuilder sb = new StringBuilder();
foreach(var c in data)
{
    sb.AppendFormat("<b>{0}</b><hr/>", c.CompanyName);
    foreach(Order o in c.Orders)
    {
        sb.AppendFormat("{0}<br/>", o.OrderID);
    }
    sb.Append("<br/><br/>");
}
Label1.Text = sb.ToString();
```

Figure 10-6 shows the result.

FIGURE 10-6 Manual representation of hierarchical data

The same query can be expressed in a tabular format, with some inevitable data redundancy, by using the *SelectMany* method on the *Table* class. Here's how to do it:

```
var data = (from c in dataContext.Customers
            where c.Country == "Spain"
            select c).SelectMany(c => c.Orders);
```

In this case, the result is a tabular data set in which each record is an order.

Deferred Loading and Prefetching

Using the LINQ syntax, you might end up modeling queries that span over multiple objects according to existing relationships between tables. This can lead to the unwanted situation of loading in memory more data than is strictly needed to accomplish a task. Linq-to-SQL tends to be lazy when it comes to retrieving objects and doesn't automatically fetch all related objects at the same time. For example, suppose you want to load customers:

```
var data = from c in dataContext.Customers
           select c;
```

Because the table Customers has a relationship to Orders, and Orders to Order Details, and Order Details to Products, and Products to Categories, does it mean that the whole Northwind database is being loaded with a single query? Of course, not. As mentioned, by default data is loaded only when strictly necessary. The following query gets orders and accesses customer information only when necessary:

```
var data = from o in dataContext.Orders
           where o.ShipVia == 3
           select o;
foreach(var o in data)
{
    // This condition is a heavy one and filters
    // out most customer records
    if (o.Freight > 300)
        SendCustomerNotification(o.Customer);
    ProcessOrder(o);
}
```

The *foreach* statement forces a query over the *Orders* table; the *if* statement, though, limits the additional retrieval of customer information for each order to only the customers that are going to receive the notification. Each time you access the *Customer* property, a new round-trip is made to SQL Server to retrieve related data.

Deferred loading can be controlled via the *DeferredLoadingEnabled* Boolean property on the data-context class. When set to *false*, the property tells Linq-to-SQL not to delay-load one-to-many and one-to-one relationships. As a result, you are responsible for physically loading all the data you need. Consider the following snippet:

```
var customers = from c in dataContext.Customers
                where c.City == "London"
                select c;

dataContext.DeferredLoadingEnabled = false;
StringBuilder sb = new StringBuilder();
foreach (var c in customers)
{
    sb.AppendFormat("Customer ID: {0}<br/>", c.CustomerID);
    sb.AppendFormat("Orders: {0}<br/>", c.Orders.Count());
}
Label1.Text = sb.ToString();
```

With deferred loading disabled, the *Orders* collection on the *Customer* object remains empty and the *Count* methods can't do more than just return zero. If you want to take control of how orders are loaded, you might want to load orders explicitly, as shown here:

```
var orders = (from o in dataContext.Orders
              where o.Customer.City == "London"
              select o).ToList();
```

This approach costs you only one roundtrip to load all orders from London customers; from now on, you can operate having the *dataContext.Orders* filled and filtering this sequence by customer ID, as the next code snippet shows:

```
StringBuilder sb = new StringBuilder();
foreach (var c in customers)
{
    sb.AppendFormat("<b>Customer ID: {0}</b><br/>", c.CustomerID);
    sb.AppendFormat("Orders: {0}<hr/>",
                    orders.Count(o => o.CustomerID == c.CustomerID));
    foreach(var o in orders)
    {
        if (o.CustomerID == c.CustomerID)
            sb.AppendFormat("{0}<br/>", o.OrderID);
    }
}
Label1.Text = sb.ToString();
```

In this way, you make only two queries—one for all customers from London, and one for all related orders.

Preloading Data

The data-context class features a *LoadOptions* property that can be used to force an early loading of data according to existing one-to-many and one-to-one relationships. The *LoadOptions* property contains an instance of the *DataLoadOptions* class. Here's how to set it:

```
DataLoadOptions options = new DataLoadOptions();
options.LoadWith<Customer>(c => c.Orders);
dataContext.LoadOptions = options;
```

The *LoadWith* method indicates the relationships you want to preload with entities of a particular type—in this case, *Customer*. Basically, you are telling the Linq-to-SQL runtime to preload orders for each customer when it is going to load information for the customer. If deferred loading is disabled, *LoadWith* is your option to ensure that related data is in place when you access properties connected to relationships such as *Orders* for the *Customer* entity and *Order_Details* for the *Order* entity.

LoadWith also instructs the Linq-to-SQL query translator to try to implement the loading of a hierarchy of tables through fewer queries by using smart forms of joins or by whatever other trick may be known. However, there's no guarantee that by using *LoadWith* you actually save roundtrips to the database. The only certain thing is that related data is eager loaded when the parent entity is loaded. For example, with a data context configured as previously shown (using the *LoadWith* method), the following query also fires a SELECT statement to populate the *Orders* property of each loaded *Customer* entity. More importantly, this happens regardless of whether you use orders records or not.

```
var data = from c in dataContext.Customers
           where c.City == "London"
           select c;
```

Along with *LoadWith*, the *DataLoadOptions* class also features the *AssociateWith* method. The *AssociateWith* method specifies filters and/or orders for a particular relationship. Filters and orders are applied regardless of whether data from relationships are eager or lazy loaded.

Linq-to-SQL Query Restrictions

Linq-to-SQL translates standard query operators of LINQ into T-SQL commands. It is key to note that LINQ operators are defined against an *ordered sequence* of elements. The T-SQL language (as well as any other SQL-based language) works with unordered sets of values. The ordering you can apply through the ORDER BY clause is merely an operation that occurs once the sequence has been obtained. In other words, you always get an unordered set that is then ordered in the way you requested. The order is not implicit in the sequence. As a result, the identity of an element descends from its values, not from its position in the sequence.

The bottom line is that certain standard LINQ operators do not work properly or are just not supported in Linq-to-SQL. For example, *Take* and *Skip* originate quite complex T-SQL statements, in fierce contrast with their inherent simplicity. Other operators such as *TakeWhile*, *SkipWhile*, *Last*, *ElementAt*, and *Reverse* are just not translated to T-SQL and are unsupported by Linq-to-SQL.

Updating Data

So far, we considered only how to use Linq-to-SQL to load data from the database into memory via the data-context object. Linq-to-SQL, though, is not just a one-way mechanism, and the object model you get through the data context can also be used to save data back to the original database.

Making Changes to the Data Context

To perform insert, update, and delete operations via Linq-to-SQL, you just add, update, and remove objects in the object model you access via the data context. It couldn't be easier and more natural. Once entity objects are available in memory, inserting, say, an order is as easy as creating a new instance of the *Order* class and adding it to the *Orders* collection of the customer. Linq-to-SQL tracks your changes to the data context, and it transmits those changes back to the database when you call the *SubmitChanges* method on the data-context object. Let's consider a simple case that shows how to edit the address of a given customer:

```
string id = "ALFKI";
Customer c = dataContext.Customers.Single(c => c.CustomerID == id);
c.Address = "123 Flowers Street";
dataContext.SubmitChanges();
```

As you can see, there are two main steps involved. First, you retrieve the entity object to update and proceed with changes. Second, you persist the updated model back to the database.

The preceding code snippet has purely illustrative purposes and therefore is a bit out of context. Let's reconsider it as you would probably integrate it in an ASP.NET page like that shown in Figure 10-7.

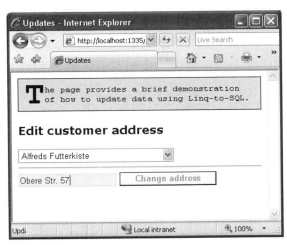

FIGURE 10-7 A sample ASP.NET page to update the customer's address

The drop-down list is initially populated using either Linq-to-SQL or a classic ASP.NET data source control. As the user selects a new customer in the list, the page automatically posts back and fills the text box with the address of the currently selected customer:

```
void DropDownList1_SelectedIndexChanged(object sender, EventArgs e)
{
    string id = DropDownList1.SelectedValue;
    Customer c = dataContext.Customers.SingleOrDefault(
                    c => c.CustomerID == id);
    TextBox1.Text = "";
    if (c != null)
        TextBox1.Text = c.Address;
}
```

The call to *SingleOrDefault* originates a database roundtrip each time you change the selection on the drop-down list. Next, the user is free to edit the content of the text box and click to persist changes, as shown here:

```
void Button1_Click(object sender, EventArgs e)
{
    string id = DropDownList1.SelectedValue;

    Customer c = dataContext.Customers.SingleOrDefault(
                        c => c.CustomerID == id);
    if (c != null)
    {
        c.Address = TextBox1.Text;
        dataContext.SubmitChanges();
    }
}
```

Also in this case, the call to *SingleOrDefault* originates a roundtrip to the database. Finally, the call to *SubmitChanges* to persist changes fires yet another roundtrip. Can some of these roundtrips be avoided in some way? I guess that there's just one possible answer to this question—caching. But it's not necessarily a great answer, as we'll learn in a moment.

Adding and Deleting Objects

The data-context object automatically tracks objects being added to the context and knows which have been updated, deleted, or added at any time. When you invoke the *SubmitChanges* method, you instruct the data-context class to transform each pending change into an update statement against the underlying database.

So to add a new record, here's what you would typically do:

```
Customer newCustomer = new Customer();
newCustomer.CustomerID = "KOEN2";
newCustomer.CompanyName = " ... ";
...
dataContext.Customers.InsertOnSubmit(newCustomer);
dataContext.SubmitChanges();
```

For insertions, the object must be an external object not already loaded in the data context. What about deleting a database record?

The record to delete must belong to the data context, either because the data context loaded it or because you previously attached it to the data context. Here's a first example in which you use the same data context to retrieve and then delete a given customer:

```
Customer koen2 = dataContext.Customers.SingleOrDefault(
                        c => c.CustomerID == "KOEN2");
if (koen2 != null)
{
    dataContext.Customers.DeleteOnSubmit(koen2);
    dataContext.SubmitChanges();
}
```

Note that after the successful execution of *SubmitChanges*, deleted objects are marked as *Deleted* in the data context but are not physically eliminated from its internal cache. Furthermore, the effect of deletion is not propagated to related objects either in the database or in memory.

Cross-Table Updates

Linq-to-SQL enables you to model cross-table relationships in the data context and also supports cross-table updates. All that you have to do is remove objects from their own *Table* objects, and *SubmitChanges* will do the rest for you. Let's see how to add a new customer and a few related orders:

```
Customer mands = new Customer();
mands.CustomerID = "MANDS";
mands.CompanyName = "Managed Design";
mands.ContactName = "Dino Esposito";
mands.Country = "Italy";
mands.City = "Milan";
mands.Address = "Via dei Tigli, 23";
dataContext.Customers.InsertOnSubmit(mands);

Order o1 = new Order();
o1.OrderID = 21221;
o1.OrderDate = new DateTime(2007, 10, 1);
o1.ShipCity = "Rome";
mands.Orders.Add(o1);

Order o2 = new Order();
o2.OrderID = 21222;
o2.OrderDate = DateTime.Now;
o2.ShipCity = "Turin";
mands.Orders.Add(o2);

// Cross-table updates
try
{
    dataContext.SubmitChanges();
    Label1.Text = String.Empty;
}
catch
{
    Label1.Text = "The insertion failed. Sorry about that.";
}
```

In terms of database statements, it involves three *INSERT*s, one for the customer and two for the orders. Let's see now what's needed to delete the new customers and related orders:

```
var orders = from o in dataContext.Orders
             where o.CustomerID == "MANDS"
             select o;
```

```
// Delete orders for a given customer
foreach(var o in orders)
    dataContext.Orders.DeleteOnSubmit(o);

// Retrieve the customer to delete
Customer mands = dataContext.Customers.SingleOrDefault(
                        c => c.CustomerID == "MANDS");
if (mands != null)
{
    dataContext.Customers.DeleteOnSubmit(mands);
    try
    {
        dataContext.SubmitChanges();
        Label1.Text = String.Empty;
    }
    catch
    {
        Label1.Text = "The deletion failed. Sorry about that.";
    }
}
```

You first delete orders and then move on to consider the customer. If you attempt to just cancel the customer, not only won't you get orders automatically cleared, but also a violation exception will be raised. Note that this is a function of the constraints placed on the tables rather than anything LINQ did while simply working with the database.

It is worth noting that it takes you three *DELETE*s to complete the operation—two deletions for the orders and one for the customer.

Optimistic Concurrency

It is even more interesting to take a look at the structure of the *DELETE* statements being used to delete entities. (As mentioned, you can use the SQL Profiler tool for the purpose.) The statement contains a huge *WHERE* clause that Linq-to-SQL has basically ordered to ensure that all properties in the entity object match the current values in the table record:

```
DELETE FROM [dbo].[Customers]
WHERE ([CustomerID] = 'MANDS') AND
      ([CompanyName] = 'Managed Design') AND
      ([ContactName] = 'Dino Esposito') AND
      ([ContactTitle] IS NULL) AND
      ([Address] = 'Via dei Tigli, 23') AND
      ([City] = 'Milan') AND
      ([Region] IS NULL) AND
      ([PostalCode] IS NULL) AND
      ([Country] = 'Italy') AND
      ([Phone] IS NULL) AND
      ([Fax] IS NULL)
```

This technique is known as *optimistic concurrency*, and it demands that before updating or deleting a record you must first investigate whether other transactions have changed any values in the record. Optimistic concurrency can be contrasted with *pessimistic concurrency*, which locks the record to avoid conflicts. It is referred to as *optimistic* because it considers it unlikely that a concurrent transaction will alter a record that another user might be using. By default, Linq-to-SQL supports optimistic concurrency.

From a database perspective, a conflict simply doesn't exist. The previous *DELETE* command is perfectly legal; it can succeed or fail, but from the database perspective there's nothing wrong or bad. Optimistic concurrency is a choice of the data access layer. So Linq-to-SQL makes *SubmitChanges* throw an exception (a LINQ exception, not a SQL exception) if it doesn't successfully delete or update a record. After a *DELETE* or *UPDATE* statement executes, if the number of affected records is zero, a conflict exception is raised.

As a developer, you can handle conflict exceptions in either of two ways.

The first option entails that you pass an extra argument to *SubmitChanges* and instruct it to continue even when there are conflict exceptions:

```
// Make sure you include the System.Data.Linq namespace
dataContext.SubmitChanges(ConflictMode.ContinueOnConflict);
```

The default value is *ConflictMode.FailOnFirstConflict*. If you choose to continue with updates, how would you know about failed commands? You explore the contents of the *ChangeConflicts* collection property on the data-context class, as shown next:

```
try
{
    dataContext.SubmitChanges(ConflictMode.ContinueOnConflict);
}

catch (ChangeConflictException e)
{
    foreach (ObjectChangeConflict occ in dataContext.ChangeConflicts)
    {
        // Recover from the conflict, for example reiterating the
        // command with a less restrictive WHERE clause or notifying
        // the user that a conflict occurred and allowing them to
        // decide what course of action to take.
    }
}
```

Properties defined on the *ObjectChangeConflict* class let you know exactly what happened, on which table, and regarding which entity object.

The second option you have to control and prevent conflicts is watering down the inherent optimism of Linq-to-SQL's concurrency model. Basically, you get back to the source code of entity classes and add an attribute called *UpdateCheck*, as shown here:

```
[Column(Storage="_CompanyName", UpdateCheck.Never)]
public string CompanyName
{
    ...
}
```

The default value for the *UpdateCheck* attribute is *Always*, and it's exactly this setting that causes each property to be added to the *WHERE* clause of *UPDATE* and *DELETE* statements. If you change the value to *Never*, a property will never be added to the *WHERE* clause. Of course, what you really want to do is preserve the *Always* setting for properties that represent key columns and perhaps choose a halfway point for important properties that you want to check but only if they are updated. In this case, you use the *WhenChanged* value for the *UpdateCheck* attribute.

Customizing Update Operations

If you weren't using LINQ, you would have certainly coded the removal of all orders for a customer in a different way, as shown in the following line of code:

```
DELETE FROM orders WHERE customerid='MANDS'
```

In this way, all orders would have been deleted from the database with a single roundtrip. In many cases, to delete an entity (say, a *Customer*) you don't need the whole object; its unique key is enough. Does this mean that we should drop LINQ to return to plain ADO.NET commands? Not necessarily.

Linq-to-SQL offers to change the default implementation of update operations on entity objects. It is as easy as overriding a method in a derived class. However, because Linq-to-SQL is built on partial classes, all that you need to do is add a partial method. Here's the list of extensions supported via partial methods by the data-context class for the *Customer* entity:

```
partial void InsertCustomer(Customer instance);
partial void UpdateCustomer(Customer instance);
partial void DeleteCustomer(Customer instance);
```

It goes without saying that methods are in the form of *InsertXxx*, *UpdateXxx*, and *DeleteXxx*, where *Xxx* is the name of an entity in the data context. Here's an example:

```
partial void DeleteCustomer(Customer instance)
{
    this.ExecuteCommand("DELETE FROM customers WHERE customerid=@id",
            instance.CustomerID);
}
```

The preceding code deletes a customer by only looking at the *CustomerID* property, regardless of anything else.

> **Note** The possibility of customizing update operations also makes it possible for you to use stored procedures instead of plain T-SQL commands to execute database operations.

Other Features

To top off the examination of Linq-to-SQL features that pertain to updating, let's briefly review what the standard behavior is as far as transactions and stored procedures are concerned.

Using Transactions

All the updates you carry through *SubmitChanges* are wrapped in a transaction. When you call the method, Linq-to-SQL verifies that the call isn't already in the scope of a transaction and that no user-started transaction has been explicitly bound to the data context. If there is no existing transaction, Linq-to-SQL then starts a local transaction and employs that transaction to execute any T-SQL commands. When all commands have been successfully terminated, Linq-to-SQL commits the transaction.

As mentioned, you are allowed to use your own *TransactionScope* object to wrap any database operations that originate out of the *SubmitChanges* method. By using an external *TransactionScope* object, you can for instance enlist non-database resources into the transaction, such as sending a Microsoft Message Queue (MSMQ) or updating the file system. When *SubmitChanges* detects that it is called to operate in the scope of an existing transaction, not only does it avoid creating a new transaction, but it also avoids closing the connection.

Finally, you can also start a transaction yourself and associate the commands of *SubmitChanges* with it. You do so by using the *Transaction* property of the data-context object. It is then up to you to commit or roll back the transaction as appropriate. If the connection string for the transaction doesn't match the connection string used for the data context, an exception is thrown.

Using Stored Procedures

What if your database has a number of powerful stored procedures that you want to use for both basic CRUD and more specific operations? As briefly hinted at earlier, you can force Linq-to-SQL to use stored procedures for basic CRUD manipulation of entity objects by defining partial methods for update operations, as the following code snippet shows:

```
partial void DeleteCustomer(Customer instance)
{
   this.ExecuteCommand("exec delete_customer ...",
         instance.CustomerID);
}
```

In addition to this, you can add stored procedures as methods to the data-context class. The O/R designer in Visual Studio 2008 greatly simplifies the task. All that you have to do is pick up the stored procedure from the Database Explorer view and drag it anywhere onto the layout of the data-context class. (See Figure 10-8.)

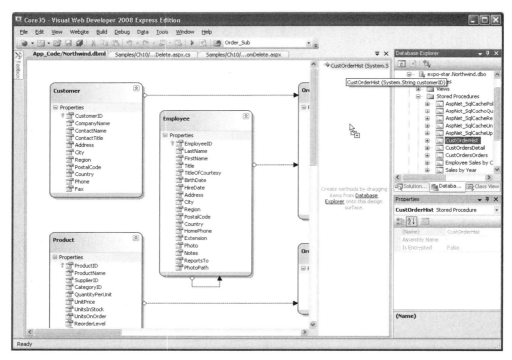

FIGURE 10-8 Adding stored procedures to the data-context class

Next, you use the stored procedure as a regular method, as shown here:

```
var orders = dataContext.CustOrderHist(customerID);
```

As for any other Linq-to-SQL operation, you can use the *var* keyword to infer the type of the result. Depending on the type, you can bind it to a data-bound control or you can loop over it using a *foreach* statement.

When the stored procedure returns multiple values or values of different types, the data-context wrapper for the stored procedure returns an *IMultipleResults* type. In this case, you use the *GetResult<T>* method to access a given result, where *T* indicates the return type of a particular result based on your knowledge of the internals of the stored procedure.

Using User-Defined Functions

User-defined functions (UDFs) are T-SQL functions defined in the database. Here's an example:

```
CREATE FUNCTION dbo.CalcDiscount(
        @unitprice money, @quantity decimal, @discount float)
RETURNS money
AS
    BEGIN
    RETURN CONVERT(money, @unitprice * @quantity * (1-@discount))
    END
```

Just like a stored procedure, a UDF can be attached to the data context and used as a method in your pages.

Conclusion

Over the years, several different query languages have been developed, each designed to target a particular data source. Popular examples are SQL for relational databases and XQuery for XML documents. Another good example is the SQL-ish dialect that the *Select* method of the ADO.NET *DataTable* class recognizes. With LINQ, developers can focus on just one set of syntax elements.

In this chapter, we kept an eye on Linq-to-SQL, which is the implementation of LINQ that works on SQL Server tables using the SQL Server ADO.NET data provider. Linq-to-SQL offers a data model that is representative of the underlying database and creates a number of classes for you through the services of a Visual Studio 2008 tool—the O/R designer.

Linq-to-SQL lets you work with objects rather than with data tables and data rows, and it also automatically resolves for you relationships between tables. The overall object model it supplies is a kind of "active record"—that is, a model in which you have an object for each table row whose interface matches closely the columns in the row. In addition, though, Linq-to-SQL also adds extra properties to track relationships and automatically expands foreign keys. So it is a bit more than just an "active record," but probably not yet an instance of the "data mapper" pattern. Active Record and Data Mapper are two popular design patterns for modeling a data source in the context of a fully object-based middle tier. Linq-to-SQL doesn't entirely comply to the requirements of either, but it still delivers an object-based model where entity classes are plain data transfer objects (only data, no behavior) and all the logic is grouped in a gateway class—the data context. The behavior required to operate on the data model is not provided through methods on entity classes (as in a regular Active Record or Data Mapper model), but is coded via LINQ queries and commands.

In the end, rather than using Linq-to-SQL to model your domain, I suggest you use Linq-to-SQL in the data access layer to replace T-SQL with objects and raise the bar of the abstraction level beyond imagination. In the middle tier, I suggest you use another set of objects to manage entity classes. The middle-tier objects can then use Linq-to-SQL classes to store data and add methods to expose any requested behavior to the presentation layer.

 ## Just the Facts

- LINQ is s part of the .NET Framework 3.5 and, as such, it is available to ASP.NET and Windows applications and services.

- A new set of keywords have been added to C# and Visual Basic .NET to support LINQ. Using these keywords, you can perform quite complex operations (such as filtering, ordering, and grouping) with a limited amount of code and over a variety of data sources: SQL Server databases, ADO.NET *DataSet* objects, XML documents, and in-memory collections.

- Linq-to-SQL is an O/R implementation used to expose the schema and contents of a SQL Server database through a set of objects.

- In Linq-to-SQL, you perform CRUD operations on any mapped database using the LINQ syntax and the persistence capabilities of the root data-context class.

- Linq-to-SQL supports transactions and stored procedures, and its classes offer a number of extensibility points for you to override most of the default behaviors.

- Linq-to-SQL is not a tool to build your middle tier. It should be seen, instead, as a powerful tool to build a data access layer using objects and a high-level query syntax, rather than using result sets and T-SQL statements.

Chapter 11
Creating Bindable Grids of Data

Data-bound controls play a key role in the development of ASP.NET applications. Data-driven controls allow you to associate the whole interface, or individual properties, with one or more columns read out of a .NET-compliant data source. We already mentioned data-bound controls in Chapter 10 and reviewed their basics. In this chapter, we'll delve into the details of a couple of extremely versatile data-bound controls that are a fixed presence in any real-world ASP.NET application—the *DataGrid* control in ASP.NET 1.x and the *GridView* control in ASP.NET 2.0 and newer versions.

Both controls render a multicolumn, templated grid and provide a largely customizable user interface with read/write options. In spite of the rather advanced programming interface and the extremely rich set of attributes, *DataGrid* and *GridView* controls simply generate an HTML table with interspersed hyperlinks to provide interactive functionalities such as sorting, paging, selection, and in-place editing.

Although they are customizable at will, grid controls feature a relatively rigid and inflexible graphical model. The data bound to a *DataGrid* or *GridView* is always rendered like a table, therefore, in terms of rows and columns. As we'll see later in the chapter, though, the contents of the cells in a column can be customizable to some extent using system-provided as well as user-defined templates.

The *DataGrid* is the principal control of most data-driven ASP.NET 1.x applications. Like all ASP.NET 1.x controls, the *DataGrid* is fully supported in ASP.NET 2.0 and newer versions, but it is partnered with a newer control that is meant to replace it in the long run. The new grid control, *GridView*, is complemented by other view controls, such as *DetailsView*, *FormView*, and only in ASP.NET 3.5 the *ListView* control. (We'll cover *ListView* in the next chapter and *DetailsView* and *FormView* in Chapter 13.) The *GridView* is a major upgrade of the ASP.NET 1.x *DataGrid* control. It provides the same basic set of capabilities, plus a long list of extensions and improvements.

In this chapter, we'll first take a look at the *DataGrid* capabilities and try to identify and discuss its major shortcomings and limitations. Then we'll consider the *GridView* control and its modified programming interface. For brand new ASP.NET 3.5 applications, choosing the *GridView* over the *DataGrid* is a no-brainer. For ASP.NET 1.x applications that are being maintained, a move to the *GridView* doesn't present any significant difficulties and such a move positions you well for future enhancements.

> **Note** I mentioned that the output of grid controls is an HTML table. It should be said that this represents just the default and most common option. By installing the CSS-friendly adapter toolkit, you can have grid controls to output HTML markup that makes no use of tables but resorts to cascading style sheet (CSS) style to define the data layout. For more information, check out the following white paper: *http://www.asp.net/cssadapters/whitepaper.aspx*. Note, though, that only the *GridView* control supports CSS adapters; the *DataGrid* always outputs HTML tables.

The *DataGrid* Control

The *DataGrid* is a column-based control that supports various types of data-bound columns, including text, templated, and command columns. You associate the control with a data source using either the *DataSource* or, in ASP.NET 2.0 and beyond, the *DataSourceID* property. The simplest way of displaying a table of data using the ASP.NET grid is as follows:

```
<asp:DataGrid runat="server" id="grid" />
```

Once the control has been placed into the page, you bind it to the data source and have it display the resulting markup.

The *DataGrid* Object Model

The *DataGrid* control provides a grid-like view of the contents of a data source. Each column represents a data source field, and each row represents a record. The *DataGrid* control supports several style and visual properties; in a more realistic scenario, the markup required to embed the control in a page is significantly larger and more complex so as to include all those attributes. In ASP.NET 2.0 and newer versions, themes can wrap control-specific visual settings and apply them seamlessly while leaving the markup as slim as possible.

Properties of the *DataGrid* Control

Table 11-1 lists the properties of the control, except those the control inherits from *Control* and *WebControl*.

TABLE 11-1 **Properties of the *DataGrid* Class**

Property	Description
AllowCustomPaging	Gets or sets whether custom paging is enabled. *AllowPaging* must be set to *true* for this setting to work.
AllowPaging	Gets or sets whether paging is enabled.
AllowSorting	Gets or sets whether sorting is enabled.
AlternatingItemStyle	Gets the style properties for alternating rows.
AutoGenerateColumns	Gets or sets whether columns are automatically created and displayed for each field in the data source. *True* by default.
BackImageUrl	Gets or sets the URL of the image to display as the background of the control.
Caption	The text to render in the control's caption. *Not available in ASP.NET 1.x.*
CaptionAlign	Alignment of the caption. *Not available in ASP.NET 1.x.*
CellPadding	Gets or sets the space (in pixels) remaining between the cell's border and the embedded text.
CellSpacing	Gets or sets the space (in pixels) remaining, both horizontally and vertically, between two consecutive cells.
Columns	Gets a collection of *DataGridColumn* objects.
CurrentPageIndex	Gets or sets the index of the currently displayed page.
DataKeyField	Gets or sets the key field in the bound data source.
DataKeys	Gets a collection that stores the key values of all records displayed as a row in the grid. The column used as the key is defined by the *DataKeyField* property.
DataMember	Indicates the specific table in a multimember data source to bind to the grid. The property works in conjunction with *DataSource*. If *DataSource* is a *DataSet* object, it contains the name of the particular table to bind.
DataSource	Gets or sets the data source object that contains the values to populate the control.
DataSourceID	Indicates the data source object to populate the control. *Not available in ASP.NET 1.x.*
EditItemIndex	Gets or sets the index of the grid's item to edit.
EditItemStyle	Gets the style properties for the item being edited.
FooterStyle	Gets the style properties for the footer section of the grid.
GridLines	Gets or sets whether all cells must have the border drawn.
HeaderStyle	Gets the style properties for the heading section of the grid.
HorizontalAlign	Gets or sets the horizontal alignment of the text in the grid.

Property	Description
Items	Gets the collection of the currently displayed items.
ItemStyle	Gets the style properties for the items in the grid.
PageCount	Gets the number of pages required to display all bound items.
PagerStyle	Gets the style properties for the paging section of the grid.
PageSize	Gets or sets the number of items to display on a single page.
SelectedIndex	Gets or sets the index of the currently selected item.
SelectedItem	Gets a *DataGridItem* object representing the selected item.
SelectedItemStyle	Gets the style properties for the currently selected item.
ShowFooter	Indicates whether the footer is displayed. *False* by default.
ShowHeader	Indicates the header is displayed. *True* by default.
UseAccessibleHeader	Indicates whether the control's header is rendered in an accessible format—that is, using <th> tags instead of <td>. *Not available in ASP.NET 1.x.*
VirtualItemCount	Gets or sets the virtual number of items in the *DataGrid* control when custom paging is used.

The characteristic traits of the *DataGrid* control are the *Columns* and *Items* collections, the style and data-binding properties. All columns in the grid are represented by an object with its own set of properties and methods. Several types of columns are available to implement the most common tasks. In general, not all rows in the bound data source are included in the HTML code for the client. The *Items* collection returns a collection of *DataGridItem* objects, one per each displayed row. The *DataGridItem* class is a specialized version of the *TableRow* class.

> **Note** In ASP.NET 2.0, a bunch of new properties make their debut to improve the usability of the control, especially for users with accessibility problems. *Caption*, *CaptionAlign*, and *UseAccessibleHeader* let you tweak the markup the control generates to make it easier for users of Assistive Technology devices to work with.

Constituent Elements of a *DataGrid*

The output of a *DataGrid* control is made of several constituent elements grouped in the *ListItemType* enumeration. Each element plays a clear role and has a precise location in the user interface of the control, as Figure 11-1 shows.

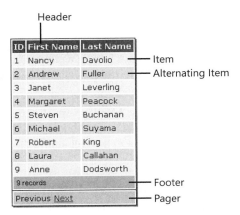

FIGURE 11-1 The layout of a *DataGrid* control.

The *DataGrid* user interface comprises the logical elements listed in Table 11-2. Each element has its own style property—that is, the set of graphical settings that are automatically applied by the control.

TABLE 11-2 Graphical Elements that Form a Data Grid

Item Type	Description
AlternatingItem	Represents a data-bound row placed in an odd position. Useful if you want to use different styles for alternating rows. *AlternatingItemStyle* is the property that lets you control the look and feel of the element.
EditItem	Represents the item currently displayed in edit mode. *EditItemStyle* lets you control the look and feel of the element.
Footer	Represents the grid's footer. The element can't be bound to a data source and is styled using the settings in the *FooterStyle* property.
Header	Represents the grid's header. The element can't be bound to a data source and is styled using the settings in the *HeaderStyle* property.
Item	Represents a data-bound row placed in an even position. Styled through the *ItemStyle* property.
Pager	Represents the pager element you use to scroll between pages. The element can't be bound to a data source and is styled using the settings in the *PagerStyle* property. The pager can be placed at the top or bottom of the grid's table and even in both places.
SelectedItem	Represents the item, or alternating item, currently selected. The property that defines its look and feel is *SelectedItemStyle*.

Each time one of the constituent elements is about to be created, the grid fires an *ItemCreated* event for you to perform some application-specific tasks. We'll return to grid events in a moment.

Data Source Rows and Displayed Rows

By design, the *DataGrid* control displays the data stored in a data source object—be it an enumerable data object or a data source control. Each row in the bound data source is potentially a row in the grid. However, this one-to-one mapping doesn't always correspond to reality. Each displayed grid row finds a place in the *Items* collection. Each element in the *Items* collection is an instance of the *DataGridItem* class—a slightly richer table row object—and supplies a *DataItem* property set to the object that corresponds to the row in the bound data source. Note that only bindable items are contained in the *Items* collection. The header, footer, and pager are not included in the collection.

The index properties of the *DataGrid* refer to the rows displayed rather than to the underlying data source. When the item with an index of 1 is selected, the second displayed item is selected, but this piece of information says nothing about the position of the corresponding source record. The data source index for the item object is stored in the *DataSetIndex* property on the *DataGridItem* class. *DataSetIndex* returns the absolute position in the overall data source of the record represented by the current item. Although functional, this method isn't especially handy in some common scenarios, such as when you want to select a row and retrieve a bunch of associated records. In such a case, you need to know the value of the key field in the underlying data source row.

The *DataKeys* collection and the *DataKeyField* property provide an effective shortcut designed specifically to work in similar situations. When you configure a *DataGrid*, you can store the name of a key field in the *DataKeyField* property. During the data-binding phase, the control extracts from the data source the values for the specified key field that correspond to the rows being displayed. As a result, the index of the selected row in the *Items* collection can be used with *DataKeys* to get the key value for the underlying data source row. Let's consider the following declaration, which refers to a grid that displays information about the employees of a company:

```
<asp:DataGrid runat="server" id="grid"
              DataKeyField="employeeid" ... >
```

To get the ID of the selected employee—to be used to implement, say, a drill-down view—you simply use the following code:

```
// empID is the key of the currently selected item
int empID = grid.DataKeys[grid.SelectedIndex];
```

The *DataKeys* collection is automatically filled by the control based on the value of the *DataKeyField* property and the bound data source.

Events of the *DataGrid* Control

The *DataGrid* control has no specific methods worth mentioning. Table 11-3 lists the events that the control fires during its life cycle.

TABLE 11-3 Events of the *DataGrid* Class

Event	Description
CancelCommand	The user clicked to cancel any updates made on the current item being edited.
DeleteCommand	The user clicked to start a delete operation on the current item.
EditCommand	The user clicked to put the current item in edit mode.
ItemCommand	The user clicked a command button within the grid control.
ItemCreated	This event occurs after a new grid item is created.
ItemDataBound	This event occurs after a grid item is bound to data.
PageIndexChanged	The user clicked to see a new page of data.
SelectedIndexChanged	The user clicked to select a different item.
SortCommand	The user clicked to start a sort operation on a column.
UpdateCommand	The user clicked to save any updates made on the current item being edited.

The *CancelCommand* and *UpdateCommand* events are fired under special circumstances—that is, when an item is being edited. (We'll cover the *DataGrid* in-place editing feature later in the chapter.) The *CancelCommand* event signals that the user clicked the Cancel button to cancel all pending changes. The *UpdateCommand* event denotes the user's intention to persist all the changes. The other command events—*EditCommand*, *DeleteCommand*, and *SortCommand*—indicate that the user required a particular action by clicking on command buttons within the user interface of the grid.

In addition to the events just listed, the *DataGrid* control fires all the standard events of Web controls, including *Load*, *Init*, *PreRender*, and *DataBinding*. In particular, you might want to write a handler for *PreRender* if you need to modify the HTML code generated for the grid. The *DataBinding* event, on the other hand, is the entry point in the grid's binding process. The event is fired as the first step before the whole binding process begins regardless of the type of object bound—be it an enumerable object or a data source control.

 Note These command events mark a key difference between the *DataGrid* and the newer *GridView* control. While the *DataGrid* is limited to firing an event to let the page know the user's intention, the *GridView* proactively handles the event by executing the configured command through the bound data source control. The *DataGrid* supports data source controls too, but the support is limited to showing read-only data.

Binding Data to the Grid

A *DataGrid* control is formed by data-bindable columns. By default, the control includes all the data source columns in the view. You can change this behavior by setting the *AutoGenerateColumns* property to *false*. In this case, only the columns explicitly listed in the *Columns* collection are displayed. The *DataGrid* control supports a variety of column types, which mostly differ from one another in how each represents the data. You are required to indicate the type of the column if you add it to the *Columns* collection; otherwise, if automatic generation is used, all columns are of the simplest type—the *BoundColumn* column type. Table 11-4 details the various types of columns supported.

TABLE 11-4 Types of Columns

Column Type	Description
BoundColumn	The contents of the column are bound to a field in a data source. Each cell displays as plain text.
ButtonColumn	Displays a button for each item in the column. The text of the button can be data-bound, and buttons have a common command name.
EditCommandColumn	Particular type of button column associated with a command named *Edit*. When in edit mode, the whole row is drawn using text boxes rather than literals.
HyperLinkColumn	Displays the contents of each item in the column as a hyperlink. The text of the hyperlink can be bound to a column in the data source or it can be static text. The target URL can be data-bound too. Clicking a hyperlink column causes the browser to jump to the specified URL.
TemplateColumn	This type displays each cell of the column following a specified ASP.NET template. It also allows you to provide custom behaviors.

Note that the *AutoGenerateColumns* property and the *Columns* collection are not mutually exclusive. If both properties are set to *true* and the collection is not empty, the grid will show the user-defined columns followed by all the ones that auto-generation would produce.

You normally bind columns using the *<columns>* tag in the body of the *<asp:datagrid>* server control, as the following code demonstrates:

```
<asp:datagrid runat="server" id="grid" ... >
   ...
  <columns>
    <asp:BoundColumn runat="server" DataField="employeeid"
        HeaderText="ID" />
    <asp:BoundColumn runat="server" DataField="firstname"
        HeaderText="First Name" />
    <asp:BoundColumn runat="server" DataField="lastname"
        HeaderText="Last Name" />
  </columns>
</asp:datagrid>
```

Alternately, you can create a new column of the desired class, fill its member properly, and then add the class instance to the *Columns* collection. Here is some code to add a *BoundColumn* object to a grid:

```
BoundColumn bc = new BoundColumn();
bc.DataField = "firstname";
bc.HeaderText = "First Name";
grid.Columns.Add(bc);
```

The order of the columns in the collection determines the order in which the columns are displayed in the *DataGrid* control.

> **Note** The *Columns* collection doesn't persist its contents to the view state, and it is empty whenever the page posts back. To preserve any dynamically added column, you need to re-add it on each and every postback.

Data-Bound Columns

All grid column types inherit from the *DataGridColumn* class and have a few common properties, such as the header text, footer and item style, and visibility flag. Table 11-5 details the properties shared by all types of columns.

TABLE 11-5 Common Properties for All Column Types

Property	Description
FooterStyle	Gets the style properties for the footer of the column
FooterText	Gets or sets the static text displayed in the footer of the column
HeaderImageUrl	Gets or sets the URL of an image to display in the header
HeaderStyle	Gets the style properties for the header of the column
HeaderText	Gets or sets the static text displayed in the header of the column
ItemStyle	Gets the style properties for the item cells of the column
SortExpression	Gets or sets the expression to sort the data in the column
Visible	Gets or sets whether the column is visible

The *BoundColumn* class represents a column type that is bound to a data field. The key properties to set up a grid column are *DataField*, which represents the name of the column to bind, and *DataFormatString*, which allows you to format the displayed text to some extent. The *ReadOnly* property has an effect only if an edit command column is added to the grid. In this case, the cells in the column are switched to edit mode according to the value of the property.

The following code snippet inserts two columns and specifies for each the header text and the source column. In addition, the second column is given a format string to make it look like a currency value with right alignment.

```
<asp:boundcolumn runat="server" datafield="quantityperunit"
    headertext="Packaging" />
<asp:boundcolumn runat="server" datafield="unitprice"
    headertext="Price" DataFormatString="{0:c}">
    <itemstyle width="80px" horizontalalign="right" />
</asp:boundcolumn>
```

Graphical settings for a column must be specified using a child style element.

HyperLink Columns

The *HyperLinkColumn* class is a column type that contains a hyperlink for each cell. The programmer can control the text of the hyperlink and the URL to navigate. Both fields can be bound to a column in the data source. The *DataTextField* takes the name of the field to use for the text of the hyperlink. *DataNavigateUrlField*, on the other hand, accepts the field that contains the URL. Another property, named *DataNavigateUrlFormatString*, defines the format of the final URL to use. By combining the two properties, you can redirect users to the same page, passing row-specific information on the query string, as shown in the following code:

```
<asp:hyperlinkcolumn runat="server" datatextfield="productname"
    headertext="Product"
    datanavigateurlfield="productid"
    datanavigateurlformatstring="productinfo.aspx?id={0}"
    target="ProductView">
    <itemstyle width="200px" />
</asp:hyperlinkcolumn>
```

The hyperlinks will point to the same page—productinfo.aspx—each with the product ID associated with the corresponding row of the bound data. The column class is responsible for building the real URL correctly.

Note By using the *DataNavigateUrlField* and *DataNavigateUrlFormatString* property together, you can make the URL of the hyperlink parametric. However, by default you are limited to just one parameter—the value of the field bound through the *DataNavigateUrlField* property. To use a hyperlink bound to any number of arguments, you should resort to templated columns or use a *GridView*.

Button Columns

The *ButtonColumn* class represents a command column and contains a user-defined button for each cell in the column. Functionally similar to hyperlink columns, button columns are different because they generate a postback event on the same URL. Although the caption of each button can be bound to a data-source column, more often than not a button column has static text displayed through all the cells.

The key idea behind the button column is that you execute a particular action after the user clicks on a row. All buttons in the column are associated with some script code that posts the page back and executes the *ItemCommand* server-side procedure. Within that procedure, you use the command name (*CommandName* property) to distinguish between multiple button columns and you use the *ItemIndex* property of the *DataGridItem* class to know about the particular row that was clicked. A reference to a *DataGridItem* object is passed through the *ItemCommand* event.

A special type of button column is the *select* column. It is a normal button column with the command name of *select*. When you click on such a column, the *DataGrid* automatically redraws the selected row using a different class of settings—those determined by the *SelectedItemStyle* property. There is no need for you to write an *ItemCommand* handler; the described behavior is built in.

```
<asp:ButtonColumn runat="server" text="Select" CommandName="Select" />
```

The style of the selected row—with, at most, one row selected at a time—is set using the *SelectedItemStyle* property. It can be as easy as the following code:

```
<selecteditemstyle backcolor="cyan" />
```

The change of the selected item is signaled with the *SelectedIndexChanged* event. However, before this event is fired, the application can handle the related *ItemCommand* event. When *SelectedIndexChanged* reaches the application, the *SelectedIndex* property indicates the new selected index.

Templated Columns

Templated columns allow you to create combinations of HTML text and server controls to design a custom layout for any cells in the column. The controls within a templated column can be bound to any combination of fields in the data source. In particular, you can group more fields in a single expression and even embellish it with HTML attributes such as bold-face or italic style. Templates are column-specific and cannot be applied to auto-generated columns. If you want more columns to share the same template, you can duplicate the code only in the ASP.NET page for each column.

A templated column is recognized by the *<TemplateColumn>* tag and rendered by the *TemplateColumn* class. The body of the tag can contain up to four different templates: *ItemTemplate*, *EditItemTemplate*, *HeaderTemplate*, and *FooterTemplate*. Just as with any other column type, a templated column can have header text and a sort expression. Templated columns, though, do not have an explicit data source field to bind. To bind a templated column to one or more data fields, you use a data-binding expression. (See Chapter 10.) In particular, you use the *Eval* method to evaluate data-bound expressions at run time and return the value properly cast. For example, the following code snippet shows a templated column that mimics the behavior of a *BoundColumn* object associated with the lastname column:

```
<asp:templatecolumn runat="server" headertext="Last Name">
    <itemtemplate>
        <asp:label runat="server" Text='<%#
            DataBinder.Eval(Container.DataItem, "lastname") %>' />
    </itemtemplate>
</asp:templatecolumn>
```

By using *DataBinder.Eval* (or simply *Eval* in ASP.NET 2.0 and beyond), you can access any number of fields in the currently bound data source. In addition, you can combine them in any order to obtain any sort of expression, which is otherwise impossible using a simpler bound or button column.

Working with the *DataGrid*

The *DataGrid* control is not simply a tool to display static data; it also provides advanced functionalities to page, sort, and edit bound data. The interaction that is established between a *DataGrid* and the host page is limited to exchanging notifications in the form of postback events. The *DataGrid* lets the page know that something happened and leaves the page free to react as appropriate. This pattern is common to most supported operations, with the notable exception of item selection. As mentioned, in fact, if you add a Select button column to the grid and define a proper style for selected items, clicking on a *select* button makes the page post back and forces the *DataGrid* to change the appearance of the corresponding row. Other operations for which the *DataGrid* simply fires an event to the page are paging, sorting, and in-place editing.

As you can see, these are relatively common operations that plenty of pages need to accomplish. If you choose to use a *DataGrid* control, be ready to write much more boilerplate code than you would with the newer *GridView* control.

Paging Through the Data Source

In real-world scenarios, the size of a data source easily exceeds the real estate of the page. Data paging is the contrivance that many applications adopt to both gain in scalability and present a more helpful page to the user. Especially on the Web, displaying only a few rows at a time is a more effective approach than downloading hundreds of records that stay hidden most of the time. The *DataGrid* control provides some built-in facilities to let the programmer easily switch to a new page according to the user's clicking.

The control needs to know how many items should be displayed per page, what type of functionality is required for the pager, and the data source to page through. In return for this, the control tracks the current page index, extracts the rows that fit into the particular page, and refreshes the user interface. Whenever the page index changes, an event is fired to the application—the *PageIndexChanged* event.

Note, however, that the host page is still responsible for ensuring that all the rows that fit into the new page are bound to the control. This holds true even if the *DataGrid* is bound to a data source control or a classic enumerable object. With a *DataGrid*, a handler for the *PageIndexChanged* event is always required. What you do in the handler might be different, though, depending on the actual data source. Here's the code you need to use if the *DataGrid* is bound to a data source control:

```
protected void grid_PageIndexChanged(
        object sender,
        DataGridPageChangedEventArgs e)
{
    grid.CurrentPageIndex = e.NewPageIndex;

    // Must be repeated to force a refresh
    grid.DataSourceID = "SqlDataSource1";
}
```

Note that you still need to reassign *DataSourceID* to trigger an internal data source changed event and cause the control to load its new data set. If the grid is bound to an enumerable object, you simply assign a new bunch of rows to the *DataSource* property.

Overall, paging is a tough feature and a potential scalability killer. If you leave grid controls in charge of handling paging more or less automatically, caching data is a must. A data source control makes it as easy as turning on the *EnableCaching* property, as you saw in Chapter 10. Caching a lot of data, though, might pose a serious problem, especially if you have to do that for each user.

DataGrid controls also support custom paging, an alternative and cost-effective approach to paging that binds to the control only the records that fit in the current page:

```
protected void grid_PageIndexChanged(
        object sender,
        DataGridPageChangedEventArgs e)
{
    grid.CurrentPageIndex = e.NewPageIndex;
    grid.DataSource = GetRecordsInPage(grid.CurrentPageIndex);
}
protected object GetRecordsInPage(int pageIndex)
{
    // Retrieve and return data that fits in the given page
    ...
}
```

As we'll see later, the *GridView* doesn't explicitly support custom paging. On the other hand, the *GridView* doesn't prevent server paging from working if it is supported by the underlying data source control or the data access layer (DAL).

Sorting Columns of Data

The *AllowSorting* property enables sorting on all or some of the *DataGrid*'s displayed columns. Just as for paging, clicking to sort data by a column doesn't really produce any visible effect unless you add a handler for the *SortCommand* event. Here's a simple handler you can use if the *DataGrid* is bound to a data source control:

```
protected void grid_SortCommand(
        object sender,
        DataGridSortCommandEventArgs e)
{
    SqlDataSource1.SelectCommand += " ORDER BY " + e.SortExpression;
    grid.DataSourceID = "SqlDataSource1";
}
```

Sorting is a potentially slow operation to accomplish and can have significant repercussions on scalability. For this reason, it is important to understand how it really works in the context of grids. In ASP.NET 1.x, you can employ in the *SortCommand* event handler only your own logic to sort. You can sort in memory using the *Sort* method of the *DataView* object (which is a very slow process, indeed); you can rely on the database sort capabilities (which is typically the fastest approach to sort data, but communication latency and network bandwidth might slow things down from the user's perspective); and sometimes you can also maintain presorted caches of data. Whatever approach you choose, you need to know what you're doing.

In ASP.NET 2.0 and beyond, data source controls tend to hide some details. If the data source control is configured to retrieve data via a *DataSet* (the default setting), sorting happens in memory via the *Sort* method. This approach is not really efficient, and it should be avoided unless you have only a few records to sort. If the data source control works via data readers and stored procedures, sorting can take place on the server and data will be returned in the correct order. In the end, sorting is a delicate operation no matter which controls you use. Only careful benchmarks and an application-specific combination of tools and options can deliver the perfect result. To get this, you need to understand how controls work internally.

Editing Existing Rows

A *DataGrid* control displays mostly read-only data. If editing is needed, you select the row to update and post a request for editing. The new page contains an edit form with input fields and links to persist or reject the changes. This pattern is probably the most effective one for editing data over the Web, and it's certainly the pattern that provides the highest level of flexibility. With *DataGrid* controls, though, a simpler model of data editing is possible. The new model is known as *in-place editing* and mimics the behavior of a Microsoft Office Excel worksheet. When you trigger the event that begins the editing phase, the visible part of the grid is redrawn and—like cells in Excel—the row selected for editing is rendered in a different way, using text-box controls instead of literals and labels. At the same time, the *DataGrid* control completes its own user interface with a couple of button links to allow you to commit or roll back changes.

In-place editing does not require much work to be completely set up, but at the same time it is not appropriate for all types of applications and not functional in all operating contexts. All in all, if you have to edit the content of single and relatively small tables that have no special validation or business logic to apply, in-place editing is extremely handy and powerful.

The key object for in-place editing is the *EditCommandColumn* class. The column adds a link button to all rows of the grid. When the link is clicked, the page posts back and the cells of the row are drawn in edit mode. How a column behaves in edit mode depends on the column type. For example, button and hyperlink columns are completely ignored in edit mode. Bound and templated columns, on the other hand, change their rendering when the row is being edited. In particular, bound columns are rendered using text boxes in place of literals, whereas templated columns display the contents of the *<EditItemTemplate>* section, if any.

As with paging and sorting, code is required to have the *DataGrid* complete an in-place editing operation too. You typically need to write three event handlers—*EditCommand*, to put the grid in edit mode; *CancelCommand*, to put the grid back in read-only mode; and *UpdateCommand*, to persist changes and refresh the grid. Handlers for *EditCommand* and *CancelCommand* are relatively simple and standard. Writing a handler for *UpdateCommand* might not be that easy, though.

Basically, the *UpdateCommand* handler must accomplish two key operations—retrieving input data and persisting changes. Both operations are hard-coded in the *GridView*, performed in collaboration with the underlying data source control, and mostly configured at design-time by the page author.

Important Admittedly, this section about *DataGrid* controls didn't get into the nitty-gritty details of how the control works and deliberately avoided describing how to implement paging, sorting, and editing properly in real-world scenarios. The reason for this approach lies in the structural difference that exists between *DataGrid* and *GridView* controls. To a large extent, the two controls provide the same set of abstract features—grid-like display, paging, sorting, editing, and templates. How each control implements individual features and binds to data is radically different. In one word, the *philosophy* behind each control is different. Now, the *GridView* control is newer, richer, and smarter, and it would probably have been the only grid control starting with ASP.NET 2.0 if it weren't for compatibility issues.

If you have an existing ASP.NET application to maintain, and you don't feel like leaping to *GridView*, you already know all the details and techniques omitted here. If you're building a new application and want to take advantage of grids, you don't need to know about *DataGrid* controls and are better off focusing entirely on *GridView* controls. The purpose of this section is to help people in the middle make a decision about which control to use while explaining why Microsoft decided to go with a new control that is designed to complement the changes in the data-binding model we explored in Chapter 10. The *GridView* control is also complemented by other view controls—specifically, *FormView*, *DetailsView*, and *ListView*—that we'll cover in the upcoming chapters.

The *GridView* Control

The *GridView* is the successor to the ASP.NET 1.x *DataGrid* control. It provides the same base set of capabilities, plus a long list of extensions and improvements. As mentioned, the *DataGrid*—which is still fully supported in ASP.NET 2.0—is an extremely powerful and versatile control. However, it has one big drawback: it requires you to write a lot of custom code, even to handle relatively simple and common operations such as paging, sorting, editing, or deleting data. The *GridView* control was designed to work around this limitation and make two-way data binding happen with as little code as possible. The control is tightly coupled to the family of new data source controls, and it can handle direct data source updates as long as the underlying data source object supports these capabilities.

This virtually codeless two-way data binding is by far the most notable feature of the new *GridView* control, but other enhancements are numerous. The control is an improvement over the *DataGrid* control because it has the ability to define multiple primary key fields, new column types, and style and templating options. The *GridView* also has an extended eventing model that allows you to handle or cancel events.

The *GridView* Object Model

The *GridView* control provides a tabular grid-like view of the contents of a data source. Each column represents a data source field, and each row represents a record. The class is declared as follows:

```
public class GridView : CompositeDataBoundControl,
                        ICallbackContainer,
                        ICallbackEventHandler
```

The base class ensures data-binding and naming-container support. The *ICallbackContainer* and *ICallbackEventHandler* interfaces provide more effective paging and sorting than is now supported. It does this through client-side, out-of-band calls that use the new script callback technology. (I'll talk more about this later, even though with the advent of AJAX it has lost most, if not all, of its original appeal.) Let's begin our tour of the *GridView* control by looking at the control's programming interface.

Properties of the *GridView* Control

The *GridView* supports a large set of properties that fall into the following broad categories: behavior, visual settings, style, state, and templates. Table 11-6 details the properties that affect the behavior of the *GridView*.

TABLE 11-6 Behavior Properties of the *GridView* Control

Property	Description
AllowPaging	Indicates whether the control supports paging.
AllowSorting	Indicates whether the control supports sorting.
AutoGenerateColumns	Indicates whether columns are automatically created for each field in the data source. The default is *true*.
AutoGenerateDeleteButton	Indicates whether the control includes a button column to let users delete the record that is mapped to the clicked row.
AutoGenerateEditButton	Indicates whether the control includes a button column to let users edit the record that is mapped to the clicked row.
AutoGenerateSelectButton	Indicates whether the control includes a button column to let users select the record that is mapped to the clicked row.
DataMember	Indicates the specific table in a multimember data source to bind to the grid. The property works in conjunction with *DataSource*. If *DataSource* is a *DataSet* object, it contains the name of the particular table to bind.
DataSource	Gets or sets the data source object that contains the values to populate the control.
DataSourceID	Indicates the bound data source control
EnableSortingAndPagingCallbacks	Indicates whether sorting and paging are accomplished using script callback functions. Disabled by default.
RowHeaderColumn	Name of the column to use as the column header. This property is designed for improving accessibility.
SortDirection	Gets the direction of the column's current sort.
SortExpression	Gets the current sort expression.
UseAccessibleHeader	Specifies whether to render *<th>* tags for the column headers instead of default *<td>* tags.

The *SortDirection* and *SortExpression* properties specify the direction and the sort expression on the column that currently determine the order of the rows. Both properties are set by the control's built-in sorting mechanism when users click a column's header. The whole sorting engine is enabled and disabled through the *AllowSorting* property. The *EnableSortingAndPagingCallbacks* property toggles on and off the control's capability of using script callbacks to page and sort without doing roundtrips to the server and changing the entire page.

Note This feature doesn't require ASP.NET AJAX Extensions 1.0, nor does it take advantage of the built-in AJAX engine available in ASP.NET 3.5. It is an AJAX-like, small, embedded framework for placing context-specific calls to the Web server using a proprietary engine based on the popular *XMLHttpRequest* object.

Each row displayed within a *GridView* control corresponds to a special type of grid item. The list of predefined types of items is nearly identical to that of the *DataGrid*, and it includes items such as the header, rows and alternating rows, footer, and pager. These items are static in the sense that they remain in place for the lifetime of the control in the application. Other types of items are active for a short period of time—the time needed to accomplish a certain operation. Dynamic items are the edit row, selected row, and *EmptyData* item. *EmptyData* identifies the body of the grid when the grid is bound to an empty data source.

Note The *GridView* control provides a few properties specifically designed for accessibility. They are *UseAccessibleHeader*, *Caption*, *CaptionAlign*, and *RowHeaderColumn*. When you set *RowHeaderColumn*, all the column cells will be rendered with the default header style (boldface type). However, *ShowHeader*, *HeaderStyle*, and other header-related properties don't affect the column indicated by *RowHeaderColumn*.

Table 11-7 details the style properties available on the *GridView* control.

TABLE 11-7 Style Properties of the *GridView* Control

Style	Description
AlternatingRowStyle	Defines the style properties for every other row in the table
EditRowStyle	Defines the style properties for the row being edited
FooterStyle	Defines the style properties for the grid's footer
HeaderStyle	Defines the style properties for the grid's header
EmptyDataRowStyle	Defines the style properties for the empty row, which is rendered when the *GridView* is bound to empty data sources
PagerStyle	Defines the style properties for the grid's pager
RowStyle	Defines the style properties for the rows in the table
SelectedRowStyle	Defines the style properties for the currently selected row

Table 11-8 lists most of the properties that affect the appearance of the control, and Table 11-9 details the templating properties.

TABLE 11-8 Appearance Properties of the *GridView* Control

Property	Description
BackImageUrl	Indicates the URL to an image to display in the background
Caption	The text to render in the control's caption
CaptionAlign	Alignment of the caption text
CellPadding	Indicates the amount of space (in pixels) between the contents of a cell and the border
CellSpacing	Indicates the amount of space (in pixels) between cells
EmptyDataText	Indicates the text to render in the control when it is bound to an empty data source
GridLines	Indicates the gridline style for the control
HorizontalAlign	Indicates the horizontal alignment of the control on the page
PagerSettings	References an object that lets you set the properties of the pager buttons
ShowFooter	Indicates whether the footer row is displayed
ShowHeader	Indicates whether the header row is displayed

The *PagerSettings* object groups together all the visual properties you can set on the pager. Many of these properties should sound familiar to *DataGrid* programmers. The *PagerSettings* class also adds some new properties to accommodate new predefined buttons (first and last pages), and it uses images instead of text in the links. (You need to figure out a trick to do the same with a *DataGrid*.)

TABLE 11-9 Templating Properties of the *GridView* Control

Template	Description
EmptyDataTemplate	Indicates the template content to be rendered when the control is bound to an empty source. This property takes precedence over *EmptyDataText* if both are set. If neither is set, the grid isn't rendered if bound to an empty data source.
PagerTemplate	Indicates the template content to be rendered for the pager. This property overrides any settings you might have made through the *PagerSettings* property.

The final block of properties—the state properties—is shown in Table 11-10. State properties return information about the internal state of the control.

TABLE 11-10 State Properties

Property	Description
BottomPagerRow	Returns a *GridViewRow* object that represents the bottom pager of the grid.
Columns	Gets a collection of objects that represent the columns in the grid. The collection is always empty if columns are auto-generated.
DataKeyNames	Gets an array that contains the names of the primary key fields for the currently displayed items.
DataKeys	Gets a collection of *DataKey* objects that represent the values of the primary key fields set in *DataKeyNames* for the currently displayed records.
EditIndex	Gets and sets the 0-based index that identifies the row currently rendered in edit mode.
FooterRow	Returns a *GridViewRow* object that represents the footer.
HeaderRow	Returns a *GridViewRow* object that represents the header.
PageCount	Gets the number of pages required to display the records of the data source.
PageIndex	Gets and sets the 0-based index that identifies the currently displayed page of data.
PageSize	Indicates the number of records to display on a page.
Rows	Gets a collection of *GridViewRow* objects that represent the data rows currently displayed in the control.
SelectedDataKey	Returns the *DataKey* object for the currently selected record.
SelectedIndex	Gets and sets the 0-based index that identifies the row currently selected.
SelectedRow	Returns a *GridViewRow* object that represents the currently selected row.
SelectedValue	Returns the explicit value of the key as stored in the *DataKey* object. Similar to *SelectedDataKey*.
TopPagerRow	Returns a *GridViewRow* object that represents the top pager of the grid.

The *GridView* is designed to leverage the new data source object model, and it works best when bound to a data source control via the *DataSourceID* property. The *GridView* also supports the classic *DataSource* property, but if you bind data in that way, some of the features (such as built-in updates and paging) become unavailable.

Events of the *GridView* Control

The *GridView* control doesn't have methods other than *DataBind*. As mentioned, though, in many situations you don't need to call methods on the *GridView* control. The data-binding process is started implicitly when you bind the *GridView* to a data source control.

Starting with ASP.NET 2.0, many controls, and the *Page* class itself, feature pairs of events of the type *doing/done*. Key operations in the control life cycle are wrapped by a pair of events—one firing before the operation takes place, and one firing immediately after the operation is completed. The *GridView* class is no exception. The list of events is shown in Table 11-11.

TABLE 11-11 Events Fired by the *GridView* Control

Event	Description
PageIndexChanging, *PageIndexChanged*	Both events occur when one of the pager buttons is clicked. They fire before and after the grid control handles the paging operation, respectively.
RowCancelingEdit	Occurs when the Cancel button of a row in edit mode is clicked, but before the row exits edit mode.
RowCommand	Occurs when a button is clicked.
RowCreated	Occurs when a row is created.
RowDataBound	Occurs when a data row is bound to data.
RowDeleting, *RowDeleted*	Both events occur when a row's Delete button is clicked. They fire before and after the grid control deletes the row, respectively.
RowEditing	Occurs when a row's Edit button is clicked but before the control enters edit mode.
RowUpdating, *RowUpdated*	Both events occur when a row's Update button is clicked. They fire before and after the grid control updates the row, respectively.
SelectedIndexChanging, *SelectedIndexChanged*	Both events occur when a row's Select button is clicked. The two events occur before and after the grid control handles the select operation, respectively.
Sorting, *Sorted*	Both events occur when the hyperlink to sort a column is clicked. They fire before and after the grid control handles the sort operation, respectively.

RowCreated and *RowDataBound* events are the same as the *DataGrid*'s *ItemCreated* and *ItemDataBound* events, with new names. They behave exactly as they do in ASP.NET 1.x. The same is true of the *RowCommand* event, which is the same as the *DataGrid*'s *ItemCommand* event.

The availability of events that announce a certain operation significantly enhances your programming power. By hooking the *RowUpdating* event, you can cross-check what is being updated and validate the new values. Likewise, you might want to handle the *RowUpdating* event to HTML-encode the values supplied by the client before they are persisted to the underlying data store. This simple trick helps you to fend off script injections.

Simple Data Binding

The following code demonstrates the simplest way to bind data to a *GridView* control. The data source object keeps the page virtually code-free.

```
<asp:ObjectDataSource ID="MySource" runat="server"
    TypeName="Core35.DAL.Customers"
    SelectMethod="LoadAll">
</asp:ObjectDataSource>
<asp:GridView runat="server" id="grid" DataSourceID="MySource"  />
```

Setting the *DataSourceID* property triggers the binding process, which runs the data source query and populates the user interface of the grid. You need not write any binding code. (Note that you still have to write the *LoadAll* method and the data access layer it calls.)

By default, the *GridView* control auto-generates enough columns to contain all the data coming through the data source. In other cases, you might want to control and style each column individually. For this to happen, the binding process should be refined a little bit.

Binding Data to a *GridView* Control

If no data source property is set, the *GridView* control doesn't render anything. If an empty data source object is bound and an *EmptyDataTemplate* template is specified, the results shown to the user have a more friendly look:

```
<asp:gridview runat="server" datasourceid="MySource">
   <emptydatatemplate>
      <asp:label runat="server">
         There's no data to show in this view.
      </asp:label>
   </emptydatatemplate>
</asp:gridview>
```

The *EmptyDataTemplate* property is ignored if the bound data source is not empty. Figure 11-2 shows the output generated by the empty template.

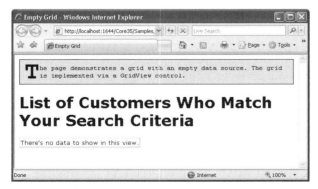

FIGURE 11-2 The *GridView* in action on an empty data source.

When you use a declared set of columns, the *AutoGenerateColumns* property of the grid is typically set to *false*. However, this is not a strict requirement—a grid can have declared and auto-generated columns. In this case, declared columns appear first. Note also that auto-generated columns are not added to the *Columns* collection. As a result, when column auto-generation is used, the *Columns* collection is typically empty.

Configuring Columns

The *Columns* property is a collection of *DataControlField* objects. The *DataControlField* object is akin to the *DataGrid*'s *DataGridColumn* object, but it has a more general name because these field objects can be reused in other data-bound controls that do not necessarily render columns. (For example, in the *DetailsView* control, the same class is used to render a row.)

You can define your columns either declaratively or programmatically. In the latter case, you just instantiate any needed data field objects and add them to the *Columns* collection. The following code adds a data-bound column to the grid:

```
BoundField field = new BoundField();
field.DataField = "companyname";
field.HeaderText = "Company Name";
grid.ColumnFields.Add(field);
```

Columns of data are displayed in the order that the column fields appear in the collection. To statically declare your columns in the *.aspx* source file, you use the *<Columns>* tag, as shown here:

```
<columns>
    <asp:boundfield datafield="customerid" headertext="ID" />
    <asp:boundfield datafield="companyname" headertext="Company Name" />
</columns>
```

Table 11-12 lists the column field classes that can be used in a *GridView* control. All the classes inherit *DataControlField*.

TABLE 11-12 Supported Column Types in *GridView* Controls

Type	Description
BoundField	Default column type. Displays the value of a field as plain text.
ButtonField	Displays the value of a field as a command button. You can choose the link or the push button style.
CheckBoxField	Displays the value of a field as a check box. It is commonly used to render Boolean values.
CommandField	Enhanced version of *ButtonField*, represents a special command such as Select, Delete, Insert, or Update. It's rarely useful with *GridView* controls; the field is tailormade for *DetailsView* controls. (*GridView* and *DetailsView* share the set of classes derived from *DataControlField*.)

Type	Description
HyperLinkField	Displays the value of a field as a hyperlink. When the hyperlink is clicked, the browser navigates to the specified URL.
ImageField	Displays the value of a field as the *Src* property of an *<img>* HTML tag. The content of the bound field should be the URL to the physical image.
TemplateField	Displays user-defined content for each item in the column. You use this column type when you want to create a custom column field. The template can contain any number of data fields combined with literals, images, and other controls.

Table 11-13 lists the main properties shared by all column types.

TABLE 11-13 Common Properties of *GridView* Columns

Property	Description
AccessibleHeaderText	The text that represents abbreviated text read by screen readers of Assistive Technology devices.
FooterStyle	Gets the style object for the column's footer.
FooterText	Gets and sets the text for the column's footer.
HeaderImageUrl	Gets and sets the URL of the image to place in the column's header.
HeaderStyle	Gets the style object for the column's header.
HeaderText	Gets and sets the text for the column's header.
InsertVisible	Indicates whether the field is visible when its parent data-bound control is in insert mode. This property does not apply to *GridView* controls.
ItemStyle	Gets the style object for the various columns' cells.
ShowHeader	Indicates whether the column's header is rendered.
SortExpression	Gets and sets the expression used to sort the grid contents when the column's header is clicked. Typically, this string property is set to the name of the bound data field.

The properties listed in the table represent a subset of the properties that each column type actually provides. In particular, each type of column defines a tailormade set of properties to define and configure the bound field. Refer to the MSDN documentation for details on the programming interface of *GridView*'s column types.

Bound Fields

The *BoundField* class represents a field that is displayed as plain text in a data-bound control such as *GridView* or *DetailsView*. To specify the field to display, you set the *DataField* property to the field's name. You can apply a custom formatting string to the displayed value by setting the *DataFormatString* property. The *NullDisplayText* property lets you specify alternative text to display should the value be *null*. Finally, by setting the *ConvertEmptyStringToNull* property to *true*, you force the class to consider empty strings as null values.

A *BoundField* can be programmatically hidden from view through the *Visible* property, while the *ReadOnly* property prevents the displayed value from being modified in edit mode. To display a caption in the header or footer sections, set the *HeaderText* and *FooterText* properties, respectively. You can also choose to display an image in the header instead of text. In this case, you set the *HeaderImageUrl* property.

Button Fields

A button field is useful to put a clickable element in a grid's column. You typically use a button field to trigger an action against the current row. A button field represents any action that you want to handle through a server-side event. When the button is clicked, the page posts back and fires a *RowCommand* event. Figure 11-3 shows a sample.

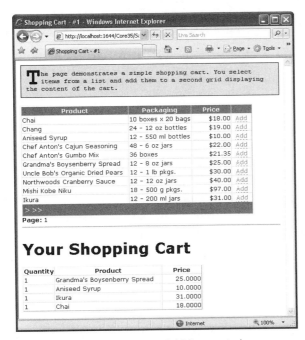

FIGURE 11-3 Button fields in a *GridView* control.

The following listing shows the markup code behind the grid in the figure:

```
<asp:GridView ID="GridView1" runat="server" DataSourceID="SqlDataSource1"
    AutoGenerateColumns="false" AllowPaging="true"
    OnRowCommand="GridView1_RowCommand">
    <HeaderStyle backcolor="gray" font-bold="true" height="200%" />
    <PagerStyle backcolor="gray" font-bold="true" height="200%" />
    <PagerSettings Mode="NextPreviousFirstLast" />
    <Columns>
        <asp:BoundField datafield="productname"
            headertext="Product" />
        <asp:BoundField datafield="quantityperunit"
            headertext="Packaging" />
        <asp:BoundField datafield="unitprice"
            headertext="Price"
            htmlencode="false"
            DataFormatString="{0:c}">
            <itemstyle width="80px" horizontalalign="right" />
        </asp:BoundField>
        <asp:ButtonField buttontype="Button" text="Add" CommandName="Add" />
    </Columns>
</asp:GridView>
```

Product information is displayed using a few *BoundField* objects. The sample button column allows you to add the product to the shopping cart. When users click the button, the *RowCommand* server event is fired. In case multiple button columns are available, the *CommandName* attribute lets you figure out which button was clicked. The value you assign to *CommandName* is any unique string that the code-behind class can understand. Here's an example:

```
void GridView1_RowCommand(object sender, GridViewCommandEventArgs e)
{
    if (e.CommandName.Equals("Add"))
    {
        // Get the index of the clicked row
        int index = Convert.ToInt32(e.CommandArgument);

        // Create a new shopping item and add it to the cart
        AddToShoppingCart(index);
    }
}
```

In the sample, the button column shows fixed text for all data items. You get this by setting the *Text* property on the *ButtonField* class. If you want to bind the button text to a particular field on the current data item, you set the *DataTextField* property to the name of that field.

You can choose different styles for the button—push, link, or image. To render the button as an image, do as follows:

```
<asp:buttonfield buttontype="Image" CommandName="Add"
    ImageUrl="/core35/images/cart.gif" />
```

To add a ToolTip to the button (or the image), you need to handle the *RowCreated* event. (I'll discuss this in more detail later in the chapter.)

> **Note** The *DataFormatString* property of the *BoundField* class doesn't work properly without the additional attribute *HtmlEncode="false"*. The reason is because ASP.NET first HTML-encodes the value of bound field and then applies the formatting. But at that point, the bound value is no longer affected by the specified format string. Enabling HTML-encoding earlier in the cycle is a security measure aimed at preventing cross-site scripting attacks.

HyperLink Fields

Hyperlink columns point the user to a different URL, optionally displayed in an inner frame. Both the text and URL of the link can be obtained from the bound source. In particular, the URL can be set in either of two ways: through a direct binding to a data source field or by using a hard-coded URL with a customized query string. You choose the direct binding if the URL is stored in one of the data source fields. In this case, you set the *DataNavigateUrlFields* property to the name of the column. In some situations, though, the URL to access is application specific and not stored in the data source. In this case, you can set the *DataNavigateUrlFormatString* property with a hard-coded URL and with an array of parameters in the query string, as follows:

```
<asp:HyperLinkField DataTextField="productname"
    HeaderText="Product"
    DataNavigateUrlFields="productid"
    DataNavigateUrlFormatString="productinfo.aspx?id={0}"
    Target="ProductView" />
```

When the user clicks, the browser fills the specified frame window with the contents of the *productinfo.aspx?id=xxx* URL, where *xxx* comes from the *productid* field. The URL can include multiple parameters. To include more data-bound values, just set the *DataNavigateUrlFields* property to a comma-separated list of field names. This behavior extends that of the *DataGrid*'s hyperlink column in that it supports multiple parameters.

The text of the hyperlink can be formatted too. The *DataTextFormatString* property can contain any valid markup and uses the {0} placeholder to reserve space for the data-bound value. (See Figure 11-4.)

FIGURE 11-4 Hyperlink fields in a *GridView* control.

Tip When choosing a target for the hyperlinked pages, you can also use any of the following standard targets: *_self*, *_parent*, *_new*.

CheckBox Fields

Although renamed, the column types we hitherto considered maintain an overall behavior that is very akin to that of analogous column types for *DataGrid*s. The *CheckBoxField* type, on the other hand, is a new entry in ASP.NET 2.0 and beyond and is limited to *GridView* and other view controls. The simplest way in which you can get a check-box column in ASP.NET 1.x (or in general for *DataGrid*s) is through templates.

The *CheckBoxField* column is a relatively simple bound column that displays a check box. You can bind it only to a data field that contains Boolean values. A valid Boolean value is a value taken from a column of type *Bit* in a SQL Server table (and analogous types in other databases) or a property of type *bool* if the control is bound to a custom collection. Any other form of binding will result in a parsing exception. In particular, you get an exception if you bind a *CheckBoxField* column to an integer property, thus implicitly assuming that 0 is false and a nonzero value is true. Figure 11-5 shows the *CheckBoxField* field type active within a *GridView* control.

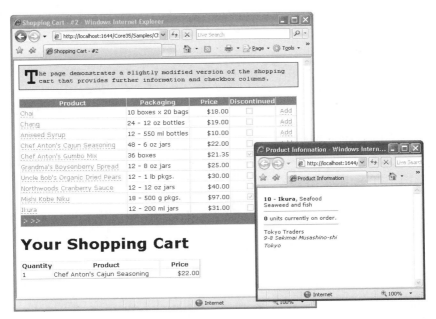

FIGURE 11-5 Check box fields in a *GridView* control.

Image Fields

The *ImageField* column type represents a field that is displayed as an image in a data-bound control. The cell contains an *<img>* element, so the underlying field must reference a valid URL. You can compose the URL at will, though. For example, you can use the *DataImageUrlField* to perform a direct binding where the content of the field fills the *Src* attribute of the *<img>* tag. Alternately, you can make the column cells point to an external page (or HTTP handler) that retrieves the bytes of the image from any source and passes them down to the browser. The following code illustrates this approach:

```
<Columns>
  <asp:ImageField DataImageUrlField="employeeid"
    DataImageUrlFormatString="showemployeepicture.aspx?id={0}"
    DataAlternateTextField="lastname">
    <ControlStyle Width="120px" />
  </asp:ImageField>
  <asp:TemplateField headertext="Employee">
    <ItemStyle Width="220px" />
    <ItemTemplate>
        <b><%# Eval("titleofcourtesy") + " " +
              Eval("lastname") + ", " +
              Eval("firstname") %></b> <br />
              <%# Eval("title")%>
              <hr />
              <i><%# Eval("notes")%></i>
    </ItemTemplate>
  </asp:templatefield>
</Columns>
```

Cells in the *ImageField* column are filled with the output of the next URL:

```
ShowEmployeePicture.aspx?id=xxx
```

Needless to say, *xxx* is the value in the *employeeid* field associated with *DataImageUrlField*. Interestingly enough, the alternate text can also be data bound. You use the *DataAlternateTextField* property. Figure 11-6 gives a sneak preview of the feature. The page in Figure 11-6 employs a template column to render the employee's information. I'll return to template columns in a moment.

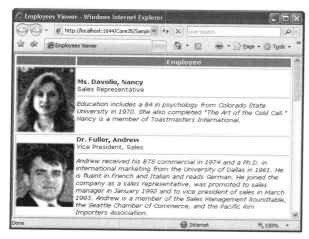

FIGURE 11-6 Image fields in a *GridView* control.

The following code demonstrates the world's simplest page to retrieve and then serve an image out of a database table:

```
void Page_Load(object sender, EventArgs e)
{
    int id = Convert.ToInt32(Request.QueryString["id"]);
    string connString = "...";
    string cmdText = "SELECT photo FROM employees WHERE employeeid=@empID";

    using (SqlConnection conn = new SqlConnection(connString))
    {
        SqlCommand cmd = new SqlCommand(cmdText, conn);
        cmd.Parameters.AddWithValue("@empID", id);
        byte[] img = null;
        conn.Open();

        try
        {
            img = (byte[])cmd.ExecuteScalar();
            if (img != null)
```

```
        {
            Response.ContentType = "image/png";
            Response.OutputStream.Write(img, EMP_IMG_OFFSET, img.Length);
        }
    }
    catch
    {
        Response.WriteFile("/proaspnet20/images/noimage.gif");
    }
    conn.Close();
}
```

The preceding code serves a standard image if the value of the field specified is *null*. You can obtain the same result by setting the *NullImageUrl* property if you're using direct binding—that is, not passing through an external page or handler.

> **Note** The EMP_IMG_OFFSET constant in the code snippet should normally be just 0. However, given the particular structure of the photo column of the Northwind's Employees database, it has to be 78. But, again, this is required only with that particular table.

Templated Fields

Figure 11-6 shows a customized column where the values of several fields are combined. This is exactly what you can get by using templates. A *TemplateField* column gives each row in the grid a personalized user interface that is completely defined by the page developer. You can define templates for various rendering stages, including the default view, in-place editing, the header, and the footer. The supported templates are listed in Table 11-14.

TABLE 11-14 Supported Templates

Template	Description
AlternatingItemTemplate	Defines the contents and appearance of alternating rows. If these items are not specified, the *ItemTemplate* is used.
EditItemTemplate	Defines the contents and appearance of the row currently being edited. This template should contain input fields and possibly validators.
FooterTemplate	Defines the contents and appearance of the row's footer.
HeaderTemplate	Defines the contents and appearance of the row's header.
ItemTemplate	Defines the default contents and appearance of the rows.

A templated view can contain anything that makes sense to the application you're building—server controls, literals, and data-bound expressions. Data-bound expressions allow you to insert values contained in the current data row. You can use as many fields as needed in a template. Notice, though, that not all templates support data-bound expressions. The header and footer templates are not data-bound, and any attempt to use expressions will result in an exception.

The following code shows how to define the item template for a product column. The column displays on two lines and includes the name of the product and some information about the packaging. You use data-bound expressions (which are discussed in Chapter 10) to refer to data fields.

```
<asp:templatefield headertext="Product">
    <itemtemplate>
        <b><%# Eval("productname")%></b> <br />
        available in <%# Eval("quantityperunit")%>
    </itemtemplate>
</asp:templatefield>
```

Figure 11-7 demonstrates template fields in action.

FIGURE 11-7 Template fields in a *GridView* control.

Note The *TemplateField* class also features an *InsertTemplate* property. However, this type of template is never used by the *GridView* control. *InsertTemplate* is used by the *FormView* control instead. As mentioned earlier, in ASP.NET, view controls share some field classes, such as *TemplateField*. As a result, *TemplateField* (and a few more classes) provides a superset of properties that serves the needs of multiple view controls. We'll cover the *FormView* control in Chapter 13.

Paging Data

The *GridView* is designed to take advantage of specific capabilities of the underlying data source control. In this way, the grid control can handle common operations on data such as sorting, paging, updating, and deleting. In general, not all data source components support all possible and feasible data operations. Data source components expose Boolean properties (such as the *CanSort* property) to signal whether they can perform a given operation.

> **Important** If a *GridView* control is bound to its data source through the *DataSource* property—that is, it doesn't leverage data source controls—its overall behavior as far as paging and other operations (for example, sorting, editing) are concerned is nearly identical to the *DataGrid* control. In this case, the *GridView* fires events and expects the binding code in the page to provide instructions and fresh data. In the remainder of the chapter, unless explicitly mentioned, we refer to a *GridView* bound to a data source control.

To some extent, the *GridView* makes transparent for the page developer the implementation of commonly required features such as sorting and paging. In most cases, you need only a fraction of the code you need with *DataGrid*; in some cases, no code at all is required. This said, don't forget what one old and wise proverb says—not all that glitters is gold. Put another way, be aware that the less code you write, the more you rely on the existing infrastructure to get things done. In doing so, you let the system make important decisions on your behalf. Paging and sorting are key operations in Web applications. You can still accept what the *GridView* does by default, but if you get to know exactly what happens under the hood, you have a better chance of diagnosing and fixing in a timely manner any performance problems that show up in the lifetime of the application.

Codeless Data Paging

The ability to scroll a potentially large set of data is an important but challenging feature for modern, distributed applications. An effective paging mechanism allows customers to interact with a database without holding resources. To enable paging on a *GridView* control, all you do is set the *AllowPaging* property to *true*. When the *AllowPaging* property is set to *true*, the grid displays a pager bar and prepares to detect a user's pager button clicks.

When a user clicks to see a new page, the page posts back, but the *GridView* traps the event and handles it internally. This marks a major difference between *GridView* and the *DataGrid* and programming model you might know from previous versions of ASP.NET. With the *GridView*, there's no need to write a handler for the *PageIndexChanged* event. The event is still exposed (and partnered with *PageIndexChanging*), but you should handle it only to perform extra actions. The *GridView* knows how to retrieve and display the requested new page. Let's take a look at the following control declaration:

```
<asp:GridView ID="GridView1" runat="server"
    DataSourceID="SqlDataSource1" AllowPaging="true" />
```

Any data *SqlDataSource1* binds to the grid is immediately pageable. As in Figure 11-8, the control displays a pager with a few predefined links (first, previous, next, and last) and automatically selects the correct subset of rows that fit in the selected page.

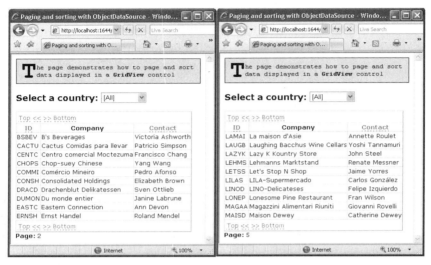

FIGURE 11-8 Moving through pages in a *GridView* control.

The default user interface you get with the *GridView* doesn't include the page number. Adding a page number label is as easy as writing a handler for the *PageIndexChanged* event:

```
protected void GridView1_PageIndexChanged(object sender, EventArgs e)
{
    ShowPageIndex();
}
private void ShowPageIndex()
{
    CurrentPage.Text = (GridView1.PageIndex + 1).ToString();
}
```

Once again, note that the *PageIndexChanged* handler is not involved with data binding or page selection as it is with *DataGrid*s. If you don't need any post-paging operation, you can blissfully omit it altogether.

What's the cost of this apparently free (and magical) paging mechanism?

The *GridView* control doesn't really know how to get a new page. It simply asks the bound data source control to return the rows that fit in the specified page. Paging is ultimately up to the data source control. When a grid is bound to a *SqlDataSource* control, paging requires that the whole data source be bound to the control. When a grid is bound to an *ObjectDataSource* control, paging depends on the capabilities of the business object you're connecting to.

Let's tackle *SqlDataSource* first. It is mandatory that you set *DataSourceMode* to *DataSet* (the default setting). This means that the whole data set is retrieved and only the few records that fit in the current page size are displayed. In an extreme scenario, you might end up down-loading 1000 records for each postback to show only 10. Things go much better if you en-able caching on *SqlDataSource* by setting *EnableCaching* to *true*. In this case, the whole data set is downloaded only once and stored in the ASP.NET cache for the specified duration. As long as the data stays cached, any page is displayed almost for free. However, a potentially large chunk of data is stored in memory. This option is therefore recommended only for rela-tively small sets of records shared by all users.

> **Tip** If you want to page records at the database level, the best that you can do is code the desired behavior in a stored procedure and bind the stored procedure to the *SelectCommand* property of the *SqlDataSource* control. In this case, turn caching off.

Moving the Burden of Paging to the DAL

As we discussed in Chapter 10, the *ObjectDataSource* control supplies a rather generic interface for paging that heavily relies on the capabilities of the underlying business and data access layers (DALs).

The key point is that you should have a paging-enabled business object. You configure the *ObjectDataSource* control based on the characteristics of your business object method. Once you have identified the select method, you overload it with a version that takes two extra parameters—the page size and start index for the page. In the end, the select method must be able to retrieve pages of records. In the declaration of the *ObjectDataSource* control, you set the *StartRowIndexParameterName* and *MaximumRowsParameterName* properties to the name of the method parameter that denotes the start index and page size, respectively.

One more step is needed to enable the *GridView* to page the data source provided by the *ObjectDataSource* control. You also need to set the *EnablePaging* property of *ObjectDataSource* to *true*:

```
<asp:ObjectDataSource ID="ObjectDataSource1" runat="server"
    EnablePaging="true"
    TypeName="Core35.DAL.Customers"
    StartRowIndexParameterName="firstRow"
    MaximumRowsParameterName="totalRows"
    SelectMethod="LoadByCountry">
    <SelectParameters>
        <asp:ControlParameter Name="country" ControlID="Countries"
            PropertyName="SelectedValue" />
    </SelectParameters>
</asp:ObjectDataSource>
```

```
<asp:GridView ID="GridView1" runat="server" AutoGenerateColumns="false"
    DataSourceID="ObjectDataSource1" AllowPaging="true"
    OnPageIndexChanged="GridView1_PageIndexChanged">
  <PagerSettings Mode="NextPreviousFirstLast" />
  <Columns>
      <asp:BoundField DataField="id" HeaderText="ID" />
      <asp:BoundField DataField="companyname" HeaderText="Company" />
      <asp:BoundField DataField="contactname" HeaderText="Contact" />
  </Columns>
</asp:GridView>
<b>Page: </b><asp:Label runat="server" ID="CurrentPage" />
```

In the preceding code, you explicitly specify only the parameters whose contents are important for the method to work. The two paging-related parameters are left to the *GridView* to set. The page size parameter is automatically bound to the *PageSize* property of the *GridView*; the first index to retrieve is determined by multiplying page size by page index. Here are the prototypes of the *LoadByCountry* method:

```
public static CustomerCollection LoadByCountry(string country) {
    LoadByCountry(country, -1, 0);
}
public static CustomerCollection LoadByCountry(string country,
        int totalRows, int firstRow) {
    // Retrieve the specified subset of records
}
```

The mechanics of *ObjectDataSource* doesn't say much about the effectiveness of the paging algorithm. How the business object actually retrieves the records in the requested page is an implementation and application-specific detail. In the sample code, *LoadByCountry* runs the original query and retrieves a data reader to the whole data set. Next, it discards all the records that don't fit in the specified range. This implementation is a good compromise between simplicity and effectiveness. It is not the best solution possible, but it's easy to implement and demonstrate. The memory consumption is limited to one record at a time, but the database returns the whole data set.

Paging Algorithms

The *GridView* doesn't support the *AllowCustomPaging* property you find on *DataGrid*s. However, customizing the paging algorithm is definitely possible. At its core, a custom paging algorithm provides a way to extract pages of records that minimizes caching of records. Ideally, you would ask the database to page the results of a particular query. Very few databases, though, support this feature. Several alternative approaches exist, with pros and cons.

A possible strategy entails creating temporary tables to select only the subset of records you really need. You build a stored procedure and pass it parameters to indicate the page size and index. Alternately, you can use nested SELECT commands and the TOP statement to retrieve all the records up to the last record in the requested page, reverse the order, and discard unneeded records. Again, the TOP clause is not common to all databases. Another possible approach based on dynamically built SQL code is discussed in the following blog post: *http://weblogs.sqlteam.com/jeffs/archive/2004/03/22/1085.aspx.*

If you can collaborate with the database administrator (DBA), you can require that an ad hoc column be added to index the queries. In this case, the DAL must guarantee that the values in the column form a regular succession of values and can be computable. The simplest way of accomplishing this is by giving the column progressive numbers.

Configuring the Pager

When the *AllowPaging* property is set to *true*, the grid displays a pager bar. You can control the characteristics of the pager to a large extent, through the *<PagerSettings>* and *<PagerStyle>* tags or their equivalent properties. The pager of the *GridView* control also supports first and last page buttons and lets you assign an image to each button. (This is also possible for *DataGrids*, but it requires a lot of code.) The pager can work in either of two modes—displaying explicit page numbers, or providing a relative navigation system. In the former case, the pager contains numeric links, one representing a page index. In the latter case, buttons are present to navigate to the next or previous page and even to the first or last page. The *Mode* property rules the user interface of the pager. Available modes are listed in the Table 11-15.

TABLE 11-15 Modes of a Grid Pager

Mode	Description
NextPrevious	Displays next and previous buttons to access the next and previous pages of the grid
NextPreviousFirstLast	Displays next and previous buttons plus first and last buttons to directly access first and last pages of the grid
Numeric	Displays numeric link buttons corresponding to the pages of the grid
NumericFirstLast	Displays numeric link buttons corresponding to the pages of the grid plus first and last buttons to directly access first and last pages of the grid

Ad hoc pairs of properties—*xxxPageText* and *xxxPageImageUrl*—let you set the labels for these buttons as desired. The *xxx* stands for any of the following: First, Last, Next, or Previous. Figure 11-9 shows a sample page in action.

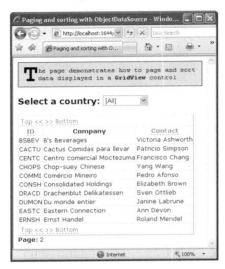

FIGURE 11-9 A pageable *GridView* with two pagers.

Depending on the size of the grid, the first and last rows in a grid might not necessarily fit in the screen real estate. To make it easier for users to page regardless of the scrollbar position, you can enable top and bottom pagers for a grid. You do this by setting the *Position* attribute on the *<PagerSettings>* element:

```
<PagerSettings Position="TopAndBottom" />
```

Other options are to display the pager only at the top or only at the bottom of the grid.

The pager of the *GridView* control can be entirely replaced with a new one, in case of need. (See Figure 11-10.) You do this by adding the *<PagerTemplate>* element to the control's declaration. Here's an example:

```
<PagerTemplate>
    <asp:Button ID="BtnFirst" runat="server" commandname="First"
        Text="First" />
    <asp:Button ID="BtnPrev" runat="server" commandname="Prev"
        Text="<<" />
    <asp:Button ID="BtnNext" runat="server" commandname="Next"
        Text=">>" />
    <asp:Button ID="BtnLast" runat="server" commandname="Last"
        Text="Last" />
</PagerTemplate>
```

To handle clicks on the buttons, you write a *RowCommand* event handler and set the page index explicitly:

```
void GridView1_RowCommand(object sender, GridViewCommandEventArgs e)
{
    if (e.CommandName == "Last")
        GridView1.PageIndex = GridView1.PageCount - 1;
    if (e.CommandName == "First")
        GridView1.PageIndex = 0;
    if (e.CommandName == "Next")
        GridView1.PageIndex ++;
    if (e.CommandName == "Prev")
        GridView1.PageIndex --;
}
```

Admittedly, this code is quite simple and should be fleshed out a little bit, at least to make it capable of disabling buttons when the first or last index is reached.

FIGURE 11-10 A pageable *GridView* with a custom pager.

Sorting Data

Sorting is a delicate, nonlinear operation that normally is quite expensive if performed on the client. Generally speaking, in fact, the best place to sort records is in the database environment because of the super-optimized code you end up running most of the time. Be aware of this as we examine the sorting infrastructure of the *GridView* control and data source controls. The *GridView* doesn't implement a sorting algorithm; instead, it relies on the data source control (or the page, if bound to an enumerable object) to provide sorted data.

Codeless Data Sorting

To enable the *GridView*'s sorting capabilities, you set the *AllowSorting* property to *true*. When sorting is enabled, the *GridView* gains the ability of rendering the header text of columns as links. You can associate each column with a sorting expression by using the *SortExpression* property. A sorting expression is any comma-separated sequence of column names. Each column name can be enriched with an order qualifier such as DESC or ASC. DESC indicates a descending order, while ASC denotes the ascending order. The ASC qualifier is the default; if the order qualifier value is omitted, the column is sorted in ascending order. The following code sets up the *GridView* column for sorting on the *productname* data source column:

```
<asp:GridView runat="server" id="MyGridView" DataSourceID="MySource"
    AllowSorting="true" AutoGenerateColumns="false">
    <Columns>
        <asp:BoundField datafield="productname" headertext="Product"
            sortexpression="productname" />
        <asp:BoundField datafield="quantityperunit"
            headertext="Packaging" />
    </Columns>
</asp:GridView>
```

Just as for paging, with a *GridView* no manually written code is required to make sorting work. If properly configured, the *GridView*'s sorting infrastructure works without further intervention and in a bidirectional way—that is, if you click on a column sorted in descending order, it is sorted in ascending order and vice versa. You need to add some custom code only if you want to implement more advanced capabilities such as showing a glyph in the header to indicate the direction. (I'll say more about that in a moment.)

Just as for paging, the main snag with sorting is how the underlying data source control implements it. Let's see what happens when the grid is bound to a *SqlDataSource* object. Other than setting *AllowSorting* to *true* and adding the sort expression to the sortable columns, no other action is required. (See Figure 11-11.)

When the user clicks to sort, the grid asks the *SqlDataSource* control to return sorted data. As mentioned, the *SqlDataSource* control returns a *DataSet* by default. If this is the case, the control retrieves the data, builds a *DataView* out of it, and calls the *DataView*'s *Sort* method. This approach works fine, but it's not exactly the fastest way you have to sort. You might still find it to be a good fit for your application, but be aware that sorting is performed using the Web server's memory. Combined with caching, both paging and sorting in memory are a feasible solution for shared and relatively small sets of records.

FIGURE 11-11 A sortable *GridView* control

Is there any chance to get pre-sorted data from the database server? The first step is to set the *DataSourceMode* property of the *SqlDataSource* control to *DataReader*. If you leave it set to *DataSet*, sorting will occur in memory. The second step requires you to write a stored procedure to retrieve data. To get data sorted, you also set the *SortParameterName* property of the data source control to the name of the stored procedure parameter that indicates the sort expression. Obviously, you need the stored procedure to build its command text dynamically to incorporate the proper *ORDER BY* clause. Here's how to modify the Northwind database's *CustOrderHist* stored procedure to make its results sortable at will:

```
CREATE PROCEDURE CustOrderHistSorted
      @CustomerID nchar(5), @SortedBy varchar(20)='total'  AS
SET QUOTED_IDENTIFIER OFF
IF @SortedBy = ''
BEGIN
   SET @SortedBy = 'total'
END

EXEC (
   'SELECT ProductName, Total=SUM(Quantity)  ' +
   'FROM Products P, [Order Details] OD, Orders O, Customers C ' +
   'WHERE C.CustomerID = "' + @CustomerID + '" ' +
   'AND C.CustomerID = O.CustomerID AND O.OrderID = OD.OrderID ' +
   'AND OD.ProductID = P.ProductID GROUP BY ProductName ' +
   'ORDER BY ' + @SortedBy)
GO
```

At this point, the grid is ready to show sorted columns of data and the burden of sorting has moved to the database management system (DBMS).

```
<asp:SqlDataSource ID="SqlDataSource1" runat="server"
    DataSourceMode="DataReader"
    ConnectionString='<%$ ConnectionStrings:NWind %>'
    SortParameterName="SortedBy"
    SelectCommand="CustOrderHistSorted"
    SelectCommandType="StoredProcedure">
  <SelectParameters>
    <asp:ControlParameter ControlID="CustList"
        Name="CustomerID" PropertyName="SelectedValue" />
  </SelectParameters>
</asp:SqlDataSource>
```

It is essential to know that sorting data on the database, as shown here, is incompatible with caching. You need to set *EnableCaching* to false, otherwise an exception is thrown. As a result, you go back to the database every time the user clicks to sort.

If you use the *DataSet* mode and enable caching, you initially get data from the database, sorted as expected, but successive sorting operations are resolved in memory. Finally, if you use the *DataSet* mode and disable caching, you still go down to the database for sorting each time. Note that this option is mentioned only for completeness: the effect is the same as using *DataReader*, but a data reader is a more efficient approach when caching is not required.

In general, the availability of the *SortParameterName* property opens up a world of possibility for sorting the contents of other data-bound controls (for example, *Repeater* and custom controls) that mostly consume data and don't require paging or caching.

Moving the Burden of Sorting to the DAL

What if you use an *ObjectDataSource* control instead? In this case, the burden of sorting should be moved to the DAL or business layer and exposed to the data source control by the programming interface of the bound business object. Let's modify the *LoadByCountry* method we considered earlier for paging and add to it a new parameter to indicate the sort expression:

```
public static CustomerCollection LoadByCountry(
    string country, int totalRows, int firstRow, string sortExpression)
{
    CustomerCollection coll = new CustomerCollection();
    using (SqlConnection conn = new SqlConnection(ConnectionString))
    {
        SqlCommand cmd;
```

```
        cmd = new SqlCommand(cmdLoadByCountry, conn);
        cmd.Parameters.AddWithValue("@country", country);
        if (!String.IsNullOrEmpty(sortExpression))
            cmd.CommandText += " ORDER BY " + sortExpression;

        conn.Open();
        SqlDataReader reader = cmd.ExecuteReader();
        HelperMethods.FillCustomerList(coll, reader, totalRows, firstRow);
        reader.Close();
        conn.Close();
    }
    return coll;
}
```

The *cmdLoadByCountry* constant represents the SQL command or stored procedure we use to retrieve data. As you can see, this implementation of the method simply adds an optional *ORDER BY* clause to the existing command. This might not be the best approach ever devised, but it certainly fits the bill of having the burden of sorting moved down to the DAL and from there to the database. At this point, you set the *SortParameterName* on the *ObjectDataSource* control to the method's parameter that determines the sorting—in this case, *sortExpression*:

```
<asp:ObjectDataSource ID="ObjectDataSource1" runat="server"
    EnablePaging="true"
    TypeName="Core35.DAL.Customers"
     SortParameterName="sortExpression"
     StartRowIndexParameterName="firstRow"
     MaximumRowsParameterName="totalRows"
     SelectMethod="LoadByCountry">
     <SelectParameters>
        ...
     </SelectParameters>
</asp:ObjectDataSource>
```

The advantage of this approach is that you take full control of the sorting machinery, and you can decide how, where, and when to implement it. You might have to write some code in your DAL for sorting, but consider that you only write highly focused code. In fact, no infrastructural code is required, as the machinery is set up for you by ASP.NET.

Note One more item worth mentioning about sorting on a *GridView* control is that you can cancel the sorting operation if need be. To do this, you write a handler for the *Sorting* event, get the event argument data (of type *GridViewSortEventArgs*), and set its *Cancel* property to *true*.

Give Users Feedback

The *GridView* control doesn't automatically add any visual element to the output that indicates the direction of the sorting. This is one of the few cases in which some coding is needed to complete sorting:

```
<script runat="server">
void GridView1_RowCreated (object sender, GridViewRowEventArgs e) {
    if (e.Row.RowType == DataControlRowType.Header)
        AddGlyph(sender as GridView, e.Row);
}

void AddGlyph(GridView grid, GridViewRow item) {
    Label glyph = new Label();
    glyph.EnableTheming = false;

    // This does assume you have this font installed. You might want to
    // consider using images in reality
    glyph.Font.Name = "webdings";
    glyph.Font.Size = FontUnit.Small;
    glyph.Text = (grid.SortDirection==SortDirection.Ascending ?"5" :"6");

    // Find the column you sorted by
    for(int i=0; i<grid.Columns.Count; i++) {
        string colExpr = grid.Columns[i].SortExpression;
        if (colExpr != "" && colExpr == grid.SortExpression)
            item.Cells[i].Controls.Add (glyph);
    }
}
</script>
```

The idea is that you write a handler for the *RowCreated* event and look for the moment when the header is created. Next you create a new *Label* control that represents the glyph you want to add. Where should the *Label* control be added?

The newly created *Label* control has font and text adequately set to generate a glyph (typically ▲ and ▼) that indicates the direction of the sorting. (The glyphs correspond to 5 and 6 in the Webdings font.) You must add it alongside the header text of the clicked column. The index of the column can be stored to the view state during the *Sorting* event. Alternately, it can simply be retrieved, comparing the current sort expression—the grid's *SortExpression* property—to the column's sort expression. Once you know the index of the column, you retrieve the corresponding table cells and add the *Label*:

```
item.Cells[i].Controls.Add (glyph);
```

The results are shown in Figure 11-12. If your page is based on a theme, the font of the *Label* control—essential for rendering the glyph correctly—might be overridden. To avoid that, you should disable theming support for the label control. The *EnableTheming* property does just that.

FIGURE 11-12 Enhancing the sorting capabilities of the *GridView* control.

Using Callbacks for Paging and Sorting

Both sorting and paging operations require a postback with subsequent full refresh of the page. In most cases, this is a heavy operation, as the page usually contains lots of graphics. To provide the user with a better experience, wouldn't it be nice if the grid could go down to the Web server, grab the new set of records, and update only a portion of the interface? Thanks to ASP.NET script callbacks—which I cover in greater detail in my other book, *Programming Microsoft ASP.NET 2.0 Applications: Advanced* Topics (Microsoft Press, 2006)—the *GridView* control is capable of offering this feature. All that you have to do is turn on the Boolean property *EnableSortingAndPagingCallbacks*.

As mentioned, the feature relies on the services of the ASP.NET script callback engine, which is designed to work also with non–Internet Explorer browsers, including Firefox, Netscape 6.x and newer, Safari 1.2, and the latest Opera browser.

Important As we'll see later in Chapter 19 and Chapter 20, the AJAX library makes this feature obsolete. Either via partial rendering or through direct calls to script services, flicker-free page updates are better implemented via AJAX than by using the ASP.NET Script Callback engine.

SqlDataSource vs. ObjectDataSource

A few considerations will help clarify when to use *SqlDataSource* and *ObjectDataSource* controls. First, remember that these data source controls are not the only two choices for developers to do sane data binding. By far, though, they are the most popular and commonly used. It is also essential to bear in mind that data binding in ASP.NET 2.0 and beyond is in no way limited to using data source controls. This said, *SqlDataSource* and *ObjectDataSource* are just tools in the ASP.NET toolbox and should be used if they're right for the job.

As I see things, *SqlDataSource* is optimized for a disconnected approach to data binding. It works at its best if you retrieve data through a *DataSet*. Only in this case are paging, sorting, and caching capabilities enabled. Of these three functionalities, only sorting is somehow replicable in data reader mode. If using *DataSet*s is fine for your application, using *SqlDataSource* is an excellent choice. It gives you ready-made solutions with mostly declarative code that is simple to write, but it's not necessarily effective in a real-world application. Put another way, using *SqlDataSource* in an application might be good for certain features, but it's hardly sufficient to power the whole DAL.

Should you instead realize that you need more control over paging and sorting operations (such as custom paging or server-side sorting), switching to *ObjectDataSource* appears to me to be a sounder idea. In this case, you start by designing and implementing a fully fledged DAL and, optionally, a business layer too. In this layer, you craft any capabilities you need to be supported from the grid—paging, sorting, or even data caching.

In addition, the *ObjectDataSource* control fully supports custom entity classes and custom collections. The support for generics in the .NET Framework makes writing custom collections a snap, and it significantly reduces the cost of writing a fully custom DAL built on made-to-measure and domain-specific objects. LINQ and related data source controls doesn't diminish the importance of *ObjectDataSource* and, especially, what lies behind it. You can use the LINQ syntax to work on data within the DAL or use LINQ as a replacement for the *SqlDataSource* control. LINQ doesn't kill the DAL; instead, it is a smart option to use to build parts of it.

Editing Data

A major strength of the *GridView* control—which makes up for a major shortcoming of the *DataGrid*—is the ability to handle updates to the data source. The *DataGrid* control provides only an infrastructure for data editing. The *DataGrid* provides the necessary user interface elements and fires appropriate events when the user modifies the value of a certain data field, but it does not submit those changes back to the data source. Developers are left with the disappointing realization that they have to write a huge amount of boilerplate code to really persist changes.

With the *GridView* control, when the bound data source supports updates, the control can automatically perform this operation, thus providing a truly out-of-the-box solution. The data source control signals its capability to update through the *CanUpdate* Boolean property.

Much like the *DataGrid*, the *GridView* can render a column of command buttons for each row in the grid. These special command columns contain buttons to edit or delete the current record. With the *DataGrid*, you must explicitly create an edit command column using a special column type—the *EditCommandColumn* class. The *GridView* simplifies things quite a bit for update and delete operations.

In-Place Editing and Updates

In-place editing refers to the grid's ability to support changes to the currently displayed records. You enable in-place editing on a grid view by turning on the *AutoGenerateEditButton* Boolean property:

```
<asp:gridview runat="server" id="GridView1" datasourceid="MySource"
    autogeneratecolumns="false" autogenerateeditbutton="true">
  ...
</asp:gridview>
```

When the *AutoGenerateEditButton* property is set to *true*, the *GridView* displays an additional column, like that shown in Figure 11-13. By clicking the Edit button, you put the selected row in edit mode and can enter new data at will.

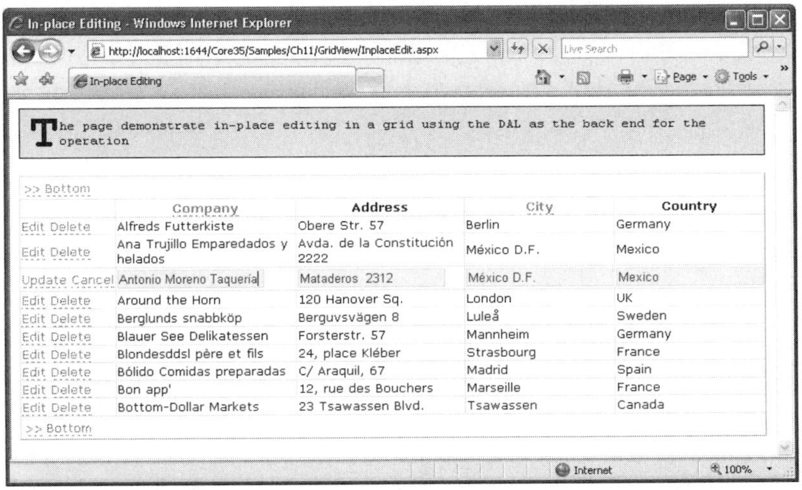

FIGURE 11-13 A *GridView* that supports in-place editing.

To abort editing and lose any changes, users simply click the *Cancel* button. The *GridView* can handle this click without any external support; the row returns to its original read-only state; and the *EditIndex* property takes back its -1 default value—meaning no row is currently being edited. But what if users click the update link? The *GridView* first fires the *RowUpdating* event and then internally checks the *CanUpdate* property on the data source control. If *CanUpdate* returns false, an exception is thrown. *CanUpdate* returns false if the data source control has no update command defined.

Suppose your grid is bound to a *SqlDataSource* object. To persist changes when the user updates, you have to design your code as follows:

```
<asp:sqldatasource runat="server" ID="EmployeesSource"
    ConnectionString="<%$ ConnectionStrings:NWind %>"
    SelectCommand="SELECT employeeid, firstname, lastname FROM employees"
    UpdateCommand="UPDATE employees SET
            firstname=@firstname, lastname=@lastname
            WHERE employeeid=@original_employeeid">
</asp:sqldatasource>
<asp:gridview runat="server" id="GridView1" datasourceid="EmployeesSource"
    AutoGenerateColumns="false"
    DataKeyNames="employeeid" AutoGenerateEditButton="true">
    <columns>
        <asp:boundfield datafield="firstname" headertext="First" />
        <asp:boundfield datafield="lastname" headertext="Last" />
    </columns>
</asp:gridview>
```

The *UpdateCommand* attribute is set to the SQL command to use to perform updates. When you write the command, you declare as many parameters as needed. However, if you stick with a particular naming convention, parameter values are automatically resolved. Parameters that represent fields to update (such as *firstname*) must match the name of *DataField* property of a grid column. The parameter used in the WHERE clause to identify the working record must match the *DataKeyNames* property—the key for the displayed records. The *original_XXX* format string is required for identity parameters. You can change this scheme if you want through the *OldValuesParameterFormatString* property on the data source control.

The successful completion of an update command is signaled throughout the grid via the *RowUpdated* event.

> **Note** The *GridView* collects values from the input fields and populates a dictionary of name/value pairs that indicate the new values for each field of the row. The *GridView* also exposes a *RowUpdating* event that allows the programmer to validate the values being passed to the data source object. In addition, the *GridView* automatically calls *Page.IsValid* before starting the update operation on the associated data source. If *Page.IsValid* returns false, the operation is canceled. This is especially useful if you're using a custom template with validators.

If the grid is bound to an *ObjectDataSource* control, things go a bit differently. The bound business object must have an update method. This method will receive as many arguments as it needs to work. You can decide to pass parameters individually or grouped in a unique data structure. This second option is preferable if you have a well-done DAL. Here's an example:

```
<asp:ObjectDataSource ID="CustomersSource" runat="server"
    TypeName="Core35.DAL.Customers"
    SelectMethod="LoadAll"
    UpdateMethod="Save"
    DataObjectTypeName="Core35.DAL.Customer">
</asp:ObjectDataSource>
<asp:GridView ID="GridView1" runat="server" DataSourceID="CustomersSource"
    DataKeyNames="id" AutoGenerateColumns="false">
    AutoGenerateEditButton="true"
    <Columns>
        <asp:BoundField DataField="companyname" HeaderText="Company" />
        <asp:BoundField DataField="street" HeaderText="Address" />
        <asp:BoundField DataField="city" HeaderText="City" />
    </Columns>
</asp:GridView>
```

The *Save* method can have the following prototype and implementation:

```
public static void Save(Customer cust)
{
    using (SqlConnection conn = new SqlConnection(ConnectionString))
    {
        SqlCommand cmd = new SqlCommand(cmdSave, conn);
        cmd.Parameters.AddWithValue("@id", cust.ID);
        cmd.Parameters.AddWithValue("@companyname", cust.CompanyName);
        cmd.Parameters.AddWithValue("@city", cust.City);
        cmd.Parameters.AddWithValue("@address", cust.Street);
        ...

        conn.Open();
        cmd.ExecuteNonQuery();
        conn.Close();
        return;
    }
}
```

The physical SQL command (or stored procedure) to run is nothing more than a classic UPDATE statement with a list of SET clauses. The *DataObjectTypeName* attribute indicates the name of a class that the *ObjectDataSource* uses for a parameter in a data operation.

Note If you set the *DataObjectTypeName* property, all data methods can either be parameterless or accept an object of the specified type. This happens regardless of whether you declaratively fill the parameters collection for the method. The *DataObjectTypeName* property takes precedence over parameter collections.

Deleting Displayed Records

From the *GridView*'s standpoint, deleting records is not much different from updating. In both cases, the *GridView* takes advantage of a data source's ability to perform data operations. You enable record deletion by specifying a value of *true* for the *AutoGenerateDeleteButton* property. The *GridView* renders a column of buttons that, if clicked, invokes the delete command for the row on the bound data source control. The data source method is passed a dictionary of key field name/value pairs that are used to uniquely identify the row to delete.

```
<asp:sqldatasource runat="server" ID="EmployeesSource"
    ConnectionString="<%$ ConnectionStrings:NWind %>"
    SelectCommand="SELECT employeeid, firstname, lastname FROM employees"
    UpdateCommand="UPDATE employees SET
            firstname=@firstname, lastname=@lastname
            WHERE employeeid=@original_employeeid"
    DeleteCommand="DELETE employees WHERE
                employeeid=@original_employeeid" />
```

The *GridView* doesn't provide any feedback about the operation that will take place. Before proceeding, it calls *Page.IsValid*, which is useful if you have a custom template with validators to check. In addition, the *RowDeleting* event gives you another chance to programmatically control the legitimacy of the operation.

The delete operation fails if the record can't be deleted because of database-specific constraints. For example, the record can't be deleted if child records refer to it through a relationship. In this case, an exception is thrown.

To delete a record through an *ObjectDataSource* control, you give your business object a couple of methods, as follows:

```
public static void Delete(Customer cust)
{
    Delete(cust.ID);
}
public static void Delete(string id)
{
    using (SqlConnection conn = new SqlConnection(ConnectionString))
    {
        SqlCommand cmd = new SqlCommand(cmdDelete, conn);
        cmd.Parameters.AddWithValue("@id", id);
        conn.Open();
        cmd.ExecuteNonQuery();
        conn.Close();
        return;
    }
}
```

Overloading the delete method is not mandatory, but it can be useful and certainly make your DAL more flexible and easier to use.

Inserting New Records

In its current form, the *GridView* control doesn't support inserting data against a data source object. This omission is a result of the *GridView* implementation and not the capabilities and characteristics of the underlying data source. In fact, all data source controls support an insert command property. As you'll see in Chapter 13, the insertion of new records is a scenario fully supported by the *DetailsView* and *FormView* control.

In older versions of ASP.NET, a common practice to make *DataGrid* controls support record insertions entails that you modify the footer or the pager to make room for empty text boxes and buttons. The *GridView* supports the same model and makes it slightly simpler through the *PagerTemplate* property as far as the pager is concerned. Modifying the contents of the footer is possible through the *RowCreated* event (which I'll say more about in a moment). Note, though, that if the grid is bound to an empty data set, the footer bar is hidden. What if you want your users to be able to add a new record to an empty grid? Resort to the *EmptyDataTemplate*, as follows:

```
<emptydatatemplate>
    <asp:label ID="Label1" runat="server">
      There's no data to show in this view.
      <asp:Button runat="server" ID="btnAddNew" CommandName="AddNew"
          Text="Add New Record" />
    </asp:label>
</emptydatatemplate>
```

To trap the user's click of the button, you write a handler for the *RowCommand* event:

```
void Gridview1_RowCommand(object sender, GridViewCommandEventArgs e)
{
    if (e.CommandName == "AddNew")
    { ... }
}
```

Advanced Capabilities

To complete the overview of the *GridView* control, we just need to take a look at a couple of common programming scenarios—drill-down and row customization. A grid presents a list of items to the user; in many cases, the user needs to select one of those items and start an operation on it. As discussed earlier, button columns exist to facilitate this task. We'll delve deeper into this topic in a moment. Row customization is another common feature, which gives you a chance to modify the standard rendering of the grid. You can edit the row layout, add or remove cells, or modify visual attributes on a per-row basis so that certain rows show up distinctly from others (for example, rows representing negative values).

Executing an Operation on a Given Row

Let's return to a problem that we briefly mentioned earlier in the chapter while discussing button columns. Imagine you're building an e-commerce application; one of your pages shows a grid of products with buttons for users to add products to their shopping cart. You add a button column and write a handler for the *RowCommand* event:

```
void GridView1_RowCommand(object sender, GridViewCommandEventArgs e)
{
    if (e.CommandName.Equals("Add"))
    {
        // Get the index of the clicked row
        int index = Convert.ToInt32(e.CommandArgument);

        // Create a new shopping item and add it to the cart
        AddToShoppingCart(index);
    }
}
```

This is where we left off earlier. Let's go one step further now and expand the code for *AddToShoppingCart*. What's the purpose of this method? Typically, it retrieves some information regarding the clicked product and stores that in the data structure that represents the shopping cart. In the sample code, the shopping cart is a custom collection named *ShoppingCart*:

```
public class ShoppingCart : List<ShoppingItem>
{
    public ShoppingCart()
    {
    }
}
```

ShoppingItem is a custom class that describes a purchased product. It contains a few properties—product ID, product name, price per unit, and quantity purchased. The shopping cart is stored in the session state and exposed through a pagewide property named *MyShoppingCart*:

```
protected ShoppingCart MyShoppingCart
{
    get
    {
        object o = Session["ShoppingCart"];
        if (o == null) {
            InitShoppingCart();
            return (ShoppingCart) Session["ShoppingCart"];
        }
        return (ShoppingCart) o;
    }
}
```

```
private void InitShoppingCart()
{
    ShoppingCart cart = new ShoppingCart();
    Session["ShoppingCart"] = cart;
}
```

At its core, the goal of *AddToShoppingCart* is merely that of creating a *ShoppingItem* object filled with the information of the clicked product. How would you retrieve that information?

As you can see, the *GridView* stores the index of the clicked row in the *CommandArgument* property of the *GridViewCommandEventArgs* structure. This information is necessary but not sufficient for our purposes. We need to translate that index into the key of the product behind the grid's row. Better yet, we need to translate the grid row index into a data set index to retrieve the data item object rendered in the clicked grid's row.

The *DataKeyNames* property of the *GridView* indicates the names of the data fields to persist in the view state to be retrieved later during postback events, such as *RowCommand*. Implemented as a string array, *DataKeyNames* is the *GridView*'s counterpart of the *DataKeyField* of *DataGrid* controls. It carries the value of the primary key for a displayed row in a *DataGrid* and a slew of properties for a *GridView*.

```
<asp:GridView ID="GridView1" runat="server"
    DataSourceID="SqlDataSource1"
    DataKeyNames="productid,productname,unitprice" ... />
```

How many fields should you list in *DataKeyNames*? Consider that every field you list there takes up some view-state space. On the other hand, if you limit yourself to storing only the primary key field, you need to run a query to retrieve all the data you need. Which approach is better depends on what you really need to do. In our sample scenario, we need to make a copy of a product that is already cached in the Web server's memory. There's no need to run a query to retrieve data we already know. To fill a *ShoppingItem* object, you need the product ID, name, and unit price:

```
private void AddToShoppingCart(int rowIndex)
{
    DataKey data = GridView1.DataKeys[rowIndex];
    ShoppingItem item = new ShoppingItem();
    item.NumberOfItems = 1;
    item.ProductID = (int) data.Values["productid"];
    item.ProductName = data.Values["productname"].ToString();
    item.UnitPrice = (decimal) data.Values["unitprice"];
    MyShoppingCart.Add(item);

    ShoppingCartGrid.DataSource = MyShoppingCart;
    ShoppingCartGrid.DataBind();
}
```

The values of the fields listed in *DataKeyNames* are packed in the *DataKeys* array—an old acquaintance for *DataGrid* developers. *DataKeys* is an array of *DataKey* objects. *DataKey*, in turn, is a sort of ordered dictionary. You access the values of the persisted fields through the *Values* collection as shown in the preceding code.

For user-interface purposes, the contents of the shopping cart are bound to a second *GridView* so that users can see what's in their basket at any time. The binding takes place through the classic *DataSource* object. Look back to Figure 11-3 for a view of this feature.

> **Caution** Each grid row gets bound to a data item—a row from the data source—only when the control is rendered out. A postback event such as *RowCommand* fires before this stage is reached. As a result, the *DataItem* property of the clicked *GridViewRow* object—where the data we need is expected to be—is inevitably null if accessed from within the *RowCommand* handler. That's why you need *DataKeyNames* and the related *DataKeys* properties.

Selecting a Given Row

A more general mechanism to select clicked rows can be implemented through a special command button—the select button. As with delete and edit buttons, you bring it on by setting the *AutoGenerateSelectButton* Boolean property. To fully take advantage of the selection feature, it is recommended that you also add a style for selected rows:

```
<asp:GridView ID="GridView1" runat="server" ... >
   <SelectedRowStyle BackColor="cyan" />
   ...
</asp:GridView>
```

When users click a select-enabled button, the page receives a more specific *SelectedIndexChanged* event. Some properties such as *SelectedIndex*, *SelectedRow*, and *SelectedDataKey* are updated too. For completeness, note that when a row is selected the page first receives a *RowCommand* event, and later it is reached by the *SelectedIndexChanged* event. When *RowCommand* fires, though, none of the select properties is updated yet.

The following code shows how to rewrite the previous example to add to the cart the product being selected:

```
protected void GridView1_SelectedIndexChanged(object sender, EventArgs e)
{
    AddToShoppingCart();
}
private void AddToShoppingCart()
{
    DataKey data = GridView1.SelectedDataKey;
```

```
ShoppingItem item = new ShoppingItem();
item.NumberOfItems = 1;
item.ProductID = (int) data.Values["productid"];
item.ProductName = data.Values["productname"].ToString();
item.UnitPrice = (decimal) data.Values["unitprice"];
MyShoppingCart.Add(item);

ShoppingCartGrid.DataSource = MyShoppingCart;
ShoppingCartGrid.DataBind();
}
```

As you can see, there's no need to pass the row index, as the corresponding *DataKey* object is served by the *SelectedDataKey* property. (See Figure 11-14.)

FIGURE 11-14 Adding the selected item to the shopping cart.

Row Customization

Want a quick example of why it's often important to render grid rows in a customized way? Take a look at Figure 11-14. The user just added to the cart a product that has been discontinued. Wouldn't it be nice if you could disable any rows matching certain criteria or, more simply, customize the row layout according to runtime conditions? Let's see how to do it.

There are two *GridView* events that are essential for the task—*RowCreated* and *RowDataBound*. The former is fired when any grid row is being created—whether it's a header, footer, item, alternating item, pager, and so on. The latter fires when the newly created row is bound to its data item—that is, the corresponding record in the bound data source. The *RowDataBound* event is not fired for all rows in the grid, but only for those that represent bound items. No event fires for the header, footer, and pager.

As a first example, let's see how to disable the Select link for rows where the *Discontinued* field returns *true*. In this case, you need a handler to *RowDataBound* because the required customization depends on the values on the bound data row. As mentioned, this information is not available yet when *RowCreated* fires.

```
void GridView1_RowDataBound(object sender, GridViewRowEventArgs e)
{
    if (e.Row.RowType == DataControlRowType.DataRow)
    {
        object dataItem = e.Row.DataItem;
        bool discontinued = (bool) DataBinder.Eval(dataItem,
            "discontinued");
        e.Row.Enabled = !discontinued;
    }
}
```

In general, you start by checking the type of the row. To be precise, this test is not strictly necessary for a *RowDataBound* event, which fires only for data rows. The data item—that is, the corresponding record—is retrieved through the *DataItem* property of the *GridViewRow* object. Next, you retrieve the field of interest and apply your logic. You might not know in advance the type of the data object bound to the row. The *DataBinder.Eval* method is a generic accessor that works through reflection and regardless of the underlying object. If you want to disable the whole row (and contained controls), you can turn off the *Enabled* property of the grid row object. To access a particular control, you need to find your way in the grid's object model. Here's how to access (and disable) the Select link alone:

```
((WebControl)e.Row.Cells[0].Controls[0]).Enabled = !discontinued;
```

This code works because in the sample grid the Select link is always the first control in the first cell of each data row. Figure 11-15 shows the previous product list with discontinued products disabled.

Once you gain access to the grid row object model, you can do virtually whatever you want.

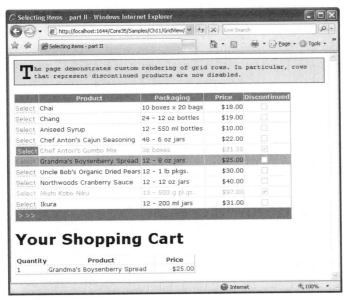

FIGURE 11-15 The rows corresponding to discontinued products are now disabled.

Conclusion

In this chapter, we examined the grid controls available in ASP.NET—*DataGrid* and the newer *GridView*. Grids are a type of component that all Web applications need to employ in one shape or another. All Web applications, in fact, at a certain point of their life cycle are called to display data. More often than not, this data is in tabular format.

As long as the data to be displayed can be articulated in rows and columns, a grid is ideal for displaying it. Such controls provide facilities to select and edit single rows, page through a bound data source, and sort views. In addition, you can customize all the cells in a column by using any data-bound template made of any combination of HTML and ASP.NET text. To top it off, a fair number of events signal to user applications the key events in the control's life cycle.

The in-place editing feature is a piece of cake to use, as it is powerful and easy to configure. Even though this type of editing—designed to resemble Excel worksheets—is not appropriate for all applications and pages, as long as you can functionally afford the feature, in-place editing can save you a lot of coding and increase productivity by at least one order of magnitude.

Why are there two grid controls in ASP.NET 2.0 and beyond? Let's state the answer clearly— the *DataGrid* control is supported mostly for backward compatibility. If you're writing a new ASP.NET application, choosing to use the *GridView* is a no-brainer. The *GridView* has a newer and more effective design and totally embraces the data-binding model of newest versions of ASP.NET. The key shortcoming of ASP.NET 1.x data binding is that it requires too much code for common, relatively boilerplate operations. This has been addressed with the introduction of data source controls. But data source controls require richer data-bound controls that are capable of working with the new model. This explains why ASP.NET now offers a brand-new control—the *GridView*—rather than just enhancing the existing *DataGrid*.

In the upcoming chapters, we'll cover controls named *ListView*, *DetailsView*, and *FormView*—the perfect complements to the *GridView*. The latter two controls, in particular, fill another hole in the ASP.NET data toolbox, as they offer a smart interface for displaying individual records.

Just The Facts

- ASP.NET comes with two grid controls—*DataGrid* and *GridView*. The *DataGrid* works like in ASP.NET 1.x, whereas the *GridView* has a newer and more effective design and totally embraces the new data-binding model of ASP.NET.

- The *GridView* supports more column types including check box and image columns.

- The *GridView* provides paging, sorting, and editing capabilities, and it relies on the bound data source control for effective implementation. If bound to an enumerable data source object (ASP.NET 1.x-style binding), it behaves like a *DataGrid* control.

- If bound to a *SqlDataSource* control, the *GridView* heavily relies on the capabilities of the *DataSet* capabilities for paging and sorting data in memory.

- If bound to a *LinqDataSource* control, the *GridView* relies on the capabilities of the specified LINQ command.

- If bound to an *ObjectDataSource* control, the *GridView* requires a fully fledged DAL that contains any custom logic for paging, sorting, and, sometimes, caching.

- Compared to the *DataGrid* control, the *GridView* provides an extended eventing model: pre/post pairs of events, the possibility of canceling ongoing operations, and more events.

- To retrieve information about a clicked row, you use the *CommandArgument* property of the event data structure to get the index and the newest version of the *DataKeys* collection to access selected field on the data item. With *DataGrid*, you can select only the primary key field and need to run a query to access row data in drill-down scenarios.

Chapter 12
Managing a List of Records

In ASP.NET 3.5, the family of data-bound controls that allow you to view bound data adds a new member—the *ListView* control. *ListView* joins *GridView*, *DetailsView*, and *FormView* to form a complete offering to developers wanting to build rich data-bound Web pages that are both functional to use and flexible enough to be quickly customized.

As a completely new control in ASP.NET, *ListView* sums up the features of multiple view controls in a single one. For example, it can be used to create a tabular view of data nearly identical to that you can obtain from a *GridView* or *DataGrid* control. At the same time, the *ListView* control can be employed to generate a multicolumn layout with the flexibility that only a general-purpose *Repeater* or, better yet, *DataList* control can offer.

The *ListView* control doesn't only have similarities with other controls; it also has a number of unique features that, when evaluated from a wider perspective, make similarities shine under a different light. *ListView* uses similarities with other controls as the starting point for building more advanced and unique capabilities that warrant it having its own space in the toolbox of ASP.NET 3.5 controls.

In this chapter, we'll focus on exploring the programming interface of the *ListView* control and its usage in a variety of common scenarios.

The *ListView* Control

The control is fully template-based and allows you to control all aspects of the user interface via templates and properties. *ListView* operates in a way that closely resembles the behavior of existing data-bound controls, such as *FormView* or *DataList*. However, unlike these controls, the *ListView* control never creates any user-interface layout. Every markup tag that the control generates is entirely under the developer's control, including header, footer, body, item, selected item, and so on.

The *ListView* control binds to any data source control and executes its set of data operations. It can page, update, insert, and delete data items in the underlying data source as long as the data source supports these operations. In most cases, no code is required to set up any of these operations. If code is required, you can also explicitly bind data to the control using the more traditional *DataSource* property and related *DataBind* method.

The rendering capabilities of the *ListView* control make it suitable for publishing scenarios where a read-only, but compelling, user interface is needed. The control also works great in editing scenarios even though it lacks some advanced features such as input validation or made-to-measure edit templates for particular types of data or foreign keys.

The *ListView* Object Model

Data binding and template support are the principal characteristics of the *ListView* control that are most obvious when you examine the control's programming model. From the programmer's perspective, the key thing to be aware of is that you need to specify at least two template properties for the *ListView* control to compile and work. They are *LayoutTemplate* and *ItemTemplate*. In addition, the overall layout template must expose a connection point to the control so that bound records can be merged into the final markup.

Properties of the *ListView* Control

The *ListView* layout supports several properties that fall into two main categories: behavior and templates. It also supports a few general ASP.NET control properties and binding properties. Table 12-1 lists the behavioral properties.

TABLE 12-1 *ListView* **Behavior Properties**

Property	Description
ConvertEmptyStringToNull	Boolean value, indicates whether empty string values are automatically converted to null values when any contents edited in the control's interface are saved back to the data source.
EditIndex	Gets or sets the index of the item being edited.
EditItem	Gets the item that is currently in edit mode within a *ListView* control. The type of the item is *ListViewItem*.
GroupItemCount	Gets or sets the number of items to display per group.
GroupPlaceholderID	Gets or sets the ID of the page element where the content for the *ListView* groups will be placed. The placeholder must be a server element flagged with the *runat* attribute. If a value for this property is not specified, a value of *groupPlaceholder* is assumed.
InsertItem	Gets the item that is currently in insert mode within a *ListView* control. The type of the item is *ListViewItem*.

Property	Description
InsertItemPosition	Gets or sets the location of the insert template. Feasible values are defined in the *InsertItemPosition* enumerated type: *FirstItem*, *LastItem*, or *None*.
ItemPlaceholderID	Gets or sets the ID of the page element that will host data-bound items. The placeholder must be a server element flagged with the *runat* attribute. If this property is not specified, a value of *ItemPlaceholder* is assumed.
Items	Gets the collection of bound items.
SelectedDataKey	Gets the data-key array of values for the selected item. This value coincides with *SelectedValue* except when multiple key fields are used.
SelectedIndex	Gets or sets the index of the currently selected item.
SelectedValue	Gets the data-key value of the first key field of the selected item.
SortDirection	Gets the sort direction of the field or fields being sorted.
SortExpression	Gets the sort expression that is associated with the field or fields being sorted.

Two properties in this list are somewhat new even to seasoned ASP.NET developers. They are *ItemPlaceholderID* and *GroupPlaceholderID*. When you are using groups to represent bound items, the group placeholder is the server-side ASP.NET control that when added to the layout template indicates where the group will be rendered. Similarly, the item placeholder indicates where bound items will be rendered. You add the item placeholder to the item template or to the group template if you are using groups.

The key thing about the *ListView* control is its full support for templates and the subsequent highly flexible rendering engine. Table 12-2 lists the templates the control supports.

TABLE 12-2 *ListView* **Template Properties**

Property	Description
AlternatingItemTemplate	Indicates the template used to render every other bound item. If this property is not specified, all items are usually rendered using the item template. The alternating item template usually contains the same controls and content as the item, but with a different style to distinguish items.
EditItemTemplate	Indicates the template to use for editing each bound item. The edit template usually contains input controls to update the values of the bound record. An edit template should also contain buttons to save and discard changes.

Property	Description
EmptyDataTemplate	Indicates the template to render when the data source bound to the ListView control is empty. When this happens, the empty data template is rendered instead of the layout template. Note, though, that the InsertItemTemplate takes precedence if InsertItemPosition is not set to None.
EmptyItemTemplate	Indicates the template to render when there are no more data items to display in the last group.
GroupSeparatorTemplate	Indicates the template used to put custom content between each group in the ListView control.
GroupTemplate	Indicates the template used to create a tiled layout for the contents of the ListView control. In a tiled layout, the items are repeated horizontally in a row according to the value of the GroupItemCount property.
InsertItemTemplate	Indicates the template to use for inserting a new data item. The insert template contains input controls to gather data to initialize a new record. An insert template should also contain buttons to save and discard changes.
ItemSeparatorTemplate	Indicates the template used to specify the content for the separator between the items of a ListView control.
ItemTemplate	Indicates the template to use to render items bound to the control.
LayoutTemplate	Indicates the template to render the root container of any contents displayed through the ListView control. This template is required.
SelectedItemTemplate	Indicates the template used to render the currently selected data item.

In addition to the properties listed in Table 12-1 and Table 12-2, the *ListView* control has a number of data-binding properties, including *DataKeyNames*, *DataSource*, *DataSourceID*, and *DataMember*.

The *DataKeyNames* property specifies the fields that represent the primary key of the data source. When you set this property declaratively, you use a comma-separated list of field names. The underlying type is an array of strings. Strictly related to *DataKeyNames* is *DataKeys*. This property contains an object that identifies the unique key for each item that is currently displayed in the *ListView* control. Through the *DataKeys* collection, you can access the individual values that form the primary key for each displayed record.

DataSource and *DataSourceID* provide two mutually exclusive ways of bringing data inside of the control. The *DataSource* property represents an enumerable collection of bindable records; the *DataSourceID* property points to a data source control in the page that does the entire job of retrieving and binding data. Starting with ASP.NET 2.0, all data controls can be bound to a data source control, but not all of them can fully leverage the capabilities of a data source control. Only view controls such as *GridView* and *DetailsView* can, for example, update the record in the data source or page and sort based on the capabilities of the under-lying data source. Older data-bound controls, such as *DataList*, support only the read-only interface of data source controls. In this regard, the *ListView* control is a specialization of the *DataList* control that does provide full support for the capabilities of the underlying data source control.

Finally, because the *ListView* control inherits from *WebControl*, it features a bunch of user-interface properties, including *Style*, *CssClass*, *SkinID*, *Visible*, and *EnableTheming*.

> **Note** The *ListView* control lacks the usual ton of style properties that characterize all other view controls in ASP.NET. The output of the *ListView* control can be styled at your leisure, but only by using cascading style sheets (CSS) directly, without even the mediation from ASP.NET themes.
>
> This is intentional for a number of reasons. First, the control benefits from the momentum that CSS-based layouts are gaining in the industry. Second, Microsoft Visual Studio 2008 comes with a superb CSS editor through which editing and attaching styles to HTML elements is a breeze. Finally, the extreme flexibility of the markup generated by the *ListView* control, would be hindered in several ways by ASP.NET themes. Themes work with entire ASP.NET controls, whereas the *ListView* control is an ASP.NET control that generates its output based on a template that is, when all is said and done, made of pure HTML you control at a fine-grained level.

Events of the *ListView* Control

The *ListView* control has no specific methods worth mentioning. Table 12-3 lists the events that the control fires during its life cycle.

TABLE 12-3   **Events of the *ListView* Class**

Event	Description
ItemCanceling	Occurs when the user requests a cancel operation, but before the control cancels the ongoing insert or edit operation.
ItemCommand	Occurs when the user clicks on any buttons found in the body of the control.
ItemCreated	Occurs when a new item in the *ListView* control is being created.
ItemDataBound	Occurs when an item is bound to its data.
ItemDeleting, ItemDeleted	The two events occur before and after, respectively, the deletion of an item. The operation is requested by the interface of the *ListView* control.
ItemEditing	Occurs when an edit operation is requested, but before the *ListView* switches to the edit template.
ItemInserting, ItemInserted	The two events occur before and after, respectively, the insertion of an item. The operation is requested by the interface of the *ListView* control.

Event	Description
ItemUpdating, ItemUpdated	The two events occur before and after, respectively, the update of an item. The operation is requested by the interface of the *ListView* control.
LayoutCreated	Occurs when the layout template is created.
PagePropertiesChanging, PagePropertiesChanged	The two events occur before and after, respectively, the properties of a page of data in the *ListView* control change. A page of data is the set of items that form a page in a paged *ListView* control. Page properties include page size and start row index.
SelectedIndexChanging, SelectedIndexChanged	The two events occur before and after, respectively, the *ListView* control handles the selection of a displayed item and switches to the selected-item template.
Sorting, Sorted	The two events occur before and after, respectively, the associated data source is sorted.

As you can see, most of the events are related to the life cycle of individual data items. You can control when an item is created, deleted, inserted, or edited. Events fire before and after a given operation is accomplished. So you find doing/done pairs of events for each fundamental operation, such as *ItemInserting/ItemInserted* or *ItemDeleting/ItemDeleted* events. You can determine which item type is being created by using the *ItemType* property on the event data structure. Feasible values are *DataItem*, *InsertItem*, and *EmptyItem*. These values belong to the *ListViewItemType* enumerated type.

The *ListView* control also features typical events of ASP.NET controls such as *Init*, *Load*, *PreRender*, *DataBinding*, and *Unload*. You can handle these event the same way you handle them for other ASP.NET controls.

> **Note** The *ItemCommand* event fires only if the original click event is not handled by a predefined method. This typically occurs if you define custom buttons in one of the templates. You do not need to handle this event to intercept any clicking on the Edit or Insert buttons.

Compared to Other View Controls

The view controls introduced with previous versions of ASP.NET solved many problems that developers were facing every day. Controls such as *GridView* and *DetailsView* make it a snap to create a list of records and even arrange a master/detail view. However, they offer limited control over the actual markup generated. Want an example? With a *GridView* control, placing a *TBODY* tag around the group of child rows is not a trivial task. And it is almost impossible to do with a *DataGrid* control, unless you resort to your most advanced skills and take on the tough task of deriving a custom grid control.

On the other hand, adapting the final markup to the actual needs would be quite a simple task if the view controls introduced with ASP.NET 2.0 provided a bit more programmatic control over the rendering process and templating. This is just one of the key capabilities you gain with the *ListView* control. As you'll see in a moment, the *ListView* control is flexible enough to render out in a tabular or tiled manner. It can be used to replace the *GridView* control, at least in relatively common situations, but also to create completely custom layouts.

This said, let's briefly compare the *ListView* control to the other view controls available in ASP.NET 3.5 to see exactly what each control can do and cannot do. Table 12-4 lists and briefly describes the view controls.

TABLE 12-4 Rich, Data-Bound View Controls in ASP.NET

Control	Description
DetailsView	Designed to represent a single record of data, the control renders out a tabular and fixed layout. You decide the fields to be rendered and their format. You can use templates to customize the appearance of individual data fields, but you can't change the overall table-based layout. The control supports in-place editing as well as insertion and deletion, and it goes down to the bound data source control for the actual data access tasks. As long as the underlying data source supports paging and sorting, the control makes these functionalities available through its own user interface.
FormView	The *FormView* control can be considered to be the fully templated version of the *DetailsView* control. It renders one record at a time, picked from the associated data source and, optionally, supplies paging buttons to navigate between records. It doesn't provide any free user interface. You have to build all of it using header, item, and footer templates. *FormView* doesn't use data control fields and requires the user to define the rendering of each item by using templates. It supports any basic data access operation its data source supports, but you have to provide ad hoc trigger buttons.
GridView	The *GridView* control provides a tabular, grid-like view of the contents of a data source. Each column represents a data source field, and each row represents a record. You can use templates to customize individual data fields, but you are forced to use the tabular representation of contents. The granularity of customizable items is the table cell. With some hard work, though, you can change the structure of the table row—for example, you can add or remove cells. You can hardly do more than this, however. Like other view controls, the *GridView* also fully supports two-way data binding.

We covered the *GridView* control in the previous chapter. We'll cover the *DetailsView* and *FormView* controls in greater detail in the next chapter, where you'll learn about their programming model and how to use them in common scenarios.

So where does the *ListView* control fit in this puzzle of data-bound controls? Like all the controls listed in Table 12-4, the *ListView* control supports two-way data binding—that is, the ability of displaying and editing the contents of the bound data source. Unlike the others, though, the *ListView* control provides the greatest flexibility as far as the generation of the markup is concerned. It is not limited to a single record like *FormView* and *DetailsView* are, and it is not limited to a tabular layout like the *GridView* is. It is essentially a repeater with rich layout capabilities (like a *DataList* control) and the two-way data-binding capabilities of other view controls.

> **Note** The *ListView* control differs from *GridView* and *DetailsView* controls in another way that I consider to be of secondary importance at this stage of the Web technology, but it's an aspect of the control still worth mentioning. Designed a few years ago and released with ASP.NET 2.0 back in 2005, the *GridView* and *DetailsView* controls provide some AJAX-like capabilities such as paging and sorting callbacks. Both controls enable developers to page or sort content using an underlying instance of the *XMLHttpRequest* browser object. As a result, a regular postback is made but the request is served differently and the user interface is not fully refreshed.
>
> The *ListView* control doesn't offer such facilities for one simple and comprehensible reason—the current availability of a true and powerful ASP.NET AJAX framework make this AJAX precursor technology unnecessary and obsolete. By using the ASP.NET AJAX framework (which you can learn more about in Chapter 19), you can enable callback-style capabilities in the *ListView* control, and you are not even limited to paging and sorting. By simply wrapping the *ListView* control in an *UpdatePanel* region, you can page, edit, or sort any contents without full page refreshes.

Simple Data Binding

You use the *ListView* control to generate any user interface that needs to be built as you iterate a collection of records. You associate data with a *ListView* control using the *DataSource* property or, better yet, using the *DataSourceID* property. In the former case, you explicitly provide the data and control any aspect of the binding process. The *DataSourceID* property connects the control to a data source component. The binding process is mostly automatic, but it works both ways—it reads and saves data. The following data source control populates a *ListView* control with customers who reside in the United States:

```
<asp:ObjectDataSource ID="ObjectDataSource1" runat="server"
        TypeName="Core35.DAL.Customers"
        SelectMethod="LoadByCountry"
        OldValuesParameterFormatString="original_{0}">
    <SelectParameters>
        <asp:Parameter DefaultValue="USA" Name="country" />
    </SelectParameters>
</asp:ObjectDataSource>
```

The data source control invokes the *LoadByCountry* method on the specified business object and makes the response available to any bound control. Let's use a *ListView* control:

```
<asp:ListView ID="ListView1" runat="server"
    DataSourceID="ObjectDataSource1"
    ItemPlaceholderID="ListViewContent">
    <LayoutTemplate>
        <div id="header">
            <h1 id="logo">Customer List</h1>
        </div>
```

```
        <div runat="server" id="ListViewContent">
           <%-- ListView contents display here --%>
        </div>
     </LayoutTemplate>
     <ItemTemplate>
        <asp:Label runat="server" ID="lblCompany" Text='<%# Eval("CompanyName") %>' />
        ,  
        <asp:Label runat="server" ID="lblCountry" Text='<%# Eval("Country") %>' />
     </ItemTemplate>
     <ItemSeparatorTemplate>
        <hr />
     </ItemSeparatorTemplate>
</asp:ListView>
```

In this example, the *ListView* control comprises three templates—layout, item, and item separator. Of the three, only the item separator template is optional. The layout template defines the overall structure of the output. The *<div>* element in the layout marked with the *runat=server* attribute represents the insertion point for a pair of item and item separator templates. The item template is finally filled with the actual data from the n.th record. The *Eval* method evaluates the specified property on the data item being currently bound. The *Eval* method works in reading; as we'll see later; the *Bind* method works also in writing.

The item markup is made of a company name and country separated by a comma, and they are vertically separated from one another by a horizontal rule. Figure 12-1 shows the final results.

FIGURE 12-1 A very simple ListView control in action

Defining the Layout of the List

Most templated ASP.NET controls provide optional header and footer templates along with a repeated and data-bound item template. Header and footer templates are instantiated only once, at the beginning and end, respectively, of the data binding loop. You can hide the header and footer, but most controls implicitly force you to think about the layout in terms of three components placed vertically—header, body, footer.

In this regard, the *ListView* control is different. It has no header or footer template, and it features just one template for the structure of the resulting markup—the layout template. If you need a header or a footer, you can easily place them in the layout. But if you need to develop the layout horizontally or in a tiled manner, the *ListView* approach makes it easier.

The layout template is mandatory in any *ListView* control and can be as simple as the code shown here:

```
<LayoutTemplate>
    <div runat="server" ID="Body">
      ...
    </div>
</LayoutTemplate>
```

Instead of the *<div>* tag, you can use a *<span>* tag or provide appropriate CSS styling if you like the output flow with the rest of the page. The layout template must contain a server-side element that acts as the insertion point for data-bound item templates. This can be an HTML element decorated with the *runat* attribute or an ASP.NET server control. The ID of this placeholder element must be passed to the *ListView*'s *ItemPlaceholderID* property.

The *LayoutTemplate* property alone is not enough, though. At the very minimum, you must also specify content for the *ItemTemplate* or *GroupTemplate* property. As mentioned, to bind to data, you use ASP.NET <%# ... %> data-binding expressions and the *Eval* or *Bind* method.

> **Note** Like any other template properties in ASP.NET controls, the template properties of the *ListView* control also can be set programmatically as well as declaratively. You can assign to a template property any managed object that implements the *ITemplate* interface. Such an object can be obtained from an ASCX user control by using the *LoadTemplate* method on the *System. Web.UI.Page* class.

Let's put the graphical flexibility of the *ListView* control through its paces by examining how to render bound data using a number of layouts.

Building a Tabular Layout

The *ListView* control is the perfect tool to build a table-based interface with more liberty than specialized controls such as *DataGrid* and *GridView* typically allow. By properly designing the layout template of a *ListView* control, you can create an outermost table and then arrange a completely custom output for the child rows. In this way, you gain control over the rows and can, for example, employ two rows per record and even give each row a different number of cells. This level of control is extremely hard to achieve with a *GridView* control, although it's not impossible. To customize the *GridView* control to this level of detail, you need to override some of its protected virtual methods. Doing this requires the creation of a new derived control whose behavior touches on parts of the internal mechanics of the grid.

A *ListView* control lets you achieve the same results, but much more comfortably and with full support from Visual Studio 2008 designers.

> **Note** Before the advent of ASP.NET 3.5, you likely used the *Repeater* control for this task. The *ListView* control weds the flexibility of a *Repeater* control with the data access capabilities of view controls.

Definition of the Overall Layout

To generate an HTML table, the *ListView* control needs to have a layout template defined as in the following code snippet:

```
<LayoutTemplate>
    <div>
        <h1 id="logo">Customer List</h1>
    </div>
    <div>
        <table>
            <thead>
                <tr>
                    <th>Company</th>
                    <th>Country</th>
                </tr>
                <tbody runat="server" id="ListViewContent">
                </tbody>
            </thead>
        </table>
    </div>
</LayoutTemplate>
```

The layout comprises two *<div>* elements, both of which are optional from a purely functional perspective. The *<div>* element, in fact, simplifies the process of styling the output, as you'll see later in this chapter. Generally, the output is made of two HTML blocks—one for the header and one for the actual data.

The layout template defines the overall markup by defining the *<table>* tag and adding a child *<thead>* tag. Next, a *<tbody>* tag wraps the child rows, each of which will be bound to a data record. In this case, the *<tbody>* tag hosts the item templates. For this reason, it features the *runat* attribute and has its own ID set as the argument of the *ItemPlaceholderID* property of the *ListView* control:

```
<asp:ListView ID="ListView1" runat="server"
    DataSourceID="ObjectDataSource1"
    ItemPlaceholderID="ListViewContent">
    ...
</asp:ListView>
```

The actual body of the resulting table is determined by the item and alternating item templates.

Definition of the Item Template

In a tabular layout, created using an HTML table, the item template can't be anything but a sequence of *<tr>* tags. Unlike with a pure grid control such as *GridView*, in a *ListView* layout you have no limitation on the number of rows per data item you can display. The following example uses two table rows per bound item:

```
<ItemTemplate>
    <tr>
        <td>
            <asp:Label runat="server" ID="lblCompany" Text='<%# Eval("CompanyName") %>' />
        </td>
        <td>
            <asp:Label runat="server" ID="lblCountry" Text='<%# Eval("Country") %>' />
        </td>
    </tr>
    <tr>
        <td colspan="2">
            <i>To contact this customer, please call <b><%# Eval("Phone") %></b></i>
        </td>
    </tr>
</ItemTemplate>
```

The first row contains two cells: one for the company name, and one for the country. The second row shows the phone number on a single-cell row. Both rows are rendered for each record bound to the *ListView* control. Figure 12-2 demonstrates the markup you obtain in this way.

FIGURE 12-2 A tabular layout built with the ListView control

As you can see in the figure, some extremely simple styles have been applied to the table items. In particular, the *<th>* tags and the *<td>* tag of the second row have been styled to show a bottom border. Style properties can be applied using CSS styles or explicit style properties, as shown here:

```
<th style="border-bottom:solid 3px black;">Company</th>
```

When comparing this sort of flexibility with the *GridView* control, the *GridView* control provides a number of free facilities, but it doesn't offer as much flexibility in design, as seen in this example. To choose between either control, you have to first evaluate your requirements and make a choice between flexibility of rendering and functions to implement.

Using Alternate Rendering for Data Items

ItemTemplate is mandatory in a *ListView* control and indicates the template to use for each bound item. The *AlternatingItemTemplate* property can be used to differentiate every other item, as shown in Figure 12-3.

FIGURE 12-3 A tabular layout built with the ListView control using an alternating item template

Most of the time, the alternating item template just features the same layout as regular items but styles it differently. However, changes to the template are allowed to any extent that can keep your users happy. The following code uses a small indentation for alternating rows:

```
<AlternatingItemTemplate>
    <tr>
        <td>
                
            <asp:Label runat="server" ID="lblCompany" Text='<%# Eval("CompanyName") %>' />
        </td>
        <td>
            <asp:Label runat="server" ID="lblCountry" Text='<%# Eval("Country") %>' />
        </td>
    </tr>
    <tr>
        <td style="border-bottom:solid 1px darkgray;" colspan="2">
                
            <i>To contact this customer, please call <b><%# Eval("Phone") %></b></i>
        </td>
    </tr>
</AlternatingItemTemplate>
```

Figure 12-4 shows the result.

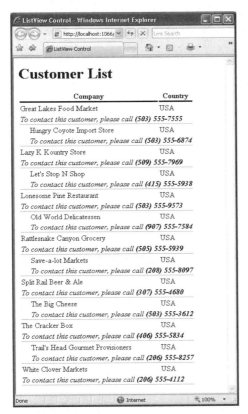

FIGURE 12-4 Using a slightly different layout for alternating items

Reflecting On the Table Layout

HTML tables are an essential, but too often abused, piece of the Web jigsaw puzzle. HTML tables were designed for presenting tabular information. And they are still great at doing this. So any developer of a Web page that needs to incorporate a matrix of data is correct in using HTML tables. The problem with tables is that they are often used to define the page layout—a task they weren't designed for. To illustrate, a grid control that uses HTML tables to output its content is more than acceptable. A tree-view control that uses HTML tables to list its contents is less desirable. It's not by mere chance that the ASP.NET team released the CSS adapter toolkit just to allow you to change the rendering engine of some controls to make them inherently more CSS-friendly. And the *TreeView* was just one of the controls whose rendering style can be modified by using the toolkit.

> **Note** Using tables for creating multicolumn layouts—which is pretty common these days in most Web sites—has a number of significant drawbacks. Tables require a lot of code (or tags if you create tables declaratively) that has little to do with the data you intend to display through them. This code is tedious to write, verbose, and difficult to maintain. Worse yet, it makes for longer downloads and slower rendering in the browsers (a factor of growing importance for wireless devices). In addition, tables tend to mix up information and layout instead of forcing you to keep them neatly separated and result in less accessible content.

Building a Flow Layout

Visual Studio 2008 provides some facilities to work with *ListView* controls. Specifically, once you have bound the control to a data source, Visual Studio queries the data source and offers to generate some templates for you. Figure 12-5 shows the related Visual Studio 2008 dialog box.

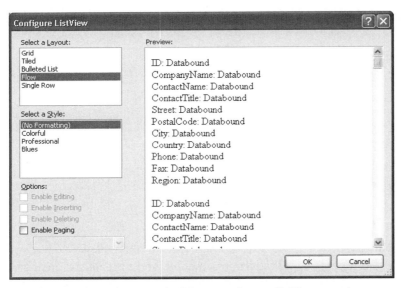

FIGURE 12-5 Visual Studio 2008 facilities to configure a ListView control

Definition of the Overall Layout

A flow layout is the simplest layout you can get. It requires only that you define a container—typically, a *<div>*—and then the markup for each record. The *ListView* control simply composes the resulting markup by concatenating the markup in a unique flow of HTML tags. Needless to say, the resulting markup can flow horizontally or vertically, depending on the tags you use (block or inline) and the CSS styles you apply.

If you're looking for a block flow layout, your *LayoutTemplate* property will probably always look as simple as the one shown here:

```
<LayoutTemplate>
    <div ID="ListViewContent" runat="server">
    </div>
</LayoutTemplate>
```

If you opt for a *<span>* tag, instead of getting a new block you get a piece of markup that flows inline with the rest of the ASP.NET page.

Definition of the Item Layout

A good example of a flowing template is the *ListView* control illustrated in Figure 12-1. Here's another example:

```
<ItemTemplate>
    <div style="float:left; padding:20px; border: solid 1px black;">
        <b>ID:</b>
        <asp:Label ID="IDLabel" runat="server" Text='<%# Eval("ID") %>' />
        <br />
        <b>CompanyName:</b>
        <asp:Label ID="CompanyNameLabel" runat="server"
            Text='<%# Eval("CompanyName") %>' />
        <br />
        <b>ContactName:</b>
        <asp:Label ID="ContactNameLabel" runat="server"
            Text='<%# Eval("ContactName") %>' />
        <br />
        <b>ContactTitle:</b>
        <asp:Label ID="ContactTitleLabel" runat="server"
            Text='<%# Eval("ContactTitle") %>' />
    </div>
</ItemTemplate>
```

The *<div>* tag normally creates a new block of markup and breaks the current flow of HTML. However, if you give it the *float:left* CSS style, it will float in the specified direction. As a result, the block of markup forms a horizontal sequence that wraps to the next line when the border of the browser's window is met. Figure 12-6 offers a preview.

> **Note** In the previous chunk of HTML markup, I used *<span>* and *<div>* tags with styles applied and also mixed CSS styles with HTML tags used for controlling the appearance of the page such as *<b>* and*
*. This approach is clearly arguable. The reason why I haven't opted for a niftier, pure CSS-based code in the snippet is clarity. By reading which CSS styles are applied to which tag, you can more easily make sense of the output depicted in Figure 12-6.

FIGURE 12-6 Using the float CSS attribute to display <div> tags as a horizontal sequence

Building a Tiled Layout

Admittedly, the output of Figure 12-6 is not really attractive, even though it contains a few elements that, if improved a bit, might lead to more compelling results. The output of Figure 12-6 shows blocks of markup that flow horizontally and wrap to the next row. However, they share no common surrounding layout. In other words, those blocks are not tiled. To build a perfectly tiled output, you need to leverage group templates.

Grouping Items

So far we've used the *ListView* control to repeat the item template for each bound record. The *GroupTemplate* property adds an intermediate (and optional) step in this rendering process. When you specify a group template, the total number of bound records is partitioned in groups and the item template is applied to the records in each group. When a group has been rendered, the control moves to the next one. Each group of records can have its own particular template—the group template—and a separator can be inserted between items and groups. How is the size of each determined? That has to be a fixed value that you set, either declaratively or programmatically, through the *GroupItemCount* property. Let's consider the following layout and group templates:

```
<LayoutTemplate>
    <table border="1">
        <tr ID="groupPlaceholder" runat="server">
        </tr>
    </table>
```

```
</LayoutTemplate>
<GroupTemplate>
    <tr>
        <td ID="itemPlaceholder" runat="server">
        </td>
    </tr>
</GroupTemplate>
```

It indicates that the final output will be an HTML table where a new row is created for each group of items. Each table row contains as many cells as the value of *GroupItemCount* sets. The default value is *1*. Note that in the preceding code snippet we're using the default names for group and item containers—that is, *groupPlaceholder* and *itemPlaceholder*. When these names are used, there's no need to set corresponding *GroupPlaceholderID* and *ItemPlaceholderID* properties on the *ListView* markup. Here's the top-level markup for a tiled layout:

```
<asp:ListView ID="ListView1" runat="server"
    DataSourceID="ObjectDataSource1" GroupItemCount="4">
    ...
</asp:ListView>
```

As an example, if you set *GroupItemCount* to *4*, you'll have rows of 4 cells each until there are less than 4 records left. And after that? What if the number of bound records is not a perfect multiple of the group item count? That's where the *EmptyItemTemplate* property fits in:

```
<EmptyItemTemplate>
        <td />
</EmptyItemTemplate>
```

This template is used to complete the group when no more data items are available. Figure 12-7 shows a typical tiled output you obtain by employing a *ListView* control.

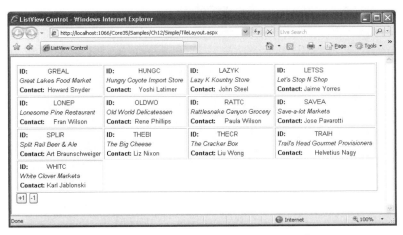

FIGURE 12-7 A 4-cell tiled layout built with the ListView control

> **Note** The *EmptyDataTemplate* property, indicates the desired output when the data source bound to the *ListView* control is empty.

Using the Group Separator Template

Each group of items can be separated by a custom block of markup defined through the *GroupSeparatorTemplate* property. Here's an example:

```
<GroupSeparatorTemplate>
    <tr>
        <td colspan='4'> </td>
    </tr>
</GroupSeparatorTemplate>
```

If you add this markup to the preceding example, you'll display a blank row in between rows with data-bound cells. It's a kind of vertical spacing.

The same can be done horizontally to separate data-bound cells within the same table row. To do so, you use the *ItemSeparatorTemplate* property instead. In both cases, the markup you put in must be consistent with the overall markup being created for the whole *ListView* control.

Modifying the Group Item Count Dynamically

The *GroupItemCount* property is read-write, meaning that you can change the size of each group programmatically based on some user actions. The following code snippet shows a pair of event handlers associated with the *Click* event of two *Button* controls:

```
protected void Button1_Click(object sender, EventArgs e)
{
    // There's no upper limit to the value of the property
    ListView1.GroupItemCount += 1;
}
protected void Button2_Click(object sender, EventArgs e)
{
    // The property can't be 2 or less
    if (ListView1.GroupItemCount >2)
        ListView1.GroupItemCount -= 1;
}
```

The *GroupItemCount* property itself can't take any value less than 1, but it has no upper limit. However, it should not accept any value larger than the actual number of data items currently bound.

As you assign a new value, the *set* modifier of the property resets the internal data-binding flag and orders a new binding operation. If you change the value of *GroupItemCount* over a postback, the *ListView* control automatically renders the updated markup back to the client. (See Figure 12-8.)

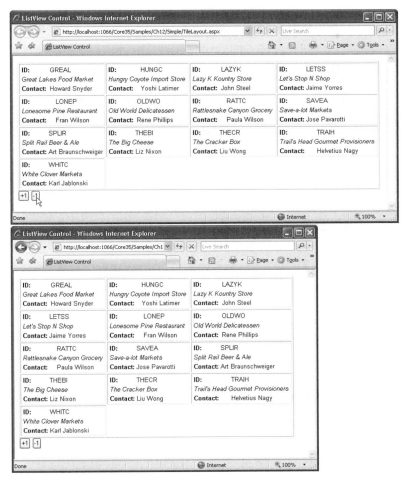

FIGURE 12-8 Changing the size of ListView groups dynamically

Note The *DataList* control offers similar layout capabilities, even though it doesn't expose a user-defined group template. The *DataList* control exposes only a few properties to let developers decide about the tiling—for example, direction, number of rows, and/or number of columns. It means that the group template is an internal property not publicly exposed and modifiable by developers. As far as tiling is concerned, compared to the *DataList* control, the *ListView* control always tiles horizontally and requires event handlers to program the output to be tiled differently.

The *ListView* control doesn't natively support more advanced capabilities—such as uneven groups of items where, for example, the association between an item and a group is based on a logical condition and not merely determined by an index. In this scenario, you could have a list where the first group contains customers whose name begins with *A* and the second group contains those beginning with *B*, and so on. You would have to provide the logic for this yourself. Let's look at this next.

Data-Driven Group Templates

The support for groups built into the *ListView* control is not data driven. In other words, the layout (groups and items) is first created and it is then bound to data. When the binding step occurs, the group template is not directly involved and you won't receive any event that tells you that a group has been either created or bound to its data.

However, this doesn't mean that your group templates must have a fixed layout and can't be dynamically populated using data from its contained items. The *ListView*'s *ItemDataBound* event is the key to obtaining output such as that shown in Figure 12-9.

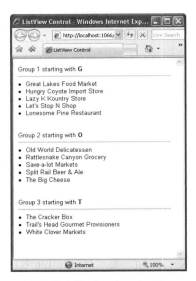

FIGURE 12-9 The header of each group is determined dynamically by looking at the bound contents

To start out, let's take a look at the overall layout template of the *ListView* control:

```
<asp:ListView ID="ListView1" runat="server"
    DataSourceID="ObjectDataSource1"
    GroupItemCount="5"
    OnItemDataBound="ListView1_ItemDataBound">
    <ItemTemplate>
        <li><%# Eval("CompanyName") %></li>
    </ItemTemplate>
```

```
    <ItemSeparatorTemplate>
        <br />
    </ItemSeparatorTemplate>

    <LayoutTemplate>
        <div id="groupPlaceholder" runat="server">
        </div>
    </LayoutTemplate>

    <GroupTemplate>
        <asp:Label runat="server" ID="groupHeader" Text="Group" />
        <hr />
        <div id="itemPlaceholder" runat="server">
        </div>
        <br /><br /><br />
    </GroupTemplate>
</asp:ListView>
```

The group template is made of a *Label* control followed by an *<hr>* tag and the list of data items. Each bound item is expressed through an *<li>* tag. Let's see how to change the *Text* property of the *groupHeader* control for each group being created. Here's the structure of the *ItemDataBound* event handler:

```
private int lastGroup = -1;
protected void ListView1_ItemDataBound(object sender, ListViewItemEventArgs e)
{
    // To assign the group a data-bound title, retrieve the data item first
    if (e.Item.ItemType == ListViewItemType.DataItem)
    {
            ListViewDataItem currentItem = (ListViewDataItem) e.Item;
            CustomizeGroupHeader((ListView) sender, currentItem);
    }
}
```

The *ListViewItemEventArgs* argument contains an *Item* property that refers to the item being bound to data. This item can be of a few types—*InsertItem*, *EmptyItem*, or *DataItem*. The list of feasible values is in the *ListViewItemType* enumerated type. In this case, we're interested only in data items—that is, regular items showing some bound data.

To put your hands on the real data being bound to the item, you need to cast the *ListView* item to the *ListViewDataItem* type, from which you can access a number of data-related properties:

```
private void CustomizeGroupHeader(ListView root, ListViewDataItem currentItem)
{
    // The type of the data item depends on the data you bound--in this case,
    // a collection of Customer objects
    Core35.DAL.Customer cust = (Core35.DAL.Customer) currentItem.DataItem;

    // Get a ListViewContainer object--the container of the group template
    Control container = currentItem.NamingContainer;
    if (container == null)
        return;
```

```
// Look up for a particular control in the group template--the Label
Label groupHeader = (Label)container.FindControl("groupHeader");
if (groupHeader == null)
    return;

// Figure out the 0-based index of current group. Note that the display index
// refers to the index of the item being bound, not the group
int groupIndex = currentItem.DisplayIndex / root.GroupItemCount;
if (groupIndex != lastGroup)
{
    // This is a new group
    lastGroup = groupIndex;

    // Update the UI
    groupHeader.Text = String.Format("Group {0} starting with <b>{1}</b>",
        groupIndex + 1,
        cust.CompanyName.Substring(0, 1).ToUpper());
}
}
```

You first get a reference to the naming container of the item. This container is the wrapper control for the group template. By using the *FindControl* method, you gain access to the *Label* control in the group template. The final step entails determining the value for the *Text* property of the *Label* control.

As mentioned, the *ListView* control doesn't provide any readymade information about groups. So you don't know about the index of the current group. The *DisplayIndex* property tells you only the index of the item being processed. Because the size of each group is fixed—and is based on the *GroupItemCount* property—you can easily obtain the 0-based index of the current group. You track the index of the current group in a global variable, and whenever a new group is found, you update the header.

Styling the List

Unlike other view controls, the *ListView* control doesn't feature the usual long list of style properties such as *HeaderStyle*, *ItemStyle*, *SelectedItemStyle*, and so forth. After a few years of industry use, Microsoft downsized the importance of style properties and their role. Today, as evidenced by the *ListView* control, in ASP.NET, CSS styles are emerging as the most effective and efficient way to modify the appearance of the markup.

Style Properties

ASP.NET controls let you set style attributes in two nonexclusive ways—using the *CssClass* property and using style properties. The *CssClass* property takes the name of a CSS class and passes it on to the *class* attribute of the root HTML tag generated for the control. More often than not, though, ASP.NET controls produce a complex markup where multiple HTML tags are rendered together but yet need to be styled differently. Although this is far from being an impossible goal to achieve with CSS styles, for a few years Microsoft pushed style properties as the way to go.

Developers are probably more inclined to use style properties than CSS styles, which require some specific skills. Anyway, style properties let you specify CSS attributes to apply to particular regions of the markup being generated. For example, the *ItemStyle* property in a *GridView* control allows you to define the colors, font, and borders of each displayed item. In the end, the value of these properties are translated to CSS attributes and assigned to the HTML tags via the *style* attribute. The developers don't have to build up any CSS skills and can leverage the Visual Studio editors and designers to get a preview.

Is there anything wrong with this approach?

The problem is that style attributes are defined as part of the page's code, and there's no clear separation between layout and style. ASP.NET themes are helpful and certainly mitigate the problem. All in all, for view controls with a relatively fixed layout, style properties—which are better if used through the intermediation of themes—are still a good option. The *ListView* control, though, is kind of an exception.

Using Cascading Style Sheets

The *ListView* control provides an unprecedented level of flexibility when it comes to generating the markup for the browser. The item that for, say, a *GridView* control can be safely identified with a table row, can be virtually anything with a *ListView* control. Add to this flexibility the new support in Visual Studio 2008 for CSS that we discovered back in Chapter 2.

The CSS designer in Visual Studio 2008 allows you to style controls and save everything back to a CSS class. So, as a developer, you always work with properties and scalar values but have them saved back to the CSS class instead of the view state.

This is another important factor to push the preference for cascading style sheets over style properties. The CSS is a separate file that is downloaded only once. Style properties, on the other hand, are saved to the view state and continually uploaded and downloaded with the page.

Cool cascading style sheets are usually developed by designers and assign a style to the vast majority of HTML tags. Often cascading style sheets incorporate layout information and influence the structure of the page they are applied to. A common trick used by cascading style sheets consists of assigning a particular ID to *<div>* tags and treating them in a special way. If you want to try some compelling cascading style sheets, navigate to *http://www.opensourcetemplates.org*.

Let's see how to radically improve the user interface of a previous *ListView*-based page with a cool CSS.

First, you explicitly link any relevant CSS file to the page (or the master page) by using the *<link>* tag. The *HtmlHead* control also allows you to load CSS files programmatically. Note that most realistic CSS files have an auxiliary folder of images that you have to set up on the production server too. The CSS file I'm using in the next example assigns a special role to *<div>* tags with the following IDs: *header*, *footer*, *page*, and *content*. The alternative is to explicitly assign a CSS class using the *class* attribute. Both ways are widely accepted. The *class* approach makes more obvious that something has been styled and what class it has been assigned to. But, in the end, it's a matter of preference. If you opt for styling via IDs, you are totally free to choose any names you want.

```
<asp:ListView ID="ListView1" runat="server"
    DataSourceID="ObjectDataSource1"
    ItemPlaceholderID="ListViewContent">
    <LayoutTemplate>
        <div id="header">
            <h1 id="logo">Customer List</h1>
        </div>
        <div id="page">
            <div id="content">
                <table>
                    <thead>
                        <tr>
                            <th>Company</th>
                            <th>Country</th>
                        </tr>
                        <tbody runat="server" id="ListViewContent">
                        </tbody>
                    </thead>
                </table>
            </div>
        </div>
        <div id="footer">
            <p id="copyright">&copy; 2007
                <b>Programming ASP.NET 3.5 Core Reference</b></p>
        </div>
    </LayoutTemplate>

    <ItemTemplate>
        <tr>
            <td><asp:Label runat="server" ID="lblName"
                    Text='<%# Eval("CompanyName") %>' /></td>
            <td><asp:Label runat="server" ID="lblCountry"
                    Text='<%# Eval("Country") %>' /></td>
        </tr>
    </ItemTemplate>
</asp:ListView>
```

The result is shown in Figure 12-10.

FIGURE 12-10 Using cascading style sheets to style the markup of a ListView control

The CSS used in the preceding example is CrystalX, available as a free download from *http://www.oswd.org/design/preview/id/3465*.

Working with the *ListView* Control

The *ListView* control makes it easy to handle common data-based operations, such as insert, update, delete, or sorting. All that you have to do is place buttons in the layout template and associate buttons with command names. Buttons can be global to the list (such as insert, sort, and page buttons) or specific to a particular item (such as update and delete buttons). Command names are just strings that are assigned to the *CommandName* property of the *Button* control.

So far, we have considered only scenarios with relatively static and noninteractive templates. It is definitely possible, though, to use the *ListView* control to create rich user interfaces that allow in-place editing, selection of items, paging, and updates back to the data source. Let's start with in-place editing.

In-Place Editing

Unlike the *GridView* control, the *ListView* control doesn't automatically generate an Edit button; nor does it automatically adapt the edit mode user interface from the item template. This responsibility falls to the developer by design. The developer is required to define an edit template that will be used to edit the contents of the selected item, in keeping with the flexible nature of the control.

Defining the Edit Item Template

The edit template is any piece of markup you intend to display to your users when they click to edit a record. It can have any layout you like and can handle data access in a variety of ways.

If you've bound the *ListView* control to a data source control—for example, an *ObjectDataSource* control—you can take advantage of the ASP.NET built-in support for two-way data binding. Simply put, you use data binding <%# ... %> expressions to bind to data, the *Eval* method for read-only operations, and the *Bind* method for full I/O operations.

The following markup defines a classic two-column table for editing some fields of a customer record:

```
<table>
    <tr>
        <td><b>ID</b></td>
        <td><asp:Label runat="server" ID="lblID" Text='<%# Eval("ID") %>' /></td>
    </tr>
    <tr>
        <td><b>Name</b></td>
        <td><asp:TextBox runat="server" ID="txtName"
            Text='<%# Bind("CompanyName") %>' /></td>
    </tr>
    <tr>
        <td><b>Country</b></td>
        <td><asp:TextBox runat="server" ID="txtCountry"
            Text='<%# Bind("Country") %>' /></td>
    </tr>
    <tr>
        <td><b>Street</b></td>
        <td><asp:TextBox runat="server" ID="txtStreet"
            Text='<%# Bind("Street") %>' /></td>
    </tr>
    <tr>
        <td><b>City</b></td>
        <td><asp:TextBox runat="server" ID="txtCity"
            Text='<%# Bind("City") %>' /></td>
    </tr>
</table>
```

Only one displayed item at a time can be in edit mode; the *EditIndex* property is used to get or set this 0-based index. If an item is being edited and the user clicks on a button to edit another one, the last-win policy applies. As a result, editing on the previous item is canceled and it's enabled on the last-clicked item.

To turn the *ListView* user interface into edit mode, you need an ad hoc button control with a command name of *Edit*:

```
<asp:Button ID="Button1" runat="server" Text="Edit" CommandName="Edit" />
```

When this button is clicked, the *ItemEditing* event fires on the server. By handling this event, you can run your own checks to ensure that the operation is legitimate. If something comes up to invalidate the call, you set the *Cancel* property of the event data structure to cancel the operation, like so:

```
protected void ListView1_ItemEditing(object sender, ListViewEditEventArgs e)
{
    // Just deny the edit operation
    e.Cancel = true;
}
```

Adding Predefined Command Buttons

An edit item template wouldn't be very helpful without at least a couple of predefined buttons to save and cancel changes. You can define buttons using a variety of controls, including *Button*, *LinkButton*, *ImageButton*, and any kind of custom control that implements the *IButtonControl* interface.

Command names are plain strings that can be assigned to the *CommandName* property of button controls. The *ListView* (and other view controls) recognizes a number of predefined command names, as listed in Table 12-5.

TABLE 12-5 Supported Command Names

Command	Description
Cancel	Cancels the current operation (edit, insert), and returns to the default view (item template)
Delete	Deletes the current record from the data source
Edit	Turns the *ListView* control into edit mode (edit item template)
Insert	Inserts a new record into the data source
Page	Moves to the next or previous page
Select	Selects the clicked item, and switches to the selected item template
Sort	Sorts the bound data source
Update	Saves the current status of the record back to the data source

The following code shows how to add a pair of Save/Cancel buttons:

```
<asp:Button ID="btnSave" runat="server" Text="Save" CommandName="Update" />
<asp:Button ID="btnCancel" runat="server" Text="Cancel" CommandName="Cancel" />
```

Any button clicking done within the context of a *ListView* control originates a server-side event—the *ItemCommand* event:

```
protected void ListView1_ItemCommand(object sender, ListViewCommandEventArgs e)
{
    // Use e.CommandName to check the command requested
}
```

Clicking buttons associated with predefined command buttons can result in subsequent, and more specific, events. For example, *ItemUpdating* and *ItemUpdated* are fired before and after, respectively, a record is updated. You can use the *ItemUpdating* event to make any last-minute check on the typed data before this data is sent to the database.

Note that before the update is made, *ListView* checks the validity of any data typed by calling the *IsValid* method on the *Page* class. If any validator is defined in the template, it is evaluated at this time.

Adding Custom Command Buttons

In the edit mode user interface, you can have custom buttons too. A custom button differs from a regular Save or Cancel button only in terms of the command name. The command name of a custom button is any name not listed in Table 12-5. Here's an example:

```
<asp:Button ID="btnMyCommand" runat="server" Text="Custom"
            CommandName="mycommand" />
```

To execute any code in response to the user's clicking on this button, all you can do is to add an *ItemCommand* event handler and check for the proper (custom) command name and react accordingly:

```
protected void ListView1_ItemCommand(object sender, ListViewCommandEventArgs e)
{
    // Check the command requested
    if (e.CommandName.Equals("MyCommand", StringComparison.OrdinalIgnoreCase))
    {
        ...
    }
}
```

Conducting the Update

When the *ListView* control is used in two-way binding mode, any update operation is conducted through the connected data source control. You define select and save methods on the data source, configure their parameters (either declaratively or programmatically), and delegate to the *ListView* control all remaining chores.

For update and delete operations, though, you need to identify the record uniquely. This is where the *DataKeyNames* property gets into the game. You use this property to define a collection of fields that form the primary key on the data source:

```
<asp:ListView ID="ListView1" runat="server"
    ...
    DataSourceID="ObjectDataSource1"
    DataKeyNames="id">
    ...
</asp:ListView>
```

In this case, the *DataKeyNames* tells the underlying data source control that the ID field on the bound record has to be used as the key. Figure 12-11 shows a sample page in action that edits the contents of the currently displayed record.

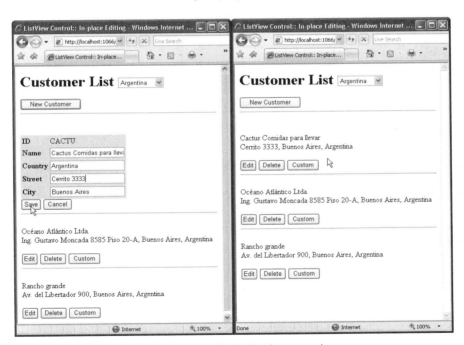

FIGURE 12-11 In-place editing in action with the ListView control

Deleting an Existing Record

As you can see, Figure 12-11 also contains a Delete button side by side with the aforementioned Edit button. Here's the full markup for *ListView*'s item template:

```
<ItemTemplate>
    <p>
        <%# Eval("CompanyName") %>
        <br />
        <%# Eval("Street") %>, <%# Eval("City") %>, <%# Eval("Country") %>
    </p>

    <asp:Button ID="btnEdit" runat="server" Text="Edit" CommandName="edit" />
    <asp:Button ID="btnDelete" runat="server" Text="Delete" CommandName="delete"
      OnClientClick="return confirm('Are you sure you want to delete this item?');" />
    <asp:Button ID="btnMyCommand" runat="server" Text="Custom" CommandName="mycommand" />
</ItemTemplate>
```

The *Delete* operation is even more crucial than an update. For this reason, you might want to be sure that deleting the record is exactly what the user wants. To start, you pop up a client-side message box in which you ask the user to confirm the operation. It is a little piece of JavaScript code that you attach to the *OnClientClick* property of a *Button* control or to the *onclick* attribute of the corresponding HTML tag. You can also use an extender control to get this, as we'll see in Chapter 19. (See Figure 12-12.)

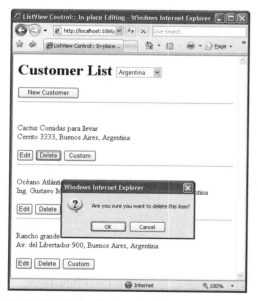

FIGURE 12-12 Confirming the deletion of the current record

There might be situations in which the user is honestly sure that all she wants is to delete the displayed record. So she happily confirms the message box. What happens next is up to you. By handling the *ItemDeleting* event, you can run your own checks and allow the operation only if all you can check is fine.

> **Note** The delete operation, as well as the update operation, requires that a proper method be defined on the data source control. For more information, check out Chapter 9.

Showing a Message Box upon Completion

Wouldn't it be nice if your application displays a message box upon the completion of an update operation? It doesn't change the effect of the operation, but it would make users feel more comfortable. In a Web scenario, you can use only JavaScript for this purpose. The trick is that you register a piece of startup script code with the postback event where you execute the update operation. In this way, the script will be executed as soon as the page is served back to the browser. From the user's perspective, this means right after the completion of the operation. Here's what you need:

```
protected void ListView1_ItemUpdated(object sender, ListViewUpdatedEventArgs e)
{
    // Display a client message box at the end of the operation
    Page.ClientScript.RegisterStartupScript(
            this.GetType(),
            "update_Script",
            "alert('You successfully updated the system.');",
            true);
}
```

Inserting New Data Items

The *ListView* control allows you to define a made-to-measure interface for adding new records to the underlying data source. You do this through the *InsertItemTemplate* property. More often than not, the insert template is nearly identical to the edit item template, except for the fields that form the primary key of the data source. These fields are normally rendered as read-only text in the edit template. Clearly they have to be editable in an insert item scenario.

Setting Up the Insert Item Template

So let's assume the following insert item template. As you can easily verify, it is the same edit item template we used in the previous example, except that a *TextBox* control is used for entering the ID of the new customer:

```
<InsertItemTemplate>
    <table style="background-color:yellow;">
        <tr>
            <td><b>ID</b></td>
            <td><asp:TextBox runat="server" ID="txtID"
                             MaxLength="5"
                             Text='<%# Bind("ID") %>' /></td>
        </tr>
        <tr>
            <td><b>Name</b></td>
            <td><asp:TextBox runat="server" ID="txtName"
                       Text='<%# Bind("CompanyName") %>' /></td>
        </tr>
        <tr>
            <td><b>Country</b></td>
            <td><asp:TextBox runat="server" ID="txtCountry"
                       Text='<%# Bind("Country") %>' /></td>
        </tr>
        <tr>
            <td><b>Street</b></td>
            <td><asp:TextBox runat="server" ID="txtStreet"
                       Text='<%# Bind("Street") %>' /></td>
        </tr>
        <tr>
            <td><b>City</b></td>
            <td><asp:TextBox runat="server" ID="txtCity"
                       Text='<%# Bind("City") %>' /></td>
        </tr>
    </table>
    <asp:Button ID="btnInsert" runat="server" Text="Add" CommandName="insert" />
    <asp:Button ID="btnCancel" runat="server" Text="Cancel" CommandName="cancel" />
</InsertItemTemplate>
```

How would you display this template? The edit item template shows up when the user clicks a button decorated with the *Edit* command name. Unfortunately, there's no equivalent *New* command name to automatically bring up the insert item template. (As you'll see in the next chapter, this is exactly what happens with the *DetailsView* and *FormView* controls.) Instead, with the *ListView* the *New* command name would be considered a custom command, handled by code you provide to activate the insert item template unless it's active by default. We'll look at the details next.

The insert item template is displayed by position. The *InsertItemPosition* property determines where the template is displayed. There are three possibilities, as shown in Table 12-6.

TABLE 12-6 Feasible Positions for the Insert Item Template

Position	Description
FirstItem	The insert item template is displayed as the first item in the list and precedes all items in the bound data source.
LastItem	The insert item template is displayed as the last item in the list and trails all items in the bound data source.
None	The insert item template is not automatically displayed. The developer is responsible for showing and hiding the template programmatically. This is the default value for the *InsertItemPosition* property.

If you leave the *InsertItemPosition* property set to its default value, no insert template is displayed, but you won't have a predefined button to bring it up. If you use any of the other two values, the template is always visible and displayed at the beginning or the end of the list. This might not be desirable in most cases. Let's see how to take programmatic control over the display of the insert template.

Taking Full Control of the Insert Template

In the layout template, you add a custom button and capture any user's click event. You can give the button any command name not listed in Table 12-5:

```
<asp:Button ID="btnNew" runat="server" Text="New Customer" CommandName="new" />
```

To handle the click on the button, you write an *ItemCommand* handler. In the event handler, you simply change the value of the *InsertItemPosition* property, as shown here:

```
protected void ListView1_ItemCommand(object sender, ListViewCommandEventArgs e)
{
    if (e.CommandName.Equals("New", StringComparison.OrdinalIgnoreCase))
    {
        ListView me = (ListView) sender;
        me.InsertItemPosition = InsertItemPosition.FirstItem;
    }
}
```

Changing the value of *InsertItemPosition* to anything but None brings up the insert item template, if any. In the insert template, you need to have a couple of predefined buttons with command names of *Insert* (to add) and *Cancel* (to abort).

It should be noted, though, that the insert item template is not automatically dismissed by the *ListView* control itself. As mentioned, this is because of the lack of built-in support for the *New* command name. In the end, this requires that you add a couple more handlers to dismiss the template when the user cancels or confirms the insertion.

The *ItemCanceling* event fires when the user hits a button associated with the *Cancel* command name. This can happen from either the edit or insert template. The event data object passed to the handler has the *CancelMode* property that is designed to help you figure out what mode is active (insert or edit) and allow you to tailor your application's response.

```
protected void ListView1_ItemCanceling(object sender, ListViewCancelEventArgs e)
{
    ListView me = (ListView) sender;

    // Dismissing the insert item template
    if (e.CancelMode == ListViewCancelMode.CancelingInsert)
    {
        me.InsertItemPosition = InsertItemPosition.None;
    }
}
```

To hide the insert item template after the new data item has been successfully appended to the data source, you use the *ItemInserted* event:

```
protected void ListView1_ItemInserted(object sender, ListViewInsertedEventArgs e)
{
    ListView me = (ListView) sender;
    me.InsertItemPosition = InsertItemPosition.None;
}
```

> **Note** The advent of AJAX and the availability of rich client-side libraries of widgets makes it possible to plan alternative ways of displaying temporary forms such as the edit or insert item templates. The AJAX Control Toolkit (which is discussed in Chapter 19 and is a free download from *http://www.asp.net/downloads*) offers a modal dialog box component for Web pages. You can incorporate the insert item template in this modal dialog box. By doing so, though, you charge yourself with the additional task of connecting to the data source and updating.

Adding a Bit of Validation

When you're going to add a new record to an existing data source, a bit of validation—much more than is generally desirable—is mandatory. Being responsible for the insert template, you can add as many validators as necessary to the markup. The *ListView* control's internal facilities then ensure that the operation is finalized only if no validator raised an error.

In particular, you might want to check whether the ID being inserted already exists in the data source. You can use a *CustomValidator* control attached to the text box:

```
<asp:TextBox runat="server" ID="txtID"
             MaxLength="5"
             Text='<%# Bind("ID") %>' />
<asp:CustomValidator runat="server" ID="CustomValidator1"
             ErrorMessage="Invalid ID"
             ControlToValidate="txtID"
             OnServerValidate="CustomValidator1_CheckID" />
```

The *CustomValidator* control fires a server-side event in which you can run code to validate the text in the input field. The server event is fired via a postback and has the following prototype:

```
protected void  CustomValidator1_CheckID(object source, ServerValidateEventArgs e)
{
    string proposedCustomerID = e.Value;
    e.IsValid = CheckIfUsed(proposedCustomerID);
}
private bool CheckIfUsed(string proposedCustomerID)
{
    Core35.DAL.Customer c = Customers.Load(proposedCustomerID);

    // The object is of type NoCustomer if no matching customer exists
    if (c is Core35.DAL.NoCustomer)
        return true;
    return false;
}
```

The *Load* method in the sample data access layer (DAL) used in this example supports the Special Case pattern. In other words, the method always returns a valid *Customer* object regardless of the value of the input *proposedCustomerID* parameter. If a customer with a matching ID can't be found, the return object is an instance of the *NoCustomer* class. Of course, *NoCustomer* is a class that derives from *Customer*.

How is this different from returning a plain *null* value or perhaps an error code? In both cases, the caller can figure out whether a matching customer exists or not. However, returning a special-case *Customer* object is inherently more informative and doesn't violate the consistency of the method—a class that inherits from *Customer* is always returned, whereas an error code is a number and *null* is a non-value.

Selecting an Item

The *SelectedItemTemplate* property allows you to assign a different template to the currently selected item in the *ListView* control. Note that only one displayed item at a time can be given the special selected template. But how would you select an item?

Triggering the Selection

The selected item template is a special case of the item template. The two templates are similar and mostly differ in terms of visual settings—for example, a different background color. The switch between the regular and selected item template occurs when the user clicks on a button with the *Select* command name. If you intend to support the selection item feature, you place a *Select* button in the item template. When this button gets clicked, the *ListView* automatically applies the new template to the clicked item. Here are some sample item and selected item templates.

```
<ItemTemplate>
    <p>
        <asp:linkbutton runat="server" Text='<%# Eval("CompanyName") %>'
            CommandName="Select" />
        <br />
        <%# Eval("Street") %>, <%# Eval("City") %>, <%# Eval("Country") %>
    </p>
</ItemTemplate>

<SelectedItemTemplate>
    <h3>
        <%# Eval("CompanyName") %>
        <br />
        <%# Eval("Street") %>, <%# Eval("City") %>, <%# Eval("Country") %>
    </h3>

    <asp:Button ID="btnEdit" runat="server" Text="Edit" CommandName="Edit" />
    <asp:Button ID="btnDelete" runat="server" Text="Delete" CommandName="Delete"
        OnClientClick="return confirm('Are you sure you want to delete this item?');" />
    <asp:Button ID="btnUnselect" runat="server" Text="Unselect" CommandName="unselect" />
</SelectedItemTemplate>
```

In addition to changing some visual settings, the selected item template can contain buttons to trigger operations on the particular item.

In Figure 12-11 shown earlier, each item features its own set of operational buttons such as Edit and Delete. This layout can be reworked to display buttons only on the selected item. To do so, you just move the buttons to the *SelectedItemTemplate* property.

In the item template, though, you need to insert a button control to trigger the selection process. You can use a push button or attach any significant text in the template to a link button:

```
<asp:linkbutton runat="server" Text='<%# Eval("CompanyName") %>' CommandName="Select" />
```

Figure 12-13 shows the result.

FIGURE 12-13 A selected item in a ListView control

Releasing the Selection

When you click the link button, the *ListView* switches the template and sets the *SelectedIndex* property accordingly. As soon as the user clicks on a different item, the selection is moved and the previously selected item regains the regular template. Is there a way to programmatically reset the selection? You bet.

All that you have to do is add a new custom button and handle its click event. In the event handler, you assign the -1 value to the *SelectedIndex* property. A value of -1 means that no items are selected. Here's the related code snippet:

```
protected void ListView1_ItemCommand(object sender, ListViewCommandEventArgs e)
{
    ListView me = (ListView) sender;
    if (e.CommandName.Equals("Unselect", StringComparison.OrdinalIgnoreCase))
        me.SelectedIndex = -1;
}
```

Note that the index of the currently selected item and the index of the item being edited are saved to the view state and persisted across postbacks. This means that if the user changes the country selection (shown in Figure 12-13), both the edit and selection indexes are retained, which might not be desirable. For example, imagine that you selected (or are editing) the second customer from Argentina. Next, the user changes to Brazil while the selected (or edit) template is on. The result is that the second customer from Brazil is displayed in selected (or edit) mode. If this behavior works for you, there's nothing to modify in the code. Otherwise, you need to reset *SelectedIndex* and *EditIndex* in any postback event outside the *ListView* control. Here's an example:

```
protected void DropDownList1_SelectedIndexChanged(object sender, EventArgs e)
{
    // The sender argument here indicates the DropDownList or any other
    // control responsible for the postback. You reference the ListView by
    // name or via a custom global member in the code-behind class of the page
    ListView1.SelectedIndex = -1;
    ListView1.EditIndex = -1;
}
```

Note From a purely architectural perspective, accessing a *ListView* control by name as in the previous example doesn't enforce a neat separation between view and presentation. Ideally, you should tell an external component—you can call it the presenter—to configure the view (in this case, the ASP.NET page) in such a way that there's no item selected or being edited. From a syntax perspective, the preceding code snippet is perfectly functional. The approach behind it, though, might become the source of maintenance trouble in the long run and in relatively large projects. With this, I'm not saying you have to avoid any code such as that just shown; at least, though, be aware of its implications.

Paging the List of Items

In ASP.NET, grid controls support data paging natively. Purely iterative controls such as *Repeater* and *DataList*, though, leave the burden of pagination entirely on the developer's capable shoulders. The *ListView* control falls somewhere in the middle of these two extreme positions. The *ListView* control doesn't have built-in paging capabilities, but it knows how to work with a new control specifically designed to enable data paging on a variety of data-bound controls. This new control, introduced in ASP.NET 3.5, is the *DataPager*.

The *DataPager* Control

The *DataPager* control is designed to add paging capabilities to a family of data-bound controls and not just the *ListView*. The support that the *DataPager* control offers to data-bound pageable controls such as the *ListView* is limited to the user interface of the pager.

You configure the *DataPager* to obtain the pager bar you like best, and then instruct the *DataPager* control to fall back to the paged control to display the specified number of data items starting at the specified position. In no case does the *DataPager* expose itself to the data source or a data source control. All that it does is communicate to the paged control the next set of records to select and display. Table 12-7 lists the properties of the *DataPager* control.

TABLE 12-7 Properties of the *DataPager* Control

Property	Description
Fields	Gets the collection of *DataPagerField* elements that form the pager bar. Elements in this collection belong to classes such as *NumericPagerField*, *TemplatePagerField*, and *NextPreviousPagerField*.
MaximumRows	Gets the maximum number of rows that the page can support.
PagedControlID	Gets and sets the ID of the control to page. This control must implement the *IPageableItemContainer* interface.
PageSize	Gets and sets the size of the page. The default value is 10.
QueryStringField	The name of the query string field for the current page index. The pager uses the query string when this property is set.
StartRowIndex	Gets the index of the first item in the data source to display.
TotalRowCount	Gets the total number of rows to page through.

Only a few of these properties can be set declaratively. They are *Fields*, *PagedControlID*, *PageSize*, and *QueryStringField*. The other properties are read-only and owe their value to the paged control and the size of the bound data source.

Using the *DataPager* Control

The following code snippet shows the typical code you use to embed a data pager in an ASP. NET page that hosts a *ListView* control:

```
<asp:DataPager ID="DataPager1" runat="server"
    PagedControlID="ListView1" PageSize="4">
    <Fields>
        <asp:NextPreviousPagerField />
    </Fields>
</asp:DataPager>
```

The *DataPager* control heralds a new model for paging data-bound controls that is quite a bit different from the model employed by *GridView* controls. The user interface for paging is not part of the control, but it can be placed anywhere in the page and even driven through the query string.

The *DataPager* control is linked to the data-bound control being paged and lets this control know about the user selection. Subsequently, the paged control adjusts its row properties and passes the information back to the data pager. Figure 12-14 shows a data pager in action.

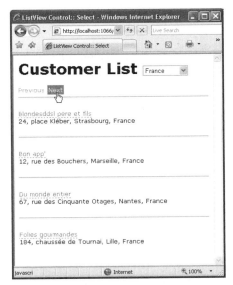

FIGURE 12-14 A data pager in action—the pager can be placed anywhere in the page

Configuring the Data Pager Fields

The user interface of the data pager control is largely customizable. You do that through the *Fields* property—a collection of *DataPagerField* objects. The property allows you to add multiple pagers of different styles. Table 12-8 lists the various options you have.

TABLE 12-8 Types of Data Pagers

Type	Description
NextPreviousPagerField	Displays a fully customizable Next/Previous user interface for the pager. You can use images or text for Next/Previous buttons and also add a First/Last pair of buttons.
NumericPagerField	Displays a fully customizable list of numeric links, one for each page. The number of pages is calculated on the page size and the total number of bound rows.
TemplatePagerField	Allows you to use a user-defined template for the pager.

All classes in Table 12-8 inherit from the same common class—*DataPagerField*. If you're OK with the default user interface of the pagers, you don't need to set any of the pager's properties. The following markup, therefore, is perfectly functional:

```
<Fields>
    <asp:NumericPagerField />
</Fields>
```

Pager fields, though, have a number of visual properties to set the CSS style of buttons, the companion text, or perhaps the images to use instead of text.

Pageable Containers

As mentioned, the data pager control doesn't handle data itself. Rather, the control is the manager of the paging user interface. For this reason, it needs to communicate with the paged control. Whenever a button in the pager is clicked to move to a given page, the pager control fires a message to the paged control and has it refresh the user interface properly.

Not all data-bound controls can be paged using a data pager. In ASP.NET 3.5, this privilege is limited to controls that implement the *IPageableItemContainer* interface. Currently, the sole control to support this interface is the *ListView* control. You can create your own custom controls to implement the interface, however. Here's the definition of the interface:

```
public interface IPageableItemContainer
{
    // Events
    event EventHandler<PageEventArgs> TotalRowCountAvailable;

    // Methods
    void SetPageProperties(int startRowIndex, int maximumRows, bool databind);

    // Properties
    int MaximumRows { get; }
    int StartRowIndex { get; }
}
```

The *PagedControlID* property on the *DataPager* control defines the linked data-bound control. Whenever the pager is acted on, it invokes the *SetPageProperties* method on the paged control through the contracted interface. In doing so, it lets the *ListView* control (or the paged control) know about the new start row to display and the size of the page. Here's the pseudocode used by the *ListView* control to support paging:

```
void SetPageProperties(int startRowIndex, int maximumRows, bool databind)
{
    if ((this._startRowIndex != startRowIndex) || (this._maximumRows != maximumRows))
    {
        PagePropertiesChangingEventArgs e;
        e = new PagePropertiesChangingEventArgs(startRowIndex, maximumRows);
        if (databind)
        {
            this.OnPagePropertiesChanging(e);
        }
        this._startRowIndex = e.StartRowIndex;
        this._maximumRows = e.MaximumRows;
        if (databind)
        {
            this.OnPagePropertiesChanged(EventArgs.Empty);
        }
    }
    if (databind)
    {
        base.RequiresDataBinding = true;
    }
}
```

PagePropertiesChanging and *PagePropertiesChanged* events are fired before and after, respectively, each paging operation.

The data pager control is normally placed outside the *ListView*'s layout. In this case, you use the *PagedControlID* property of the data pager to specify the paged control. However, if the *PagedControlID* property is not specified, the data pager assumes that its naming container is the paged control (as long as it implements the *IPageableItemContainer* interface). What does this mean to you? It means you can embed the data pager in the layout template of the *ListView* control and avoid setting the *PagedControlID* property on the pager explicitly.

Sorting the List

The data bound to the *ListView* control can be sorted using a button in the layout template with the command name of *Sort*:

```
<LayoutTemplate>
    <asp:Button ID="btnSort" runat="server" Text="Sort"
            CommandName="Sort"
            CommandArgument="companyname" />
</LayoutTemplate>
```

You specify the sort expression and the initial sort direction using the *CommandArgument* property of the button. You use *asc* and *desc* to indicate the desired direction. Multiple sorting fields can be listed as well. The sorting automatically reverses from ascending to descending and vice versa as you click. The *ListView*'s *SortExpression* and *SortDirection* read-only properties tell you at any time about the current status of the sort.

Conclusion

The *ListView* control adds the benefits of ASP.NET view controls (such as the *GridView* or *DetailsView* control) to classic repeater data-bound controls such as *DataList*. The resulting control weds the extreme layout flexibility of a *DataList* or *Repeater* control with the power of two-way data binding of data source controls.

The *ListView* control can be used to implement virtually any reporting and publishing scenarios you can imagine. The distinct layout template gives you total control over the HTML being generated and the style it must have. Various item templates (regular, alternate, edit, selected, insert) let you decide about the markup to output for each possible state of the control.

Finally, the *ListView* control is a pageable control. Unlike other view controls, though, the *ListView* control binds to an external pager control—the new *DataPager* control. The connection between the two controls is a new interface introduced in ASP.NET 3.5—the *IPageableItemContainer* interface. As a result, each data-bound control with this interface can be paged without incorporating the logic to page.

ListView and *DataPager* controls are the only new server controls in ASP.NET 3.5, but they add functionality that was missing or implemented in a less-than-optimal way.

Well, to be honest, other new controls show up in ASP.NET 3.5 that weren't available with ASP.NET 2.0—I'm talking about ASP.NET AJAX controls for partial rendering. These controls, available previously through the ASP.NET AJAX Extensions 1.0 release, have been incorporated in ASP.NET 3.5. We'll cover these controls in Chapter 19.

For now, let's just stay focused on view controls and get ready to dig out the features of *DetailsView* and *FormView* controls.

 ## Just the Facts

■ Overall, the *ListView* control is an enhanced version of the *DataList* control. It repeats a user-defined template over the bound data source.

■ The *ListView* control fully supports data source controls and two-way data binding.

- The layout template defines the surrounding markup for the data items and gives developers total freedom as far the HTML markup is concerned and CSS styles.

  The *ListView* control doesn't offer any style properties; instead, it entirely relies on CSS classes for styling.

- The *ListView* control supports a tiled layout and the ability to group items. However, item grouping is based only on numeric partitions and not logical conditions. This means that you can create a group every, say, five customer records, but not a group with all customer records where the name begins with, say, *A*.

- The *ListView* control supports in-place editing and insertion of new items through custom templates.

- The *ListView* control supports a new model for paging its bound data. Instead of relying on a built-in paging engine, it relies on the services of an external pager control.

- Unlike other view controls, the *ListView* control lacks any feature related to ASP.NET callbacks. Instead, you can use ASP.NET AJAX partial rendering to refresh more quickly and cleanly the control's user interface over postbacks.

- The *DataPager* control is a new control in ASP.NET 3.5 that provides the user interface for paging any controls that implement the *IPageableItemContainer* interface. In ASP.NET 3.5, only the *ListView* control implements this interface.

Managing Views of a Record

Many applications need to work on a single record at a time. Old versions of ASP.NET had no built-in support for this scenario. For example, creating a single record view is possible in ASP.NET 1.x, but it requires some coding and, possibly, a custom control. You have to fetch the record, bind its fields to a data-bound form, and optionally provide paging buttons to navigate between records. Displaying the contents of a single record is a common and necessary practice when you build master/detail views. Typically, the user selects a master record from a list or a grid, and the application drills down to show all the available fields. In ASP.NET 2.0 and newer versions, the *DetailsView* control fulfills this role and is the ideal complement to the *DataGrid*, *GridView*, and ListView controls that we examined in Chapter 11 and Chapter 12.

The *DetailsView* control deliberately doesn't support templates. A fully templated details-view control is the *FormView* control, which we'll also cover in this chapter.

The *DetailsView* Control

The *DetailsView* is a data-bound control that renders a single record at a time from its associated data source, optionally providing paging buttons to navigate between records. It is similar to the Form View of a Microsoft Access database and is typically used for updating and inserting records in a master/detail scenario.

The *DetailsView* control binds to any data source control and executes its set of data operations. It can page, update, insert, and delete data items in the underlying data source as long as the data source supports these operations. In most cases, no code is required to set up any of these operations. You can customize the user interface of the *DetailsView* control by choosing the most appropriate combination of data fields and styles in much the same way that you do with the *GridView*.

Finally, note that although the *DetailsView* is commonly used as an update and insert interface, it does not perform any input validation against the data source schema, nor does it provide any schematized user interface such as foreign key field drop-down lists or made-to-measure edit templates for particular types of data.

The *DetailsView* Object Model

The *DetailsView* is to a single record what a *GridView* is to a page of records. Just as the grid lets you choose which columns to display, the *DetailsView* allows you to select a subset of fields to display in read-only or read/write fashion. The rendering of the *DetailsView* is largely customizable using templates and styles. The default rendering consists of a vertical list of rows, one for each field in the bound data item. *DetailsView* is a composite data-bound control and acts as a naming and binding container. Much like the *GridView*, the *DetailsView* control also supports out-of-band calls for paging through the *ICallbackContainer* and *ICallbackEventHandler* interfaces. Here's the declaration of the control class:

```
public class DetailsView : CompositeDataBoundControl,
                           IDataItemContainer,
                           ICallbackContainer,
                           ICallbackEventHandler,
                           INamingContainer
```

The typical look and feel of the control is shown in Figure 13-1.

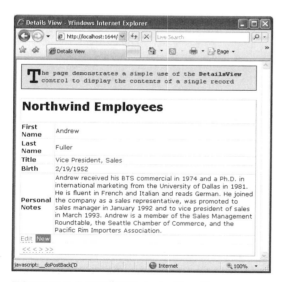

FIGURE 13-1 A *DetailsView* control in action.

The control is formed by a few main areas—a header, field rows, a pager bar, a command bar, and a footer.

Properties of the *DetailsView*

The *DetailsView* layout supports several properties that fall into the following categories: behavior, appearance, style, state, and templates. Table 13-1 lists the behavioral properties.

TABLE 13-1 *DetailsView* **Behavior Properties**

Property	Description
AllowPaging	Indicates whether the control supports navigation.
AutoGenerateDeleteButton	Indicates whether the command bar includes a Delete button. The default is *false*.
AutoGenerateEditButton	Indicates whether the command bar includes an Edit button. The default is *false*.
AutoGenerateInsertButton	Indicates whether the command bar includes an Insert button. The default is *false*.
AutoGenerateRows	Indicates whether the control auto-generates the rows. The default is *true*—all the fields of the record are displayed.
DataMember	Indicates the specific table in a multimember data source to bind to the control. The property works in conjunction with *DataSource*. If *DataSource* is a *DataSet* object, it contains the name of the particular table to bind.
DataSource	Gets or sets the data source object that contains the values to populate the control.
DataSourceID	Indicates the bound data source control.
DefaultMode	Indicates the default display mode of the control. It can be any value from the *DetailsViewMode* enumeration (read-only, insert, edit).
EnablePagingCallbacks	Indicates whether client-side callback functions are used for paging operations.
PagerSettings	Gets a reference to the *PagerSettings* object that allows you to set the properties of the pager buttons.
UseAccessibleHeader	Determines whether to render *<th>* tags for the column headers instead of default *<td>* tags.

The *DefaultMode* property determines the initial working mode of the control and also the mode that the control reverts to after an edit or insert operation is performed.

The output generated by the *DetailsView* control is a table in which each row corresponds to a record field. Additional rows represent special items such as the header, footer, pager, and new command bar. The command bar is a sort of toolbar where all the commands available on the record are collected. Auto-generated buttons go to the command bar.

The user interface of the control is governed by a handful of visual properties, which are listed in Table 13-2.

TABLE 13-2 *DetailsView* **Appearance Properties**

Property	Description
BackImageUrl	Indicates the URL to an image to display in the background
Caption	The text to render in the control's caption
CaptionAlign	Alignment of the caption
CellPadding	Gets or sets the space (in pixels) remaining between the cell's border and the embedded text
CellSpacing	Gets or sets the space (in pixels) remaining, both horizontally and vertically, between two consecutive cells
EmptyDataText	Indicates the text to render in the control when bound to an empty data source
FooterText	Indicates the text to render in the control's footer
Gridlines	Indicates the gridline style for the control
HeaderText	Indicates the text to render in the control's header
HorizontalAlign	Indicates the horizontal alignment of the control on the page

The properties listed in the table apply to the control as a whole. You can program specific elements of the control's user interface by using styles. The supported styles are listed in Table 13-3.

TABLE 13-3 *DetailsView* **Style Properties**

Property	Description
AlternatingRowStyle	Defines the style properties for the fields that are displayed for each even-numbered row
CommandRowStyle	Defines the style properties for the command bar
EditRowStyle	Defines the style properties of individual rows when the control renders in edit mode
EmptyDataRowStyle	Defines the style properties for the displayed row when no data source is available
FieldHeaderStyle	Defines the style properties for the label of each field value
FooterStyle	Defines the style properties for the control's footer
HeaderStyle	Defines the style properties for the control's header
InsertRowStyle	Defines the style properties of individual rows when the control renders in insert mode
PagerStyle	Defines the style properties for the control's pager
RowStyle	Defines the style properties of the individual rows

The *DetailsView* control can be displayed in three modes, depending on the value—*ReadOnly*, *Insert*, or *Edit*—of the *DetailsViewMode* enumeration. The read-only mode is the default display mode in which users see only the contents of the record. To edit or add a new record, users must click the corresponding button (if any) on the command bar. Such buttons must be explicitly enabled on the command bar through the *AutoGenerateXxxButton* properties. Each mode has an associated style. The current mode is tracked by the *CurrentMode* read-only property.

Other state properties are listed in Table 13-4.

TABLE 13-4 *DetailsView* **State Properties**

Property	Description
BottomPagerRow	Returns a *DetailsViewRow* object that represents the bottom pager of the control.
CurrentMode	Gets the current mode for the control—any of the values in the *DetailsViewMode* enumeration. The property determines how bound fields and templates are rendered.
DataItem	Returns the data object that represents the currently displayed record.
DataItemCount	Gets the number of items in the underlying data source.
DataItemIndex	Gets or sets the index of the item being displayed from the underlying data source.
DataKey	Returns the *DataKey* object for the currently displayed record. The *DataKey* object contains the key values corresponding to the key fields specified by *DataKeyNames*.
DataKeyNames	An array specifying the primary key fields for the records being displayed. These keys are used to uniquely identify an item for update and delete operations.
Fields	Returns the collection of *DataControlField* objects for the control that was used to generate the *Rows* collection.
FooterRow	Returns a *DetailsViewRow* object that represents the footer of the control.
HeaderRow	Returns a *DetailsViewRow* object that represents the header of the control.
PageCount	Returns the total number of items in the underlying data source bound to the control.
PageIndex	Returns the 0-based index for the currently displayed record in the control. The index is relative to the total number of records in the underlying data source.
Rows	Returns a collection of *DetailsViewRow* objects representing the individual rows within the control. Only data rows are taken into account.
SelectedValue	Returns the value of the key for the current record as stored in the *DataKey* object.
TopPagerRow	Returns a *DetailsViewRow* object that represents the top pager of the control.

If you're not satisfied with the default control rendering, you can use certain templates to better adapt the user interface to your preferences. Table 13-5 details the supported templates.

TABLE 13-5 *DetailsView* **Template Properties**

Property	Description
EmptyDataTemplate	The template for rendering the control when it is bound to an empty data source. If set, this property overrides the *EmptyDataText* property.
FooterTemplate	The template for rendering the footer row of the control.
HeaderTemplate	The template for rendering the header of the control. If set, this property overrides the *HeaderText* property.
PagerTemplate	The template for rendering the pager of the control. If set, this property overrides any existing pager settings.

As you can see, the list of templates is related to the layout of the control and doesn't include any template that influences the rendering of the current record. This is by design. For more ambitious template properties, such as *InsertTemplate* or perhaps *ItemTemplate*, you should resort to the *FormView* control, which is the fully templated sibling of the *DetailsView* control.

The *DetailsView* control has only one method, *ChangeMode*. As the name suggests, the *ChangeMode* method is used to switch from one display mode to the next.

```
public void ChangeMode(DetailsViewMode newMode)
```

This method is used internally to change views when a command button is clicked.

Events of the *DetailsView*

The *DetailsView* control exposes several events that enable the developer to execute custom code at various times in the life cycle. The event model is similar to that of the *GridView* control in terms of supported events and because of the pre/post pair of events that characterize each significant operation. Table 13-6 details the supported events.

TABLE 13-6 **Events of the *DetailsView* Control**

Event	Description
ItemCommand	Occurs when any clickable element in the user interface is clicked. This doesn't include standard buttons (such as Edit, Delete, and Insert), which are handled internally, but it does include custom buttons defined in the templates.
ItemCreated	Occurs after all the rows are created.
ItemDeleting, ItemDeleted	Both events occur when the current record is deleted. They fire before and after the record is deleted.

Event	Description
ItemInserting, ItemInserted	Both events occur when a new record is inserted. They fire before and after the insertion.
ItemUpdating, ItemUpdated	Both events occur when the current record is updated. They fire before and after the row is updated.
ModeChanging, ModeChanged	Both events occur when the control switches to a different display mode. They fire before and after the mode changes.
PageIndexChanging, PageIndexChanged	Both events occur when the control moves to another record. They fire before and after the display change occurs.

The *ItemCommand* event fires only if the original click event is not handled by a predefined method. This typically occurs if you define custom buttons in one of the templates. You do not need to handle this event to intercept any clicking on the Edit or Insert buttons.

Simple Data Binding

Building a record viewer with the *DetailsView* control is easy and quick. You just drop an instance of the control onto the Web form, bind it to a data source control, and add a few decorative settings. The following listing shows the very minimum that's needed:

```
<asp:DetailsView runat="server" id="RecordView"
    DataSourceID="MySource"
    HeaderText="Employees">
</asp:DetailsView>
```

When the *AllowPaging* property is set to *true*, a pager bar is displayed for users to navigate between bound records. As you'll see in more detail later, this works only if multiple records are bound to the control. Here's a more realistic code snippet—the code behind the control in Figure 13-2:

```
<asp:ObjectDataSource ID="RowDataSource" runat="server"
    TypeName="Core35.DAL.Employees"
    SelectMethod="LoadAll">
</asp:ObjectDataSource>

<asp:DetailsView ID="RecordView" runat="server"
    DataSourceID="RowDataSource" AllowPaging="true"
    HeaderText="Northwind Employees"
    AutoGenerateRows="false">
    <PagerSettings Mode="NextPreviousFirstLast" />
    <Fields>
        <asp:BoundField DataField="firstname" HeaderText="First Name" />
        <asp:BoundField DataField="lastname" HeaderText="Last Name" />
        <asp:BoundField DataField="title" HeaderText="Title" />
        <asp:BoundField DataField="birthdate" HeaderText="Birth"
            HtmlEncode="false"
            DataFormatString="{0:d}" />
    </Fields>
</asp:DetailsView>
```

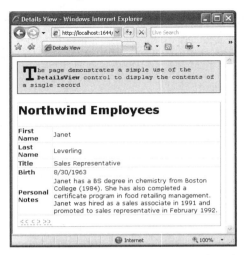

FIGURE 13-2 A *DetailsView* control to explore the results of a query.

Binding Data to a *DetailsView* Control

A *DetailsView* control is formed by data-bindable rows—one for each field in the displayed data item. By default, the control includes all the available fields in the view. You can change this behavior by setting the *AutoGenerateRows* property to *false*. In this case, only the fields explicitly listed in the *Fields* collection are displayed. Just as grids do, the *DetailsView* control can have both declared and auto-generated fields. In this case, declared fields appear first and auto-generated fields are not added to the *Fields* collection. The *DetailsView* supports the same variety of field types as the *GridView*. (See Chapter 11.)

If no data source property is set, the *DetailsView* control doesn't render anything. If an empty data source object is bound and an *EmptyDataTemplate* template is specified, the results shown to the user have a more friendly look:

```
<asp:DetailsView runat="server" datasourceid="MySource">
   <EmptyDataTemplate>
      <asp:label runat="server">
         There's no data to show in this view.
      </asp:label>
   </EmptyDataTemplate>
</asp:DetailsView>
```

The *EmptyDataTemplate* property is ignored if the bound data source is not empty. If you simply plan to display a message to the user, you can more effectively resort to the *EmptyDataText* property. Plain text properties, in fact, are faster than templates.

Fields can be defined either declaratively or programmatically. If you opt for the latter, instantiate any needed data field objects and add them to the *Fields* collection, as shown in the following code snippet:

```
BoundField field = new BoundField();
field.DataField = "companyname";
field.HeaderText = "Company Name";
detailsView1.Fields.Add(field);
```

Rows in the control's user interface reflect the order of fields in the *Fields* collection. To statically declare your columns in the *.aspx* source file, you use the *<Fields>* tag.

> **Note** If you programmatically add fields to the control, be aware of the view state. The field is not automatically added to the view state and won't be there the next time the page posts back. (This is the same snag we found in a previous chapter for the columns of a *GridView* or *DataGrid* control.) If some fields have to be added programmatically all the time, you put the code in the *Page_Load* event handler. If field insertion is conditional, after adding fields you write a custom flag to the view state. In *Page_Load*, you then check the view state flag and, if it is set, you add fields as expected.

Controlling the Displayed Fields

Just as grid controls can display only a selected range of columns, the *DetailsView* control can display only a subset of the available fields for the current record. As mentioned, you disable the automatic generation of all fields by setting the *AutoGenerateRows* property to *false*. Then you declare as many fields as needed under the *<Fields>* element, as shown here:

```
<asp:detailsview>
    ...
    <fields>
        <asp:boundfield datafield="firstname" headertext="First Name" />
        <asp:boundfield datafield="lastname" headertext="Last Name" />
        <asp:boundfield datafield="title" headertext="Position" />
    </fields>
</asp:detailsview>
```

The *HeaderText* attribute refers to the label displayed alongside the field value. You can style this text using the *FieldHeaderStyle* property. The following code makes field labels appear in boldface type:

```
<FieldHeaderStyle Font-Bold="true" />
```

To improve the readability of displayed data, you select the field type that best suits the data to display. For example, Boolean data is better displayed through *CheckBoxField* rows, whereas URLs render the best via *HyperLinkField*. Admittedly, the list is not exhaustive, but the main issues won't show up until you turn on the record in edit mode. By default, in fact, in edit or insert mode the content of the field is displayed using a text box, which is great for many data types but not for all. For example, what if your users need to edit a date? In this case, the *Calendar* control would be far more appropriate. However, you can't use templates to modify the default rendering because the *DetailsView* control doesn't support data-bound templates on rows. You should resort to the *FormView* control if template support is an unavoidable necessity.

Paging Through Bound Data

The *DetailsView* control is designed to display one record at a time, but it allows you to bind multiple records. In a master/detail scenario, you really need to bind a single record. In a record-viewer scenario, you might find it useful to bind the whole cached data source and have the control to page through. The following paragraph details the rules for paging in the *DetailsView* control.

No paging is allowed if *AllowPaging* is set to *false* (the default setting). If *AllowPaging* is turned on, paging is allowed only if more than one record is bound to the control. When paging is possible, the pager is displayed to let users select the next record to view. Just as for grids, the pager can provide numeric links to the various records (the first, the third, the last, and so forth) as well as relative hyperlinks to the first, previous, next, or last record. The *PagerSettings* type determines the attributes and behavior of the pager bar. *PagerStyle*, on the other hand, governs the appearance of the pager.

The *DetailsView* paging mechanism is based on the *PageIndex* property, which indicates the index of the current record in the bound data source. Clicking any pager button updates the property; the control does the data binding and refreshes the view. *PageCount* returns the total number of records available for paging. Changing the record is signaled by a pair of events—*PageIndexChanging* and *PageIndexChanged*.

The *PageIndexChanging* event allows you to execute custom code before the *PageIndex* actually changes—that is, before the control moves to a different record. You can cancel the event by setting the *Cancel* property of the event argument class to *true*:

```
void PageIndexChanging(object sender, DetailsViewPageEventArgs e)
{
    e.Cancel = true;
}
```

Note that when the event fires you don't have much information about the new record being displayed. You can read everything about the currently displayed record, but you know only the index of the next one. To retrieve details of the current record, you proceed as you would with *GridView*s and use the *DataKey* property:

```
DataKey data = DetailsView1.DataKey;
string country = (string) data.Values["country"];
if (country == "Mexico" || country == "USA" || country == "Brazil")
{
    ...
}
```

To be able to use the *DataKey* property within data-bound events, you must set the *DataKeyNames* property to the comma-separated list of fields you want to be persisted in the view state and exposed by the *DataKey* structure later:

```
<asp:DetailsView ID="DetailsView1" runat="server"
   DataKeyNames="id, country"
   ...
/>
```

It is essential that *DataKeyNames* contains public properties of the bound data type. In other words, *id* and *country* must be record fields if the *DetailsView* control is bound to a *DataSet* or *DataTable*. They must be property names if the *DetailsView* control is bound to a custom collection via *ObjectDataSource*.

There's no easy way to look up the next record from within the *PageIndexChanging* event. The simplest thing you can do is cache the data set bound to the *DetailsView*, get a reference to the cached data, and select in that list the record that corresponds to the index of the next page.

> **Note** Paging with the *DetailsView* control is subject to the same paging issues for *GridView* and *DataGrid* that we examined in the previous chapter. If you bind the control to *SqlDataSource*, you're better off caching the data source; if you bind to *ObjectDataSource*, it is preferable that you use business objects that page themselves through the data source.

Paging via Callbacks

Paging is normally implemented through a server-side event and requires a full page refresh. The *DetailsView* control provides the *EnablePagingCallbacks* property to specify whether paging operations are performed using client-side callback functions.

Paging callbacks are based on ASP.NET script callbacks, and when they are enabled, they prevent the need to post the page back to the server. At the same time, new data for the requested page is retrieved through an out-of-band call. The control is responsible for grabbing the server data and refreshing its own user interface on browsers that support a Dynamic HTML–compliant document object model.

For a developer, turning on the client paging feature couldn't be easier. You just set the *EnablePagingCallbacks* property to *true* and you're done.

> **Note** As mentioned for the *GridView* control in Chapter 11, script callbacks are a functionality completely replaced by AJAX and partial rendering. We'll cover this in Chapter 18.

Creating Master/Detail Views

In versions prior to ASP.NET 2.0, implementing master/detail views is not particularly hard to do, but it's certainly not automatic and codeless. In ASP.NET 2.0 and beyond, combining the *DetailsView* control with another data-bound control such as the *GridView* or *DropDownList* greatly simplifies the creation of master/detail views of data. The master control (such as the *GridView*) selects one particular record in its own data source, and that record becomes the data source for a *DetailsView* control in the same form. Let's see how.

Drill Down into the Selected Record

A typical master/detail page contains a master control (such as a *GridView*) and a detail control (such as a *DetailsView*), each bound to its own data source. The trick is in binding the detail control to a data source represented by the currently selected record. The following code snippet shows the configuration of the "master" block. It consists of a *GridView* bound to a pageable *ObjectDataSource*:

```
<asp:ObjectDataSource ID="CustomersDataSource" runat="server"
    EnablePaging="true"
    StartRowIndexParameterName="firstRow"
    MaximumRowsParameterName="totalRows"
    TypeName="Core35.DAL.Customers"
    SelectMethod="LoadAll">
</asp:ObjectDataSource>
<asp:GridView ID="GridView1" runat="server"
    DataSourceID="CustomersDataSource"
    DataKeyNames="id"
    AllowPaging="True"
    AutoGenerateSelectButton="True"
    AutoGenerateColumns="False">
    <PagerSettings Mode="NextPreviousFirstLast" />
    <Columns>
        <asp:BoundField DataField="CompanyName" HeaderText="Company" />
        <asp:BoundField DataField="Country" HeaderText="Country" />
    </Columns>
</asp:GridView>
```

The grid shows a Select column for users to select the record to drill down into. However, you don't need to handle the corresponding *SelectedIndexChanged* event for the details view to kick in. The following code shows the "detail" block of the master/detail scheme:

```
<asp:ObjectDataSource ID="RowDataSource" runat="server"
    TypeName="Core35.DAL.Customers"
    SelectMethod="Load">
    <SelectParameters>
        <asp:ControlParameter Name="id" ControlID="GridView1"
            PropertyName="SelectedValue" />
    </SelectParameters>
</asp:ObjectDataSource>
```

```
<asp:DetailsView ID="DetailsView1" runat="server"
    HeaderText="Customer Details"
    EmptyDataText="No customer currently selected"
    DataSourceID="RowDataSource"
    AutoGenerateRows="False"
    AutoGenerateInsertButton="True"
    AutoGenerateDeleteButton="True"
    AutoGenerateEditButton="True">
    <Fields>
        <asp:BoundField DataField="ID" HeaderText="ID" />
        <asp:BoundField DataField="CompanyName" HeaderText="Company" />
        <asp:BoundField DataField="ContactName" HeaderText="Contact" />
        <asp:BoundField DataField="Street" HeaderText="Address" />
        <asp:BoundField DataField="City" HeaderText="City" />
        <asp:BoundField DataField="Country" HeaderText="Country" />
    </Fields>
</asp:DetailsView>
```

The *DetailsView* control is bound to the return value of the *Load* method on the *Customer* data access layer (DAL) class. The *Load* method requires an argument to be the ID of the customer. This parameter is provided by the grid through its *SelectedValue* property. Whenever the user selects a new row in the grid, the *SelectedValue* property changes (as discussed in Chapter 11), the page posts back, and the *DetailsView* refreshes its user interface accordingly. No code should be written in the code-behind class for this to happen.

Figure 13-3 shows the page in action when no row is selected in the grid. This is a great example for understanding the importance of the empty data row template.

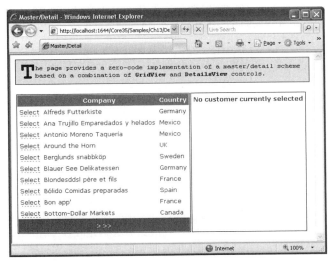

FIGURE 13-3 A no-code implementation of a master/detail scheme based on a combination of *GridView* and *DetailsView* controls.

Figure 13-4 shows the two controls in action when a record is selected.

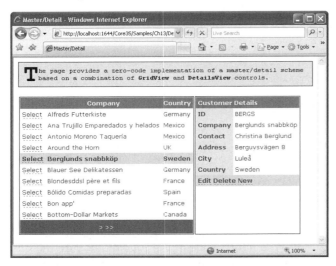

FIGURE 13-4 The *DetailsView* control shows the details of the selected customer.

Note that the internal page mechanics places a call to the *Load* method at all times, even when the page first loads and there's no record selected in the grid. Even when there's no record selected, the *Load* method is passed the value of the *SelectedValue* property on the grid—which is null. What happens in this case? It depends on the implementation of the *Load* method. If *Load* can handle null input values and degrades gracefully, nothing bad happens and the page displays the empty data template. Otherwise, you typically get a runtime exception from the ADO.NET infrastructure in charge of retrieving data because of the invalid parameter you provided to the method. Here's a good code sequence to use for methods with data source controls:

```
public static Customer Load(string id)
{
    if (String.IsNullOrEmpty(id))
        return null;
    ...
}
```

Caching Issues

The preceding scheme for master/detail pages is easy to understand and arrange. Furthermore, you can design it through a full point-and-click metaphor directly in the Microsoft Visual Studio integrated development environment (IDE) without writing a single line of code. Could you possibly ask for more? Actually, what you should do is ensure that it works the way you want it to. Let's delve a bit deeper into this type of automatic master/detail binding.

The grid is bound to a list of customers as returned by the data source control. As you would expect, this list is cached somewhere. If you use *SqlDataSource*, you can control caching to some extent through a bunch of properties. If you use *ObjectDataSource* as in the previous example, you have no caching at all unless you instruct the *Load* method or, more generally, you instruct your DAL and business layer to cache data. All the data bound to the grid is retrieved from the database whenever the grid is paged or sorted. But there's more.

When the user selects a given record, the *DetailsView* gets bound to a particular record whose details are retrieved through another query. This repeated query might or might not be necessary. It might not be necessary if you're building a master/detail scheme on a single table (Customers, in this case) and if the "master" control already contains all the data. In the previous example, the *LoadAll* method that populates the grid returns a collection based on the results of *SELECT [fields] FROM customers*. In light of this, there would be no need for the *DetailsView* to run a second query to get details that could already be available, if only they were cached.

In summary, *ObjectDataSource* doesn't inherently support caching unless you use ADO.NET data containers. Generally speaking, caching is a performance booster if the overall size of cached data is limited to hundreds of records. If you can't get caching support from the data source control, build it in the business objects you use. If you use *SqlDataSource*, or *ObjectDataSource* with ADO.NET objects, enable caching, but keep an eye on the size of the cached data. And in all cases, use the SQL Server profiler (or similar tools if you use other database management systems) to see exactly when data is being retrieved from the database.

Working with Data

A detailed view like that of the *DetailsView* control is particularly useful if users can perform basic updates on the displayed data. Basic updates include editing and deleting the record, as well as inserting new records. The *DetailsView* command bar gathers all the buttons needed to start data operations. You tell the control to create those buttons by setting to *true* the following properties: *AutoGenerateEditButton* (for updates), *AutoGenerateDeleteButton* (for deletions), and *AutoGenerateInsertButton* for (adding new records).

Editing the Current Record

As with the *GridView*, data operations for the *DetailsView* control are handled by the bound data source control, as long as the proper commands are defined and a key to identify the correct record to work on is indicated through the *DataKeyNames* property. Let's test *SqlDataSource* first:

```
<asp:SqlDataSource runat="server" id="SqlDataSource1"
    ConnectionString="<%$ ConnectionStrings:NWind %>"
    SelectCommand="SELECT * FROM customers"
    UpdateCommand="UPDATE customers SET
                companyname=@companyname, contactname=@contactname,
                city=@city, country=@country
             WHERE customerid=@original_customerid"
    DeleteCommand="DELETE customers WHERE customerid=@original_customerid"
/>
```

```
<asp:DetailsView ID="DetailsView1" runat="server"
    DataKeyNames="customerid"
    DataSourceID="SqlDataSource1"
    AllowPaging="True"
    AutoGenerateRows="False"
    HeaderText="Customers"
    AutoGenerateEditButton="True"
    AutoGenerateDeleteButton="True">
    <PagerSettings Mode="NextPreviousFirstLast" />
    <Fields>
        <asp:BoundField DataField="CompanyName" HeaderText="Company" />
        <asp:BoundField DataField="ContactName" HeaderText="Contact" />
        <asp:BoundField DataField="City" HeaderText="City" />
        <asp:BoundField DataField="Country" HeaderText="Country" />
    </Fields>
</asp:DetailsView>
```

The *SqlDataSource* must expose SQL commands (or stored procedures) for deleting and updating records. Once this has been done, the *DetailsView* control does all the rest. Users click to edit or delete the current record and the control ultimately calls upon the underlying data source to accomplish the action.

Figure 13-5 shows the changed user interface of the *DetailsView* control when it works in edit mode. Note that in edit mode, the default set of buttons in the command is replaced by a pair of update/cancel buttons.

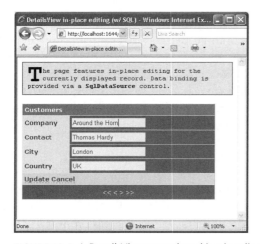

FIGURE 13-5 A *DetailsView* control working in edit mode.

If you attach the *DetailsView* control to an *ObjectDataSource* control, make sure you properly bind the update and delete methods of the business object:

```
<asp:ObjectDataSource runat="server" id="ObjectDataSource1"
    TypeName="Core35.DAL.Customers"
    SelectMethod="LoadAll"
    DeleteMethod="Delete"
    UpdateMethod="Save"
    DataObjectTypeName="Core35.DAL.Customer"
/>
```

The *DataKeyNames* property must be set to the name of the public property that represents the key for identifying the record to delete or update.

Deleting the Current Record

Although the delete operation can be pre- and post-processed by a pair of events such as *ItemDeleting/ItemDeleted*, there's not much a page author can do to give users a chance to recall an inadvertently started delete operation. The bad news is that unlike other data-bound controls, the *DetailsView* doesn't offer easy-to-use events and properties for you to override default behaviors. You might think that the *ItemCreated* event is the right place to handle the interception of the command bar creation and add some script code to the delete button. *ItemCreated* is still the right (the only, actually) entry point in the control's machinery, but adding a client-side message box to the delete button is a difficult challenge.

ItemCreated fires whenever a *DetailsView* row is being created, but it doesn't supply additional information about the newly created row. Furthermore, the command row is not exposed through a direct property as is the case with a pager, header, and footer. A trick is needed to access the row representing the command bar. If you turn tracing on and snoop into the contents of the *Rows* collection while debugging, you can easily figure out that the *Rows* collection contains as many elements as there are data rows in the control, plus one. The extra row is actually the command bar. You get it with the following code:

```
protected void DetailsView1_ItemCreated(object sender, EventArgs e)
{
    if (DetailsView1.FooterRow != null)
    {
        int commandRowIndex = DetailsView1.Rows.Count-1;
        DetailsViewRow commandRow = DetailsView1.Rows[commandRowIndex];
        ...
    }
}
```

To be sure that your code kicks in when the command bar exists, you check the *FooterRow* property for nullness. The footer row is always created regardless of whether it is displayed or not; in addition, it is always created after all the data rows have been created. The command bar is the last row in the *Rows* collection and is an object of type *DetailsViewRow*—a special type of table row. The row contains a cell—an internal object of type *DataControlFieldCell*—which in turn contains edit, delete, and insert buttons. The tracing tool reveals that buttons are not plain buttons, but instances of the internal *DataControlLinkButton* class, a class derived from *LinkButton*. You get the cell with the following code:

```
DataControlFieldCell cell;
cell = (DataControlFieldCell) commandRow.Controls[0];
```

At this point, you're pretty much done. What remains for you to do is loop through all the child controls of the cell and get a reference to all link buttons. How can you distinguish the delete button from the edit button? What if one of these controls is not enabled? Link buttons have the *CommandName* property, which assigns them a characteristic and unique name—Delete, Edit, or New for the data operations we're interested in here. Have a look at the following code:

```
protected void DetailsView1_ItemCreated(object sender, EventArgs e)
{
    if (DetailsView1.FooterRow != null)
    {
        int commandRowIndex = DetailsView1.Rows.Count-1;
        DetailsViewRow commandRow = DetailsView1.Rows[commandRowIndex];

        DataControlFieldCell cell;
        cell = (DataControlFieldCell) commandRow.Controls[0];
        foreach(Control ctl in cell.Controls)
        {
            LinkButton link = ctl as LinkButton;
            if (link != null)
            {
                if (link.CommandName == "Delete")
                {
                    link.ToolTip = "Click here to delete";
                    link.OnClientClick = "return confirm('Do you really want
                                          to delete this record?');";
                }
                else if (link.CommandName == "New")
                {
                    link.ToolTip = "Click here to add a new record";
                }
                else if (link.CommandName == "Edit")
                {
                    link.ToolTip = "Click here to edit the current record";
                }
            }
        }
    }
}
```

Once you have received a valid reference to the link button that represents, say, the delete button, you can do whatever you want—for example, add a ToolTip and a Javascript confirm popup. (See Figure 13-6.)

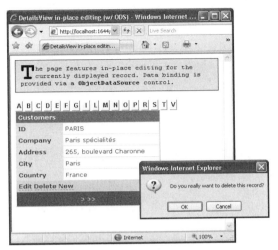

FIGURE 13-6 A popup asking for confirmation before you delete the current record.

Inserting a New Record

The process of adding a new record is much like the process for editing or deleting. You add an insert command in the bound data source control and enable the insert button on the *DetailsView* control. Here is a valid insert command:

```
<asp:SqlDataSource ID="SqlDataSource1" runat="server"
    EnableCaching="true"
    ConnectionString='<%$ ConnectionStrings:NWind %>'
    SelectCommand="SELECT employeeid, firstname, lastname, title, hiredate
                FROM employees"
    InsertCommand="INSERT INTO employees
                (firstname, lastname, title, hiredate) VALUES
                (@firstname, @lastname, @title, @hiredate)"
/>
<asp:DetailsView ID="DetailsView1" runat="server"
    AllowPaging="true"
    DataSourceID="SqlDataSource1"
    AutoGenerateInsertButton="true"
    HeaderText="Employee Details" >
    <PagerSettings Mode="NextPreviousFirstLast" />
</asp:DetailsView>
```

Figure 13-7 shows how it works.

FIGURE 13-7 A *DetailsView* control working in insert mode.

When you implement the insert command, you should pay attention to primary keys. In particular, the preceding command doesn't specify the primary key (*employeeid*) because, in this example, the underlying database auto-generates values for the field. Generally, for a database that accepts user-defined keys, you should provide a validation mechanism in the page before you push the new record. Once again, all this code is best placed in the DAL and bound to *DetailsView* through an *ObjectDataSource* control. I'll say more on input data validation in a moment.

Templated Fields

The *DetailsView* control doesn't support edit and insert templates to change the layout of the control entirely. When editing the contents of a data source, you either go through the standard layout of the user interface—a vertical list of header/value pairs—or resort to another control, such as the *FormView* or a custom control. Designed to be simple and effective, the *DetailsView* turns out to be somewhat inflexible and hard to hook up. As seen earlier, walking your way through the internal object model of the *DetailsView* control is not impossible. The real problem, though, is forcing the control to play by rules that it hasn't set.

You can change, instead, the way in which a particular field is displayed within the standard layout. For example, you can use a *Calendar* control to render a date field, or a *DropDownList* control to display multiple options. To do this, you employ the *TemplateField* class, as we did for grid controls. By using a *TemplateField* class to render a data field, you are free to use any layout you like for view, edit, and insert operations, as shown here:

```
<asp:TemplateField HeaderText="Country">
    <ItemTemplate>
        <asp:literal runat="server" Text='<%# Eval("country") %>' />
    </ItemTemplate>
```

```
    <EditItemTemplate>
        <asp:dropdownlist ID="DropDownList1" runat="server"
            datasourceid="CountriesDataSource"
            selectedvalue='<%# Bind("country") %>' />
    </EditItemTemplate>
</asp:TemplateField>
```

The field *Country* is rendered through a literal in view mode, and turns to a data-bound drop-down list control in edit mode. The bound data source control is responsible for providing all the displayable countries. The *Bind* operator is like *Eval* except that it writes data back to the data source—this is the power of ASP.NET two-way data binding. (See Chapter 10.) Figure 13-8 shows a sample page.

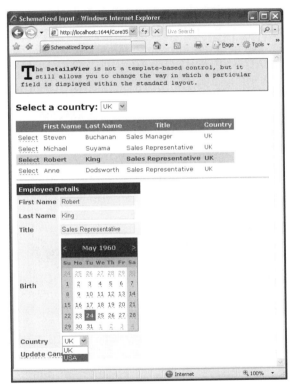

FIGURE 13-8 Templated fields in a *DetailsView* control.

Adding Validation Support

By using templated fields, you can also add any validator control you need and add it where you need it. What if you don't want templated fields? Limited to validator controls, there's an alternate approach. In this way, you still use *BoundField* controls to render fields, but you attach validators to them programmatically.

You start by adding an *ItemCreated* event handler to the *DetailsView* control in the page, as follows:

```
protected void DetailsView1_ItemCreated(object sender, EventArgs e)
{
    if (DetailsView1.CurrentMode == DetailsViewMode.ReadOnly)
        return;
    if (DetailsView1.FooterRow == null)
        return;

    AddRequiredFieldValidator(0, "First name required");
    AddRequiredFieldValidator(1, "Last name required");
}
```

First you ensure the control is in edit mode and all the data rows have been created. Next, you assume you know the ordinal position of the fields you want to modify. (This is a reasonable assumption, as we're not designing a general-purpose solution, but simply adjusting a particular ASP.NET page that we created.)

The *AddRequiredFieldValidator* method takes the index of the field you want to validate and the message to display in case the field is left blank. It instantiates and initializes a validator, and then adds it to the corresponding cell, as in the following code:

```
void AddRequiredFieldValidator(int rowIndex, string msg)
{
    // Retrieve the data row to extend
    const int DataCellIndex = 1;
    DetailsViewRow row = DetailsView1.Rows[rowIndex];

    // Get the second cell--the first contains the label
    DataControlFieldCell cell;
    cell = (DataControlFieldCell) row.Cells[DataCellIndex];

    // Initialize the validator
    RequiredFieldValidator req = new RequiredFieldValidator();
    req.Text = String.Format("<span title='{0}'>*</span>", msg);

    // Get the ID of the TextBox control to validate
    string ctlID = cell.Controls[0].UniqueID;
    int pos = ctlID.LastIndexOf("$");
    if (pos < 0)
      return;
    string temp = ctlID.Substring(pos + 1);
    req.ControlToValidate = temp;

    // Insert the validator
    cell.Controls.Add(req);
}
```

You retrieve the data row to extend with a validator control and get a reference to its second cell. A *DetailsView* row has two cells—one for the field header and one for the field value. In edit/insert mode, the second cell contains a *TextBox* control.

The validator control—a *RequiredFieldValidator* in this example—requires some behavior settings (say, the message to display). More importantly, it requires the ID of the control to validate. Nobody knows the ID of the dynamically generated *TextBox* control. However, you can get a reference to the control and read the *UniqueID* property, and here's why that's important.

The *DetailsView* is a naming container, which means that it prefixes the names of contained controls. For example, an internal *TextBox* named, say, *clt01* is publicly known as *DetailsView1$clt01*, where *DetailsView1* is the ID of the *DetailsView* control. You need to pass the real control's ID to the validator. That's why the preceding code locates the last occurrence of the $ symbol and discards all that precedes it. The equivalent of *ctl01* is finally assigned to the *ControlToValidate* property of the validator, and the validator is added to the cell.

You have added a new control with its own behavior, and you have no need to interact with the remainder of the host control. In this case, it works just fine, as shown in Figure 13-9.

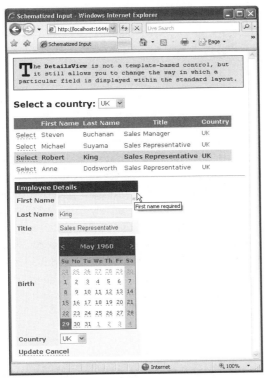

FIGURE 13-9 Validation support added to a *DetailsView* control.

The preceding code always displays an asterisk to signal an incomplete field. The actual text is wrapped by a *<span>* tag to include a ToolTip. This is arbitrary; you can configure the validator control at your leisure.

Validating Without Validators

So far we considered two different scenarios for validating data manipulated with the *DetailsView* control. In the first, you employ templates and explicitly add validator controls. In the second, you stick to nontemplated bound fields but use a slick piece of code to add validators programmatically. It is important to mention that there's also a simpler, and perhaps more natural, way of approaching the problem of validating data—using events.

You write a handler for the *ItemUpdating* event (*ItemInserting* or *ItemDeleting* for insert and delete operations, respectively), check the new values and cancel the operation if there's something wrong. The following code ensures that the *title* field contains one of two hard-coded strings:

```
void DetailsView1_ItemUpdating(object sender, DetailsViewUpdateEventArgs e)
{
    string title = (string) e.NewValues["title"];
    if (!title.Equals("Sales Representative") &&
        !title.Equals("Sales Manager"))
    {
        e.Cancel = true;
    }
}
```

The *NewValues* dictionary you get through the event data contains new values as edited by the user; the *OldValues* dictionary contains the original data. What's the difference between this approach and validators? *ItemUpdating* (and similar events) are run on the server during the postback event. Validators can catch patently invalid input data already on the client. However, a golden rule of validation states that you should never rely on client-side validation only. You should always do some validation on the server, so performance is not the issue here. The event-based approach is easier to set up and is ideal for quick pages where you don't bother using a more advanced and templated user interface. Validators are a more complete toolkit for validation and, of course, include a control for server-side validation as we saw in Chapter 4. The validation-without-validators scheme can be applied for any view controls—*DetailsView*, *FormView*, and *GridView*.

The *FormView* Control

FormView is a new data-bound control that can be considered the templated version of the *DetailsView*. It renders one record at a time, picked from the associated data source and, optionally, provides paging buttons to navigate between records. Unlike the *DetailsView* control, *FormView* doesn't use data control fields and requires the user to define the rendering of each item by using templates. The *FormView* can support any basic operation its data source provides.

Note that the *FormView* requires you to define everything through templates, and not just the things you want to change. The *FormView* has no built-in rendering engine and is limited to printing out the user-defined templates.

The *FormView* Object Model

Two functional aspects mark the difference between *FormView* and *DetailsView*. First, the *FormView* control has properties such as *ItemTemplate*, *EditItemTemplate*, and *InsertItemTemplate* that—as we've seen thus far—the *DetailsView* lacks entirely. Second, the *FormView* lacks the command row—that is, a sort of toolbar where available functions are grouped. The graphical layout of a *FormView* control is completely customizable using templates. Therefore, each template will include all command buttons needed by the particular record.

The control's definition is shown in the following code:

```
public class FormView : CompositeDataBoundControl,
                        IDataItemContainer,
                        INamingContainer
```

As you can see, *FormView* has the same root and implements the same interfaces as *DetailsView* except for the interfaces related to ASP.NET script callbacks.

Members of the *FormView* Control

The *FormView* control exposes many of the properties that we've seen already for the *DetailsView* control. This aspect is no surprise, as the two controls serve as two sides of the same coin—a record viewer control—one with and one without templates. Only the templates and related styles mark the difference between *FormView* and *DetailsView*. You can refer to Table 13-1 through Table 13-6 for the complete list of properties and events supported by the *FormView* control.

Supported Templates

The output of the *FormView* control is exclusively based on templates. This means that you always need to specify the item template at a very minimum. Table 13-7 shows the list of data-bound supported templates.

TABLE 13-7 Templates of the *FormView* Control

Template	Description
EditItemTemplate	The template to use when an existing record is being updated
InsertItemTemplate	The template to use when a new record is being created
ItemTemplate	The template to use when an existing record is rendered for viewing only

It's not a coincidence that the *FormView* templates match the three feasible states of the control—ReadOnly, Edit, and Insert. You use *ItemTemplate* to define the control's layout when in view mode. You use *EditItemTemplate* to edit the contents of the current record, and you use *InsertItemTemplate* to add a new record.

In addition to these templates, the control features the same set of templates offered by the *DetailsView*—that is, *HeaderTemplate*, *FooterTemplate*, and the other templates listed in Table 13-5.

Supported Operations

Because the user interface of the control is largely defined by the page author, you cannot expect a *FormView* control to understand the click on a particular button and act accordingly. For this reason, the *FormView* control exposes a few publicly callable methods to trigger common actions, such as those listed in Table 13-8.

TABLE 13-8 Methods of the *FormView* Control

Method	Description
ChangeMode	Changes the working mode of the control from the current one to any of the modes defined in the *FormViewMode* type—ReadOnly, Edit, or Insert.
DeleteItem	Deletes the current record in the *FormView* control from the data source.
InsertItem	Inserts the current record in the data source. The *FormView* control must be in insert mode when this method is called; otherwise, an exception is thrown.
UpdateItem	Updates the current record in the data source. The *FormView* control must be in edit mode when this method is called; otherwise, an exception is thrown.

Both *InsertItem* and *UpdateItem* require a Boolean indicating whether or not input validation should be performed. In this context, performing validation simply means that any validator controls you might have in the template will be called. If no validators are found, no other form of validation ever occurs. The *InsertItem* and *UpdateItem* methods are designed to start a basic operation from within controls in any of the supported templates. You don't have to pass the record to insert, the values to update, or the key of the record to delete. The *FormView* control knows how to retrieve that information internally in much the same way the *DetailsView* does.

The *DeleteItem*, *InsertItem*, and *UpdateItem* methods let you define your own delete, insert, and edit user interface and attach it to the standard data-binding model of ASP.NET controls. In the *DetailsView* control, this association is implicit because the user interface is relatively static and fixed; in the *FormView*, the same association must be explicitly defined in light of the totally customizable user interface.

Binding Data to a *FormView* Control

Let's see how to use templates to configure and run a *FormView* control in a sample ASP. NET Web page. All templates must contain everything needed to accomplish tasks—user interface elements and command buttons. The control itself provides the pager bar and the surrounding table.

Header, Footer, and Pager

The final output of the *FormView* control takes the form of an HTML table with a header and footer row, plus an optional row for the pager. Just like the *DetailsView*, the *FormView* control provides templates for the header and footer; unlike the *DetailsView*, though, it doesn't provide simpler and handy text properties such as *HeaderText* and *FooterText*.

```
<asp:FormView ID="FormView1" runat="server"
     AllowPaging="true"
     DataSourceID="CustomersDataSource">
     <PagerSettings Mode="NextPreviousFirstLast" />

   <HeaderTemplate>
       <h1>Customer Viewer</h1>
   </HeaderTemplate>

   <FooterTemplate>
       <h3>Courtesy of "Programming ASP.NET"</h3>
   </FooterTemplate>
</asp:FormView>
```

The pager is dual in the sense that you can have the control to render it as the settings established through *PagerSettings* and *PagerStyle* properties dictate, or create it from scratch via the *PagerTemplate* property.

Displaying Data

The following code snippet shows the typical layout of the code you write to embed a *FormView* in your pages:

```
<asp:FormView ID="FormView1" runat="server"
    DataSourceId="CustomersDataSource" AllowPaging="true">
    <ItemTemplate>
      ...
    </ItemTemplate>
    <EditItemTemplate>
      ...
    </EditItemTemplate>
    < InsertItemTemplate >
      ...
    </InsertItemTemplate>
</asp:FormView>
```

The following code generates the page shown in Figure 11-9:

```
<asp:FormView runat="server" id="FormView1"
     DataKeyNames="employeeid"
     DataSourceID="MySource" AllowPaging="true">
    <ItemTemplate>
        <table style="border:solid 1px black;" width="100%">
        <tr>
            <td bgcolor="yellow" width="50px" align="center">
                <b><%# Eval("id") %></b></td>
            <td bgcolor="lightyellow" >
                <b><%# Eval("companyname") %></b></td>
        </tr>
        </table>
        <table style="font-family:Verdana;font-size:8pt;">
          <tr>
            <td><b>Contact</b></td>
            <td><%# Eval("contactname") %></td>
          </tr>
          <tr>
            <td><b>City</b></td>
            <td><%# Eval("city") %></td>
          </tr>
          <tr>
            <td valign="top"><b>Country</b></td>
            <td><%# Eval("country") %></td>
          </tr>
          </table>
          <br />
          <asp:Button ID="EditButton" runat="server" CommandName="Edit"
                     Text="Edit" />
      </ItemTemplate>
</asp:FormView>
```

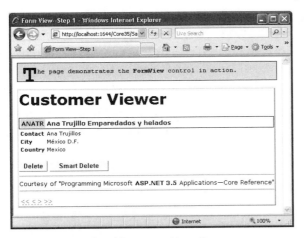

FIGURE 13-10 A *FormView* control in action.

All the markup you place in the *ItemTemplate* is rendered in a table cell that spans two columns. As mentioned, the overall layout of the *FormView* is a table.

```
<td colspan="2">
   ...
</td>
```

If you want to obtain a tabular output, feel free to define an inner table, as in the preceding code.

The Edit button is added using a classic *<asp:Button>* button with the Edit command name. The command name will cause the *FormView* to automatically switch from the read-only mode to edit mode and display using the edit item template, if any is defined. You can use any button control with whatever command name and caption you like. If it doesn't change mode automatically, you call *ChangeMode* and the other methods supported by the *FormView* control.

The *Eval* Function

How can you insert data fields in a template? You resort to data-binding expressions and, in particular, use the *Eval* function:

```
<td><%# Eval("city") %></td>
```

As mentioned in Chapter 10, *Eval* exists in two forms, one of which is also supported in ASP. NET 1.x. The two forms are functionally equivalent, as one of them is implemented in terms of the other. The first form you can use is the following:

```
<%# DataBinder.Eval(Container.DataItem, "city")%>
```

The static function *Eval* on the *DataBinder* class uses reflection to parse and evaluate a data-binding expression against an object at run time. The object it works with is the data item object from the bound data source that corresponds to the record being rendered. Most of the time, the data-binding expression will be the name of a property on the data item bound to a row. The *Eval* function has a third overload to specify a format string.

In ASP.NET 2.0 and beyond, a similar function is available that has a more compact syntax—the *Eval* function defined on the *TemplateControl* class and inherited by all ASP.NET pages. *Eval* is an instance function and accepts only the data-binding expression, and optionally a format string. The *Eval* function ends up calling into the *DataBinder.Eval* function.

The *Eval* is useful only in read-only, one-way data-binding scenarios. For implementing real two-way data binding, an extension to *Eval* is required—the *Bind* function, which we'll discuss in a moment.

Editing Data

To edit bound records, you define an ad hoc edit template through the *EditItemTemplate* property. You can place on the form any combination of input controls, including validators. You are not limited to using text boxes and can unleash your imagination to build the user interface.

How do you retrieve values to update the bound record? You enable two-way binding by using the newest *Bind* function in lieu of *Eval*.

The Edit Template

The following code snippet shows a sample *TextBox* control bound to the *companyname* property of the data source. This is the key difference between item and edit item templates.

```
<asp:TextBox runat="server" Text='<%# Bind("companyname") %>' />
```

The following code snippet shows a sample edit template. It contains quite a few standard text boxes but also a data-bound drop-down list.

```
<EditItemTemplate>
  <table style="border:solid 1px black;" width="100%">
  <tr>
  <td bgcolor="yellow" align="center">
      <b><%# Eval("id") %></b></td>
      <td bgcolor="lightyellow">
      <asp:textbox runat="server" text='<%# Bind("companyname") %>' /></td>
  </tr>
  </table>
  <table style="font-family:Verdana;font-size:8pt;">
```

```
<tr>
    <td><b>Contact</b></td>
    <td><%# Eval("contactname") %></td>
</tr>
<tr>
    <td><b>Address</b></td><td>
    <asp:textbox runat="server" text='<%# Bind("street") %>' /></td>
</tr>
<tr>
    <td><b>City</b></td>
    <td><asp:textbox runat="server" text='<%# Bind("city") %>' /></td>
</tr>
<tr>
    <td valign="top"><b>Country</b></td>
    <td><asp:dropdownlist runat="server"
            datasourceid="CountriesDataSource"
            selectedvalue='<%# Bind("country") %>' /></td>   </tr>
</table>
<br />
<asp:Button runat="server" CommandName="Update" Text="Update" />
<asp:Button runat="server" CommandName="Cancel" Text="Cancel" />
</EditItemTemplate>
```

You use *Eval* to populate control properties not involved in the update process. Wherever you need two-way data binding—that is, read/write capabilities—you use the *Bind* function instead of *Eval*, with the same syntax. For text boxes, you bind the *Text* property; for drop-down lists, you typically bind the *SelectedValue* property. Other controls would bind to their respective data properties. For example, when using a *Calendar* control you would bind to its *SelectedDate* property.

How would you populate a data-bound drop-down list? You would do it by using another data source control, properly configured and parameterized to retrieve its data based on any input that proves necessary. In the sample code, you bind the drop-down list with all possible countries. Similarly, you might bind an employee ID field to the list of all employees from an external, foreign data source.

At last, bear in mind that the edit template must contain buttons to save changes. These are ordinary buttons with specific command names—*Update* to save and *Cancel* to abort. Buttons trigger update commands whose details are stored in the associated data source object. You can choose any text for the captions as long as you don't change the command names. If you want to modify the command names, be prepared to handle the *ItemCommand* event on the *FormView* and call the *UpdateItem* method in response.

Figure 13-11 demonstrates the output of this code.

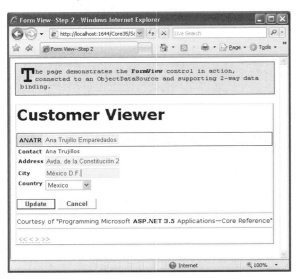

FIGURE 13-11 A *FormView* control running in edit mode.

For the update command to work, the *DataKeyNames* property must be set on the *FormView* to identify the key field. For deleting a record, just add a button with the *Delete* command name and configure the underlying data source control.

The *Bind* Function

How does the *Bind* function work? The function stores the value of the bound control property into a collection of values that the *FormView* control automatically retrieves and uses to compose the parameter list of the edit command.

The argument passed to *Bind* must match the name of a parameter in the update command or method or one of the properties on the type used as an argument to the update method. This is the case in the example shown earlier, where the update method takes an instance of the *Core35.DAL.Customer* class. An exception is raised if no parameter match is found.

The Insert Template

The *InsertItemTemplate* property allows you to define the input layout when a new record is being added. To avoid confusion, an insert template should not be much different from an edit template. At the same time, you should be aware that edit and insert are distinct operations with different requirements. For example, an insert template should provide default values to controls wherever that is acceptable, and it should display neutral or null values elsewhere.

To start an insert operation, you also need a button with a command name of *New*. Clicking on this button will force the *FormView* control to change its mode to Insert and render the

contents defined for the insert template. The insert template should also provide a couple of
Update/Cancel buttons with the same command names discussed for edit operations.

When the Function Is Not Supported

Both *DetailsView* and *FormView* controls expose some predefined operations—such as
Insert, Edit, and Delete. As we've seen thus far, these operations are implemented inside the
data source control bound to the view control. What if, say, the *Edit* function is enabled on
the *FormView* control but not supported by the underlying data source control? When this
happens, a *NotSupportedException* exception is thrown and the application fails.

It's hard to imagine a team of developers who release some production code with an Edit
button associated with a non-updateable data source. However, checking if a requested
function is available is a good measure to make any application more robust and stable.
The following code demonstrates this feature:

```
if (e.CommandName == "Edit")
{
   IDataSource obj = (IDataSource) FindControl(FormView1.DataSourceID);
   DataSourceView view = obj.GetView("DefaultView");
   if (!view.CanUpdate)
   {
     Response.Write("Sorry, you can't update");
     return;
   }
   else
     FormView1.UpdateItem();
}
```

The code retrieves the data source control and obtains a reference to its default data source
view object. At this point, it checks whether the requested functionality is available. You
can place this code in the *ItemCommand* event handler of any view controls—*DetailsView*,
FormView, or *GridView*. Note that all ASP.NET built-in data source controls have only one
view, named *DefaultView*.

Conclusion

Starting with ASP.NET 2.0, the developer's toolbox for data-binding operations is definitely
richer and more complete than in previous versions. You not only have a new and radically
revised grid control, but you also have two other controls to manage views of a single record.
There's nothing like this in ASP.NET 1.x.

The *DetailsView* and *FormView* controls are two sides of the same coin. Both offer a user interface to see the contents of a single record. In both cases, the user interface is largely customizable and associated with predefined data operations such as delete, update, and insert.
Bound to a data source control, both *DetailsView* and *FormView* can manage an underlying
data source effectively without forcing developers to write ad hoc code. (Well, this is not

entirely true. If you expose your data source through a DAL—as recommended for large systems—you have to write that code at least.)

The key difference between *DetailsView* and *FormView* lies in the support for templates. The former is perhaps a richer control with good basic support for templates limited to individual fields, and it has a relatively rich set of styles and visual properties. If you want to create your own form to edit and insert records, you should use the *FormView* control. If you do so, though, forget about standard rendering—a form view, in fact, is 100-percent templated and requires you to specify every single byte of markup.

With this chapter, we conclude the second part of the book—the part devoted to data access and related tools. Starting with the next chapter, we'll begin a new trip in the ASP.NET infrastructure, one that shows you how to make pages and applications run.

 ## Just The Facts

- Both the *DetailsView* and *FormView* controls render a single record at a time from the associated data source, optionally providing paging buttons to navigate between records.

- Both the *DetailsView* and *FormView* controls lend themselves very well to implement master/detail views.

- The *DetailsView* control has a fixed tabular layout and is formed by a few main areas—header, field rows, pager bar, command bar, and footer.

- The *FormView* control has areas such as header, footer, pager plus a completely templated item area. You can define a custom form to render the contents of a single record.

- The *DetailsView* control typically uses text boxes to render fields. If a particular field defines a template, any markup can be displayed. This feature is useful for representing dates and foreign keys through ad hoc controls such as calendars and drop-down lists.

- Both the *DetailsView* and *FormView* controls support basic I/O operations such as insert, delete, and update. If bound to data source controls such as *ObjectDataSource* or *SqlDataSource*, they leverage the capabilities of the bound data source control to execute data-binding operations.

- Both the *DetailsView* and *FormView* controls support two-way data binding, through which data can not only be automatically read from a bound data source but also written back.

- During updates and insertions, validation is possible in either of two ways. If templates are used, you can insert validator controls to sanitize the input both on the client and the server. If templates are not used, you can intercept events fired by *DetailsView* and *FormView* as well as control values being passed, and modify them at will or just cancel the operation.

Programming Microsoft® ASP.NET 3.5

Part III
ASP.NET Infrastructure

Chapter 14
The HTTP Request Context

There are various steps involved in having the ASP.NET worker process serve an incoming HTTP request . The request is assigned to the *aspnet_isapi.dll* ISAPI extension which, in turn, hands it over to the HTTP runtime pipeline. The entry point in the ASP.NET pipeline is the *HttpRuntime* class. A new instance of this class is created for each request, governs its overall execution, and generates the response text for the browser. Upon instantiation, the *HttpRuntime* class performs a number of initialization tasks, the first of which is the creation of a wrapper object to encapsulate all the HTTP-specific information available about the request. The newly created object—an instance of the *HttpContext* class—is then passed along to the pipeline and is used by the various modules to access intrinsic worker objects such as *Request*, *Response*, and *Server*.

In this chapter, we'll first review the startup process of the ASP.NET application and then move on to examine the various objects that form the context of the HTTP request. If you're a former Web developer new to ASP.NET, some material in this chapter might sound familiar, especially as we discuss old acquaintances such as *Request* and *Response*. Although these objects are much more feature-rich and powerful than in, say, classic ASP, they should be considered lower-level tools; their use is necessary and unavoidable only in a relatively small number of situations. In general, too-frequent use of these objects in your code should be considered an alarm bell warning you of possible nonoptimal use of the ASP.NET programming toolkit.

Initialization of the Application

Once the context for the request is created, the *HttpRuntime* class sets up an ASP.NET application object to carry out the request. An ASP.NET application consists of an instance of the *HttpApplication* class that we briefly met in Chapter 3. *HttpApplication* is a *global.asax*-derived object that handles all HTTP requests directed to a particular virtual folder.

An ASP.NET running application is wholly represented by its virtual folder and optionally by the *global.asax* file. The virtual folder name is a sort of key that the HTTP runtime uses to selectively identify which of the running applications should take care of the incoming request. The *global.asax* file, if present, contains settings and code for responding to application-level events raised by ASP.NET or by registered HTTP modules that affect the application.

The particular *HttpApplication* selected is responsible for managing the entire lifetime of the request it is assigned to. That instance of *HttpApplication* can be reused only after the request has been completed. If no *HttpApplication* object is available, either because the application has not been started yet or all valid objects are busy, a new *HttpApplication* is created and pooled.

Properties of the *HttpApplication* Class

Although the *HttpApplication* provides a public constructor, user applications never need to create instances of the *HttpApplication* class directly. The ASP.NET runtime infrastructure always does the job for you. As mentioned, instances of the class are pooled and, as such, can process many requests in their lifetime, but always one at a time. Should concurrent requests arrive for the same application, additional instances are created. Table 14-1 lists the properties defined for the class.

TABLE 14-1 *HttpApplication* **Properties**

Property	Description
Application	Instance of the *HttpApplicationState* class. It represents the global and shared state of the application. It is functionally equivalent to the ASP intrinsic *Application* object.
Context	Instance of the *HttpContext* class. It encapsulates in a single object all HTTP-specific information about the current request. Intrinsic objects (for example, *Application* and *Request*) are also exposed as properties.
Modules	Gets the collection of modules that affect the current application.
Request	Instance of the *HttpRequest* class. It represents the current HTTP request. It is functionally equivalent to the ASP intrinsic *Request* object.
Response	Instance of the *HttpResponse* class. It sends HTTP response data to the client. It is functionally equivalent to the ASP intrinsic *Response* object.
Server	Instance of the *HttpServerUtility* class. It provides helper methods for processing Web requests. It is functionally equivalent to the ASP intrinsic *Server* object.

Property	Description
Session	Instance of the *HttpSessionState* class. It manages user-specific data. It is functionally equivalent to the ASP intrinsic *Session* object.
User	An *IPrincipal* object that represents the user making the request.

The *HttpApplication* is managed by the ASP.NET infrastructure, so how can you take advantage of the fairly rich, public programming interface of the class? The answer is that properties and, even more, overridable methods and class events can be accessed and programmatically manipulated in the *global.asax* file. (We'll return to *global.asax* in a moment.)

Application Modules

The property *Modules* returns a collection of application-wide components providing ad hoc services. An HTTP module component is a class that implements the *IHttpModule* interface. Modules can be considered the managed counterpart of ISAPI filters; they are kind of request interceptors with the built-in capability of modifying the overall context of the request being processed. The .NET Framework defines a number of standard modules, as listed in Table 14-2. Custom modules can be defined too. I cover this particular aspect of HTTP programming in Chapter 18.

TABLE 14-2 ASP.NET Modules

Module	Description
AnonymousIdentification	Assigns anonymous users a fake identity. *Not installed in ASP.NET 1.x.*
FileAuthorization	Verifies that the remote user has Windows NT permissions to access the requested resource.
FormsAuthentication	Enables applications to use forms authentication.
OutputCache	Provides page output caching services.
PassportAuthentication	Provides a wrapper around Passport authentication services.
Profile	Provides user profile services. *Not installed in ASP.NET 1.x.*
RoleManager	Provides session-state services for the application. *Not installed in ASP.NET 1.x.*
ScriptModule	Used to implement page methods in AJAX pages. *Not installed in ASP.NET 2.0.*
SessionState	Provides session-state services for the application.
UrlAuthorization	Provides URL-based authorization services to access specified resources.
WindowsAuthentication	Enables ASP.NET applications to use Windows and Internet Information Services (IIS)-based authentication.

The list of default modules is defined in the *machine.config* file. The modules listed in *machine.config* are available to all applications. By creating a proper *web.config* file, you can also create an application-specific list of modules. (Configuration is covered in *Programming Microsoft ASP.NET 2.0 Applications: Advanced Topics*.)

Methods of the *HttpApplication* Class

The methods of the *HttpApplication* class can be divided into two groups—operational methods and event handler managers. The *HttpApplication* operational methods are described in Table 14-3.

TABLE 14-3 *HttpApplication* Operational Methods

Method	Description
CompleteRequest	Sets an internal flag that causes ASP.NET to skip all successive steps in the pipeline and directly execute *EndRequest*. Mostly useful to HTTP modules.
Dispose	Overridable method, cleans up the instance variables of all registered modules once the request has been served. At this time, *Request*, *Response*, *Session*, and *Application* are no longer available.
GetVaryByCustomString	Overridable method, provides a way to set output caching based on a custom string for all pages in the application. (We'll say more about output page caching in Chapter 16.)
Init	Overridable method that executes custom initialization code after all modules have been linked to the application to serve the request. You can use it to create and configure any object that you want to use throughout the request processing. At this time, *Request*, *Response*, *Session*, and *Application* are not yet available.

Note that the *Init* and *Dispose* methods are quite different from well-known event handlers such as *Application_Start* and *Application_End*.

Init executes for every request directed to the Web application, whereas *Application_Start* fires only once in the Web application's lifetime. *Init* indicates that a new instance of the *HttpApplication* class has been initialized to serve an incoming request; *Application_Start* denotes that the first instance of the *HttpApplication* class has been created to start up the Web application and serve its very first request. Likewise, *Dispose* signals the next termination of the request processing but not necessarily the end of the application. *Application_End* is raised only once, when the application is being shut down.

> **Note** The lifetime of any resources created in the *Init* method is limited to the execution of the current request. Any resource you allocate in *Init* should be disposed of in *Dispose*, at the latest. If you need persistent data, resort to other objects that form the application or session state.

In addition to the operational methods in Table 14-3, a few other *HttpApplication* methods are available to register asynchronous handlers for application-level events. These methods are of little interest to user applications and are used only by HTTP modules to hook up the events generated during the request's chain of execution.

Events of the *HttpApplication* Class

Table 14-4 describes the event model of the *HttpApplication* class—that is, the set of events that HTTP modules, as well as user applications, can listen to and handle.

TABLE 14-4 *HttpApplication* **Events**

Event	Description
AcquireRequestState, PostAcquireRequestState	Occurs when the handler that will actually serve the request acquires the state information associated with the request. *The post event is not available in ASP.NET 1.x.*
AuthenticateRequest, PostAuthenticateRequest	Occurs when a security module has established the identity of the user. *The post event is not available in ASP.NET 1.x.*
AuthorizeRequest, PostAuthorizeRequest	Occurs when a security module has verified user authorization. *The post event is not available in ASP.NET 1.x.*
BeginRequest	Occurs as soon as the HTTP pipeline begins to process the request.
Disposed	Occurs when the *HttpApplication* object is disposed of as a result of a call to *Dispose*.
EndRequest	Occurs as the last event in the HTTP pipeline chain of execution.
Error	Occurs when an unhandled exception is thrown.
PostMapRequestHandler	Occurs when the HTTP handler to serve the request has been found. *The event is not available in ASP.NET 1.x.*
PostRequestHandlerExecute	Occurs when the HTTP handler of choice finishes execution. The response text has been generated at this point.
PreRequestHandlerExecute	Occurs just before the HTTP handler of choice begins to work.
PreSendRequestContent	Occurs just before the ASP.NET runtime sends the response text to the client.
PreSendRequestHeaders	Occurs just before the ASP.NET runtime sends HTTP headers to the client.
ReleaseRequestState, PostReleaseRequestState	Occurs when the handler releases the state information associated with the current request. *The post event is not available in ASP.NET 1.x.*
ResolveRequestCache, PostResolveRequestCache	Occurs when the ASP.NET runtime resolves the request through the output cache. *The post event is not available in ASP.NET 1.x.*
UpdateRequestCache, PostUpdateRequestCache	Occurs when the ASP.NET runtime stores the response of the current request in the output cache to be used to serve subsequent requests. *The post event is not available in ASP.NET 1.x.*

To handle any of these events asynchronously, an application will use the corresponding method whose name follows a common pattern: *AddOnXXXAsync*, where *XXX* stands for the event name. To hook up some of these events in a synchronous manner, an application will define in the *global.asax* event handler procedures with the following signature:

```
public void Application_XXX(object sender, EventArgs e)
{
    // Do something here
}
```

Of course, the *XXX* placeholder must be replaced with the name of the event from Table 14-4. All the events in the preceding table provide no event-specific data. You can also use the following simpler syntax without losing additional information and programming power:

```
public void Application_XXX()
{
    // Do something here
}
```

In addition to the events listed in Table 14-4, in *global.asax* an application can also handle *Application_Start* and *Application_End*. When ASP.NET is about to fire *BeginRequest* for the very first time in the application lifetime, it makes *Application_Start* precede it. *EndRequest* will happen at the end of every request to an application. *Application_End* occurs outside the context of a request, when the application is ending.

Application events are fired in the following sequence:

1. *BeginRequest*   The ASP.NET HTTP pipeline begins to work on the request. This event reaches the application after *Application_Start*.

2. *AuthenticateRequest*   The request is being authenticated. All the internal ASP.NET authentication modules subscribe to this event and attempt to produce an identity. If no authentication module produced an authenticated user, an internal default authentication module is invoked to produce an identity for the unauthenticated user. This is done for the sake of consistency so that code doesn't need to worry about null identities.

3. *PostAuthenticateRequest*   The request has been authenticated. All the information available is stored in the *HttpContext*'s *User* property.

4. *AuthorizeRequest*   The request authorization is about to occur. This event is commonly handled by application code to do custom authorization based on business logic or other application requirements.

5. *PostAuthorizeRequest*   The request has been authorized.

6. *ResolveRequestCache*   The ASP.NET runtime verifies whether returning a previously cached page can resolve the request. If a valid cached representation is found, the request is served from the cache and the request is short-circuited, calling only any registered *EndRequest* handlers.

7. *PostResolveRequestCache*   The request can't be served from the cache, and the procedure continues. An HTTP handler corresponding to the requested URL is created at this point. If the requested resource is an *.aspx* page, an instance of a page class is created.

8. *PostMapRequestHandler*   The event fires when the HTTP handler corresponding to the requested URL has been successfully created.

9. *AcquireRequestState*   The module that hooks up this event is willing to retrieve any state information for the request. A number of factors are relevant here: the handler must support session state in some form, and there must be a valid session ID.

10. *PostAcquireRequestState*   The state information (such as *Application*, *Session*) has been acquired.

11. *PreRequestHandlerExecute*   This event is fired immediately prior to executing the handler for a given request. The handler does its job and generates the output for the client.

12. *PostRequestHandlerExecute*   This event is raised when the handler has generated the response text.

13. *ReleaseRequestState*   This event is raised when the handler releases its state information and prepares to shut down. This event is used by the session state module to update the dirty session state if necessary.

14. *PostReleaseRequestState*   The state, as modified by the page execution, has been persisted. Any relevant response filtering is done at this point. (I'll say more about this topic later.)

15. *UpdateRequestCache*   The ASP.NET runtime determines whether the generated output, now also properly filtered by registered modules, should be cached to be reused with upcoming identical requests.

16. *PostUpdateRequestCache*   The page has been saved to the output cache if it was configured to do so.

17. *EndRequest*   This event fires as the final step of the HTTP pipeline. The control passes back to the *HttpRuntime* object, which is responsible for the actual forwarding of the response to the client. At this point, the text has not been sent yet.

Another pair of events can occur during the request, but in a nondeterministic order. They are *PreSendRequestHeaders* and *PreSendRequestContent*. The *PreSendRequestHeaders* event informs the *HttpApplication* object in charge of the request that HTTP headers are about to be sent. The event normally fires after *EndRequest* but not always. For example, if buffering is turned off, the event gets fired as soon as some content is going to be sent to the client. Finally, with the *PreSendRequestContent* event, the *HttpApplication* object in charge of the request learns that the response body is about to be sent. Speaking of nondeterministic application events, it must be said that a third nondeterministic event is, of course, *Error*.

The *global.asax* File

The *global.asax* file is used by Web applications to handle some application-level events raised by the ASP.NET runtime or by registered HTTP modules. The *global.asax* file is optional. If it is missing, the ASP.NET runtime environment simply assumes you have no application or module event handlers defined. To be functional, the *global.asax* file must be located in the root directory of the application. Only one *global.asax* file per application is accepted. Any *global.asax* files placed in subdirectories are simply ignored. Note that Microsoft Visual Studio doesn't list *global.asax* in the items you can add to the project if there already is one.

Compiling *global.asax*

When the application is started, *global.asax*, if present, is parsed into a source class and compiled. The resultant assembly is created in the temporary directory just as any other dynamically generated assembly would be. The following listing shows the skeleton of the C# code that ASP.NET generates for any *global.asax* file:

```
namespace ASP
{
    public class global_asax : System.Web.HttpApplication
    {
        //
        // The source code of the "global.asax" file is flushed
        // here verbatim. For this reason, the following code
        // in global.asax would generate a compile error.
        //      int i;
        //      i = 2;  // can't have statements outside methods
        //
    }
}
```

The class is named *ASP.global_asax* and is derived from the *HttpApplication* base class. In most cases, you deploy *global.asax* as a separate text file; however, you can also write it as a class and compile it either in a separate assembly or within your project's assembly. The class source code must follow the outline shown earlier and, above all, must derive from *HttpApplication*. The assembly with the compiled version of *global.asax* must be deployed in the application's *Bin* subdirectory.

Note, though, that even if you isolate the logic of the *global.asax* file in a precompiled assembly, you still need to have a (codeless) *global.asax* file that refers to the assembly, as shown in the following code:

```
<%@ Application Inherits="Core35.Global" %>
```

We'll learn more about the syntax of *global.asax* in the next section, "Syntax of *global.asax*." With a precompiled global application file, you certainly don't risk exposing your source code over the Web to malicious attacks. However, even if you leave it as source code, you're somewhat safe.

The *global.asax* file, in fact, is configured so that any direct URL request for it is automatically rejected by Internet Information Services (IIS). In this way, external users cannot download or view the code it contains. The trick that enables this behavior is the following line of code, excerpted from *machine.config*:

```
<add verb="*" path="*.asax" type="System.Web.HttpForbiddenHandler" />
```

ASP.NET registers with IIS to handle .asax resources, but then it processes those direct requests through the *HttpForbiddenHandler* HTTP handler. As a result, when a browser requests an *.asax* resource, an error message is displayed on the page, as shown in Figure 14-1.

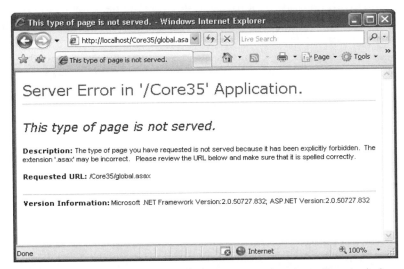

FIGURE 14-1 Direct access to forbidden resources, such as *.asax files, results in a server error.

> **Tip** You can duplicate that line in your application's *web.config* file and block direct access to other types of resources specific to your application. For this trick to work, though, make sure that the resource type is redirected to ASP.NET at the IIS level. In other words, you must first register *aspnet_isapi.dll* to handle those files in the IIS metabase and then ask ASP.NET to block any requests. You accomplish this through the IIS manager applet from the Control Panel.

When the *global.asax* file of a running application is modified, the ASP.NET runtime detects the change and prepares to shut down and restart the application. It waits until all pending requests are completed and then fires the *Application_End* event. When the next request from a browser arrives, ASP.NET reparses and recompiles the *global.asax* file, and again raises the *Application_Start* event.

Syntax of *global.asax*

Four elements determine the syntax of the *global.asax* file. They are: application directives, code declaration blocks, server-side *<object>* tags, and server-side includes. These elements can be used in any order and number to compose a *global.asax* file.

Application Directives

The *global.asax* file supports three directives: *@Application*, *@Import*, and *@Assembly*. The *@Import* and *@Assembly* directives work as we saw in Chapter 3. The *@Import* directive imports a namespace into an application; the *@Assembly* directive links an assembly to the application at compile time.

The *@Application* directive supports a few attributes—*Description*, *Language*, and *Inherits*. *Description* can contain any text you want to use to describe the behavior of the application. This text has only a documentation purpose and is blissfully ignored by the ASP.NET parser. *Language* indicates the language being used in the file. The *Inherits* attribute indicates a code-behind class for the application to inherit. It can be the name of any class derived from the *HttpApplication* class. The assembly that contains the class must be located in the *Bin* subdirectory of the application.

Code Declaration Blocks

A *global.asax* file can contain code wrapped by a *<script>* tag. Just as for pages, the *<script>* tag must have the *runat* attribute set to *server*. The *language* attribute indicates the language used throughout:

```
<script language="C#" runat="server">
    ...
</script>
```

If the *language* attribute is not specified, ASP.NET defaults to the language set in the configuration, which is Microsoft Visual Basic. The source code can also be loaded from an external file, whose virtual path is set in the *Src* attribute. The location of the file is resolved using *Server.MapPath*—that is, starting under the physical root directory of the Web application.

```
<script language="C#" runat="server" src="somecode.aspx.cs" />
```

In this case, any other code in the declaration *<script>* block is ignored. Notice that ASP.NET enforces syntax rules on the *<script>* tag. The *runat* attribute is mandatory, and if the block has no content the *Src* must be specified.

Server-Side <*object*> Tags

The server-side <*object*> tag lets you create new objects using a declarative syntax. The <*object*> tag can take three forms, as shown in the following lines of code, depending on the specified reference type:

```
<object id="..." runat="server" scope="..." class="..." />
<object id="..." runat="server" scope="..." progid="..." />
<object id="..." runat="server" scope="..." classid="..." />
```

In the first case, the object is identified by the name of the class and assembly that contains it. In the last two cases, the object to create is a COM object identified by the program identifier (*progid*) and the 128-bit CLSID, respectively. As one can easily guess, the *classid*, *progid*, and *class* attributes are mutually exclusive. If you use more than one within a single server-side <*object*> tag, a compile error is generated. Objects declared in this way are loaded when the application is started.

The *scope* attribute indicates the scope at which the object is declared. The allowable values are defined in Table 14-5. Unless otherwise specified, the server-side object is valid only within the boundaries of the HTTP pipeline that processes the current request. Other settings that increase the object's lifetime are *application* and *session*.

TABLE 14-5 Feasible Scopes for Server-Side <*object*> Tags

Scope	Description
pipeline	Default setting, indicates the object is available only within the context of the current HTTP request
application	Indicates the object is added to the *StaticObjects* collection of the *Application* object and is shared among all pages in the application
session	Indicates the object is added to the *StaticObjects* collection of the *Session* object and is shared among all pages in the current session

Server-Side Includes

An #*include* directive inserts the contents of the specified file as-is into the ASP.NET file that uses it. The directive for file inclusion can be used in *global.asax* pages as well as in *.aspx* pages. The directive must be enclosed in an HTML comment so that it isn't mistaken for plain text to be output verbatim:

```
<!-- #include file="filename" -->
<!-- #include virtual="filename" -->
```

The directive supports two mutually exclusive attributes—*file* and *virtual*. If the *file* attribute is used, the file name must be a relative path to a file located in the same directory or in a subdirectory; the included file cannot be in a directory above the file with the #*include* directive.

With the *virtual* attribute, the file name can be indicated by using a full virtual path from a virtual directory on the same Web site.

> **Note** This technique might sound a bit outdated in the dazzling world of ASP.NET 3.5 with AJAX onboard and awaiting for the even more futuristic features of Silverlight. However, if used for what it is supposed to do—inserting the content of a server-side file—it can be helpful even in ASP.NET 3.5. For example, it can be used to build text-heavy pages that contain a lot of relatively static text. Keeping this text on a separate resource might make it easier to manage and maintain.

Static Properties

If you define static properties in the *global.asax* file, they will be accessible for reading and writing by all pages in the application:

```
<script language="C#" runat="server">
    public static int Counter = 0;
</script>
```

The *Counter* property defined in the preceding code works like an item stored in *Application*—namely, it is globally visible across pages and sessions. Consider that concurrent access to *Counter* is not serialized; on the other hand, you have a strong-typed, direct global item whose access speed is much faster than retrieving the same piece of information from a generic collection such as *Application*.

To access the property from a page, you must use the *ASP.global_asax* qualifier, shown here:

```
Response.Write(ASP.global_asax.Counter.ToString());
```

If you don't particularly like the *ASP.global_asax* prefix, you can alias it as long as you use C#. Add the following code to a C#-based page (or code-behind class) for which you need to access the globals:

```
using Globals = ASP.global_asax;
```

The preceding statement creates an alias for the *ASP.global_asax* class (or whatever name your *global.asax* class has). The alias—*Globals* in this sample code—can be used throughout your code wherever *ASP.global_asax* is accepted.

```
Response.Write(Globals.Counter.ToString());
```

> **Important** You can use the *global.asax* file to handle any event exposed by the modules called to operate on the request. Handlers for events exposed by an HTTP module must have a name that conforms to the following scheme: *ModuleName_EventName*. The module name to use is defined in the *<httpModules>* section of the configuration file.

Tracking Errors and Anomalies

When an error occurs, displaying a friendly page to the user is only half the job a good programmer should do. The second half of the work consists of sending appropriate notifications to the system administrator—if possible, in real time. A great help is the *Error* event of the *HttpApplication* object, as we already saw in Chapter 5. Write an *Application_Error* event handler in your *global.asax* file, and the system will call it back whenever an unhandled error occurs in the application—either in the user code, a component's code, or ASP.NET code.

In the *Application_Error* event handler, you first obtain specific information about the error and then implement the tracking policy that best suits your needs—for example, e-mailing the administrator, writing to the Windows Event Log, or dumping errors to a text file. The *Server.GetLastError* method returns an *Exception* object that represents the unhandled exception you want to track down. URL information is contained in the *Request* object, and even session or application state is available.

The following code demonstrates how to write an *Application_Error* event handler in *global.asax* to report run-time anomalies to the Event Log. An example of this code in action is shown in Figure 14-2. The code retrieves the last exception and writes out available information to the event log. Note that the *ToString* method on an exception object returns more information than the *Message* property. Additional information includes the stack trace.

```
<%@ Import Namespace="System.Diagnostics" %>
<%@ Import Namespace="System.Text" %>

<script language="C#" runat="server">
void Application_Error(object sender, EventArgs e)
{
    // Obtain the URL of the request
    string url = Request.Path;

    // Obtain the Exception object describing the error
    Exception error = Server.GetLastError();

    // Build the message --> [Error occurred. XXX at url]
    StringBuilder text = new StringBuilder("Error occurred. ");
    text.Append(error.ToString());
    text.Append(" at ");
    text.Append(url);

    // Write to the Event Log
    EventLog log = new EventLog();
    log.Source = "Core35 Log";
    log.WriteEntry(text.ToString(), EventLogEntryType.Error);
}
</script>
```

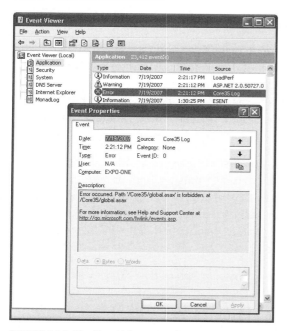

FIGURE 14-2 The Event Viewer tracks an error on an ASP.NET application.

Your code doesn't necessarily have to create the event source. If the source specified in the *Source* property does not exist, it will be created before writing to the event log. The *WriteEntry* method takes care of that. Windows provides three log files: Application, Security, and System, which is reserved for device drivers. The *Log* property of the *EventLog* class gets and sets the log file to use. It is Application by default.

Caution To create new event logs, applications should use the static method *CreateEventSource* on the *EventLog* class. Note, though, that ASP.NET applications can't create new event logs because the running account (ASPNET or NETWORK SERVICE) doesn't have enough permissions. If you want your ASP.NET application to use a custom log, create that at setup time.

The *HttpContext* Class

During the various steps of the request's chain of execution, an object gets passed along from class to class—this object is the *HttpContext* object. *HttpContext* encapsulates all the information available about an individual HTTP request that ASP.NET is going to handle. The *HttpContext* class is instantiated by the *HttpRuntime* object while the request processing mechanism is being set up. Next, the object is flowed throughout the various stages of the request's lifetime, as Figure 14-3 demonstrates.

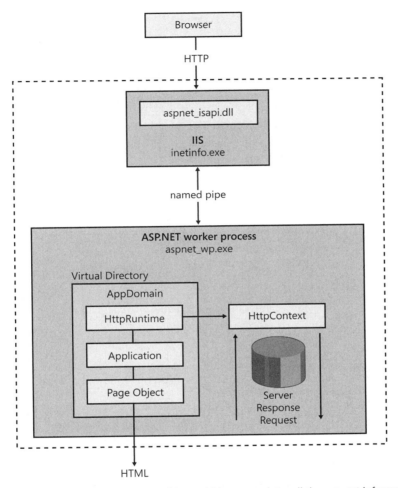

FIGURE 14-3 The *HttpContext* object, which encapsulates all the request information and is passed along through the HTTP pipeline until the client response is generated.

Properties of the *HttpContext* Class

Table 14-6 enumerates all the properties exposed by the *HttpContext* class. The class represent a single entry point for a number of intrinsic objects such as classic ASP's intrinsics and ASP.NET-specific *Cache* and *User* objects.

TABLE 14-6 *HttpContext* Properties

Property	Description
AllErrors	Gets an array of *Exception* objects, each of which represents an error that occurred while processing the request.
Application	Gets an instance of the *HttpApplicationState* class, which contains the global and shared states of the application.
ApplicationInstance	Gets or sets the *HttpApplication* object for the current request. The actual type is the *global.asax* code-behind class. Make a cast to access public properties and methods you might have defined in *global.asax*.
Cache	Gets the ASP.NET *Cache* object for the current request.
Current	Gets the *HttpContext* object for the current request.
CurrentHandler	Gets the handler for the request that is currently being executed by the application. It is a read-only property that returns the value stored in *Handler. Not supported in ASP.NET 1.x.*
Error	Gets the first exception (if any) that has been raised while processing the current request.
Handler	Gets or sets the HTTP handler for the current request.
IsCustomErrorEnabled	Indicates whether custom error handling is enabled for the current request.
IsDebuggingEnabled	Indicates whether the current request is in debug mode.
Items	Gets a name/value collection (hash table) that can be used to share custom data and objects between HTTP modules and HTTP handlers during the request lifetime.
PreviousHandler	Gets the last handler before the current request was executed. *Not supported in ASP.NET 1.x.*
Profile	Gets the object that represents the profile of the current user. *Not supported in ASP.NET 1.x.*
Request	Gets an instance of the *HttpRequest* class, which represents the current HTTP request.
Response	Gets an instance of the *HttpResponse* class, which sends HTTP response data to the client.
Server	Gets an instance of the *HttpServerUtility* class, which provides helper methods for processing Web requests.
Session	Gets an instance of the *HttpSessionState* class, which manages session-specific data.
SkipAuthorization	Gets or sets a Boolean value that specifies whether the URL-based authorization module will skip the authorization check for the current request. This is *false* by default. It is mostly used by authentication modules that need to redirect to a page that allows anonymous access.

Property	Description
Timestamp	Gets a *DateTime* object that represents the initial timestamp of the current request.
Trace	Gets the *TraceContext* object for the current response.
User	Gets or sets the *IPrincipal* object that represents the identity of the user making the request.

The *Current* property is a frequently used static member that returns the *HttpContext* object for the request being processed.

The *Items* property is a dictionary object—a hash table, to be exact—that can be used to share information between the modules and handlers involved with the particular request. By using this property, each custom HTTP module or handler can add its own information to the *HttpContext* object serving the request. The information stored in *Items* is ultimately made available to the page. The lifetime of this information is limited to the request.

Methods of the *HttpContext* Class

Table 14-7 lists the methods specific to the *HttpContext* class.

TABLE 14-7 *HttpContext* Methods

Method	Description
AddError	Adds an exception object to the *AllErrors* collection.
ClearError	Clears all errors for the current request.
GetAppConfig	Returns requested configuration information for the current application. The information is collected from *machine.config* and the application's main *web.config* files. *Marked as obsolete in ASP.NET 2.0.*
GetConfig	Returns requested configuration information for the current request. The information is collected at the level of the requested URL, taking into account any child *web.config* files defined in subdirectories. *Marked as obsolete in ASP.NET 2.0.*
GetGlobalResourceObject	Loads a global resource. *Not available in ASP.NET 1.x.*
GetLocalResourceObject	Loads a local, page-specific resource. *Not available in ASP.NET 1.x.*
GetSection	Returns requested configuration information for the current request. *Not available in ASP.NET 1.x.*
RewritePath	Mostly for internal use; overwrites URL and query string of the current *Request* object.

Starting with ASP.NET 2.0, the *GetSection* method replaces *GetConfig*, which has been marked as obsolete and should not be used. If you have old code using *GetConfig*, just change the name of the method. The prototype is the same. Also, *GetAppConfig* is marked as obsolete in ASP.NET 2.0 and beyond. It has been replaced by *GetWebApplicationSection*, a static member of the new *WebConfigurationManager* class. Also, in this case, no changes are required to be made to the prototype. Let's spend a few more words to dig out some interesting characteristics of other methods of the *HttpContext* class.

URL Rewriting

The *RewritePath* method lets you change the URL of the current request on the fly, thus performing a sort of internal redirect. As a result, the displayed page is the one you set through *RewritePath*; the page shown in the address bar remains the originally requested one. The change of the final URL takes place on the server and, more importantly, within the context of the same call. *RewritePath* should be used carefully and mainly from within the *global.asax* file. If you use *RewritePath* in the context of a postback event, you can experience some view-state troubles.

```
protected void Application_BeginRequest(object sender, EventArgs e)
{
    HttpContext context = HttpContext.Current;
    object o = context.Request["id"];
    if (o != null)
    {
        int id = (int) o;
        string url = GetPageUrlFromId(id);
        context.RewritePath(url);
    }
}
protected string GetPageUrlFromId(int id)
{
    // Return a full URL based on the input ID value.
    ...
}
```

The preceding code rewrites a URL such as *page.aspx?id=1234* to a specific page whose real URL is read out of a database or a configuration file.

Loading Resources Programmatically

In Chapter 2, we discussed expressions allowed in ASP.NET 2.0 pages to bind control properties to embedded global or local resources. The *$Resources* and *meta:resourcekey* expressions for global and local resources, respectively, work only at design time. What if you need to generate text programmatically that embeds resource expressions, instead? Both the *Page* and *HttpContext* classes support a pair of programmatic methods to retrieve the content of resources embedded in the application.

GetGlobalResourceObject retrieves a global resource—that is, a resource defined in an *.resx* file located in the *App_GlobalResources* special folder. *GetLocalResourceObject* does the same for an *.resx* file located in the *App_LocalResources* special folder of a given page.

```
msg1.Text = (string) HttpContext.GetGlobalResourceObject(
    "Test", "MyString");
msg2.Text = (string) HttpContext.GetLocalResourceObject(
    "/Core35/Samples/Ch02/ResPage.aspx", "PageResource1.Title");
```

The first parameter you pass to *GetGlobalResourceObject* indicates the name of the *.resx* resource file without an extension; the second parameter is the name of the resource to retrieve. As for *GetLocalResourceObject*, the first argument indicates the virtual path of the page; the second is the name of the resource.

The *Server* Object

In the all-encompassing container represented by the *HttpContext* object, a few popular objects also find their place. Among them are *Server*, *Request*, and *Response*. They are old acquaintances for ASP developers and, indeed, they are feature-rich elements of the ASP.NET programming toolkit. The set of properties and methods still makes these objects a fundamental resource for developers. Let's learn more about them, starting with the *Server* object.

The functionality of the ASP intrinsic *Server* object in ASP.NET is implemented by the *HttpServerUtility* class. An instance of the type is created when ASP.NET begins to process the request and is then stored as part of the request context. The bunch of helper methods that *HttpServerUtility* provides are publicly exposed to modules and handlers—including *global. asax*, pages, and Web services—through the *Server* property of the *HttpContext* object. In addition, to maintain ASP.NET coding as close as possible to the ASP programming style, several other commonly used ASP.NET objects also expose their own *Server* property. In this way, developers can use in the code, say, *Server.MapPath* without incurring compile errors.

Properties of the *HttpServerUtility* Class

This class provides two properties, named *MachineName* and *ScriptTimeout*. The *MachineName* property returns the machine name, whereas *ScriptTimeout* gets and sets the time in seconds that a request is allowed to be processed. This property accepts integers and defaults to 90 seconds; however, it is set to a virtually infinite value if the page runs with the attribute *debug=true*, as shown here:

```
this.Server.ScriptTimeout = 30000000;
```

The *ScriptTimeout* property is explicitly and automatically set in the constructor of the dynamically created class that represents the page.

Methods of the *HttpServerUtility* Class

Table 14-8 lists all methods exposed by the *HttpServerUtility* class. As you can see, they constitute a group of helper methods that come in handy at various stages of page execution. The class provides a couple of methods to create instances of COM components and a few others to deal with errors. Another group of methods relates to the decoding and encoding of content and URLs.

TABLE 14-8 Methods of the *Server* Object

Method	Description
ClearError	Clears the last exception that was thrown for the request.
CreateObject	Creates an instance of the specified COM object.
CreateObjectFromClsid	Creates an instance of the COM object identified by the specified CLSID. The class identifier is expressed as a string.
Execute	Passes control to the specified page for execution. The child page executes like a subroutine. The output can be retained in a writer object or automatically flushed in the parent response buffer.
GetLastError	Returns the last exception that was thrown.
HtmlDecode	Decodes a string that has been encoded to eliminate invalid HTML characters. For example, it translates *<* into <.
HtmlEncode	Encodes a string to be displayed in a browser. For example, it encodes < into *<*.
MapPath	Returns the physical path that corresponds to the specified virtual path on the Web server.
Transfer	Works as a kind of server-side redirect. It terminates the execution of the current page and passes control to the specified page. Unlike *Execute*, control is not passed back to the caller page.
UrlDecode	Decodes a string encoded for HTTP transmission to the server in a URL. The decoded string can be returned as a string or output to a writer.
UrlEncode	Encodes a string for HTTP transmission to a client in a URL. The encoded string can be returned as a string or output to a writer.
UrlPathEncode	Encodes only the path portion of a URL string, and returns the encoded string. This method leaves the query string content intact.

HTML and URL encoding are ways of encoding characters to ensure that the transmitted text is not misunderstood by the receiving browser. HTML encoding, in particular, replaces <, >, &, and quotes with equivalent HTML entities such as *<*, *>*, *&*, and *"*. It also encodes blanks, punctuation characters, and in general, all characters not allowed in an

HTML stream. On the other hand, URL encoding is aimed at fixing the text transmitted in URL strings. In URL encoding, the same critical characters are replaced with different character entities than in HTML encoding.

Starting with ASP.NET 2.0, two new static methods have been added to encode and decode a token. The *UrlTokenEncode* method accepts a byte array containing Base64 data and converts it into a URL-encoded token. *UrlTokenDecode* does the reverse.

Embedding Another Page's Results

The *Execute* method allows you to consider an external page as a subroutine. When the execution flow reaches the *Server.Execute* call, control is passed to the specified page. The execution of the current page is suspended, and the external page is spawned. The response text generated by the child execution is captured and processed according to the particular overload of *Execute* that has been used. Table 14-9 lists the overloads of the *Execute* method.

TABLE 14-9 Overloads of the *Execute* Method

Overload	Description
Execute(string);	You pass the URL of the page, and the response text is automatically embedded in the main page.
Execute(string, TextWriter);	The response text is accumulated in the specified text writer.
Execute(string, bool);	The same description as for previous item, except that you can choose whether to preserve the *QueryString* and *Form* collections. *True* is the default setting.
Execute(IHttpHandler, TextWriter, bool);	You indicate the HTTP handler to transfer the current request to. The response is captured by the text writer.
Execute(string, TextWriter, bool);	The response text is captured by the specified text writer, and the *QueryString* and *Form* collections are either preserved or not preserved, as specified.

Note that ASP.NET 1.x supports only the first two overloads listed in Table 14-9.

It is important to note that if a *TextWriter* object is specified, the response text of the child execution is accumulated into the writer object so that the main page output can be used later at will. Figure 14-4 shows this in action—the main page generates the bold-faced text, while the child page's output is shown in normal font sandwiched between the main page output.

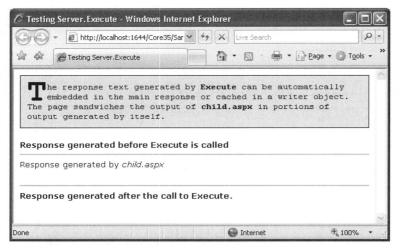

FIGURE 14-4 The response text generated by *Execute*, which can be automatically embedded in the main response or cached in a writer object.

The source code for the main page in Figure 14-4 is as follows:

```
void Page_Load(object sender, EventArgs e)
{
    StringBuilder builder = new StringBuilder();
    builder.Append("<b>Response generated before
                    Execute is called</b><hr/>");

    StringWriter writer = new StringWriter();
    Server.Execute("child.aspx", writer);
    builder.Append(writer.ToString());

    builder.Append("<hr/><b>Response generated after
                    the call to Execute.</b>");

    Label1.Text = builder.ToString();
}
```

It's interesting to look at the internal implementation of the *Execute* method. Both the main and child pages are run by the same *HttpApplication* object as if they were the same request. What happens within the folds of *Execute* is a sort of context switch. First, the method obtains an HTTP handler from the application factory to serve the new request. The original handler of the main request is cached and replaced with the new handler. The spawned page inherits the context of the parent; when finished, any modification made to *Session* or *Application* is immediately visible to the main page.

The handler switching makes the whole operation extremely fast, as there's no need to create a new object to serve the request. When the child page returns, the original handler is restored. The execution of the main page continues from the point at which it was stopped, but it uses the context inherited from the child page.

> **Caution** ASP.NET directly calls the handler indicated by the *Execute* method without reapplying any authentication and authorization logic. If your security policy requires clients to have proper authorization to access the resource, the application should force reauthorization. You can force reauthorization by using the *Response.Redirect* method instead of *Execute*. When *Redirect* is called, the browser places a new request in the system, which will be authenticated and authorized as usual by IIS and ASP.NET. As an alternative, you can verify whether the user has permission to call the page by defining roles and checking the user's role before the application calls the *Execute* method.

Server-Side Redirection

The *Transfer* method differs from the *Execute* method in that it terminates the current page after executing the specified page. The new page runs as if it was the originally requested one. The *Transfer* method has the following overloads:

```
public void Transfer(string);
public void Transfer(string, bool);
public void Transfer(IHttpHandler, bool);
```

The string parameter indicates the destination URL. The Boolean parameter indicates what to do with regard to the *QueryString* and *Form* collections. If *true*, the collections are preserved; otherwise, they are cleared and made unavailable to the destination page (which is the recommended approach). Starting with ASP.NET 2.0, you can also directly indicate the HTTP handler to invoke, with the same security issues that were mentioned for *Execute*.

All the code that might be following the call to *Transfer* in the main page is never executed. In the end, *Transfer* is just a page redirect method. However, it is particularly efficient for two reasons. First, no roundtrip to the client is requested, as is the case, for example, with *Response.Redirect*. Second, the same *HttpApplication* that was serving the caller request is reused, thus limiting the impact on the ASP.NET infrastructure.

Late-Bound COM Objects

The *HttpServerUtility* class provides you with the ability to create late-bound COM objects in much the same way you do in ASP. The methods are *CreateObject* and *CreateObjectFromClsid*. Objects can be created either from the string representation of the class CLSID or from the progID. The following code creates an instance of a COM component using the CLSID:

```
' Only in VB (and in non-strict mode) can you call methods
' on an Object variable beyond the members of the Object class.
' The code here will work written in C#, but it will hardly be usable
Dim strClsid As String = "42754580-16b7-11ce-80eb-00aa003d7352"
Dim comObj As Object = Server.CreateObject(strClsid)
```

When assigned to a variable declared of type *Object*, an object is said to be *late bound*—as opposed to early-bound, strongly typed objects. Late-bound objects can hold references to any object, but they lack many advantages of early-bound objects. Early-bound objects should be used whenever possible because they are significantly faster than late-bound objects and provide strong type checking, thus making your code easier to develop, read, and maintain.

Primarily for backward-compatibility reasons, you might sometimes create late-bound instances of COM objects. Using COM objects in ASP.NET applications is a common necessity in real-world projects. The best way to import COM functionality in .NET applications entails the use of managed wrappers—special classes that expose the type library of the COM class as a .NET class. Managed wrappers are usually created by Visual Studio .NET when you reference a COM object in your project.

> **Note** A command-line utility is also available should you need to generate the class assembly using a particular namespace, language, or file name that is different from those automatically set by Visual Studio .NET. The utility is the Type Library Importer (*tlbimp.exe*), and it is located in the installation path of Visual Studio .NET.

Although it's not an especially effective approach, the *Server.CreateObject* method can be used to create a late-bound instance of a COM component. The ideal language for late binding is Visual Basic .NET; however, bear in mind that late binding is supported only if the *Strict* option is *Off* (the default).

The following code shows how to fill an ADO *Recordset* object using the ASP programming style:

```
<%@ Page Language="VB" AspCompat="true" %>

<script runat="server">
Sub Page_Load(sender as object, e as EventArgs)
    Dim rs As Object = Server.CreateObject("ADODB.Recordset")
    rs.Open("SELECT firstname, lastname FROM employees", _
        "PROVIDER=sqloledb;DATABASE=northwind;SERVER=(local);" + _
        "UID=...;PWD=...;")

    Dim sb As StringBuilder = New StringBuilder("")
    While Not rs.EOF
        sb.Append(rs.Fields("lastname").Value.ToString())
        sb.Append(", ")
        sb.Append(rs.Fields("firstname").Value.ToString())
        sb.Append("<br/>")
        rs.MoveNext
    End While

    Response.Write(sb.ToString())
End Sub
</script>
```

Note the use of the *AspCompat* attribute in the *@Page* directive. Apartment-threaded COM components can be created only in ASP.NET pages that have the *AspCompat* attribute set to *true*. Before an attempt to create the object is made, the *CreateObject* method checks the threading model of the component. If the page is already working in ASP compatibility mode—that is, the *AspCompat* attribute is *true*—the object is created, regardless of the threading model of the component. If the *AspCompat* attribute is set to *false* (the default), *CreateObject* reads the threading model of the COM component from the registry. If the threading model is *apartment* or no threading model is specified, an exception is thrown; otherwise, the object is successfully created.

Note also that the use of the *AspCompat* attribute is not strictly necessary with the ADO library because the ADO library supports both the apartment and free-threading models.

> **Note** COM components developed using Visual Basic 6.0 need the *AspCompat* attribute to be used in ASP.NET pages because they typically use the single-threaded apartment (STA) model. This situation is detected, and an exception is thrown.
>
> Note, though, that if your code instantiates the COM object through a managed wrapper (instead of creating the instance using *CreateObject*), the runtime will no longer be able to detect the apartment nature of the component and does not throw an exception. A managed wrapper saves you from a run-time exception but not from the need of setting *AspCompat* to *true*.

The Importance of *AspCompat*

Running STA components in a multithreaded apartment (MTA) environment such as ASP. NET is strongly discouraged for performance reasons. The *AspCompat* attribute is designed specifically to avoid this critical situation. Let's see how and why.

To process HTTP requests, normally ASP.NET uses a pool of threads from an MTA. Objects in an MTA execute on any thread and allow any number of methods to occur simultaneously. Single-threaded apartment COM components (that is, all VB6 COM components) execute on the particular thread in which they were created and allow only one method to execute at a time. Until special countermeasures are taken, when you run an STA component in an MTA environment continued thread switching is likely to happen. More importantly, a thread switch can happen only when the particular thread in the pool that can serve the STA component is available. As you can see, this situation is heralding poor performance issues, and possibly even a deadlock.

By setting the *AspCompat* attribute to *true*, you force ASP.NET to use an STA thread pool to accommodate the COM object on a per-page basis. In this case, both the caller thread and the callee component live in the same apartment and extra overhead is involved. As a matter of fact, ASP.NET pages that contain STA COM components run better in STA mode than in an otherwise generally faster MTA mode.

Because the *AspCompat* attribute is processed after the instance of the page class is created, you should also avoid creating instances of STA COM objects in the page constructor. If you don't avoid this, the page will be served by an MTA thread regardless of the value of *AspCompat* and you'll probably experience poor performance.

Setting *AspCompat* to *true* has another advantage—it makes ASP's intrinsic objects (*ObjectContext*, *Request*, *Response*, and so on) available to the COM component. ASP.NET creates unmanaged ASP intrinsic objects and passes them to the COM components used in the page.

The *HttpResponse* Object

In ASP.NET, the HTTP response information is encapsulated in the *HttpResponse* class. An instance of the class is created when the HTTP pipeline is set up to serve the request. The instance is then linked to the *HttpContext* object associated with the request and exposed via the *Response* property. The *HttpResponse* class defines methods and properties to manipulate the text that will be sent to the browser. Although user-defined ASP.NET code never needs to use the *HttpResponse* constructor, looking at it is still useful to get the gist of the class:

```
public HttpResponse(TextWriter writer);
```

As you can see, the constructor takes a writer object, which will then be used to accumulate the response text. All calls made to *Response.Write* (and similar output methods) are resolved in terms of internal calls to the specified writer object.

Properties of the *HttpResponse* Class

All properties of the class are grouped and described in Table 14-10. You set a few of these properties to configure key fields on the HTTP response packet, such as content type, character set, page expiration, and status code.

TABLE 14-10 *HttpResponse* Properties

Property	Description
Buffer	Indicates whether the response text should be buffered and sent only at the end of the request. This property is deprecated and provided only for backward compatibility with classic ASP. ASP.NET applications should instead use *BufferOutput*.
BufferOutput	Gets or sets a Boolean value that indicates whether response buffering is enabled. The default is *true*.
Cache	Gets the caching policy set for the page. The caching policy is an *HttpCachePolicy* object that can be used to set the cache-specific HTTP headers for the current response.

Property	Description
CacheControl	Sets the *Cache-Control* HTTP header. Acceptable values are *Public*, *Private*, or *No-Cache*. The property is deprecated in favor of *Cache*.
Charset	Gets or sets a string for the HTTP character set of the output stream. If set to *null*, it suppresses the *Content-Type* header.
ContentEncoding	Gets or sets an object of type *Encoding* for the character encoding of the output stream.
ContentType	Gets or sets the string that represents the Multipurpose Internet Mail Extensions (MIME) type of the output stream. The default value is *text/html*.
Cookies	Gets a collection (*HttpCookieCollection*) object that contains instances of the *HttpCookie* class generated on the server. All the cookies in the collection will be transmitted to the client through the *set-cookie* HTTP header.
Expires	Gets or sets the number of minutes before a page cached on a browser expires. Provided for compatibility with ASP, the property is deprecated in favor of *Cache*.
ExpiresAbsolute	Gets or sets the absolute date and time at which the page expires in the browser cache. Provided for compatibility with ASP, the property is deprecated in favor of *Cache*.
Filter	Gets or sets a filter *Stream* object through which all HTTP output is directed.
IsClientConnected	Indicates whether the client is still connected.
IsRequestBeingRedirected	Indicates whether the request is being redirected. *Not available in ASP. NET 1.x.*
Output	Gets the writer object used to send text out.
OutputStream	Gets the *Stream* object used to output binary data to the response stream.
RedirectLocation	Gets or a sets a string for the value of the *Location* header.
Status	Sets the string returned to the client describing the status of the response. Provided for compatibility with ASP, the property is deprecated in favor of *StatusDescription*.
StatusCode	Gets or sets an integer value for the HTTP status code of the output returned to the client. The default value is *200*.
StatusDescription	Gets or sets the HTTP status string, which is a description of the overall status of the response returned to the client. The default value is *OK*.
SuppressContent	Gets or sets a Boolean value that indicates whether HTTP content should be sent to the client. This is set to *false* by default; if it is set to *true*, only headers are sent.

As you can see, a few of the *HttpResponse* properties are provided only for backward compatibility with classic ASP. In some cases (for example, *BufferOutput*), the property has just been renamed; in other cases, the deprecated properties have been replaced by a more general and powerful APIs. This is certainly the case for cache and expiration properties.

Setting the Response Cache Policy

The response object has three properties dedicated to controlling the ability of the page being sent to the browser to be cached. The *Expires* and *ExpiresAbsolute* properties define relative and absolute times at which the page cached on the client expires and is no longer used by the browser to serve a user request. In fact, if the user navigates to a currently cached page, the cached version is displayed and no roundtrip occurs to the server. A third property somehow related to page caching is *CacheControl*. The property sets a particular HTTP header—the *Cache-Control* header. The *Cache-Control* header controls how a document is to be cached across the network. These properties represent the old-fashioned programming style and exist mostly for compatibility with classic ASP applications.

In ASP.NET, all caching capabilities are grouped in the *HttpCachePolicy* class. With regard to page caching, the class has a double role. It provides methods for both setting cache-specific HTTP headers and controlling the ASP.NET page output cache. In this chapter, we're mostly interested in the HTTP headers, and we'll keep page output caching warm for Chapter 16.

To set the visibility of a page in a client cache, use the *SetCacheability* method of the *HttpCachePolicy* class. To set an expiration time, use the *SetExpires* method, which takes for input an absolute *DateTime* object. Finally, to set a lifetime for the cached page, pass to *SetExpires* the current time plus the desired interval.

> **Note** In the case of conflicting cache policies, ASP.NET maintains the most restrictive settings. For example, if a page contains two controls that set the *Cache-Control* header to *public* and *private*, the most restrictive policy will be used. In this case, *Cache-Control: Private* is what will be sent to the client.

Setting an Output Filter

In ASP.NET, a new component makes its debut—the *response filter*. A response filter is a *Stream*-derived object associated with the *HttpResponse* object. It monitors and filters any output being generated by the page. If you set the *Filter* property with the instance of a class derived from *Stream*, all output being written to the underlying HTTP writer first passes through your output filter.

The custom filter, if any, is invoked during the *HttpResponse*'s *Flush* method before the actual text is flushed to the client. An output filter is useful for applying the final touches to the markup, and it is sometimes used to compact or fix the markup generated by controls.

Building a response filter is a matter of creating a new stream class and overriding some of the methods. The class should have a constructor that accepts a *Stream* object. In light of this, a response filter class is more a wrapper stream class than a purely inherited stream class. If you simply try to set *Response.Filter* with a new instance of, say, *MemoryStream* or *FileStream*, an exception is thrown.

The following listing shows how to create a stream class that works as a response filter. For simplicity, the class inherits from *MemoryStream*. You might want to make it inherit from *Stream*, but in this case you need to override (because they are abstract) a number of methods, such as *CanRead*, *CanWrite*, *CanSeek*, and *Read*. The class converts lowercase characters to uppercase ones.

```
public class MyFilterStream : MemoryStream
{
    private Stream m_Stream;

    public MyFilterStream(Stream filterStream)
    {
        m_Stream = filterStream;
    }

    // The Write method actually does the filtering
    public override void Write(byte[] buffer, int offset, int count)
    {
        // Grab the output as a string
        string buf = UTF8Encoding.UTF8.GetString(buffer, offset, count);

        // Apply some changes
        // Change lowercase chars to uppercase
        buf = buf.ToUpper();

        // Write the resulting string back to the response stream
        byte[] data = UTF8Encoding.UTF8.GetBytes(buf.ToString());
        m_Stream.Write(data, 0, data.Length);
    }
}
```

Use the following code to associate this output filter with the *Response.Filter* property. Here's a sample page:

```
void Page_Load(object sender, EventArgs e)
{
    Response.Filter = new MyFilterStream(Response.Filter);
}
```

Figure 14-5 shows a page that uses the sample filter.

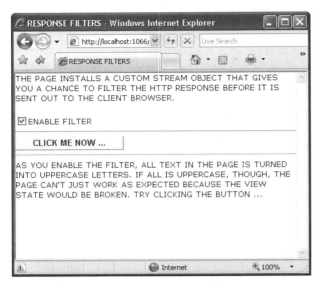

FIGURE 14-5 A page that uses a response filter to turn uppercase characters on.

Response filters provide an interesting opportunity for developers to build more powerful applications, but I caution you to be careful when considering this option. As the sample demonstrates, changing the case of the entire output is not a smart move. If done without care, the change ends up affecting the view state and the internal script code, both of which consist of case-sensitive text, seriously compromising the functionality of the page. Second, filters must be activated on a per-page basis. If you need to filter all the pages in a Web site, you're better off writing an HTTP module.

Methods of the *HttpResponse* Class

Table 14-11 lists all the methods defined on the *HttpResponse* class.

TABLE 14-11 *HttpResponse* **Methods**

Method	Description
AddCacheDependency	Adds an array of cache dependencies to make the cached page output invalid if any dependency gets broken. In the array, you can have any class that inherits from *CacheDependency*. *Not available in ASP.NET 1.x.*
AddCacheItemDependencies	Adds an array of strings representing names of items in the ASP. NET *Cache*. When any of the specified items vary, the cached page output becomes invalid.
AddCacheItemDependency	Description is the same as for the previous item, except that *AddCacheItemDependency* adds a single cache item name.

Method	Description
AddFileDependencies	Adds a group of file names to the collection of file names on which the current page is dependent. When any of the files are modified, the cached output of the current page is deemed invalid.
AddFileDependency	Adds a single file name to the collection of file names on which the current page is dependent. If the file is modified, the cached output of the current page becomes invalid.
AddHeader	Adds an HTTP header to the output stream. It is provided for compatibility with previous versions of ASP. In ASP.NET, you should use *AppendHeader*.
AppendCookie	Adds an HTTP cookie to the cookie collection.
AppendHeader	Adds an HTTP header to the output stream.
AppendToLog	Adds custom log information to the IIS log file.
ApplyAppPathModifier	Adds a session ID to the specified virtual path, and returns the result. It is mostly used with cookieless sessions to construct absolute *HREF*s for hyperlinks.
BinaryWrite	Writes binary characters to the HTTP output stream. It is subject to failures with very large files. (See the references to this method later in the chapter.)
Clear	Clears all content output from the buffer stream.
ClearContent	Calls into *Clear*.
ClearHeaders	Clears all headers from the buffer stream.
Close	Closes the socket connection with the client.
End	Sends all buffered text to the client, stops execution, and raises the end event for the request.
Flush	Sends all currently buffered output to the client.
Pics	Appends a PICS-Label HTTP header to the output. PICS stands for *Platform for Internet Content Selection* and is a World Wide Web Consortium (W3C) standard for rating pages. Any string is acceptable as long as it doesn't exceed 255 characters.
Redirect	Redirects a client to a new URL. Needs a roundtrip.
RemoveOutputCacheItem	A static method that takes a file system path and removes from the cache all cached items associated with the specified path.
SetCookie	Updates an existing cookie in the cookie collection.
TransmitFile	Just like *BinaryWrite* and *WriteFile*, it writes the specified file directly to the output stream. You can safely use *TransmitFile* regardless of the size of the file that you want to transmit. *Available in ASP.NET 1.x through the Service Pack 1.*

Method	Description
Write	Writes content to the underlying output stream. The method can write a string, a single character, or an array of characters, as well as an object. In this case, though, what gets written is the output of the object's *ToString* method.
WriteFile	Writes the specified file (or a portion of it) directly to the output stream. The file can be identified with its path or a Win32 handle (an *IntPtr* object). It is subject to failures with very large files. (See the references to this method later in the chapter.)
WriteSubstitution	Allows fragments of a page to be substituted and sent to the output cache. (We'll cover this method in more detail in Chapter 16.) *Not available in ASP.NET 1.x.*

Output Caching Features

The *HttpResponse* class has several methods to make the page response it represents dependent on files or cache item changes. The methods *AddFileDependency* and *AddCacheItemDependency* (and their versions that handle multiple dependencies) make the page response invalid when the specified file(s) or cached item(s) are modified.

This is a simple form of programmatic page output caching, not as powerful as the API that we'll examine in Chapter 16, but still worth a look. The API discussed in Chapter 16 is superior because it allows you to control how the page response is cached, assigning also the cached output a duration and perhaps a location.

Starting with ASP.NET 2.0 the new method *AddCacheDependency* completes the offering, as it gives you the possibility to make the page response dependent on any dependency object available to your application, including custom dependency objects. See Chapter 16 for more details on custom dependency objects.

Large File Transmission

As you can see, there are three methods for writing potentially large chunks of data down to the output stream—*BinaryWrite*, *WriteFile*, and *TransmitFile*. The *TransmitFile* method was introduced years ago through a hot-fix package for ASP.NET 1.x, as documented in Microsoft KnowledgeBase article KB823409. It was later incorporated in the .NET Framework 1.x SP1 and newer versions of ASP.NET. In summary, *TransmitFile* is the most stable and reliable of the three methods, although you won't notice any significant difference for most files.

Both the *WriteFile* and *BinaryWrite* methods seem perfect for streaming binary data down to the client. However, both can put the Web server memory under pressure if called to work on very large files. Why? It's because both methods load the entire data block (the contents of the file or the byte array) into the Web server's memory. For large files, this can cause severe problems that can culminate in the recycling of the ASP.NET process. The *TransmitFile* method is designed to elegantly work around the problem. It sends output directly from a file to the ASP.NET ISAPI extension and then down to the client, without passing a humongous string to the ISAPI extension.

> **Note** Although *TransmitFile* makes large file downloads more stable than ever and fixes the problem of recycling, it is far from being a full solution to the problem of tracking and resuming large file downloads. For example, if a download fails, for whatever reason, *TransmitFile* can start it again only from the beginning. The article found at the following Web site discusses a better approach to the problem: *http://www.devx.com/dotnet/Article/22533*.

The *HttpRequest* Object

The *HttpRequest* object groups all the information contained in the HTTP packet that represents the incoming Web request. The contents of the various HTTP headers, the query string, or the form's input fields, path, and URL information are organized in a series of collections and other ad hoc objects for easy and effective programmatic access. The *HttpRequest* object is populated as soon as ASP.NET begins working on a Web request, and it's made available through the *Request* property of *HttpContext*.

HttpRequest exposes a fair number of properties and is one of the objects that has been more significantly enriched in the transition from ASP to ASP.NET.

Properties of the *HttpRequest* Class

The class properties can be categorized into three groups based on the type of information they contain: the type of the request, client data, and connection.

Information About the Request

Table 14-12 lists the properties that define the type of request being issued.

TABLE 14-12 Properties Describing the Request Type

Property	Description
AcceptTypes	Gets an array of strings denoting the list of MIME types supported by the client for the specified request.
AnonymousID	Indicates the ID of the anonymous user, if any. The identity refers to the string generated by the *AnonymousIdentification* module and has nothing to do with the identify of the IIS anonymous user. *Not available in ASP.NET 1.x.*
Browser	Gets an *HttpBrowserCapabilities* object that contains information about the capabilities of the client's browser.
ContentEncoding	Gets or sets an *Encoding* object that represents the client's character set. If specified, this property overrides the ASP.NET default encoding.
ContentLength	Gets the length in bytes of the content sent by the client.
ContentType	Gets or sets the MIME content type of the incoming request.
CurrentExecutionFilePath	Gets the current virtual path of the request even when the client is redirected to another page via *Execute* or *Transfer*. The *FilePath* property, on the other hand, always returns the path to the originally requested page.
FilePath	Gets the virtual path of the current request. The path doesn't change in cases of server-side page redirection.
HttpMethod	Gets a string that denotes the HTTP method used for the request. Values are *GET*, *POST*, or *HEAD*.
RequestType	Gets or sets a string that denotes the HTTP command used to issue the request. It can be *GET* or *POST*.
TotalBytes	Gets the total number of bytes in the input stream. This property differs from *ContentLength* in that it also includes headers.
UserAgent	Gets a string that identifies the browser. This property gets the raw content of the user agent header.

The anonymous ID is usually transmitted through a cookie (default name is *.ASPXANONYMOUS*) and serves the purpose of giving an identity to nonauthenticated users, mainly for user profile functions. The anonymous ID is a GUID and is transmitted as clear text. It doesn't play any relevant role with authentication and security; it is merely a way to track nonregistered users as they move around the site. (See Chapter 5 for profiles and Chapter 17 for user authentication.)

Initially, *CurrentExecutionFilePath* and *FilePath* share the same content—the requested URL. However, in cases of server-side redirects, the value of *CurrentExecutionFilePath* is automatically updated. You should check *CurrentExecutionFilePath* for up-to-date information about the target URL.

The *HttpBrowserCapabilities* object groups in a single place values that identify a fair number of browser capabilities, including support for ActiveX controls, scripting languages, frames, cookies, and more. When the request arrives, the user agent information is used to identify the requesting browser and an instance of the *HttpBrowserCapabilities* class is created and populated with browser-specific information. The information is in no way dynamically set by the browser; instead, it is retrieved from an offline server-side repository.

> **Note** The *Browser* property also supports mobile scenarios in version 1.1 of the .NET Framework and newer versions. In this case, the actual object returned is of class *MobileCapabilities*—an *HttpBrowserCapabilities*-derived class. When you obtain the *Browser* property reference, you should cast it as a *MobileCapabilities* class if you are interested in the mobile browser capabilities.

Information from the Client

Table 14-13 lists the *HttpRequest* properties that expose the client data that ASP.NET pages might want to use for server-side processing. The following table includes, for example, cookies, forms, and query string collections.

TABLE 14-13 Properties Describing the Client Data

Property	Description
ClientCertificate	Gets an *HttpClientCertificate* object with information on the client's security certificate settings, if any. The certificate object wraps up information such as number, validity, and issuer of the certificate.
Cookies	Gets a collection representing all cookies sent by the client. A cookie is identified by the *HttpCookie* object.
Files	Gets a collection of client-uploaded files. The property requires the HTTP *Content-Type* header to be set to *multipart/form-data*.
Filter	Gets or sets a *Stream*-based object through which all HTTP input passes when received. The filtered input is anything read via *InputStream*.
Form	Gets a name-value collection filled with the values of the input fields in the form posted. The collection is populated when the *Content-Type* header is either *application/x-www-form-urlencoded* or *multipart/form-data*.
Headers	Gets a name-value collection filled with all the header values in the request.
InputStream	Gets a *Stream* object representing the contents of the incoming HTTP content body.
Params	Gets a name-value collection that is a union of four other similar collections: *QueryString*, *Form*, *ServerVariables*, and *Cookies*.
QueryString	Gets a name-value collection containing all the query string variables sent by the client.

Property	Description
ServerVariables	Gets a name-value collection filled with a collection of Web server–defined variables.
UserHostAddress	Gets the Internet Protocol (IP) address of the remote client.
UserHostName	Gets the Domain Name System (DNS) name of the remote client.
UserLanguages	Gets an array of strings denoting the list of the languages accepted by the client for the specified request. The languages are read from the Accept-Language header.

The *Params* collection combines four different but homogeneous collections—*QueryString*, *Form*, *ServerVariables*, and *Cookies*—and it replicates the information contained in each of them. The collections are added in the following order: *QueryString*, *Form*, *Cookies*, and finally *ServerVariables*.

Information About the Connection

Table 14-14 lists the properties that relate to the open connection.

TABLE 14-14 Properties Describing the Connection

Property	Description
ApplicationPath	Gets the virtual path of the current application.
IsAuthenticated	Indicates whether or not the user has been authenticated.
IsLocal	Indicates if it is a local request. *Not available in ASP.NET 1.x.*
IsSecureConnection	Indicates whether the connection is taking place over a Secure Sockets Layer (SSL) using HTTPS.
LogonUserIdentity	Gets an object representing the Windows identity of the current user as logged at the IIS gate. *Not available in ASP.NET 1.x.*
Path	Gets the virtual path of the current request.
PathInfo	Gets additional path information for the requested resource, if any. The property returns any text that follows the URL.
PhysicalApplicationPath	Gets the file system path of the current application's root directory.
PhysicalPath	Gets the physical file system path corresponding to the requested URL.
RawUrl	Gets the raw URL of the current request.
Url	Gets the *Uri* object that represents the URL of the current request.
UrlReferrer	Gets the *Uri* object that represents the URL from which the current request originated.

The *Uri* class provides an object representation of a Uniform Resource Identifier (URI)—a unique name for a resource available on the Internet. The *Uri* class provides easy access to the parts of the URI as well as properties and methods for checking host, loopback, ports, and DNS.

The server variables set in the *ServerVariables* collection are decided by the run-time environment that processes the request. The information packed in the collection is for the most part excerpted from the HTTP worker request object; another part contains Web server–specific information. The *ServerVariables* collection is just a friendly name/value model to expose that information.

Methods of the *HttpRequest* Class

Table 14-15 lists all methods exposed by the *HttpRequest* class.

TABLE 14-15 *HttpRequest* **Methods**

Method	Description
BinaryRead	Performs a binary read from the current input stream. The method lets you specify the number of bytes to read and returns an array of bytes. The method is provided for compatibility with ASP. ASP. NET applications should read from the stream associated with the *InputStream* property.
MapImageCoordinates	Maps an incoming image-field form parameter to x/y coordinate values.
MapPath	Maps the specified virtual path to a physical path on the Web server.
SaveAs	Saves the current request to a file disk with or without headers. This method is especially useful for debugging.
ValidateInput	Performs a quick, nonexhaustive check to find potentially dangerous input data in the request.

Saving the Request to Disk

The *SaveAs* method lets you create a file to store the entire content of the HTTP request. Note that the storage medium can only be a disk file; no stream or writer can be used. Because ASP.NET by default isn't granted write permissions, this method causes an access denied exception unless you take ad hoc measures. Granting the ASP.NET account full control over the file to be created (or over the whole folder) is one of the possible ways to successfully use the *SaveAs* method. The following listing shows possible content that *SaveAs* writes to disk:

```
GET /Core35/Samples/Ch14/Misc/TestFilter.aspx HTTP/1.1Connection: Keep-Alive
Accept: */*
Accept-Encoding: gzip, deflate
```

```
Accept-Language: it,en-us;q=0.5
Cookie: .ASPXANONYMOUS=AGzHqyVAyAEkAAAAO ... MWE3YZreWoYt-jkSc_RwU169brWNTIw1
Host: localhost:1066
User-Agent: Mozilla/4.0 (compatible; MSIE 7.0; Windows NT 5.2; .NET CLR 1.1.4322; .NET CLR
2.0.50727; .NET CLR 3.0.04506.30; .NET CLR 3.0.04506.590; .NET CLR 3.0.04506.648; .NET CLR
3.5.21022)
UA-CPU: x86
```

If the intercepted request is a *POST*, instead, you'll find posted values at the bottom of the string.

Validating Client Input

A golden rule of Web security claims that all user input is evil and should always be filtered and sanitized before use. The *@Page* directive has an attribute—*ValidateRequest*—that automatically blocks postbacks that contain potentially dangerous data. This feature is not the silver bullet of Web input security, but it helps detect possible problems. From a general security perspective, you're better off replacing the automatic input validation with a strong, application-specific validation layer.

The automatic input validation feature—*ValidateRequest*—is enabled by default and implemented via a call to the *HttpRequest*'s *ValidationInput* method. *ValidateInput* can be called by your code if the validation feature is not enabled. Request validation works by checking all input data against a hard-coded list of potentially dangerous data. The contents of the collections *QueryString*, *Form*, and *Cookies* are checked during request validation.

Conclusion

In this chapter, we covered some basic objects that are the foundation of ASP.NET programming—*Server*, *Response*, *Request*, and others. An ASP.NET application is represented by an instance of the *HttpApplication* class properly configured by the contents of the *global.asax* file. And both the *HttpApplication* class and the *global.asax* file found their space in this chapter too.

While discussing the interface of the objects that generate the context of an HTTP request, we reviewed in detail some specific programming issues such as the instantiation of late-bound COM objects, server-side page redirection, and the setup of response filters. In the next chapter, we'll discuss an important topic related to Web applications and ASP.NET—state management. Fundamentally, Web applications are stateless, but ASP.NET provides various mechanisms for maintaining application state and caching pages.

Just the Facts

- Any ASP.NET request is served by making it flow through a pipeline of internal components. The entry point in the ASP.NET pipeline is the *HttpRuntime* class.

- *HttpRuntime* creates an object that represents the context of the request—the *HttpContext* class. An instance of this class accompanies the request for its entire lifetime.

- The HTTP context of a request is enriched with references to the intrinsic worker objects, such as *Request*, *Response*, and *Server*. In addition, it references the session state, ASP.NET cache, tracer, and identity object.

- The execution of the request is governed by a pooled *HttpApplication* object. An instance of this class is created based on the contents of the *global.asax* file, if any.

- *HttpApplication* makes the request flow through the pipeline along with its associated HTTP context so that registered HTTP modules can intercept the request, consume any contained information, and add new information if needed.

- Modules can fire their own events, and the *global.asax* file is the place where page authors can put code to catch application-level events.

- Standard intrinsic objects such as *Request*, *Response*, and *Server* look like their classic ASP counterparts, but they provide some specific functionalities. For example, *Response* manages file downloads and filters page output; *Request* allows you to manage the incoming request and its values.

Chapter 15
ASP.NET State Management

All real-world applications of any shape and form need to maintain their own state to serve users' requests. ASP.NET applications are no exception. However, unlike other types of applications, they need special system-level tools to achieve the result. The reason for this peculiarity lies in the stateless nature of the underlying protocol that Web applications still rely upon. As long as HTTP remains the transportation protocol for the Web, all applications will run into the same trouble—figuring out the most effective way to persist state information.

Application state is a sort of blank container that each application and programmer can fill with whatever piece of information makes sense to persist: from user preferences to global settings, from worker data to hit counters, from lookup tables to shopping carts. This extremely variegated mess of data can be organized and accessed according to a number of different usage patterns. Typically, all the information contributing to the application state is distributed in various layers, each with its own settings for visibility, programmability, and lifetime.

ASP.NET provides state management facilities at four levels: application, session, page, and request. Each level has its own special container object, which is a topic we'll cover in this chapter. In this chapter, we'll explore the *HttpApplicationState*, *HttpSessionState*, and *ViewState* objects, which provide for application, session, and page state maintenance, respectively. In the next chapter, we'll dive into the *Cache* object. In Chapter 14, you will recall, we covered the *HttpContext* object, which is the primary tool used to manage state and information across the entire request lifetime. The context of the request is different from all other state objects in that the request has a limited lifetime but passes through the entire pipeline of objects processing an HTTP request.

The Application's State

Table 15-1 summarizes the main features of the various state objects.

TABLE 15-1 State Management Objects at a Glance

Object	Lifetime	Data Visibility	Location
Cache	Implements an automatic scavenging mechanism, and periodically clears less frequently used contents	Global to all sessions	Does not support Web farm or Web garden scenarios
HttpApplicationState	Created when the first request hits the Web server, and released when the application shuts down	Same as for *Cache*	Same as for *Cache*
HttpContext	Spans the entire lifetime of the individual request	Global to the objects involved with the request	Same as for *Cache*
HttpSessionState	Created when the user makes the first request, and lasts until the user closes the session	Global to all requests issued by the user who started the session	Configurable to work on Web farms and gardens
ViewState	Represents the calling context of each page being generated	Limited to all requests queued for the same page	Configurable to work on Web farms and gardens

In spite of their quite unfamiliar names, the *HttpApplicationState* and *HttpSessionState* objects are state facilities totally compatible with classic Active Server Pages (ASP) intrinsic objects such as *Application* and *Session*. Ad hoc properties known as *Application* and *Session* let you use these objects in much the same way you did in ASP.

> **Note** In this chapter, we'll review several objects involved, at various levels, with the state management. We won't discuss cookies in detail, but cookies are definitely useful for storing small amounts of information on the client. The information is sent with the request to the server and can be manipulated and re-sent through the response. The cookie is a text-based structure with simple key/value pairs, and it consumes no resources on the server. In e-commerce applications, for example, cookies are the preferred way of storing user preferences. In addition, cookies have a configurable expiration policy. The downside of cookies is their limited size (browser-dependent, but seldom greater than 8 KB) and the fact that the user can disable them.

Note In Chapter 21,"Silverlight and Rich Internet Applications," we'll address some of the features announced for Silverlight 2.0—the Microsoft' flagship product to build rich Internet applications. Among other things, Silverlight 2.0 (not yet released even in Beta at the time of this writing) is expected to support the .NET Framework isolated storage API. The API allows developers to save data to files located in a specified file system subtree. In this regard, isolated storage can be compared to cookies for its ability to persist data to the client. Unlike cookies, any content saved to isolated storage is never uploaded and is not accessible from the server.

The *HttpApplicationState* object makes a dictionary available for storage to all request handlers invoked within an application. In classic ASP, only pages have access to the application state; this is no longer true in ASP.NET, in which all HTTP handlers and modules can store and retrieve values within the application's dictionary. The application state is accessible only within the context of the originating application. Other applications running on the system cannot access or modify the values.

An instance of the *HttpApplicationState* class is created the first time a client requests any resource from within a particular virtual directory. Each running application holds its own global state object. The most common way to access application state is by means of the *Application* property of the *Page* object. Application state is not shared across either a Web farm or Web garden.

Properties of the *HttpApplicationState* Class

The *HttpApplicationState* class is sealed and inherits from a class named *NameObjectCollectionBase*. In practice, the *HttpApplicationState* class is a collection of pairs, each made of a string key and an object value. Such pairs can be accessed either using the key string or the index. Internally, the base class employs a hashtable with an initial capacity of zero that is automatically increased as required. Table 15-2 lists the properties of the *HttpApplicationState* class.

TABLE 15-2 *HttpApplicationState* **Properties**

Property	Description
AllKeys	Gets an array of strings containing all the keys of the items currently stored in the object.
Contents	Gets the current instance of the object. But wait! What this property returns is simply a reference to the application state object, not a clone. Provided for ASP compatibility.
Count	Gets the number of objects currently stored in the collection.
Item	Indexer property, provides read/write access to an element in the collection. The element can be specified either by name or index. Accessors of this property are implemented using *Get* and *Set* methods.
StaticObjects	Gets a collection including all instances of all objects declared in *global.asax* using an *<object>* tag with the *scope* attribute set to *Application*.

Note that static objects and actual state values are stored in separate collections. The exact type of the static collection is *HttpStaticObjectsCollection*.

Methods of the *HttpApplicationState* Class

The set of methods that the *HttpApplicationState* class features are mostly specialized versions of the typical methods of a name/value collection. As Table 15-3 shows, the most significant extension entails the locking mechanism necessary to serialize access to the state values.

TABLE 15-3 *HttpApplicationState* **Methods**

Method	Description
Add	Adds a new value to the collection. The value is boxed as an *object*.
Clear	Removes all objects from the collection.
Get	Returns the value of an item in the collection. The item can be specified either by key or index.
GetEnumerator	Returns an enumerator object to iterate through the collection.
GetKey	Gets the string key of the item stored at the specified position.
Lock	Locks writing access to the whole collection. No concurrent caller can write to the collection object until *UnLock* is called.
Remove	Removes the item whose key matches the specified string.
RemoveAll	Calls *Clear*.
RemoveAt	Removes the item at the specified position.
Set	Assigns the specified value to the item with the specified key. The method is thread-safe, and the access to the item is blocked until the writing is completed.
UnLock	Unlocks writing access to the collection.

Note that the *GetEnumerator* method is inherited from the base collection class and, as such, is oblivious to the locking mechanism of the class. If you enumerate the collection using this method, each returned value is obtained through a simple call to one of the *get* methods on the base *NameObjectCollectionBase* class. Unfortunately, that method is not aware of the locking mechanism needed on the derived *HttpApplicationState* class because of the concurrent access to the application state. As a result, your enumeration would not be thread-safe. A better way to enumerate the content of the collection is by using a *while* statement and the *Get* method to access an item. Alternatively, you could lock the collection before you enumerate.

State Synchronization

Note that all operations on *HttpApplicationState* require some sort of synchronization to ensure that multiple threads running within an application safely access values without incurring deadlocks and access violations. The writing methods, such as *Set* and *Remove*, as well as the *set* accessor of the *Item* property implicitly apply a writing lock before proceeding. The *Lock* method ensures that only the current thread can modify the application state. The *Lock* method is provided to apply the same writing lock around portions of code that need to be protected from other threads' access.

You don't need to wrap a single call to *Set*, *Clear*, or *Remove* with a lock/unlock pair of statements—those methods, in fact, are already thread-safe. Using *Lock* in these cases will only have the effect of producing additional overhead, increasing the internal level of recursion.

```
// This operation is thread-safe
Application["MyValue"] = 1;
```

Use *Lock* instead if you want to shield a group of instructions from concurrent writings:

```
// These operations execute atomically
Application.Lock();
int val = (int) Application["MyValue"];
if (val < 10)
    Application["MyValue"] = val + 1;
Application.UnLock();
```

Reading methods such as *Get*, the *get* accessor of *Item*, and even *Count* have an internal synchronization mechanism that, when used along with *Lock*, will protect them against concurrent and cross-thread readings and writings:

```
// The reading is protected from concurrent read/writes
Application.Lock();
int val = (int) Application["MyValue"];
Application.UnLock();
```

You should always use *Lock* and *UnLock* together. However, if you omit the call to *UnLock*, the likelihood of incurring a deadlock is not high because the .NET Framework automatically removes the lock when the request completes or times out, or when an unhandled error occurs. For this reason, if you handle the exception, consider using a *finally* block to clear the lock or expect to face some delay while ASP.NET clears the lock for you when the request ends.

Tradeoffs of Application State

Instead of writing global data to the *HttpApplicationState* object, you could use public members within the *global.asax* file. Compared to entries in the *HttpApplicationState* collection, a global member is preferable because it is strongly typed and does not require a hashtable access to locate the value. On the other hand, a global variable is not synchronized per se and must be manually protected. You have to use language constructs to protect access to these members—for example, the C# *lock* operator or, in Visual Basic .NET, the *SyncLock* operator. We demonstrated global members in Chapter 14.

Memory Occupation

Whatever form you choose for storing the global state of an application, some general considerations apply about the opportunity of storing data globally. For one thing, global data storage results in permanent memory occupation. Unless explicitly removed by the code, any data stored in the application global state is removed only when the application shuts down. On one end, putting a few megabytes of data in the application's memory speeds up access; on the other hand, doing this occupies valuable memory for the entire duration of the application.

For this reason, it is extremely important that you consider using the *Cache* object (which is discussed further in the next chapter) whenever you have the need for globally shared data. Unlike data stored with *Application* and global members, data stored in the ASP.NET *Cache* is subject to an automatic scavenging mechanism that ensures that the data is removed when a too high percentage of virtual memory is being consumed. In addition, the *Cache* object has a lot of other beneficial features that we'll explore in the next chapter. The bottom line is that the *Cache* object was introduced specifically to mitigate the problem of memory occupation and to replace the *Application* object.

Concurrent Access to Data

Storing data globally is also problematic because of locking. Synchronization is necessary to ensure that concurrent thread access doesn't cause inconsistencies in the data. But locking the application state can easily become a performance hit that leads to nonoptimal use of threads. The application global state is held in memory and never trespasses the machine's boundaries. In multimachine and multiprocessor environments, the application global state is limited to the single worker process running on the individual machine or CPU. As such, it is not something really global. Finally, the duration of the data in memory is at risk because of possible failures in the process or, more simply, because of the ASP.NET process recycling. If you're going to use the application state feature and plan to deploy the application in a Web farm or Web garden scenario, you're probably better off dropping global state in favor of database tables. At the very least, you should wrap your global data in smart proxy objects that check for the existence of data and refill it if it's not there, for whatever reason. Here's a quick snapshot:

```
// Retrieve data
public object GetGlobalData(string entry)
{
    object o = Application[entry];
    if (o == null)
    {
        // TODO:: Reload the data from its source
        ...

        // Return data
        return Application[entry];
    }
    return o;
}
```

The Session's State

The *HttpSessionState* class provides a dictionary-based model of storing and retrieving session-state values. Unlike *HttpApplicationState*, this class doesn't expose its contents to all users operating on the virtual directory at a given time. Only the requests that originate in the context of the same session—that is, generated across multiple page requests made by the same user—can access the session state. The session state can be stored and published in a variety of ways, including in a Web farm or Web garden scenario. By default, though, the session state is held within the ASP.NET worker process.

Compared to *Session*, the intrinsic object of ASP, the ASP.NET session state is nearly identical in use, but it's significantly richer in functionality and radically different in architecture. In addition, it provides some extremely handy facilities—such as support for cookieless browsers, Web farms, and Web gardens—and the capability of being hosted by external processes, including Microsoft SQL Server. In this way, ASP.NET session management can provide an unprecedented level of robustness and reliability.

Starting with ASP.NET 2.0, developers can create custom data stores for session state. For example, if you need the robustness that a database-oriented solution can guarantee but you work with Oracle databases, you need not install SQL Server as well. By writing a piece of additional code, you can support an Oracle session data store while using the same *Session* semantics and classes.

The extensibility model for session state offers two options: customizing bits and pieces of the existing ASP.NET session state mechanism (for example, creating an Oracle session provider or a module controlling the generation of the ID), and replacing the standard session state HTTP module with a new one. The former option is easier to implement but provides a limited set of features you can customize. The latter option is more complicated to code but provides the greatest flexibility.

The Session-State HTTP Module

Regardless of the internal implementation, the programmer's application programming interface (API) for session state management is just one—the old acquaintance known as the *Session* object. It was a COM object in classic ASP that was instantiated in the *asp.dll* ISAPI extension and injected into the memory space of the ActiveX Scripting engine called to parse and process the *.asp* script. It is a collection object in ASP.NET, living behind the *Session* property of the *Page* class. The exact type is *HttpSessionState*; it's a class that's not further inheritable and that implements *ICollection* and *IEnumerable*. An instance of this class is created during the startup of each request that requires session support. The collection is filled with name/value pairs read from the specified medium and attached to the context of the request—the *HttpContext* class. The *Page*'s *Session* property just mirrors the *Session* property of the *HttpContext* class.

If developers can simply work with one object—the *Session* object—regardless of other details, most of the credit goes to an HTTP module that governs the process of retrieving and storing session state with some help from special provider objects. The ASP.NET module in charge of setting up the session state for each user connecting to an application is an HTTP module named *SessionStateModule*. Structured after the *IHttpModule* interface, the *SessionStateModule* object provides session-state services for ASP.NET applications.

Although, as an HTTP module, it is required to supply a relatively simple programming interface—the *IHttpModule* interface contracts only for *Init* and *Dispose* methods—*SessionStateModule* does perform a number of quite sophisticated tasks, most of which are fundamental for the health and functionality of the Web application. The session-state module is invoked during the setup of the *HttpApplication* object that will process a given request and is responsible for either generating or obtaining a unique session ID string and for storing and retrieving state data from a state provider—for example, SQL Server or the Web server's memory.

State Client Managers

When invoked, the session-state HTTP module reads the settings in the *<sessionState>* section of the *web.config* file and determines what the expected state client manager is for the application. A state client manager is a component that takes care of storing and retrieving data of all currently active sessions. The *SessionStateModule* component queries the state client manager to get the name/value pairs of a given session.

In ASP.NET, there are four possibilities for working with the session state. The session state can be stored locally in the ASP.NET worker process; the session state can be maintained in an external, even remote, process named *aspnet_state.exe*; and the session state can be managed by SQL Server and stored in an ad hoc database table. The fourth option entails you storing the sessions in a custom component. Table 15-4 briefly discusses the various options.

TABLE 15-4 State Client Providers

Mode	Description
Custom	The values for all the sessions are stored in a custom data store. *Not available in ASP.NET 1.x.*
InProc	The values for all the sessions are maintained as live objects in the memory of the ASP.NET worker process (*aspnet_wp.exe* or *w3wp.exe* in Microsoft Windows Server 2003 and beyond). This is the default option.
Off	Session state is disabled, and no state client provider is active.
SQLServer	The values for all the sessions are serialized and stored in a SQL Server table. The instance of SQL Server can run either locally or remotely.
StateServer	The values for all the sessions are serialized and stored in the memory of a separate system process (*aspnet_state.exe*). The process can also run on another machine. Session values are deserialized into the session dictionary at the beginning of the request. If the request completes successfully, state values are serialized into the process memory and made available to other pages.

The *SessionStateMode* enum type lists the available options for the state client provider. The *InProc* option is by far the fastest possible in terms of access. However, bear in mind that the more data you store in a session, the more memory is consumed on the Web server, which increases the risk of performance hits. If you plan to use any of the out-of-process solutions, the possible impact of serialization and deserialization should be carefully considered. We'll discuss this aspect in detail later in the chapter starting in the "Persist Session Data to Remote Servers" section.

The session-state module determines the state provider to use based on what it reads out of the *<sessionState>* section of the *web.config* file. Next, it instantiates and initializes the state provider for the application. Each provider continues its own initialization, which is quite different depending on the type. For example, the SQL Server state manager opens a connection to the given database, whereas the out-of-process manager checks the specified TCP port. The *InProc* state manager, on the other hand, stores a reference to the callback function that will be used to fire the *Session_End* event. (I'll discuss this further in the section "Lifetime of a Session.")

All state providers expose a common set of methods to communicate with the caller. The schema is outlined in Figure 15-1.

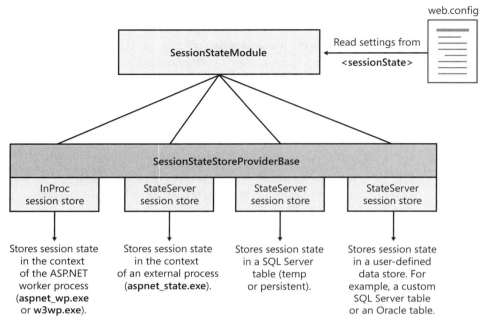

FIGURE 15-1 *SessionStateModule* and its child-state client managers.

> **Note** All the actual state provider objects derive from a base class—*SessionStateStoreProvi-derBase*. In ASP.NET 1.x, on the other hand, all state providers implement a common interface, named *IStateClientManager*. This interface has been lost in the transition to version 2.0, a victim of the refactoring process and the advent of the provider model. (See Chapter 1.) However, the switch to base classes, from interfaces, is a pervasive design choice that affects the entire ASP. NET Framework.

Creating the *HttpSessionState* Object

The state module is responsible for retrieving and attaching the session state to the context of each request that runs within the session. The session state is available only after the *HttpApplication.AcquireRequestState* event fires, and it gets irreversibly lost after the *HttpApplication.ReleaseRequestState* event. Subsequently, this means that no state is still available when *Session_End* fires.

The session module creates the *HttpSessionState* object for a request while processing the *HttpApplication.AcquireRequestState* event. At this time, the *HttpSessionState* object—a sort of collection—is given its session ID and the session dictionary. The session dictionary is the actual collection of state values that pages will familiarly access through the *Session* property.

If a new session is being started, such a data dictionary is simply a newly created empty object. If the module is serving a request for an existing session, the data dictionary will be filled by deserializing the contents supplied by the currently active session state provider. At the end of the request, the current content of the dictionary, as modified by the page request, is flushed back to the state provider through a serialization step. The whole process is depicted in Figure 15-2.

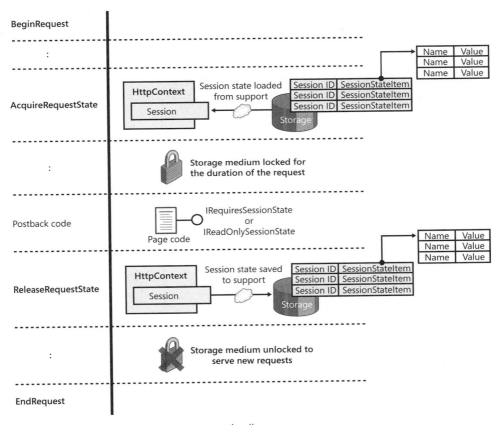

FIGURE 15-2 The session state management timeline.

Synchronizing Access to the Session State

So when your Web page makes a call into the *Session* property, it's actually accessing a local, in-memory copy of the data. What if other pages (in the same session) attempt to concurrently access the session state? In that case, the current request might end up working on inconsistent data or data that isn't up to date.

To avoid that, the session state module implements a reader/writer locking mechanism and queues the access to state values. A page that has session-state write access will hold a writer lock on the session until the request finishes. A page gains write access to the session state by setting the *EnableSessionState* attribute on the *@Page* directive to *true*. A page that has session-state read access—for example, when the *EnableSessionState* attribute is set to *ReadOnly*—will hold a reader lock on the session until the request finishes.

If a page request sets a reader lock, other concurrently running requests cannot update the session state but are allowed to read. If a page request sets a writer lock on the session state, all other pages are blocked regardless of whether they have to read or write. For example, if two frames attempt to write to *Session*, one of them has to wait until the other finishes. Figure 15-3 shows the big picture.

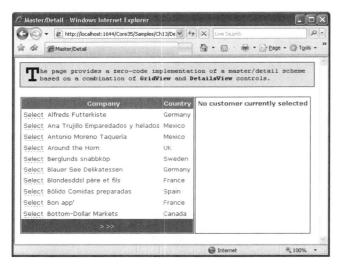

FIGURE 15-3 Page access to the session state is synchronized, and a serialization/deserialization layer ensures that each request is served an up-to-date dictionary of values, stored at the application's convenience.

Tip Concurrent access to the session state is not very common in reality. It might happen if you have a multiframe page or if your users work with two copies of the same page or multiple pages of the same application at the same time. It also happens when you use session-enabled HTTP handlers to serve embedded resources such as images or CSS files. By default, you are protected against concurrent accesses. However, declaring the exact use of the session state that a page is going to make (read/write, readonly, or no use) is an excellent form of optimization. You do this through the *EnableSessionState* attribute on the *@Page* directive.

Properties of the *HttpSessionState* Class

The *HttpSessionState* class is defined in the *System.Web.SessionState* namespace. It is a generic collection class and implements the *ICollection* interface. The properties of the *HttpSessionState* class are listed in Table 15-5.

TABLE 15-5 *HttpSessionState* **Properties**

Property	Description
CodePage	Gets or sets the code page identifier for the current session.
Contents	Returns a reference to *this* object. Provided for ASP compatibility.
CookieMode	Details the application's configuration for cookieless sessions. Declared to be of type *HttpCookieMode*. (I'll discuss this in more detail later.) *Not available in ASP.NET 1.x.*
Count	Gets the number of items currently stored in the session state.
IsCookieless	Indicates whether the session ID is embedded in the URL or stored in an HTTP cookie. It's more specific than *CookieMode*.
IsNewSession	Indicates whether the session was created with the current request.
IsReadOnly	Indicates whether the session is read-only. The session is read-only if the *EnableSessionState* attribute on the *@Page* directive is set to the keyword *ReadOnly*.
IsSynchronized	Returns *false*. (See references to this later in the chapter.)
Item	Indexer property, provides read/write access to a session-state value. The value can be specified either by name or index.
Keys	Gets a collection of the keys of all values stored in the session.
LCID	Gets or sets the locale identifier (LCID) of the current session.
Mode	Gets a value denoting the state client manager being used. Acceptable values are listed in Table 15-4.
SessionID	Gets a string with the ID used to identify the session.
StaticObjects	Gets a collection including all instances of all objects declared in *global.asax* using an *<object>* tag with the *scope* attribute set to *Session*. Note that you cannot add objects to this collection from within an ASP.NET application—that is, programmatically.
SyncRoot	Returns a reference to *this* object. (See references to this later in the chapter.)
Timeout	Gets or sets the minutes that the session module should wait between two successive requests before terminating the session.

The *HttpSessionState* class is a normal collection class because it implements the *ICollection* interface, but synchronization-wise it is a very special collection class. As mentioned, the synchronization mechanism is implemented in the *SessionStateModule* component, which guarantees that at most one thread will ever access the session state. However, because *HttpSessionState* implements the *ICollection* interface, it must provide an implementation for both *IsSynchronized* and *SyncRoot*. Note that *IsSynchronized* and *SyncRoot* are collection-specific properties for synchronization and have nothing to do with the session synchronization discussed previously. They refer to the ability of the collection class (*HttpSessionState* in this case) to work in a synchronized manner. Technically speaking, the *HttpSessionState* is not synchronized, but access to session state is.

Methods of the *HttpSessionState* Class

Table 15-6 shows all the methods available in the *HttpSessionState* class. They mostly have to do with the typical operations on a collection. In this sense, the only exceptional method is *Abandon*, which causes the session to be canceled.

TABLE 15-6 *HttpSessionState* **Methods**

Method	Description
Abandon	Sets an internal flag that instructs the session module to cancel the current session.
Add	Adds a new item to the session state. The value is boxed in an *object* type.
Clear	Clears all values from the session state.
CopyTo	Copies the collection of session-state values to a one-dimensional array, starting at the specified index in the array.
GetEnumerator	Gets an enumerator to loop through all the values in the session.
Remove	Deletes an item from the session-state collection. The item is identified by the key.
RemoveAll	Calls *Clear*.
RemoveAt	Deletes an item from the session-state collection. The item is identified by position.

When running the procedure to terminate the current request, the session-state module checks an internal flag to verify whether the user ordered that the session be abandoned. If the flag is set—that is, the *Abandon* method was called—any response cookie is removed and the procedure to terminate the session is begun. Notice, though, that this does not necessarily mean that a *Session_End* event will fire.

First, the *Session_End* event fires only if the session mode is *InProc*; second, the event does not fire if the session dictionary is empty and no real session state exists for the application. In other words, at least one request must have been completed for the *Session_End* to fire when the session is closed either naturally or after a call to *Abandon*.

Working with a Session's State

Now that you have grabbed hold of the session state basics, we can sharpen our skills by looking into more technically relevant aspects of session state management. Handling session state is a task that can be outlined in three steps: assigning a session ID, obtaining session data from a provider, and stuffing it into the context of the page. As mentioned, the session state module governs the execution of all these tasks. In doing so, it takes advantage of a couple of additional components: the session ID generator and session state provider. In ASP.NET 2.0 and beyond, both can be replaced with custom components, as we'll discuss later. For now, let's tackle some of the practical issues you face when working with session state.

Identifying a Session

Each active ASP.NET session is identified using a 120-bit string made only of URL-allowed characters. Session IDs are guaranteed to be unique and randomly generated to avoid data conflicts and prevent malicious attacks. Obtaining a valid session ID algorithmically from an existing ID is virtually impossible. In ASP.NET 1.x, the generator of the session ID is a system component buried in the framework and invisible from outside. In ASP.NET, it has become a customizable component that developers can optionally replace.

> **Note** An old proverb reminds us that nothing should be done only because it is doable. This motto is particularly apt here as we talk about parts of the session state management that are customizable in ASP.NET. These subsystems, such as the session ID generator, should be customized only with good reason and with certainty that it won't make things worse or lower the level of security. I'll return to this point in a moment with more details.

Generating the Session ID

A session ID is 15 bytes long by design (15x8 = 120 bits). The session ID is generated using the Random Number Generator (RNG) cryptographic provider. The service provider returns a sequence of 15 randomly generated numbers. The array of numbers is then mapped to valid URL characters and returned as a string.

If the session contains nothing, a new session ID is generated for each request and the session state is not persisted to the state provider. However, if a *Session_Start* handler is used, the session state is always saved, even if empty. For this reason, and especially if you're not using the in-process session provider, define *Session_Start* handlers with extreme care and only if strictly necessary.

In contrast, the session ID remains the same after a nonempty session dictionary times out or is abandoned. By design, even though the session state expires, the session ID lasts until the browser session is ended. This means that the same session ID is used to represent multiple sessions over time as long as the browser instance remains the same.

Session Cookies

The *SessionID* string is communicated to the browser and then returned to the server application in either of two ways: using a cookie or a modified URL. By default, the session-state module creates an HTTP cookie on the client, but a modified URL can be used—especially for cookieless browsers—with the *SessionID* string embedded. Which approach is taken depends on the configuration settings stored in the application's *web.config* file. By default, session state uses cookies.

A cookie is really nothing more than a text file placed on the client's hard disk by a Web page. In ASP.NET, a cookie is represented by an instance of the *HttpCookie* class. Typically, a cookie has a name, a collection of values, and an expiration time. In addition, you can configure the cookie to operate on a particular virtual path and over secure connections (for example, HTTPS).

> **Important** ASP.NET 2.0 (and newer versions) takes advantage of the HTTP-only feature for session cookies on the browsers that support it. For example, it is supported on Internet Explorer 6.0 SP1 or with Windows XP SP2 installed. The HTTP-only feature prevents cookies from being available to client-side script, thus raising a barrier against potential cross-site scripting attacks aimed at stealing session IDs.

When cookies are enabled, the session-state module actually creates a cookie with a particular name and stores the session ID in it. The cookie is created as the following pseudocode shows:

```
HttpCookie sessionCookie;
sessionCookie = new HttpCookie("ASP.NET_SessionId", sessionID);
sessionCookie.Path = "/";
```

ASP.NET_SessionId is the name of the cookie, and the *SessionID* string is its value. The cookie is also associated with the root of the current domain. The *Path* property describes the relative URL that the cookie applies to. A session cookie is given a very short expiration term and is renewed at the end of each successful request. The cookie's *Expires* property indicates the time of day on the client at which the cookie expires. If not explicitly set, as is the case with session cookies, the *Expires* property defaults to *DateTime.MinValue*—that is, the smallest possible unit of time in the .NET Framework.

> **Note** A server-side module that needs to write a cookie adds an *HttpCookie* object to the *Response.Cookies* collection. All cookies found on the client and associated with the requested domain are uploaded and made available for reading through the *Request.Cookies* collection.

Cookieless Sessions

For the session state to work, the client must be able to pass the session ID to the server application. How this happens depends on the configuration of the application. ASP.NET applications define their session-specific settings through the *<sessionState>* section of the configuration file. To decide about the cookie support, you set the *cookieless* attribute to one of the values in Table 15-7. The listed values belong to the *HttpCookieMode* enumerated type.

TABLE 15-7 *HttpCookieMode* Enumerated Type

Mode	Description
AutoDetect	Use cookies only if the requesting browser supports cookies.
UseCookies	Use cookies to persist the session ID regardless of whether or not the browser supports cookies. This is the default option.
UseDeviceProfile	Base the decision on the browser's capabilities as listed in the device profile section of the configuration file.
UseUri	Store the session ID in the URL regardless of whether the browser supports cookies or not. Use this option if you want to go cookieless no matter what.

When *AutoDetect* is used, ASP.NET queries the browser to determine whether it supports cookies. If the browser supports cookies, the session ID is stored in a cookie; otherwise, the session ID is stored in the URL. When *UseDeviceProfile* is set, on the other hand, the effective capabilities of the browser are not checked. For the session HTTP module to make the decision about cookies or URL, the declared capabilities of the browser are used, as they result from the *SupportsRedirectWithCookie* property of the *HttpBrowserCapabilities* object. Note that even though a browser can support cookies, a user might have disabled cookies. In this case, session state won't work properly.

> **Note** In ASP.NET 1.x, you have fewer options to choose from. The *cookieless* attribute of the *<sessionState>* section can accept only a Boolean value. To disable cookies in sessions, you set the attribute to *true*.

With cookie support disabled, suppose that you request a page at the following URL:

```
http://www.contoso.com/test/sessions.aspx
```

What is displayed in the browser's address bar is slightly different and now includes the session ID, as shown here:

```
http://www.contoso.com/test/(S(5ylg0455mrvws1uz5mmaau45))/sessions.aspx
```

When instantiated, the session-state module checks the value of the *cookieless* attribute. If the value is *true*, the request is redirected (HTTP 302 status code) to a modified virtual URL that includes the session ID just before the page name. When processed again, the request embeds the session ID. A special ISAPI filter—the *aspnet_filter.exe* component—preprocesses the request, parses the URL, and rewrites the correct URL if it incorporates a session ID. The detected session ID is also stored in an extra HTTP header, named *AspFilterSessionId*, and retrieved later.

Issues with Cookieless Sessions

Designed to make stateful applications also possible on a browser that does not support cookies or on one that does not have cookies enabled, cookieless sessions are not free of issues. First, they cause a redirect when the session starts and whenever the user follows an absolute URL from within an application's page.

When cookies are used, you can clear the address bar, go to another application, and then return to the previous one and retrieve the same session values. If you do this when session cookies are disabled, the session data is lost. This feature is not problematic for postbacks, which are automatically implemented using relative URLs, but it poses a serious problem if you use links to absolute URLs. In this case, a new session will always be created. For example, the following code breaks the session:

```
<a runat="server" href="/test/sessions.aspx">Click</a>
```

Is there a way to automatically mangle absolute URLs in links and hyperlinks so that they incorporate session information? You can use the following trick, which uses the *ApplyAppPathModifier* method of the *HttpResponse* class:

```
<a href='<% =Response.ApplyAppPathModifier("test/page.aspx")%>' >Click</a>
```

The *ApplyAppPathModifier* method takes a string representing a relative URL and returns an absolute URL, which embeds session information. This trick is especially useful when you need to redirect from an HTTP page to an HTTPS page, where the full, absolute address is mandatory. Note that *ApplyAppPathModifier* returns the original URL if session cookies are enabled and if the path is an absolute path.

> **Caution** You can't use <%...%> code blocks in server-side expressions—that is, expressions flagged with the *runat=server* attribute. It works in the preceding code because the *<a>* tag is emitted verbatim, being devoid of the *runat* attribute. Code blocks mentioned here have nothing to do with data binding expressions <%# ... %> which are perfect legal and even desirable in server-side code. The reason why you can't use <%...%> code blocks in server-side expressions is that the presence of the *runat* attribute forces the creation of a server object that is not designed for handling code blocks.

Cookieless Sessions and Security

Another issue regarding the use of cookieless sessions is connected with security. Session hijacking is one of the most popular types of attacks and consists in accessing an external system through the session ID generated for another, legitimate user. Try this: set your application to work without cookies and visit a page. Grab the URL with the session ID as it appears in the browser's address bar, and send it immediately in an e-mail to a friend. Have your friend paste the URL in his or her own machine and click Go. Your friend will gain access to your session state as long as the session is active. The session ID is certainly not well-protected information (and probably couldn't work otherwise). For the safety of a system, an unpredictable generator of IDs is key because it makes it difficult to guess a valid session ID. With cookieless sessions, the session ID is exposed in the address bar and visible to all. For this reason, if you are storing private or sensitive information in the session state, it is recommended that you use Secure Sockets Layer (SSL) or Transport Layer Security (TLS) to encrypt any communication between the browser and server that includes the session ID.

In addition, you should always provide users the ability to log out and call the *Abandon* method when they think security has been breached in this way. This contrivance reduces the amount of time available for anybody getting to use your session ID to exploit data stored in the session state. And, speaking of security, it is important that you configure the system to avoid the reuse of expired session IDs when cookieless sessions are used. This behavior is configurable in ASP.NET through the *<sessionState>* section, as you can read in the following section.

Configuring the Session State

The *<sessionState>* section has grown significantly in the transition from ASP.NET 1.x to ASP. NET 2.0. Here's how it looks now:

```
<sessionState
    mode="Off|InProc|StateServer|SQLServer|Custom"
    timeout="number of minutes"
    cookieName="session cookie name"
    cookieless="http cookie mode"
    regenerateExpiredSessionId="true|false"
    sqlConnectionString="sql connection string"
    sqlCommandTimeout="number of seconds"
    allowCustomSqlDatabase="true|false"
    useHostingIdentity="true|false"
    partitionResolverType=""
    sessionIDManagerType="custom session ID generator"
    stateConnectionString="tcpip=server:port"
    stateNetworkTimeout="number of seconds"
    customProvider="custom provider name">
    <providers>
        ...
    </providers>
</sessionState>
```

Table 15-8 details goals and characteristics of the various attributes. Note that only *mode*, *timeout*, *stateConnectionString*, and *sqlConnectionString* are identical to ASP.NET 1.x. The attribute *cookieless* also exists in ASP.NET 1.x but accepts Boolean values. All the others are supported only in ASP.NET 2.0 and newer versions.

TABLE 15-8 *<sessionState>* **Attributes**

Mode	Description
allowCustomSqlDatabase	If *true*, enables specifying a custom database table to store session data instead of using the standard *ASPState*.
cookieless	Specifies how to communicate the session ID to clients.
cookieName	Name of the cookie, if cookies are used for session Ids.
customProvider	The name of the custom session state store provider to use for storing and retrieving session state data.
mode	Specifies where to store session state.
partitionResolverType	Indicates type and assembly of the partition resolver component to be loaded to provide connection information when session state is working in *SQLServer* or *StateServer* mode. If a partition resolver can be correctly loaded, *sqlConnectionString* and *stateConnectionString* attributes are ignored.
regenerateExpiredSessionId	When a request is made with a session ID that has expired, if this attribute is *true*, a new session ID is generated; otherwise, the expired one is revived. The default is *false*.
sessionIDManagerType	Null by default. If set, it indicates the component to use as the generator of session IDs.
sqlCommandTimeout	Specifies the number of seconds a SQL command can be idle before it is canceled. The default is 30.
sqlConnectionString	Specifies the connection string to SQL Server.
stateConnectionString	Specifies the server name or address and port where session state is stored remotely.
stateNetworkTimeout	Specifies the number of seconds the TCP/IP network connection between the Web server and the state server can be idle before the request is canceled. The default is 10.
timeout	Specifies the number of minutes a session can be idle before it is abandoned. The default is 20.
useHostingIdentity	*True* by default. It indicates that the ASP.NET process identity is impersonated when accessing a custom state provider or the *SQLServer* provider configured for integrated security.

In addition, the child *<providers>* section lists custom session-state store providers. ASP.NET session state is designed to enable you to easily store user session data in different sources, such as a Web server's memory or SQL Server. A store provider is a component that manages the storage of session state information and stores it in alternative media (for example, Oracle) and layout. We'll return to this topic later in the chapter.

Lifetime of a Session

The life of a session state begins only when the first item is added to the in-memory dictionary. The following code demonstrates how to modify an item in the session dictionary. "MyData" is the key that uniquely identifies the value. If a key named "MyData" already exists in the dictionary, the existing value is overwritten.

```
Session["MyData"] = "I love ASP.NET";
```

The *Session* dictionary generically contains *object* types; to read data back, you need to cast the returned values to a more specific type:

```
string tmp = (string) Session["MyData"];
```

When a page saves data to *Session*, the value is loaded into an in-memory dictionary—an instance of an internal class named *SessionDictionary*. (See Figure 15-2 to review session state loading and saving.) Other concurrently running pages cannot access the session until the ongoing request completes.

The *Session_Start* Event

The session startup event is unrelated to the session state. The *Session_Start* event fires when the session-state module is servicing the first request for a given user that requires a new session ID. The ASP.NET runtime can serve multiple requests within the context of a single session, but only for the first of them does *Session_Start* fire.

A new session ID is created and a new *Session_Start* event fires whenever a page is requested that doesn't write data to the dictionary. The architecture of the session state is quite sophisticated because it has to support a variety of state providers. The overall schema entails that the content of the session dictionary is serialized to the state provider when the request completes. However, to optimize performance, this procedure really executes only if the content of the dictionary is not empty. As mentioned earlier, though, if the application defines a *Session_Start* event handler, the serialization takes place anyway.

The *Session_End* Event

The *Session_End* event signals the end of the session and is used to perform any clean-up code needed to terminate the session. Note, though, that the event is supported only in *InProc* mode—that is, only when the session data is stored in the ASP.NET worker process.

For *Session_End* to fire, the session state has to exist first. That means you have to store some data in the session state and you must have completed at least one request. When the first value is added to the session dictionary, an item is inserted into the ASP.NET cache—the aforementioned *Cache* object that we'll cover in detail in the next chapter. The behavior is specific to the in-process state provider; neither the out-of-process state server nor the SQL Server state server work with the *Cache* object.

However, much more interesting is that the item added to the cache—only one item per active session—is given a special expiration policy. You'll also learn more about the ASP.NET cache and related expiration policies in the next chapter. For now, it suffices to say that the session-state item added to the cache is given a sliding expiration, with the time interval set to the session timeout. As long as there are requests processed within the session, the sliding period is automatically renewed. The session-state module resets the timeout while process-ing the *EndRequest* event. It obtains the desired effect by simply performing a read on the cache! Given the internal structure of the ASP.NET *Cache* object, this evaluates to renewing the sliding period. As a result, when the cache item expires, the session has timed out.

An expired item is automatically removed from the cache. As part of the expiration policy for this item, the state-session module also indicates a remove callback function. The cache au-tomatically invokes the remove function which, in turn, fires the *Session_End* event.

> **Note** The items in *Cache* that represent the state of a session are not accessible from outside the *system.web* assembly and can't even be enumerated, as they are placed in a system-reserved area of the cache. In other words, you can't programmatically access the data resident in another session or even remove it.

Why Does My Session State Sometimes Get Lost?

Values parked in a *Session* object are removed from memory either programmatically by the code or by the system when the session times out or it is abandoned. In some cases, though, even when nothing of the kind seemingly happens, the session state gets lost. Is there a rea-son for this apparently weird behavior?

When the working mode is *InProc*, the session state is mapped in the memory space of the AppDomain in which the page request is being served. In light of this, the session state is subject to process recycling and AppDomain restarts. The ASP.NET worker process is periodi-cally restarted to maintain an average good performance; when this happens, the session state is lost. Process recycling depends on the percentage of memory consumption and maybe the number of requests served. Although cyclic, no general estimate can be made regarding the interval of the cycle. Be aware of this when designing your session-based, in-process application. As a general rule, bear in mind that the session state might not be there when you try to access it. Use exception handling or recovery techniques as appropriate for your application.

Consider that some antivirus software might be marking the *web.config* or *global.asax* file as modified, thus causing a new application to be started and subsequently causing the loss of the session state. This holds true also if you or your code modify the timestamp of those files or alter the contents of one of the special folders, such as *Bin* or *App_Code*.

> **Note** What happens to the session state when a running page hits an error? Will the current dictionary be saved, or is it just lost? The state of the session is not saved if, at the end of the request, the page results in an error—that is, the *GetLastError* method of the *Server* object returns an exception. However, if in your exception handler you reset the error state by calling *Server. ClearError*, the values of the session are saved regularly as if no error ever occurred.

Persist Session Data to Remote Servers

The session state loss problem that we mentioned earlier for *InProc* mode can be neatly solved by employing either of the two predefined out-of-process state providers— *StateServer* and *SQLServer*. In this case, though, the session state is held outside the ASP.NET worker process and an extra layer of code is needed to serialize and deserialize it to and from the actual storage medium. This operation takes place whenever a request is processed.

The need of copying session data from an external repository into the local session dictionary might tax the state management process to the point of causing a 15 percent to 25 percent decrease in performance. Note, though, that this is only a rough estimate, and it's closer to the minimum impact rather than to the maximum impact. The estimate, in fact, does not fully consider the complexity of the types actually saved into the session state.

> **Caution** When you get to choose an out-of-process state provider (for example, *StateServer* and *SQLServer*), be aware that you need to set up the runtime environment before putting the application in production. This means either starting a Windows service for *StateServer* or configuring a database for *SQLServer*. No preliminary work is needed if you stay with the default, in-process option.

State Serialization and Deserialization

When you use the *InProc* mode, objects are stored in the session state as live instances of classes. No real serialization and deserialization ever takes place, meaning that you can actually store in *Session* whatever objects (including COM objects) you have created and access them with no significant overhead. The situation is less favorable if you opt for an out-of-process state provider.

In an out-of-process architecture, session values are to be copied from the native storage medium into the memory of the AppDomain that processes the request.

A serialization/deserialization layer is needed to accomplish the task and represents one of the major costs for out-of-process state providers. How does this affect your code? First, you should make sure that only serializable objects are ever stored in the session dictionary; otherwise, as you can easily imagine, the session state can't be saved and you'll sustain an exception, moreover.

To perform the serialization and deserialization of types, ASP.NET uses two methods, each providing different results in terms of performance. For basic types, ASP.NET resorts to an optimized internal serializer; for other types, including objects and user-defined classes, ASP. NET makes use of the .NET binary formatter, which is slower. Basic types are *string*, *DateTime*, *Guid*, *IntPtr*, *TimeSpan*, *Boolean*, *byte*, *char*, and all numeric types.

The optimized serializer—an internal class named *AltSerialization*—employs an instance of the *BinaryWriter* object to write out one byte to denote the type and then the value. While reading, the *AltSerialization* class first extracts one byte, detects the type of the data to read, and then resorts to a type-specific method of the *BinaryReader* class to take data. The type is associated to an index according to an internal table, as shown in Figure 15-4.

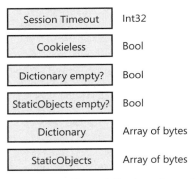

Session Timeout	Int32
Cookieless	Bool
Dictionary empty?	Bool
StaticObjects empty?	Bool
Dictionary	Array of bytes
StaticObjects	Array of bytes

FIGURE 15-4 The serialization schema for basic types that the internal *AltSerialization* class uses.

Note While Booleans and numeric types have a well-known size, the length of a string can vary quite a bit. How can the reader determine the correct size of a string? The *BinaryReader. ReadString* method exploits the fact that on the underlying stream the string is always prefixed with the length, encoded as an integer seven bits at a time. Values of the *DateTime* type, on the other hand, are saved by writing only the total number of ticks that form the date and are read as an *Int64* type.

As mentioned, more complex objects are serialized using the relatively slower *BinaryFormatter* class as long as the involved types are marked as serializable. Both simple and complex types use the same stream, but all nonbasic types are identified with the same type ID. The performance-hit range of 15 percent to 25 percent is a rough estimate based on the assumption that basic types are used. The more you use complex types, the more the overhead grows, and reliable numbers can be calculated only by testing a particular application scenario.

In light of this, if you plan to use out-of-process sessions, make sure you store data effectively. For example, if you need to persist an instance of a class with three string properties, performancewise you are *probably* better off using three different slots filled with a basic type rather than one session slot for which the binary formatter is needed. Better yet, you can use a type converter class to transform the object to and from a string format. However, understand that this is merely a guideline to be applied case by case and with a grain of salt.

> **Caution** In classic ASP, storing an ADO Recordset object in the session state was a potentially dangerous action because of threading issues. Fortunately, in ASP.NET no thread-related issues exist to cause you to lose sleep. However, you can't just store any object to *Session* and be happy. If you use an out-of-process scheme, you ought to pay a lot of attention to storing *DataSet* objects. The reason has to do with the serialization process of the *DataSet* class. Because the *DataSet* is a complex type, it gets serialized through the binary formatter. The serialization engine of the *DataSet*, though, generates a lot of XML data and turns out to be a serious flaw, especially for large applications that store a large quantity of data. In fact, you can easily find yourself moving megabytes of data for each request. Just avoid *DataSet* objects in ASP.NET 1.x out-of-process sessions and opt for plain arrays of column and row data. In ASP.NET 2.0, set the *RemotingFormat* property before you store it.

Storing Session Data

When working in *StateServer* mode, the entire content of the *HttpSessionState* object is serialized to an external application—a Microsoft Windows NT service named *aspnet_state. exe*. The service is called to serialize the session state when the request completes. The service internally stores each session state as an array of bytes. When a new request begins processing, the array corresponding to the given session ID is copied into a memory stream and then deserialized into an internal session state item object. This object really represents the contents of the whole session. The *HttpSessionState* object that pages actually work with is only its application interface.

As mentioned, nonbasic types are serialized and deserialized using the system's binary formatter class, which can handle only classes explicitly marked to be serializable. This means that COM objects, either programmatically created or declared as static objects with a session scope in *global.asax*, can't be used with an out-of-process state provider. The same limitation applies to any nonserializable object.

Configuring the *StateServer* Provider

Using out-of-process storage scenarios, you give the session state a longer life and your application greater robustness. Out-of-process session-state storage basically protects the session against Internet Information Services (IIS) and ASP.NET process failures. By separating the session state from the page itself, you can also much more easily scale an existing application to Web farm and Web garden architectures. In addition, the session state living in an external process eliminates at the root the risk of periodically losing data because of process recycling.

As mentioned, the ASP.NET session-state provider is a Windows NT service named *aspnet_state.exe*. It normally resides in the installation folder of ASP.NET:

```
%WINDOWS%\Microsoft.NET\Framework\[version]
```

As usual, note that the final directory depends on the .NET Framework version you're actually running. Before using the state server, you should make sure that the service is up and running on the local or remote machine used as the session store. The state service is a constituent part of ASP.NET and gets installed along with it, so you have no additional setup application to run.

By default, the state service is stopped and requires a manual start. You can change its configuration through the properties dialog box of the service, as shown in Figure 15-5.

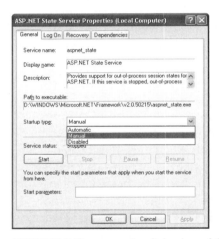

FIGURE 15-5 The properties dialog box of the ASP.NET state server.

An ASP.NET application needs to specify the TCP/IP address of the machine hosting the session-state service. The following listing shows the changes that need to be made to the *web.config* file to enable the remote session state:

```
<configuration>
    <system.web>
        <sessionState
            mode="StateServer"
            stateConnectionString="tcpip=MyMachine:42424" />
    </system.web>
</configuration>
```

Note that the value assigned to the *mode* attribute is case sensitive. The format of the *stateConnectionString* attribute is shown in the following line of code. The default machine address is 127.0.0.1, while the port is 42424.

```
stateConnectionString="tcpip=server:port"
```

The server name can be either an IP address or a machine name. In this case, though, non-ASCII characters in the name are not supported. Finally, the port number is mandatory and cannot be omitted.

Important The state server doesn't offer any authentication barrier to requestors, meaning that anyone who can get access to the network is potentially free to access session data. To protect session state and make sure that it is accessed only by the Web server machine, you can use a firewall, IPSec policies, or a secure net 10.X.X.X so external attackers couldn't gain direct access. Another security-related countermeasure consists of changing the default port number. To change the port, you edit the *Port* entry under the registry key: *HKEY_LOCAL_MACHINE\SYSTEM\CurrentControlSet\Services\aspnet_state\Parameters*. Writing the port in the *web.config* file isn't enough.

The ASP.NET application attempts to connect to the session-state server immediately after loading. The *aspnet_state* service must be up and running; otherwise, an HTTP exception is thrown. By default, the service is not configured to start automatically. The state service uses .NET Remoting to move data back and forth.

Note The ASP.NET state provider runs under the ASP.NET account. The account, though, can be configured and changed at will using the Service Control Manager interface. The state service is slim and simple and does not implement any special features. It is limited to holding data and listens to the specified port for requests to serve. In particular, the service isn't cluster-aware (that is, it doesn't provide a failover monitor to be error tolerant) and can't be used in a clustered world when another server takes on the one that fails.

Finally, note that by default the state server listens only to local connections. If the state server and Web server live on different machines, you need to enable remote connections. You do this through another entry in the same registry key as mentioned earlier. The entry is *AllowRemoteConnection*, and it must be set to a nonzero value.

Persist Session Data to SQL Server

Maintaining the session state in an external process certainly makes the whole ASP.NET application more stable. Whatever happens to the worker process, the session state is still there, ready for further use. If the service is paused, the data is preserved and automatically retrieved when the service resumes. Unfortunately, if the state provider service is stopped or if a failure occurs, the data is lost. If robustness is key for your application, drop the *StateServer* mode in favor of *SQLServer*.

Performance and Robustness

When ASP.NET works in *SQLServer* mode, the session data is stored in a made-to-measure database table. As a result, the session data survives even SQL Server crashes, but you have to add higher overhead to the bill. *SQLServer* mode allows you to store data on any connected machine, as long as the machine runs SQL Server 7.0 or newer. Besides the different medium, the storage mechanism is nearly identical to that described for remote servers. In particular, the serialization and deserialization algorithm is the same, only it's a bit slower because of the characteristics of storage. When storing data of basic types, the time required to set up the page's *Session* object is normally at least 25 percent higher than in an *InProc* scenario. Also in regard to this issue, the more complex types you use, the more time it will take to manage the session data.

> **Note** When you get to make a decision between state server or SQL server storage, consider the fact that SQL Server is cluster-aware, which makes a solution based on it more robust and reliable than one based on a state server.

Configuring Session State for SQL Server Support

To use SQL Server as the state provider, enter the following changes in the *<sessionState>* section of the *web.config* file:

```
<configuration>
  <system.web>
    <sessionState
       mode="SQLServer"
       sqlConnectionString="server=127.0.0.1;integrated security=SSPI;" />
  </system.web>
</configuration>
```

In particular, you need to set the *mode* attribute (which is case sensitive) to *SQLServer* and specify the connection string through the *sqlConnectionString* attribute. Note that the *sqlConnectionString* attribute string must provide for a user ID, password, and server name. It cannot contain, though, tokens such as *Database* and *Initial Catalog*, unless a custom database is enabled using *allowCustomSqlDatabase*, as mentioned in Table 15-8. You can specify a SQL Server *Initial Catalog* database name or use the SQL Server Express *attachDBFileName* to point to an MDB file in the connection string only if the *allowCustomSqlDatabase* configuration setting is enabled. If that is disabled, any attempts to specify these settings in the connection string will result in an exception.

> **Note** The connection string for an out-of-process session state implementation (both *SQLServer* and *StateServer*) can also be specified referring to a connection string defined in the *<connectionStrings>* section. The session state module first attempts to look up a connection string from the *<connectionStrings>* section with the name specified in the appropriate *<sessionState>* attribute; if it is not found, the session state attempts to use the specified string directly.

As for credentials to access the database, you can either use User ID and passwords or resort to integrated security.

> **Note** Whatever account you use to access session state in SQL Server, make sure that it is granted the *db_datareader* and *db_datawriter* permissions at the very least. Note also that to configure the SQL Server environment for storing session state, administrative privileges are required, as a new database and stored procedures need to be created.

Session state in SQL Server mode supports the specification of a custom command timeout value (in seconds) to accommodate slow-responding-server scenarios. You control it through the *sqlCommandTimeout* attribute, as mentioned in Table 15-8.

Creating the SQL Server Data Store

ASP.NET provides two pairs of scripts to configure the database environment by creating any needed tables, stored procedures, triggers, and jobs. The scripts in the first pair are named *InstallSqlState.sql* and *UninstallSqlState.sql*. They create a database called *ASPState* and several stored procedures. The data, though, is stored in a couple tables belonging to the TempDB database. In SQL Server, the TempDB database provides a storage area for temporary tables, temporary stored procedures, and other temporary working storage needs. This means that the session data is lost if the SQL Server machine is restarted.

The second pair consists of the scripts *InstallPersistSqlState.sql* and *UninstallPersistSqlState.sql*. Also in this case, an *ASPState* database is created, but the tables are persistent because they are created within the same database. All scripts are located in the following path:

```
%SystemRoot%\Microsoft.NET\Framework\[version]
```

> **Important** These script files are included for backward compatibility only. You should use *aspnet_regsql.exe* to install and uninstall a SQL session state. Among other things, the newest *aspnet_regsql.exe* supports more options, such as using a custom database table.

The tables that get created are named ASPStateTempApplications and ASPStateTempSessions. Figure 15-6 shows a view of the session database in SQL Server.

FIGURE 15-6 The *ASPState* database in SQL Server Enterprise Manager

The ASPStateTempApplications table defines a record for each currently running ASP.NET application. The table columns are listed in Table 15-9.

TABLE 15-9 The ASPStateTempApplications Table

Column	Type	Description
AppId	Int	Indexed field. It represents a sort of auto-generated ID that identifies a running application using the *SQLServer* session mode.
AppName	char(280)	Indicates the application ID of the AppDomain running the application. It matches the contents of the *AppDomainAppId* property on the *HttpRuntime* object.

The ASPStateTempSessions table stores the actual session data. The table contains one row for each active session. The structure of the table is outlined in Table 15-10.

TABLE 15-10 The ASPStateTempSessions Table

Column	Type	Description
SessionId	Char(88)	Indexed field. It represents the session ID.
Created	DateTime	Indicates the time at which the session was created. It defaults to the current date.
Expires	DateTime	Indicates the time at which the session will expire. This value is normally the time at which the session state was created plus the number of minutes specified in *Timeout*. Note that *Created* refers to the time at which the session started, whereas *Expires* adds minutes to the time in which the first item is added to the session state.

Column	Type	Description
Flags	int	Indicates action flags—initialize items or none—from the *SessionStateActions* enum. *Not available in ASP.NET 1.x.*
LockCookie	int	Indicates the number of times the session was locked— that is, the number of accesses.
LockDate	DateTime	Indicates the time at which the session was locked to add the last item. The value is expressed as the current Universal Time Coordinate (UTC).
LockDateLocal	DateTime	Like the previous item, except that this one expresses the system's local time. *Not available in ASP.NET 1.x.*
Locked	bit	Indicates whether the session is currently locked.
SessionItemLong	Image	Nullable field, represents the serialized version of a session longer than 7000 bytes.
SessionItemShort	VarBinary(7000)	Nullable field. It represents the values in the specified session. The layout of the bytes is identical to the layout discussed for *StateServer* providers. If more than 7000 bytes are needed to serialize the dictionary, the *SessionItemLong* field is used instead.
Timeout	int	Indicates the timeout of the session in minutes.

The column *SessionItemLong*, contains a long binary block of data. Although the user always works with image data as if it is a single, long sequence of bytes, the data is not stored in that format. The data is stored in a collection of 8-KB pages that aren't necessarily located next to each other.

When installing the SQL Server support for sessions, a job is also created to delete expired sessions from the session-state database. The job, which is shown in Figure 15-7, is named *ASPState_Job_DeleteExpiredSessions*, and the default configuration makes it run every minute. You should note that the SQLServerAgent service needs to be running for this to work.

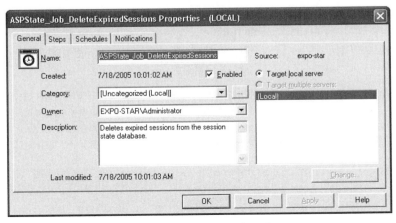

FIGURE 15-7 The SQL Server job to delete expired sessions.

Reverting to the Hosting Identity

In ASP.NET 1.x, credentials used to access the SQL Server stored session state depend on the connection string. If explicitly provided, the user name and password are used to access the database. Otherwise, if integrated security is requested, the account of the currently logged-in client is used. This approach clashes with the *StateServer* state provider, which uses the ASP.NET identity to do its job. More importantly, though, it poses some administrative issues for intranet sites using client impersonation. In these cases, in fact, you have to grant access to the database to every client account that might be making calls.

In ASP.NET 2.0 and newer versions, the *useHostingIdentity* attribute (shown in Table 15-8) lets you decide about the identity to be effectively used. Breaking the ASP.NET 1.x behavior, when the *SQLServer* state provider is used with integrated security the identity is that impersonated by ASP.NET. It will typically be ASPNET or NETWORK SERVICE or any other account impersonated by the ASP.NET worker process through the *<identity>* section of the configuration file. This simplifies the administrative experience for intranet sites, requiring that only the ASP.NET account be granted access to protected and critical resources. The *useHostingIdentity* attribute defaults to *true*, which enables you to revert to the ASP.NET identity before making calls to the *SQLServer* session state provider. This will also happen if a custom provider is used.

> **Note** If you're using Windows integrated authentication to access SQL Server, reverting to the host identity is the most recommended option, for security reasons. Otherwise, it is advisable that you create a specific account and grant it only rights to execute session state stored procedures and access related resources.

Session State in a Web Farm Scenario

ASP.NET applications designed to run in a Web farm or Web garden hardware configuration cannot implement an in-process session state. The *InProc* mode won't work on a Web farm because a distinct worker process will be running on each connected machine, with each process maintaining its own session state. It doesn't even work on a Web garden because multiple worker processes will be running on the same machine.

Keeping all states separate from worker processes allows you to partition an application across multiple worker processes even when they're running on multiple computers. In both Web farm and Web garden scenarios, there can be only one *StateServer* or *SQLServer* process to provide session-state management.

If you're running a Web farm, make sure you have the same *<machineKey>* in all your Web servers. (More details can be found in the article "How To: Configure MachineKey in ASP.NET 2.0", found at *http://msdn2.microsoft.com/en-us/library/ms998288.aspx*)

In addition, for the session state to be maintained across different servers in the Web farm, all applications should have the same application path stored in the IIS metabase. This value is set as the AppDomain application ID and identifies a running application in the ASP.NET state database. (See Knowledge Base article Q325056 for more details.)

In ASP.NET 2.0, partition resolvers have been introduced to let a session state provider partition its data onto multiple back-end nodes. This allows you to scale session state on large Web farms, according to a custom, user-defined load-balancing scheme. A partition provider is a component that supplies the connection string (the actual string, not the pointer to a string in the *web.config* file) to the session state that is used to access data, overriding any other settings in the *<sessionState>* section.

Customizing Session State Management

Since its beginning, the ASP.NET session state was devised to be an easy-to-customize and extensible feature. For various reasons, in ASP.NET 1.x it came out with a high degree of customization but a total lack of extensibility. In ASP.NET 2.0, the session state subsystem was refactored to allow developers to replace most of the functionalities—a characteristic that is often referred to as *session state pluggability*. In ASP.NET 3.5, you find the same set of capabilities as in the previous version.

All things considered, you have the following three options to customize session state management:

- You can stay with the default session state module but write a custom state provider to change the storage medium (for example, to a non–SQL Server database or a different table layout). In doing so, you also have the chance to override some of the helper classes (mostly collections) that are used to bring data from the store to the *Session* object and back.

- You can stay with the default session state module but replace the session ID generator. But hold on! The algorithm that generates session IDs is a critical element of the application, as making session IDs too easy for attackers to guess can lead straight to session-hijacking attacks. Nonetheless, this remains a customizable aspect of session state that, properly used, can make your application even more secure.

- You can unplug the default session state module and roll your own. Technically possible also in ASP.NET 1.x, this option should be used as a last resort. Obviously, it provides the maximum flexibility, but it is also extremely complicated and is recommended only if strictly necessary and if you know exactly what you're doing. We won't cover this topic in the book.

The first option—the easiest and least complicated of all—addresses most of the scenarios for which some custom session management is desirable. So let's tackle it first.

Building a Custom Session State Provider

A session state provider is the component in charge of serving any data related to the current session. Invoked when the request needs to acquire state information, it retrieves data from a given storage medium and returns that to the module. Invoked by the module when the request ends, it writes the supplied data to the storage layer. As mentioned, ASP.NET supports three state providers, as listed in Table 15-11.

TABLE 15-11 Default State Providers

Name	Class	Storage Medium
InProc	*InProcSessionStateStore*	Stores data as live objects in the ASP.NET *Cache*.
StateServer	*OutOfProcSessionStateStore*	Stores data as serialized objects to the memory of a Windows service named *aspnet_state.exe*.
SQLServer	*SqlSessionStateStore*	Stores data as serialized objects into a SQL Server database.

In ASP.NET 2.0, you can write your own state provider class that uses the storage medium of your choice. Note that the default state providers also make use of various helper classes to move data around. In your custom provider, you can replace these classes too, or just stick to the standard ones.

Defining the Session State Store

A state provider (also often referred to as a *session state store*) is a class that inherits from *SessionStateStoreProviderBase*. The main methods of the interface are listed in Table 15-12.

TABLE 15-12 Methods of the *SessionStateStoreProviderBase* Class

Method	Description
CreateNewStoreData	Creates an object to contain the data of a new session. It should return an object of type *SessionStateStoreData*.
CreateUninitializedItem	Creates a new and uninitialized session in the data source. The method is called when an expired session is requested in a cookie-less session state. In this case, the module has to generate a new session ID. The session item created by the method prevents the next request with the newly generated session ID from being mistaken for a request directed at an expired session.
Dispose	Releases all resources (other than memory) used by the state provider.
EndRequest	Called by the default session state module when it begins to handle the *EndRequest* event.

Method	Description
GetItem	Returns the session item matching the specified ID from the data store. The session item selected is locked for read. The method serves requests from applications that use a read-only session state.
GetItemExclusive	Returns the session item matching the specified ID from the data store and locks it for writing. Used for requests originated by applications that use a read-write session state.
Initialize	Inherited from the base provider class, performs one-off initialization.
InitializeRequest	Called by the default session state module when it begins to handle the *AcquireRequestState* event.
ReleaseItemExclusive	Unlocks a session item that was previously locked by a call to the *GetItemExclusive* method.
RemoveItem	Removes a session item from the data store. Called when a session ends or is abandoned.
ResetItemTimeout	Resets the expiration time of a session item. Invoked when the application has session support disabled.
SetAndReleaseItemExclusive	Writes a session item to the data store.
SetItemExpireCallback	The default module calls this method to notify the data store class that the caller has registered a *Session_End* handler.

Classes that inherit the *SessionStateStoreProviderBase* class work with the default ASP.NET session state module and replace only the part of it that handles session-state data storage and retrieval. Nothing else in the session functionality changes.

Locking and Expiration

Can two requests for the same session occur concurrently? You bet. Take a look at Figure 15-3. Requests can arrive in parallel—for example, from two frames or when a user works with two instances of the same browser, the second of which is opened as a new window. To avoid problems, a state provider must implement a locking mechanism to serialize access to a session. The session state module determines whether the request requires read-only or read-write access to the session state and calls *GetItem* or *GetItemExclusive* accordingly. In the implementation of these methods, the provider's author should create a reader/writer lock mechanism to allow multiple concurrent reads but prevent writing on locked sessions.

Another issue relates to letting the session state module know when a given session has expired. The session state module calls the method *SetItemExpireCallback* when there's a *Session_End* handler defined in *global.asax*. Through the method, the state provider receives a callback function with the following prototype:

```
public delegate void SessionStateItemExpireCallback(
    string sessionID, SessionStateStoreData item);
```

It has to store that delegate internally and invoke it whenever the given session times out. Supporting expiration callbacks is optional and, in fact, only the InProc provider actually supports it. If your custom provider is not willing to support expiration callbacks, you should instruct the *SetItemExpireCallback* method to return *false*.

> **Note** A provider that intends to support cookieless sessions must also implement the *CreateUninitialized* method to write a blank session item to the data store. More precisely, a *blank session item* means an item that is complete in every way except that it contains no session data. In other words, the session item should contain the session ID, creation date, and perhaps lock IDs, but no data. ASP.NET 2.0 generates a new ID (in cookieless mode only) whenever a request is made for an expired session. The session state module generates the new session ID and redirects the browser. Without an uninitialized session item marked with a newly generated ID, the new request will again be recognized as a request for an expired session.

Replacing the Session Data Dictionary

SessionStateStoreData is the class that represents the session item—that is, a data structure that contains all the data that is relevant to the session. *GetItem* and *GetItemExclusive*, in fact, are defined to return an instance of this class. The class has three properties: *Items*, *StaticObjects*, and *Timeout*.

Items indicates the collection of name/values that will ultimately be passed to the page through the *Session* property. *StaticObjects* lists the static objects belonging to the session, such as objects declared in the *global.asax* file and scoped to the session. As the name suggests, *Timeout* indicates how long, in minutes, the session state item is valid. The default value is 20 minutes.

Once the session state module has acquired the session state for the request, it flushes the contents of the *Items* collection to a new instance of the *HttpSessionStateContainer* class. This object is then passed to the constructor of the *HttpSessionState* class and becomes the data container behind the familiar *Session* property.

The *SessionStateStoreData* class is used in the definition of the base state provider class, meaning that you can't entirely replace it. If you don't like it, you can inherit a new class from it, however. To both the session module and state provider, the container of the session items is merely a class that implements the *ISessionStateItemCollection* interface. The real class being used by default is *SessionStateItemCollection*. You can replace this class with your own as long as you implement the aforementioned interface.

> **Tip** To write a state provider, you might find helpful the methods of the *SessionStateUtility* class. The class contains methods to serialize and deserialize session items to and from the storage medium. Likewise, the class has methods to extract the dictionary of data for a session and add it to the HTTP context and the *Session* property.

Registering a Custom Session State Provider

To make a custom session state provider available to an application, you need to register it in the *web.config* file. Suppose you have called the provider class *SampleSessionStateProvider* and compiled it to *MyLib*. Here's what you need to enter:

```
<system.web>
    <sessionState mode="Custom"
      customProvider="SampleSessionProvider">
      <providers>
        <add name="SampleSessionProvider"
          type="SampleSessionStateProvider, MyLib" />
      </providers>
    </sessionState>
</system.web>
```

The name of the provider is arbitrary but necessary. To force the session state module to find it, set the *mode* attribute to *Custom*.

Generating a Custom Session ID

To generate the session ID, ASP.NET 2.0 uses a special component named *SessionIDManager*. Technically speaking, the class is neither an HTTP module nor a provider. More simply, it is a class that inherits from *System.Object* and implements the *ISessionIDManager* interface. You can replace this component with a custom component as long as the component implements the same *ISessionIDManager* interface. To help you decide whether you really need a custom session ID generator, let's review some facts about the default module.

The Default Behavior

The default session ID module generates a session ID as an array of bytes with a crypto-graphically strong random sequence of 15 values. The array is then encoded to a string of 24 URL-accepted characters, which is what the system will recognize as the session ID.

The session ID can be round-tripped to the client in either an HTTP cookie or a mangled URL, based on the value of the *cookieless* attribute in the *<sessionState>* configuration section. Note that when cookieless sessions are used, the session ID module is responsible for adding the ID to the URL and redirecting the browser. The default generator redirects the browser to a fake URL like the following one:

```
http://www.contoso.com/test/(S(session_id))/page.aspx
```

In ASP.NET 1.x, the fake URL is slightly different and doesn't include the *S(...)* delimiters. How can a request for this fake URL be served correctly? In the case of a cookieless session, the Session ID module depends on a small and simple ISAPI filter (*aspnet_filter.dll*, which is also available to ASP.NET 1.x) to dynamically rewrite the real URL to access. The request is served correctly, but the path on the address bar doesn't change. The detected session ID is placed in a request header named *AspFilterSessionId*.

A Homemade Session ID Manager

Now that we've ascertained that a session ID manager is a class that implements *ISessionIDManager*, you have two options: build a new class and implement the interface from the ground up, or inherit a new class from *SessionIDManager* and override a couple of virtual methods to apply some personalization. The first option offers maximum flexibility; the second is simpler and quicker to implement, and it addresses the most compelling reason you might have to build a custom session ID generator—to supply your own session ID values.

Let's start by reviewing the methods of the *ISessionIDManager* interface, which are shown in Table 15-13.

TABLE 15-13 Methods of the *ISessionIDManager* Interface

Method	Description
CreateSessionID	Virtual method. It creates a unique session identifier for the session.
Decode	Decodes the session ID using *HttpUtility.UrlDecode*.
Encode	Encodes the session ID using *HttpUtility.UrlEncode*.
Initialize	Invoked by the session state immediately after instantiation; performs one-time initialization of the component.
InitializeRequest	Invoked by the session state when the session state is being acquired for the request.
GetSessionID	Gets the session ID from the current HTTP request.
RemoveSessionID	Deletes the session ID from the cookie or from the URL.
SaveSessionID	Saves a newly created session ID to the HTTP response.
Validate	Confirms that the session ID is valid.

If you plan to roll your own completely custom session ID generator, bear in mind the following points:

- The algorithm you choose for ID generation is a critical point. If you don't implement strong cryptographic randomness, a malicious user can guess a valid session ID when the same session is still active, thus accessing some user's data. (This is known as *session hijacking*.) A good example of a custom session ID algorithm is one that returns a globally unique identifier (GUID).

- You can choose to support cookieless sessions or not. If you do, you have to endow the component with the ability to extract the session ID from the HTTP request and redirect the browser. You probably need an ISAPI filter or HTTP module to preprocess the request and enter appropriate changes. The algorithm you use to store session IDs without cookies is up to you.

If you are absolutely determined to have the system use your session IDs, you derive a new class from *SessionIDManager* and override two methods: *CreateSessionID* and *Validate*. The former returns a string that contains the session ID. The latter validates a given session ID to ensure it conforms to the specification you set. Once you have created a custom session ID module, you register it in the configuration file. Here's how to do it:

```
<sessionState
    sessionIDManagerType="Samples.MyIDManager, MyLib" />
</sessionState>
```

Session State Performance Best Practices

State management is a necessary evil. By enabling it, you charge your application with an extra burden. The September 2005 issue of MSDN Magazine contains an article with the ASP.NET team's coding best practices to reduce the performance impact of session state on Web applications.

The first guideline is disabling session state whenever possible. However, to prevent the session from expiring, the HTTP module still marks the session as active in the data store. For out-of-process state servers, this means that a roundtrip is made. Using a custom session ID manager returning a null session ID for requests that are known not to require session state is the best way to work around this issue and avoid the overhead entirely. (Write a class that inherits from *SessionIDManager* and overrides *GetSessionID*.)

The second guideline entails minimizing contention on session data by avoiding frames and downloadable resources served by session-enabled handlers.

The third guideline relates to data serialization and deserialization. You should always use simple types and break complex classes into arrays of simple properties, at least as far as session management is concerned. In other words, I'm not suggesting that you should factor out your DAL classes—just change the way you serialize them into the session store. An alternate approach entails building a custom serialization algorithm that is optimized for session state storage. Breaking a class into various properties, with each stored in a session slot, is advantageous because of the simple types being used, but also because the extreme granularity of the solution minimizes the data to save in case of changes. If one property changes, only one slot with a simple type is updated instead of a single slot with a complex type.

The View State of a Page

ASP.NET pages supply the *ViewState* property to let applications build a call context and retain values across two successive requests for the same page. The view state represents the state of the page when it was last processed on the server. The state is persisted—usually, but not necessarily, on the client side—and is restored before the page request is processed.

By default, the view state is maintained as a hidden field added to the page. As such, it travels back and forth with the page itself. Although it is sent to the client, the view state does not represent, nor does it contain, any information specifically aimed at the client. The information stored in the view state is pertinent only to the page and some of its child controls and is not consumed in any way by the browser.

Using the view state has advantages and disadvantages that you might want to carefully balance prior to making your state management decision. First, the view state does not require any server resources and is simple to implement and use. Because it's a physical part of the page, it's fast to retrieve and use. This last point, that in some respects is a strong one, turns into a considerable weakness as soon as you consider the page performance from a wider perspective.

Because the view state is packed with the page, it inevitably charges the HTML code transferred over HTTP with a few extra kilobytes of data—useless data, moreover, from the browser's perspective. A complex real-world page, especially if it does not even attempt to optimize and restrict the use of the view state, can easily find 20 KB of extra stuff packed in the HTML code sent out to the browser.

In summary, the view state is one of the most important features of ASP.NET, not so much because of its technical relevance but because it allows you to benefit from most of the magic of the Web Forms model. Used without strict criteria, though, the view state can easily become a burden for pages.

The *StateBag* Class

The *StateBag* class is the class behind the view state that manages the information that ASP.NET pages and controls want to persist across successive posts of the same page instance. The class works like a dictionary and, in addition, implements the *IStateManager* interface. The *Page* and *Control* base classes expose the view state through the *ViewState* property. So you can add or remove items from the *StateBag* class as you would with any dictionary object, as the following code demonstrates:

```
ViewState["FontSize"] = value;
```

You should start writing to the view state only after the *Init* event fires for the page request. You can read from the view state during any stage of the page life cycle, but not after the page enters rendering mode—that is, after the *PreRender* event fires.

View State Properties

Table 15-14 lists all the properties defined in the *StateBag* class.

TABLE 15-14 **Properties of the *StateBag* Class**

Property	Description
Count	Gets the number of elements stored in the object.
Item	Indexer property. It gets or sets the value of an item stored in the class.
Keys	Gets a collection object containing the keys defined in the object.
Values	Gets a collection object containing all the values stored in the object.

Each item in the *StateBag* class is represented by a *StateItem* object. An instance of the *StateItem* object is implicitly created when you set the *Item* indexer property with a value or when you call the *Add* method. Items added to the *StateBag* object are tracked until the view state is serialized prior to the page rendering. Items serialized are those with the *IsDirty* property set to *true*.

View State Methods

Table 15-15 lists all the methods you can call in the *StateBag* class.

TABLE 15-15 **Methods of the *StateBag* Class**

Method	Description
Add	Adds a new *StateItem* object to the collection. If the item already exists, it gets updated.
Clear	Removes all items from the current view state.
GetEnumerator	Returns an object that scrolls over all the elements in the *StateBag*.
IsItemDirty	Indicates whether the element with the specified key has been modified during the request processing.
Remove	Removes the specified object from the *StateBag* object.

The *IsItemDirty* method represents an indirect way to call into the *IsDirty* property of the specified *StateItem* object.

> **Note** The view state for the page is a cumulative property that results from the contents of the *ViewState* property of the page plus the view state of all the controls hosted in the page.

Common Issues with View State

Architecturally speaking, the importance of the view state cannot be denied, as it is key to setting up the automatic state management feature of ASP.NET. A couple of hot issues are connected to the usage of the view state, however. Most frequently asked questions about the view state are related to security and performance. Can we say that the view state is inherently secure and cannot be tampered with? How will the extra information contained in the view state affect the download time of the page? Let's find out.

Encrypting and Securing

Many developers are doubtful about using the view state specifically because it is stored in a hidden field and left on the client at the mercy of potential intruders. Although the data is stored in a hashed format, there's no absolute guarantee that it cannot be tampered with. The first comment I'd like to make in response to this is that the view state as implemented in ASP.NET is inherently more secure than any other hidden fields you might use (and that you were likely using, say, in old classic ASP applications). My second remark is that only data confidentiality is at risk. While this is a problem, it is minor compared to code injection.

Freely accessible in a hidden field named __VIEWSTATE, the view state information is, by default, hashed and Base64 encoded. To decode it on the client, a potential attacker must accomplish a number of steps, but the action is definitely possible. Once decoded, though, the view state reveals only its contents—that is, confidentiality is at risk. However, there's no way an attacker can modify the view state to post malicious data. A tampered view state, in fact, is normally detected on the server and an exception is thrown.

For performance reasons, the view state is not encrypted. If needed, though, you can turn the option on by acting on the *web.config* file, as follows:

```
<machineKey validation="3DES" />
```

When the validation attribute is set to 3DES, the view-state validation technique uses 3DES encryption and doesn't hash the contents.

Machine Authentication Check

As mentioned in Chapter 3, the *@Page* directive contains an attribute named *EnableViewStateMac*, whose only purpose is making the view state a bit more secure by detecting any possible attempt at corrupting the original data. When serialized, and if *EnableViewStateMac* is set to *true*, the view state is appended with a validator hash string based on the algorithm and the key defined in the *<machineKey>* section of the configuration file. The resulting array of bytes, which is the output of the *StateBag*'s binary serialization plus the hash value, is Base64 encoded. By default, the encryption algorithm to calculate the hash is SHA1, and the encryption and decryption keys are auto-generated and stored in the

Web server machine's Local Security Authority (LSA) subsystem. The LSA is a protected component of Windows NT, Windows 2000, Windows Server 2003, and Windows XP. It provides security services and maintains information about all aspects of local security on a system.

If *EnableViewStateMac* is *true*, when the page posts back, the hash value is extracted and used to verify that the returned view state has not been tampered with on the client. If it has been, an exception is thrown. The net effect is that you might be able to read the contents of the view state, but to replace it you need the encryption key, which is in the Web server's LSA. The *MAC* in the name of the *EnableViewStateMac* property stands for *Machine Authentication Check*, which is enabled by default. If you disable the attribute, an attacker could alter the view-state information on the client and send a modified version to the server and have ASP.NET blissfully use that tampered-with information.

To reinforce the security of the view state, in ASP.NET 1.1 the *ViewStateUserKey* property has been added to the *Page* class. The property evaluates to a user-specific string (typically, the session ID) that is known on the server and hard to guess on the client. ASP.NET uses the content of the property as an input argument to the hash algorithm that generates the MAC code.

Size Thresholds and Page Throughput

My personal opinion is that you should be concerned about the view state, but not for the potential security holes it might open in your code—it can let hackers exploit only existing holes. You should be more concerned about the overall performance and responsiveness of the page. Especially for feature-rich pages that use plenty of controls, the view state can reach a considerable size, measured in KB of data. Such an extra burden taxes all requests, in downloads and uploads, and ends up creating serious overhead for the application as a whole.

What would be a reasonable size for an ASP.NET page? And for the view state of a page? Let's take a look at a sample page that contains a grid control bound to about 100 records (the Customers table in the Northwind database of SQL Server):

```
<html>
<head runat="server">
    <title>Measure Up Your ViewState</title>
</head>
<script language="javascript">
function ShowViewStateSize()
{
    var buf = document.forms[0]["__VIEWSTATE"].value;
    alert("View state is " + buf.length + " bytes");
}
</script>
```

```
<body>
    <form id="form1" runat="server">
        <input type="button" value="Show View State Size"
               onclick="ShowViewStateSize()">
        <asp:SqlDataSource ID="SqlDataSource1" runat="server"
               SelectCommand="SELECT companyname, contactname, contacttitle
                              FROM customers"
               ConnectionString="<%$ ConnectionStrings:LocalNWind %>">
        <asp:DataGrid ID="grid" runat="server"
               DataSourceID="SqlDataSource1" />
    </form>
</body>
</html>
```

In ASP.NET 2.0 and beyond, the total size of the page is about 20 KB. The view state alone, though, takes up about 11 KB. If you port the same page back to ASP.NET 1.x, results are even worse. The whole page amounts to 28 KB, while the view state alone amounts to a burdensome 19 KB. Two conclusions can be drawn from these numbers:

- Starting with ASP.NET 2.0, the view-state field appears to be more compact. (I'll discuss this in more detail later in the chapter.)

- The view state takes up a large share of the downloaded bytes for the page. You won't be too far from the truth if you estimate the view-state size to be about 60 percent of the entire page size.

What can you do about this? First, let's play with some numbers to determine a reasonable goal for view-state size in our applications. You should endeavor to keep a page size around 30 KB, to the extent that is possible of course. For example, the Google home page is less than 4 KB. The home page of *http://www.asp.net* amounts to about 50 KB. The Google site is not written with ASP.NET, so nothing can be said about the view state. But what about the view-state size of the home of *http://www.asp.net*? Interestingly enough, that page has only 1 KB of view state. On the other hand, the page *http://www.asp.net/ControlGallery/default. aspx?Category=7&tabindex=0* is larger than 130 KB, of which 10 KB is view state. (This page has been redesigned lately; a few months ago, I measured it to be 500 KB in size, with 120 KB of view state!)

The ideal size for a view state is around 7 KB; it is optimal if you can keep it down to 3 KB or so. In any case, the view state, regardless of its absolute size, should never exceed 30 percent of the page size.

Note   Where do these numbers come from? "From my personal experience," would perhaps be a valid answer, but not necessarily a good and exhaustive one. Let's put it this way: the smallest you can keep a page is the best size. To me, 30 KB looks like a reasonable compromise, because most things can be stuffed into that size. Clearly, if you have 250 items to display, your page size can grow up to 1 MB or so. In the end, having a smaller or larger view state is a design choice and is mostly application-specific. Within these boundaries, though, a few guidelines can be stated. The most important guideline is not so much that view state should be limited to a few KB, but that it should take a minimal percentage of the overall page size. Which percentage? Being the view-state helper, I'd say no more than 25 percent or 30 percent at the most. But here I'm just throwing out numbers using a bit of common sense. If you can disable the view state altogether, do it. At the very least, you should avoid storing there the avoidable items that don't change often and are easily cached on the server, such as a long list of countries.

Programming Web Forms Without View State

By default, the view state is enabled for all server controls; however, this doesn't mean that you strictly need it all the time and for all controls. The use of the view-state feature should be carefully monitored because it can hinder your code. View state saves you from a lot of coding and, more importantly, makes coding simpler and smarter. However, if you find you're paying too much for this feature, drop view state altogether and reinitialize the state of the size-critical controls at every postback. In this case, disabling view state saves processing time and speeds up the download process.

Disabling View State

You can disable the view state for an entire page by using the *EnableViewState* attribute of the *@Page* directive. Although this is not generally a recommended option, you should definitely consider it for read-only pages that either don't post back or don't need state to be maintained.

```
<% @Page EnableViewState="false" %>
```

A better approach entails disabling the view state only for some of the controls hosted in the page. To disable it on a per-control basis, set the *EnableViewState* property of the control to *false*, as shown here:

```
<asp:datagrid runat="server" EnableViewState="false">
    ...
</asp:datagrid>
```

While developing the page, you can keep the size of the view state under control by enabling tracing on the page. The tracer doesn't show the total amount of the view state for the page, but it lets you form a precise idea of what each control does. In Figure 15-8, the page contains a relatively simple *DataGrid* control. As you can see, the cells of the grid take up a large part of the view state. The *TableCell* control, in particular, strips the view state of all its user interfaces, including text, column, and row-span style attributes.

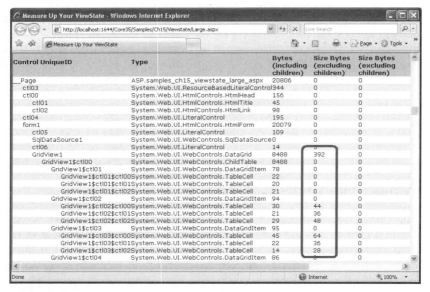

Control UniqueID	Type	Bytes (including children)	Size Bytes (excluding children)	Size Bytes (excluding children)
Page	ASP.samples_ch15_viewstate_large_aspx	20806	0	0
ctl03	System.Web.UI.ResourceBasedLiteralControl	344	0	0
ctl00	System.Web.UI.HtmlControls.HtmlHead	156	0	0
ctl01	System.Web.UI.HtmlControls.HtmlTitle	45	0	0
ctl02	System.Web.UI.HtmlControls.HtmlLink	98	0	0
ctl04	System.Web.UI.LiteralControl	195	0	0
form1	System.Web.UI.HtmlControls.HtmlForm	20079	0	0
ctl05	System.Web.UI.LiteralControl	109	0	0
SqlDataSource1	System.Web.UI.WebControls.SqlDataSource	0	0	0
ctl06	System.Web.UI.LiteralControl	14	0	0
GridView1	System.Web.UI.WebControls.DataGrid	8488	392	0
GridView1$ctl00	System.Web.UI.WebControls.ChildTable	8488	0	0
GridView1$ctl01	System.Web.UI.WebControls.DataGridItem	78	0	0
GridView1$ctl01$ctl00	System.Web.UI.WebControls.TableCell	22	0	0
GridView1$ctl01$ctl01	System.Web.UI.WebControls.TableCell	20	0	0
GridView1$ctl01$ctl02	System.Web.UI.WebControls.TableCell	21	0	0
GridView1$ctl02	System.Web.UI.WebControls.DataGridItem	94	0	0
GridView1$ctl02$ctl00	System.Web.UI.WebControls.TableCell	30	44	0
GridView1$ctl02$ctl01	System.Web.UI.WebControls.TableCell	21	36	0
GridView1$ctl02$ctl02	System.Web.UI.WebControls.TableCell	29	48	0
GridView1$ctl03	System.Web.UI.WebControls.DataGridItem	95	0	0
GridView1$ctl03$ctl00	System.Web.UI.WebControls.TableCell	45	64	0
GridView1$ctl03$ctl01	System.Web.UI.WebControls.TableCell	22	36	0
GridView1$ctl03$ctl02	System.Web.UI.WebControls.TableCell	14	28	0
GridView1$ctl04	System.Web.UI.WebControls.DataGridItem	86	0	0

FIGURE 15-8 All controls, including child controls, contribute to the view state burden.

Note Like all other data-bound controls, the *DataGrid* doesn't store its data source in the view state. However, the data source bound to the control has some impact on the view-state size. Each constituent control in the overall data-bound user interface takes up some view state for its settings. The number of child controls (for example, rows and columns in a *DataGrid*) obviously depend on the data source.

Determining When to Disable View State

Let's briefly recap what view state is all about and what you might lose if you ban it from your pages. View state represents the current state of the page and its controls just before the page is rendered to HTML. It is then serialized to a hidden field and downloaded to the client. When the page posts back, the view state—a sort of call context for the page request—is recovered from the hidden field, deserialized, and used to initialize the server controls in the page and the page itself. However, as pointed out in Chapter 3, this is only the first half of the story.

After loading the view state, the page reads client-side posted information and uses those values to override most of the settings for the server controls. Applying posted values overrides some of the settings read from the view state. You understand that in this case, and only for the properties modified by posted values, the view state represents an extra burden.

Let's examine a typical case and suppose you have a page with a text box server control. What you expect is that when the page posts back, the text box server control is automatically assigned the value set on the client. Well, to meet this rather common requirement, you *don't* need view state. Let's consider the following page:

```
<% @Page language="c#" %>
<form runat="server">
    <asp:textbox runat="server" enableviewstate="false"
         id="theInput" readonly="false" text="Type here" />
    <asp:checkbox runat="server" enableviewstate="false"
          id="theCheck" text="Check me" />
    <asp:button runat="server" text="Click" onclick="OnPost" />
</form>
```

Apparently, the behavior of the page is stateful even if view state is disabled for a couple of controls. The reason lies in the fact that you are using two server controls—*TextBox* and *CheckBox*—whose key properties—*Text* and *Checked*—are updated according to the values set by the user. For these properties, posted values override any setting that view state might have set. As a result, as long as you're simply interested in persisting these properties you don't need view state at all.

Likewise, you don't need view state for all control properties that are set at design-time in the *.aspx* file and are not expected to change during the session. The following code illustrates this point:

```
<asp:textbox runat="server" id="TextBox1" Text="Some text"
             MaxLength="20" ReadOnly="true" />
```

You don't need view state to keep the *Text* property of a *TextBox* up to date; you do need view state to keep up to date, say, *ReadOnly* or *MaxLength*, as long as these properties have their values changed during the page lifetime. If the two properties are constant during the page lifetime, you don't need view state for them either.

So when is view state really necessary?

View state is necessary whenever your page requires that accessory control properties (other than those subject to posted values) are updated during the page lifetime. In this context, "updated" means that their original value changes—either the default value or the value you assign to the property at design-time. Consider the following form:

```
<script runat="server">
    void Page_Load(object sender, EventArgs e)
    {
       if (!IsPostBack)
           theInput.ReadOnly = true;
    }
</script>
```

```
<form id="form1" runat="server">
    <asp:textbox runat="server" id="theInput" text="Am I read-only?" />
    <asp:button ID="Button1" runat="server" text="Click" onclick="OnPost" />
</form>
```

When the page is first loaded, the text box becomes read-only. Next, you click the button to post back. If view state is enabled, the page works as expected and the text box remains read-only. If view state is disabled for the text box, the original setting for the *ReadOnly* property is restored—in this case, *false*.

In general, you can do without view state whenever the state can be deduced either from the client or from the runtime environment. In contrast, doing without view state is hard whenever state information can't be dynamically inferred and you can't ensure that all properties are correctly restored when the page posts back. This is exactly what view state guarantees at the cost of extra bytes when downloading and uploading. To save those bytes, you must provide an alternate approach.

> **Tip** You can enable and disable the view state programmatically for the page as well as individual controls by using the Boolean *EnableViewState* property.

Disabling the view state can also create subtler problems that are difficult to diagnose and fix, especially if you're working with third-party controls or, in general, controls for which you have source code access. Some ASP.NET controls, in fact, might save to the view state not just properties that are officially part of the programming interface (and that can be set accordingly), but also behavioral properties that serve internal purposes and are marked as protected or even private. Unfortunately, for these controls, you do not have the option of disabling the view state. But ASP.NET 2.0 and newer versions come to the rescue with *control state*.

Changes in the ASP.NET View State

Two important changes occurred to the view-state implementation starting with ASP.NET 2.0. As a result, two major drawbacks have been fixed, or at least greatly mitigated. The size of the view state is significantly reduced as a result of a new serialization format. The contents of the view state have been split into two states: classic view state and control state. Unlike the classic view state, the control state can't be disabled programmatically and is considered a sort of private view state for a control. This feature is ideal for developers building third-party ASP.NET controls, as it helps them to keep critical persistent properties out of the reach of end page developers.

The Serialization Format

In Figure 15-9, you see the same page running under ASP.NET 1.x (the bottom window) and ASP.NET 2.0 or ASP.NET 3.5 (the top window). A client-side button retrieves the view-state string and calculates its length. The JavaScript code needed is pretty simple:

```
<script language="javascript">
    function ShowViewStateSize() {
        var buf = document.forms[0]["__VIEWSTATE"].value;
        alert("View state is " + buf.length + " bytes");
    }
</script>
```

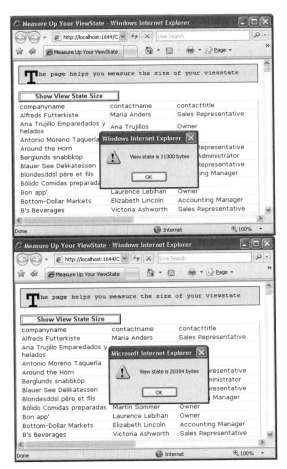

FIGURE 15-9 The overall view state size obtained scriptwise.

As you can see, the size of the view state for the same page is quite different, and significantly smaller, in newer versions of ASP.NET. Let's see why.

The contents persisted to the view state are ultimately the results of the serialization process applied to an object graph. The object graph results from the hierarchical concatenation of the view state of each individual control participating in the page's construction. The data going to the view state is accumulated in tuples made of special containers such as *Pair* and *Triplet*. *Pair* and *Triplet* are extremely simple classes containing two and three members, respectively, of type *object*. Each object is serialized to the stream according to various rules:

- Simple types such as strings, dates, bytes, characters, Booleans, and all types of numbers are written as is to a binary stream.

- Enum types and *Color*, *Type*, and *Unit* dictionary objects are serialized in a way that is specific to the type.

- All other objects are checked to see whether there's a type converter object to convert them to a string. If there is, the type converter is used.

- Objects that lack a type converter are serialized through the binary formatter. If the type is not serializable, an exception is thrown.

- *Pair*, *Triplet*, and *ArrayList* objects are recursively serialized.

The resulting stream is hashed (or encrypted, based on configuration settings), Base64 encoded, and then persisted to the hidden field. This is more or less what happens already in ASP.NET 1.x. So where's the difference?

The difference is all in a little detail lying in the folds of type serialization. The type of each member being serialized is identified with a byte—exactly, nonprintable characters in the 1 through 50 range. In ASP.NET 1.x, printable characters—such as <, >, l, s, l, and a few more—were used for the same purpose. This change brings two benefits—a smaller size and a little more speed in deserialization.

> **Note** The class behind the new serialization format of the ASP.NET 2.0 view state is a new type of formatter object—the *ObjectStateFormatter* class. Specifically designed in ASP.NET 2.0 to serialize and deserialize object graphs to and from a binary writer, the class is a yet another .NET formatter object, as it also implements the *IFormatter* interface. In ASP.NET 2.0 and beyond, the *ObjectStateFormatter* class replaces the *LosFormatter* class used in ASP.NET 1.x. *LosFormatter* writes to a text writer. This change is not an optimization per se, but it allows a number of other improvements. For example, it allows indexing of strings and more compact storage, as non-string values (such as numbers and Booleans) are written as binaries and take up much less space.

The Control State

It is not uncommon for a server control to persist information across postbacks. For example, consider what happens to a *DataGrid* control modified to support autoreverse sorting. When the user clicks to sort by a column, the control compares the current sort expression and the new sort expression. If the two are equivalent, the sort direction is reversed. How does the *DataGrid* track the current sort direction? If you don't place the sort direction property in the control's view state, it will be lost as soon as the control renders to the browser.

This kind of property is not intended to be used for plain configurations such as pager style or background color. It has an impact on how the control works. What if the control is then used in a page that has the view state disabled? In ASP.NET 1.x, the control feature just stops working. Private or protected properties that are to be persisted across two requests should not be placed in the view state. In ASP.NET 1.x, you can use the session state, the ASP.NET cache, or perhaps another, custom hidden, field.

In ASP.NET 2.0 and beyond, the *control state* is a special data container introduced just to create a sort of protected zone inside the classic view state. It is safer to use the control state than the view state because application-level and page-level settings cannot affect it. If your existing custom control has private or protected properties stored in the view state, you should move all of them to the control state. Anything you store in the control state remains there until it is explicitly removed. Also the control state is sent down to the client and up-loaded when the page posts back. The more data you pack into it, the more data is moved back and forth between the browser and the Web server. You should use control state, but you should do so carefully.

Programming the Control State

The implementation of the control state is left to the programmer, which is both good and bad. It is bad because you have to manually implement serialization and deserialization for your control's state. It is good because you can control exactly how the control works and tweak its code to achieve optimal performance in the context in which you're using it. The page's infrastructure takes care of the actual data encoding and serialization. The control state is processed along with the view state information and undergoes the same treatment as for serialization and Base64 encoding. The control state is also persisted within the same view state's hidden field. The root object serialized to the view state stream is actually a *Pair* object that contains the control state as the first element and the classic view state as the second member.

There's no ready-made dictionary object to hold the items that form the control state. You no longer have to park your objects in a fixed container such as the *ViewState* state bag—you can maintain control-state data in plain private or protected members. Among other things, this means that access to data is faster because it is more direct and is not mediated by a dictionary object. For example, if you need to track the sort direction of a grid, you can do so using the following variable:

```
private int _sortDirection;
```

In ASP.NET 1.x, you resort to the following:

```
private int _sortDirection
{
   get {
      object o = ViewState["SortDirection"];
      if (o == null)  return 0;
      return (int) o;
   }
   set {ViewState["SortDirection"] = value;)
}
```

To restore control state, the *Page* class invokes the *LoadControlState* on all controls that have registered with the page object as controls that require control state. The following pseudo-code shows the control's typical behavior:

```
private override void LoadControlState(object savedState)
{
    // Make a copy of the saved state.
    // You know what type of object this is because
    // you saved it in the SaveControlState method.
    object[] currentState = (object[]) savedState;
    if (currentState == null)
        return;

    // Initialize any private/protected member you stored
    // in the control state. The values are packed in the same
    // order and format you stored them in the SaveControlState method.
    _myProperty1 = (int) currentState[0];
    _myProperty2 = (string) currentState[1];
    ...
}
```

The *LoadControlState* method receives an object identical to the one you created in *SaveControlState*. As a control developer, you know that type very well and can use this knowledge to extract any information that's useful for restoring the control state. For example, you might want to use an array of objects in which every slot corresponds to a particular property.

The following pseudocode gives you an idea of the structure of the *SaveControlState* method:

```
private override object SaveControlState()
{
    // Declare a properly sized array of objects
    object[] stateToSave = new Object[...];

    // Fill the array with local property values
    stateToSave[0] = _myProperty1;
    stateToSave[1] = _myProperty2;
    ...

    // Return the array
    return stateToSave;
}
```

You allocate a new data structure (such as a *Pair*, a *Triplet*, an array, or a custom type) and fill it with the private properties to persist across postbacks. The method terminates, returning this object to the ASP.NET runtime. The object is then serialized and encoded to a Base64 stream. The class that you use to collect the control state properties must be serializable. We'll return to the topic of control state in my book *Programming Microsoft ASP.NET 2.0 Applications: Advanced Topics* (Microsoft Press, 2006).

Keeping the View State on the Server

As discussed so far, there's one major reason to keep the view state off the client browser. The more stuff you pack into the view state, the more time the page takes to download and upload because the view state is held in a hidden field. It is important to note that the client-side hidden field is not set in stone, but is simply the default storage medium where the view state information can be stored. Let's see how to proceed to save the view state on the Web server in the sample file.

> **Important** Before we go any further in discussing the implementation of server-side view state, there's one key aspect you should consider. You should guarantee that the correct view-state file will be served to each page instance the user retrieves via the browser's history. This is not an issue as long as each page contains its own view state. But when the view state is stored elsewhere, unless you want to disable Back/Forward functionality, you should provide a mechanism that serves the "right" view state for the instance of a given page that the user is reclaiming. At a minimum, you need to make copies of the view state for about 6 to 8 instances. As you can see, what you save in the roundtrip is lost in server's memory or server-side I/O operations. All in all, keeping the view state on the client and inside of the page is perhaps the option that works better in the largest number of scenarios. If the view state is a problem, you have only one way out: reducing its size.

The *LosFormatter* Class

To design an alternative storage scheme for the view state, we need to put our hands on the string that ASP.NET stores in the hidden field. The string will be saved in a server-side file and read from where the page is being processed. The class that ASP.NET 1.x actually uses to serialize and deserialize the view state is *LosFormatter*.

The *LosFormatter* class has a simple programming interface made of only two publicly callable methods—*Serialize* and *Deserialize*. The *Serialize* method writes the final Base64 representation of the view state to a *Stream* or *TextWriter* object:

```
public void Serialize(Stream stream, object viewState);
public void Serialize(TextWriter output, object viewState);
```

The *Deserialize* method builds an object from a stream, a *TextReader* object, or a plain Base64 string:

```
public object Deserialize(Stream stream);
public object Deserialize(TextReader input);
public object Deserialize(string input);
```

The *LosFormatter* class is the entry point in the view-state internal mechanism. By using it, you can be sure everything will happen exactly as in the default case and, more importantly, you're shielded from any other details.

The *ObjectStateFormatter* Class

As mentioned, the *LosFormatter* class is replaced by *ObjectStateFormatter* starting with ASP. NET 2.0. *LosFormatter* is still available for compatibility reasons, however. The new serializer writes to a binary writer, whereas *LosFormatter* writes to a text writer. *LosFormatter* needs to turn everything to a string for storage, while *ObjectStateFormatter* capitalizes on the underlying binary model and writes out just bytes. As a result, *ObjectStateFormatter* serializes the same object graph into roughly half the size, and spends about half as much time in the serialization and deserialization process.

The *Serialize* method of *ObjectStateFormatter* writes the final Base64 representation of the view state to a *Stream* or a string object:

```
public string Serialize(Object graph);
public void Serialize(Stream stream, Object graph);
```

The *Deserialize* method of *ObjectStateFormatter* builds an object from a stream or a plain Base64 string:

```
public object Deserialize(Stream stream);
public object Deserialize(string input);
```

Creating a View-State-Less Page

The *Page* class provides a couple of protected virtual methods that the run time uses when it needs to deserialize or serialize the view state. The methods are named *LoadPageStateFromPersistenceMedium* and *SavePageStateToPersistenceMedium*:

```
protected virtual void SavePageStateToPersistenceMedium(object viewState);
protected virtual object LoadPageStateFromPersistenceMedium();
```

If you override both methods, you can load and save view-state information from and to anything. In particular, you can use a storage medium that is different from the hidden field used by the default implementation. Because the methods are defined as protected members, the only way to redefine them is by creating a new class and making it inherit from *Page*. The following code gives you an idea of the default behavior of *LoadPageStateFromPersistenceMedium*:

```
string m_viewState = Request.Form["__VIEWSTATE"];
ObjectStateFormatter m_formatter = new ObjectStateFormatter();
StateBag viewStateBag = m_formatter.Deserialize(m_viewState);
```

The structure of the page we're going to create is as follows:

```
public class ServerViewStatePage : Page
{
    protected override
        object LoadPageStateFromPersistenceMedium()
    { ... }
    protected override
        void SavePageStateToPersistenceMedium(object viewState)
    { ... }
}
```

Saving the View State to a Web Server File

The tasks accomplished by the *SavePageStateToPersistenceMedium* method are easy to explain and understand. The method takes a string as an argument, opens the output stream, and calls into the *LosFormatter* serializer:

```
protected override
void SavePageStateToPersistenceMedium(object viewStateBag)
{
    string file = GetFileName();
    StreamWriter sw = new StreamWriter(file);
    ObjectStateFormatter m_formatter = new ObjectStateFormatter();
    m_formatter.Serialize(sw, viewStateBag);
    sw.Close();
    return;
}
private string GetFileName()
{
    // Return the desired filename.
    ...
}
```

How should we choose the name of the file to make sure that no conflicts arise? The view state is specific to a page request made within a particular session. So the session ID and the request URL are pieces of information that can be used to associate the request with the right file. Alternatively, you could give the view state file a randomly generated name and persist it in a custom hidden field within the page. Note that in this case you can't rely on the __VIEWSTATE hidden field because when overriding the methods, you alter the internal procedure that would have created it.

The *GetFileName* function in the preceding code could easily provide the file a unique name according to the following pattern:

```
SessionID_URL.viewstate
```

Notice that for an ASP.NET application to create a local file, you must give the ASP.NET account special permissions on a file or folder. I suggest creating a new subfolder to contain all the view-state files. Deleting files for expired sessions can be a bit tricky, and a Windows service is probably the tool that works best. A Windows service, after all, can auto-start on reboot and because it runs autonomously from the ASP.NET application it can clean out files in any case.

Loading the View State from a Web Server File

In our implementation, the *LoadPageStateFromPersistenceMedium* method determines the name of the file to read from, extracts the Base64 string, and calls *ObjectStateFormatter* to deserialize:

```
protected override object LoadPageStateFromPersistenceMedium()
{
    object viewStateBag;

    string file = GetFileName();
    try {
        StreamReader sr = new StreamReader(file);
        string m_viewState = sr.ReadToEnd();
        sr.Close();
    }
    catch {
        throw new HttpException("The View State is invalid.");
    }
    ObjectStateFormatter m_formatter = new ObjectStateFormatter();

    try {
        viewStateBag = m_formatter.Deserialize(m_viewState);
    }
    catch {
        throw new HttpException("The View State is invalid.");
    }
    return viewStateBag;
}
```

To take advantage of this feature to keep view state on the server, you only need to change the parent class of the page code file to inherit from *ServerViewStatePage*:

```
public partial class TestPage : ServerViewStatePage
{
}
```

Figure 15-10 shows the view-state files created in a temporary folder on the Web server machine.

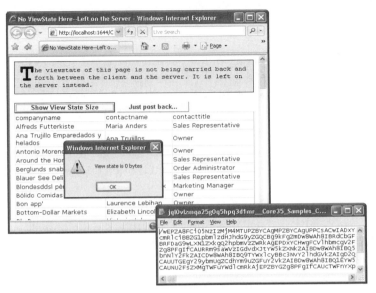

FIGURE 15-10 View state files created on the server. The folder must grant write permissions to the ASP.NET account.

The page shown in Figure 15-10 enables view state, but no hidden field is present in its client-side code.

Conclusion

Although HTTP is a stateless protocol, Web applications can't just do without certain forms of state. Moreover, state management is a hot topic for all real-world Web applications. Setting up an effective and efficient solution for state management is often the difference between an application being scalable or nonscalable.

One of the most-used forms of state is session state—that is, the state specific to a user and valid as long as that user works with the application. You can store session data in the memory of the ASP.NET worker process as well as in external processes, and even in a SQL Server table or in custom state provider. In spite of the radically different options, the top-level programming interface is identical. More importantly, the ASP.NET session state can be persisted in a Web farm or Web garden scenario as well.

In the next chapter, we'll deal with another extremely powerful form of state container—the *Cache* object.

Just the Facts

- Compared to the intrinsic *Session* object of classic ASP, the ASP.NET session state is nearly identical in use, but it's significantly richer in functionality and radically different in architecture.

- There are four possibilities for working with the session state. The session state can be stored locally in the ASP.NET worker process; the session state can be maintained in a remote process; the session state can be managed by SQL Server and stored in an ad hoc database table. Finally, a fourth option is added in ASP.NET 2.0 that allows you to store the sessions in a custom component.

- The session state subsystem was refactored to allow developers to replace most of the bits and pieces of functionality—a characteristic that is often referred to as *session state pluggability*.

- By default, the view state is enabled for all server controls; however, this doesn't mean that you absolutely need it all the time and for all controls. The use of the view-state feature should be carefully monitored because it can hinder your code and unduly bloat your pages.

- Starting with ASP.NET 2.0, the size of the view state is significantly reduced as a result of a new binary serialization format.

- The contents of the view state have been split into two states: classic view state and control state. Unlike the classic view state, the control state can't be disabled programmatically and is considered a sort of private view state for a control.

Chapter 16
ASP.NET Caching

Caching is the system's, or the application's, ability to save frequently used data to an intermediate storage medium. An intermediate storage medium is any support placed in between the application and its primary data source that lets you persist and retrieve data more quickly than with the primary data source. In a typical Web scenario, the canonical intermediate storage medium is the Web server's memory, whereas the data source is the back-end data management system. Obviously, you can design caching around the requirements and characteristics of each application, thus using as many layers of caching as needed to reach your performance goals.

In ASP.NET, caching comes in two independent but not exclusive flavors—caching application data, and caching the output of served pages. Page-output caching is the quickest way to take advantage of cache capabilities. You don't need to write code; you just configure it at design-time and go. For pages that don't get stale quickly (and also for pages that reclaim "live" data), page-output caching is a kind of free performance booster. To build an application-specific caching subsystem, you use the caching application programming interface (API) that lets you store data in a global, system-managed object—the *Cache* object. This approach gives you the greatest flexibility, but you need to learn a few usage patterns to stay on the safe side. Let's tackle application data first.

Caching Application Data

Centered around the *Cache* object, the ASP.NET caching API is much more than simply a container of global data shared by all sessions like the *Application* object that I briefly discussed in the previous chapter. Preserved for backward compatibility with classic ASP applications, the *Application* intrinsic object presents itself as a global container of data with an indexer property and a user-callable locking mechanism. The *Cache* object is a smarter and thread-safe container that can automatically remove unused items, support various forms of dependencies, and optionally provide removal callbacks and priorities.

The *Application* object is maintained for backward compatibility with legacy applications; new ASP.NET applications should use the *Cache* object.

The *Cache* Class

The *Cache* class is exposed by the *System.Web.Caching* namespace and is a new entry in the set of tools that provide state management in ASP.NET. The *Cache* class works like an applicationwide repository for data and objects, but this is the only aspect that it has in common with the *HttpApplicationState* class, as we'll see in a moment.

An instance of the *Cache* class is created on a per-AppDomain basis and remains valid until that AppDomain is up and running. The current instance of the application's ASP.NET cache is returned by the *Cache* property of the *HttpContext* object or the *Cache* property of the *Page* object.

Cache and Other State Objects

In spite of their common goal—to serve as a global data repository for ASP.NET applications—*Cache* and *HttpApplicationState* classes are quite different. *Cache* is a thread-safe object and does not require you to explicitly lock and unlock before access. All critical sections in the internal code are adequately protected using synchronization constructs. Another key difference with the *HttpApplicationState* class is that data stored in *Cache* doesn't necessarily live as long as the application does. The *Cache* object lets you associate a duration as well as a priority with any of the items you store.

Any cached item can be configured to expire after a specified number of seconds, freeing up some memory. By setting a priority on items, you help the *Cache* object select which items can be safely disposed of in case of memory shortage. Items can be associated with various types of dependencies, such as the timestamp of one or more files and directories, changes on other cached items, database table changes, and external events. When something happens to break the link, the cached item is invalidated and is no longer accessible by the application.

Both *Cache* and *HttpApplicationState* are globally visible classes and span all active sessions. However, neither works in a Web farm or Web garden scenario; in general, they don't work outside the current AppDomain.

> **Note**   When more than one AppDomain is involved (for example, in a Web farm), presumably all AppDomains would contain the same cached data, assuming that the cached information is not dynamic. Unlike with session state, this isn't as troubling because the assumption is that applicationwide static values can be read upon initialization and cache timeout. If the cached information is dynamic, that's a different story. In that case, you should consider a global cross-machine container, as we'll discuss shortly.

The *Cache* object is unique in its capability to automatically scavenge the memory and get rid of unused items. Aside from that, it provides the same dictionary-based and familiar programming interface as *Application* and *Session*. Unlike *Session*, the *Cache* class does not store data on a per-user basis. Furthermore, when the session state is managed in-process, all currently running sessions are stored as distinct items in the ASP.NET *Cache*.

> **Note** If you're looking for a global repository object that, like *Session*, works across a Web farm or Web garden architecture, you might become frustrated. No such object exists in the .NET Framework. To build a cross-machine container, you need to resort to a shared and remote resource, such as an external service or perhaps an installation of Microsoft SQL Server or another database. This means that each access to data will require serialization and is subject to network latency. In general, this scheme is complex enough to invalidate most of the advantages you get from data caching. As far as caching is involved, the tradeoff to evaluate is accessing ready-made data versus running the query to fetch a fresh copy of desired data. ASP.NET provides an effective infrastructure for caching data locally because that is what you need most of the time. Adding to the infrastructure to cover farms is up to you.

Properties of the *Cache* Class

The *Cache* class provides a couple of properties and public fields. The properties let you count and access the various items. The public fields are internal constants used to configure the expiration policy of the cache items. Table 16-1 lists and describes them all.

TABLE 16-1 *Cache* **Class Properties and Public Fields**

Property	Description
Count	Gets the number of items stored in the cache
Item	An indexer property that provides access to the cache item identified by the specified key
NoAbsoluteExpiration	A static constant that indicates a given item will never expire
NoSlidingExpiration	A static constant that indicates sliding expiration is disabled for a given item

The *NoAbsoluteExpiration* field is of the *DateTime* type and is set to the *DateTime.MaxValue* date—that is, the largest possible date defined in the .NET Framework. The *NoSlidingExpiration* field is of the *TimeSpan* type and is set to *TimeSpan.Zero*, meaning that sliding expiration is disabled. We'll say more about sliding expiration shortly.

The *Item* property is a read/write property that can also be used to add new items to the cache. If the key specified as the argument of the *Item* property does not exist, a new entry is created. Otherwise, the existing entry is overwritten.

```
Cache["MyItem"] = value;
```

The data stored in the cache is generically considered to be of type *object*, whereas the key must be a case-sensitive string. When you insert a new item in the cache using the *Item* property, a number of default attributes are assumed. In particular, the item is given no expiration policy, no remove callback, and a normal priority. As a result, the item will stay in the cache indefinitely, until programmatically removed or until the application terminates. To specify any extra arguments and exercise closer control on the item, use the *Insert* method of the *Cache* class instead.

Methods of the *Cache* Class

The methods of the *Cache* class let you add, remove, and enumerate the items stored. Methods of the *Cache* class are listed and described in Table 16-2.

TABLE 16-2 *Cache* Class Methods

Method	Description
Add	Adds the specified item to the cache. It allows you to specify dependencies, expiration and priority policies, and a remove callback. The call fails if an item with the same key already exists. The method returns the object that represents the newly added item.
Get	Retrieves the value of the specified *n* item from the cache. The item is identified by key. The method returns *null* if no item with that key is found. (This method is used to implement the *get* accessor of the *Item* property.)
GetEnumerator	Returns a dictionary enumerator object to iterate through all the valid items stored in the cache.
Insert	Inserts the specified item into the cache. *Insert* provides several overloads and allows you to specify dependencies, expiration and priority policies, and a remove callback. The method is void and, unlike *Add*, overwrites an existing item having the same key as the item being inserted. (This method is used to implement the *set* accessor of the *Item* property.)
Remove	Removes the specified item from the cache. The item is identified by the key. The method returns the instance of the object being removed or *null* if no item with that key is found.

Both the *Add* and *Insert* methods don't accept null values as the key or the value of an item to cache. If null values are used, an exception is thrown. You can configure sliding expiration for an item for no longer than one year. Otherwise, an exception will be raised. Finally, bear in mind that you cannot set both sliding and absolute expirations on the same cached item.

Note *Add* and *Insert* work in much the same way, but a couple of differences make it worthwhile to have both on board. *Add* fails (but no exception is raised) if the item already exists, whereas *Insert* overwrites the existing item. In addition, *Add* has just one signature, while *Insert* provides several different overloads.

An Interior View

The *Cache* class inherits from *Object* and implements the *IEnumerable* interface. It is a wrapper around an internal class that acts as the true container of the stored data. The real class used to implement the ASP.NET cache varies depending on the number of affinitized CPUs. If only one CPU is available, the class is *CacheSingle*; otherwise, it is *CacheMultiple*. In both cases, items are stored in a hashtable and there will be a distinct hashtable for each CPU. It turns out that *CacheMultiple* manages an array of hashtables. Figure 16-1 illustrates the architecture of the *Cache* object.

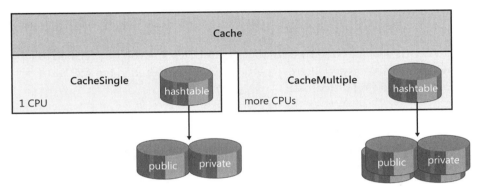

FIGURE 16-1 The internal structure of the ASP.NET cache.

The hashtable is divided into two parts—public and private elements. In the public portion of the hashtable are placed all items visible to user applications. System-level data, on the other hand, goes in the private section. The cache is a resource extensively used by the ASP.NET runtime itself; system items, though, are neatly separated by application data and there's no way an application can access a private element on the cache.

The *Cache* object is mostly a way to restrict applications to read from, and write to, the public segment of the data store. *Get* and *set* methods on internal cache classes accept a flag to denote the public attribute of the item. When called from the *Cache* class, these internal methods always default to the flag that selects public items.

The hashtable containing data is then enhanced and surrounded by other internal components to provide a rich set of programming features. The list includes the implementation of a least recently used (LRU) algorithm to ensure that items can be removed if the system runs short of memory, dependencies, and removal callbacks.

Caution On a multiprocessor machine with more than one CPU affinitized with the ASP.NET worker process, each processor ends up getting its own *Cache* object. The various cache objects are not synchronized. In a Web garden configuration, you can't assume that users will return to the same CPU (and worker process) on subsequent requests. So the status of the ASP.NET cache is not guaranteed to be aligned with what the same page did last time.

Working with the ASP.NET *Cache*

An instance of the *Cache* object is associated with each running application and shares the associated application's lifetime. The cache holds references to data and proactively verifies validity and expiration. When the system runs short of memory, the *Cache* object automatically removes some little-used items and frees valuable server resources. Each item when stored in the cache can be given special attributes that determine a priority and an expiration policy. All these are system-provided tools to help programmers control the scavenging mechanism of the ASP.NET cache.

Inserting New Items in the Cache

A cache item is characterized by a handful of attributes that can be specified as input arguments of both *Add* and *Insert*. In particular, an item stored in the ASP.NET *Cache* object can have the following properties:

- **Key**   A case-sensitive string, it is the key used to store the item in the internal hashtable the ASP.NET cache relies upon. If this value is null, an exception is thrown. If the key already exists, what happens depends on the particular method you're using: *Add* fails, while *Insert* just overwrites the existing item.

- **Value**   A non-null value of type *Object* that references the information stored in the cache. The value is managed and returned as an *Object* and needs casting to become useful in the application context.

- **Dependencies**   Object of type *CacheDependency*, tracks a physical dependency between the item being added to the cache and files, directories, database tables, or other objects in the application's cache. Whenever any of the monitored sources are modified, the newly added item is marked obsolete and automatically removed.

- **Absolute Expiration Date**   A *DateTime* object that represents the absolute expiration date for the item being added. When this time arrives, the object is automatically removed from the cache. Items not subject to absolute expiration dates must use the *NoAbsoluteExpiration* constants representing the farthest allowable date. The absolute expiration date doesn't change after the item is used in either reading or writing.

- **Sliding Expiration**   A *TimeSpan* object, represents a relative expiration period for the item being added. When you set the parameter to a non-null value, the expiration-date parameter is automatically set to the current time plus the sliding period. If you explicitly set the sliding expiration, you cannot set the absolute expiration date too. From the user's perspective, these are mutually exclusive parameters. If the item is accessed before its natural expiration time, the sliding period is automatically renewed.

- **Priority**   A value picked out of the *CacheItemPriority* enumeration, denotes the priority of the item. It is a value ranging from *Low* to *NotRemovable*. The default level of priority is *Normal*. The priority level determines the importance of the item; items with a lower priority are removed first.

■ **Removal Callback**   If specified, indicates the function that the ASP.NET *Cache* object calls back when the item will be removed from the cache. In this way, applications can be notified when their own items are removed from the cache no matter what the reason is. As mentioned in Chapter 15, when the session state works in *InProc* mode, a removal callback function is used to fire the *Session_End* event. The delegate type used for this callback is *CacheItemRemoveCallback*.

There are basically three ways to add new items to the ASP.NET *Cache* object—the *set* accessor of the *Item* property, the *Add* method, and the *Insert* method. The *Item* property allows you to indicate only the key and the value. The *Add* method has only one signature that includes all the aforementioned arguments. The *Insert* method is the most flexible of all options and provides the following four overloads:

```
public void Insert(string, object);
public void Insert(string, object, CacheDependency);
public void Insert(string, object, CacheDependency, DateTime, TimeSpan);
public void Insert(string, object, CacheDependency, DateTime, TimeSpan,
    CacheItemPriority, CacheItemRemovedCallback);
```

The following code snippet shows the typical call that is performed under the hood when the *Item* set accessor is used:

```
Insert(key, value, null, Cache.NoAbsoluteExpiration,
    Cache.NoSlidingExpiration, CacheItemPriority.Normal, null);
```

If you use the *Add* method to insert an item whose key matches that of an existing item, no exception is raised, nothing happens, and the method returns *null*.

Removing Items from the Cache

All items marked with an expiration policy, or a dependency, are automatically removed from the cache when something happens in the system to invalidate them. To programmatically remove an item, on the other hand, you resort to the *Remove* method. Note that this method removes any item, including those marked with the highest level of priority (*NotRemovable*). The following code snippet shows how to call the *Remove* method:

```
object oldValue = Cache.Remove("MyItem");
```

Normally, the method returns the value just removed from the cache. However, if the specified key is not found, the method fails and *null* is returned, but no exception is ever raised.

When items with an associated callback function are removed from the cache, a value from the *CacheItemRemovedReason* enumeration is passed on to the function to justify the operation. The enumeration includes the values listed in Table 16-3.

TABLE 16-3 The *CacheItemRemovedReason* Enumeration

Reason	Description
DependencyChanged	Removed because the associated dependency changed.
Expired	Removed because expired.
Removed	Programmatically removed from the cache using *Remove*. Notice that a *Removed* event might also be fired if an existing item is replaced either through *Insert* or the *Item* property.
Underused	Removed by the system to free memory.

If the item being removed is associated with a callback, the function is executed immediately after having removed the item.

Tracking Item Dependencies

Items added to the cache through the *Add* or *Insert* method can be linked to an array of files and directories as well as to an array of existing cache items, database tables, or external events. The link between the new item and its cache dependency is maintained using an instance of the *CacheDependency* class. The *CacheDependency* object can represent a single file or directory or an array of files and directories. In addition, it can also represent an array of cache keys—that is, keys of other items stored in the *Cache*—and other custom dependency objects to monitor—for example, database tables or external events.

The *CacheDependency* class has quite a long list of constructors that provide for the possibilities listed in Table 16-4.

TABLE 16-4 The *CacheDependency* Constructor List

Constructor	Description
String	A file path—that is, a URL to a file or a directory name
String[]	An array of file paths
String, DateTime	A file path monitored starting at the specified time
String[], DateTime	An array of file paths monitored starting at the specified time
String[], String[]	An array of file paths, and an array of cache keys
String[], String[], CacheDependency	An array of file paths, an array of cache keys, and a separate *CacheDependency* object
String[], String[], DateTime	An array of file paths and an array of cache keys monitored starting at the specified time
String[], String[], CacheDependency, DateTime	An array of file paths, an array of cache keys, and a separate instance of the *CacheDependency* class monitored starting at the specified time

Any change in any of the monitored objects invalidates the current item. It's interesting to note that you can set a time to start monitoring for changes. By default, monitoring begins right after the item is stored in the cache. A *CacheDependency* object can be made dependent on another instance of the same class. In this case, any change detected on the items controlled by the separate object results in a broken dependency and the subsequent invalidation of the present item.

> **Note** Starting with ASP.NET 2.0, cache dependencies underwent some significant changes and improvements in. In previous versions, the *CacheDependency* class was sealed and not further inheritable. As a result, the only dependency objects you could work with were those linking to files, directories, or other cached items. Now, the *CacheDependency* class is inheritable and can be used as a base to build custom dependencies. In addition, ASP.NET 2.0 and newer versions come with a built-in class to monitor database tables for changes. We'll examine custom dependencies shortly.

In the following code snippet, the item is associated with the timestamp of a file. The net effect is that any change made to the file that affects the timestamp invalidates the item, which will then be removed from the cache.

```
CacheDependency dep = new CacheDependency(filename);
Cache.Insert(key, value, dep);
```

Bear in mind that the *CacheDependency* object needs to take file and directory names expressed through absolute file system paths.

Defining a Removal Callback

Item removal is an event independent from the application's behavior and control. The difficulty with item removal is that because the application is oblivious to what has happened, it attempts to access the removed item later and gets only a null value back. To work around this issue, you can either check for the item's existence before access is attempted or, if you think you need to know about removal in a timely manner, register a callback and reload the item if it's invalidated. This approach makes particularly good sense if the cached item just represents the content of a tracked file or query.

The following code-behind class demonstrates how to read the contents of a Web server's file and cache it with a key named "MyData." The item is inserted with a removal callback. The callback simply re-reads and reloads the file if the removal reason is *DependencyChanged*.

```csharp
void Load_Click(object sender, EventArgs e)
{
    AddFileContentsToCache("data.xml");
}
void Read_Click(object sender, EventArgs e)
{
    object data = Cache["MyData"];
    if (data == null)
    {
        contents.Text = "[No data available]";
        return;
    }
    contents.Text = (string) data;
}
void AddFileContentsToCache(string fileName)
{
    string file = Server.MapPath(fileName);
    StreamReader reader = new StreamReader(file);
    string buf = reader.ReadToEnd();
    reader.Close();

    // Create and display the contents
    CreateAndCacheItem(buf, file);
    contents.Text = Cache["MyData"].ToString();
}
void CreateAndCacheItem(object buf, string file)
{
    CacheItemRemovedCallback removal;
    removal = new CacheItemRemovedCallback(ReloadItemRemoved);

    CacheDependency dep = new CacheDependency(file);
    Cache.Insert("MyData", buf, dep, Cache.NoAbsoluteExpiration,
        Cache.NoSlidingExpiration, CacheItemPriority.Normal, removal);
}
void ReloadItemRemoved(string key, object value,
        CacheItemRemovedReason reason)
{
    if (reason == CacheItemRemovedReason.DependencyChanged)
    {
        // At this time the item has been removed. We get fresh data and
        // re-insert the item
        if (key == "MyData")
            AddFileContentsToCache("data.xml");

        // This code runs asynchronously with respect to the application,
        // as soon as the dependency gets broken. To test it, add some
        // code here to trace the event
    }
}
void Remove_Click(object sender, EventArgs e)
{
    Cache.Remove("MyData");
}
```

Figure 16-2 shows a sample page to test the behavior of the caching API when dependencies are used. If the underlying file has changed, the *dependency-changed* event is notified and the new contents are automatically loaded. So the next time you read from the cache you get fresh data. If the cached item is removed, any successive attempt to read returns *null*.

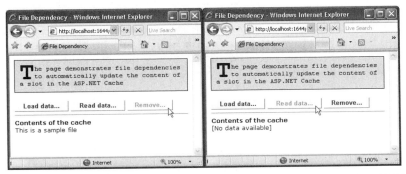

FIGURE 16-2 A sample page to test the behavior of removal callbacks in the ASP.NET cache.

Note that the item removal callback is a piece of code defined by a user page but automatically run by the *Cache* object as soon as the removal event is fired. The code contained in the removal callback runs asynchronously with respect to the page. If the removal event is related to a broken dependency, the *Cache* object will execute the callback as soon as the notification is detected.

If you add an object to the *Cache* and make it dependent on a file, directory, or key that doesn't exist, the item is regularly cached and marked with a dependency as usual. If the file, directory, or key is created later, the dependency is broken and the cached item is invalidated. In other words, if the dependency item doesn't exist, it's virtually created with a null timestamp or empty content.

> **Note** Once an item bound to one or more dependencies is removed from the cache, it stops monitoring for changes. Further changes to, say, the underlying file won't be caught just because the item is no longer in the cache. You can verify this behavior by loading some data as in Figure 16-2. Next, you click *Remove* to dispose of the item and modify the underlying file. Later, if you try to re-read the item it'll return *null* because the element is no longer in the cache.

To define a removal callback, you first declare a variable of type *CacheItemRemovedCallback*. Next, you instantiate this member with a new delegate object with the right signature.

```
CacheItemRemovedCallback removal;
removal = new CacheItemRemovedCallback(ReloadItemRemoved);
```

The *CacheDependency* object is simply passed the *removal* delegate member, which executes the actual function code for the *Cache* object to call back.

> **Tip** If you define a removal callback function through a static method, you avoid an instance
> of the class that contains the method to be kept in memory all the time to support the callback.
> Static methods (that is, *Shared* methods according to the Microsoft Visual Basic .NET jargon) are
> callable on a class even when no instance of the class has been created. Note, though, that this
> choice raises other issues as far as trying to use the callback to re-insert a removed item. In this
> case, therefore, you reasonably need to access a method on the page class, which is not permit-
> ted from within a static member. To work around this issue, you create a static field, say *ThisPage*,
> and set it to the page object (the *this* keyword in C# or *Me* in Visual Basic .NET) during the
> *Page_Init* event. You then invoke any object-specific method through the static *ThisPage*
> member, even from within a static method.

Setting the Item's Priority

Each item in the cache is given a priority—that is, a value picked up from the
CacheItemPriority enumeration. A priority is a value ranging from *Low* (lowest) to
NotRemovable (highest), with the default set to *Normal*. The priority is supposed to
determine the importance of the item for the *Cache* object. The higher the priority is, the
more chances the item has to stay in memory even when the system resources are going
dangerously down.

If you want to give a particular priority level to an item being added to the cache, you have
to use either the *Add* or *Insert* method. The priority can be any value listed in Table 16-5.

TABLE 16-5 Priority Levels in the *Cache* Object

Priority	Value	Description
Low	1	Items with this level of priority are the first items to be deleted from the cache as the server frees system memory.
BelowNormal	2	Intermediate level of priority between *Normal* and *Low*.
Normal	3	Default priority level. It is assigned to all items added using the *Item* property.
Default	3	Same as *Normal*.
AboveNormal	4	Intermediate level of priority between *Normal* and *High*.
High	5	Items with this level of priority are the last items to be removed from the cache as the server frees memory.
NotRemovable	6	Items with this level of priority are never removed from the cache. Use this level with extreme care.

The *Cache* object is designed with two goals in mind. First, it has to be efficient and built
for easy programmatic access to the global repository of application data. Second, it has
to be smart enough to detect when the system is running low on memory resources and

to clear elements to free memory. This trait clearly differentiates the *Cache* object from *HttpApplicationState*, which maintains its objects until the end of the application (unless the application itself frees those items). The technique used to eliminate low-priority and seldom-used objects is known as *scavenging*.

Controlling Data Expiration

Priority level and changed dependencies are two of the causes that could lead a cached item to be automatically garbage-collected from the *Cache*. Another possible cause for a premature removal from the *Cache* is infrequent use associated with an expiration policy. By default, all items added to the cache have no expiration date, neither absolute nor relative. If you add items by using either the *Add* or *Insert* method, you can choose between two mutually exclusive expiration policies: absolute and sliding expiration.

Absolute expiration is when a cached item is associated with a *DateTime* value and is removed from the cache as the specified time is reached. The *DateTime.MaxValue* field, and its more general alias *NoAbsoluteExpiration*, can be used to indicate the last date value supported by the .NET Framework and to subsequently indicate that the item will never expire.

Sliding expiration implements a sort of relative expiration policy. The idea is that the object expires after a certain interval. In this case, though, the interval is automatically renewed after each access to the item. Sliding expiration is rendered through a *TimeSpan* object—a type that in the .NET Framework represents an interval of time. The *TimeSpan.Zero* field represents the empty interval and is also the value associated with the *NoSlidingExpiration* static field on the *Cache* class. When you cache an item with a sliding expiration of 10 minutes, you use the following code:

```
Insert(key, value, null, Cache.NoAbsoluteExpiration,
    TimeSpan.FromMinutes(10), CacheItemPriority.Normal, null);
```

Internally, the item is cached with an absolute expiration date given by the current time plus the specified *TimeSpan* value. In light of this, the preceding code could have been rewritten as follows:

```
Insert(key, value, null, DateTime.Now.AddMinutes(10),
    Cache.NoSlidingExpiration, CacheItemPriority.Normal, null);
```

However, a subtle difference still exists between the two code snippets. In the former case— that is, when sliding expiration is explicitly turned on—each access to the item resets the absolute expiration date to the time of the last access plus the time span. In the latter case, because sliding expiration is explicitly turned off, any access to the item doesn't change the absolute expiration time.

Statistics About Memory Usage

Immediately after initialization, the *Cache* collects statistical information about the memory in the system and the current status of the system resources. Next, it registers a timer to invoke a callback function at one-second intervals. The callback function periodically updates and reviews the memory statistics and, if needed, activates the scavenging module. Memory statistics are collected using a bunch of Win32 API functions to obtain information about the system's current usage of both physical and virtual memory.

The *Cache* object classifies the status of the system resources in terms of low and high pressure. Each value corresponds to a different percentage of occupied memory. Typically, low pressure is in the range of 15 percent to 40 percent, while high pressure is measured from 45 percent to 65 percent of memory occupation. When the memory pressure exceeds the guard level, seldom-used objects are the first to be removed according to their priority.

Practical Issues

Caching is a critical factor for the success of a Web application. Caching mostly relates to getting quick access to prefetched data that saves you roundtrips, queries, and any other sort of heavy operations. Caching is important also for writing, especially in systems with a high volume of data to be written. By posting requests for writing to a kind of intermediate memory structure, you decouple the main body of the application from the service in charge of writing. Some people call this a *batch update*, but in the end it is nothing more than a form of caching for data to write.

The caching API provides you with the necessary tools to build a bullet-proof caching strategy. When it comes to this, though, a few practical issues arise.

Should I Cache or Should I Fetch?

There's just one possible answer to this question—it depends. It depends on the characteristics of the application and the expected goals. For an application that must optimize throughput and serve requests in the shortest possible amount of time, caching is essential. The quantity of data you cache and the amount of time you cache it are the two parameters you need to play with to arrive at a good solution.

Caching is about reusing data, so data that is not often used in the lifetime of the application is not a good candidate for the cache. In addition to being frequently used, cacheable data is also general-purpose data rather than data that is specific to a request or a session. If your application manages data with these characteristics, cache them with no fear.

Caching is about memory, and memory is relatively cheap. However, a bad application design can easily drive the application to unpleasant out-of-memory errors regardless of the cost of a memory chip. On the other hand, caching can boost the performance just enough to ease your pain and give you more time to devise a serious refactoring.

Sometimes you face users who claim an absolute need for live data. Sure, data parked in the cache is static, unaffected by concurrent events, and not fully participating in the life of the application. Can your users afford data that has not been updated for a few seconds? With a few exceptions, the answer is, "Sure, they can." In a canonical Web application, there's virtually no data that can't be cached at least for a second or two. No matter what end users claim, caching can realistically be applied to the vast majority of scenarios. Real-time systems and systems with a high degree of concurrency (for example, a booking application) are certainly an exception, but most of the time a slight delay of one or two seconds can make the application run faster under stress conditions without affecting the quality of the service.

In the end, you should be considering caching all the time and filter it out in favor of direct data access only in very special situations. As a practical rule, when users claim they need live data, you should try with a counterexample to prove to them that a few seconds of delay are still acceptable and maximize hardware and software investments.

Fetching to get the real data is an option, but it's usually the most expensive one. If you choose that option, make sure you really need it. Accessing cached data is faster if the data you get in this way makes sense to the application. On the other hand, be aware that caching requires memory. If abused, it can lead to out-of-memory errors and performance hits.

Building a Wrapper Cache Object

As mentioned, no data stored in the ASP.NET cache is guaranteed to stay there when a piece of code attempts to read it. For the safety of the application, you should never rely on the value returned by the *Get* method or the *Item* property. The following pattern keeps you on the safe side:

```
object data = Cache["MyData"];
if (data != null)
{
    // The data is here, process it
    ...
}
```

The code snippet deliberately omits the *else* branch. What should you do if the requested item is *null*? You can abort the ongoing operation and display a friendly message to the user, or you can perhaps reload the data with a new fetch. Whatever approach you opt for, it will probably not work for just any piece of data you can have in the cache. You'll most likely need to decide on a case by case basis how best to reload the cache.

When it comes to building a cache layer, you're better off thinking in a domain-based way. You should avoid caching data as individual elements, with the key being the only clue to retrieve the element later. You can build a helper class with domain-specific properties bound to cache entries. Here's an example.

```
public static class MyCache
{
   protected static class MyCacheEntries
   {
      public const string Customers = "Customers";
   }

   public static CustomerCollection Customers
   {
      get
      {
         object o = HttpContext.Current.Cache[MyCacheEntries.Customers];
         if (o == null)
         {
            HttpContext.Current.Trace.Warn("Empty cache--reloading...");
            LoadCustomers();
            o = HttpContext.Current.Cache[MyCacheEntries.Customers];
         }
         return (CustomerCollection) o;
      }
   }

   protected static void LoadCustomers()
   {
      // Get data
      CustomerCollection coll = ProAspNet20.DAL.Customers.LoadAll();

      // Set the item (5 seconds duration)
      HttpContext.Current.Cache.Insert(MyCacheEntries.Customers, coll,
         null, DateTime.Now.AddSeconds(5), Cache.NoSlidingExpiration);
   }
}
```

The *MyCache* class defines a property named *Customers* of type *CustomerCollection*. The contents of this property comes from the sample Data Access Layer (DAL) we discussed in Chapter 10, and it's stored in the cache for a duration of 5 seconds. The *Customers* property hides all the details of the cache management and ensures the availability of valid data to host pages. If the cached item is not there because it has expired (or it has been removed), the *get* accessor of the property takes care of reloading the data.

> **Note** If you move the preceding code to a non-code-behind class, you can't access the ASP. NET cache object using the plain *Cache* keyword. ASP.NET has no intrinsic objects like classic ASP, meaning that all objects you invoke must be public or reachable properties on the current class or its parent. Just as we did in the previous example of the *MyCache* class, you need to qualify the cache using the static property *HttpContext.Current*.

A caller page needs only the following code to populate a grid with the results in the cache:

```
CustomerCollection data = MyCache.Customers;
CustomerList.DataTextField = "CompanyName";
CustomerList.DataValueField = "ID";
CustomerList.DataSource = data;
CustomerList.DataBind();
```

By writing a wrapper class around the specific data you put into the cache, you can more easily implement a safe pattern for data access that prevents null references and treats each piece of data appropriately. In addition, the resulting code is more readable and easy to maintain.

> **Note** This approach is potentially more powerful than using the built-in cache capabilities of data source controls. First and foremost, such a wrapper class encapsulates all the data you need to keep in the cache and not just the data bound to a control. Second, it gives you more control over the implementation—you can set the priority and removal callback, implement complex dependencies, and choose the name of the entry. Next, it works with any data and not just with ADO.NET objects, as is the case with *SqlDataSource* and *ObjectDataSource*. You can use this approach instead while building your own DAL so that you come up with a bunch of classes that support caching to bind to data source controls. If your pages are quite simple (for example, some data bound to a grid or other data-bound controls) and you're using only *DataSet* or *DataTable*, the caching infrastructure of data source controls will probably suit your needs.

Enumerating Items in the Cache

Although most of the time you simply access cached items by name, you might find it useful to know how to enumerate the contents of the cache to list all stored public items. As mentioned, the *Cache* class is a sort of collection that is instantiated during the application's startup. Being a collection, its contents can be easily enumerated using a *for..each* statement. The following code shows how to copy the current contents of the ASP.NET cache to a newly created *DataTable* object:

```
private DataTable CacheToDataTable()
{
    DataTable dt = CreateDataTable();
    foreach(DictionaryEntry elem in HttpContext.Current.Cache)
        AddItemToTable(dt, elem);
    return dt;
}
private DataTable CreateDataTable()
{
    DataTable dt = new DataTable();
    dt.Columns.Add("Key", typeof(string));
    dt.Columns.Add("Value", typeof(string));
    return dt;
}
```

```
private void AddItemToTable(DataTable dt, DictionaryEntry elem)
{
    DataRow row = dt.NewRow();
    row["Key"] = elem.Key.ToString();
    row["Value"] = elem.Value.ToString();
    dt.Rows.Add(row);
}
```

The *DataTable* contains two columns, one for the key and one for the value of the item stored. The value is rendered using the *ToString* method, meaning that the string and numbers will be loyally rendered but objects will typically be rendered through their class name.

> **Important** When you enumerate the items in the cache, only two pieces of information are available—the key and value. From a client page, there's no way to read the priority of a given item or perhaps its expiration policy. When you enumerate the contents of the *Cache* object, a generic *DictionaryEntry* object is returned with no property or method pointing to more specific information. To get more information, you should consider using the .NET Reflection API.
>
> Also note that because the *Cache* object stores data internally using a hashtable, the enumerator returns contained items in an apparently weird order, neither alphabetical nor time-based. The order in which items are returned, instead, is based on the internal hash code used to index items.

Clearing the Cache

The .NET Framework provides no method on the *Cache* class to programmatically clear all the content. The following code snippet shows how to build one:

```
public void Clear()
{
    foreach(DictionaryEntry elem in Cache)
    {
        string s = elem.Key.ToString();
        Cache.Remove(s);
    }
}
```

Even though the ASP.NET cache is implemented to maintain a neat separation between the application's and system's items, it is preferable that you delete items in the cache individually. If you have several items to maintain, you might want to build your own wrapper class and expose one single method to clear all the cached data.

Cache Synchronization

Whenever you read or write an individual cache item, from a threading perspective you're absolutely safe. The ASP.NET *Cache* object guarantees that no other concurrently running threads can ever interfere with what you're doing. If you need to ensure that multiple operations on the *Cache* object occur atomically, that's a different story. Consider the following code snippet:

```
int counter = -1;
object o = Cache["Counter"];
if (o == null)
{
    // Retrieve the last good known value from a database
    // or return a default value
    counter = RetrieveLastKnownValue();
}
else
{
    counter = (int) Cache["Counter"];
    counter ++;
    Cache["Counter"] = counter;
}
```

The *Cache* object is accessed repeatedly in the context of an atomic operation—incrementing a counter. Although individual accesses to *Cache* are thread-safe, there's no guarantee that other threads won't kick in between the various calls. If there's potential contention on the cached value, you should consider using additional locking constructs, such as the C# *lock* statement (*SyncLock* in Visual Basic .NET).

Important Where should you put the lock? If you directly lock the *Cache* object, you might run into trouble. ASP.NET uses the *Cache* object extensively and directly locking the *Cache* object might have a serious impact on the overall performance of the application. However, most of the time ASP.NET doesn't access the cache via the *Cache* object; rather, it accesses the direct data container—that is the *CacheSingle* or *CacheMultiple* class. In this regard, a lock on the *Cache* object probably won't affect many ASP.NET components; regardless, it's a risk that personally I wouldn't like to take. By locking the *Cache* object, you also risk blocking HTTP modules and handlers active in the pipeline, as well as other pages and sessions in the application that need to use cache entries different from the ones you want to serialize access to.

The best way out seems to be using a synchronizer—that is, an intermediate but global object that you lock before entering in a piece of code sensitive to concurrency:

```
lock(yourSynchronizer) {
    // Access the Cache here. This pattern must be replicated for
    // each access to the cache that requires serialization.
}
```

The synchronizer object must be global to the application. For example, it can be a static member defined in the *global.asax* file.

Per-Request Caching

Although you normally tend to cache only global data and data of general interest, to squeeze out every little bit of performance you can also cache per-request data that is long-lived even though it's used only by a particular page. You place this information in the *Cache* object.

Another form of per-request caching is possible to improve performance. Working information shared by all controls and components participating in the processing of a request can be stored in a global container for the duration of the request. In this case, though, you might want to use the *Items* collection on the *HttpContext* class (discussed in Chapter 14) to park the data because it is automatically freed up at the end of the request and doesn't involve implicit or explicit locking like *Cache*.

Designing a Custom Dependency

Let's say it up front: writing a custom cache dependency object is no picnic. You should have a very good reason to do so, and you should carefully design the new functionality before proceeding. As mentioned, from ASP.NET 2.0 onward the *CacheDependency* class is inheritable—you can derive your own class from it to implement an external source of events to invalidate cached items.

The base *CacheDependency* class handles all the wiring of the new dependency object to the ASP.NET cache and all the issues surrounding synchronization and disposal. It also saves you from implementing a start-time feature from scratch—you inherit that capability from the base class constructors. (The start-time feature allows you to start tracking dependencies at a particular time.)

Let's start reviewing the original limitations of *CacheDependency* that have led to removing the *sealed* attribute on the class, making it fully inheritable.

What Cache Dependencies Cannot Do in ASP.NET 1.x

In ASP.NET 1.x, a cached item can be subject to four types of dependencies: time, files, other items, and other dependencies. The ASP.NET 1.x *Cache* object addresses many developers' needs and has made building in-memory collections of frequently accessed data much easier and more effective. However, this mechanism is not perfect, nor is it extensible.

Let's briefly consider a real-world scenario. What type of data do you think a distributed data-driven application would place in the ASP.NET *Cache*? In many cases, it would simply be the results of a database query. But unless you code it yourself—which can really be tricky—the object doesn't support database dependency. A database dependency would invalidate a cached result set when a certain database table changes. In ASP.NET 1.x, the *CacheDependency* class is sealed and closed to any form of customization that gives developers a chance to invalidate cached items based on user-defined conditions.

As far as the *Cache* object is concerned, the biggest difference between ASP.NET 1.x and newer versions is that newer versions support custom dependencies. This was achieved by making the *CacheDependency* class inheritable and providing a made-to-measure *SqlCacheDependency* cache that provides built-in database dependency limited to SQL Server 7.0 and later.

Extensions to the *CacheDependency* Base Class

To fully support derived classes and to facilitate their integration into the ASP.NET caching infrastructure, a bunch of new public and protected members have been added to the *CacheDependency* class. They are summarized in Table 16-6.

TABLE 16-6 New Members of the *CacheDependency* Class

Member	Description
DependencyDispose	Protected method. It releases the resources used by the class.
GetUniqueID	Public method. It retrieves a unique string identifier for the object.
NotifyDependencyChanged	Protected method. It notifies the base class that the dependency represented by this object has changed.
SetUtcLastModified	Protected method. It marks the time when a dependency last changed.
UtcLastModified	Public read-only property. It gets the time when the dependency was last changed. This property also exists in version 1.x, but it is not publicly accessible.

As mentioned, a custom dependency class relies on its parent for any interaction with the *Cache* object. The *NotifyDependencyChanged* method is called by classes that inherit *CacheDependency* to tell the base class that the dependent item has changed. In response, the base class updates the values of the *HasChanged* and *UtcLastModified* properties. Any cleanup code needed when the custom cache dependency object is dismissed should go into the *DependencyDispose* method.

Getting Change Notifications

As you might have noticed, nothing in the public interface of the base *CacheDependency* class allows you to insert code to check whether a given condition—the heart of the dependency—is met. Why is this? The *CacheDependency* class was designed to support only a limited set of well-known dependencies—against changes to files or other items.

To detect file changes, the *CacheDependency* object internally sets up a file monitor object and receives a call from it whenever the monitored file or directory changes. The *CacheDependency* class creates a *FileSystemWatcher* object and passes it an event handler. A similar approach is used to establish a programmatic link between the *CacheDependency* object and the *Cache* object and its items. The *Cache* object invokes a *CacheDependency* internal method when one of the monitored items changes. What does this all mean to the developer?

A custom dependency object must be able to receive notifications from the external data source it is monitoring. In most cases, this is really complicated if you can't bind to existing notification mechanisms (such as file system monitor or SQL Server 2005 notifications). When the notification of a change in the source is detected, the dependency uses the parent's infrastructure to notify the cache of the event. We'll consider a practical example in a moment.

The *AggregateCacheDependency* Class

Starting with ASP.NET 2.0, not only can you create a single dependency on an entry, you can also aggregate dependencies. For example, you can make a cache entry dependent on both a disk file and a SQL Server table. The following code snippet shows how to create a cache entry, named *MyData*, that is dependent on two different files:

```
// Creates an array of CacheDependency objects
CacheDependency dep1 = new CacheDependency(fileName1);
CacheDependency dep2 = new CacheDependency(fileName2);
CacheDependency deps[] = {dep1, dep2};

// Creates an aggregate object
AggregateCacheDependency aggDep = new AggregateCacheDependency();
aggDep.Add(deps);
Cache.Insert("MyData", data, aggDep)
```

Any custom cache dependency object, including *SqlCacheDependency*, inherits *CacheDependency*, so the array of dependencies can contain virtually any type of dependency.

The *AggregateCacheDependency* class is built as a custom cache dependency object and inherits the base *CacheDependency* class.

A Cache Dependency for XML Data

Suppose your application gets some key data from a custom XML file and you don't want to access the file on disk for every request. So you decide to cache the contents of the XML file, but still you'd love to detect changes to the file that occur while the application is up and running. Is this possible? You bet. You arrange a file dependency and you're done.

In this case, though, any update to the file that modifies the timestamp is perceived as a critical change. As a result, the related entry in the cache is invalidated and you're left with no choice other than re-reading the XML data from the disk. The rub here is that you are forced to re-read everything even if the change is limited to a comment or to a node that is not relevant to your application.

Because you want the cached data to be invalidated only when certain nodes change, you create a made-to-measure cache dependency class to monitor the return value of a given XPath expression on an XML file.

Note If the target data source provides you with a built-in and totally asynchronous notification mechanism (such as the command notification mechanism of SQL Server 2005), you just use it. Otherwise, to detect changes in the monitored data source, you can only poll the resource at a reasonable rate.

Designing the *XmlDataCacheDependency* Class

To better understand the concept of custom dependencies, think of the following example. You need to cache the inner text of a particular node in an XML file. You can define a custom dependency class that caches the current value upon instantiation and reads the file periodically to detect changes. When a change is detected, the cached item bound to the dependency is invalidated.

Note Admittedly, polling might not be the right approach for this particular problem. Later on, in fact, I'll briefly discuss a more effective implementation. Be aware, though, that polling is a valid and common technique for custom cache dependencies.

A good way to poll a local or remote resource is through a timer callback. Let's break the procedure into a few steps:

1. The custom *XmlDataCacheDependency* class gets ready for the overall functionality. It initializes some internal properties and caches the polling rate, file name, and XPath expression to find the subtree to monitor.

2. After initialization, the dependency object sets up a timer callback to access the file periodically and check contents.

3. In the callback, the return value of the XPath expression is compared to the previously stored value. If the two values differ, the linked cache item is promptly invalidated.

There's no need for the developer to specify details on how the cache dependency is broken or set up. The *CacheDependency* class in ASP.NET 2.0 takes care of it entirely.

> **Note** If you're curious to know how the *Cache* detects when a dependency is broken, read on. When an item bound to a custom dependency object is added to the *Cache*, an additional entry is created and linked to the initial item. *NotifyDependencyChanged* simply dirties this additional element which, in turn, invalidates the original cache item. Figure 16-3 illustrates the connections.

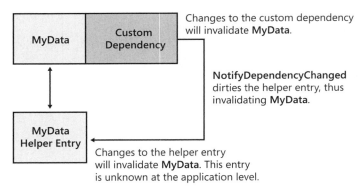

FIGURE 16-3 Custom dependencies use helper cache entries to invalidate any items under their control.

Implementing the Dependency

The following source code shows the core implementation of the custom *XmlDataCacheDependency* class:

```
public class XmlDataCacheDependency : CacheDependency
{
    // Internal members
    static Timer _timer;
    int _pollSecs = 10;
    string _fileName;
    string _xpathExpression;
    string _currentValue;

    public XmlDataCacheDependency(string file, string xpath, int pollTime)
    {
        // Set internal members
        _fileName = file;
        _xpathExpression = xpath;
        _pollSecs = pollTime;

        // Get the current value
        _currentValue = CheckFile();

        // Set the timer
        if (_timer == null) {
            int ms = _pollSecs * 1000;
            TimerCallback cb = new TimerCallback(XmlDataCallback);
            _timer = new Timer(cb, this, ms, ms);
        }
    }
}
```

```
public string CurrentValue
{
    get { return _currentValue; }
}

public void XmlDataCallback(object sender)
{
    // Get a reference to THIS dependency object
    XmlDataCacheDependency dep = (XmlDataCacheDependency) sender;

    // Check for changes and notify the base class if any are found
    string value = CheckFile();
    if (!String.Equals(_currentValue, value))
        dep.NotifyDependencyChanged(dep, EventArgs.Empty);
}

public string CheckFile()
{
    // Evaluates the XPath expression in the file
    XmlDocument doc = new XmlDocument();
    doc.Load(_fileName);
    XmlNode node = doc.SelectSingleNode(_xpathExpression);

    return node.InnerText;
}

protected override void DependencyDispose()
{
    // Kill the timer and then proceed as usual
    _timer.Dispose();
    _timer = null;
    base.DependencyDispose();
}
}
```

When the cache dependency is created, the file is parsed and the value of the XPath expression is stored in an internal member. At the same time, a timer is started to repeat the operation at regular intervals. The return value is compared against the value stored in the constructor code. If the two are different, the *NotifyDependencyChanged* method is invoked on the base *CacheDependency* class to invalidate the linked content in the ASP.NET *Cache*.

Testing the Custom Dependency

How can you use this dependency class in a Web application? It's as easy as it seems—you just use it in any scenario where a *CacheDependency* object is acceptable. For example, you create an instance of the class in the *Page_Load* event and pass it to the *Cache.Insert* method:

```
protected const string CacheKeyName = "MyData";
protected void Page_Load(object sender, EventArgs e)
{
    if (!IsPostBack)
    {
```

```
        // Create a new entry with a custom dependency
        XmlDataCacheDependency dep = new XmlDataCacheDependency(
            Server.MapPath("employees.xml"),
            "MyDataSet/NorthwindEmployees/Employee[employeeid=3]/lastname",
            1);
        Cache.Insert(CacheKeyName, dep.CurrentValue, dep);
    }

    // Refresh the UI
    Msg.Text = Display();
}
```

You write the rest of the page as usual, paying close attention to accessing the specified
Cache key. The reason for this is that because of the dependency, the key could be null.
Here's an example:

```
protected string Display()
{
    object o = Cache[CacheKeyName];
    if (o == null)
        return "[No data available--dependency broken]";
    else
        return (string) o;
}
```

The *XmlDataCacheDependency* object allows you to control changes that occur on a file and
decide which are relevant and might require you to invalidate the cache. The sample dependency uses XPath expressions to identify a subset of nodes to monitor for changes. For
simplicity, only the first node of the output of the XPath expression is considered. The sample
XPath expression monitors in the sample *employees.xml* file the *lastname* node of the subtree
where *employeeid=3*:

```
<MyDataSet>
    <NorthwindEmployees>
        ...
        <Employee>
            <employeeid>3</employeeid>
            <lastname>Leverling</lastname>
            <firstname>Janet</firstname>
            <title>Sales Representative</title>
        </Employee>
        ...
    </NorthwindEmployees>
</MyDataSet>
```

The XML file, the cache dependency object, and the preceding sample page produce the
output shown in Figure 16-4.

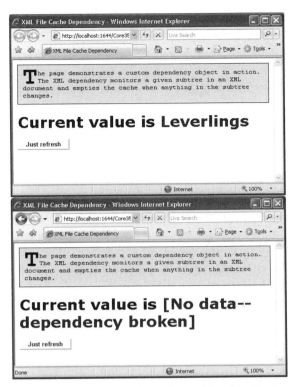

FIGURE 16-4 The custom dependency object in action in a sample page.

The screen shot at the top is what users see when they first invoke the page. The page at the bottom is what they get when the cached value is invalidated because of a change in the monitored node of the XML file. Note that changes to other nodes, except *lastname* where *employeeid=3*, are blissfully ignored and don't affect the cached value.

> **Note** I decided to implement polling in this sample custom dependency because polling is a pretty common, often mandatory, approach for custom dependencies. However, in this particular case polling is not the best option. You could set a *FileSystemWatcher* object and watch for changes to the XML file. When a change is detected, you execute the XPath expression to see whether the change is relevant for the dependency. Using an asynchronous notifier, if available, results in much better performance.

SQL Server Cache Dependency

Many ASP.NET applications query some data out of a database, cache it, and then manage to serve a report to the user. Binding the report to the data in the cache will both reduce the time required to load each report and minimize traffic to and from the database. What's the problem, then? With a report built from the cache, if the data displayed is modified in the database, users will get an out-of-date report. If updates occur at a known or predictable rate, you can set an appropriate duration for the cached data so that the report gets automatically refreshed at regular intervals. However, this contrivance just doesn't work if serving live data is critical for the application or if changes occur rarely and, worse yet, randomly. In the latter case, whatever duration you set might hit the application in one way or the other. A too-long duration creates the risk of serving outdated reports to end users which, in some cases, could undermine the business; a too-short duration burdens the application with unnecessary queries.

A database dependency is a special case of custom dependency that consists of the automatic invalidation of some cached data when the contents of the source database table changes. Not directly supported by the framework in ASP.NET 1.x, database dependencies are a native feature starting with ASP.NET 2.0. In ASP.NET 2.0 and beyond, you find an ad hoc class—*SqlCacheDependency*—that inherits *CacheDependency* and supports dependencies on SQL Server tables. More precisely, the class is compatible with MSDE, SQL Server 7.0, and subsequent SQL Server versions (including SQL Server 2005).

Under the Hood of Database Dependencies

With the notable exception of SQL Server 2005, no database today offers listening features to detect when relevant changes occur. This means that on SQL Server 7.0, SQL Server 2000, and non-SQL Server databases you must create a database-level infrastructure that makes table changes emerge, allows them to be captured, and notifies the ASP.NET cache of the changes.

In the past several years, a few techniques have been investigated by the ASP.NET team and developers in the community. None of the techniques is perfect, but all are worth a look if you plan to implement database cache invalidation in ASP.NET 1.x applications.

A database cache invalidation system is based on two key elements—a mechanism to detect changes on the database, and a mechanism to notify ASP.NET of the changes. To detect changes, triggers are the most commonly used technique. You need to have a trigger active on each table in a database that you want to monitor for changes. The trigger captures insertions, deletions, and updates on a table and does something with them. What exactly it does depends on the second mechanism you implement. Various approaches have been tested over time:

- An extended stored procedure invokes an application-specific HTTP handler (which is simpler than a plain page). The handler receives the key of the cache item that has been invalidated and removes it from the cache.

- An extended stored procedure modifies the timestamp of a disk file that the cached data is dependent upon.

Although some people don't particularly like the use of triggers, as I see things the real issue here is the use of extended stored procedures. They have to be written in C++ and deployed manually to SQL Server. Furthermore, they require administrative permissions because they run external programs and introduce potentially serious blocking issues. The extended stored procedure can't return until the HTTP call or the file modification is complete. What if the Web server takes a long time to respond? What if the file is locked? In the end, the database will be affected and the flow of information from it or to it might be slowed down. These solutions might work great for small applications with no scalability concerns, but they are not ideal for large, real-world sites.

> **Tip** If you don't like triggers, you might want to try T-SQL checksum functions. The following query returns a value that varies when changes are made to a table record:
>
> ```
> SELECT CHECKSUM_AGG(BINARY_CHECKSUM(*)) FROM Customers
> ```
>
> Checksum functions are reasonably fast but don't work with reference columns such as text and image. The advantage of checksum functions is that all you need to deploy on the database is a stored procedure to wrap the query just shown.

Extended stored procedures implement a push model, where the database backend pushes changes to the ASP.NET application. The reverse approach is also possible—a pull model based on polling—which is the foundation of the ASP.NET implementation of database cache invalidation.

The database to be monitored is equipped with triggers and a helper table with one record for each monitored table. Triggers update the helper table whenever the corresponding table is modified. A custom component placed in the ASP.NET cache polls this helper table looking for changes—and because it's a very small table, results are likely to be paged in SQL Server's memory for the fastest performance. When the polling component detects a change in the table, it will invalidate the linked cache item with the data used by the application.

> **Note** To implement database dependencies in ASP.NET 1.x, you start by creating a custom *CacheDependency* class along the lines of the *CacheDependency* class available in ASP.NET 2.0 and beyond. This abstract class will start a timer in the constructor and call an overridable method—say, *HasChanged*—to check for changes. The user-defined *DatabaseCacheDependency* class inherits from *CacheDependency* and overrides *HasChanged* to query against the helper table of change notifications (or checksums). To insert data in the cache bound to this dependency object, you resort to a helper method that extends the *Insert* method of the native *Cache* object. Basically, your helper insert method will create a pair of cache entries—one for the real data, and one for the dependency object polling for data. The two entries are linked so that changes to the entry with the dependency invalidate the one with real data. Details and sample code are available at *http://msdn.microsoft.com/msdnmag/issues/04/07/CuttingEdge*.

Enabling Database Dependencies

In ASP.NET 2.0 and beyond, database dependencies are implemented through the *SqlCacheDependency* class. The class works with SQL Server 7.0, SQL Server 2000, and the newer SQL Server 2005. To make it work with SQL Server 2005, much less setup work is required. Let's tackle SQL Server 7.0 and SQL Server 2000 first.

For the *SqlCacheDependency* class to work correctly, any tables that you want to monitor for changes must have notifications enabled. Enabling notifications entails administrative changes to the database that must be accomplished before the application is published. Changes include creating ad hoc triggers and stored procedures to handle any incoming UPDATE, INSERT, or DELETE statements.

You use the command-line tool *aspnet_regsql* to do any required offline work. You first enable notifications on the database, and next do the same on one or more of the database tables. Run the following command to enable notifications on the Northwind database for the local installation of SQL Server:

```
aspnet_regsql.exe -S (local) -U YourUserName -P YourPassword
                  -d Northwind -ed
```

Run the following command to enable notification on the *Customers* table:

```
aspnet_regsql.exe -S (local) -U YourUserName -P YourPassword
                  -d Northwind -et -t Customers
```

The first command adds a new table to the database whose name is *AspNet_SqlCacheTablesForChangeNotification*. In addition, a bunch of stored procedures and triggers are added. Note that you need to specify a login with enough permissions to perform all the operations.

The second command adds a trigger to the specified table and a new record to *AspNet_SqlCacheTablesForChangeNotification* that refers to the specified table. Here's the trigger:

```
CREATE TRIGGER dbo.[Customers_AspNet_SqlCacheNotification_Trigger]
ON [Customers]
FOR INSERT, UPDATE, DELETE AS BEGIN
  SET NOCOUNT ON
  EXEC dbo.AspNet_SqlCacheUpdateChangeIdStoredProcedure N'Customers'
END
```

Figure 16-5 provides a view of the structure of the change notification table. This table contains one record for each monitored table.

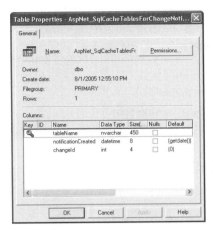

FIGURE 16-5 The structure of the *AspNet_SqlCacheTablesForChangeNotification* table.

The trigger executes the following stored procedure whenever a change occurs on the monitored table. As a result, the *changeId* column for the table is modified.

```
BEGIN
   UPDATE dbo.AspNet_SqlCacheTablesForChangeNotification WITH (ROWLOCK)
     SET changeId = changeId + 1
     WHERE tableName = @tableName
END
```

To finalize the setup of *SqlCacheDependency*, you need to add the following script to the application's *web.config* file:

```
<system.web>
  <caching>
    <sqlCacheDependency enabled="true" pollTime="1000" >
      <databases>
        <add name="Northwind" connectionStringName="NWind" />
      </databases>
    </sqlCacheDependency>
  </caching>
</system.web>
```

The *pollTime* attribute indicates (in milliseconds) the interval of the polling. In the preceding sample, any monitored table will be checked every second. Under the *<databases>* node, you find a reference to monitored databases. The *name* attribute is used only to name the dependency.. The *connectionStringName* attribute points to an entry in the *<connectionStrings>* section of the *web.config* file and denotes the connection string to access the database.

> **Note** In addition to using the *aspnet_regsql* command-line tool, you can use a program-
> ming interface to create the runtime environment that allows database cache dependencies
> for SQL Server 7 and SQL Server 2000. The following code enables the Northwind database for
> notifications:
>
> ```
> SqlCacheDependencyAdmin.EnableNotifications("Northwind");
> ```
>
> You add a table to the list of monitored tables with the following code:
>
> ```
> SqlCacheDependencyAdmin.EnableTableForNotifications(
>     "Northwind", "Employees");
> ```
>
> The *SqlCacheDependencyAdmin* class also has methods to disable previously enabled
> dependencies.

Let's see now how to create and use a *SqlCacheDependency* object.

Taking Advantage of SQL Server Dependencies

The *SqlCacheDependency* class has two constructors. The first takes a *SqlCommand* object,
and the second accepts two strings—the database name and the table name. The constructor that accepts a *SqlCommand* is intended for use only with SQL Server 2005; the other is
designed for dependencies that involve older versions of SQL Server. Functionally speaking,
the two are equivalent.

The following code creates a SQL Server dependency and binds it to a cache key:

```
protected void AddToCache(object data)
{
    string database = "Northwind";
    string table = "Customers";
    SqlCacheDependency dep = new SqlCacheDependency(database, table);
    Cache.Insert("MyData", data, dep);
}
protected void Page_Load(object sender, EventArgs e)
{
    if (!IsPostBack)
    {
        // Get some data to cache
        CustomerCollection data = Customers.LoadByCountry("USA");

        // Cache with a dependency on Customers
        AddToCache(data);
    }
}
```

The data in the cache can be linked to any data-bound control, as follows:

```
CustomerCollection data = null;
object o = Cache["MyData"];
if (o != null)
    data = (CustomerCollection)o;
else
    Trace.Warn("Null data");

CustomerList.DataTextField = "CompanyName";
CustomerList.DataSource = data;
CustomerList.DataBind();
```

When the database is updated, the *MyData* entry is invalidated and, as for the sample implementation provided here, the listbox displays empty.

> **Important** You get notification based on changes in the table as a whole. In the preceding code, we're displaying a data set that results from the following:
>
> ```
> SELECT * FROM customers WHERE country='USA'
> ```
>
> If, say, a new record is added to the *Customers* table, you get a notification no matter what the value in the *country* column is. The same happens if a record is modified or deleted where the *country* column is not USA.
>
> SQL Server 2005 offers a finer level of control and can notify applications only of changes to the database that modify the output of a specific command.

Once you are set up for table notifications, pages that use a *SqlDataSource* control can implement a smarter form of caching that monitors the bound table for changes and reloads data in case of changes:

```
<asp:SqlDataSource ID="SqlDataSource1" runat="server"
    ConnectionString="<%$ ConnectionStrings:NWind %>"
    SelectCommand="SELECT * FROM Customers"
    EnableCaching="true"
    SqlCacheDependency="Northwind:Customers">
</asp:SqlDataSource>
```

You set the *SqlCacheDependency* property to a string of the form *Database:Table*. The first token is the name of the database dependency as set in the *<databases>* section. The second token is the name of the table to monitor. You can also define multiple dependencies, separating each pair with a semi-colon:

```
<asp:SqlDataSource ID="SqlDataSource1" runat="server"
    EnableCaching="true"
    SqlCacheDependency="Northwind:Customers;Pubs:Authors"
    ...
/>
```

Note that caching must be enabled for the feature to work.

> **Note** Although I've mentioned only *SqlDataSource*, the *SqlCacheDependency* property also works with *ObjectDataSource* as long as *ObjectDataSource* returns data through ADO.NET objects.

Cache Dependencies in SQL Server 2005

As mentioned, the *SqlCacheDependency* class has two constructors, one of which takes a *SqlCommand* object as its sole argument. This constructor is used to create *SqlCacheDependency* objects for SQL Server 2005 databases. Here's how to use it:

```
protected void AddToCache()
{
    SqlConnection conn = new SqlConnection(
        ConfigurationManager.ConnectionStrings["NWind05"].ConnectionString);
    SqlCommand cmd = new SqlCommand(
        "SELECT * FROM Customers WHERE country='USA'",
        conn);

    SqlDataAdapter adapter = new SqlDataAdapter(cmd);
    DataTable data = new DataTable();
    adapter.Fill(data);

    SqlCacheDependency dep = new SqlCacheDependency(cmd);
    Cache.Insert("MyData", data, dep);
}
```

Note that with SQL Server 2005 no setup work is needed and no external objects must be added to the database. No triggers, stored procedures, and notification tables are needed.

SQL Server 2005 incorporates a made-to-measure component that monitors changes at a finer level than was possible in earlier versions. This component takes a command object and tracks all the ongoing changes to detect whether something happened to modify the result set returned by the command. When this happens, the component pushes new information to the listening object. This mechanism relies on the ADO.NET *SqlDependency* class that we discussed back in Chapter 7.

So when you instantiate a *SqlCacheDependency* object and have it guard a given command, a *SqlDependency* object wraps the command and fires an event when a change is detected. In turn, the *SqlCacheDependency* catches the event and invalidates the cached item. Figure 16-6 illustrates the data flow.

Invalidates the linked cache item

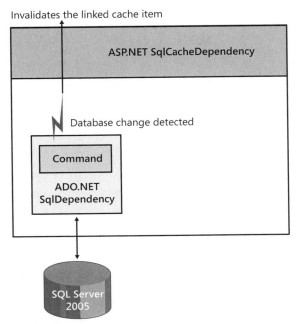

FIGURE 16-6 The internal implementation of *SqlCacheDependency* when used with SQL Server 2005.

Note The SQL Server 2005 implementation of database cache invalidation is clearly the best possible because it leverages a new infrastructure built in the database. ASP.NET applications receive an asynchronous notification of changes, which is good for performance and poses no blocking issues. Also, no setup is necessary for the feature to work. The SQL Server 7.0 and SQL Server 2000 implementation of the same feature relies on polling and requires some setup work. The ASP.NET team made the SQL dependency setup as smooth as possible, but it still requires an administrative login to get into the database to create triggers, tables, and stored procedures. This might be a problem if you're not allowed full access to the database or if you're working in an ISP scenario. Is polling the best possible option for detecting changes? All things considered, polling is a necessity when there's no built-in notification mechanism in the database. And polling a small table is more efficient than repeatedly running a query. Finally, polling doesn't suffer from blocking issues as do approaches built on extended stored procedures, and it also works great in Web farms and Web gardens. In the end, the ASP.NET team determined that polling was the best option for the broadest number of ASP.NET applications willing to support database cache invalidation.

Caching ASP.NET Pages

There are many situations where it is acceptable for a page response to be a little stale if this brings significant performance advantages. Want an example? Think of an e-commerce application and its set of pages for the products catalog. These pages are relatively expensive to create because they could require one or more database calls and likely some form of data join. All things considered, a page like this could easily cost you a few million CPU cycles. Why should you regenerate this same page a hundred times per second? Product pages tend to remain the same for weeks and are rarely updated more than once per day. Whatever the refresh rate is for the pages, there's little value in regenerating them on a per-request basis.

A much better strategy is to create the page once, cache it somewhere, and give the page output a maximum duration. Once the cached page becomes stale, the first incoming request will be served in the standard way, running the page's code, and the new page output will be cached for another period until it also becomes stale.

ASP.NET page output caching is the feature that allows you to cache page responses so that following requests can be satisfied without executing the page; instead, the requests are satisfied by simply returning the cached output. Output caching can take place at two levels—entire pages or portions of the page. Page caching is smart enough to let you save distinct output based on the requesting URL, query string or form parameters, and even custom strings.

Easy to set up and terrifically effective, output caching can either be configured declaratively through the *@OutputCache* directive or programmatically through an API built around the *HttpCachePolicy* class.

Important Page output caching is simply a way to have the application serve more pages more quickly. It has nothing to do with sophisticated caching strategies or elegant code design. In other words, it will enable your application to serve pages faster, but it won't necessarily make the application more efficient and scalable. With page output caching, you can certainly reduce the workload on the server as pages are cached downstream. Finally, be aware that page output caching works only for anonymous content. Requests for cached pages are served by Internet Information Services (IIS) 6.0 directly or by the ASP.NET worker process under IIS 5.0. In any case, a page request never reaches stages in the ASP.NET pipeline where it can be authenticated, which is a strategy employed to prevent access to protected content.

The *@OutputCache* Directive

Caching the output of a page is as easy as defining an *@OutputCache* directive at the top of the page. The directive accepts a handful of attributes, a couple of which—*Duration* and *VaryByParam*—are mandatory. The *Duration* attribute indicates in seconds how long the system should cache the page output. The *VaryByParam* attribute allows you to vary the cached output depending on the *GET* query string or form *POST* parameters. The following declaration will cache the page for one minute regardless of any *GET* or *POST* parameters:

```
<%@ OutputCache Duration="60" VaryByParam="None" %>
```

For frequently requested pages and relatively static pages, the *@OutputCache* directive is a real performance booster. With a shorter duration, even limited to one second or two, it provides a way to speed up the entire application.

The *@OutputCache* directive consists of six attributes that indicate the location of the cache, its duration, and the arguments to use to vary page caching. The list of supported attributes is shown in Table 16-7. Note that the directive can be applied to both pages (*.aspx*) and user controls (*.ascx*). Some of the attributes are valid in one case but not the other.

TABLE 16-7 Attributes of the *@OutputCache* Directive

Attribute	Applies to	Description
CacheProfile	Page	Associates a page with a group of output caching settings specified in the *web.config* file (More later). *Not supported in ASP.NET 1.x.*
Duration	Page, User control	The time, in seconds, that the page or user control is cached.
Location	Page	Specifies a valid location to store the output of a page. The attribute takes its value from the *OutputCacheLocation* enumeration.
NoStore	Page	Indicates whether to send a *Cache-Control:no-store* header to prevent additional storage of the page output. *Not supported in ASP.NET 1.x.*
Shared	User control	Indicates whether the user control output can be shared with multiple pages. It is *false* by default.
SqlDependency	Page, User control	Indicates a dependency on the specified table on a given SQL Server database. Whenever the contents of the table changes, the page output is removed from the cache. *Not supported in ASP.NET 1.x.*
VaryByControl	User control	A semicolon-separated list of strings that represent properties of the user control. Each distinct combination of values for the specified properties will originate a distinct copy of the page in the cache.
VaryByCustom	Page, User control	A semicolon-separated list of strings that lets you maintain distinct cached copies of the page based on the browser type or user-defined strings.
VaryByHeader	Page	A semicolon-separated list of HTTP headers.
VaryByParam	Page, User control	A semicolon-separated list of strings representing query string values sent with *GET* method attributes, or parameters sent using the *POST* method.

Note that the *VaryByParam* attribute is mandatory. If you omit it, a runtime exception is always thrown. However, if you don't need to vary by parameters, set the attribute to *None*. The empty string is not an acceptable value for the *VaryByParam* attribute.

Choosing a Duration for the Page Output

When the output caching service is active on a page, the *Duration* attribute indicates the number of seconds that the caching system will maintain an HTML-compiled version of the page. Next, requests for the same page, or for an existing parameterized version of the page, will be serviced while bypassing most of the ASP.NET pipeline. As mentioned, this process has two important repercussions—no authentication is possible and no code is run, meaning that no page events are fired and handled and no state is updated. The implementation of output caching varies with the ASP.NET process model in use. (See Chapter 3 for details on the ASP.NET process models.)

With the IIS 5.0 process model, any request for an ASP.NET page is always handed over to the worker process, assigned to an *HttpApplication* object, and processed by the pipeline. The ASP.NET pipeline includes an HTTP module named *OutputCacheModule* that captures two application-level events related to output caching—*ResolveRequestCache* and *UpdateRequestCache*. In particular, the module uses the *ResolveRequestCache* event handler to short-circuit the processing of requests for pages that have been cached. In the end, the request is hooked by the HTTP module and served by returning the copy of the page stored in the cache. When the page is being generated, *OutputCacheModule* grabs the output of the pages marked with the *@OutputCache* directive and stores it internally for further use. The output of the page is stored in a private slot of the ASP.NET *Cache* object. Setting the *Duration* attribute on a page sets an expiration policy for the HTTP response generated by the ASP.NET runtime. The output is cached by the module for exactly the specified number of seconds. In the meantime, all the incoming requests that hit one of the cached pages are serviced by the module rather than by the ASP.NET pipeline.

With the IIS 6.0 process model, the output caching mechanism is integrated in the Web server, resulting in much better performance and responsiveness, thanks to the IIS 6.0 *kernel caching*. When enabled, this feature makes it possible for IIS to intercept the output of a page generated by ASP.NET. A copy of the page output is then cached by the IIS kernel. Incoming requests for an ASP.NET page are filtered by a kernel-level driver (*http.sys*) and examined to see whether they match cached pages. If so, the output is served to callers directly from kernel-level code without even bothering the worker process and the ASP.NET pipeline. If you have any ASP.NET applications and are still considering an upgrade to IIS 6.0, this is a great reason to do it as soon as possible. Note that this facility in IIS 6.0 is used by ASP.NET since version 1.1 to host the output cache. So, when using the output cache directive in ASP.NET 1.1 and ASP.NET 2.0 (or newer) applications, your responses are being served from the kernel cache. See the sidebar "Inside IIS 6.0 Kernel Caching" for more performance details.

A fair value for the *Duration* attribute depends on the application, but it normally doesn't exceed 60 seconds. This value usually works great, especially if the page doesn't need to be updated frequently. A short duration (say, 1 second) can be useful for applications that claim live data all the time.

Inside IIS 6.0 Kernel Caching

IIS 6.0 employs an ad hoc component to cache the dynamically generated response to a request in the kernel. This feature has tremendous potential and can dramatically improve the performance of a Web server, as long as enough of the content being served is cacheable. What's the performance gain you can get?

According to the numbers provided with the IIS 6.0 technical documentation, an application using the kernel cache returns a throughput of over ten times the throughput you would get in the noncached case. Additionally, the latency of responses is dramatically better. The following table compares caching in IIS 6.0 kernel mode and user-mode caching to caching as implemented by the ASP.NET runtime in IIS 5.0. (Note that TTFB stands for "time to first byte" while TTLB stands for "time to last byte" for serving the page in question.)

	User-Mode	Kernel-Mode
Requests/Sec	1,394	15,416
TTFB/TTLB (msec)	70.82/70.97	3.39/4.02
User Mode CPU %	76.57%	0.78%
Kernel Mode CPU %	22.69%	99.22%
System Calls/Sec	20,110	2,101
Network Util (KB/Sec)	6,153	68,326
Context Switches/Sec	2,621	6,261

Source: *http://www.microsoft.com/technet/prodtechnol/windowsserver2003/technologies/webapp/iis/iis6perf.mspx*

The numbers in the preceding table provide you with an idea of the results, but the results will vary according to the amount of work and size of the response. The bottom line, though, is that leveraging the kernel cache can make a dramatic difference in the performance of an application. The great news for ASP.NET developers is that no code changes are required to benefit from kernel caching, except for the *@OutputCache* directive.

On a high-volume Web site, an output cache duration of only one second can make a significant difference for the overall throughput of a Web server. There's more to know about kernel caching, though. First and foremost, kernel caching is available only for pages requested through a *GET* verb. No kernel caching is possible on postbacks.

> Furthermore, pages with *VaryByParam* and *VaryByHeader* attributes set are also not stored in the kernel cache. Finally, note that ASP.NET Request/Cache performance counters will not be updated for pages served by the kernel cache.

Choosing a Location for the Page Output

The output cache can be located in various places, either on the client that originated the request or the server. It can also be located on an intermediate proxy server. The various options are listed in Table 16-8. They come from the *OutputCacheLocation* enumerated type.

TABLE 16-8 Output Cache Locations

Location	Cache-Control	Description
Any	*Public*	The HTTP header *Expires* is set according to the duration set in the *@OutputCache* directive. A new item is placed in the ASP.NET *Cache* object representing the output of the page.
Client	*Private*	The output cache is located on the browser where the request originated. The HTTP header *Expires* is set according to the duration set in the *@OutputCache* directive. No item is created in the ASP.NET *Cache* object.
DownStream	*Public*	The output cache can be stored in any HTTP cache-capable devices other than the origin server. This includes proxy servers and the client that made the request. The HTTP header *Expires* is set according to the duration set in the *@OutputCache* directive. No item is created in the ASP.NET *Cache* object.
None	*No-Cache*	The HTTP header *Expires* is not defined. The *Pragma* header is set to *No-Cache*. No item is created in the ASP.NET *Cache* object.
Server	*No-Cache*	The HTTP header *Expires* is not defined. The *Pragma* header is set to *No-Cache*. A new item is placed in the ASP.NET *Cache* object to represent the output of the page.
ServerAndClient		The data can be stored at the origin server (creating an item in the ASP.NET *Cache*) or on the receiving client.

A page marked with the *@OutputCache* directive also generates a set of HTTP headers, such as *Expires* and *Cache-Control*. Downstream proxy servers such as Microsoft ISA Server understand these headers and cache the page along the way. In this way, for the duration of the output, requests for the page can be satisfied even without reaching the native Web server.

In particular, the *Expires* HTTP header is used to specify the time when a particular page on the server should be updated. Until that time, any new request the browser receives for the resource is served using the local, client-side cache and no server round-trip is ever made. When specified and not set to *No-Cache*, the *Cache-Control* HTTP header typically takes values such as *public* or *private*. A value of *public* means that both the browser and the proxy servers can cache the page. A value of *private* prevents proxy servers from caching the page; only the browser will cache the page. The *Cache-Control* is part of the HTTP 1.1 specification and is supported only by Internet Explorer 5.5 and higher.

If you look at the HTTP headers generated by ASP.NET when output caching is enabled, you'll notice that sometimes the *Pragma* header is used—in particular, when the location is set to *Server*. In this case, the header is assigned a value of *No-Cache*, meaning that client-side caching is totally disabled both on the browser side and the proxy side. As a result, any access to the page is resolved through a connection.

> **Note** To be precise, the *Pragma* header set to *No-Cache* disables caching only over HTTPS channels. If used over nonsecure channels, the page is actually cached but marked as expired.

Let's examine the client and Web server caching configuration when each of the feasible locations is used.

- **Any**   This is the default option. This setting means that the page can be cached everywhere, including in the browser, the server, and any proxies along the way. The *Expires* header is set to the page's absolute expiration time as determined by the *Duration* attribute; the *Cache-Control* header is set to *public*, meaning that the proxies can cache if they want and need to. On the Web server, a new item is placed in the *Cache* object with the HTML output of the page. In summary, with this option the page output is cached everywhere. As a result, if the page is accessed through the browser before it expires, no round-trip is ever made. If, in the same timeframe, the page is refreshed—meaning that server-side access is made anyway—the overhead is minimal, the request is short-circuited by the output cache module, and no full request processing takes place.

- **Client**   The page is cached only by the browser because the *Cache-Control* header is set to *private*. Neither proxies nor ASP.NET stores a copy of it. The *Expires* header is set according to the value of the *Duration* attribute.

- **DownStream**   The page can be cached both on the client and in memory of any intermediate proxy. The *Expires* header is set according to the value of the *Duration* attribute, and no copy of the page output is maintained by ASP.NET.

- **None**   Page output caching is disabled both on the server and on the client. No *Expires* HTTP header is generated, and both the *Cache-Control* and the *Pragma* headers are set to *No-Cache*.

- **Server** The page output is exclusively cached on the server, and its raw response is stored in the *Cache* object. The client-side caching is disabled. No *Expires* header is created, and both the *Cache-Control* and *Pragma* headers are set to *No-Cache*.

- **ServerAndClient** The output cache can be stored only at the origin server or at the requesting client. Proxy servers are not allowed to cache the response.

Adding a Database Dependency to Page Output

The *SqlDependency* attribute is the *@OutputCache* directive's interface to the *SqlCacheDependency* class that we discussed earlier. When the *SqlDependency* attribute is set to a *Database:Table* string, a SQL Server cache dependency object is created. When the dependency is broken, the page output is invalidated and the next request will be served by pushing the request through the pipeline as usual. The output generated will be cached again.

```
<% @OutputCache Duration="15" VaryByParam="none"
                SqlDependency="Northwind:Employees" %>
```

A page that contains this code snippet has its output cached for 15 seconds or until a record changes in the Employees table in the Northwind database. Note that the Northwind string here is not the name of a database—it's the name of an entry in the *<databases>* section of the configuration file. That entry contains detailed information about the connection string to use to reach the database. You can specify multiple dependencies by separating multiple *Database:Table* pairs with a semicolon in the value of the *SqlDependency* attribute.

> **Note** A user control is made cacheable in either of two ways: by using the *@OutputCache* directive, or by defining the *PartialCaching* attribute on the user control's class declaration in the code-behind file, as follows:
>
> ```
> [PartialCaching(60)]
> public partial class CustomersGrid : UserControl {
>    ...
> }
> ```
>
> The *PartialCaching* attribute allows you to specify the duration and values for the *VaryByParam*, *VaryByControl*, and *VaryByCustom* parameters.

The *HttpCachePolicy* Class

The *HttpCachePolicy* class is a programming interface alternative to using the *@OutputCache* directive. It provides direct methods to set cache-related HTTP headers, which you could also control to some extent by using the members of the *HttpResponse* object.

Properties of the *HttpCachePolicy* Class

Table 16-9 shows the properties of the *HttpCachePolicy* class.

TABLE 16-9 *HttpCachePolicy* **Class Properties**

Property	Description
VaryByHeaders	Gets an object of type *HttpCacheVaryByHeaders*, representing the list of all HTTP headers that will be used to vary cache output
VaryByParams	Gets an object of type *HttpCacheVaryByParams*, representing the list of parameters received by a *GET* or *POST* request that affect caching

When a cached page has several vary-by headers or parameters, a separate version of the page is available for each HTTP header type or parameter name.

Methods of the *HttpCachePolicy* Class

Table 16-10 shows the methods of the *HttpCachePolicy* class.

TABLE 16-10 *HttpCachePolicy* **Class Methods**

Method	Description
AddValidationCallback	Registers a callback function to be used to validate the page output in the server cache before returning it.
AppendCacheExtension	Appends the specified text to the *Cache-Control* HTTP header. The existing text is not overwritten.
SetAllowResponseInBrowserHistory	When this setting is *true*, the response is available in the browser's History cache, regardless of the *HttpCacheability* option set on the server.
SetCacheability	Sets the *Cache-Control* HTTP header to any of the values taken from the *HttpCacheability* enumeration type.
SetETag	Sets the *ETag* header to the specified string. The *ETag* header is a unique identifier for a specific version of a document.
SetETagFromFileDependencies	Sets the *ETag* header to a string built by combining and then hashing the last modified date of all the files upon which the page is dependent.
SetExpires	Sets the *Expires* header to an absolute date and time.
SetLastModified	Sets the *Last-Modified* HTTP header to a particular date and time.
SetLastModifiedFromFileDependencies	Sets the *Last-Modified* HTTP header to the most recent timestamps of the files upon which the page is dependent.

Method	Description
SetMaxAge	Sets the *max-age* attribute on the *Cache-Control* header to the specified value. The sliding period cannot exceed one year.
SetNoServerCaching	Disables server output caching for the current response.
SetNoStore	Sets the *Cache-Control: no-store* directive.
SetNoTransforms	Sets the *Cache-Control: no-transforms* directive.
SetOmitVaryStar	If set to *true*, causes *HttpCachePolicy* to ignore the * value in *VaryByHeaders*. Not supported by ASP.NET 1.x.
SetProxyMaxAge	Sets the *Cache-Control: s-maxage* header.
SetRevalidation	Sets the *Cache-Control* header to either *must-revalidate* or *proxy-revalidate*.
SetSlidingExpiration	Sets cache expiration to *sliding*. When cache expiration is set to *sliding*, the *Cache-Control* header is renewed at each response.
SetValidUntilExpires	Specifies whether the ASP.NET cache should ignore HTTP *Cache-Control* headers sent by some browsers to evict a page from the cache. If this setting is *true*, the page stays in the cache until it expires.
SetVaryByCustom	Sets the *Vary* HTTP header to the specified text string.

Most methods of the *HttpCachePolicy* class let you control the values of some HTTP headers that relate to the browser cache. The *AddValidationCallback* method, on the other hand, provides a mechanism to programmatically check the validity of page output in the server cache before it is returned from the cache.

Server Cache-Validation Callback

Before the response is served from the ASP.NET cache, all registered handlers are given a chance to verify the validity of the cached page. If at least one handler marks the cached page as invalid, the entry is removed from the cache and the request is served as if it were never cached. The signature of the callback function looks like this:

```
public delegate void HttpCacheValidateHandler(
    HttpContext context,
    object data,
    ref HttpValidationStatus validationStatus
);
```

The first argument denotes the context of the current request, whereas the second argument is any user-defined data the application needs to pass to the handler. Finally, the third argument is a reference to a value from the *HttpValidationStatus* enumeration. The callback sets this value to indicate the result of the validation. Acceptable values are *IgnoreThisRequest*,

Invalid, and *Valid*. In the case of *IgnoreThisRequest*, the cached resource is not invalidated but the request is served as if no response was ever cached. If the return value is *Invalid*, the cached page is not used and gets invalidated. Finally, if the return value is *Valid*, the cached response is used to serve the request.

Caching Multiple Versions of a Page

Depending on the application context from which a certain page is invoked, the page might generate different results. The same page can be called to operate with different parameters, can be configured using different HTTP headers, can produce different output based on the requesting browser, and so forth.

ASP.NET allows you to cache multiple versions of a page response; you can distinguish versions by *GET* and *POST* parameters, HTTP headers, browser type, custom strings, and control properties.

Vary By Parameters

To vary output caching by parameters, you can use either the *VaryByParam* attribute of the *@OutputCache* directive or the *VaryByParams* property on the *HttpCachePolicy* class. If you proceed declaratively, use the following syntax:

```
<% @OutputCache Duration="60" VaryByParam="employeeID" %>
```

Note that the *VaryByParam* attribute is mandatory; if you don't want to specify a parameter to vary cached content, set the value to *None*. If you want to vary the output by all parameters, set the attribute to *. When the *VaryByParam* attribute is set to multiple parameters, the output cache contains a different version of the requested document for each specified parameter. Multiple parameters are separated by a semicolon. Valid parameters to use are items specified on the *GET* query string or parameters set in the body of a *POST* command.

If you want to use the *HttpCachePolicy* class to define caching parameters, first set the expiration and the cacheability of the page using the *SetExpires* and *SetCacheability* methods. Next, set the *VaryByParams* property as shown here:

```
Response.Cache.SetExpires(DateTime.Now.AddSeconds(60));
Response.Cache.SetCacheability(HttpCacheability.Public);
Response.Cache.VaryByParams["employeeid;lastname"] = true;
```

This code snippet shows how to vary page output based on the employee ID and the last name properties. Note that the *Cache* property on the *HttpResponse* class is just an instance of the *HttpCachePolicy* type.

Dealing with Postback Pages

Most ASP.NET pages do postbacks. The page in Figure 16-7 (*sqldepoutputcache.aspx*) is no exception. The page has two key features: it is dependent on changes to the Customers table in the Northwind database, and it has a cache duration of 30 seconds. Furthermore, the drop-down list (named *Countries*) has auto-postback functionality and places a *POST* request for the same page whenever you change the selection.

FIGURE 16-7 To properly cache pages that post back, you need to vary them by one or more parameters.

With *VaryByParam* set to *None*, you'll wait 30 seconds (or whatever the cache duration is) to have your country selection processed. It is a bit frustrating: no matter which selection you make, it is blissfully ignored and the same page is displayed. Worse yet, if you test the page under the Visual Studio .NET Web Development server, after a couple of attempts you get a "page not found" error. If you test the page under IIS, you are repeatedly served the same page response, regardless of the selection made.

Two points clearly emerge from this discussion. First, pages with static content are a better fit for caching than interactive pages. Second, the postback mechanism returns a bunch of form parameters. You need to vary the cached copies of the page by the most critical of them. The sample page in Figure 16-7 has a few hidden fields (try snooping in its HTML source), such as __VIEWSTATE and __LASTFOCUS, and the drop-down list. Varying by view state makes no sense at all, but varying by the selected countries is exactly what we need:

```
<%@ OutputCache VaryByParam="Countries" Duration="30"
                SqlDependency="Northwind:Customers" %>
```

The directive stores each country-specific page for 30 seconds unless a change occurs in the Customers database. In such a case, all the cached versions of the page will be invalidated.

The bottom line is that enabling page output caching might not be painless for interactive pages. It is free of pain and charge for relatively static pages like those describing a product, a customer, or some news.

> **Caution** A cached ASP.NET page is served more quickly than a processed page, but not as quickly as a static HTML page. However, the response time is nearly identical if the ASP.NET page is kernel-cached in IIS 6.0. Unfortunately, IIS 6.0 doesn't store in its kernel-level cache ASP.NET pages requested via a POST verb and, more importantly, pages with *VaryByParam* or *VaryByHeader*. In the end, postback pages have very few chances to be cached in the IIS kernel. They are cached in the ASP.NET *Cache*, in downstream caching servers, or both.

Vary By Headers

The *VaryByHeader* attribute and the *HttpCachePolicy*'s *VaryByHeaders* property allow you to cache multiple versions of a page, according to the value of one or more HTTP headers that you specify.

If you want to cache pages by multiple headers, include a semicolon-delimited list of header names. If you want to cache a different version of the page for each different header value, set the *VaryByHeader* attribute to an asterisk *. For example, the following declaration caches for one-minute pages based on the language accepted by the browser. Each language will have a different cached copy of the page output.

```
<%@ OutputCache Duration="60" VaryByParam="None"
    VaryByHeader="Accept-Language" %>
```

If you opt for a programmatic approach, here's the code to use that leverages the *VaryByHeaders* property of the *HttpCachePolicy* class:

```
Response.Cache.VaryByHeaders["Accept-Language"] = true;
```

If you want to programmatically vary the pages in the cache by all HTTP header names, use the *VaryByUnspecifiedParameters* method of the *HttpCacheVaryByHeaders* class:

```
HttpCacheVaryByHeaders.VaryByUnspecifiedParameters();
```

The preceding code is equivalent to using the asterisk with the *VaryByHeader* attribute.

Vary By Custom Strings

The *VaryByCustom* attribute in the *@OutputCache* directive allows you to vary the versions of page output by the value of a custom string. The string you assign to the *VaryByCustom* attribute simply represents the description of the algorithm employed to vary page outputs. The string is then passed to the *GetVaryByCustomString* method, if any, in the *global.asax* file. The method takes the string and returns another string that is specific to the request. Let's examine a concrete example—varying pages by the type of device that requests the page. You use, say, the string *device* with the *VaryByCustom* attribute:

```
<%@ OutputCache Duration="60" VaryByParam="None" VaryByCustom="device" %>
```

Next, you add your application-specific *GetVaryByCustomString* method in the *global.asax* file. Here's a possible implementation:

```
public override string GetVaryByCustomString(HttpContext context, string custom)
{
    if (custom == "device")
        return context.Request.Browser.Type;
    return base.GetVaryByCustomString(context, custom);
}
```

The output of the page is varied by user agent string. You can use any other custom information as long as the information is available through the *HttpContext* class. You can't use information that is known only when the page is loaded, such as the theme. Custom information gathered by a custom HTTP module might be used if the HTTP module parks the information in the *Items* collection of the *HttpContext* object, and as long as the HTTP module is triggered before the request to resolve the page output cache is made.

Nicely enough, the feature described above—varying pages by user agent strings—is natively available since ASP.NET 1.0. The only difference is that it uses the keyword *browser* instead of *device*. In other words, the following code is perfectly acceptable and leverages the implementation of *GetVaryByCustomString* on the base *HttpApplication* class:

```
<%@ OutputCache Duration="60" VaryByParam="None" VaryByCustom="browser" %>
```

You use the *SetVaryByCustom* method on the *HttpCachePolicy* class if you don't like the declarative approach:

```
Response.Cache.SetVaryByCustom("browser");
```

Caching Portions of ASP.NET Pages

The capability of caching the output of Web pages adds a lot of power to your programming arsenal, but sometimes caching the entire content of a page is not possible or it's just impractical. Some pages, in fact, are made of pieces with radically different features as far as cacheability is concerned. In these situations, being able to cache portions of a page is an incredible added value.

If caching the entire page is impractical, you can always opt for partial caching. Partial caching leverages the concept of ASP.NET user controls—that is, small, nested pages that inherit several features of the page. In particular, user controls can be cached individually based on the browser, *GET* and *POST* parameters, and the value of a particular set of properties.

We'll cover user controls in detail in my other book *Programming Microsoft ASP.NET 2.0 Applications: Advanced Topics* (Microsoft Press, 2006), but a quick introduction is in order for the purpose of partial caching.

What's a User Control, Anyway?

A user control is a Web form saved to a distinct file with an *.ascx* extension. The similarity between user controls and pages is not coincidental. You create a user control in much the same way you create a Web form, and a user control is made of any combination of server and client controls sewn together with server and client script code. Once created, the user control can be inserted in an ASP.NET page like any other server control. ASP.NET pages see the user control as an atomic, encapsulated component and work with it as with any other built-in Web control.

The internal content of the user control is hidden to the host page. However, the user control can define a public programming interface and filter access to its constituent controls via properties, methods, and events.

User controls and pages have so much in common that transforming a page, or a part of it, into a user control is no big deal. You copy the portion of the page of interest to a new *.ascx* file and make sure the user control does not contain any of the following tags: *<html>*, *<body>*, or *<form>*. You complete the work by associating a code-behind file (or a *<script runat="server">* block) to code the expected behavior of the user control. Finally, you add a *@Control* directive in lieu of the *@Page* directive. Here's an example of a user control:

```
<%@ Control Language="C#" CodeFile="Message.ascx.cs" Inherits="Message" %>
<span style="color:<%= ForeColor%>"><%= Text%></span>
```

Here's the related code-behind class:

```
public partial class Message : System.Web.UI.UserControl
{
    public string ForeColor;
    public string Text;
}
```

To insert a user control into an ASP.NET page, you drag it from the project onto the Web form, when in design mode. Visual Studio .NET registers the user control with the page and prepares the environment for you to start adding code.

```
<%@ Page Language="C#" CodeFile="Test.aspx.cs" Inherits="TestUserCtl" %>
<%@ Register Src="Message.ascx" TagName="Message" TagPrefix="x" %>
<html><body>
    <form id="form1" runat="server">
        <x:Message ID="Message1" runat="server" />
    </form>
</body></html>
```

In the page code-behind class, you work the *Message1* variable as you would do with any other server control:

```
protected void Page_Load(object sender, EventArgs e)
{
    Message1.ForeColor = "blue";
    Message1.Text = "Hello world";
}
```

Caching the Output of User Controls

User controls are not only good at modularizing your user interface, they're also great at caching portions of Web pages. User controls, therefore, fully support the *@OutputCache* directive, although they do so with some differences with ASP.NET pages, as outlined in Table 16-7.

A page that contains some dynamic sections cannot be cached entirely. What if the page also contains sections that are both heavy to compute and seldom updated? In this case, you move static contents to one or more user controls and use the user control's *@OutputCache* directive to set up output caching.

To make a user control cacheable, you declare the *@OutputCache* attribute using almost the same set of attributes we discussed earlier for pages. For example, the following code snippet caches the output of the control that embeds it for one minute:

```
<% @OutputCache Duration="60" VaryByParam="None" %>
```

The *Location* attribute is not supported because all controls in the page share the same location. So if you need to specify the cache location, do that at the page level and it will work for all embedded controls. The same holds true for the *VaryByHeader* attribute.

The output of a user control can vary by custom strings and form parameters. More often, though, you'll want to vary the output of a control by property values. In this case, use the new *VaryByControl* attribute.

Vary by Controls

The *VaryByControl* attribute allows you to vary the cache for each specified control property. For user controls, the property is mandatory unless the *VaryByParam* attribute has been specified. You can indicate both *VaryByParam* and *VaryByControl*, but at least one of them is required.

The following user control displays a grid with all the customers in a given country. The country is specified by the user control's *Country* property.

```
<%@ Control Language="C#" CodeFile="CustomersGrid.ascx.cs"
        Inherits="CustomersGridByCtl" %>
<%@ OutputCache Duration="30" VaryByControl="Country" %>

<h3><%= DateTime.Now.ToString() %></h3>
<asp:ObjectDataSource ID="ObjectDataSource1" runat="server"
    TypeName="Core35.DAL.Customers"
    SelectMethod="LoadByCountry">
</asp:ObjectDataSource>

<asp:GridView ID="GridView1" runat="server" AutoGenerateColumns="false">
    <Columns>
        <asp:BoundField DataField="ID" HeaderText="ID" />
        <asp:BoundField DataField="CompanyName" HeaderText="Company" />
        <asp:BoundField DataField="ContactName" HeaderText="Contact" />
        <asp:BoundField DataField="Country" HeaderText="Country" />
    </Columns>
</asp:GridView>
```

Here is the code file of the user control:

```
public partial class CustomersGridByCtl : System.Web.UI.UserControl
{
    public string Country;

    protected void Page_Load(object sender, EventArgs e)
    {
        if (!String.IsNullOrEmpty(Country))
        {
            ObjectDataSource1.SelectParameters.Add("country", Country);
            GridView1.DataSourceID = "ObjectDataSource1";
        }
    }
}
```

The @*OutputCache* directive caches a different copy of the user control output based on the different values of the *Country* property. Figure 16-8 shows it in action.

The strings you assign to *VaryByControl* can be properties of the user controls as well as ID property values for contained controls. In this case, you'll get a distinct cached copy for each distinct combination of property values on the specified control.

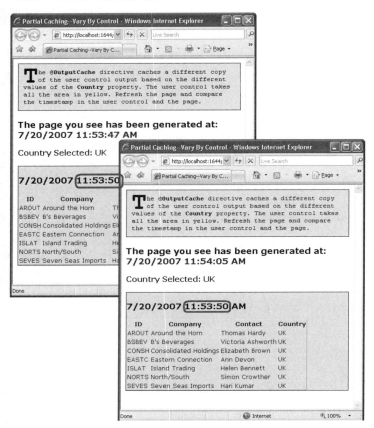

FIGURE 16-8 Two pages created in different moments use the same user control output, as you can see from the creation time of the grid.

The *Shared* Attribute

In Figure 16-8, you see two instances of the same page sharing the cached output of a user control. Try the following simple experiment. Make a plain copy of the page (say, *page1.aspx*) and give it another name (say, *page2.aspx*). You should have two distinct pages that generate identical output. In particular, both pages contain an instance of the same cacheable user control. Let's say that the cache duration of the user control is 30 seconds.

As the next step of the experiment, you open both pages at different times while the cache is still valid. Let's say you open the second page ten seconds later than the first. Interestingly enough, the two pages are no longer sharing the same copy of user control output, as Figure 16-9 documents.

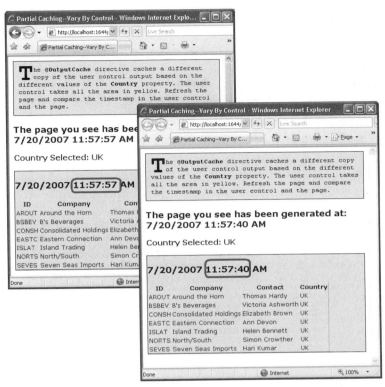

FIGURE 16-9 Distinct pages don't automatically share the output of the same user control.

By default, distinct pages don't share the output of the same cacheable user control. Each page will maintain its own copy of the user control response, instead. Implemented to guarantee total separation and avoid any sort of conflicts, this feature is far more dangerous than one might think at first. It might lead to flooding the Web server memory with copies and copies of the user control responses—one for each varying parameter or control property and one set for each page that uses the control.

To allow distinct pages to share the same output of a common user control, you need to set the *Shared* attribute to *true* in the user control's *@OutputCache* directive:

```
<%@ OutputCache Duration="30" VaryByParam="None" Shared="true" %>
```

Tip To avoid memory problems, you should put a limit on the total amount of memory available to IIS. It is set to 60 percent of the physical memory, but you should keep it under 800 MB per Microsoft recommendations. Setting the IIS 6.0 Maximum Used Memory parameter is important especially if output cache is used aggressively. You'll set the parameter on a per-application-pool basis by selecting the IIS 6.0 application pool where your application is configured to run and opening its Properties dialog box.

Fragment Caching in Cacheable Pages

If you plan to cache user controls—that is, you're trying for partial caching—it's probably because you just don't want to, or cannot, cache the entire page. However, a good question to ask is: what happens if user controls are cached within a cacheable page?

Both the page and the controls are cached individually, meaning that both the page's raw response and the control's raw responses are cached. However, if the cache duration is different, the page duration wins and user controls are refreshed only when the page is refreshed.

A cacheable user control can be embedded both in a cacheable page and in a wrapper cacheable user control.

> **Warning** Cacheable user controls should be handled with extreme care in the page's code. Unlike regular controls, a user control marked with the *@OutputCache* directive is not guaranteed to be there when your code tries to access it. If the user control is retrieved from the cache, the property that references it in the code-behind page class is just *null*.
>
> ```
> if (CustomerGrid1 != null)
>     CustomerGrid1.Country = "USA";
> ```
>
> To avoid bad surprises, you should always check the control reference against the *null* value before executing any code.

Advanced Caching Features

The output caching subsystem has also a few other cool features to offer. They are caching profiles and post-cache substitution. In brief, caching profiles let you save a block of output caching-related settings to the configuration file. Post-cache substitution completes the ASP.NET offering as far as output caching is concerned. In addition to saving the entire page or only fragments of the page, you can now also cache the entire page except for a few regions.

Caching Profiles

The *@OutputCache* directive for pages supports the *CacheProfile* string attribute, which references an entry under the *<outputCacheProfiles>* section in the *web.config* file:

```
<caching>
    <outputCacheSettings>
        <outputCacheProfiles>
            <add name="..." enabled="true|false" duration="..."
                location="..." sqlDependency="..."
                varyByCustom="..." varyByControl="..."
```

```
                    varyByHeader="..." varyByParam="..."
                              noStore=true|false"
            />
        </outputCacheProfiles>
    </outputCacheSettings>
</caching>
```

Basically, by defining a named entry in the *<add>* section you can store in the configuration file all the cache-related settings to be applied to the page. Instead of specifying the same set of parameters for each page over and over again, you can put them in the *web.config* file and reference them by name. In this way, you can also modify settings for a number of pages without touching the source files.

```
<%@ OutputCache CacheProfile="MySettings" %>
```

In the preceding code, the application has a *MySettings* entry in the *<outputCacheProfiles>* section and doesn't need any additional attribute in the *@OutputCache* directive. As you can see, the attributes of the *<add>* node match the attributes of the *@OutputCache* directive.

Post-Cache Substitution

With user controls, you can cache only certain portions of ASP.NET pages. With post-cache substitution, you can cache the whole page except specific regions. For example, using this mechanism, an *AdRotator* control can serve a different advertisement on each request even if the host page is cached.

To use post-cache substitution, you place a new control—the *<asp:substitution>* control—at the page location where content should be substituted, and you set the *MethodName* property of the control to a callback method. Here's a quick example:

```
<form id="form1" runat="server">
    <h3>The output you see has been generated at:
        <%=DateTime.Now.ToString() %> and is valid for 30 seconds</h3>
    <hr />
    This content is updated regularly
    <h2><asp:Substitution ID="Substitution1" runat="server"
            MethodName="WriteTimeStamp" /></h2>
    <hr />
    This is more static and cached content
    <asp:Button runat="server" Text="Refresh" />
</form>
```

Figure 16-10 shows the page in action.

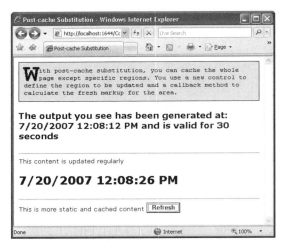

FIGURE 16-10 The fragment of the page between the two horizontal lines is updated regularly at each postback; the rest of the page is retrieved from the cache.

The *MethodName* property must be set to the name of a static method that can be encapsulated in an *HttpResponseSubstitutionCallback* delegate, as follows:

```
public static string WriteTimeStamp(HttpContext context)
{
    return DateTime.Now.ToString();
}
```

Whatever string the method returns will be rendered out and becomes the output of the *Substitution* control. Note also that the callback method must be static and thread-safe. The *HttpContext* parameter to the method can be used to retrieve request parameters such as query string variables, authentication information, or personalization details.

You can also set up post-cache substitution programmatically through the *WriteSubstitution* method of the *HttpResponse* object:

```
Response.WriteSubstitution(
    new HttpResponseSubstitutionCallback(WriteTimeStamp));
```

The preceding call inserts a sort of placeholder in the response, which will be replaced with the output of the method. This trick allows the *AdRotator* control in ASP.NET 2.0 to automatically display a new banner even on cached pages.

The use of post-cache substitution automatically enables server caching for the page output. If the page is configured for client output caching, the setting is ignored. The reason for this change lies in the fact that markup editing is necessarily a server-side operation. In addition, a page that makes use of post-cache substitution can't rely on IIS 6.0 kernel mode caching because ASP.NET needs to do some work before the page can be served to the user. In light of this, the page can't just be served by IIS without first involving ASP.NET.

> **Note** The *Substitution* control can also be used in pages that don't use output caching. In this case, the substitution callback will be called at rendering time to contribute to the response. You can think of the *Substitution* control as a server-side control that has the capability of expanding a placeholder to some server-side processed results.

For performance reasons, you should also avoid calling the *Substitution* control from within the callback. If you do so, the callback will maintain a reference to the control and the page containing the control. As a result, the page instance won't be garbage-collected until the cached content expires.

Conclusion

The ability to store in memory chunks of frequently accessed data becomes a winning factor in the building of scalable Web applications that handle significant volumes of data. Instead of continuously connecting to the database server, locking records, and consuming one of the available connection channels, you can simply read the results needed from some block of memory. This scenario delineates caching as an asset for any application. Well, not just any, as we discussed—but certainly for many.

Caching is rather a double-edged sword, and if abused or misused, it can easily morph into an insidious weakness. This typically happens when the quantity of memory-held information grows uncontrolled and beyond a reasonable threshold. Aside from the performance repercussions, the theoretical possibility that the data stored in the cache can grow uncontrolled also opens up security concerns. A denial-of-service (DoS) attack, in fact, might succeed in flooding the Web server's memory with useless data if the caching subsystem is not well designed.

Caching is mostly about memory. In the short run, you can perhaps even find that some good caching improves the overall performance enough to appease your customer or your boss. I'm not at all claiming that caching can fix design holes, but caching can sometimes put a patch on nonoptimal performance and allow you time to rethink and refactor the application properly.

Caching is an essential feature to consider for all serious Internet applications. To build high-performance applications, a fundamental guideline is "cache as much as you can." However, be aware that there's a threshold you should never exceed. The more aggressive you are with caching, the more you should be concerned about the invisible memory threshold that suddenly turns good things into bad things.

In ASP.NET, caching comes in two complementary forms—page output caching and the *Cache* object. The former is a relatively quick and simple approach to serve static pages bypassing the ASP.NET pipeline. The latter is the tip of a comprehensive caching API designed to let you place a caching layer inside your business or data tier.

Just the Facts

- Caching is the system's, or the application's, ability to save frequently used data to an intermediate storage medium. In ASP.NET, caching comes in two independent but not exclusive flavors—caching application data, and caching the output of served pages.

- To cache application data, you use the *Cache* object, a global container of data with a dictionary-based API and the capabilities of automatically scavenging the memory and getting rid of unused items.

- Items added to the cache can be linked to an array of files and directories as well as to an array of existing cache items, database tables, or external custom events. Whenever files, folders, existing cache items, and database tables are modified, or whenever the external event fires, the item automatically becomes stale and is removed from memory.

- Page output caching is the ability of saving the raw HTML of a page to a location on the client, the server, or a downstream proxy server. Cached pages can be given a duration and vary in terms of query and form parameters, HTTP headers, and custom strings.

- When the IIS 6.0 process model is enabled, the output caching mechanism is integrated into the Web server. Incoming requests for an ASP.NET page are filtered by a kernel-level driver and examined to see whether they match cached pages.

- By creating user controls, you can cache only a portion of an ASP.NET page.

- Starting with ASP.NET 2.0, new caching features are available, such as post-cache substitution. Post-cache substitution lets you cache the entire page except for a few regions.

Chapter 17
ASP.NET Security

Many developers have learned on their own that security is not a feature that can be added to existing applications or introduced late in the development stage. Security is inherently tied to the functions of an application and should be planned as one of the first features, very early at the design level.

By nature, Web applications are subject to several types of attacks whose damage and impact can vary quite a bit, depending on the characteristics of the application itself. The most secure Web application is the application that actually resists attacks, not the application just designed to. Security is a rather intricate puzzle whose solution varies from one application to another. The important thing to remember is that, more often than not, security is manifested through a successful mix of application-level and system-level measures.

ASP.NET simplifies programming secure applications by providing a built-in infrastructure that supplies application-level protection against unauthorized access to Web pages. Be aware, though, that this kind of security is only one side of the coin. A really secure Web site is especially well protected against server attacks, which can sneakily be used to scale the highest protective walls of the application logic.

In this chapter, we will discuss the security context of ASP.NET, including its relationship with server-side Internet Information Services (IIS) authentication mechanisms and best coding practices to fend off Web attacks.

Where the Threats Come From

The concept of security implies the presence of an enemy we're protecting against. In Table 17-1, you find summarized the most common types of Web attacks.

TABLE 17-1 Common Web Attacks

Attack	Description
Cross-site scripting (XSS)	Untrusted user input is echoed to the page.
Denial of service (DoS)	The attacker floods the network with fake requests, overloading the system and blocking regular traffic.
Eavesdropping	The attacker uses a sniffer to read unencrypted network packets as they are transported on the network.
Hidden-field tampering	The attacker compromises unchecked (and trusted) hidden fields stuffed with sensitive data.
One-click	Malicious HTTP posts are sent via script.
Session hijacking	The attacker guesses or steals a valid session ID and connects over another user's session.
SQL injection	The attacker inserts malicious input that the code blissfully concatenates to form dangerous SQL commands.

The bottom line is that whenever you insert any sort of user input into the browser's markup you potentially expose yourself to a code-injection attack (that is, any variations of SQL injection and XSS). In addition, sensitive data should never be sent across the wire (let alone as clear text) and must be stored safely on the server.

If there's a way to write a bulletproof and tamper-resistant application, it can only consist of the combination of the following aspects:

- Coding practices: data validation, type and buffer length checking, and antitampering measures

- Data access strategies: using roles to ensure the weakest possible account is used on the server to limit server resource access, and using stored procedures or, at least, parameterized commands

- Effective storage and administration: no sending of critical data down to the client, using hashed values to detect manipulation, authenticating users and protecting identities, and applying rigorous policies for passwords

As you can see from this list, a secure application can result only from the combined efforts of developers, architects, and administrators. Don't imagine that you can get it right otherwise.

The ASP.NET Security Context

From an application point of view, security is mostly a matter of authenticating users and authorizing actions on the system's resources. ASP.NET provides a range of authentication and authorization mechanisms implemented in conjunction with IIS, the .NET Framework, and the underlying security services of the operating system. The overall security context of an ASP.NET application is composed of three distinct levels:

- The IIS level associates a valid security token with the sender of the request. The security token is determined according to the current IIS authentication mechanism.

- The ASP.NET worker process level determines the identity of the thread in the ASP.NET worker process serving the request. If enabled, impersonation settings can change the security token associated with the thread. The identity of the process model is determined by settings in the configuration file or the IIS metabase, according to the process model in use.

- The ASP.NET pipeline level gets the credentials of the application-specific user who is using the application. The way this task is accomplished depends on the application settings in the configuration files for authentication and authorization. A common setting for most ASP.NET applications is choosing to use Forms Authentication.

Among other things, the identity of the ASP.NET worker process influences access to local files, folders, and databases.

Who Really Runs My ASP.NET Application?

When an ASP.NET request arrives at the Web server machine, IIS picks it up and assigns the request to one of its pooled threads. IIS runs under the SYSTEM account—the most powerful account in Windows. From this point forward when processing this request, the three security contexts of ASP.NET applications I mentioned execute, one after the other.

IIS Thread Security Context

The thread that physically handles the request impersonates an identity according to the current IIS authentication settings: Basic, Digest, Integrated Windows, or anonymous. If the site is configured for anonymous access, the identity impersonated by the thread is the one you set through the dialog box shown in Figure 17-1. By default, it is named *IUSR_xxx*, where *xxx* stands for the machine name. (The dialog box is the Properties dialog box of the IIS administrative manager application.)

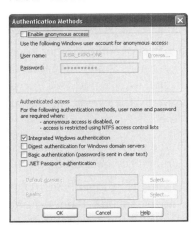

FIGURE 17-1 Enabling anonymous access and editing authentication methods for the site.

Basic authentication is an HTTP standard supported by virtually any browser. With this type of authentication, a request bounces back with a particular HTTP status code that the browser understands as a demand to display a standard dialog box to request the user's credentials. The information gathered is sent to IIS, which attempts to match it with any of the Web server's accounts. Because credentials are sent out as Base64-encoded text, essentially in clear text, Basic authentication is recommended only for use over HTTPS secure channels.

Digest authentication differs from Basic authentication mostly because it hashes credentials before sending. Digest authentication is an HTTP 1.1 feature and, as such, is not supported by some old browsers. In addition, on Windows 2000 it requires the password to be stored on the server with reversible encryption. This is no longer a requirement with Windows Server 2003. Both Basic and Digest authentication work well through firewalls and proxy servers.

Integrated Windows authentication sets up a conversation between the browser and the Web server. The browser passes the credentials of the currently logged-on user, who is not required to type anything. The user needs to have a valid account on the Web server or in a trusted domain to be successfully authenticated. The authentication can take place through the NTLM challenge/response method or by using Kerberos. The technique has limited browser support and is impractical in the presence of firewalls. It is designed for intranet use.

Note Yet another type of authentication mode exists and is based on certificates. You can use the Secure Sockets Layer (SSL) security features of IIS and use client certificates to authenticate users requesting information on your Web site. SSL checks the contents of the certificate submitted by the browser for the user during the logon. Users obtain client certificates from a trusted third-party organization. In an intranet scenario, users can also get their certificate from an authority managed by the company itself.

After authentication, the thread dispatches the request to the appropriate external module. For an ASP.NET request, what happens depends on the process model in use within the application.

Worker Process Security Context

In the IIS 5.0 process model, the IIS thread hands the request out to *aspnet_isapi.dll* which, in turn, starts the *aspnet_wp.exe* worker process. In the IIS 6.0 process model, the request is queued to the application pool that hosts the ASP.NET application and picked up by the copy of the *w3wp.exe* IIS worker process that serves the application pool. What is the identity of the worker process?

If the IIS 5.0 process model is used, the worker process runs under the guise of the ASPNET account. ASPNET is a local account created when the .NET Framework is installed. It has the least set of privileges required for its role and is far less powerful than the SYSTEM account. You can change the identity to an existing account through the following section in *machine. config*:

```
<processModel userName="..." password="..." />
```

If the IIS 6.0 process model is used, the worker process has the identity of the NETWORK SERVICE account. You can change it through the dialog box shown in Figure 17-2. In the IIS administrative manager, you select the application pool of choice and click to see its properties. NETWORK SERVICE has the same limited set of privileges as ASPNET and is a new built-in account in Windows Server 2003 and Windows XP.

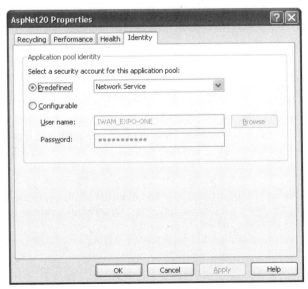

FIGURE 17-2 Setting the default identity of the worker process serving an application pool in IIS 6.0.

Inside the worker process, a pooled thread will pick up the request to serve it. What's the identity of this thread? If impersonation is disabled in the ASP.NET application, this thread will inherit the identity of the worker process. This is what happens by default. If impersonation is enabled, the worker thread will inherit the security token passed by IIS. You enable impersonation in the *web.config* file as follows:

```
<impersonation enabled="true" />
```

There's more to say about ASP.NET impersonation, particularly about the extended form of impersonation where a fixed identity is specified. We'll discuss this further in a moment.

When impersonation is active, the worker process account doesn't change. The worker process still compiles pages and reads configuration files using the original account. Impersonation is used only with the code executed within the page and not for all the preliminary steps that happen before the request is handed to the page handler. For example, this means that any access to local files or databases occur using the impersonated account, not the worker process's account.

ASP.NET Pipeline Security Context

The third security context indicates the identity of the user making the request. The point here is authenticating the user and authorizing access to the page and its embedded resources. Obviously, if the requested page is freely available no further step is performed; the page output is generated and served to the user.

To protect pages against unauthorized access, an ASP.NET application needs to define an authentication policy—Windows, Passport, or Forms. Authentication modules hook up requests for protected pages and manage to obtain the user's credentials. The user is directed to the page only if the credentials are deemed valid and authorize access to the requested resource.

Changing the Identity of the ASP.NET Process

In a situation in which you want to change the default ASP.NET account to give it more privileges, how should you proceed? Is it preferable to create a custom account and use it for the worker process, or should you opt for the worker process to impersonate a fixed identity?

> **Note** You can hardly create a new, functional account with less than the privileges granted to ASPNET or NETWORK SERVICE. If you give it a try, make sure you pass through a careful testing phase and ensure it really works for your application.

Setting the Process Account

Using the *<processModel>* section (for the IIS 5.0 process model) or using the dialog box shown in Figure 17-2 (for the IIS 6.0 process model) are the only ways to change the real identity of the ASP.NET process. If you change the process identity, all threads in the process will use this as the base identity and no extra work is needed on thread switches. More importantly, you should make sure the new account has at least full permissions on the *Temporary ASP.NET Files* folder. (Review carefully the list of permissions granted to the standard ASP.NET accounts, which you can find in the "Privileges of the ASP.NET Default Account" section.)

Alternately, you can require the worker process to impersonate a fixed identity through the *<identity>* section of the *web.config* file. Note that when fixed impersonation is used, every worker thread processing a request needs to impersonate the specified account. Impersonation must be performed for each thread switch because a thread switch event takes the thread identity back to the process identity.

Impersonating a Fixed Identity

To impersonate a fixed identity, you first define the user account and then add a setting to the *web.config* file. The following snippet shows an example:

```
<identity impersonate="true"
    userName="MyAspNetAccnt" password="ILoveA$p*SinceVer3.0" />
```

As mentioned earlier, impersonation doesn't really change the *physical* identity of the process running ASP.NET. More simply, all threads serving in the context of the ASP.NET worker process always impersonate a given user for the duration of the application.

Impersonating a fixed identity is different from classic, per-request impersonation such as impersonating the identity of the Windows user making the request. *Per-request impersonation* refers to the situation in which you enable impersonation without specifying a fixed identity. In this case, the security token with identity information is created by IIS and inherited by the worker process. When a fixed identity is involved, the security token must be generated by the ASP.NET worker process. When running under a poorly privileged account, though, the ASP.NET worker process sometimes lacks the permission to do that.

Inside the Fixed Impersonation Feature

A process running under a nonadministrator account cannot impersonate a specific account on Windows 2000 unless you grant it appropriate privileges. Under Windows 2000, a process requires the *Act As Part Of The Operating System* privilege to impersonate a fixed identity. This is indeed a strong and powerful privilege that, for security reasons, nonadministrator process accounts such as ASPNET and NETWORK SERVICE generally will not have.

The requirement disappears with Windows XP and Windows Server 2003, which makes it possible for processes lacking the *Act As Part Of The Operating System* privilege to impersonate a given identity.

In ASP.NET 1.1, though, impersonating a fixed identity is possible also under Windows 2000 machines and IIS 5.0. The ASP.NET 1.1 runtime plays some tricks to re-vector the call back to the *aspnet_isapi.dll* module, which is running inside IIS 5.0 and under the SYSTEM account. Basically, the ASP.NET 1.1 ISAPI extension creates the security token and duplicates it in the memory space of the worker process. In this way, ASP.NET 1.1 supports fixed impersonation without requiring the *Act As Part Of The Operating System* privilege on the worker process account.

In the end, expect to have troubles with fixed impersonation only if you're still running ASP.NET 1.0 applications under Windows 2000. In this case, for the impersonation to work you need to run your ASP.NET applications under the SYSTEM account, with all the security repercussions that this entails.

Impersonating Through the Anonymous Account

A third possibility to change the identity of the ASP.NET worker process is by impersonating through the anonymous account. The idea is that the ASP.NET application grants access to anonymous users, and the anonymous account is configured to be the desired account for the application.

In this case, the application uses per-request impersonation and the ASP.NET code executes as the impersonated account. The process account remains set to ASPNET or NETWORK SERVICE, which means that you don't have to worry about replicating into the new account the minimum set of permissions on folders that allow ASP.NET to work.

Privileges of the ASP.NET Default Account

Of all the possible user rights assignments, ASPNET and NETWORK SERVICE are granted only the following five:

- Access this computer from the network
- Deny logon locally
- Deny logon through Terminal Services
- Log on as a batch job
- Log on as a service

In addition, the accounts are given some NTFS permissions to operate on certain folders and create temporary files and assemblies. The folders involved are these:

- **.NET Framework Root Folder**   This folder contains some .NET Framework system assemblies that ASP.NET must be able to access. The physical folder is normally *Microsoft.NET\Framework\[version]* and is located under the Windows folder. ASP.NET has only read and list permissions on this folder.

- **Temporary ASP.NET Files**   This folder represents the file system subtree in which all temporary files are generated. ASP.NET is granted full control over the entire subtree.

- **Global Assembly Cache**   ASP.NET needs to gain read permissions on the assemblies in the global assembly cache (GAC). The GAC is located in the *Windows\Assembly\GAC* folder. The GAC folder is not visible in Windows Explorer, but you can view the installed assemblies by opening the *Windows\Assembly* folder.

- **Windows System Folder**   The ASP.NET process needs to access and read the *System32* Windows folder to load any necessary Win32 DLLs.

- **Application Root Folder**   The ASP.NET process needs to access and read the files that make up the Web application. The folder is typically located under *Inetpub\wwwroot*.

- **Web Site Root**   ASP.NET might have the need to scan the root of the Web server— typically, *Inetpub\wwwroot*—looking for configuration files to read.

An ASP.NET application running under an account that lacks some of these permissions might fail. Granting at least all these permissions is highly recommended for all accounts used for fixed account impersonation.

The Trust Level of ASP.NET Applications

ASP.NET applications are made of managed code and run inside the common language runtime (CLR). In the CLR, running code is assigned to a security zone based on the evidence it provides about its origin—for example, the originating URL. Each security zone corresponds to a set of permissions. Each set of permissions correspond to a trust level. By default, ASP.NET applications run from the MyComputer zone with full trust. Is this default setting just evil?

An ASP.NET application runs on the Web server and doesn't hurt the user that connects to it via the browser. An ASP.NET application cannot be consumed in other ways than through the browser. So why do several people feel cold shivers down their spine as they think of ASP.NET full trust?

The problem is not with the ASP.NET application itself, but with the fact that it is publicly exposed over the Internet—one of the most hostile environments for computer security you can imagine. Should a fully trusted ASP.NET account be hijacked, a hacker could perform restricted actions from within the worker thread. In other words, a publicly exposed fully trusted application is a potential platform for hackers to launch attacks. The less an application is trusted, the more secure that application happens to be.

The *<trust>* Section

By default, ASP.NET applications run unrestricted and are allowed to do whatever their account is allowed to do. The actual security restrictions that sometimes apply to ASP.NET applications (for example, the inability to write files) are not a sign of partial trust, but more simply the effect of the underprivileged account under which ASP.NET applications normally run.

By tweaking the *<trust>* section in the root *web.config* file, you can configure code access security permissions for a Web application and decide whether it has to run fully or partially trusted:

```
<trust level="Medium" originUrl="" />
```

Table 17-2 describes the levels of trust available.

TABLE 17-2 Levels Permitted in the *<trust>* Section

Level	Description
Full	Applications run fully trusted and can execute arbitrary native code in the process context in which they run. This is the default setting.
High	Code can use most permissions that support partial trust. This level is appropriate for applications you want to run with least privilege to mitigate risks.
Medium	Code can read and write its own application directories and can interact with databases.
Low	Code can read its own application resources but can't interact with resources located outside of its application space.
Minimal	Code can't interact with any protected resources. Appropriate for nonprofessional hosting sites that simply intend to support generic HTML code and highly isolated business logic.

Note Web applications and Web services built using .NET Framework version 1.0 always run with unrestricted code access permissions. Configurable levels listed in Table 17-2 do not apply to ASP.NET 1.0 applications.

Admittedly, restricting the set of things an application can do might be painful at first. However, in the long run (read, if you don't just give up and deliver the application) it produces better and safer code.

Note The *<trust>* section supports an attribute named *originUrl*. The attribute is a sort of misnomer. If you set it, the specified URL is granted the permission to access an HTTP resource using either a *Socket* or *WebRequest* class. The permission class involved with this is *WebPermission*. Of course, the Web permission is granted only if the specified *<trust>* level supports that. *Medium* and higher trust levels do.

ASP.NET Permissions

Let's review in more detail the permission granted to ASP.NET applications when the various trust levels are applied. Key ASP.NET permissions for each trust level are outlined in Table 17-3.

TABLE 17-3 Main Permissions in ASP.NET Trust Levels

	High	Medium	Low	Minimal
FileIO	Unrestricted	Read/Write to application's space	Read	None
IsolatedStorage	Unrestricted	ByUser	ByUser (maximum of 1 MB)	None
Printing	DefaultPrinting	*Same as High*	None	None
Security	Assertion, Execution, ControlThread, ControlPrincipal	*Same as High*	Execution	Execution
SqlClient	Unrestricted	Unrestricted (no blank password allowed)	None	None
Registry	Unrestricted	None	None	None
Environment	Unrestricted	None	None	None
Reflection	ReflectionEmit	None	None	None
Socket	Unrestricted	None	None	None
Web	Unrestricted	Connect to origin host, if configured	*Same as Medium*	None

More detailed information about the permissions actually granted to the default trust levels are available in the security configuration files for each level. The name of the file for each level is stored in the *<trustLevel>* section.

In the end, full-trust applications run unrestricted. High-trust applications have read/write permission for all the files in their application space. However, the physical access to files is still ruled by the NTFS access control list on the resource. High-trust applications have unrestricted access to Microsoft SQL Server but not, for example, to OLE DB classes. (The *OleDbPermission* and other managed provider permissions are denied to all but fully trusted applications.) Reflection calls are denied with the exception of those directed at classes in the *System.Reflection.Emit* namespace.

Medium applications have unrestricted access to SQL Server, but only as long as they do not use blank passwords for accounts. The *WebPermission* is granted to both medium- and low-trust applications, but it requires that the URL be configured in the *<trust>* section through the *originUrl* attribute. Low-trust applications have read-only permission for files in their application directories. Isolated storage is still permitted but limited to a 1-MB quota.

A rule of thumb is that *Medium* trust should be fine for most ASP.NET applications and applying it shouldn't cause significant headaches, provided that you don't need to access legacy Component Object Model (COM) objects or databases exposed via OLE DB providers.

Granting Privileges Beyond the Trust Level

What if one of the tasks to perform requires privileges that the trust level doesn't grant? There are two basic approaches. The simplest approach is to customize the policy file for the trust level and add any permissions you need. The solution is easy to implement and doesn't require code changes. It does require administrator rights to edit the security policy files. From a pure security perspective, it is not a great solution, as you're just adding to the whole application the permissions you need for a particular method of a particular page or assembly.

The second approach requires a bit of refactoring but leads to better and safer code. The idea is to sandbox the server-side code and make it delegate to external components (for example, serviced components or command-line programs) the execution of any tasks that exceed the application's permission set. Obviously, the external component will be configured to have all required permissions.

Note Code sandboxing is the only option you have if your partially trusted ASP.NET application is trying to make calls into an assembly that doesn't include the *AllowPartiallyTrustedCallers* attribute. For more information on programming for medium trust, check out the contents at the following URL: *http://msdn2.microsoft.com/en-us/library/ms998341.aspx*.

ASP.NET Authentication Methods

Depending on the type of the requested resource, IIS might or might not be able to handle the request itself. If the resource needs the involvement of ASP.NET (for example, it is an *.aspx* file), IIS hands the request over to ASP.NET along with the security token of the authenticated, or anonymous, user. What happens next depends on the ASP.NET configuration.

ASP.NET supports three types of authentication methods: Windows, Passport, and Forms. A fourth possibility is None, meaning that ASP.NET does not even attempt to perform its own authentication and completely relies on the authentication already carried out by IIS. In this case, anonymous users can connect and resources are accessed using the default ASP.NET account.

You choose the ASP.NET authentication mechanism using the *<authentication>* section in the root *web.config* file. Child subdirectories inherit the authentication mode chosen for the application. By default, the authentication mode is set to Windows. Let's briefly examine the Windows and Passport authentication and reserve wider coverage for the most commonly used authentication method—Forms authentication.

Windows Authentication

When using Windows authentication, ASP.NET works in conjunction with IIS. The real authentication is performed by IIS, which uses one of its authentication methods: Basic, Digest, or Integrated Windows. When IIS has authenticated the user, it passes the security token on to ASP.NET. When in Windows authentication mode, ASP.NET does not perform any further authentication steps and limits its use of the IIS token to authorizing access to the resources.

Typically, you use the Windows authentication method in intranet scenarios when the users of your application have Windows accounts that only can be authenticated by the Web server. Let's assume that you configured the Web server to work with the Integrated Windows authentication mode and that you disabled anonymous access. The ASP.NET application works in Windows authentication mode. What happens when a user connects to the application? First, IIS authenticates the user (popping up a dialog box if the account of the local user doesn't match any accounts on the Web server or in trusted domain) and then hands the security token over to ASP.NET.

Using ACLs to Authorize Access

In most cases, Windows authentication is used in conjunction with file authorization—via the *FileAuthorizationModule* HTTP module. User-specific pages in the Web application can be protected from unauthorized access by using access control lists (ACLs) on the file. When ASP.NET is about to access a resource, the *FileAuthorizationModule* HTTP module is called into action. File authorization performs an ACL check on ASP.NET files using the caller's identity. This means that, say, the user Joe will never be able to access an *.aspx* page whose ACL doesn't include an entry for him.

Note, though, that file authorization does not require impersonation at the ASP.NET level and, more importantly, works regardless of whether the impersonation flag is turned on. There's good news and bad news in this statement. The good news is that once you've set an appropriately configured ACL on an ASP.NET resource, you're pretty much done. Nobody will be able to access the resource without permission. But what about non-ASP.NET resources such as local files?

For example, how can you protect an HTML page from unauthorized access? The first consideration is that an HTML page rarely needs to be protected against access. If you need to protect a page, the page very likely also executes some server-side code. Implementing it as *.aspx* is more useful anyway. That said, by design HTML pages are not protected from unauthorized access because they are not processed by the ASP.NET pipeline. If you want to protect it, the best thing you can do is rename the page to *.aspx* so that it is processed by the ASP.NET runtime.

Note HTML pages and other resources can still be protected using NTFS permissions. If particular constraints are set on a file using NTFS permissions, there's no way the file can be accessed by anyone lacking proper rights.

Alternately, you can rename the page to a custom extension and write a lightweight Internet Server Application Programming Interface (ISAPI) extension (or a managed HTTP handler) to implement a made-to-measure authorization mechanism. I discuss HTTP handlers in Chapter 18.

Note Windows authentication also works with URL authorization implemented by the HTTP module named *URLAuthorizationModule*. This module allows or denies access to URL resources to certain users and roles. (We'll talk more about URL authorization later while discussing Forms authentication.)

Passport Authentication

Passport authentication is a Microsoft-centralized authentication service. Passport provides a way to authenticate users coming across all the sites that participate in the initiative. Users need to do a single logon and, if successfully authenticated, they can then freely move through all the member sites. In addition to the single logon service, Passport also offers core profile services for member sites.

ASP.NET provides the *PassportAuthenticationModule* HTTP module to set up authentication for Web applications hosted by Passport member sites. When an HTTP request hits a

Passport-enabled Web site, the HTTP module verifies whether or not the request contains a valid Passport ticket. If not, the Web server returns the status code 302 and redirects the client to the Passport Logon service. The query string contains properly encrypted information about the original request. The client issues a GET request to the logon server and passes the supplied query string. At this point, the Passport logon server prompts the client with an HTML logon form. After the user has filled out the form, the form is posted back to the logon server over an SSL-secured channel.

The logon server uses the form information to authenticate the user and, if successful, creates a Passport ticket. Next, the user is redirected to the original URL and the ticket is passed, encrypted, in the query string. Finally, the browser follows the redirect instruction and again requests the original Passport-protected resource. This time, though, the request contains a valid ticket so that the *PassportAuthenticationModule* will allow the request to pass.

> **Note** The .NET Framework 3.0 contains a new technology that can be used with ASP.NET Web sites to authenticate users: Windows CardSpace. Any page that includes the Identity Selector object, uses the identity cards of the connected user to send credentials to the server. Each can manage its own cards by using the Windows CardSpace applet in the Control Panel of a Windows Vista machine (or any other client machine equipped with the .NET Framework 3.0 or later versions.) The Identity Selector is an *<object>* tag of type *application/x-informationcard*. By requesting the value property of this object, you force an enabled browser (i.e., Internet Explorer 7.0) to bring up the CardSpace applet. The user then picks up the right card to send. The server-side login page will then access the content of the card and makes any necessary checks to authorize the request. If widely accepted, Windows CardSpace would be the perfect tool for authentication over the Internet. For more information, you can read the MSDN online documentation for Windows CardSpace. A good place to start is the Windows CardSpace Web site at *http://cardspace.netfx3.com/*.

Using Forms Authentication

Both Windows and Passport authentication are seldom practical for real-world Internet applications. Windows authentication is based on Windows accounts and NTFS ACL tokens and, as such, assumes that clients are connecting from Windows-equipped machines. Useful and effective in intranet and possibly in some extranet scenarios, Windows authentication is simply unrealistic in more common situations because the Web application users are required to have Windows accounts in the application's domain. The same conclusion applies to Passport authentication, although for different reasons. Passport is not free, requires the implementation of serious security measures (that are not free and that you don't necessarily need at all sites), and makes sense mostly for e-commerce and co-branded Web sites.

So what is the ideal authentication mechanism for real Web developers? A Web programming best practice recommends that you place some relatively boilerplated code on top of each nonpublic page and redirect the user to a login page. In the login page, the user is prompted for credentials and redirected to the originally requested page, if successfully authenticated. All this code is not exactly rocket science, but it's still code that you have to write yourself and use over and over again.

Forms authentication is just the ASP.NET built-in infrastructure to implement the aforementioned pattern for login. Today, Forms authentication is the ideal—I would say, the only—choice whenever you need to collect user credentials and process them internally—for example, against a database of user accounts. The login pattern implemented by Forms authentication doesn't look radically different from Windows and Passport authentication. The key difference is that with Forms authentication everything happens under the strict control of the application.

You set up an ASP.NET application for Forms authentication by tweaking its root *web.config* file. You enter the following script:

```
<system.web>
    <authentication mode="Forms">
        <forms loginUrl="login.aspx" />
    </authentication>
    <authorization>
        <deny users="?" />
    </authorization>
</system.web>
```

The *<authentication>* section indicates the URL of the user-defined login form. ASP.NET displays the form only to users who have explicitly been denied access in the *<authorization>* section. The *?* symbol indicates any anonymous, unauthenticated users. Note that the anonymous user here is not the IIS anonymous user but simply a user who has not been authenticated through your login form.

All blocked users are redirected to the login page, where they are asked to enter their credentials.

> **Note** The Forms authentication mechanism protects any ASP.NET resource located in a folder for which Forms authentication and authorization is enabled. Note that only resource types explicitly handled by ASP.NET are protected. The list includes *.aspx*, *.asmx*, and *.ashx* files, but not plain HTML pages or classic ASP pages. In IIS 7.0, though, you are given the tools to change this by setting a Web server-level web.config file where you assign new resources to the ASP.NET standard HTTP handler.

Forms Authentication Control Flow

Form-based authentication is governed by an HTTP module implemented in the *FormsAuthenticationModule* class. The behavior of the component is driven by the contents of the *web.config* file. When the browser attempts to access a protected resource, the module kicks in and attempts to locate an authentication ticket for the caller. In ASP.NET 1.x, a ticket is merely a cookie with a particular (and configurable) name. In ASP.NET 2.0 and newer versions, it can be configured to be a value embedded in the URL (cookieless Forms authentication).

If no valid ticket is found, the module redirects the request to a login page. Information about the originating page is placed in the query string. The login page is then displayed. The programmer creates this page, which, at a minimum, contains text boxes for the user-name and the password and a button for submitting credentials. The handler for the button click event validates the credentials using an application-specific algorithm and data store. If the credentials are authenticated, the user code redirects the browser to the original URL. The original URL is attached to the query string of the request for the login page, as shown here:

```
http://YourApp/login.aspx?ReturnUrl=original.aspx
```

Authenticating a user means that an authentication ticket is issued and attached to the request. When the browser places its second request for the page, the HTTP module retrieves the authentication ticket and lets the request pass.

Let's see how form-based authentication works in practice and consider a scenario in which users are not allowed to connect anonymously to any pages in the application. The user types the URL of the page, say *welcome.aspx*, and goes. As a result, the HTTP module redi-rects to the login page any users for which an authentication ticket does not exist, as shown in Figure 17-3.

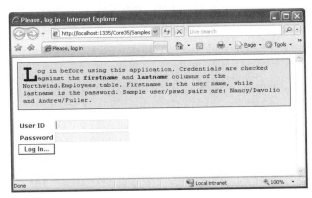

FIGURE 17-3 The login page of the sample application.

Important There are inherent security concerns that arise with Forms authentication related to the fact that any data is transmitted as clear text . Unfortunately, with today's browser tech-nology these potential security concerns can be removed only by resorting to secure channels (HTTPS). I'll return to this topic later in the "General Security Issues" section.

Collecting Credentials Through Login

The layout of a login page is nearly the same—a couple of text boxes for the user name and password, a button to confirm, and perhaps a label to display error messages. However, you can make it as complex as needed and add as many graphics as appropriate. The user enters the credentials, typically in a case-sensitive way, and then clicks the button to log on. When the login page posts back, the following code runs:

```
void LogonUser(object sender, EventArgs e)
{
    string user = userName.Text;
    string pswd = passWord.Text;

    // Custom authentication
    bool bAuthenticated = AuthenticateUser(user, pswd);
    if (bAuthenticated)
        FormsAuthentication.RedirectFromLoginPage(user, false);
    else
        errorMsg.Text = "Sorry, yours seems not to be a valid account.";
}
```

The event handler retrieves the strings typed in the user name and password fields and calls into a local function named *AuthenticateUser*. The function verifies the supplied credentials and returns a Boolean value. If the user has been successfully authenticated, the code invokes the *RedirectFromLoginPage* static method on the *FormsAuthentication* class to inform the browser that it's time to issue a new request to the original page.

The *RedirectFromLoginPage* method redirects an authenticated user back to the originally requested URL. It has two overloads with the following prototypes:

```
public static void RedirectFromLoginPage(string, bool);
public static void RedirectFromLoginPage(string, bool, string);
```

The first argument is the name of the user to store in the authentication ticket. The second argument is a Boolean value that denotes the duration of the cookie, if any, being created for the authentication ticket. If this argument is *true*, the cookie is given a duration that equals the number of minutes set by the *timeout* attribute (which is 30 minutes by default). In this way, you get a cookie that persists across browser sessions. Otherwise, your authentication cookie will last for the current session only. Finally, the third argument optionally specifies the cookie path.

Authenticating the User

The authenticating algorithm—that is, the code inside the *AuthenticateUser* method seen earlier—is entirely up to you. For example, you might want to check the credentials against a database or any other user-defined storage device. The following listing shows a function that compares the user name and password against the *firstname* and *lastname* columns of the Northwind Employees table in SQL Server:

```
private bool AuthenticateUser(string username, string pswd)
{
    // Performs authentication here
    string connString = "...";
    string cmdText = "SELECT COUNT(*) FROM employees " +
                     "WHERE firstname=@user AND lastname=@pswd";

    int found = 0;
    using(SqlConnection conn = new SqlConnection(connString))
    {
        SqlCommand cmd = new SqlCommand(cmdText, conn);
        cmd.Parameters.Add("@user",
            SqlDbType.NVarChar, 10).Value = username;
        cmd.Parameters.Add("@pswd",
            SqlDbType.NVarChar, 20).Value = pswd;
        conn.Open();
        found = (int)cmd.ExecuteScalar();
        conn.Close();
    }
    return (found > 0);
}
```

The query is configured to return an integer that represents the number of rows in the table that match the specified user name and password. Notice the use of typed and sized parameters in the SQL command as a line of defense against possible injection of malicious code. Notice also that the SQL code just shown does not support strong passwords because the SQL = operator in the *WHERE* clause doesn't perform case-sensitive comparisons. To make provisions for that, you should rewrite the command as follows:

```
SELECT COUNT(*) FROM employees WHERE
    CAST(RTRIM(firstname) AS VarBinary)=CAST(RTRIM(@user) AS VarBinary)
    AND
    CAST(RTRIM(lastname) AS VarBinary)=CAST(RTRIM(@pswd) AS VarBinary)
```

The *CAST* operator converts the value into its binary representation, while the *RTRIM* operator removes trailing blanks.

Figure 17-4 shows the page of the application once the user has been successfully authenticated.

FIGURE 17-4 The user has been authenticated, and his name shows up in the user interface.

The *welcome.aspx* page has the following, fairly simple, source code:

```
<%@ Page Language="C#" CodeFile="Welcome.aspx.cs" Inherits="Welcome" %>
<html><body>
    <form id="form1" runat="server">
    <h1>Welcome, <%= User.Identity.Name %></h1>
    </form>
</body></html>
```

Signing Out

While an explicit sign-in is always required by Web sites that need authentication, an explicit sign-out is less common but legitimate nonetheless. The Forms authentication module provides an explicit method to sign out. The *SignOut* method on the *FormsAuthentication* class takes no argument and resets the authentication ticket. In particular, when cookies are used, the *SignOut* method removes the current ticket from the *Cookies* collection of the current *HttpResponse* object and replaces it with an empty and expired cookie.

After you call *SignOut*, you might want to redirect the application to another page—for example, the home page. To do this, you don't have to redirect the browser, but as long as the page is publicly accessible, you can use the more efficient *Server.Transfer* method that we described in Chapter 14:

```
void Signout(object sender, EventArgs e)
{
    FormsAuthentication.SignOut();
    Server.Transfer("home.aspx");
}
```

Starting with ASP.NET 2.0, the *FormsAuthentication* class has a new method— *RedirectToLoginPage*—that provides the described functionality, except that it uses *Response.Redirect* instead of *Server.Transfer*.

We've just covered the basics of Forms authentication, but we've not yet covered the programming application programming interface (API) we find in ASP.NET in any detail. Before we get to this, it is important that you take a look at the methods of the *FormsAuthentication* class and the configurable parameters you find in the *web.config* file. After this, I'll move on to introduce the membership API and role management.

The *FormsAuthentication* Class

The *FormsAuthentication* class supplies some static methods that you can use to manipulate authentication tickets and execute basic authentication operations. You typically use the *RedirectFromLoginPage* method to redirect an authenticated user back to the originally requested URL; likewise, you call *SignOut* to remove the authentication ticket for the current user. Other methods and properties are for manipulating and renewing the ticket and the associated cookie.

Properties of the *FormsAuthentication* Class

Table 17-4 lists the properties of the *FormsAuthentication* class. As you can see, many of them deal with cookie naming and usage and expose the content of configuration attributes in the *<forms>* section. We'll look at the underpinnings of the *<forms>* XML configuration element in the next section. All the properties of the *FormsAuthentication* class shown in the table are static.

TABLE 17-4 **Properties of the *FormsAuthentication* Class**

Property	Description
CookieDomain	Returns the domain set for the authentication ticket. This property is equal to the value of the *domain* attribute in the *<forms>* section. *Not supported in ASP.NET 1.x.*
CookieMode	Indicates whether Forms authentication is implemented with or without cookies. *Not supported in ASP.NET 1.x.*
CookiesSupported	Returns *true* if the current request supports cookies. *Not supported in ASP.NET 1.x.*
DefaultUrl	Returns the URL for the page to return after a request has been successfully authenticated. Matches the *defaultUrl* attribute in the *<forms>* section. *Not supported in ASP.NET 1.x.*
EnableCrossAppRedirects	Indicates whether redirects can span different Web applications. *Not supported in ASP.NET 1.x.*
FormsCookieName	Returns the configured cookie name used for the current application. The default name is *.ASPXAUTH*.
FormsCookiePath	Returns the configured cookie path used for the current application. The default is the root path /.

Property	Description
LoginUrl	Returns the configured or default URL for the login page. Matches the *loginUrl* attribute in the *<forms>* section. *Not supported in ASP.NET 1.x.*
RequireSSL	Indicates whether a cookie must be transmitted using only HTTPS.
SlidingExpiration	Indicates whether sliding expiration is enabled.

Most of the properties are initialized with the values read from the *<forms>* configuration section of the *web.config* file when the application starts up.

Methods of the *FormsAuthentication* Class

Table 17-5 details the methods supported by the *FormsAuthentication* class. All the methods listed in the table are static.

TABLE 17-5 Methods of the *FormsAuthentication* Class

Method	Description
Authenticate	Attempts to validate the supplied credentials against those contained in the configured *<credentials>* section. (I'll say more about this later.)
Decrypt	Given a valid authentication ticket, it returns an instance of the *FormsAuthenticationTicket* class.
Encrypt	Produces a string containing the printable representation of an authentication ticket. The string contains, encoded to URL-compliant characters, the user's credentials optionally hashed and encrypted.
GetAuthCookie	Creates an authentication ticket for a given user name.
GetRedirectUrl	Returns the redirect URL for the original request that caused the redirect to the login page.
HashPasswordForStoringInConfigFile	Given a password and a string identifying the hash type, the method hashes the password for storage in the *web.config* file.
Initialize	Initializes the *FormsAuthentication* class.
RedirectFromLoginPage	Redirects an authenticated user back to the originally requested URL.
RedirectToLoginPage	Performs a redirect to the configured or default login page. *Not supported in ASP.NET 1.x.*
RenewTicketIfOld	Conditionally updates the sliding expiration on an authentication ticket.
SetAuthCookie	Creates an authentication ticket, and attaches it to the outgoing response. It does not redirect to the originally requested URL.
SignOut	Removes the authentication ticket.

The *Initialize* method is called only once in the application's lifetime and initializes the properties in Table 17-4 by reading the configuration file. The method also gets the cookie values and encryption keys to be used for the application.

Not available to ASP.NET 1.x applications, *RedirectToLoginPage* fills a hole in the programming interface of the *FormsAuthentication* class. The method is useful when a user signs out and you want to redirect her to the login page afterwards. When this happens, the method figures out what the login page is and calls *Response.Redirect*.

> **Note** In spite of their names, in ASP.NET both the *GetAuthCookie* method and the *SetAuthCookie* method get and set an authentication ticket, whatever it means to the application. If the application is configured to do Forms authentication in a cookieless manner, the two methods read and write ticket information from and to the URL of the request. They read and write a cookie if the authentication method is configured to use cookies.

Configuration of *Forms* Authentication

Although ASP.NET Forms authentication is fairly simple to understand, it still provides a rich set of options to deal with to fine-tune the behavior of the authentication mechanism. Most of the settable options revolve around the use of cookies for storing the authentication ticket. All of them find their place in the *<forms>* section under the *<authentication>* section.

The *<forms>* Section

Forms authentication is driven by the contents of the *<forms>* section child of the *<authentication>* section. The overall syntax is shown here:

```
<forms name="cookie"
    loginUrl="url"
    protection="All|None|Encryption|Validation"
    timeout="30"
    requireSSL="true|false"
    slidingExpiration="true|false"
    path="/"
    enableCrossAppsRedirects="true|false"
    cookieless="UseCookies|UseUri|AutoDetect|UseDeviceProfile"
    defaultUrl="url"
    domain="string">
</forms>
```

The various attributes are described in Table 17-6.

TABLE 17-6 Attributes for *Forms* Authentication

Attribute	Description
cookieless	Defines if and how cookies are used for authentication tickets. Feasible values are *UseCookies*, *UseUri*, *AutoDetect*, and *UseDeviceProfile*. *Not supported in ASP.NET 1.x.*
defaultUrl	Defines the default URL to redirect after authentication. The default is *default.aspx*. *Not supported in ASP.NET 1.x.*
domain	Specifies a domain name to be set on outgoing authentication cookies. (I'll say more about this later.) *Not supported in ASP.NET 1.x.*
enableCrossAppRedirects	Indicates whether users can be authenticated by external applications when authentication is cookieless. The setting is ignored if cookies are enabled. When cookies are enabled, cross-application authentication is always possible. (I'll cover more issues related to this as we go along.) *Not supported in ASP.NET 1.x.*
loginUrl	Specifies the URL to which the request is redirected for login if no valid authentication cookie is found.
name	Specifies the name of the HTTP cookie to use for authentication. The default name is *.ASPXAUTH*.
path	Specifies the path for the authentication cookies issued by the application. The default value is a slash (/). Note that some browsers are case-sensitive and will not send cookies back if there is a path case mismatch.
protection	Indicates how the application intends to protect the authentication cookie. Feasible values are *All*, *Encryption*, *Validation*, and *None*. The default is *All*.
requireSSL	Indicates whether an SSL connection is required to transmit the authentication cookie. The default is *false*. If *true*, ASP.NET sets the *Secure* property on the authentication cookie object so that a compliant browser does not return the cookie unless the connection is using SSL. *Not supported in ASP.NET 1.0.*
slidingExpiration	Indicates whether sliding expiration is enabled. The default is *false*, meaning that the cookie expires at a set interval from the time it was originally issued. The interval is determined by the *timeout* attribute. *Not supported in ASP.NET 1.0.*
timeout	Specifies the amount of time, in minutes, after which the authentication cookie expires. The default value is 30.

The *defaultUrl* attribute lets you set the default name of the page to return after a request has been successfully authenticated. This URL is hard-coded to *default.aspx* in ASP.NET 1.x and has been made configurable in ASP.NET 2.0 and newer versions. But isn't the URL of the return page embedded in the query string, in the *ReturnUrl* parameter? So when is *defaultUrl* useful?

If a user is redirected to the login page by the authentication module, the *ReturnUrl* variable is always correctly set and the value of *defaultUrl* is blissfully ignored. However, if your page contains a link to the login page, or if it needs to transfer programmatically to the login page (for example, after the current user has logged off), you are responsible for setting the *ReturnUrl* variable. If it is not set, the URL stored in the *defaultUrl* attribute will be used.

Cookie-Based Forms Authentication

In ASP.NET 1.x, Forms authentication is exclusively based on cookies. The content of the authentication ticket is stored in a cookie named after the value of the *name* attribute in the *<forms>* section. The cookie contains any information that helps to identify the user making the request.

By default, a cookie used for authentication lasts 30 minutes and is protected using both data validation and encryption. Data validation ensures that the contents of the cookie have not been tampered with along the way. Encryption uses the Rijndael encryption algorithm to scramble the content. You can force it to use DES or 3DES if you like, however.

When validation is turned on, the cookie is created by concatenating a validation key with the cookie data, computing a Machine Authentication Code (MAC) and appending the MAC to the outgoing cookie. The validation key, as well as the hash algorithm to use for the MAC, are read out of the *<machineKey>* section in the *web.config* file. The same section also specifies the cryptographic key for when encryption is enabled.

> **Important** When you create a new ASP.NET application with Microsoft Visual Studio 2008, the default *web.config* file added to the application might not include most of the settings mentioned in this chapter and earlier in the book. It is interesting to note that both the *web.config* file in the application's root and any others you might have in subdirectories override the settings defined in the *machine.config* file. Installed with ASP.NET, *machine.config* contains a default value for each possible section and attribute in the configuration scheme. Therefore, if any given setting is not set (or overridden) in your *web.config* file, that configurable parameter will be set when you run your ASP.NET application using the default value found in *machine.config*.

Cookieless Forms Authentication

Using cookies requires some support from the client browser. In ASP.NET 1.x, cookies are mandatory if you want to take advantage of the built-in authentication framework. Starting with ASP.NET 2.0, the core API also supports cookieless semantics. More precisely, the whole API has been reworked to make it expose a nearly identical programming interface but also support dual semantics—cookied and cookieless.

In ASP.NET 2.0 and beyond, when cookieless authentication is on the ticket it is incorporated into the URL in much the same way as for cookieless sessions. Figure 17-5 provides an example.

FIGURE 17-5 Cookieless Forms authentication in action.

The URL of the page served to an authenticated user follows the pattern shown here:

```
http://YourApp/(F(XYZ...1234))/samples/default.aspx
```

The ticket, properly encoded to an URL-compliant alphabet, is inserted in the URL right after the server name.

> **Note** No matter which settings you might have for validation and encryption, or whether your authentication scheme is cookied or cookieless, the information stored in the authentication ticket is encoded so that it is not immediately human-readable. Forms authentication uses a URI-safe derivative of the Base64 encoding that carries six bits of encoding per character.

Cookieless authentication requires an ISAPI filter to intercept the request, extract the ticket, and rewrite the correct path to the application. The filter also exposes the authentication ticket as another request header. The same *aspnet_filter.dll* component that we saw in Chapter 15 for cookieless sessions is used to parse the URL when cookieless authentication is used. To avoid confusion, each extra piece of information stuffed in the URL is wrapped by unique delimiters: *S(...)* for a session ID and *F(...)* for an authentication ticket. The filter extracts the information, removes URL adornments, and places the ticket information in a header named *AspAuthenticationTicket*.

Options for Cookieless Authentication

To enable cookieless authentication, you set the *cookieless* attribute in the *<forms>* section of the configuration file to a particular value. The attribute specifies if and how cookies are used to store the authentication ticket. It can take any of the values listed in Table 17-7.

TABLE 17-7 Values for the *cookieless* Attribute

Value	Description
AutoDetect	Uses cookies if the browser has cookie support currently enabled. It uses the cookieless mechanism otherwise.
UseCookie	Always uses cookies, regardless of the browser capabilities.
UseDeviceProfile	Uses cookies if the browser supports them, and uses the cookieless mechanism otherwise. When this option is used, no attempt is made to check whether cookie support is really enabled for the requesting device. This is the default option.
UseUri	Never uses cookies, regardless of the browser capabilities.

There's a subtle difference between *UseDeviceProfile* and *AutoDetect*. Let's make it clear with an example. Imagine a user making a request through Internet Explorer 6.0. The browser does have support for cookies as reported in the browser capabilities database installed with ASP.NET. However, a particular user might have disabled cookies support for her own browser. *AutoDetect* can correctly handle the latter scenario and opts for cookieless authentication. *UseDeviceProfile* doesn't probe for cookies being enabled, and it stops at what's reported by the capabilities database. It will wrongly opt for cookied authentication, causing an exception to be thrown.

For compatibility with ASP.NET 1.x, the default value for the *cookieless* attribute is *UseDeviceProfile*. You should consider changing it to *AutoDetect*.

> **Note** When assigning a value to the *cookieless* attribute in the *<forms>* section, pay attention at how you type any of the feasible values in Table 17-7. Case does matter here—for instance, *UseUri* is a different thing than *useuri*. Only the first will work.

Advanced Forms Authentication Features

Let's tackle a few less obvious issues that might arise when working with Forms authentication.

Applications to Share Authentication Cookies

HTTP cookies support a *path* attribute to let you define the application path the cookie is valid within. Pages outside of that path cannot read or use the cookie. If the path is not set explicitly, it defaults to the URL of the page creating the cookie. For authentication cookies, the path defaults to the root of the application so that it is valid for all pages in the application. So far so good.

Already in ASP.NET 1.x, two applications in the same Internet domain can share their own authentication cookies, implementing a sort of single sign-on model. Typically, both applications provide their own login pages, and users can log on using any of them and then freely navigate between the pages of both. For this to happen, you only have to ensure that some settings in the root *web.config* files are the same for both applications. In particular, the settings for the *name*, *protection*, and *path* attributes in the *<forms>* section must be identical. Moreover, a *<machineKey>* section should be added to both *web.config* files with explicit validation and decryption keys:

```
<machineKey
    validationKey="C50B3C89CB21F4F1422FF158A5B42D0…E"
    decryptionKey="8A9BE8FD67AF6979E7D20198C…D"
    validation="SHA1" />
```

Read Knowledge Base article 312906 (located at *http://support.microsoft.com/default. aspx?scid=kb;en-us;312906*) for suggestions on how to create machine keys. Note that by default, validation and decryption keys are set to *AutoGenerate*. The keyword indicates that a random key has been generated at setup time and stored in the Local Security Authority (LSA). LSA is a Windows service that manages all the security on the local system. If you leave the *AutoGenerate* value, each machine will use distinct keys and no shared cookie can be read.

Applications running in the same domain can share authentication cookies also in ASP.NET 2.0 and newer versions. This happens also between an ASP.NET 1.x and ASP.NET 2.0 or ASP. NET 3.5 application as long as they are hosted in the same domain. Cookie sharing is impossible between ASP.NET 1.0 applications and applications written with any successive version of ASP.NET.

Suppose now you run two ASP.NET Web sites named *www.contoso.com* and *blogs.contoso. com*. Each of these sites generates authentication cookies not usable by the other. This is because, by default, authentication cookies are associated with the originating domain. All HTTP cookies, though, support a *domain* attribute, which takes the flexibility of their *path* attribute to the next level. If set, the *domain* attribute indicates the domain the cookie is valid for. Cookies can be assigned to an entire Internet domain, a subdomain, or even multiple subdomains.

Starting with ASP.NET 2.0, the *domain* attribute in the *<forms>* section determines the value of the *domain* attribute on the authentication cookie being created.

```
<forms domain="contoso.com" />
```

Add the preceding script to the *web.config* file of the Web sites named *www.contoso.com* and *blogs.contoso.com* and you'll have them share the authentication cookies (provided the client browser recognizes the *domain* attribute of the cookie, which most modern browsers are bound to do).

The effect of the setting is that the primary domain (www) and any other subdomains will be able to handle each other's authentication cookies, always with the proviso that their *web. config* files are synchronized on the machine key values.

> **Note** Setting the *domain* attribute doesn't cause anything to be emitted into the authentication ticket; it simply forces all Forms authentication methods to properly set the *domain* property on each issued or renewed ticket. The attribute is ignored if cookieless authentication is used. The domain attribute of the *<forms>* section takes precedence over the domain field used in the *<httpCookies>* section and is valid for all cookies created in the ASP.NET application.

External Applications to Authenticate Users

Forms authentication also supports having the login page specified in another application in the same Web site:

```
<forms loginUrl="/anotherApp/login1.aspx" />
```

The two applications must have identical machine keys configured for this to work. If the application is using cookied authentication tickets, no additional work is necessary. The authentication ticket will be stored in a cookie and sent back to the original application.

In ASP.NET 2.0 and beyond, if cookieless authentication is used, some extra work is required to enable the external application to authenticate for us. You need to set the *enableCrossAppRedirects* attribute in *<forms>* in the *web.config* file of both applications.

```
<forms ... enableCrossAppRedirects="true" />
```

Upon successful authentication, the ticket is generated and attached to a query string parameter to be marshaled back to the original application. Figure 17-6 shows an example.

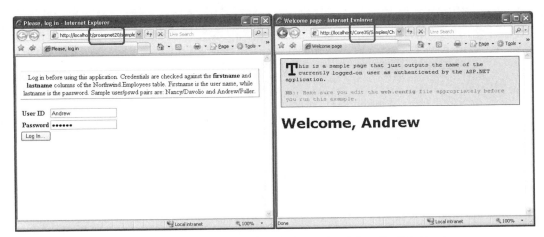

FIGURE 17-6 Another application performs the authentication and serializes the ticket back.

If the *enableCrossAppRedirects* attribute is missing and cookieless authentication is used, the external application will throw an exception.

> **Note** To run this example, ensure that the *<machineKey>* section in the *web.config* file of both applications contains the same values. They are to be explicit keys, not just the *AutoGenerate* command.

Forms Authentication and Secured Sockets

A hacker who manages to steal a valid authentication ticket is in a position to perpetrate a replay attack for the lifetime of the ticket—which might be for as long as 50 years if you choose to create persistent tickets with an old version of ASP.NET! To mitigate the risk of replay attacks, you can perform authentication over a secured socket.

This means that first you must deploy your login page on an HTTPS-capable server, and second you need to set the *requireSSL* attribute to *true* in the *<forms>* section. This setting causes the ASP.NET application to enable the *Secure* attribute on the HTTP cookie being created. When the *Secure* attribute is set, compliant browsers send back only the cookie containing the ticket over a resource that is protected with SSL. In this way, you can still use a broad cookie scope, such as the whole application ('/') while providing a reasonable security level for the ticket in transit.

If you don't want to use SSL to protect the ticket, the best you can do to alleviate the risk of replay attacks is set the shortest lifetime for the authentication ticket to a value that is reasonable for the application. Even if the ticket is intercepted, there won't be much time remaining for the attacker to do his or her (bad) things.

> **Tip** What if you don't want to be bound to a fixed time for the ticket expiration, but still don't want to leave perpetual tickets around? You can make the application emit persistent tickets, but change the validation and encryption keys in the *web.config* file when you think it is about time to renew all the tickets. A change in the *web.config* file will restart the application, and the new cryptographic parameters will make issued tickets invalid.

As a final note regarding SSL, consider the following. If *requireSSL* is set and the user attempts to log in on a request not made over SSL, an exception is thrown, as shown in Figure 17-7. If *requireSSL* is set and an authentication cookie (a possibly stolen one at that) is provided over a non-SSL request, no exception is thrown; however, the cookie is wiped out and a regular login page is displayed through the browser.

Note that if the same happens with cookieless authentication, no protocol check is made and the request is served to the user...or the attacker.

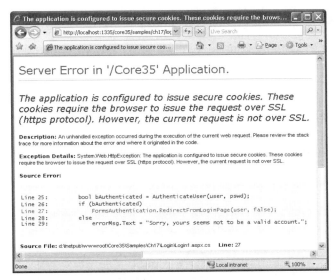

FIGURE 17-7 An application configured to issue secure cookies can accept requests only over SSL.

General Security Issues

Functionally speaking, Forms authentication is the most appropriate authentication method for Web and ASP.NET applications. However, a few general security issues shouldn't pass without comment.

To start with, Forms authentication credentials are sent out as clear text from the client. SSL can be used to protect the communication, but in the end Forms authentication is as weak as the IIS Basic authentication.

As mentioned, a stolen authentication cookie can be used to plan replay attacks as long as it is valid. This risk can be partially mitigated by reducing the lifetime of the ticket. Requiring an SSL connection for the cookie transmission resolves the issue if cookied authentication is used, but not if a cookieless solution is employed.

Finally, Forms authentication is based on application code, which is good and bad news at the same time. It is good because you can keep everything under control. It is bad because any bug you leave in your code opens a security hole. A way to mitigate the risk of vulnerabilities stemming from incorrect code is to resort to the membership API in ASP.NET 2.0 and beyond.

The Membership and Role Management API

In ASP.NET 2.0 and beyond, the core of Forms authentication is the same as in ASP.NET 1.x. Most of the tricks and techniques you have learned remain valid and usable. The most notable change to Forms authentication in ASP.NET 2.0 and newer versions is the introduction of a complementary API—the membership API. The membership API provides a set of classes to let you manage users and roles. Partnered with the *FormsAuthentication* class, the new *Membership* and *Roles* classes form a complete security toolkit for ASP.NET developers. The *Membership* class supplies methods to manage user accounts—for adding or deleting a new user and editing any associated user information such as e-mail address and password. The *Roles* class creates and manages associations between users and roles.

What does the expression "managing user accounts" mean exactly? Simply put, it states that the *Membership* class knows how to create a new user or change his or her password. How do you create a user? Typically, you add a new record to some sort of data store. If that's the case, who is in charge of deciding which data store to use and how to actually write the new user information? These tasks represent the core functionality the membership API is designed to provide.

The membership API doesn't bind you to a fixed data store and data scheme. Quite the reverse, I'd say. It leaves you free to choose any data store and scheme you want, but it binds you to a fixed API through which users and roles are managed. The membership API is based on the provider model (discussed in Chapter 1), and it delegates to the selected provider the implementation of all the features defined by the API itself.

The *Membership* Class

Centered around the *Membership* static class, the membership API shields you from the details of how the credentials and other user information are retrieved and compared. The *Membership* class contains a few methods that you use to obtain a unique identity for each connected user. This information can also be used with other ASP.NET services, including role-based function enabling and personalization.

Among the members of the class are methods for creating, updating, and deleting users, but not methods for managing roles and programmatically setting what a user can and cannot do. For that you'll have to turn to the *Roles* class, which we'll cover later.

The *Membership* class defaults to a provider that stores user information in a SQL Express database in a predefined format. If you want to use a custom data store (such as a personal database), you can create your own provider and just plug it in.

The Programming Interface of the *Membership* Class

Table 17-8 lists the properties exposed by the *Membership* class.

TABLE 17-8 Properties of the *Membership* Class

Property	Description
ApplicationName	A string to identify the application. Defaults to the application's root path.
EnablePasswordReset	Returns *true* if the provider supports password reset.
EnablePasswordRetrieval	Returns *true* if the provider supports password retrieval.
MaxInvalidPasswordAttempts	Returns the maximum number of invalid password attempts allowed before the user is locked out.
MinRequiredNonAlphanumericCharacters	Returns the minimum number of punctuation characters required in the password.
MinRequiredPasswordLength	Returns the minimum required length for a password.
PasswordAttemptWindow	Returns the number of minutes in which a maximum number of invalid password or password answer attempts are allowed before the user is locked out.
PasswordStrengthRegularExpression	Returns the regular expression that the password must comply with.
Provider	Returns an instance of the provider being used.
Providers	Returns the collection of all registered providers.
RequiresQuestionAndAnswer	Returns *true* if the provider requires a password question/answer when retrieving or resetting the password.
UserIsOnlineTimeWindow	Number of minutes after the last activity for which the user is considered on line.

The *Provider* property returns a reference to the membership provider currently in use. As you'll see in a moment, the provider is selected in the configuration file. ASP.NET comes with a couple of predefined providers that target MDF files in SQL Server Express and Active Directory. However, many more membership providers are in the works from Microsoft and third-party vendors, or you can even derive your own. You can obtain the list of installed providers for a given application through the *Providers* collection.

All properties are static and read-only. All of them share a pretty simple implementation. Each property just accesses the corresponding member on the current provider, as shown here:

```
public static int PasswordAttemptWindow
{
   get
   {
      Membership.Initialize();
      return Membership.Provider.PasswordAttemptWindow;
   }
}
```

As the name suggests, the *Initialize* method ensures that the internal structure of the *Membership* class is properly initialized and that a reference to the provider exists.

The class supports fairly advanced functionality, such as estimating the number of users currently using the application. It uses the value assigned to the *UserIsOnlineTimeWindow* property to determine this number. A user is considered on line if he has done something with the application during the previous time window. The default value for the *UserIsOnlineTimeWindow* property is 15 minutes. After 15 minutes of inactivity, a user is considered off line.

Table 17-9 details the methods supported by the *Membership* class. This list clarifies the tasks the class accomplishes.

TABLE 17-9 Methods of the *Membership* Class

Member	Description
CreateUser	Creates a new user and fails if the user already exists. The method returns a *MembershipUser* object representing any available information about the user.
DeleteUser	Deletes the user corresponding to the specified name.
FindUsersByEmail	Returns a collection of *MembershipUser* objects whose e-mail address corresponds to the specified e-mail.
FindUsersByName	Returns a collection of *MembershipUser* objects whose user name matches the specified username.
GeneratePassword	Generates a random password of the specified length.
GetAllUsers	Returns a collection of all users.
GetNumberOfUsersOnline	Returns the total number of users currently on line.
GetUser	Retrieves the *MembershipUser* object associated with the current or specified user.
GetUserNameByEmail	Obtains the user name that corresponds to the specified e-mail. If more users share the same e-mail, the first is retrieved.

Member	Description
UpdateUser	Takes a *MembershipUser* object and updates the information stored for user.
ValidateUser	Authenticates a user by using supplied credentials.

Setting Up Membership Support

To build an authentication layer based on the membership API, you start by choosing the default provider and establish the data store. In the simplest case, you can stay with the default predefined provider, which saves user information in a local MDF file in SQL Server 2005 Express.

The Web Site Administration Tool (WSAT) in Visual Studio provides a user interface for creating and administering the registered users of your application. Figure 17-8 provides a glimpse of the user interface.

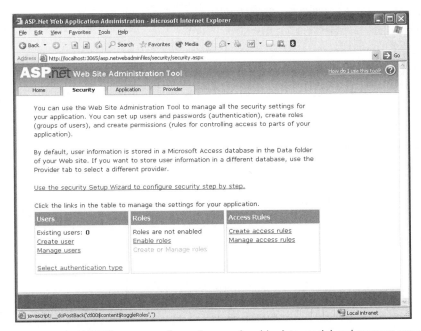

FIGURE 17-8 WSAT lets you configure the membership data model and manage users offline.

To add a new user or to edit properties of an existing one, you use the links shown in the figure. When you edit the properties of a new user, you use the page in Figure 17-9.

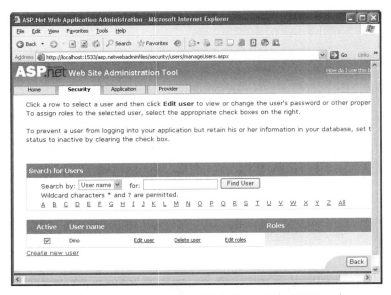

FIGURE 17-9 Choosing a user to edit or delete through the WSAT tool.

Validating Users

At this point, we're ready to write some code that uses the membership API. Let's start with the most common operation—authenticating credentials. Using the features of the membership subsystem, you can rewrite the code in the login page you saw previously to authenticate a user as follows:

```
void LogonUser(object sender, EventArgs e)
{
    string user = userName.Text;
    string pswd = passWord.Text;

    if (Membership.ValidateUser(user, pswd))
        FormsAuthentication.RedirectFromLoginPage(user, false);
    else
        errorMsg.Text = "Sorry, yours seems not to be a valid account.";
}
```

This code doesn't look much different from what you would write for an ASP.NET 1.x application, but there's one big difference: the use of the built-in *ValidateUser* function. Here is the pseudocode of this method as it is implemented in the *system.web* assembly:

```
public static bool ValidateUser(string username, string password)
{
    return Membership.Provider.ValidateUser(username, password);
}
```

As you can see, all the core functionality that performs the authentication lives in the provider. What's nice is that the name of the provider is written in the *web.config* file and can be changed without touching the source code of the application. The overall schema is illustrated in Figure 17-10.

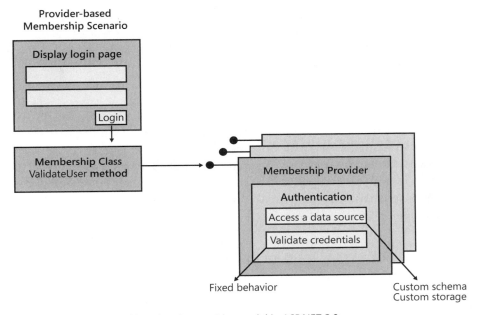

FIGURE 17-10 Membership using the provider model in ASP.NET 2.0.

Managing Users and Passwords

The *Membership* class provides easy-to-use methods for creating and managing user data. For example, to create a new user programmatically, all you do is place a call to the *CreateUser* method:

```
Membership.CreateUser(userName, pswd);
```

To delete a user, you call the *DeleteUser* method:

```
Membership.DeleteUser(userName);
```

You can just as easily get information about a particular user by using the *GetUser* method. The method takes the username and returns a *MembershipUser* object:

```
MembershipUser user = Membership.GetUser("DinoE");
```

Once you've got a *MembershipUser* object, you know all you need to know about a particular user, and you can, for example, programmatically change the password (or other user-specific information). An application commonly needs to execute several operations on passwords, including changing the password, sending a user her password, or resetting the password, possibly with a question/answer challenge protocol. Here is the code that changes the password for a user:

```
MembershipUser user = Membership.GetUser("DinoE");
user.ChangePassword(user.GetPassword(), newPswd);
```

To use the *ChangePassword* method, you must pass in the old password. In some cases, you might want to allow users to simply reset their password instead of changing it. You do this by using the *ResetPassword* method:

```
MembershipUser user = Membership.GetUser("DinoE");
string newPswd = user.ResetPassword();
```

In this case, the page that calls *ResetPassword* is also in charge of sending the new password to the user—for example, via e-mail. Both the *GetPassword* and *ResetPassword* methods have a second overload that takes a string parameter. If specified, this string represents the answer to the user's "forgot password" question. The underlying membership provider matches the supplied answer against the stored answers; if a user is identified, the password is reset or returned as appropriate.

> **Note** It goes without saying that the ability to reset the password, as well as support for the password's question/answer challenge protocol, is specific to the provider. You should note that not all the functions exposed by the membership API are necessarily implemented by the underlying provider. If the provider does not support a given feature, an exception is thrown if the method is invoked.

The Membership Provider

The beauty of the membership model lies not merely in the extremely compact code you need to write to validate or manage users but also in the fact that the model is abstract and extensible. For example, if you have an existing data store filled with user information, you can integrate it with the membership API without much effort. All you have to do is write a custom data provider—that is, a class that inherits from *MembershipProvider* which, in turn, inherits from *ProviderBase*:

```
public class MyAppMembershipProvider : MembershipProvider
{
    // Implements all abstract members of the class and, if
    // needed, defines custom functionality
    ...
}
```

This approach can be successfully employed to migrate existing authentication code to newer versions of ASP.NET applications and, perhaps more importantly, to link a custom and existing data store to the membership API. We'll return to this subject in a moment.

The *ProviderBase* Class

All the providers used in ASP.NET—not just membership providers—implement a common set of members: the members defined by the *ProviderBase* class. The class comes with one method, *Initialize*, and one property, *Name*. The *Name* property returns the official name of the provider class. The *Initialize* method takes the name of the provider and a name/value collection object packed with the content of the provider's configuration section. The method is supposed to initialize its internal state with the values just read out of the *web.config* file.

The *MembershipProvider* Class

Many of the methods and properties used with the *Membership* class are actually implemented by calling into a corresponding method or property in the underlying provider. It comes as no surprise then that many of the methods listed in Table 17-10, which are defined by the *MembershipProvider* base class, support the functions you saw in Table 17-9 that are implemented by the dependent *Membership* class. However, note that Table 17-9 and Table 17-10 are very similar but not identical.

TABLE 17-10 Methods of the *MembershipProvider* Class

Method	Description
ChangePassword	Takes a username in addition to the old and new password and changes the user's password.
ChangePasswordQuestionAndAnswer	Takes a username and password and changes the pair of question/answer challenges that allows reading and changing the password.
CreateUser	Creates a new user account, and returns a *MembershipUser*-derived class. The method takes the username, password, and e-mail address.
DeleteUser	Deletes the record that corresponds to the specified username.
FindUsersByEmail	Returns a collection of membership users whose e-mail address corresponds to the specified e-mail.
FindUsersByName	Returns a collection of membership users whose username matches the specified username.
GetAllUsers	Returns the collection of all users managed by the provider.

Method	Description
GetNumberOfUsersOnline	Returns the number of users that are currently considered to be on line.
GetPassword	Takes the username and the password's answer and returns the current password for the user.
GetUser	Returns the information available about the specified username.
GetUserNameByEmail	Takes an e-mail address, and returns the corresponding username.
ResetPassword	Takes the username and the password's answer, and resets the user password to an auto-generated password.
UpdateUser	Updates the information available about the specified user.
ValidateUser	Validates the specified credentials against the stored list of users.

All these methods are marked as *abstract virtual* in the class (*must-inherit, overridable* in Visual Basic .NET jargon). The *MembershipProvider* class also features a few properties. They are listed in Table 17-11.

TABLE 17-11 Properties of the *MembershipProvider* Class

Property	Description
ApplicationName	Returns the provider's nickname.
EnablePasswordReset	Indicates whether the provider supports password reset.
EnablePasswordRetrieval	Indicates whether the provider supports password retrieval.
MaxInvalidPasswordAttempts	Returns the maximum number of invalid password attempts allowed before the user is locked out.
MinRequiredNonAlphanumericCharacters	Returns the minimum number of punctuation characters required in the password.
MinRequiredPasswordLength	Returns the minimum required length for a password.
PasswordAttemptWindow	Returns the number of minutes in which a maximum number of invalid password attempts are allowed before the user is locked out.
PasswordStrengthRegularExpression	Returns the regular expression that the password must comply with.
RequiresQuestionAndAnswer	Indicates whether the provider requires a question/answer challenge to enable password changes.
RequiresUniqueEmail	Indicates whether the provider is configured to require a unique e-mail address for each user name.

Extending the Provider's Interface

The provider can also store additional information with each user. For example, you can derive a custom class from *MembershipUser*, add any extra members, and return an instance of that class via the standard *GetUser* method of the membership API.

To use the new class, you cast the object returned by *GetUser* to the proper type, as shown here:

```
MyCompanyUser user = (MyCompanyUser) Membership.GetUser(name);
```

In addition to the members listed in Table 17-10 and Table 17-11, a custom membership provider can add new methods and properties. These are defined outside the official schema of the provider base class and are therefore available only to applications aware of this custom provider.

```
MyCompanyProvider prov = (MyCompanyProvider) Membership.Provider;
```

> **Note** The *Providers* collection property allows you to use a dynamically selected provider:
>
> ```
> MembershipProvider prov = Membership.Providers["ProviderName"];
> ```
>
> This feature allows applications to support multiple providers simultaneously. For example, you can design your application to support a legacy database of users through a custom provider, while storing new users in a standard SQL Server 2005 table. In this case, you use different membership providers for different users.

A Custom Provider for ASP.NET 1.x Code

Earlier in the chapter, we discussed a few sample pages using the Employees table in the SQL Server 2000 Northwind database as the data store for user accounts. Let's turn this into a membership provider and register it with the WSAT tool:

```
public class MyMembershipProvider : MembershipProvider
{
    public MyMembershipProvider()
    {
    }
    public override bool ChangePassword(string username,
        string oldPassword, string newPassword)
    {
        // If you don't intend to support a given method
        // just throw an exception
        throw new NotSupportedException();
    }

    ...
```

```
public override bool ValidateUser(string username, string password)
{
    return AuthenticateUser(username, password);
}

private bool AuthenticateUser(string username, string pswd)
{
    // Place here any analogous code you may have in your
    // ASP.NET 1.x application
}
}
```

You define a new class derived from *MembershipProvider*. In this class definition, you have to override all the members in Table 17-10 and Table 17-11. If you don't intend to support a given method or property, for that method just throw a *NotSupportedException* exception. For the methods you do plan to support—which for the previous example included only *ValidateUser*—you write the supporting code. At this point, nothing prevents you from reusing code from your old application. There are two key benefits with this approach: you reuse most of your code (perhaps with a little bit of refactoring), and your application now embraces the new membership model of ASP.NET version 2.0 and later.

Generally speaking, when writing providers there are three key issues to look at: lifetime of the provider, thread-safety, and atomicity. The provider is instantiated as soon as it proves necessary but only once per ASP.NET application. This fact gives the provider the status of a stateful component, but at the price of protecting that state from cross-thread access. A provider is not thread-safe, and it will be your responsibility to guarantee that any critical data is locked before use. Finally, some functions in a provider can be made of multiple steps. Developers are responsible for ensuring atomicity of the operations either through database transactions (whenever possible) or through locks. For more information, refer to *http://msdn2.microsoft.com/en-us/library/aa479030.aspx*.

Configuring a Membership Provider

You register a new provider through the *<membership>* section of the *web.config* file. The section contains a child *<providers>* element under which additional providers are configured:

```
<membership>
    <providers>
        <add name="MyMembershipProvider"
             type="ProAspNet20.MyMembershipProvider" />
    <providers>
</membership>
```

You can change the default provider through the *defaultProvider* attribute of the *<membership>* section. Figure 17-11 shows the new provider in WSAT.

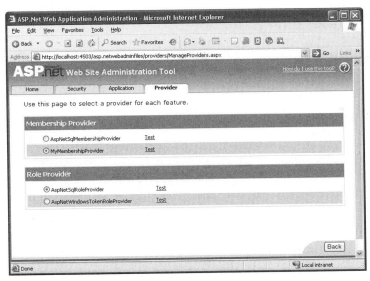

FIGURE 17-11 WSAT reflects a newly added ` provider.

With the new provider in place, the code to verify credentials reduces to the following code, which is the same as you saw earlier in the chapter:

```
void LogonUser(object sender, EventArgs e)
{
    string user = userName.Text;
    string pswd = passWord.Text;
    if (Membership.ValidateUser(user, pswd))
        FormsAuthentication.RedirectFromLoginPage(user, false);
    else
        errorMsg.Text = "Sorry, yours seems not to be a valid account.";
}
```

There's more than just this with the membership API. Now a login page has a relatively standard structure and a relatively standard code attached. At least in the simplest scenarios, it can be reduced to a composite control with no binding code. This is exactly what security controls do. Before we get to cover this new family of server controls, though, let's review roles and their provider-based management.

Managing Roles

Roles in ASP.NET simplify the implementation of applications that require authorization. A role is just a logical attribute assigned to a user. An ASP.NET role is a plain string that refers to the logical role the user plays in the context of the application. In terms of configuration, each user can be assigned one or more roles. This information is attached to the identity object, and the application code can check it before the execution of critical operations.

For example, an application might define two roles—Admin and Guest, each representative of a set of application-specific permissions. Users belonging to the Admin role can perform tasks that other users are prohibited from performing.

> **Note** Assigning roles to a user account doesn't add any security restrictions by itself. It is the responsibility of the application to ensure that authorized users perform critical operations only if they are members of a certain role.

In ASP.NET, the role manager feature simply maintains the relationship between users and roles. ASP.NET 1.1 has no built-in support for managing roles. You can attach some role information to an identity, but this involves writing some custom code. Checking roles is easier, but ASP.NET 2.0 makes the whole thing significantly simpler.

> **Note** The Role Management API, although it consists of different methods and properties, works like the Membership API from a mechanical standpoint. Many of the concepts you read in the previous section also apply to role management.

The Role Management API

The role management API lets you define roles as well as specify programmatically which users are in which roles. The easiest way to configure role management, define roles, add users to roles, and create access rules is to use WSAT. (See Figure 17-11.) You enable role management by adding the following script to your application's *web.config* file:

```
<roleManager enabled="true" />
```

You can use roles to establish access rules for pages and folders. The following *<authorization>* block states that only *Admin* members can access all the pages controlled by the *web.config* file:

```
<configuration>
<system.web>
    <authorization>
        <allow roles="Admin" />
        <deny users="*" />
    </authorization>
</system.web>
<configuration>
```

The order in which you place <*allow*> and <*deny*>tags is important. Permissions and denies are processed in the order in which they appear in the configuration file.

WSAT provides a visual interface for creating associations between users and roles. If necessary, you can instead perform this task programmatically by calling various role manager methods. The following code snippet demonstrates how to create the Admin and Guest roles and populate them with usernames:

```
Roles.CreateRole("Admin");
Roles.AddUsersToRole("DinoE", "Admin");
Roles.CreateRole("Guest");
string[] guests = new string[2];
guests[0] = "JoeUsers";
guests[1] = "Godzilla";
Roles.AddUsersToRole(guests, "Guest")
```

At run time, information about the logged-in user is available through the HTTP context *User* object. The following code demonstrates how to determine whether the current user is in a certain role and subsequently enable specific functions:

```
if (User.IsInRole("Admin"))
{
      // Enable functions specific to the role
      ...
}
```

When role management is enabled, ASP.NET 2.0 looks up the roles for the current user and binds that information to the *User* object. This same feature had to be manually coded in ASP.NET 1.x.

Note In ASP.NET 1.x, you typically cache role information on a per-user basis through a cookie or for all users in a custom *Cache* entry. In both cases, you do this when the application starts by handling the *Application_Start* event in the *global.asax* file. After that, you write a *get* function to read role information from the store and call it wherever required.

The *Roles* Class

When role management is enabled, ASP.NET creates an instance of the *Roles* class and adds it to the current request context—the *HttpContext* object. The *Roles* class features the methods listed in Table 17-12.

TABLE 17-12 Methods of the *Roles* Class

Method	Description
AddUsersToRole	Adds an array of users to a role.
AddUsersToRoles	Adds an array of users to multiple roles.
AddUserToRole	Adds a user to a role.
AddUserToRoles	Adds a user to multiple roles.
CreateRole	Creates a new role.
DeleteCookie	Deletes the cookie that the role manager used to cache all the role data.
DeleteRole	Deletes an existing role.
FindUsersInRole	Retrieves all the user names in the specified role that match the provider user name string. The user names found are returned as a string array.
GetAllRoles	Returns all the available roles.
GetRolesForUser	Returns a string array listing the roles that a particular member belongs to.
GetUsersInRole	Returns a string array listing the users that belong to a particular role.
IsUserInRole	Determines whether the specified user is in a particular role.
RemoveUserFromRole	Removes a user from a role.
RemoveUserFromRoles	Removes a user from multiple roles.
RemoveUsersFromRole	Removes multiple users from a role.
RemoveUsersFromRoles	Removes multiple users from multiple roles.
RoleExists	Returns *true* if the specified role exists.

Table 17-13 lists the properties available in the *Roles* class. All the properties are static and read-only. They owe their value to the settings in the *<roleManager>* configuration section.

TABLE 17-13 Properties of the *Roles* Class

Property	Description
ApplicationName	Returns the provider's nickname.
CacheRolesInCookie	Returns *true* if cookie storage for role data is enabled.
CookieName	Specifies the name of the cookie used by the role manager to store the roles. Defaults to *.ASPXROLES*.
CookiePath	Specifies the cookie path.

Property	Description
CookieProtectionValue	Specifies an option for securing the roles cookie. Possible values are All, Clear, Hashed, and Encrypted.
CookieRequireSSL	Indicates whether the cookie requires SSL.
CookieSlidingExpiration	Indicates whether the cookie has a fixed expiration time or a sliding expiration.
CookieTimeout	Returns the time, in minutes, after which the cookie will expire.
CreatePersistentCookie	Creates a role cookie that survives the current session.
Domain	Indicates the domain of the role cookie.
Enabled	Indicates whether role management is enabled.
MaxCachedResults	Indicates the maximum number of roles that can be stored in a cookie for a user.
Provider	Returns the current role provider.
Providers	Returns a list of all supported role providers.

Some methods in the *Roles* class need to query continuously for the roles associated with a given user, so when possible, the roles for a given user are stored in an encrypted cookie. On each request, ASP.NET checks to see whether the cookie is present; if so, it decrypts the role ticket and attaches any role information to the *User* object. By default, the cookie is a session cookie and expires as soon as the user closes the browser.

Note that the cookie is valid only if the request is for the current user. When you request role information for other users, the information is read from the data store using the configured role provider.

> **Note** Role management passes through the role manager HTTP module. The module is responsible for adding the appropriate roles to the current identity object, such as the *User* object. The module listens for the *AuthenticateRequest* event and does its job. This is exactly the kind of work you need to code for yourself in ASP.NET 1.x.

The Role Provider

For its I/O activity, the role manager uses the provider model and a provider component. The role provider is a class that inherits the *RoleProvider* class. The schema of a role provider is not much different from that of a membership provider. Table 17-14 details the members of the *RoleProvider* class.

TABLE 17-14 Methods of the *RoleProvider* Class

Method	Description
AddUsersToRoles	Adds an array of users to multiple roles.
CreateRole	Creates a new role.
DeleteRole	Deletes the specified role.
FindUsersInRole	Returns the name of users in a role matching a given user name pattern.
GetAllRoles	Returns the list of all available roles.
GetRolesForUser	Gets all the roles a user belongs to.
GetUsersInRole	Gets all the users who participate in the given role.
IsUserInRole	Indicates whether the user belongs to the role.
RemoveUsersFromRoles	Removes an array of users from multiple roles.
RoleExists	Indicates whether a given role exists.

You can see the similarity between some of these methods and the programming interface of the *Roles* class. As we've seen for membership, this is not just coincidental.

ASP.NET ships with a few built-in role providers—*SqlRoleProvider* (default), *WindowsTokenRoleProvider*, and *AuthorizationStoreRoleProvider*. The *SqlStoreProvider* class stores role information in the same MDF file in SQL Server 2005 Express as the default membership provider. For *WindowsTokenRoleProvider*, role information is obtained based on the settings defined for the Windows domain (or Active Directory) the user is authenticating against. This provider does not allow for adding or removing roles. The *AuthorizationStoreRoleProvider* class manages storage of role information for an authorization manager (AzMan) policy store. Supported on Windows Server 2003, Windows XP Professional, and Windows 2000 Server, AzMan is a separate Windows download that enables you to group individual operations together to form tasks. You can then authorize roles to perform specific tasks, individual operations, or both. AzMan provides an MMC snap-in to manage roles, tasks, operations, and users. Role information is stored in a proper policy store, which can be an XML file, an Active Directory, or an ADAM server.

 Note To learn more about AzMan, check the article at *http://msdn2.microsoft.com/en-us/library/ms998336.aspx*. You can download AzMan from *http://windowsupdate.microsoft.com*, as it is part of most service packs.

Custom role providers can be created deriving from *RoleProvider* and registered using the child *<providers>* section in the *<roleManager>* section. Note that the process for doing so is nearly identical to the process you saw for the custom membership provider we explored previously.

Security-Related Controls

In addition to the membership and role management APIs, ASP.NET from version 2.0 onward offers several server controls that make programming security-related aspects of a Web application easier than ever: *Login*, *LoginName*, *LoginStatus*, *LoginView*, *PasswordRecovery*, *ChangePassword*, and *CreateUserWizard*. These are composite controls, and they provide a rich, customizable user interface. They encapsulate a large part of the boilerplate code and markup you would otherwise have to write repeatedly for each Web application you developed. Figure 17-12 offers a comprehensive view of the membership platform and illustrates the role of the login controls.

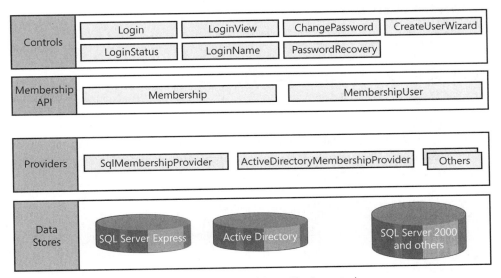

FIGURE 17-12 The big picture of ASP.NET membership and login controls.

The *Login* Control

An application based on the Forms authentication model always needs a login page. Aside from the quality of the graphics, all login pages look alike. They contain a couple of text boxes (for username and password), a button to validate credentials, plus perhaps a Remember Me check box, and possibly links to click if the user has forgotten his or her password or needs to create a new account. The *Login* control provides all this for free, including the ability to validate the user against the default membership provider.

Setting Up the *Login* Control

The *Login* control is a composite control that provides all the common user interface elements of a login form. Figure 17-13 shows the default user interface of the control. To use it, you simply drop the control from the toolbox onto the Web form, or you just type the following code:

```
<asp:login runat="server" id="MyLoginForm" />
```

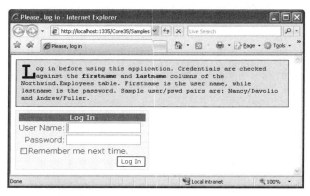

FIGURE 17-13 The *Login* control in action.

The *Login* control also has optional user-interface elements for functions such as password reminder, new user registration, help link, error messages, and a custom action in case of a successful login. When you drop the control onto a Visual Studio 2008 form, the AutoFormat verb lets you choose among a few predefined styles, as in Figure 17-14.

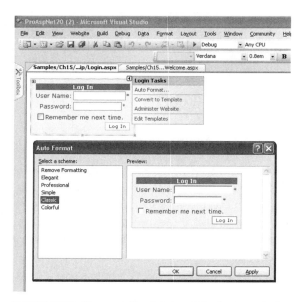

FIGURE 17-14 The predefined styles of the *Login* control.

The appearance of the control is fully customizable through templates and style settings. All user-interface text messages are also customizable through properties of the class.

The Programming Interface of the Control

The control is modularized, and each constituent part can be individually customized. The parts include the Username and Password text boxes, the Submit button, the button to create a new user, the Remember Me check box, and instructions with guidance to the user.

If you don't like the standard user interface of the control, you can define your own template too:

```
<asp:login runat="server" id="MyLoginForm">
    <layouttemplate>
        ...
    </layouttemplate>
</asp:login>
```

Your template can include new elements, and you can recycle default components. To do the latter, you should use the same ID for the controls as in the default template. To simplify this operation, right-click on the control in the Visual Studio designer, choose Convert To Template, and switch to the Source view. The markup you see is the default template of the control expressed as ASP.NET code. Use it as a starting point for creating your own template.

Events of the Control

The *Login* control fires the server events listed in Table 17-15.

TABLE 17-15 Events of the *Login* Control

Event	Description
Authenticate	Fires when a user is authenticated.
LoggedIn	Fires when the user logs in to the site after a successful authentication.
LoggingIn	Fires when a user submits login information but before the authentication takes place. At this time, the operation can still be canceled.
LoginError	Fires when a login error is detected.

In most common cases, though, you don't need to handle any of these events, nor will you likely find it necessary to programmatically access any of the numerous properties of the control.

The most common use for the *Login* control is to use it as a single-control page to set up the user interface of the login page for use with Forms authentication. The control relies entirely on the membership API (and the selected provider) to execute standard operations, such as validating credentials, displaying error messages, and redirecting to the originally requested page in the case of a successful login.

If you have a provider with custom capabilities that you want to be reflected by the *Login* control, you need to modify the layout to add new visual elements bound to a code-behind method. In the code-behind method, you invoke the custom method on the custom provider.

The *LoginName* Control

The *LoginName* control is an extremely simple but useful server control. It works like a sort of label control and displays the user's name on a Web page:

```
<asp:loginname runat="server" />
```

The control captures the name of the currently logged-in user from the *User* intrinsic object and outputs it using the current style. Internally, the control builds a dynamic instance of a *Label* control, sets fonts and color accordingly, and displays the text returned by the following expression:

```
string name = HttpContext.Current.User.Identity.Name;
```

The *LoginName* control has a pretty slim programming interface that consists of only one property—*FormatString*. *FormatString* defines the format of the text to display. It can contain only one placeholder, as shown here:

```
myLogin.FormatString = "Welcome, {0}";
```

If *Dino* is the name of the current user, the code generates a "Welcome, Dino" message.

The *LoginStatus* Control

The *LoginStatus* control indicates the state of the authentication for the current user. Its user interface consists of a link button to log in or log out, depending on the current user logon state. If the user is acting as an anonymous user—that is, he or she never logged in—the control displays a link button to invite the user to log in. Otherwise, if the user successfully passed through the authentication layer, the control displays the logout button.

Setting Up the *LoginStatus* Control

The *LoginStatus* control is often used in conjunction with the *LoginName* control to display the name of the current user (if any), plus a button to let the user log in or out. The style, text, and action associated with the button changes are conveniently based on the authentication state of the user.

The following code creates a table showing the name of the current user and a button to log in or log out:

```
<table width="100%" border="0"><tr>
    <td>
        <asp:loginname runat="server" FormatString="Welcome, {0}" />
    </td>
    <td align="right">
        <asp:loginstatus runat="server" LogoutText="Log off" />
    </td>
  </tr>
</table>
```

Figure 17-15 shows the results. The first screen shot demonstrates a page that invites a user to log in, while the second shows the *LoginName* and *LoginStatus* controls working together in the case of a logged-in user. To detect whether the current user is authenticated and adapt the user interface, you can use the *IsAuthenticated* property of the *User* object:

```
void Page_Load(object sender, EventArgs e)
{
    if (User.Identity.IsAuthenticated)
        // Adjust the UI by outputting some text to a label
        Msg.Text = "Enjoy more features";
    else
        Msg.Text = "Login to enjoy more features.";
}
```

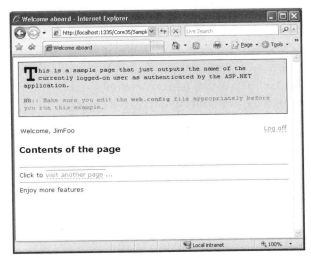

FIGURE 17-15 The *LoginStatus* control invites a user who is not currently logged in to log in; next, it displays more features reserved to registered users.

The Programming Interface of the Control

Although the *LoginStatus* control is quite useful in its default form, it provides a bunch of properties and events that you can use to configure it. The properties are listed in Table 17-16.

TABLE 17-16 Properties of the *LoginStatus* Control

Property	Description
LoginImageUrl	Gets or sets the URL of the image used for the login link.
LoginText	Gets or sets the text used for the login link.
LogoutAction	Determines the action taken when a user logs out of a Web site. Possible values are *Refresh*, *Redirect*, and *RedirectToLoginPage*. *Refresh* reloads the current page with the user logged out. The other two values redirect the user to the logout page or the login page, respectively.
LogoutImageUrl	Gets or sets the URL of the image used for the logout button.
LogoutPageUrl	Gets or sets the URL of the logout page.
LogoutText	Gets or sets the text used for the logout link.

The control also features a couple events—*LoggingOut* and *LoggedOut*. The former fires before the user clicks to log off. The latter is raised immediately after the logout process has completed.

The *LoginView* Control

The *LoginView* control allows you to aggregate the *LoginStatus* and *LoginName* controls to display a custom user interface that takes into account the authentication state of the user as well as the user's role or roles. The control, which is based on templates, simplifies creation of a user interface specific to the anonymous or connected state and particular roles to which they are assigned. In other words, you can create as many templates as you need, one per state or per role.

The Programming Interface of the Control

Table 17-17 lists the properties of the user interface of the *LoginView* control.

TABLE 17-17 Properties of the *LoginView* Class

Property	Description
AnonymousTemplate	Gets or sets the template to display to users who are not logged in to the application.
LoggedInTemplate	Gets or sets the template to display to users who are logged in to the application.
RoleGroups	Returns the collection of templates defined for the supported roles. Templates can be declaratively specified through the *<roleGroups>* child tag.

Note that the *LoggedInTemplate* template is displayed only to logged-in users who are not members of one of the role groups specified in the *RoleGroups* property. The template (if any) specified in the *<roleGroups>* tag always takes precedence.

The *LoginView* control also fires the *ViewChanging* and *ViewChanged* events. The former reaches the application when the control is going to change the view (such as when a user logs in). The latter event fires when the view has changed.

Creating a Login Template

The *LoginView* control lets you define two distinct templates to show to anonymous and logged-in users. You can use the following markup to give your pages a common layout and manage the template to show when the user is logged in:

```
<asp:loginview runat="server">
   <anonymoustemplate>
      <table width="100%" border="0"><tr><td>
         To enjoy more features,
         <asp:loginstatus runat="server">
      </td></tr></table>
   </anonymoustemplate>
   <loggedintemplate>
      <table width="100%" border="0"><tr>
         <td><asp:loginname runat="server" /></td>
         <td align="right"><asp:loginstatus runat="server" /></td>
      </tr></table>
   </loggedintemplate>
</asp:loginview>
```

Basically, the *LoginView* control provides a more flexible, template-based programming interface to distinguish between logged-in and anonymous scenarios, as we did in the previous example by combining *LoginStatus* and *LoginName*.

Creating Role-Based Templates

The *LoginView* control also allows you to define blocks of user interface to display to all logged-in users who belong to a particular role. As mentioned, these templates take precedence over the *<loggedintemplate>* template, if both apply.

```
<asp:loginview runat="server">
   <rolegroups>
      <asp:rolegroup roles="Admin">
         <contenttemplate>
            ...
         </contenttemplate>
      </asp:rolegroup>
```

```
    <asp:rolegroup roles="Guest">
       <contenttemplate>
          ...
       </contenttemplate>
    </asp:rolegroup>
  </rolegroups>
</asp:loginview>
```

The content of each *<contenttemplate>* block is displayed only to users whose role matches the value of the *roles* attribute. You can use this feature to create areas in a page whose contents are strictly role-specific. For the *LoginView* control to work fine, role management must be enabled, of course. The control uses the default provider.

The *PasswordRecovery* Control

The *PasswordRecovery* control is another server control that wraps a common piece of Web user interface into an out-of-the-box component. The control represents the form that enables a user to recover or reset a lost password. The user will receive the password through an e-mail message sent to the e-mail address associated with his or her account.

The control supports three views, depending on the user's password recovery stage, as follows. The first view is where the user provides the user name and forces the control to query the membership provider for a corresponding membership user object. The second view is where the user must provide the answer to a predetermined question in order to obtain or reset the password. Finally, the third view is where the user is informed of the success of the operation.

Requirements for Password Retrieval

For the control to work properly, you must first ensure that the selected membership provider supports password retrieval. The password retrieval also requires that the provider defines a *MembershipUser* object and implements the *GetUser* methods. Remember that the membership provider decides how to store passwords: clear text, hashed, or encrypted.

If passwords are stored as hashed values, the control doesn't work. Hash algorithms are not two-way algorithms. In other words, the hash mechanism is great at encrypting and comparing passwords, but it doesn't retrieve the clear text. If you plan to use the *PasswordRecovery* control, you must ensure that the provider stores password as clear text or encrypted data.

Retrieving a Password

The *PasswordRecovery* control supports a child element named *MailDefinition*:

```
<asp:passwordrecovery runat="server">
   <maildefinition from="admin@contoso.com" />
</asp:passwordrecovery>
```

The *<MailDefinition>* element configures the e-mail message and indicates the sender as well as the format of the body (text or HTML), priority, subject, and carbon-copy (CC). For the same settings, you can also use a bunch of equivalent properties on the associated *Framework* class and set values programmatically.

If the user who has lost the password has a question/answer pair defined, the *PasswordRecovery* control changes its user interface to display the question and ask for the answer before the password is retrieved and sent back. Figure 17-16 demonstrates the behavior of the control.

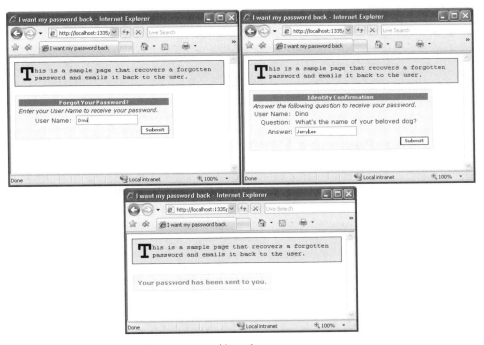

FIGURE 17-16 The *PasswordRecovery* control in action.

The control first asks the user to provide the user name; next it retrieves associated information and displays the security question, if any is defined for the user. Finally, if an e-mail address is known, the control sends a message with details, as in Figure 17-17. Bear in mind that you need to have proper e-mail settings in the *web.config* file, specifically in the *<system.net>* section, as below:

```
<system.net>
  <mailSettings>
    <smtp deliveryMethod="Network">
      <network host="your.smtp.server" />
    </smtp>
  </mailSettings>
</system.net>
```

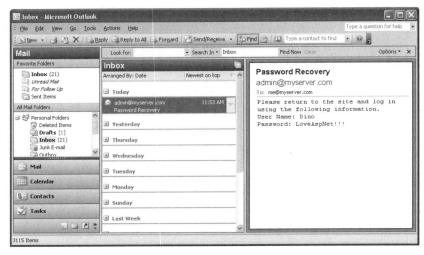

FIGURE 17-17 The e-mail message with password information.

The *ChangePassword* Control

The *ChangePassword* control provides an out-of-the-box and virtually codeless solution that enables end users to change their password to the site. The control supplies a modifiable and customizable user interface and built-in behaviors to retrieve the old password and save a new one:

```
<asp:ChangePassword ID="ChangePassword1" runat="server" />
```

The underlying API for password management is the same membership API we discussed earlier in this chapter.

User Authentication

The *ChangePassword* control will work in scenarios where a user might or might not be already authenticated. However, note that the User Name text box is optional. If you choose not to display the user name and still permit nonauthenticated users to change their password, the control will always fail.

If the user is not authenticated but the User Name text box is displayed, the user will be able to enter his or her user name, current password, and new password at the same time.

Password Change

The change of the password is performed using the *ChangePassword* method on the *MembershipUser* object that represents the user making the attempt. Note that the provider might pose an upper limit to the invalid attempts to change or reset the password. If set, this limit affects the *ChangePassword* control. The control won't work any longer once the limit has been exceeded.

Once the password has been successfully changed, the control can send—if properly configured—a confirmation e-mail to the user, as shown in Figure 17-18.

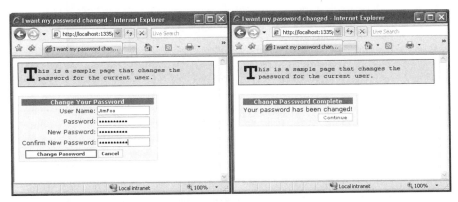

FIGURE 17-18 The *ChangePassword* control in action.

The e-mail message is configured through the same *<MailDefinition>* element we saw earlier for the *PasswordRecovery* control.

The *Continue* button points the page with the control to a new destination URL to let users continue working. If you don't set the *ContinuePageDestinationUrl* property, clicking the button simply refreshes the current page.

The *CreateUserWizard* Control

The *CreateUserWizard* control is designed to provide a native functionality for creating and configuring a new user using the membership API. The control offers a basic behavior that the developer can extend to send a confirmation e-mail to the new user and add steps to the wizard to collect additional information, such as address, phone number, or perhaps roles.

Customization is supported in two ways: by customizing one of the default steps, and by adding more user-defined steps. Figure 17-19 shows the control in action in the Create User page of the WSAT tool.

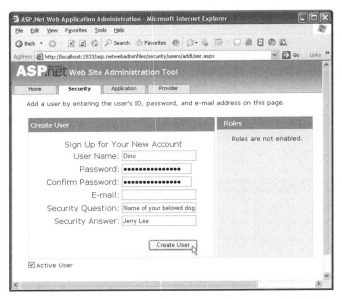

FIGURE 17-19 The *CreateUserWizard* control in action within WSAT.

The difference between this control and the *CreateUser* method on the membership provider is that the method just adds the user name and password. The wizard provides a user inter-face and lets you add more information in a single shot.

Resources to Write Attack-Resistant Code

How can we design and code secure ASP.NET applications? First of all, security is strictly related to the application's usage, its popularity, and the type of users who connect to it and work with it. Paradoxically, a poorly secured application that isn't attractive to hackers can be perceived as being much more secure than a well-armored applica-tion with just one loophole or two. Successful attacks are possible through holes in the system-level and application-level security apparatus. When it comes to security, don't look for a magic wand to do the job for you. Security is a state of mind, and insecu-rity is often the result of loose coding styles, if not true programming laziness. Never blindly trust anything regarding Web and ASP.NET security. Always keep in mind that security for Web applications is mostly about raising the bar higher and higher to make it hard for bad guys to jump over.

The following Patterns & Practices links can help you find great information to fend off most common types of attacks and implement effective input validation in ASP.NET applications:

- **How To—Protect from Injection Attacks in ASPNET**
  http://msdn2.microsoft.com/en-us/library/Bb355989.aspx

- **How To—Use Regular Expressions to Constrain Input in ASP.NET**
  http://msdn2.microsoft.com/en-us/library/ms998267.aspx

- **How To—Protect from SQL Injection in ASP.NET**
  http://msdn2.microsoft.com/en-us/library/ms998271.aspx

- **How To—Prevent Cross-Site Scripting in ASP.NET**
  http://msdn2.microsoft.com/en-us/library/ms998274.aspx

Conclusion

There are three layers of security wrapped around ASP.NET applications: the IIS layer, the ASP.NET worker process layer, and the application layer. As a developer, you can configure parameters in the first two levels, but you are totally responsible for planning and implementing the third one. Forms authentication is the most reasonable approach to protecting pages from unauthorized access in an Internet-exposed application. The most reasonable approach for an intranet application is integrated Windows authentication. Although it's not perfect, Forms authentication is broadly used because it is simple to understand and functional. In ASP.NET 2.0 and newer versions, Forms authentication is partnered with the membership API.

The membership API doesn't change the way in which Forms authentication works, it simply adds new and powerful tools for developers. If you're writing a new ASP.NET application, there's no reason for not implementing authentication through the membership API and its auxiliary classes and server controls. If you're migrating an existing application, you should try to embrace the newest API by refactoring your code to make it fully reusable.

Is this enough to claim that an ASP.NET application is secure? Unfortunately not. Secure software requires knowledgeable IT personnel, but no software can ever be considered secure if the network is not at least as secure. Likewise, secure software requires knowledgeable developers, because proper administration is useless and ineffective when the code lays itself open to malicious and injurious attacks. Administration is and remains the primary bedrock of security; however, even a wise and restrictive policy can't do much if developers and architects build inherently insecure code.

To achieve security for any piece of software exposed over the Web, you must enforce network and application security. Network threats to guard against include denial of service (DoS), spoofing, and eavesdropping. Bad effects of these attacks include theft of passwords and other critical data, request floods, and an undesired understanding of internal network topologies by potential attackers. Examples of threats aimed at the application, instead, include the notorious SQL injection threat and cross-site scripting (XSS). As an ASP.NET developer, you should apply at least one key rule all the time: don't trust user input.

Just the Facts

- The ASP.NET worker process runs under a weak account named ASPNET or NETWORK SERVICE, depending on the process model in use. None of these accounts has administrative privileges.

- You can change the worker process account, but you should at least give the new account full permissions on the folders where the ASP.NET runtime creates temporary files.

- Forms authentication is the most common way of protecting ASP.NET pages and resources from unauthorized access in an Internet application. It works by attaching an authentication ticket to the request to prove the identity of the user; an HTTP module intercepts any requests and checks for that.

- Membership API complements Forms authentication by decoupling the page code and the code that works with user information. This second type of code is isolated in a provider component that can be plugged into and out of the configuration file.

- The role management API provides a rich API to manage roles. It also provides an HTTP module that uses a provider to extract role information for the user and that attaches that information to the request.

- The membership API is integrated with Visual Studio .NET through the WSAT tool, and it gives administrators a tool to manage users and roles offline.

- The membership API is linked to a new family of controls for common login-related operations, such as password recovery and change, user creation, and login display.

- Secure applications depend on secure coding practices that prevent common attacks. The key rule to apply all the time is, "Don't trust user input." Sanitizing any data the user inserts in the application is key, and validation controls and coded validation rules can raise the security bar much higher to prevent attackers from being successful in their attempts.

Chapter 18
HTTP Handlers and Modules

HTTP modules and HTTP handlers are fundamental pieces of the ASP.NET architecture. HTTP handlers and modules are truly the building blocks of the .NET Web platform. Any requests for an ASP.NET managed resource is always resolved by an HTTP handler and passes through a pipeline of HTTP modules. After the handler has processed the request, the request flows back through the pipeline of HTTP modules and is finally transformed into markup for the caller.

An HTTP handler is the component that actually takes care of serving the request. It is an instance of a class that implements the *IHttpHandler* interface. The *ProcessRequest* method of the interface is the central console that governs the processing of the request. For example, the *Page* class—the base class for all ASP.NET run-time pages—implements the *IHttpHandler* interface, and its *ProcessRequest* method is responsible for loading and saving the view state and for firing the well-known set of page events, including *Init*, *Load*, *PreRender*, and the like.

ASP.NET maps each incoming HTTP request to a particular HTTP handler. A special breed of component—named the *HTTP handler factory*—provides the infrastructure for creating the physical instance of the handler to service the request. For example, the *PageHandlerFactory* class parses the source code of the requested *.aspx* resource and returns a compiled instance of the class that represents the page. An HTTP handler is designed to process one or more URL extensions. Handlers can be given an application or machine scope, which means they can process the assigned extensions within the context of the current application or all applications installed on the machine. Of course, this is accomplished by making changes to either the machine-wide *web.config* file or a local *web.config* file, depending on the scope you desire.

HTTP modules are classes that implement the *IHttpModule* interface and handle runtime events. There are two types of public events that a module can deal with. They are the events raised by *HttpApplication* (including asynchronous events) and events raised by other HTTP modules. For example, *SessionStateModule* is one of the built-in modules provided by

ASP.NET to supply session-state services to an application. It fires the *End* and *Start* events that other modules can handle through the familiar *Session_End* and *Session_Start* signatures.

HTTP handlers and HTTP modules have the same functionality as ISAPI extensions and ISAPI filters, respectively, but with a much simpler programming model. ASP.NET allows you to create custom handlers and custom modules. Before we get into this rather advanced aspect of Web programming, a review of the Internet Information Services (IIS) extensibility model is in order because this model determines what modules and handlers can do and what they cannot do.

Note ISAPI stands for Internet Server Application Programming Interface and represents the protocol by means of which IIS talks to external components. The ISAPI model is based on a Microsoft Win32 unmanaged dynamic-link library (DLL) that exports a couple of functions. This model is significantly expanded in IIS 7.0 and largely matches the ASP.NET extensibility model, which is based on HTTP handlers and modules. I'll return to this topic shortly.

Quick Overview of the IIS Extensibility API

A Web server is primarily a server application that can be contacted using a bunch of Internet protocols, such as HTTP, File Transfer Protocol (FTP), Network News Transfer Protocol (NNTP), and the Simple Mail Transfer Protocol (SMTP). IIS—the Web server included with the Microsoft Windows operating system—is no exception.

A Web server generally also provides a documented application programming interface (API) for enhancing and customizing the server's capabilities. Historically speaking, the first of these extension APIs was the Common Gateway Interface (CGI). A CGI module is a new application that is spawned from the Web server to service a request. Nowadays, CGI applications are almost never used in modern Web applications because they require a new process for each HTTP request. As you can easily understand, this approach is rather inadequate for high-volume Web sites and poses severe scalability issues. IIS supports CGI applications, but you will seldom use this feature unless you have serious backward-compatibility issues. More recent versions of Web servers supply an alternate and more efficient model to extend the capabilities of the module. In IIS, this alternative model takes the form of the ISAPI interface.

The ISAPI Model

When the ISAPI model is used, instead of starting a new process for each request, IIS loads an ISAPI component—namely, a Win32 DLL—into its own process. Next, it calls a well-known entry point on the DLL to serve the request. The ISAPI component stays loaded until IIS is shut down and can service requests without any further impact on Web server activity. The downside to such a model is that because components are loaded within the Web server process, a single faulty component can tear down the whole server and all installed applications. Starting with IIS 4.0, though, some countermeasures have been taken to address this problem. Before the advent of IIS 6.0, you were allowed to set the protection level of a newly installed application choosing from three options: low, medium, and high.

If you choose a low protection, the application (and its extensions) will be run within the Web server process (*inetinfo.exe*). If you choose medium protection, applications will be pooled together and hosted by an instance of a different worker process (*dllhost.exe*). If you choose high protection, each application set to High will be hosted in its own individual worker process (*dllhost.exe*).

Web applications running under IIS 6.0 are grouped in pools, and the choice you can make is whether you want to join an existing pool or create a new one. Figure 18-1 shows the dialog box picking the application pool of choice in IIS 6.0 and Microsoft Windows Server 2003.

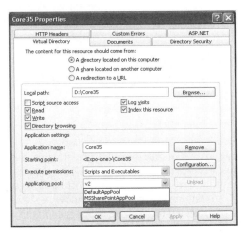

FIGURE 18-1 Configuring the protection level of Web applications in IIS 6.0 under Windows Server 2003.

All applications in a pool share the same run-time settings and the same worker process—*w3wp.exe*.

Illustrious Children of the ISAPI Model

The ISAPI model has another key drawback—the programming model. An ISAPI component represents a compiled piece of code—a Win32 DLL—that retrieves data and writes HTML code to an output console. It has to be developed using C or C++, it should generate multi-threaded code, and it must be written with extreme care because of the impact that bugs or runtime failures can have on the application.

A while back, Microsoft attempted to encapsulate the ISAPI logic in the Microsoft Foundation Classes (MFC), but even though the effort was creditable, it didn't pay off very well. MFC tended to bring more code to the table than high-performance Web sites would perhaps like, and worse, the resulting ISAPI extension DLL suffered from a well-documented memory leak.

Active Server Pages (ASP), the predecessor of ASP.NET, is, on the other hand, an example of a well-done ISAPI application. ASP is implemented as an ISAPI DLL (named *asp.dll*) registered to handle HTTP requests with an *.asp* extension. The internal code of the ASP ISAPI extension DLL parses the code of the requested resource, executes any embedded script code, and builds the page for the browser.

As of IIS 6.0, any functionality built on top of IIS must be coded according to the guidelines set by the ISAPI model. ASP and ASP.NET are no exceptions. Today, the whole ASP.NET platform works closely with IIS, but it is not part of it. The *aspnet_isapi.dll* core component is the link between IIS and the ASP.NET runtime environment. When a request for *.aspx* resources comes in, IIS passes the control to *aspnet_isapi.dll*, which in turn hands the request to the ASP. NET pipeline inside an instance of the common language runtime (CLR).

As of this writing, to extend IIS you can write a Win32 DLL only with a well-known set of entry points. This requirement ceases to exist with IIS 7.0, which is scheduled to ship with Windows 2008 Server.

> **Note** A good place to learn about IIS 7.0 and find good scripts and code snippets is *http://www.iis.net*. IIS 7.0 is also part of Windows Vista, but that is not particularly relevant here in the context of an ASP.NET book. Although you can certainly develop part of your Web site on a Windows Vista machine, it is simply out of question that you use Windows Vista as a Web server to host a site. Although fully functional, the IIS 7.0 that has shipped with Windows Vista can be seen as a live tool to experiment and test. The "real" IIS 7.0 for Web developers and administrators will ship in 2008 with Windows 2008 Server.

Structure of ISAPI Components

An ISAPI extension is invoked through a URL that ends with the name of the DLL that implements the function, as shown in the following URL:

```
http://www.contoso.com/apps/hello.dll
```

The DLL must export a couple of functions—*GetExtensionVersion* and *HttpExtensionProc*. The *GetExtensionVersion* function sets the version and the name of the ISAPI server extension. When the extension is loaded, the *GetExtensionVersion* function is the first function to be called. *GetExtensionVersion* is invoked only once and can be used to initialize any needed variables. The function is expected to return *true* if everything goes fine. In the case of errors, the function should return *false* and the Web server will abort loading the DLL and put a message in the system log.

The core of the ISAPI component is represented by the *HttpExtensionProc* function. The function receives basic HTTP information regarding the request (for example, the query string and the headers), performs the expected action, and prepares the response to send back to the browser.

> **Note** Certain handy programming facilities, such as the session state, are abstractions the ISAPI programming model lacks entirely. The ISAPI model is a lower level programming model than, say, ASP or ASP.NET.

The ISAPI programming model is made of two types of components—ISAPI extensions and ISAPI filters.

ISAPI Extensions

ISAPI extensions are the IIS in-process counterpart of CGI applications. As mentioned, an ISAPI extension is a DLL that is loaded in the memory space occupied by IIS or another host application. Because it is a DLL, only one instance of the ISAPI extension needs to be loaded at a time. On the downside, the ISAPI extension must be thread-safe so that multiple client requests can be served simultaneously. ISAPI extensions work in much the same way as an ASP or ASP.NET page. It takes any information about the HTTP request and prepares a valid HTTP response.

Because the ISAPI extension is made of compiled code, it must be recompiled and reloaded at any change. If the DLL is loaded in the Web server's memory, the Web server must be stopped. If the DLL is loaded in the context of a separate process, only that process must be stopped. Of course, when an external process is used, the extension doesn't work as fast as it could when hosted in-process, but at least it doesn't jeopardize the stability of IIS.

ISAPI Filters

ISAPI filters are components that intercept specific server events before the server itself handles them. Upon loading, the filter indicates what event notifications it will handle. If any of these events occur, the filter can process them or pass them on to other filters.

You can use ISAPI filters to provide custom authentication techniques or to automatically redirect requests based on HTTP headers sent by the client. Filters are a delicate gear in the IIS machinery. They can facilitate applications and let them take control of customizable aspects of the engine. For this same reason, though, ISAPI filters can also degrade performance if not written carefully. Filters, in fact, can run only in-process. Filters can be loaded for the Web server as a whole or for specific Web sites.

ISAPI filters can accomplish tasks such as implementing custom authentication schemes, compression, encryption, logging, and request analysis. The ability to examine, and if necessary modify, both incoming and outgoing streams of data makes ISAPI filters very powerful and flexible. This last sentence shows the strength of ISAPI filters but also indicates their potential weakness, which is that they will hinder performance if not written well.

Changes in IIS 7.0

ASP.NET 1.0 was originally a self-contained, brand new runtime environment bolted onto IIS 5.0. With the simultaneous release of ASP.NET 1.1 and IIS 6.0, the Web development and server platforms have gotten closer and started sharing some services, such as process recycling and output caching. The advent of ASP.NET 2.0 and newer versions hasn't changed anything, but the release of IIS 7.0 will.

A Unified Runtime Environment

In a certain way, IIS 7.0 represents the unification of the ASP.NET and IIS platforms. HTTP handlers and modules, the runtime pipeline, and configuration files will become constituent elements of a common environment. The whole IIS internal pipeline has been componentized to originate a distinct and individually configurable component. A new section will be added to the *web.config* schema of ASP.NET applications to configure the IIS environment.

Put another way, it will be as if the ASP.NET runtime expanded to incorporate and replace the surrounding Web server environment. It's hard to say whether things really went this way or whether it was the other way around. As a matter of fact, the same concepts and instruments you know from ASP.NET are available in IIS 7.0 at the Web server level.

To illustrate, on Windows 2008 Server (and for testing purposes, also on a Windows Vista machine) you can use Forms authentication to protect access to any resources available on the server and not just ASP.NET-specific resources. You might already know that static resources such as HTML pages and JPG images are not served by ASP.NET by default; as such, they're not subject to the authentication rules you set for the application. Where IIS 7.0 is supported, you can now define a handler for some specific and static resources and be sure that IIS will use your code to serve those resources.

Managed ISAPI Extensions and Filters

Today if you want to take control of an incoming request in any version of IIS older than version 7.0, you have no choice other than writing a C or C++ DLL, using either MFC or perhaps the ActiveX Template Library (ATL). More comfortable HTTP handlers and modules are an ASP.NET-only feature, and they can be applied only to ASP.NET-specific resources and only after the request has been authenticated by IIS and handed over to ASP.NET.

In IIS 7.0, you can write HTTP handlers and modules to filter *any* requests and implement any additional features using .NET code for whatever resources the Web server can serve. More precisely, you'll continue writing HTTP handlers and modules as you do today for ASP.NET, except that you will be given the opportunity to register them for any file type. Needless to say, old-style ISAPI extensions will still be supported, but unmanaged extensions and filters will likely become a thing of the past. I'll demonstrate IIS 7.0 handlers later in the chapter.

Writing HTTP Handlers

ASP.NET comes with a small set of built-in HTTP handlers. There is a handler to serve ASP.NET pages, one for Web services, and yet another to accommodate .NET Remoting requests for remote objects hosted by IIS. Other helper handlers are defined to view the tracing of individual pages in a Web application (*trace.axd*) and to block requests for prohibited resources such as *.config* or *.asax* files. Starting with ASP.NET 2.0, you also find a handler (*webresource. axd*) to inject assembly resources and script code into pages. In ASP.NET 3.5, the *scriptresource.axd* handler has been added as a more refined tool to inject script code and AJAX capabilities into Web pages.

You can write custom HTTP handlers whenever you need ASP.NET to process certain requests in a nonstandard way. The list of useful things you can do with HTTP handlers is limited only by your imagination. Through a well-written handler, you can have your users invoke any sort of functionality via the Web. For example, you could implement click counters and any sort of image manipulation, including dynamic generation of images, server-side caching, or obstructing undesired linking to your images.

> **Note** An HTTP handler can either work synchronously or operate in an asynchronous way. When working synchronously, a handler doesn't return until it's done with the HTTP request. An asynchronous handler, on the other hand, launches a potentially lengthy process and returns immediately after. A typical implementation of asynchronous handlers are asynchronous pages. Later in this chapter, though, we'll take a look at the mechanics of asynchronous handlers, of which asynchronous pages are a special case.

Conventional ISAPI extensions and filters should be registered within the IIS metabase. In contrast, HTTP handlers are registered in the *web.config* file if you want the handler to participate in the HTTP pipeline processing of the Web request. In a manner similar to ISAPI extensions, you can also invoke the handler directly via the URL.

The *IHttpHandler* Interface

Want to take the splash and dive into HTTP handler programming? Well, your first step is getting the hang of the *IHttpHandler* interface. An HTTP handler is just a managed class that implements that interface. More specifically, a synchronous HTTP handler implements the *IHttpHandler* interface; an asynchronous HTTP handler, on the other hand, implements the *IHttpAsyncHandler* interface. Let's tackle synchronous handlers first.

The contract of the *IHttpHandler* interface defines the actions that a handler needs to take to process an HTTP request synchronously.

Members of the *IHttpHandler* Interface

The *IHttpHandler* interface defines only two members—*ProcessRequest* and *IsReusable*, as shown in Table 18-1. *ProcessRequest* is a method, whereas *IsReusable* is a Boolean property.

TABLE 18-1 Members of the *IHttpHandler* Interface

Member	Description
IsReusable	This property gets a Boolean value indicating whether the HTTP runtime can reuse the current instance of the HTTP handler while serving another request.
ProcessRequest	This method processes the HTTP request.

The *IsReusable* property on the *System.Web.UI.Page* class—the most common HTTP handler in ASP.NET—returns *false*, meaning that a new instance of the HTTP request is needed to serve each new page request. You typically make *IsReusable* return *false* in all situations where some significant processing is required that depends on the request payload. Handlers used as simple barriers to filter special requests can set *IsReusable* to *true* to save some CPU cycles. I'll return to this subject with a concrete example in a moment.

The *ProcessRequest* method has the following signature:

```
void ProcessRequest(HttpContext context);
```

It takes the context of the request as the input and ensures that the request is serviced. In the case of synchronous handlers, when *ProcessRequest* returns, the output is ready for forwarding to the client.

A Very Simple HTTP Handler

Again, an HTTP handler is simply a class that implements the *IHttpHandler* interface. The output for the request is built within the *ProcessRequest* method, as shown in the following code:

```
using System.Web;

namespace Core35.Components
{
    public class SimpleHandler : IHttpHandler
    {
        // Override the ProcessRequest method
        public void ProcessRequest(HttpContext context)
        {
            context.Response.Write("<H1>Hello, I'm an HTTP handler</H1>");
        }
```

```
        // Override the IsReusable property
        public bool IsReusable
        {
            get { return true; }
        }
    }
}
```

You need an entry point to be able to call the handler. In this context, an entry point into the handler's code is nothing more than an HTTP endpoint—that is, a public URL. The URL must be a unique name that IIS and the ASP.NET runtime can map to this code. When registered, the mapping between an HTTP handler and a Web server resource is established through the *web.config* file:

```
<configuration>
    <system.web>
        <httpHandlers>
            <add verb="*" path="hello.aspx"
                type="Core35.Components.SimpleHandler" />
        </httpHandlers>
    </system.web>
</configuration>
```

The *<httpHandlers>* section lists the handlers available for the current application. These settings indicate that *SimpleHandler* is in charge of handling any incoming requests for an endpoint named *hello.aspx*. Note that the URL *hello.aspx* doesn't have to be a physical resource on the server; it's simply a public resource identifier. The *type* attribute references the class and assembly that contains the handler. It's canonical format is *type[,assembly]*. You omit the assembly information if the component is defined in the *App_Code* or other reserved folders.

> **Note** If you enter the settings shown earlier in the global *web.config* file, you will register the *SimpleHandler* component as callable from within all Web applications hosted by the server machine.

If you invoke the *hello.aspx* URL, you obtain the results shown in Figure 18-2.

FIGURE 18-2 A sample HTTP handler that answers requests for *hello.aspx*.

The technique discussed here is the quickest and simplest way of putting an HTTP handler to work, but there is more to know about registration of HTTP handlers and there are many more options to take advantage of. Now let's consider a more complex example of an HTTP handler.

An HTTP Handler for Quick Data Reports

With their relatively simple programming model, HTTP handlers give you a means of interacting with the low-level request and response services of IIS. In the previous example, we returned only constant text and made no use of the request information. In the next example, we'll configure the handler to intercept and process only requests of a particular type and generate the output based on the contents of the requested resource.

The idea is to build an HTTP handler for custom *.sqlx* resources. A SQLX file is an XML document that expresses the statements for one or more SQL queries. The handler grabs the information about the query, executes it, and finally returns the result set formatted as a grid. Figure 18-3 shows the expected outcome.

FIGURE 18-3 A custom HTTP handler in action.

To start, let's examine the source code for the *IHttpHandler* class.

> **Warning** Take this example for what it really is—merely a way to process a custom XML file with a custom extension doing something more significant than outputting a "hello world" message. *Do not* take this handler as a realistic prototype for exposing your Microsoft SQL Server databases over the Web.

Building a Query Manager Tool

The HTTP handler should get into the game whenever the user requests an *.sqlx* resource. Assume for now that the system knows how to deal with such a weird extension, and focus on what's needed to execute the query and pack the results into a grid. To execute the query, at a minimum, we need the connection string and the command text. The following text illustrates the typical contents of an *.sqlx* file:

```
<queries>
  <query connString="DATABASE=northwind;SERVER=localhost;UID...;">
    SELECT firstname, lastname, country FROM employees
  </query>
  <query connString="DATABASE=northwind;SERVER=localhost;UID=...;">
    SELECT companyname FROM customers WHERE country='Italy'
  </query>
</queries>
```

The XML document is formed by a collection of *<query>* nodes, each containing an attribute for the connection string and the text of the query.

The *ProcessRequest* method extracts this information before it can proceed with executing the query and generating the output:

```
class SqlxData
{
    public string ConnectionString;
    public string QueryText;
}

public class QueryHandler : IHttpHandler
{
    public void ProcessRequest(HttpContext context)
    {
        // Parses the SQLX file
        SqlxData[] data = ParseFile(context);

        // Create the output as HTML
        StringCollection htmlColl = CreateOutput(data);

        // Output the data
        context.Response.Write("<html><head><title>");
        context.Response.Write("QueryHandler Output");
        context.Response.Write("</title></head><body>");
        foreach (string html in htmlColl)
        {
            context.Response.Write(html);
            context.Response.Write("<hr />");
        }
        context.Response.Write("</body></html>");
    }
```

```
    // Override the IsReusable property
    public bool IsReusable
    {
        get { return true; }
    }


    ...
}
```

The *ParseFile* helper function parses the source code of the *.sqlx* file and creates an instance of the *SqlxData* class for each query found:

```
private SqlxData[] ParseFile(HttpContext context)
{
    XmlDocument doc = new XmlDocument();
    string filePath = context.Request.Path;
    using (Stream fileStream = VirtualPathProvider.OpenFile(filePath))  {
        doc.Load(fileStream);
    }

    // Visit the <mapping> nodes
    XmlNodeList mappings = doc.SelectNodes("queries/query");
    SqlxData[] descriptors = new SqlxData[mappings.Count];
    for (int i=0; i < descriptors.Length; i++)
    {
        XmlNode mapping = mappings[i];
        SqlxData query = new SqlxData();
        descriptors[i] = query;

        try {
            query.ConnectionString =
                mapping.Attributes["connString"].Value;
            query.QueryText = mapping.InnerText;
        }
        catch {
            context.Response.Write("Error parsing the input file.");
            descriptors = new SqlxData[0];
            break;
        }
    }
    return descriptors;
}
```

The *SqlxData* internal class groups the connection string and the command text. The information is passed to the *CreateOutput* function, which will actually execute the query and generate the grid:

```
private StringCollection CreateOutput(SqlxData[] descriptors)
{
    StringCollection coll = new StringCollection();

    foreach (SqlxData data in descriptors)
    {
```

```
    // Run the query
    DataTable dt = new DataTable();
    SqlDataAdapter adapter = new SqlDataAdapter(data.QueryText,
        data.ConnectionString);
    adapter.Fill(dt);


    // Error handling
    ...

    // Prepare the grid
    DataGrid grid = new DataGrid();
    grid.DataSource = dt;
    grid.DataBind();

    // Get the HTML
    string html = Utils.RenderControlAsString(grid);
    coll.Add(html);
    }
    return coll;
}
```

After executing the query, the method populates a dynamically created *DataGrid* control. In ASP.NET pages, the *DataGrid* control, like any other control, is rendered to HTML. However, this happens through the care of the special HTTP handler that manages *.aspx* resources. For *.sqlx* resources, we need to provide that functionality ourselves. Obtaining the HTML for a Web control is as easy as calling the *RenderControl* method on an HTML text writer object. This is just what the helper method *RenderControlAsString* does:

```
static class Utils
{
    public static string RenderControlAsString(Control ctl)
    {
        StringWriter sw = new StringWriter();
        HtmlTextWriter writer = new HtmlTextWriter(sw);
        ctl.RenderControl(writer);
        return sw.ToString();
    }
}
```

Note An HTTP handler that needs to access session-state values must implement the *IRequiresSessionState* interface. Like *INamingContainer*, it's a marker interface and requires no method implementation. Note that the *IRequiresSessionState* interface indicates that the HTTP handler requires read and write access to the session state. If read-only access is needed, use the *IReadOnlySessionState* interface instead.

Registering the Handler

An HTTP handler is a class and must be compiled to an assembly before you can use it. The assembly must be deployed to the *Bin* directory of the application. If you plan to make this handler available to all applications, you can copy it to the global assembly cache (GAC). The next step is registering the handler with an individual application or with all the applications running on the Web server. You register the handler in the configuration file:

```
<system.web>
  <httpHandlers>
    <add verb="*"
      path="*.sqlx"
      type= "Core35.Components.QueryHandler,Core35Lib" />
  </httpHandlers>
</system.web>
```

You add the new handler to the *<httpHandlers>* section of the local or global *web.config* file. The section supports three actions: *<add>*, *<remove>*, and *<clear>*. You use *<add>* to add a new HTTP handler to the scope of the *.config* file. You use *<remove>* to remove a particular handler. Finally, you use *<clear>* to get rid of all the registered handlers. To add a new handler, you need to set three attributes—*verb*, *path*, and *type*—as shown in Table 18-2.

TABLE 18-2 Attributes Needed to Register an HTTP Handler

Attribute	Description
Verb	Indicates the list of the supported HTTP verbs—for example, *GET*, *PUT*, and *POST*. The wildcard character (*) is an acceptable value and denotes all verbs.
Path	A wildcard string, or a single URL, that indicates the resources the handler will work on—for example, **.aspx*.
Type	Specifies a comma-separated class/assembly combination. ASP.NET searches for the assembly DLL first in the application's private *Bin* directory and then in the system global assembly cache.

These attributes are mandatory. An optional attribute is also supported—*validate*. When *validate* is set to *false*, ASP.NET delays as much as possible loading the assembly with the HTTP handler. In other words, the assembly will be loaded only when a request for it arrives. ASP.NET will not try to preload the assembly, thus catching any error or problem with it.

So far, you have correctly deployed and registered the HTTP handler, but if you try invoking an *.sqlx* resource, the results you produce are not what you'd expect. The problem lies in the fact that so far you configured ASP.NET to handle only *.sqlx* resources, but IIS still doesn't know anything about them!

A request for an *.sqlx* resource is handled by IIS *before* it is handed to the ASP.NET ISAPI extension. If you don't register *some* ISAPI extension to handle ..sqlx resource requests, IIS will treat each request as a request for a static resource and serve the request by sending back the source code of the .sqlx file. The extra step required is registering the *.sqlx* extension with the IIS 6.0 metabase such that requests for .sqlx resources are handed off to ASP.NET, as shown in Figure 18-4.

FIGURE 18-4 Registering the *.sqlx* extension with the IIS 6.0 metabase.

The dialog box in the figure is obtained by clicking on the properties of the application in the IIS 6.0 manager and then the configuration of the site. To involve the HTTP handler, you must choose *aspnet_isapi.dll* as the ISAPI extension. In this way, all *.sqlx* requests are handed out to ASP.NET and processed through the specified handler. Make sure you select *aspnet_isapi.dll* from the folder of the ASP.NET version you plan to use.

> **Caution** In Microsoft Visual Studio, if you test a sample *.sqlx* resource using the local embedded Web server, nothing happens that forces you to register the *.sqlx* resource with IIS. This is just the point, though. You're not using IIS! In other words, if you use the local Web server, you have no need to touch IIS; you do need to register any custom resource you plan to use with IIS before you get to production.

Registering the Handler with IIS 7.0

If you run IIS 7.0, you don't strictly need to change anything through the IIS Manager. You can add a new section to the *web.config* file and specify the HTTP handler also for static resources that would otherwise be served directly by IIS. Here's what you need to enter:

```
<system.webServer>
    <add verb="*"
        path="*.sqlx"
        type="Core35.Components.QueryHandler, Core35Lib" />
</system.webServer>
```

The new section is a direct child of the root tag *<configuration>*. Without this setting, IIS can't recognize the page and won't serve it up. The configuration script instructs IIS 7.0 to forward any **.sqlx* requests to your application, which knows how to deal with it.

The Picture Viewer Handler

Let's examine another scenario that involves custom HTTP handlers. Thus far, we have explored custom resources and realized how important it is to register any custom extensions with IIS.

To speed up processing, IIS claims the right of personally serving some resources that typically form a Web application without going down to a particular ISAPI extension. The list includes static files such as images and HTML files. What if you request a GIF or a JPG file directly from the address bar of the browser? IIS retrieves the specified resource, sets the proper content type on the response buffer, and writes out the bytes of the file. As a result, you'll see the image in the browser's page. So far so good.

What if you point your browser to a virtual folder that contains images? In this case, IIS doesn't distinguish the contents of the folder and returns a list of files, as shown in Figure 18-5.

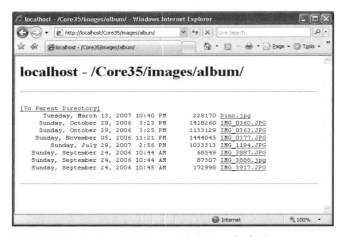

FIGURE 18-5 The standard IIS-provided view of a folder.

Wouldn't it be nice if you could get a preview of the contained pictures, instead?

Designing the HTTP Handler

To start out, you need to decide how you would let IIS know about your wishes. You can use a particular endpoint that, appended to a folder's name, convinces IIS to yield to ASP.NET and provide a preview of contained images. Put another way, the idea is binding our picture viewer handler to a particular endpoint—say, *folder.axd*. As mentioned earlier in the chapter, a fixed endpoint for handlers doesn't have to be an existing, deployed resource. You make the *folder.axd* endpoint follow the folder name, as shown here:

```
http://www.contoso.com/images/folder.axd
```

The handler will process the URL, extract the folder name, and select all the contained pictures.

> **Note** In ASP.NET, the *.axd* extension is commonly used for endpoints referencing a special service. *Trace.axd* for tracing and *WebResource.axd* for script and resources injection are examples of two popular uses of the extension. In particular, the *Trace.axd* handler implements the same logic described here. If you append its name to the URL, it will trace all requests for pages in that application.

Implementing the HTTP Handler

The picture viewer handler returns a page composed of a multirow table showing as many images as there are in the folder. Here's the skeleton of the class:

```
class PictureViewerInfo
{
    public PictureViewerInfo() {
        DisplayWidth = 200;
        ColumnCount = 3;
    }
    public int DisplayWidth;
    public int ColumnCount;
    public string FolderName;
}

public class PictureViewerHandler : IHttpHandler
{
    // Override the ProcessRequest method
    public void ProcessRequest(HttpContext context)
    {
        PictureViewerInfo info = GetFolderInfo(context);
        string html = CreateOutput(info);

        // Output the data
        context.Response.Write("<html><head><title>");
        context.Response.Write("Picture Web Viewer");
        context.Response.Write("</title></head><body>");
        context.Response.Write(html);
        context.Response.Write("</body></html>");
    }
```

```
    // Override the IsReusable property
    public bool IsReusable
    {
        get { return true; }
    }
    ...
}
```

Retrieving the actual path of the folder is as easy as stripping off the *folder.axd* string from
the URL and trimming any trailing slashes or backslashes. Next, the URL of the folder is
mapped to a server path and processed using the .NET Framework API for files and folders:

```
private ArrayList GetAllImages(string path)
{
    string[] fileTypes = { "*.bmp", "*.gif", "*.jpg", "*.png" };
    ArrayList images = new ArrayList();
    DirectoryInfo di = new DirectoryInfo(path);
    foreach (string ext in fileTypes)
    {
        FileInfo[] files = di.GetFiles(ext);
        if (files.Length > 0)
            images.AddRange(files);
    }
    return images;
}
```

The *DirectoryInfo* class provides some helper functions on the specified directory; for example, the *GetFiles* method selects all the files that match the given pattern. Each file is wrapped
by a *FileInfo* object. The method *GetFiles* doesn't support multiple search patterns; to search
for various file types, you need to iterate for each type and accumulate results in an array list
or equivalent data structure.

After you get all the images in the folder, you move on to building the output for the
request. The output is a table with a fixed number of cells and a variable number of rows
to accommodate all selected images. The image is not downloaded as a thumbnail, but it
is more simply rendered in a smaller area. For each image file, a new *<img>* tag is created
through the *Image* control. The *width* attribute of this file is set to a fixed value (say, 200
pixels), causing most modern browsers to automatically resize the image. Furthermore, the
image is wrapped by an anchor that links to the same image URL. As a result, when the user
clicks on an image, the page refreshes and shows the same image at its natural size.

```
string CreateOutputForFolder(PictureViewerInfo info)
{
    ArrayList images = GetAllImages(info.FolderName);
    Table t = new Table();

    int index = 0;
    bool moreImages = true;
```

```
while (moreImages)
{
    TableRow row = new TableRow();
    t.Rows.Add(row);
    for (int i = 0; i < info.ColumnCount; i++)
    {
        TableCell cell = new TableCell();
        row.Cells.Add(cell);

        // Create the image
        Image img = new Image();
        FileInfo fi = (FileInfo)images[index];
        img.ImageUrl = fi.Name;
        img.Width = Unit.Pixel(info.DisplayWidth);

        // Wrap the image in an anchor so that a larger image
        // is shown when the user clicks
        HtmlAnchor a = new HtmlAnchor();
        a.HRef = fi.Name;
        a.Controls.Add(img);
        cell.Controls.Add(a);

        // Check whether there are more images to show
        index++;
        moreImages = (index < images.Count);
        if (!moreImages)
            break;
    }
}
}
```

You might want to make the handler accept some optional query string parameters, such as width and column count. These values are packed in an instance of the helper class *PictureViewerInfo* along with the name of the folder to view. Here's the code to process the query string of the URL to extract parameters if any are present:

```
PictureViewerInfo info = new PictureViewerInfo();
object p1 = context.Request.Params["Width"];
object p2 = context.Request.Params["Cols"];
if (p1 != null)
    Int32.TryParse((string)p1, out info.DisplayWidth);
if (p2 != null)
    Int32.TryParse((string)p2, out info.ColumnCount);
```

Figure 18-6 shows the handler in action.

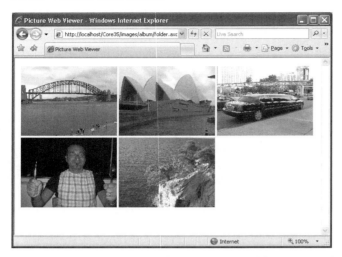

FIGURE 18-6 The picture viewer handler in action with a given number of columns and width.

Registering the handler is easy too. You just add the following script to the *web.config* file:

```
<add verb="*" path="folder.axd"
     type="Core35.Components.PictureViewerHandler,Core35Lib" />
```

You place the assembly in the GAC and move the configuration script to the global *web.config* to extend the settings to all applications on the machine.

Serving Images More Effectively

Any page we get from the Web today is topped with so many images and is so well conceived and designed that often the overall page looks more like a magazine advertisement than an HTML page. Looking at the current pages displayed by portals, it's rather hard to imagine there ever was a time—and it was only seven or eight years ago—when one could create a Web site by using only a text editor and some assistance from a friend who had a bit of familiarity with Adobe PhotoShop.

In spite of the wide use of images on the Web, there is just one way in which a Web page can reference an image—by using the HTML *<img>* tag. By design, this tag points to a URL. As a result, to be displayable within a Web page, an image must be identifiable through a URL and its bits should be contained in the output stream returned by the Web server for that URL.

In many cases, the URL points to a static resource such as a GIF or JPEG file. In this case, the Web server takes the request upon itself and serves it without invoking external components. However, the fact that many *<img>* tags on the Web are bound to a static file does not mean there's no other way to include images in Web pages.

Where else can you turn to get images aside from picking them up from the server file system? For example, you can load images from a database or you can generate or modify them on the fly just before serving the bits to the browser.

Loading Images from Databases

The use of a database as the storage medium for images is controversial. Some people have good reasons to push it as a solution; others tell you bluntly they would never do it and that you shouldn't either. Some people can tell you wonderful stories of how storing images in a properly equipped database was the best experience of their professional life. With no fear that facts could perhaps prove them wrong, other people will confess that they would never use a database again for such a task.

The facts say that all database management systems (DBMS) of a certain reputation and volume have supported binary large objects (BLOB) for quite some time. Sure, a BLOB field doesn't necessarily contain an image—it can contain a multimedia file or a long text file— but overall there must be a good reason for having this BLOB support in SQL Server, Oracle, and similar popular DBMS systems!

To read an image from a BLOB field with ADO.NET, you execute a *SELECT* statement on the column and use the *ExecuteScalar* method to catch the result and save it in an array of bytes. Next, you send this array down to the client through a binary write to the response stream. Let's write an HTTP handler to serve a database-stored image:

```
public class DbImageHandler : IHttpHandler
{
    public void ProcessRequest(HttpContext ctx)
    {
        // Ensure the URL contains an ID argument that is a number
        int id = -1;
        bool result = Int32.TryParse(ctx.Request.QueryString["id"], out id);
        if (!result)
            ctx.Response.End();

        string connString = "...";
        string cmdText = "SELECT photo FROM employees WHERE employeeid=@id";

        // Get an array of bytes from the BLOB field
        byte[] img = null;
        SqlConnection conn = new SqlConnection(connString);
        using (conn)
        {
            SqlCommand cmd = new SqlCommand(cmdText, conn);
            cmd.Parameters.AddWithValue("@id", id);
            conn.Open();
            img = (byte[])cmd.ExecuteScalar();
            conn.Close();
        }
```

```
        // Prepare the response for the browser
        if (img != null)
        {
            ctx.Response.ContentType = "image/jpeg";
            ctx.Response.BinaryWrite(img);
        }
    }

    public bool IsReusable
    {
        get { return true; }
    }
}
```

There are quite a few assumptions made in this code. First, we assume that the field named *photo* contains image bits and that the format of the image is JPEG. Second, we assume that images are to be retrieved from a fixed table of a given database through a predefined connection string. Finally, we're assuming that the URL to invoke this handler includes a query string parameter named *id*.

Notice the attempt to convert the value of the *id* query parameter to an integer before proceeding. This simple check significantly reduces the surface attack for malicious users by verifying that what is going to be used as a numeric ID is really a numeric ID. Especially when you're inoculating user input into SQL query commands, filtering out extra characters and wrong data types is a fundamental measure for preventing attacks.

The *BinaryWrite* method of the *HttpResponse* object writes an array of bytes to the output stream.

> **Warning** If the database you're using is Northwind (as in the preceding example), an extra step might be required to ensure that the images are correctly managed. For some reason, the SQL Server version of the Northwind database stores the images in the *photo* column of the Employees table as OLE objects. This is probably because of the conversion that occurred when the database was upgraded from the Microsoft Access version. As a matter fact, the array of bytes you receive contains a 78-byte prefix that has nothing to do with the image. Those bytes are just the header created when the image was added as an OLE object to the first version of Access. Although the preceding code works like a champ with regular BLOB fields, it must undergo the following modification to work with the *photo* field of the Northwind.Employees database:
>
> ```
> Response.OutputStream.Write(img, 78, img.Length);
> ```
>
> Instead of using the *BinaryWrite* call, which doesn't let you specify the starting position, use the code shown here.

A sample page to test BLOB field access is shown in Figure 18-7. The page lets users select an employee ID and post back. When the page renders, the ID is used to complete the URL for the ASP.NET *Image* control.

```
string url = String.Format("dbimage.axd?id={0}",
                           DropDownList1.SelectedValue);
Image1.ImageUrl = url;
```

FIGURE 18-7 Downloading images stored within the BLOB field of a database.

An HTTP handler must be registered in the *web.config* file and bound to a public endpoint. In this case, the endpoint is *dbimage.axd* and the script to enter in the configuration file is shown next:

```
<httpHandlers>
    <add verb="*" path="dbimage.axd"
         type="Core35.Components.DbImageHandler,Core35Lib"/>
</httpHandlers>
```

> **Note** The preceding handler clearly has a weak point: it hard-codes a SQL command and the related connection string. This means that you might need a different handler for each different command or database to access. A more realistic handler would probably use an external and configurable database-specific provider. Such a provider can be as simple as a class that implements an agreed interface. At a minimum, the interface will supply a method to retrieve and return an array of bytes. Alternatively, if you want to keep the ADO.NET code in the handler itself, the interface will just supply members that specify the command text and connection string. The handler will figure out its default provider from a given entry in the *web.config* file.

Serving Dynamically Generated Images

Isn't it true that an image is worth thousands of words? Many financial Web sites offer charts and, more often than not, these charts are dynamically generated on the server. Next, they are served to the browser as a stream of bytes and travel over the classic response output stream. But can you create and manipulate server-side images? For these tasks, Web applications normally rely on ad hoc libraries or the graphic engine of other applications (for example, Microsoft Office applications).

ASP.NET applications are different and, to some extent, luckier. ASP.NET applications, in fact, can rely on a powerful and integrated graphic engine capable of providing an object model for image generation. This server-side system is GDI+, and contrary to what some people might have you believe, GDI+ is fair game for generating images on the fly for ASP.NET applications.

As its name suggests, GDI+ is the successor of GDI, the Graphics Device Interface included with versions of the Windows operating system that shipped before Windows XP. The .NET Framework encapsulates the key GDI+ functionalities in a handful of managed classes and makes those functions available to Web, Windows Forms, and Web service applications.

Most of the GDI+ services belong to the following categories: 2D vector graphics and imaging. 2D vector graphics involve drawing simple figures such as lines, curves, and polygons. Under the umbrella of imaging are functions to display, manipulate, save, and convert bitmap and vector images. Finally, a third category of functions can be identified—typography, which includes the display of text in a variety of fonts, sizes, and styles. Having the goal of creating images dynamically, we are most interested in drawing figures and text and in saving the work as JPEGs or GIFs.

In ASP.NET, writing images to disk might require some security adjustments. Normally, the ASP.NET runtime runs under the aegis of the *NETWORK SERVICE* user account. In the case of anonymous access with impersonation disabled—which are the default settings in ASP.NET— the worker process lends its own identity and security token to the thread that executes the user request of creating the file. With regard to the default scenario, an access denied exception might be thrown if *NETWORK SERVICE* lacks writing permissions on virtual directories— a pretty common situation.

ASP.NET and GDI+ provide an interesting alternative to writing files on disk without changing security settings: in-memory generation of images. In other words, the dynamically generated image is saved directly to the output stream in the needed image format or in a memory stream.

Writing Copyright Notes on Images

GDI+ supports quite a few image formats, including JPEG, GIF, BMP, and PNG. The whole collection of image formats is in the *ImageFormat* structure from the *System.Drawing* namespace. You can save a memory-resident *Bitmap* object to any of the supported formats by using one of the overloads of the *Save* method:

```
Bitmap bmp = new Bitmap(file);
...
bmp.Save(outputStream, ImageFormat.Gif);
```

When you attempt to save an image to a stream or disk file, the system attempts to locate an encoder for the requested format. The encoder is a GDI+ module that converts from the native format to the specified format. Note that the encoder is a piece of unmanaged code that lives in the underlying Win32 platform. For each save format, the *Save* method looks up the right encoder and proceeds.

The next example wraps up all the points we touched on. This example shows how to load an existing image, add some copyright notes, and serve the modified version to the user. In doing so, we'll load an image into a *Bitmap* object, obtain a *Graphics* for that bitmap, and use graphics primitives to write. When finished, we'll save the result to the page's output stream and indicate a particular MIME type.

The sample page that triggers the example is easily created, as shown in the following listing:

```
<html>
<body>
    <img id="picture" src="dynimage.axd?url=images/pic1.jpg" />
</body>
</html>
```

The page contains no ASP.NET code and displays an image through a static HTML *<img>* tag. The source of the image, though, is an HTTP handler that loads the image passed through the query string, and then manipulates and displays it. Here's the source code for the *ProcessRequest* method of the HTTP handler:

```
public void ProcessRequest (HttpContext context)
{
    object o = context.Request["url"];
    if (o == null)
    {
        context.Response.Write("No image found.");
        context.Response.End();
        return;
    }

    string file = context.Server.MapPath((string)o);
    string msg = ConfigurationManager.AppSettings["CopyrightNote"];
    if (File.Exists(file))
    {
        Bitmap bmp = AddCopyright(file, msg);
        context.Response.ContentType = "image/jpeg";
        bmp.Save(context.Response.OutputStream, ImageFormat.Jpeg);
        bmp.Dispose();
    }
    else
    {
        context.Response.Write("No image found.");
        context.Response.End();
    }
}
```

Note that the server-side page performs two different tasks indeed. First, it writes copyright text on the image canvas; next, it converts whatever the original format was to JPEG:

```
Bitmap AddCopyright(string file, string msg)
{
    // Load the file and create the graphics
    Bitmap bmp = new Bitmap(file);
    Graphics g = Graphics.FromImage(bmp);

    // Define text alignment
    StringFormat strFmt = new StringFormat();
    strFmt.Alignment = StringAlignment.Center;

    // Create brushes for the bottom writing
    // (green text on black background)
    SolidBrush btmForeColor = new SolidBrush(Color.PaleGreen);
    SolidBrush btmBackColor = new SolidBrush(Color.Black);

    // To calculate writing coordinates, obtain the size of the
    // text given the font typeface and size
    Font btmFont = new Font("Verdana", 7);
    SizeF textSize = new SizeF();
    textSize = g.MeasureString(msg, btmFont);

    // Calculate the output rectangle and fill
    float x = ((float) bmp.Width-textSize.Width-3);
    float y = ((float) bmp.Height-textSize.Height-3);
    float w = ((float) x + textSize.Width);
    float h = ((float) y + textSize.Height);
    RectangleF textArea = new RectangleF(x, y, w, h);
    g.FillRectangle(btmBackColor, textArea);

    // Draw the text and free resources
    g.DrawString(msg, btmFont, btmForeColor, textArea);
    btmForeColor.Dispose();
    btmBackColor.Dispose();
    btmFont.Dispose();
    g.Dispose();

    return bmp;
}
```

Figure 18-8 shows the results.

Note that the additional text is part of the image the user downloads on her client browser. If the user saves the picture by using the *Save Picture As* menu from the browser, the text (in this case, the copyright note) is saved along with the image.

FIGURE 18-8 A server-resident image has been modified before being displayed.

Note What if the user requests the JPG file directly from the address bar? And what if the image is linked by another Web site or referenced in a blog post? In these cases, the original image is served without any further modification. Why is it so? As mentioned, for performance reasons IIS serves static files, such as JPG images, directly without involving any external module, including the ASP.NET runtime. The HTTP handler that does the trick of adding a copyright note is therefore blissfully ignored when the request is made via the address bar or a hyperlink. What can you do about it?

In IIS 6.0, you must register the JPG extension as an ASP.NET extension for a particular application using the IIS Manager as shown in Figure 18-4. In this case, each request for JPG resources is forwarded to your application and resolved through the HTTP handler.

In IIS 7.0, things are even simpler for developers. All that you have to do is add the following lines to the application's *web.config* file:

```
<system.webServer>
    <handlers>
        <add verb="*"
             path="*.jpg"
             type="Core35.Components.DynImageHandler,Core35Lib" />
    </handlers>
</system.webServer>
```

The *system.webServer* section is a direct child of the root *configuration* node.

Advanced HTTP Handler Programming

HTTP handlers are not a tool for everybody. They serve a very neat purpose: changing the way a particular resource, or set of resources, is served to the user. You can use handlers to filter out resources based on runtime conditions or to apply any form of additional logic to the retrieval of traditional resources such as pages and images. Finally, you can use HTTP handlers to serve certain pages or resources in an asynchronous manner.

For HTTP handlers, the registration step is key. Registration enables ASP.NET to know about your handler and its purpose. Registration is required for two practical reasons. First, it serves to ensure that IIS forwards the call to the correct ASP.NET application. Second, it serves to instruct your ASP.NET application on the class to load to "handle" the request. As mentioned, you can use handlers to override the processing of existing resources (for example, *hello. aspx*) or to introduce new functionalities (for example, *folder.axd*). In both cases, you're invoking a resource whose extension is already known to IIS—the *.axd* extension is registered in the IIS metabase when you install ASP.NET. In both cases, though, you need to modify the *web.config* file of the application to let the application know about the handler.

By using the ASHX extension and programming model for handlers, you can also save yourself the *web.config* update and deploy a new HTTP handler by simply copying a new file in a new or existing application's folder.

Deploying Handlers as ASHX Resources

An alternative way to define an HTTP handler is through an *.ashx* file. The file contains a special directive, named *@WebHandler*, that expresses the association between the HTTP handler endpoint and the class used to implement the functionality. All *.ashx* files must begin with a directive like the following one:

```
<%@ WebHandler Language="C#" Class="Core35.Components.YourHandler" %>
```

When an *.ashx* endpoint is invoked, ASP.NET parses the source code of the file and figures out the HTTP handler class to use from the *@WebHandler* directive. This automation removes the need of updating the *web.config* file. Here's a sample *.ashx* file. As you can see, it is the plain class file plus the special *@WebHandler* directive:

```
<%@ WebHandler Language="C#" Class="MyHandler" %>

using System.Web;

public class MyHandler : IHttpHandler {

    public void ProcessRequest (HttpContext context) {
        context.Response.ContentType = "text/plain";
        context.Response.Write("Hello World");
    }
```

```
    public bool IsReusable {
        get {
            return false;
        }
    }
}
```

Note that the source code of the class can either be specified inline or loaded from any of the assemblies referenced by the application. When *.ashx* resources are used to implement an HTTP handler, you just deploy the source file, and you're done. Just as for XML Web services, the source file is loaded and compiled only on demand. Because ASP.NET adds a special entry to the IIS metabase for *.ashx* resources, you don't even need to enter changes to the Web server configuration.

Resources with an *.ashx* extension are handled by an HTTP handler class named *SimpleHandleFactory*. Note that *SimpleHandleFactory* is actually an HTTP handler factory class, not a simple HTTP handler class. We'll discuss handler factories in a moment.

The *SimpleHandleFactory* class looks for the *@WebHandler* directive at the beginning of the file. The *@WebHandler* directive tells the handler factory the name of the HTTP handler class to instantiate once the source code has been compiled.

Important You can build HTTP handlers both as regular class files compiled to an assembly and via *.ashx* resources. There's no significant difference between the two approaches except that *.ashx* resources, like ordinary ASP.NET pages, will be compiled on the fly upon the first request.

Prevent Access to Forbidden Resources

If your Web application manages resources of a type that you don't want to make publicly available over the Web, you must instruct IIS not to display those files. A possible way to accomplish this consists of forwarding the request to *aspnet_isapi* and then binding the extension to one of the built-in handlers—the *HttpForbiddenHandler* class:

```
<add verb="*" path="*.xyz" type="System.Web.HttpForbiddenHandler" />
```

Any attempt to access an *.xyz* resource results in an error message being displayed. The same trick can also be applied for individual resources served by your application. If you need to deploy, say, a text file but do not want to take the risk that somebody can get to them, add the following:

```
<add verb="*" path="yourFile.txt" type="System.Web.HttpForbiddenHandler" />
```

Should It Be Reusable or Not?

In a conventional HTTP handler, the *ProcessRequest* method takes the lion's share of the over-all set of functionality. The second member of the *IHttpHandler* interface—the *IsReusable* property—is used only in particular circumstances. If you set the *IsReusable* property to return *true*, the handler is not unloaded from memory after use and is repeatedly used. Put another way, the Boolean value returned by *IsReusable* indicates whether the handler object can be pooled.

Frankly, most of the time it doesn't really matter what you return—be it *true* or *false*. If you set the property to return *false*, you require that a new object be allocated for each request. The simple allocation of an object is not a particularly expensive operation. However, the initialization of the handler might be costly. In this case, by making the handler reusable, you save much of the overhead. If the handler doesn't hold any state, there's no reason for not making it reusable.

In summary, I'd say that *IsReusable* should be always set to *true*, except when you have instance properties to deal with or properties that might cause trouble if used in a concur-rent environment. If you have no initialization tasks, it doesn't really matter whether it re-turns *true* or *false*. As a margin note, the *System.Web.UI.Page* class—the most popular HTTP handler ever—sets its *IsReusable* property to *false*.

The key point to make is the following. Who's really using *IsReusable* and, subsequently, who really cares about its value?

Once the HTTP runtime knows the HTTP handler class to serve a given request, it simply instantiates it—no matter what. So when is the *IsReusable* property of a given handler taken into account? Only if you use an HTTP handler factory—that is, a piece of code that dynami-cally decides which handler should be used for a given request. An HTTP handler factory can query a handler to determine whether the same instance can be used to service multiple requests and thus optionally create and maintain a pool of handlers.

ASP.NET pages and ASHX resources are served through factories. However, none of these factories ever checks *IsReusable*. Of all the built-in handler factories in the whole ASP.NET platform, very few check the *IsReusable* property of related handlers. So what's the bottom line?

As long as you're creating HTTP handlers for AXD, ASHX, or perhaps ASPX resources, be aware that the *IsReusable* property is blissfully ignored. Do not waste your time trying to figure out the optimal configuration. Instead, if you're creating an HTTP handler factory to serve a set of resources, whether or not to implement a pool of handlers is up to you and *IsReusable* is the perfect tool for the job.

But when should you employ an HTTP handler factory? In all situations in which the HTTP handler class for a request is not uniquely identified. For example, for ASPX pages, you don't know in advance which HTTP handler type you have to use. The type might not even exist (in which case, you compile it on the fly). The HTTP handler factory is used whenever you need to apply some logic to decide which is the right handler to use. In other words, you need an HTTP handler factory when declarative binding between endpoints and classes is not enough.

HTTP Handler Factories

An HTTP request can be directly associated with an HTTP handler or with an HTTP handler factory object. An HTTP handler factory is a class that implements the *IHttpHandlerFactory* interface and is in charge of returning the actual HTTP handler to use to serve the request. The *SimpleHandlerFactory* class provides a good example of how a factory works. The factory is mapped to requests directed at *.ashx* resources. When such a request comes in, the factory determines the actual handler to use by looking at the *@WebHandler* directive in the source file.

In the .NET Framework, HTTP handler factories are used to perform some preliminary tasks on the requested resource prior to passing it on to the handler. Another good example of a handler factory object is represented by an internal class named *PageHandlerFactory*, which is in charge of serving *.aspx* pages. In this case, the factory handler figures out the name of the handler to use and, if possible, loads it up from an existing assembly.

HTTP handler factories are classes that implement a couple of methods on the *IHttpHandlerFactory* interface—*GetHandler* and *ReleaseHandler*, as shown in Table 18-3.

TABLE 18-3 Members of the *IHttpHandlerFactory* Interface

Method	Description
GetHandler	Returns an instance of an HTTP handler to serve the request
ReleaseHandler	Takes an existing HTTP handler instance and frees it up or pools it

The *GetHandler* method has the following signature:

```
public virtual IHttpHandler GetHandler(HttpContext context,
    string requestType, string url, string pathTranslated);
```

The *requestType* argument is a string that evaluates to *GET* or *POST*—the HTTP verb of the request. The last two arguments represent the raw URL of the request and the physical path behind it. The *ReleaseHandler* method is a mandatory override for any class that implements *IHttpHandlerFactory*; in most cases, it will just have an empty body.

The following listing shows a sample HTTP handler factory that returns different handlers based on the HTTP verb (*GET* or *POST*) used for the request:

```
class MyHandlerFactory : IHttpHandlerFactory
{
    public IHttpHandler GetHandler(HttpContext context,
        string requestType, String url, String pathTranslated)
    {
        // Feel free to create a pool of HTTP handlers here
        if(context.Request.RequestType.ToLower() == "get")
            return (IHttpHandler) new MyGetHandler();
        else if(context.Request.RequestType.ToLower() == "post")
            return (IHttpHandler) new MyPostHandler();
        return null;
    }

    public void ReleaseHandler(IHttpHandler handler)
    {
        // Nothing to do
    }
}
```

When you use an HTTP handler factory, it's the factory, not the handler, that needs to be registered with the ASP.NET configuration file. If you register the handler, it will always be used to serve requests. If you opt for a factory, you have a chance to decide dynamically and based on runtime conditions which handler is more appropriate for a certain request. In doing so, you can use the *IsReusable* property of handlers to implement a pool.

Asynchronous Handlers

An asynchronous HTTP handler is a class that implements the *IHttpAsyncHandler* interface. The system initiates the call by invoking the *BeginProcessRequest* method. Next, when the method ends, a callback function is automatically invoked to terminate the call. In the .NET Framework, the sole *HttpApplication* class implements the asynchronous interface. The members of *IHttpAsyncHandler* interface are shown in Table 18-4.

TABLE 18-4 Members of the *IHttpAsyncHandler* Interface

Method	Description
BeginProcessRequest	Initiates an asynchronous call to the specified HTTP handler
EndProcessRequest	Terminates the asynchronous call

The signature of the *BeginProcessRequest* method is as follows:

```
IAsyncResult BeginProcessRequest(HttpContext context,
    AsyncCallback cb, object extraData);
```

The *context* argument provides references to intrinsic server objects used to service HTTP requests. The second parameter is the *AsyncCallback* object to invoke when the asynchronous method call is complete. The third parameter is a generic cargo variable that contains any data you might want to pass to the handler.

> **Note** An *AsyncCallback* object is a delegate that defines the logic needed to finish process-
> ing the asynchronous operation. A delegate is a class that holds a reference to a method. A
> delegate class has a fixed signature, and it can hold references only to methods that match that
> signature. A delegate is equivalent to a type-safe function pointer or a callback. As a result, an
> *AsyncCallback* object is just the code that executes when the asynchronous handler has com-
> pleted its job.

The *AsyncCallback* delegate has the following signature:

```
public delegate void AsyncCallback(IAsyncResult ar);
```

It uses the *IAsyncResult* interface to obtain the status of the asynchronous operation. To illustrate the plumbing of asynchronous handlers, I'll show you the pseudocode that the HTTP
runtime employs when it deals with asynchronous handlers. The HTTP runtime invokes the
BeginProcessRequest method as illustrated by the following pseudocode:

```
// Sets an internal member of the HttpContext class with
// the current instance of the asynchronous handler
context.AsyncAppHandler = asyncHandler;

// Invokes the BeginProcessRequest method on the asynchronous HTTP handler
asyncHandler.BeginProcessRequest(context, OnCompletionCallback, context);
```

The *context* argument is the current instance of the *HttpContext* class and represents
the context of the request. A reference to the HTTP context is also passed as the custom data sent to the handler to process the request. The *extraData* parameter in the
BeginProcessRequest signature is used to represent the status of the asynchronous operation.
The *BeginProcessRequest* method returns an object of type *HttpAsyncResult*—a class that
implements the *IAsyncResult* interface. The *IAsyncResult* interface contains a property named
AsyncState that is set with the *extraData* value—in this case, the HTTP context.

The *OnCompletionCallback* method is an internal method. It gets automatically triggered
when the asynchronous processing of the request terminates. The following listing illustrates
the pseudocode of the *HttpRuntime* private method:

```
// The method must have the signature of an AsyncCallback delegate
private void OnHandlerCompletion(IAsyncResult ar)
{
    // The ar parameter is an instance of HttpAsyncResult
    HttpContext context = (HttpContext) ar.AsyncState;

    // Retrieves the instance of the asynchronous HTTP handler
    // and completes the request
    IHttpAsyncHandler asyncHandler = context.AsyncAppHandler;
    asyncHandler.EndProcessRequest(ar);

    // Finalizes the request as usual
    ...
}
```

The completion handler retrieves the HTTP context of the request through the *AsyncState* property of the *IAsyncResult* object it gets from the system. As mentioned, the actual object passed is an instance of the *HttpAsyncResult* class—in any case, it is the return value of the *BeginProcessRequest* method. The completion routine extracts the reference to the asynchronous handler from the context and issues a call to the *EndProcessRequest* method:

```
void EndProcessRequest(IAsyncResult result);
```

The *EndProcessRequest* method takes the *IAsyncResult* object returned by the call to *BeginProcessRequest*. As implemented in the *HttpApplication* class, the *EndProcessRequest* method does nothing special and is limited to throwing an exception if an error occurred.

Implementing Asynchronous Handlers

Asynchronous handlers essentially serve one particular scenario—when the generation of the markup is subject to lengthy operations, such as time-consuming database stored procedures or calls to Web services. In these situations, the ASP.NET thread in charge of the request is stuck waiting for the operation to complete. Because the thread is a valuable member of the ASP.NET thread pool, lengthy tasks are potentially the perfect scalability killer. However, asynchronous handlers are here to help.

The idea is that the request begins on a thread-pool thread, but that thread is released as soon as the operation begins. In *BeginProcessRequest*, you typically create your own thread and start the lengthy operation. *BeginProcessRequest* doesn't wait for the operation to complete; therefore, the thread is returned to the pool immediately.

There are a lot of tricky details that this bird's-eye description just omitted. In the first place, you should strive to avoid a proliferation of threads. Ideally, you should use a custom thread pool. Furthermore, you must figure out a way to signal when the lengthy operation has terminated. This typically entails creating a custom class that implements *IAsyncResult* and returning it from *BeginProcessRequest*. This class embeds a synchronization object—typically a *ManualResetEvent* object—that the custom thread carrying the work will signal upon completion.

In the end, building asynchronous handlers is definitely tricky and not for novice developers. Very likely, you are more interested in asynchronous pages than in asynchronous HTTP handlers—that is, the same mechanism but applied to *.aspx* resources. In this case, the "lengthy task" is merely the *ProcessRequest* method of the *Page* class. (Obviously, you configure the page to execute asynchronously only if the page contains code that might start I/O-bound and potentially lengthy operations.)

Starting with ASP.NET 2.0, you find ad hoc support for building asynchronous pages more easily and comfortably. An introductory but still practical chapter on asynchronous pages can be found in my book *Programming ASP.NET Applications—Advanced Topics* (Microsoft Press, 2006).

Warning I've seen several ASP.NET developers using an *.aspx* page to serve markup other than HTML markup. This is not a good idea. An .aspx resource is served by quite a rich and sophisticated HTTP handler—the *System.Web.UI.Page* class. The *ProcessRequest* method of this class entirely provides for the page life cycle as we know it—*Init*, *Load*, and *PreRender* events, as well as rendering stage, view state, and postback management. Nothing of the kind is really required if you only need to retrieve and return, say, the bytes of an image.

Writing HTTP Modules

So we've learned that any incoming requests for ASP.NET resources are handed over to the worker process for the actual processing within the context of the CLR. In IIS 6.0, the worker process is a distinct process from IIS, so if one ASP.NET application crashes, it doesn't bring down the whole server.

ASP.NET manages a pool of *HttpApplication* objects for each running application and picks up one of the pooled instances to serve a particular request. These objects are based on the class defined in your *global.asax* file, or on the base *HttpApplication* class if *global.asax* is missing. The ultimate goal of the *HttpApplication* object in charge of the request is getting an HTTP handler.

On the way to the final HTTP handler, the *HttpApplication* object makes the request pass through a pipeline of HTTP modules. An HTTP module is a .NET Framework class that implements the *IHttpModule* interface. The HTTP modules that filter the raw data within the request are configured on a per-application basis within the *web.config* file. All ASP.NET applications, though, inherit a bunch of system HTTP modules configured in the global *web.config* file.

Generally speaking, an HTTP module can pre-process and post-process a request, and it intercepts and handles system events as well as events raised by other modules. The highly-configurable nature of ASP.NET makes it possible for you to also write and register your own HTTP modules and make them plug into the ASP.NET runtime pipeline, handle system events, and fire their own events.

The *IHttpModule* Interface

The *IHttpModule* interface defines only two methods—*Init* and *Dispose*. The *Init* method initializes a module and prepares it to handle requests. At this time, you subscribe to receive notifications for the events of interest. The *Dispose* method disposes of the resources (all but memory!) used by the module. Typical tasks you perform within the *Dispose* method are closing database connections or file handles.

The *IHttpModule* methods have the following signatures:

```
void Init(HttpApplication app);
void Dispose();
```

The *Init* method receives a reference to the *HttpApplication* object that is serving the request. You can use this reference to wire up to system events. The *HttpApplication* object also features a property named *Context* that provides access to the intrinsic properties of the ASP.NET application. In this way, you gain access to *Response*, *Request*, *Session*, and the like.

Table 18-5 lists the events that HTTP modules can listen to and handle.

TABLE 18-5 *HttpApplication* **Events**

Event	Description
AcquireRequestState, PostAcquireRequestState	Occurs when the handler that will actually serve the request acquires the state information associated with the request. *The post event is not available in ASP.NET 1.x.*
AuthenticateRequest, PostAuthenticateRequest	Occurs when a security module has established the identity of the user. *The post event is not available in ASP.NET 1.x.*
AuthorizeRequest, PostAuthorizeRequest	Occurs when a security module has verified user authorization. *The post event is not available in ASP.NET 1.x.*
BeginRequest	Occurs as soon as the HTTP pipeline begins to process the request.
Disposed	Occurs when the *HttpApplication* object is disposed of as a result of a call to *Dispose*.
EndRequest	Occurs as the last event in the HTTP pipeline chain of execution.
Error	Occurs when an unhandled exception is thrown.
PostMapRequestHandler	Occurs when the HTTP handler to serve the request has been found. *The event is not available in ASP.NET 1.x.*
PostRequestHandlerExecute	Occurs when the HTTP handler of choice finishes execution. The response text has been generated at this point.
PreRequestHandlerExecute	Occurs just before the HTTP handler of choice begins to work.
PreSendRequestContent	Occurs just before the ASP.NET runtime sends the response text to the client.
PreSendRequestHeaders	Occurs just before the ASP.NET runtime sends HTTP headers to the client.
ReleaseRequestState, PostReleaseRequestState	Occurs when the handler releases the state information associated with the current request. *The post event is not available in ASP.NET 1.x.*

Event	Description
ResolveRequestCache, *PostResolveRequestCache*	Occurs when the ASP.NET runtime resolves the request through the output cache. *The post event is not available in ASP.NET 1.x.*
UpdateRequestCache, *PostUpdateRequestCache*	Occurs when the ASP.NET runtime stores the response of the current request in the output cache to be used to serve subsequent requests. *The post event is not available in ASP.NET 1.x.*

All these events are exposed by the *HttpApplication* object that an HTTP module receives as an argument to the *Init* method.

A Custom HTTP Module

Let's begin coming to grips with HTTP modules by writing a relatively simple custom module named *Marker* that adds a signature at the beginning and end of each page served by the application. The following code outlines the class we need to write:

```
using System;
using System.Web;

namespace Core35.Components
{
    public class MarkerModule : IHttpModule
    {
        public void Init(HttpApplication app)
        {
            // Register for pipeline events
        }

        public void Dispose()
        {
            // Nothing to do here
        }
    }
}
```

The *Init* method is invoked by the *HttpApplication* class to load the module. In the *Init* method, you normally don't need to do more than simply register your own event handlers. The *Dispose* method is, more often than not, empty. The heart of the HTTP module is really in the event handlers you define.

Wiring Up Events

The sample *Marker* module registers a couple of pipeline events. They are *BeginRequest* and *EndRequest*. *BeginRequest* is the first event that hits the HTTP application object when the request begins processing. *EndRequest* is the event that signals the request is going to be terminated, and it's your last chance to intervene. By handling these two events, you can write custom text to the output stream before and after the regular HTTP handler—the *Page*-derived class.

The following listing shows the implementation of the *Init* and *Dispose* methods for the sample module:

```
public void Init(HttpApplication app)
{
    // Register for pipeline events
    app.BeginRequest += new EventHandler(OnBeginRequest);
    app.EndRequest += new EventHandler(OnEndRequest);
}

public void Dispose()
{
}
```

The *BeginRequest* and *EndRequest* event handlers have a similar structure. They obtain a reference to the current *HttpApplication* object from the sender and get the HTTP context from there. Next, they work with the *Response* object to append text or a custom header:

```
public void OnBeginRequest(object sender, EventArgs e)
{
    HttpApplication app = (HttpApplication) sender;
    HttpContext ctx = app.Context;

    // More code here
    ...

    // Add custom header to the HTTP response
    ctx.Response.AppendHeader("Author", "DinoE");

    // PageHeaderText is a constant string defined elsewhere
    ctx.Response.Write(PageHeaderText);
}

public void OnEndRequest(object sender, EventArgs e)
{
    // Get access to the HTTP context
    HttpApplication app = (HttpApplication) sender;
    HttpContext ctx = app.Context;

    // More code here
    ...

    // Append some custom text
    // PageFooterText is a constant string defined elsewhere
    ctx.Response.Write(PageFooterText);
}
```

OnBeginRequest writes standard page header text and also adds a custom HTTP header. *OnEndRequest* simply appends the page footer. The effect of this HTTP module is visible in Figure 18-9.

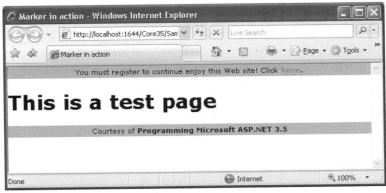

FIGURE 18-9 The *Marker* HTTP module adds a header and footer to each page within the application

Registering with the Configuration File

You register a new HTTP module by adding an entry to the *<httpModules>* section of the configuration file. The overall syntax of the *<httpModules>* section closely resembles that of HTTP handlers. To add a new module, you use the *<add>* node and specify the *name* and *type* attributes. The *name* attribute contains the public name of the module. This name is used to select the module within the *HttpApplication*'s *Modules* collection. If the module fires custom events, this name is also used as the prefix for building automatic event handlers in the *global.asax* file:

```
<system.web>
  <httpModules>
    <add name="Marker"
         type="Core35.Components.MarkerModule,Core35Lib" />
  </httpModules>
</system.web>
```

The *type* attribute is the usual comma-separated string that contains the name of the class and the related assembly. The configuration settings can be entered into the application's configuration file as well as into the global *web.config* file. In the former case, only pages within the application are affected; in the latter case, all pages within all applications are processed by the specified module.

The order in which modules are applied depends on the physical order of the modules in the configuration list. You can remove a system module and replace it with your own that provides a similar functionality. In this case, in the application's *web.config* file you use the *<remove>* node to drop the default module and then use *<add>* to insert your own. If you want to completely redefine the order of HTTP modules for your application, you can clear all the default modules by using the *<clear>* node and then re-register them all in the order you prefer.

> **Note** HTTP modules are loaded and initialized only once, at the startup of the application. Unlike HTTP handlers, they apply to just any requests. So when you plan to create a new HTTP module, you should first wonder whether its functionality should span all possible requests in the application. Is it possible to choose which requests an HTTP module should process? The *Init* method is called only once in the application's lifetime; but the handlers you register are called once for each request. So to operate only on certain pages, you can do as follows:
>
> ```
> public void OnBeginRequest(object sender, EventArgs e)
> {
>     HttpApplication app = (HttpApplication) sender;
>     HttpContext ctx = app.Context;
>     if (!ShouldHook(ctx))
>         return;
>     ...
> }
> ```
>
> *OnBeginRequest* is your handler for the *BeginRequest* event. The *ShouldHook* helper function returns a Boolean value. It is passed the context of the request—that is, any information that is available on the request. You can code it to check the URL as well as any HTTP content type and headers.

Accessing Other HTTP Modules

The sample just discussed demonstrates how to wire up pipeline events—that is, events fired by the *HttpApplication* object. But what about events fired by other modules? The *HttpApplication* object provides a property named *Modules* that gets the collection of modules for the current application.

The *Modules* property is of type *HttpModuleCollection* and contains the names of the modules for the application. The collection class inherits from the abstract class *NameObjectCollectionBase*, which is a collection of pairs made of a string and an object. The string indicates the public name of the module; the object is the actual instance of the module. To access the module that handles the session state, you need code like this:

```
SessionStateModule sess = app.Modules["Session"];
sess.Start += new EventHandler(OnSessionStart);
```

As mentioned, you can also handle events raised by HTTP modules within the *global.asax* file and use the *ModuleName_EventName* convention to name the event handlers. The name of the module is just one of the settings you need to define when registering an HTTP module.

The Page Refresh Feature

Let's examine a practical situation in which the ability to filter the request before it gets processed by an HTTP handler helps to implement a feature that would otherwise be impossible. The postback mechanism has a nasty drawback—if the user refreshes the currently displayed page, the last action taken on the server is blindly repeated. If a new record was added as a result of a previous posting, for example, the application would attempt to insert an identical record upon another postback. Of course, this results in the insertion of identical records and should result in an exception. This snag has existed since the dawn of Web programming and was certainly not introduced by ASP.NET. To implement nonrepeatable actions, some countermeasures are required to essentially transform any critical server-side operation into an *idempotency*. In algebra, an operation is said to be *idempotent* if the result doesn't change regardless of how many times you execute it. For example, take a look at the following SQL command:

```
DELETE FROM employees WHERE employeeid=9
```

You can execute the command 1000 consecutive times, but only one record at most will ever be deleted—the one that satisfies the criteria set in the WHERE clause. Consider this command, instead:

```
INSERT INTO employees VALUES (...)
```

Each time you execute the command, a new record might be added to the table. This is especially true if you have auto-number key columns or nonunique columns. If the table design requires that the key be unique and specified explicitly, the second time you run the command a SQL exception would be thrown.

Although the particular scenario we considered is typically resolved in the data access layer (DAL), the underlying pattern represents a common issue for most Web applications. So the open question is, how can we detect whether the page is being posted as the result of an explicit user action or because the user simply hit F5 or the page refresh () toolbar button?

The Rationale Behind Page Refresh Operations

The page refresh action is a sort of internal browser operation for which the browser doesn't provide any external notification in terms of events or callbacks. Technically speaking, the page refresh consists of the "simple" reiteration of the latest request. The browser caches the latest request it served and reissues it when the user hits the page refresh key or button. No browsers that I'm aware of provide any kind of notification for the page refresh event—and if there are any that do, it's certainly not a recognized standard.

In light of this, there's no way the server-side code (for example, ASP.NET, classic ASP, or ISAPI DLLs) can distinguish a refresh request from an ordinary submit or postback request. To help ASP.NET detect and handle page refreshes, you need to build surrounding machinery that makes two otherwise identical requests look different. All known browsers implement the refresh by resending the last HTTP payload sent; to make the copy look different from the original, any extra service we write must add more parameters and the ASP.NET page must be capable of catching them.

I considered some additional requirements. The solution should not rely on session state and should not tax the server memory too much. It should be relatively easy to deploy and as unobtrusive as possible.

Outline of the Solution

The solution is based on the idea that each request will be assigned a ticket number and the HTTP module will track the last-served ticket for each distinct page it processes. If the number carried by the page is lower than the last-served ticket for the page, it can only mean that the *same* request has been served already—namely, a page refresh. The solution consists of a couple of building blocks: an HTTP module to make preliminary checks on the ticket numbers, and a custom page class that automatically adds a progressive ticket number to each served page. Making the feature work is a two-step procedure: first, register the HTTP module; second, change the base code-behind class of each page in the relevant application to detect browser refreshes.

The HTTP module sits in the middle of the HTTP runtime environment and checks in every request for a resource in the application. The first time the page is requested (when not posting back), there will be no ticket assigned. The HTTP module will generate a new ticket number and store it in the *Items* collection of the *HttpContext* object. In addition, the module initializes the internal counter of the last-served ticket to 0. Each successive time the page is requested, the module compares the last-served ticket with the page ticket. If the page ticket is newer, the request is considered a regular postback; otherwise, it will be flagged as a page refresh. Table 18-6 summarizes the scenarios and related actions.

TABLE 18-6 Scenarios and Actions

Scenario	Action
Page has no ticket associated: ■ No refresh	Counter of the last ticket served is set to 0. The ticket to use for the next request of the current page is generated and stored in *Items*.
Page has a ticket associated: ■ Page refresh occurs if the ticket associated with the page is lower than the last served ticket	Counter of the last ticket served is set with the ticket associated with the page. The ticket to use for the next request of the current page is generated and stored in *Items*.

Some help from the page class is required to ensure that each request—except the first—comes with a proper ticket number. That's why you need to set the code-behind class of each page that intends to support this feature to a particular class—a process that we'll discuss in a moment. The page class will receive two distinct pieces of information from the HTTP module—the next ticket to store in a hidden field that travels with the page, and whether or not the request is a page refresh. As an added service to developers, the code-behind class will expose an extra Boolean property—*IsRefreshed*—to let developers know whether or not the request is a page refresh or a regular postback.

> **Important** The *Items* collection on the *HttpContext* class is a cargo collection purposely created to let HTTP modules pass information down to pages and HTTP handlers in charge of physically serving the request. The HTTP module we employ here sets two entries in the *Items* collection. One is to let the page know whether the request is a page refresh; another is to let the page know what the next ticket number is. Having the module pass the page the next ticket number serves the purpose of keeping the page class behavior as simple and linear as possible, moving most of the implementation and execution burden on to the HTTP module.

Implementation of the Solution

There are a few open points with the solution I just outlined. First, some state is required. Where do you keep it? Second, an HTTP module will be called for each incoming request. How do you distinguish requests for the same page? How do you pass information to the page? How intelligent do you expect the page to be?

It's clear that each of these points might be designed and implemented in a different way than shown here. All design choices made to reach a working solution here should be considered arbitrary, and they can possibly be replaced with equivalent strategies if you want to rework the code to better suit your own purposes. Let me also add this disclaimer: I'm not aware of commercial products and libraries that fix this reposting problem. In the past couple of years, I've been writing articles on the subject of reposting and speaking at various user groups. The version of the code presented in this next example incorporates the most valuable suggestions I've collected along the way. One of these suggestions is to move as much code as possible into the HTTP module, as mentioned in the previous note.

The following code shows the implementation of the HTTP module:

```
public class RefreshModule : IHttpModule
{
    public void Init(HttpApplication app) {
        app.BeginRequest += new EventHandler(OnAcquireRequestState);
    }
    public void Dispose() {
    }
    void OnAcquireRequestState(object sender, EventArgs e) {
        HttpApplication app = (HttpApplication) sender;
        HttpContext ctx = app.Context;
        RefreshAction.Check(ctx);
        return;
    }
}
```

The module listens to the *BeginRequest* event and ends up calling the *Check* method on the helper *RefreshAction* class:

```
public class RefreshAction
{
    static Hashtable requestHistory = null;

    // Other string constants defined here
    ...

    public static void Check(HttpContext ctx) {
        // Initialize the ticket slot
        EnsureRefreshTicket(ctx);

        // Read the last ticket served in the session (from Session)
        int lastTicket = GetLastRefreshTicket(ctx);

        // Read the ticket of the current request (from a hidden field)
        int thisTicket = GetCurrentRefreshTicket(ctx, lastTicket);

        // Compare tickets
        if (thisTicket > lastTicket ||
        (thisTicket==lastTicket && thisTicket==0)) {
            UpdateLastRefreshTicket(ctx, thisTicket);
            ctx.Items[PageRefreshEntry] = false;
        }
        else
            ctx.Items[PageRefreshEntry] = true;
    }

    // Initialize the internal data store
    static void EnsureRefreshTicket(HttpContext ctx)
    {
        if (requestHistory == null)
            requestHistory = new Hashtable();
    }

    // Return the last-served ticket for the URL
    static int GetLastRefreshTicket(HttpContext ctx)
    {
        // Extract and return the last ticket
        if (!requestHistory.ContainsKey(ctx.Request.Path))
            return 0;
        else
            return (int) requestHistory[ctx.Request.Path];
    }

    // Return the ticket associated with the page
    static int GetCurrentRefreshTicket(HttpContext ctx, int lastTicket)
    {
        int ticket;
        object o = ctx.Request[CurrentRefreshTicketEntry];
        if (o == null)
            ticket = lastTicket;
        else
            ticket = Convert.ToInt32(o);
```

```
        ctx.Items[RefreshAction.NextPageTicketEntry] = ticket + 1;
        return ticket;
    }

    // Store the last-served ticket for the URL
    static void UpdateLastRefreshTicket(HttpContext ctx, int ticket)
    {
        requestHistory[ctx.Request.Path] = ticket;
    }
}
```

The *Check* method performs the following actions. It compares the last-served ticket with the ticket (if any) provided by the page. The page stores the ticket number in a hidden field that is read through the *Request* object interface. The HTTP module maintains a hashtable with an entry for each distinct URL served. The value in the hashtable stores the last-served ticket for that URL.

> **Note** The *Item* indexer property is used to set the last-served ticket instead of the *Add* method because *Item* overwrites existing items. The *Add* method just returns if the item already exists.

In addition to creating the HTTP module, you also need to arrange a page class to use as the base for pages wanting to detect browser refreshes. Here's the code:

```
// Assume to be in a custom namespace
public class Page : System.Web.UI.Page
{
    public bool IsRefreshed {
        get {
            HttpContext ctx = HttpContext.Current;
            object o = ctx.Items[RefreshAction.PageRefreshEntry];
            if (o == null)
                return false;
            return (bool) o;
        }
    }

    // Handle the PreRenderComplete event
    protected override void OnPreRenderComplete(EventArgs e) {
        base.OnPreRenderComplete(e);
        SaveRefreshState();
    }

    // Create the hidden field to store the current request ticket
    private void SaveRefreshState() {
        HttpContext ctx = HttpContext.Current;
        int ticket = (int) ctx.Items[RefreshAction.NextPageTicketEntry];
        ClientScript.RegisterHiddenField(
            RefreshAction.CurrentRefreshTicketEntry,
            ticket.ToString());
    }
}
```

The sample page defines a new public Boolean property *IsRefreshed* that you can use in code in the same way you would use *IsPostBack* or *IsCallback*. It overrides *OnPreRenderComplete* to add the hidden field with the page ticket. As mentioned, the page ticket is received from the HTTP module through an ad hoc (and arbitrarily named) entry in the *Items* collection.

Figure 18-10 shows a sample page in action. Let's take a look at the source code of the page.

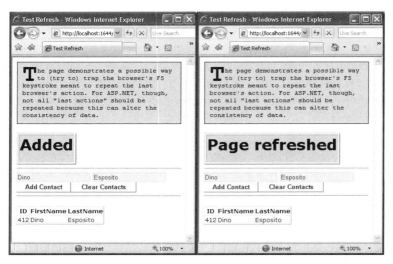

FIGURE 18-10 The page doesn't repeat a sensitive action if the user refreshes the browser's view.

```
public partial class TestRefresh : Core35.Components.Page
{
    protected void AddContactButton_Click(object sender, EventArgs e)
    {
        Msg.InnerText = "Added";
        if (!this.IsRefreshed)
            AddRecord(FName.Text, LName.Text);
        else
            Msg.InnerText = "Page refreshed";

        BindData();
    }
    ...
}
```

The *IsRefreshed* property lets you decide what to do when a postback action is requested. In the preceding code, the *AddRecord* method is not invoked if the page is refreshing. Needless to say, *IsRefreshed* is available only with the custom page class presented here. The custom page class doesn't just add the property, it also adds the hidden field, which is essential for the machinery to work.

Conclusion

HTTP handlers and HTTP modules are the building blocks of the ASP.NET platform. ASP.NET includes several predefined handlers and HTTP modules, but developers can write handlers and modules of their own to perform a variety of tasks. HTTP handlers, in particular, are faster than ordinary Web pages and can be used in all circumstances in which you don't need state maintenance and postback events. To generate images dynamically on the server, for example, an HTTP handler is more efficient than a page.

Everything that occurs under the hood of the ASP.NET runtime environment occurs because of HTTP handlers. When you invoke a Web page or an ASP.NET Web service method, an appropriate HTTP handler gets into the game and serves your request. At the highest level of abstraction, the behavior of an HTTP handler closely resembles that of an ISAPI extension. While the similarity makes sense, a key difference exists. HTTP handlers are managed and CLR-resident components. The CLR, in turn, is hosted by the worker process. An ISAPI extension, on the other hand, is a Win32 library that can live within the IIS process. In the ASP.NET process model, the *aspnet_isapi* component is a true ISAPI extension that collects requests and dispatches them to the worker process. ASP.NET internally implements an ISAPI-like extensibility model in which HTTP handlers play the role of ISAPI extensions in the IIS world. This model changes in IIS 7.0, at which point managed HTTP modules and extensions will also be recognized within the IIS environment.

HTTP modules are to ISAPI filters what HTTP handlers are to ISAPI extensions. HTTP modules are good at performing a number of low-level tasks for which tight interaction and integration with the request/response mechanism is a critical factor. Modules are sort of interceptors that you can place along an HTTP packet's path, from the Web server to the ASP.NET runtime and back. Modules have read and write capabilities, and they can filter and modify the contents of both inbound and outbound requests.

Just the Facts

- HTTP handlers and modules are like classic ISAPI extensions and filters except that they are managed components and provide a much simpler, less error-prone programming model.

- An HTTP handler is the ASP.NET component in charge of handling a request. In the end, an ASP.NET page is just an instance of an HTTP handler.

- HTTP handlers are classes that implement the *IHttpHandler* interface and take care of processing the payload of the request.

- HTTP modules are classes that implement the *IHttpModule* interface and listen to application-level events.

- Custom HTTP handlers and modules must be registered with the application, or all applications in the server machine, through special sections in the *web.config* file.

Part IV
ASP.NET AJAX Extensions

Chapter 19
Partial Rendering: The Easy Way to AJAX

Gone are the days when a Web application could be architected and implemented as a collection of related and linked pages. The incredible success of the Internet has whetted people's appetite for Web-related technology beyond imagination. Over the years, the users' demand for ever more powerful and Web-exposed applications and services led architects and developers to incorporate more and more features into the server platform and client browser. As a result, the traditional pattern of Web applications is becoming less adequate every day. A radical change in the design and programming model cannot be further delayed.

AJAX is a relatively new acronym that stands for *Asynchronous JavaScript and XML*. Coined in 2005, it is a sort of blanket term used to describe highly interactive and responsive Web applications. What's the point here? Weren't Web applications created about a decade ago specifically to be "interactive," "responsive," and deployed over a unique tool called the browser? So what's new today?

At the current state of the art, the industry needs more than just an improved and more powerful platform devised along the traditional guidelines and principles of Web applications—a true paradigm shift is required. AJAX is the incarnation of a new paradigm for the next generation of Web applications that is probably destined to last for at least the next decade.

To address the demand for more powerful features and a framework to support them, in January 2007 Microsoft released a separate framework—the ASP.NET AJAX Extensions. When this framework is installed on top of ASP.NET 2.0, developers can add AJAX capabilities to any new and existing Web sites written with ASP.NET. In ASP.NET 3.5, the ASP.NET AJAX Extensions framework has been slightly enhanced and fully incorporated in the main framework. As a result, once you upgrade to ASP.NET 3.5 you have AJAX capabilities out of the box and don't need the services of ASP.NET AJAX Extensions any longer. At the same time,

ASP.NET 3.5 Web sites and ASP.NET 2.0 Web sites equipped with ASP.NET AJAX Extensions can happily live and run side by side on the same Web server.

In this chapter, I'll first dig deeper into the motivation for and driving force behind AJAX. Next, I'll review the AJAX features you find in ASP.NET 3.5, focusing on what appears to be the easiest route to AJAX in ASP.NET systems—partial rendering. In the next chapter, I'll consider the use of ad hoc server-side services to more evenly distribute the workload between the client and the server.

> **Note** Most books, articles, and documentation tend to use the expressions "Web site" and "Web application" interchangeably. My books and articles are no exception. In the majority of situations, using the two expressions as synonyms is acceptable. It should be noted, though, that strictly speaking "Web site" and "Web application" mean two distinct things. In particular, a *Web site* is a collection of Web pages and auxiliary resources hosted on a Web server accessible via the Internet or local area network (LAN). A *Web application* is an application that provides a Web front end and is accessed via the Internet or LAN. The two concepts differ if we consider a Web site made of plain HTML pages and images. But as we move on to consider a dynamic Web site whose pages are generated dynamically on the server, the difference between a Web site and application begins to blur. A server application that reaches its users over the Internet often needs a Web-based presentation layer—that is, one or more Web sites. The distinction becomes important when working with AJAX because we're no longer simply transferring Web pages but also lower-level data. As defined, Web sites deal only with pages and other resources (such as images), whereas Web applications have the added capability to transfer information other than pure pages or resources. It's this "other information" we're interested in when working with AJAX.

The ASP.NET AJAX Infrastructure

From a developer-oriented perspective, AJAX collectively refers to a set of development components, tools, and techniques for creating highly interactive Web applications that give users an overall better experience. According to the AJAX paradigm, Web applications work by exchanging data rather than pages with the Web server. From a user perspective, this means that faster roundtrips occur and, more importantly, page loading is quicker and the need for refreshing the page entirely is significantly reduced.

As a result, a Web application tends to look like a classic desktop Microsoft Windows application and can invoke server code from the client, run and control server-side asynchronous tasks, and feature a strongly responsive and nonflickering user interface. An AJAX application can have a number of features that minimize user frustration, provide timely feedback about what's going on, and deliver great mashed-up content. (Hold on! This doesn't mean AJAX Web applications are the same as desktop applications; they simply allow for a few more desktop-like features.)

Note AJAX applications have a number of plusses but also a few drawbacks. Overall, choosing an AJAX application rather than a classic Web application is simply a matter of weighing the trade-offs. An AJAX application certainly gives users continuous feedback and never appears held up by some remote operation. On the other hand, AJAX applications are not entirely like desktop applications, and their capabilities in terms of graphics, multimedia, and hardware control are not as powerful as in a regular (smart) client. In the end, AJAX applications are just one very special breed of a Web application; as such, they might require some code refactoring to deliver the expected performance and results.

We are all witnessing and contributing to an interesting and unique phenomenon—the Web is undergoing an epochal change right before our eyes as a result of our actions. Ten years ago, the Web was in its infancy and based on an infrastructure that was simple, ubiquitous, and effective. Ten years of Web evolution has resulted in the building of a thick layer of abstraction on the server side, but it hasn't changed the basic infrastructure—HTTP protocol and pages. The original infrastructure, which was the chief factor for the rapid success of the Web model of applications, is still there.

In fact, the next generation of Web applications will still be based on the HTTP protocol and pages. However, the contents of pages and the capabilities of the server-side and client-side machinery will change to provide a significantly richer user experience.

The Hidden Engine of AJAX

Today Web applications work by submitting user-filled forms to the Web server and displaying the markup returned by the Web server. The client-to-server communication employs the HTTP protocol and is usually conducted by the browser. The new model that AJAX heralds simply employs an alternate and scriptable tool to conduct the HTTP communication with the Web server. The benefit is that the page that triggers the call remains up and running and refreshes its document object model (DOM) with the freshly downloaded data. No page replacement occurs, and the overall user experience is smooth and continual.

The Classic Browser-Led Model

Using the local Domain Name System (DNS) resolver in the operating system, the browser resolves the requested URL to an IP address and opens a socket. An HTTP packet travels over the wire to the given destination. The packet includes the form and all its fields. The request is captured by the Web server and typically forwarded to an internal module for further processing. At the end of the process, an HTTP response packet is prepared and the return value for the browser is inserted in the body. If the response contains an HTML page, the browser replaces the current contents entirely with the new chunk of markup.

While the request is being processed on the server, the "old" page is frozen but still displayed to the client user. As soon as the "new" page is downloaded, the browser clears the display and renders the page.

This model was just fine in the beginning of the Web age when pages contained little more than formatted text, hyperlinks, and some images. The success of the Web has prompted users to ask for increasingly more powerful features, and it has led developers and designers to create more sophisticated services and graphics. The net effect is that pages are heavy and cumbersome—even though we still insist on calling them "rich" pages. Regardless of whether they're rich or just cumbersome, these are the Web pages of today's applications. And nobody really believes that we're going to return to the scanty and spartan HTML pages of a decade ago.

Given the current architecture of Web applications, each user action requires a complete redraw of the page. Subsequently, richer and heavier pages render slowly and, as a result, produce a good deal of flickering. Projected to the whole set of pages in a large, portal-like application, this mechanism is just perfect for unleashing the frustrations of the poor end user.

The New Out-of-Band Model

The chief factor that enables AJAX functionality in a Web page is the ability to issue *out-of-band* HTTP requests. In this context, an out-of-band call indicates an HTTP request placed using a component different from the browser. The out-of-band call is triggered via script by an HTML page event and is served by a proxy component. In AJAX frameworks, the proxy component is based on the *XMLHttpRequest* object.

> **Note** About a decade ago, there was a team at Microsoft working on a technology called Remote Scripting (RS). RS never reached the stage of a version 1.0 but had a lot in common with today's AJAX hidden engine. In RS, the proxy component was a Java applet managing the browser-to-server communication.

XMLHttpRequest is a browser's object that is scriptable through JavaScript. It sends a regular HTTP request to the specified URL and waits, either synchronously or asynchronously, for it to be fully served. When the response data is ready, the proxy invokes a user-defined JavaScript callback to refresh any portion of the page that needs updating. Figure 19-1 provides a graphical overview of the model.

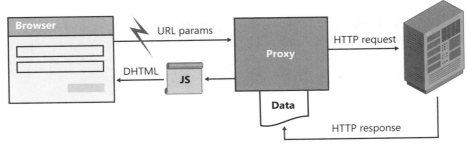

FIGURE 19-1 Out-of-band calls are sent through a proxy component, and a JavaScript callback is used to update any portion of the page affected by returned data

All browsers know how to replace an old page with a new page; until a few years ago, though, not all of them provided an object model to represent the current contents of the page. (Today, I can hardly mention a single modern, commercially available browser that doesn't expose a read/write page DOM.) For browsers that supply an updatable object model for HTML pages, the JavaScript callback function can refresh specific portions of the old page, thus making them look updated, without a full reload.

Exactly what are the capabilities required of a browser to run AJAX functionalities? As mentioned, a browser needs to provide two key capabilities: a proxy mechanism to make client code able to place out-of-band HTTP calls, and an updatable DOM. And both capabilities must be achieved through standard and globally accepted interfaces.

There's a World Wide Web Consortium (W3C) ratified standard for the updatable DOM. A W3C standard for the proxy component is currently being developed. It takes the form of the existing *XMLHttpRequest* object and is devised as an interface exposed by the browser to allow script code to perform HTTP client functionality, such as submitting form data or loading data from a remote Web site. The latest working draft is available at *http://www.w3.org/ TR/XMLHttpRequest*.

In addition, browsers must support JavaScript and, preferably, cascading style sheets (CSS).

The Role of the HTML Document Object Model

The page Document Object Model (DOM) is the specification that defines a platform- and language-neutral interface for accessing and updating the contents, structure, and style of HTML and XML documents. As a recognized standard ratified by the W3C committee, the DOM is now supported by virtually all browsers. The DOM provides a standard set of objects for representing the constituent elements of HTML and XML documents. All together, these objects form a standard interface for accessing and manipulating child elements of HTML pages and, more in general, XML documents.

The DOM application programming interface (API) renders the displayed page as a tree-based structure. For a Web page, each node maps to an object that represents an HTML tag.

The object, therefore, has properties and methods that can be applied to an HTML tag. There are three fundamental operations you can accomplish on a node: find the node (including related nodes such as children, parent, or sibling nodes), create a node, and manipulate a node. Identifying a particular node is easy as long as the page author knows the ID of the corresponding element.

The W3C DOM consists of three levels that indicate, for the browser, three different levels of adherence to the standard. For more information, take a look at *http://www.w3.org/DOM*.

From Dynamic HTML to the Standard DOM

About ten years ago, with Internet Explorer 4.0, Microsoft introduced a proprietary object model named Dynamic HTML (DHTML) to enable page authors to update the current page dynamically using JavaScript. The success of DHTML led to the definition of a standard document object model—the W3C's DOM. Quite obviously, the DOM evolved from DHTML and became much more generalized than DHTML.

Today most browsers support a mix of DOM and DHTML. Which one should you use? In particular, to update some contents, should you obtain a reference to the textual child node of the node that matches the intended HTML tag (the DOM way) or just grab a reference to a node and use the *innerHTML* property as you would do in the DHTML way? Likewise, to add a new element, should you create a new element or just stuff in a chunk of updated HTML via *innerHTML*? Admittedly, one of the most interesting debates in the community is whether to use DHTML to manipulate pages or opt for the cleaner approach propounded by the DOM API.

The key fact is that the DOM API is significantly slower than using *innerHTML*. If you go through the DOM to generate some user interface dynamically, you have to create every element, append each into the proper container, and then set properties. The alternative only entails that you define the HTML you want and render it into the page using *innerHTML*. The browser, then, does the rest by rendering your markup into direct graphics.

Overall, DHTML and DOM manipulation are both useful depending on the context. There are many Web sites that discuss performance tests, and DHTML is always the winner. Anyway, DOM is still perfectly fast as long as you use it the right way—that is, create HTML fragments and append them to the proper container only as the final step.

Note The inclusion of a standard API to edit the currently displayed page is a key factor in the success of AJAX. Although the first working frameworks for AJAX-like remote scripting date back to a decade ago, the limited support that browsers have had for dynamic document changes through most of this time period slowed down the adoption of such technologies in the industry. Until now. With the HTML DOM becoming a widely supported standard and the availability of a mature tool for remote calls such as *XMLHttpRequest*, AJAX is ready for prime time.

The *XMLHttpRequest* Object

Created by Microsoft and adopted soon thereafter by Mozilla, the *XMLHttpRequest* object is fully supported these days by the majority of Web browsers. The implementation can significantly differ from one browser to the next, even though the top-level interface is nearly identical. For this reason, a W3C committee is at work with the goal of precisely documenting a minimum set of interoperable features based on existing implementations. An excellent presentation on the component can be found here: *http://developer.mozilla.org/en/docs/ XMLHttpRequest*.

> **Note** The *XMLHttpRequest* object originally shipped as a separate component with Internet Explorer 5.0 back in the spring of 1999. It is a native component of all Microsoft operating systems that have shipped since. In particular, you'll certainly find it installed on all machines that run Windows 2000, Windows XP, and newer operating systems.

When the *XMLHttpRequest* object was first released, the Component Object Model (COM) was ruling the world at Microsoft. The extensibility model of products and applications was based on COM and implemented through COM components. In the late 1990s, the right and natural choice was to implement this new component as a reusable automation COM object, named *Microsoft.XmlHttp*.

COM objects are external components that require explicit permission to run inside of a Web browser. In particular, to run the *XMLHttpRequest* object, and subsequently enable any AJAX functionality built on top of it, at a minimum a client machine needs to accept ActiveX components marked safe for scripting. (See Figure 19-2.)

The *XMLHttpRequest* object is certainly a safe component, but to enable it users need to decrease their security settings and accept any other component "declared" safe for scripting that is around the Web sites they visit.

Mozilla adopted *XMLHttpRequest* immediately after its first release with Internet Explorer 5.0. However, in Mozilla-equipped browsers, the *XMLHttpRequest* object is part of the browser's object model and doesn't rely on external components. Put another way, a Mozilla browser such as Firefox publishes its own *XMLHttpRequest* object into the scripting engine and never uses the COM component, even when the COM component is installed on the client machine and is part of the operating system.

FIGURE 19-2 The property window used to change the security settings in Internet Explorer

As a result, in Mozilla browsers, *XMLHttpRequest* looks like a native JavaScript object and can be instantiated through the classic *new* operator:

```
// The object name requires XML in capital letters
var proxy = new XMLHttpRequest();
```

When the browser is Internet Explorer (up to version 6.0), the *XMLHttpRequest* object is instantiated using the *ActiveXObject* wrapper, as shown here:

```
var proxy = new ActiveXObject("Microsoft.XmlHttp");
```

Generally, AJAX-style frameworks check the current browser and then decide which route to take.

Implemented as a COM component for historical reasons on Internet Explorer browsers, the *XMLHttpRequest* object has finally become a browser object with Internet Explorer 7.0. All potential security concerns are removed at the root. Needless to say, implemented as a browser object, the *XMLHttpRequest* functionality is somewhat safer, at least in the sense it doesn't require users to change their security settings for the browser.

Using the *XMLHttpRequest* Object

The *XMLHttpRequest* object is designed to perform one key operation: sending an HTTP request. The request can be sent either synchronously or asynchronously. The following bit of code shows the programming interface of the object as it results from the W3C working draft at the time of this writing:

```
interface XMLHttpRequest
{
  function onreadystatechange;
  readonly unsigned short readyState;
  void open(string method, string url);
  void open(string method, string url, bool async);
  void open(string method, string url, bool async, string user);
  void open(string method, string url, bool async,
            string user, string pswd);
  void setRequestHeader(string header, string value);
  void send(string data);
  void send(Document data);
  void abort();
  string getAllResponseHeaders();
  string getResponseHeader(string header);
  string responseText;
  Document responseXML;
  unsigned short status;
  string statusText;
};
```

Using the component is a two-step operation. First, you open a channel to the URL and specify the method (GET, POST, or other) to use and whether you want the request to execute asynchronously. Next, you set any required header and send the request. If the request is a POST, you pass to the *send* method the body of the request.

The *send* method returns immediately in the case of an asynchronous operation. You write an *onreadystatechange* function to check the status of the current operation and, using that function, figure out when it is done. The following code shows how to carry on a POST request using the *XMLHttpRequest* object:

```
var xmlRequest, e;
try
{
    xmlRequest = new XMLHttpRequest();
}
catch(e)
{
    try
    {
        xmlRequest = new ActiveXObject("Microsoft.XMLHTTP");
    }
    catch(e)
    {
    }
}
```

```
// Prepare for a synchronous POST request
var body = null;  // An empty request body this time...
xmlRequest.open("POST", pageUrl, false);
xmlRequest.setRequestHeader("Content-Type",
                            "application/x-www-form-urlencoded");
xmlRequest.send(body);
```

In a synchronous call, the *send* method returns when the response has been fully downloaded and parsed by the object. You can access it as a plain string using the *responseText*
property. If the response is an XML stream, you can have it exposed as an XML DOM object
using the *responseXml* property.

> **Important** If you're going to use ASP.NET AJAX or any other AJAX-like framework for building
> your applications, you'll hardly hear anything about the *XMLHttpRequest* object, much less use
> it directly in your own code. An AJAX framework completely encapsulates this object and shields
> page authors and application designers from it. You don't need to know about *XMLHttpRequest*
> to write great AJAX applications, no matter how complex and sophisticated they are. However,
> knowing the fundamentals of *XMLHttpRequest* can lead you to a better and more thorough
> understanding of the platform and to more effective diagnoses of problems.

The Microsoft AJAX JavaScript Library

Most of the power of AJAX resides on the client and is strictly related to the browser's and
platform's client-side functionality. No AJAX capability would ever be possible without a client-side engine; and this engine can only be written in JavaScript. Such a script code governs
the execution of out-of-band calls and often kicks in and replaces regular postbacks with
AJAX postbacks. Moreover, no AJAX functionality would ever be possible without JavaScript
and a standard (and rich) DOM. The DOM, though, is not enough.

The DOM represents the programming gateway to the page constituent elements, but it
is not designed to provide programming facilities such as those you can find in a general-
purpose library. Normally, the script tools you can leverage to consume objects and contents
from the DOM are those provided by the JavaScript language. Not exactly a powerful toolkit.
Enter the Microsoft AJAX JavaScript library.

The AJAX extensions to ASP.NET silently leverages the Microsoft AJAX JavaScript library for
all of its built-in features. The library, though, is also available to page authors to code their
own JavaScript page-specific functions.

The Microsoft AJAX library is written in JavaScript, although with a strong sense of object-
orientation. The JavaScript language does support objects and allow the creation of custom
objects. It does not, however, support full object-orientedness because it has no native
concept of true object inheritance. Nonetheless, even excluding true object orientation,
JavaScript is still a modern and suitable language that can be used to build a class framework

à la the .NET Framework. ASP.NET AJAX takes the JavaScript language to the next level by adding some type-system extensions and the notions of namespace and inheritance. In addition, the ASP.NET AJAX JavaScript supports interfaces and enumerations, and it has a number of helper functions to manipulate strings and arrays.

These extensions are coded using the base set of instructions that characterize the core JavaScript language, and they're persisted to a set of *.js* files. These *.js* files are not installed as distinct files on the Web server when you install ASP.NET. They are embedded as resources into the ASP.NET AJAX assembly—*system.web.extensions*. If you want them available as distinct files (for example, for your home perusal), go to *http://msdn2.microsoft.com/en-us/asp.net/bb944808.aspx*, check the license agreement, and get them as a single downloaded compressed file.

Let's now dig out some of these extensions to the JavaScript language and briefly explore the features of the built-in classes. For more information, you can have a look at Chapter 2 of my *Introducing ASP.NET AJAX* books from Microsoft Press.

Important The Microsoft AJAX JavaScript library is self-contained in the *.js* files you get from the aforementioned URL. This means that you can embed these files in any Web page and enjoy the object-oriented features of JavaScript regardless of whether or not ASP.NET AJAX is being used to power the page. For example, you can use the *<script>* tag to include all required JavaScript files in a PHP or classic ASP page and enjoy the advanced capabilities of the Microsoft AJAX JavaScript library.

JavaScript Language Extensions

The JavaScript language features a set of built-in objects, including *Function, Object, Boolean, Array, Number,* and *String*. All intrinsic objects have a read-only property named *prototype*. You use the *prototype* property to provide a base set of functionality shared by any new instance of an object of that class. New functionality can be added to the class prototype inside of an application to extend and improve the capabilities of a given class. This is exactly what the Microsoft AJAX library does.

Type information is the most important aspect of the JavaScript language that has been enhanced. Aside from instances of the base types, everything else in JavaScript is a plain *object*. With the library extensions, you have a type information system that is similar to the .NET Framework. The following code now works and displays "Person" instead of a generic "object" string:

```
var p = new Person("Dino", "Esposito");
alert(Object.getTypeName(p));
```

But where does the *getTypeName* method come from? It is a new method defined on the native JavaScript *Object* type. The Microsoft AJAX library contains code that defines new objects and extends existing JavaScript objects with additional functionality. Table 19-1 lists the main global objects defined in the library.

TABLE 19-1 Top-Level Objects in the Microsoft AJAX Library

Property	Description
Array	Extends the native *Array* object. This object groups static methods to add, insert, remove, and clear elements of an array. It also includes static methods to enumerate elements and check whether a given element is contained in the array.
Boolean	Extends the native *Boolean* object. This object defines a static *parse* method to infer a Boolean value from a string or any expression that evaluates to a Boolean value.
Date	Extends the native *Date* object with a couple of instance methods: *localeFormat* and *format*. These methods format the date using the locale or invariant culture information.
Error	Defines a static *create* method to wrap the JavaScript *Error* object and add a richer constructor to it. This object incorporates a couple of properties—*message* and *name*—to provide a description of the error that occurred and identify the error by name. A number of built-in error objects are used to simulate exceptions. In this case, the *name* property indicates the name of the exception caught.
Function	Extends the native *Function* object. This object groups methods to define classes, namespaces, delegates, and a bunch of other object-oriented facilities.
Number	Extends the native *Number* object. This object defines a static *parse* method to infer a numeric value from a string or any expression that evaluates to a numeric value. In addition, it supports a pair of static formatting methods: *localeFormat* and *format*.
Object	Extends the native *Object* object. This object groups methods to read type information, such as the type of the object being used.
RegExp	Wraps the native *RegExp* object.
String	Extends the native *String* object. This object groups string manipulation methods, such as trim methods and *endsWith* and *startsWith* methods. In addition, it defines static *localeFormat* and *format* methods that are close relatives of the *String.Format* method of the managed *String* type.

After the Microsoft AJAX library has been added to the application, the following code will work just fine:

```
var s = "Dino";
alert(s.startsWith('D'));
```

The native JavaScript *String* object doesn't feature either a *startsWith* or an *endsWith* method; the extended AJAX *String* object does.

One of the most common mistakes made when writing script code inside of Web pages is to use direct access to HTML elements instead of resorting to the *getElementById* method of the DOM. Suppose you have a text box element named *TextBox1* in your client page. The following script code won't work on all browsers:

```
alert(TextBox1.value);
```

The correct form ratified by the W3C paper for the HTML DOM standards is shown here:

```
alert(document.getElementById("TextBox1").value);
```

The correct form is clearly more verbose and bothersome to write over and over again. The Microsoft AJAX library comes to the rescue with the *$get* global function. Simply put, the *$get* function is a shortcut for the *document.getElementById* function. If the Microsoft AJAX library is in use, the following expression is fully equivalent to the one just shown:

```
alert($get("TextBox1").value);
```

The *$get* function has two overloads. If you call *$get* passing the sole ID, the function falls back into *document.getElementById*. Alternatively, you can specify a container as the second argument, as shown here:

```
var parent = $get("Div1");
$get("TextBox1", parent);
```

If the container element supports the *getElementById* method, the function returns the output of *element.getElementById*; otherwise, the *$get* function uses the DOM interface to explore the contents of the subtree rooted in the element to locate any node with the given ID.

Object-Oriented Extensions: Namespaces

In JavaScript, the *Function* object is the main tool you use to combine code with properties and forge new components. In the Microsoft AJAX library, the *Function* object is extended to incorporate type information, as well as namespaces, inheritance, interfaces, and enumerations.

A namespace provides a way of grouping and classifying types belonging to a library. A namespace is not a type itself, but it adds more information to the definition of each type it contains to better qualify the type. By default, all custom JavaScript functions belong to the global space of names. In the Microsoft AJAX library, you can associate a custom function with a particular namespace, for purely organizational reasons. When declaring a custom type in the Microsoft AJAX library, you can do as follows:

```
Type.registerNamespace("Core35");
Core35.Person = function Core35$Person(firstName, lastName)
{
    this._firstName = firstName;
    this._lastName = lastName;
}

// Define the body of members
function Core35$Person$ToString() {
    return this._lastName + ", " + this._firstName;
}
...

// Define the prototype of the class
Core35.Person.prototype = {
    ToString:       Core35$Person$ToString,
    get_FirstName: Core35$Person$get_FirstName,
    set_FirstName: Core35$Person$set_FirstName,
    get_LastName:  Core35$Person$get_LastName,
    set_LastName:  Core35$Person$set_LastName
}

// Register the class, extending our own IntroAjax Person class
IntroAjax.Person.registerClass("Core35.Person");
```

The *Type.registerNamespace* method adds the specified namespace to the runtime environment. In a way, the *registerNamespace* method is equivalent to using the *namespace {...}* construct in C# or the *Namespace .. End Namespace* construct in Microsoft Visual Basic.

The *Core35.Person* function defined following the namespace declaration describes a *Person* type in the *Core35* namespace. Finally, the newly defined function must be registered as a class with the Microsoft AJAX library framework. You use the *registerClass* method on the current function. The *registerClass* method is defined in the prototype of the *Function* object; as such, it is inherited by all functions. Internally, the *registerClass* method sets the *_typeName* property of the function to the first parameter of the method—the actual name of the class.

The *registerClass* method takes a number of parameters. The first parameter is mandatory, and it indicates the public name that will be used to expose the JavaScript function as a class. Additional and optional parameters are the parent class, if there is any, and any interface implemented by the class.

Note In the definition of a new class, you can use an anonymous function or a named function. In terms of syntax, both solutions are acceptable. The convention , though, is that you opt for named functions and name each function after its fully qualified name, replacing the dot symbol (.) with a dollar symbol ($).

Object-Oriented Extensions: Inheritance

Let's define a new class, *Citizen*, that extends *Person* by adding a couple of properties: an address and a national identification number. Here's the skeleton of the code you need:

```
// Declare the class
Core35.Citizen = function Core35$Citizen(firstName, lastName, id)
{
   ...
}

// Define the prototype of the class
Core35.Citizen.prototype = {
   ...
}

// Register the class
Core35.Citizen.registerClass("Core35.Citizen", Core35.Person);
```

Note that the first argument of *registerClass* is a string, but the second one has to be an object reference. Let's flesh out this code a bit.

In the constructor, you'll set some private members and call the base constructor to initialize the members defined on the base class. The *initializeBase* method (defined on *Function*) retrieves and invokes the base constructor:

```
Core35.Citizen = function Core35$Citizen(firstName, lastName, id)
{
    Core35.Citizen.initializeBase(this, [firstName, lastName]);
    this._id = id;
    this._address = "";
}
```

You pass *initializeBase* the reference to the current object as well as an array with any parameters that the constructor to call requires. You can use the *[...]* notation to define an array inline. If you omit the *[...]* notation, be ready to handle a parameter count exception.

Quite often, developers derive a class because they need to add new members or alter the behavior of an existing method or property. Object-oriented languages define a proper keyword to flag members as overridable. How is that possible in JavaScript? By simply adding a member to the class prototype, you mark it as overridable in derived classes. In addition, if the member already exists on the base class, it is silently overridden in the new one. Here's the prototype of the *Citizen* class:

```
Core35.Citizen.prototype =
{
    ToString:     Core35$Citizen$ToString,
    get_ID:       Core35$Citizen$get_ID,
    get_Address:  Core35$Citizen$get_Address,
    set_Address:  Core35$Citizen$set_Address
}
```

The class has a read-only *ID* property and a read-write *Address* property. Furthermore, it overrides the *ToString* method defined in the parent class:

```
function Core35$Citizen$ToString()
{
    var temp = Core35.Citizen.callBaseMethod(this, 'ToString');
    temp += "   [" + this._id + "]";
    return temp;
}
```

You use *callBaseMethod* to invoke the same method on the parent class. Defined on the *Function* class, the *callBaseMethod* method takes up to three parameters: the instance, the name of the method, plus an optional array of arguments for the base method.

As mentioned earlier, the *ToString* method on the *Person* class returns a *LastName, FirstName* string. The *ToString* method on the *Citizen* class returns a string in the following format: *LastName, FirstName [ID]*.

Object-Oriented Extensions: Interfaces

Finally, an interface describes a group of related behaviors that are typical of a variety of classes. In general, an interface can include methods, properties, and events; in JavaScript, it contains only methods.

Keeping in mind the constraints of the JavaScript language, to define an interface you create a regular class with a constructor and a prototype. The constructor and each prototyped method, though, will just throw a not-implemented exception. Here's the code for the sample *Sys.IDisposable* built-in interface:

```
Type.registerNamespace("Sys");
Sys.IDisposable = function Sys$IDisposable()
{
    throw Error.notImplemented();
}
function Sys$IDisposable$dispose()
{
    throw Error.notImplemented();
}
Sys.IDisposable.prototype =
{
    dispose: Sys$IDisposable$dispose
}
Sys.IDisposable.registerInterface('Sys.IDisposable');
```

The following statement registers the *Citizen* class, makes it derive from *Person*, and implements the *IDisposable* interface:

```
Core35.Citizen.registerClass('Core35.Citizen',
        Core35.Person, Sys.IDisposable);
```

To implement a given interface, a JavaScript class simply provides all methods in the interface and lists the interface while registering the class:

```
function Core35$Citizen$dispose
{
   this._id = "";
   this._address = "";
}

Core35.Citizen.prototype =
{
   dispose: Core35$Citizen$dispose
   ...
}
```

Note, though, that you won't receive any runtime error if the class that declares to implement a given interface doesn't really support all the methods.

If a class implements multiple interfaces, you simply list all required interfaces in the *registerClass* method as additional parameters. Here's an example:

```
Sys.Component.registerClass('Sys.Component', null,
      Sys.IDisposable,
      Sys.INotifyPropertyChange,
      Sys.INotifyDisposing);
```

As you can see, in this case you don't have to group interfaces in an array.

The Application Core Component

The AJAX client library is made up of three main logical layers: JavaScript extensions, core framework classes, and user-interface (UI) framework classes. (See Figure 19-3.)

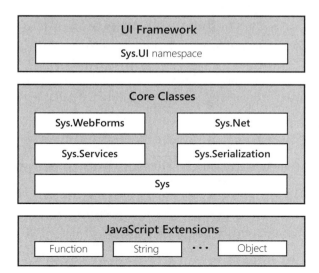

FIGURE 19-3 A graphical view of the Microsoft AJAX JavaScript library

As mentioned, JavaScript extensions add new methods and capabilities to native JavaScript objects and enable registration methods to simulate object-oriented constructs such as classes, namespaces, inheritance, and interfaces. The UI framework includes base components to define client behaviors, controls, DOM elements, and input devices such as keyboard and mouse buttons. The core framework classes form a sort of base library that incorporates a set of commonly used classes for event handling, string manipulation, Web services, debugging, and network operations.

The execution of each ASP.NET AJAX page is controlled by an application object that is instantiated in the body of the library. The application object is an instance of a private class—the *Sys._Application* class. Whenever an ASP.NET AJAX page is loaded in the browser, an instance of the *Sys._Application* class is promptly created and assigned to the *Sys.Application* object:

```
Sys.Application = new Sys._Application();
```

In addition, each ASP.NET AJAX page is injected with the following script code:

```
<script type="text/javascript">
<!--
    Sys.Application.initialize();
// -->
</script>
```

This code is placed immediately after the closing tag of the page's form, and it commands the loading of any script files registered for loading with the page's script manager. As a result, the *Sys.Application* object is the nerve center of the ASP.NET AJAX page.

 Note JavaScript has no notion of private members; therefore, private members are conventionally indicated by the underscore symbol (_) prefixing their names.

The *Sys.Application* object serves one main purpose: providing access to page components. Its *findComponent* method scrolls the runtime hierarchy of Microsoft AJAX components for the current page until it finds a component with a matching ID. The method has two possible prototypes:

```
Sys._Application.findComponent(id);
Sys._Application.findComponent(id, parent);
```

The former overload takes the ID of the component, uses it to look up the component, and then navigates the hierarchy all the way down from the root. When a non-null *parent* argument is specified, the search is restricted to the subtree rooted in the context object. The *id* parameter must be a string; the *parent* parameter must be a Microsoft AJAX library object. The method returns the object that matches the ID, or it returns null if no such object is found.

The Microsoft AJAX library also supports a shortcut for retrieving runtime components—the *$find* method. The *$find* method is an alias for *findComponent*:

```
var $find = Sys.Application.findComponent;
```

You can use this method to locate all components created by server controls and extenders, as well as by your own JavaScript code. You can't use *$find* to locate DOM elements; for DOM elements, you must resort to *$get*.

When a page using the Microsoft AJAX library page first loads up, the *load* event is fired for the client code to perform any required initialization. Note that the event refers to the page lifetime, not the application lifetime. So whenever a classic postback occurs, you receive a new *load* event. You don't receive such events for any AJAX-style postback conducted via *XMLHttpRequest*. Likewise, the *unload* event is fired when the page is unloaded.

The *load* event occurs after a page has been loaded and initialized completely. For such a page, the *load* event is preferable to the browser's *onload* for initialization purposes. Only when you get the Microsoft AJAX library *load* event, therefore, can you be sure that the page is ready for user interaction. The *unload* event occurs just before the Microsoft AJAX library runtime releases the page and all of its resources. For the sake of the application's stability, you should use this event instead of the browser's *onunload* event for clean-up tasks.

The easiest way to define *load* and *unload* handlers is by means of predefined function names: *pageLoad* and *pageUnload*. These functions need to be global and parameterless:

```
<script type="text/JavaScript" language="JavaScript">
    function pageLoad()
    {
        alert("Being loaded");
    }
    function pageUnload()
    {
        alert("Being unloaded");
    }
</script>
```

Because this piece doesn't directly call into any of the Microsoft AJAX library objects—including *Sys.Application*—you can safely place it everywhere, even at the top of the page.

The Network Stack

AJAX libraries in general, and ASP.NET AJAX Extensions in particular, owe their growing popularity to their ability to execute out-of-band Web requests from the client. In particular, ASP.NET AJAX extensions allow you to invoke Web service methods as well as static methods defined on the code-behind page class. This ability leverages the networking support built into the Microsoft AJAX library.

In the Microsoft AJAX library, a remote request is represented by an instance of the *Sys.Net.WebRequest* class. Table 19-2 lists the properties of the class.

TABLE 19-2 Properties of the *Sys.Net.WebRequest* class

Property	Description
body	Gets and sets the body of the request
executor	Gets and sets the Microsoft AJAX library object that will take care of executing the request
headers	Gets the headers of the request
httpVerb	Gets and sets the HTTP verb for the request
timeout	Gets and sets the timeout, if any, for the request
url	Gets and sets the URL of the request

The *WebRequest* class defines the *url* property to get and set the target URL and the *headers* property to add header strings to the request. If the request is going to be a POST, you set the body of the request through the *body* property. A request executes through the method *invoke*. The *completed* event informs you about the completion of the request.

Each Web request is executed through an internal class—the Web request manager—that employs an "executor" to open the socket and send the packet. All executors derive from a common base class—the *Sys.Net.WebRequestExecutor* class.

The Microsoft AJAX library defines just one HTTP executor—the *Sys.Net.XMLHttpExecutor* class. As the name suggests, this executor uses the popular *XMLHttpRequest* object to execute the HTTP request.

> **Note** All AJAX libraries are associated with the *XMLHttpRequest* browser object. So what else could an executor be other than a reference to the *XMLHttpRequest* browser object? In general, an HTTP executor is any means you can use to carry out a Web request. An alternative executor might be based on HTTP frames. The idea is to use a dynamically created inline frame to download the response of a given request and then parse that result into usable objects.

DOM Events

Building cross-browser compatibility for events is not an easy task. Internet Explorer has its own eventing model, and so do Firefox and Safari. For this reason, the event model of the Microsoft AJAX library is a new abstract API that joins together the standard W3C API and the Internet Explorer nonextensible model. The new API is closely modeled after the standard W3C API.

In addition to using different method names (*add/removeEventListener* is for Firefox, and *attach/detachEvent* is for Internet Explorer), browsers differ in the way they pass event data down to handlers. In Internet Explorer, an event handler receives its data through the global *window.event* object; in Firefox, the event data is passed as an argument to the handler. In the Microsoft AJAX library, event handlers receive a parameter with proper event data.

Another significant difference is in the way mouse and keyboard events are represented. The Microsoft AJAX library abstracts away any differences between browsers by providing ad hoc enumerated types, such as *Sys.UI.Key* and *Sys.UI.MouseButton*. Here's some sample code:

```
function button1_Click(e)
{
  if (e.button === Sys.UI.MouseButton.leftButton)
  {
    ...
  }
}
function keyboard_EnterPressed(e)
{
  if (e.keyCode === Sys.UI.Key.enter)
  {
    ...
  }
}
```

The Microsoft AJAX library provides a shorthand notation to create DOM event hookups and removal. For example, you can use the *$addHandler* and *$removeHandler* aliases to add and remove a handler. Here's the syntax:

```
$addHandler(element, "eventName", handler);
$removeHandler(element, "eventName", handler);
```

In many cases, you'll want to hook up several handlers to a DOM event for a component. Rather than manually creating all the required delegates and related handlers, you can use a condensed syntax to add and remove multiple handlers:

```
initialize: function()
{
   var elem = this.get_element();
   $addHandlers(
        elem,
        {[
            'mouseover': this._mouseHoverHandler,
            'mouseout': this._mouseOutHandler,
            'focus', this._focusHandler,
            'blur', this_blurHandler
        ]},
        this);
}
```

The *$clearHandlers* alias, conversely, removes all handlers set for a particular DOM element in a single shot.

If you write a component and wire up some events, it is essential that you clear all handlers when the component is unloaded, or even earlier, if you don't need the handler any longer. For example, you should do that from the component's *dispose* method to break circular references between your JavaScript objects and the DOM. Correctly applied, this trick easily prevents nasty memory leaks.

> **Note** You won't receive any event data if you bind the handler via markup—for example, by setting the *onclick* attribute of an *<input>* tag. Everything said here applies only to event handlers added via methods (and aliases) of the *Sys.UI.DomEvent* class. Events bound through attributes are still processed, but you have to resort to your knowledge of the browser's event model to correctly grab associated information.

Other Facilities

The Microsoft AJAX library contains a number of other miscellaneous components to provide additional facilities to ASP.NET AJAX developers.

The *Sys.StringBuilder* class adds advanced text manipulation capabilities to ASP.NET AJAX pages. As the name suggests, the class mimics the behavior of the managed *StringBuilder* class defined in the .NET Framework. When you create an instance of the builder object, you specify initial text. The builder caches the text in an internal array by using an element for each added text or line. The *Sys.StringBuilder* object doesn't accept objects other than non-null strings. The *toString* method composes the text by using the join method of the JavaScript array class.

The Microsoft AJAX library *String* class is also enriched with a format method that mimics the behavior of the *Format* method on the .NET Framework *String* class:

```
alert(String.format("Today is: {0}", new Date()));
```

You define placeholders in the format string using *{n}* elements. The real value for placeholders is determined by looking at the *n*.th argument in the format method call.

Another class that is worth mentioning is the *Sys._Debug* class. An instance of this internal class is assigned to the *Sys.Debug* global object:

```
Sys.Debug = new Sys._Debug();
```

In your pages, you use the *Sys.Debug* object to assert conditions, break into the debugger, or trace text. For example, the *traceDump* method writes the contents of the specified object in a human-readable format in the Microsoft AJAX library trace area. The trace area is expected to be a *<textarea>* element with an ID of *traceConsole*. You can place this element anywhere in the page:

```
<textarea id="traceConsole" cols="40" rows="10" />
```

The *traceDump* method accepts two parameters, as shown here:

```
Sys.Debug.traceDump(object, name)
```

The *name* parameter indicates descriptive text to display as the heading of the object dump. The text can contain HTML markup. Figure 19-4 shows the results.

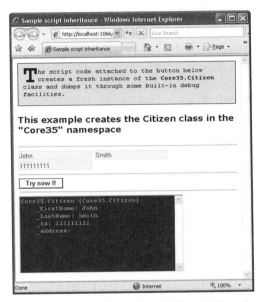

FIGURE 19-4 The Microsoft AJAX library debugging tracer in action

The Script Manager Control

The main control in the server infrastructure of ASP.NET AJAX is the *ScriptManager* control and its twin, the *ScriptManagerProxy* control. You will find just one instance of the *ScriptManager* control in each ASP.NET AJAX page. No AJAX capabilities can be enabled in ASP.NET pages that lack a reference to one *ScriptManager* control. The *ScriptManagerProxy* control is used only in master pages scenarios to reference the original script manager from content pages. (See Chapter 6 for more information about master pages.)

The *ScriptManager* control manages and delivers script resources, thus enabling client scripts to make use of the JavaScript type system extensions and other JavaScript features that we covered earlier in this chapter. The *ScriptManager* control also enables features such as partial-page rendering and Web service and page method calls. The following code shows the simplest and most common way to insert the script manager in an ASP.NET page:

```
<asp:ScriptManager runat="server" ID="ScriptManager1" />
```

The control produces no user interface, works exclusively on the server, and doesn't add any extra bytes to the page download.

Properties of the *ScriptManager* Control

The *ScriptManager* control features a number of properties for you to configure its expected behavior. Table 19-3 details the supported properties.

TABLE 19-3 Properties of *ScriptManager*

Property	Description
AllowCustomErrorsRedirect	Indicates whether custom error redirects will occur during an asynchronous postback. The property is set to *true* by default.
AsyncPostBackErrorMessage	Gets and sets the error message to be sent to the client when an unhandled exception occurs on the server during an asynchronous postback. If this property is not set, the native exception's message will be used.
AsyncPostBackSourceElementID	Gets the ID of the server control that triggered the asynchronous postback. If there's no ongoing asynchronous postback, the property is set to the empty string.
AsyncPostBackTimeout	Gets and sets the timeout period in seconds for asynchronous postbacks. A value of zero indicates no timeout. The property is set to *90* by default.
AuthenticationService	Gets an object through which you can set preferences for the client-side authentication service.
EnablePageMethods	Indicates whether static page methods on an ASP.NET page can be called from client script. The property is set to *false* by default.
EnablePartialRendering	Indicates whether partial rendering is enabled for the page. The property is set to *true* by default.
EnableScriptGlobalization	Indicates whether the *ScriptManager* control renders script in the client that supports parsing and formatting of culture-specific information. The property is set to *false* by default.
EnableScriptLocalization	Indicates whether the *ScriptManager* control retrieves script files for the current culture, if they exist. The property is set to *false* by default.
IsDebuggingEnabled	Indicates whether the debug versions of client script libraries will be rendered. The *debug* attribute on the *@Page* directive doesn't affect this property.
IsInAsyncPostBack	Indicates whether the current page request is due to an asynchronous postback.
LoadScriptsBeforeUI	Indicates whether scripts are loaded before or after markup for the page UI is loaded.
ProfileService	Gets an object through which you can set preferences for the client-side profile service.

Property	Description
RoleService	Gets an object through which you can set preferences for the client-side role service. *This property is not available in ASP.NET AJAX Extensions for ASP.NET 2.0.*
ScriptMode	Gets and sets the type (debug or retail) of scripts to load when more than one type is available. Possible values come from the *ScriptMode* enumeration type: *Auto*, *Inherit*, *Debug*, or *Release*. The default value is *Auto*, meaning that the type of script is determined on the fly.
ScriptPath	Indicates that scripts should be loaded from this path instead of from assembly Web resources.
Scripts	Gets a collection of script references that the *ScriptManager* control should include in the page.
Services	Gets a collection of service references that the *ScriptManager* control should include in the page.
SupportsPartialRendering	Indicates whether a particular browser or browser version can support partial page rendering. If this property is set to *false*, regardless of the value of the *EnablePartialRendering* property, no partial rendering will be supported on the page. The property is set to *true* by default.

The script manager is the nerve center of any ASP.NET AJAX pages and does all the work that is necessary to make AJAX features function as expected. Enabling AJAX features mostly means injecting the right piece of script in the right place. The script manager saves ASP.NET developers from dirtying their hands with JavaScript.

Methods of the *ScriptManager* Control

Table 19-4 lists the methods defined on the *ScriptManager* control.

TABLE 19-4 Methods of *ScriptManager*

Method	Description
GetCurrent	Static method, returns the instance of the *ScriptManager* control active on the current page.
GetRegisteredArrayDeclaration	Static method, returns a read-only collection of *ECMAScript* array declarations that were previously registered with the page. *This method is not available in ASP.NET AJAX Extensions for ASP.NET 2.0.*
GetRegisteredClientScriptBlocks	Static method, returns a read-only collection of client script blocks that were previously registered with the *ScriptManager* control. *This method is not available in ASP.NET AJAX Extensions for ASP.NET 2.0.*

Method	Description
GetRegisteredDisposeScripts	Static method, returns a read-only collection of dispose scripts that were previously registered with the page. *This method is not available in ASP.NET AJAX Extensions for ASP.NET 2.0.*
GetRegisteredExpandoAttributes	Static method, returns a read-only collection of custom (expando) attributes that were previously registered with the page. *This method is not available in ASP.NET AJAX Extensions for ASP.NET 2.0.*
GetRegisteredHiddenFields	Static method, returns a read-only collection of hidden fields that were previously registered with the page. *This method is not available in ASP.NET AJAX Extensions for ASP.NET 2.0.*
GetRegisteredOnSubmitStatements	Static method, returns a read-only collection of *onsubmit* statements that were previously registered with the page. *This method is not available in ASP.NET AJAX Extensions for ASP.NET 2.0.*
GetRegisteredStartupScripts	Static method, returns a read-only collection of startup scripts that were previously registered with the page. *This method is not available in ASP.NET AJAX Extensions for ASP.NET 2.0.*
RegisterArrayDeclaration	Static method, ensures that an *ECMAScript* array is emitted in a partial rendering page.
RegisterAsyncPostBackControl	Takes note that the specified control can trigger an asynchronous postback event from within an updatable panel.
RegisterClientScriptBlock	Static method, ensures that the specified script is emitted in a partial rendering page.
RegisterClientScriptInclude	Static method, ensures that the markup to import an external script file through the *src* attribute of the *<script>* tag is emitted in a partial rendering page.
RegisterClientScriptResource	Static method, ensures that the markup to import an external script from the page's resources is emitted in a partial rendering page.
RegisterDataItem	Registers a string of data that will be sent to the client along with the output of a partially rendered page.
RegisterDispose	Registers controls that require a client script to run at the end of an asynchronous postback to dispose of client resources.
RegisterExpandoAttribute	Static method, ensures that the markup to import a custom, nonstandard attribute is emitted in a partial rendering page.
RegisterExtenderControl	Registers an extender control with the current ASP.NET AJAX page.

Method	Description
RegisterHiddenField	Static method, ensures that the specified hidden field is emitted in a partial rendering page.
RegisterOnSubmitStatement	Static method, ensures that that client-side script associated with the form's *OnSubmit* event is emitted in a partial rendering page.
RegisterPostBackControl	Takes note that the specified control can trigger a full postback event from within an updatable panel.
RegisterScriptControl	Registers a script control with the current ASP.NET AJAX page.
RegisterScriptDescriptors	Registers a script descriptor with the current ASP.NET AJAX page.
RegisterStartupScript	Static method, ensures that client-side script is emitted at the end of the *<form>* tag in a partial rendering page. In this way, the script will execute as the page refresh is completed.
SetFocus	Allows you to move the input focus to the specified client element after an asynchronous postback.

All static methods emit some form of script and markup in the client page. These static methods are the AJAX counterpart of similar methods defined on the page's *ClientScript* object that you should know from ASP.NET 2.0. The static *RegisterXXX* methods on the *ScriptManager* class ensure that the given piece of script and markup is properly emitted only once in each partial update of the ASP.NET AJAX page. Similarly, other nonstatic *RegisterXXX* methods should be seen as tools to emit proper script code in ASP.NET AJAX pages—especially script code that is associated with custom controls.

> **Note** Script registration is an old feature of ASP.NET, in spite of the slight changes that occurred in the transition from version 1.x to 2.0. To most developers, script registration is a pretty neat and clear feature. However, the advent of ASP.NET AJAX extensions mixed things up a little bit. What's the difference between *RegisterXXX* methods in the *ScriptManager* control and the page's *ClientScript* object, which is an instance of the *ClientScriptManager* class?
>
> *ClientScriptManager*'s and *ScriptManager*'s registration methods serve the same purpose but in radically different scenarios. You need to use the *ScriptManager*'s methods only if you need to emit script code during an AJAX partial rendering postback operation. An AJAX partial rendering postback operation is processed by the runtime as usual, except for the rendering stage. At this time, the markup is generated and any registered script is emitted. Because during AJAX postbacks the *ScriptManager* is responsible for the markup rendering, it's the *ScriptManager* that needs to know about registered scripts to emit. If you stick to using *ClientScriptMananager*'s methods in an AJAX page, you risk that no script will be emitted during the refresh of an updatable panel. As a result, a portion of your page might display strange and weird behaviors.

Events of the *ScriptManager* Control

Table 19-5 details the two events fired by the *ScriptManager* control.

TABLE 19-5 Events of *ScriptManager*

Event	Description
AsyncPostBackError	Occurs when an exception goes unhandled on the server during an asynchronous postback.
ResolveScriptReference	Occurs when the *ScriptManager* control is going to resolve a script reference.

Both events are much more than mere notifications of something that has happened on the server. Both give you good chances to intervene effectively in the course of the application. For example, by handling the *ResolveScriptReference* event, you can change the location from where the script is going to be downloaded on the client:

```
protected void ResolveScript(object sender, ScriptReferenceEventArgs e)
{
    // Check Path or Name on the e.Script object based on what you've put in Scripts.
    // Next, you specify the real file to load
    if (String.Equals(e.Script.Path, "personal.js", StringComparison.OrdinalIgnoreCase))
        e.Script.Path = "person.js";
}
```

By handling the *AsyncPostBackError* event, you can edit the error message being returned to the client. Here's an example:

```
protected void AsyncPostBackError(object sender, AsyncPostBackErrorEventArgs e)
{
        ScriptManager sm = sender as ScriptManager;

        if (Request.UserHostAddress == "127.0.0.1")
        {
            sm.AsyncPostBackErrorMessage = String.Format(
                "<b>An error occurred. <br/>{0}<b>",
                e.Exception.Message);
        }
        else
        {
            sm.AsyncPostBackErrorMessage = String.Format(
                "<b>An error occurred. <br/>{0}<b>",
                "Please contact your Web master.");
        }
}
```

When executed locally, the client-side error message appears as you see in Figure 19-5.

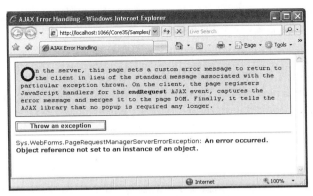

FIGURE 19-5 An error occurred during a partial rendering operation

What if you don't like to display the message directly in the page popups and want to redirect the user to an error page instead? In this case, you configure the page to use the traditional error-handling mechanism for ASP.NET pages. You configure the *<customErrors>* section in the *web.config* file and indicate HTML error pages to reach in case of specific errors. (See Chapter 5.) This behavior is fully supported by ASP.NET AJAX and can be disabled by setting to *false* the value of the *AllowCustomErrorRedirects* property of the *ScriptManager* object.

> **Note** When an exception is thrown during a partial rendering operation, the HTTP request returns a regular HTTP 200 status code, but instead of including the updated markup, it includes a full description of the error. In ASP.NET AJAX Extensions for ASP.NET 2.0, the default error handler pops up a client-side message box with the exception message or any text you assign to the *AsyncPostBackErrorMessage* property. In ASP.NET 3.5, on the other hand, you get a JavaScript exception.

The *ScriptManagerProxy* Control

Only one instance of the *ScriptManager* control can be added to an ASP.NET AJAX page. However, there are two ways in which you can do this. You can add it directly on the page using the *<asp:ScriptManager>* tag or indirectly by importing a component that already contains a script manager. Typically, you can accomplish the second alternative by importing a user control, creating a content page for a master page, or authoring a nested master page.

What if a content page needs to add a new script reference to the manager? In this case, you need a reference to the script manager. Although it's defined in the master page (or in a user control), the script manager might not be publicly exposed to the content page. You can use the static method *GetCurrent* on the class *ScriptManager* to get the right instance:

```
// Retrieve the instance of the ScriptManager active on the page
sm = ScriptManager.GetCurrent(this.Page);
```

The *ScriptManagerProxy* class saves you from this sort of coding. In general, in cases where you need features of the *ScriptManager* control but lack a direct reference to it, you can instead include a *ScriptManagerProxy* control in the content page.

You can't have two script managers in the context of the same page; however, you can have a script manager and a proxy to retrieve it. The *ScriptManagerProxy* control enables you to add scripts and services to nested components, and it enables partial page updates in user controls and nested master pages. When you use the proxy, the *Scripts* and *Services* collections on the *ScriptManager* and *ScriptManagerProxy* controls are merged at runtime.

> **Note** The *ScriptManagerProxy* class is a very simple wrapper around the *GetCurrent* method of the *ScriptManager* class, and its programming interface is not an exact clone of the *ScriptManager*. From within the proxy, you have access only to a limited number of properties, including *Scripts*, *Services*, *AuthenticationService*, *RoleService*, and *ProfileService*. If you need to modify anything else, refer to the *GetCurrent* static method of the *ScriptManager* class.

Script Binding and Loading

By extensively relying on client capabilities, ASP.NET AJAX requires a lot of script code. The framework itself links a lot of code, as do custom controls and actual user pages. The only HTML-supported way of linking script files is the *<script>* tag and its *src* attribute. The *ScriptManager* control can be used to save yourself the direct manipulation of quite a few *<script>* tags and also obtain richer features, such as built-in management of localized scripts.

You use the *Scripts* collection to tell the *ScriptManager* about the scripts you want to add to the page. The collection can be accessed either declaratively or programmatically. In addition to the user-requested scripts, the *ScriptManager* control automatically emits in the client page any ASP.NET AJAX required script. This means that, as a page developer, you don't have to worry about linking the Microsoft AJAX library or any other ASP.NET AJAX native feature. The following example illustrates the script loading model you can use to load optional and custom scripts:

```
<asp:ScriptManager runat="server" ID="ScriptManager1">
  <Scripts>
    <asp:ScriptReference
        Name="YourCompany.ScriptLibrary.CoolUI.js"
        Assembly="YourCompany.ScriptLib" />
    <asp:ScriptReference
        Path="~/Scripts/MyLib.js" />
  </Scripts>
</asp:ScriptManager>
```

Table 19-6 lists the properties of the *ScriptReference* class by means of which you can control the loading of scripts.

TABLE 19-6 Events of *ScriptManager*

Property	Description
Assembly	Indicates the assembly that contains in its resources the script to download on the client.
IgnoreScriptPath	Boolean value, indicates whether the *ScriptPath* value optionally set at the top *ScriptManager* level has to be ignored. This property is set to *false* by default.
Name	Name of the script to download on the client.
NotifyScriptLoaded	Boolean value, indicates whether the script resource loader should automatically append a script-loaded notification statement to let the *Sys.Application* object know when the script is loaded. This property is set to *true* by default.
Path	Indicates the server path where the script to download on the client can be found.
ResourceUICultures	A comma-delimited string of valid user-interface cultures supported by the path.
ScriptMode	Specifies the algorithm for choosing between the debug and release versions of the script file. If no debug version exists, the *ScriptReference* class automatically falls back to release code. Feasible values for the property come from the *ScriptMode* enumeration type.

You can reference script files, including ASP.NET AJAX system scripts, either from an assembly or from a disk file. There's a benefit in using disk files. You gain something in performance because less work is required to load the script in memory directly from a file. We'll see how to reference from disk the principal ASP.NET AJAX script file—*MicrosoftAjax.js*—which alone contains two-thirds of the Microsoft AJAX library. The technique is also valid for any custom script file, however.

Normally, you don't take care of *MicrosoftAjax.js*—you just find it downloaded care of the script manager. If you examine the HTML source of an ASP.NET AJAX page, you can hardly find a reference to such a file. Here's what you find instead:

```
<script src="/Core35/ScriptResource.axd?d=...&amp;t=..."
        type="text/javascript">
</script>
```

Script references obtained from embedded Web resources are served by the *ScriptResource.axd* HTTP handler. In ASP.NET AJAX, this handler replaces an old acquaintance, the *WebResource.axd* handler—a native component of ASP.NET 2.0. What's the difference? In addition to serving script references, the *ScriptResource.axd* handler also appends any localized JavaScript resource types for the file.

To load a system file from disk, or to load a manually modified version of a system script file, you create a directory structure that roots under a custom folder the following subdirectories:

```
System.Web.Extensions\3.5.0.0
```

Now set the *ScriptPath* property on *ScriptManager* to a custom parent folder specific to your application. Say, you call it *JS*:

```
<asp:ScriptManager ID="ScriptManager1" runat="server" ScriptPath="~/JS" />
```

All of a sudden, the *MicrosoftAjax.js* script file is now referenced as shown here:

```
<script
    src="~/JS/System.Web.Extensions/3.5.0.0/MicrosoftAjax.js"
    type="text/javascript">
</script>
```

Needless to say, your pages will fail if no such script files can be found in the specified directory path.

Handling Debug and Release Script Files

One of the additional free services offered by *ScriptManager* that isn't offered by the classic *<script>* tag is the ability to automatically link debug or release script files, as appropriate. ASP.NET uses a special naming convention to distinguish between debug and release script files. Given a release script file named *script.js*, its debug version is expected to be filed as *script.debug.js*.

In general, the main difference between debug and release scripts is that the release scripts remove unnecessary blank characters, comments, trace statements, and assertions. Normally the burden of switching the links to debug and release scripts is left to the developer.

The *ScriptManager* control takes on this burden and, based on the aforementioned naming convention, distinguishes between debug and release scripts. The *ScriptManager* control picks debug scripts when the *debug* attribute of the *<compilation>* section in the *web.config* file is *true*.

Localized Scripts

Script files can have localizable elements such as text strings for messages and user-interface elements. When the *EnableScriptLocalization* property is set to *true* and a UI culture is properly set in the page, the script manager automatically retrieves script files for the current culture, if any.

Localization is driven by the *UICulture* attribute in the *@Page* directive and the *UICulture* property in the *Page* class:

```
<%@ Page Language="C#" UICulture="it-IT" ... %>
```

This information is not enough for the *ScriptManager* to pick up localized scripts, if any. You also need to specify which UI cultures you intend to support for each referenced script. You indicate the supported cultures through the *ResourceUICultures* property on individual script references. The property is a comma-separated string of culture symbols. Here's an example:

```
<asp:ScriptManager ID="ScriptManager1" runat="server" EnableScriptLocalization="true">
    <Scripts>
        <asp:ScriptReference Path="Person.js" ResourceUICultures="it-IT" />
    </Scripts>
</asp:ScriptManager>
```

Note that *ResourceUICultures* is ignored if the *Path* attribute is not specified on the script reference tag.

At this point, if the page requires a script named *person.js* and the UI culture is set to *it-IT*, the *ScriptManager* object attempts to retrieve a script file named *person.it-IT.js* from the same path.

Script Globalization

Globalization is a programming feature that refers to the code's ability to support multiple cultures. A request processed on the server has a number of ways to get and set the current culture settings. For example, you can use the *Culture* attribute on the *@Page* directive, the *Culture* property on the *Page* class, or perhaps the *<globalization>* section in the *web.config* file. How can you access the same information on the client from JavaScript?

When the *EnableScriptGlobalization* property is *true*, the *ScriptManager* emits proper script code that sets up a client-side global *Sys.CultureInfo* object that JavaScript classes can consume to display their contents in a culture-based way. Only a few methods and a few JavaScript objects support globalization. In particular, it will work for the *localeFormat* method of *Date*, *String*, and *Number* types. Custom JavaScript classes, though, can be made global by simply calling into these methods or accepting a *Sys.CultureInfo* object in their signatures.

Note For more information about script loading and script-related features in ASP.NET AJAX pages, refer to Chapter 3 of my book *Introducing ASP.NET AJAX* (Microsoft Press, 2007).

Selective Page Updates with Partial Rendering

AJAX is not a particular technology or product. It refers to a number of client features, and related development techniques, that make Web applications look like desktop applications. AJAX doesn't require any plug-in modules either and is not browser specific. Virtually any browser released in the past five years can serve as a great host for AJAX-based applications. AJAX development techniques revolve around one common software element—the *XMLHttpRequest* object. The availability of this object in the object model of most browsers is the key to the current ubiquity and success of AJAX applications. In addition to *XMLHttpRequest*, a second factor contributes to the wide success of AJAX—the availability of a rich document object model in virtually any browser.

Based on this quick assay of the AJAX paradigm, the programming model of AJAX applications seem to be clear and unquestionable. You write code that captures client-side events, conduct an operation on the server via *XMLHttpRequest*, get the results, and update the user interface. All the client-side programming is done through JavaScript. This model is a real performance booster when applied to individual features or bottlenecks in existing pages, but it's hard to scale to a large application because it proves quite expensive in terms of skills to acquire and time to implement.

It is the downside of the loudly requested change of paradigm for Web applications. When it comes to rewriting Web applications for AJAX, nearly all aspects of the application need to be redesigned, refactored, and rewritten. Opting for AJAX all the way might be too much for too many companies; and it's not a step to take with a light heart.

Today you do much of your ASP.NET programming using server controls. A server control normally emits HTML markup. In an AJAX scenario, a server control emits markup plus some script code to support AJAX requests. This is not exactly the loudly requested change of paradigm, but it is a good compromise between the today's Web and AJAX. Most third-party vendors prepared their own offering based on this idea. They just provide you with a new set of controls that supply a server and client programming model and manage any browser-to-server communication for you.

But what if you aren't using any third-party library? Should you write new AJAX-enabled controls yourself? An AJAX server control can be the AJAX version of a traditional server control—for example, an AJAX-enabled drop-down list that supports client insertions and moves them back to the server without a full-page postback. But it can also be a generic control container that takes care of refreshing all of its children without a full-page postback. Enter partial rendering.

ASP.NET partial rendering works according to this idea. It provides a new container control—the *UpdatePanel* control—that you use to surround portions of existing pages, or portions of new pages developed with the usual programming model of ASP.NET 2.0. A postback that originates within any of these updatable regions is managed by the *UpdatePanel* control and updates only the controls in the region.

The *UpdatePanel* Control

In ASP.NET AJAX, partial rendering is the programming technique centered around the *UpdatePanel* control. In ASP.NET, the *UpdatePanel* control represents the shortest path to AJAX. It allows you to add effective AJAX capabilities to sites written according to the classic programming model of ASP.NET 2.0. As a developer, you have no new skills to learn, except the syntax and semantics of the *UpdatePanel* control. The impact on existing pages is very limited, and the exposure to JavaScript is very limited, and even null in most common situations.

You might wonder how partial rendering differs from classic postbacks. The difference is in how the postback is implemented—instead of letting the browser perform a full-page refresh, the *UpdatePanel* control intercepts any postback requests and sends an out-of-band request for fresh markup to the same page URL. Next, it updates the DOM tree when the response is ready. Let's investigate the programming interface of the control.

The *UpdatePanel* Control at a Glance

The *UpdatePanel* control is a container control defined in the *System.Web.Extensions* assembly. It belongs specifically to the *System.Web.UI* namespace. The control class is declared as follows:

```
public class UpdatePanel : Control
{
   ...
}
```

Although it's logically similar to the classic ASP.NET *Panel* control, the *UpdatePanel* control differs from the classic panel control in a number of respects. In particular, it doesn't derive from *Panel* and, subsequently, it doesn't feature the same set of capabilities as ASP.NET panels, such as scrolling, styling, wrapping, and content management.

The *UpdatePanel* control derives directly from *Control*, meaning that it acts as a mere AJAX-aware container of child controls. It provides no user-interface-related facilities. Any required styling and formatting should be provided through the child controls. In contrast, the control sports a number of properties to control page updates and also exposes a client-side object model. Consider the following classic ASP.NET code:

```
<asp:GridView ID="GridView1" runat="server"
    DataSourceID="ObjectDataSource1"
    AllowPaging="True"
    AutoGenerateColumns="False" Width="450px">
    <Columns>
        <asp:BoundField DataField="ID" HeaderText="ID">
            <ItemStyle Width="70px" />
        </asp:BoundField>
        <asp:BoundField DataField="CompanyName" HeaderText="Company">
            <ItemStyle Width="300px" />
        </asp:BoundField>
        <asp:BoundField DataField="Country" HeaderText="Country">
            <ItemStyle Width="80px" />
        </asp:BoundField>
    </Columns>
</asp:GridView>
<asp:ObjectDataSource ID="ObjectDataSource1" runat="server"
    TypeName="Core35.DAL.Customers"
    SelectMethod="LoadAll" />
```

This code causes a postback each time you click to view a new page, edit a record, or sort by a column. As a result, the entire page is redrawn even though the grid is only a small fragment of it. With partial rendering, you take the preceding markup and just wrap it with an *UpdatePanel* control, as shown here:

```
<asp:UpdatePanel ID="UpdatePanel1" runat="server">
    <ContentTemplate>
        . . .
    </ContentTemplate>
</asp:UpdatePanel>
```

In addition, you need to add a *ScriptManager* control to the page. That's the essence of partial rendering. And it magically just works. Well, not just magically, but it works.

> **Note** From this simple but effective example, you might be led to think that it suffices that you surround the whole body of the page with an *UpdatePanel* control and you're done. If you do, it certainly works. It might not be particularly efficient though. In the worst case, you need the same bandwidth as you do with classic ASP.NET; however, you still give your users an infinitely better experience because only a portion of the page actually refreshes.
>
> As we'll learn in the rest of the chapter, partial rendering offers a number of attributes to optimize the overall behavior and performance. However, the majority of users are more than happy with the sole effect of a partial page rendering.

The Programming Interface of the Control

Table 19-7 details the properties defined on the *UpdatePanel* control that constitute the aspects of the control's behavior that developers can govern.

TABLE 19-7 **Properties of the *UpdatePanel* Control**

Property	Description
ChildrenAsTriggers	Indicates whether postbacks coming from child controls will cause the *UpdatePanel* to refresh. This property is set to *true* by default. When this property is *false*, postbacks from child controls are ignored. You can't set this property to *false* when the *UpdateMode* property is set to *Always*.
ContentTemplate	A template property, defines what appears in the *UpdatePanel* when it is rendered.
ContentTemplateContainer	Retrieves the dynamically created template container object. You can use this object to programmatically add child controls to the *UpdatePanel*.
IsInPartialRendering	Indicates whether the panel is being updated as part of an asynchronous postback. Note that this property is designed for control developers. Page authors should just ignore it.
RenderMode	Indicates whether the contents of the panel will be rendered as a block *<div>* tag or as an inline *<span>* tag. The feasible values for the property—*Block* and *Inline*—are defined in the *UpdatePanelRenderMode* enumeration. The default is *Block*.
UpdateMode	Gets or sets the rendering mode of the control by determining under which conditions the panel gets updated. The feasible values—*Always* and *Conditional*—come from the *UpdatePanelUpdateMode* enumeration. The default is *Always*.
Triggers	Defines a collection of trigger objects, each representing an event that causes the panel to refresh automatically.

A bit more explanation is needed for the *IsInPartialRendering* read-only Boolean property. It indicates whether the contents of an *UpdatePanel* control are being updated. From this description, it seems to be a fairly useful property. Nonetheless, if you read its value from within any of the handlers defined in a code-behind class, you'll find out that the value is always *false*.

As mentioned, *IsInPartialRendering* is a property designed for control developers only. So it is assigned its proper value only at rendering time—that is, well past the *PreRender* event you can capture from a code-behind class. Developers creating a custom version of the *UpdatePanel* control will likely override the *Render* method. From within this context, they can leverage the property to find out whether the control is being rendered in a full-page refresh or in a partial rendering operation.

As a page author, if you just need to know whether a portion of a page is being updated as a result of an AJAX postback, you use the *IsInAsyncPostBack* Boolean property on the *ScriptManager* control.

> **Note** Like any other ASP.NET AJAX feature, partial rendering requires a *ScriptManager* control in the page. It is essential, though, that the *EnablePartialRendering* property on the manager be set to *true*—which is the default case. If this property is set to *false*, the *UpdatePanel* control works like a regular panel.

Populating the Panel Programmatically

The content of an updatable panel is defined through a template property—the *ContentTemplate* property. Just like any other template property in ASP.NET controls, *ContentTemplate* can be set programmatically. Consider the following page fragment:

```
<asp:ScriptManager ID="ScriptManager1" runat="server" />
<asp:UpdatePanel ID="UpdatePanel1" runat="server">
    <%-- Left empty deliberately. Will be filled out programmatically --%>
</asp:UpdatePanel>
```

In the *PreInit* event of the code-behind page, you can set the *ContentTemplate* programmatically, as shown here:

```
protected void Page_PreInit(object sender, EventArgs e)
{
    // You could also read the URL of the user control from a configuration file
    string ascx = "customerview.ascx";
    UpdatePanel1.ContentTemplate = this.LoadTemplate(ascx);
}
```

You are not allowed to set the content template past the *PreInit* event. However, at any time before the rendering stage, you can add child controls programmatically. In ASP.NET, to add or remove a child control, you typically use the *Controls* property of the parent control, as shown here:

```
UpdatePanel1.Controls.Add(new LiteralControl("Test"));
```

If you try to add a child control programmatically to the *Controls* collection of an *UpdatePanel*—as in the preceding code snippet—all that you get is a runtime exception. You should use the *ContentTemplateContainer* property instead. The reason is that what you really want to do is add or remove controls to the content template, not to the *UpdatePanel* directly. That's why *Controls* doesn't work and you have to opt for the actual container of the template. The following code shows how to populate the content template programmatically:

```
public partial class Samples_Ch19_Partial_Dynamic : System.Web.UI.Page
{
    private Label Label1;

    protected void Page_Load(object sender, EventArgs e)
    {
        UpdatePanel upd = new UpdatePanel();
        upd.ID = "UpdatePanel1";

        // Define the button
        Button button1 = new Button();
        button1.ID = "Button1";
        button1.Text = "What time is it?";
        button1.Click += new EventHandler(Button1_Click);

        // Define the literals
        LiteralControl lit = new LiteralControl("<br>");

        // Define the label
        Label1 = new Label();
        Label1.ID = "Label1";
        Label1.Text = "[time]";

        // Link controls to the UpdatePanel
        upd.ContentTemplateContainer.Controls.Add(button1);
        upd.ContentTemplateContainer.Controls.Add(lit);
        upd.ContentTemplateContainer.Controls.Add(Label1);

        // Add the UpdatePanel to the list of form controls
        this.Form.Controls.Add(upd);
    }

    protected void Button1_Click(object sender, EventArgs e)
    {
        Label1.Text = DateTime.Now.ToShortTimeString();
    }
}
```

You can add an *UpdatePanel* control to the page at any time in the life cycle. Likewise, you can add controls to an existing panel at any time. However, you can't set the content template programmatically past the page's *PreInit* event.

Master Pages and Updatable Regions

You can safely use *UpdatePanel* controls from within master pages. Most of the time, the use of updatable panels is easy and seamless. There are a few situations, though, that deserve a bit of further explanation.

If you add a *ScriptManager* control to a master page, partial rendering is enabled by default for all content pages. In addition, initial settings on the script manager are inherited by all content pages. What if you need to change some of the settings (for example, add a new script file or switch on script localization) for a particular content page? You can't have a new script manager, but you need to retrieve the original one defined on the master page.

In the content page, you can declaratively reference a *ScriptManagerProxy* and change some of its settings. The proxy retrieves the script manager currently in use and applies changes to it.

The *ScriptManagerProxy* control, though, is mostly designed to let you edit the list of scripts and services registered with the manager in a declarative manner, and it doesn't let you customize, say, error handling or script localization. You can do the same (and indeed much more) by programmatically referencing the script manager in the master page. Here's how:

```
protected void Page_Init(object sender, EventArgs e)
{
    // Work around the limitations in the API of the ScriptManagerProxy control
    ScriptManager.GetCurrent(this).EnableScriptLocalization = true;
}
```

In the content page, you create a handler for the page's *Init* event, retrieve the script manager instance using the static *GetCurrent* method on the *ScriptManager* class, and apply any required change.

User Controls and Updatable Regions

User controls provide an easy way to bring self-contained, auto-updatable AJAX components into an ASP.NET page. Because each page can have at most one script manager, you can't reasonably place the script manager in the user control. That would work and make the user control completely self-contained, but it would also limit you to using exactly one instance of the user control per page. On the other hand, the *UpdatePanel* control requires a script manager. Multiple script managers, or the lack of at least one script manager, will cause an exception.

The simplest workaround is that you take the script manager out of the user control and place it in the host page. User controls therefore assume the presence of a script manager, and they use internally as many updatable panels as needed:

```
<asp:ScriptManager runat="server" ID="ScriptManager1" />
<x:Clock runat="server" ID="Clock1" />
<hr />
<x:Clock runat="server" ID="Clock2" />
```

> **Note** You can't call *Response.Write* from within a postback event handler (for example, *Button1_Click*) that gets called during an asynchronous AJAX postback. If you do so, you'll receive a client exception stating that the message received from the server could not be parsed. In general, calls to *Response.Write*—but also response filters, HTTP modules, or server tracing (*Trace=true*)—modify the stream returned to the client by adding explicit data that alters the expected format.

Optimizing the Usage of the *UpdatePanel* Control

Partial rendering divides the page into independent regions, each of which controls its own postbacks and refreshes without causing, or requiring, a full-page update. This behavior is desirable when only a portion—and perhaps only a small portion—of the page needs to change during a postback. Partial updates reduce screen flickering and allow you to create more interactive Web applications. An ASP.NET page can contain any number of *UpdatePanel* controls.

An *UpdatePanel* control refreshes its content under the following conditions:

- When another *UpdatePanel* control in the same page refreshes

- When any of the child controls originates a postback (for example, a button click or a change of selection in a drop-down list with *AutoPostBack=true*)

- When handling a postback event the page invokes the *Update* method on the *UpdatePanel* control

- When the *UpdatePanel* control is nested inside another *UpdatePanel* control and the parent update panel is updated

- When any of the trigger events for the *UpdatePanel* occur

You can control these conditions through a number of properties such as *UpdateMode*, *ChildrenAsTriggers*, and the collection *Triggers*. To minimize the total number of postbacks and the amount of data being roundtripped, you should pay a lot of attention to the values you assign to these properties. Let's delve deeper into this topic.

Configuring for Conditional Refresh

By default, all updatable panels in a page are synchronized and refresh at the same time. To make each panel refresh independently from the others, you change the value of the *UpdateMode* property. The default value is *Always*, meaning that the panel's content is updated on every postback that originates from anywhere in the page, from inside and outside the updatable region.

By changing the value of the *UpdateMode* property to *Conditional*, you instruct the updatable panel to update its content only if it is explicitly ordered to refresh. This includes calling the *Update* method, intercepting a postback from a child control, or any of the events declared as triggers.

Normally, any control defined inside of an *UpdatePanel* control acts as an implicit trigger for the panel. You can stop all child controls from being triggers by setting the value of *ChildrenAsTriggers* to *false*. In this case, a button inside an updatable panel, if clicked, originates a regular full postback.

What if you want only a few controls within an *UpdatePanel* to act as triggers? You can define them as triggers of a particular *UpdatePanel*, or you can use the *RegisterAsyncPostBackControl* method on the *ScriptManager* class.

The *RegisterAsyncPostBackControl* method enables you to register controls to perform an asynchronous postback instead of a synchronous postback, which would update the entire page. Here is an example of the *RegisterAsyncPostBackControl* method:

```
protected void Page_Load(object sender, EventArgs e)
{
    ScriptManager1.RegisterAsyncPostBackControl(Button1);
}
```

The control object you pass as an argument will be a control not included in any updatable panels and not listed as a trigger. The effects of the postback that originates from the control differ with regard to the number of *UpdatePanel* controls in the page. If there's only one *UpdatePanel* in the page, the script manager can easily figure out which one to update. The following code shows a page whose overall behavior may change if one or two *UpdatePanel* controls are used.

```
protected void Button1_Click(object sender, EventArgs e)
{
    // If there's only one UpdatePanel in the page, and it includes this Label control,
    // the panel is refreshed automatically.
    Label1.Text = "Last update at:  " + DateTime.Now.ToLongTimeString();

    // This Label control, not included in any UpdatePanel, doesn't have its UI
    // refreshed. Its state, though, is correctly updated.
    Label2.Text = "Last update at:  " + DateTime.Now.ToLongTimeString();
}
```

When multiple panels exist, to trigger the update you have to explicitly invoke the *Update* method on the panel you want to refresh:

```
protected void Button1_Click(object sender, EventArgs e)
{
    Label1.Text = "Last update at:  " + DateTime.Now.ToLongTimeString();
    UpdatePanel1.Update();
}
```

All controls located inside of an *UpdatePanel* control are automatically passed as an argument to the *RegisterAsyncPostBackControl* method when *ChildrenAsTriggers* is *true*.

> **Note** A postback that originates from within an *UpdatePanel* control is often referred to as an *asynchronous postback* or an *AJAX postback*. Generally, these expressions are used to reference a postback conducted via a script taking advantage of *XMLHttpRequest*.

Programmatic Updates

We have already mentioned the *Update* method quite a few times. It's time we learn more about it, starting with its signature:

```
public void Update()
```

The method doesn't take any special action itself, but is limited to requiring that the child controls defined in the content template of the *UpdatePanel* control be refreshed. By using the *Update* method, you can programmatically control when the page region is updated in response to a standard postback event or perhaps during the initialization of the page.

An invalid operation exception can be thrown from within the *Update* method in a couple of well-known situations. One situation is if you call the method when the *UpdateMode* property is set to *Always*. The exception is thrown in this case because a method invocation prefigures a conditional update—you do it when you need it—which is just the opposite of what the *Always* value of the *UpdateMode* property indicates. The other situation in which the exception is thrown is when the *Update* method is called during or after the page's rendering stage.

So when should you get to use the *Update* method in your pages?

You resort to the method if you have some server logic to determine whether an *UpdatePanel* control should be updated as the side effect of an asynchronous postback—whether it is one that originated from another *UpdatePanel* in the page or a control registered as an asynchronous postback control.

Using Triggers

As mentioned, you can associate an *UpdatePanel* control with a list of server-side events. Whenever a registered event is triggered over a postback, the panel is updated. Triggers can be defined either declaratively or programmatically. You add an event trigger declaratively using the *<Triggers>* section of the *UpdatePanel* control:

```
<asp:UpdatePanel runat="server" ID="UpdatePanel1">
    <ContentTemplate>
        ...
    </ContentTemplate>
```

```
<Triggers>
    <asp:AsyncPostBackTrigger
        ControlID="DropDownList1"
        EventName="SelectedIndexChanged" />
</Triggers>
</asp:UpdatePanel>
```

You need to specify two pieces of information for each trigger—the ID of the control to monitor, and the name of the event to catch. It is essential to note that the *AsyncPostBackTrigger* component can catch only server-side events. Both *ControlID* and *EventName* are string properties. For example, the panel described in the previous code snippet is refreshed when any of the controls in the page posts back (that is, its UpdateMode property defaults to *Always*) or when the selection changes on a drop-down list control named *DropDownList1*.

Note Keep in mind that we're talking about server-side events here. This implies that, in the previous example, the *DropDownList1* control must have *AutoPostBack* equals to *true* in order to fire a postback.

The event associated with the *AsyncPostBackTrigger* component triggers an asynchronous AJAX postback on the *UpdatePanel* control. As a result, the host page remains intact except for the contents of the referenced panel and its dependencies, if any. Usually, the *AsyncPostBackTrigger* component points to controls placed outside the *UpdatePanel*. However, if the panel has the *ChildrenAsTriggers* property set to *false*, it could make sense for you to define an embedded control as the trigger. In both cases, when a control that is a naming container is used as a trigger, all of its child controls that cause postback behave as triggers.

Note You can also add triggers programmatically by using the *Triggers* collection of the *UpdatePanel* control. The collection accepts instances of the *AsyncPostBackTrigger* class.

Full Postbacks from Inside Updatable Panels

By default, all child controls of an *UpdatePanel* that post back operate as implicit asynchronous postback triggers. You can prevent all of them from triggering a panel update by setting *ChildrenAsTriggers* to *false*. Note that when *ChildrenAsTriggers* is *false* postbacks coming from child controls are processed as asynchronous postbacks and they modify the state of involved server controls, but they don't update the user interface of the panel.

There might be situations in which you need to perform full, regular postbacks from inside an *UpdatePanel* control in response to a control event. In this case, you use the *PostBackTrigger* component, as shown here:

```
<asp:UpdatePanel runat="server" ID="UpdatePanel1">
   <ContentTemplate>
      ...
   </ContentTemplate>
   <Triggers>
      <asp:AsyncPostBackTrigger ControlID="DropDownList1"
         EventName="SelectedIndexChanged" />
      <asp:PostBackTrigger ControlID="Button1" />
   </Triggers>
</asp:UpdatePanel>
```

The preceding panel features both synchronous and asynchronous postback triggers. The panel is updated when the user changes the selection on the drop-down list; the whole host page is refreshed when the user clicks the button.

A *PostBackTrigger* component causes referenced controls inside an *UpdatePanel* control to perform regular postbacks. These triggers must be children of the affected *UpdatePanel*.

The *PostBackTrigger* object doesn't support the *EventName* property. If a control with that name is causing the form submission, the ASP.NET AJAX client script simply lets the request go as usual. The ASP.NET runtime then figures out which server postback event has to be raised for the postback control by looking at its implementation of *IPostBackEventHandler*.

 Note When should you use a *PostBackTrigger* component to fire a full postback from inside an updatable panel? If you need, say, a button to refresh a given panel, why not list the *Click* event of the button as an asynchronous trigger and leave the button outside the panel? Especially when complex and templated controls are involved, it might not be easy to separate blocks of user interface in distinct panels and single controls. So the easiest, and often the only, solution is wrapping a whole block of user interface in an updatable panel. If a single control in this panel needs to fire a full postback, you need to use the *PostBackTrigger* component.

Practical Steps for Adopting Updatable Panels

The *UpdatePanel* control works with the idea of limiting the refresh of the page to only the portions of it that are touched by the postback. A clear mapping between user actions and portions of the page that are updated consequently is key to successfully adopting the *UpdatePanel* control in an ASP.NET site.

The first practical step for successfully migrating page behavior to partial rendering entails that you, given the expected behavior of the page, identify the portions of the page subject to refresh. If you have, say, a complex table layout but only a small fragment of only one cell changes in the page lifetime, there's no reason to keep the whole table in an *UpdatePanel* control. Only the server-side control that displays the modifiable text should be wrapped by the panel.

The portions of the page that you should consider to be candidates to be wrapped by an *UpdatePanel* control should be as small as possible. They also should include the minimum amount of markup and ASP.NET controls.

The second step consists of associating each candidate region with a list of refresh conditions. You basically answer the question, *"When does this region get updated?"* After you have compiled a list of candidate regions, and for each you have a list of refresh events, you're pretty much done.

The final step is mapping this information to *UpdatePanel* controls and triggers. If all the regions you have identified are disjointed, you're fine. If not, you use properties and triggers on the *UpdatePanel* control to obtain the expected page behavior, thereby minimizing the impact of postbacks and page flickering.

If needed, updatable panels can be nested. There's no syntax limitation to the levels of nesting allowed. Just consider that any nested panel refreshes when its parent is refreshed regardless of the settings.

Let's be honest. It might not be a trivial task, and getting a disjoint set of regions is not always possible. However, given the number of properties supported by the *UpdatePanel* control, there's always room for a good compromise between user experience and performance.

Giving Feedback to the User

A partial rendering operation still requires a postback; it still uploads and downloads the view state and fires the well-known page life cycle on the server. The benefits of an asynchronous postback lie in the fact that no full-page refresh is required and only a smaller amount of HTML markup is returned to the client. An asynchronous postback might still take a few seconds to complete if the server operation is a lengthy one.

The mechanics of the asynchronous postback keeps the displayed page up and running. So the biggest improvement of AJAX—the continuous feel with the page—can become its major weakness if not handled properly. Having the computer engaged in a potentially long task might be problematic. Will the user resist the temptation of reclicking that button over and over again? Will the user patiently wait for the results to show up? Finally, will the user be frustrated and annoyed by waiting without any clue of what's going on? After all, if the page is sustaining a full postback, the browser itself normally provides some user feedback that this is happening. Using ASP.NET AJAX, the callback doesn't force a regular full postback and the browser's visual feedback system is not called upon to inform the user things are happening.

In the end, AJAX and partial rendering let developers arrange pages that provide "continuous feel" to users and increased responsiveness. The continuous experience, however, raises new issues. Feedback should be given to users to let them know that an operation is taking place. In addition, user-interface elements should be disabled if the user would start new operations by clicking on the element.

ASP.NET AJAX supplies the *UpdateProgress* control to display a templated content while any of the panels in the page are being refreshed.

The *UpdateProgress* Control

The *UpdateProgress* control is designed to provide any sort of feedback on the browser while one or more *UpdatePanel* controls are being updated. If you have multiple panels in the page, you might want to find a convenient location in the page for the progress control or, if possible, move it programmatically to the right place with respect to the panel being updated. You can use cascading style sheets (CSSs) to style and position the control at your leisure.

The user interface associated with an *UpdateProgress* control is displayed and hidden by the ASP.NET AJAX framework and doesn't require you to do any work on your own. The *UpdateProgress* control features the properties listed in Table 19-8.

TABLE 19-8 Properties of the *UpdateProgress* Control

Property	Description
AssociatedUpdatePanelID	Gets and sets the ID of the *UpdatePanel* control that this control is associated with.
DisplayAfter	Gets and sets the time in milliseconds after which the progress template is displayed. Set to *500* by default.
DynamicLayout	Indicates whether the progress template is dynamically rendered in the page. Set to *true* by default.
ProgressTemplate	Indicates the template displayed during an asynchronous postback that is taking longer than the time specified through the *DisplayAfter* property.

An *UpdateProgress* control can be bound to a particular *UpdatePanel* control. You set the binding through the *AssociatedUpdatePanelID* string property. If no updatable panel is specified, the progress control is displayed for any panels in the page. The user interface of the progress bar is inserted in the host page when the page is rendered. However, it is initially hidden from view using the CSS *display* attribute.

When set to none, the CSS *display* attribute doesn't display a given HTML element and reuses its space in the page so that other elements can be shifted up properly. When the value of the *display* attribute is toggled on, existing elements are moved to make room for the new element.

If you want to reserve the space for the progress control and leave it blank when no update operation is taking place, you just set the *DynamicLayout* property to *false*.

Composing the Progress Screen

The ASP.NET AJAX framework displays the contents of the *ProgressTemplate* property while waiting for a panel to update. You can specify the template either declaratively or programmatically. In the latter case, you assign the property any object that implements the *ITemplate* interface. For the former situation, you can easily specify the progress control's markup declaratively, as shown in the following code:

```
<asp:UpdateProgress runat="server" ID="UpdateProgress1">
    <ProgressTemplate>
        ...
    </ProgressTemplate>
</asp:UpdateProgress>
```

You can place any combination of controls in the progress template. However, most of the time, you'll probably just put some text there and an animated GIF. (See Figure 19-6.)

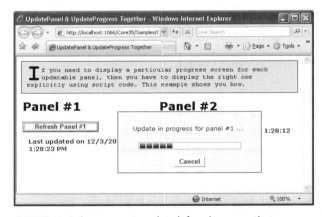

FIGURE 19-6 A progress template informing users that some work is occurring on the server

Note that the *UpdateProgress* control is not designed to be a gauge component, but rather a user-defined panel that the *ScriptManager* control shows before the panel refresh begins and that it hides immediately after its completion.

Important If you're looking for a real gauge bar to monitor the progress of a server-side task, partial rendering and the *UpdateProgress* control are not the right tools. As we'll see later in the chapter, polling is one of the main drawbacks of partial rendering and polling is unavoidable for monitoring server tasks from the client.

Client-Side Events for Richer Feedback

Each asynchronous postback is triggered on the client via script. The entire operation is conducted by the *PageRequestManager* client object, which invokes, under the hood, the *XMLHttpRequest* object. What kind of control do developers have on the underlying operation? If you manage *XMLHttpRequest* directly, you have full control over the request and response. But when these key steps are managed for you, there's not much you can do unless the request manager supports an eventing model.

The *Sys.WebForms.PageRequestManager* object provides a few events so that you can customize handling of the request and response. Table 19-9 lists the supported events that signal the main steps around an AJAX postback that partially update a page. The events are listed in the order in which they fire to the client page.

TABLE 19-9 Properties of the *UpdateProgress* Control

Event	Event Argument	Description
initializeRequest	*InitializeRequestEventArgs*	Occurs before the request is prepared for sending
beginRequest	*BeginRequestEventArgs*	Occurs before the request is sent
pageLoading	*PageLoadingEventArgs*	Occurs when the response has been acquired but before any content on the page is updated
pageLoaded	*PageLoadedEventArgs*	Occurs after all content on the page is refreshed as a result of an asynchronous postback
endRequest	*EndRequestEventArgs*	Occurs after an asynchronous postback is finished and control has been returned to the browser

To register an event handler, you use the following JavaScript code:

```
var manager = Sys.WebForms.PageRequestManager.getInstance();
manager.add_beginRequest(OnBeginRequest);
```

The prototype of the event handler method—*OnBeginRequest* in this case—is shown here:

```
function beginRequest(sender, args)
```

The real type of the *args* object, though, depends on the event data structure. By using any of these events, you can control in more detail the steps of an asynchronous request. Let's dig out more.

The *initializeRequest* event is the first in the client life cycle of an asynchronous request. The life cycle begins at the moment in which a postback is made that is captured by the *UpdatePanel*'s client-side infrastructure. You can use the *initializeRequest* event to evaluate the postback source and do any additional required work. The event data structure is the *InitializeRequestEventArgs* class. The class features three properties—*postBackElement*, *request*, and *cancel*.

The *postBackElement* property is read-only and evaluates to a *DomElement* object. It indicates the DOM element that is responsible for the postback. The *request* property (read-only) is an object of type *Sys.Net.WebRequest* and represents the ongoing request. Finally, *cancel* is a read-write Boolean property that can be used to abort the request before it is sent.

Immediately after calling the *initializeRequest* handler, if any, the *PageRequestManager* object aborts any pending async requests. Next, it proceeds with the *beginRequest* event and then sends the packet.

When the response arrives, the *PageRequestManager* object first processes any returned data and separates hidden fields, updatable panels and whatever pieces of information are returned from the server. Once the response data is ready for processing, the *PageRequestManager* object fires the *pageLoading* client event. The event is raised after the server response is received but before any content on the page is updated. You can use this event to provide a custom transition effect for updated content or to run any clean-up code that prepares the panels for the next update. The event data is packed in an instance of the class *PageLoadingEventArgs*. The class has three properties: *panelsUpdating*, *panelsDeleting*, and *dataItems*. The first two are arrays and list the updatable panels to be updated and deleted, respectively.

The *pageLoaded* event is raised after all content on the page is refreshed. You can use this event to provide a custom transition effect for updated content, such as flashing or highlighting updated contents. The event data is packed in the class *PageLoadedEventArgs*, which has three properties: *panelsUpdated*, *panelsDeleted*, and *dataItems*. The first two are arrays and list the updatable panels that were just updated and deleted, respectively.

The *endRequest* event signals the termination of the asynchronous request. You receive this event regardless of the success or failure of the asynchronous postback.

Disabling Visual Elements During Updates

If you want to prevent users from generating more input while a partial page update is being processed, you can also consider disabling the user interface—all or in part. To do so, you write handlers for *beginRequest* and *endRequest* events:

```
<script type="text/javascript">
function pageLoad()
{
    var manager = Sys.WebForms.PageRequestManager.getInstance();
    manager.add_beginRequest(OnBeginRequest);
    manager.add_beginRequest(OnEndRequest);
}
</script>
```

You typically use the *beginRequest* event to modify the user interface as appropriate and notify the user that the postback is being processed:

```
// Globals
var currentPostBackElem;

function OnBeginRequest(sender, args)
{
    // Get the reference to the button click (i.e., btnStartTask)
    currentPostBackElem = args.get_postBackElement();
    if (typeof(currentPostBackElem) === "undefined")
        return;
    if (currentPostBackElem.id.toLowerCase() === "btnStartTask")
    {
        // Disable the button
        $get("btnStartTask").disabled = true;
    }
}
```

The *beginRequest* handler receives event data through the *BeginRequestEventArgs* data structure—the *args* formal parameter. The class features only two properties—*request* and *postBackElement*. The properties have the same characteristics of analogous properties on the aforementioned *InitializeRequestEventArgs* class.

In the preceding code snippet, I disable the clicked button to prevent users from repeatedly clicking the same button.

At the end of the request, any temporary modification to the user interface must be removed. So animations must be stopped, altered styles must be restored, and disabled controls must be re-enabled. The ideal place for all these operations is the *endRequest* event. The event passes an *EndRequestEventArgs* object to handlers. The class has a few properties, as described in Table 19-10.

TABLE 19-10 Properties of the *EndRequestEventArgs* Control

Property	Description
dataItems	Returns the client-side dictionary packed with server-defined data items for the page or the control that handles this event. (More on registering data items later.)
Error	Returns an object of type *Error* that describes the error (if any) that occurred on the server during the request.
errorHandled	Gets and sets a Boolean value that indicates whether the error has been completely handled by user code. If this property is set to *true* in the event handler, no default error handling will be executed by the ASP.NET AJAX client library. We saw an example of this property in Chapter 3.
Response	Returns an object of type *Sys.Net.WebRequestExecutor* that represents the executor of the current request. Most of the time, this object will be an instance of *Sys.Net.XMLHttpExecutor*. For more information, refer to Chapter 2.

As you can see, when the *endRequest* event occurs there's no information around about the client element that fired the postback. If you need to restore some user interface settings from inside the *endRequest* event handler, you might need a global variable to track which element caused the postback:

```
function OnEndRequest(sender, args)
{
    if (typeof(currentPostBackElem) === "undefined")
        return;
    if (currentPostBackElem.id.toLowerCase() === "btnStartTask")
    {
        $get("btnStartTask").disabled = false;
    }
}
```

Wouldn't it be nice if you could visually notify users that a certain region of the screen has been updated? As we've seen, partial rendering improves the user experience with pages by eliminating a good number of full refreshes. If you look at it from the perspective of the average user, though, a partial page update doesn't have a clear start and finish like a regular Web roundtrip. The user doesn't see the page redrawn and might not notice changes in the user interface. A good pattern is employing a little animation to show the user what has really changed with the latest operation. You can code this by yourself using the pair of *beginRequest* and *endRequest* events, or you can resort to a specialized component—an *UpdatePanel* extender control—as we'll see in a moment.

Important The *disabled* HTML attribute works only on *INPUT* elements. It has no effect on hyperlinks and *<a>* tags. If you plan to use *LinkButton* controls, you have to resort to other JavaScript tricks to disable the user interface. One possible trick is temporarily replacing the onclick handler of the hyperlink with a return value of *false*. Another effective trick might be to cover the area to be disabled with a partially opaque *DIV*.

Aborting a Pending Update

A really user-friendly system always lets its users cancel a pending operation. How can you obtain this functionality with an *UpdateProgress* control? The progress template is allowed to contain an abort button. The script code injected in the page will monitor the button and stop the ongoing asynchronous call if it's clicked. To specify an abort button, you add the following to the progress template:

```
<input type="button" onclick="abortTask()" value="Cancel" />
```

In the first place, the button has to be a client-side button. So you can express it either through the *<input>* element or the *<button>* element for the browsers that support this element. If you opt for the *<input>* element, the *type* attribute must be set to *button*. The script code you wire up to the *onclick* event is up to you, but it will contain at least the following instructions:

```
<script type="text/JavaScript">
function abortTask()
{
    var manager = Sys.WebForms.PageRequestManager.getInstance();
    if (manager.get_isInAsyncPostBack())
        manager.abortPostBack();
}
</script>
```

You retrieve the instance of the client *PageRequestManager* object active in the client page and check whether an asynchronous postback is going on. If so, you call the *abortPostBack* method to stop it.

 Important Canceling an ongoing update in this way is equivalent to closing the connection with the server. No results will ever be received, and no updates will ever occur on the page. However, canceling the update is a pure client operation and has no effect over what's happening on the server. If the user started a destructive operation, the client-side *Cancel* button can just do nothing to stop that operation on the server.

Light and Shade of Partial Rendering

Partial rendering is definitely the easiest way to add AJAX capabilities to an ASP.NET Web site. It has a relatively low impact on the structure of existing pages, doesn't require significant new skills, doesn't require exposure to JavaScript, and leaves the application model intact. Advocates of a pure AJAX approach might say that there's no AJAX at all in partial rendering. And such a statement is not false, indeed.

Haven't we said that AJAX is key because it propounds a new programming paradigm for building Web applications? And now we're back to giving kudos to partial rendering—an approach that admittedly maintains the old programming model of classic Web applications? What's the point?

Overall, partial rendering is only one possible way to approach AJAX. It preserves most of your current investments and is relatively cheap to implement. Partial rendering just adds AJAX capabilities to your pages. It doesn't constitute a true AJAX application. There's no architectural new point in partial rendering. It's a great technique to quickly update legacy applications, and it is an excellent choice when you lack the time, skills, or budget to move on and redesign the application. But in a good number of cases, an improved user interface and optimized rendering is all that your users demand. So partial rendering would perfectly fit in.

On the other hand, building true AJAX applications where all the presentation logic lives on the client written in JavaScript is not trivial either, no matter how much help third-party libraries might offer.

In the end, you should be aware of the structural limitations that partial rendering has. You might want to start with partial rendering to improve your pages and then move on to other, more purely AJAX, solutions to fix particular bottlenecks that still remain. My advice is that a pure AJAX approach where a lot of JavaScript is involved is a solution that should be considered carefully. And that you should have good reasons for both adopting or refusing it.

> **Note** Why is it so darned hard to write pure AJAX applications? AJAX applications are all about the client, and the client is JavaScript and HTML. Both have significant limitations in light of the complexity of applications these days. JavaScript is an interpreted language, and it does not have a particularly modern syntax. Additionally, JavaScript is subject to the implementation that browsers provide. So a feature might be flaky in one browser and super-optimized in another. Originally born as a document format, HTML is used more as an application delivery format. But for this purpose, HTML is simply inadequate because it lacks strong and built-in graphics and layout capabilities. Silverlight 2.0 with its embedded common language runtime (CLR), support for managed languages, and full support for Windows Presentation Foundation (WPF) seems to address both issues.

Issues with Concurrent Calls

Partial rendering has a number of positives, but it also has a couple of key drawbacks. In particular, it doesn't support concurrent asynchronous postbacks. This means that you are not allowed to have two asynchronous postbacks going on at the same time. Partial rendering bypasses the standard browser's mechanism that handles an HTTP request. It hooks up the *submit* event of the form, cuts the standard browser handler out, and finally places the HTTP request using *XMLHttpRequest*.

The request that reaches the Web server differs from a regular ASP.NET request only for an extra HTTP header. The request sends in the contents of the posting form, including the view-state hidden field. The response is not pure HTML but represents a text record where each field describes the new status of a page element—update panels, hidden fields, scripts to run on loading.

As you can see, the underlying model of partial rendering is still the model of classic ASP.NET pages. It is a sort of stop-and-go model where the users posts back, waits for a while, and then receives a new page. While waiting for the next page, there's not much the user can do. Only one server operation per session occurs at a time. Partial rendering is only a smarter way of implementing the old model.

From a technical standpoint, the major factor that prevents multiple asynchronous postbacks is the persistence of the view-state information. When two requests go, both send out the same copy of the view state, but each reasonably returns a different view state. Which one has to be good for the page then?

Is dropping the view state entirely an option, at least for asynchronous postbacks? Whatever way you look at it, dropping the view state increases the amount of JavaScript needed for each page. The view state allows you to keep the server logic in C# or Visual Basic .NET and generate the user interface through server controls. This is not to say, though, that another approach isn't possible. Anyway, partial rendering works this way.

Whenever a request for an asynchronous postback is raised, the *PageRequestManager* class checks whether another operation is pending. If so, by default, it silently kills the ongoing request to make room for the new one—a *last-win* discipline.

This fact has a clear impact on developers. In fact, you should always modify the user interface to ensure that users can't start a second operation before the first is terminated. Otherwise, the first operation is aborted in favor of the second. This happens in any case, even when the two operations are logically unrelated.

Note When concurrent calls are necessary, you should consider moving that page (if not the whole application) to a more AJAX-oriented design. Alternatively, you can consider implementing that feature within the page using some of the features covered in the next chapter, such as page methods or script services.

Issues with Polling

Among other things, AJAX pages are popular because they can bring on the client information in a timely manner. A page starts polling a remote URL, grabs fresh information, and returns it to the client for the actual display. Implemented via partial rendering, polling is subject to being interrupted when the user starts a new partial rendering operation to restart automatically at the end.

If this is not a problem for you, you can use the new *Timer* server control, as shown here:

```
<asp:Timer ID="Timer1" runat="server" Enabled="true" Interval="1000" ontick="Timer1_Tick" />
<asp:Button ID="Button1" runat="server" Text="Start task" onclick="Button1_Click" />
<asp:UpdateProgress ID="UpdateProgress1" runat="server" DynamicLayout="false">
    <ProgressTemplate>
        <img src="loading.gif" />
    </ProgressTemplate>
</asp:UpdateProgress>

<asp:UpdatePanel ID="UpdatePanel1" runat="server">
    <ContentTemplate>
        <asp:Label ID="Label1" runat="server" />
    </ContentTemplate>
    <Triggers>
        <asp:AsyncPostBackTrigger ControlID="Button1" EventName="Click" />
    </Triggers>
</asp:UpdatePanel>

<hr />

<asp:UpdatePanel ID="UpdatePanel2" runat="server">
    <ContentTemplate>
        <asp:Label ID="lblClock" runat="server" />
    </ContentTemplate>
    <Triggers>
        <asp:AsyncPostBackTrigger ControlID="Timer1" EventName="Tick" />
    </Triggers>
</asp:UpdatePanel>
```

The *Timer* control is the server counterpart of a client timer created using the *window.setTimeout* method. In the preceding code, the *Timer* control causes a postback every second as specified by the *Interval* property. The postback fires the *Tick* event. By using the timer as the trigger of an updatable panel, you can refresh the content of the panel periodically. In the code, the second *UpdatePanel* control just renders out a digital clock:

```
protected void Timer1_Tick(object sender, EventArgs e)
{
    // Update the clock
    lblClock.Text = DateTime.Now.ToString();
}
```

As in Figure 19-7, the clock stops working while the remote task triggered by the other button is still running.

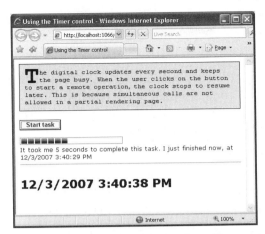

FIGURE 19-7 Multiple calls are not allowed in a partial rendering page

The AJAX Control Toolkit

In addition to partial rendering, developers can use *control extenders* to add a predefined client-side behavior to new and existing ASP.NET controls. A client-side behavior is a block of JavaScript code that adds a new capability to the markup generated by a given ASP.NET control. An extender is basically a server control that emits proper script code—the client behavior—to enhance how a given ASP.NET control behaves on the client. An extender is not simply a custom control derived from an existing control. Rather, it represents a general behavior—such as auto-completion, focus management, generation of popups, and dragga-bility—that can be declaratively applied to various target control types.

For the time being, there's no way to add rich capabilities and functionalities to the Web client other than by crafting good and tricky JavaScript code. Control extenders offer a suitable model, but other frameworks are available too, including Dojo (*http://www.dojotoolkit.org*) and Gaia (*http://www.ajaxwidgets.com*). Plus suites of controls are available from large endors such as ComponentArt (*http://www.componentart.com*), Infragistics (*http://www.infragistics. com*), and Telerik (*http://www.telerik.com*).

The AJAX Control Toolkit (ACT) is a shared-source library of Web controls specifically de-signed for ASP.NET. It is not included in the ASP.NET 3.5 platform and should be downloaded separately. You can get it from *http://www.asp.net/ajax/ajaxcontroltoolkit*.

Enhancing Controls with Extenders

ASP.NET comes with a fairly rich collection of built-in controls. In addition, plenty of custom controls are available for developers from third-party vendors, from community projects, and even from contributions by volunteers. If you still can't find the control you are looking for, you typically write one yourself or buy a new specialized control that extends the original control and adds the desired behavior. Object orientation, of course, encourages this approach.

All in all, it's rare that you need to write a completely new control yourself. More often, your control will derive from an existing ASP.NET control. Blindly using inheritance for building specialized versions of controls might not be a wise choice, though. Even in relatively small projects, in fact, it can lead straight to a proliferation of controls.

ASP.NET control extenders go in the opposite direction. First and foremost, an extender control is a server control itself. An extender represents a logical behavior that can be attached to one or more control types to extend their base capabilities. Extenders decouple controls from behaviors and make it possible to extend existing controls with new behaviors.

From a technology point of view, ASP.NET AJAX and extenders are not strictly related. In theory, one could develop extenders for ASP.NET 1.1 and ASP.NET 2.0 that work without AJAX extensions. In practice, though, ACT provides some interesting facilities for writers of extender controls—specifically, base classes and, more importantly, the Microsoft AJAX library for developing JavaScript functionalities more comfortably.

Extenders at a Glance: the *TextBoxWatermark* Control

To better understand the goals and characteristics of control extenders, let's briefly consider the behavior encapsulated by one of the extenders contained in the ACT—the *TextBoxWatermark* extender.

A text box watermark is a string of text that is displayed in an empty text box as a guide to the user. This help text is stripped off when the text box is submitted and is automatically removed as the user starts typing in the field. Likewise, it is automatically re-inserted when the user wipes out any text in the text box. You start by linking the ACT assembly to the project and then place an extendee *TextBox* control in the page:

```
<%@ Register Assembly="AjaxControlToolkit" Namespace="AjaxControlToolkit" TagPrefix="act" %>
...
<asp:TextBox ID="TextBox1" runat="server" />
```

Later in the ASPX source, you add a new control—the *TextBoxWatermarkExtender* control:

```
<act:TextBoxWatermarkExtender runat="server" ID="TextBoxWatermark1"
    TargetControlID="TextBox1"
    WatermarkText="Type First Name Here"
    WatermarkCssClass="watermarked" />
```

The watermark extender targets the specified control ID and adds a new behavior to it. The behavior is further configured using a few public properties on the extender control, such as *WatermarkText* and *WatermarkCssClass* in the previous example.

In particular, the watermark behavior injects script code that hooks up three HTML events: *onfocus*, *onblur*, and *onkeypress*. In its initialization stage, the injected script also sets a new style and default text for the target text box if the body of the field is empty. When the text box gets the input focus, the event handler promptly removes the watermark text and restores the original style. As the user types, the handler for *onkeypress* ensures that the current text box is watermarked. Finally, when the input field loses the focus—the *onblur* event—the handler sets the watermark back if the content of the field is the empty string.

> **Note** To add a watermark behavior to an ASP.NET *TextBox*, you use the aforementioned extender control. Alternatively, if you feel comfortable with ASP.NET control development and JavaScript, you can develop a custom *TextBox* control and use a client-side code fragment to achieve the same results.

Creating a New Extender Control

ASP.NET 3.5 doesn't include any concrete implementation of an extender. However, it defines the base class from which all custom extenders, as well as all extenders in the ACT, derive. This class is named *ExtenderControl*. You can create your own extenders starting from this class; it is not recommended, though. Why is it so? There's an easier and faster way that leverages the extensions available in the ACT library.

The following code shows the source code of the focus extender control. The sample extender adds to its target control a highlighting behavior that changes the appearance of the control when this gets focused:

```
using AjaxControlToolkit;
...
namespace Core35
{
    [TargetControlType(typeof(Control))]
    [ClientScriptResource("Core35.FocusBehavior", "focusBehavior.js")]
    public class FocusExtender : AjaxControlToolkit.ExtenderControlBase
    {
        [ExtenderControlProperty]
        [RequiredProperty]
        public string HighlightCssClass
        {
            get { return GetPropertyValue("HighlightCssClass", ""); }
            set { SetPropertyValue("HighlightCssClass", value); }
        }

        [ExtenderControlProperty]
        public string NoHighlightCssClass
        {
            get { return GetPropertyValue("NoHighlightCssClass", ""); }
            set { SetPropertyValue("NoHighlightCssClass", value); }
        }
    }
}
```

The *TargetControlType* attribute indicates the type of controls this behavior can be attached to. The *ClientScriptResource* attribute indicates the name of the script class to inject in the client page and its source file. The base class is *ExtenderControlBase*, which is defined in the ACT library.

All that you do with managed code is define the set of properties that developers can customize on the both the server and the client. Each property must be decorated with the *ExtenderControlProperty* attribute and, optionally, the *RequiredProperty* attribute.

The property is not directly responsible for the persistence of its assigned value. It is limited to getting and setting the value through the *GetPropertyValue* and *SetPropertyValue* methods of the base class. These stock methods take care of persistence.

The core part of an AJAX extender control is its JavaScript code. Here's the JavaScript code you need for the focus extender:

```
Type.registerNamespace('Core35');

Core35.FocusBehavior = function(element)
{
    Core35.FocusBehavior.initializeBase(this, [element]);

    this._highlightCssClass = null;
    this._nohighlightCssClass = null;
}

Core35.FocusBehavior.prototype =
{
    initialize : function() {
        Core35.FocusBehavior.callBaseMethod(this, 'initialize');
        this._onfocusHandler = Function.createDelegate(this, this._onFocus);
        this._onblurHandler = Function.createDelegate(this, this._onBlur);
        $addHandlers(this.get_element(),
                    { 'focus' : this._onFocus,
                      'blur' : this._onBlur },
                    this);
        this.get_element().className = this._nohighlightCssClass;
    },
    dispose : function() {
        $clearHandlers(this.get_element());
        Core35.FocusBehavior.callBaseMethod(this, 'dispose');
    },
    _onFocus : function(e) {
        if (this.get_element() && !this.get_element().disabled) {
            this.get_element().className = this._highlightCssClass;
        }
    },
    _onBlur : function(e) {
        if (this.get_element() && !this.get_element().disabled) {
            this.get_element().className = this._nohighlightCssClass;
        }
    },
```

```
get_highlightCssClass : function() {
    return this._highlightCssClass;
},
set_highlightCssClass : function(value) {
    if (this._highlightCssClass !== value) {
        this._highlightCssClass = value;
        this.raisePropertyChanged('highlightCssClass');
    }
},
get_nohighlightCssClass : function() {
    return this._nohighlightCssClass;
},
set_nohighlightCssClass : function(value) {
    if (this._nohighlightCssClass !== value) {
        this._nohighlightCssClass = value;
        this.raisePropertyChanged('nohighlightCssClass');
    }
}
}
}

// Optional descriptor for JSON serialization
Core35.FocusBehavior.descriptor = {
    properties: [   {name: 'highlightCssClass', type: String},
                    {name: 'nohighlightCssClass', type: String} ]
}

// Register the class as a type that inherits from Sys.UI.Control.
Core35.FocusBehavior.registerClass('Core35.FocusBehavior', Sys.UI.Behavior);
```

The script for the extender is centered around a couple of handlers for *focus* and *blur* DOM events. In the *focus* handler, the code sets the CSS class for the target element. In the *blur* handler, it resets the CSS class.

> **Tip** The easiest way to create extenders is to use the facilities of the ACT. You run the VSI file in the toolkit download, set up the templates, and then click *"Add AJAX Control Extender"* from the Visual Studio 2008 Solution Explorer to obtain a scaffold for the extender and the behavior.

In a test page, all that you have to do is register the ACT assembly and the assembly that contains the focus extender and then go with the following code:

```
<asp:TextBox ID="TextBox1" runat="server" EnableTheming="false" />
<act:FocusExtender ID="FocusExtender1" runat="server"
        TargetControlID="TextBox1"
        NoHighlightCssClass="LowLightTextBox"
        HighlightCssClass="HighLight" />
```

You can attach the focus extender behavior to virtually all ASP.NET controls and, for each control, you can specify the CSS class to use to render the control as highlighted and normal. Bear in mind that you need to disable theming to make sure that CSS styles you apply through the extender take precedence over any other style set via themes. Figure 19-8 shows the extender in action.

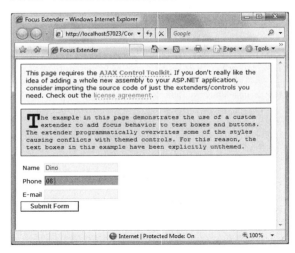

FIGURE 19-8 The focus behavior in action

Extenders in the ACT

Table 19-11 lists the components available in the ACT. Note that the full name of the extender class contains an "Extender" suffix that I omitted in the table for brevity. So, for example, there will be no *CollapsiblePanel* component in the ACT assembly; you will find a *CollapsiblePanelExtender* control instead.

TABLE 19-11 Extenders in the ACT

Control	Description
AlwaysVisibleControl	Pins a control to a corner of the page, and keeps it floating over the page background as the user scrolls or resizes the page. You use this extender to make sure that, say, a given panel shows up at the top-left corner of the page regardless of the scroll position or the size of the browser window.
Animation	Provides a specialized framework for adding animation effects to controls hosted in ASP.NET pages. You associate client-side events of the target control with one or more of the predefined animation effects.
AutoComplete	Associated with a text box, provides a list of suggestions for the text to type in the field.
Calendar	Attached to a text box, the extender provides client-side date-picking functionality with customizable date format and pop-up control.

Control	Description
CascadingDropDown	Associated with a *DropDownList* control. This extender automatically populates the list with data retrieved from a Web service method. The nice thing about this extender is that you can create a hierarchy of drop-down lists and have the extender automatically populate child drop-down lists based on the current selections in any of the previous lists in the hierarchy, if any.
CollapsiblePanel	Adds collapsible sections to a Web page. This extender can be used only with panel controls—that is, with the ASP.NET *Panel* control or any class derived from it. You let the extender know which panel in the page acts as the header and which panel provides the contents that collapse and expand.
ConfirmButton	Associated with a button control. This extender adds a confirmation JavaScript dialog box to the click event of the button. The extender is supported on any class that implements the *IButtonControl* interface, including *Button*, *LinkButton*, and *ImageButton*.
DragPanel	Associated with panel controls. This extender adds drag-and-drop capabilities so that you can move the panel around the page. You can specify the contents to move as well as the handle that, if pressed, triggers the dragging operation.
DropDown	The extender provides a mouse-over link to open a drop-down panel.
DropShadow	Adds drop shadows to any control available on the page. With this extender, you can specify the opacity and width of the shadow.
DynamicPopulate	Updates the contents of a control with the result of a Web service or page method call.
FilteredTextBox	Lets users enter text in a *TextBox* control that matches a given set of valid characters.
HoverMenu	Displays the contents of an associated panel control when the mouse hovers next to a given control. You can associate this extender with any ASP.NET control. The extender works as a kind of specialized and extremely flexible ToolTip.
ListSearch	Enables users to search for an item in a list by typing some of the characters.
MaskedEdit	Lets users enter text in a *TextBox* control according to a given input layout.
ModalPopup	Associated with a control that can fire a client-side *onclick* event (typically, buttons and hyperlinks), this extender implements a classic modal dialog box without using HTML dialog boxes. Basically, it displays the contents of a given panel and prevents the user from interacting with the rest of the page.

Control	Description
MutuallyExclusiveCheckBox	Associated with *CheckBox* controls, this extender lets you define logical groups of check boxes so that users can select only one in each group.
NoBot	Applies some *anti-bot* techniques to input forms. Bots, or robot applications, are software applications that run automated tasks over the Internet. For example, bots are used to fill input forms and submit ad hoc values.
NumericUpDown	Associated with text box controls, this extender allows you to click automatically displayed buttons to enter the next/previous value in the field. It works with numbers, custom lists, and Web service methods.
PagingBulletedList	Associated with *BulletedList* controls, this extender groups all items bound to the list and organizes them in client-side sorted pages.
PasswordStrength	Associated with text box controls used to type a password, this extender provides visual feedback on the strength of the password being typed.
PopupControl	Transforms the contents of a given panel into a pop-up window without using HTML dialog boxes. You can associate this extender with any control that can fire any of the following client-side events: *onfocus*, *onclick*, and *onkeydown*.
ResizableControl	Attaches to any page element, and allows the user to resize the element using a handle placed at the lower-right corner of the control.
RoundedCorners	Adds a background panel to any ASP.NET control so that the control appears with rounded corners. The overall height of the original control changes slightly.
Slider	Extends a *TextBox* control with a slider user interface.
SlideShow	Associated with *Image* controls, it can be used to transition images automatically when hosted on a page.
TextBoxWatermark	Associated with *TextBox* controls. This extender adds sample or prompt text, called a "watermark," that illustrates the type of text the user is expected to enter in the field. For example, the watermark might say, "Type your name here." The watermark text disappears as soon as the user starts typing and reappears if the text box becomes empty.
ToggleButton	Associated with *CheckBox* controls. This extender enables you to use custom images to render the check buttons. You can use different images to indicate the selected and cleared states.
UpdatePanelAnimation	Plays animations during key steps of a partial update. You can use the extender to animate the page both while the panel is being updated and when the update has completed.

Control	Description
ValidatorCallout	Works on top of ASP.NET validators, and improves their user interface. In particular, the extender displays a yellow callout with the error message.

As you can probably guess, some extenders listed in the table require rich browser capabilities, whereas others are just a smart piece of JavaScript code attached to a block of markup elements. Note that all these features work in a cross-browser way. I'll return to some of the aforementioned extenders with code samples and more details in a moment. For more complete documentation, please refer to *http://www.asp.net/ajax/ajaxcontroltoolkit/samples*.

Controls in the ACT

Along with all the extenders listed in Table 19-11, the ACT also supplies a few traditional server controls with rich capabilities: the *Accordion*, *Rating*, *ReorderList*, and *TabContainer* controls.

The *Accordion* control allows you to provide multiple collapsible panes and display only one at a time. When the user clicks a new pane, the currently displayed pane is collapsed to leave room for the new one.

The *Rating* control provides an intuitive user interface to let users select the number of stars that represents their rating of a given subject. The control is the wrapped-up version of the user interface that several Web sites provide to let users rate published items.

A data-bound control, *ReorderList*, allows its child elements to be reordered on the client using drag-and-drop functionality. To move an item in the list, the user drags the item's handle up to its new position. At the end of the operation, the control posts back so that the new status of the data source can be recorded.

Finally, the *TabContainer* control is a purely client-side container of tabbed forms.

You use any of these controls in the same way you would use any native ASP.NET server controls.

Improving the User Interface with Input Extenders

In a perfect world where architects design applications in strict accordance with requirements and keeping the user's satisfaction in mind, each logical data type features its own set of input controls. In general, money, days of the week, ages, and quantities are all data represented with numbers. However, each of these logical data types might need a different user interface. The same can be said for URLs, paths, IP addresses, and dates.

Both in Windows and the Web, user interfaces are built by composing controls together. The original toolbox of controls, though, is not particularly rich in either Windows/WPF or ASP.NET. Input controls for Windows Forms are still based on the original windows in Win32. Input controls for Web pages are little more than wrappers for the HTML *<input>* element.

The need for effective input controls is even higher today, now that AJAX is taking root. The more work a page can do on the client, the better the overall experience is for the user. The user experience is widely improved because of saved postbacks but also because of the increased interactivity, dynamic data formatting, and validation that ad hoc input components can guarantee. As a result, input controls should be more interactive than ever. ACT extenders can help a lot.

Motivation for Input Facilities

As mentioned, in HTML there's one primary element for accepting data—the *<input>* element. You use it for numbers, strings, dates, currency values, and so forth. So what if you need numeric input to be restricted to a specific range of values?

You can leave the user free of typing any values and then enforce this business rule through a server-side validation layer. Although server-side validation shouldn't be avoided (for the safety of data), it would be even better if you could start yelling at wrong data as it's entered into the input box.

JavaScript code is required to check values and ensure they comply with expected types and formats. In some cases, a specialized user interface also is required to make the user feel more comfortable. Here's where some ad hoc input extenders fit in. Let's start with the *Slider* and *NumericUpDown* extenders. Both force users to enter only numbers that fall in a given range.

The *Slider* Extender

The *Slider* extender hides its associated *TextBox* and replaces it with a graphical slider moving through discrete steps within a minimum and maximum interval. The underlying *TextBox* can always be set programmatically to any value you want. Note, though, that the assigned value must be compatible with the numeric range set via the slider; otherwise, the slider will silently fix it. Let's consider the following example:

```
<act:SliderExtender runat="server" ID="SliderExtender1"
    TargetControlID="txtYourIncome"
    Minimum="0"
    Maximum="200000"
    Steps="41"
    BoundControlID="lblIncomeAsText" />
```

The slider applies to a *TextBox* control named *txtYourIncome* and ensures it is visually assigned a value in the range 0 through 200,000. The *Steps* property indicates how many discrete steps should be provided. The preceding setting lets the slider jump by 5000 every time.

> **Note** Why is *Steps* is set to a weird 41 value, when a value of 40 would have probably looked better? Correctly, 40 is what you get by dividing 200,000 by 5000. However, the property *Steps* counts the number of steps ranging from 0 to 200000. You have to add one more tick to be able to select 0 first and then values every 5000.

If you programmatically set the slider on the server, the value is first converted to a number and then mapped to the nearest step value. If you pass in a string (that is, not a number), the slider ignores it and defaults to the initial value of the range. If you set the value of the underlying text box on the client via JavaScript, the value is correctly recognized over the next postback, but it is not immediately reflected by the user interface. To programmatically change the value in the slider from within the client, use the following code:

```
$find("SliderExtender1").set_Value(145678);
```

Why should you opt for *$find* instead of *$get*? As mentioned, the *$get* function is shorthand for *document.getElementById* and looks only for DOM elements. The *$find* function stands for *Sys.Application.findComponent* and applies to any component of the Microsoft AJAX Library that has been programmatically created.

The *BoundControlID* property refers to a DOM element that dynamically displays the current slider value. In most cases, you'll use a *<span>* tag or a *Label* control for this purpose. Internally, the slider distinguishes between *<input>* and any other HTML elements. It sets the *value* property in the former case; otherwise, it uses the *innerHTML* property of the matching DOM element.

> **Tip** The slider script hides the underlying *TextBox*. For this reason, it is recommended that you hide the text box declaratively using CSS styles to avoid any flashing when the page loads up. Finally, be aware that regular text boxes are displayed inline, whereas slider boxes are positioned through blocks.

Figure 19-9 shows a few input extenders in action in a sample page.

FIGURE 19-9 Input extenders in action

The *NumericUpDown* Extender

The *NumericUpDown* extender selects the next/previous value in a bound list of possible values. Despite what the name implies, *NumericUpDown* is not just a tool for specifying numeric quantities. The *RefValues* property allows you to list values to move through:

```
<act:NumericUpDownExtender ID="UpDown1" runat="server"
    Width="200"
    RefValues="None;1;2;3;4;5;More than 5;"
    TargetControlID="Children" />
```

NumericUpDown has the ability to retrieve reference values from a remote service. The service is invoked asynchronously each time the user clicks the up or down buttons. The service must be script-callable and include methods with the following signature:

```
public int YourMethod(int current, string tag)
```

You configure the extender to use the remote service through the *ServiceDownPath*, *ServiceDownMethod*, *ServiceUpPath*, and *ServiceUpMethod* properties. Finally, the up and down buttons don't have to be auto-generated via script. They can be buttons already defined in the page and referenced through the *TargetButtonDownID* and *TargetButtonUpID* properties.

The *FilteredTextBox* Extender

Preventing user mistakes involves controlling the input by filtering out undesired characters, invalid expressions, or data of the wrong type. Using the standard *TextBox* control, you enforce proper input by validating it on the server, where you can check whether the input string can be converted to a given data type. Extenders simply save you from writing the JavaScript code required to make checks on the client.

The *FilteredTextBox* extender prevents a user from entering invalid characters into a text box. It basically adds JavaScript that hooks up the keyboard activity and filters out undesired keystrokes. You can configure the extender to refuse certain characters or to ensure that only specified characters are accepted. You use the *FilterMode* property for this setting: it accepts only *ValidChars* and *InvalidChars* as its value:

```
<act:FilteredTextBoxExtender ID="Filtered1" runat="server"
    TargetControlID="YourAge"
    FilterMode="ValidChars"
    FilterType="Numbers" />
```

The *FilterType* property determines the type of filter to apply—only numbers, only lowercase or uppercase, and a custom set of characters. It should be noted that a *TextBox* with a watermark can't be filtered to accept numeric values only. The filter layer, in fact, automatically clears any watermark text you set.

The *Calendar* Extender

Using the calendar extender, you make it virtually impossible for users to type anything other than a date. ASP.NET comes with a server *Calendar* control, but a calendar extender is really different, as it builds its user interface entirely on the client, works entirely on the client, and generates no postbacks at all as the user navigates to find the month and day. Furthermore, if a given browser doesn't support JavaScript, the old text box is displayed.

```
<act:CalendarExtender ID="CalendarExtender1" runat="server"
    TargetControlID="Birth"
    Format="dd/MM/yyyy" />
```

The preceding code snippet is sufficient to display a popup calendar as the associated text box receives the focus. As an alternative, you can display the popup when the user clicks a page button. The ID of the button is set through the *PopupButtonID* property. The *Format* property indicates the format of the date as it will be written to the text box when the user dismisses the calendar popup. (See Figure 19-10.)

FIGURE 19-10 The *Calendar* extender in action

The *Calendar* extender is good for date-picking functionality; it is not as good for real calendaring functionality.

The *MaskedEdit* Extender

Would you really use the *Calendar* extender to pick a date that represents a birth date? It is an option and, all in all, it is one of the best options you have. But it is not the perfect choice. Why is that so? A date that represents a birth date would reasonably require you to navigate a few years back to find the right day. A popup calendar is great to pick close dates; it loses part of its appeal as it is employed to pick up just any date. To some extent, we're back to square one—using a text box to have users enter a date. This raises a number of new issues—involving formatting, locales, and separators.

When we start reasoning about data formatting and locales, *Date* is not the only critical data type. Currency, numbers, special strings such as URLs, disk paths, phone numbers, and e-mail addresses are all great examples of data types for which a specialized and masked input field is desirable. In ASP.NET, the *MaskedEdit* extender is a component that when attached to a *TextBox* control allows you to control input in a number of common scenarios.

You can use the *MaskedEdit* extender to enter numbers, dates, times, and date/times. The extender decides its output based on given culture settings. The following code snippet shows the typical way to use the extender with a text box that accepts a date:

```
<asp:TextBox runat="server" ID="TextBox1" />
<act:MaskedEditExtender ID="MaskedEditExtender1" runat="server"
    TargetControlID="TextBox1"
    Mask="99/99/9999"
    MaskType="Date" />
```

You define an input mainly through two properties: *Mask* and *MaskType*. The full list of properties is shown in Table 19-12.

TABLE 19-12 **Properties of the *MaskedEdit* Extender**

Property	Default	Description
AcceptAMPM	False	Boolean property, indicates whether an AM/PM symbol should be used when representing a time.
AcceptNegative	None	Indicates whether a negative sign (-) is required for negative values. Feasible values come from the *MaskedEditShowSymbol* enumeration: *None*, *Left*, *Right*.
AutoComplete	True	Boolean property, indicates whether empty mask characters not specified by the user must be automatically filled in.
AutoCompleteValue	""	Indicates the default character to use when *AutoComplete* is enabled.
Century	1900	Indicates the century to use when a date mask has only two digits for the year.
ClearMaskOnLostFocus	True	Boolean property, indicates whether to remove the mask when the *TextBox* loses the input focus.
ClearTextOnInvalid	False	Boolean property, indicates whether to clear the *TextBox* when the user has entered invalid text.
ClipboardEnabled	True	Boolean property, indicates whether to allow copy/paste with the clipboard.
ClipboardText	""	Indicates the prompt text to use when a clipboard paste is performed.
CultureName	""	Gets and sets the name of the culture to use.
DisplayMoney	None	Indicates whether the currency symbol is displayed. Feasible values come from the *MaskedEditShowSymbol* enumeration: *None*, *Left*, *Right*.
ErrorTooltipCssClass	""	Gets and sets the CSS class for the ToolTip message.
ErrorTooltipEnabled	False	Boolean property, indicates whether to show a ToolTip message when the mouse hovers over a *TextBox* with invalid content.

Property	Default	Description
Filtered	*""*	Gets and sets the list of valid characters for the mask type when the "C" placeholder is specified
InputDirection	*LeftToRight*	Indicates the text input direction. Feasible values come from the *MaskedEditInputDirection* enumeration: *LeftToRight, RightToLeft*.
Mask	*""*	Specifies the mask of characters that is acceptable to the extender.
MaskType	*""*	Indicates the mask type using any of the values defined by the *MaskedEditType* enumeration.
MessageValidatorTip	*True*	Boolean property, indicates whether a help message is displayed as the user types in the *TextBox*.
OnBlurCssNegative	*""*	Gets and sets the CSS class used when the *TextBox* loses the input focus and contains a negative value.
OnFocusCssClass	*""*	Gets and sets the CSS class used when the *TextBox* receives the input focus.
OnFocusCssNegative	*""*	Gets and sets the CSS class used when the *TextBox* gets the input focus and contains a negative value.
OnInvalidCssClass	*""*	Gets and sets the CSS class used when the text is not valid.
PromptCharacter	_	Gets and sets the prompt character being used for unspecified mask characters
UserDateFormat	*None*	Indicates a particular date format. Feasible values are defined by the *MaskedEditUserDateFormat* enumeration.
UserTimeFormat	*None*	Indicates a particular time format. Feasible values are defined by the *MaskedEditUserTimeFormat* enumeration.

The *MaskType* property selects a general pattern from a predefined list—the *MaskedEditType* enumeration:

```
public enum MaskedEditType
{
    None,
    Date,
    Number,
    Time,
    DateTime
}
```

By selecting a mask type, you inform the extender that the target control is going to accept a number, a date, a time, or both. The *Mask* property (of string type) indicates the physical sequence of characters that form a valid input for the text box. For example, *"5/4/08"* and *"04-05-2008"* are both valid dates, but they use different input masks.

To build a mask, you use a few predefined symbols as placeholders. The list of supported symbols is in Table 19-13. For example, the "999,999.99" mask makes your code accept a number with a decimal separator and, at most, a one thousand separator.

TABLE 19-13 Symbols Supported by the *MaskedEdit* Extender

Symbol	Description
9	Indicates a numeric character
L	Indicates a letter
$	Indicates a letter or a blank
C	Indicates a custom case-sensitive character as defined by the *Filtered* property
A	Indicates a letter or a custom character as defined by the *Filtered* property
N	Indicates a numeric or custom character as defined by the *Filtered* property
?	Indicates any character
/	Indicates a date separator according to the current culture
:	Indicates a time separator according to the current culture
.	Indicates a decimal separator according to the current culture
,	Indicates a thousand separator according to the current culture
\	Indicates an escape character
{	Indicates the initial delimiter for repetition of masks
}	Indicates the final delimiter for repetition of masks

The appearance of the currency symbol is controlled by the *DisplayMoney* property, and each character to type is represented by a prompt. The default prompt is the underscore, but you can change it via the *PromptCharacter* property.

For dates, you can also use extra properties such as *AcceptAMPM*, *Century*, and even a custom user format in addition to the predefined formats defined by the *MaskedEditUserDateFormat* enumeration:

```
public enum MaskedEditUserDateFormat
{
    None,
    DayMonthYear,
    DayYearMonth,
    MonthDayYear,
    MonthYearDay,
    YearDayMonth,
    YearMonthDay
}
```

Many of the settings that influence the formatting applied by the *MaskedEdit* extender descend from the current culture. The *CultureName* property indicates the culture to apply. Note that this setting overrides the culture setting defined for the page through the *UICulture* attribute in the *@Page* directive.

While the masked extender provides dynamic formatting capabilities, an additional component—the masked validator—ensures that any text typed can be successfully parsed back to the expected type:

```
<act:MaskedEditValidator ID="MaskedEditValidator1" runat="server"
    ControlExtender="MaskedEditExtender1"
    ControlToValidate="TextBox1"
    IsValidEmpty="False"
    EmptyValueMessage="Number is required "
    InvalidValueMessage="Number is invalid" />
```

The *MaskedEditValidator* control is a custom validator that you optionally attach to the *MaskedEdit* extender so that the content of the edited *TextBox* is carefully verified. The validator ensures that the text matches the mask. The validator performs server and client validation, and it can be associated with a validation group, just like any other ASP.NET validator control.

The *Text* property of a masked *TextBox* returns formatted text. For a date, the property returns something like "05/04/2008"; for a number input field, the property returns text like "3,500.00". The currency symbol is not included in the *Text* property, even though it is shown to the user in the page.

How can you parse the value returned by *Text* into the logical data type—be it a date or a decimal? You can use the static *Parse* method on the *DateTime* and *Decimal* types, but you must pay due attention to the culture you use. For example, "05/04/2008" can be either the 4th of May (US culture) or the 5th of April (European culture).

The issue is that there's no guaranteed matching between the culture used by the input page and the server page. The risk is that users type the date according to the European culture and have it processed on the server as a US culture data. Worse yet, the 3500 value entered using, say, Italian decimal and thousand separators in a numeric text box ("3.500,00") might throw an exception because the parser of the *Decimal* type defaults to the US culture where commas and the dot are reversed. You have to work around these issues programmatically.

The key fact to remember is that extenders default to the *en-us* culture unless the *CultureName* property is explicitly set. On the server, instead, the system defaults to the value of the *UICulture* property on the *Page* class. In your code-behind class, you first obtain a *CultureInfo* object that reflects the culture used for the user interface of the *MaskedEdit* extender. You can proceed as shown here:

```
string culture = "en-us";
if (!String.IsNullOrEmpty(MaskedEditExtender1.CultureName))
    culture = MaskedEditExtender1.CultureName;
CultureInfo info = new CultureInfo(culture);
```

Next, you call the *Parse* method, specifying a format provider based on the selected culture:

```
NumberFormatInfo numberInfo = info.NumberFormat;
DateTimeFormatInfo dateInfo = info.DateTimeFormat;
DateTime when = DateTime.Parse(txtBirthDate.Text, dateInfo);
decimal amount = Decimal.Parse(txtAmount.Text, numberInfo);
```

Figure 19-11 shows the behavior of a page that uses the it-IT culture in the masked editor but an en-US culture on the server. The preceding code snippet performs the trick of transforming dates correctly.

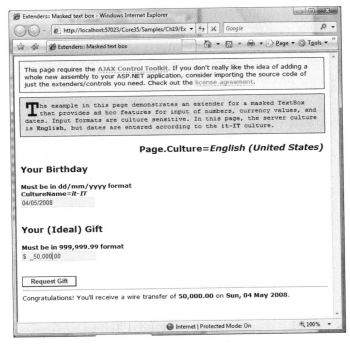

FIGURE 19-11 The *MaskedEdit* extender in action

The *AutoComplete* Extender

Auto-completion consists of the program's ability to predict the word the user is typing from the first few characters he or she has just entered. In Internet Explorer, for example, auto-completion keeps track of any text you type in the address bar and form fields and offers suggestions whenever you're typing again in a similar control. This feature is entirely browser-led and can just be turned on and off for *<input>* and *<form>* tags by setting the *autocomplete* attribute to *off*. Note, though, that the *autocomplete* attribute is not a standard HTML attribute, although today nearly all browsers do recognize and support it.

The *AutoComplete* extender in the ACT provides a similar behavior for *TextBox* controls, but it makes the developer responsible for all the logic that provides possible words to the user. The extender creates a drop-down panel, much like a drop-down list, and positions it right at the bottom of the text box. Here's how to associate an auto-complete extender with a text box:

```
<act:AutoCompleteExtender runat="server" ID="AutoComplete1"
    TargetControlID="TextBox1"
    MinimumPrefixLength="3"
    ServicePath="Suggestions.asmx"
    ServiceMethod="GetSuggestions" />
```

The extender is bound to a Web service or WCF service that actually provides the words to populate the drop-down list. The *MinimumPrefixLength* property instructs the control when to place a call to the Web service—for example, only when the user has typed at least the specified number of characters. The text already typed in will be used as input for the specified Web service method. The response is used to populate the drop-down list.

The *EnableCaching* Boolean property can also be turned on. If you do so, typing the same prefix more than once results in a single call to the Web service. Furthermore, depending on the way the Web service retrieves its data, you also can enable caching on the server to save some extra roundtrips to a database or another remote data store. Table 19-14 shows the full list of properties supported by the extender.

TABLE 19-14 Properties of the *AutoComplete* Extender

Property	Description
Animations	Sets animations to be played when the flyout is shown and hidden.
CompletionInterval	Gets and sets the number of milliseconds after which the extender gets suggestions using the bound Web service.
CompletionListCssClass	Indicates the CSS class used to style the completion list flyout.
CompletionListHighlightedItemCssClass	Indicates the CSS class used to style the highlighted item in the completion list flyout.
CompletionListItemCssClass	Indicates the CSS class used to style the item in the completion list flyout.
CompletionSetCount	Gets and sets the number of suggestions to get from the bound Web service. Default is 10.
ContextKey	String property, indicates any page or user-specific information to pass to the bound Web service.
DelimiterCharacters	Indicates one or more characters that the extender will use to tokenize the text-box content. The Web service will then use the last of these token to provide suggestions. Not set by default.

Property	Description
EnableCaching	Boolean property, indicates whether client-side caching is enabled. *True* by default.
FirstRowSelected	Boolean property, indicates whether the first option in the list will be automatically selected. *False* by default.
MinimumPrefixLength	Gets and sets the minimum number of characters in the text-box buffer that trigger the bound Web service. Default is *3*.
ServiceMethod	Gets and sets the name of the method to invoke on the bound Web service.
ServicePath	Gets and sets the URL of the bound Web service.
UseContextKey	Boolean property, indicates whether the value of the *ContextKey* property should be used, if specified. *False* by default.

A Web service that works with the *AutoComplete* extender is an ASP.NET AJAX script service. It looks nearly the same as a regular ASP.NET Web service, except that its class must be decorated with the *ScriptService* attribute. If you employ a Web service that lacks the attribute, each request to the associated ASMX endpoint originates an HTTP 500 error.

```
[ScriptService]
public class SuggestionService : WebService
{
   :
}
```

The name of any public method on the class that is flagged with the *WebMethod* attribute can be successfully assigned to the *ServiceMethod* property of the extender. A method that provides suggestions must have the following signature:

```
[WebMethod]
public string[] GetCustomerIDs(string prefixText, int count)
```

The first argument is the prefix text to generate suggestions. It matches the current content of the text box and its length is not smaller than the value of the *MinimumPrefixLength* property. The *count* parameter indicates how many suggestions are to be provided. The value of the *count* parameter comes from the value of the *CompletionSetCount* property. The return value is always packed as an array of strings. Because of the *ScriptService* attribute, any communication between the server and client occurs through JSON strings.

You can leverage any supported attributes on Web service methods that will make the call go faster. For example, the *CacheDuration* attribute on the *WebMethod* attribute forces the service to cache internally for the specified duration the response of the method call. Likewise, you can enable session state if it's strictly required by the logic the method implements. See Figure 19-12.

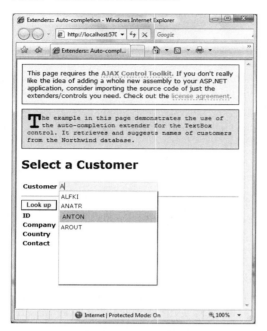

FIGURE 19-12 The *AutoComplete* extender in action

We'll return to the topic of script services and WCF services in the next chapter and discuss the full source for this example.

Adding Safe Popup Capabilities to Web Pages

Dialog boxes are plain windows and can work with or without modality. A *modal window* is a window that disables entirely any visual elements underneath it. The user can't take any action on the current application until he or she dismisses the modal window. The most popular Web counterpart of dialog boxes are popups.

The internal object model of most Web browsers already provides a native API to manage popups, and it supplies methods to open and close such windows with and without modality. Largely abused by some Web sites, popups are blocked by most client browsers and are no longer a valid option to drill down information over the Web. However, this doesn't mean that modal dialog boxes are definitely banned from Web applications.

It is essential to come up with a different implementation of dialog boxes that is as effective as modal popups and totally hassle-free for end users. The problem with classic popups is that they are just additional browser windows adorned with a different set of styles and fully controlled via script. A truly modal Web window, instead, provides you with the same modal effect of classic popups, but it leverages the page's object model rather than the browser's object model.

In the ACT, you find a number of extenders to provide popup functionalities. The most compelling is the *ModalPopup* extender.

The *ModalPopup* Extender

The *ModalPopup* extender adds modality to a piece of markup—typically, a panel. Bound to a button control, it pops up the specified panel and disables the underlying page. Any clicking on anything other than the elements in the topmost panel is lost and never reaches the intended target. *ModalPopup* performs a smart trick by adding an invisible *<div>* tag to cover the entire browser window. This layer swallows any user action and stops it from reaching underlying controls. With clever CSS coding, you can add some nice effects, such as graying out anything underneath the top-most panel, as shown in Figure 19-13.

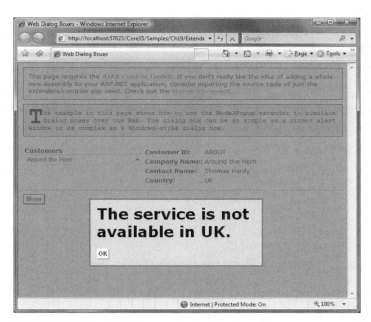

FIGURE 19-13 The *ModalPopup* extender in action

The modal popup extender just takes the markup generated by a server-side ASP.NET panel and shows and hides it as the user clicks on a linked HTML element. Initially styled to be hidden, the markup used for the dialog box is downloaded on the client when the host page is loaded and then shown and hidden on demand.

You start by defining a panel to provide the user interface, and then you add a button control to trigger the display of the dialog box:

```
<asp:Button runat="server" ID="btnViewMore" Text="More" />
<asp:Panel runat="server" ID="pnlViewCustomer">
    <div style="margin:10px">
        <h1>The service is not available in <span id="lblCountry"></span>.</h1>
        <asp:Button runat="server" ID="viewBox_OK" Text="OK" />
    </div>
</asp:Panel>
```

Next, you set up the extender and specify the target control ID and the popup control ID:

```
<act:ModalPopupExtender ID="ModalPopupExtender1" runat="server"
    TargetControlID="btnViewMore"
    PopupControlID="pnlViewCustomer"
    BackgroundCssClass="modalBackground"
    OkControlID="viewBox_OK"
    OnOkScript="allSet()" />
```

The target control ID of a modal popup extender is the ID of the server control that, when clicked, causes the dialog box to pop up. The popup control ID is the ID of the server control that provides the content for the dialog box.

The *OkControlID* property allows you to identify a button control in the popup panel to be used to dismiss the panel with an OK answer. When the panel is dismissed using the OK button, the associated *OnOkScript* JavaScript function, if any is present, is executed:

```
<script>
function allSet()
{
    ...
}
</script>
```

The content of the popup panel can be initialized before display on both the client and the server. On the client, you register a handler for the *showing* event:

```
function pageLoad(sender, args)
{
    $find("ModalPopupExtender1").add_showing(onModalShowing);
}
function onModalShowing(sender, args)
{
    $get("pnlViewCustomer").style.backgroundColor = "yellow";
}
```

On the server, you do it in the code associated with the *Click* event of the trigger button. However, in this case the popup panel must be wrapped in an *UpdatePanel* and brought up programmatically from the server:

```
protected void btnEditText_Click(object sender, EventArgs e)
{
    // Initialize the controls in the panel used as the UI of the dialog box
    InitDialog();

    // The panel markup has already been served to the page. To edit it,
    // you need to wrap the panel's content in an UpdatePanel region and
    // update the panel once you make any changes
    popupPanel.Update();

    // Inject the script to show the dialog as the page is loaded in the browser.
    ModalPopupExtender1.Show();
}
```

There's another trick that contributes to making this code work. The *ModalPopup* extender is bound to an invisible button so that it can never be brought up via the user interface. If you bind the popup to a visible push button, the *Click* server event will never be fired and you have no way to initialize the control in the popup panel. For more information and details on Web dialog boxes, you might want to read the March 2008 installment of my "Cutting Edge" column in MSDN Magazine.

The *PopupControl* Extender

The *PopupControl* extender differs from *ModalPopup* because it can be dismissed by simply clicking outside. The *PopupControl* extender can be attached to any HTML element that fires the *onclick*, *onfocus*, or *onkeydown* events. The ultimate goal of the extender is to display a pop-up window that shows additional content, such as a calendar on a text box in which the user is expected to enter a date. The contents of the pop-up panel are expressed through a *Panel* control, and they can contain ASP.NET server controls as well as static text and HTML elements:

```
<asp:textbox runat="server" ID="txtInvoiceDate" />
<asp:panel runat="server" ID="Panel1">
    ...
</asp:panel>
<act:PopupControlExtender ID="PopupExtender1" runat="server"
        TargetControlID="txtInvoiceDate"
        PopupControlID="Panel1"
        Position="Bottom" />
```

The *TargetControlID* property points to the control that triggers the popup, whereas *PopupControlID* indicates the panel to display. The *Position* property sets the position of the panel—either at the top, left, right, or bottom of the parent control. Additional properties are *OffsetX* and *OffsetY*, which indicate the number of pixels to offset the popup from its position, as well as *CommitProperty* and *CommitScript*, which can be used to assign values to the target control.

The pop-up window will probably contain some interactive controls and post back. For this reason, you might want to insert it within an *UpdatePanel* control so that it can perform server-side tasks without refreshing the whole page. Typically, the popup will be dismissed after a postback—for example, after the user has selected a date in a *Calendar* control. The *Calendar* control in this case fires the *SelectionChanged* event on the server:

```
protected void Calendar1_SelectionChanged(object sender, EventArgs e)
{
    PopupExtender1.Commit(Calendar1.SelectedDate.ToShortDateString());
}
```

The *Commit* method sets the default property of the associated control to the specified value. If you want to control which (nondefault) property is set on the target when the popup is dismissed, use the *CommitProperty* property. Likewise, you use the *CommitScript* property to indicate the JavaScript function to execute on the client after setting the result of the popup.

> **Note** An extender can't be placed in an *UpdatePanel* that is different than the control it extends. If the extended control is incorporated in an *UpdatePanel*, the extender should also be placed in the updatable panel. If you miss this, you get a runtime exception.

The *HoverMenu* Extender

The *HoverMenu* extender is similar to the *PopupControl* extender and can be associated with any ASP.NET control. Both extenders display a pop-up panel to display additional content, but they do it for different events. The *HoverMenu*, in particular, pops up its panel when the user moves the mouse cursor over the target control. The panel can be displayed at a position specified by the developer. It can be at the left, right, top, or bottom of the target control. In addition, the control can be given an optional CSS style so that it looks like it is in a highlighted state. (See Figure 19-14.)

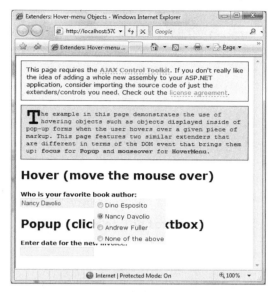

FIGURE 19-14 The *ModalPopup* extender in action

The *HoverMenu* extender is good for implementing an auto-display context menu for virtually every ASP.NET control instance and for providing tips to fill in some input fields. In Figure 19-14, for example, when the user hovers the cursor over the text box, a list of suggestions appears to simplify the work:

```
<asp:TextBox ID="TextBox1" runat="server" />
<asp:Panel ID="Panel1" runat="server" CssClass="popupMenu">
    <asp:RadioButtonList ID="RadioButtonList1" runat="server" AutoPostBack="true"
        OnSelectedIndexChanged="RadioButtonList1_SelectedIndexChanged">
        <asp:ListItem Text="Dino Esposito"></asp:ListItem>
        <asp:ListItem Text="Nancy Davolio"></asp:ListItem>
        <asp:ListItem Text="Andrew Fuller"></asp:ListItem>
        <asp:ListItem Value="" Text="None of the above"></asp:ListItem>
    </asp:RadioButtonList>
</asp:Panel>

<act:HoverMenuExtender ID="HoverMenu1" runat="server"
    TargetControlID="TextBox1"
    HoverCssClass="hoverPopupMenu"
    PopupControlID="Panel1"
    PopupPosition="Right" />
```

The *Panel1* control defines a list of radio buttons, each containing a suggestion for filling the text box. The *HoverMenu* extender targets the text box control and defines *Panel1* as its dynamic pop-up panel. The *PopupPosition* property indicates the position of the panel with respect to the target control. Likewise, other properties not shown in the previous example code, such as *OffsetX* and *OffsetY*, define the desired offset of the panel. The *PopDelay* sets the time (in milliseconds) to pass between the mouse movement and the display of the panel. The *HoverCssClass* can optionally be used to give the text box a different style when the hover menu is on. It is interesting to look at the CSS class associated with the panel:

```
.popupMenu
{
    position:absolute;
    visibility:hidden;
    background-color:#F5F7F8;
}
.hoverPopupMenu
{
    background-color:yellow;
}
```

Just as for the *PopupControl* extender, to take full advantage of the *HoverMenu* extender you need to place extended controls inside of an *UpdatePanel* control. In this way, whenever the user clicks a radio button, the panel posts back asynchronously and fires the *SelectedIndexChanged* event on the server:

```
void RadioButtonList1_SelectedIndexChanged(object sender, EventArgs e)
{
    TextBox1.Text = RadioButtonList1.SelectedValue;
}
```

The server-side event handler will then just update the text in the text box, as shown in Figure 19-14.

The *TabContainer* Control

Multiple views are a common feature in most pages. They group information in tabs and let users click to display only a portion of the information available. In ASP.NET, the *MultiView* control provides an effective shortcut to this feature. But it requires a postback to update the page when the user selects a new tab. In the ACT, the *TabContainer* control provides a free AJAX version of the multiview control.

The *TabContainer* control includes a list of child *TabPanel* objects you can access programmatically via the *Tabs* collection. You add one *<TabPanel>* tag for each desired tab and configure it at will. Here's an example:

```
<act:TabContainer runat="server" ID="TabContainer1">
    <act:TabPanel runat="server" ID="TabPanel1" HeaderText="Your Tab">
        <ContentTemplate>
            <h3>Some text here</h3>
        </ContentTemplate>
    </act:TabPanel>
    ...
</act:TabContainer>
```

All tabs are given the same size, and you can control the size designation through the *Width* and *Height* properties of the container. The height you set refers to the body of tags and doesn't include the header.

You can add some script code to run when the user selects a new tab. You can wrap up all the code in a page-level JavaScript function and bind the name of the function to the *OnClientActiveTabChanged* property of the tab container. The following code writes the name of the currently selected tab to a page element (originally, an ASP.NET *Label* control) named *CurrentTab*:

```
<script type="text/javascript">
    function ActiveTabChanged(sender, e)
    {
        var tab = $get('<%=CurrentTab.ClientID%>');
        tab.innerHTML = sender.get_activeTab().get_headerText();
    }
</script>
```

Note the usage of code blocks in JavaScript. In this way, the client ID of the label is merged in the script regardless of whether the page is a regular page or a content page (with a hierarchy of parent controls and naming containers). Figure 19-15 shows the control in action.

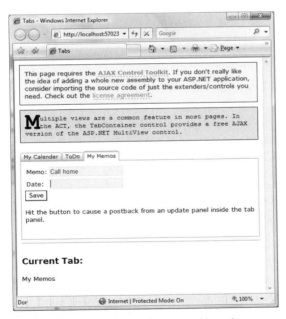

FIGURE 19-15 The *TabContainer* control in action

Conclusion

Partial rendering provides an excellent compromise between the need to implement asynchronous and out-of-band functionality and the desire to use the same familiar ASP.NET application model. As you've seen in this chapter, any ASP.NET page can be easily transformed into an ASP.NET AJAX page. You divide the original page into regions and assign each markup region to a distinct *UpdatePanel* control. From that point on, each updatable region can be refreshed individually through independent and asynchronous calls that do not affect the rest of the page. The current page remains up and active while regions are updated.

Partial rendering doesn't embody the loudly demanded change of paradigm for Web applications. It is limited to making the current Web model more efficient and effective by silently adding more script code and using this script code to hook up some standard browser procedures.

Partial rendering is the quickest way to AJAX and a profitable one too, as long as you are aware of its inherent limitations and know when to choose differently. A different aspect that AJAX-powered pages have when compared to classic ASP.NET pages is the use of more responsive and interactive controls.

No matter how many controls you have in your arsenal, you'll likely always be lacking just the one that is crucial for your current work. That's why the extensibility model of ASP.NET has been so successful over the years, and that's why so many component vendors crowd the market with excellent product offerings.

Anyway, always deriving new controls from existing ones might not necessarily be a wise strategy. A new control is required for a significant piece of server and client code that can be used to back up a good chunk of user interface. If you only need to filter the values in a text box, a custom text box control is hardly the best option. But until the arrival of extenders and the AJAX Control Toolkit, there was no other way out.

With control extenders, you define the concept of a "behavior" and work with it as a distinct entity, set apart from classic server controls. Extenders are server controls, but they work on top of bound controls and improve their overall capabilities by adding a new behavior.

Partial rendering and extenders in the ACT offer a powerful framework for authoring richer pages today, and it requires only limited new skills. True AJAX, though, requires an architectural switch. An AJAX application is articulated in two layers—the front end and back end. For the front end, you mostly have JavaScript and Silverlight in the near future. (I'll cover Silverlight in Chapter 21.) For the back end, you need services. And services are just the topic of the next chapter.

Just the Facts

- AJAX is a term that collectively refers to a set of development components, tools, and techniques for creating highly interactive Web applications that give users an overall better experience.

- AJAX pages work by making out-of-band calls to the Web server using the *XMLHttpRequest* object—a component designed to perform one key operation: —sending an HTTP request either synchronously or asynchronously.

- AJAX raises the need for a more powerful JavaScript language. Entirely written in —standard JavaScript, the Microsoft AJAX Library delivers a richer environment in which to write client-side code with a strong sense of object-orientation.

- Any ASP.NET AJAX page needs a reference to one *ScriptManager* control. The *ScriptManager* control manages and delivers script resources and enables partial-page rendering and Web service and page method calls.

- Partial rendering divides the page into independent regions, each of which controls its own postbacks and refreshes without causing a full-page update.

- You can safely use *UpdatePanel* controls from within master pages and user controls. *UpdatePanel* controls can be nested too.

- The mechanics of asynchronous postbacks keeps the displayed page up and running all the time. Subsequently, users must be prevented from clicking anywhere so that they don't start new (and unwanted) operations.

- Partial rendering is only one possible way to approach AJAX. It preserves most of your current investments and is relatively cheap to implement. Partial rendering adds AJAX capabilities to your pages but doesn't change its basic architecture.

- The AJAX Control Toolkit is a shared-source library of Web controls specifically designed to enhance ASP.NET control. It is not included in the ASP.NET 3.5 platform and should be downloaded separately.

- An ACT extender control represents a logical behavior that can be attached to one or more control types to extend their base capabilities. Extenders decouple controls from behaviors and make it possible to extend existing controls with new behaviors.

Chapter 20
AJAX-Enabled Web Services

The sense of continuity that end users feel when working with AJAX pages, as opposed to the traditional stop-and-go of classic Web pages, is a big step forward for the usability of any application. It is beneficial to users, but it also leads architects and developers to plan more ambitious features and, in the end, to deliver better and richer applications.

At the highest level of abstraction, Web applications are client/server applications that require an Internet connection between the two layers. This connection, though, is incorporated in the special client application—the browser. And the browser clears the user interface before updating the screen with the results of a server operation. To make the usability of Web applications grow as close as possible to that of desktop applications, the overall software platform must fulfill two key requirements. One is a client-side infrastructure that allows for opening and managing the Internet connection with the server. The other requirement is the availability of a public and known programming interface on the server.

The AJAX paradigm is as easy to understand and embrace as it is challenging to implement effectively. The availability of powerful tools and technologies to simplify the development of such applications is a key factor. For the needs of the –server-side of an AJAX application, we do have solid options in the form of ASP.NET Web services and Windows Communication Foundation (WCF) services. As far as the presentation layer is concerned, though, we need to run some client-side code to format data and update the user interface. Because the client is the browser, JavaScript is the only possible programming language. But JavaScript has a number of limitations (performance and leaks in some browser implementations) that make it unfit in scenarios where the client-side is really thick and akin to a smart client. In addition, all that JavaScript can do is target the document object model (DOM). This might not be sufficient to raise the user experience to the level that is required. In a nutshell, this is the big challenge of today's Web platform.

In this chapter, I'll review the technologies for building an AJAX server architecture for ASP.NET applications. For the presentation layer, I'll stick to JavaScript. In the next chapter, I'll review the opportunities being offered by the Silverlight platform for rich Internet client development.

Implementing the AJAX Paradigm

According to the AJAX paradigm, Web applications work by exchanging data rather than pages with the Web server. An AJAX page sends a request with some input arguments and receives a response with some return values. The code in the client browser orchestrates the operation, gets the data, and then updates the user interface. From a user perspective, this means that faster roundtrips occur and, more importantly, page loading is quicker and the need to refresh the page entirely is significantly reduced.

As a result, a Web application tends to look like a classic desktop Microsoft Windows application. It is allowed to invoke server code from the client and run and control server-side asynchronous tasks, and it features a strongly responsive and nonflickering user interface.

Moving Away from Partial Rendering

As we saw in the previous chapter, partial rendering replaces classic full postbacks with partial postbacks that update only a portion of the requesting page. An AJAX postback is more lightweight than a full postback, but a drawback is that the AJAX postback is still a request that moves view state, event validation data, and any other input fields you might have around the page. Also, the AJAX postback is still a request that goes through the full server-side page life cycle. It differs from a regular ASP.NET postback only because it has a custom rendering phase and, of course, returns only a portion of the whole page markup. Put another way, an AJAX postback is definitely faster and much more beneficial than regular postbacks, but it's still subject to a number of constraints. And, more importantly, it doesn't fit just any scenario. To fully enjoy the benefits of AJAX, we have to move past partial rendering and rewrite our applications to use full-fledged behind-the-scenes asynchronous communication and user interface updates.

The Flip Side of Partial Rendering

This isn't to suggest that partial rendering is inherently bad or wrong. There are two opposite forces that apply to the Web. One is the force of evolution signified by AJAX that is geared toward the adoption of new technologies and patterns. The other is the force of continuity that tends to make things evolve without disrupting the neat flow from past to present. In the case of AJAX, the force of continuity is exemplified by ASP.NET partial rendering.

With ASP.NET partial rendering, there's nothing really new architecturally speaking. It's just the same ASP.NET model revamped through a set of tricky solutions that make page rendering smarter and, more importantly, limited to the fragments of the page that really need a refresh.

Partial rendering has inherent limitations and should be considered a short-term solution for adding AJAX capabilities to legacy applications. This said, we can't ignore that a significant share of today's Web applications just need a bit of facelift to look better and run faster. In this regard, partial rendering is the perfect remedy.

The ASP.NET AJAX Emerging Model

The ASP.NET application model based on postback and view state is, technologically speaking, probably a thing of the past. Of course, this doesn't mean that thousands of pages will be wiped out tomorrow and that hundreds of applications must be rewritten in the upcoming months. More simply, a superior model for Web applications is coming out that is more powerful, both technologically and architecturally, and able to serve today's demand for enhancing and enriching the user experience.

The AJAX emerging model is based on two layers—a client –application layer and a server –application layer. The –client layer sends requests to the –server layer and the server layer sends back responses. Server endpoints are identified through URLs and expose data feeds—mostly JavaScript Object Notation (JSON) data streams—to the client. The –server layer is only a façade that receives calls and forwards them to the business layer of the application. Figure 20-1 depicts the entire model.

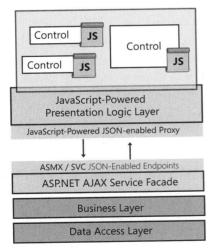

FIGURE 20-1 The ASP.NET AJAX emerging model for Web applications

Let's drill down a bit more in the client layer and –server layer of true AJAX applications for the ASP.NET platform.

Designing the –Client Layer of an ASP.NET AJAX Application

The –client layer manages the user interface and incorporates the presentation logic. How would you code the presentation logic? Using which language or engine? And using which delivery format? For the client layer to really be cross-browser capable, you should use JavaScript and HTML. However, by using JavaScript and HTML you can hardly provide the innovative, immersive, and impressive user experience that many categories of applications loudly demand.

Limits of JavaScript

JavaScript was not designed to back up the presentation logic of Web pages. Originally, it was a small engine added to one of the first versions of Netscape Navigator with the sole purpose of making HTML pages more interactive. Today, it is being used for more ambitious tasks, but it's still nearly the same relatively simple engine created a decade ago.

JavaScript is an interpreted, dynamic-binding, and weakly-typed language with first-class functions. It was influenced by many languages and was designed to look like a simpler form of Java so that it would be easy to use for nonexpert Web page authors.

Worse yet, JavaScript is subject to the browser's implementation of the engine. The result is that the same language feature provides different performance on different browsers and might be flawed on one browser while working efficiently on others. This limitation makes it difficult to write good, cross-browser JavaScript code and justifies the love/hate relationship (well, mostly hate) that many developers have with the language.

Enriching JavaScript

When you move towards AJAX-based architectures, you basically move some of the workload to the client. But on the Web, the client is the browser and JavaScript is currently the sole programming option you have. How can you get a richer and more powerful JavaScript?

At the end of the day, JavaScript has two main drawbacks: it is an interpreted language (significantly slower than a compiled language) and is not fully object oriented. Extending JavaScript is not as easy and affordable as it might seem. Being so popular, any radical change to the language risks breaking a number of applications. But, on the other hand, radical changes are required to meet the upcoming challenges of AJAX.

There exists a proposed standard for JavaScript 2.0 that is discussed in a paper you can download at *http://www.mozilla.org/js/language/evolvingJS.pdf*. And at *http://developer. mozilla.org/presentations/xtech2006/javascript*, you can read Brendan Eich's considerations regarding the feature set in JavaScript 2.0. (Brendan Eich is the inventor of the language.)

It is key to note that the proposed standard is intended, among other things, to achieve better support for programs assembled from components and packaged. Time will tell, however, if and how JavaScript will undergo a facelift. As a matter of fact, from the AJAX perspective JavaScript is at the same time a pillar of the Web but also one of its key bottlenecks.

Using ad hoc libraries (for example, the Microsoft AJAX library) and widgets (for example, Dojo, Gaia), you can mitigate some of the JavaScript development issues and still deploy richer applications. Honestly, there's not much you can do to improve the performance of heavyweight JavaScript pages.

The real turning point for empowering the Web presentation layer is Silverlight 2.0. Silverlight is a cross-platform browser plug-in that brings a fraction of the power of the common language runtime (CLR) and .NET Framework to the browser, including support for managed languages. I'll cover Silverlight in the next chapter.

Limits of the HTML Markup Language

Today's Web pages use HTML to express their contents. But what's HTML, exactly? Is it a document format? Or is it rather an application delivery format? Or is it none of the above? If you look back at the origins of the Web, you should conclude that HTML is a document format designed to contain information, some images and, more importantly, links to other documents.

Today, we use HTML pages with tables, cascading style sheet (CSS) styles, and lots of images for the pictures they contain and to add compelling separators and rounded borders to otherwise ugly and squared blocks of markup. If you're looking for a document format, HTML is outdated because it lacks a number of composing and packaging capabilities that you find, for example, in the Microsoft Office Open XML formats. If you're looking for an application-delivery format, HTML lacks a rich layout model, built-in graphics, and media capabilities.

Just as for JavaScript, though, getting rid of HTML is not a decision to make with a light heart because HTML is popular and used in a wide variety of applications (not just Web pages). Embedding richer content in a thin HTML wrapper might be a good compromise. And, again, Silverlight with its full support for the XAML language and the Windows Presentation Foundation (WPF) engine is the real turning point.

What About AJAX-Specific Controls?

The programming model of ASP.NET pages based on server controls gained wide acceptance and proved to be quite helpful in the past. How are server controls affected by the aforementioned limitations of JavaScript and HTML, and what's the impact of Silverlight on them?

All in all, server controls are orthogonal to JavaScript, HTML, and even Silverlight. Server controls are the programming tools used to generate the delivery format of the application. They can generate HTML as well as XAML (eXtended Application Markup Language, which is the language of Silverlight), and they can support JavaScript as well as Silverlight or managed languages.

Today, a number of commercial products exist to take the user interface of Web applications to the next level. They are all made of a collection of rich and smart server controls that generate HTML and JavaScript. This is to say that it's not by using Telerik or ComponentArt or Infragistics that you work around the issues that slow down the implementation of the AJAX paradigm in the today's Web. Rather, more is required.

A set of lower level tools is required to enlarge the browser's capabilities. This can be obtained in two ways: new browser technology or cross-platform browser extensions (for example., plug-ins). The first option is a utopian plan that would take years to be effective. The second option is what you get with Silverlight.

Designing the –Server Layer of ASP.NET AJAX Applications

There are situations in which the partial-rendering model is not appropriate and other situations in which it is just perfect. When the client requires that a specific operation be executed on the server with no frills and in a purely stateless manner, you should consider options other than partial rendering. Enter remote server method calls.

Making a call to a remote server requires that a public, well-known application programming interface (API) be exposed and made accessible from JavaScript or whatever other programming technology you have available in the browser (for example, Silverlight).

As Figure 20-1 shows, the –server layer of an AJAX application is made of services. But which services?

A Service-Oriented –Server-Side Architecture

The –server layer is easy to devise. It is made of services, and on the ASP.NET platform this can only mean XML Web services or WCF services. Hold on, though. You should take the preceding statement literally because the involvement of XML Web services might take you in the wrong direction.

In the context of ASP.NET AJAX, XML Web services are instrumental to the definition of a public, contract-based API that JavaScript (or Silverlight) code can invoke. It doesn't necessarily mean that you can call just any WS-* Web services from an AJAX client. In the context of ASP.NET AJAX, I suggest you think of Web services as a sort of application-specific façade to expose some server-side logic to a JavaScript (or Silverlight) client.

To be invoked from within an ASP.NET AJAX page, the remote service must meet a number of requirements, the strictest of which relate to the location of the endpoint and underlying platform. AJAX-enabled services must be hosted in the same domain from which the call is made. This means that a Web service must be an ASP.NET XML Web service (an .asmx endpoint) and must be hosted in an IIS application on the same Web server as the ASP. NET application.

From the client, you can't just call any Web services on Earth regardless of location and platform. This is a security measure; not a technical limitation.

In summary, there are three ways to define services for the –server layer of an ASP.NET AJAX application:

- ASP.NET XML Web services with an .asmx endpoint

- WCF services with an .svc endpoint

- Page methods with an .aspx endpoint defined on the same page that calls them

In the rest of the chapter, we'll delve deep into these three options.

Note The term "service" is a bit overused and often abused. In AJAX, a service indicates a piece of code that is local to the application (resident on the domain of the application) and exposes functionalities to the client. In the end, services used by AJAX applications tend not to use Simple Object Access Protocol (SOAP) to communicate (they use JSON) and are not necessarily autonomous services in the service-oriented architecture (SOA) sense. They are instead bound to the platform and the domain where they're hosted. Based on this, they can hardly be called WS-* Web services or SOA services.

REST Services

The ideal service for AJAX applications is centered around the idea of data and resources to expose to Web clients. It is reachable over HTTP and requires that clients use URLs (and optionally HTTP headers) to access data and command operations. Clients interact with the service using HTTP verbs such as GET, POST, PUT, and DELETE. Put another way, the URL represents a resource and the HTTP verb describes the action you want to take on the resource. Data exchanged in those interactions is represented in simple formats such as JSON and plain XML, or even in syndication formats such RSS and ATOM.

A service with these characteristics is a Representational State Transfer (REST) service. For more information on the definition of REST, have a look at the original paper that describes the vision behind it. You can find it at the following URL: *http://www.ics.uci.edu/~fielding/ pubs/dissertation/top.htm*.

Microsoft is currently working on a new generation of data services for the ASP.NET platform that fully embodies REST principles. Such data services are slated to be part of the .NET Framework 3.5 Service Pack 1, which is scheduled to ship sometime in 2008. Meanwhile, you can get the flavor of it using the latest Community Technology Preview (CTP) of the ASP.NET 3.5 Extensions toolkit.

Data Serialization

Needless to say, the communication between browser and remote services occurs over the HTTP protocol. But what about the content of the packets? An AJAX call consist of some data that is passed as arguments to the invoked service method and some data that is returned as the output. How is this data serialized?

The common serialization format that can be understood on both ends is JavaScript Object Notation (JSON). You can learn more on syntax and purposes of JSON at *http://www.json.org*.

JSON is a text-based format specifically designed to move the state of an object across tiers. It is natively supported by JavaScript in the sense that a JSON-compatible string can be evaluated to a JavaScript object through the JavaScript *eval* function. However, if the JSON string represents the state of a custom object, it's your responsibility to ensure that the definition of the corresponding class is available on the client.

The ASP.NET AJAX network stack takes care of creating JSON strings for each parameter to pass remotely. On the server, ad hoc formatter classes receive the data and use .NET reflection to populate matching managed classes. On the way back, .NET managed objects are serialized to JSON strings and sent over. The script manager is called to guarantee that proper classes referenced in the JSON strings—the Web service proxy class—exist on the client. The nicest thing is that all this machinery is transparent to programmers.

The JSON format describes the state of the object as shown here:

```
{"ID"="ALFKI", "Company":"Alfred Futterkiste"}
```

The string indicates an object with two properties—*ID* and *Company*—and their respective, text-serialized values. If a property is assigned a nonprimitive value—say, a custom object—the value is recursively serialized to JSON.

JSON vs. XML

For years, XML has been touted as the lingua franca of the Web. Now that AJAX has become a key milestone for the entire Web, XML is pushed to the side in favor of JSON as far as data representation over the Web is concerned. Why is that?

Essentially, JSON is slightly simpler and more appropriate for the JavaScript language than XML. Although it might be arguable whether JSON is easier to understand than XML for humans—this is just my thought, by the way—it is certainly easier than XML for a machine to process. No such thing as an XML parser is required for JSON. Everything you need to parse the text is built into the JavaScript language. JSON is also less verbose than XML and less ambitious too.

JSON is not perfect either. The industrial quantity of commas and quotes it requires makes it a rather quirky format. But can you honestly say that XML is more forgiving?

With JSON, you also gain a key architectural benefit at a relatively low cost. You reason in terms of objects everywhere. On the server, you define your entities and implement them as classes in your favorite managed language. When a service method needs to return an instance of any class, the state of the object is serialized to JSON and travels over the wire. On the client, the JSON string is received and processed, and its contents are loaded into an array, or a kind of mirror JavaScript object, with the same interface as the server class. The interface of the class is inferred from the JSON stream. In this way, both the service and the client page code use the same logical definition of an entity—or, more precisely, of the entity's data transfer object (DTO).

It goes without saying that, from a purely technical standpoint, the preservation of the data contract doesn't strictly require JSON to be implemented. You could get to the same point using XML as well. In that case, though, you need to get yourself an XML parser that can be used from JavaScript.

Parsing some simple XML text in JavaScript might not be an issue, but getting a full-blown parser is another story completely. Performance and functionality issues will likely lead to a proliferation of similar components with little in common. And then you must decide whether such a JavaScript XML parser should support things such as namespaces, schemas, whitespaces, comments, and processing instructions.

As I see it, for the sake of compatibility you will end up with a subset of XML limited to nodes and attributes. At that point, it is merely a matter of choosing between the "angle brackets" of XML and the "curly brackets" of JSON. Additionally, JSON has a free parser already built into the JavaScript engine—the aforementioned function *eval*.

Web Services for ASP.NET AJAX Applications

Let's start examining the steps required to build an ASP.NET AJAX service using an *.asmx* endpoint. The service is part of a server layer that your pages interact with using JavaScript.

Web Services as Application-Specific Services

ASP.NET doesn't just let you call into any SOAP-based Web services from JavaScript. When you take advantage of AJAX extensions for ASP.NET, you use JavaScript to place calls into some server code within the boundaries your own application and domain. In some way, the application server code must be exposed to the client. The way in which this happens depends on the capabilities of the platform. In ASP.NET 2.0 with AJAX Extensions installed, you can rely only on ASP.NET XML Web services local to the application (as modified to return JSON data). In ASP.NET 3.5, you can also employ WCF services. External Web services—those being services outside your application's domain—cannot be invoked directly from the client for security reasons, neither in ASP.NET 2.0 nor ASP.NET 3.5. This is by design.

By default, ASP.NET Web services work by sending and receiving SOAP packets instead of JSON packets and expose their contract using a Web Services Description Language (WSDL) document. What about ASP.NET XML Web services working in the context of an AJAX application?

The *web.config* file of an ASP.NET AJAX application can modify the HTTP handler that receives *.asmx* requests and redirect these calls to an HTTP handler that understands JSON streams. (I'll return to this point with more details later in the chapter.) This means that an ASP.NET XML Web service can be a dual service and can be able to accept and serve both SOAP and JSON requests. Acting at the configuration level, though, you can disable any SOAP support and hide any WSDL file for public discovery of the service functionalities.

And since I'll be referring to JSON-enabled ASP.NET Web services, from this point forward I'll drop the "XML" since we won't be working with SOAP and XML when invoking ASP.NET Web services. ASP.NET Web services for AJAX applications do not use any SOAP messages.

Defining the Remote API

A contract is used to specify what the server-side endpoints expose to callers. If you plan to implement the service as an ASP.NET Web service, an explicit contract is not strictly required. A contract, instead, is mandatory if you opt for a WCF service in ASP.NET 3.5. All in all, designing the public API as an interface produces cleaner code, which is never a bad thing. When you're done with the interface of the server API, you proceed with the creation of a class that implements the interface. Finally, you publish the remote API and let the ASP.NET AJAX runtime manage calls from the client.

For ASP.NET Web services, you define the contract through a plain interface that groups methods and properties for the server API. Here's an example of a simple service that returns the current time on the server:

```
using System;
public interface ITimeService
{
    DateTime GetTime();
    string GetTimeFormat(string format);
}
```

The contract exposes two methods: *GetTime* and *GetTimeFormat*. These methods form the server API that can be called from within the client.

Warning You are on your own when implementing a given interface in an ASP.NET Web service. There's no automatic runtime check to enforce the requirement that exactly those methods are exposed by the server API.

Implementing the Contracted Interface

After you have defined the server API you want to invoke from the client, you implement it in a class and then bind the class to a publicly addressable endpoint.

An ASP.NET Web service is usually implemented through a .NET class that derives from the *WebService* base class. Here's an example:

```
using System.Web.Services;
public class TimeService : WebService, ITimeService
{
    ...
}
```

To direct the Web service to support a given interface, you simply add the interface type to the declaration statement and implement corresponding methods in the body of the class.

Note that deriving from the *WebService* base class is optional and serves primarily to gain the service direct access to common ASP.NET objects, such as *Application* and *Session*. If you don't need direct access to the intrinsic ASP.NET objects, you can still create an ASP.NET Web service without deriving from the *WebService* class. In this case, you can still use ASP.NET intrinsics through the *HttpContext* object.

Publishing the Contract

Now that we have defined the formal contract and implementation of the server API of an ASP.NET AJAX application, one more step is left—publishing the contract. How do you do that?

Publishing the contract means making the server API visible to the JavaScript client page and, subsequently, enabling the JavaScript client page to place calls to the server API. From the client page, you can invoke any object that is visible to the JavaScript engine. In turn, the JavaScript engine sees any class that is linked to the page. In the end, publishing a given server contract means generating a JavaScript proxy class that the script embedded in the page can command.

When the server API is implemented through a Web service, you register the Web service with the script manager control of the ASP.NET AJAX page. In addition, you add a special HTTP handler for *.asmx* requests in the application's *web.config* file.

Let's expand upon the topic of AJAX Web services development by exploring a few examples.

Remote Calls via Web Services

Web services provide a natural environment for hosting server-side code that needs to be called in response to a client action such as clicking a button. The set of Web methods in the service refers to pieces of code specific to the application.

Creating an AJAX Web Service

A Web service made to measure for an ASP.NET AJAX application is similar to any other ASP.NET Web service you might write for whatever purposes. Two peripheral aspects, though, delineate a clear difference between ASP.NET AJAX Web services and traditional ASP.NET XML Web services.

First and foremost, when working with ASP.NET AJAX Web services, you design the contract of an ASP.NET AJAX Web service to fit the needs of a particular application rather than to configure the behavior of a public service. The target application is also the host of the Web service. Second, you must use a new attribute to decorate the class of the Web service that is not allowed on regular ASP.NET XML Web services.

The effect of this is, in the end, that an ASP.NET AJAX Web service might have a double public interface: the JSON-based interface consumed by the hosting ASP.NET AJAX application, and the classic SOAP-based interface exposed to any clients, from any platforms, that can reach the service URL.

The *ScriptService* Attribute

To create an ASP.NET AJAX Web service, you first set up a standard ASP.NET Web service project. Next, you import the *System.Web.Script.Services* namespace:

```
using System.Web.Script.Services;
```

The attribute that establishes a key difference between ASP.NET XML Web services and ASP. NET AJAX Web services is the *ScriptService* attribute. You apply the attribute to the service class declaration, as shown here:

```
namespace Core35.WebServices
{
    [WebService(Namespace = "http://core35.book/")]
    [WebServiceBinding(ConformsTo = WsiProfiles.BasicProfile1_1)]
    [ScriptService]
    public class TimeService : System.Web.Services.WebService, ITimeService
    {
        ...
    }
}
```

The *ScriptService* attribute indicates that the service is designed to accept calls from JavaScript-based client proxies. If the Web service lacks the attribute, an exception is thrown on the server when you attempt to place calls from your AJAX-enabled client. Figure 20-2 shows the message that is returned when an AJAX page links to a service not flagged with the attribute.

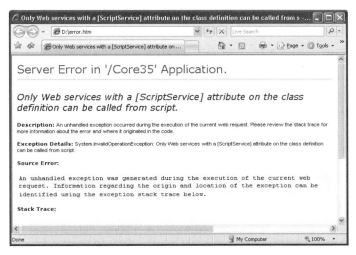

FIGURE 20-2 The result of an ASP.NET AJAX page referencing a nonscriptable service

More precisely, the page shown in the figure is never displayed to any end users. The markup comes with an HTTP 500 error code when access is attempted to a nonscriptable Web service from JavaScript. To get the screen shot in Figure 20-2, I intercepted the HTTP 500 response, saved the body to a local file, and displayed the HTML file in a browser.

The internal ASP.NET machinery refuses to process any calls directed at ASP.NET AJAX Web services that lack the *ScriptService* attribute.

Important You should avoid exposing sensitive pieces of the middle tier to the public without a well-configured security barrier. It is recommended, then, that you add to the Web service only methods that form a sort of user interface–level business logic, where no critical task is accomplished. In addition, you should consider adding a validation layer in the body of Web methods and perhaps using network-level tools to monitor calling IP addresses and, if needed, block some of them. Finally, you can consider SSL/TLS even. That won't preclude unauthorized use, but it helps with snooping when the use is authorized.

Blocking SOAP Clients

Once created, an AJAX Web service is published as an ASMX resource. By default, it's a public URL and can be consumed by AJAX clients, as well as discovered and consumed by SOAP clients and tools. But you can opt to disable SOAP clients and tools altogether. Just enter the following configuration settings to the *web.config* of the ASP.NET application that hosts the service:

```
<webServices>
   <protocols>
      <clear />
   </protocols>
</webServices>
```

This simple setting disables any protocols defined for ASP.NET Web services (in particular, SOAP) and lets the service reply only to JSON requests. Note that with these settings on, you can no longer call the Web service through the browser's address bar for a quick test. Likewise, you can't ask for the WSDL by adding the *?wsdl* suffix to the URL.

Defining Methods for a Web Service

Public methods of the Web service class decorated with the *WebMethod* attribute can be invoked from the client page. Any method is invoked using the HTTP POST verb and return its values as a JSON object. You can change these default settings on a per-method basis by using an optional attribute—*ScriptMethod*.

The *ScriptMethod* attribute features three properties, as described in Table 20-1.

TABLE 20-1 **Properties of the *ScriptMethod* Attribute**

Property	Description
ResponseFormat	Specifies whether the response will be serialized as JSON or as XML. The default is JSON, but the XML format can come in handy when the return value of the method is an *XmlDocument* object. In this case, because *XMLHttpRequest* has the native ability to expose the response as an XML DOM, using JSON you save unnecessary serialization and deserialization overhead.
UseHttpGet	Indicates whether an HTTP GET verb should be used to invoke the Web service method. The default is *false*, meaning that the POST verb is used. The GET verb poses some security issues, especially when sensitive data is being transmitted. All the data, in fact, is stored in the URL and is visible to everybody.
XmlSerializeString	Indicates whether all return types, including strings, are serialized as XML. The default is *false*. The value of the property is ignored when the response format is JSON.

Because of the repercussions it might have on security and performance, the *ScriptMethod* attribute should be used very carefully. The following code uses the attribute without specifying nondefault settings:

```
[WebMethod]
[ScriptMethod]
public DateTime GetTime()
{
    ...
}
```

The *WebMethod* attribute is required; the *ScriptMethod* attribute is optional. You should use the *ScriptMethod* attribute only when you need to change some of the default settings. In general, you should have very good reasons to use the *ScriptMethod* attribute.

Registering AJAX Web Services

To place calls to an ASP.NET Web service from the client, all that you need is the *XMLHttpRequest* object, the URL of the target Web service, and the ability to manage JSON streams. For convenience, all this functionality is wrapped up in a JavaScript proxy class that mirrors the remote API. The JavaScript proxy is automatically generated by the ASP.NET AJAX framework and injected into the client page.

To trigger the built-in engine that generates any required JavaScript proxy and helper classes, you register the AJAX Web service with the script manager control of each page where the Web service is required. You can achieve this both declaratively and programmatically. Here's how to do it declaratively from page markup:

```
<asp:ScriptManager ID="ScriptManager1" runat="server">
    <Services>
        <asp:ServiceReference Path="~/WebServices/TimeService.asmx" />
    </Services>
</asp:ScriptManager>
```

You add a *ServiceReference* tag for each Web service bound to the page and set the *Path* attribute to a relative URL for the *.asmx* resource. Each service reference automatically produces an extra *<script>* block in the client page. The URL of the script points to a system HTTP handler that, under the hood, invokes the following URL:

```
~/WebServices/TimeService.asmx/js
```

The */js* suffix appended to the Web service URL instructs the ASP.NET AJAX runtime to generate the JavaScript proxy class for the specified Web service. If the page runs in debug mode, the suffix changes to */jsdebug* and a debug version of the proxy class is emitted.

By default, the JavaScript proxy is linked to the page via a *<script>* tag and thus requires a separate download. You can also merge any needed script to the current page by setting the *InlineScript* attribute of the *ServiceReference* object to *true*. The default value of *false* is

helpful if browser caching is enabled and multiple Web pages use the same service reference. In this case, therefore, only one additional request is executed, regardless of how many
pages need the proxy class. A value of *true* for the *InlineScript* property reduces the number
of network requests at the cost of consuming a bit more bandwidth. This option is preferable
when there are many service references in the page and most pages do not link to the same
services.

To register AJAX Web services programmatically, you add the following code, preferably in
the *Page_Load* event of the page's code-behind class:

```
ServiceReference service = new ServiceReference();
service.Path = "~/WebServices/TimeService.asmx";
ScriptManager1.Services.Add(service);
```

Whatever route you take, to invoke the Web service you need to place a call to the proxy
class using JavaScript. The proxy class has the same name as the Web service class and the
same set of methods. We'll return to this topic in a moment.

Configuring ASP.NET Applications to Host AJAX Web Services

To enable Web service calls from within ASP.NET AJAX applications, you need to add the
following script to the application's *web.config* file and register a special HTTP handler for
.asmx requests:

```
<httpHandlers>
   <remove verb="*" path="*.asmx" />
   <add verb="*" path="*.asmx"
       type="System.Web.Script.Services.ScriptHandlerFactory" />
   ...
</httpHandlers>
```

This setting is included in the default *web.config* file that Microsoft Visual Studio 2008 creates
for you when you create an AJAX-enabled Web project.

A handler factory determines which HTTP handler is in charge of serving a given set of
requests. The specialized ASP.NET AJAX Web service handler factory for *.asmx* requests
distinguishes JSON calls made by script code from ordinary Web service calls coming from
SOAP-based clients, including ASP.NET and Windows Forms applications. JSON-based requests are served by a different HTTP handler, whereas regular SOAP calls take the usual
route in the ASP.NET pipeline.

Consuming AJAX Web Services

A referenced ASP.NET AJAX Web service is exposed to the JavaScript code as a class with the
same name as the server class, including namespace information. As we'll see in a moment,
the proxy class is a singleton and exposes static methods for you to call. No instantiation is

required, which saves time and makes the call trigger more quickly. Let's take a look at the JavaScript proxy class generated from the public interface of an AJAX Web service.

The Proxy Class

To understand the structure of a JavaScript proxy class, we'll consider what the ASP.NET AJAX runtime generates for the aforementioned *timeservice.asmx* Web service. In the following example, the full name of the Web service class is *Core35.WebServices.TimeService*, and therefore it is the name of the JavaScript proxy as well. Here's the first excerpt from the script injected into the client page for the time Web service:

```
Type.registerNamespace('Core35.WebServices');
Core35.WebServices.TimeService = function()
{
    Core35.WebServices.TimeService.initializeBase(this);
    this._timeout = 0;
    this._userContext = null;
    this._succeeded = null;
    this._failed = null;
}
Core35.WebServices.TimeService.prototype =
{
    GetTime : function(succeededCallback, failedCallback, userContext)
    {
        return this._invoke(Core35.WebServices.TimeService.get_path(),
                    'GetTime', false, {}, succeededCallback,
                    failedCallback, userContext);
    },
    GetTimeFormat : function(timeFormat, succeededCallback,
                            failedCallback, userContext)
    {
        return this._invoke(Core35.WebServices.TimeService.get_path(),
                    'GetTimeAsFormat', false, {format:timeFormat},
                    succeededCallback, failedCallback, userContext);
    }
}
Core35.WebServices.TimeService.registerClass(
        Core35.WebServices.TimeService',
        Sys.Net.WebServiceProxy);
Core35.WebServices.TimeService._staticInstance = new Core35.WebServices.TimeService();
```

As you can see from the prototype, the *TimeService* class has two methods—*GetTime* and *GetTimeFormat*—the same two methods defined as Web methods in the server-side Web service class. Both methods have an extended signature that encompasses additional parameters other than the standard set of input arguments (as defined by the server-side methods). In particular, you see two callbacks to call—one for the success of the call, and one for failure—and an object that represents the context of the call. Internally, each method on the proxy class yields to a private member of the parent class—*Sys.Net.WebServiceProxy*—that uses *XMLHttpRequest* to physically send bytes to the server.

The last statement in the preceding code snippet creates a global instance of the proxy class. The methods you invoke from within your JavaScript to execute remote calls are defined around this global instance, as shown here:

```
Core35.WebServices.TimeService.GetTime = function(
        onSuccess,onFailed,userContext)
{
   Core35.WebServices.TimeService._staticInstance.GetTime(
        onSuccess, onFailed, userContext);
}

Core35.WebServices.TimeService.GetTimeFormat = function(
        format, onSuccess, onFailed, userContext)
{
    Core35.WebServices.TimeService._staticInstance.GetTimeFormat(
        format, onSuccess, onFailed, userContext);
}
```

The definition of the proxy class is completed with a few public properties, as described in Table 20-2.

TABLE 20-2 Static Properties on a JavaScript Proxy Class

Property	Description
path	Gets and sets the URL of the underlying Web service
timeout	Gets and sets the duration (in seconds) before the method call times out
defaultSucceededCallback	Gets and sets the default JavaScript callback function to invoke for a successful call
defaultFailedCallback	Gets and sets the default JavaScript callback function, if any, to invoke for a failed or timed-out call
defaultUserContext	Gets and sets the default JavaScript object, if any, to be passed to success and failure callbacks

If you set a "default succeeded" callback, you don't have to specify a "succeeded" callback in any successive call as long as the desired callback function is the same. The same holds true for the failed callback and the user context object. The user context object is any JavaScript object, filled with any information that makes sense to you, that gets automatically passed to any callback that handles the success or failure of the call.

Note The JavaScript code injected for the proxy class uses the *path* property to define the URL to the Web service. You can change the property programmatically to redirect the proxy to a different URL.

Executing Remote Calls

A Web service call is an operation that the page executes in response to a user action such as a button click. Here's the typical way of attaching some JavaScript to a client button click:

```
<input type="button" value="Get Time" onclick="getTime()" />
```

The button, preferably, is a client button, but it can also be a classic server-side *Button* object submit button as long as it sets the *OnClientClick* property to a piece of JavaScript code that returns *false* to prevent the alternative default submit action:

```
<asp:Button ID="Button1" runat="server" Text="Button"

            OnClientClick="getTime();return false;" />
```

The *getTime* function collects any required input data and then calls the desired static method on the proxy class. If you plan to assign default values to callbacks or the user context object, the best place to do it is in the *pageLoad* function. As discussed in Chapter 19, "Partial Rendering: The Easy Way to AJAX," the *pageLoad* function is invoked when the client page ASP.NET AJAX tree has been fully initialized, and precisely because of this it is more reliable than the browser's *onload* event.

```
<script language="javascript" type="text/javascript">
    function pageLoad()
    {
        Core35.WebServices.TimeService.set_defaultFailedCallback(methodFailed);
    }
    function getTime()
    {
        Core35.WebServices.TimeService.GetTimeFormat(
            "ddd, dd MMMM yyyy [hh:mm:ss]", methodComplete);
    }
    function methodComplete(results, context, methodName)
    {
        $get("Label1").innerHTML = results;
    }
    function methodFailed(errorInfo, context, methodName)
    {
        $get("Label1").innerHTML = String.format(
            "Execution of method '{0}' failed because of the
             following:\r\n'{1}'",
            methodName, errorInfo.get_message());
    }
</script>
```

Because the Web service call proceeds asynchronously, you need callbacks to catch up both in the case of success and failure. The signature of the callbacks is similar, but the internal format of the results parameter can change quite a bit:

```
function method(results, context, methodName)
```

Table 20-3 provides more details about the various arguments.

TABLE 20-3 Arguments for JavaScript Web Service Callback Functions

Argument	Description
results	Indicates the return value from the method in the case of success. In the case of failure, a JavaScript *Error* object mimics the exception that occurred on the server during the execution of the method.
context	The user context object passed to the callback.
methodName	The name of the Web service method that was invoked.

Based on the previous code, if the call is successful the *methodCompleted* callback is invoked to update the page. The result is shown in Figure 20-3.

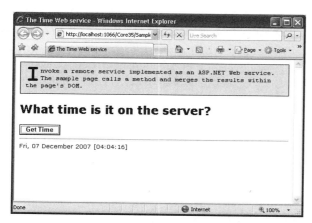

FIGURE 20-3 A remote call made from the client

Error Handling

The "failed" callback kicks in when an exception occurs on the server during the execution of the remote method. In this case, the HTTP response contains an HTTP 500 error code (internal error) and the body of the response looks like the following:

```
{"message":"Exception thrown for testing purposes",
 "stackTrace":"  at Core35.WebServices.MyDataService.Throw() in
            d:\\Core35\\App_Code\\Services\\MyDataService.cs:line
            62","ExceptionType":"System.InvalidOperationException"}
```

On the client, the server exception is exposed through a JavaScript *Error* object dynamically built based on the message and a stack trace received from the server. This *Error* object is exposed to the "failed" callback via the results argument. You can read back the message and stack trace through *message* and *stackTrace* properties on the *Error* object.

You can use a different error handler callback for each remote call, or you can designate a default function to be invoked if one is not otherwise specified. However, ASP.NET AJAX still defines its own default callback, which is invoked when it gets no further information from the client developer. The system-provided error handler callback simply pops up a message box with the message associated with the server exception. If you define your own "failed" callback, you can avoid message boxes and incorporate any error message directly in the body of the page.

Giving User Feedback

A remote call might take a while to complete because the operation to execute is fairly heavy or just because of the network latency. In any case, you might feel the need to show some feedback to the user to let her know that the system is still working. In the previous chapter, we saw that the Microsoft AJAX library has a built-in support for an intermediate progress screen and also a client-side eventing model. Unfortunately, this functionality is limited to calls that originate within updatable panels. For classic remote method calls, you have to personally take care of any user feedback.

You bring up the wait message, the animated GIF, or whatever else you need just before you call the remote method:

```
function takeaWhile()
{
    // In this example, the Feedback element is a <span> tag
    $get("Feedback").innerHTML = "Please, wait ...";
    Core35.WebServices.MySampleService.VeryLengthyTask(
        methodCompletedWithFeedback, methodFailedWithFeedback);
}
```

In the "completed" callback, you reset the user interface first and then proceed:

```
function methodCompletedWithFeedback(results, context, methodName)
{
    $get("Feedback").innerHTML = "";
    ...
}
```

Note that you should also clear the user interface in the case of errors. In addition to showing some sort of wait message to the user, you should also consider that other elements in the page might need to be disabled during the call. If this is the case, you need to disable them before the call and restore them later.

Handling Timeouts

A remote call that takes a while to complete is not necessarily a good thing for the application. Keep in mind that calls that work asynchronously for the client are not necessarily asynchronous for the ASP.NET runtime. In particular, note that when you make a client call to an

.asmx Web service, you are invoking the *.asmx* directly. For this request, only a synchronous handler is available in the ASP.NET runtime. This means that regardless of how the client perceives the ongoing call, an ASP.NET thread is entirely blocked (waiting for results) until the method is done. To mitigate the impact of lengthy AJAX methods on the application scalability, you can set a timeout:

```
Core35.WebServices.MySampleService.set_timeout(3000);
```

The *timeout* attribute is global and applies to all methods of the proxy class. This means that if you want to time out only one method call, you have to reset the timeout for all calls you're making from the page. To reset the timeout, you just set the timeout property to zero:

```
Core35.WebServices.MySampleService.set_timeout(0);
```

When the request times out, there's no response received from the server. It's simply a call that is aborted from the client. After all, you can't control what's going on with the server. The best you can do is abort the request on the client and take other appropriate measures, such as having the user try again later.

Considerations for AJAX-Enabled Web Services

Now that we know how to tackle AJAX-enabled Web services, it would be nice to spend some time reflecting on some other aspects of them—for example, why use local services?

Why Local Web Services?

To make sure you handle AJAX Web services the right way, think of them as just one possible way of exposing a server API to a JavaScript client. You focus on the interface that must be exposed and then choose between ASP.NET Web services, WCF services, and page methods for its actual implementation. Looking at it from this angle, you might find it to be quite natural that the Web service has to be hosted in the same ASP.NET AJAX application that is calling it.

But why can't you just call into any SOAP-based Web services out there? There are two main reasons: security and required support for JSON serialization.

For security reasons, browsers tend to stop script-led cross-site calls. (Not all scripts are benevolent.) Most browsers bind scripted requests to what is often referred to as the "same origin policy." Defined, it claims that no documents can be requested via script that have a different port, server, or protocol than the current page. In light of this, you can use the *XMLHttpRequest* object to place asynchronous calls as long as your request hits the same server endpoint that served the current page.

Because of the cross-site limitations of *XMLHttpRequest* in most browsers, ASP.NET doesn't allow you to directly invoke a Web service that lives on another IIS server or site. Without this limitation, nothing would prevent you from invoking a Web service that is resident on any platform and Web server environment, but then your users are subject to potential security threats from less scrupulous applications. With this limitation in place, though, an additional issue shows up: the inability of your host ASP.NET AJAX environment to build a JavaScript proxy class for the remote, non–ASP.NET AJAX Web service.

> **Note** Because of the impact that blocked cross-site calls have on general AJAX development, a new standard might emerge in the near future to enable such calls from the browser. It might be desirable that the client sends the request and dictates the invoked server accept or deny cross-site calls made via *XMLHttpRequest*. As of this writing, though, the possibility of direct cross-site calls from AJAX clients (not just ASP.NET AJAX Extensions) remains limited to the use of IFRAMEs and finds no built-in support in ASP.NET 3.5.

Why JSON-Based Web Services?

A call to a Web service hosted by the local ASP.NET AJAX application is not conducted using SOAP as you might expect. SOAP is XML-based, and parsing XML on the client is very expensive in terms of memory and processing resources. It means that an XML parser must be available in JavaScript, and an XML parser is never an easy toy to build and manage, especially using a relatively lightweight tool such as JavaScript. So a different format is required to pack messages to be sent and unpack messages just received. Like SOAP and XML schemas together, though, this new format must be able to serialize an object's public properties and fields to a serial text-based format for transport. The format employed by ASP.NET AJAX Web services is JSON.

The client-side ASP.NET AJAX network stack takes care of creating JSON strings for each parameter to pass remotely. The JavaScript class that does that is called *Sys.Serialization. JavaScriptSerializer*. On the server, ad hoc formatter classes receive the data and use .NET reflection to populate matching managed classes. On the way back, .NET managed objects are serialized to JSON strings and sent over. The script manager is called to guarantee that proper classes referenced in the JSON strings—the Web service proxy class—exist on the client.

Runtime Support for JSON-Based Web Services

As a developer, you don't necessarily need to know much about the JSON format. You normally don't get close enough to the heart of the system to directly manage JSON strings. However, a JSON string represents an object according to the following sample schema:

```
{
 "__type":"IntroAjax.Customer",
 "ID":"ANATR",
 "ContactName":"Ana Trujillo"
 ...
}
```

You'll find a number of comma-separated tokens wrapped in curly brackets. Each token is, in turn, a colon-separated string. The left part, in quotes, represents the name of the property; the right part, in quotes, represents the serialized version of the property value. If the property value is not a primitive type, it gets recursively serialized via JSON. If the object is an instance of a known type (that is, it is not an untyped JavaScript associative array), the class name is inserted as the first piece of information associated with the __*type* property. Any information being exchanged between an ASP.NET AJAX client and an ASP.NET AJAX Web service is serialized to the JSON format.

To the actual Web service, the transport format is totally transparent—be it SOAP, JSON, plain-old XML (POX), or whatever else. The runtime infrastructure takes care of deserializing the content of the message and transforms it into valid input for the service method. The ASP.NET AJAX runtime recognizes a call directed to an AJAX Web service because of the particular value of the *Content-Type* request header. Here's an excerpt from the Microsoft AJAX client library where the header is set:

```
request.get_headers()['Content-Type'] = 'application/json; charset=utf-8';
```

The value of this header is used to filter incoming requests and direct them to the standard ASP.NET XML Web service HTTP handler or to the made-to-measure ASP.NET AJAX Web service handler that will do all the work with the JSON string.

WCF Services for ASP.NET AJAX Applications

Starting with ASP.NET 3.5, you can use Windows Communication Foundation to build AJAX-callable services. Overall, the developer's experience is mostly the same whether you use ASP.NET Web services or WCF services. Instead, the richness of the WCF platform—specifically designed to generate and support software services—is a no-brainer. A good question, then, is, "Why weren't WCF services available in ASP.NET AJAX pages before ASP.NET 3.5?"

Before the availability of the .NET Framework 3.5, the WCF platform had no built-in support for taking JSON as input and returning it as output. So what's does the .NET Framework 3.5 really do in the area of WCF? It basically empowers WCF to support JSON serialization. Now WCF services can optionally output JSON, and not always SOAP envelopes, over HTTP. All that you have to do is configure an endpoint to use the *webHttpBinding* binding model and enable Web scripting through a new attribute. I'll provide more detail about this in a moment.

Building a Simple WCF Service

Having always been a huge fan of the bottom-up approach to things, I just can't learn anything new without first testing it in a very simple scenario that then evolves as quickly as possible into a more realistic one. So let's simply create a new Web site in Visual Studio 2008, click to add a new WCF service item, and name the item *TimeService*.

Rewriting *TimeService* as a WCF Service

After confirming the operation, you find your project extended with a service endpoint (say, *timeservice.svc*) and its related code-behind file placed in the *App_Code* folder—say, *wcftimeservice.cs*. In addition, the *web.config* file is modified, too, to provide registration and discovery information for the service being created.

You might want to define the contract for the service by using an interface. This is not strictly required, but it is helpful and also gives you the possibility of implementing multiple contracts in the same actual class.

```
namespace Core35.Services.Wcf
{
    // Contract
    [ServiceContract(Namespace = "Core35.Services", Name="WcfTimeService")]
    public interface ITimeService
    {
        [OperationContract]
        DateTime GetTime();

        [OperationContract]
        string GetTimeFormat(string format);
    }
}
```

In the example, the *ITimeService* interface represents the contract of the service. The *ServiceContract* attribute marks the contract, whereas the *OperationContract* attribute indicates methods. In simpler cases, you can just define a class that is both the contract and implementation. If you do so, you use the *ServiceContract* and *OperationContract* attributes directly in the class.

Pay attention to the *Namespace* and *Name* properties of the *ServiceContract* attribute. They gain additional importance in AJAX-enabled WCF services, as we'll see in a moment. The following code shows a class that implements the *ITimeService* contract:

```
using System;
using System.Runtime.Serialization;
using System.ServiceModel;
using System.ServiceModel.Activation;
using System.ServiceModel.Web;

namespace Core35.Services.Wcf
{
    [AspNetCompatibilityRequirements(
            RequirementsMode=AspNetCompatibilityRequirementsMode.Allowed)]
    public class TimeService : ITimeService
    {
        public DateTime GetTime()
        {
            return DateTime.Now;
        }
```

```
        public string GetTimeFormat(string format)
        {
                return DateTime.Now.ToString(format);
        }
    }
}
```

In the end, the *TimeService* class exposes a couple of public endpoints—named *GetTime* and *GetTimeFormat*.

Registering the Service

The endpoint to reach the methods on this interface are defined in an SVC file, like the *timeservice.svc* file shown next:

```
<%@ ServiceHost Debug="true"
                Service="Core35.Services.Wcf.TimeService"
                CodeBehind="~/App_Code/WcfTimeService.cs" %>
```

The service host, whether it is running in debug or release mode, indicates the location of the source files and the type that implements the service. If the code for the service is placed inline in the SVC file, you must indicate an additional *Language* attribute.

The final step before you can test the service is registering its usage in the *web.config* file of the host ASP.NET application. Here's what you need to have:

```
<system.serviceModel>
    <behaviors>
      <endpointBehaviors>
         <behavior name="TimeServiceAspNetAjaxBehavior">
            <enableWebScript />
         </behavior>
      </endpointBehaviors>
    </behaviors>
    <serviceHostingEnvironment aspNetCompatibilityEnabled="true" />
    <services>
       <service name="Core35.Services.Wcf.TimeService">
          <endpoint address=""
                    behaviorConfiguration="TimeServiceAspNetAjaxBehavior"
                    binding="webHttpBinding"
                    contract="Core35.Services.Wcf.ITimeService" />
       </service>
    </services>
</system.serviceModel>
```

First, you register the list of behaviors for endpoints. In doing so, you define a behavior for your service—named *TimeServiceAspNetAjaxBehavior*—and state that it accepts requests from the Web via script. The *enableWebScript* element is logically equivalent to the *ScriptService* attribute you use to decorate a Web service class for the same purpose.

Next, you list the services hosted by the current ASP.NET application. This preceding *web.config* file has just one service coded in the class *Core35.Services.Wcf.TimeService* with one endpoint using the *ITimeService* contract and the *webHttpBinding* binding model. The *name* attribute must be set to the type of the class implementing the service.

Testing the Service

The service is pretty much all set. How would you use it from the *<script>* section of a client ASP.NET page? The steps required from a developer aren't much different from those required to invoke a Web service. You start by registering the service with the script manager using the SVC endpoint:

```
<asp:ScriptManager ID="ScriptManager1" runat="server">
    <Services>
        <asp:ServiceReference Path="~/TimeService.svc" />
    </Services>
</asp:ScriptManager>
```

When processing the markup, the *ScriptManager* control triggers additional requests to generate and download the JavaScript proxy class for the specified WCF service. The client page uses the proxy class to place calls.

The proxy class is named after the *Namespace* and *Name* properties of the *ServiceContract* attribute of the contract. If you leave the parameters to their default values, the JavaScript proxy class is named *Tempuri.org.ITimeService*, where *Tempuri.org* is the default namespace and the interface name is the default name of the contract.

There's no relationship between the name of the service class and JavaScript proxy class, not even when you use the same class to provide both the contract and implementation of the service. The name of the JavaScript proxy class depends on namespace and name of the service contract. It is common to assign the namespace a unique URI, such as *http://www. Core35-Book.com*. In this case, the name of the proxy class comes out a bit mangled, like *http. www.Core35Book.com*. It is recommended, therefore, that you use plain strings to name the namespace of a contract being used in an AJAX-enabled WCF service.

Let's assume the following, instead:

```
[ServiceContract(Namespace = "Core35.Services", Name="WcfTimeService")]
```

In this case, the following JavaScript can be used to invoke the method *GetTimeFormat*:

```
<script language="javascript" type="text/javascript">
    function getTime()
    {
        Core35.Services.WcfTimeService.GetTimeFormat(
            "dd-mm-yyyy [hh:mm:ss]", onMethodCompleted);
    }

    function onMethodCompleted(results)
    {
        $get("lblCurrentTime").innerText = results;
    }
</script>
```

```
<form id="Form1" runat="server">
    <asp:ScriptManager ID="ScriptManager1" runat="server">
        <Services>
            <asp:ServiceReference Path="~/Services/TimeService.svc" />
        </Services>
    </asp:ScriptManager>

    <h1>What time is on the server? Set your clock...</h1>
    <input type="button" value="Get time" onclick="getTime()" />
    <hr />
    <asp:Label runat="server" ID="lblCurrentTime" />
</form>
```

The JavaScript proxy class is made of static methods whose name and signature match the prototype of the WCF service endpoints. In addition, and like the ASP.NET AJAX Web services, each JavaScript proxy method supports a bunch of additional parameters—callback functions to handle the success or failure of the operation.

ASP.NET Compatibility Modes

When you create a new WCF service for ASP.NET AJAX, the service class is also decorated by default by the *AspNetCompatibilityRequirements* attribute, which deserves a few words of its own.

```
[AspNetCompatibilityRequirements(
        RequirementsMode=AspNetCompatibilityRequirementsMode.Allowed)]
public class TimeService : ITimeService
{
    :
}
```

Although they are designed to be transport independent, when WCF services are employed in the context of an ASP.NET AJAX application, they might actually work in a manner very similar to ASMX services. By using the *AspNetCompatibilityRequirements* attribute, you state your preference of having WCF and ASMX services work according to the same model. One practical repercussion of this setting is that when a WCF service is activated, the runtime checks declared endpoints and ensures that all of them use the Web HTTP binding model.

Their compatibility with ASMX services enables WCF services to access, for example, the *HttpContext* object and subsequently other ASP.NET intrinsic objects. The compatibility is required at two levels. The first level is in the *web.config* file, where you use the following:

```
<system.serviceModel>
  :
  <serviceHostingEnvironment aspNetCompatibilityEnabled="true" />
</system.serviceModel>
```

Second, developers need to explicitly choose the compatibility mode for a given WCF service by using the service *AspNetCompatibilityRequirements* attribute.

Building a Less Simple Service

In Chapter 19, we discussed the *AutoComplete* extender to provide suggestions to users typing into a text box. The extender calls into a service to receive an array of suggestions. The service can be either a scriptable Web service or an AJAX-enabled WCF service. Let's see what it takes to create a helper WCF service for the *AutoComplete* extender.

The *Suggestions* Service

A service for the auto-complete extender can have any number of operations, but all have the same prototype. Here's a possible contract:

```
[ServiceContract(Namespace = "Core35.Services", Name = "SuggestionService")]
public interface ISuggestionService
{
    [OperationContract]
    string[] GetCustomerNames(string prefixText, int count);

    [OperationContract]
    string[] GetCustomerIDs(string prefixText, int count);
}
```

The implementation contains the code to query for customer names and ID and, optionally, for some server-side caching. Here's a fragment of the service class:

```
[AspNetCompatibilityRequirements(
     RequirementsMode = AspNetCompatibilityRequirementsMode.Allowed)]
public class SuggestionService : ISuggestionService
{
    public string[] GetCustomerIDs(string prefixText, int count)
    {
        int i=0;
        DataView data = GetData();
        data = FilterDataByID(data, prefixText);
        string [] suggestions = new string[data.Count];

        foreach (DataRowView row in data) {
            suggestions[i++] = row["customerID"].ToString();
        }

        return suggestions;
    }

    // Other methods here
    ...
}
```

The next step is creating the endpoint for the service. Let's call it *suggestions.svc*:

```
<%@ ServiceHost
    Service="Core35.Services.Wcf.SuggestionService"
    CodeBehind="~/App_Code/WcfSuggestionService.cs" %>
```

At this point, you link the auto-complete extender to the WCF service, as shown next:

```
<act:AutoCompleteExtender runat="server" ID="AutoCompleteExtender1"
    ...
    ServicePath="~/Services/Suggestions.svc"
    ServiceMethod="GetCustomerIDs" />
```

One more step is left—publishing the contract in a service host. For an AJAX-enabled WCF service, the host is Microsoft Internet Information Services (IIS). However, you still need to publish the endpoint.

Service Without Configuration

Publishing a given contract means binding the contract to a public endpoint. This usually requires adding a new *<service>* block in the *web.config* file under the *<services>* section, as shown here:

```
<services>
    <service name="Core35.Services.Wcf.SuggestionService">
        <endpoint behaviorConfiguration="StandardServiceAspNetAjaxBehavior"
                  binding="webHttpBinding"
                  contract="Core35.Services.Wcf.ISuggestionService" />
    </service>
</services>
```

The key thing to notice is that AJAX-enabled WCF services can also be deployed without configuration. All that you have to do is add a new *Factory* attribute to the *@ServiceHost* directive in the SVC file:

```
<%@ ServiceHost
    Factory="System.ServiceModel.Activation.WebScriptServiceHostFactory"
    Service="Core35.Services.Wcf.SuggestionService"
    CodeBehind="~/App_Code/WcfSuggestionService.cs" %>
```

By taking this approach, you do not need to make changes in the *web.config* file, and creating a WCF service for AJAX pages is as easy as creating the class and defining the endpoint.

Data Contracts

Any nonprimitive data to be sent or received over WCF methods must be marked with the *DataContract* attribute. Imagine you have the following service:

```
[ServiceContract(Namespace = "Core35.Services.Wcf")]
[AspNetCompatibilityRequirements(
        RequirementsMode = AspNetCompatibilityRequirementsMode.Allowed)]
public class CustomerService
{
    [OperationContract]
    public CustomerDTO LookupCustomer(string id)
    {
```

```
NorthwindDataContext context = new NorthwindDataContext();
var data = (from c in context.Customers
            where c.CustomerID == id
            select c).SingleOrDefault();
if (data != null)
{
    CustomerDTO dto = new CustomerDTO((Customer)data);
    return dto;
}
else
    return null;
}
}
```

The method *LookupCustomer* is expected to return a custom object. This object must be decorated with ad hoc *DataContract* attributes:

```
namespace Core35.Services.Wcf
{
    [DataContract]
    public class CustomerDTO
    {
        private Customer _c;
        public CustomerDTO(Customer c)
        {
            this._c = c;
        }

        [DataMember]
        public string CustomerID
        {
            get { return _c.CustomerID; }
            set { _c.CustomerID = value; }
        }

        ...
    }
}
```

In this particular case, the class being used over WCF is a data-transfer object (DTO)—that is, a helper class that moves the content of domain model objects across tiers.

> **Note** Could you directly use the *Customer* class obtained from Linq-to-SQL? Yes, as long as the class and its members are flagged with the *DataContract* and *DataMember* attributes. Linq-to-SQL classes as generated by the Visual Studio 2008 O/R designer are kind of anemic objects (only data, no behavior) and, as such, they are just perfect as DTOs. However, you need to make sure that they contain the right *DataContract* and *DataMember* attributes. You can add these attributes automatically by setting the *SerializationMode* property of the data context class to *Unidirectional*. (See Chapter 10, "The Linq-to-SQL Programming Model.")

Remote Calls via Page Methods

As we've seen, Web and WCF services are simple and effective ways of implementing a server API. When the ASP.NET AJAX runtime engine has generated the proxy class, you're pretty much done and can start calling methods as if they were local to the client. Web and WCF services, though, are not free of issues. They require an extra layer of code and additional files or assembly references to be added to the project. Is this a big source of concern for you? If so, consider that you have an alternative—page methods.

Introducing Page Methods

Page methods are simply public, static methods exposed by the code-behind class of a given page and decorated with the *WebMethod* attribute. The runtime engine for page methods and AJAX-enabled Web services is nearly the same. Using page methods saves you from the burden of creating and publishing a service; at the same time, though, it binds you to having page-scoped methods that can't be called from within a page different from the one where they are defined. We'll return later to the pros and cons of page methods. For now, let's just learn more about them.

Defining a Page Method

Public and static methods defined on a page's code-behind class and flagged with the *WebMethod* attribute transform an ASP.NET AJAX page into a Web service. Here's a sample page method:

```
public class TimeServicePage : System.Web.UI.Page
{
    [WebMethod]
    public static DateTime GetTime()
    {
        return DateTime.Now;
    }
}
```

You can use any data type in the definition of page methods, including .NET Framework types as well as user-defined types. All types will be transparently JSON-serialized during each call.

> **Note** The page class where you define methods might be the direct code-behind class or, better yet, a parent class. In this way, in the parent class you can implement the contract of the public server API and keep it somewhat separated from the rest of event handlers and methods that are specific to the page life cycle and behavior. Because page methods are required to be *static* (*shared* in Microsoft Visual Basic .NET), you can't use the syntax of interfaces to define the contract. You have to resort to abstract base classes.

Alternatively, you can define Web methods as inline code in the *.aspx* source file as follows (and if you use Visual Basic, just change the type attribute to *text/VB*):

```
<script type="text/C#" runat="server">
    [WebMethod]
    public static DateTime GetTime()
    {
        return DateTime.Now;
    }
</script>
```

Note that page methods are specific to a given ASP.NET page. Only the host page can call its methods. Cross-page method calls are not supported. If they are critical for your scenario, I suggest that you move to using Web or WCF services.

Enabling Page Methods

When the code-behind class of an ASP.NET AJAX page contains *WebMethod*-decorated static methods, the runtime engine emits a JavaScript proxy class nearly identical to the class generated for a Web service. You use a global instance of this class to call server methods. The name of the class is hard-coded to *PageMethods*. We'll return to the characteristics of the proxy class in a moment.

Note, however, that page methods are not enabled by default. In other words, the *PageMethods* proxy class that you use to place remote calls is not generated unless you set the *EnablePageMethods* property to *true* in the page's script manager:

```
<asp:ScriptManager runat="server" ID="ScriptManager1" EnablePageMethods="true" />
```

For the successful execution of a page method, the ASP.NET AJAX application must have the *ScriptModule* HTTP module enabled in the *web.config* file:

```
<httpModules>
  <add name="ScriptModule"
      type="System.Web.Handlers.ScriptModule, System.Web.Extensions" />
</httpModules>
```

Among other things, the module intercepts the application event that follows the loading of the session state, executes the method, and then serves the response to the caller. Acquiring session state is the step that precedes the start of the page life cycle. For page method calls, therefore, there's no page life cycle and child controls are not initialized and processed.

Why No Page Life Cycle?

In the early days of ASP.NET AJAX (when it was code-named Atlas), page methods were instance methods and required view state and form fields to be sent with every call. The sent view state was the last known good view state for the page—that is, the view state downloaded to the client. It was common for developers to expect that during the page method execution, say, a *TextBox* was set to the same text just typed before triggering the remote call. Because the sent view state was the last known good view state, that expectation was just impossible to meet. At the same time, a large share of developers was also complaining that the view state was being sent at all during page method calls. View state is rarely small, which serves to increase the bandwidth and processing requirements for handling page methods.

In the end, ASP.NET AJAX extensions require static methods and execute them just before starting the page life cycle. The page request is processed as usual until the session state is retrieved. After that, instead of the page method call going through the page life cycle, the HTTP module kicks in, executes the method via reflection, and returns.

Coded in this way, the execution of a remote page method is quite effective and nearly identical to having a local Web service up and running. The fact that static methods are used and no page life cycle is ever started means one thing to you—you can't programmatically access page controls and their properties.

Consuming Page Methods

The collection of page methods is exposed to the JavaScript code as a class with a fixed name—*PageMethods*. The schema of this class is similar to the schema of proxy classes for AJAX-enabled Web services. The class lists static methods and doesn't require any instantiation on your own. Let's take a look at the *PageMethods* class.

The Proxy Class

Unlike the proxy class for Web services, the *PageMethods* proxy class is always generated as inline script in the body of the page it refers to. That's a fairly obvious choice given the fixed naming convention in use; otherwise, the name of the class should be different for each page. Here's the source code of the *PageMethods* class for a page with just one Web method, named *GetTime*:

```
<script type="text/javascript">
var PageMethods = function()
{
    PageMethods.initializeBase(this);
    this._timeout = 0;
    this._userContext = null;
    this._succeeded = null;
    this._failed = null;
}
PageMethods.prototype =
{
    GetTime:function(succeededCallback, failedCallback, userContext)
        {
            return this._invoke(PageMethods.get_path(),
                    'GetTime', false, {}, succeededCallback,
                    failedCallback, userContext);
        }
```

```
}
PageMethods.registerClass('PageMethods', Sys.Net.WebServiceProxy);
PageMethods._staticInstance = new PageMethods();

PageMethods.set_path = function(value) {
    var e = Function._validateParams(arguments,
                                     [{name: 'path', type: String}]);
    if (e) throw e;
    PageMethods._staticInstance._path = value;
}
PageMethods.get_path = function() {
    return PageMethods._staticInstance._path;
}
PageMethods.set_timeout = function(value) {
    var e = Function._validateParams(arguments,
                                     [{name: 'timeout', type: Number}]);
    if (e) throw e;
    if (value < 0)
       throw Error.argumentOutOfRange('value', value,
                                      Sys.Res.invalidTimeout);
    PageMethods._staticInstance._timeout = value;
}
PageMethods.get_timeout = function() {
    return PageMethods._staticInstance._timeout;
}
PageMethods.set_defaultUserContext = function(value) {
    PageMethods._staticInstance._userContext = value;
}
PageMethods.get_defaultUserContext = function() {
    return PageMethods._staticInstance._userContext;
}
PageMethods.set_defaultSucceededCallback = function(value) {
    var e = Function._validateParams(arguments,
                    [{name: 'defaultSucceededCallback', type: Function}]);
    if (e) throw e;
    PageMethods._staticInstance._succeeded = value;
}
PageMethods.get_defaultSucceededCallback = function() {
    return PageMethods._staticInstance._succeeded;
}
PageMethods.set_defaultFailedCallback = function(value) {
    var e = Function._validateParams(arguments,
        [{name: 'defaultFailedCallback', type: Function}]);
    if (e) throw e;
    PageMethods._staticInstance._failed = value;
}
PageMethods.get_defaultFailedCallback = function() {
    return PageMethods._staticInstance._failed;
}

PageMethods.set_path("/Core35/Ch20/CallPageMethod.aspx");
PageMethods.GetTime = function(onSuccess,onFailed,userContext) {
    PageMethods._staticInstance.GetTime(onSuccess,onFailed,userContext);
}
</script>
```

As you can see, the structure of the class is nearly identical to the proxy class of an AJAX Web service. You can define default callbacks for success and failure, user context data, path, and timeout. A singleton instance of the *PageMethods* class is created, and all callable methods are invoked through this static instance. No instantiation whatsoever is required.

Executing Page Methods

The *PageMethods* proxy class has as many methods as there are Web methods in the code-behind class of the page. In the proxy class, each mapping method takes the same additional parameters you would find with a Web service method: completed callback, failed callback, and user context data. The completed callback is necessary to update the page with the results of the call. The other parameters are optional. The following code snippet shows a locally-defined *getTime* function bound to a client event handler. The function calls a page method and leaves the *methodCompleted* callback the burden of updating the user interface as appropriate.

```
function getTime()
{
    PageMethods.GetTime(methodCompleted);
}
function methodCompleted(results, context, methodName)
{
    // Format the date-time object to a more readable string
    var displayString = results.format("ddd, dd MMMM yyyy");
    $get("Label1").innerHTML = displayString;
}
```

The signature of a page method callback is exactly the same as the signature of an AJAX Web service proxy. The role of the *results*, *context*, and *methodName* parameters is the same as described in Table 20-3.

Timeout, error handling, and user feedback are all aspects of page methods that require the same programming techniques discussed earlier for Web service calls.

> **Note** From page methods, you can access session state, the ASP.NET *Cache*, and *User* objects, as well as any other intrinsic objects. You can do that using the *Current* property on *HttpContext*. The HTTP context is not specific to the page life cycle and is, instead, a piece of information that accompanies the request from the start.

Page Methods vs. AJAX-Enabled Services

From a programming standpoint, no difference exists between service methods and page methods. Performance is nearly identical. A minor difference is the fact that page methods are always emitted as inline JavaScript, whereas this aspect is configurable for services.

Web services are publicly exposed over the Web and, as such, they're publicly callable by SOAP-based clients (unless the protocol is disabled). A method exposed through a Web or WCF service is visible from multiple pages; a page method, conversely, is scoped to the page that defines it. On the other hand, a set of page methods saves you from the additional work of developing a service.

Whatever choice you make, it is extremely important that you don't call any critical business logic from page and service methods. Both calls can be easily replayed by attackers and have no additional barrier against one-click and replay attacks. Normally, the view state, when spiced up with user key values, limits the range of replay attacks. As mentioned, though, there's no view state involved with page and Web service method calls, so even this small amount of protection isn't available for these specific cases. However, if you limit your code to calling UI-level business logic from the client, you should be fine.

> **Note** I repeatedly mentioned that AJAX-enabled services, including Web services, are to be considered local to the application. They are in fact application services implemented as ASP.NET Web services because of the lack of alternatives. With ASP.NET 3.5, though, you have the possibility of using WCF services. What if you want to incorporate data coming from a classic WS-* Web service? You can't invoke the Web service directly from the client, but nothing prevents you from making a server-to-server call using the networking API of the .NET Framework.

Conclusion

ASP.NET offers two approaches to AJAX: partial rendering and scriptable services. Of the two, partial rendering is the one with some hidden costs. Although it can still achieve better performance than classic postbacks, partial rendering moves a lot of data around. In the worst cases, the savings in terms of markup are negligible compared to the quantity of bytes moved. On the other hand, AJAX was developed around the idea of making stateless server-side calls from the client and updating the page via the DOM.

Here's where scriptable services fit in. No hidden costs are buried in this model. As in a classic SOAP-powered Web service call, you send in only input data required by the method being invoked and receive only the return value. Traffic is minimal, and no view state or other hidden fields (for example, event validation) are roundtripped. On the down side, remote method calls require JavaScript skills. You control the execution of the method via JavaScript and use a JavaScript callback to incorporate the results in the page.

You need a server API to plan and execute client-to-server direct calls. How do you expose this API? Using a contract that is often implemented through a plain interface. How do you implement such a server API? There are various options: as a local, application-specific Web service, as an AJAX-enabled WCF service, or through page methods. In all cases, the ASP.NET

AJAX client page is enriched with a system-generated proxy class to make calling the server easy and effective.

Once you have a back end based on services, you orchestrate calls to endpoints from the client browser using whatever programming language the browser provides. JavaScript might not always be optimal; Silverlight 2.0 is just around the corner.

In the next chapter, I'll examine the characteristics of a rich browser plug-in—that is, Silverlight 2.0—and also have a look at the less powerful, but still quite useful, Silverlight 1.0.

 ## Just the Facts

- To definitely move away from postbacks, you need the ability to execute server calls from the client. JavaScript and *XMLHttpRequest* provide this ability.

- You need a standard and reliable way of defining the server API—contract-based services are the right way to go.

- ASP.NET AJAX allows you to define the server API using AJAX-enabled versions of ASP.NET Web services and WCF services.

- In the context of a single page, you can also use page methods—namely, public and static methods defined on the code-behind class of a page.

- WCF services are not supported in versions of ASP.NET AJAX older than version 3.5.

- In the latest version of ASP.NET, WCF services can be auto-configurable and don't require you to edit the *web.config* file for IIS to host them successfully.

Chapter 21
Silverlight and Rich Internet Applications

The user's demand for rich Internet-based applications (RIA) is continual and growing; and it can hardly be satisfied with traditional Web tools, techniques, and tricks. The adoption of the AJAX (Asynchronous JavaScript and XML) paradigm is definitely a quantum leap. AJAX solves many problems, but it also raises new ones and brings into focus existing, but partially latent, issues.

One of the most important new issues that AJAX brings up is the development of a rich user interface. In a classic Web scenario, the set of tools you can employ to build a user interface includes the browser's Document Object Model (DOM), cascading style sheet (CSS), and then JavaScript to glue things together. By combining styles, blocks, images, text, and client-side event handlers, smart developers can serve users an attractive and sometimes stunning user interface. Thankfully, most of the underlying technologies (for example, DOM, CSS, JavaScript) are now stabilized and well understood; so Web developers find it easy to arrange even sophisticated user interfaces that work on a variety of browsers on different platforms.

Traditional Web user interfaces, though, are limited to the browser's rendering capabilities and a set of standard HTML tags. To get beyond this point, you need to add power to the browser and possibly in a cross-platform manner. It's not, however, a matter of making one particular browser support a larger and richer set of HTML features. A cross-browser and cross-platform solution to empower or replace the browser's rendering engine is required. For years, Adobe Flash served just this purpose. When a rich, animated, gorgeous, and interactive interface is required, some developers resort to Flash—a cross-platform plug-in that, hosted in the browser, actually replaces the native rendering engine.

The Microsoft answer to users' demands for ad hoc tools for building rich Internet applications is Silverlight. Silverlight places itself in the same product area as Flash, but it is not a standalone product. It comes up with strong connections to ASP.NET AJAX, Windows Presentation Foundation (WPF), the .NET Framework 3.x, and the Expression suite of products. It represents the new Microsoft way of building a compelling user interface for Web applications in a cross-browser and cross-platform scenario. A browser plug-in, Silverlight focuses on .NET Web applications that need media support and sophisticated forms of interactivity.

Silverlight Fast Facts

Formerly code-named *WPF/Everywhere*, Silverlight is a free browser plug-in that is currently available for the Microsoft Windows and Apple Macintosh platforms under the following operating systems:

- Windows Server 2003, Windows Vista, Windows XP, Windows 2000
- Macintosh OS X 10.4.8 and newer for both Power PC–based and Intel-based hardware

Silverlight supports all major browsers available on these platforms (Mozilla Firefox, Netscape Navigator, Apple Safari, Internet Explorer) and offers a consistent experience all the way through.

> **Note** As you can see, there's currently no support for Linux and mobile systems. However, this is not necessarily a situation destined to last for too long. Silverlight support for Linux systems is coming through the efforts of the Mono group. You can read more on the progress by visiting *http://www.mono-project.com/moonlight*. Support for mobile systems is being experimented with at this time.

Named after the idea of lighting up the Web, Silverlight has its real mission explained even more clearly by the code-name WPF/Everywhere. That's what Silverlight really does: it brings the power of WPF—the presentation subsystem of the .NET Framework 3.x—to the Web. Let's learn more about some key Silverlight facts.

Versions of Silverlight

Silverlight is for Web applications and, perhaps in the future, for mobile applications. You use Silverlight to enhance HTML and ASP.NET pages—essentially adding more interactivity, rich text and graphics, and, above all, media capabilities.

There are two versions of Silverlight available with different functionalities and purposes. Silverlight 1.0 is essentially a rendering engine where the support for WPF is limited to two-dimensional (2D) graphics, animation, and media elements. Silverlight 2.0 is the version that provides full WPF support along with an impressive number of programming features.

Silverlight 1.0

Released in September 2007, Silverlight 1.0 is only the vanguard of the Microsoft platform for RIA development. As mentioned, in this version the support for the native WPF document format—the Extensible Application Markup Language (XAML)—is limited to a small subset of tags. You have no data-binding and input features, limited layout capabilities, and no styling. There's support for canvas, basic shapes, gradients, coloring, text blocks, animation, and media playing. In addition, you find an eventing model and, more importantly, a XAML-based document object model is exposed to the hosting page. In this way, you can create some JavaScript functions to handle events from XAML elements and to drive the interaction between XAML elements and page DOM elements.

Although Microsoft is building the new Download Center using Silverlight 1.0, this version of Silverlight is mostly aimed at replacing ActiveX-based media players in current pages and at offering an alternate engine for building and displaying small animations and advertisements in Web pages. Figure 21-1 shows a preview of the new Download Center being built with Silverlight 1.0.

FIGURE 21-1 The new and Silverlight-based Web site for downloading Microsoft products

The plug-in for Silverlight 1.0 is a very small one and measures 1.37 MB in total. Furthermore, it supports auto-installation and points you to the home Web site for automatic download when you navigate to a page that requires the plug-in. (See Figure 21-2.)

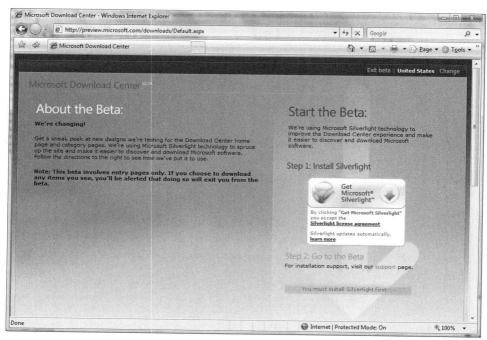

FIGURE 21-2 The interface displayed to users when the Silverlight plug-in is required

Note, though, that the Silverlight plug-in can also be installed offline. You download and save it locally and then run the setup at your earliest convenience. In this case, you don't need to be connected to the network during the setup. It is also possible to distribute the plug-in via CD in large organizations or in all scenarios where network access is limited.

Silverlight 2.0

In the course of 2008, Microsoft is expected to release a second, and largely richer, version of Silverlight. This new version will contain all the features already available in Silverlight 1.0, plus a long list of additions. In particular, Silverlight 2.0 embeds a shrink-wrapped version of the common language runtime (CLR) and an implementation of the upcoming Dynamic Language Runtime (DLR). This means that Silverlight will be able to process compiled code written in a number of managed languages, including C#, Visual Basic .NET, and Managed Jscript. In addition, new dynamic languages will be supported too, such as Python and, likely, Ruby.

Managed code will have access to a notable subset of the .NET Framework that includes Linq-to-Objects and Linq-to-XML; a rich network stack to work with Really Simple Syndication (RSS), "plain old XML" (POX), and JavaScript Object Notation (JSON) data feeds; a comprehensive base class library; and, last but not least, a set of user-interface (UI) controls specifically designed using ASP.NET server controls as a model. We'll return to Silverlight 2.0 programming later in the chapter.

Silverlight and Flash

What kind of applications or pages can you write with Silverlight? You should bear in mind that Silverlight doesn't overcome any of the structural limitations of the Web browser, such as hardware control or file I/O. You should think of Silverlight as a tool to build a rich front end for your Web applications, with or without AJAX capabilities.

You can embed a Silverlight object in existing pages, or you can take a single Silverlight object to cover the whole client area of the browser. In both cases, a comparison with Adobe Flash can't be avoided. Without beating around the bush, Silverlight 1.0 and Flash are direct competitors. Both have pros and cons, and both need to evolve into something different and more programmable to serve as the host technology for a more powerful Web presentation layer.

Programmability

Flash was not designed to be a developer tool. Rather, it is a design tool that developed a programming model. The lack of a proper programming language and development tools is evident as you move up in complexity to create a significant application. Flash is frame oriented, which is great for creating animation, but which turns out to be a real pain in the neck if you try to do something different. On the other hand, Silverlight is built on a more solid foundation—the development tools and languages that thousands of developers are familiar with.

A single project in Visual Studio 2008 can contain all the code for the server components and the client user interface. If you need a special graphics tool, an Expression Blend project can author the markup you need in such a way that it is ready to import into Visual Studio 2008 for further retouching or integration in the project.

Reach and Adoption

As it has already been available for years, Flash is clearly much better positioned as far as adoption is concerned. Silverlight is currently supported on all Windows platforms starting with Windows 2000 Server and Mac. It has not been released yet on Linux, but the porting is under development. It might simply be a matter of time and market penetration. There are no reasons for not having Silverlight on any reasonable platforms. In terms of functionality, there isn't much that Flash does that Silverlight can't do.

Audio/Video

Silverlight supports Windows Media Video (WMV) and Windows Media Audio (WMA) video and audio formats, and it supports the industry-standard VC-1 codec for video. How can you produce these movies? For example, you can use Windows Movie Maker—a part of Windows XP and Windows Vista. If you don't like it, you can always resort to the free Encoder SDK for producing WMA and WMV files. On the other hand, Flash supports multiple video formats, but producing them is not free and requires licensing.

Animation and Graphics

Flash's animation engine is based on transformation matrices. To move an element around, you apply a matrix to it on a per-frame basis. To animate the element for a given number of seconds, you first have to calculate how many frames it will take to move the element for the given interval. Silverlight, instead, supports the WPF animation model. This model is time based instead of frame based. This means that the Silverlight animation model allows you to define the start and end condition of the animation and just takes you there without matrices and frames.

Silverlight stores its graphics objects using XAML—a text-based declarative markup language. You edit XAML files in Visual Studio 2008 or by using any text editors, including Notepad. With Flash, instead, you create your graphics objects using a binary file format for handling, for which you can optionally license a software development kit (SDK).

Note Flash itself is evolving into a richer platform more specifically designed to handle RIA scenarios. For more information, you might want to check out the Flex Web site at *http://www. flex.org*. Flex is a direct competitor to Silverlight 2.0. Flex, however, still inherits some of the limitations of Flash. It does have an improved animation engine, but it still requires that you use ActionScript to code. In addition, it currently requires a Java application server. A porting to the .NET Framework has been announced.

Hosting Silverlight in Web Pages

A Silverlight page is centered on a XAML file. You can build this source file using two development tools—Expression Blend, Visual Studio 2008, or both. Mostly targeted to designers, Expression Blend allows you to create interactive user interfaces and media-rich experiences. With Visual Studio 2008, instead, developers can author XAML script by typing and make it even richer by adding both script and managed code.

A Silverlight page is a Web page that incorporates one or more instances of the Silverlight plug-in. The Silverlight plug-in can be the only element contained in the host page, or the page can contain other ASP.NET controls and HTML literals. The host page can be an HTML, ASP.NET, or even ASP.NET AJAX page.

The Silverlight Engine

To have the Silverlight plug-in active in a Web page, you need to accomplish a few tasks. First, you need to embed the plug-in in the page. Second, you need to run some script code to initialize the plug-in. Third, you need to point the plug-in to the target document it has to display.

This overall set of steps can be executed in different ways and might require you to create some ad hoc JavaScript code or use readymade ASP.NET controls to emit the script code for you. As of ASP.NET 3.5, there are no server controls available to initialize Silverlight while saving you from direct JavaScript exposure. The situation, though, is expected to improve soon—specifically, by the time Service Pack 1 for the .NET Framework 3.5 is released.

The Silverlight Object

The Silverlight plug-in is a binary application hosted by the browser and designed to display the output of a XAML document. The binary application takes different forms based on the target platform and might require different tricks and tags to be successfully embedded in different browsers.

When you install the Silverlight product on a client machine, the binary application is installed and registered with the local system. The Silverlight plug-in is perceived by the browser as an external object to instantiate. To drive the plug-in, Microsoft makes available a helper script file as part of the Silverlight SDK. This file is named *Silverlight.js*. As a developer, you need to copy this file somewhere in your Web site and link it to any Web pages that require Silverlight functionality. You can link *Silverlight.js* using either the old faithful *<script>* tag or the *Scripts* section of the *ScriptManager* control. Following is an example of using the *<script>* tag:

```
<script type="text/javascript" src="Silverlight.js"></script>
```

If you're creating an ASP.NET AJAX page, you can link it through the *Scripts* section of the *ScriptManager* control:

```
<asp:ScriptManager ID="ScriptManager1" runat="server">
    <Scripts>
        <asp:ScriptReference Path="Silverlight.js" />
    </Scripts>
</asp:ScriptManager>
```

The file contains an object named *Silverlight* that contains, essentially, methods to test whether the plug-in is installed and to generate the markup that will incorporate the plug-in in the page. A Web page can contain multiple instances of the Silverlight plug-in, each bound to a different XAML document.

The Script-Behind File

Every Silverlight-powered Web page contains a script function that creates and initializes each instance of the plug-in. The name of the function is arbitrary. The content, on the other hand, takes the following form:

```
function createSilverlightHost()
{
    Silverlight.createObject(
        "page.xaml",
        document.getElementById("SilverlightControlHost"),
        "SilverlightControl1",
        {
            width:'300',
            height:'200',
            version:'1.0'
        },
        {
            onError:null,
            onLoad:null
        },
        null);
}
```

The *createObject* method takes care of embedding the plug-in in the current page as a child of the specified parent element. The parent of the plug-in is the element specified as the second argument of the method. In the preceding example, the plug-in will be inserted in the host page as a child of a DOM element named *SilverlightControlHost*. Most of the time, this element is a *<span>* or *<div>* tag. In particular, it will be a *<span>* tag if you want the plug-in to flow with the rest of the page. It will be a *<div>* tag if you want the plug-in to display as a distinct block in the HTML page.

By convention, the initialization script is persisted in a sort of script-behind file, which is a JavaScript file with the same name as the related page, plus the *.js* extension—for example, *testpage.aspx.js*. Such a script file collects all JavaScript functions that are necessary to the page; for Silverlight-powered pages, there are always quite a few JavaScript functions to track.

Note In a relatively large project where multiple pages use Silverlight, you might want to supply a parametric version of the *createSilverlightHost* that can be reused by multiple pages. Having this alternative available is another good reason for storing the function in a separate JavaScript file instead of embedding it inline in the page.

Where do you invoke the initialization script? A common approach entails that you call the function from within the body of the tag destined to host the Silverlight plug-in, as shown next:

```
<div id="SilverlightControlHost">
    <script type="text/javascript">
        createSilverlightHost();
    </script>
</div>
```

In this way, the script is processed as soon as the browser reaches it during the parsing of the page markup. In ASP.NET AJAX pages, you can call the function from the *pageLoad* function that signals the readiness of a page based on the Microsoft client library for AJAX. (See Chapter 19, "Partial Rendering: The Easy Way to AJAX.")

```
<script type="text/javascript">
    function pageLoad()
    {
        createSilverlightHost();
    }
</script>
```

The script-behind file needs to be linked to the host page in the usual way—either using the *<script>* tag or the *<Scripts>* section of the *ScriptManager* control.

Embedding the Silverlight Object

The *createObject* method of the Silverlight browser object generates the markup for embedding the plug-in in the current browser. How Silverlight is actually embedded in the browser depends on the browser itself. For example, for Safari the *<embed>* tag is used; for all other browsers, the *<object>* tag is used. In both cases, the application type is *application/x-silverlight*. Here's what you might get for Internet Explorer given the previous settings:

```
<object type="application/x-silverlight"
        id="SilverlightControl1"
        width="300"
        height="200"
    <param name="source" value="page.xaml" />
</object>
```

Figure 21-3 shows the dynamic structure of the page document object model once the Silverlight plug-in has been instantiated.

FIGURE 21-3 The DOM of an HTML page that contains the Silverlight plug-in

The ID of the *<object>* tag is determined by another parameter specified in the call to *createObject*. This ID is extremely important because it represents your gateway to programming the content of the Silverlight plug-in.

The API of the *Silverlight* browser is centered on a few static methods: *createObject*, *createObjectEx*, and *isInstalled*. Other methods are available, too, but these are the methods you will more likely use in your coding.

Checking the Installed Version

As the name suggest, the *isInstalled* method gets a string that represents a version number and returns a Boolean answer:

```
if (!Silverlight.isInstalled("1.0"))
    alert("Please, install version 1.0.");
```

Note that the version checked is the minimum version that is checked. In other words, if you have Silverlight 2.0 installed and check for version 1.0, you'll always get a positive answer. You can use this function to disable some features of your pages that require a newer version of the plug-in. The version number is made of four values, as here:

```
versionMajor.versionMinor.buildNumber.revisionNumber
```

However, you normally use only major and minor version numbers.

Instantiating the Silverlight Object

Both *createObject* and *createObjectEx* create a new instance of the Silverlight plug-in and embed it in a Web page. The methods perform the same task, but each one features a different signature. The *createObject* function has the following signature:

```
Silverlight.createObject =
    function(source, parentElement, id, properties, events, initParams, userContext)
    {
      ...
    }
```

Table 21-1 details the various arguments.

TABLE 21-1 Arguments of the *createObject* Function

Parameter	Description
source	Indicates the XAML file providing the content.
parentElement	Indicates the DOM element that will host the Silverlight plug-in. You normally use an empty *<div>* or *<span>* tag for this.
id	Indicates the ID of the Silverlight instance being created. If multiple engines are being used in the same page, it's your responsibility to assign each a unique ID.
properties	Indicates an array of properties to be set on the engine. You set properties using a string-based notation *{prop1:value, ... , propN:value}*. All values are of type *String*. Supported properties are listed in Table 21-2.
events	Indicates an array of events to be handled from within the engine. You set event handlers using a string-based notation *{event1:handler, ..., eventN:handler}*. Supported events are listed in Table 21-3.
initParams	Indicates an optional array of user-defined initialization values to be set on the plug-in's properties. You set these properties using a string-based notation *{prop1:value, ... , propN:value}*. All values are of type *String*.
userContext	Indicates an optional object that will be passed as a parameter to the *load* event handler function for the current instance of Silverlight.

The method automatically detects the underlying browser and determines which technique should be used to instantiate the plug-in. If the plug-in isn't installed, the *createObject* method displays information to the user on how to install it.

The Silverlight engine can be personalized through the set of properties listed in Table 21-2.

TABLE 21-2 Properties Supported by the Silverlight Engine

Property	Description
background	Indicates the background color of the region that displays the Silverlight content. This property is set to white by default.
enableHtmlAccess	Indicates whether the content hosted in the Silverlight control has access to the browser's DOM. This property is set to *true* by default.
frameRate	Indicates the maximum number of frames to render per second. This property is set to 24 by default.
height	Indicates the height of the rectangular region that displays the Silverlight content. The value you set is assumed to be in pixels, but a percentage is also acceptable. This property is set to 0 by default.
ignoreBrowserVer	Determines whether to disable checking for supported Silverlight browsers and browser versions. A value of *true* means that any browser can attempt to display the Silverlight-based application. The default value is *false*, however, which means that only supported Silverlight browsers can display the application. This property can be used only via the *initParams* collection and doesn't have a corresponding runtime property for programmatic access.
inplaceInstallPrompt	Indicates which in-place install prompt should appear if the specified version of the Silverlight control is not installed on the browser. When this property is set to *false*, the standard prompt appears, linking users to the Silverlight download page. When this property is set to *true*, a different prompt appears that lets users install Silverlight in place. This property is set to *false* by default.
isWindowless	Indicates whether the control displays in a windowless manner. When this property is set to *true*, the background property's alpha value (if any) is used to blend the color with the HTML page. The final effect is that the content of Silverlight is more smoothly merged with the page. This property is set to *false* by default.
version	Indicates the Silverlight version required to run the application. The value is compared with the version of the currently installed Silverlight runtime, and the result of the operation determines whether the install prompt is displayed.
width	Indicates the width of the rectangular region that displays the Silverlight content. The value you set is assumed to be in pixels, but a percentage is also acceptable. This property is set to 0 by default.

As you can easily figure out, most of these properties are optional. However, in a realistic page you might want to give an explicit value to *width* and *height*. For Silverlight 2.0 pages, you might want to also indicate a version higher than 1.0.

These properties are used to initialize the Silverlight plug-in, but only a few of them can be retrieved at run time. In particular, you use the *settings* collection on the Silverlight plug-in to retrieve the values of *isWindowless*, *background* and *enableHtmlAccess*. The corresponding runtime properties take the following names: *Windowless*, *Background*, and *EnableHtmlAccess*. (I'll discuss this in more detail later.)

 Note The Silverlight plug-in is hosted in a portion of the container page. However, you can request that the plug-in expand to cover the full browser client area. You get this behavior by setting the *width* and *height* properties to 100%.

The Silverlight plug-in fires a couple of events during its life cycle. Events are listed in Table 21-3.

TABLE 21-3 Events Fired by the Silverlight Plug-in

Event	Description
load	Occurs when the Silverlight plug-in is fully loaded and all the elements in the XAML document are loaded and parsed.
error	Occurs when a parser or runtime error is detected. A default handler is provided to display a message box with a standard error message.

To instantiate the Silverlight plug-in, you also have a second option—using the *createObjectEx* method. Let's take a look at the signature:

```
Silverlight.createObjectEx(propArray)
```

Compared to *createObject*, the method *createObjectEx* doesn't support additional features; it supports only a somewhat different syntax that basically groups all possible individual parameters in a single object. Here's a sample usage of the method:

```
Silverlight.createObjectEx(
    {
        source: 'page.xaml',
        parentElement:document.getElementById("host"),
        id:'SilverlightControl1',
        properties:
        {
            width:'300',
            height:'200',
            inplaceInstallPrompt:false,
            background:'white',
            isWindowless:'false',
            version:'1.0'
        },
        events:
        {
            onError:null,
            onLoad:null
        },
        initParams:null,
        context:null
    }
);
```

The main advantage of using *createObjectEx* is that you don't have to remember the exact position of a given parameter but can resort to a JSON dictionary to package all accepted parameters.

> **Note** As mentioned, the *isWindowless* parameter defaults to *false*, which is a good setting from a pure performance standpoint. However, if you want a transparent background for the Silverlight area, you must set *isWindowless* to *true*. Likewise, if you want to overlay an HTML element on top of the Silverlight plug-in, you must set *isWindowless* to *true*. This is because a windowed control always has a *z-index* of 1 and sits on top of everything else.

Initialization of the Plug-in

The *load* event occurs after the XAML content in the Silverlight plug-in has completely loaded. For this reason, no handler for this event can be attached after the plug-in initialization. Note that the *load* event occurs after any *Loaded* event defined in the source XAML for a user-interface element (for example, *Canvas*, *TextBlock*, or *Rectangle*) has been processed. Here's a sample handler for the *load* event:

```
function pluginLoaded(sender, userContext, rootElement)
{
    alert("Initializing: " + sender.id);
}
```

The *sender* argument identifies the Silverlight plug-in that invoked the event. The *userContext* argument indicates any custom data object specified in *createObject* that you want to send to the event handler. Finally, *rootElement* indicates the root element of the XAML document displayed in the plug-in. Often, this element is a *Canvas*.

When multiple Silverlight plug-ins are defined in the same page, you can use different *load* handlers. There might be situations, though, in which you like to reuse the same handler. In this case, you use the *id* property of the *sender* argument to figure out which plug-in has just been initialized.

Error Handling

To handle any Silverlight errors that occur on your page, you set the *onError* property when you create the plug-in using either *createObject* or *createObjectEx*. The *error* event handler is used for errors that occur during the parsing or loading of the XAML document, runtime errors, and any other errors that are not handled using a *try/catch* block.

The file *Silverlight.js* defines a default *error* event handler that ends up displaying a dialog box like the one you get when you encounter a scripting error in the browser. Figure 21-4 shows a preview.

FIGURE 21-4 The default error handler in Silverlight

Needless to say, you can create your own error handler and assign it to the *onError* property in the *events* parameter of *createObject* or *createObjectEx*. The *error* event handler takes two parameters, as in the following code snippet:

```
function onErrorOccurred(sender, args)
{
    ...
}
```

The *sender* argument represents the object that the error occurred on. The *args* argument is an object of type *ParserErrorEventArgs* or *RuntimeErrorEventArgs*, depending on the type of error. The event data structure returns information about the error type, message, and code. A parser error adds information about the XAML element and position in the file. A runtime error also indicates the method where the error occurred. Here's a sample error handler:

```
function onErrorOccurred(sender, args)
{
    var msg = "Silverlight Error: \n\n";
    msg += "Error Type:    " + args.errorType + "\n";
    msg += "Error Message: " + args.errorMessage + "\n";
    msg += "Error Code:    " + args.errorCode + "\n";
    alert(msg);
}
```

The error event is raised only if the exception is not handled in the code. If you want to wrap some JavaScript code that relates to Silverlight elements in a *try/catch* block, the catch block will receive an error object that contains only a descriptive message and no other information.

Defining XAML Content

The primary goal of the Silverlight plug-in is showing XAML content within a browser on a variety of platforms. XAML is a declarative XML-based language used in Windows Presentation Foundation (WPF) as a language to define user-interface elements, data binding, eventing, and other features. XAML is also used in Windows Workflow Foundation (WF) to persist the definition of a workflow.

Elements of the XAML markup language map directly to CLR objects, and anything that is implemented in XAML can also be expressed using a traditional .NET language such as C#. The main advantage of XAML is the reduced complexity needed for tools to process the content. XAML documents are typically authored using design and developer tools, including Microsoft Expression Blend and Visual Studio 2008. The following code snippet shows a classic "Hello XAML" document:

```
<Canvas xmlns="http://schemas.microsoft.com/client/2007"
    xmlns:x="http://schemas.microsoft.com/winfx/2006/xaml">
    <TextBlock>
        Hello XAML from the Web
    </TextBlock>
</Canvas>
```

To process any XAML content within a Web browser, the availability of a Silverlight plug-in is essential. Current Web browsers, in fact, don't know how to handle a XAML document. For XAML documents, today Web browsers can't do (yet?) what most of them do for XML or RSS data—that is, represent the content in a graphical way using built-in templates.

Downloading XAML Documents

The content for a Silverlight plug-in is passed as an argument to the *createObject* or *createObjectEx* method used to initialize the plug-in. The argument name is *source*, as shown next:

```
Silverlight.createObjectEx(
    {
        source: 'page.xaml',
            ...
    }
    ...
);
```

At run time, you can get and set the URL of the XAML source through the *source* property of the plug-in object:

```
document.getElementById("SilverlightControl1").source = "../xaml/hello1.xaml";
```

If you use a static XAML document, you need to have it deployed to the Web server. The XAML content is downloaded to the client and cached as any other Web resource. Next, the plug-in parses the content and converts it into an object model. Finally, the content is rendered into the browser.

Figure 21-5 shows the aforementioned "Hello XAML" document in action. In the sample code, the *load* event has also been hooked up to display some runtime information, such as the installed version, source, and size of the current plug-in.

FIGURE 21-5 A "Hello XAML" document in a Silverlight-powered browser

Inline XAML

The XAML content can also be embedded in the Web page using a special *<script>* tag with a type of *text/xaml*. From the browser's perspective, this content is nothing more than a data island and, as such, it is blissfully ignored when it comes to render the page.

```
<script type="text/xaml" id="xamlContent">
    <?xml version="1.0"?>
    <Canvas xmlns="http://schemas.microsoft.com/client/2007">
    <TextBlock
      Canvas.Left="20"
      FontSize="18"
      Loaded="setDate">
    </TextBlock>
    </Canvas>
</script>
<script type="text/javascript">
  function setDate(sender, args)
  {
     sender.text += Date();
  }
</script>
```

The first *<script>* element defines the XAML content embedded in the page; the second *<script>* element defines a handler for the *Loaded* event of the *TextBlock*. In this way, the content of the XAML data island is entirely determined programmatically on the client.

How can you bind this chunk of XAML markup to the Silverlight plug-in?

You give the *<script>* tag that contains the inline XAML a unique ID and use that ID prefixed by # as the URL of the document, as shown here:

```
Silverlight.createObjectEx(
    {
        source: '#xamlContent',
        ...
    }
    ...
);
```

It is key to note that the *<script>* tag with the inline XAML content must precede the HTML element that contains the Silverlight plug-in. The XAML just shown appears in Figure 21-6.

FIGURE 21-6 A page with some inline XAML whose content is determined at run time

Dynamically Generated XAML

You use a URL to reference a XAML document from within a Silverlight plug-in. The URL can point to a statically uploaded resource or to an HTTP handler. (See Chapter 18.) that returns a *text/xaml* stream. The code for the HTTP handler is fairly simple:

```csharp
<%@ WebHandler Language="C#" Class="XamlGen" %>

using System;
using System.Web;

public class XamlGen : IHttpHandler
{
    public void ProcessRequest (HttpContext context)
    {
        context.Response.ContentType = "text/xaml";
        context.Response.Write(
            "<Canvas xmlns='http://schemas.microsoft.com/client/2007' " +
            "xmlns:x='http://schemas.microsoft.com/winfx/2006/xaml'>" +
            "<TextBlock Foreground='lime'><Run>XAML content</Run><LineBreak/>" +
            "<Run>[generated at " + DateTime.Now + "]</Run>" +
            "</TextBlock></Canvas>");
    }

    public bool IsReusable
    {
        get {return true;}
    }
}
```

Figure 21-7 shows the page in action.

FIGURE 21-7 Using an HTTP handler to generate XAML content dynamically

XAML content can also be created (or downloaded) on demand and attached to the existing XAML content in the Silverlight plug-in. You parse the content to an object hierarchy using the *createFromXaml* method on the *content* property of the plug-in. Attached to the *load* event of a plug-in, the following function adds a dynamically created *TextBlock* to the current content. As mentioned, the content property represents the gateway to the content of any XAML element hosted in Silverlight.

```
function loaded(sender, userContext, rootElement)
{
    var xaml = '<TextBlock Foreground="white" Canvas.Top="50" Text="Click for more" />';
    textBlock = sender.content.createFromXaml(xaml);

    // Add the XAML fragment as a child of the root Canvas object.
    rootElement.children.add(textBlock);
}
```

The new XAML subtree is added using the *children* property just like browser DOM elements.

> **Note** The *Downloader* is a Silverlight object that provides the ability to download application data—such as XAML, media, or JavaScript content—on demand in response to application needs. This behavior is in contrast to providing the entire application content when the plug-in is instantiated. Any downloaded content can be rendered in the plug-in without having to refresh the entire Web page. The *Downloader* object supports monitoring the progress of the data transfer and can be used in the background to preload content that might be requested later.

The XAML Syntax in Silverlight

Depending on the version of Silverlight you support, you can have a XAML document with a different set of tags. Silverlight 1.0 supports a small subset of the entire XAML syntax, limiting use to a few elements, such as *media*, *rectangle*, *canvas*, *textblock*, and a few more. Silverlight 2.0, which will be released in the course of 2008, is expected to support the full range of XAML elements, thus making it possible to have 100-percent WPF programming over the Web.

Syntax Highlights

XAML is an XML-based language whose tags are used to declare objects in the WPF framework and set their properties. To define an object, you use opening and closing tags and add attributes to set the value of a property:

```
<Canvas xmlns="http://schemas.microsoft.com/client/2007"
        xmlns:x="http://schemas.microsoft.com/winfx/2006/xaml">
   <Rectangle Width="100" Height="100" Fill="Blue" />
</Canvas>
```

Some object properties can also be set using an element-based syntax, especially when they're going to take a nonprimitive value type. To use an element-based syntax, you create XML elements for the property that you want to set, as follows:

```
<Canvas xmlns="http://schemas.microsoft.com/client/2007"
        xmlns:x="http://schemas.microsoft.com/winfx/2006/xaml">
  <Rectangle Width="100" Height="100">
    <Rectangle.Fill>
      <LinearGradientBrush>
        <GradientStop Offset="0.0" Color="Red" />
        <GradientStop Offset="1.0" Color="Blue" />
      </LinearGradientBrush>
    </Rectangle.Fill>
  </Rectangle>
</Canvas>
```

In this case, you're filling the rectangle using a linear gradient brush that ranges from red to blue. Using this technique, the value of the *Fill* property is not merely a solid color as in the previous example. It is, rather, a gradient brush object that needs a more complex initialization than just a color name.

XAML also includes a facility for attaching event handlers to objects in the markup. You provide the name of the event as an attribute name and the name of the handler as its value. The XAML parser reads the handler name and creates a delegate for it:

```
<Canvas xmlns="http://schemas.microsoft.com/client/2007"
        xmlns:x="http://schemas.microsoft.com/winfx/2006/xaml"
        Loaded="onLoaded">
    . . .
</Canvas>
```

In Silverlight 1.0, the handler (the *onLoaded* function in the example) can only be a JavaScript function. In Silverlight 2.0, it can be a function written in a managed language such as C#. In this case, the function will be incorporated in the XAML code-behind class.

The *Canvas* Object

In XAML, the *Canvas* is an object designed to contain and position shapes and objects. In Silverlight 1.0, it is the main container element. Subsequently, every XAML document designed for Silverlight 1.0 contains at least one *Canvas*; and often a *Canvas* is used as the root element. A *Canvas* can contain any number of objects, even other *Canvas* objects.

To position an object in a *Canvas*, you set the *Canvas.Left* and *Canvas.Top* properties on the child object. The following example composes three *Ellipse* elements by placing each 30 pixels from the left and 30 pixels from the top of the Canvas. Each *Ellipse* object is also given a thick border and filled with a solid brush.

```
<Canvas
    xmlns="http://schemas.microsoft.com/client/2007"
    xmlns:x="http://schemas.microsoft.com/winfx/2006/xaml"
    Width="200" Height="200"
    Background="LimeGreen">
  <Ellipse
      Canvas.Left="5" Canvas.Top="5" Canvas.ZIndex="1"
      Height="200" Width="200"
      Stroke="Black" StrokeThickness="10" Fill="Silver" />
  <Ellipse
      Canvas.Left="50" Canvas.Top="50" Canvas.ZIndex="3"
      Height="200" Width="200"
      Stroke="Black" StrokeThickness="10" Fill="DeepSkyBlue" />
  <Ellipse
      Canvas.Left="95" Canvas.Top="95" Canvas.ZIndex="2"
      Height="200" Width="200"
      Stroke="Black" StrokeThickness="10" Fill="Lime" />
</Canvas>
```

Figure 21-8 shows the output of the XAML document after it is embedded in a sample ASP. NET page.

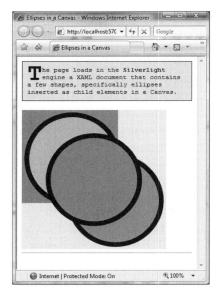

FIGURE 21-8 Shapes in a XAML document

The *ZIndex* property of the *Canvas* object lets you decide which element appears on top of others. The element with the highest z-index is displayed in front.

You size XAML elements using the *Width* and *Height* properties. Sizes are intended to be in pixels, and percentage sizes are not supported. Both *Width* and *Height* default to zero if you do not set them explicitly. Note that this default behavior also applies to the Silverlight plug-in; so if you omit an explicit size all that you have is a 0x0 container for the XAML document.

When a child object exceeds the size of the parent, it is not clipped. Any XAML document gets clipped, instead, if its rendering expands over the declared size of the Silverlight plug-in. The size of the document and the size of the plug-in area are two distinct and independent settings.

Let's see how to create more complex shapes and how to paint with solid colors, gradients, and images.

Graphics and Shapes

In addition to the *Ellipse* object, Silverlight 1.0 also supports other shape elements, such as *Rectangle, Line, Polygon, Polyline*, and *Path*.

A *Polygon* is a closed shape with an arbitrary number of sides, while a *Polyline* is a series of connected lines that might or might not form a closed shape. The *Path* element can be used to represent complex shapes that include curves and arcs. The following example creates a few shapes. (See Figure 21-9.)

```
<Canvas
   xmlns="http://schemas.microsoft.com/client/2007"
   xmlns:x="http://schemas.microsoft.com/winfx/2006/xaml"
   Width="300" Height="300">

   <Polyline Points="150, 150 150, 250 250, 250 250, 150"
      Stroke="Gray" StrokeThickness="5"
      Canvas.ZIndex="3" />

   <Polygon Points="10,10 10,110 110,110 110,10"
      Stroke="Blue" StrokeThickness="10" Fill="LightBlue" />

   <Path Data="M 0,200 L 100,200 50,50z"
      Stroke="LightYellow" Fill="Yellow"
      Canvas.Left="150" Canvas.Top="70" />
</Canvas>
```

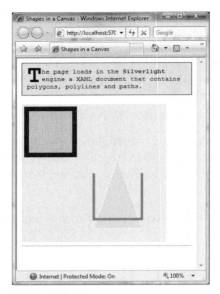

FIGURE 21-9 More complex shapes in a XAML document

To use a *Path* element, you need to get familiar with a special syntax to set the *Data* property. Each letter in the text indicates a command. For example, *M* indicates the starting point, *z* is the ending point, and *L* is a drawing command that renders a line between the specified points. A number of other drawing commands exist to draw curves and other types of lines. The full syntax is described at the following Web site: *http://msdn2.microsoft.com/en-us/ library/bb412389.aspx*.

To fill and outline a shape, you use a brush object. There are a few types of brush objects that you can use: *SolidColorBrush*, *LinearGradientBrush*, *RadialGradientBrush*, and *ImageBrush*.

The *ImageBrush* object uses an image to fill the assigned area. The image is stretched to fill the entire shape, but you can use the *Stretch* property to control how the brush stretches its image.

The *SolidColorBrush* object paints an area with a solid color. You can specify the color by name, such as LimeGreen or Yellow, or by using a hexadecimal notation for the red, green, and blue values of a color, and optionally its transparency. An example is "#0033FF". If you want to add an alpha value, or opacity, you add a leading value, which gives you a final format of #*aarrggbb*.

Gradient brushes fill the area with different colors and apply color transitions in specified points, named *gradient stops*. Most gradients use only two stops, but you can add as many gradient stops as you need. Silverlight supports both linear and radial gradients. A linear gradient is represented by the *LinearGradientBrush* object, which paints a gradient along a line. By default, the line stretches from the upper-left corner to the lower-right corner of the painted object. A radial gradient—the *RadialGradientBrush* object—paints a gradient along a circle centered on the area being painted. In both cases, you can customize the parameters.

The following code shows how to transition the fill of an ellipse from white to a deep blue hue:

```
<Ellipse
   Canvas.Left="50" Canvas.Top="50" Canvas.ZIndex="3"
   Height="200" Width="200"
   Stroke="Black" StrokeThickness="10">
   <Ellipse.Fill>
        <LinearGradientBrush>
            <GradientStop Offset="0.00" Color="White"/>
            <GradientStop Offset="1.00" Color="DeepSkyBlue"/>
        </LinearGradientBrush>
    </Ellipse.Fill>
</Ellipse>
```

In addition you can combine gradients with an opacity mask, as done for the first ellipse in Figure 21-10.

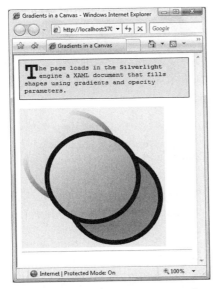

FIGURE 21-10 Gradients to fill XAML shapes

The *OpacityMask* property gains you control over the alpha value of different portions of an element. As a result, you can make an element fade along the line of a linear gradient. To determine which parts of an element are faded, you use a brush. The brush is mapped to the element, and the alpha channel of each of the brush's pixels is then used to figure out the resulting opacity of the corresponding pixels in the element. Typical brushes that you use to create an opacity mask are *LinearGradientBrush* and *RadialGradientBrush*. The transparency effect in Figure 21-10 has been obtained using the following code:

```
<Ellipse
   Canvas.Left="5" Canvas.Top="5" Canvas.ZIndex="1"
   Height="200" Width="200"
   Stroke="Black" StrokeThickness="10" Fill="Silver">
     <Ellipse.OpacityMask>
         <LinearGradientBrush>
             <GradientStop Offset="0.25" Color="#00000000" />
             <GradientStop Offset="1" Color="#FF000000" />
         </LinearGradientBrush>
     </Ellipse.OpacityMask>
</Ellipse>
```

Clipping and Transforming

Another interesting feature is clipping, which you control via the *Clip* property. The property indicates which region of the element should be drawn, and everything that falls outside the region is clipped. You specify the drawing region using a *Geometry* object such as a *RectangleGeometry*. Other geometry objects can be expressed using a *Path*, a *Line*, or an *Ellipse*.

```
<Ellipse Height="200" Width="200"
   Canvas.Left="30" Canvas.Top="30" Canvas.ZIndex="2"
   Stroke="Black" StrokeThickness="10" Fill="Blue">
     <Ellipse.Clip>
         <RectangleGeometry Rect="0, 0, 100, 100"/>
     </Ellipse.Clip>
</Ellipse>
<Ellipse Height="200" Width="200" Canvas.Left="30" Canvas.Top="30"
   Stroke="Black" StrokeThickness="10" Fill="Blue" Opacity="0.3">
</Ellipse>
```

The code snippet shows two overlapping ellipses. The top-most ellipse is clipped using rectangular geometry; the underlying ellipse is given an opacity value to show which part of the top-most ellipse has been cut off. (See Figure 21-11.)

Graphic shapes can be manipulated and moved around to obtain new and more complex shapes. You apply transforms to shapes using the *RenderTransform* property. In particular, you use the *RotateTransform* behavior to rotate an object by a specified degree, as shown next:

```
<Rectangle Height="100" Width="100" Canvas.Left="70" Canvas.Top="10" Fill="Blue">
   <Rectangle.RenderTransform>
     <RotateTransform Angle="45"/>
   </Rectangle.RenderTransform>
</Rectangle>
```

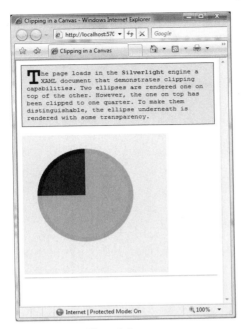

FIGURE 21-11 Clipped shapes

The *SkewTransform* behavior skews an object by the specified amount along the X axis, the Y axis, or both. *ScaleTransform* enlarges or shrinks an object horizontally or vertically by the specified amount. Finally, *TranslateTransform* moves an object horizontally or vertically by the specified amount. You can combine multiple transforms by using the *TransformGroup* object. Figure 21-12 shows the effect of the following changes applied to the ellipses of Figure 21-8:

```
<Canvas Width="510" Height="250"
  xmlns="http://schemas.microsoft.com/client/2007"
  xmlns:x="http://schemas.microsoft.com/winfx/2006/xaml">
    <Canvas>
      <Ellipse
        Canvas.Left="5" Canvas.Top="5" Canvas.ZIndex="1"
        Height="200" Width="200"
        Stroke="Black" StrokeThickness="10" Fill="Silver" />
      <Ellipse
        Canvas.Left="50" Canvas.Top="50" Canvas.ZIndex="3"
        Height="200" Width="200"
        Stroke="Black" StrokeThickness="10" Fill="DeepSkyBlue" />
      <Ellipse
        Canvas.Left="95" Canvas.Top="95" Canvas.ZIndex="2"
        Height="200" Width="200"
        Stroke="Black" StrokeThickness="10" Fill="Lime" />
```

```
        <Canvas.RenderTransform>
          <TransformGroup>
            <TranslateTransform X="-30" Y="40" />
            <SkewTransform AngleX="15" />
            <ScaleTransform ScaleX="1.5" ScaleY="0.6" />
          </TransformGroup>
        </Canvas.RenderTransform>
      </Canvas>
    </Canvas>
```

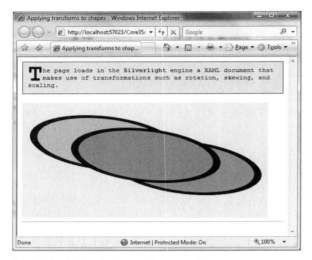

FIGURE 21-12 Applying transforms to shapes

Animation

Silverlight 1.0 allows you to animate user-interface elements using XAML instructions. To start out, you need to assign a unique name to elements that need be animated. You use the *x:Name* property:

```
<Ellipse x:Name="Lime" ... />
```

Next, you define an event that triggers the animation of the named objects. To define an event trigger, you use the *EventTrigger* object and associate it with a list of actions. An animation is defined by a storyboard:

```
<Canvas.Triggers>
    <EventTrigger RoutedEvent="Canvas.Loaded">
        <EventTrigger.Actions>
            <BeginStoryboard>
                <!-- Storyboard goes here -->
            </BeginStoryboard>
        </EventTrigger.Actions>
    </EventTrigger>
</Canvas.Triggers>
```

Given the preceding code, the animation begins when the *Loaded* event is fired for the *Canvas*. In Silverlight, you animate objects by defining a range of values for one or more properties. The system takes care of changing values in the range, thus animating the object.

You have to specify the object that is the target of the animation and the property being animated. You can also optionally indicate duration for the animation and whether the animation has to be repeated. Based on the data type of the property being animated, a few different types of animation classes have been defined. You have *DoubleAnimation* for double types, *ColorAnimation* for colors, and *PointAnimation* for varying the value of a *Point* property between two target values using linear interpolation. You should note that the WPF full syntax supports much larger set animation components. Only these three types are supported in Silverlight 1.0. Among other things, this means that you can't use animation on integer properties such as *ZIndex*.

The following code produces an animation to get the same content of Figure 21-12. The three ellipses are named after their fill color (*Silver*, *DeepSkyBlue*, and *Lime*). In particular, the width of the three ellipses is animated from 0 to the actual value in just one second. At the same time, the *Left* or *Top* property ranges from a value outside the canvas to the actual position.

```
<Storyboard>
  <DoubleAnimation
    Storyboard.TargetName="DeepSkyBlue"
    Storyboard.TargetProperty="(Width)"
    From="0" Duration="0:0:1" />
  <DoubleAnimation
    Storyboard.TargetName="Silver"
    Storyboard.TargetProperty="(Width)"
    From="0" Duration="0:0:1" />
  <DoubleAnimation
    Storyboard.TargetName="Lime"
    Storyboard.TargetProperty="(Width)"
    From="0" Duration="0:0:1" />
  <DoubleAnimation
    Storyboard.TargetName="Lime"
    Storyboard.TargetProperty="(Canvas.Left)"
    From="-20" Duration="0:0:1" />
  <DoubleAnimation
    Storyboard.TargetName="Silver"
    Storyboard.TargetProperty="(Canvas.Left)"
    From="-20" Duration="0:0:1" />
  <DoubleAnimation
    Storyboard.TargetName="DeepSkyBlue"
    Storyboard.TargetProperty="(Canvas.Top)"
    From="-20" Duration="0:0:1" />
</Storyboard>
```

On the *Storyboard* object, the *TargetName* and *TargetProperty* properties identify the object and property being animated, respectively. Figure 21-13 shows a frame of the preceding animation.

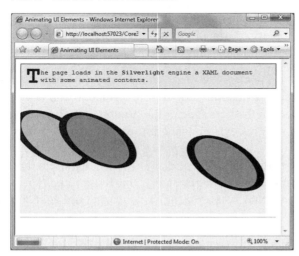

FIGURE 21-13 An ongoing animation

What we considered so far is the simplest type of Silverlight animation, also known as a *From/To/By* animation. A second type of animation is supported, and its name is *key-frame* animation. Both types animate the value of a target property. However, while a From/To/By animation creates a transition between two values, a key-frame animation creates transitions among any number of target values.

The following code snippet shows a storyboard where you move a rectangle around the area and the animation runs each step at a given time. Key-frame and double animations can be combined and occur simultaneously. In the following example, in fact, the rectangle *MyRect* gets wider as it is being moved:

```
<Storyboard>
  <DoubleAnimationUsingKeyFrames
    Storyboard.TargetName="MyAnimatedTranslateTransform"
    Storyboard.TargetProperty="X"
    Duration="0:0:10">
      <LinearDoubleKeyFrame Value="0" KeyTime="0:0:0" />
      <LinearDoubleKeyFrame Value="350" KeyTime="0:0:2" />
      <LinearDoubleKeyFrame Value="50" KeyTime="0:0:7" />
      <LinearDoubleKeyFrame Value="200" KeyTime="0:0:8" />
  </DoubleAnimationUsingKeyFrames>
  <DoubleAnimation
    Storyboard.TargetName="MyRect"
    Storyboard.TargetProperty="(Width)"
    To="150"
    Duration="0:0:1" />
</Storyboard>
```

Note Animations can be controlled programmatically using a scripting object model. In particular, you can start, stop, and pause animations using JavaScript code.

Text

Silverlight 1.0 allows you to add text to your documents using the *TextBlock* element. The simplest way to display some text in a Silverlight 1.0 plug-in is the following:

```
<Canvas xmlns="http://schemas.microsoft.com/client/2007">
  <TextBlock>Hello, world!</TextBlock>
</Canvas>
```

You can specify a number of font attributes, including the font family, size, style, weight, and stretch. Downloadable fonts, which are downloaded and installed on demand can also be used.

The text associated with a *TextBlock* element can be expressed as inline content or assigned to the *Text* property. The text can be broken into pieces using the *Run* and *LineBreak* elements. In particular, the *Run* object is a text element that represents a discrete section of formatted or unformatted text. The *LineBreak* object represents an explicit new line. You typically use the *Run* element when you need to apply different settings to portions of text.

```
<TextBlock Canvas.Left="25" Canvas.Top="10" FontFamily="Verdana"
  FontWeight="Bold" Text="PROGRAMMING ASP.NET 3.5">
    <LineBreak/>
    <Run Foreground="Teal" FontFamily="Verdana" FontSize="24">
       Core Reference
    </Run>
    <LineBreak/>
    <Run Foreground="Teal" FontFamily="Verdana" FontSize="18"
      FontStyle="Italic">
       Dino Esposito,
    </Run>
    <Run Foreground="SteelBlue" FontFamily="Verdana" FontSize="18">
       Microsoft Press, 2008
    </Run>
</TextBlock>
```

To color the text, you can use a solid color set through the *Foreground* property or gradient brush, as shown here:

```
<TextBlock Text=" ... ">
    <TextBlock.Foreground>
        <LinearGradientBrush StartPoint="0,0" EndPoint="1,1">
            <GradientStop Color="Red" Offset="0.0" />
            <GradientStop Color="Orange" Offset="0.2" />
            <GradientStop Color="Yellow" Offset="0.4" />
            <GradientStop Color="Green" Offset="0.6" />
            <GradientStop Color="Blue" Offset="0.8" />
            <GradientStop Color="Violet" Offset="1.0" />
        </LinearGradientBrush>
    </TextBlock.Foreground>
    <TextBlock.RenderTransform>
            <ScaleTransform ScaleY="2.0" />
    </TextBlock.RenderTransform>
</TextBlock>
```

Text can further be styled using rotation and scaling. In particular, scaling can be a better approach than font size to choose the right height of the text.

Multimedia

Silverlight 1.0 can play media content without the support of any external player. You add media content to a page via the *MediaElement* object:

```
<Canvas xmlns="http://schemas.microsoft.com/client/2007" Width="300" Height="300">
  <MediaElement Source="FedExpress.wmv" Width="300" Height="300" />
</Canvas>
```

The *MediaElement* object can play WMV, WMA, MP3 files, and files encoded with VC-1 regardless of the file extension. *MediaElement* also supports playlists in the form of Advanced Stream Redirector (ASX) and on-demand and live streaming from a Windows Media server.

The media object can be controlled programmatically and started, stopped, and paused at will. In Silverlight 1.0, this code can be written only in JavaScript.

The Silverlight Object Model

The content of a XAML file doesn't have to be static and read only. With some JavaScript code, for example, you can make it react to runtime events. The script code can affect it in either of two ways. First, the script code can be embedded in the XAML and essentially handle events raised by XAML elements. Second, the script code is part of the host page and is used to get and set values on the public properties of XAML elements.

Silverlight Programming Fundamentals

Even in the simplified version of XAML you have in Silverlight 1.0, the XAML language is a real application-delivery format and a much more powerful option than a simple document format such as HTML. With XAML, you can easily embed graphics and media capabilities in your pages, thus making up for two of the major points of weakness of HTML.

Even the full syntax of XAML, though, is limited without user-defined code to script the object model of the user-interface elements. When hosted in a Silverlight plug-in, the XAML content originates a document object model that developers and designers can consume to catch events and trigger special behaviors.

At the same time, when the *enableHtmlAccess* property is enabled on the plug-in object, the XAML document object model is made visible to HTML DOM elements, meaning that any page-level JavaScript code can dynamically alter both the structure and the content of the XAML document.

Referencing Objects

The Silverlight plug-in is referenced just like any other HTML element in the page. The ID of the Silverlight plug-in is defined as an argument to the *createObject* or *createObjectEx* methods used to instantiate it. Once you know this ID, the following code can be used to get a reference to the plug-in:

```
var plugin = document.getElementById("SilverlightControl1");
```

In an ASP.NET AJAX page, you can also use the popular *$get* shorthand:

```
var plugin = $get("SilverlightControl1");
```

The content of the document hosted in the plug-in is reached through the *content* property:

```
var root = plugin.content;
```

Finally, the *findName* method can be used to find a particular element in the XAML document regardless of the position. The method performs a recursive search in the specified subtree:

```
var textBlock = plugin.content.findName("status");
```

The preceding line looks for an element named *status* located anywhere in the XAML document. Note that if you call the method *findName* on content, you conduct a search on the full document. If you call *findName* on a child object, you then conduct the search on the XAML subtree rooted in the specified object. The *findName* method can retrieve only XAML elements with a unique given name. You name an element using the *x:Name* attribute in the source XAML.

The Silverlight Eventing Model

The events you can catch on Silverlight's user-interface elements are listed in Table 21-4. The list includes mouse and keyboard input, plus a couple of other events. In addition, *Image* and *MediaElement* objects fire their own specific events.

TABLE 21-4 Events Common to User Interface Elements

Event	Description
Loaded	Occurs when the element is loaded
MouseEnter	Occurs when the mouse cursor enters the area of a particular XAML object
MouseLeave	Occurs when the mouse cursor leaves the area of a particular XAML object
MouseLeftButtonDown	Occurs when the mouse left button is pressed down but before it is released
MouseLeftButtonUp	Occurs when the mouse left button is released after being pressed

Event	Description
MouseMove	Occurs when the mouse cursor is moved over an area where it previously entered
KeyDown	Occurs when the key is pressed while the content has focus
KeyUp	Occurs when the key is released while the content has focus
GotFocus	Occurs when an object gets focus
LostFocus	Occurs when an object loses focus

It should be noted that *KeyDown*, *KeyUp*, *GotFocus*, and *LostFocus* events can be handled only on the root *Canvas* object. Handlers defined elsewhere will be ignored. Handlers for mouse and loading events, on the other hand, can be defined on any XAML element.

Writing Event Handlers

To define handlers for these events, you can use an attribute-oriented syntax or go through the Silverlight object model. If you opt for an attribute-oriented syntax, you do as in the following code snippet:

```
<Canvas MouseLeftButtonDown="media_stop"
  Canvas.Left="10" Canvas.Top="265">
    <Rectangle Stroke="Black"
      Height="30" Width="55" RadiusX="5" RadiusY="5">
      <Rectangle.Fill>
        <RadialGradientBrush GradientOrigin="0.75,0.25">
          <GradientStop Color="Orange" Offset="0.0" />
          <GradientStop Color="Red" Offset="1.0" />
        </RadialGradientBrush>
      </Rectangle.Fill>
    </Rectangle>
    <TextBlock Canvas.Left="5" Canvas.Top="5">Stop</TextBlock>
</Canvas>
```

The *Canvas* object defines a handler for the left button click through the *MouseLeftButtonDown* attribute. The *media_stop* name in the code snippet is the name of a JavaScript function that will be invoked as the user clicks. In Silverlight 1.0, XAML handlers can be written only in JavaScript; in Silverlight 2.0, this code can also be written using a managed language.

```
function media_stop(sender, args)
{
    sender.findName("media").stop();
}
```

The code snippet retrieves the XAML element named *media* and invokes its *stop* method. For the *MediaElement*, this means stopping the movie being played.

You can also add an event handler using the *addEventListener* method, as shown here:

```
var entertoken1;
var leavetoken1;
function onLoaded(sender, eventArgs)
{
    textBlock = sender.findName("Status");
    entertoken1 = textBlock.addEventListener("MouseEnter", onMouseEnter);
    leavetoken1 = textBlock.addEventListener("MouseLeave", onMouseLeave);
}
```

If you want to remove the handler at some point, you use the *removeEventListener* method:

```
function removeEvents()
{
    textBlock.removeEventListener("MouseEnter", entertoken1);
    textBlock.removeEventListener("MouseLeave", leavetoken1);
}
```

To remove a particular handler, you need to pass the token returned to you when you first added the handler.

Accessing Properties of XAML Elements

The *findName* method is a powerful general-purpose tool to help you get a reference to a particular element at any level of nesting. However, when working within an event handler, the *sender* parameter provides you with a reference to the object that triggered the event. For example, in the following code for the *MouseEnter* event, the *sender* parameter returns the object currently underneath the mouse. The statement then just sets the property *stroke* on the XAML user-interface element.

```
function mouse_enter(sender, args)
{
    sender.stroke = "orange";
}
```

Using mouse events, you can detect any element the XAML is made of and dynamically configure its properties. You can use the classic dot (.) notation for direct properties, such as *stroke* on a XAML user-interface element. Alternatively, you can use the *getValue* and *setValue* methods to read and write properties:

```
function mouse_enter(sender, args)
{
    if (sender.getValue("stroke") !== "orange")
        sender.setValue("stroke", "orange");
}
```

Let's briefly consider the following XAML snippet that inspired Figure 21-12:

```
<Ellipse x:Name="Ellipse1"
    MouseEnter="mouse_enter" MouseLeave="mouse_leave"
    Canvas.Left="40" Canvas.Top="40" Canvas.ZIndex="3"
    Stroke="Black" StrokeThickness="5">
</Ellipse>
```

Direct properties of the sample *Ellipse* are *Stroke* and *StrokeThickness*. What about *Canvas. Left* or *Canvas.ZIndex*? These are attached properties and require a different syntax to be set programmatically:

```
function mouse_enter(sender, args)
{
    sender["Canvas.ZIndex"] = 100;
}
```

If you opt for the dot (.) syntax, you need to use square brackets to reach a particular element named *Canvas.ZIndex* in the array of attached properties for the object. If you stick to the *setValue* syntax, you just reach a property in the usual way:

```
sender.setValue("Canvas.ZIndex", 100);
```

In this case, the *setValue* method hides the difference between direct and attached properties.

> **Note** In WPF you have *direct* and *attached* properties. Direct properties are regular properties defined on the class and managed by the class. When a caller sets a direct property on a class, the class knows what to do and does it. An attached property, instead, is a property exposed by class A, but associated with an instance of class B. As a developer, you assign a value to the property on an instance of class B, but the code that actually uses that information is defined on class A. In a certain way, an attached property decorates an instance of a class so that another class— typically a container class—can better manipulate it. To illustrate, consider a *Button* and a custom *Panel*. Let's say that your custom *Panel* has the ability of animating a buttons when the mouse hovers. How would you enable this extra capability? The *Button* doesn't know about animation and doesn't know how to handle it. On the other hand, the custom *Panel* needs to know whether it has to animate a given button or not. In this case, the custom *Panel* would define an attached Boolean property so that developers can attach it to any child button. It is transparent for the *Button* class, but decorates the *Button* in a way that the custom *Panel* understands.

Scripting and Animation Together

One of the scenarios in which Silverlight 1.0 excels is in creating little animations for Web pages. Whether you have to play a short movie or just run some advertisements, Silverlight 1.0 can help and save your users from installing additional media players. If you move up to Silverlight for your Web site, with a single plug-in you can have media and graphics capabilities, and you can create simple animations and relatively simple advertisement spots without the costs of hiring an expert professional.

Many Web pages today host some advertisements. They are storyboards that run periodically as the user visits the page. Most of them are created as Flash animations and require an ad hoc engine to play. Creating a Flash animation might not be that easy and definitely requires an expert. With Silverlight, you have the additional option of engaging your most creative developers.

As we saw earlier in the "The XAML Syntax in Silverlight" section, you can create animations by defining a storyboard. A storyboard is ultimately a collection of animation objects that work by moving around, fading, and styling constituent XAML elements. With script code, you can handle mouse events, thus making the animation more interactive, and hide and display parts of it according to the user movements. For example, Figure 21-14 shows a logo with three ellipses, each representing an activity— writing, training, and consulting—of a fictional company named Contoso Solutions.

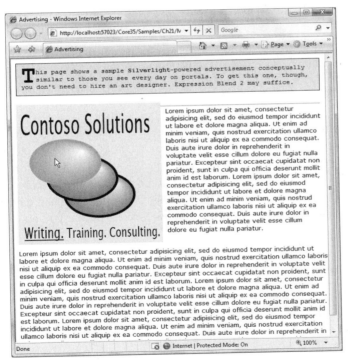

FIGURE 21-14 A relatively simple advertisement created with some scripting and animation

The following script brings up the ellipse underneath the mouse, decorates the text corresponding to the ellipse, and shows some descriptive text.

```
function bringToTheFront(element, flag)
{
    // Flag is a Boolean to indicate whether you highlight or un-highlight
    if (flag)
    {
        // Cache the current z-index, and change the current level
        cache_zIndex = element["Canvas.ZIndex"];
        element["Canvas.ZIndex"] = highest_zIndex;
    }
    else
    {
        element["Canvas.ZIndex"] = cache_zIndex;
    }
}
```

At the same time, you can remove the border and change the gradient color to augment the effect of highlighting.

The constituent ellipses reach their final position at the end of a simple animation that makes each ellipse move from a position outside the document. Each time the user clicks on the Silverlight document, the animation is played again:

```
function animateLogo(sender, args)
{
    // sender is the root Canvas where we define the click handler.
    // The "logoAnimation" element is the storyboard in the document.
    sender.findName("logoAnimation").begin();
}
```

The full source for this demo is in the *ad.xaml* file you can find in the source code of the book. If you take a look at it, you'll realize that it takes quite a bit of JavaScript code to make it work. Creating a small and relatively simple animation for Silverlight 1.0, therefore, needs JavaScript coding. That's a good point to keep in mind and a good reason to look forward to Silverlight 2.0. (Why? The more logic you put in the client, the more you can gain in performance by using a compiled language. And you can use languages that you may be more familiar with than JavaScript.)

Resizing the Silverlight Area

Some nice advertisements you find in Web sites today expand their area when the user moves the mouse over them. Typically, they expand to drill down and show more to the user. Can you do the same in Silverlight? You bet. All you need to do is resize the Silverlight area, as in the following code:

```
function enlargeWindow(sender, args)
{
    slPlugin = document.getElementById("SilverlightControl1");
    slPlugin.width = 330;
    slPlugin.height = 400;
}
```

You should use absolute measures for width and height and avoid relative measures such as increasing or decreasing the current value by a delta. Using absolute measures puts you on the safe side regardless of the user interaction with the mouse and the browser's way of managing those events. With a relative delta, it could happen that the *MouseLeave* event is not fired because the user moves the mouse too quickly or even lifts it up enough to confuse the browser. In case of relative sizing, the dimensions of the plug-in could be incorrect.

When you resize the plug-in, normally the rest of the page shifts to make room for it. Some players hosted in modern Web sites, instead, overlay the page with their content. Getting this effect is kind of unrelated to the Silverlight content. It is obtained by using absolute positioning for the Silverlight host and other page elements:

```
<span id="SilverlightHost" style="position:absolute;float:left;border:solid 1px black;">
    <script type="text/javascript">
        createSilverlightPlugIn();
    </script>
</span>
```

Figure 21-15 shows the result. When the user hovers over any of the ellipses, the plug-in expands and shows an additional message about the selected company's assets.

FIGURE 21-15 The Silverlight plug-in overlays the page when its window is dynamically resized

Note In Chapter 19, we mentioned the ability of the *ScriptManager* control to support script localization. Used in the page shown in Figure 21-15, that feature would give you the chance of showing a localized advertisement. In the XAML document, you define a placeholder for the descriptive text at the bottom and set it via script. In this way, a localized script would localize the overall animation. Simple and effective.

Introducing Silverlight 2.0

As mentioned, Silverlight 1.0 supports a small subset of the XAML syntax. The next version of Silverlight, to be released in 2008, promises to do much more. For one thing, it has been announced that it will support the full XAML syntax. In addition, it will feature a significantly revised architecture that incorporates a shrink-wrapped version of the CLR and the new Dynamic Language Runtime (DLR)—a hot new component of the .NET Framework 4.0.

The embedded CLR makes it possible for developers to write managed code to power up a XAML document. In other words, a large share of the code we wrote in JavaScript in this chapter could be rewritten in C#, Visual Basic .NET, or IronPython in Silverlight 2.0.

The object model available to developers is a Silverlight-adapted version of the .NET Framework. It contains classes to handle exceptions, work with sockets, make HTTP requests to endpoints, parse and create XML, support LINQ for objects and XML documents, and perform local file I/O limited to isolated storage.

The resulting page is not like a desktop form, but it will let you code your way in a nearly identical manner. The resulting page is still a sandboxed page with all the inherent restrictions of a typical browser page, but it is coded using managed and compiled languages. This makes it possible, at last, to move some of the server workload to the thick and rich client.

The Visual Studio 2008 Template Project

The easiest way to create a Silverlight 2.0 project is by using the tools created for Visual Studio 2008. Once installed, the tools make available a new project type for Silverlight 2.0 that serves up a ready-to-use environment. Once you finish up the work and get the final version of the page, you deploy it to the production server. The project you create and edit is entirely local, meaning that you test it on an HTML page and load it as a disk page.

The project adds a few predefined references for the assemblies required by Silverlight 2.0. Table 21-5 lists these assemblies.

TABLE 21-5 Silverlight 2.0 Assemblies

Assembly	Description
Agclr	Contains the Silverlight 2.0 implementation of the CLR
MsCorLib	Contains the core library of the .NET Framework
System.Core	Contains the core subset of the .NET Framework classes supported by Silverlight
System.Silverlight	Contains the new classes added just for the Silverlight runtime
System.Xml.Core	Contains the core library for XML data manipulation

The XAML file added to the project contains a code-behind class that can be written in C# or Visual Basic .NET. The code in this class can address any class in the preceding assemblies. The code-behind class is compiled to an assembly and downloaded to the client along with the source XAML.

The XAML Code-Behind Class

When you host a Silverlight 2.0 page in a Web application, all assemblies found in the *ClientBin* folder of the server are downloaded to the client. Additional assemblies required by your code-behind class must be copied to the *ClientBin* folder also. The following code shows the root of a XAML document in Silverlight 2.0:

```
<Canvas x:Name="parentCanvas"
  xmlns="http://schemas.microsoft.com/client/2007"
  xmlns:x="http://schemas.microsoft.com/winfx/2006/xaml"
  x:Class="Ad2.Page;assembly=ClientBin/Ad2.dll"
  Loaded="Page_Loaded"
  Width="300"
  Height="300">
  ...
</Canvas>
```

There are two aspects of this code snippet that are worth noting. First, you should note the new *x:Class* attribute. The attribute indicates the .NET Framework type used to back up the XAML document. The attribute plays the same role as the *Inherits* attribute in a classic Web page. The assembly property in the value of the *x:Class* attribute indicates the assembly that contains the class.

The second important aspect relates to the *Loaded* attribute. On the surface, the attribute is nearly identical to the *Loaded* attribute in Silverlight 1.0. However, there's an important change under the hood. *Page_Loaded* now refers to a method in the code-behind class and is written in a managed language instead of JavaScript.

> **Note** In Silverlight 2.0, you define event handlers for user-interface elements using the same
> syntax as in Silverlight 1.0. However, names of event handlers now refer to methods defined in
> the code-behind class and are made of managed code instead of JavaScript.

The Object Model

Working with the Silverlight object model in C# is overall similar to JavaScript but with some
scattered changes made possible by the different nature of the C# language. First and foremost, you work with classes. This means that you can store references to various XAML elements in private members and reuse them across the code. Here's the typical structure of the
handler of the *Loaded* event for the root object:

```
public partial class Page : Canvas
{
    private Canvas _canvas;
    private Ellipse _writing, _training, _consulting;
    ...

    public void Page_Loaded(object sender, EventArgs e)
    {
        // Required to initialize variables (defined on the base class)
        InitializeComponent();

        // Cache member references to ellipses in the XAML
        _canvas = sender as Canvas;
        _writing = _canvas.FindName("e_Writing") as Ellipse;
        _training = _canvas.FindName("e_Training") as Ellipse;
        _consulting = _canvas.FindName("e_Consulting") as Ellipse;
        ...
    }
    ...
}
```

You use the cached member references in the various event handlers of the class. Among
other things, this means that you save some CPU cycles by saving yourself a lot of *FindName*
calls.

When you define an event handler in the XAML source, you specify only the name of the
handler. However, it is required that the corresponding method be given the correct signature. The following code snippet shows handlers for the *MouseEnter* and *MouseLeave* events:

```
public void _writing_MouseEnter(object sender, MouseEventArgs e)
{
    ...
}
public void _writing_MouseLeave(object sender, EventArgs e)
{
    ...
}
```

You can also register event handlers programmatically, as shown here:

```
_elem.MouseLeftButtonUp += new MouseEventHandler(_elem_MouseLeftButtonUp);
```

In an event handler, you typically change the value of properties and modify the XAML tree as appropriate.

Reading and Writing Properties

The Silverlight object model serves you strongly typed objects with typed properties. You can set direct properties using the classic dot (.) notation, as shown next:

```
ellipse.Stroke = _hiliteBrush;
gradient.Color = _hiliteColor;
msg.FontSize += 2;
msg.TextDecorations = TextDecorations.Underline;
```

It goes without saying that if you use variables to assign values to properties, the type must match. It should be noted that the *Stroke* and *Fill* property are of type *Brush* and not *Color*. At the same time, the Silverlight *Color* type is not the same *Color* type of the .NET Framework *System.Drawing* namespace. You typically create a color using the RGB notation:

```
_hiliteColor = Color.FromRgb(255, 128, 0);
```

How can you set attached properties such as *Canvas.ZIndex*? You use a special notation represented by a static property on the class named after the original property, followed by the "Property" suffix:

```
ellipse.SetValue(Canvas.ZIndexProperty, 100);
```

To set an attached property in C#, you use the *SetValue* method.

> **Note** In the book's sample code, you also will find a Silverlight 2.0 version of the advertisement document featured in Figure 21-15.

Accessing the HTML DOM

Managed languages can be used for event handlers defined within a XAML document, but they can also be used to define a handler for an HTML element. Imagine you have the following HTML markup in a page that also hosts a Silverlight 2.0 plug-in:

```
<input type="button" value="Switch to Italian" id="btnSwitchLang" />
```

As you can see, the input button has no *onclick* handler defined. The great news is that you also can use C# managed code for the *onclick* handler of an HTML *<input>* tag. In this case, though, you attach the handler programmatically from the XAML code-behind class:

```
using System.Windows.Browser;
...
HtmlDocument _document = HtmlPage.Document;
HtmlElement _btnSwitchLang = _document.GetElementByID("btnSwitchLang");
_btnSwitchLang.AttachEvent("onclick", new EventHandler(btnSwitchLang_Click));
```

The *btnSwitchLang_Click* method is a regular C# method in the XAML code-behind class with the signature of a click event handler:

```
private void btnSwitchLang_Click(object sender, EventArgs e)
{
    // Set the innerHTML property of a <span> named Label1
    HtmlElement label1 = _document.GetElementByID("Label1");
    label1.SetProperty("innerHTML", "Done.");
}
```

You use the *SetProperty* method on an *HtmlElement* object to set a DOM property. You use the *SetAttribute* method to set an attribute. Figure 21-16 shows the Silverlight 2.0 version of the advertisement sample we previously built for Silverlight 1.0 entirely in JavaScript. It doesn't show up in the figure, but it's been done all in C#, runs on the client, and never posts back.

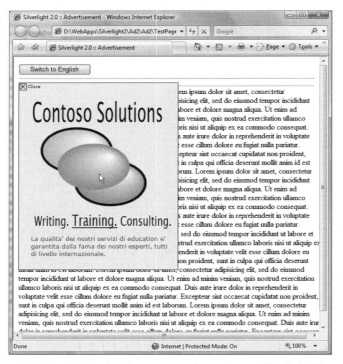

FIGURE 21-16 The advertisement sample running on Silverlight 2.0

Conclusion

Microsoft Silverlight is a cross-browser, cross-platform plug-in for building rich Internet applications that works on Windows and Mac platforms and is coming to Linux too. Silverlight is designed to make Web applications (and, in particular, ASP.NET applications) become desktop-like applications that are deployed over the Web. Silverlight is designed to bring the Windows Presentation Foundation (WPF) application delivery format (XAML) to the Web.

With its limited XAML support, Silverlight 1.0 can help you only in a limited number of scenarios as far as user experience is concerned. However, Silverlight 1.0 does the few things it has been designed for very well. In this chapter, we've illustrated a concrete example of how to build a little animation that can be used as an advertisement.

The next version of Silverlight (to be released in the course of 2008) is even more compelling and enticing. With Silverlight 2.0 on board, your Web applications will take advantage of a shrink-wrapped version of the .NET common language runtime, which means you will have support for managed languages and a lightweight version of the .NET Framework that includes features such as isolated storage, LINQ, sockets, exceptions, and an XML reader/writer application programming interface (API). In addition, Silverlight supports the full WPF set of features. In this chapter, we only scratched the surface of the topic using the limited information available at the time of this writing. If I can give you a piece of advice, it would be to learn as much as possible about WPF and XAML programming. In one way or another, they'll play a key role in the near future of the Web. Maybe even more fundamental than AJAX itself.

As usual, time will tell.

Just the Facts

- Silverlight is a browser plug-in that enables Web pages to host rich XAML documents.
- Silverlight 1.0 recognizes and supports only a small subset of the XAML syntax limited to 2D vector graphics, media capabilities, and text.
- Silverlight 2.0, to be released in 2008, supports the full XAML syntax and embeds a core version of the .NET Framework and the CLR.
- You add interactivity to Silverlight documents using JavaScript in version 1.0 and managed languages in version 2.0.
- Silverlight media capabilities are self-contained and don't rely on external players of any kind.
- You can access the Silverlight-hosted document using an object model compatible with JavaScript and accessible from within the HTML DOM.

- Silverlight 1.0 is great at authoring small animations and advertisements.

- Silverlight 2.0 represents an essential turning point and a key milestone for architects, as it enables them to use a new pattern for the presentation layer of multitier Web systems.

- Silverlight doesn't represent a replacement for AJAX, but it can work with or without AJAX in HTML and ASP.NET pages.

Index

A

I

Dino Esposito

Dino Esposito is a Web architect and a trainer based in Rome, Italy. Dino specializes in Microsoft Web technologies, including ASP.NET AJAX and Silverlight, and spends most of his time teaching and consulting across Europe, Australia, and the United States.

Over many years, Dino developed hands-on experience and skills in architecting and building distributed systems for banking and insurance companies in industry contexts where the demand for security, optimization, performance, scalability, and interoperability is dramatically high.

Every month at least five different magazines and Web sites around the world publish Dino's articles covering topics ranging from Web development to data access, and from software best practices to Web services. In addition to being a prolific author, Dino writes the monthly "Cutting Edge" column for MSDN Magazine and the ASP.NET-2-The-Max newsletter for Dr. Dobb's Journal. Considered an authoritative and knowledgeable expert in Web applications built with .NET technologies, Dino contributes to Microsoft's content platform for developers and IT consultants. Check out his articles on a variety of MSDN Developer Centers such as ASP.NET, security, and data access.

Dino has written an array of books, most of which are considered state-of-the-art in their respective areas. His most recent books are *Introducing Microsoft ASP.NET AJAX* (Microsoft Press, 2007), and *Programming Microsoft ASP.NET 2.0 Applications—Advanced Topics (*Microsoft Press, 2006).

Dino regularly speaks at industry conferences all over the world (Microsoft TechEd, Microsoft DevDays, DevConnections, DevWeek, Basta) and local technical conferences and meetings in Europe and the United States.

Dino lives near Rome and plays tennis at least twice a week.

What do you think of this book?

We want to hear from you!

Do you have a few minutes to participate in a brief online survey?

Microsoft is interested in hearing your feedback so we can continually improve our books and learning resources for you.

To participate in our survey, please visit:

www.microsoft.com/learning/booksurvey/

...and enter this book's ISBN-10 or ISBN-13 number (located above barcode on back cover*). As a thank-you to survey participants in the United States and Canada, each month we'll randomly select five respondents to win one of five $100 gift certificates from a leading online merchant. At the conclusion of the survey, you can enter the drawing by providing your e-mail address, which will be used for prize notification only.

Thanks in advance for your input. Your opinion counts!

* Where to find the ISBN on back cover

ISBN-13: 000-0-0000-0000-0
ISBN-10: 0-0000-0000-0

0 000000 000000

00000

Example only. Each book has unique ISBN.

Microsoft *Press*

www.microsoft.com/learning/booksurvey/